The Law of
Higher Education

William A. Kaplin

Barbara A. Lee

The Law of Higher Education

A Comprehensive Guide to Legal Implications of Administrative Decision Making

VOLUME II

FOURTH EDITION

JOSSEY-BASS
A Wiley Imprint
www.josseybass.com

Published by Jossey-Bass
A Wiley Imprint
989 Market Street, San Francisco, CA 94103-1741   www.josseybass.com

Jossey-Bass books and products are available through most bookstores. To contact Jossey-Bass directly call our Customer Care Department within the U.S. at 800-956-7739, outside the U.S. at 317-572-3986, or fax 317-572-4002.

Jossey-Bass also publishes its books in a variety of electronic formats. Some content that appears in print may not be available in electronic books.

ISBN-10: 0-7879-8656-9
ISBN-13: 978-0-7879-8656-8

Library of Congress Cataloging-in-Publication Data

Kaplin, William A.
   The law of higher education / William A. Kaplin, Barbara A. Lee. — 4th ed.
     v. cm.
   Includes bibliographical references and index.
   Contents: Overview of higher education law—Legal planning and dispute resolution—The college and its trustees and officers—The college and its employees—Nondiscrimination and affirmative action in employment—Faculty employment issues—Faculty academic freedom and freedom of expression—Rights and responsibilities of individual students—Rights and responsibilities of student organizations and their members—Local governments and the local community—The college and the state government—The college and the federal government—The college and the education associations (on website)—The college and the business/industrial community (on website).
    ISBN-10: 0-7879-8659-3 (cloth)
    ISBN-13: 978-0-7879-8659-9 (cloth)
   1. Universities and colleges—Law and legislation—United States. 2. School management and organization—Law and legislation—United States. 3. Universities and colleges—United States—Administration.   I. Lee, Barbara A.   II. Title.
    KF4225.K36 2006
    344.73'074—dc22
                       2006010076

Printed in the United States of America
FIRST EDITION
HB Printing   10 9 8 7 6 5 4 3 2 1

Contents

15 The College and the Business/Industrial Community 1591

9

Rights and Responsibilities of Individual Students

Sec. 9.1. Disciplinary and Grievance Systems

9.1.1. Overview. Colleges and universities develop codes of student conduct (discussed in Section 9.2) and standards of academic performance (discussed in Section 9.3), and expect students to conform to those codes and standards. Sections 9.1 through 9.4 discuss student challenges to institutional attempts to discipline students for violations of these codes and standards. Section 9.1 presents the guidelines for disciplinary and grievance systems that afford students appropriate statutory and constitutional protections. Section 9.2 analyzes the courts' responses to student challenges to colleges' disciplinary rules and regulations, emphasizing the different standards that public and private institutions must meet. Section 9.3 addresses "academic" matters, such as students' challenges to grades, graduates' challenges to degree revocation, students' allegations of sexual harassment by faculty, and the special issues raised by students with disabilities who request accommodations of an academic nature. Section 9.4 reviews the guidelines courts have developed in reviewing challenges to the *procedures* used by colleges when they seek to discipline or expel a student for either social or academic misconduct.

Section 9.5 discusses a variety of legal limitations on institutions' authority to discipline students for social or academic misconduct, with particular attention to the differences between public and private institutions. Sections 9.5 and 9.6 focus on the parameters of student free speech and expressive conduct, with special emphasis on student protests, free speech zones, and the phenomenon of "hate speech." Section 9.7 addresses federal (and some state) protections for the privacy of student records and the interplay between such protections and state open records and open meetings laws. (The latter laws are also discussed in Section 12.5.)

9.1.2. Establishment of systems.

Postsecondary institutions have extensive authority to regulate both the academic and the nonacademic activities and behavior of students. This power is summarized in an often-cited judicial statement:

> In the field of discipline, scholastic and behavioral, an institution may establish any standards reasonably relevant to the lawful missions, processes, and functions of the institution. It is not a lawful mission, process, or function of . . . [a public] institution to prohibit the exercise of a right guaranteed by the Constitution or a law of the United States to a member of the academic community in the circumstances. Therefore, such prohibitions are not reasonably relevant to any lawful mission, process, or function of . . . [a public] institution.
>
> Standards so established may apply to student behavior on and off the campus when relevant to any lawful mission, process, or function of the institution. By such standards of student conduct the institution may prohibit any action or omission which impairs, interferes with, or obstructs the missions, processes, and functions of the institution.
>
> Standards so established may require scholastic attainments higher than the average of the population and may require superior ethical and moral behavior. In establishing standards of behavior, the institution is not limited to the standards or the forms of criminal laws ["General Order on Judicial Standards of Procedure and Substance in Review of Student Discipline in Tax-Supported Institutions of Higher Education," 45 F.R.D. 133, 145 (W.D. Mo. 1968)].

It is not enough, however, for an administrator to understand the extent and limits of institutional authority. The administrator must also skillfully implement this authority through various systems for the resolution of disputes concerning students. Such systems should include procedures for processing and resolving disputes, substantive standards or rules to guide the judgment of the persons responsible for dispute resolution, and mechanisms and penalties with which decisions are enforced. The procedures, standards, and enforcement provisions should be written and made available to all students. Dispute resolution systems, in their totality, should create a two-way street; that is, they should provide for complaints by students against other members of the academic community as well as complaints against students by other members of the academic community.

The choice of structures for resolving disputes depends on policy decisions made by administrators, preferably in consultation with representatives of various interests within the institution. Should a single system cover both academic and nonacademic disputes, or should there be separate systems for different kinds of disputes? Should there be a separate disciplinary system for students, or should there be a broader system covering other members of the academic community as well? Will the systems use specific and detailed standards of student conduct, or will they operate on the basis of more general rules and policies? To what extent will students participate in establishing the rules governing their *no purely disciplinary function*

how much detail should it go into

conduct? To what extent will students, rather than administrators or faculty members, be expected to assume responsibility for reporting or investigating violations of student conduct codes or honor codes? To what extent will students take part in adjudicating complaints by or against students? What kinds of sanctions can be levied against students found to have been engaged in misconduct? Can the students be fined, made to do volunteer work on campus, suspended or expelled from the institution, given a failing grade in a course or denied a degree, or required to make restitution? To what extent will the president, provost, or board of trustees retain final authority to review decisions concerning student misconduct?

Devices for creating dispute resolution systems may include honor codes or codes of academic ethics; codes of student conduct; bills of rights, or rights and responsibilities, for students or for the entire academic community; the use of various legislative bodies, such as a student or university senate; a formal judiciary system for resolving disputes concerning students; the establishment of grievance mechanisms for students, such as an ombuds system or a grievance committee; and mediation processes that provide an alternative or supplement to judiciary and grievance mechanisms. On most campuses, security guards or some other campus law enforcement system may also be involved in the resolution of disputes and regulation of student behavior.

Occasionally, specific procedures or mechanisms will be required by law. Constitutional due process, for instance, requires the use of certain procedures before a student is suspended or dismissed from a public institution (see Section 9.4). The Title IX regulations (Section 13.5.3) and the Family Educational Rights and Privacy Act (FERPA) regulations (Section 9.7.1) require both public and private institutions to establish certain procedures for resolving disputes under those particular statutes. Even when specific mechanisms or procedures are not required by law, the procedures or standards adopted by an institution will sometimes be affected by existing law. A public institution's rules regarding student protest, for instance, must comply with First Amendment strictures protecting freedom of speech (Section 9.5). And its rules regarding administrative access to or search of residence hall rooms, and the investigatory techniques of its campus police, must comply with Fourth Amendment strictures regarding search and seizure (Section 8.4.2). Though an understanding of the law is thus crucial to the establishment of disciplinary and grievance systems, the law by no means rigidly controls such systems' form and operation. To a large extent, the kind of system adopted will depend on the institution's history and campus culture.

Fair and accessible dispute resolution systems, besides being useful administrative tools in their own right, can also insulate institutions from lawsuits. Students who feel that their arguments or grievances will be fairly considered within the institution may forgo resort to the courts. If students ignore internal mechanisms in favor of immediate judicial action, the courts may refer the students to the institution. Under the "exhaustion-of-remedies" doctrine (see Section 2.2.2.4), courts may require plaintiffs to exhaust available remedies within the institution before bringing the complaint to court. In *Pfaff v. Columbia-Greene Community*

College, 472 N.Y.S.2d 480 (N.Y. App. Div. 1984), for example, the New York courts dismissed the complaint of a student who had sued her college, contesting a C grade entered in a course, because the college had an internal appeal process and the student "failed to show that pursuit of the available administrative appeal would have been fruitless."

9.1.3. *Codes of student conduct.* Three major issues are involved in the drafting or revision of codes of student conduct: the type of conduct the code will encompass, the procedures to be used when infractions of the code are alleged, and the sanctions for code violations.

Codes of student conduct typically proscribe both academic and social misconduct, whether or not the misconduct violates civil or criminal laws, and whether or not the misconduct occurs on campus. Academic misconduct may include plagiarism, cheating, forgery, or alteration of institutional records. In their review of sanctions for academic misconduct, and of the degree of procedural protection required for students accused of such misconduct, courts have been relatively deferential (see Section 9.4.3).

Social misconduct may include disruption of an institutional function (including teaching and research) and abusive or hazing behavior (but limitations on speech may run afoul of free speech protections, as discussed in Section 9.6). It may also encompass conduct that occurs off campus,[1] particularly if the misconduct also violates criminal law and the institution can demonstrate that the restrictions are directly related to its educational mission or the campus community's welfare (*Krasnow v. Virginia Polytechnic Institute*, 551 F.2d 591 (4th Cir. 1977); *Wallace v. Florida A&M University*, 433 So. 2d 600 (Fla. Dist. Ct. App. 1983)).

Sanctions for code violations may range from a warning to expulsion, with various intermediate penalties, such as suspension or community service requirements. Students who are expelled may seek injunctive relief under the theory that they will be irreparably harmed; some courts have ruled that injunctive relief is not appropriate for sanctions short of expulsion (*Boehm v. University of Pennsylvania School of Veterinary Medicine*, 573 A.2d 575 (Pa. Super. Ct. 1990), but see *Jones v. Board of Governors*, 557 F. Supp. 263 (W.D.N.C.), *affirmed*, 704 F.2d 713 (4th Cir. 1983)). Students at public institutions may assert constitutional claims related to deprivation of a property and/or liberty interest (see Section 6.6.2), while students at both public and private institutions may file actions based on contract law.

If a code of conduct defines the offenses for which a student may be penalized by a public institution, that code must comply with constitutional due process requirements concerning vagueness. The requirement is a minimal one: the code must be clear enough for students to understand the standards with which their conduct must comply, and it must not be susceptible to arbitrary enforcement. A public institution's code of conduct must also comply with the constitutional

---

[1]Cases and authorities are collected in Dale R. Agthe, Annot., "Misconduct of College or University Students Off Campus as Grounds for Expulsion, Suspension, or Other Disciplinary Action," 28 A.L.R.4th 463.

doctrine of overbreadth in any area where the code could affect First Amendment rights. Basically, this doctrine requires that the code not be drawn so broadly and vaguely as to include protected First Amendment activity along with behavior subject to legitimate regulation (see Sections 9.5.2 & 9.6). Finally, a public institution's student conduct code must comply with a general requirement of evenhandedness; that is, the code cannot arbitrarily discriminate in the range and types of penalties, or in the procedural safeguards, afforded various classes of offenders. *Paine v. Board of Regents of the University of Texas System*, 355 F. Supp. 199 (W.D. Tex. 1972), *affirmed per curiam*, 474 F.2d 1397 (5th Cir. 1973), concerned such discriminatory practices. The institution had given students convicted of drug offenses a harsher penalty and fewer safeguards than it gave to all other code offenders, including those charged with equally serious offenses. The court held that this differential treatment violated the equal protection and due process clauses.

The student codes of conduct at some institutions include an "honor code" that requires fellow students to report cheating or other misconduct that they observe. In *Vargo v. Hunt*, 581 A.2d 625 (Pa. Super. 1990), a state appellate court affirmed the ruling of a trial court that a student's report of cheating by a fellow student was subject to a conditional privilege. The Allegheny College honor code explicitly required students to report "what appears to be an act of dishonesty in academic work" to an instructor or a member of the honor committee. When Ms. Hunt reported her suspicions that Mr. Vargo was cheating, he was charged with, and later found guilty of, a violation of the disciplinary code, was suspended from the college for one semester, and received a failing grade in the course. Vargo then sued Hunt for defamation. The court ruled that Hunt had acted within the boundaries of the honor code and had not communicated the allegedly defamatory information beyond the appropriate individuals, and that the academic community had a common interest in the integrity of the academic process.

Sometimes a state law requires students to report wrongdoing on campus. A Texas anti-hazing law contains provisions that require anyone who has "firsthand knowledge of the planning of a specific hazing incident . . . or firsthand knowledge that a specific hazing incident has occurred," to report the incident to a college official (§ 37.152, Tex. Educ. Code). Failure to do so can result in a fine or imprisonment. Students charged with failure to report hazing, as well as with hazing and assault, challenged the law, arguing that compliance with the reporting provisions of the law required them to incriminate themselves in the alleged hazing incident, a violation of their Fifth Amendment rights. In *The State of Texas v. Boyd*, 2 S.W.3d 752 (Ct. App. Tex. 1999), a state appellate court affirmed the ruling of a trial court that held this provision of the law unconstitutional. The Court of Criminal Appeals of Texas, however, reversed, noting that the anti-hazing law also provides for immunity from prosecution for anyone who testifies for the prosecution in such a case (38 S.W.3d 155 (Tex. Crim. App. 2001)).

As noted above, codes of conduct can apply to the off-campus actions as well as the on-campus activity of students. But the extension of a code to off-campus activity can pose significant legal and policy questions. In the *Paine* case above, the institution automatically suspended students who had been put on probation by the criminal courts for possession of marijuana. The court invalidated the suspensions partly because they were based on an off-campus occurrence (court probation) that did not automatically establish a threat to the institution. More recent cases, however, suggest that courts are more likely to uphold the suspension or expulsion of students who were arrested and found guilty of a criminal offense, in particular drug possession or use. (See, for example, *Krasnow v. Virginia Polytechnic Institute,* 551 F.2d 591 (4th Cir. 1977); *Sohmer v. Kinnard,* 535 F. Supp. 50 (D. Md. 1982).) In *Woodis v. Westark Community College,* 160 F.3d 435 (8th Cir. 1998), the plaintiff, a nursing student expelled from the college after she pleaded *nolo contendere* to a charge of attempting to obtain a controlled substance with a forged prescription, asserted that the college's code of conduct was unconstitutionally vague. She also argued that the college's disciplinary procedure denied her procedural due process because the vice president of student affairs had too much discretion to determine the punishment for students who violated the code. A trial court awarded summary judgment to the college, and the student appealed.

The college's code stated that students were expected to "conduct themselves in an appropriate manner and conform to standards considered to be in good taste at all times" (160 F.3d at 436). The code also required students to "obey all federal, state, and local laws." The appellate court therefore rejected the student's vagueness claim, ruling that drug offenses are criminal violations, and that she was on notice that criminal conduct was also a violation of college policy. With respect to the student's due process claim, the court also rejected the student's claim and affirmed the ruling of the trial court that had used the principles developed in *Esteban v. Central Missouri State College* (Section 9.2.2): adequate notice, a clear indication of the charges against the student, and a hearing that provides an opportunity for the student to present her side of the case. Even if the vice president's discretion had been too broad (an issue that the court did not determine), the student had the right to appeal the vice president's decision to an independent disciplinary board and also to the president. The student had also been given a second hearing after her *nolo contendere* plea, at which she was permitted to consult with counsel, examine the evidence used against her, and participate in the hearing. These procedures provided the student with sufficient due process protections to meet the *Esteban* standard.

The degree to which the institution can articulate a relationship between the off-campus misconduct and the interests of the campus community will improve its success in court. In the *Woodis* case discussed above, the fact that it was a nursing student who had used a forged prescription very likely strengthened the institution's argument that her off-campus conduct was relevant to institutional interests. In *Ray v. Wilmington College,* 667 N.E.2d 39 (Ohio Ct. App. 1995), for instance, the court stated:

> An educational institution's authority to discipline its students does not necessarily stop at the physical boundaries of the institution's premises. The institution has the prerogative to decide that certain types of off-campus conduct [are] detrimental to the institution and to discipline a student who engages in that conduct [667 N.E.2d at 711].

As long as the college can articulate a reasonable relationship between the off-campus misconduct and the well-being of the college community, reviewing courts will not overturn a disciplinary action unless they find that the action was arbitrary, an abuse of discretion, or a violation of a student's constitutional rights. And if the college includes language in its student code of conduct specifying that off-campus conduct that affects the well-being of the college community is expressly covered by the code of conduct, defending challenges to discipline for off-campus misconduct may be more successful.

(For legal and policy analysis of the institution's authority to regulate student misconduct off campus, see Gary Pavela (ed.), "Responding to Student Misconduct Off-Campus," Parts I & II, *Synfax Weekly Report*, December 13, 1999, and December 20, 1999. Part II (December 20, 1999), at page 927, makes the point that the policy issues regarding off-campus conduct are more difficult than the legal issues, and questions the extension of campus codes of conduct to off-campus settings.)

To avoid problems in this area, administrators should ascertain that an off-campus act has a direct detrimental impact on the institution's educational functions before using that act as a basis for disciplining students. (See, for example, the Opinion of the Attorney General of Maryland, upholding the right of the state university to discipline "for off-campus conduct detrimental to the interests of the institution, subject to the fundamental constitutional safeguards that apply to all disciplinary actions by educational officials" (74 *Opinions of the Attorney General* 1, Opinion No. 89-002 (Md. 1989)).)

Private institutions not subject to the state action doctrine (see Section 1.5.2) are not constitutionally required to follow these principles regarding student codes. Yet the principles reflect basic notions of fairness, which can be critical components of good administrative practice; thus, administrators of private institutions may wish to use them as policy guides in formulating their codes.

A question that colleges and universities, irrespective of control, may wish to consider is whether the disciplinary code should apply to student organizations as well as to individual students. Should students be required to assume collective responsibility for the actions of an organization, and should the university impose sanctions, such as withdrawal of institutional recognition, on organizations that violate the disciplinary code? (For a model student disciplinary code that includes student organizations within its ambit, see Edward N. Stoner & John Wesley Lowery, "Navigating Past the 'Spirit of Insubordination': A 21st Century Model for a Student Conduct Code with a Model Hearing Script," 31 *J. Coll. & Univ. Law* 1 (2004).)

(For additional information about honor codes and other resources, see the Center for Academic Integrity Web site at http://www.academicintegrity.org. A useful publication designed to assist institutions in evaluating their disciplinary rules and procedures is "Reviewing Your Student Discipline Policy: A Project Worth the Investment," available from United Educators at http://www.ue.org. For a student-oriented analysis of appropriate disciplinary procedures, see *Guide to Due Process and Fair Procedure on Campus*, published by the Foundation for Individual Rights in Education, and available at http://www.thefireguides.org.)

9.1.4. Judicial systems.

Judicial systems that adjudicate complaints of student misconduct must be very sensitive to procedural safeguards. The membership of judicial bodies, the procedures they use,[2] the extent to which their proceedings are open to the academic community, the sanctions they may impose, the methods by which they may initiate proceedings against students, and provisions for appealing their decisions should be set out in writing and made generally available within the institution.

Whenever the charge could result in a punishment as serious as suspension, a public institution's judicial system must provide the procedures required by the due process clause (see Section 9.4.2). The focal point of these procedures is the hearing at which the accused student may present evidence and argument concerning the charge. The institution, however, may wish to include preliminary stages in its judicial process for more informal disposition of complaints against students. The system may provide for negotiations between the student and the complaining party, for instance, or for preliminary conferences before designated representatives of the judicial system. Full due process safeguards need not be provided at every such preliminary stage. *Andrews v. Knowlton,* 509 F.2d 898 (2d Cir. 1975), dealt with the procedures required at a stage preceding an honor code hearing. The court held that due process procedures were not required at that time because it was not a "critical stage" that could have a "prejudicial impact" on the final determination of whether the student violated the honor code. Thus, administrators have broad authority to construct informal preliminary proceedings—as long as a student's participation in such stages does not adversely affect his or her ability to defend the case in the final stage.

Although the due process requirements for student disciplinary systems are relatively modest (see Sections 9.1.2 & 9.1.3), public institutions that do not follow their own rules and regulations may face charges of constitutional due process violations. Depending on the severity of the deviation from the rules, the courts may side with the student. For example, in *University of Texas Medical School v. Than,* 901 S.W.2d 926 (Tex. 1995), the Texas Supreme Court ruled that a medical student's procedural due process rights were violated when members of the hearing board that subsequently recommended his dismissal for academic dishonesty inspected the testing location without allowing Than to be present.

A question receiving increased attention is whether the judicial system will permit the accused student to have an attorney present. Several models are possible: (1) neither the college nor the student will have attorneys; (2) attorneys may be present to advise the student but may not participate by asking questions or making statements; or, (3) attorneys may be present and participate fully in questioning and making opening and closing statements. A federal appellate court was asked to rule on whether a judicial system at Northern Illinois University that followed the second model—attorney present but a nonparticipant—violated

---

[2]Cases and authorities related to student judicial procedures are collected in Jay M. Zitter, Annot., "Admissibility of Hearsay Evidence in Student Disciplinary Proceedings," 30 A.L.R.4th 935.

a student's due process rights. In *Osteen v. Henley*, 13 F.3d 221 (7th Cir. 1993), the court wrote:

> Even if a student has a constitutional right to *consult* counsel . . . we don't think he is entitled to be represented in the sense of having a lawyer who is permitted to examine or cross-examine witnesses, to submit and object to documents, to address the tribunal, and otherwise to perform the traditional function of a trial lawyer. To recognize such a right would force student disciplinary proceedings into the mold of adversary litigation. The university would have to hire its own lawyer to prosecute these cases and no doubt lawyers would also be dragged in—from the law faculty or elsewhere—to serve as judges. The cost and complexity of such proceedings would be increased, to the detriment of discipline as well as of the university's fisc [13 F.3d at 225].

The court then, citing *Mathews v. Eldridge* (see Section 6.7.2.3), balanced the cost of permitting lawyers to participate against the risk of harm to students if lawyers were excluded. Concluding that the risk of harm to students was "trivial," the court refused to rule that attorneys were a student's constitutional right.

Occasionally, a campus judicial proceeding may involve an incident that is also the subject of criminal court proceedings. The same student may thus be charged in both forums at the same time. In such circumstances, the postsecondary institution is not legally required to defer to the criminal courts by canceling or postponing its proceedings. As held in *Paine* (Section 9.1.4) and other cases, even if the institution is public, such dual prosecution is not double jeopardy because the two proceedings impose different kinds of punishment to protect different kinds of state interests. The Constitution's double jeopardy clause applies only to successive criminal prosecutions for the same offense. Nor will the existence of two separate proceedings necessarily violate the student's privilege against self-incrimination. In several cases—for instance, *Grossner v. Trustees of Columbia University*, 287 F. Supp. 535 (S.D.N.Y. 1968)—courts have rejected student requests to stay campus proceedings on this ground pending the outcome of criminal trials. One court emphasized, however, that if students in campus proceedings "are forced to incriminate themselves . . . and if that testimony is offered against them in subsequent criminal proceedings, they can then invoke . . . [Supreme Court precedents] in opposition to the offer" (*Furutani v. Ewigleben*, 297 F. Supp. 1163 (N.D. Cal. 1969)). In another case, the court rejected as speculative a student's claim that his being identified in campus disciplinary proceedings would jeopardize the fairness of his criminal trial (*Nzuve v. Castleton State College*, 335 A.2d 321 (Vt. 1975)).

The Supreme Court of Maine has addressed the issue of double jeopardy in a situation in which a student was subject to criminal and college penalties for an offense he committed. In *State of Maine v. Sterling*, 685 A.2d 432 (Me. 1996), Sterling, a football team member and recipient of an athletic scholarship, had assaulted a teammate on campus. The university held a hearing under the student conduct code, determined Sterling had violated the code, and suspended him for the summer. In addition, the football coach withdrew the portion of Sterling's scholarship that covered room and board. Shortly thereafter, criminal charges were brought against Sterling. He pleaded not guilty and filed a motion to dismiss the criminal charges, stating that the prosecution of the criminal complaint constituted double jeopardy because he had already received a penalty through the revocation of his scholarship. A trial court agreed, and dismissed the criminal proceedings. The state appealed.

The Supreme Court of Maine reversed, determining that the withdrawal of the scholarship was not a punishment because it was done to further the purposes of the student disciplinary code and to protect the integrity of the public educational system. The court explained that protection from double jeopardy was available if each of three requirements were met:

1. the sanction in each forum was for the same conduct;
2. the non-criminal sanction and the criminal prosecution were imposed in separate proceedings; and
3. the non-criminal sanction constitutes punishment [685 A.2d at 434].

Although Sterling's situation satisfied elements 1 and 2, the court refused to characterize the withdrawal of the scholarship as "punishment," stating that the scholarship was a privilege that could be withdrawn for valid reasons.

A Wisconsin appellate court addressed a similar issue in *City of Oshkosh v. Winkler*, 557 N.W.2d 464 (Wis. Ct. App. 1996). Winkler, a student at the University of Wisconsin-Oshkosh, was arrested by the city police for participating in a student riot near the university campus. The university also filed charges against Winkler under its disciplinary code. He was found guilty by a Student Conduct Hearing Committee and placed on disciplinary probation. When the city attempted to prosecute Winkler under its disorderly conduct ordinance, Winkler claimed that the criminal prosecution was barred by the double jeopardy doctrine. A trial court ruled in Winkler's favor, and the city appealed.

The city had argued that the university's student conduct code was not punitive but designed to maintain order on campus, and thus the double jeopardy doctrine did not apply in Winkler's case. Although some provisions of the university's code of conduct were very similar to the language of the Oshkosh ordinances prohibiting disorderly conduct, the appellate court refused to apply the double jeopardy standard. It noted that Wisconsin's administrative code requires the university system to "identify basic standards of nonacademic conduct necessary to protect the community" (Wis. Adm. Code § UWS 17.01 (1966)). Thus, the university's sanction was not punitive, according to the court, but was designed to maintain institutional order.

The court in *Winkler* relied, in part, on an opinion of the U.S. Supreme Court in *United States v. Halper*, 490 U.S. 435 (1989), which stated that if both the civil and the criminal proceedings were punitive in nature, then the double jeopardy doctrine was triggered. However, in *Hudson v. United States*, 522 U.S. 93 (1997), the U.S. Supreme Court criticized the method of analysis used in *Halper*. In an opinion to which five Justices subscribed, and in which there were four separate concurring opinions, the Court held that bank officers who had been assessed civil monetary penalties by the Office of the Comptroller of the Currency could also be indicted for criminal violations based on the same transactions for which they had been assessed civil penalties. The majority stated that, despite the fact that civil monetary penalties had a deterrent effect, they could not be construed as so punitive that they had the effect of a criminal sanction because they were not disproportionate to the nature of the misconduct. *Hudson* suggests that it may now be more difficult for students to claim double jeopardy, particularly if the noncriminal proceeding occurs before the criminal proceeding (as is often the case in campus disciplinary actions). As always, those institutions that can demonstrate that their student codes of conduct and judicial systems are designed for educational purposes and to maintain order rather than to punish will be in the best position to defend against double jeopardy claims, whether they are used in the campus disciplinary case or a criminal matter.

While neither double jeopardy nor self-incrimination need tie the administrator's hands, administrators may nevertheless choose, for policy reasons, to delay or dismiss particular campus proceedings when the same incident is in the criminal courts. It is possible that the criminal proceedings will adequately protect the institution's interests. Or, as *Furutani* and *Nzuve* suggest, student testimony at a campus proceeding could create evidentiary problems for the criminal court.

If a public institution proceeds with its campus action while the student is subject to charges still pending in criminal court, the institution may have to permit the student to have a lawyer with him or her during the campus proceedings. In *Gabrilowitz v. Newman*, 582 F.2d 100 (1st Cir. 1978), a student challenged a University of Rhode Island rule that prohibited the presence of legal counsel at campus disciplinary hearings. The student obtained an injunction prohibiting the university from conducting the hearing without permitting the student the advice of counsel. The appellate court, affirming the lower court's injunction order, held that when a criminal case based on the same conduct giving rise to the disciplinary proceeding is pending in the courts, "the denial to [the student] of the right to have a lawyer of his own choice to consult with and advise him during the disciplinary proceeding would deprive [him] of due process of law."

The court emphasized that the student was requesting the assistance of counsel to consult with and advise him during the hearing, not to conduct the hearing on the student's behalf. Such assistance was critical to the student because of the delicacy of the legal situation he faced:

> Were the appellee to testify in the disciplinary proceeding, his statement could be used as evidence in the criminal case, either to impeach or as an admission if he did not choose to testify. Appellee contends that he is, therefore, impaled on the horns of a legal dilemma: if he mounts a full defense at the disciplinary hearing without the assistance of counsel and testifies on his own behalf, he might jeopardize his defense in the criminal case; if he fails to fully defend himself or chooses not to testify at all, he risks loss of the college degree he is within weeks of receiving, and his reputation will be seriously blemished [582 F.2d at 103].

If a public institution delays campus proceedings, and then uses a conviction in the criminal proceedings as the basis for its campus action, the institution must take care to protect the student's due process rights. In the *Paine* case, a university rule required the automatic two-year suspension of any student convicted of a narcotics offense. The court held that the students must be given an opportunity to show that, despite their conviction and probation, they posed "no substantial threat of influencing other students to use, possess, or sell drugs or narcotics." Thus, a criminal conviction does not automatically provide the basis for suspension; administrators should still ascertain that the conviction has a detrimental impact on the campus, and the affected student should have the opportunity to make a contrary showing.

Given the deferential review by courts of the outcomes of student disciplinary proceedings (assuming that the student's constitutional or contractual rights have been protected), student challenges to these proceedings are usually unsuccessful. Even if the student is eventually exonerated, the institution that follows its rules and provides procedural protections will very likely prevail in subsequent litigation. For example, a state trial court rejected a student's attempt to state a negligence claim against a university for subjecting him to disciplinary proceedings for an infraction he did not commit. In *Weitz v. State of New York*, 696 N.Y.S.2d 656 (Ct. Claims N.Y. 1999), the plaintiff was an innocent bystander during a brawl in his residence hall that involved individuals who did not live in the residence hall. In addition to claims of negligence with respect to the security of the residence hall, the student claimed that the university was negligent in prosecuting him for violating the institution's code of conduct when he had not done so. The court noted that there was no cause of action in New York for negligent prosecution, and that it could find no public policy reason for creating such a cause of action simply because the student charged with a violation was ultimately found to be innocent.

Sec. 9.2. *Disciplinary Rules and Regulations*

9.2.1. Overview. Postsecondary institutions customarily have rules of conduct or behavior that students are expected to follow. It has become increasingly common to commit these rules to writing and embody them in codes of conduct that are binding on all students (see Section 9.1.3). Although the trend toward written codes is a sound one, legally speaking, because it gives students fairer notice of what is expected from them and often results in a better-conceived and administered system, written rules also provide a specific target to aim at in a lawsuit.

Students have challenged institutional attempts to discipline them by attacking the validity of the rule they allegedly violated or by attacking the nature of the disciplinary proceeding that determined that the alleged violation occurred. This Section discusses student challenges to the validity of institutional rules and regulations; Section 9.4 discusses challenges to the procedures used by colleges to determine whether, in fact, violations have occurred.

9.2.2. Public institutions. In public institutions, students frequently contend that the rules of conduct violate some specific guarantee of the Bill of

Rights, as made applicable to state institutions by the Fourteenth Amendment (see Section 1.5.2). These situations, the most numerous of which implicate the free speech and press clauses of the First Amendment, are discussed in Section 9.1 and various other Sections of this chapter. In other situations, the contention is a more general one: that the rule is so vague that its enforcement violates due process; that is (as was noted in Section 9.1.3), the rule is unconstitutionally "vague" or "void for vagueness."

Soglin v. Kauffman, 418 F.2d 163 (7th Cir. 1969), is illustrative. The University of Wisconsin had expelled students for attempting to block access to an off-campus recruiter as a protest against the Vietnam War. The university had charged the students under a rule prohibiting "misconduct" and argued in court that it had inherent power to discipline, which need not be exercised through specific rules. Both the U.S. District Court and the U.S. Court of Appeals held that the misconduct policy was unconstitutionally vague. The appellate court reasoned:

> The inadequacy of the rule is apparent on its face. It contains no clues which could assist a student, an administrator, or a reviewing judge in determining whether conduct not transgressing statutes is susceptible to punishment by the university as "misconduct."
>
> . . . We do not require university codes of conduct to satisfy the same rigorous standards as criminal statutes. We only hold that expulsion and prolonged suspension may not be imposed on students by a university simply on the basis of allegations of "misconduct" without reference to any preexisting rule which supplies an adequate guide [418 F.2d at 167–68].

While similar language about vagueness is often found in other court opinions, the actual result in *Soglin* (the invalidation of the rule) is unusual. Most university rules subjected to judicial tests of vagueness have survived, sometimes because the rule at issue is less egregious than the "misconduct" rule in *Soglin,* sometimes because a court accepts the "inherent power to discipline" argument raised by the *Soglin* defendants and declines to undertake any real vagueness analysis, and sometimes because the student conduct at issue was so contrary to the judges' own standards of decency that they tended to ignore the defects in the rules in light of the obvious "defect" in behavior. *Esteban v. Central Missouri State College,* 415 F.2d 1077 (8th Cir. 1969), the case most often cited in opposition to *Soglin,* reveals all three of these distinctions. In this case, students contested their suspension under a regulation prohibiting "participation in mass gatherings which might be considered as unruly or unlawful." In upholding the suspension, the court emphasized the need for "flexibility and reasonable breadth, rather than meticulous specificity, in college regulations relating to conduct" and recognized the institution's "latitude and discretion in its formulation of rules and regulations." The approach has often been followed in later cases—for instance, in *Jenkins v. Louisiana State Board of Education,* 506 F.2d 992 (5th Cir. 1975), where the court upheld a series of regulations dealing with disorderly assembly and disturbing the peace on campus.

In addition to *procedural* due process challenges, institutional rules and their application may be challenged under *substantive* due process theories. Such challenges are possible when the institution may have violated fundamental privacy rights of a student or may have acted arbitrarily or irrationally (see generally William Kaplin, *American Constitutional Law* (Carolina Academic Press, 2004), Ch. 11, Secs. B & C). The latter argument, for instance, has been made in situations in which a college or school has enacted "zero tolerance" rules with respect to possession of controlled substances and weapons, a practice that requires punishment for possession despite the factual circumstances. In *Seal v. Morgan,* 229 F.3d 567 (6th Cir. 2000), a high school student was expelled after a knife was found in the glove compartment of his car. The student said that the knife belonged to a friend, and that he was not aware that the knife was in the car. Under the school's zero tolerance rules, the student was expelled anyway. The trial and appellate courts rejected the school district's argument that the serious problem of weapons at school justified its summary action, stating that if the student had been unaware that he was "in possession" of a knife, then he could not have used it to harm anyone. Thus, said the court, the expulsion without an opportunity to determine if the student had actual knowledge of his "possession" was a violation of substantive due process. The court remanded the case for trial on the issue of the student's credibility.

Despite the outcome in *Seal,* courts are reluctant to create new substantive due process protections, particularly where students have remedies under other legal theories. For example, in *Dacosta v. Nwachukwa,* 304 F.3d 1045 (11th Cir. 2002), *cert. denied,* 538 U.S. 908 (2003), an instructor at the Georgia Military College injured a student when he shoved her and slammed a door in her face. The student filed a claim under 42 U.S.C. § 1983 (see Section 4.7.4 of this book), asserting a breach of her substantive due process rights. Noting that the student had a cause of action against the instructor for intentional battery, a tort under Georgia law, the court ruled that the instructor was protected by qualified immunity from constitutional claims.

Although the judicial trend suggests that most rules and regulations will be upheld, administrators should not assume that they have a free hand in promulgating codes of conduct. *Soglin* signals the institution's vulnerability when it has no written rules at all or when the rule provides no standard to guide conduct. And even the *Esteban* court warned: "We do not hold that any college regulation, however loosely framed, is necessarily valid." To avoid such pitfalls, disciplinary rules should provide standards sufficient to guide both the students in their conduct and the disciplinarians in their decision making. A rule will likely pass judicial scrutiny if the standard "conveys sufficiently definite warning as to the proscribed conduct when measured by common understanding and practices" (*Sword v. Fox,* 446 F.2d 1091 (4th Cir. 1971), upholding a regulation that "demonstrations are forbidden in any areas of the health center, inside any buildings, and congregating in the locations of fire hydrants"). Regulations need not be drafted by a lawyer—in fact, student involvement in drafting may be valuable to ensure an expression of their "common understanding"—but it would usually be wise to have a lawyer play a general advisory role in the process.

Once the rules are promulgated, institutional officials have some latitude in interpreting and applying them, as long as the interpretation is reasonable.

In *Board of Education of Rogers, Ark. v. McCluskey*, 458 U.S. 966 (1982), a public school board's interpretation of one of its rules was challenged as unreasonable. The board had held that its rule against students being under the influence of "controlled substances" included alcoholic beverages. The U.S. Supreme Court, quoting *Wood v. Strickland* (see Section 4.7.4), asserted that "federal courts [are] not authorized to construe school regulations" unless the board's interpretation "is so extreme as to be a violation of due process" (458 U.S. at 969–70).

9.2.3. Private institutions.

Private institutions, not being subject to federal constitutional constraints (see Section 1.5.2), have even more latitude than public institutions do in promulgating disciplinary rules. Courts are likely to recognize a broad right to make and enforce rules that is inherent in the private student-institution relationship or to find such a right implied in some contractual relationship between student and school. Under this broad construction, private institutional rules will not be held to specificity standards such as those in *Soglin* (discussed in Section 9.2.2). Thus, in *Dehaan v. Brandeis University*, 150 F. Supp. 626 (D. Mass. 1957), the court upheld the plaintiff's suspension for misconduct under a policy where the school "reserves the right to sever the connection of any student with the university for appropriate reason"; and in *Carr v. St. John's University, New York*, 231 N.Y.S.2d 410 (N.Y. App. Div. 1962), *affirmed*, 187 N.E.2d 18 (N.Y. 1962), the courts upheld the dismissal of four students for off-campus conduct under a regulation providing that "in conformity with the ideals of Christian education and conduct, the university reserves the right to dismiss a student at any time on whatever grounds the university judges advisable."

Despite the breadth of such cases, the private school administrator, like his or her public counterpart, should not assume a legally free hand in promulgating disciplinary rules. Courts can now be expected to protect private school students from clearly arbitrary disciplinary actions (see Section 1.5.3). When a school has disciplinary rules, courts may overturn administrators' actions taken in derogation of the rules. And when there is no rule, or if the applicable rule provides no standard of behavior, courts may overturn suspensions for conduct that the student could not reasonably have known was wrong. Thus, in *Slaughter v. Brigham Young University*, 514 F.2d 622 (10th Cir. 1975), though the court upheld the expulsion of a graduate student for dishonesty under the student code of conduct, it first asked "whether the . . . [expulsion] was arbitrary" and indicated that the university's findings would be accorded a presumption of correctness only "if the regulations concerned are reasonable [and] if they are known to the student or should have been." To avoid such situations, private institutions may want to adhere to much the same guidelines for promulgating rules as are suggested above for public institutions, despite the fact that they are not required by law to do so.

9.2.4. Disciplining students with psychiatric illnesses.

Research conducted in 2002 indicated that the number of students seeking help for psychiatric disorders has increased dramatically on college campuses (Erica Goode,

"More in College Seek Help for Psychological Problems," *New York Times,* February 3, 2003, p. A11). Students with mental or psychological disabilities are protected against discrimination by the Rehabilitation Act and the Americans With Disabilities Act (ADA) (see Sections 8.2.4.3. & 13.5.4, and for student employees, Section 5.2.5). Yet a student's misconduct may disrupt campus activities, or the student may be dangerous to herself or to other students, faculty, or administrators. Opinion is divided among educators and mental health professionals as to whether students suffering from mental disorders who violate the institution's code of student conduct should be subject to the regular disciplinary procedure or should be given a "medical withdrawal" if their presence on campus becomes disruptive or dangerous.[3]

Several issues arise in connection with mentally ill students who are disruptive or dangerous. If campus counseling personnel have gained information from a student indicating that he or she is potentially dangerous, the teachings of *Tarasoff v. Regents of the University of California* (Section 4.7.2 of this book) and its progeny (as well as many state statutes codifying *Tarasoff*) regarding a duty to warn the potential target(s) of the violence would apply. If administrators or faculty know that the student is potentially dangerous and that student subsequently injures someone, negligence claims based on the foreseeability of harm may arise (Section 3.3.2). On the other hand, potential violations of the federal Family Educational Rights and Privacy Act (discussed in Section 9.7.1) could also be implicated if institutional officials routinely warned a student's family or others of medical or psychological conditions.

Furthermore, college counseling staff may face tort claims for their alleged negligence in treating or advising students with psychiatric disorders (see, for example, *Williamson v. Liptzin,* 539 S.E.2d 313 (N.C. 2000), in which the court rejected the claim by a student who shot two individuals that the negligence of the university psychiatrist who treated him was the proximate cause of his criminal acts and subsequent injuries). Or the student may claim that disclosure by a counselor of his psychiatric condition constitutes "malpractice" (see *Jarzynka v. St. Thomas University School of Law,* 310 F. Supp. 2d 1256 (S.D. Fla. 2004), in which the court rejected the plaintiff's malpractice claim because the counselor was not a mental health therapist).

Federal and state disability discrimination laws require colleges and universities, as places of public accommodation, to provide appropriate accommodations for otherwise qualified students with disabilities. But if a student's misconduct is related to the nature of the disability, and the conduct would otherwise violate the college's code of student conduct, administrators must face a difficult choice. This issue was addressed squarely in a case that has implications for higher education even though it involves a private elementary school. In *Bercovitch v. Baldwin School,* 133 F.3d 141 (1st Cir. 1998), a student with attention deficit disorder (ADD) performed acceptably in his studies, but consistently violated the school's code of conduct. The school made numerous

---

[3]Cases and authorities are collected in J. M. Zitter, Annot., "Physical or Mental Illness as Basis of Dismissal of Student from School, College or University," 17 A.L.R.4th 519.

attempts to accommodate his disruptive behavior even before it was aware of the diagnosis of ADD. After the diagnosis and medication, the student's disruptive behavior continued, and the school suspended the student. The parents brought a claim under Title III of the Americans With Disabilities Act. Although a trial court ruled that the school had to reinstate the student and make greater efforts to accommodate him, the appellate court disagreed. The student was not otherwise qualified for ADA purposes if he could not comply with the school's code of conduct, said the court. Furthermore, the student's disorder did not qualify for protection under the ADA because it did not substantially limit his ability to learn. (The court explained that this private school was not subject to the Individuals With Disabilities Education Act (IDEA) (20 U.S.C. § 1400 *et seq.*), as are public schools, and had no obligation to provide an individualized educational plan or to provide accommodations that modified its disciplinary code or its academic programs.)[4]

But if a court determines that following the rules is an essential function of being a student, then the student may not be "otherwise qualified" and thus unprotected by disability discrimination law. A federal trial court rejected the claim of a graduate student that the university should have considered his learning disability when enforcing its code of conduct against him. In *Childress v. Virginia Commonwealth University,* 5 F. Supp. 2d 384 (E.D. Va. 1998), the plaintiff was charged with multiple violations of the honor code when he committed several acts of plagiarism. The honor board found him guilty of the violations and recommended his expulsion. The student appealed, but his appeal was denied and he was expelled from the university. He filed discrimination claims under the Americans With Disabilities Act and Section 504 of the Rehabilitation Act.

The court assumed without deciding that the plaintiff had a learning disability that qualified for protection under the ADA and Section 504. The court then turned to the issue of whether the plaintiff was a qualified individual with a disability—whether he could perform the essential functions of a graduate student. The court determined that complying with the honor code was an essential function of being a graduate student. Furthermore, said the court, the honor board had taken the plaintiff's disability into consideration when determining whether he had violated the honor code, thus complying with the ADA's requirement that an individualized determination be made as to whether the individual is qualified. (For another case decided in a similar fashion, see *El Kouni v. Trustees of Boston University,* 169 F. Supp. 2d 1 (D. Mass. 2001).)

Students with disabilities who challenge disciplinary sanctions as discriminatory must establish that the college was aware of the student's disability and that the discipline resulted from that knowledge. In *Rosenthal v. Webster*

---

[4]On the other hand, if a student has a record of otherwise acceptable academic performance and behavior, and the alleged code violation is not a serious one, a court may require the school to take the disability into consideration when determining whether to discipline the student. In *Thomas v. Davidson Academy,* 846 F. Supp. 611 (M.D. Tenn. 1994), a federal trial court enjoined a private secondary school from expelling a student with an autoimmune disorder for misconduct related to an injury she incurred at school. The court ruled that the student's prior good academic and disciplinary record established that she was "otherwise qualified," and that her expulsion was an ADA violation.

University, 2000 U.S. App. LEXIS 23733 (8th Cir. 2000) (unpublished), a federal appellate court rejected a student's ADA and Rehabilitation Act claims that the university discriminated against him on the basis of his bipolar disorder by suspending him. The court found that the university was not aware of his disability before it suspended him, but took that action because the plaintiff had carried a gun onto campus and had threatened to use it.

These cases suggest that the courts will follow the analysis used by the U.S. Supreme Court in the *Sutton* trilogy (see Section 5.2.5). If other courts rule that the ability to comply with a reasonable code of conduct is an "essential function" of being a student, then students whose misconduct is linked to their disability will have considerable difficulty demonstrating that they should be exempt from that code of conduct under the ADA or Section 504.

Given the potential for constitutional claims at public institutions and discrimination and contract claims at all institutions, administrators who are considering disciplinary action against a student with a mental or emotional disorder should provide due process protections (see Section 9.4.2). If the student has violated the institution's code of conduct and is competent to participate in the hearing, some experts recommend subjecting the student to the same disciplinary proceedings that a student without a mental or emotional impairment would receive (see, for example, Gary Pavela, *The Dismissal of Students with Mental Disorders* (College Administration Publications, 1985)). If the student is a danger to himself/herself or others, summary suspension may be appropriate, but postsuspension due process or contractual protections should be provided if possible. (For an analysis of the issues facing public colleges and universities in these circumstances, and recommended actions, see Jeanette DiScala, Steven G. Olswang, & Carol S. Niccolls, "College and University Responses to the Emotionally or Mentally Impaired Student," 19 *J. Coll. & Univ. Law* 17 (1992).)

Sec. 9.3. Grades, Credits, and Degrees

9.3.1. Overview. Fewer legal restrictions pertain to an institution's application of academic standards to students than to its application of behavioral standards. Courts are more deferential to academia when evaluation of academic work is the issue, believing that such evaluation resides in the expertise of the faculty rather than the court.

Despite the fact that judicial review of academic judgments is more deferential than judicial review of discipline for student misconduct, courts hold institutions to their rules, policies, and procedures, and examine the foundations for the academic decision to determine whether it is based on academic standards. Faculty and administrators should ensure that they can document the basis for their academic judgments, that they follow institutional rules and procedures, and that the student is fully informed of his or her rights with respect to opportunities for appealing the decision.

9.3.2. Awarding of grades and degrees.
When a student alleges that a grade has been awarded improperly or a degree has been denied unfairly, the

courts must determine whether the defendant's action reflected the application of academic judgment or an arbitrary or unfair application of institutional policy. In one leading case, *Connelly v. University of Vermont*, 244 F. Supp. 156 (D. Vt. 1965), a medical student challenged his dismissal from medical school. He had failed the pediatrics-obstetrics course and was excluded, under a College of Medicine rule, for having failed 25 percent or more of his major third-year courses. The court described its role, and the institution's legal obligation, in such cases as follows:

> Where a medical student has been dismissed for a failure to attain a proper standard of scholarship, two questions may be involved; the first is, was the student in fact delinquent in his studies or unfit for the practice of medicine? The second question is, were the school authorities motivated by malice or bad faith in dismissing the student, or did they act arbitrarily or capriciously? In general, the first question is not a matter for judicial review. However, a student dismissal motivated by bad faith, arbitrariness, or capriciousness may be actionable. . . .
>
> This rule has been stated in a variety of ways by a number of courts. It has been said that courts do not interfere with the management of a school's internal affairs unless "there has been a manifest abuse of discretion or where [the school officials'] action has been arbitrary or unlawful" . . . or unless the school authorities have acted "arbitrarily or capriciously" . . . or unless they have abused their discretion . . . or acted in "bad faith" [citations omitted].
>
> The effect of these decisions is to give the school authorities absolute discretion in determining whether a student has been delinquent in his studies, and to place the burden on the student of showing that his dismissal was motivated by arbitrariness, capriciousness, or bad faith. The reason for this rule is that, in matters of scholarship, the school authorities are uniquely qualified by training and experience to judge the qualifications of a student, and efficiency of instruction depends in no small degree upon the school's faculty's freedom from interference from other noneducational tribunals. It is only when the school authorities abuse this discretion that a court may interfere with their decision to dismiss a student [244 F. Supp. at 159–60].

The plaintiff had alleged that his instructor decided before completion of the course to fail him regardless of the quality of his work. The court held that these allegations met its requirements for judicial review. They therefore stated a cause of action, which if proven at trial would justify the entry of judgment against the college.

In 1975, a federal appeals court issued an important reaffirmation of the principles underlying the *Connelly* case. *Gaspar v. Bruton*, 513 F.2d 843 (10th Cir. 1975), concerned a nursing student who had been dismissed for deficient performance in clinical training. In rejecting the student's suit against the school, the court held that:

> [t]he courts are not equipped to review academic records based upon academic standards within the particular knowledge, experience, and expertise of academicians. Thus, when presented with a challenge that the school authorities

suspended or dismissed a student for failure re: academic standards, the court may grant relief, as a practical matter, only in those cases where the student presents positive evidence of ill will or bad motive [513 F.2d at 850–51].

The U.S. Supreme Court has twice addressed the subject of the standard of review of academic judgments. It first considered this subject briefly in *Board of Curators of the University of Missouri v. Horowitz,* 435 U.S. 78 (1978) (discussed in Section 9.4.3). A dismissed medical student claimed that the school applied stricter standards to her because of her sex, religion, and physical appearance. Referring particularly to *Gaspar v. Bruton,* the Court rejected the claim in language inhospitable to substantive judicial review of academic decisions:

> A number of lower courts have implied in dictum that academic dismissals from state institutions can be enjoined if "shown to be clearly arbitrary or capricious." . . . Courts are particularly ill equipped to evaluate academic performance. The factors discussed . . . with respect to procedural due process [see Section 9.4.3] speak *a fortiori* here and warn against any such judicial intrusion into academic decision making [435 U.S. at 91–92].

In a case in which the Court relied heavily on *Horowitz,* a student filed a substantive due process challenge to his academic dismissal from medical school. The student, whose entire record of academic performance in medical school was mediocre, asserted that the school's refusal to allow him to retake the National Board of Medical Examiners examination violated his constitutional rights because other students had been allowed to retake the exam. In *Regents of the University of Michigan v. Ewing,* 474 U.S. 214 (1985), the Court assumed without deciding the issue that Ewing had a property interest in continued enrollment in medical school. The Court noted that it was not the school's procedures that were under review—the question was "whether the record compels the conclusion that the University acted arbitrarily in dropping Ewing from the Inteflex program without permitting a reexamination" (474 U.S. at 225). The court then stated:

> Ewing's claim, therefore, must be that the University misjudged his fitness to remain a student in the Inteflex program. The record unmistakably demonstrates, however, that the faculty's decision was made conscientiously and with careful deliberation, based on an evaluation of the entirety of Ewing's academic career [474 U.S. at 225].

Citing *Horowitz,* the Court emphasized:

> When judges are asked to review the substance of a genuinely academic decision, such as this one, they should show great respect for the faculty's professional judgment. Plainly, they may not override it unless it is such a substantial departure from accepted academic norms as to demonstrate that the person or committee responsible did not actually exercise professional judgment [474 U.S. at 225].

Citing *Keyishian* (discussed in Section 7.1.1), the Court reminded the parties that concerns about institutional academic freedom also limited the nature of judicial review of substantive academic judgments.

Although the result in *Ewing* represents the standard to be used by lower courts, the Court's willingness to assume the existence of a property or liberty interest is questionable in light of a subsequent Supreme Court ruling. In *Siegert v. Gilley*, 500 U.S. 226 (1991), the Court ruled that when defendants who are state officials or state agencies raise a defense of qualified immunity (see Section 4.7.4), federal courts must determine whether a property or liberty interest was "clearly established" at the time the defendant acted. Applying *Siegert*, the Supreme Court of Hawaii in *Soong v. University of Hawaii*, 825 P.2d 1060 (Haw. 1992), ruled that a student had no clearly established substantive constitutional right to continued enrollment in an academic program.

The *Ewing* case has guided courts in subsequent challenges to academic dismissals of students. In *Frabotta v. Meridia Huron Hospital School*, 657 N.E.2d 816 (Ohio Ct. App. 1995), a nursing student who was dismissed six days prior to graduation challenged her dismissal as arbitrary and capricious, and a violation of her due process and equal protection guarantees. The court, citing *Ewing*, stated:

> Courts should not intervene in academic decision-making where a student is dismissed unless the dismissal is clearly shown to be arbitrary and capricious. . . . In this case, Frabotta was dismissed because of her failing performance in the clinical portion of her Nursing 303 class. . . . Thus, there is no dispute that Frabotta's dismissal was clearly an academic decision. It being an academic decision, Frabotta had the burden of proving that the decision was arbitrary and capricious [657 N.E.2d at 819].

Simply because the student believed she deserved a second chance, or an additional opportunity to improve her performance, did not render the school's actions either arbitrary or capricious, according to the court, nor was the school's refusal to give her additional opportunities to improve her performance a denial of due process. The student had been warned of her deficiencies, said the court; even though the school cut short her opportunity to improve her performance, that was a subjective, academic judgment that the court could not overturn absent clear evidence of bad faith on the part of the instructor.[5]

A Texas appellate court did find considerable evidence of bad faith on the part of faculty members who voted to dismiss a doctoral student on purported academic grounds. In *Alcorn v. Vaksman*, 877 S.W.2d 390 (Tex. Ct. App. 1994), an *en banc* court upheld the findings of a trial court that several faculty members had voted to dismiss Vaksman from the doctoral program at the University of Houston not because of poor academic performance but because of his unpopular ideas and his tendency to publicize those ideas. Vaksman had never been informed that his academic performance was sufficiently poor to justify

---

[5]Although *Ewing* may protect an institution against constitutional challenges if a student is dismissed just prior to graduation, one student used contract law to receive damages for forgone income when he was dismissed for academic reasons just prior to graduation. See *Sharik v. Southeastern University of the Health Sciences*, 780 So. 2d 136 (Fla. Dist. Ct. App. 2000), *rev. dismissed*, 822 So. 2d 1290 (Fla. 2002), discussed in Section 8.1.3.

any academic sanction, and he had not been given an opportunity to discuss the alleged academic deficiencies with the graduate committee that recommended his dismissal. In addition to ordering the university to reinstate Vaksman to the doctoral program in history and pay him $32,500 in actual damages, the trial judge ordered the two faculty members, the department chair, and a member of the graduate committee, who voted to dismiss Vaksman, to pay $10,000 each toward the damage award. The appellate court held that, although the university's officers were immune from liability for money damages in their official capacities, the actions of the two faculty members, whose conduct "intentionally inflicted emotional distress" upon Vaksman, were not taken in good faith and, thus, the award of individual judgments against the two faculty members was appropriate.

Courts may resolve legal questions concerning the award of grades, credits, or degrees not only by applying standards of arbitrariness or bad faith but also by applying the terms of the student-institution contract (Section 8.1.3). A 1979 Kentucky case, *Lexington Theological Seminary v. Vance,* 596 S.W.2d 11 (Ky. Ct. App. 1979), illustrates the deference that may be accorded postsecondary institutions—especially church-related institutions—in identifying and construing the contract. The case also illustrates the problems that may arise when institutions attempt to withhold academic recognition from students because of their homosexuality.

The Lexington Theological Seminary, a seminary training ministers for the Disciples of Christ and other denominations, had denied Vance, a student who had successfully completed all his academic requirements, a Master of Divinity degree because of his admitted homosexuality. Three years after he first enrolled, he advised the dean of the school and the president of the seminary of his homosexuality. In January 1976, the student was informed that his degree candidacy would be deferred until he completed one additional course. In May 1976, after he had successfully completed the course, the faculty voted to grant the Master of Divinity degree. The seminary's executive committee, however, voted not to approve the faculty recommendation, and the board of trustees subsequently ratified the committee's decision. The student brought suit, seeking conferral of the degree.[6]

The trial court dealt with the suit as a contract case and held that the seminary had breached its contract with the plaintiff student. The Kentucky Court of Appeals, although it overruled the trial court, also agreed to apply contract principles to the case: "The terms and conditions for graduation from a private college or university are those offered by the publications of the college at the time of enrollment and, as such, have some of the characteristics of a contract."

The appellate court relied on various phrases from the seminary's catalog—such as "Christian ministry," "gospel transmitted through the Bible," "servants of the Gospel," "fundamental character," and "display traits of character and personality which indicate probable effectiveness in the Christian ministry"—that it

---

[6]See generally Annot., "Student's Right to Compel School Officials to Issue Degree, Diploma, or the Like," 11 A.L.R.4th 1182.

determined to be contract terms. It held that these terms created "reasonably clear standards" and interpreted them to permit the seminary to bar a homosexual student from receiving a degree. The court found that the seminary, being a religious institution preparing ministers to preach the gospel, had "a most compelling interest" in allowing only "persons possessing character of the highest Christian ideals" to graduate and that it had exercised sound discretion in denying the degree.

The court's reasoning sparked a strong dissenting opinion, which examined not only the language in the seminary catalog but also the conduct of the seminary's dean, president, and faculty. To the dissenting judge, "Since neither the dean, the president, nor the faculty understood the catalogue to clearly exclude homosexuals, their view certainly cloud[ed] any contrary meaning." The dissent also argued that the language used in the catalog was not sufficiently clear: "In the future, the board should consider revising the catalogue to be more explicit on what is meant by 'fundamental character.' The board might also make it clear that applications for degree candidacy will not only be 'evaluated by the faculty' but will also be reviewed by the board."

The *Lexington Theological Seminary* case illustrates that courts may resolve questions of academic credits or degrees by viewing the school catalog as a contract binding on both student and institution. The majority opinion also illustrates the flexibility that courts may accord postsecondary institutions in drafting and interpreting this contract, and the special deference that may be accorded church-related institutions in enforcing terms dealing with morality. The dissent in this case, however, deserves as much attention as the majority opinion. It cautions administrators against construing ambiguous catalog or policy language in a way that is inconsistent with their prior actions (see Section 1.4.2.3) and illustrates the potential for ambiguity that resides in general terms such as "fundamental character." Even if administrators could confidently expect broad deference from the courts, the dissent's cautions are still valuable as suggestions for how institutions can do better, of their own accord rather than through judicial compulsion, in ordering their own internal affairs. Statements in the catalog reserving the institution's right to make changes in programs, graduation requirements, or grading policy provide important protections in breach of contract claims (see, for example, *Bender v. Alderson-Broaddus College*, 575 S.E.2d 112 (W. Va. 2002), in which the court rejected a nursing student's claim that the college's decision to change its grading policy was arbitrary and capricious).

An example of a court's refusal to defer to a college's interpretation of its catalog and policy documents is *Russell v. Salve Regina College*, 890 F.2d 484 (1st Cir. 1989). Sharon Russell had been asked to withdraw from the nursing program at the college because the administrators believed her obesity was unsatisfactory for a nursing student. Russell's academic performance in all but one course was satisfactory or better; the instructor in one clinical course gave her a failing grade, which the jury found was related to her weight, not to her performance. Although the nursing program's rules specified that failing a clinical course would result in expulsion, the college promised Russell that she could remain in the program if she would sign a contract promising to lose weight on a regular basis. She did so, and attended Weight Watchers during that year, but did not lose weight. At the end of her junior year, Russell was asked to withdraw from Salve Regina, and she transferred to a nursing program at another college, where she was required to repeat her junior year because of a two-year residency requirement. She completed her nursing degree, but in five years rather than four.

Although the trial judge dismissed her tort claims of intentional infliction of emotional distress and invasion of privacy (stemming from administrators' conduct regarding her obesity), the contract claim had been submitted to the jury, which had found for Russell and had awarded her approximately $144,000. On appeal, the court discussed the terms of the contract:

> From the various catalogs, manuals, handbooks, etc., that form the contract between student and institution, the district court, in its jury charge, boiled the agreement between the parties down to one in which Russell on the one hand was required to abide by disciplinary rules, pay tuition, and maintain good academic standing, and the College on the other hand was required to provide her with an education until graduation. The court informed the jury that the agreement was modified by the "contract" the parties signed during Russell's junior year. The jury was told that, if Russell "substantially performed" her side of the bargain, the College's actions constituted a breach [890 F.2d at 488].

The college had objected to the trial court's use of commercial contract principles of substantial performance rather than using a more deferential approach, such as was used in *Slaughter v. Brigham Young University* (discussed in Sections 9.2.3 & 9.4.4). But the appellate court disagreed, noting that the college's actions were based not on academic judgments but on a belief that the student's weight was inappropriate, despite the fact that the college knew of the student's obesity when it admitted her to both the college and the nursing program:

> Under the circumstances, the "unique" position of the College as educator becomes less compelling. As a result, the reasons against applying the substantial performance standard to this aspect of the student-college relationship also become less compelling. Thus, Salve Regina's contention that a court cannot use the substantial performance standard to compel an institution to graduate a student merely because the student has completed 124 out of 128 credits, while correct, is inapposite. The court may step in where, as here, full performance by the student has been hindered by some form of impermissible action [890 F.2d at 489].

Unlike the student in the *Lexington Theological Seminary* case, Russell was not asking the court to award her a degree; she was asking for contract damages, which included one year of forgone income (while she attended the other college for the extra year). The appellate court found that this portion of the award, $25,000, was appropriate.[7]

---

[7]The U.S. Supreme Court subsequently reversed and remanded the appellate court's decision (499 U.S. 255 (1991)); on remand the appellate court reinstated its prior judgment and opinion (938 F.2d 315 (1st Cir. 1991)).

Although infrequent, challenges to grades or examination results have been brought by students. For example, in *Olsson v. Board of Higher Education of the City of New York,* 402 N.E.2d 1150 (N.Y. 1980), a student had not passed a comprehensive examination and therefore had not been awarded the M.A. degree for which he had been working. He claimed that his professor had misled him about the required passing grade on the examination. The professor had meant to say that a student must score three out of a possible five points on four of the five questions; instead, the professor said that a student must pass three of five questions. The student invoked the "estoppel" doctrine—the doctrine that justifiable reliance on a statement or promise estops the other from contradicting it if the reliance led directly to a detriment or injustice to the promisee. He argued that (1) he had justifiably relied on the professor's statement in budgeting both his study and test time, (2) he had achieved the grade the professor had stated was necessary, and (3) injustice would result if the university was not estopped from denying the degree.

The trial court and the intermediate appellate court both accepted the student's argument. The state's highest appellate court, however, did not. Deferring to the academic judgment of the institution, and emphasizing that the institution had offered the student an opportunity to retake the exam, the court refused to grant a "degree by estoppel." Although conceding that principles of apparent authority and agency law would be relevant in a noneducational context, the court stated that:

> such hornbook rules cannot be applied mechanically where the "principal" is an educational institution and the result would be to override a determination concerning a student's academic qualifications. Because such determinations rest in most cases upon the subjective professional judgment of trained educators, the courts have quite properly exercised the utmost restraint in applying traditional legal rules to disputes within the academic community. . . .
>
> This judicial reluctance to intervene in controversies involving academic standards is founded upon sound considerations of public policy. When an educational institution issues a diploma to one of its students, it is, in effect, certifying to society that the student possesses all of the knowledge and skills that are required by his chosen discipline. In order for society to be able to have complete confidence in the credentials dispensed by academic institutions, however, it is essential that the decisions surrounding the issuance of these credentials be left to the sound judgment of the professional educators who monitor the progress of their students on a regular basis. Indeed, the value of these credentials from the point of view of society would be seriously undermined if the courts were to abandon their longstanding practice of restraint in this area and instead began to utilize traditional equitable estoppel principles as a basis for requiring institutions to confer diplomas upon those who have been deemed to be unqualified [402 N.E.2d at 1152–53].

Although the court refused to apply the estoppel doctrine to the particular facts of this case, it indicated that in other, more extreme, circumstances estoppel could apply to problems concerning grading and other academic judgments. The court compared Olsson's situation to that of the plaintiff in *Blank v. Board of Higher Education of the City of New York,* 273 N.Y.S.2d 796 (see Section 3.2.2), in which the student had completed all academic requirements for his bachelor's degree but had not spent his final term "in residence." The student demonstrated reliance on the incorrect advice of several advisers and faculty members, and had failed only to satisfy a technical requirement rather than an academic one. The court explained:

> The outstanding feature which differentiates *Blank* from the instant case is the unavoidable fact that in *Blank* the student unquestionably had fulfilled the academic requirements for the credential he sought. Unlike the student here, the student in *Blank* had demonstrated his competence in the subject matter to the satisfaction of his professors. Thus, there could be no public policy objection to [the court's] decision to award a "diploma by estoppel" [402 N.E.2d at 1154].[8]

The *Olsson* case thus provides both an extensive justification of "academic deference"—that is, judicial deference to an educational institution's academic judgments—and an extensive analysis of the circumstances in which courts, rather than deferring, should invoke estoppel principles to protect students challenging academic decisions. Synthesizing its analysis, the court concluded:

> It must be stressed that the judicial awarding of an academic diploma is an extreme remedy which should be reserved for the most egregious of circumstances. In light of the serious policy considerations which militate against judicial intervention in academic disputes, the courts should shun the "diploma by estoppel" doctrine whenever there is some question as to whether the student seeking relief has actually demonstrated his competence in accordance with the standards devised by the appropriate school authorities. Additionally, the courts should be particularly cautious in applying the doctrine in cases such as this, where a less drastic remedy, such as retesting, may be employed without seriously disrupting the student's academic or professional career [402 N.E.2d at 1154].

A challenge to grades in two law school courses provided the New York courts with an opportunity to address another issue similar to that in *Olsson*—the standard of review to be used when students challenge particular grades. In *Susan M v. New York Law School,* 544 N.Y.S.2d 829 (N.Y. App. Div. 1989), *reversed,* 556 N.E.2d 1104 (N.Y. 1990), a law student dismissed for inadequate academic performance sought judicial review of her grades in her constitutional law and corporations courses. The student claimed that she had received poor grades because of errors made by the professors in both courses. In the constitutional law

---

[8]Another case in which the court ordered the award of a degree is *Kantor v. Schmidt,* 423 N.Y.S.2d 208 (N.Y. App. Div. 1979), a *mandamus* proceeding under New York law. The State University of New York at Stony Brook had withheld the degree because the student had not made sufficient progress, within established time limits, toward completion of the degree. A New York trial court ordered the defendant to award a B.A. degree to the student because the university had not complied with the state commissioner of education's regulations on student progress and informing students of progress. The appellate court affirmed but, on reargument, vacated its decision and dismissed the appeal as moot (432 N.Y.S.2d 156 (1980)).

course, she alleged, the professor gave incorrect instructions on whether the exam was open book; in the corporations course, the professor evaluated a correct answer as incorrect. The law school asserted that these allegations were beyond judicial review because they were a matter of professional discretion.

Although Susan M's claims were dismissed by the trial court, the intermediate appellate court disagreed with the law school's characterization of both grade disputes as beyond judicial review. It agreed that the dispute over the constitutional law examination was "precisely the type of professional, educational judgment the courts will not review" (544 N.Y.S.2d at 830); but the student's claim regarding her answer in the corporations exam, for which she received no credit, was a different matter. The court ruled that the student's allegation that the professor's decision had been arbitrary and capricious required the court to determine whether the professor's justification for giving the student no credit for one of her answers was "rational." The court remanded this issue to the law school for further consideration of petitioner's grade in the corporations course. The law school appealed, and the state's highest court unanimously reversed the appellate division's holding, reinstating the outcome in the trial court.

The court strongly endorsed the academic deference argument made by the law school, stating in the opinion's first paragraph: "Because [the plaintiff's] allegations are directed at the pedagogical evaluation of her test grades, a determination best left to educators rather than the courts, we conclude that her petition does not state a judicially cognizable claim" (556 N.E.2d at 1105). After reviewing the outcomes in earlier challenges to the academic determinations of colleges and universities, the state's highest court stated:

> As a general rule, judicial review of grading disputes would inappropriately involve the courts in the very core of academic and educational decision making. Moreover, to so involve the courts in assessing the propriety of particular grades would promote litigation by countless unsuccessful students and thus undermine the credibility of the academic determinations of educational institutions. We conclude, therefore, that, in the absence of demonstrated bad faith, arbitrariness, capriciousness, irrationality or a constitutional or statutory violation, a student's challenge to a particular grade or other academic determination relating to a genuine substantive evaluation of the student's academic capabilities, is beyond the scope of judicial review [556 N.E.2d at 1107].

Concluding that the plaintiff's claims concerned substantive evaluation of her academic performance, the court refused to review them.

Students' attempts to challenge course requirements have also met with judicial rejection. In *Altschuler v. University of Pennsylvania Law School,* 1997 U.S. Dist. LEXIS 3248 (S.D.N.Y. March 21, 1997), *affirmed without opinion,* 201 F.3d 430 (3d Cir. 1999), for example, a law student who had just graduated challenged a failing grade he received in his first year. The grade resulted from the plaintiff's refusal to argue a "mock" case in a legal writing class on the grounds of moral and ethical objections. The plaintiff claimed that the professor "promised" him that he could argue and brief the opposite side but later retracted her promise. When the plaintiff refused to argue the assigned side, he received a failing grade in the course. The court dismissed all contract and tort claims based on the failing grade, saying that the professor's "breach of promise" was an academic decision, which had been reviewed by a faculty committee and found to be appropriate. (For a more recent and successful challenge to a course requirement on first amendment grounds, see the *Axson-Flynn* case, discussed in Section 8.1.4.)

In *Disesa v. St. Louis Community College,* 79 F.3d 92 (8th Cir. 1996), the court rejected a student's challenge to a particular grade based on alleged "administrative deficiencies" in the testing process, including typographical errors in the materials and test questions, testing on materials not covered in class, an inability to review quizzes after they were graded, and arbitrary implementation of a class policy prohibiting erasure marks. Despite the plaintiff's argument that these were not "academic" decisions per se, the court disagreed and deferred to the college's actions.

Courts also have refused to review certain challenges to grades on the basis that the claims were "frivolous." (See, for example, *Banks v. Dominican College,* 35 Cal. App. 4th 1545 (1995) (granting $18,000 in sanctions against the plaintiff); and *Dilworth v. Dallas Community College Dist.,* 81 F.3d 616 (5th Cir. 1996) (finding there was no controversy sufficient to rise to the level of federal jurisdiction).) But in *Sylvester v. Texas Southern University,* 957 F. Supp. 944 (S.D. Tex. 1997), a federal district court ordered a law student's grade changed to a "Pass" from a D because the law school had not followed its procedures for adjudicating a grade dispute.

The law school's rules provided that, if a student appealed a grade to the Academic Standing Committee, the committee was required to review the disputed grade. Neither the professor who gave the disputed grade nor the Academic Standing Committee complied with university regulations. The court criticized the institution and the professor for flouting the institution's own policies and procedures: "Between active manipulation and sullen intransigence, the faculty, embodying arbitrary government, have mistreated a student confided to their charge. This violates their duty to conduct the public's business in a rationally purposeful manner" (957 F. Supp. at 947).

The type of "bad faith" referred to in *Susan M* and its progeny is often alleged in the context of a retaliation claim. In *Ross v. Saint Augustine's College,* 103 F.3d 338 (4th Cir. 1996), a federal appeals court upheld a jury award of $180,000 against a college for harassing an honors student who testified on behalf of a professor in a reverse discrimination suit against the institution. The court held that Leslie Ross "experienced a sudden reversal of fortune at Saint Augustine's College" when her grade point average fell from 3.69/4.0 to 2.2/4.0. The administration called a sudden student body meeting to impeach Ross as class president, and ultimately Ross was not able to graduate. Although the case involved only monetary damages, there is no indication that courts would afford deference to the academic decisions made under those circumstances had the student challenged the college's failure to award her a degree. (For additional cases in which students challenged specific course grades using retaliation theories, see *Davis v. Goode*, 995 F. Supp. 82 (E.D.N.Y. 1998) (court denied college's motion for summary judgment); and *Mostaghim v. Fashion Institute of Technology*, 2002 U.S. Dist. LEXIS 10968 (S.D.N.Y. 2002), *affirmed*, 57 Fed. Appx. 497 (2d Cir. 2003) (court rejected student's claim that course requirement to design women's wear rather than men's wear constituted a Title IX violation, and that his subsequent grade of C and suspension from the institution were a form of retaliation under Title IX).)

(For a summary of legal challenges to academic judgments and a review of the *Susan M* case, see Note, "Student Challenges to Grades and Academic Dismissals: Are They Losing Battles?" 18 *J. Coll. & Univ. Law* 577 (1992). See also F. Faulkner, "Judicial Deference to University Decisions Not to Grant Degrees, Certificates, and Credit—The Fiduciary Alternative," 40 *Syracuse L. Rev.* 837 (1990); and T. A. Schweitzer, "'Academic Challenge' Cases: Should Judicial Review Extend to Academic Evaluations of Students?" 41 *Am. U. L. Rev.* 267 (1992). *Susan M* is also humorously reviewed in verse by R. E. Rains in 40 *J. Legal Educ.* 485 (1990), and 43 *J. Legal Educ.* 149 (1993).)

Although students apparently may not obtain academic credentials through litigation, they occasionally obtain them fraudulently, either by claiming degrees from "diploma mills" or by altering transcripts to make it appear that they completed a degree. (For analysis of this issue, see J. Van Tol, "Detecting, Deterring and Punishing the Use of Fraudulent Academic Credentials: A Play in Two Acts," 29 *Santa Clara L. Rev.* 1 (1990).)

Finally, a college or university may decide not to award a degree, even if the student has completed all academic requirements satisfactorily, because the student has violated the institution's disciplinary code. (For cases rejecting students' challenges to the denial of their degrees on these grounds, see *Harwood v. Johns Hopkins University*, 747 A.2d 205 (Ct. App. Md. 2000), discussed in Section 8.1.3; and *Dinu v. Harvard College*, 56 F. Supp. 2d 129 (D. Mass. 1999).)

9.3.3. Degree revocation.

Generally, both public and private colleges and universities have authority to revoke improperly awarded degrees when good cause for doing so, such as discovery of fraud or misrepresentation, is shown.[9] Public institutions must afford the degree recipient notice and an opportunity for a hearing before making a decision on whether to revoke a degree, following due process guidelines (see Section 9.4.2). Private institutions, although generally not subject to constitutional requirements, are subject to contract law, and generally must use procedures that will protect the degree recipient from potentially arbitrary or capricious conduct by the institution (see Section 9.4.4).

Degree revocations by both public and private institutions have been challenged in lawsuits. In *Waliga v. Board of Trustees of Kent State University*, 488 N.E.2d 850 (Ohio 1986), the Ohio Supreme Court upheld the university's right to rescind a degree. Two individuals had been awarded baccalaureate degrees, one in 1966 and one in 1967, from Kent State University. University officials

---

[9]Cases and authorities are collected in Lori J. Henkel, Annot., "College's Power to Revoke Degree," 57 A.L.R.4th 1243.

discovered, more than ten years later, discrepancies such as credits granted for courses the students never took, and grades on official records different from those reported by course professors. The university rescinded the degrees on the grounds that the students had not completed the appropriate number of credits for graduation.

The students sought a declaratory judgment on the university's power to rescind a degree. The Ohio Supreme Court found such power under two theories. First, the court interpreted Ohio law as permitting any action necessary for operating the state university unless such action was expressly prohibited by statute. As long as a fair hearing had been held, the university had the power to rescind a degree procured by fraud. Second, the court addressed the significance of the public's confidence in the integrity of degrees awarded by colleges and universities:

> Academic degrees are a university's certification to the world at large of the recipient's educational achievement and the fulfillment of the institution's standards. To hold that a university may never withdraw a degree, effectively requires the university to continue making a false certification to the public at large of the accomplishment of persons who in fact lack the very qualifications that are certified [488 N.E.2d at 852].

Just as a university has the power to refuse to confer a degree if a student does not complete the requirements for graduation, it also has the power, the court ruled, to rescind a degree awarded to a student who did not complete those requirements.

Given an institution's power to rescind a degree, what procedural protections must the institution give the student? If the institution is public, the Fourteenth Amendment's due process clause may require certain protections, particularly if the court finds a property interest in the student's possession of the degree. In *Crook v. Baker*, 813 F.2d 88 (6th Cir. 1987), a federal appeals court addressed this issue.

After awarding Crook an M.A. in geology, the University of Michigan determined that the data he had used in his master's thesis were fabricated, and notified him that a hearing would be held to determine whether the degree should be revoked. Crook filed a complaint in federal court, asserting that the university lacked the power to rescind a degree and, if such power were present, that the procedures used by the university violated his due process rights because they did not permit him to cross-examine witnesses.

The court first considered whether the university had the power to rescind the degree. Summarizing the opinion in *Waliga* at some length, the court determined that "there is nothing in Michigan constitutional, statutory or case law that indicates that the Regents do not have the power to rescind the grant of a degree" (813 F.2d at 92), and noted that the state constitution gave the university significant independence in educational matters.

Turning to the student's procedural claims, the court applied the teachings of *Goss v. Lopez* (Section 9.4.2) to evaluate the sufficiency of the procedural protections afforded Crook. Although the trial court had ruled that the hearing violated Crook's right to due process, the appellate court found that the university had given Crook sufficient notice of the charges against him and that the hearing—at which he was permitted to have counsel present, to present witnesses in his behalf, and to respond to the charges against him—complied with the requirements of *Goss.* The appellate court characterized the hearing as "informal," in that hearing panel members asked questions and neither the university nor Crook was permitted to ask questions of the witnesses. Citing its earlier opinion in *Frumkin v. Board of Trustees* (see Section 6.7.2.3), the court found that Crook had no procedural due process right to have his attorney examine and cross-examine witnesses, and that the procedures provided by the university were sufficient for due process purposes.

Crook had also claimed violation of his substantive due process rights, alleging no rational basis for the rescission of his degree. Citing *Ewing* (see Section 9.3.1), the court found that the hearing committee had exercised professional judgment and that the committee's determination that Crook's data were fabricated was neither arbitrary nor capricious.

Waliga and *Crook* establish the power of a public institution to rescind a degree, and *Crook* discusses the type of procedural protection required to meet constitutional due process standards. When private institutions are involved, however, constitutional requirements typically do not apply. Unless the institution can meet the "state action" test (see Section 1.5.2), constitutional protections are not available to the student (*Imperiale v. Hahnemann University,* 966 F.2d 125 (3d Cir. 1992)).

In a lawsuit filed against Claremont University Center by a student whose doctoral degree was revoked on the grounds that his dissertation was plagiarized, a California appellate court analyzed the university's actions under a deferential standard of review—whether or not the university abused its discretion. In *Abalkhail v. Claremont University Center,* 2d Civ. No. B014012 (Cal. Ct. App. 1986), the court detailed the procedures used to determine whether the degree should be revoked. The university had received a report that portions of the dissertation might have been plagiarized, and it appointed a committee of investigation to determine whether plagiarism had occurred and degree revocation was warranted.

After the committee concluded that plagiarism might have occurred, the graduate school dean informed Abalkhail that a hearing would be held and described the procedures that would be followed. Abalkhail did not receive a copy of the letter that instigated the investigation until the day of the hearing, but he was given the opportunity to respond to the charges against him and was asked if there were additional procedures necessary to give him a fair hearing. The hearing committee met again with Abalkhail to inform him of additional evidence against him and to permit him to respond to that evidence by a particular time. After the time for response had elapsed, the committee found that much of Abalkhail's dissertation was plagiarized and recommended that his degree be rescinded. The university did so, and Abalkhail filed a complaint, alleging deprivation of due process and fairness protections.

Applying the California common law doctrine of fair procedures required of nonprofit groups, the court ruled that Abalkhail was entitled to "the minimum requisites of procedural fairness" (2d Civ. No. B014012 at 15). These "minimum requisites" included notice of the charges and the probable consequences of a finding that the charges would be upheld, a fair opportunity to present his position, and a fair hearing. These had been provided to the plaintiff, according to the court.

(For analysis of *Waliga, Crook,* and *Abalkhail,* see B. Reams, Jr., "Revocation of Academic Degrees by Colleges and Universities," 14 *J. Coll. & Univ. Law* 283 (1987). For a case in which a court confirmed a public university's right to revoke a degree for criminal misconduct (embezzlement) but allowed breach of contract and other claims to go forward because of alleged procedural due process violations, see *Goodreau v. Rector and Visitors of the University of Virginia,* 116 F. Supp. 2d 694 (W.D. Va. 2000).)

Although institutions of higher education appear to have the authority to revoke degrees, the revocation must be an act of the same entity that has the authority to award the degree. In *Hand v. Matchett,* 957 F.2d 791 (10th Cir. 1992), a federal appellate court affirmed a federal trial court's award of summary judgment to a former student who challenged his degree revocation. The Board of Regents of New Mexico State University had not acted on the degree revocation, but had delegated that decision to the graduate dean and, when the student appealed the dean's decision, to the executive vice president. Although the university had developed a procedure that involved both faculty and external experts in the determination that the plaintiff's dissertation had been plagiarized, the court, interpreting New Mexico law, said that the board could not delegate its authority to revoke a degree to a subordinate individual or body.

9.3.4. *Sexual harassment of students by faculty members.*

Whether one is addressing students' sexual harassment complaints against faculty members, as in this Section, or students' sexual harassment complaints against other students (as in Section 8.1.5),[10] it is important to begin with a general understanding of what type of behaviors constitute sexual harassment.[11] The following definitions and examples will provide a foundation for this understanding.

In guidelines issued by the U.S. Department of Education, sexual harassment is defined as "unwelcome [verbal, nonverbal, or physical] conduct of a sexual nature" ("Revised Sexual Harassment Guidance: Harassment of Students by School Employees, Other Students, or Third Parties," Part II, (January 19, 2001), available at http://www.ed.gov/offices/OCR/archives/index.html). In two studies by the American Association of University Women (AAUW), sexual harassment is defined as "unwanted and unwelcome sexual behavior [both physical and nonphysical] that interferes with the [victim's] life" (*Hostile Hallways: The AAUW Survey on*

[*strong definition*]

---

[10]Other types of harassment may also create problems on campus and become the subject of internal complaints or litigation. The most important of these other types of harassment are discussed at the end of this subsection.

[11]When a student's sexual harassment complaint against a faculty member concerns the faculty member's classroom statements or classroom conduct, academic freedom arguments may also come into play. This problem is discussed in Section 7.2.2, most specifically with reference to the *Cohen, Silva,* and *Bonnell* cases.

Sexual Harassment in America's Schools (AAUW Education Foundation, 1993), 6, 8; see also *Hostile Hallways: Bullying, Teasing, and Sexual Harassment in School* (AAUW Education Foundation, 2001), 9–11). And in a report by the National Coalition for Women and Girls in Education, sexual harassment is defined as "unwanted and unwelcome sexual behavior that creates a hostile environment, limiting full access to education" (*Title IX at 30: Report Card on Gender Equity,* June 2002, 40). Examples of sexual harassment, from the above sources, include: sexual advances; requests for sexual favors; sexual taunting; spreading sexual rumors; drawing graffiti of a sexual nature; making jokes, gestures, or comments of a sexual nature; showing sexually explicit photographs or illustrations; sending sexual notes or messages; pulling clothing down or off in a sexual way; forced kissing; touching, grabbing, or pinching in a sexual way; flashing; and intentionally brushing up against someone, blocking someone's path, or cornering someone in a sexual way. Consistent with the three general definitions, such behaviors must be "unwelcome" before they would be considered to be sexual harassment.

Harassment victims can be both male and female, just as perpetrators are both female and male. Moreover, sexual harassment can occur not only when the victim and perpetrator are of the opposite sex but also when they are of the same sex. Thus, as the Education Department's Sexual Harassment Guidance emphasizes, a female's harassment of another female or a male's harassment of another male is sexual harassment whenever the harasser's conduct is sexual in nature ("Revised Sexual Harassment Guidance," Part III).

Sexual harassment by faculty members (or other employees) may be divided into two categories: "*quid pro quo* harassment" and "hostile environment harassment." The Education Department's Sexual Harassment Guidance, for instance, distinguishes the categories as follows:

> *Quid pro quo* harassment occurs if a teacher or other employee conditions an educational decision or benefit on the student's submission to unwelcome sexual conduct, [regardless of whether] the student resists and suffers the threatened harm or submits and avoids the threatened harm. . . .
>
> By contrast, [hostile environment] harassment . . . does not explicitly or implicitly condition a decision or benefit on submission to sexual conduct [but does nevertheless] limit a student's ability to participate in or benefit from the school's program based on sex.
>
> Teachers and other employees can engage in either type of harassment. Students . . . are not generally given responsibility over other students and, thus, generally can only engage in hostile environment harassment ["Revised Sexual Harassment Guidance," Part V.A].

Student complaints alleging harassment by a faculty member may implicate grades in two basic ways. In the first way, akin to *quid pro quo* harassment, a student may complain that she was denied a deserved grade because she refused the instructor's sexual advances, or that she was awarded a grade only after having submitted unwillingly to the instructor's advances. In *Crandell v. New York College of Osteopathic Medicine,* 87 F. Supp. 2d 304 (S.D.N.Y. 2000), for example, a female medical student claimed she was harassed by a medical resident who supervised her in a six-week rotation at a teaching hospital. She claimed she was subjected to numerous sexual comments, incidents of touching, and a threat to give her a failing grade for the rotation if she did not spend time with him on a regular basis. In context, the student interpreted this demand to be sexual in nature. The court determined that this conduct constituted *quid pro quo* harassment. (The *Alexander v. Yale University* case, discussed below, is also this type of case.) In the second way, akin to hostile environment harassment, a student may complain that she received (or is in danger of receiving) a low grade because the instructor's sexual conduct has interfered with her ability to do her course work. In *Hayut v. State University of New York,* 352 F.3d 733 (2d Cir. 2003), for example, a student was in an undergraduate political science course in which the professor gave her the nickname "Monica," in light of "her supposed physical resemblance to Monica Lewinsky, a former White House intern who at that time was attaining notoriety for her involvement in a widely-covered sex scandal with then-President William Clinton." The professor's "use of this nickname persisted even after [the student] requested that he stop. Despite her protestations, [the professor] would occasionally, in dramatic fashion, attempt to locate [the student] in the classroom by sitting in front of his desk and screaming the name 'Monica.'" His comments "occurred at least once per class period throughout the rest of the semester." His conduct "was not limited to using the 'Monica' nickname, but included other comments as well. These added context to the nickname by associating [the student] with some of the more sordid details of the Clinton/Lewinsky scandal." The student claimed that the "Monica" comments "humiliat[ed] her in front of her peers, caus[ed] her to experience difficulty sleeping, and ma[de] it difficult for her to concentrate in school and at work." The court determined that, on these facts, a reasonable jury could conclude that the professor's actions constituted hostile environment sexual harassment. (See also *Kracunas and Pallett v. Iona College,* 119 F.3d 80 (2d Cir. 1997).) This second type of claim may also extend to situations when the student is harassed for having received a low grade, as in *Kadiki v. Virginia Commonwealth University,* 892 F. Supp. 746 (E.D. Va. 1995), where a professor spanked a student; or when a low grade precedes rather than follows the harassment (see *Kracunas and Pallett v. Iona College,* 119 F.3d 80 (2d Cir. 1997)); or when the harasser is a patient, client, or coworker in a clinical or internship setting, rather than the instructor (see, for example, *Murray v. New York University College of Dentistry,* 57 F.3d 243 (2d Cir. 1995)).

In such situations, students may assert sex discrimination claims under Title IX of the Education Amendments of 1972 (see Section 13.5.3 of this book) or under a comparable state civil rights law. Section 1983 claims (see Sections 3.5 & 4.7.4 of this book) alleging a violation of the federal equal protection clause may also be brought in some circumstances. In addition, if the student works for the college or university and is harassed by a supervisor or coworker, the student may assert an employment discrimination claim under Title VII (see Section 5.2.1 of this book) or the state's fair employment statute.[12] (See, for

---

[12]Various tort and contract claims may also be brought under state law, as discussed later in this subsection.

example, *Karibian v. Columbia University,* 14 F.3d 773 (2d Cir. 1994), where the university was held liable for the sexual harassment of a student employee by her supervisor; and see also *Lipsett v. University of Puerto Rico,* 864 F.2d 881 (1st Cir. 1988).) Depending on the source of law used, claims may be assertable against the college or university itself, against the alleged harasser(s), or against other institutional employees who have some role in supervising the alleged harasser or protecting against harassment on campus.

For all such claims, it is important, as a threshold matter, to focus on the claim's legal elements. The case of *Waters v. Metropolitan State University,* 91 F. Supp. 2d 1287 (D. Minn. 2000), provides a good shorthand description of these elements that would fit most statutes that cover hostile environment sexual harassment. According to that case, challenged conduct must have been "unwelcome," it must have been "based on sex," and it must have been "sufficiently severe as to alter the conditions of [the student's] education and create an abusive educational environment" (91 F. Supp. 2d at 1291). Further specificity on these elements is provided by the excellent analysis of Judge Calabresi in *Hayut v. State University of New York,* 352 F.3d 733 (2d Cir. 2003) (discussed above and below in this subsection), in which he carefully reviewed the severity requirement, a related pervasiveness requirement, the "on the basis of sex" or "because of sex" requirement, and the hostile or abusive educational environment requirement, as they applied to the student's claim in that case (352 F.3d at 746–49). The court in *Hayut* also reviewed the requirement that the educational environment be hostile not only from the victim's subjective perspective but also from the objective perspective of a reasonable person or reasonable fact finder (352 F.3d at 746). In addition, the court demonstrated how Title VII still provides important guidance for making hostile environment determinations under Title IX and Section 1983, even though Title IX's standards for determining institutional liability for an employee's acts are different from Title VII's (352 F.3d at 744).

First Amendment free speech law sometimes must also be taken into account in determining the parameters of sexual harassment,[13] since sexual harassment (whether of the *quid pro quo* or the hostile environment variety) is usually effectuated in large part through the spoken or written word or by symbolic gestures. This was strikingly true in the *Hayut* case, as well as in other cases cited above. Because much of the conduct alleged to be harassment is also expressive conduct, institutions and faculty members may seek to defend themselves against harassment claims by asserting that the challenged conduct is protected by the First Amendment. The cases discussed in Section 7.2.2 of this book, especially

---

[13]Free exercise and establishment issues may also become involved in sexual harassment cases when the defendant is a religious institution or a religious figure. For an example, see *Bollard v. California Providence of the Society of Jesus,* 196 F.3d 940 (9th Cir. 1999), in which a student priest alleged that his instructor, his superior priest, had sexually harassed him while he was attending the seminary. The defendant argued that the free exercise and establishment clauses compelled the court to dismiss the case; the appellate court disagreed, because religious reasons for the harassment and religious doctrine were not involved in the case, nor would a decision in the plaintiff's favor interfere with the defendant's freedom to select its ministers.

the *Silva, Cohen,* and *Bonnell* cases, all present such issues in the context of academic freedom claims; and these cases, taken together, do provide some First Amendment protection for faculty members. This does not mean, however, that there is a viable free speech issue whenever a harasser uses expression as part of the harassment. In some cases, *Hayut* being a major example, the faculty member's classroom comments are so far removed from any legitimate purpose that a free expression claim becomes marginalized or is not even addressed in the case (352 F.3d at 745–49). (See generally Sangree, "Title VII Prohibitions Against Hostile Environment Sexual Harassment and the First Amendment: No Collision in Sight," 47 *Rutgers L. Rev.* 461 (1995).)

The case of *Trejo v. Shoben*, 319 F.3d 878 (7th Cir. 2003), illustrates how courts may summarily dismiss free speech claims when they arise in contexts concerning a faculty member's conduct with respect to students. In this case, a professor had been denied reappointment, largely on the basis of various complaints and charges against him that suggested a "pattern of unwelcome, inappropriate, boorish behavior." The professor's oral statements were a major component of much of this behavior. For example, at an academic conference, while attending a private dinner party along with his graduate students, the professor made extended statements about "pregnancy, orgasms, and extramarital affairs and went on to advocate sex outside marriage. . . ."

The professor had also accompanied his statements with "the use of hand gestures to demonstrate various parts of the female anatomy." At the same conference, he made various "sexually charged comments in the presence of male and female professors and students." In addition, on and around the campus, the professor had extended "unwelcome invitations" to his graduate students to meet with him to play cards or engage in other activities, and had made various sexual comments about his female graduate students. The professor claimed that his various comments were protected speech under the First Amendment. The court rejected this contention. Regarding the academic conference, the court determined that the professor's "statements were simply parts of a calculated type of speech designed to further [his] private interest in attempting to solicit female companionship . . ."; and that "the record is barren of any evidence besides Trejo's self-serving statements that [his] remarks were designed to serve any truly pedagogic purpose." Regarding other comments by the professor, on and off campus, the court determined that they were primarily "casual, idle, and flirtatious chit-chat. . . ." The court concluded that these comments, and the comments at the academic conference, "were focused almost exclusively on matters of private concern" and did not merit protection either under the *Pickering/Connick* line of cases or under *Keyishian* (see Sections 7.1.1 & 7.1.4).

Of the various types of harassment claims, Title IX claims have received the greatest attention from the courts. Title IX harassment claims are the primary focus of the rest of this Section. Such claims are assertable only against institutions, and not against their individual officers or employees (see Section 13.5.9). In an early case, *Alexander v. Yale University,* 631 F.2d 178 (2d Cir. 1980), five female students alleged that Yale's practices and procedures for dealing with sexual harassment of students violated Title IX of the Education Amendments of 1972. One of the plaintiffs alleged that a faculty member had "offered to give her a grade of 'A' in the course in exchange for her compliance with his sexual demands" and that, when she refused, he gave her a C, which "was not the result of a fair evaluation of her academic work, but the result of her failure to accede to [the professor's] sexual demands." The remaining plaintiffs made other allegations concerning acts of harassment and the inadequacies of campus procedures to deal with them. The district court entered judgment for Yale, and the U.S. Court of Appeals affirmed. With the exception of the lowered-grade claim of one plaintiff, all the various claims and plaintiffs were dismissed for technical reasons: the plaintiffs had graduated and their claims were therefore "moot"; Yale had already adopted procedures for dealing with sexual harassment and thus, in effect, had already granted the primary remedy requested in the suit; other claims of harm were too "speculative" or "uncertain." The lowered-grade claim was dismissed because the plaintiff, at trial, did not prove the allegations.

Although all claims were rejected, the *Alexander* litigation by no means shut the door on Title IX actions alleging that the integrity of grading or other academic processes has been compromised by a faculty member's sexual harassment of students. Both the district and appellate courts made clear that the grade claim was a "justiciable claim for relief under Title IX." A denial or threatened denial of earned academic awards would be a deprivation of an educational benefit protected by Title IX; and when imposed for sexual reasons, that deprivation becomes sex discrimination prohibited by Title IX. As the district court held, and the appellate court quoted with apparent approval, "[A]cademic advancement conditioned upon submission to sexual demands constitutes sex discrimination in education" (459 F. Supp. at 4; 631 F.2d at 182).

Nevertheless, the lower courts in cases after *Alexander* expressed differing views on when, and the extent to which, Title IX would cover sexual harassment. It was not until 1992 that the U.S. Supreme Court resolved this matter in *Franklin v. Gwinnett County Public Schools,* 503 U.S. 60 (1992). The plaintiff, a high school student in Georgia, sued the school board under Title IX, seeking relief from both hostile environment and *quid pro quo* sexual harassment by a teacher. Her complaint alleged that the teacher, also a sports coach, had harassed her continually beginning in the fall of her sophomore year. The student accused the teacher of engaging her in sexually oriented conversations, forcibly kissing her on the mouth on school property, telephoning her at home, and asking her to see him socially. She also alleged that during her junior year, this teacher went to her class, asked the classroom teacher to excuse her, and then took her to a private office where he raped her. According to the student's complaint, school officials and teachers were aware of these occurrences, and although the school board eventually investigated them, it took no action to stop the harassment and agreed to let the teacher resign in return for dropping all harassment charges.

The student filed a complaint with the U.S. Department of Education's Office for Civil Rights (OCR), which investigated her charges. OCR determined that verbal and physical sexual harassment had occurred, and that the school district had violated the student's Title IX rights. But OCR concluded that, because the teacher and the school principal had resigned and the school had implemented a grievance procedure, the district was in compliance with Title IX. The student then went to federal court, and ultimately the U.S. Supreme Court ruled in her favor. (The Court's reasoning and legal analysis are further discussed in Section 13.5.9.) The teacher's actions were sexual harassment, and the district, in failing to intervene, had intentionally discriminated against her, in violation of Title IX.

The *Franklin* case clearly established that sexual harassment, including hostile environment harassment, may be the basis for a sex discrimination claim under Title IX, and that student victims of harassment by a teacher may sue their schools for money damages under Title IX. But other important issues remained unresolved by the Court's *Franklin* opinion—in particular the issue of when, and under what theories, courts would hold schools and colleges liable for money damages under Title IX for a faculty member's or other employee's sexual harassment of a student. In *Franklin,* the school administrators had actual knowledge of the teacher's misconduct. The Supreme Court did not address whether a school could be found liable only if it had such actual knowledge of the misconduct but failed to stop it, or whether a school could be liable even absent actual knowledge because an employee's intentional discrimination could be imputed to the school. (Under agency law, the employer may be held responsible for the unlawful conduct of its agent (called *respondeat superior*) even if the employer does not have actual knowledge of the conduct; see Section 2.1 of this book.)[14]

The institutional liability questions left open by *Franklin* were extensively discussed in the lower courts in *Franklin*'s aftermath. No pattern emerged; different courts took different approaches in determining when liability would accrue to an educational institution for the actions of its teachers or other employees. Some courts determined that an educational institution could be vicariously liable on the basis of common law agency principles of *respondeat superior* (see, for example, *Kracunas and Pallett v. Iona College,* 119 F.3d 80 (2d Cir. 1997)). Other courts determined that an educational institution should be liable under a constructive notice, or "knew or should have known," standard (see, for example, *Doe v. Petaluma School District,* 949 F. Supp. 1415 (N.D. Cal. 1996)); or could be liable only in certain narrow circumstances where it had knowledge of the harassment and failed to respond (see, for example, *Rosa H. v. San Elizario*

---

[14]Another unresolved issue after *Franklin* was whether plaintiffs must always show that the discrimination (the sexual harassment) was intentional, or whether unintentional discrimination may also be actionable upon a showing of discriminatory effect or impact (see Section 13.5.7.2). Although *Franklin* did not address this issue, federal district courts in cases subsequent to *Franklin* generally required that plaintiffs demonstrate intentional discrimination. See, for example, *R.L.R. v. Prague Public School District I-103,* 838 F. Supp 1526 (W.D. Okla. 1993). The U.S. Supreme Court's later decision in *Alexander v. Sandoval,* discussed in Sections 13.5.7.2 and 13.5.9, appears to resolve this point, requiring intentional discrimination.

Independent School District, 106 F.3d 648 (5th Cir. 1997) (harassment)); or should not be liable at all, at least for hostile environment harassment (see *Bougher v. University of Pittsburgh*, 713 F. Supp. 139 (W.D. Pa. 1989), *affirmed on other grounds*, 882 F.2d 74 (3rd Cir. 1989)). The U.S. Department of Education also weighed in on these liability issues. The department's Office for Civil Rights published the first version of its sexual harassment guidelines ("Sexual Harassment Guidance: Harassment of Students by School Employees, Other Students, or Third Parties," 62 Fed. Reg. 12034 (March 13, 1997), also available at http://www.ed.gov/about/offices/list/ocr/docs/sexhar00.html). The Guidance provided that liability for harassment by teachers or other employees of a school or college should be governed by agency principles:

> A school will . . . be liable for hostile environment sexual harassment by its employees . . . if the employee—(1) acted with apparent authority (i.e., because of the school's conduct, the employee reasonably appears to be acting on behalf of the school, whether or not the employee acted with authority); or (2) was aided in carrying out the sexual harassment of students by his or her position of authority with the institution . . . [62 Fed. Reg. at 12039].

The U.S. Supreme Court resolved these Title IX liability issues in *Gebser v. Lago Vista Independent School District*, 524 U.S. 274 (1998), where the issue was the extent to which "a school district may be held liable in damages in an implied right of action under Title IX . . . for the sexual harassment of a student by one of the district's teachers." In a 5-to-4 decision, the Court majority held that Title IX damages liability is based neither on common law agency principles of *respondeat superior* nor upon principles of constructive notice. Distinguishing Title IX from Title VII of the Civil Rights Act of 1964 (Section 5.2.1 of this book), which does utilize such principles, the Court insisted that "[i]t would 'frustrate the purposes' of Title IX to permit a damages recovery against a school district for a teacher's sexual harassment of a student based on [such] principles . . . , i.e., without actual notice to a school district official" (524 U.S. at 285). Thus, the Court held that students may not recover damages from a school district under Title IX for teacher-student sexual harassment "unless an official [of the school district], who at a minimum, has authority to address the alleged discrimination and to institute corrective measures on the [district's] behalf has actual knowledge of discrimination and fails adequately to respond" (524 U.S. at 276). Moreover, the official's response to the harassment:

> . . . must amount to deliberate indifference to discrimination. The administrative enforcement scheme presupposes that an official who is advised of a Title IX violation refuses to take action to bring the recipient into compliance. The premise, in other words, is an official decision by the recipient not to remedy the violation. That framework finds a rough parallel in the standard of deliberate indifference. Under a lower standard, there would be a risk that the recipient would be liable in damages not for its own official decision but instead for its employees' independent actions [524 U.S. at 290].

Putting aside the U.S. Department of Education's Sexual Harassment Guidance (see above) that had applied agency principles to teacher-student sexual harassment, the Court made clear that it would listen only to Congress (and not to the Department of Education) on these questions: "[U]ntil Congress speaks directly on the subject . . . , we will not hold a school district liable in damages under Title IX for a teacher's sexual harassment of a student absent actual notice and deliberate indifference" (524 U.S. at 292). In so doing, and in contrast with its methodology in other situations (see, for example, *Martin v. Occupational Safety and Health Review Commission,* 499 U.S. 144 (1991)), the Court refused to accord any deference to the decisions of the administrative agency authorized to implement the statute, as Justice Stevens emphasized in his dissent (524 U.S. at 300).

Applying these principles to the student's claim, the Court determined that the student had not met the standards and therefore affirmed the lower court's entry of summary judgment for the school district. In reaching this decision, the Court acknowledged that the school district had not implemented any sexual harassment policy or any grievance procedure for enforcing such a policy as required by the Department of Education's regulations (34 C.F.R. §§ 106.8(b) & 106.9(a)). But the Court nevertheless held that the school district's failure in this regard was not evidence of "actual notice and deliberate indifference," nor did this failure "itself constitute 'discrimination' under Title IX" (524 U.S. at 292).

Four Justices vigorously dissented from the majority's holdings in *Gebser.* Point by point, the dissenting Justices refuted the majority's reasons for rejecting the application of agency principles under Title IX and for concluding that Title IX is based upon a different model of liability than Title VII. In addition, the dissenting Justices provided an extended argument to the effect that the refusal to provide meaningful protection for students subjected to harassment flies in the face of the purpose and meaning of Title IX. According to Justice Stevens:

> Congress included the prohibition against discrimination on the basis of sex in Title IX [in order] to induce school boards to adopt and enforce practices that will minimize the danger that vulnerable students will be exposed to such odious behavior. The rule that the Court has crafted creates the opposite incentive. As long as school boards can insulate themselves from knowledge about this sort of conduct, they can claim immunity from damages liability. Indeed, the rule that the Court adopts would preclude a damages remedy even if every teacher at the school knew about the harassment but did not have "authority to institute corrective measures on the district's behalf." *Ante,* at 277.

> * * * *

> As a matter of policy, the Court ranks protection of the school district's purse above the protection of immature high school students. . . . Because those students are members of the class for whose special benefit Congress enacted Title IX, that policy choice is not faithful to the intent of the policymaking branch of our Government [524 U.S. at 300–301, 306 (Stevens, J. dissenting); see generally 524 U.S. at 293–306 (Stevens, J., dissenting)].

The *Gebser* case thus establishes a two-part standard for determining institutional liability in damages for a faculty member's (or other employee's) sexual harassment of a student:[15]

1. An official of the school district: (a) must have had "actual knowledge" of the harassment; and (b) must have authority to "institute corrective measures" to resolve the harassment problem.

2. If such an official did have actual knowledge, then the official: (a) must have "fail[ed] to adequately respond" to the harassment; and (b) must have acted with "deliberate indifference."

In these respects, the *Gebser* test stands in stark contrast to the liability standards under Title VII. In two cases decided in the same court term as the *Gebser* case, the Supreme Court determined that liability under Title VII is based upon agency principles and a *respondeat superior* model of liability (*Faragher v. City of Boca Raton,* 524 U.S. 775 (1998); and *Burlington Industries v. Ellerth,* 524 U.S. 742 (1998), both discussed in Section 5.3.3.3). Thus, under Title VII, but not under Title IX, an employer may be liable in damages for a supervisor's acts of harassment even though the employer did not have either actual knowledge or constructive notice of the harassment. It is therefore much more difficult for students to meet the Title IX liability standards than it is for employees to meet the Title VII standards, and consequently students have less protection against harassment under Title IX than employees have under Title VII. While Title IX, as a spending statute, is structured differently from Title VII, a regulatory statute, and while courts interpreting and applying Title IX are not bound by Title VII judicial precedents and administrative guidelines, the result in *Gebser* nevertheless seems questionable. Students may be at a more vulnerable age than many employees, and may be encouraged by the academic environment to have more trust in teachers than would usually be the case with supervisors in the work environment. It is thus not apparent, either as a matter of policy or of law, why students should receive less protection from harassment under Title IX than employees do under Title VII.

In practice, the *Gebser* two-part liability standard provides scant opportunity for student victims of harassment to succeed with Title IX damages actions against educational institutions. The difficulty of proving "actual knowledge" is compounded by the difficulty of proving "deliberate indifference" (see, for example, *Wills v. Brown University,* 184 F.3d 20 (1st Cir. 1999)). In addition, since "actual knowledge" must be possessed by an official with authority to take corrective

---

[15]*Gebser* standards may also be applicable to student-student harassment in certain narrow circumstances in which the institution has granted a student some kind of authority over other students. In *Morse v. Regents of the University of Colorado,* 154 F.3d 1124 (10th Cir. 1998), for instance, the court applied *Gebser* to a Title IX claim against the university brought by female Reserve Officer Training Corps (ROTC) cadets who were allegedly harassed by a higher-ranking male cadet. The university could be liable for the actions of the male cadet, said the court, if he was "acting with authority bestowed by" the university-sanctioned ROTC program.

action, there are difficulties in proving that the officials or employees whom the victim notified had such authority.[16] In *Liu v. Striuli*, 36 F. Supp. 2d 452, 465–66 (D.R.I. 1999), for instance, a court applying *Gebser* rejected a graduate student's Title IX claim because neither the director of financial aid nor the director of the graduate history department, whom the student had notified, had "supervisory authority" over the alleged harasser. Therefore neither official had authority to correct the alleged harassment. Similarly, in *Delgado v. Stegall*, 367 F.3d 668 (7th Cir. 2004), a student confided to a professor that she had been harassed by another professor and had also discussed the matter with a counselor. But her Title IX harassment claim failed because neither the professor nor the counselor had authority to take corrective action, and neither they nor the student had reported the harassment to a university official who did have such authority.

In *Hayut v. State University of New York*, 352 F.3d 733 (2d Cir. 2003), the court had no difficulty determining that a jury could conclude that a professor's classroom behavior was "hostile educational environment sexual harassment." But the university was not liable for the professor's misconduct because its authorized officials did not have knowledge of the harassment until after it had ceased. The student plaintiff also could not meet the deliberate indifference test. Although the court acknowledged that "deliberate indifference may be found . . . when remedial action only follows after a 'lengthy and unjustified delay,'" there was no such delay in this case. Once the student did report the alleged harassment to the dean, the dean's response thereafter was timely and adequate.

In *Oden v. Northern Marianas College*, 284 F.3d 1058 (9th Cir. N. Mariana Islands 2002), the plaintiff-student did have evidence of a lengthy delay, but her Title IX claim failed nevertheless. The student had complained to college officials that her music professor had sexually harassed her on various occasions with various inappropriate acts. Once the student had reported the harassment, college personnel helped the student draft a formal internal complaint, provided counseling for her, began an investigation, and took other actions, culminating in a hearing by the college's Committee on Sexual Harassment, which determined that the professor's actions constituted sexual harassment. The student, dissatisfied with various aspects of the college's response, filed her Title IX suit, claiming that the college had acted with deliberate indifference. Her primary contention was that almost ten months had passed between the date of her formal complaint to the date of her hearing. In the context of the various actions that the college had taken in responding to the student's harassment allegations, the court declined to consider the delay as deliberate indifference:

> Although there was a lengthy delay, there were also valid reasons for the
> delay: [the College] had a number of administrative hurdles to jump, including

---

[16]It is important that institutions do not overemphasize such technical questions concerning legal liability. In resolving students' harassment complaints through campus grievance mechanisms, for instance, the primary focus of attention should be on whether harassment occurred, not on whether the institution could be liable in court if it did occur. Moreover, much of the institution's policy and practice regarding sexual harassment may be driven more by educational and ethical concerns than by legal concerns, as discussed later in this subsection.

the formation of a sexual harassment hearing committee; [the student] had difficulty retaining an attorney; and . . . had relocated to the State of New Mexico.
At most, [the College] is guilty of bureaucratic sluggishness. We decline to
equate bureaucratic sluggishness with "deliberate indifference," especially
where the school authorities began turning their bureaucratic wheels immediately after being notified of the alleged misconduct [284 F.3d at 1061].[17]

In the *Delgado* case (above), although the court rejected the student's claim,
it did provide clarification of the actual notice standard that could prove helpful to student victims in subsequent cases. Specifically, the court explained that
the university could have been liable under Title IX if university officials had
foreknowledge that the alleged harasser (the professor) had harassed *other*
students. It was not necessary, for purposes of the "actual knowledge" requirement, that officials knew of the professor's harassment of the plaintiff (the
complaining student). "So if, for example, [the professor] had been known to
be a serial harasser, [university officials] might well be found to have had a
sufficient approximation to actual knowledge that [the plaintiff] would
be harassed." This argument did not work for the student in this case
because, even though the professor "had made advances to three other woman
students, . . . they had never filed complaints" (367 F.3d at 670). The professor
therefore "was not known by anyone in the university administration . . . to be
harassing other students" (367 F.3d at 672).

On the other hand, although the new *Gebser* standards are very difficult for
plaintiffs to meet, these standards do not create an insurmountable barrier
for students challenging a faculty member's harassment. For example, in
Chontos v. Rhea, 29 F. Supp. 2d 931 (N.D. Ind. 1998), a student filed a Title IX
claim against Indiana University, claiming that a professor of physical education had forcibly kissed and fondled her. The university had received three other
complaints about this professor from three different women students over the
prior seven years. After the first incident, he received a written reprimand and
was warned that if he repeated the behavior he could be fired. After the second
incident, the professor was sent for psychological counseling, but the university
did not follow up to ascertain whether the counseling was successful. After the
third incident (which, in contrast to the others, was limited to verbal harassment), the faculty member was told to "clean up his act." A sealed report was
placed in his personnel file, but no disciplinary action was taken. After the
fourth incident, which was the subject of this litigation, he was suspended and
offered the choice of a dismissal proceeding or resignation. The professor
resigned with full benefits. Ruling that a reasonable jury could find that the
university was deliberately indifferent, the court rejected the university's motion
for summary judgment. With respect to the university's defense that the
students did not want to pursue formal complaints, which meant that, under
university rules, they would not confront the professor in a formal termination

---

[17]The judgment in this case was later vacated by the U.S. Supreme Court on technical grounds
having nothing to do with the lower court's analysis of the sexual harassment issues (*Oden v.
Northern Marianas College*, 539 U.S. 924 (2003)).

hearing, the court replied that the university had other sanctions available short of dismissal, but chose "to do nothing."

The *Gebser* court did not utilize the distinction between *quid pro quo* harassment and hostile environment harassment that previous courts had sometimes invoked. Although the *Gebser* liability standard clearly applies to hostile environment claims, it is not entirely clear whether it would apply in the same way to *quid pro quo* harassment—or, as courts increasingly put it, to harassment that involves a "tangible" adverse action against the victim. Thus, it is not entirely clear whether earlier cases applying a different liability standard (easier for plaintiffs to meet) to *quid pro quo* claims (see, for example, *Kadiki v. Virginia Commonwealth University*, above) are still good law. So far, the answer is apparently "No." The court in *Burtner v. Hiram College*, 9 F. Supp. 2d 852 (N.D. Ohio 1998), *affirmed without opinion*, 194 F.3d 1311 (6th Cir. 1999), applied the *Gebser* actual knowledge standard to both types of harassment; the court in *Liu v. Striuli*, 36 F. Supp. 2d 452 (D.R.I. 1999), applied the actual notice standard to *quid pro quo* harassment; and the court in *Klemencic v. Ohio State University*, 10 F. Supp. 2d 911 (S.D. Ohio 1998), *affirmed*, 263 F. 3d 504 (6th Cir. 2001), applied the actual notice and the deliberate indifference standards to *quid pro quo* harassment. Similarly, in the administrative realm, the Department of Education's Sexual Harassment Guidance "moves away from specific labels for types of sexual harassment," using the distinction between *quid pro quo* and hostile environment harassment only for explanatory purposes ("Revised Sexual Harassment Guidance," Part V.A, and Preamble, under "Harassment by Teachers and Other School Personnel").

After *Gebser*, lawsuits against institutions for money damages are not the only way students may enforce their Title IX rights. There are two other ways: (1) suing the institution in court and seeking injunctive or declaratory relief rather than money damages;[18] and (2) in lieu of or in addition to suit, filing an administrative complaint against the institution with the U.S. Department of Education and seeking administrative compliance. (See generally William Kaplin, "A Typology and Critique of Title IX Sexual Harassment Law After *Gebser* and *Davis*," 26 *J. Coll. & Univ. Law* 615, 632–34, 636–38 (2000).) The first alternative, since it does not itself seek monetary damages, is apparently not directly governed by the *Gebser* case—whose factual context is limited to monetary liability and whose legal rationale seems dependent on the negative impact of monetary damage awards upon educational institutions. It is therefore not clear what the liability standard would be for a Title IX harassment claim seeking only injunctive or declaratory relief. Even if the actual knowledge standard did apply, it would likely be easily met, since the lawsuit itself would

---

[18]Title IX suits for monetary, injunctive, or declaratory relief are suits against the institution, not against individuals. See, for example, *Soper v. Hoben*, 195 F. 3d 845 (6th Cir. 1999), discussed in Section 13.5.3. Suits against individuals for sexual harassment may be brought under Section 1983 (see Section 4.7.4.1 of this book) if the individuals are acting under color of law; see Laura Oren, "Section 1983 and Sex Abuse in Schools: Making a Federal Case of It," 72 *Chi-Kent L. Rev.* 747 (1997).

have provided such notice well before the court would order the institution to comply with Title IX.

The second alternative—the administrative complaint—is apparently not governed at all by *Gebser*. In the administrative process, the U.S. Department of Education is presumably free to use standards of institutional noncompliance that differ from the *Gebser* liability standards, as long as its standards are consistent with the nondiscrimination prohibitions in the Title IX statute and regulations. Since the institution would always receive notice of its noncompliance and the opportunity to make appropriate adjustments before any administrative penalty is imposed, and since an administrative proceeding would never result in a monetary damages remedy against the institution, it appears that the U.S. Department of Education may continue to apply its own Sexual Harassment Guidance (see above) to administrative complaints, compliance investigations, and fund cut-off hearings (see *Gebser* at 287, 292). Indeed, in the aftermath of *Gebser* and the successor *Davis* case on peer sexual harassment (see Section 8.1.5), the department issued a revised guidance (66 Fed. Reg. 5512 (January 2001)) that reaffirms the department's own separate standards that it had first articulated in the 1997 Guidance (above). (See "Revised Sexual Harassment Guidance: Harassment of Students by School Employees, Other Students, or Third Parties," 66 Fed. Reg. 5512 (January 19, 2001), available at http://www.ed.gov/offices/OCR/archives/shguide/index.html.)

Colleges and universities have considerable leeway in fulfilling their legal obligations under the *Gebser* case (as well as the *Davis* case that deals with peer harassment; see Section 8.1.5). The monetary liability standards in these cases are not onerous and should be viewed as the minimum or floor—not the full extent—of the institution's responsibilities regarding sexual harassment. The standards for injunction and declaratory relief cases may be a bit stricter for institutions, but these cases are seldom pursued by students (see Section 13.5.9). The standards for compliance in the Department of Education's Sexual Harassment Guidance are stricter for institutions but nevertheless leave considerable discretion in the hands of institutions. Thus, as is true in other legal contexts as well, educational and ethical standards can be as important as Title IX legal standards in guiding institutional planning, and nonlegal solutions to campus problems can be as viable as legal solutions—or more so.

Since sexual harassment can do substantial harm to the victims and have substantial adverse consequences for the campus community, and since sexual harassment is such a sensitive matter to deal with, institutions will likely engage in considerable institutional planning and educational programming. A highly pertinent perspective and useful starting point for doing so is contained in the "Preamble" accompanying the Department of Education's Revised Sexual Harassment Guidance. The Preamble emphasizes that a central concern of Title IX is whether schools can recognize when harassment has occurred and take "prompt and effective action calculated to end the harassment, prevent its recurrence, and, as appropriate, remedy its effects" ("Revised Sexual

Harassment Guidance," Preamble, under "Enduring Principles from the 1997 Guidance," available at http://www.ed.gov/offices/OCR/archives/shguide/index.html). In this regard, the preamble makes two key points. First,

> If harassment has occurred, doing nothing is always the wrong response. However, depending on the circumstances, there may be more than one right way to respond. The important thing is for school employees or officials to pay attention to the school environment and not to hesitate to respond to sexual harassment in the same reasonable, commonsense manner as they would to other types of serious misconduct [Id.].

Second, it is critically important:

> [to have] well-publicized and effective grievance procedures in place to handle complaints of sex discrimination, including sexual harassment complaints. . . . Strong policies and effective grievance procedures are essential to let students and employees know that sexual harassment will not be tolerated and to ensure that they know how to report it [Id.; see also Parts V.D & X of Revised Sexual Harassment Guidance].

[handwritten margin note: Yale has explicit detailed well publicized procedure]

Following these two key points, there are numerous initiatives that colleges and universities might undertake. They include educational programs for students; workshops and other training programs for instructors, staff, and leaders of student organizations; counseling and support programs for victims; counseling programs for perpetrators; and alternative dispute resolution programs that provide mediation and other nonadversarial means for resolving some sexual harassment complaints. Institutions should also make sure that sexual harassment is covered clearly and specifically in their student disciplinary codes and faculty ethics codes. It is equally important to ensure that *retaliation* against persons complaining of sexual harassment is clearly covered and prohibited in such codes. In addition, institutions should make sure that mechanisms are in place for protecting the confidentiality of students who report that they—or others—have been sexually harassed (see "Revised Sexual Harassment Guidance," Part VII.B); and for protecting the due process rights and free speech rights of anyone accused of harassment. Through such initiatives, colleges and universities can work out harassment problems in a multifaceted manner that lessens the likelihood of lawsuits against them in court. Effectuating such initiatives will require good teamwork between administrators and college counsel (see Section 2.4.2).

(For further guidance, see Judith Brandenburg, *Confronting Sexual Harassment: What Schools and Colleges Can Do* (Teachers College Press,1997), especially 49–82; Susan Hippensteele & Thomas C. Pearson, "Responding Effectively to Sexual Harassment: Victim Advocacy, Early Intervention, and Problem Solving," *Change*, January–February 1999, 48–53; and "Sexual Harassment: Suggested Policy and Procedures for Handling Complaints," in *AAUP Policy Documents and Reports* (9th ed., 2001), 113–15, which includes due process protections for the accused and provides for a faculty committee as fact finder.

Another related decision institutions may face in drafting and enforcing sexual harassment policies is whether to prohibit all sexual relationships between students and faculty members, consensual or not. Proponents of a total ban argue that the unequal power relationships between student and faculty member mean that no relationship is truly consensual. Opponents of total bans, on the other hand, argue that students are usually beyond the legal age for consent, and that institutions may infringe on constitutional rights of free association or risk invasion of privacy claims if they attempt to regulate the personal lives of faculty and students. (For discussion of this difficult issue, see R. Carlson, "Romantic Relationships Between Professors and Their Students: Morality, Ethics, and Law," 42 S. Tex. L. Rev. 493 (2001); M. Chamallas, "Consent, Equality and the Legal Control of Sexual Conduct," 61 S. Cal. L. Rev. 777 (1988); P. DeChiara, "The Need for Universities to Have Rules on Consensual Sexual Relationships Between Faculty Members and Students," 21 Columbia J.L. & Soc. Probs. 137 (1988); and E. Keller, "Consensual Amorous Relationships Between Faculty and Students: The Constitutional Right to Privacy," 15 J. Coll. & Univ. Law 21 (1988).)

Sexual harassment claims may also be brought under Section 1983, which is used to enforce the Fourteenth Amendment equal protection clause against both institutions and individuals (see Laura Oren, "Section 1983 and Sex Abuse in Schools: Making a Federal Case of It," 72 Chi-Kent L. Rev. 747 (1997)). Unlike Title IX claims, Section 1983 claims can be brought only against public institutions and individuals employed by public institutions. Moreover, claims against the institution can succeed only if the challenged actions were taken pursuant to an established institutional policy or custom (see Section 3.5 of this book). Claims against individuals can succeed only if the plaintiff can defeat the qualified immunity defense typically asserted by individuals who are Section 1983 defendants (see Section 4.7.4). In Oona R.S. v. McCaffrey, 143 F.3d 473 (9th Cir. 1998), for instance, a student who was allegedly harassed by a student teacher used Section 1983 to sue school officials who were allegedly responsible for permitting the harassment. The court held that the student had stated a valid equal protection claim for gender discrimination and rejected the officials' qualified immunity defense.

In Hayut v. State University of New York, 352 F.3d 733 (2d Cir. 2003), a student filed a Section 1983 claim against a professor whom she alleged had harassed her and against three administrators whom she claimed were supervisors of the professor at the time of the harassment. The court acknowledged that a hostile environment sexual harassment claim may also be an equal protection claim that can be brought under Section 1983 if the professor and the supervisors were acting "under color of law" (see Section 3.5 of this book). Since the student's evidence concerning the professor's classroom conduct was sufficient to sustain a Section 1983 claim, the appellate court reversed the district court's entry of summary judgment in the professor's favor. The student's failure to report the professor's harassment to a supervisor until after the course was over was not fatal to the student's claim. "Given the power disparity between teacher and student a factfinder could reasonably conclude that a student-victim's inaction, or counter-intuitive reaction does not reflect the true impact of objectionable conduct. . . . 'What students will silently endure is not the measure of what a college must tolerate'" (*Hayut*, 352 F.3d at 749, quoting *Vega v. Miller* 273 F.3d 460, 468 (2d Cir. 2001)). Regarding the administrators, however, the appellate court affirmed summary judgment in their favor because the student had not introduced any evidence of their "personal involvement" in the harassment. To bring a Section 1983 claim against supervisory personnel for the actions of a subordinate, the plaintiff must have shown that the supervisors participated in the harassment, failed to take corrective action after being notified of the harassment, created "a policy or custom to foster the unlawful conduct," committed "gross negligence in supervising subordinates" who commit the harassment, or are deliberately indifferent "to the rights of others by failing to act on information regarding the [harassment]."

In *Lipsett v. University of Puerto Rico,* above, the plaintiff also sued university officials under Section 1983 in their individual capacities (see Section 4.7.4 of this book). The court held that individuals can be liable for a subordinate's actions (including harassment) in certain circumstances:

> A state official . . . can be held liable . . . if (1) the behavior of such subordinates results in a constitutional violation and (2) the official's action or inaction was "affirmative[ly] link[ed]," *Oklahoma City v. Tuttle*, 471 U.S. 808 . . . (1985), to that behavior in the sense that it could be characterized as "supervisory encouragement, condonation, or acquiescence" *or* "gross negligence amounting to deliberate indifference" [864 F.2d at 902].

Since the plaintiff had discussed the harassment numerous times with the dean, the director of surgery, and the director of the surgical residency program, the court concluded that "supervisory encouragement" could be found and that Section 1983 liability could attach.

Another possibility for a student harassment victim is a claim brought under a state nondiscrimination law. In *Smith v. Hennepin County Technical Center,* 1988 U.S. Dist. LEXIS 4876 (D. Minn. 1988), two students brought suit under Minnesota's statute, charging their instructor in a dental laboratory with offensive touching and retaliation when they complained of his conduct. The court ruled that, under the state law, the, plaintiff must show that "she was subject to unwelcome harassment," that "the harassment was based on sex," and that "the harassment had the purpose or effect of unreasonably interfering with her education or created an intimidating, hostile, or offensive learning environment." In addition, using the federal Title VII law by analogy, the court determined that the educational institution would be liable for the acts of its employees if it "knew or should have known of the harassment and failed to take proper remedial action." Because the instructor was an employee of the institution, the court ruled that the institution would be directly liable for his acts of its employee if it should have known of them and could have prevented them through the exercise of reasonable care.

State tort law claims challenging harassment can be brought against both institutions and individual employees, either public or private, but public institutions and their officials will sometimes be immune from suit (see Section 3.3.1). The types of tort claims that could cover harassment include intentional (or negligent) infliction of emotional distress, assault, battery, negligent hiring, negligent supervision, and negligent retention. In *Chontos v. Rhea*, 29 F. Supp. 2d 931 (N.D. Ind. 1998), for example, the court allowed a student to proceed with a negligent retention claim against a university based on the university's awareness of a professor's prior harassment of students. But in *Wills v. Brown University*, 184 F.3d 20 (1st Cir. 1999), the court determined that a student complaining of a professor's harassment had not established viable claims of intentional infliction or negligent hiring against the university.

Contract claims are also a possibility. In *George v. University of Idaho*, 822 P.2d 549 (Idaho Ct. App. 1991), a law student, who had ended a consensual relationship with a law professor, filed a breach of contract claim against the university, asserting that the professor's efforts to resume the relationship, and his retaliation in the form of actions disparaging her character within the law school and the legal community, constituted breach of an implied contract. The court denied summary judgment for the university, noting the existence of several questions of fact concerning the nature and scope of the university's responsibility to the student. First of all, the court noted, the university had an implied contract with the student—as evidenced by the university's sexual harassment policy and by its statement in the faculty handbook that it would "fulfill its responsibilities in pursuit of the academic goals and objectives of all members of the university community." Furthermore, when the student brought the professor's actions to the attention of the school, a written agreement had been executed, in which the professor promised to stop harassing the plaintiff if she would drop claims against him and the law school. The court found that the university had an obligation under that agreement independent of its implied contract with the plaintiff, an obligation that extended beyond her graduation, to take reasonable measures to enforce the agreement.

Sexual harassment, of course, is not the only form of harassment that is a problem on college campuses or that may be actionable under the law. It is, however, the type of harassment most often associated with problems concerning grades and credits earned by students, and the type of harassment that is most often addressed in court opinions. Other forms of harassment, all of which would apparently fall within the scope of pertinent civil rights statutes, include racial harassment, harassment on the basis of national origin, harassment of students with disabilities, and harassment on the basis of age. Regarding racial harassment, the U.S. Department of Education has determined that it is within the scope of Title VI, and has issued guidelines for dealing with racial harassment issues under that statute. See *Racial Incidents and Harassment Against Students at Educational Institutions: Investigative Guidance*, 59 Fed. Reg. 11448 (March 10, 1994). This Guidance preceded the Sexual Harassment Guidance that is discussed above, and it articulates liability standards in a slightly different way; but the policy is still comparable to the sexual harassment guidance, and like that Guidance, its standards are much tougher on institutions than the judicial standards for sexual harassment articulated in the *Gebser* case.

Another form of harassment that has created substantial problems for colleges and universities, as well as elementary and secondary schools, is harassment on the basis of sexual orientation. As indicated at the beginning of this Section, same-sex harassment may sometimes be covered under Title IX as a form of sexual harassment. In other circumstances, it now seems clear that same-sex harassment is also covered by the equal protection clause of the Fourteenth Amendment, in which case victims of such harassment in public postsecondary institutions may use Section 1983 (see above) to sue individual instructors, administrators, staff persons, and other students who have participated in the harassment. In two public school cases concerning peer harassment, two federal courts of appeals have ruled that local school personnel may be held personally liable for failing to protect gay students from persistent patterns of peer harassment, including verbal and physical abuse (see *Nabozny v. Podlesny*, 92 F.3d 446 (7th Cir. 1996); and *Flores v. Morgan Hill Unified School District*, 324 F.3d 1130 (9th Cir. 2003)).

9.3.5. *Evaluating students with disabilities*

9.3.5.1 Overview. As noted in Section 8.2.4.3, the Rehabilitation Act and the Americans With Disabilities Act of 1990 require colleges and universities to provide reasonable accommodations for students with disabilities. Although the laws do not require institutions to change their academic criteria for disabled students, institutions may need to change the format of tests; to provide additional time, or readers or aides, to help students take examinations; or to change minor aspects of course requirements.

Lawsuits filed by students who assert that a college or university has not accommodated their disabilities have mushroomed. Although courts have addressed claims involving a wide range of disabilities, the largest proportion involve alleged learning disabilities and academic accommodations, such as additional time on tests (or a different test format), waiver of required courses or prerequisites, and, in some cases, waiver of certain portions of the curriculum. Students in elementary and secondary education have been entitled to accommodations for physical, psychological, and learning disorders since the 1975 enactment of the Education for All Handicapped Children Act (Pub. L. No. 94-142), which was renamed the Individuals With Disabilities Education Act (IDEA) in 1990 and was most recently amended by the Individuals With Disabilities Education Improvement Act of 2004, Pub. L. No. 108-446. The IDEA is codified in 20 U.S.C. §§ 1400 *et seq.* Many of the students who have received special services and other accommodations under this law are now enrolled in college and, due to their experiences with IDEA services, may have heightened expectations about receiving services at the postsecondary level as well.[19]

Although the IDEA does not apply to a disabled student once he or she has completed high school or has reached the age of twenty-one (whichever occurs

---

[19]According to a report published in 2000, approximately one out of every eleven college students reports having a disability. Of those, 41 percent reported a learning disability (American Council on Education, "More College Freshmen Report Disabilities, New ACE Study Shows," 49 *Higher Educ. & Nat'l. Aff.* 2 (January 17, 2000), available at http://www.ace.net.edu, cited in Laura Rothstein, "Disability Law and Higher Education: A Road Map for Where We've Been and Where We May Be Heading," 63 *Maryland L. Rev.* 122 (2004)).

first), such students continue to be protected in higher education by Section 504 of the Rehabilitation Act of 1973 and by the Americans With Disabilities Act (ADA). As is the case with disputes over the admission of students with disabilities (see Section 8.2.4.3), issues related to classroom accommodations, testing issues, and accommodations for licensing examinations have expanded in recent years, in part because of the expectations and aspirations of students who have grown up with IDEA.

In 2001, the U.S. Supreme Court ruled that the employment provisions of the ADA are subject to Eleventh Amendment immunity in *University of Alabama v. Garrett*, 531 U.S. 356 (2001) (discussed in Section 5.2.5). This means that public institutions cannot be sued for money damages under the ADA in federal court. Federal appellate courts have applied the reasoning of *Garrett* to lawsuits brought against a university under Title II of the ADA, which forbids discrimination by places of public accommodation. For example, in *Robinson v. University of Akron School of Law*, 307 F.3d 409 (6th Cir. 2002), the student brought claims under both the ADA and the Rehabilitation Act, alleging that the law school had failed to provide accommodations to which the student was entitled as a result of his learning disability. The court ruled that the university had waived sovereign immunity against Rehabilitation Act claims, but that it was protected from ADA suits in federal court under the result in *Garrett*. (For a similar ruling, see *Shepard v. Irving*, 77 Fed. Appx. 615 (4th Cir. 2003) (unpublished).)

9.3.5.2. The concept of disability. In order to receive the protections of either Section 504 or the ADA, the student must demonstrate that he or she has a disability that meets the statutory requirements. The ADA defines disability as "a physical or mental impairment that substantially limits one or more of the major life activities" of the individual, or "a record of such an impairment," or "being regarded as having such an impairment" (42 U.S.C. § 12102(2)). Whether or not an individual is disabled for ADA purposes is to be determined on an individualized basis (29 C.F.R. § 1630.21(j)). The definition of disability used in Section 504 is the same as the ADA definition (34 C.F.R. § 104.3(j)). Although most cases do not involve this issue (in contrast to employment litigation under the ADA, in which a frequent employer defense is that the individual's disorder does not meet the ADA definition—see Section 5.2.5), it is useful to remember that the institution is entitled to inquire into the nature of the disability, to require documentation of the disability, and to reach its own determination as to whether the disorder is a disability that requires accommodation under the ADA or Section 504.

Courts evaluating whether students met the laws' definition of disability initially struggled with the issue of whether an individual whose disability was mitigated, fully or in part, by either medication or self-accommodation was entitled to reasonable accommodations under the law. For example, in *McGuinness v. University of New Mexico School of Medicine*, 170 F.3d 974 (10th Cir. 1998), a federal appellate court considered whether a medical student with test anxiety in math and chemistry classes was disabled for ADA purposes. The student had challenged his marginal first-year grades but refused to retake the exams or repeat the first year of instruction. Although the medical school did not dispute the student's claim that he had an "anxiety disorder," the court emphasized that "[j]ust as eyeglasses correct impaired vision, so that it does not constitute a disability under the ADA, an adjusted study regimen can mitigate the effects of test anxiety" (170 F.3d at 979). The court then ruled that this disorder did not meet the ADA definition of disability because it did not substantially limit one or more major life activities.

The question of whether to consider "mitigating measures" in determining whether an individual has an ADA-protected disability was resolved by three decisions announced by the U.S. Supreme Court in 1999. In *Sutton v. United Air Lines*, 527 U.S. 471; *Murphy v. United Parcel Service*, 527 U.S. 516; and *Albertson's v. Kirkingburg*, 527 U.S. 555 (1999) (all discussed in Section 5.2.5), the Court addressed the employment discrimination claims of three individuals under the ADA. In each of these cases, the individual had a disorder that could be minimized or corrected by a device (such as prescription lenses) or by medication. The Court ruled that such "mitigating measures" must be taken into account in determining whether the individuals were disabled. Although the trio of cases is in the employment context, the Court interpreted the ADA's definition of "disability," which applies to all titles of the ADA.

The potential fallout of these three cases is illustrated by *New York State Board of Law Examiners v. Bartlett*, 527 U.S. 1031 (1999). Bartlett had sought accommodations in taking the New York State Bar Examination because of her learning disabilities. The board of law examiners had refused to provide those accommodations because they had found that Bartlett's self-accommodations had permitted her to read at an average level. The U.S. Court of Appeals for the Second Circuit had followed the Equal Employment Opportunity Commission (EEOC) Guidance that required the determination of a disability to be made without regard to mitigating measures, and found that Bartlett's learning disorder qualified as a disability for purposes of the ADA. It had remanded the case to the trial court to determine what accommodations should be provided and the damages due Bartlett (*Bartlett v. New York State Board of Law Examiners*, 156 F.3d 321 (2d Cir. 1998)). The board appealed, and the U.S. Supreme Court vacated the appellate court's decision and remanded it for further consideration in light of the three ADA cases it had recently decided. On remand, the trial court that had originally heard the case determined that Bartlett's dyslexia substantially limited her in the major life activities of reading and working, and that she was entitled to reasonable accommodations in the form of double the normally allotted time to take the bar examination, the use of a computer, additional accommodations, and compensatory damages (2001 U.S. Dist. LEXIS 11926 (S.D.N.Y. 2001)).

Despite the eventual outcome in *Bartlett*, the Supreme Court's rulings in the mitigation cases have made it more difficult for students whose disabilities are somehow mitigated to state ADA claims. For example, in *Gonzales v. National Board of Medical Examiners*, 225 F.3d 620 (6th Cir. 2000), *cert. denied*, 532 U.S. 1038 (2001), a federal appellate court rejected a medical student's request for a preliminary injunction to force the National Board of Medical Examiners to allow him extra time on a licensing examination. The court ruled that the student did not meet the ADA's definition of disability because he had performed successfully without accommodation on other timed standardized tests.

Similarly, a surgical resident's subsequent academic and professional success after being dismissed from a residency program by the University of Cincinnati persuaded a court that he was not disabled. In *Swanson v. University of Cincinnati*, 268 F.3d 307 (6th Cir. 2001), the federal appellate court rejected the former resident's ADA and Rehabilitation Act claims against the university, observing that the limitations posed by his depression were not the reason for his termination from the residency program, and his subsequent success at another university's residency program demonstrated that his depression did not substantially limit his ability to work.

The ADA also protects students against discrimination when they are erroneously regarded as disabled. In *Lee v. Trustees of Dartmouth College*, 958 F. Supp. 37 (D.N.H. 1997), a student contended that his professors and academic advisors regarded him as disabled and caused him to be dismissed from his medical residency. The plaintiff, a resident in neurosurgery, developed a disorder that mimicked the symptoms of multiple sclerosis (MS). Although the resident provided medical documentation that his condition was not MS, and also disputed the defendants' contention that he could not perform surgery, he was dismissed from the residency program. The court found that the medical school had not followed its own procedures, which included a meeting with the student to discuss his performance problems and a three-month probationary period. In addition, said the court, issues of material fact existed as to whether the defendants regarded the plaintiff as disabled and as to whether he could perform the physical demands of the neurosurgical residency. The summary judgment motion of the defendants was denied. (For a case in which an appellate court ruled that the university had regarded a student as disabled but had not discriminated against that student, see *Betts v. Rector and Visitors of the University of Virginia*, 198 F. Supp. 2d 787 (W.D. Va. 2002).)

In addition to satisfying the laws' definition of disability, students must also be able to demonstrate that they are "qualified" to meet the institution's academic standards. For example, regulations implementing Section 504 of the Rehabilitation Act define a "qualified" individual with a disability as one who "meets the academic and technical standards requisite to admission or participation" (34 C.F.R. § 104.3(l)(3)). *Zukle v. Regents of the University of California*, 166 F.3d 1041 (9th Cir. 1999), addresses this issue. Zukle, a medical student who had learning disabilities and who had received numerous accommodations but still could not meet the school's academic standards, was unable to convince the court that she could meet the eligibility requirements of the medical school, even with reasonable accommodations. The court ruled that the student's requested accommodation—lengthening the time during which she could complete her medical degree—would lower the school's academic standards, which is not required by either the ADA or the Rehabilitation Act (see Section 9.3.5.4).

9.3.5.3. Notice and documentation of disabilities. Courts have generally ruled that, unless the institution has knowledge of the student's disability, there is no duty to accommodate. For example, in *Goodwin v. Keuka College*, 929 F.

Supp. 90 (W.D.N.Y. 1995), the plaintiff alleged that she had been improperly terminated from an occupational therapy program due to her mental disability. Under the school's policy, if a student failed to complete two field placements, he or she was automatically terminated from the program. The school policy also provided that a student would automatically fail a field placement if he or she left the assignment without prior permission. After failing one field assignment, passing another, and having a third incomplete, the plaintiff walked off her fourth field assignment after an argument with her supervisor. Nearly three weeks later, the plaintiff sent a letter to the college explaining that she was seeking an evaluation to determine if she had a learning disability and was eligible for accommodation. The college responded that she had been terminated from the program based on her actions, not on the basis of any disability. Although the plaintiff subsequently produced a psychiatric report that she did have a disability, the college refused to reinstate her. The court dismissed the plaintiff's suit, finding that she could not make out a *prima facie* case under either the Rehabilitation Act or the ADA because she could not allege she was dismissed on the basis of her disability. For a school to dismiss a student based on her disability, it must first be aware of that disability.

In addition to the institution having knowledge of the disability, courts have ruled that the ADA requires the student to demonstrate that the university has actually denied a specific request for an accommodation. In *Tips v. Regents of Texas Tech University,* 921 F. Supp. 1515 (N.D. Tex. 1996), the court dismissed the plaintiff's claim because it found that she had not requested the accommodation. After examining the relevant legislative history and regulations, the court held that the duty to accommodate is triggered only upon a request by (or on behalf of) the disabled student. Because the plaintiff did not make her request for accommodation until after her dismissal from the program, the court held that the plaintiff could not make out a case of disability discrimination. A similar result was reached in *Gill v. Franklin Pierce Law Center,* discussed in 8.2.4.3. And in *Scott v. Western State University College of Law,* 1997 U.S. App. LEXIS 9089 (9th Cir. 1997) (unpublished), the appellate court affirmed a trial court's summary judgment on behalf of the law school. The college had dismissed Scott for academic reasons after his first year of law school. After he was dismissed, Scott asserted that he had a disability. The court ruled that the law school's action was unrelated to Scott's disability, since it had no notice of the alleged disability, and that, furthermore, Scott was not "otherwise qualified" for Rehabilitation Act purposes.

Institutions are entitled to require students who seek accommodation to provide recent documentation from a qualified health care provider or other appropriate diagnostician not only of the disability, but also the restrictions or limitations placed on the student by the disability. This issue arose in a widely publicized case, *Guckenberger v. Boston University,* 957 F. Supp. 306 (D. Mass. 1997) (*Guckenberger I*), which ultimately resulted in three lengthy opinions by the district court. Students asserted that Boston University's new policy requiring students to present recent (no more than three years old) documentation of learning disabilities was in violation of state and federal nondiscrimination laws.

They also challenged the evaluation and appeal procedure for requesting academic accommodations, as well as the university's "blanket prohibition" against course substitutions for mathematics and foreign language requirements. Furthermore, the students claimed that negative comments by the university's president about learning-disabled students had created a hostile learning environment for them.

The district court granted class action certification to the plaintiffs (all students with learning disabilities and/or attention deficit disorders currently enrolled at Boston University), thus avoiding mootness concerns. In addition, the court examined the viability of a "hostile academic environment" claim based on disability, concluding that such a claim was possible, but that the allegations of the plaintiffs' complaint fell short of such a claim. Although statements made by the university's president may have been offensive, the court considered the First Amendment concerns at hand and found that these remarks were not "sufficiently directed" toward the plaintiffs to constitute a hostile academic environment.

In a subsequent opinion, *Guckenberger v. Boston University,* 974 F. Supp. 106 (D. Mass. 1997) (*Guckenberger II*), the district court addressed the plaintiffs' claims that the university violated the ADA and Section 504 by requiring students with learning disabilities to be retested every three years by a physician, a clinical psychologist, or a licensed psychologist; and by refusing to modify the requirement that students in the College of Arts and Sciences complete one semester of mathematics and four semesters of a foreign language. The court ruled that the university's previous policy and its application had, in several respects, violated the disability discrimination laws. But the university had changed its policy and some of its practices after the litigation began, and some of those changes had cured some of the violations.

The court ruled that requiring new documentation of a learning disability every three years, without regard to whether the updated information was medically necessary, violated the law because the requirements screened out or tended to screen out students with specific disabilities, and because the university did not demonstrate that the requirements were necessary to provide educational services or accommodations. The university's new policy permits a waiver of the three-year retesting regulation when medically unnecessary; this change, said the court, cured the violation.

The court also ruled that the university's requirement that it would accept documentation only from professionals with certain types of doctorates violated the law because professionals with other degrees (doctorates in education and certain master's degrees) were also qualified to assess individuals for learning disabilities. The court did note, however, that for the assessment of attention deficit disorder, it was appropriate to require that the assessor have a doctorate.

The university's decision to implement the policy in the middle of the academic year, without advance notice to affected students, also violated the ADA and Section 504, according to the court. Furthermore, the court ruled that the president and his staff, who lacked "experience or expertise in diagnosing learning disabilities or in fashioning appropriate accommodations" (974 F. Supp. at

118) had personally administered the policy on the basis of "uninformed stereo-types about the learning disabled." The university's new policy, which delegated the evaluation of accommodation requests to a licensed psychologist, cured that violation. (The third *Guckenberger* opinion is discussed in Section 9.3.5.4 below.)

9.3.5.4. Requests for programmatic or instructional accommodations.[20] Although both Section 504 and the ADA require colleges and universities to provide reasonable accommodations to qualified disabled students, they need not do so if the accommodation will fundamentally alter the nature of the academic program (see *Southeastern Community College v. Davis,* Section 8.2.4.3).[21]

The question of how much change is required arose in *Wynne v. Tufts University School of Medicine,* 976 F.2d 791 (1st Cir. 1992). A medical student dismissed on academic grounds asserted that the medical school had refused to accommodate his learning disability by requiring him to take a multiple choice test rather than an alternative that would minimize the impact of his learning disability. Initially, the trial court granted summary judgment for Tufts, but the appellate court reversed on the grounds that the record was insufficient to enable the court to determine whether Tufts had attempted to accommodate Wynne and whether Tufts had evaluated the impact of the requested accommodation on its academic program (932 F.2d 19 (1st Cir. 1991, *en banc*)).

On remand, the university provided extensive evidence to the trial court that it had permitted Wynne to repeat his first year of medical school, had paid for the neuropsychological testing of Wynne that had identified his learning disabilities, and had provided him with tutors, note takers, and other assistance. It had permitted him to take make-up examinations for courses he failed, and had determined that there was not an appropriate alternative method of testing his knowledge in the biochemistry course.

On the strength of the school's evidence of serious consideration of alternatives to the multiple choice test, the district court again awarded summary judgment for Tufts, and the appellate court affirmed. In deferring to the school's judgment on the need for a certain testing format, the court said:

> [T]he point is not whether a medical school is "right" or "wrong" in making program-related decisions. Such absolutes rarely apply in the context of subjective decision-making, particularly in a scholastic setting. The point is that Tufts, after undertaking a diligent assessment of the available options, felt itself obliged to make "a professional, academic judgment that [a] reasonable accommodation [was] simply not available" [976 F.2d at 795].

---

[20]Cases and other authorities are collected at Richard E. Kaye, Annot., "What Constitutes Reasonable Accommodation Under Federal Statutes Protecting Rights of Disabled Individual, as Regards Educational Program or School Rules as Applied to Learning Disabled Student," 166 A.L.R. Fed. 503.

[21]For the pertinent regulations on accommodation, see 28 C.F.R. § 35.130(h)(7) (ADA Title II), 28 C.F.R. §36.302(a) (ADA Title III), and 34 C.F.R. § 104.44 (Section 504). For the pertinent regulations defining "qualified" disabled student, see 28 C.F.R. § 35.104 (ADA Title II) and 34 C.F.R. § 104.3(k)(4) (Section 504).

Given the multiple forms of assistance that Tufts had provided Wynne, and its ability to demonstrate that it had evaluated alternate test forms and determined that none would be an appropriate substitute for the multiple choice format, the court was satisfied that the school had satisfied the requirements of the Rehabilitation Act.

In *Halasz v. University of New England,* 816 F. Supp. 37 (D. Maine 1993), a federal trial court relied on *Wynne* to review the challenge of a student, dismissed from the University of New England on academic grounds, that the school had failed to provide him with necessary accommodations and had discriminated against him on the basis of his disability. The school had a special program for students with learning disabilities who lacked the academic credentials necessary for regular admission to the university. The program provided a variety of support services for these students, and gave them an opportunity for regular admission to the university after they completed the special one-year program. Despite the special services, such as tutoring, taped texts, untimed testing, and readers for some of his classes, the plaintiff was unable to attain an academic record sufficient for regular admission to the university. His performance in the courses and tests that he took during his year in the special program indicated, the university alleged, that he was not an "otherwise qualified" student with a disability and thus was not protected by the Rehabilitation Act. The university was able to demonstrate the academic rationale for its program requirements and to show that the plaintiff had been given the same amount and quality of assistance that had been given to other students who later were offered admission to the university's regular academic program.

The decisions in *Wynne* and *Halasz* demonstrate the significance of an institution's consideration of potential accommodations for students with disabilities. Given the tendency of courts to defer to academic judgments, but to hold colleges and universities to strict procedural standards, those institutions that can demonstrate, as could Tufts, that they gave careful consideration to the student's request, and reached a decision on *academic* grounds that the accommodation was either unnecessary or unsuitable, should be able to prevail against challenges under either the Rehabilitation Act or the ADA.

The scope of the accommodation requirement was also addressed in the *Guckenberger* trilogy (Section 9.3.5.3), and the case is particularly instructive because of the court's scrutiny of the process used by the university to make an academic determination concerning the requested accommodations. The students had challenged the university's refusal to waive the foreign language requirement in the College of Arts and Sciences, or to permit substitution of other courses taught in English, as a violation of the ADA. In *Guckenberger II,* the court agreed in principle that the university was not required to lower its academic standards or require substantial alteration of academic programs. The court found, however, that the university had not even considered the alternatives suggested by the students (or any other alternatives) that would have provided an appropriate accommodation while maintaining academic standards and programmatic integrity. Said the court: "[T]he University simply relied on the status quo as the rationale" (974 F. Supp. at 115). The court awarded damages for breach of contract and emotional distress to several of the students whose accommodations were delayed or denied because of the policy and its application by university officials. It also ordered the university to develop a "deliberative procedure" for considering whether other courses could be substituted for the foreign language requirement of the liberal arts college without fundamentally altering the nature of its liberal arts degree program.

The university turned to a faculty committee that advised the dean of arts and sciences on curricular and programmatic issues. That committee heard the views of some of the student plaintiffs during its deliberations; no administrators were committee members, nor did they attend the meetings. At the conclusion of its deliberations, the committee stated that the foreign language requirement was "fundamental to the nature of the liberal arts degree at Boston University" and recommended against permitting course substitutions as an alternative to the foreign language requirement. The president accepted the committee's recommendation. Then, in a third ruling, *Guckenberger v. Boston University,* 8 F. Supp. 2d 82 (D. Mass. 1998) (*Guckenberger III*), the court ruled that the university had complied with its order, approved the procedure that had been used, and dismissed the plaintiffs' challenge to the process and the outcome of the committee's work.

In determining whether the university used the appropriate process and standards to decide whether a requested accommodation was reasonable, the district court in *Guckenberger III* looked to the opinion of the U.S. Court of Appeals for the First Circuit in *Wynne v. Tufts University School of Medicine,* discussed earlier in this subsection.

> "If the institution submits undisputed facts demonstrating that the relevant officials within the institution considered alternative means, their feasibility, cost and effect on the academic program, and came to a rationally justifiable conclusion that the available alternatives would result either in lowering academic standards or requiring substantial program alteration, the court could rule as a matter of law that the institution had met its duty of seeking reasonable accommodation" [8 F. Supp. 2d at 87, quoting *Wynne I* at 26].

The *Guckenberger III* court first engaged in fact finding to determine whether Boston University had exercised "reasoned deliberation." It examined who the decision makers were, whether the deliberative group addressed why the foreign language requirement was unique, and whether it considered possible alternatives to the requirement. Although the committee had not kept minutes of its meetings in the past, it had been ordered by the court to do so; review of those minutes was an important factor in the court's determination. The minutes reflected that the committee had discussed why the foreign language requirement was important, and why alternatives to the foreign language requirement would not meet the goals which the requirement was enacted to fulfill. The committee was insulated from those officials whose comments and decisions had been criticized by the court in earlier rulings, and the committee gave students an opportunity to provide information and their perspective on the issue. The court concluded that "the Committee's reliance on only its own academic judgment and the input of College students was reasonable and in keeping with the nature of the decision" (8 F. Supp. 2d at 87–88).

The court then evaluated "whether the facts add up to a professional, academic judgment that reasonable accommodation is simply not available" (8 F. Supp. 2d at 89, quoting *Wynne I* at 27–28). Despite the fact that the committee did not consult external experts, and the fact that many elite universities, such as Harvard, Yale, and Columbia, have no similar foreign language requirement, the court ruled that the process used was appropriate and the outcome was rationally justifiable. The court stated:

> [S]o long as an academic institution rationally, without pretext, exercises its deliberate professional judgment not to permit course substitutions for an academic requirement in a liberal arts curriculum, the ADA does not authorize the courts to intervene even if a majority of other comparable academic institutions disagree [8 F. Supp. 2d at 90].

Determinations of whether accommodation requests would fall short of fundamental academic standards must be based on professional academic judgments.

Much of the litigation concerning conflicts between the accommodations sought by the student and the accommodations the institution is willing to grant occur with medical students or other students for whom a clinical experience is required. Most federal courts are deferential to a determination by faculty or academic administrators that a requested accommodation is either inappropriate for educational reasons or that the student cannot satisfactorily complete the required curriculum even with accommodation. For example, in *Zukle v. The Regents of the University of California,* 166 F.3d 1041 (9th Cir. 1999), the court treated as a matter of first impression the question of "judicial deference to an educational institution's academic decisions in ADA and Rehabilitation Act cases" (166 F.3d at 1047). Although the Tenth Circuit had rejected a deferential approach in *Pushkin v. Regents of the University of Colorado* (Section 8.2.4.3), the Ninth Circuit determined that deference was appropriate, following the lead of the First, Second, and Fifth Circuits. In *Zukle,* a medical student with learning disorders that made reading slow and difficult, requested to be relieved of the requirement to complete several of her clinical rotations until after other academic requirements had been completed. The medical school refused. The court ruled that the medical school had offered the plaintiff "all of the accommodations that it normally offers learning disabled students," such as double time on exams, note-taking services, and textbooks on audiocassettes. But Zukle's request that she delay the completion of several clinical rotations and retake a portion of them at a later time was a "substantial alteration" of the curriculum, and thus the medical school was not required to acquiesce to her request. Because the student could not demonstrate that she could meet the academic requirements of the medical school, even with the accommodations it did provide, the court ruled that she was not qualified, and thus had not established a *prima facie* case of disability discrimination.

In a somewhat similar case from the Sixth Circuit, the court ruled that the Ohio College of Podiatric Medicine (OPM) had provided sufficient accommodations for a student. In *Kaltenberger v. Ohio College of Podiatric Medicine,* 162

F.3d 432 (6th Cir. 1998), the plaintiff challenged her academic dismissal on ADA grounds. The student had not performed well academically during her first semester at OPM, and sought a diagnosis for possible learning disorders. She was eventually diagnosed with attention deficit/hyperactive disorder (ADHD). Although by the time the student was properly diagnosed she had been dismissed for academic reasons, she appealed the dismissal on the grounds that she had ADHD, and she was reinstated to a five-year program that provided a lighter course load. She was also provided with the five accommodations that the diagnosing professional had recommended for the student. The student did not take advantage of several of the accommodations (individual tutoring, additional academic counseling), and continued to perform poorly in courses she was required to retake. She was dismissed at the end of her second academic year. As in *Zukle,* the Sixth Circuit deferred to the academic judgment of the plaintiff's professors and advisors. It rejected the plaintiff's assertion that she should be allowed to substitute less demanding courses for the required curriculum, and ruled that the college had provided sufficient reasonable accommodations to the student.

Another Ninth Circuit case addressed the standard used by courts to review an institution's claim that it could not provide academic accommodations. In *Wong v. Regents of the University of California,* 192 F.3d 807 (9th Cir. 1999), a medical student with learning disabilities had been dismissed on academic grounds, primarily because he had difficulties completing his clinical rotations successfully. The trial court had ruled that accommodations provided by the university were reasonable, and that the plaintiff was not qualified to continue as a medical student. The appellate court disagreed.

Although the medical school dean had approved several accommodations for the student over a period of years, he had rejected the student's final accommodation requests. The court explained the standard of review appropriate to accommodation decisions of academic institutions:

> In the typical disability discrimination case in which a plaintiff appeals a district court's entry of summary judgment in favor of the defendant, we undertake this reasonable accommodation analysis ourselves as a matter of course, examining the record and deciding whether the record reveals questions of fact as to whether the requested modification substantially alters the performance standards at issue or whether the accommodation would allow the individual to meet those requirements. In a case involving assessment of the standards of an academic institution, however, we abstain from an in-depth, de novo analysis of suggested accommodations that the school rejected if the institution demonstrates that it conducted such an inquiry itself and concluded that the accommodations were not feasible or would not be effective [192 F.3d at 818].

Because the university had not submitted evidence that the dean had made a reasoned determination that the accommodations requested by Wong were unreasonable, particularly since they were very similar to earlier accommodations that the dean had approved, and given the fact that the prior accommodations enabled Wong to perform very well (circumstances very different from those in *Zukle*), the court refused to defer to the university's determination "because it did not demonstrate that it conscientiously exercised professional judgment in considering the feasibility" of the requested accommodations. The court then addressed the issue of Wong's qualifications to continue as a medical student. Again the court rejected the deferential standard of review, because "the school's system for evaluating a learning disabled student's abilities and its own duty to make its program accessible to such individuals fell short of the standards we require to grant deference . . ." (192 F.3d at 823). Because Wong had performed well when given additional time to prepare for each clinical rotation, the court ruled that he should be allowed to establish at trial that he was qualified.

The court concluded with some advice to institutions, and a warning:

> The deference to which academic institutions are entitled when it comes to the ADA is a double-edged sword. It allows them a significant amount of leeway in making decisions about their curricular requirements and their ability to structure their programs to accommodate disabled students. On the other hand, it places on an institution the weighty responsibility of carefully considering each disabled student's particular limitations and analyzing whether and how it might accommodate that student in a way that would allow the student to complete the school program without lowering academic standards or otherwise unduly burdening the institution. . . . We will not sanction an academic institution's decision to refuse to accommodate a disabled student and subsequent dismissal of that student when the record contains facts from which a reasonable jury could conclude that the school made those decisions for arbitrary reasons unrelated to its academic standards [192 F.3d at 826].[22]

On remand, the trial court determined that the student was not disabled (an issue that the earlier opinions had not addressed) because he had been able to achieve earlier academic success without accommodations; the appellate court affirmed that ruling (379 F.3d 1097 (1994)).

In another case, *Doe v. University of Maryland Medical System Corporation,* 50 F.3d 1261 (4th Cir. 1995), an HIV-infected neurosurgical resident had rejected the medical school's proposed accommodation and attempted to force the school to permit him to continue performing surgery. The third-year resident was stuck with a needle while treating an HIV-positive patient, and the resident later tested HIV-positive himself. The hospital permanently suspended Doe from surgical practice, offering him residencies in pathology and psychiatry. Doe rejected these alternatives and filed claims under the Rehabilitation Act and the ADA. The court ruled that he was not otherwise qualified because he

---

[22]After the appellate court ruling, but before remanded case came to trial, the U.S. Supreme Court released its opinion in *Toyota Motor Mfg. Kentucky, Inc. v. Williams,* 534 U.S. 184 (2002), which interpreted the ADA's definition of "disability" very narrowly. The trial court determined that, under the *Toyota* standard, Wong was not disabled because his overall academic performance prior to the final year of medical school had been very successful, and the appellate court affirmed, thus ending Wong's case (379 F.3d 1097 (9th Cir. 2004)).

posed a significant risk to patient safety that could not be eliminated by reasonable accommodation, and that the accommodations proposed by the medical school were reasonable.

As is the case with ADA claims by employees, students may ask to "telecommute" to college. In *Maczaczyj v. State of New York,* 956 F. Supp. 403 (W.D.N.Y. 1997), a federal trial court was asked to order Empire State College to permit the plaintiff to "attend" required weekend class sessions by telephone from his home, an accommodation that the college had refused to allow. The plaintiff, who suffered from panic attacks (a psychiatric disorder), had rejected the offer of the program faculty to modify certain program requirements, such as excusing him from social portions of the class sessions, providing an empty room for him to use when he became agitated, allowing him to bring along a friend of his choice, and allowing him to select the location on campus where the sessions would take place. The court credited the college's argument that attendance was required for pedagogical reasons, and that the course was not designed to be delivered through distance learning or telecommunication technologies. Finding that telephone "attendance" would therefore not be the academic equivalent of the required class sessions, the court denied the plaintiff's request.

As study abroad programs become more popular, students with disabilities have sought to participate, and many institutions have worked to accommodate the individualized needs of students with mobility or other impairments. Although the Office of Civil Rights, U.S. Department of Education has ruled that Section 504 of the Rehabilitation Act and Title II of the ADA do not apply outside the United States,[23] students have attempted to state both federal and state law claims challenging their institutions' alleged failure to accommodate them on study abroad trips.

In *Bird v. Lewis & Clark College,* 303 F.3d 1015 (9th Cir. 2002), *cert. denied,* 538 U.S. 923 (2003), a student who used a wheelchair participated in the college's study abroad program in Australia after college representatives assured her and her parents that she would be fully accommodated. Although the college made numerous accommodations for the student, she was unable to participate in several activities with her classmates, and sued the college upon her return, claiming ADA violations and breach of the college's fiduciary duty to her, a state law claim. The college argued that neither Section 504 nor Title III of the ADA had extraterritorial application (see Section 13.5.7.6), but the court did not rule on that issue because it determined that the college had reasonably accommodated the student. However, the court affirmed the jury's finding that the college breached its fiduciary duty to the student, based upon the assurances and representations that the college had made to the student and her parents, and its award of $5,000 in damages.

As the court opinions (particularly *Guckenberger* and *Wong*) in this Section illustrate, process considerations are of great importance in administering the institution's system for reviewing student requests for accommodation.

---

[23]OCR Region VIII, Case #08012047, December 3, 2001 (Arizona State University).

The institution will need to consider such requests on an individualized, case-by-case basis. Documentation that is submitted by students or obtained by the institution will need to be prepared or evaluated by professionals with appropriate credentials. Determinations of whether accommodation requests would fall short of fundamental academic standards must be based on professional judgments of faculty and academic administrators. On the other hand, once the institution can show that it has in effect, and has relied upon, a process meeting these requirements, it can expect to receive considerable deference from the courts if its determination is challenged (see especially the *Zukle* case).

This area of the law continues to develop rapidly. Although the 1999 decisions of the U.S. Supreme Court (Section 9.3.5.2 above) clarify one aspect of the ADA's interpretation, and other cases in Section 9.3.5 clarify other aspects, many other issues related to students with disabilities remain. How substantial must a requested change in an academic program be before it is considered an undue hardship for the institution? What should be the institution's response if a faculty member argues that a requested accommodation infringes his or her academic freedom rights? Can an institution require a student to receive counseling or to take medication as part of the accommodation agreement? These and other issues will challenge administrators, faculty, and university counsel as they seek to act within the ADA's requirements while maintaining the academic integrity of their programs.

Sec. 9.4. Procedures for Suspension, Dismissal, and Other Sanctions

9.4.1. Overview. As Sections 9.2 and 9.3 indicate, both public and private postsecondary institutions have the clear right to dismiss, suspend, or impose lesser sanctions on students for behavioral misconduct or academic deficiency. But just as that right is limited by the principles set out in those Sections, so it is also circumscribed by a body of procedural requirements that institutions must follow in effecting disciplinary or academic sanctions. These procedural requirements tend to be more specific and substantial than the requirements set out above, although they do vary depending on whether behavior or academics is involved and whether the institution is public or private (see Section 1.5.2).

At the threshold level, whenever an institution has established procedures that apply to the imposition of sanctions, the law will usually require that these procedures be followed. In *Woody v. Burns*, 188 So. 2d 56 (Fla. 1966), for example, the court invalidated an expulsion from a public institution because a faculty committee had "circumvented . . . [the] duly authorized [disciplinary] committee and arrogated unto itself the authority of imposing its own penalty for appellant's misconduct." And in *Tedeschi v. Wagner College*, 49 N.Y.2d 652 (N.Y. 1980), New York's highest court invalidated a suspension from a private institution, holding that "when a university has adopted a rule or guideline establishing the procedure to be followed in relation to suspension or expulsion, that procedure must be substantially observed."

There are three exceptions, however, to this "follow the rules" principle. *First,* an institution may be excused from following its own procedures if the student knowingly and freely waives his or her right to them, as in *Yench v. Stockmar,* 483 F.2d 820 (10th Cir. 1973), where the student neither requested that the published procedures be followed nor objected when they were not. *Second,* deviations from established procedures may be excused when they do not disadvantage the student, as in *Winnick v. Manning,* 460 F.2d 545 (2d Cir. 1972), where the student contested the school's use of a panel other than that required by the rules, but the court held that the "deviations were minor ones and did not affect the fundamental fairness of the hearing." And *third,* if an institution provides more elaborate protections than constitutionally required, failure to provide nonrequired protections may not imply constitutional violations (see Section 9.4.3).

This Section focuses on challenges to the fairness of the procedures that colleges use to determine whether a student has violated a campus rule or code of conduct, as well as the fairness of the sanction, if any, levied against the student. Because public colleges are subject to constitutional regulation as well as statutory and common law, disciplinary decisions at public colleges are discussed separately from those at private colleges. And sanctions based on student academic misconduct are discussed separately for public institutions from those based upon student social (or criminal) misconduct, although the distinctions between academic and disciplinary sanctions seem to be blurring as some courts are viewing academic misconduct as behavior rather than as a violation of academic standards, and are applying standards developed in student discipline cases to academic misconduct cases.

(For a thoughtful critique of college disciplinary procedures and suggestions for enhancing the fairness of such discipline, see Curtis J. Berger & Vivian Berger, "Academic Discipline: A Guide to Fair Process for the University Student," 99 *Columbia L. Rev.* 289 (1999).)

9.4.2. Public institutions: Disciplinary sanctions.

State institutions may be subject to state administrative procedure acts, state board of higher education rules, or other state statutes or administrative regulations specifying particular procedures for suspensions or expulsions. In *Mary M. Clark,* 473 N.Y.S.2d 843 (N.Y. App. Div. 1984), the court refused to apply New York State's Administrative Procedure Act to a suspension proceeding at State University of New York-Cortland; but in *Mull v. Oregon Institute of Technology,* 538 P.2d 87 (Or. 1975), the court applied that state's administrative procedure statutes to a suspension for misconduct and remanded the case to the college with instructions to enter findings of fact and conclusions of law as required by one of the statutory provisions.

The primary external source of procedural requirements for public institutions, however, is the due process clause of the federal Constitution, which prohibits the government from depriving an individual of life, liberty, or property without certain procedural protections.[24] Since the early 1960s, the concept of procedural due process has been one of the primary legal forces shaping the

---

[24]Cases are collected in Daniel A. Klein, Annot., "Expulsion, Dismissal, Suspension, or Other Discipline of Student of Public School, College, or University as Violating Due Process Clause of Federal Constitution's Fourteenth Amendment—Supreme Court Cases," 88 L. Ed. 2d 1015.

administration of postsecondary education. For purposes of due process analysis, courts typically assume, without deciding, that a student has a property interest in continued enrollment at a public institution (see, for example, *Marin v. University of Puerto Rico,* 377 F. Supp. 613, 622 (D.P.R. 1974)). One court stopped short of finding a property interest, but said that the Fourteenth Amendment "gives rights to a student who faces expulsion for misconduct at a tax-supported college or university" (*Henderson State University v. Spadoni,* 848 S.W.2d 951 (Ark. Ct. App. 1993). As did the court in *Marin,* the U.S. Supreme Court has assumed a property interest in continued enrollment in a public institution (for example, in *Ewing* and *Horowitz,* discussed in Sections 9.3.1 and 9.4.3 respectively), but has not yet directly ruled on this point.

A landmark 1961 case on suspension procedures, *Dixon v. Alabama State Board of Education,* 294 F.2d 150 (5th Cir. 1961), is still very instructive. Several black students at Alabama State College had been expelled during a period of intense civil rights activity in Montgomery, Alabama. The students, supported by the National Association for the Advancement of Colored People (NAACP), sued the state board, and the court faced the question "whether [the] due process [clause of the Fourteenth Amendment] requires notice and some opportunity for hearing before students at a tax-supported college are expelled for misconduct." On appeal this question was answered in the affirmative, with the court establishing standards by which to measure the adequacy of a public institution's expulsion procedures:

> The notice should contain a statement of the specific charges and grounds which, if proven, would justify expulsion under the regulations of the board of education. The nature of the hearing should vary depending upon the circumstances of the particular case. The case before us requires something more than an informal interview with an administrative authority of the college. By its nature, a charge of misconduct, as opposed to a failure to meet the scholastic standards of the college, depends upon a collection of the facts concerning the charged misconduct, easily colored by the point of view of the witnesses. In such circumstances, a hearing which gives the board or the administrative authorities of the college an opportunity to hear both sides in considerable detail is best suited to protect the rights of all involved. This is not to imply that a full-dress judicial hearing, with the right to cross-examine witnesses, is required. Such a hearing, with the attending publicity and disturbance of college activities, might be detrimental to the college's educational atmosphere and impractical to carry out. Nevertheless, the rudiments of an adversary proceeding may be preserved without encroaching upon the interests of the college. In the instant case, the student should be given the names of the witnesses against him and an oral or written report on the facts to which each witness testifies. He should also be given the opportunity to present to the board, or at least to an administrative official of the college, his own defense against the charges and to produce either oral testimony or written affidavits of witnesses in his behalf. If the hearing is not before the board directly, the results and findings of the hearing should be presented in a report open to the student's inspection. If these rudimentary elements of fair play are followed in a case of misconduct of this particular type, we feel that the requirements of due process of law will have been fulfilled [294 F.2d at 158–59].

Since the *Dixon* case, courts at all levels have continued to recognize and extend the due process safeguards available to students charged by college officials with misconduct. Such safeguards must now be provided for all students in publicly supported schools, not only before expulsion, as in *Dixon,* but before suspension and other serious disciplinary action as well (unless the student is a danger to the campus community and must be removed, in which case a postremoval hearing would be required). In 1975, the U.S. Supreme Court itself recognized the vitality and clear national applicability of such developments when it held that even a secondary school student faced with a suspension of less than ten days is entitled to "*some* kind of notice and . . . *some* kind of hearing" (*Goss v. Lopez,* 419 U.S. 565, 579 (1975)).

Although the Court in *Goss* was not willing to afford students the right to a full-blown adversary hearing (involving cross-examination, written transcripts, and representation by counsel), it set out minimal requirements for compliance with the due process clause. The Court said:

> We do not believe that school authorities must be totally free from notice and hearing requirements. . . . [T]he student [must] be given oral or written notice of the charges against him and, if he denies them, an explanation of the evidence the authorities have and an opportunity to present his side of the story. The [Due Process] Clause requires at least these rudimentary precautions against unfair or mistaken findings of misconduct and arbitrary exclusion from school [419 U.S. at 581].

In cases subsequent to *Goss,* most courts have applied these "minimal" procedural standards and, for the most part, have ruled in favor of the college.

Probably the case that has set forth due process requirements in greatest detail and, consequently, at the highest level of protection, is *Esteban v. Central Missouri State College,* 277 F. Supp. 649 (W.D. Mo. 1967) (see also later litigation in this case, discussed in Section 9.2.2 above). The plaintiffs had been suspended for two semesters for engaging in protest demonstrations. The lower court held that the students had not been accorded procedural due process and ordered the school to provide the following protections for them:

1. A written statement of the charges, for each student, made available at least ten days before the hearing;

2. A hearing before the person(s) having power to expel or suspend;

3. The opportunity for advance inspection of any affidavits or exhibits the college intends to submit at the hearing;

4. The right to bring counsel to the hearing to advise them (but not to question witnesses);

5. The opportunity to present their own version of the facts, by personal statements as well as affidavits and witnesses;

6. The right to hear evidence against them and question (personally, not through counsel) adverse witnesses;

7. A determination of the facts of each case by the hearing officer, solely on the basis of the evidence presented at the hearing;

8. A written statement of the hearing officer's findings of fact; and

9. The right, at their own expense, to make a record of the hearing.

The judicial imposition of specific due process requirements rankles many administrators. By and large, courts have been sufficiently sensitive to avoid such detail in favor of administrative flexibility (see, for example, *Moresco v. Clark,* 473 N.Y.S.2d 843 (N.Y. App. Div. 1984); *Henson v. Honor Committee of the University of Virginia,* 719 F.2d 69 (4th Cir. 1983), discussed in Section 9.4.2.2). Yet for the internal guidance of an administrator responsible for disciplinary procedures, the *Esteban* requirements provide a useful checklist. The listed items not only suggest the outer limits of what a court might require but also identify those procedures most often considered valuable for ascertaining facts where they are in dispute. Within this framework of concerns, the constitutional focus remains on the notice-and-opportunity-for-hearing concept of *Dixon.*

Although the federal courts have not required the type of protection provided at formal judicial hearings, deprivations of basic procedural rights can result in judicial rejection of an institution's disciplinary decision. In *Weidemann v. SUNY College at Cortland,* 592 N.Y.S.2d 99 (N.Y. App. Div. 1992), the court annulled the college's dismissal of a student who had been accused of cheating on an examination, and ordered a new hearing. Specifically, the court found these procedural defects:

1. Evidence was introduced at the hearing of which the student was unaware.

2. The student was not provided the five-day written notice required by the student handbook about evidence supporting the charges against him, and had no opportunity to defend against that evidence.

3. The hearing panel contacted a college witness after the hearing and obtained additional evidence without notifying the student.

4. The student was given insufficient notice of the date of the hearing and the appeal process.

5. The student was given insufficient notice (one day) of his right to appeal.

6. The student's attorney had advised college officials of these violations, but the letter had been ignored.

In addition to possible due process problems listed above, a long delay between the time a student is charged and the date of the hearing may disadvantage the student. Although a federal trial court rejected a student's claim that a nine-month delay in scheduling his disciplinary hearing was a denial of due process (*Cross v. Rector and Visitors of the University of Virginia,* 84 F. Supp.

2d 740 (W.D. Va. 2000), *affirmed without opinion,* 2000 U.S. App. LEXIS 22017 (August 28, 2000)), ensuring that hearings are held in a timely fashion should discourage such due process claims.

A case brought against Indiana University is illustrative of both notice and hearing aspects of the student disciplinary process. In *Reilly v. Daly,* 666 N.E.2d 439 (Ind. App. 1996), a student who was dismissed from the university for cheating claimed a variety of constitutional violations. Reilly, a student at Indiana University School of Medicine, was accused of cheating on a final examination by two professors who believed she had been copying from another student.

The professors compared the test papers of the two students. A statistician advised the professors that there was 1 chance in 200,000 that Reilly and the other student could have had the same incorrect answers on their multiple choice questions without cheating having occurred. The professors gave Reilly an F on the exam, sending her a letter that outlined the suspicious behavior and the statistical comparisons. Reilly sent a letter of protest to the professors, who reaffirmed their decision. Reilly was permitted to bring a lawyer with her to meet with the professors to rebut their charges. As a result of that meeting, the professors had a second statistical analysis run on the two test papers, which resulted in a lower, but still significantly high probability that the similarities were not a result of chance.

Because Reilly had received a grade of F in another course, also as the result of cheating on a final exam, she was informed that she was entitled to a hearing before the Student Promotions Committee prior to dismissal from medical school. She was permitted the assistance of her attorney and was allowed to present her version of the facts. The committee voted to recommend her dismissal. Reilly appealed the committee's decision, but it reaffirmed its recommendation. The dean then dismissed Reilly from medical school.

In court, Reilly alleged that the university denied her due process and equal protection. The alleged due process violations were her lack of opportunity to question the course professors at the hearing, the vagueness of a rule that forbids "the appearance of cheating," and the committee's failure to use the "clear and convincing" standard of proof. The court did not address whether the dismissal was on academic or disciplinary grounds because it found that the medical school had afforded her sufficient due process for either type of dismissal. Even had the dismissal been on disciplinary grounds, said the court, she had no right to formally cross-examine her accusers; she was fully aware of the evidence against her; and she had been given the opportunity to discuss it with the professors.

The court disposed of the vagueness claim by noting that Reilly had been dismissed because the committee had determined that she cheated, so the "appearance of cheating" rule was irrelevant to her dismissal. And the court stated that only "substantial evidence" was necessary to uphold the dismissal; the committee was not required to use the "clear and convincing" standard of proof.

Reilly also challenged her dismissal on equal protection grounds, asserting that students in other units of the university were given certain rights that she, as a medical student, was not, including the right to cross-examine witnesses and the use of the clear and convincing evidence standard. The court noted that the equal protection clause does not require that all persons be treated identically, but only that an individual be treated the same as "similarly situated" persons. Reilly was treated the same as other medical students, said the court; she was not "similarly situated" to undergraduates or students in the law school. The court affirmed the trial court's denial of the preliminary injunction sought by Reilly.

Because of the potential for constitutional or other claims, administrators should ensure that the staff who handle disciplinary charges against students, and the members of the hearing panels who determine whether the campus code of conduct have been violated, are trained in the workings of the disciplinary system and the protections that must be afforded students. Judicial review of the outcomes of disciplinary hearings is typically deferential *if* the institution has followed its own procedures carefully, and if those procedures comport with constitutional requirements.

9.4.2.1. Notice. Notice should be given of both the conduct with which the student is charged and the rule or policy that allegedly proscribes the conduct.[25] The charges need not be drawn with the specificity of a criminal indictment, but they should be "in sufficient detail to fairly enable . . . [the student] to present a defense" at the hearing (*Jenkins v. Louisiana State Board of Education,* 506 F.2d 992 (5th Cir. 1975)), holding notice in a suspension case to be adequate, particularly in light of information provided by the defendant subsequent to the original notice). Factual allegations not enumerated in the notice may be developed at the hearing if the student could reasonably have expected them to be included.

There is no clear constitutional requirement concerning how much advance notice the student must have of the charges. As little as two days before the hearing has been held adequate (*Jones v. Tennessee State Board of Education,* 279 F. Supp. 190 (M.D. Tenn. 1968), *affirmed,* 407 F.2d 834 (6th Cir. 1969); see also *Nash v. Auburn University,* 812 F.2d 655 (11th Cir. 1987)). *Esteban* required ten days, however, and in most other cases the time has been longer than two days. In general, courts handle this issue case by case, asking whether the amount of time was fair under all the circumstances. And, of course, if the college's written procedures for student discipline provide for deadlines for notice to be given, or provide periods of time for the student to prepare for the hearing, those procedures should be followed in order to avoid potential breach of contract or constitutional claims.

9.4.2.2. Hearing. The minimum requirement is that the hearing provide students with an opportunity to speak in their own defense and explain their side of the story. Since due process apparently does not require an open or a public hearing, the institution has the discretion to close or partially close the hearing or to leave the choice to the accused student. But courts usually will accord students

---

[25]Cases and authorities are collected at E. H. Schopler, Annot., "Right of Student to Hearing on Charges Before Suspension or Expulsion from Educational Institution," 58 A.L.R.2d 903.

the right to hear the evidence against them and to present oral testimony or, at minimum, written statements from witnesses. Formal rules of evidence need not be followed. Cross-examination, the right to counsel, the right to a transcript, and an appellate procedure have generally not been constitutional essentials, but where institutions have voluntarily provided these procedures, courts have often cited them approvingly as enhancers of the hearing's fairness.

When the conduct with which the student is charged in the disciplinary proceeding is also the subject of a criminal court proceeding, the due process obligations of the institution will likely increase. Since the student then faces additional risks and strategic problems, some of the procedures usually left to the institution's discretion may become constitutional essentials. In *Gabrilowitz v. Newman*, 582 F.2d 100 (1st Cir. 1978) (discussed in Section 9.1.4), for example, the court required that the institution allow the student to have a lawyer present to advise him during the disciplinary hearing.

The person(s) presiding over the disciplinary proceedings and the person(s) with authority to make the final decision must decide the case on the basis of the evidence presented and must, of course, weigh the evidence impartially. Generally the student must show malice, bias, or conflict of interest on the part of the hearing officer or panel member before a court will make a finding of partiality. In *Blanton v. State University of New York*, 489 F.2d 377 (2d Cir. 1973), the court held that—at least where students had a right of appeal—due process was not violated when a dean who had witnessed the incident at issue also sat on the hearing committee. And in *Jones v. Tennessee State Board of Education*, 279 F. Supp. 190 (M.D. Tenn. 1968), *affirmed*, 407 F.2d 834 (6th Cir. 1969), the court even permitted a member of the hearing committee to give evidence against the accused student, in the absence of proof of malice or personal interest. But other courts may be less hospitable to such practices, and it would be wise to avoid them whenever possible.

A federal appellate court considered the question of the neutrality of participants in the hearing and discipline process. In *Gorman v. University of Rhode Island*, 837 F.2d 7 (1st Cir. 1988), a student suspended for a number of disciplinary infractions charged that the university's disciplinary proceedings were defective in several respects. He asserted that two students on the student-faculty University Board on Student Conduct were biased against him because of earlier encounters; that he had been denied the assistance of counsel at the hearing; that he had been denied a transcript of the hearing; and that the director of student life had served as adviser to the board and also had prepared a record of the hearing, thereby compromising the board's independence.

Finding no evidence that Gorman was denied a fair hearing, the court commented:

> [T]he courts ought not to extol form over substance, and impose on educational institutions all the procedural requirements of a common law criminal trial. The question presented is not whether the hearing was ideal, or whether its procedure could have been better. In all cases the inquiry is whether, under the particular circumstances presented, the hearing was fair, and accorded the individual the essential elements of due process [837 F.2d at 16].

In some cases, the institution may determine that a student must be removed from campus immediately for his or her own safety or the safety of others. Even if the institution determines that a student is dangerous and that a summary suspension is needed, the student's due process rights must be addressed. While case law on these points has been sparse, the U.S. Supreme Court's 1975 ruling in *Goss v. Lopez* explains that:

> [a]s a general rule notice and hearing should precede removal of the student from school. We agree . . . , however, that there are recurring situations in which prior notice and hearing cannot be insisted upon. Students whose presence poses a continuing danger to persons or property or an ongoing threat of disrupting the academic process may be immediately removed from school . . . [and notice and hearing] should follow as soon as practicable [419 U.S. at 583 (1975)].

In *Ashiegbu v. Williams,* 1997 U.S. App. LEXIS 32345 (6th Cir. 1997) (unpublished), a student from Ohio State University (OSU) alleged that he had been called to the office of the vice president for student affairs, handed a letter stating that he was being suspended "because of a continuing pattern of threats and disruptions to the OSU community," and ordered not to return to campus until he had obtained both a psychiatric evaluation and OSU's consent to his return. Ruling that the indefinite suspension was the equivalent of a permanent expulsion, the court stated that the vice president should have provided Ashiegbu with notice, an explanation of the evidence against him, and an opportunity to present his side of the story. The court also ruled that Ashiegbu had the right to a preexpulsion (but not necessarily a presuspension) hearing. Given these due process violations, the appellate court ruled that the trial court's dismissal of Ashiegbu's civil rights action was improper.

On the other hand, a federal trial court rejected a student's claim that his suspension prior to a hearing violated due process guarantees. In *Hill v. Board of Trustees of Michigan State University,* 182 F. Supp. 2d 621 (W.D. Mich. 2001), Hill, a Michigan State University student, was caught on videotape participating in a riot after a basketball game and vandalizing property. Because Hill was already on probation for recent violations of the alcohol policy, an administrator suspended Hill and offered him a hearing before a student-faculty hearing panel the following week. The court ruled that the administrator was justified in using his emergency power of suspension prior to a hearing because of Hill's violent conduct, and that the subsequent hearing held a week later, at which Hill was represented by counsel who participated in the questioning, was timely and impartial.

Some victims of alleged violence by fellow students, or other witnesses, may be reluctant to actually "face" the accused, and have requested that either they or the accused be allowed to sit behind screens in order not to be seen by the accused. In *Gomes v. University of Maine System,* 304 F. Supp. 2d 117 (D. Maine 2004), the university had suspended two students for allegedly committing a sexual assault. The students challenged their suspensions on both substantive and procedural due process grounds. Although the trial court awarded summary judgment to the university on the students' substantive due process claims, finding that the university's decision was within the protections of the Fourteenth Amendment, it refused to side with the university on the students' procedural due process claims. The students and their attorneys had been required to sit behind screens so that neither the students nor their attorneys could see the accuser or the hearing panel. The court agreed with the students that such a walling off could have interfered with their counsels' ability to cross-examine witnesses, and ruled that the procedural due process claim would have to be tried.

(For analyses of student rights in disciplinary hearings, see J. M. Picozzi, "University Disciplinary Process: What's Fair, What's Due and What You Don't Get," 96 *Yale L.J.* 2132 (1987); and D. R. Richmond, "Students' Right to Counsel in University Disciplinary Proceedings," 15 *J. Coll. & Univ. Law* 289 (1989).)

When students are accused of academic misconduct, such as plagiarism or cheating, conduct issues become mixed with academic evaluation issues (compare the *Napolitano* case in Section 9.4.4). Courts typically require some due process protections for students suspended or dismissed for academic misconduct, but not elaborate ones. For example, in *Easley v. University of Michigan Board of Regents,* 853 F.2d 1351 (6th Cir. 1988), the court found no constitutional deprivation in a law school's decision to suspend a student for one year after finding that he had plagiarized a course paper. The school had given the student an opportunity to respond to the charges against him, and the court also determined that the student had no property interest in his law degree because he had not completed the degree requirements.

But in *Jaksa v. Regents of the University of Michigan,* 597 F. Supp. 1245 (E.D. Mich. 1984), a trial court noted that a student challenging a one-semester suspension for cheating on a final examination had both a liberty interest and a property interest in continuing his education at the university. Applying the procedural requirements of *Goss v. Lopez,* the court ruled that the student had been given a meaningful opportunity to present his version of the situation to the hearing panel. It rejected the student's claims that due process was violated because he was not allowed to have a representative at the hearing, was not given a transcript, could not confront the student who charged him with cheating, and was not provided with a detailed statement of reasons by the hearing panel.

If an institution has developed due process procedures for investigating allegations of plagiarism or other forms of academic misconduct on the part of faculty, their use when graduate students are accused of academic misconduct should protect them from constitutional claims. In *Pugel v. Board of Trustees of the University of Illinois,* 378 F.3d 659 (7th Cir. 2004), the university initiated an investigation of data that a graduate student had submitted to a scholarly journal and had presented at a conference. The university used its standard investigative process, submitting the issue to an "Inquiry Team," which issued a report recommending that a full investigation be conducted. The investigation concluded that the graduate student had fabricated data in her article and presentation. The university had notified the student at the beginning of the investigative process. After receiving the report of the Inquiry Team, an Investigation Panel was created that held hearings at which the student was permitted to testify and to present witnesses to testify on her behalf. Her doctor testified that she had attention deficit/hyperactivity disorder (ADHD) and thus was not guilty of academic misconduct. The Investigative Panel concluded that the student had committed academic misconduct. The next level of review was the chancellor, who concurred with the panel's conclusions and dismissed the student from the university. She appealed that decision to the president of the university, who denied her appeal on all grounds but one—the severity of the sanction. He referred that issue to the Senate Committee on Student Discipline, which met and determined that the sanction was warranted. The lawsuit followed. The trial court dismissed the student's constitutional claims, and the appellate court affirmed, stating that the student had been given ample notice, an opportunity to be heard and to clear her name, and three opportunities to appeal the outcome of the hearing.

Although the appellate court cited *Goss* as authority for somewhat less formal procedures than required by *Loudermill* (see Section 6.7.2.3), it noted that dismissal from graduate school was a more severe sanction than the discipline at issue in *Goss,* and thus required procedural protections more extensive than those outlined in *Goss.* Nevertheless, according to the court, the student received appropriate notice and a pretermination hearing, both of which fully complied with procedural due process requirements.

9.4.3. Public institutions: Academic sanctions.

As noted above, the Fourteenth Amendment's due process clause also applies to students facing suspension or dismissal from publicly supported schools for deficient academic performance. But even though academic dismissals may be even more damaging to students than disciplinary dismissals, due process affords substantially less protection to students in the former situation. Courts grant less protection because they recognize that they are less competent to review academic evaluative judgments than factually based determinations of misconduct and that hearings and the attendant formalities of witnesses and evidence are less meaningful in reviewing grading than in determining misconduct.

Gaspar v. Bruton, 513 F.2d 843 (10th Cir. 1975), was apparently the first case to provide any procedural due process rights to a student facing an academic suspension or dismissal. The plaintiff was a forty-four-year-old high school graduate pursuing practical nurse training in a vocational-technical school. After completing more than two-thirds of the program, she was dismissed for deficient performance in clinical training. She had been on probation for two months owing to such deficiencies and had been informed that she would be dismissed if they were not corrected. When they were not, she was notified of dismissal in a conference with the superintendent and some of her instructors and was subsequently offered a second conference and an opportunity to question other staff and faculty members who had participated in the dismissal decision.

The trial and appellate courts upheld the dismissal, rejecting the student's contention that before dismissal she should have been confronted with and allowed to challenge the evidence supporting the dismissal and permitted to present evidence in her defense. Although the appellate court recognized a "property interest" in continued attendance, it held that school officials had only minimal due process obligations in this context:

> We hold that school authorities, in order to satisfy due process prior to termination or suspension of a student for deficiencies in meeting minimum academic performance, need only advise that student with respect to such deficiencies in any form. All that is required is that the student be made aware prior to termination of his failure or impending failure to meet those standards [513 F.2d at 850–51].

More significant protection was afforded in *Greenhill v. Bailey*, 519 F.2d 5 (8th Cir. 1975), where another U.S. Court of Appeals invalidated a medical student's dismissal because he had not been accorded procedural due process. The school had dismissed the student for "lack of intellectual ability or insufficient preparation" and had conveyed that information to the liaison committee of the Association of American Medical Colleges, where it was available to all other medical schools. The court ruled that:

> the action by the school in denigrating Greenhill's intellectual ability, as distinguished from his performance, deprived him of a significant interest in liberty, for it admittedly "imposed on him a stigma or other disability that foreclose[s] his freedom to take advantage of other . . . opportunities" [*Board of Regents v. Roth*, 408 U.S. at 573, 92 S. Ct. at 2707].

The next year the same U.S. Court of Appeals extended its *Greenhill* ruling in another medical school case, *Horowitz v. Board of Curators of the University of Missouri*, 538 F.2d 1317 (8th Cir. 1976). But on appeal, the U.S. Supreme Court clipped this court's wings and put an apparent halt to the development of procedural due process in academic disputes (*Board of Curators of the University of Missouri v. Horowitz*, 435 U.S. 78 (1978)). The university had dismissed the student, who had received excellent grades on written exams, for deficiencies in clinical performance, peer and patient relations, and personal hygiene. After several faculty members repeatedly expressed dissatisfaction with her clinical work, the school's council on evaluation recommended that Horowitz not be allowed to graduate on time and that, "absent radical improvement" in the remainder of the year, she be dropped from the program. She was then allowed to take a special set of oral and practical exams, administered by practicing physicians in the area, as a means of appealing the council's determination. After receiving the results of these exams, the council reaffirmed its recommendation. At the end of the year, after receiving further clinical reports on Horowitz, the council recommended that she be dropped from school. The school's coordinating committee, then the dean, and finally the provost for health sciences affirmed the decision.

Though there was no evidence that the reasons for the dismissal were conveyed to the liaison committee, as in *Greenhill*, the appellate court held that

"Horowitz's dismissal from medical school will make it difficult or impossible for her to obtain employment in a medically related field or to enter another medical school." The court concluded that dismissal would so stigmatize the student as to deprive her of liberty under the Fourteenth Amendment and that, under the circumstances, the university could not dismiss the student without providing "a hearing before the decision-making body or bodies, at which she shall have an opportunity to rebut the evidence being relied upon for her dismissal and accorded all other procedural due process rights."

The Supreme Court found it unnecessary to decide whether Horowitz had been deprived of a liberty or property interest. Even assuming she had, Horowitz had no right to a hearing:

> Respondent has been awarded at least as much due process as the Fourteenth Amendment requires. The school fully informed respondent of the faculty's dissatisfaction with her clinical progress and the danger that this posed to timely graduation and continued enrollment. The ultimate decision to dismiss respondent was careful and deliberate. These procedures were sufficient under the due process clause of the Fourteenth Amendment. We agree with the district court that respondent was afforded full procedural due process by the [school]. In fact, the court is of the opinion, and so finds, that the school went beyond [constitutionally required] procedural due process by affording [respondent] the opportunity to be examined by seven independent physicians in order to be absolutely certain that their grading of the [respondent] in her medical skills was correct [435 U.S. at 85].

The Court relied on the distinction between academic and disciplinary cases that lower courts had developed in cases prior to *Horowitz*, finding that distinction to be consistent with its own due process pronouncements, especially in *Goss v. Lopez* (Section 9.4.2):

> The Court of Appeals apparently read *Goss* as requiring some type of formal hearing at which respondent could defend her academic ability and performance. . . .
> A school is an academic institution, not a courtroom or administrative hearing room. In *Goss,* this Court felt that suspensions of students for disciplinary reasons have a sufficient resemblance to traditional judicial and administrative fact finding to call for a "hearing" before the relevant school authority. . . .
> Academic evaluations of a student, in contrast to disciplinary determinations, bear little resemblance to the judicial and administrative fact-finding proceedings to which we have traditionally attached a full hearing requirement. In *Goss,* the school's decision to suspend the students rested on factual conclusions that the individual students had participated in demonstrations that had disrupted classes, attacked a police officer, or caused physical damage to school property. The requirement of a hearing, where the student could present his side of the factual issue, could under such circumstances "provide a meaningful hedge against erroneous action." The decision to dismiss respondent, by comparison, rested on the academic judgment of school officials that she did not have the necessary clinical ability to perform adequately as a medical doctor and was

making insufficient progress toward that goal. Such a judgment is by its nature more subjective and evaluative than the typical factual questions presented in the average disciplinary decision. Like the decision of an individual professor as to the proper grade for a student in his course, the determination whether to dismiss a student for academic reasons requires an expert evaluation of cumulative information and is not readily adapted to the procedural tools of judicial or administrative decision making [435 U.S. at 85–90].

Horowitz signals the Court's lack of receptivity to procedural requirements for academic dismissals. Clearly, an adversary hearing is not required. Nor are all the procedures used by the university in *Horowitz* required, since the Court suggested that Horowitz received more due process than she was entitled to. But the Court's opinion does not say that no due process is required. Due process probably requires the institution to inform the student of the inadequacies in performance and their consequences on academic standing. Apparently, due process also generally requires that the institution's decision making be "careful and deliberate." For the former requirements, courts are likely to be lenient on how much information or explanation the student must be given and also on how far in advance of formal dismissal the student must be notified. For the latter requirement, courts are likely to be very flexible, not demanding any particular procedure but rather accepting any decision-making process that, overall, supports reasoned judgments concerning academic quality. Even these minimal requirements would be imposed on institutions only when their academic judgments infringe on a student's "liberty" or "property" interest.

Since courts attach markedly different due process requirements to academic sanctions than to disciplinary sanctions, it is crucial to be able to place particular cases in one category or the other. The characterization required is not always easy. The *Horowitz* case is a good example. The student's dismissal was not a typical case of inadequate scholarship, such as poor grades on written exams; rather, she was dismissed at least partly for inadequate peer and patient relations and personal hygiene. It is arguable that such a decision involves "fact finding," as in a disciplinary case, more than an "evaluative," "academic judgment." Indeed, the Court split on this issue: five Justices applied the "academic" label to the case, two Justices applied the "disciplinary" label or argued that no labeling was appropriate, and two Justices refused to determine either which label to apply or "whether such a distinction is relevant." (For an analysis of *Horowitz,* and a criticism of its deference to the university's academic judgment, see W. G. Buss, "Easy Cases Make Bad Law: Academic Expulsion and the Uncertain Law of Procedural Due Process," 65 *Iowa L. Rev.* 1 (1979).)

Two federal appellate courts weighed in on the "academic" side in cases involving mixed issues of misconduct and poor academic performance. In *Mauriello v. University of Medicine and Dentistry of New Jersey,* 781 F.2d 46 (3d Cir. 1986), the court ruled that the dismissal of a medical student who repeatedly failed to produce thesis data was on academic rather than disciplinary grounds. And in *Harris v. Blake,* 798 F.2d 419 (10th Cir. 1986), in reviewing a student's involuntary withdrawal for inadequate grades, the court held that a professor's letter to a student's file, charging the student with incompetent performance (including absence from class) and unethical behavior in a course, concerned academic rather than disciplinary matters.

Although there is no bright line separating the type of "academic" conduct to which a deferential standard of review should be applied from academic misconduct (such as cheating) to which due process protections should be provided, the Supreme Court of Texas has provided some guidance. In *University of Texas Medical School at Houston v. Than*, 901 S.W.2d 926 (Tex. 1995), a medical student, Than, was dismissed for allegedly cheating on an examination. The University of Texas (UT) Medical School provided Than with the opportunity to challenge his dismissal before a hearing board. Than's hearing itself met due process requirements, but at the hearing's end, the hearing officer and the medical school official, who presented the case against Than, inspected the room in which the test had been administered. Than was not allowed to accompany them; he asserted that this decision was a denial of due process. The court said:

> UT argues that Than's dismissal was not solely for disciplinary reasons, but was for academic reasons as well, thus requiring less stringent procedural due process than is required under *Goss* for disciplinary actions. . . . This argument is specious. Academic dismissals arise from a failure to attain a standard of excellence in studies whereas disciplinary dismissals arise from acts of misconduct. . . . Than's dismissal for academic dishonesty unquestionably is a disciplinary action for misconduct [901 S.W.2d at 931].

The court ruled that the exclusion of Than from the posthearing inspection violated his procedural due process rights.

A federal district court rejected the contentions of a defendant college that it was not required to follow its disciplinary procedures in cases of expulsion for "academic misconduct." In *Siblerud v. Colorado State Board of Agriculture*, 896 F. Supp. 1506 (D. Colo. 1995), Robert Siblerud, a former student who was trying to complete his dissertation, was dismissed from the Ph.D. program in physiology after he twice submitted manuscripts to journals that included a footnote in which he represented himself as a student. He was not given a hearing, but was permitted to appeal his dismissal by using the graduate school's grievance process. Although the graduate school committee was divided, the provost affirmed the dismissal. Siblerud asserted that his dismissal was disciplinary, not academic, and the trial court agreed. Although the case was dismissed because the claim was time barred, the judge criticized the university's handling of the situation and characterized it as a disciplinary action, rather than one sounding in academic judgment.

The boundary between academic and disciplinary dismissals, examined in *Siblerud* and *Than*, was also at issue in a 1999 U.S. Court of Appeals case. In *Wheeler v. Miller*, 168 F.3d 241 (5th Cir. 1999), the plaintiff had been dismissed from a doctoral program after receiving four grades of C and failing two sets of oral examinations. The program director gave the student two opportunities to remediate his academic deficiencies, but the student was unable to do so. The appellate court upheld the grant of summary judgment to the university, ruling that Wheeler's due process claim was without merit because "the school's decision to terminate him from the doctoral program was careful and deliberate, following a protracted series of steps to rate [his] academic performance, identify and inform him of his weak performance, and . . . provide [him] with a specially tailored remedial plan" (168 F.3d at 248). These actions were not disciplinary, but designed to help him overcome his prior academic failure. To Wheeler's claim that one professor gave him a C in a course because he fell asleep in class, turned in assignments late, and exhibited behavior that caused her to question his commitment to school psychology, the court responded that these issues were academic ones and were not conduct for which he was being disciplined.

In many cases an academic dismissal decision is based on both academic failure and problematic behavior, particularly for students in professional or clinical programs.[26] Observing that courts have struggled with the academic/disciplinary distinction and that students deserve to be given a reasonable opportunity to respond to charges whether the context be academic or disciplinary failure, one commentator suggests that a "consolidated" standard that is sensitive to the type of expertise required of the decision-maker be adopted by the courts (Fernand N. Dutile, "Disciplinary Versus Academic Sanctions in Higher Education: A Doomed Dichotomy?" 29 *J. Coll. & Univ. Law* 619 (2003)).

When dismissal or other serious sanctions depend more on disputed factual issues concerning conduct than on expert evaluation of academic work, the student should be accorded procedural rights akin to those for disciplinary cases (Section 9.4.2), rather than the lesser rights for academic deficiency cases. Of course, even when the academic label is clearly appropriate, administrators may choose to provide more procedural safeguards than the Constitution requires. Indeed, there may be good reason to provide some form of hearing prior to academic dismissal whenever the student has some basis for claiming that the academic judgment was arbitrary, in bad faith, or discriminatory (see Section 9.3.1). The question for the administrator, therefore, is not merely what procedures are constitutionally required but also what procedures would make the best policy for the particular institution.

Overall, two trends are emerging from the reported decisions in the wake of *Horowitz*. First, litigation challenging academic dismissals has usually been decided in favor of the institutions. Second, courts have read *Horowitz* as a case whose message has meaning well beyond the context of constitutional due process and academic dismissal. Thus, *Horowitz* also supports the broader concept of "academic deference," or judicial deference to the full range of an academic institution's academic decisions. Both trends help insulate postsecondary institutions from judicial intrusion into their academic evaluations of students

---

[26]See, for example, *Ku v. State of Tennessee*, 322 F.3d 431 (6th Cir. 2003), in which a student was dismissed for failing a required test, for his "lack of professional demeanor with his colleagues," and for being "a possible risk to patients in a clinical setting." The court ruled that the dismissal was for academic reasons and that fully informing the student of the "faculty's dissatisfaction with the student's academic progress," and a "careful and deliberate" decision process, were sufficient to meet due process requirements.

by members of the academic community. But just as surely, these trends emphasize the institution's own responsibilities to deal fairly with students and others and to provide appropriate internal means of accountability regarding institutional academic decision making.

9.4.4. Private institutions.
Federal constitutional guarantees of due process do not bind private institutions unless their imposition of sanctions falls under the state action doctrine explained in Section 1.5.2. But the inapplicability of constitutional protections, as Sections 9.2 and 9.3 suggest, does not necessarily mean that the student stands procedurally naked before the authority of the school.

The old view of a private institution's authority is illustrated by *Anthony v. Syracuse University*, 231 N.Y.S. 435 (N.Y. App. Div. 1928), where a student's dismissal was upheld even though "no adequate reason [for it] was assigned by the university authorities." The court held that "no reason for dismissing need be given," though the institution "must . . . have a reason" that falls within its dismissal regulations. "Of course, the university authorities have wide discretion in determining what situation does and what does not fall within . . . [its regulations], and the courts would be slow indeed in disturbing any decision of the university authorities in this respect."

In more recent times, however, many courts have become faster on the draw with private schools. In *Carr v. St. John's University, New York* (see Section 9.2.3), a case limiting the impact of *Anthony* within New York State, the court indicated, although ruling for the university, that a private institution dismissing a student must act "not arbitrarily but in the exercise of an honest discretion based on facts within its knowledge that justify the exercise of discretion." In subsequently applying this standard to a discipline case, another New York court ruled that "the college or university's decision to discipline that student [must] be predicated on procedures which are fair and reasonable and which lend themselves to a reliable determination" (*Kwiatkowski v. Ithaca College*, 368 N.Y.S.2d 973 (N.Y. Sup. Ct. 1975)).

A federal appellate court has made it clear that private colleges and universities are not held to the same constitutional standards as are public institutions, even if state law requires them to promulgate disciplinary rules. In *Albert v. Carovano*, 851 F.2d 561 (2d Cir. 1988), students suspended by Hamilton College for occupying the college's administration building brought constitutional claims under a state action theory (see Section 1.5.2). Section 6450 of New York's Education Law required all institutions of higher education to adopt disciplinary rules, and to file them with the state, which the college had done. Although the college's rules and disciplinary procedures provided for a judiciary board that would review the charges and evidence and determine the sanctions to be levied, the procedures also reserved to the president the right to dispense with the written procedures. In dealing with the students, who continued to occupy the building even after the college had secured a court order enjoining the occupation, the president suspended them effective at the end of the semester, but invited them to state in writing their views on the situation to either the trustees or himself. The students demanded a hearing before the judiciary board, which was not granted. The lawsuit ensued.

The *en banc* court provided a lengthy discussion of the state action doctrine. In this case, it noted, the state law required that the disciplinary rules be placed on file, but the state had made no attempt to evaluate the rules or to ensure that the colleges followed them. Given the lack of state action, the plaintiffs' constitutional claims were dismissed. The court remanded for further consideration the students' claim that the college's selective enforcement of its disciplinary regulations violated Section 1981's prohibitions against race discrimination (see Section 8.2.4.1).

As is true for public institutions, judges are more likely to require private institutions to provide procedural protections in the misconduct area than in the academic sphere. For example, in *Melvin v. Union College,* 600 N.Y.S.2d 141 (N.Y. App. Div. 1993), a breach of contract claim, a state appellate court enjoined the suspension of a student accused of cheating on an examination; the court took this action because the college had not followed all the elements of its written disciplinary procedure. But in *Ahlum v. Administrators of Tulane Educational Fund,* 617 So. 2d 96 (La. Ct. App. 1993), the appellate court of another state refused to enjoin Tulane University's suspension of a student found guilty of sexual assault. Noting that the proper standard of judicial review of a private college's disciplinary decisions was the "arbitrary and capricious" standard, the court upheld the procedures used and the sufficiency of the factual basis for the suspension. Since the court determined that Tulane's procedures exceeded even the due process protections required in *Goss v. Lopez,* it did not attempt to determine the boundaries of procedural protections appropriate for the disciplinary actions of private colleges and universities. A similar result was reached in *In re Rensselaer Society of Engineers v. Rensselaer Polytechnic Institute,* 689 N.Y.S.2d 292 (N.Y. App. Div. 1999), in which the court ruled that "judicial scrutiny of the determination of disciplinary matters between a university and its students, or student organizations, is limited to determining whether the university substantially adhered to its own published rules and guidelines for disciplinary proceedings so as to ascertain whether its actions were arbitrary or capricious" (689 N.Y.S.2d at 295).

In an opinion extremely deferential to a private institution's disciplinary procedure, and allegedly selective administrative enforcement of the disciplinary code, a federal appellate court refused to rule that Dartmouth College's suspension of several white students violated federal nondiscrimination laws. In *Dartmouth Review v. Dartmouth College,* 889 F.2d 13 (1st Cir. 1989), the students alleged that the college's decision to charge them with disciplinary code violations, and the dean's refusal to help them prepare for the hearing (which was promised in the student handbook), were based on their race. The court disagreed, stating that unfairness or inconsistency of administrative behavior did not equate to racial discrimination, and, since they could not demonstrate a causal link between their race and the administrators' conduct, the students' claims failed.

The emerging legal theory of choice for students challenging disciplinary or academic sanctions levied by private colleges is the contract theory. In

Boehm v. University of Pennsylvania School of Veterinary Medicine, 573 A.2d 575 (Pa. Super. Ct. 1990), the court, after reviewing case law, legal scholarship, and other sources, concluded that:

> [a] majority of the courts have characterized the relationship between a private college and its students as contractual in nature. Therefore, students who are being disciplined are entitled only to those procedural safeguards which the school specifically provides. . . . The general rule, therefore, has been that where a private university or college establishes procedures for the suspension or expulsion of its students, substantial compliance with those established procedures must be had before a student can be suspended or expelled [573 A.2d at 579].

In *Fellheimer v. Middlebury College,* 869 F. Supp. 238 (D. Vt. 1994), a student challenged his suspension for a violation of a "disrespect for persons" provision of the college's code of student conduct. The student had been charged with raping a fellow student. The hearing board found him not guilty of that charge, but guilty of the disrespect charge, a charge of which he had never received notice. The college accepted the hearing board's determination and suspended Fellheimer for a year, requiring him to receive counseling prior to applying for readmission. Fellheimer then filed a breach of contract claim (Section 8.1.3), based upon his theory that the student handbook, which included the code of conduct, was a contract. The court agreed, ruling that the college was contractually bound to provide whatever procedural safeguards the college had promised to students.[27]

Although the court rejected Fellheimer's argument that the college had promised to provide procedural protections "equivalent to those required under the Federal and State constitutions," the handbook's language did promise "due process. . . . The procedures outlined [in the handbook] are designed, however, to assure fundamental fairness, and to protect students from arbitrary or capricious disciplinary action" (869 F. Supp. at 243–44). Fellheimer, thus, did not have constitutional due process rights, but he did have the contractual right to be notified of the charges against him. He had never been told that there were two charges against him, nor was he told what conduct would violate the "disrespect for persons" language of the handbook. Therefore, the court ruled, the hearing was "fundamentally unfair." The court refused to award Fellheimer damages until the college decided whether it would provide him with another hearing that cured the violation of the first hearing. It also rejected his emotional distress claim, ruling that, with the exception of the notice violation, the college substantially complied with its own procedures and thus its conduct was neither extreme nor outrageous.

On the other hand, the Massachusetts Supreme Court, while assuming that the student handbook was a contract, rejected a student's claim based on alleged

---

[27]Cases and authorities are collected at Claudia G. Catalano, "Liability of Private School or Educational Institution for Breach of Contract Arising from Expulsion or Suspension of Student,"47 A.L.R.5th 1.

violations of the handbook's provisions regarding student disciplinary hearings. In *Schaer v. Brandeis University*, 735 N.E.2d 373 (Mass. 2000), a student suspended after being found guilty of raping a fellow student challenged the discipline on the grounds that the institution's failure to follow its own policies and procedures was a breach of contract. The student had alleged that the university failed to investigate the rape charge, and that the disciplinary board did not make a record of the hearing, admitted irrelevant evidence and excluded relevant evidence, failed to apply the "clear and convincing evidence" standard set out in the student code, and failed to follow the institution's policies regarding instructing the hearing board on due process in a disciplinary hearing. Although the trial court had dismissed his complaint, the intermediate appellate court reversed and remanded, ruling that the college had made several procedural errors that had prejudiced Schaer and that could have constituted a breach of contract.

The college appealed, and the state's highest court, assuming without deciding that a contractual relationship existed between Schaer and Brandeis, ruled in a 3-to-2 opinion that Schaer had not stated a claim for which relief could be granted. The majority took particular exception to the intermediate appellate court's criticism of the conduct of the hearing and the admission of certain evidence, saying:

> It is not the business of lawyers and judges to tell universities what statements they may consider and what statements they must reject. . . . A university is not required to adhere to the standards of due process guaranteed to criminal defendants or to abide by rules of evidence adopted by courts [735 N.E.2d at 380, 381].

Two of the five justices dissented vigorously, stating that "students should not be subject to disciplinary procedures that fail to comport with the rules promulgated by the school itself" (735 N.E.2d at 381), and that Schaer's allegations were sufficient to survive the motion to dismiss. The sharp differences of opinion in *Schaer* suggest that some courts will more closely scrutinize colleges' compliance with their own disciplinary rules and regulations.

Two trial court opinions on breach of contract claims by students challenging the outcomes of disciplinary hearings demonstrate the importance of careful drafting of procedural rules. In *Millien v. Colby College*, 2003 Maine Super. LEXIS 183 (Maine Super. Ct., Kennebec Co., August 15, 2003), the court rejected a student's breach of contract claim, in part because of a strong reservation of rights clause in the student handbook (see Section 8.1.3). The student complained that an additional appeal board not mentioned in the student handbook had reversed an earlier hearing panel decision in the student's favor. The court said that the handbook was not the only source of a potential contractual relationship between the college and the student, and ruled that the student was attempting to use a breach of contract claim to invite the court to review the merits of the appeal board's ruling, which the court refused to do.

But in *Ackerman v. President and Trustees of the College of Holy Cross*, 2003 Mass. Super. LEXIS 111 (Super. Ct. Mass. at Worcester, April 1, 2003), the court ordered a student reinstated pending a hearing before the campus hearing board. Citing *Schaer,* the court closely read the words of the student handbook. Because the handbook provided that disciplinary charges against a student that could result in suspension would "normally" be heard by the hearing board, failure to provide the student a hearing under such circumstances could be a breach of contract.

Given the tendency of courts to find a contractual relationship between the college and the student with respect to serious discipline (suspension, expulsion), it is very important that administrators and counsel review student codes of conduct and published procedures for disciplinary hearings. Terms such as "due process," "substantial evidence," and "just cause" should not be used unless the private college intends to provide a hearing that will meet each of these standards. Protocols should be developed for staff who interview students charged with campus code violations, especially if the charges have the potential to support criminal violations. Members of campus hearing boards should be trained and provided with guidelines for the admission of evidence, for the evaluation of potentially biased testimony, for assigning the burden of proof between the parties (see Section 2.2.3.6), for determining the evidentiary standard that the board should follow in making its decision (see Section 2.2.3.5), and for determining what information should be in the record of the proceeding or in the board's written ruling.

Even the most conscientious training of staff and hearing board members may not prevent alleged unfairness in the disciplinary process. The case of *Williams v. Lindenwood University,* 288 F.3d 349 (8th Cir. 2002), is instructive. Williams, an African American student, was expelled from the university for violating its alcohol policies and other school rules at a party. Three other students who had also violated the rules were expelled and then reinstated (two were white, one African American), but Williams was not reinstated because the dean determined that he had created a dangerous situation by "bringing criminals and gang members" to campus and because he had hosted the party. Williams brought race discrimination and breach of contract claims against the university. Although the trial court granted the university's motion for summary judgment, the federal appellate court reversed, ruling that the student's evidence that racially derogatory remarks by the dean of students (who recommended the expulsion), the university's president, and the dean of admissions (who made the negative readmission decision) raised sufficient issues of material fact to permit a fact finder to conclude that racial discrimination was a motive for the university's refusal to readmit the plaintiff.

In reviewing determinations of academic performance, rather than disciplinary misconduct, the courts have crafted lesser procedural requirements for private colleges. As is also true for public institutions, however, the line between academic and disciplinary cases may be difficult to draw. In *Napolitano v. Trustees of Princeton University,* 453 A.2d 263 (N.J. Super. Ct. App. Div. 1982), the court reviewed the university's withholding of a degree, for one year, from a student whom a campus committee had found guilty of plagiarizing a term paper. In upholding the university's action, the court determined that the problem was one "involving academic standards and not a case of violation of rules of conduct." In so doing, the court distinguished "academic disciplinary actions" from disciplinary actions involving other types of "misconduct," according greater deference to the institution's decisions in the former context and suggesting that lesser "due process" protection was required. The resulting dichotomy differs from the "academic/disciplinary" dichotomy delineated in Section 9.4.3 and suggests the potential relevance of a third, middle category for "academic disciplinary" cases. Because such cases involve academic standards, courts should be sufficiently deferential to avoid interference with the institution's expert judgments on such matters; however, because such cases may also involve disputed factual issues concerning student conduct, courts should afford greater due process rights than they would in academic cases involving only the evaluation of student performance.

The Supreme Court of Iowa addressed the question of whether a medical student's dismissal for failure to successfully complete his clinical rotations was on academic or disciplinary grounds. In *Lekutis v. University of Osteopathic Medicine,* 524 N.W.2d 410 (Iowa 1994), the student had completed his coursework with the highest grades in his class and had scored in the 99th percentile in standardized tests. The student had serious psychological problems, however, and had been hospitalized several times while enrolled in medical school. During several clinical rotations, his instructors had found his behavior bizarre, inappropriate, and unprofessional, and gave him failing grades. He was eventually dismissed from medical school.

The court applied the *Ewing* standard, reviewing the evidence to determine whether the medical school faculty "substantially departed from accepted academic norms [or] demonstrated an absence of professional judgment" (524 N.W.2d at 413). Although some evaluations had been delayed, the court found that the staff did not treat the student in an unfair or biased way, and that there was considerable evidence of his inability to interact appropriately with patients and fellow medical staff.

While the doctrinal bases for procedural rights in the public and private sectors are different, and while the law accords private institutions greater deference, the cases discussed in this Section demonstrate that courts are struggling with the notion that students who attend private colleges are entitled to something less than the notice and opportunity to be heard that are central to the concept of due process that students at public colleges enjoy. Because many student affairs personnel view student conduct codes and the disciplinary process as part of the educational purpose of the institution (rather than as law enforcement or punishment for a "crime"), the language of the student handbook and other policy documents should reflect that purpose and make clear the rights of the accused student, the disciplinary board, and the institution itself.

Sec. 9.5. *Student Protests and Freedom of Speech*

9.5.1. *Student free speech in general.* Student free speech issues arise in many contexts on the campus as well as in the local community. Issues

regarding protests and demonstrations were among the first to receive extensive treatment from the courts, and these cases served to develop many of the basic general principles concerning student free speech (see below). Issues regarding student protests and demonstrations also remain among the most difficult for administrators and counsel, both legally and strategically. Subsections 9.5.3 through 9.5.5 and 9.5.7 below therefore focus on these First Amendment issues and the case law in which they have been developed and resolved. Other important free speech developments, of more recent origin, concern matters such as student communication via posters and leaflets (discussed in subsection 9.5.6 below), hate speech (discussed in Section 9.6), student communication via campus computer networks (discussed in Section 8.5.1), students' freedom to refrain from supporting student organizations whose views they oppose (discussed in Sections 10.1.2 & 10.1.3), and student academic freedom (discussed in Section 8.1.4). The closely related topic of students' freedom of the press is discussed in Section 10.3.

Freedom of expression for students is protected mainly by the free speech and press provisions in the First Amendment of the U.S. Constitution, which applies only to "public" institutions (see *Coleman v. Gettysburg College,* 335 F. Supp. 2d 586 (M.D. Pa. 2004), and see generally Section 1.5.2 of this book). In some situations, student freedom of expression may also be protected by state constitutional provisions (see Section 1.4.2.1 and the *Schmid* case in Section 11.6.3) or by state statutes (see, for example, Cal. Educ. Code §§ 66301 & 76120 (public institutions) and § 94367 (private institutions)). As the California statutes and the *Schmid* case both illustrate, state statutes and constitutional provisions sometimes apply to private as well as public institutions. In 1998, Congress also attempted to extend First Amendment free speech protections to students in private institutions by adding a new provision to the Higher Education Act. This provision, which applies to all institutions receiving federal financial assistance, appears as Section 112, "Protection of Student Speech and Association Rights," of the Higher Education Amendments of 1998, Pub. L. No. 105-244, 112 Stat. 1581, 1591 (October 7, 1998), codified at 20 U.S.C. § 1011a. The provision has had minimal impact, however, because it has no enforcement mechanism and, in effect, merely states the "sense of Congress" on this matter.

Student freedom of expression may also be protected by the institution's own bill of rights or other internal rules (see Section 1.4.2.3) in both public and private institutions. By this means, private institutions may consciously adopt First Amendment norms that have been developed in the courts and that bind public institutions, so that these norms sometimes become operative on private as well as public campuses. The following discussion focuses on these First Amendment norms and the case law in which they have been developed.

In a line of cases arising mainly from the campus unrest of the late 1960s and early 1970s, courts have affirmed that students have a right to protest and demonstrate peacefully—a right that public institutions may not infringe. This right stems from the free speech clause of the First Amendment as reinforced by that Amendment's protection of "the right of the people peaceably to assemble, and to petition the Government for a redress of grievances." The keystone case is *Tinker v. Des Moines Independent Community School District,* 393 U.S. 503 (1969). Several high school students had been suspended for wearing black armbands to school to protest the United States' Vietnam War policy. The U.S. Supreme Court ruled that the protest was a nondisruptive exercise of free speech and could not be punished by suspension from school. The Court made clear that "First Amendment rights, applied in light of the special characteristics of the school environment, are available to teachers and students" and that students "are possessed of fundamental rights which the state must respect, just as they themselves must respect their obligations to the State."

Though *Tinker* involved secondary school students, the Supreme Court soon applied its principles to postsecondary education in *Healy v. James,* 408 U.S. 169 (1972), discussed further in Section 9.1.1. The *Healy* opinion carefully notes the First Amendment's important place on campus:

> State colleges and universities are not enclaves immune from the sweep of the First Amendment. . . . [T]he precedents of this Court leave no room for the view that . . . First Amendment protections should apply with less force on college campuses than in the community at large. Quite to the contrary, "The vigilant protection of constitutional freedoms is nowhere more vital than in the community of American schools" (*Shelton v. Tucker,* 364 U.S. 479, 487 (1960)). The college classroom with its surrounding environs is peculiarly the "marketplace of ideas," and we break no new constitutional ground in reaffirming this Nation's dedication to safeguarding academic freedom [408 U.S. at 180–81].

In the *Tinker* case (above), the Court also made clear that the First Amendment protects more than just words; it also protects certain "symbolic acts" that are performed "for the purpose of expressing certain views." The Court has elucidated this concept of "symbolic speech" or "expressive conduct" in a number of subsequent cases; see, for example, *Virginia v. Black,* 538 U.S. 343, 358 (2003) (cross burning is symbolic speech); *Texas v. Johnson,* 491 U.S. 397, 404 (1989) (burning the American flag is symbolic speech). Lower courts have applied this concept to higher education and students' rights. In *Burnham v. Ianni,* 119 F.3d 668 (8th Cir. 1997) (*en banc*), for example, the dispute concerned two photographs that students had posted in a display case outside a departmental office (for further details, see Section 9.5.2 below). Citing *Tinker,* the court noted that the posting of the photographs was "expressive behavior" that "qualifies as constitutionally protected speech." According to the court:

> Nonverbal conduct constitutes speech if it is intended to convey a particularized message and the likelihood is great that the message will be understood by those who view it, regardless of whether it is actually understood in a particular instance in such a way. *Spence* [*v. Washington,* 418 U.S. 405, 411 (1969)]. [The two professors], through their photographs, were attempting, at least in part, to convey and advocate their scholarly and professorial interests in military history and in military weaponry's part in their vocation. [The two students], as well, were attempting to show their creativeness and interest in the scope of the

teaching mission of the history department. The display was [the students']
idea; they organized and exhibited it. Because these messages sufficiently satisfy
the *Spence* test, the photographs and the display qualify as speech. *Id.* And,
we do not understand that [the chancellor] disputes this conclusion [119 F. 3d
at 674].

The free speech protections for students are at their peak when the speech
takes place in a "public forum"—that is, an area of the campus that is, traditionally or by official policy, available to students, the entire campus community, or the general public for expressive activities. Since the early 1980s, the
public forum concept has become increasingly important in student freedom of
expression cases. The concept and its attendant "public forum doctrine" are discussed in Section 9.5.2 below.

Although *Tinker, Healy,* and *Widmar* apply the First Amendment to the campus just as fully as it applies to the general community, the cases also make
clear that academic communities are "special environments," and that "First
Amendment rights . . . [must be] applied in light of the special characteristics
of the school environment" (*Tinker* at 506). In this regard, "[a] university differs in significant respects from public forums such as streets or parks or even
municipal theaters. A university's mission is education, and decisions of this
Court have never denied a university's authority to impose reasonable regulations compatible with that mission upon the use of its campus and facilities"
(*Widmar v. Vincent,* 454 U.S. 263, 268, n.5 (1981)). The interests that academic
institutions may protect and promote, and the nature of threats to these interests, may thus differ from the interests that may exist for other types of entities
and in other contexts. Therefore, although First Amendment principles do apply
with full force to the campus, their application may be affected by the unique
interests of academic communities.

Moreover, colleges and universities may assert and protect their interests in
ways that create limits on student freedom of speech. The *Tinker* opinion recognizes "the need for affirming the comprehensive authority of the States and
of school officials, consistent with fundamental constitutional safeguards, to
prescribe and control conduct in the schools" (at 507). That case also emphasizes that freedom to protest does not constitute freedom to disrupt: "[C]onduct
by the student, in class or out of it, which for any reason—whether it stems
from time, place, or type of behavior—materially disrupts classwork or involves
substantial disorder or invasion of the rights of others is . . . not immunized by
the constitutional guarantee of freedom of speech" (at 513). *Healy* makes the
same points.

9.5.2. The "public forum" concept. As indicated in Section 9.5.1 above,
student expressive activities undertaken in a "public forum" receive more protection under the First Amendment than expressive activities undertaken in or
on other types of government property. The public forum concept is therefore
a key consideration in many disputes about freedom of speech on campus as
well as in the local community.

Public forum issues arise, or may arise, when government seeks to regulate "private speech" activities that take place on its own property.[28] The "public forum doctrine" provides help in resolving these types of issues. The general questions addressed by the public forum doctrine are (1) whether a government's status as *owner, proprietor,* or *manager* of the property affords it additional legal rationales (beyond traditional rationales such as incitement, fighting words, obscenity, or defamation) for regulating speech that occurs on this property; and (2) whether the free speech rights of the speaker may vary depending on the *character* of the government property on which the speech occurs. In other words, can government regulate speech on its own property that it could not regulate elsewhere and, if so, does the constitutionality of such speech regulations depend on the character of the government property at issue? These questions are sometimes framed as *access* questions: To what extent do private individuals have a First Amendment *right of access* to government property for purposes of expressive activity?

Since the right of access is based in the First Amendment, and since the property involved must be government property, public forum issues generally arise only at public colleges and universities. Such issues could become pertinent to a private college or university, however, if its students were engaging, or planning to engage, in speech activities on public streets or sidewalks that cut through or are adjacent to the private institution's campus; or if its students were using other government property in the vicinity of the campus for expressive purposes.

The basic question is whether the property is "forum" property; some, but not all, government property will fit this characterization. The U.S. Supreme Court's cases reveal three categories of forum property: (1) the "traditional" public forum; (2) the "designated" public forum; and (3) the "nonpublic" forum.[29] Government property that does not fall into any of these three categories is considered to be "nonforum" property, that is, "not a forum at all" (*Arkansas Educational Television Comm'n. v. Forbes,* 523 U.S. 666, 678 (1998)). For such property, the government, in its capacity as owner, proprietor, or manager, may exclude all private speech activities from the property and preserve the property solely for its intended governmental purposes.

Courts have long considered public streets and parks, as well as sidewalks and town squares, to be traditional public forums. A traditional public forum is

---

[28]"Private speech" is the speech of private individuals who are expressing their own ideas rather than those of the government. Private speech may be contrasted to "government speech," by which government conveys its own message through its own officials or employees, or through private entities that government subsidizes for the purpose of promoting the governmental message. See *Rosenberger v. Rectors and Visitors of University of Virginia,* 515 U.S. 819, 833 (1995); and see generally William Kaplin, *American Constitutional Law* (Carolina Academic Press, 2004), Chap. 11, Sec. F. Student speech is typically considered to be private speech, as it was in the *Rosenberger* case.

[29]See generally *Perry Education Association v. Perry Local Educator's Association,* 460 U.S. 37, 44–46 (1983); *Cornelius v. NAACP Legal Defense and Education Fund,* 473 U.S. 788, 800–802 (1985); *Arkansas Educational Television Comm'n. v. Forbes,* 523 U.S. 666, 677–78 (1998).

generally open to all persons to speak on any subjects of their choice. The government may impose restrictions regarding the "time, place, or manner" of the expressive activity in a public forum, so long as the restrictions are content neutral and otherwise meet the requirements for such regulations (see Section 9.5.3). But the government cannot exclude a speaker from the forum based on content or otherwise regulate the content of forum speech unless the exclusion or regulation "is necessary to serve a compelling state interest and . . . is narrowly drawn to achieve that interest" (*Arkansas Educational Television Comm'n.,* 523 U.S. at 677, quoting *Cornelius,* 473 U.S. at 800). (See generally Susan Williams, "Content Discrimination and the First Amendment," 139 *U. Pa. L. Rev.* 615 (1991).) The traditional public forum category may also include a subcategory called "new forum" property or (ironically) "nontraditional forum" property that, according to some Justices, encompasses property that is the functional equivalent of, or a modern analogue to, traditional forum property.[30]

A designated public forum, in contrast to a traditional public forum, is government property that the government has, by its own intentional action, designated to serve the purposes of a public forum. Designated forum property may be land or buildings that provide physical space for speech activities, but it also may include different forms of property, such as bulletin boards, space in print publications, or (as in *Rosenberger,* above) even a student activities fund that a university uses to subsidize expressive activities of student groups. A designated forum may be just as open as a traditional forum, or access may be limited to certain classes of speakers (for example, students at a public university) or to certain classes of subject matter (for example, curriculum-related or course-related subjects). The latter type of designated forum is called a "limited public forum" or a "limited designated forum." (See *Widmar v. Vincent,* 454 U.S. 263 (1981) (discussed in Section 10.1.5).) Thus, unlike traditional public forums, which must remain open to all, governments retain the choice of whether to open or close a designated forum as well as the choice of whether to limit the classes of speakers or classes of topics for the forum. However, for speakers who fall within the classes of speakers and topics for which the forum is designated, the constitutional rules are the same as for a traditional forum. Government may impose content-neutral time, place, and manner requirements on the speaker but may not regulate the content of the speech (beyond the original designation of permissible topics) unless it meets the compelling interest standard set out above. In addition, if government does limit the forum by designating permissible classes of speakers and topics, its distinction between the classes must be "reasonable in light of the purpose served by the forum" (*Cornelius,* 473 U.S. at 806) and must also be viewpoint neutral (*Rosenberger,* 515 U.S. at 829–30; see generally *Good News Club v. Milford Central School,* 533 U.S. 98, 106–7 (2001)). As the Court explained in *Rosenberger:* "In determining whether the . . . exclusion of a class of speech is legitimate, we have observed a distinction between . . . content discrimination, which may be permissible . . . and viewpoint discrimination,

---

[30]See especially *International Society for Krishna Consciousness, Inc. v. Lee,* 505 U.S. 672, 697–99 (1992) (Kennedy, J., concurring in the judgment).

which is presumed impermissible when directed against speech otherwise within the forum's limitations" (515 U.S. at 829–30).

A nonpublic forum, in contrast to a traditional or designated forum, is open neither to persons in general nor to particular classes of speakers. It is open only on a selective basis for individual speakers. In other words, "the government allows selective access for individual speakers rather than general access for a class of speakers" (*Arkansas Educational Television Comm'n. v. Forbes*, 523 U.S. 666, 679 (1998)). Governments have more rationales for prohibiting or regulating speech activities in nonpublic forums, and governmental authority to exclude or regulate speakers is correspondingly greater, than is the case for traditional and designated forums. (See, for example, *International Society for Krishna Consciousness v. Lee*, 505 U.S. 672 (1992).) A reasonableness requirement and the viewpoint neutrality requirement, however, do limit government's discretion in selecting individual speakers and regulating their speech in a nonpublic forum. The constitutional requirements for a nonpublic forum, therefore, are similar to the requirements that apply to the government's designation of classes of speakers and topics for a limited designated forum. The nonpublic forum, however, is not subject to the additional strict requirements, noted above, that apply to a limited designated forum when government regulates the speech of persons who fall within classes designated for the forum.

When the public forum doctrine is applied to a public institution's campus, its application will vary depending on the type of property at issue. The entire grounds of a campus would not be considered to be public forum property, nor would all of the buildings and facilities. (For analysis of this point, see *Roberts v. Haragan*, 346 F. Supp. 2d 853, 860–63 (N.D. Tex. 2004).) Even for a particular part of the grounds, or a particular building or facility, part of it may be a public forum while other parts are not. Thus, a public institution need not, and typically does not, open all of its grounds or facilities to expressive uses by students or others. In *State of Ohio v. Spingola*, 736 N.E.2d 48 (Ohio 1999), for example, the court considered Ohio University's uses of its College Green—"an open, square-shaped area surrounded on three sides by academic buildings." The court first held that "the green is not a traditional public forum" because "it does not possess the characteristics inherent in" such a forum, nor was there evidence that students or others had "traditionally used the green for public assembly and debate." As to the remaining two options for characterizing the green, the court held that part of the green was in the designated forum category and part (the part called "The Monument") was in the nonpublic forum category. The university "may designate portions of the green as a nontraditional public forum, but keep other areas of the green as nonpublic forums." Since the university had done so, it could exclude demonstrators or other speakers from using the nonpublic forum parts of the green (specifically, the Monument) for their expressive activities.

Public forum property is not limited to grounds, as in *Spingola*, or to rooms in buildings, or comparable physical space. It may also be, for instance, a bulletin board (see Section 9.5.6 below), a table used for distribution of fliers, or a display case. In *Burnham v. Ianni*, 119 F.3d 668 (8th Cir. 1997) (*en banc*), for example, two students in the history department at the University of Minnesota at Duluth (UMD) had prepared a photographic display of the history faculty's professional interests. The display included a photograph of Burnham dressed in a coonskin cap and holding a .45-caliber military pistol, and a photograph of another professor wearing a cardboard laurel wreath and holding a Roman short sword. The display case was located in a public hallway outside the history department offices and classrooms. Asserting reasons relating to campus safety, the university's chancellor (Ianni) ordered the two photographs removed from the display case.

In the ensuing lawsuit, the two students, along with the two faculty members, claimed that the removal of the photographs violated their free speech rights. The chancellor argued that the display case was a "nonpublic forum" that the university could regulate subject only to a reasonableness test that the chancellor's actions had met. A seven-judge majority of the U.S. Court of Appeals, sitting *en banc,* rejected this argument; three judges dissented. According to the majority:

> In this case the nature of the forum makes little difference. Even if the display case was a nonpublic forum, . . . [the] Supreme Court has declared that "the State may reserve [a nonpublic] forum for its intended purposes, communicative or otherwise, as long as the regulation on speech is reasonable and not an effort to suppress expression merely because public officials oppose the speaker's view." Perry [*Education Ass'n. v. Perry Local Educator's Ass'n.*, 460 U.S. 37, 46]. . . . Here we find that the suppression was unreasonable both in light of the purpose served by the forum and because of its viewpoint-based discrimination.
>
> The display case was designated for precisely the type of activity for which the [plaintiff students and professors] were using it. It was intended to inform students, faculty and community members of events in and interests of the history department. The University was not obligated to create the display case, nor did it have to open the case for use by history department faculty and students. However, once it chose to open the case, it was prevented from unreasonably distinguishing among the types of speech it would allow within the forum. Since the purpose of the case was the dissemination of information about the history department, the suppression of exactly that type of information was simply not reasonable.
>
> We recognize that UMD "may legally preserve the property under its control for the use to which it is dedicated." *Lamb's Chapel* [*v. Center Moriches Union Free School District*, 508 U.S. 384, at 390 (1993)]. However, as the Supreme Court has stated:
>
>> [A]lthough a speaker may be excluded from a nonpublic forum if he wishes to address a topic not encompassed within the purpose of the forum . . . or if he is not a member of the class of speakers for whose especial benefit the forum was created . . . , the government violates the First Amendment when it denies access to a speaker solely to suppress the point of view he espouses on an otherwise includible subject. Id. at 394 (quoting *Cornelius v. NAACP Legal Defense & Educ. Fund, Inc.*, 473 U.S. 788, 806 (1985)).

The suppression of this particular speech was also viewpoint-based discrimination. As the Supreme Court has noted, in determining whether the government may legitimately exclude a class of speech to preserve the limits of a forum, we have observed a distinction between, on the one hand, content discrimination, which may be permissible if it preserves the purposes of that limited forum, and, on the other hand, viewpoint discrimination, which is presumed impermissible when directed against speech otherwise within the forum's limitations. *Rosenberger v. Rector & Visitors of Univ. of Virginia*, 515 U.S. 819, 830 (1995) (citing *Perry*, 460 U.S. at 46). As *Rosenberger* illustrates, what occurred here was impermissible. The photographs of [the professors] expressed the plaintiffs' view that the study of history necessarily involves a study of military history, including the use of military weapons. Because other persons on the UMD campus objected to this viewpoint, or, at least, to allowing this viewpoint to be expressed in this particular way, [the chancellor] suppressed the speech to placate the complainants. To put it simply, the photographs were removed because a handful of individuals apparently objected to the plaintiffs' views on the possession and the use of military-type weapons and especially to their exhibition on campus even in an historical context. Freedom of expression, even in a nonpublic forum, may be regulated only for a constitutionally valid reason; there was no such reason in this case [119 F.3d at 676; compare 119 F.3d at 685 (McMillan, J., dissenting)].

The public forum concept is complex, and there is considerable debate among judges and commentators concerning its particular applications—including its applications to the campus. Characterizing the property at issue, and assigning it to its appropriate category, requires careful analysis of institutional policies and practices against the backdrop of the case law. Administrators should therefore work closely with counsel whenever public forum issues may become pertinent to decision making concerning student expression on campus. And counsel should be cautious in working with lower court opinions on the public forum doctrine, since it is not unusual for the U.S. Supreme Court precedents to be misconstrued or the analysis to be otherwise garbled in these opinions.

9.5.3. Regulation of student protest.

9.5.3. Regulation of student protest. It is clear, under the U.S. Supreme Court's decisions in *Tinker* and *Healy* (see Section 9.5.1 above), that postsecondary institutions may promulgate and enforce rules that prohibit disruptive group or individual protests. Lower courts have upheld disruption regulations that meet the *Tinker/Healy* guidelines. In *Khademi v. South Orange Community College District*, 194 F. Supp. 2d 1011 (C.D. Cal. 2002), for example, the court cited *Tinker* in affirming the proposition that "the [college] has a compelling state interest in preventing 'the commission of unlawful acts on community college premises' and 'the substantial disruption of the orderly operation of the community college'" (194 F. Supp. 2d at 1027, quoting Cal. Educ. Code § 76120). Students may be suspended if they violate such rules by actively participating in a disruptive demonstration—for example, entering the stands during a college football game and "by abusive and disorderly acts and conduct" depriving the spectators "of the right to see and enjoy the game in peace and with safety to themselves" (*Barker v. Hardway,* 283 F. Supp. 228 (S.D. W. Va. 1968), *affirmed,* 399 F.2d 638 (4th Cir. 1968)), or physically blocking entrances to campus buildings and preventing personnel or other students from using the buildings (*Buttny v. Smiley,* 281 F. Supp. 280 (D. Colo. 1968)).[31]

The critical problem in prohibiting or punishing disruptive protest activity is determining when the activity has become sufficiently disruptive to lose its protection under *Tinker* and *Healy.* In *Shamloo v. Mississippi State Board of Trustees,* 620 F.2d 516 (5th Cir. 1980), for example, the plaintiffs, Iranian nationals who were students at Jackson State University, had participated in two on-campus demonstrations in support of the regime of Ayatollah Khomeini in Iran. The university disciplined the students for having violated campus regulations that required advance scheduling of demonstrations and other meetings or gatherings. When the students filed suit, claiming that the regulations and the disciplinary action violated their First Amendment rights, the defendant argued that the protests were sufficiently disruptive to lose any protection under the First Amendment. The appellate court asked whether the demonstration had "materially and substantially interfered with the requirements of appropriate discipline in the operation of the school"—the standard developed in an earlier Fifth Circuit case and adopted by the U.S. Supreme Court in *Tinker.* Applying this standard to the facts of the case, the court rejected the defendant's claim:

> There was no testimony by the students or teachers complaining that the demonstration was disrupting and distracting. Shamloo testified that he did not think any of the classes were disrupted. Dr. Johnson testified that the demonstration was quite noisy. Dr. Smith testified that he could hear the chanting from his office and that, in his opinion, classes were being disrupted. The only justification for his conclusion is that there are several buildings within a close proximity of the plaza that students may have been using for purposes of study or for classes. There is no evidence that he received complaints from the occupants of these buildings.
>
> The district court concluded that "the demonstration had a disruptive effect with respect to other students' rights." But this is not enough to conclude that the demonstration was not protected by the First Amendment. The court must also conclude (1) that the disruption was a *material* disruption of classwork or (2) that it involved *substantial* disorder or invasion of the rights of others. It must constitute a *material* and *substantial* interference with discipline. The district court did not make such a conclusion and we certainly cannot, especially in light of the conflicting evidence found in the record. We cannot say that the demonstration did not constitute activity protected under the First Amendment [620 F.2d at 522].

As *Shamloo* suggests, and *Tinker* states expressly, administrators seeking to regulate protest activity on grounds of disruption must base their action

---

[31]Cases are collected in Sheldon R. Shapiro, Annot., "Participation of Student in Demonstration on or Near Campus as Warranting Expulsion or Suspension from School or College," 32 A.L.R.3d 864.

on something more substantial than mere suspicion or fear of possible disruption:

> Undifferentiated fear or apprehension of disturbance is not enough to over-come the right to freedom of expression. Any departure from absolute regi-mentation may cause trouble. Any variation from the majority's opinion may inspire fear. Any word spoken, in class, in the lunchroom, or on the campus, that deviates from the views of another person may start an argument or cause disturbance. But our Constitution says we must take this risk (*Terminiello v. Chicago,* 337 U.S. 1 (1949)); and our history says that it is this sort of hazardous freedom—this kind of openness—that is the basis of our national strength and of the independence and vigor of Americans who grow up and live in this relatively permissive, often disputatious, society [*Tinker,* 393 U.S. at 508–9].

Yet substantial disruption need not be a *fait accompli* before administrators can take action. It is sufficient that administrators have actual evidence on which they can "reasonably . . . forecast" that substantial disruption is imminent (*Tinker,* 393 U.S. at 514).

In addition to determining that the protest is or will become disruptive, it is also important to determine whether the disruption is or will be created by the pro-testers themselves or by onlookers who are reacting to the protestors' message or presence. "[T]he mere possibility of a violent reaction to . . . speech is . . . not a constitutional basis on which to restrict [the] right to speech. . . . The First Amendment knows no heckler's veto" (*Lewis v. Wilson,* 253 F.3d 1077, 1081–82 (8th Cir. 2001)). In *Stacy v. Williams,* 306 F. Supp. 963 (N.D. Miss. 1969), for exam-ple, the court struck down a regulation limiting off-campus speakers at Mississippi state colleges because it allowed for such a "heckler's veto." The court empha-sized that "one simply cannot be restrained from speaking, and his audience cannot be prevented from hearing him, unless the feared result is likely to be engendered by what the speaker himself says or does." Thus, either the protest-ers themselves must engage in conduct that is disruptive, as in *Barker* and *But-tney* above, or their own words and acts must be "directed to inciting or producing imminent" disruption by others and "likely to produce" such disruption (*Brandenburg v. Ohio,* 395 U.S. 444 (1969)), before an administrator may stop the protest or discipline the protesters. Where the onlookers rather than the pro-testers create the disruption, the administrator's proper recourse is against the onlookers.

Besides adopting regulations prohibiting disruptive protest, public institutions may also promulgate "reasonable regulations with respect to the time, the place, and the manner in which student groups conduct their speech-related activities" (*Healy,* 408 U.S. at 192–93). Students who violate such regulations may be disciplined even if their violation did not create substantial disruption. As applied to speech in a public forum, however, such regulations may cover only those times, places, or manners of expression that are "basically incompatible with the normal activity of a particular place at a particular time" (*Grayned v. Rockford,* 408 U.S. 104, 116 (1972)). Incompatibility must be determined by the physical impact of the speech-related activity on its surroundings and not by the content or viewpoint of the speech as such.

The *Shamloo* case (above) also illustrates the requirement that time, place, and manner regulations be "content neutral." The campus regulation at issue provided that "all events sponsored by student organizations, groups, or individual students must be registered with the director of student activities, who, in cooperation with the vice-president for student affairs, approves activities of a wholesome nature." In validating this regulation, the court reasoned that:

> regulations must be reasonable as limitations on the time, place, and manner of the protected speech and its dissemination (*Papish v. Board of Curators of the University of Missouri*, 410 U.S. 667 . . . (1973); *Healy v. James*, 408 U.S. 169 (1972)). Disciplinary action may not be based on the disapproved *content* of the protected speech (*Papish*, 410 U.S. at 670). . . .
>
> The reasonableness of a similar university regulation was previously addressed by this court in *Bayless v. Martine*, 430 F.2d 872, 873 (5th Cir. 1970). In *Bayless* ten students sought injunctive relief from their suspension for violating a university regulation. The regulation in *Bayless* created a Student Expression Area that could be reserved forty-eight hours in advance for any nonviolent purpose. All demonstrations similar to the one held by the Iranian students were regulated to the extent that they could only be held at the Student Expression Area "between the hours of 12:00 noon to 1:00 P.M. and from 5:00 to 7:00 P.M." but there was no limitation on the content of the speech. This court noted that the requirement of forty-eight hours advance notice was a reasonable method to avoid the problem of simultaneous and competing demonstrations and it also provided advance warning of the possible need for police protection. This court upheld the validity of the regulation as a valid exercise of the right to adopt and enforce reasonable nondiscriminatory regulations as to the time, place, and manner of a demonstration.
>
> There is one critical distinction between the regulation examined in *Bayless* and the Jackson State regulation. The former made no reference to the *content* of the speech that would be allowed in the Student Expression Area. As long as there was no interference with the flow of traffic, no interruption of the orderly conduct of university affairs, and no obscene material, the students were not limited in what they could say. Apparently, the same cannot be said with respect to the Jackson State regulations, which provide that only "activities of a *wholesome* nature" will be approved. And if a demonstration is not approved, the students participating may be subjected to disciplinary action, including the possibility of dismissal.
>
> Limiting approval of activities only to those of a "wholesome" nature is a regulation of *content* as opposed to a regulation of time, place, and manner. Dr. Johnson testified that he would disapprove a student activity if, in his opinion, the activity was unwholesome. The presence of this language converts what might have otherwise been a reasonable regulation of time, place, and manner into a restriction on the content of speech. Therefore, the regulation appears to be unreasonable on its face [620 F.2d at 522–23].

Since *Shamloo,* various U.S. Supreme Court cases have elucidated the First Amendment requirements applicable to time, place, and manner regulations of speech in a public forum. *Clark v. Community for Creative Non-Violence,* 468 U.S. 288 (1984), and *Ward v. Rock Against Racism,* 491 U.S. 781 (1989), are particularly important precedents. In *Clark,* the Court upheld National Park Service regulations limiting protests in the parks. The Court noted that these regulations were "manner" regulations and upheld them because they conformed to this three-part judicial test: (1) "they are justified without reference to the content of the regulated speech . . . , (2) they are narrowly tailored to serve a significant governmental interest, and . . . (3) they leave open ample alternative channels for communication of the information" (468 U.S. at 293, numbering added). In *Ward,* the Court upheld a New York City regulation applicable to a bandstand area in Central Park. The Court affirmed that the city had a substantial interest in regulating noise levels in the bandstand area to prevent annoyance to persons in adjacent areas. It then refined the first two parts of the *Clark* test:

> [A] regulation of the time, place, or manner of protected speech must be narrowly tailored to serve the government's legitimate, content-neutral interests but . . . need not be the least restrictive or least intrusive means of doing so. Rather, the requirement of narrow tailoring is satisfied "so long as the . . . regulation promotes a substantial government interest that would be achieved less effectively absent the regulation" (quoting *United States v. Albertini,* 472 U.S. 675, 689 (1985)).

The overall effect of this *Ward* refinement is to create a more deferential standard, under which it is more likely that courts will uphold the constitutionality of time, place, and manner regulations of speech.

One particular type of time, place, and manner regulation that has been a focus of attention in recent years is the "free speech zone" or "student speech zone." (See generally Thomas Davis, Note, "Assessing Constitutional Challenges to University Free Speech Zones Under Public Forum Doctrine," 79 *Ind. L.J.* 267 (2004).) The 1970 case of *Bayless v. Martine,* discussed in the *Shamloo* case above, provides an early example. The court in *Bayless* upheld the creation of what Southwest Texas State University called a "Student Expression Area." Another example of this regulatory technique is found in *Auburn Alliance for Peace and Justice v. Martin,* 684 F. Supp. 1072 (M.D. Alabama 1988), *affirmed without opinion,* 853 F.2d 931 (11th Cir. 1988) (see Section 9.5.4 below), in which Auburn University had created, and the court upheld, the campus "Open Air Forum."

A more recent and more extended example is found in *Burbridge v. Sampson,* 74 F. Supp. 2d 940 (C.D. Cal. 1999), and *Khademi v. South Orange County Community College District,* 194 F. Supp. 2d 1011 (C.D. Cal. 2002)—twin cases involving student challenges to the free speech zones on the same community college campus. Under the district's free speech policies, three "preferred areas" were set aside for speech activities that involved twenty or more persons or would involve the use of amplification equipment. None of these three areas included the area in front of the student center, which was an "historically popular" place for speech activities and the "most strategic location on campus"

(74 F. Supp. 2d at 951). In *Burbridge,* the court issued a preliminary injunction against enforcement of the preferred areas regulations because they were content-based prior restraints that did not meet a standard of strict scrutiny and were also overbroad (74 F. Supp. 2d at 949–52). Subsequently, the community college district amended its regulations, and students again challenged them. In *Khademi,* the court held that the new preferred areas regulations violated the students' free speech rights because they granted the college president "unlimited discretion" to determine what expressive activities would be permitted in the preferred areas (194 F. Supp. 2d at 1030).

Free speech zones sometimes have been implemented by requirements that students reserve the zone in advance, as in *Bayless, Auburn Alliance, Burbridge,* and *Khademi;* or that students obtain prior approval for any use outside the hours specified in the institutional policy, as in *Auburn Alliance.* Any such regulatory system would have to meet the prior approval requirements in Section 9.5.4 below. In addition, even if the institution does not employ any prior approval requirement, the free speech zone must meet the requirements of the U.S. Supreme Court's public forum cases (Section 9.5.2 above), including the three-part test for time, place, and manner regulations established in *Clark v. Community for Creative Non-Violence* (above). Free speech zones will raise serious difficulties under these requirements in at least two circumstances. *First,* if the institution's regulations allow free speech only in the approved zone or zones, and if other parts of the campus that are unavailable for certain speech activities are considered traditional public forums, serious issues will arise because traditional public forum property cannot be entirely closed off to expressive uses. *Second,* if some but not all of the other campus areas that are public forums (besides the free speech zone or zones) are left open for some or all expressive activity, other serious issues may arise under the *Clark/Ward* three-part test (above). Specifically, there could be problems concerning (1) whether the institution selected other areas to be open and closed, or limited the expressive activity in the other open areas, on a content-neutral basis; (2) whether the closings of certain forum areas (or the limitations imposed on certain areas) were narrowly tailored to serve substantial interests of the institution; and (3) whether the areas that remain open are sufficient to provide "ample alternative channels for communication." In *Roberts v. Haragan,* 2004 WL 2203130 (N.D. Tex. 2004), pp. 11–12, for example, the court invalidated provisions of a Texas Tech interim policy regulating speech in campus areas outside of six "forum areas" designated by the policy because these provisions of the policy were not "narrowly tailored." (See also *Mason v. Wolf,* 356 F. Supp. 2d 1147 (D. Colo. 2005).)

Postsecondary administrators who are drafting or implementing protest regulations must be attentive not only to the various judicial requirements just discussed but also to the doctrines of "overbreadth" and "vagueness" (also discussed in Sections 6.6.1, 9.1.3, 9.2.2, & 9.6). The overbreadth doctrine provides that regulations of speech must be "narrowly tailored" to avoid sweeping within their coverage speech activities that would be constitutionally protected under the First Amendment. The vagueness doctrine provides that regulations of conduct must be sufficiently clear so that the persons to be regulated can understand what is required or prohibited and conform their conduct accordingly. Vagueness principles apply more stringently when the regulations deal with speech-related activity: "'Stricter standards of permissible statutory vagueness may be applied to a statute having a potentially inhibiting effect on speech; a man may the less be required to act at his peril here, because the dissemination of ideas may be the loser'" (*Hynes v. Mayor and Council of Oradell,* 425 U.S. 610, 620 (1976), quoting *Smith v. California,* 361 U.S. 147, 151 (1959)). In the *Shamloo* case (above), the court utilized both doctrines in invalidating campus regulations prohibiting demonstrations that are not "of a wholesome nature." Regarding the vagueness doctrine, the court reasoned that:

[t]he restriction on activities other than those of a "wholesome" nature raises the additional issue that the Jackson State regulation may be void for vagueness. . . . An individual is entitled to fair notice or a warning of what constitutes prohibited activity by specifically enumerating the elements of the offense (*Smith v. Goguen,* 415 U.S. 566 . . . (1974)). The regulation must not be designed so that different officials could attach different meaning to the words in an arbitrary and discriminatory manner (*Smith v. Goguen, supra*). But, of course, we cannot expect "mathematical certainty" from our language (*Grayned v. City of Rockford,* 408 U.S. 104 . . . (1972)). The approach adopted by this court with respect to university regulations is to examine whether the college students would have any "difficulty in understanding what conduct the regulations allow and what conduct they prohibit" [quoting *Jenkins v. Louisiana State Board of Education,* 506 F.2d 992, 1004 (5th Cir. 1975)].

The requirement that an activity be "wholesome" before it is subject to approval is unconstitutionally vague. The testimony revealed that the regulations are enforced or not enforced depending on the purpose of the gathering or demonstration. Dr. Johnson admitted that whether or not something was wholesome was subject to interpretation and that he, as the Vice-President of Student Affairs, and Dr. Jackson, Director of Student Activities, could come to different conclusions as to its meaning. . . . The regulation's reference to wholesome activities is not specific enough to give fair notice and warning. A college student would have great difficulty determining whether or not his activities constitute prohibited unwholesome conduct. The regulation is void for vagueness [620 F.2d at 523–24].

The time, place, and manner tests and the overbreadth and vagueness doctrines, as well as principles concerning "symbolic" speech, all played an important role in another leading case, *Students Against Apartheid Coalition v. O'Neil,* 660 F. Supp. 333 (W.D. Va. 1987), and 671 F. Supp. 1105 (W.D. Va. 1987), *affirmed,* 838 F.2d 735 (4th Cir. 1988). At issue in this case was a University of Virginia (UVA) regulation prohibiting student demonstrations against university policies on investment in South Africa. In the first phase of the litigation, students challenged the university's policy prohibiting them from constructing shanties—flimsy structures used to protest apartheid conditions in South Africa— on the university's historic central grounds, "the Lawn." The federal district court held that the university's policy created an unconstitutional restriction on symbolic expression in a public forum. Specifically, the court declared that the "current lawn use regulations . . . are vague, are too broad to satisfy the University's legitimate interest in esthetics, and fail to provide the plaintiffs with a meaningful alternative channel for expression."

UVA subsequently revised its policy to tailor it narrowly to the achievement of the university's goals of historic preservation and aesthetic integrity. The students again brought suit to enjoin the enforcement of the new policy on the same constitutional grounds they had asserted in the first suit. The case was heard by the same judge, who this time held in favor of the defendant university and upheld the revised policy. The court determined that the amended policy applied only to "structures," as narrowly defined in the policy; that the policy restricted such structures from only a small section of the Lawn; and that the policy focused solely on concerns of architectural purity. Applying the *Clark* test, the court held that:

> [UVA] may regulate the symbolic speech of its students to preserve and protect the Lawn area as an architectural landmark. To be constitutionally permissible, the regulation must be reasonable in time, place and manner. The revised Lawn Use Policy lies within the constitutional boundaries of the first amendment. The new policy is content-neutral, precisely aimed at protecting the University's esthetic concern in architecture, and permits students a wide array of additional modes of communication. The new policy is also sufficiently detailed to inform students as to the types of expression restricted on the Lawn [671 F. Supp. at 1108].

On appeal by the students, the U.S. Court of Appeals for the Fourth Circuit agreed with the reasoning of the district court and affirmed its decision.

The *O'Neil* case, together with the *Shamloo, Burbridge,* and *Khademi* cases (above), serve to illuminate pitfalls that administrators will wish to avoid in devising and enforcing their own campus's demonstration regulations. The *O'Neil* litigation also provides a good example of how to respond to and resolve problems concerning the validity of campus regulations.

9.5.4. Prior approval of protest activities.

Sometimes institutions have attempted to avoid disruption and disorder on campus by requiring that protest activity be approved in advance and by approving only those activities that will not pose problems. Under this strategy, a protest would be halted, or its participants disciplined, not because the protest was in fact disruptive or violated reasonable time, place, and manner requirements but merely because it had not been approved in advance. Administrators at public institutions should be extremely leery of such a strategy. A prior approval system constitutes a "prior restraint" on free expression—that is, a temporary or permanent prohibition of expression imposed before the expression has occurred rather than a punishment imposed afterward. Prior restraints "are the most serious and the least tolerable infringement of First Amendment rights" (*Nebraska Press Ass'n. v. Stuart,* 427 U. S. 539, 559 (1976)).

Hammond v. South Carolina State College, 272 F. Supp. 947 (D.S.C. 1967), provides a classic example of prior restraint. The defendant college had a rule providing that "the student body is not to celebrate, parade, or demonstrate on the campus at any time without the approval of the Office of the President." Several students were expelled for violating this rule after they held a demonstration for which they had not obtained prior approval. The court found the rule to be "on its face a prior restraint on the right to freedom of speech and the right to assemble" and held the rule and the expulsions under it to be invalid.

Khademi v. South Orange County Community College District, 194 F. Supp. 2d 1011 (C.D. Cal. 2002), provides a more recent example consistent with *Hammond*. The court in *Khademi* invalidated four provisions of the community college district's regulations concerning student use of certain campus grounds and buildings for expressive purposes. Three of these provisions required students to obtain a reservation of the property in advance of any such use; and the other provision required an advance reservation for certain uses of amplification equipment. The decision of whether to grant a reservation was within the sole discretion of the college's president. The court held that these provisions were prior restraints because:

> they condition expression in certain areas of the District's campuses upon approval of the administration. . . . The four sections identified here delegate completely unfettered discretion to the campus president to permit or prohibit expression. . . . Because these provisions provide the presidents with absolutely no standards to guide their decisions, they are unconstitutional and must be stricken [194 F. Supp. 2d at 1023].

The courts have not asserted, however, that all prior restraints on expression are invalid. In *Healy v. James* (Sections 9.5.1 & 10.1), the U.S. Supreme Court stated the general rule this way: "While a college has a legitimate interest in preventing disruption on campus, which under circumstances requiring the safeguarding of that interest may justify . . . [a prior] restraint, a 'heavy burden' rests on the college to demonstrate the appropriateness of that action" (408 U.S. at 184). More recently, the Court has made clear that prior restraints that are "content neutral"—based only on the time, place, and manner of the protest activity and not on the message it is to convey—are subject to a lesser burden of justification and will usually be upheld. The key case is *Thomas v. Chicago Park District*, 534 U.S. 316 (2002), in which the Court upheld a requirement that groups of fifty or more persons, and persons using sound amplification equipment, must obtain a permit before using the public parks. This "licensing scheme . . . is not subject-matter censorship, but content-neutral time, place, and manner regulation . . . ," said the Court. "The Park District's ordinance does not authorize a licensor to pass judgment on the content of speech: None of the [thirteen] grounds for denying a permit has anything to do with what a speaker might say" (534 U.S. at 322). Although *Thomas* is not a higher education case, courts have applied the same principles to public colleges and universities. In *Auburn Alliance for Peace and Justice v. Martin*, 684 F. Supp. 1072 (M.D. Ala. 1988), *affirmed without opinion*, 853 F.2d 931 (11 Cir. 1988), for instance, the trial and appellate courts upheld the facial validity of Auburn's regulations for the "Open Air Forum," an area of the campus designated as a public forum for demonstrations; and also held that the university's denial of a student-faculty group's request for weeklong, round-the-clock use of this forum was an appropriate means of implementing time, place, and manner requirements.

If a prior restraint system would permit the decision maker to consider the message to be conveyed during the protest activity, however, it will be considered to be "content based," and the "heavy burden" requirement of *Healy* clearly applies. To be justifiable under *Healy* and more recent cases, such a prior consideration of content must apparently be limited to factors that would likely create a substantial disruption on campus. It is therefore questionable whether a content-based prior approval mechanism could be applied to small-scale protests that have no reasonable potential for disruption. Also in either case, prior approval regulations would have to contain a clear definition of the protest activity to which they apply, precise standards to limit the administrator's discretion in making approval decisions, and procedures for ensuring an expeditious and fair decision-making process. Administrators must always assume the burden of proving that the protest activity would violate a reasonable time, place, or manner regulation or would cause substantial disruption.[32] Given these complexities, prior approval requirements may invite substantial legal challenges. Administrators should carefully consider whether and when the prior approval strategy is worth the risk. There are always alternatives: disciplining students who violate regulations prohibiting disruptive protest; disciplining students who violate time, place, or manner requirements; or using injunctive or criminal processes, as set out in Section 9.5.5 below.

9.5.5. Court injunctions and criminal prosecutions.

When administrators are faced with a mass disruption that they cannot end by discussion, negotiation, or threat of disciplinary action, they may want to seek judicial assistance. A court injunction terminating the demonstration is one option. Arrest and criminal prosecution is the other.[33] Although both options involve critical tactical considerations and risks, commentators favor the injunction for most situations, primarily because it provides a more immediate judicial forum for resolving disputes and because it shifts the responsibility for using law enforcement officials from administrators to the court. Injunctions may also be used in some instances to enjoin future disruptive conduct, whereas criminal prosecutions are limited to punishing past conduct. The use of the injunctive process does not legally foreclose the possibility of later criminal prosecutions; and injunctive orders or criminal prosecutions do not legally prevent the institution

---

[32]These prior restraint requirements have been established in bits and pieces in various court cases. *Healy* is a leading case on burdens of proof. *Kunz v. New York,* 340 U.S. 290 (1951), *Shuttlesworth v. Birmingham,* 394 U.S. 147 (1969), and *Forsyth County v. Nationalist Movement,* 505 U.S. 123 (1992), are leading cases on standards to guide administrative discretion. *Southeastern Promotions v. Conrad,* 420 U.S. 546 (1975), is a leading case on procedural requirements.

[33]Cases are collected in Sheldon R. Shapiro, Annot., "Participation of Student in Demonstration on or Near Campus as Warranting Imposition of Criminal Liability for Breach of Peace, Disorderly Conduct, Trespass, Unlawful Assembly, or Similar Offense," 32 A.L.R.3d 551.

from initiating student disciplinary proceedings. Under U.S. Supreme Court precedents, none of these combinations would constitute double jeopardy. (For other problems regarding the relationship between criminal prosecutions and disciplinary proceedings, see Section 9.1.4.)

The legality of injunctions or criminal prosecutions depends on two factors. First, the conduct at issue must be unlawful under state law. To warrant an injunction, the conduct must be an imminent or continuing violation of property rights or personal rights protected by state statutory law or common law; to warrant a criminal conviction, the conduct must violate the state criminal code. Second, the conduct at issue must not constitute expression protected by the First Amendment. Both injunctive orders and criminal convictions are restraints on speech-related activity and would be tested by the principles discussed in Section 9.5.3 concerning the regulation of student protest. Since injunctions act to restrain future demonstrations, they may operate as prior restraints on expression and would also be subject to the First Amendment principles described in Section 9.5.4.

The U.S. Supreme Court has now provided substantial guidance on how to analyze the validity of court injunctions against protest activities. In *Schenck v. Pro-Choice Network of Western New York*, 519 U.S. 357 (1997), and its predecessor case *Madsen v. Women's Health Center*, 512 U.S. 753 (1994), the Court considered the validity of multifaceted injunctions limiting protest activity in the vicinity of abortion clinics. In each case, the Court acknowledged that the challenged injunctions were restraints on speech-related activity and thus subject to First Amendment analysis. Also in both cases, however, the Court acknowledged that the particular injunctions at issue were content-neutral rather than content-based injunctions and thus not subject to "strict scrutiny" review. Generally, content-neutral regulations of speech are subject to a less rigorous "time, place, and manner" scrutiny. But in *Madsen* the Court determined for the first time that its "standard time, place, and manner analysis is not sufficiently rigorous" for purposes of reviewing content-neutral injunctions. The Court thus established a new test to apply: "whether the challenged provisions of the injunction burden no more speech than necessary to serve a significant government interest" (*Madsen*, 512 U.S. at 765). The *Schenck* case reaffirms and applies this same test, using it (as the *Madsen* Court did) to invalidate some parts of the injunction at issue but uphold other parts.

The protest activities in *Schenck* included what the lower court called "constructive blockades" as well as "sidewalk counseling." The blockades, as described by the lower court, consisted of "demonstrating and picketing around the entrances of the clinics, and . . . harassing patients and staff entering and leaving the clinics" (519 U.S. at 365). Included in the blockades were "attempts to intimidate or impede cars from entering the parking lots, congregating in driveway entrances, and crowding around, yelling at, grabbing, pushing, and shoving people entering and leaving the clinics" (519 U.S. at 365). The sidewalk counseling was "aggressive" and included "occasional shoving and elbowing, trespassing into clinic buildings to continue counseling . . . and blocking of doorways and driveways" (519 U.S. at 365).

Two types of injunctive provisions were the particular focus of the Court in *Schenck*: the "fixed buffer zones" provisions and the "floating buffer zones" provisions. The fixed zones provisions banned the protesters from demonstrating within 15 feet of the driveways and doorways of the abortion clinics. The floating zones provisions banned the protesters from approaching within "a normal conversational distance" of individuals arriving at or departing from the clinics in order to leaflet or otherwise communicate messages to them. Using the new test from *Madsen*, the *Schenck* Court invalidated the floating buffer zones, even though they prohibited "classic forms of speech," because "they burden more speech than is necessary to serve the relevant governmental interests" (519 U.S. at 377). Focusing on the dynamics of ingress to and egress from the clinics, the Court reasoned that, given the nature of the floating zones, "it would be quite difficult for a protester who wishes to engage in peaceful expressive activities to know how to remain in compliance with the injunction. This lack of certainty leads to a substantial risk that much more speech will be burdened than the injunction by its terms prohibits" (519 U.S. at 378). For the same reasons, the *Schenck* Court also invalidated the injunction provisions creating floating buffer zones around vehicles entering and leaving the clinic facilities.

In contrast, the Court in *Schenck* upheld the fixed buffer zones provisions because:

> these buffer zones are necessary to ensure that people or vehicles trying to enter or exit the clinic property or clinic parking lots can do so. . . . [T]he record shows that protesters purposefully or effectively blocked or hindered people from entering and exiting the clinic doorways, from driving up to and away from clinic entrances, and from driving in and out of clinic parking lots [519 U.S. at 380].

Many of the dynamics of entry and exit described by the Court may be similar to those for entering and leaving campus buildings, roadways, parking areas, and other facilities. Much campus protest activity—or other expressive activity such as religious proselytizing—may also use tactics or have effects similar to those of the blockades and sidewalk counseling in *Schenck*. The *Schenck* and *Madsen* opinions, therefore, may often be the primary guidance for higher educational institutions considering injunctions as a means to manage campus protests and demonstrations.

When the assistance of the court is requested, public and private institutions are on the same footing. Since the court, rather than the institution, will ultimately impose the restraint, and since the court is clearly a public entity subject to the Constitution, both public and private institutions' use of judicial assistance must comply with First Amendment requirements. Also, for both public and private institutions, judicial assistance depends on the same technical requirements regarding the availability and enforcement of injunctions and the procedural validity of arrests and prosecutions.

9.5.6. Posters and leaflets. Students routinely communicate by posters or fliers posted on campus and by leaflets or handbills distributed on campus. This means of communication is a classic exercise of free speech; "the distribution of leaflets, one of the 'historical weapons in the defense of liberty' is at the core of the activity protected by the First Amendment" (*Giebel v. Sylvester*, 244 F.3d 1182, 1189 (9th Cir. 2001), quoting *Schneider v. State of New Jersey*, 308 U.S. 147, 162 (1939)).[34] The message need not be in the form of a protest, nor need it even express an opinion, to be protected. "[E]ven if [speech] is merely informative and does not actually convey a position on a subject matter," First Amendment principles apply (*Giebel*, 244 F.3d at 1187). Among the most pertinent of these principles are those concerning "public forums" (see subsection 9.5.2 above). If posters appear on a bulletin board, wall, or other surface that is a public forum—usually meaning a *designated* public forum—these communications will receive strong First Amendment protection in public institutions. Similarly, if leaflets are distributed in an area that is a public forum, the communication will be strongly protected.

In *Khademi v. South Orange County Community College District*, 194 F. Supp. 2d 1011 (C.D. Cal. 2002), for example, the court considered the constitutionality of Board Policy 8000 ("BP 8000") under which the district regulated student expression on its two campuses. Some of the regulations included in BP 8000 applied specifically to the posting and distribution of written materials. BP 8000 was based upon, and served to implement, a California statute (Cal. Educ. Code § 76120, discussed in Section 9.5.1 above) that directed community college districts to implement regulations protecting student freedom of expression, including "the use of bulletin boards [and] the distribution of printed materials or petitions. . . ." Section 76120, however, also listed certain exceptions to First Amendment protection, such as expression that causes "substantial disruption of the orderly operation of the community college." One part of BP 8000 gave the district the absolute right to review writings after they are posted to determine if they comply with Section 76120. This part of BP 8000 also authorized the district to remove any writing that violates Section 76120 and to order persons to stop distributing any material found to violate Section 76120. The court in *Khademi* found that these parts of BP 8000 were "content-based" restrictions on student speech in the public forum and thus would be permissible only if they "are necessary to further a compelling interest . . . and are narrowly drawn to achieve that end" (194 F. Supp. at 1026, quoting *Burbridge v. Sampson*, 74 F. Supp. 2d 940, 950 (C.D. Cal. 1999). Applying this strict scrutiny standard, the court determined that the district had not demonstrated "a compelling interest justifying the examination of the content of student expression to root out all speech prohibited by § 76120," and that "the blanket enforcement of § 76120 is not narrowly tailored to those interests that the court finds compelling" (194 F. Supp. 2d at 1027, citing the *Tinker* case). The court therefore ruled that the regulations on student writings violated the First Amendment.

---

[34]*Schneider* is one of the foundational cases on the free speech clause and leafleting, and is usually paired with another leafleting case decided one year earlier: *Lovell v. Griffin*, 303 U.S. 444 (1938). Other key U.S. Supreme Court cases on leafleting are *Talley v. California*, 362 U.S. 60 (1960), discussed below; *Heffron v. International Society for Krishna Consciousness*, 452 U.S. 640 (1981); and *Lee v. International Society for Krishna Consciousness*, 505 U.S. 830 (1992).

If the place of posting or distribution is a "nonpublic forum" rather than a public forum, the communication may be protected to a lesser degree—but it will usually be very difficult for students to prevail in such cases. In *Desyllas v. Bernstine*, 351 F.3d 934 (9th Cir. 2003), for example, a student at Portland State University (PSU) challenged the university's alleged removal of his fliers announcing a press conference. The court determined that the campus areas that were approved for posting under the university's "Bulletin Board Posting Policy" are designated public forums; and that campus areas not approved for posting "are not designated public fora because the university did not intend to open them for expression, as manifested by the university's . . . Policy." The student's fliers were posted in unapproved areas, which the court considered to be nonpublic forums. The university could therefore remove them if the action "is reasonable," that is, "consistent with preserving the property" for its intended purposes, and is "not based on the speaker's viewpoint."[35] The university's action met the second requirement because there was no proof that the defendants had selectively removed the student's fliers "while allowing others to remain" or that the university's action "was motivated by a desire to stifle [the student's] particular perspective or opinion." The second requirement was met because:

> [t]he hallways, doorways and columns of the PSU campus are designated off-limits to fliers primarily for aesthetic reasons. The university's policy states that handbills shall not be posted in those areas because doing so causes damage. Widner's removal of Desyllas's press conference fliers, along with other fliers posted on the columns near Smith Center, is consistent with the university's purpose to preserve the appearance of campus structures [351 F.3d at 944].

Even if the place of posting or distribution is a public forum (traditional or designated), there is still some room for public colleges and universities to regulate these activities and to remove nonconforming posters and terminate nonconforming leafleting. To be valid, such regulations and enforcement actions must be not only "viewpoint neutral" (see *Desyllas*, above; and see also *Giebel v. Sylvester*, above, 244 F.3d at 1188–89) but also "content neutral," meaning that they must be based only on the "time, place, and manner" of the posting or distribution and not on the subject matter or information expressed. The three-part test that the U.S. Supreme Court has crafted for time, place, and manner regulations of speech is discussed in Section 9.5.3 above with reference to *Clark v. Community for Creative Non-Violence* and *Ward v. Rock Against Racism*. Permissible types of time, place, and manner regulations may include prior institutional approvals for postings and leafleting on campus, so long as the approval process "does not authorize [the decision maker] to pass judgment on the content of the speech" (*Thomas v. Chicago Park District*, 534 U.S. 316 (2002)) and otherwise meets the three-part test.

---

[35]The court was quoting from its own prior opinion in *DiLoreto v. Downey Unified School District Board of Education*, 196 F.3d 958, 965, 967 (9th Cir. 1999). The court also relied on *Rosenberger v. Rector and Visitors of University of Virginia*, 515 U.S. 819 (1995), which is discussed in Sections 10.1.4 and 10.3.2 of this book.

In addition to such content-neutral regulations, the institution may also, in narrow circumstances, regulate the content of posters and handbills in a public forum. The two most likely possibilities are regulations concerning obscenity and defamation (see generally Sections 10.3.4 & 10.3.5). These types of regulations, called "content-based" regulations, must be very clear and specific, such that they meet constitutional requirements regarding "overbreadth" and "vagueness," as discussed in Section 9.5.3 above. Such regulations must also usually be implemented without using a prior approval process, since a prior approval process that takes the content of the speech into account will often be considered to be an unconstitutional prior restraint (see Section 9.5.4 above).

One problematic type of poster and handbill regulation is a requirement that posters and handbills identify the student or student organization that sponsors, or that distributed, the message. From one perspective, if such a requirement is applied across the board to all postings and distributions, the requirement is a content-neutral requirement that will be upheld if it meets the three-part test. From another perspective, however, such a requirement could "chill" the expression of controversial viewpoints, and to that extent could be considered to be a "content-based" regulation. The U.S. Supreme Court took the latter approach in the classic case of *Talley v. California*, 362 U.S. 60 (1960), in which it invalidated a city ordinance requiring that all handbills include the name and address of the speaker. The Court reasoned that such an identification requirement could lead to "fear of reprisal" that would "deter perfectly peaceful discussions of public matters of importance." The Court thus, in effect, recognized a right to anonymous speech. At the same time, however, the Court left some room carefully drafted identification requirements that can be shown to be necessary to the prevention of fraud, libel, or other similar harms. In *Spartacus Youth League v. Board of Trustees of Illinois Industrial University*, 502 F. Supp. 789 (N.D. Ill. 1980), the court relied on *Talley* in upholding some of the institution's identification requirements for handbills and postings while invalidating others (502 F. Supp. at 803–4).

9.5.7. *Protests in the classroom.*

Student protest occasionally occurs in the classroom during class time. In such circumstances, general First Amendment principles will continue to apply. But the institution's interests in maintaining order and decorum are likely to be stronger than when the protest occurs in other areas of the campus, and student free speech interests are likely to be lessened because the classroom during class time is usually not considered a "public forum" (see *Bishop v. Aronov*, 926 F.2d 1066, 1071 (11th Cir. 1991); and see generally Section 9.5.2 above). If the speech is by class members and is pertinent to the class discussion and subject matter of the course, it would usually be protected if it is not expressed in a disruptive manner. Moreover, if the classroom protest is by students enrolled in the course, and is silent, passive, and nondisruptive—like the black armband protest in *Tinker v. Des Moines School District* (Section 9.5.1 above)—it will usually be protected by the First Amendment even if it is not pertinent to the class. Otherwise, however, courts will not usually protect classroom protest.

In *Salehpour v. University of Tennessee,* 159 F.3d 199 (6th Cir. 1998), for instance, the court rejected the free speech claim of a first-year dental student, a native of Iran with American citizenship who was studying dentistry as a second career. The student disagreed with a "last row rule" imposed by two professors who prohibited first-year students from occupying the last row of seats in their classrooms. The student addressed his concerns about this rule to the professors and to the associate dean; he also protested the rule, on several occasions, by sitting in the last row in the professors' classes and remaining there after being asked to change seats. Ultimately the school took disciplinary action against the student, and he filed suit claiming that the school had retaliated against him for exercising his free speech rights. The court rejected this claim because:

> [the student's] expression appears to have no intellectual content or even discernable purpose, and amounts to nothing more than expression of a personal proclivity designed to disrupt the educational process. . . . The rights afforded to students to freely express their ideas and views without fear of administrative reprisal, must be balanced against the compelling interest of the academicians to educate in an environment that is free of purposeless distractions and is conducive to teaching. Under the facts of this case, the balance clearly weighs in favor of the University [159 F.3d at 208].

The court relied on the *Tinker* case to support its reasoning, especially the passage in the opinion about "conduct by the student, in class or out of it, which . . . materially disrupts classwork . . ." (see Section 9.5.1 above).

As for students who are not class members, their rights to protest inside a classroom, or immediately outside, during class time are no greater than, and will often be less than, the rights of class members. Students who are not enrolled in the course would not likely have any right to be present in the classroom. Moreover, the presence of uninvited non-class members in the classroom during class time would be likely to create "a material disruption" of the class within the meaning of the *Tinker* case. And protest activity outside the classroom would often create noise that is projected into the classroom or would block ingress and egress to the classroom, thereby also creating a "material disruption" within the meaning of *Tinker.* In *Furumoto v. Lyman,* 362 F. Supp. 1267 (N.D. Cal. 1973), an example drawn from the civil rights era, students who were not class members had entered the classroom of Professor William Shockley at Stanford University. The uninvited students challenged the professor's views on eugenics, which the students claimed were racist views; the students did not leave the classroom when asked to do so; and the scheduled business for the class was not completed. After campus hearings, the students were indefinitely suspended. Citing the *Tinker* case, the court rejected the students' argument that the suspension violated their First Amendment free speech rights. The court also upheld the validity of the Stanford campus disruption policy (362 F. Supp. at 1280–84), which provided that "[i]t is a violation of University policy for a member of the . . . student body to (1) prevent or disrupt the effective carrying out of a University function . . . , such as lectures [or] meetings. . . ."[36]

(For further discussion of students' free speech rights in the classroom, see Section 8.1.4 of this book ("Student Academic Freedom").)

Sec. 9.6. Speech Codes and the Problem of Hate Speech[37]

9.6.1. Hate speech and the campus. Since the late 1980s, colleges and universities have frequently confronted the legal, policy, and political aspects of "hate speech" and its potential impacts on equal educational opportunity for targeted groups and individuals. Responding to racist, anti-Semitic, homophobic, and sexist incidents on campus, as well as to developments in the courts, institutions have enacted, revised, and sometimes revoked policies for dealing with these problems. (For state-by-state and institution-by institution summaries of such policies, see http://www.speechcodes.org, a Web site maintained by the Foundation for Individual Rights in Education (FIRE); and for analysis of particular institutional policies on harassing and abusive behavior directed against minority group members, see Richard Page & Kay Hunnicutt, "Freedom for the Thought We Hate: A Policy Analysis of Student Speech Regulation at America's Twenty Largest Public Universities," 21 *J. Coll. & Univ. Law* 1, 38–56 (1994).) Typically, institutional policies have been directed at harassment, intimidation, or other abusive behavior targeting minority groups. When such harassment, intimidation, or abuse has been conveyed by the spoken, written, or digitalized word, or by symbolic conduct, difficult legal and policy issues have arisen concerning students' free speech and press rights.

Beginning in the mid-1990s, after the courts had decided a number of cases limiting postsecondary institutions' authority to regulate hate speech (see subsection 9.6.2 below), and institutions had responded by developing more nuanced policies for dealing with hate speech, there was a period of relative quiet regarding these issues. In the aftermath of the terrorist attacks of September 11, 2001, however, and in light of continuing terrorist threats against the United States, the war in Iraq, and continuing violence associated with the Israeli/Palestinian conflict, the debate and controversy about hate speech and campus speech codes reemerged. (See, for example, Katherine Mangan, "Proposal for Speech Code at Harvard Law School Sets Off Debate," *Chron. Higher*

[handwritten margin note: collision between free expression and bans against "hate speech" of punishment]

---

[36]In an earlier part of its opinion, the court had concluded that, Stanford being a private university, its action did not constitute "state action" for purposes of applying the First Amendment (see Section 1.5.2). The court's First Amendment analysis, therefore, was an alternative analysis showing that the plaintiffs would lose "[e]ven if state action were present in this case" (362 F. Supp. at 1280).

[37]Some portions of this Section were extracted and adapted (without further attribution) from William Kaplin, "A Proposed Process for Managing the First Amendment Aspects of Campus Hate Speech," 63 *J. Higher Educ.* 517 (1992), copyright © 1992 by the Ohio State University Press; and from William Kaplin, "Hate Speech on the College Campus: Freedom of Speech and Equality at the Crossroads," 27 *Land & Water L. Rev.* 243 (1992), copyright © 1992 by the University of Wyoming. All rights reserved.

Educ., December 6, 2002, A37; Judith Rodin, "We Must Defeat Hate, Not Simply Ban It," *Chron. Higher Educ.,* November 1, 2002, A14.) Renewed concerns over "political correctness" on campus, and a push for an "Academic Bill of Rights" (see Section 8.1.4 of this book) also provided stimulus for the renewed debate about speech codes.[38]

"Hate speech" is an imprecise catch-all term that generally includes verbal and written words and symbolic acts that convey a grossly negative assessment of particular persons or groups based on their race, gender, ethnicity, religion, sexual orientation, or disability. Hate speech is thus highly derogatory and degrading, and the language is typically coarse. The purpose of the speech is more to humiliate or wound than it is to communicate ideas or information. Common vehicles for such speech include epithets, slurs, insults, taunts, and threats. Because the viewpoints underlying hate speech may be considered "politically incorrect," the debate over hate speech codes has sometimes become intertwined with the political correctness phenomenon on American campuses (see, for example, the *Levin* case in Section 7.3).

Hate speech is not limited to a face-to-face confrontation or shouts from a crowd. It takes many forms. It may appear on T-shirts, posters, classroom blackboards, bulletin boards (physical or virtual) or Web logs, or in flyers and leaflets, phone calls, letters, or e-mail messages. It may be a cartoon appearing in a student publication or a joke told on a campus radio station or at an after-dinner speech, a skit at a student event, an anonymous note slipped under a dormitory door, graffiti scribbled on a wall or sidewalk, or a posting in an electronic chat room. It may be conveyed through defacement of posters or displays; through symbols such as burning crosses, swastikas, KKK insignia, and Confederate flags; and even through themes for social functions, such as blackface Harlem parties or parties celebrating white history week.

When hate speech is directed at particular individuals, it may cause real psychic harm to those individuals and may also inflict pain on the broader class of persons who belong to the group denigrated by the hate speech. Moreover, the feelings of vulnerability, insecurity, and alienation that repeated incidents of hate speech can engender in the victimized groups may prevent them from taking full advantage of the educational, employment, and social opportunities on the campus and may undermine the conditions necessary for constructive dialogue with other persons or groups. Ultimately, hate speech may degrade the intellectual environment of the campus, thus harming the entire academic community.

---

[38]Similar issues may arise concerning the hate speech of faculty members and staff members. See, for example, *Dambrot v. Central Michigan University,* 55 F.3d 1177 (6th Cir. 1995); *Barrett v. University of Colorado Health Sciences Center,* 61 Fair Empl. Prac. Cases 369 (Colo. 1993). Institutions will generally have more constitutional leeway to regulate faculty and staff hate speech than they do for student hate speech; see the *Pickering/Connick* line of cases in Section 7.1.1 of this book, and see also *Martin v. Parrish* and *Bonnell v. Lorenzo* in Section 7.2.2 and *Jeffries v. Harleston* in Section 7.5. In the faculty cases, students may be targets of the alleged hate speech. Their rights as victims, rather than as speakers, would then be at stake. See Sections 7.2.2, 8.1.4, and 9.3.4 for perspectives on students' rights as the victims of hate speech and harassing speech.

Since hate speech regulations may prohibit and punish particular types of messages, they may raise pressing free expression issues not only for public institutions (see Section 1.5.2) but also for private institutions that are subject to state constitutional provisions or statutes employing First Amendment norms (see Section 9.5.1 above) or that voluntarily adhere to First Amendment norms. The free expression values that First Amendment norms protect may be in tension with the equality values that institutions seek to protect by prohibiting hate speech. The courts have decided a number of important cases implicating these values since 1989, as discussed in the next subsection.

9.6.2. The case law on hate speech and speech codes. Some of the hate speech cases have involved college or university speech codes; others have involved city ordinances or state statutes that covered hate speech activities or that enhanced the penalties for conduct undertaken with racist or other biased motivations. All of the college and university cases except one are against public institutions; the exception—the *Corry* case discussed below—provides an instructive illustration of how hate speech issues can arise in private institutions.

The U.S. Supreme Court's 1992 decision in *R.A.V. v. City of St. Paul,* 505 U.S. 377 (1992), addresses the validity of a city ordinance directed at hate crimes. This ordinance made it a misdemeanor to place on public or private property any symbol or graffiti that one reasonably knew would "arouse anger, alarm or resentment in others on the basis of race, color, creed, religion or gender." R.A.V., a juvenile who had set up and burned a cross in the yard of a black family, challenged the ordinance as overbroad (see Section 9.5.3 of this book). The lower courts upheld the validity of the statute by narrowly construing it to apply only to expression that would be considered fighting words or incitement. The U.S. Supreme Court disagreed and invalidated the ordinance, but the majority opinion by Justice Scalia did not use overbreadth analysis. Instead, it focused on the viewpoint discrimination evident in the ordinance and invalidated the ordinance because its restriction on speech content was too narrow rather than too broad:

> Although the phrase in the ordinance, "arouses anger, alarm or resentment in others," has been limited by the Minnesota Supreme Court's construction to reach only those symbols or displays that amount to "fighting words," the remaining, unmodified terms make clear that the ordinance applies only to "fighting words" that insult, or provoke violence, "on the basis of race, color, creed, religion or gender." Displays containing abusive invective, no matter how vicious or severe, are permissible unless they are addressed to one of the specified disfavored topics. Those who wish to use "fighting words" in connection with other ideas—to express hostility, for example, on the basis of political affiliation, union membership, or homosexuality—are not covered. The First Amendment does not permit St. Paul to impose special prohibitions on those speakers who express views on disfavored subjects [505 U.S. at 391].

The Court did note several narrow exceptions to this requirement of view-point neutrality but found that the St. Paul ordinance did not fall into any of these narrow exceptions (505 U.S. at 386–90). The Court also determined that the city could not justify its narrow viewpoint-based ordinance. The city did have a compelling interest in promoting the rights of those who have tradition-ally been subject to discrimination. But because a broader ordinance without the viewpoint-based restriction would equally serve this interest, the law was not "reasonably necessary" to the advancement of the interest and was thus invalid.

The Supreme Court visited the hate speech problem again in *Wisconsin v. Mitchell,* 508 U.S. at 476 (1993). At issue was the constitutionality of a state law that enhanced the punishment for commission of a crime when the victim was intentionally selected because of his "race, religion, color, disability, sexual orientation, national origin or ancestry" (Wis. Stat. § 939.645(1)(b)). The state had applied the statute to a defendant who, with several other black males, had seen and discussed a movie that featured a racially motivated beating and thereupon had brutally assaulted a white male. Before the attack, the defendant had said, among other things, "There goes a white boy; go get him." A jury convicted the defendant of aggravated battery, and the court enhanced his sentence because his actions were racially motivated.

The Court unanimously upheld the statute because it focused on the defendant's motive, traditionally a major consideration in sentencing. Unlike the *R.A.V.* case, the actual crime was not the speech or thought itself, but the assault—"conduct unprotected by the First Amendment." Moreover, the statute did not permit enhancement of penalties because of "mere disagreement with offenders' beliefs or biases" but rather because "bias-inspired conduct . . . is thought to inflict greater individual and societal harm." The Court did caution, moreover, "that a defendant's abstract beliefs, however obnoxious to most people, may not be taken into consideration by a sentencing judge." Thus, in order for a penalty-enhancing statute to be constitutionally applied, the prosecution must show more than the mere fact that a defendant is, for example, a racist. Such evidence alone would most likely be considered irrelevant and unduly prejudicial by a trial judge. Instead, the prosecution must prove that the defendant's racism motivated him to commit the particular crime; there must be a direct connection between the criminal act and a racial motive. This showing will generally be difficult to make and may necessitate direct evidence such as that in *Mitchell,* where the defendant's own contemporaneous statements indicated a clear and immediate intent to act on racial or other proscribed grounds.

In *Virginia v. Black,* 538 U.S. 343 (2003), the U.S. Supreme Court considered the constitutionality of a state statute prohibiting the use of a particular "symbol of hate": cross burnings (538 U.S. at 357). The Virginia statute at issue made it a crime to burn a cross in public with "an intent to intimidate a person or group of persons" (Va. Code Ann. § 18.2-423). In its opinion, the Court considered the First Amendment status of "true threats," a concept that arose from the earlier case of *Watts v. United States,* 394 U.S. 705 (1969) and was further developed in *R.A.V* (505 U.S. at 388). Consistent with those cases, the Court in *Virginia v.*

Black reaffirmed that "the First Amendment . . . permits a state to ban a 'true threat'" and defined a true threat as a statement "where the speaker means to communicate a serious expression of an intent to commit an act of unlawful violence to a particular individual or group of individuals" (538 U.S. at 359). The Court then determined that intimidation may be included within the category of true threats, so long as the intimidation is limited to statements in which "a speaker directs a threat to a person or a group of persons with the intent of placing the victim in fear of bodily harm or death" (538 U.S. at 360). According to the Court, such intentional statements, whether termed as threats or intimidation, are "constitutionally proscribable" and thus outside the scope of the First Amendment (538 U.S. at 365). Applying these principles to the cross burning, the Court determined that "the burning of a cross is symbolic expression," but it is also "a particularly virulent form of intimidation." The Court therefore upheld the constitutionality of Section 18.2-423's prohibition of cross burning because a "ban on cross burning carried out the intent to intimidate is fully consistent with our holding in *R.A.V.* and is proscribable under the First Amendment" (538 U.S. at 363).[39]

Although no case involving campus hate speech has yet reached the U.S. Supreme Court, there have been several important cases in the lower courts. The first was *Doe v. University of Michigan,* 721 F. Supp. 852 (E.D. Mich. 1989). The plaintiff, a graduate student, challenged the university's hate speech policy, whose central provision prohibited "[a]ny behavior, verbal or physical, that stigmatizes or victimizes an individual on the basis of race, ethnicity, religion, sex, sexual orientation, creed, national origin, ancestry, age, marital status, handicap, or Vietnam-era veteran status." The policy prohibited such behavior if it "[i]nvolves an express or implied threat to" or "[h]as the purpose or reasonably foreseeable effect of interfering with" or "[c]reates an intimidating, hostile, or demeaning environment" for individual pursuits in academics, employment, or extracurricular activities. This prohibition applied to behavior in "educational and academic centers, such as classroom buildings, libraries, research laboratories, recreation and study centers." Focusing on the wording of the policy and the way in which the university interpreted and applied this language, the court held that the policy was unconstitutionally overbroad on its face because its wording swept up and sought to punish substantial amounts of constitutionally protected speech. In addition, the court held the policy to be unconstitutionally vague on its face. This fatal flaw arose primarily from the words "stigmatize" and "victimize" and the phrases "threat to" or "interfering with," as applied to an individual's academic pursuits—language that was so vague that students would not be able to discern what speech would be protected and what would be prohibited.

---

[39]The Court declined, however, to uphold the constitutionality of another provision in the Virginia cross-burning statute that made the burning itself *prima facie* evidence of an intent to intimidate. The Court splintered on its treatment of this particular provision, but ultimately a majority determined that the provision, as interpreted by the trial court's jury instruction, was unconstitutional because it served to make all cross burnings a crime even though some burnings could be engaged in as "core political speech" rather than as intimidation (538 U.S. at 365 (plurality opinion of Justice O'Connor)).

Similarly, in *UWM Post, Inc. v. Board of Regents of the University of Wisconsin System,* 774 F. Supp. 1163 (E.D. Wis. 1991), the court utilized both overbreadth and vagueness analysis to invalidate a campus hate speech regulation. The regulation applied to "racist or discriminatory comments, epithets, or other expressive behavior directed at an individual" and prohibited any such speech that "intentionally" (1) "demean[s]" the race, sex, or other specified characteristics of the individual, and (2) "create[s] an intimidating, hostile, or demeaning environment for education." The court held this language to be overbroad because it encompassed many types of speech that would not fall within any existing exceptions to the principle that government may not regulate the content of speech. Regarding vagueness, the court rejected the plaintiffs' argument that the phrase "discriminatory comments, epithets, or other expressive behavior" and the word "demean" were vague. But the court nevertheless held the regulation unconstitutionally vague because another of its provisions, juxtaposed against the language quoted above, created confusion as to whether the prohibited speech must actually demean the individual and create a hostile educational environment, or whether the speaker must only *intend* those results and they need not actually occur.

A third case, *Iota Xi Chapter of Sigma Chi Fraternity v. George Mason University,* 993 F.2d 386 (4th Cir. 1993), was decided (unlike *Doe* and *UWM Post*) after the U.S. Supreme Court's decision in *R.A.V. v. City of St. Paul.* In this case a fraternity had staged an "ugly woman contest" in which one member wore blackface, used padding and women's clothes, and presented an offensive caricature of a black woman. After receiving numerous complaints about the skit from other students, the university imposed heavy sanctions on the fraternity. The fraternity, relying on the First Amendment, sought an injunction that would force the school to lift the sanctions. The trial court granted summary judgment for the fraternity, and the appellate court affirmed the trial court's ruling.

Determining that the skit was "expressive entertainment" or "expressive conduct" protected by the First Amendment, and that the sanctions constituted a content-based restriction on this speech, the court applied reasoning similar to that in *R.A.V.*:

> The mischief was the University's punishment of those who scoffed at its goals of racial integration and gender neutrality, while permitting, even encouraging, conduct that would further the viewpoint expressed in the University's goals and probably embraced by a majority of society as well. . . .
>
> The University, however, urges us to weigh Sigma Chi's conduct against the substantial interests inherent in educational endeavors. . . . The University certainly has a substantial interest in maintaining an environment free of discrimination and racism, and in providing gender-neutral education. Yet it seems equally apparent that it has available numerous alternatives to imposing punishment on students based on the viewpoints they express. We agree wholeheartedly that it is the University officials' responsibility, even their obligation, to achieve the goals they have set. On the other hand, a public university has many constitutionally permissible means to protect female and minority students. We must emphasize, as have other courts, that "the manner of [its action] cannot

consist of selective limitations upon speech." [*R.A.V.*, 505 U.S. at 392] . . . The First Amendment forbids the government from "restrict[ing] expression because of its message [or] its ideas." *Police Department v. Mosley*, 408 U.S. 92, 95 (1972). The University should have accomplished its goals in some fashion other than silencing speech on the basis of its viewpoint [993 F.2d at 393].[40]

In *Corry v. Stanford University*, No. 740309 (Cal. Superior Ct., Santa Clara Co., February 27, 1995), a state trial court judge invalidated Stanford's Policy on Free Expression and Discriminatory Harassment. Since Stanford is a private university, the First Amendment did not directly apply to the case, but it became applicable through a 1992 California law, the "Leonard Law" (Cal. Educ. Code § 94367) that subjects private institutions' student disciplinary actions to the strictures of the First Amendment. Applying U.S. Supreme Court precedents such as *Chaplinsky v. New Hampshire*, 315 U.S. 568 (1942) (the "fighting words" case), and *R.A.V. v. City of St. Paul* (above), the court held that the Stanford policy did *~ 1047* not fall within the scope of the "fighting words" exception to the First Amendment's application and also constituted impermissible "viewpoint discrimination" within the meaning of *R.A.V.* Stanford did not appeal. The court's opinion in *Corry* is thoughtfully "described and critiqued" in an article by one of the primary drafters of the Stanford policy (see Thomas C. Grey, "How to Write a Speech Code Without Really Trying: Reflections on the Stanford Experience," 29 *U.C. Davis L. Rev.* 891 (1996) (esp. at 896–97 & 910–31)).

The more recent disputes about hate speech and speech codes, especially in the aftermath of 9/11 (see beginning of this Section), have been more varied than the earlier disputes exemplified by the *Doe v. University of Michigan* case and the *UWM Post, Inc. v. Board of Regents* case discussed above. (See, for example, Harvey Silverglate & Greg Lukianoff, "Speech Codes: Alive and Well at Colleges," *Chron. Higher Educ.*, August 1, 2003, B7; and compare Robert O'Neil, " . . . but Litigation Is the Wrong Response," *Chron. Higher Educ.*, August 1, 2003, B9.) These newer disputes may not focus only on hate speech directed against minority groups as such, but instead may concern other types of speech considered hurtful to individuals or detrimental to the educational process. In *Bair v. Shippensburg University*, 280 F. Supp. 2d 357 (M.D. Pa. 2003), for example, the plaintiffs successfully challenged speech policies that not only prohibited "acts of intolerance directed at others for ethnic, racial, gender, sexual orientation, physical, lifestyle, religious, age, and/or political characteristics," but also prohibited communications that "provoke, harass, intimidate, or harm another" (regardless of that other's identity), and "acts of intolerance that demonstrate malicious intentions towards others" (regardless of the other's identity). The court ruled that

---

[40]In a strong concurring opinion, one judge agreed with the decision only because the university had "tacitly approv[ed]" of the skit without giving any indication that the fraternity would be punished, and then imposed sanctions only after the skit had been performed. More generally, the concurring judge asserted that the university had "greater authority to regulate expressive conduct within its confines as a result of the unique nature of the educational forum" (see Section 9.5.2 of this book) and therefore could regulate certain offensive speech that interferes with its ability to "provide the optimum conditions for learning" and thus "runs directly counter to its mission."

such language made the university's speech policies unconstitutionally overbroad. Similarly, the institutional policies involved in these more recent disputes may not be hate speech codes as such, but instead may be speech policies covering a broader range of expression, or conduct codes focusing primarily on behavior and only secondarily on expression, or mission statements drawn from various institutional documents, or even unwritten policies and ad hoc decisions implicating expression. In the *Bair* case (above), for example, the provisions being challenged were found in the preamble to and various sections of the Code of Conduct, and in the university's Racism and Cultural Diversity Policy.[41] And the settings in which the more recent disputes arise may be more particularized than in the earlier disputes. The setting, for example, may be student speech in the classroom (see Gary Pavela, "Classroom 'Hate Speech' Codes," Parts I & II, *Synfax Weekly Report,* October 11 and October 18, 2004), or student speech on the institution's computer network (see Section 8.5).

The four earlier campus cases, combined with *R.A.V., Mitchell,* and *Virginia v. Black,* demonstrate the exceeding difficulty that any public institution would face if it attempted to promulgate hate speech regulations that would survive First Amendment scrutiny. Read against the backdrop of other Supreme Court cases on freedom of speech, both before and after *R.A.V.,* the hate speech cases reflect and confirm five major free speech principles, that together, severely constrain the authority of government to regulate hate speech.

Under the first free speech principle—the "content discrimination" principle—regulations of the content of speech (that is, regulations of the speaker's subject matter or message) are suspect. As the U.S. Supreme Court has frequently stated, "[A]bove all else, the First Amendment means that government has no power to restrict expression because of its message, its ideas, its subject matter, or its content. . . . There is an 'equality of status in the field of ideas,' and government must afford all points of view an equal opportunity to be heard" (*Police Department v. Mosley,* 408 U.S. 92, 95–96 (1972), quoting A. Meiklejohn, *Political Freedom: The Constitutional Powers of the People* (1948; reprinted by Greenwood Press, 1979), 27). This principle applies with extra force whenever a government restricts a speaker's message because of its *viewpoint* rather than merely because of the subject matter being addressed. As the *R.A.V.* case makes clear, and as other cases such as *Rosenberger v. Rector and Visitors of University of Virginia* (see Section 10.1.5) have confirmed, "viewpoint discrimination" against private speakers is virtually always unconstitutional (see *R.A.V.,* 505 U.S. at 391–92). In addition to *R.A.V.,* the *Iota Xi Chapter* case and the *Corry* case above also rely on viewpoint discrimination analysis.

Under the second free speech principle—the "emotive content" principle— the emotional content as well as the cognitive content of speech is protected

---

[41]The court in the *Bair* case issued a preliminary injunction against the enforcement of the challenged speech provisions. Subsequently, the parties settled the case, with the university agreeing to rewrite portions of its conduct code and diversity policy. See Eric Hoover, "Shippensburg U. Agrees to Change Conduct Code in Settlement with Advocacy Group," *Chron. Higher Educ.,* March 5, 2004, A31.

from government regulation. As the U.S. Supreme Court explained in *Cohen v. California,* 403 U.S. 15 (1971):

> [M]uch linguistic expression serves a dual communicative function: it conveys not only ideas capable of relatively precise, detached explication, but otherwise inexpressible emotions as well. In fact, words are often chosen as much for their emotive as their cognitive force. We cannot sanction the view that the Constitution, while solicitous of the cognitive content of individual speech, has little or no regard for that emotive function which, practically speaking, may often be the more important element of the overall message [403 U.S. at 26].

Under the third free speech principle—the "offensive speech" principle—speech may not be prohibited merely because persons who hear or view it are offended by the message. In a flag-burning case, *Texas v. Johnson,* 491 U.S. 397 (1989), the U.S. Supreme Court reaffirmed that "[i]f there is a bedrock principle underlying the First Amendment, it is that the government may not prohibit the expression of an idea simply because society finds the idea itself offensive or disagreeable."

Woodward

Under the fourth free speech principle—the "overbreadth and vagueness" principle—government may not regulate speech activity with provisions whose language is either overbroad or vague and would thereby create a "chilling effect" on the exercise of free speech rights. As the U.S. Supreme Court has stated: "Because First Amendment freedoms need breathing space to survive, government may regulate in the area only with narrow specificity" (*NAACP v. Button,* 371 U.S. 415, 433 (1963)). The concurring opinion in *R.A.V.* also provides an instructive example of how overbreadth analysis applies to hate speech regulations (505 U.S. at 397–415 (White, J., concurring)). The speech codes in the *Doe, UWM Post,* and *Bair* cases were all invalidated on overbreadth grounds, and the first three of the cases were invalidated on vagueness grounds as well. Another good example comes from *Dambrot v. Central Michigan University,* 55 F.3d 1177 (6th Cir. 1995), in which the appellate court invalidated the defendant university's "discriminatory harassment policy" on its face. Since the policy expressly applied to "verbal behavior," "written literature," and the use of "symbols, [epithets], or slogans," it clearly covered First Amendment speech. But the policy's language did not clearly specify when such speech would be considered "discriminatory harassment" and thus be prohibited. The policy was therefore unconstitutionally overbroad and unconstitutionally vague. (Although *Dambrot* concerned a basketball coach's speech rather than a student's speech, its overbreadth and vagueness analysis is equally applicable to student hate speech policies.)

Application of the overbreadth doctrine to speech codes may sometimes be combined with public forum analysis (see Section 9.5.2 above). Restrictions on student speech in a public forum are more likely to be found unconstitutional than restrictions on speech in a nonpublic forum; thus, the more public forum property a speech code covers, the more vulnerable it may be to an overbreadth challenge. In *Roberts v. Haragan,* 2004 WL 2203130 (N.D. Tex. 2004), for instance, the court determined that the "application of [Texas Tech University's] Speech Code to the public forum areas on campus would suppress [substantial amounts of] speech that, no matter how offensive," is protected by the First Amendment. The court therefore held the Speech Code to be "unconstitutional as to the public forum areas of the campus." In addition, since the policy covered only certain "racial or ethnic content" and left untouched other harassing speech, it constituted "impermissible viewpoint discrimination" within the meaning of *R.A.V. v. St. Paul* (see discussion of first free speech principle above).

And under the fifth free speech principle—the "underbreadth" principle—when government regulates what is considered an unprotected type, or proscribable category, of speech—for example, fighting words or obscenity—it generally may not restrict expression of certain topics or viewpoints in that unprotected area without also restricting expressions of other topics and viewpoints within that same area. For example, if government utilizes the "fighting words" rationale for regulation, it must generally regulate all fighting words or none; it cannot selectively regulate only fighting words that convey disfavored messages. This principle, sometimes called the "underbreadth" principle, is an addition to First Amendment jurisprudence derived from the *R.A.V.* case. There is an exception to this principle created by the *R.A.V.* case, however, that permits regulation of a portion or "subset" of the proscribable category if the regulation focuses on the most serious occurrences of this type of speech and does so in a way that does not involve viewpoint discrimination. The Court in *Virginia v. Black* (above) invoked this exception when using the true threats or intimidation category of proscribable speech to uphold the Virginia cross-burning statute. "[A] State [may] choose to prohibit only those forms of intimidation that are most likely to inspire fear of bodily harm," the Court reasoned; therefore, "[i]nstead of prohibiting all intimidating messages Virginia may choose to regulate this subset of intimidating messages in light of cross burning's long and pernicious history as a signal of impending violence" (538 U.S. at 344; compare 538 U.S. at 380–387 (Souter J., dissenting in part)).

9.6.3. Guidelines for dealing with hate speech on campus. In light of the imposing barriers to regulation erected by the five free speech principles in subsection 9.6.2 above, it is critical that institutions (public and private alike) emphasize *nonregulatory* approaches for dealing with hate speech. Such approaches do not rely on the prohibition of certain types of speech or the imposition of involuntary sanctions on transgressors, as do regulatory approaches. Moreover, nonregulatory initiatives may reach or engage a wider range of students than regulatory approaches can. They also may have more influence on student attitudes and values and may be more effective in creating an institutional environment that is inhospitable to hate behavior. Thus, nonregulatory initiatives may have a broader and longer-range impact on the hate speech problem. Nonregulatory initiatives may also be more in harmony with higher education's mission to foster critical examination and dialogue in the search for truth. (See generally S. Sherry, "Speaking of Virtue: A Republican Approach to

University Regulation of Hate Speech," 75 *Minn. L. Rev.* 933, 934–36, 942–44 (1991).) Nonregulatory initiatives, moreover, do not raise substantial First Amendment issues. For these reasons, institutions should move to regulatory options only if they are certain that nonregulatory initiatives cannot suitably alleviate existing or incipient hate speech problems.

In addition to nonregulatory initiatives, institutions may regulate hate *conduct* or *behavior* (as opposed to speech) on their campuses. Hateful impulses that manifest themselves in such behavior or conduct are not within the constitutional protections accorded speech (that is, the use of words or symbols to convey a message). Examples include kicking, shoving, spitting, throwing objects at persons, trashing rooms, and blocking pathways or entryways. Since such behaviors are not speech, they can be aggressively prohibited and punished in order to alleviate hate problems on campus.

If an institution also deems it necessary to regulate speech itself, either in formulating general policies or in responding to particular incidents, it should first consider the applicability or adaptability of regulations that are already in or could readily be inserted into its general code of student conduct. The question in each instance would be whether a particular type of disciplinary regulation can be applied to some particular type of hate speech without substantially intruding on free speech values and without substantial risk that a court would later find the regulation's application to hate speech unconstitutional. Under this selective incremental approach, much hate speech must remain unregulated because no type of regulation could constitutionally reach it. But some provisions in conduct codes might be applied to some hate speech. The following discussion considers five potential types of such regulations. Any such regulation must be drafted with language that would meet the overbreadth and vagueness requirements discussed under the fourth free speech principle in subsection 9.6.2 above.

First, when hate speech is combined with nonspeech actions in the same course of behavior, institutions may regulate the nonspeech elements of behavior without violating the First Amendment. A campus building may be spray-painted with swastikas; homophobic graffiti may be chalked on a campus sidewalk; a KKK insignia may be carved into the door of a dormitory room; a student may be shoved or spit on in the course of enduring verbal abuse. All these behaviors convey a hate message and therefore involve speech; but all also have a nonspeech element characterizable as destruction of property or physical assault. While the institution cannot prohibit particular messages, it can prohibit harmful acts; such acts therefore may be covered under neutral regulations governing such nonspeech matters as destruction and defacement of property or physical assaults of persons.

Second, institutions may regulate the time or place at which hate speech is uttered or the manner in which it is uttered, as long as they use neutral regulations that do not focus on the content or viewpoint of the speech. For example, an institution could punish the shouting of racial epithets in a dormitory quadrangle in the middle of the night, as long as the applicable regulation would also cover (for example) the shouting of cheers for a local sports team at the same location and time.

Third, institutions may regulate the content of hate speech that falls within one of the various exceptions to the principle forbidding content-based restrictions on speech. Thus, institutions may punish hate speech that constitutes a "true threat" or intimidation, as provided in *Virginia v. Black* (subsection 9.6.2 above), and may prohibit hate speech (and other speech) that constitutes fighting words, obscenity, incitement, or private defamation. (For an example of a higher education case adopting the fighting words rationale, see *State v. Hoshijo ex rel. White,* 76 P.3d 550, 564–65 (Hawaii Sup. Ct. 2003).) Any such regulation, however, must comply with the "underbreadth" principle, the fifth principle set out in subsection 9.6.2 above. Under this principle, an institution could not have a specific hate speech code prohibiting (for example) "fighting words" directed at minority group members, but it could have a broader regulation that applies to hate speech constituting fighting words as well as to all other types of fighting words.

Fourth, institutions probably may regulate hate speech that occurs on or is projected onto private areas, such as dormitory rooms or library study carrels, and thereby infringes on substantial privacy interests of individuals who legitimately occupy these places. For First Amendment purposes, such private areas are not considered "public forums" open to public dialogue (see Section 9.5.2); and the persons occupying such places may be "captive audiences" who cannot guard their privacy by avoiding the hate speech (see *Frisby v. Schultz,* 487 U.S. 474 (1988)). For these two reasons, it is likely that hate speech of this type could be constitutionally reached under provisions dealing generally with unjustified invasions of students' personal privacy, so long as the regulation does not constitute viewpoint discrimination (see the first free speech principle discussed in subsection 9.6.2 above).

Fifth, institutions probably may regulate hate speech that furthers a scheme of racial or other discrimination. If a fraternity places a sign in front of its house reading "No blacks allowed here," the speech is itself an act of discrimination, making it unlikely that black students would seek to become members of that fraternity. When such speech is an integral element of a pattern of discriminatory behavior, institutions should be able to cover it and related actions under a code provision prohibiting discrimination on the basis of identifiable group characteristics such as race, sex, or ethnicity. The *R.A.V.* majority opinion itself apparently supports such a rationale when it suggests that the nondiscrimination requirements of Title VII (the federal employment discrimination statute) could constitutionally be applied to sexual harassment accomplished in part through speech (505 U.S. at 409–10).

In addition to these five bases for regulating hate speech, institutions may also—as was suggested above—devise enhanced penalties under their conduct codes for hate *behavior* or *conduct* (such as the racially inspired physical attack in *Wisconsin v. Mitchell* above) that does not itself involve speech. An offense that would normally merit a semester of probation, for instance, might be punished by a one-semester suspension upon proof that the act was undertaken for racial reasons. Institutions must proceed most cautiously, however. The delicate inquiry into the perpetrator's motives that penalty enhancement requires is usually the domain of courts, lawyers, and expert witnesses, guided by formal procedures and rules of evidence as well as a body of precedent. An institution should not consider itself equipped to undertake this type of inquiry unless its disciplinary system has well-developed fact-finding processes and substantial assistance from legal counsel or a law-trained judicial officer. Institutions should also assure themselves that the system's "judges" can distinguish between the perpetrator's actual motivation for the offense (which is a permissible basis for the inquiry) and the perpetrator's thoughts or general disposition (which, under *Mitchell,* is an impermissible consideration).

Sec. 9.7. Student Files and Records

9.7.1. Family Educational Rights and Privacy Act (FERPA). The Family Educational Rights and Privacy Act of 1974 (20 U.S.C. § 1232g), popularly known as FERPA (or sometimes as the Buckley Amendment, after its principal senatorial sponsor), places significant limitations on colleges' disclosure and handling of student records. The Act and its implementing regulations, 34 C.F.R. Part 99, apply to all public and private educational agencies or institutions that receive federal funds from the U.S. Department of Education or whose students receive such funds (under the Federal Family Education Loan program, for example) and pay them to the agency or institution (34 C.F.R. § 99.1).[42] While FERPA does not invalidate common law or state statutory law applicable to student records (see Section 9.7.2 below), the regulations are so extensive and detailed that they are the predominant legal consideration in dealing with student records.[43]

FERPA establishes three basic rights for college students: the rights (1) to inspect their own education records; (2) to request that corrections to the records be made if the information in them was recorded inaccurately (and, if the school refuses, the right to a hearing by the school to determine whether the records should be corrected); and (3) to restrict the access of others (in some cases including even the students' own parents[44]) to personally identifiable records unless one of a number of enumerated exceptions is at issue. The regulations also require colleges to notify students annually of their rights under FERPA, and they provide

---

[42]Cases and authorities are collected in John E. Theuman, Annot., "Validity, Construction, and Application of Family Educational Rights and Privacy Act of 1974 (20 U.S.C.S. § 1232g)," 112 A.L.R. Fed. 1.

[43]The FERPA regulations provide that "[i]f an educational agency or institution determines that it cannot comply with the Act or [regulations] due to a conflict with State or local law, it shall notify the [Family Policy Compliance] Office within 45 days, giving the text and citation of the conflicting law" (34 C.F.R. § 99.61). Where such conflict exists, the federal law will take precedence unless the institution is willing to relinquish federal funding (see generally *Rosado v. Wyman,* 397 U.S. 397, 420–23 (1970)). The federal government would, however, allow a period of negotiation and encourage the institution to seek an official interpretation of the state law compatible with FERPA or an amendment of the state law.

[44]If a student is a dependent for federal income tax purposes, the institution may, but is not required to, disclose the student's education records to the student's parents.

a procedure for complaints to be filed with the Department of Education if a student believes that the college has not complied with FERPA.[45]

The Family Policy Compliance Office (FPCO) of the Education Department is charged with the development, interpretation, and enforcement of FERPA regulations. The FPCO maintains a Web site that provides an overview of FERPA at http://www.ed.gov/policy/gen/guid/fpco/ferpa/index.html. The Web site also contains the FERPA legislation and its implementing regulations at http://www.ed.gov/policy/gen/leg/edpicks.jhtml?src = ln (for the legislation) and http://www.ed.gov/policy/gen/reg/ferpa/index.html (for the regulations).

The education records that are protected under FERPA's quite broad definition are all "those records that are (1) [d]irectly related to a student; and (2) [m]aintained by an educational agency or institution or by a party acting for the agency or institution" (20 U.S.C. § 1232g(a)(4)(A); 34 C.F.R. § 99.3).[46] This section of the regulations contains five exceptions to this definition, which exclude from coverage certain personal and private records of institutional personnel,[47] certain campus law enforcement records, certain student employment records, certain records regarding health care, and "records . . . [such as certain alumni records] that only contain information about an individual after he or she is no longer a student at [the] . . . institution." There is also a partial exception for "directory information," which is exempt from the regulations' nondisclosure requirements under certain conditions (34 C.F.R. § 99.37).

Following a flurry of litigation concerning access by the press to campus law enforcement records involving students (considered, under FERPA's earlier definition, to be student education records and thus protected), Congress passed the Higher Education Amendments of 1992 (Pub. L. No. 102-325, codified at 20 U.S.C. § 1232g(a)(4)(B)(ii)), which amended FERPA to exclude from the definition of "education records" records that are both created and maintained by a law enforcement unit of an educational agency or institution for the purpose of law enforcement. This change enables institutions, under certain circumstances, to disclose information about campus crime contained in law enforcement unit records to parents, the media, other students, and

---

[45]The current regulations remove the previous rule that institutions adopt a formal written student records policy (although institutions may wish to retain their policies to help avoid inconsistent practices with respect to student records) (61 Fed. Reg. at 59295). An appendix to the 1996 amendments to the regulations includes a model notice of rights under FERPA for postsecondary institutions to use. The language of the model notice is advisory only and not part of the regulations (61 Fed. Reg. at 59297).

[46]It is important to recognize that the definition of "education record" is broader than a record of grades or student discipline. For example, student course evaluation scores for courses taught by graduate students fall within the definition of "education record." Therefore, posting student course evaluation scores for these instructors, either physically or on a Web site, would arguably be a violation of FERPA.

[47]For example, in *Klein Independent School District v. Mattox*, 830 F.2d 576 (5th Cir. 1987), a school district had been asked, under the Texas open records law, to produce the college transcript of one of its teachers. The court ruled that, since the teacher was an employee, not a student, of the school district, FERPA did not protect her transcript from disclosure as required under the Texas law, even though it would have protected her transcript from disclosure by her college.

other law enforcement agencies. Regulations specifying institutional responsibilities with respect to law enforcement records under FERPA are codified at 34 C.F.R. § 99.8.

Although FERPA provides substantial protection for the privacy of student records, it has been amended numerous times to address public (and parental) concerns about campus safety and the shield that FERPA provided to alleged student perpetrators of violent crimes, as well as various other issues and concerns. FERPA regulations currently list fifteen exceptions to the requirement of prior consent before the release of a personally identifiable education record (34 C.F.R. § 99.31). Several of these exceptions are discussed below.

In one such instance, the Education Department revised the FERPA regulations to clarify the definition of a disciplinary record and to specify the conditions for its release. Disciplinary records generally are considered "education records" and are thus subject to FERPA's limitations on disclosure. However, the revised regulations permit the institution to disclose to the victim of an "alleged perpetrator of a crime of violence or non-forcible sex offense" the "final results" of a disciplinary proceeding involving the student accused of the crime (34 C.F.R. § 99.31(a)(13)).[48] Prior to this amendment, student press groups had sought access to disciplinary records, in some cases successfully, under state open records laws (see the discussion of *The Red and the Black* case, Section 12.5.3). The regulations also allow the institution to disclose the "final results" of a disciplinary proceeding to the general public if the student who is the subject of the proceeding is an "alleged perpetrator of a crime of violence or non-forcible sex offense" *and* the institution determines that the student has violated one or more institutional rules and policies. Under either exception, the institution may not disclose the names of other witnesses, including the alleged victim, without the relevant student's or students' consent (34 C.F.R. § 99.31(a)(14)).[49] Because of the specificity of these exceptions to the nondisclosure rule, most disciplinary records will still be protected by FERPA and may be disclosed only with permission of the student.

In 1994, Congress amended FERPA to permit disclosure to teachers and other school officials at *other* institutions of information about a disciplinary action taken against a student for behavior that posed a significant risk to the student or to others.[50] FERPA also permits an institution to disclose information otherwise protected by FERPA in order to comply with a judicial order or a lawfully issued subpoena, as long as either the institution makes a "reasonable effort" to notify the parent or eligible student of the order or subpoena in advance or the subpoena is for law enforcement purposes and prohibits disclosure on its face (34 C.F.R. § 99.31(a)(9)(ii)).

---

[48]In 1990, the Student Right-to-Know and Campus Security Act, discussed in Section 8.6.3, amended FERPA to permit this disclosure to the student victim of a violent crime. The FERPA regulations were amended in 1995 (60 Fed. Reg. 3464 (January 17, 1995)).

[49]The Higher Education Amendments of 1998 (Pub. L. No. 105-244, October 7, 1998) amended FERPA to permit this disclosure (20 U.S.C. § 1232g(b)(6)(C)).

[50]Improving America's Schools Act of 1994 (IASA) (Pub. L. No. 103-382, enacted October 20, 1994).

The USA PATRIOT Act (Pub. L. No. 107-56; 115 Stat. 272, October 26, 2001) (discussed in Section 13.2.4 of this book) amended FERPA to permit an institution to disclose, without informing the student or seeking the student's consent, information about the student in response to an *ex parte* order issued by a court at the request of the U.S. Attorney General or his designee. In order to obtain such a court order, the Attorney General must demonstrate the need for this information in order to further investigation or prosecution of terrorism crimes as specified in 18 U.S.C. §§ 2332b(g)(5)(B) and 2331. The USA PATRIOT Act also amends the recordkeeping provisions of FERPA (20 U.S.C. § 1232g(b)(4); 34 C.F.R. § 99.32); the institution is not required to record the disclosure of information in a student's education record in response to an *ex parte* order issued under the circumstances described above. (An explanation of the USA PATRIOT Act amendments and other exceptions to the requirement of student notice and consent is contained in a technical assistance letter of April 12, 2002, from the Director of the Family Policy Compliance Office. It can be found at http://www.ed.gov/policy/gen/guid/fpco/pdf/htterrorism.pdf.)

Another FERPA exception allows colleges to give a student's parents or guardian information concerning the student's violation of laws or institutional policies governing the use or possession of alcohol or illegal drugs if the student is under twenty-one years of age, and if the college has determined that the student's conduct constituted a disciplinary violation (34 C.F.R. § 99.31(a)(15).[51] (For an assessment of the impact of this FERPA exception in reducing underage student drinking, see Leo Reisberg, "2 Years After Colleges Started Calling Home, Administrators Say Alcohol Policy Works," *Chron. Higher Educ.*, January 19, 2001, A34–36.)

The Campus Sex Crimes Prevention Act (§ 1601 of the Victims of Trafficking and Violence Protection Act of 2000, Pub. L. 106-386) amends FERPA to permit the release of information provided to the college concerning sex offenders whom the law requires to register. This amendment to FERPA is codified at 20 U.S.C. § 1232g(b)(7).[52] Interpretive Guidance regarding this legislation and its implications for colleges may be found at http://www.ed.gov/offices/OM/fpco.

The key to success in dealing with FERPA is a thorough understanding of the implementing regulations. Administrators should keep copies of the regulations at their fingertips and should not rely on secondary sources to resolve particular problems. Counsel should review the institution's record-keeping policies and practices, and every substantial change in them, to ensure compliance with the regulations. Administrators and counsel should work together to maintain appropriate legal forms to use in implementing the regulations, such as forms for a student's waiver of his or her rights under the Act or regulations, forms for securing a student's consent to release personally identifiable information from

---

[51]Higher Education Amendments of 1998, codified at 20 U.S.C. § 1232g(i).

[52]A provision of the Student Right-to-Know Law and Campus Security Act (discussed in Section 8.6.3) requires colleges to include in their annual security reports, effective October 1, 2003, a discussion of how information concerning registered sex offenders living, working, or attending classes in the community may be found.

his or her records (34 C.F.R. § 99.30), and forms for notifying parties to whom information is disclosed of the limits on the use of that information (34 C.F.R. § 99.34). Questions concerning the interpretation or application of the regulations may be directed to the Family Policy Compliance Office at the U.S. Department of Education at http://FERPA@ED.gov.

A useful reference for FERPA compliance is Steven J. McDonald, *The Family Educational Rights and Privacy Act (FERPA): A Legal Compendium* (2d ed., National Association of College and University Attorneys, 2002). This compendium includes the statute and regulations, sample forms and policies, technical assistance letters from the Family Policy Compliance Office, and a list of additional resources.

Since FERPA has been in effect, litigation about disclosure of education records and questions about who has access, and to what types of records, have proliferated. For example, students at Harvard University who wished to examine the comments that admissions staff had made about them on "summary sheets" filed a complaint with the Department of Education when Harvard denied their request. Harvard had told the students that the summary sheets were kept in a file separate from the student's academic records, that they included direct quotes from confidential letters of recommendation, and that they had no further significance once a student was admitted. Therefore, Harvard believed that these documents were not accessible under FERPA.

In an advisory letter, reprinted in 22 *Coll. Law Dig.* 299 (July 16, 1992), the Department of Education ruled that the students had a right to examine the summary sheets. Applying FERPA's broad definition of an "education record" (documents containing information related to a student that are maintained by an educational agency (20 U.S.C. § 1232g(a)(4)(A)), the Department of Education determined that the summary sheets met that definition. However, the department ruled that the university could redact from the documents any excerpts specifically derived from confidential letters of recommendation if the student had waived his or her right of access to these letters.

In 2002, the U.S. Supreme Court ruled that there is no private right of action under FERPA, putting an end to more than two decades of litigation over that issue. In *Gonzaga University v. Doe*, 536 U.S. 273 (2002), the Court ruled 7 to 2 that Congress had not created a private right of action under FERPA, and also ruled that the law created no personal rights enforceable under 42 U.S.C. § 1983. Doe, a former education student at Gonzaga University, a private institution in the State of Washington, had sued Gonzaga in state court, alleging violation of his FERPA rights for a communication between a university administrator and the state agency responsible for teacher certification. In that communication, the university administrator alleged that Doe had committed certain sex-based offenses against a fellow student, despite the fact that the alleged victim had not filed a complaint and no determination had been made as to the truth of the allegations, which the administrator had overheard from a third party. Doe also sued Gonzaga and the administrator under tort and contract theories. A jury found for Doe, awarding him more than $1 million in compensatory and punitive damages, including $450,000 in damages on the FERPA claim.

The Washington Court of Appeals reversed the outcome at the trial level, but, in *Doe v. Gonzaga University*, 24 P.3d 390 (Wash. 2001), the Washington Supreme Court reversed yet again, ruling that, although FERPA did not create a private cause of action, its nondisclosure provisions provided a right enforceable under Section 1983. Since the lower courts were divided as to the existence of FERPA's enforceability under Section 1983, the U.S. Supreme Court granted *certiorari* to resolve the conflict.

The Court compared the language of FERPA with that of Titles VI and IX (discussed in this book, Sections 13.5.2 & 13.5.3 respectively), which provide that "no person" shall be subject to discrimination. In FERPA, however, Congress focused on the obligation of the Secretary of Education to withhold federal funds from any institution that failed to comply with the law's nondisclosure provisions. This language, said the Court, did not confer the type of "individual entitlement" that can be enforced through Section 1983, citing *Cannon v. University of Chicago* (discussed in Section 13.5.9), a case that found a private right of action under Title IX. Furthermore, said the Court, FERPA provides for penalties for institutions that have a "policy or practice" of permitting the release of education records, rather than penalties for a single act of noncompliance. Furthermore, said the Court, FERPA's creation of an administrative enforcement mechanism through the Secretary of Education demonstrates that Congress did not intend for the law to create an individual right, either under FERPA itself or through Section 1983. The Court reversed the Washington Supreme Court's ruling.[53]

(For a discussion of *Gonzaga* and *Owasso,* and a review of non-FERPA-based privacy issues with respect to student records, see Margaret L. O'Donnell, "FERPA: Only a Piece of the Privacy Puzzle," 29 *J. Coll. & Univ. Law* 679 (2003).)

A perennial issue that colleges face is whether the use of Social Security numbers as identifiers of students violates FERPA. Although an earlier ruling by a federal court[54] established that students could challenge the use of Social Security numbers as identification numbers on class rosters, identification cards, meal tickets, and other university documents under Section 1983 (a position since rejected by the U.S. Supreme Court in *Gonzaga*), the FPCO has taken the position that the use of even partial Social Security numbers to publicly post student grades is a FERPA violation (Letter re: Hunter College, FPCO May 29, 2001, available at http://www.ed.gov/policy/gen/guid/fpco/doc/hunter.doc). A New York law prohibits any public or private school or university from displaying a student's Social Security number for posting of grades, on class rosters, on student identification cards, in student directories, or for other purposes unless specifically authorized or required by law (N.Y.C.L.S. Educ. § 2-b (2003)).

---

[53]In a case decided a few months before *Gonzaga,* the U.S. Supreme Court ruled that peer grading in a classroom setting does not violate FERPA's nondisclosure requirements because unrecorded grades are not education records (*Owasso Independent School District v. Falvo,* 534 U.S. 426 (2002)). The issue of whether FERPA provided for a private right of action was not before the court in *Owasso.*

[54]*Krebs v. Rutgers, The State University of New Jersey,* 797 F. Supp. 1246 (D.N.J. 1992).

9.7.2. State law. In a majority of states, courts now recognize a common law tort of invasion of privacy, which, in some circumstances, protects individuals against the public disclosure of damaging private information about them and against intrusions into their private affairs. A few states have similarly protected privacy with a statute or constitutional provision. Although this body of law has seldom been applied to educational record-keeping practices, the basic legal principles appear applicable to record-keeping abuses by postsecondary institutions. This body of right-to-privacy law could protect students against abusive collection and retention practices where clearly intrusive methods are used to collect information concerning private affairs. In *White v. Davis,* 533 P.2d 222 (Cal. 1975) (see Section 11.5), for example, the court held that undercover police surveillance of university classes and meetings violated the right to privacy because "no professor or student can be confident that whatever he may express in class will not find its way into a police file." Similarly, right-to-privacy law could protect students against abusive dissemination practices that result in unwarranted public disclosure of damaging personal information.

In addition to this developing right-to-privacy law, many states also have statutes or administrative regulations dealing specifically with record keeping. These include subject access laws, open record or public record laws, and confidentiality laws. Such laws usually apply only to state agencies, and a state's postsecondary institutions may or may not be considered state agencies subject to record-keeping laws (see Section 12.5.3). Occasionally a state statute deals specifically with postsecondary education records. A Massachusetts statute, for instance, makes it an "unfair educational practice" for any "educational institution," including public and private postsecondary institutions, to request information or make or keep records concerning certain arrests or misdemeanor convictions of students or applicants (Mass. Gen. Laws Ann. ch. 151C, § 2(f)).

Since state laws on privacy and records vary greatly from state to state, administrators should check with counsel to determine the law in their particular state. Since state open records requirements may occasionally conflict with FERPA regulations, counsel must determine whether any such conflict exists. While there have been several cases involving the conflict between FERPA's confidentiality requirements and the demands of state public records laws, there is little agreement as to how a public institution can comply with both laws.

If a case is not brought under FERPA, but instead asserts only state law claims, federal courts may not have subject matter jurisdiction (Section 2.2.2.1). In *Gannett River States Publishing Corp. v. Mississippi State University,* 945 F. Supp. 128 (S.D. Miss. 1996), the federal district court refused to hear an action based on the Mississippi Public Records Act (Miss. Code Ann. §§ 25-61-1 through 25-61-17). The plaintiff had filed suit for disclosure of records in state court, but the university had removed the action to federal court based on federal question jurisdiction. The university argued that the plaintiff's claims were federal in nature because it was FERPA that prevented the release of the records sought; even the plaintiff's complaint explicitly mentioned FERPA and disputed its applicability to the records at hand. The federal court rejected this argument and remanded the case back to state court. Citing long-established precedents concerning federal jurisdiction, the court held that state law, not FERPA, was the basis for the plaintiff's claim, and the suit thus did not "arise under" federal law. The references to FERPA did not convert the matter from one of federal law to one of state law; mentioning FERPA in the complaint was simply an "anticipation" of the university's defense. This case is an interesting reminder to institutional defendants that, in the absence of diversity jurisdiction, the substance of the plaintiff's complaint may determine the forum in which disclosure issues are decided.

Several state courts have ruled that public records laws trump the confidentiality provisions of FERPA, particularly with respect to disciplinary proceedings. Although the changes to FERPA made by the 1998 Higher Education Amendments will allow colleges to release limited information concerning the outcomes of student disciplinary hearings (Section 9.7.1), the law still does not provide for the complete release of transcripts, documentary evidence, or other records that meet FERPA's definition of "education records." Thus, the outcomes in the cases discussed below are still relevant to college administrators and, until and unless FERPA is once again amended, colleges may have to walk a tightrope in attempting to comply with conflicting state laws regarding public records and public meetings.

In a case whose rationale is similar to the *Red and Black* case (discussed in Section 12.5.3), a Connecticut appellate court addressed a claim under Connecticut's Freedom of Information law that audiotapes of a student disciplinary hearing were public records and thus subject to disclosure. In *Eastern Connecticut State University v. Connecticut Freedom of Information Commission*, No. CV96-0556097, 1996 Conn. Super. LEXIS 2554 (Conn. Super., September 30, 1996), a faculty member who had filed disciplinary charges against a student enrolled in his class requested audiotapes of the hearing that had been held to adjudicate those charges. The college had refused, citing FERPA's provision that protects records of disciplinary hearings from disclosure unless the student consents. Although the state Freedom of Information Commission (FOIC) had found the hearings to fall squarely within FERPA's protection, it also found that the faculty member had a legitimate educational interest in the student's behavior and thus was entitled to the information under another FERPA provision (20 U.S.C. § 1232g(h); 34 C.F.R. § 99.3). The court held that FERPA did not prevent a state legislature from enacting a law providing for access to public records, and that FERPA does not prohibit disclosing the student records, but that nondisclosure is "merely a precondition for federal funds." Taken to its logical conclusion, this ruling would elevate the interest of the public in access to public records over the ability of the state institution to be eligible to receive federal funds. (This unpublished opinion does not discuss an earlier Connecticut case, *University of Connecticut v. FOI Comm'n.* (discussed in Section 12.5.3), whose outcome was quite different.)

A second state court differed sharply with the result in the *Eastern Connecticut State University* case. In *Shreveport Professional Chapter of the Society of Professional Journalists v. Louisiana State University*, No. 393, 334 (1st Judicial Dist. Ct. Caddo Parish, La., March 4, 1994) (unpublished opinion at 17), the court found that the results of a disciplinary hearing concerning theft of student government funds by student government members were more like education records (protected by FERPA) than law enforcement records (not protected by FERPA). The court rejected the plaintiffs' claim that FERPA did not prohibit disclosure of disciplinary hearing records, stating: "[T]he intent of Congress to withhold millions of federal dollars from universities that violate [FERPA] is ample prohibition, regardless of how the word 'prohibit' is construed by the plaintiffs." Although the court determined that the disciplinary hearing records were subject to the state's public records act, the court ruled that, given FERPA's requirements, the state constitution provided for an implied exception in the law for college disciplinary hearings. Distinguishing *Red and Black* (discussed in Section 12.5.3) on several grounds, the court held that the records should not be disclosed.

Despite the clarity of the FERPA regulations that include disciplinary records within the definition of education record, a lengthy legal battle pitting state courts against their federal counterparts resulted, eventually, in a determination that FERPA's privacy protections trumped state open records laws. In the state court litigation, the Supreme Court of Ohio held in *State ex rel Miami Student v. Miami University*, 680 N.E.2d 956 (Ohio 1997), that university disciplinary records are not education records under FERPA. The editor of the university's student newspaper had sought student disciplinary records, redacted of the students' names, Social Security numbers, and student identification numbers, or any other information that would identify individual students. The university provided the information but, in addition to the redactions that the editor had agreed to, also deleted information on the sex and age of the accused individuals, the date, time and location of the incidents, and memoranda, statements by students, and the disposition of some of the proceedings. The editor sought a writ of *mandamus* from the state supreme court. As in *Colonial School District,* the majority opinion did not cite or analyze the 1995 amendments to the FERPA regulations (Section 9.7.1) or, for that matter, any of the implementing regulations. Instead, the opinion analyzed the *Red and Black* case and determined that disciplinary records were not related to "student academic performance, financial aid, or scholastic probation," and thus could be disclosed without violating FERPA. Noting that the public records act was intended to be interpreted broadly, the court also noted that crime on campus was a serious problem and that the public should have access to the information requested by the student editor.

One justice dissented from the court's ruling that the information sought was not an education record, stating that the court's conclusion was "clearly contrary to the history, language and intent of FERPA." Noting that the *Red and Black* case was decided prior to the 1995 amendments (in which the Secretary of Education explicitly included disciplinary records within the definition of education records), the judge noted that *Shreveport* was a more recent analysis of the conflict, suggesting that it was the better authority.

The U.S. Supreme Court denied *certiorari* in the *Miami Student* case (522 U.S. 1022 (1997)). The U.S. Department of Education then brought a claim in a federal district court in Ohio, seeking to enjoin the colleges from complying with the state supreme court's ruling to release the disciplinary records. The federal court issued the requested injunction, stating that the disciplinary records at issue clearly met the FERPA definition of "education records" and that the Ohio Supreme Court's interpretation of FERPA as pertaining only to academic records was incorrect (*United States v. Miami University*, No. C2:98-0097, February 12, 1998).

The federal district court then permitted the addition of the *Chronicle of Higher Education* as a codefendant to argue that disciplinary records are law enforcement records, rather than education records, and that FERPA does not preempt the Ohio Public Records Act (John Lowery, "Balancing Students' Right to Privacy and the Public's Right to Know," *Synthesis: Law and Policy in Higher Education*, Vol. 10, no. 2 (Fall 1998), 715).

The *Chronicle* asked the court to dismiss the Education Department's lawsuit for lack of subject matter jurisdiction, arguing that the department lacked standing to bring the action. The trial court ruled that FERPA expressly gave the Secretary of Education standing to enforce the law (20 U.S.C. § 1232g(f)), including enforcement by litigation (*United States of America v. The Miami University and The Ohio State University*, 91 F. Supp. 2d 1132 (S.D. Ohio 2000)). Additionally, said the court, the Secretary of Education had the authority to sue the recipients of federal funds to force them to comply with the terms of funding programs, one of which is compliance with FERPA. And, third, the court rejected the *Chronicle*'s argument that FERPA does not prohibit colleges from releasing education records, but rather merely authorizes the Department of Education to withdraw federal funding from an institution that does not comply with FERPA. The court stated that the inclusion in the statute of several enforcement mechanisms, in addition to termination of funds for FERPA violations, demonstrated that Congress intended that the law apply directly to colleges. The federal district court also made an explicit ruling that student disciplinary records are education records under FERPA. Denying the *Chronicle*'s motion to dismiss and awarding summary judgment to the Department of Education, the federal court issued a permanent injunction against Miami University and Ohio State University, forbidding the further release of student disciplinary records.

The intervening party, the *Chronicle of Higher Education*, appealed, and the U.S. Court of Appeals for the Sixth Circuit affirmed (294 F.3d 797 (6th Cir. 2002)). The *Chronicle* asserted that the Department of Education lacked standing to bring the action seeking to enjoin the release of the records, challenged the lower court's ruling as an implicit decision that FERPA preempts state open records laws, and asserted that the lower court was incorrect in ruling that disciplinary records were education records within the meaning of FERPA. The *Chronicle* also argued that FERPA violates the First Amendment because it limits access to otherwise publicly available records.

The appellate court ruled that the Department of Education had standing to seek the injunction on the same grounds that the trial court had relied upon. Furthermore, said the court, the Ohio Supreme Court's ruling that disciplinary records were not education records was incorrect; despite that ruling, the Ohio court had allowed Miami to redact all personally identifiable information from the records before disclosing them, an action that complied with FERPA's requirements. The federal appellate court relied on the numerous exceptions to FERPA's prohibition against disclosure of education records to conclude that disciplinary records were, in fact, still included within the law's definition of education record, a result that complies with the position of the FPCO. With respect to the First Amendment claim, the court explained that student disciplinary proceedings were not criminal trials, and therefore, jurisprudence related to the public's access to criminal trials was not applicable to disciplinary hearings in which students lacked the panoply of protections available to litigants in the courts. Student disciplinary hearings at both universities were closed to the public, and press or public access to such hearings would complicate, not aid, the educational purpose that the hearings were designed to further. The court rejected the *Chronicle*'s First Amendment claims. The court noted that the *Chronicle* could request student disciplinary records from which all individually identifying information had been redacted, as FERPA would not prohibit the release of such information.

Despite the first ruling of the federal trial court in the Miami University case (enjoining the release of the records prior to trial), the Court of Appeals of Maryland followed the lead of the Ohio Supreme Court. In *Kirwan v. The Diamondback,* 721 A.2d 196 (Md. Ct. App. 1998), the Maryland court ruled that Maryland's Public Information Act (Maryland Code § 10-611-28) authorizes the disclosure of information sought from the university by the student newspaper. The newspaper was seeking correspondence and parking violation records involving the basketball coach and several student players, which the university refused to provide. The university asserted that the parking violation records related to the coach were personnel records, which the law exempted from disclosure, and that the parking violation records related to the students were education records, protected from disclosure by FERPA. The court rejected both of the university's defenses.

The court held that the parking violation records of the student athletes were not education records because Congress had intended only that records related to a student's academic performance be covered by FERPA. In addition to attempting to protect student privacy through FERPA, said the court:

> Congress intended to prevent educational institutions from operating in secrecy. Prohibiting disclosure of any document containing a student's name would allow universities to operate in secret, which would be contrary to one of the policies behind [FERPA]. Universities could refuse to release information about criminal activity on campus if students were involved, claiming that this information constituted education records, thus keeping very important information from other students, their parents, public officials, and the public [721 A.2d at 204].

The court upheld the ruling of the trial court that the university was required to release the information sought by the student newspaper.

But another state appellate court has ruled that, despite its finding that the "Undergraduate Court" at the University of North Carolina was a "public body" under North Carolina's Open Meetings Law (N.C. Gen. Stat. § 143-318.9 *et seq.*), that body was entitled to hold closed disciplinary hearings in order to comply with the dictates of FERPA. In *DTH Publishing Corp. v. The University of North Carolina at Chapel Hill,* 496 S.E.2d 8 (N.C. Ct. App. 1998), the court applied language in the Open Meetings Law that allowed a public body to hold a closed session, if it was necessary, to prevent the disclosure of information that is "privileged or confidential." The university had argued that FERPA's prohibition of the nonconsensual release of personally identifiable student records rendered the records of student disciplinary hearings "privileged and confidential" for the purposes of state law. The court distinguished the *Miami Student* case, noting that the Ohio court had only ordered the release of "statistical data" from which student names had been deleted, and which included the location of the incident, age and sex of the student, nature of the offense, and the type of discipline imposed, but had not ordered the release of records from specific disciplinary hearings. The court also rejected arguments by the student newspaper that the state and federal constitutions required that judicial proceedings be open to the public, stating that the Undergraduate Court was not the type of court contemplated by these constitutions, and that there was no history at the university of open disciplinary hearings.

In *Caledonian-Record Publishing Company, Inc. v. Vermont State College,* 833 A.2d 1273 (Vt. 2003), Vermont's highest court was asked to decide whether the press could have access to the daily security logs, student disciplinary records, and student disciplinary hearings at Lyndon State College and the entire Vermont State College System under the state's Open Meeting Law and Public Records Act. The colleges provided the daily security logs compiled by their campus police departments, but refused to provide the requested student disciplinary records or to allow access to student disciplinary hearings.

The court found that Vermont's Public Records Act exempts "student records at educational institutions funded wholly or in part by state revenue" (1 V.S.A. § 317(c)(11)) from disclosure. Because the plaintiffs had stated that they did not want to attend the hearings, but only to have access to the minutes or other records of the hearings, the court did not reach the issue of whether the media should be allowed to attend student disciplinary hearings. It also found that minutes or other records documenting the proceedings and outcome of student disciplinary hearings also fit the definition of "student records," and thus were exempted from disclosure.

9.7.3. The Federal Privacy Act.
The Privacy Act of 1974 (88 Stat. 1896, partly codified in 5 U.S.C. § 552a) applies directly to federal government agencies and, with two exceptions discussed below, does not restrict postsecondary education institutions. The Act accords all persons—including students, faculty members, and staff members—certain rights enforceable against the federal government regarding information about them in federal agency files, whether

collected from a postsecondary institution or from any other source. The Act grants the right to inspect, copy, and correct such information and limits its dissemination by the agency. Regulations implementing the Privacy Act are found at 34 C.F.R. Part 5b.[55]

Section 7 of the Act prohibits federal, state, and local government agencies from requiring persons to disclose their Social Security numbers. This provision applies to public but not to private postsecondary institutions (see the *Krebs* case in Section 9.7.1, which also discusses when an institution is considered a state agency for purposes of this provision) and thus may prevent public institutions from requiring either students or employees to disclose their Social Security numbers if they meet this definition. The two exceptions to this nondisclosure requirement permit an institution to require disclosure (1) where it is required by some other federal statute and (2) where the institution maintains "a system of records in existence and operating before January 1, 1975, if such disclosure was required under statute or regulation adopted prior to such date to verify the identity of an individual" (88 Stat. 1896 at 1903).

The second provision of the Act potentially relevant to some postsecondary institutions is Section 3(m) (5 U.S.C. § 552a(m)), which applies the Act's requirements to government contractors who operate record-keeping systems on behalf of a federal agency pursuant to the contract.

(A reference guide to the Federal Freedom of Information Act and the Federal Privacy Act is published regularly by the U.S. Department of Justice. A description of this guide, *The Freedom of Information Act Guide and Privacy Act Overview,* and information on obtaining it, are available at http://www.usdoj.gov/oip/foiapost/2004foiapost2.htm.)

Many states have enacted privacy laws that regulate the actions of public colleges and universities, and sometimes private colleges as well. Administrators should consult with counsel for updated information on the existence of, or changes in, state privacy laws. For example, at least eight states prohibit the use of Social Security numbers by public agencies, which some of these laws define to include colleges and universities.

Selected Annotated Bibliography

General

Kaplin, William A. *American Constitutional Law: An Overview, Analysis, and Integration* (Carolina Academic Press, 2004). In Chapters 11 and 12, this book presents the foundational due process and free expression principles, and the leading U.S. Supreme Court cases, that undergird students' federal constitutional rights. Chapter 14, Section E, provides an introduction to state constitutional rights regarding due process and freedom of expression.

---

[55]Cases and authorities are collected at George K. Chamberlin, Annot., "Applicability of § 3(b) of Privacy Act of 1974 (5 U.S.C.A. § 552a(b)), Requiring Individual's Consent to Disclosure of Agency Records Maintained on Individual, to Disclosure of Information Otherwise Known to Federal Agency or Official," 52 A.L.R. Fed. 579.

Sec. 9.1 (Disciplinary and Grievance Systems)

Bach, Jason L. "Students Have Rights, Too: The Drafting of Student Conduct Codes," 2003 *BYU Educ. & L.J.* 1 (2003). Suggests a series of factors to be considered in drafting codes of student conduct; criticizes those who argue that formal due process protections are not necessary for campus judicial hearings; analyzes the procedural and substantive due process rights of students charged with violations of campus codes of student conduct.

Baker, Thomas R. "Criminal Sanctions for Student Misconduct: Double Jeopardy Litigation in the 1990s," 130 *West's Educ. L. Rep.* 1 (1998). Discusses the problem of dealing with students whose campus code violation is also a criminal violation, and judicial responses to student attempts to challenge on-campus or criminal proceedings under the double jeopardy theory.

Dannels, Michael. *From Discipline to Development: Rethinking Student Conduct in Higher Education.* ASHE-ERIC Higher Education Report, Vol. 25, no. 2 (ERIC Clearinghouse on Higher Education, 1997). Reviews the history of student discipline, examines the characteristics of students who violate disciplinary codes, and the role of institutions in preventing or facilitating student misconduct. Suggests models of student disciplinary codes and judicial proceedings that contribute to student development as well as improving conduct.

Jameson, Jessica Katz. "Diffusion of a Campus Innovation: Integration of a New Student Dispute Resolution Center into the University," 16 *Mediation Q.* 129 (1998). Proposes guidelines for integrating dispute resolution programs into a college's existing culture while keeping in mind the educational and mediation goals of such programs.

Pavela, Gary. "Applying the Power of Association on Campus: A Model Code of Academic Integrity," 24 *J. Coll. & Univ. Law* 97 (1997). Discusses the use of honor codes at colleges and universities; proposes a model honor code. Includes a list of Ten Principles of Academic Integrity.

Pavela, Gary. "Limiting the Pursuit of Perfect Justice on Campus: A Proposed Code of Student Conduct," 6 *J. Coll. & Univ. Law* 137 (1980). A well-drafted sample code, including standards of conduct and hearing procedures, with comprehensive annotations explaining particular provisions and cites to relevant authorities. The code represents an alternative to the procedural complexities of the criminal justice model. See also Pavela's "Model Code of Student Conduct," available at http://www.collegepubs.com.

Pavela, Gary. "Therapeutic Paternalism and the Misuse of Mandatory Psychiatric Withdrawals on Campus," 9 *J. Coll. & Univ. Law* 101 (1982–83). Analyzes the pitfalls associated with postsecondary institutions' use of "psychiatric withdrawals" of students. Pitfalls include violations of Section 504 (on disability discrimination) and of students' substantive and procedural due process rights. The article concludes with "Policy Considerations," including the limits of psychiatric diagnosis, the danger of substituting a "therapeutic" approach as a solution for disciplinary problems, and the "appropriate uses for a psychiatric withdrawal policy." For a later monograph adapted from this article, with model standards and procedures, hypothetical case studies, and a bibliography, see Gary Pavela, *The Dismissal of Students with Mental Disorders: Legal Issues, Policy Considerations, and Alternative Responses* listed in Section 9.4.

Picozzi, James M. "University Disciplinary Process: What's Fair, What's Due, and What You Don't Get," 96 *Yale L.J.* 2132 (1987). Written by a defendant in a student disciplinary case. Provides a critical review of case law and institutional grievance procedures, concluding that the minimal due process protections endorsed by the courts are insufficient to protect students' interests.

U.S. District Court, Western District of Missouri (*en banc*). "General Order on Judicial Standards of Procedure and Substance in Review of Student Discipline in Tax-Supported Institutions of Higher Education," 45 *Federal Rules Decisions* 133 (1968). A set of guidelines promulgated for the use of this district court in deciding students' rights cases. The guidelines are similarly useful to administrators and counsel seeking to comply with federal legal requirements.

Sec. 9.2 (Disciplinary Rules and Regulations)

Brown, Valerie L. (ed.). *Student Disciplinary Issues: A Legal Compendium* (National Association of College and University Attorneys, 1997). A collection of law review articles, institutional policies, judicial opinions, and conference outlines related to student disciplinary rules and disciplinary systems. Issues related to both academic and nonacademic misconduct are included. A list of additional resources is also provided.

Faulkner, Janet E., & Tribbensee, Nancy E. *Student Disciplinary Issues: A Legal Compendium* (National Association of College & University Attorneys, 2004). Collects articles, NACUA outlines, institutional policies, reports, and statutes related to (1) student due process and contract rights; (2) sanctions; (3) disclosure of conduct records, and (4) model codes of student conduct.

Munsch, Martha Hartle, & Schupansky, Susan P. *The Dismissal of Students with Mental Disabilities* (National Association of College and University Attorneys, 2003). Provides guidance on upholding the institution's academic and disciplinary standards while complying with the laws protecting students with disabilities. Reviews applicable federal law; includes a question-and-answer section on common issues that arise when dealing with student misconduct related to a psychiatric or learning disability.

Zirkel, Perry A. "Disciplining Students for Off-Campus Misconduct: Ten Tips," 163 *West's Educ. L. Rep.* 551 (2002). Discusses the problems inherent in applying student codes of conduct to off-campus misconduct, and provides suggestions for avoiding legal liability.

See the Selected Annotated Bibliography for Section 9.1.

Sec. 9.3 (Grades, Credits, and Degrees)

Babbitt, Ellen M. (ed.). *Accommodating Students with Learning and Emotional Disabilities* (National Association of College and University Attorneys, 2005). Includes statutes, regulations, agency guidance, and Supreme Court decisions concerning students with learning and emotional disabilities; general principles of ADA analysis; special issues, with a particular focus on accommodating learning and emotional disabilities at professional schools, in athletics and for off-site and distance learning programs; and an extensive collection of additional resources, Web sites, and other materials.

Center for Academic Integrity. *The Fundamental Values of Academic Integrity* (Center for Academic Integrity, 1999). Describes the purpose and functions of the center, which is affiliated with the Kenan Ethics Program at Duke University. The center is a consortium of 200 colleges and universities, and 500 individual members, established "to identify and affirm the values of academic integrity and to promote their achievement in practice." Further information is available at http://www. academicintegrity.org.

Flygare, Thomas J. *Students with Learning Disabilities: New Challenges for Colleges and Universities* (2d ed., National Association of College and University Attorneys, 2002). Discusses the development of institutional policies for dealing with students with learning disabilities, ensuring that admissions materials are reviewed for accessibility, and the process of determining which accommodations are appropriate.

Francis, Leslie Pickering. *Sexual Harassment as an Ethical Issue in Academic Life* (Rowan & Littlefield, 2001). Explores sexual harassment from ethical, legal, and policy perspectives. Part One of the book contains seven chapters on various topics prepared by the author; Part Two contains selected excerpts from the pertinent writings of other authors. There is also a chapter containing "illustrative" sexual harassment policies from various public and private postsecondary institutions, and a "Selected Bibliography" of sources. Reviewed at 28 *J. Coll. & Univ. Law* 243 (2001).

Johnston, Robert Gilbert, & Oswald, Jane D. "Academic Dishonesty: Revoking Academic Credentials," 32 *J. Marshall L. Rev.* 67 (1998). Develops a "model code" for colleges and universities to guide them in the event that student academic misconduct is discovered after a degree is conferred. Includes discussion of due process protections and strategies for minimizing the risk of judicial rejection of the college's degree revocation.

Kibler, William L., Nuss, Elizabeth M., Peterson, Brent G., & Pavela, Gary. *Academic Integrity and Student Development* (College Administration Publications, 1988). Examines student academic dishonesty from several perspectives: student development, methods for preventing academic dishonesty, and the legal issues related to student dishonesty. A model code of academic integrity and case studies are included in the appendix.

Leonard, James. "Judicial Deference to Academic Standards Under Section 504 of the Rehabilitation Act and Titles II and III of the Americans With Disabilities Act," 75 *Nebraska L. Rev.* 27 (1996). Examines the role of judicial deference to academic decisions in Section 504 and ADA actions involving claims that a student is "otherwise qualified" to participate in a program. Reviews the constitutional and common law principles used by courts in deferring to academic decisions. Argues that deference to academic decisions is justified because courts are not competent to determine the appropriateness of academic standards.

Note, "Toward Reasonable Equality: Accommodating Learning Disabilities Under the Americans With Disabilities Act," 111 *Harv. L. Rev.* 1560 (1998). Provides background information on learning disabilities; reviews a range of approaches taken by courts in reviewing claims individuals with learning disabilities, and provides suggestions for evaluating claims by individuals with learning disabilities.

Schweitzer, Thomas A. "'Academic Challenge' Cases: Should Judicial Review Extend to Academic Evaluations of Students?" 41 *Am. U. L. Rev.* 267 (1992). Compares judicial review of student discipline cases with "academic challenge" cases (in which the student challenges an academic decision made by the institution). Provides a thorough and penetrating analysis of a variety of challenges to academic decisions, including degree revocation.

Wilhelm, Suzanne. "Accommodating Mental Disabilities in Higher Education: A Practical Guide to ADA Requirements," 32 *J. Law & Educ.* 217 (2003). Reviews the requirements of the ADA with respect to accommodating students with mental disorders; suggests guidelines and policies for accommodating these students.

Zirkel, Perry A., & Hugel, Paul S. "Academic Misguidance in Colleges and Universities," 56 *West's Educ. L. Rptr.* 709 (1989). Discusses the legal and practical implications of erroneous or inadequate academic advice by faculty and administrators. Reviews four legal theories used by students to seek damages when they are harmed, allegedly by "misguidance," and concludes that most outcomes favor the institution, not the student.

See the Neiger entry in the Selected Annotated Bibliography for Section 13.5 and the Paludi entry for Section 6.4.

Sec. 9.4 (*Procedures for Suspension, Dismissal, and Other Sanctions*)

Berger, Curtis J., & Berger, Vivian. "Academic Discipline: A Guide to Fair Process for the University Student," 99 *Columbia L. Rev.* 289 (1999). Argues that due process protections for students at private colleges should not differ from those for students attending public colleges, applying the contractual doctrine of the implied covenant of good faith and fair dealing as the contractual equivalent of constitutional due process.

Cole, Elsa Kircher. *Selected Legal Issues Relating to Due Process and Liability in Higher Education* (Council of Graduate Schools, 1994). A pamphlet designed for faculty and academic advisors that reviews the basics of due process in dealing with academic misconduct or discipline problems. Also covers termination of faculty, scientific misconduct, and privacy of student records.

Ford, Deborah L., & Strope, John L., Jr. "Judicial Responses to Adverse Academic Decisions Affecting Public Postsecondary Institution Students Since *Horowitz* and *Ewing*," 110 *West's Educ. L. Rptr.* 517 (1996). Discusses judicial review of institutions' judgments regarding student academic performance, noting under what circumstances courts will defer to those judgments.

Jennings, Eileen K., & Strope, John L., Jr. "Procedural Due Process in Academia: *Board of Curators v. Horowitz* Seven Years Later," 28 *West's Educ. L. Rptr.* 973 (1986). Reviews the outcome of *Horowitz* and discusses the required elements of due process in academic dismissals.

Paterson, Brent G., & Kibler, William L. (eds.). *The Administration of Campus Discipline: Student, Organization and Community Issues* (College Administration Publications, 1998). A collection of articles by student judicial affairs scholars, college attorneys, and student affairs professionals. Includes a model code for student discipline, a discussion of the differences between the criminal justice system and campus judicial systems, and a review of federal restrictions on the disclosure of student judicial records. Reviews issues related to adjudicating a variety of specific student conduct issues, issues related to disciplining student organizations, and academic misconduct issues. Includes ten case studies of student misconduct suitable for training programs.

Pavela, Gary. *The Dismissal of Students with Mental Disorders: Legal Issues, Policy Considerations, and Alternative Responses* (College Administration Publications, 1985). Reviews the protections provided by the Rehabilitation Act of 1973 (Section 504) for students with mental disabilities. Recommends elements of an appropriate policy for psychiatric withdrawal, and provides a checklist for responding to students with mental disorders. Includes a case study about a disruptive student and suggests an appropriate institutional response. For related work by the same author, see Pavela, "Therapeutic Paternalism," entry for Section 9.1.

Stevens, Ed. *Due Process and Higher Education: A Systemic Approach to Fair Decision Making.* ASHE-ERIC Higher Education Report, Vol. 27, no. 2 (ERIC Clearinghouse on Higher Education, 1999). Reviews the development and refinement of due process in higher education for both academic and disciplinary sanctions. Suggests how policies and practices may be developed and monitored to ensure compliance with due process protections and requirements.

See Faulkner and Tribbensee entry for Section 9.2.

Sec. 9.5 (Student Protests and Freedom of Speech)

Blasi, Vincent. "Prior Restraints on Demonstrations," 68 *Mich. L. Rev.* 1482 (1970). A comprehensive discussion of First Amendment theory and case law and the specific manner in which the law bears on the various components of a student demonstration.

Herman, Joseph. "Injunctive Control of Disruptive Student Demonstrations," 56 *Va. L. Rev.* 215 (1970). Analyzes strategic, constitutional, and procedural issues concerning the use of injunctions to control disruptive student protest.

Sec. 9.6 (Speech Codes and the Problem of Hate Speech)

Byrne, J. Peter. "Racial Insults and Free Speech Within the University," 79 *Georgetown L.J.* 399 (1991). Author argues that, to protect "the intellectual values of academic discourse," universities may regulate racial (and other similar) insults on campuses even if the state could not constitutionally enact and enforce the same type of regulation against society at large. He asserts, however, that public universities may not use such regulations "to punish speakers for advocating any idea in a reasoned manner." Article analyzes the evolution of relevant constitutional law and examines polices enacted at the University of Wisconsin, the University of Michigan, and Stanford University. Author was a member of a committee to formulate a "student speech and expression policy" at Georgetown University.

Coleman, Arthur L., & Alger, Jonathan R. "Beyond Speech Codes: Harmonizing Rights of Free Speech and Freedom from Discrimination on University Campuses," 23 *J. Coll. & Univ. Law* 91 (1996). Describes how an educational environment that is free from discrimination and therefore conducive to learning is mutually supportive of an educational environment in which a free and robust exchange of ideas takes place. The article provides a comprehensive review of free speech law, including the *R.A.V.* case, as well as antidiscrimination law. By applying this law to scenarios likely to arise in colleges and universities, article attempts to display how the goals of these two legal areas need not be mutually exclusive in the higher education setting.

Dry, Murray. "Hate Speech and the Constitution," 11 *Const. Comment.* 501 (1994–95). Analyzes the U.S. Supreme Court's decisions in *R.A.V. v. St. Paul* and *Wisconsin v. Mitchell.* Seeks to explain the purported conflict between the two opinions of the Court as they impact colleges and universities.

Grey, Thomas C. "How to Write a Speech Code Without Really Trying: Reflections on the Stanford Experience," 29 *U.C. Davis L. Rev.* 891 (1996). Provides a lively and thought-provoking critique of *Corry v. Stanford University,* the unreported case invalidating Stanford's policy on Free Expression and Discriminatory Harassment; and of *R.A.V. v. St. Paul* and *Chaplinsky v. New Hampshire,* the main U.S. Supreme Court precedents applied in *Corry.* Also includes the background of the Stanford policy's adoption, an analysis of the "politics" of campus hate speech, and the full text of the Stanford policy and the "Fundamental Standard" of which it was a part. A companion article—Elena Kagan, "When a Speech Code Is a Speech Code: The Stanford Policy and the Theory of Incidental Restraints," 29 *U.C. Davis* 957 (1996)—provides a counterpoint to Professor Grey's article.

Heumann, Milton, & Church, Thomas W., with Redlawsk, David (eds.). *Hate Speech on Campus* (Northeastern University Press, 1997). Divided into three parts—Cases, Case Studies, and Commentary—with the editors providing a general introduction to the book and an introduction to each of the three parts. Covers basic free speech and hate speech history and principles, and provides focused analysis pertaining to the campus setting. Includes discussion of several universities' codes and regulations, as well as the potential advantages and dangers of regulating speech on campus. The Commentary section presents a variety of viewpoints and concerns.

Kaplin, William. "A Proposed Process for Managing the Free Speech Aspects of Campus Hate Speech," 63 *J. Higher Educ.* 517 (1992). Describes a process for dealing with "hate speech" while preserving individuals' rights to free speech. Identifies key principles of First Amendment law that circumscribe the institution's discretion to deal with hate speech, suggests regulatory options that may be implemented consistent with these principles, and emphasizes the need to consider nonregulatory options prior to considering regulatory options.

Lawrence, Charles R., III. "If He Hollers Let Him Go: Regulating Racist Speech on Campus," 1990 *Duke L.J.* 431 (1990). Develops an argument for the constitutionality of hate speech regulations based on an interpretation of *Brown v. Board of Education,* calls for carefully drafted hate speech regulations on the campuses, explores the injurious nature of hate speech, and criticizes the position of free speech libertarians.

Massaro, Toni M. "Equality and Freedom of Expression: The Hate Speech Dilemma," 32 *Wm. & Mary L. Rev.* 211 (1991). Summarizes theoretical and practical aspects of the hate speech debate; critiques the approaches of "civil liberties theorists," "civil rights theorists," and "accommodationists"; and reviews various narrow approaches to regulating campus hate speech.

Shiell, Timothy C. *Campus Hate Speech on Trial* (University Press of Kansas, 1998). A thorough exploration, by a philosopher, of the arguments for and against campus speech codes. Includes an analysis of recent experience with speech codes, both in and out of court; a proposal for a narrow regulatory response to campus hate speech; and some broader perspectives on campus speech problems generally. Reviewed by Robert O'Neil in *Academe* (January–February 1999), 65–66.

Strossen, Nadine. "Regulating Racist Speech on Campus: A Modest Proposal?" 1990 *Duke L.J.* 484 (1990). Reviews the First Amendment principles and doctrines applicable to campus hate speech regulations; responds to Charles Lawrence's advocacy of hate speech regulations (see entry above); and argues that "prohibiting racist speech would not effectively counter, and could even aggravate, the underlying problem of racism," and that "means consistent with the first amendment can promote racial equality more effectively than can censorship." Includes substantial discussion of ACLU policies and activities regarding hate speech.

Sunstein, Cass. "Liberalism, Speech Codes, and Related Problems," *Academe* (July–August 1993), 14. Traces the tension between academic freedom and hate speech and relates hate speech regulation to the "low-value speech" versus "high-value speech" dichotomy developed in U.S. Supreme Court precedents. Author's primary purpose is to "defend the constitutionality of narrowly drawn restrictions on hate speech, arguing in the process against the broader versions that have become popular in some institutions." (This is a condensed version of a lecture that is included in the Menand entry in the Selected Annotated Bibliography for Section 7.1.)

Sec. 9.7 (Student Files and Records)

American Association of Collegiate Registrars and Admissions Officers. *The AACRAO 2001 FERPA Guide* (AACRAO, 2001). Provides an overview of the Act and discusses specific issues and problems that college administrators have encountered. Includes a discussion of the changes in FERPA compliance resulting from amendments to the FERPA regulations in 2000.

Daggett, Lynn M. "Bucking up *Buckley I:* Making the Federal Student Records Statute Work," 46 *Cath. U. L. Rev.* 617 (1997). Reviews the history and enforcement of FERPA. Recommends a series of amendments to the law with respect to dealing with student violations of institutional substance abuse policies.

McDonald, Steven J. (ed.). *The Family Educational Rights and Privacy Act (FERPA): A Legal Compendium* (2d ed., National Association of College and University Attorneys, 2002). Includes legislative and regulatory histories of FERPA, more than 30 of the most important technical assistance letters from the Education Department, and journal articles, outlines, memos, sample institutional policies and forms, and an annotated bibliography.

O'Donnell, Margaret L. "FERPA: Only a Piece of the Puzzle," 29 *J. Coll. & Univ. Law* 679 (2003). Reviews two U.S. Supreme Court cases involving FERPA, and discusses how institutions of higher education might apply FERPA to digital records. Discusses a range of institutional options with respect to protecting the privacy of student records.

Rosenzweig, Ethan M. "Please Don't Tell: The Question of Confidentiality in Student Disciplinary Records Under FERPA and the Crime Awareness and Campus Security Act," 51 *Emory L.J.* 447 (2002). Discusses the conflict between FERPA and the Campus Security Act; argues that student disciplinary processes and outcomes should be protected by FERPA; suggests strategies for accommodating the requirements of both laws.

Sidbury, Benjamin F. "*Gonzaga University v. Doe* and Its Implications: No Right to Enforce Student Privacy Rights Under FERPA," 29 *J. Coll. & Univ. Law* 655 (2003).

Discusses the U.S. Supreme Court's *Gonzaga* case; addresses compliance with FERPA regulations, and reviews alternative remedies available to students for allegedly unauthorized release of student education records.

Tribbensee, Nancy. *The Family Educational Rights and Privacy Act: A General Overview* (National Association of College and University Attorneys, 2002). A brief review in question-and-answer format of the most common issues related to FERPA. Designed for faculty and staff with a limited knowledge of student records law. Includes discussion of directory information, which records are protected by FERPA, access to student records by faculty and campus officials, and disclosure of student education records.

10

Rights and Responsibilities of Student Organizations and Their Members

Sec. 10.1. Student Organizations

10.1.1. The right to organize. Student organizations provide college students with the opportunity to learn leadership skills, to supplement their formal education with extracurricular academic programming, and to pursue diverse nonacademic interests. While there are therefore many good reasons for institutions to support, and students to join, student organizations, it is also true—at least at public institutions—that students have a legal right to organize and join campus groups, and that administrators have a legal obligation to permit them to do so. Specifically, students in public postsecondary institutions have a general right to organize; to be recognized officially whenever the school has a policy of recognizing student groups;[1] and to use meeting rooms, bulletin boards, computer terminals, and similar facilities open to campus groups. Occasionally a state statute will accord students specific organizational rights (see *Student Ass'n. of the University of Wisconsin-Milwaukee v. Baum*, 246 N.W.2d 622 (Wis. 1976), discussed in Section 3.2.3). More generally, organizational rights are protected by the freedom of expression and freedom of association guarantees of the First Amendment. Public institutions retain authority, however, to withhold or revoke recognition in certain instances and to regulate evenhandedly the organizational use of campus facilities. While students at private institutions do not have a constitutional right to organize (see *Jackson v. Strayer College* at end of this subsection), many private institutions nevertheless provide organizational rights to

---

[1] See the cases and authorities collected in Dag E. Ytreberg, Annot., "Student Organization Registration Statement, Filed with Public School or State University or College, as Open to Inspection by Public," 37 A.L.R.3d 1311.

students through institutional regulations; in such circumstances, the private institution's administrators may choose to be guided by First Amendment principles, as set out below, in their relations with student organizations.

The balance between the organization's rights and the institution's authority was struck in *Healy v. James,* 408 U.S. 169 (1972), the leading case in the field.[2] *Healy* concerned a state college's denial of a student organization's request for recognition. The request for recognition as a local Students for a Democratic Society (SDS) organization had been approved by the student affairs committee at Central Connecticut State College, but the college's president denied recognition, asserting that the organization's philosophy was antithetical to the college's commitment to academic freedom and that the organization would be a disruptive influence on campus. The denial of recognition had the effect of prohibiting the student group from using campus meeting rooms and campus bulletin boards and placing announcements in the student newspaper. The U.S. Supreme Court found the president's reasons insufficient under the facts to justify the extreme effects of nonrecognition on the organization's ability to "remain a viable entity" on campus and "participate in the intellectual give and take of campus debate." The Court therefore overruled the president's decision and remanded the case to the lower court, ruling that the college had to recognize the student group if the lower court determined that the group was willing to abide by all reasonable campus rules.

The associational rights recognized in *Healy* are not limited to situations where recognition is the issue. In *Gay Students Organization of the University of New Hampshire v. Bonner,* 509 F.2d 652 (1st Cir. 1974), for instance, the plaintiff, Gay Students Organization (GSO), was an officially recognized campus organization. After it sponsored a dance on campus, the state governor criticized the university's policy regarding GSO; in reaction, the university announced that GSO could no longer hold social functions on campus. GSO filed suit, and the federal appeals court found that the university's new policy violated the students' freedom of association and expression.[3] *Healy* was the controlling precedent, even though GSO had not been denied recognition:

> [T]he Court's analysis in *Healy* focused not on the technical point of recognition or nonrecognition, but on the practicalities of human interaction. While the Court concluded that the SDS members' right to further their personal beliefs

---

[2]The later case of *Widmar v. Vincent,* discussed in subsection 10.1.5 below, affirms many of the principles of *Healy* and adds important new guidance on the particular question of when a student group may have access to meeting rooms and other campus facilities. See also *Gay Student Services v. Texas A&M University,* 737 F.2d 1317, 1331–33 (5th Cir. 1984), in which the court used *Widmar's* "public forum" analysis in invalidating the defendant's refusal to recognize the plaintiff groups; and *Rosenberger v. Rector and Visitors of the University of Virginia* (discussed in subsection 10.1.5), which extends *Widmar* to protection of student access to institutional funds available to student groups.

[3]Cases and authorities are collected in Jean F. Rydstrom, Annot., "Validity, Under First Amendment and 42 U.S.C. § 1983, of Public College or University's Refusal to Grant Formal Recognition to, or Permit Meetings of, Student Homosexual Organizations on Campus," 50 A.L.R. Fed. 516.

had been impermissibly burdened by nonrecognition, this conclusion stemmed from a finding that the "primary impediment to free association flowing from nonrecognition is the denial of use of campus facilities for meetings and other appropriate purposes." The ultimate issue at which inquiry must be directed is the effect which a regulation has on organizational and associational activity, not the isolated and for the most part irrelevant issue of recognition per se [509 F.2d at 658–59].

Healy and related cases reveal three broad bases on which public institutions may decline to recognize, or limit the recognition of, particular student organizations without violating associational rights. *First,*

> [A] college administration may impose a requirement . . . that a group seeking official recognition affirm in advance its willingness to adhere to reasonable campus law. Such a requirement does not impose an impermissible condition on the students' associational rights. Their freedom to speak out, to assemble, or to petition for changes in school rules is in no sense infringed. It merely constitutes an agreement to conform to reasonable standards respecting conduct. This is a minimal requirement, in the interest of the entire academic community, of any group seeking the privilege of official recognition [*Healy,* 408 U.S. at 193].

Such standards of conduct, of course, must not themselves violate the First Amendment or other constitutional safeguards. Recognition, for instance, could not be conditioned on the organization's willingness to abide by a rule prohibiting all peaceful protest demonstrations on campus (see Section 9.5.3) or requiring all student-run newspaper articles to be approved in advance by the administration (see Section 10.3.3). But as long as campus rules avoid such pitfalls, student organizations must comply with them, just as individual students must. If the organization refuses to agree in advance to obey campus law, recognition may be denied until such time as the organization does agree. If a recognized organization violates campus law, its recognition may be suspended or withdrawn for a reasonable period of time.

Second, "[a]ssociational activities need not be tolerated where they . . . interrupt classes, or substantially interfere with the opportunity of other students to obtain an education" (*Healy,* 408 U.S. at 189). Thus, administrators may also deny recognition to a group that would create substantial disruption on campus, and they may revoke the recognition of a group that has created such disruption. In either case, the institution has the burden of demonstrating with reasonable certainty that substantial disruption will or did in fact result from the organization's actions—a burden that the college failed to meet in *Healy.* This burden is a heavy one, because "denial of recognition [is] a form of prior restraint" of First Amendment rights (*Healy,* 408 U.S. at 184).

Third, the institution may act to prevent organizational activity that is itself illegal under local, state, or federal laws, as well as activity that "is directed to inciting or producing imminent lawless action and is likely to incite or produce such action" (*Brandenburg v. Ohio,* 395 U.S. 444, 447 (1969), quoted in *Healy,* 408 U.S. at 188). While the GSO case (above) specifically supported this basis for regulation, the court found that the institution had not met its burden of demonstrating that the group's activities were illegal or inciting. A similar conclusion was reached in *Gay Lib v. University of Missouri,* 558 F.2d 848 (8th Cir. 1977), *reversing* 416 F. Supp. 1350 (W.D. Mo. 1976). The trial court found, on the basis of the university's expert evidence, that recognition of the student group would lead to "increased homosexual activities, which . . . includes sodomy [as] one of the most prevalent forms of sexual expression in homosexuality." Relying on this finding and on the fact that sodomy is an illegal activity that can be prohibited, the trial court upheld the university's refusal to recognize the group. Overruling the trial court, the appellate court held that the university's proof was insufficient to demonstrate that the student organization intended to breach university regulations or advocate or incite imminent lawless acts. At most, the group intended peaceably to advocate the repeal of certain criminal laws—expression that constitutionally could not be prohibited. Thus, the appellate court concluded that the university's denial of recognition impermissibly penalized the group's members because of their status rather than their conduct. (To the same effect, see *Gay Activists Alliance v. Board of Regents of University of Oklahoma,* 638 P.2d 1116 (Okla. 1981); and see generally Note, "The Rights of Gay Student Organizations," 10 *J. Coll. & Univ. Law* 397 (1983–84).)

All rules and decisions regarding student organizations should be supportable on one or more of these three regulatory bases. Administrators should apply the rules evenhandedly, carefully avoiding selective applications to particular groups whose views or goals they find to be repugnant (see discussion immediately below). Decisions under the rules should be based on a sound factual assessment of the impact of the group's activity rather than on speculation or on what the U.S. Supreme Court has called "undifferentiated fear or apprehension" (*Tinker v. Des Moines Independent Community School District,* 393 U.S. 503, 508 (1969)). Decisions denying organizational privileges should be preceded by "some reasonable opportunity for the organization to meet the University's contentions" or "to eliminate the basis of the denial" (*Wood v. Davison,* 351 F. Supp. 543, 548 (N.D. Ga. 1972)). If a student committee makes decisions about recognizing student organizations, or the student government devises regulations for its operations or those of recognized student organizations, they are subject to the same First Amendment restrictions as the institution itself (see the *Southworth* litigation discussed in subsection 10.1.3 below). Keeping these points in mind, administrators can retain substantial yet sensitive authority over the recognition of student groups.

If a public institution denies funding to a student group because of the views its members espouse, it is a clear violation of constitutional free speech protections, even if a student government committee rather than an institutional official makes the decision. In *Gay and Lesbian Students Ass'n. v. Gohn,* 850 F.2d 361 (8th Cir. 1988), a committee of the student senate denied funds to an organization that provided education about homosexuality. The court, noting that the administration had upheld the committee's denial of funding, said: "The University need not supply funds to student organizations; but once having decided to do so, it is bound by the First Amendment to act without regard to the content of the ideas being expressed" (850 F.2d at 362). After *Rosenberger v. Rector and Visitors of the University of Virginia,* 515 U.S. 819 (1995), these same general rules apply to an institution's decisions regarding the funding of student religious organizations (see Section 10.1.5 of this book).

In a leading post-*Rosenberger* case, a federal appeals court invalidated the attempt of the Alabama legislature to deny funding to student organizations and other groups that advocate on behalf of homosexuality. In *Gay Lesbian Bisexual Alliance v. Pryor,* 110 F.3d 1543 (11th Cir. 1997), *affirming Gay Lesbian Bisexual Alliance v. Sessions,* 917 F. Supp. 1548 (M.D. Ala. 1996), the Alabama law at issue prohibited colleges and universities from using "public funds or public facilities . . . to, directly or indirectly, sanction, recognize, or support the activities or existence of any organization or group that fosters or promotes a lifestyle or actions prohibited by the sodomy and sexual misconduct laws (Ala. Code § 16-1-28(a)). The law also declared that no student organization (or other campus group) that uses public funds or facilities "shall permit or encourage its members or encourage other persons to engage in any such unlawful acts or provide information or materials that explain how such acts may be engaged in or performed" (Ala. Code § 16-1-28(b)). Confronted with this law, the University of South Alabama denied funding for, and withheld recognition from, the Gay and Lesbian Bisexual Alliance (GLBA). The Alliance then sued the university's president and dean of students as well as the state attorney general.

The federal district court held the entire law unconstitutional, despite subsection (c) of the law, which provided that the law "shall not apply to any organization or group whose activities are limited solely to the political advocacy of a change in the sodomy and sexual misconduct laws of this state." Relying almost exclusively on the U.S. Supreme Court's decision in *Rosenberger,* the court held the Alabama statute to be "naked viewpoint discrimination" that violated the free speech clause and emphasized that:

> [a] viewpoint may include not only *what* a person says but *how* she says it. For example, as the defendants admitted at oral argument, the State does not seek to ban discussion about sexually transmitted diseases; rather, it only seeks to limit how such diseases may be discussed. In other words, the State seeks to impose its viewpoint on how the discussion may proceed [917 F. Supp. at 1554 (emphasis in the original)].

The district court was not persuaded by the state's argument that it was simply deterring crime, that is, homosexual acts. Quoting from *Healy v. James* (above), which in turn quoted *Brandenberg v. Ohio* (above), the court ruled that the statute did not draw the required distinction between mere advocacy and incitement. (In a separate reported decision, *Gay Lesbian Bisexual Alliance v. Sessions,* 917 F. Supp. 1558 (M.D. Ala. 1996), the district court reiterated and expounded upon its prior opinion and refused to limit its prior judgment or to stay the decision pending appeal.)

The U.S. Court of Appeals for the Eleventh Circuit affirmed the district court. Relying heavily on *Rosenberger,* the appellate court characterized the funding system for student organizations at the University of South Alabama (USA) as a limited public forum:

> [The law] as applied to GLBA clearly runs afoul of . . . *Rosenberger.* USA's limited public forum does not prohibit discussion of the sodomy or sexual misconduct laws in general. Rather, based on [the law], USA prohibited funding to GLBA based on the Attorney General's unsupported assumption that GLBA fosters or promotes a violation of the sodomy or sexual misconduct laws. The statute discriminates against one particular viewpoint because state funding of groups which foster or promote compliance with the sodomy or sexual misconduct laws remains permissible. This is blatant viewpoint discrimination [110 F.3d at 1549].

Given their detailed application of *Rosenberger,* the opinions in *Gay Lesbian Bisexual Alliance* provide extensive guidance for both administrators and student groups. In particular, the opinions illustrate how the *Rosenberger* case joins with the *Healy* case to enhance the constitutional protection of student organizations at public postsecondary institutions. In light of this impact of *Rosenberger,* there is now an even stronger basis for the decisions in earlier cases such as the *GSO* case and the *Gay Lib* case above.

Although students at public colleges typically have a constitutionally protected right to organize, such is not the case for students at private colleges. In *Jackson v. Strayer College,* 941 F. Supp. 192 (D.D.C. 1996), *affirmed,* 1997 WL 411656 (D.C. Cir. 1997), for example, the court dismissed a student's constitutional claims based on allegations that the college had obstructed his efforts to form a student government. The court held that federal constitutional protections do not extend to the formation of a private college student government; in the absence of "state action" (see Section 1.5.2), the alleged actions of the college could not constitute a First Amendment violation. Furthermore, the court held that the student's First Amendment "peaceful assemblage" claim failed because the college's campus is private property upon which students have no constitutional right to assemble that they may assert against the college.

Some private institutions, however, are subject to state or local civil rights laws that may serve to prohibit various forms of discrimination against students. In such circumstances, student organizations in private institutions, or their members, may have some statutory protection for their right to organize. The case of *Gay Rights Coalition of Georgetown University Law Center v. Georgetown University,* 536 A.2d 1 (D.C. 1987), illustrates such statutory protection and also examines the difficult freedom of religion issues that may arise when these statutory protections are asserted against religiously affiliated institutions.

In the *Gay Rights Coalition* case, two student gay rights groups sought official recognition from the university. The university refused, citing Catholic doctrine that condemns homosexuality. Denial of recognition meant that the groups could not use the university's facilities or its mailing and labeling services, could not have a mailbox in the student activities office, and could not request university funds. The student group sued under a District of Columbia law (D.C. Code § 1-2520) that outlaws discrimination (in the form of denying access to facilities and services) on the basis of sexual orientation (among other characteristics). The university defended its actions on the grounds of free exercise of religion. The appellate court issued seven separate opinions, which—although none attracted a majority of the judges—reached a collective result of not requiring the university to recognize the groups but requiring it to give the group access to facilities, services, and funding.

By severing the recognition process from the granting of access to university facilities and funding, the court avoided addressing the university's constitutional claim with regard to recognition. In interpreting the D.C. statute, the court found no requirement that "one private actor . . . 'endorse' another" (536 A.2d at 5). For that reason, Georgetown's denial of recognition to the student groups did not violate the statute. But the statute did require equal treatment, according to the court. And, the court concluded, the District of Columbia's compelling interest in eradicating discrimination based on sexual preference outweighed any burden on the university's freedom of religion that providing equal access would impose. (For a critical analysis of this case and the conflicts it embodies, see F. N. Dutile, "God and Gays at Georgetown: Observations on *Gay Rights Coalition of Georgetown University Law Center v. Georgetown University*," 15 *J. Coll. & Univ. Law* 1 (1988).[4])

10.1.2. The right not to join, or associate, or subsidize.

The right-to-organize concept in subsection 10.1.1 above has a flip side. Students often are organized into large associations representing all students, all undergraduate students, all graduate students, or the students of a particular school (for example, the law school). Typically these associations are recognized by the institution as student governments. Mandatory student activities fees are often collected by the institution and channeled to the student government association. The student government may then allocate (or the institution may allocate) portions of the mandatory fee collections to other recognized student organizations that do not represent the student body but serve special purposes—for example, minority and foreign student associations, gay and lesbian student alliances, social action groups, sports clubs, academic interest

---

[4]In the wake of the *Gay Rights Coalition* case, the U.S. Congress, which has legislative jurisdiction over the District of Columbia, passed The Nation's Capitol Religious Liberty and Academic Freedom Act, 102 Stat. 2269 (1988). The law provided that the District government would not receive further appropriations unless it adopted legislation authorizing religiously affiliated institutions to deny endorsement or benefits in a situation like that in the *Gay Rights Coalition* case. The constitutionality of the law was challenged by D.C. City Council members in *Clarke v. United States*, 886 F.2d 404 (D.C. Cir. 1989). Although a panel of the appellate court affirmed a trial court's ruling that the law was an unconstitutional burden on the free speech of city council members (*Clarke v. United States*, 886 F.2d 404 (D.C. Cir. 1989)), the full court vacated the panel opinion as moot in *Clarke v. United States*, 915 F.2d 699 (D.C. Cir. 1990) (*en banc*), because the appropriation act had expired. The next year's appropriations act did not contain a funding limitation because Congress used its power under the District of Columbia Self-Government and Governmental Reorganization Act (Pub. L. No. 93-198 (1973)) to amend the District of Columbia law directly to permit religious institutions to discriminate on the basis of sexual orientation.

societies (premed society, French club, and so forth), religious organizations, and student publications. In public colleges and universities, such arrangements may raise various issues under the First Amendment. Regarding student government associations, the primary focus of concern has been whether institutions may require that students be members of the association or that they pay the activities fee that supports the association. Regarding recognized special purpose organizations, the primary focus of concern has been whether the institution may require students to have any relationship with student organizations that they would prefer to avoid, and especially whether institutions may require students to pay the portions of their activities fees that are allocated to particular organizations if the students object to the views that the organization espouses. The issues regarding mandatory fee allocations for student organizations are discussed in subsections 10.1.3 and 10.1.5 below, and issues regarding mandatory fee allocations for student publications are discussed in Section 10.3.2.

An early case, *Good v. Associated Students of the Univ. of Washington*, 542 P.2d 762 (Wash. 1975), distinguished between a university's requirement that students be *members* of the student government and a requirement that students pay a mandatory student activities fee that supports the student government. The student government in the *Good* case, the Associated Students of the University of Washington (ASUW), was a nonprofit organization representing all of the university's students. The university required all students to be members. The court held that this requirement violated the First Amendment freedom of association (see Section 10.1.1 above) because "[f]reedom to associate carries with it a corresponding right to not associate." According to the court:

> [W]e have no hesitancy in holding that the state, through the university, may not compel membership in an association, such as the ASUW, which purports to represent all the students at the university. . . . [The ASUW] expends funds for political and economic causes to which the dissenters object and promotes and espouses political, social and economic philosophies which the dissenters find repugnant to their own views. There is no room in the First Amendment for such absolute compulsory support, advocation and representation. . . . Thus we hold that the university may not mandate membership of a student in the ASUW [542 P.2d at 768].

The mandatory fee requirement, however, was not unconstitutional; the university could collect, and the ASUW could use, the mandatory fees so long as the ASUW did not "become the vehicle for the promotion of one particular viewpoint, political, social, economic or religious" (542 P.2d at 769).

Since the *Good* case, it has been generally accepted that public institutions may not require students to be members of the student government association or any other student extracurricular organization (see, for example, *Carroll v. Blinken*, 957 F.2d 991, 1003 (2d Cir. 1992)). But for many years there were continuing disputes and uncertainties concerning mandatory student fee systems until the U.S. Supreme Court finally ruled on the matter in 2000, as discussed in the next subsection.

10.1.3. Mandatory student activities fees.

Throughout the 1970s, 1980s, and 1990s, the state courts and lower federal courts decided numerous cases on mandatory student activities fees in public colleges and universities. These cases presented a variety of constitutional challenges to entire systems for funding student organizations (see, for example, *Smith v. Regents of the Univ. of California,* 844 P.2d 500 (Cal. 1993)), to the use of mandatory fees by student governments (see, for example, *Smith v. Regents of the Univ. of California,* 65 Cal. Rptr. 2d 813 (Cal. Ct. App. 1997)), and to the allocations of fees to particular student organizations (see, for example, *Rounds v. Oregon State Board of Higher Education,* 166 F.3d 1032 (9th Cir. 1999)). Other cases presented statutory challenges to public institutions' authority regarding particular aspects of student fee systems (see *Cortes v. State of Florida, Board of Regents,* 655 So. 2d 132 (Fla. Dist. Ct. App. 1995); *Smith v. Regents of the Univ. of California* (above), 844 P.2d at 851)). At least one case, *Associated Students of the Univ. of California at Riverside v. Regents of the Univ. of California,* 1999 WL 13711 (N.D. Cal 1999), turned the issues around—presenting a challenge by students who favored, rather than opposed, mandatory student fees, but who objected to a particular limitation on the use of the fees.

Finally, after such cases had bounced around the lower courts for many years, the constitutionality of mandatory student activities fees finally reached the U.S. Supreme Court in *Board of Regents of University of Wisconsin System v. Southworth,* 529 U.S. 217 (2000). The Court's ruling in *Southworth,* and a follow-up ruling by the U.S. Court of Appeals on remand (*Southworth v. Board of Regents of University of Wisconsin System,* 307 F.3d 566 (7th Cir. 2002)), serve to resolve most of the inconsistencies among lower court opinions and to establish a single analytical approach for freedom of speech and freedom of association issues concerning public institutions' imposition of mandatory student fees.

The *Southworth* case was brought by a group of students at the Madison campus who objected to the university's collection and allocation of mandatory fees, insofar as the fees were allocated to student organizations that expressed "political and ideological" views with which the objecting students disagreed. The student plaintiffs claimed that this use of the fees violated their First Amendment right to be free from governmental compulsion to support speech conflicting with their personal views and beliefs. When the case reached the U.S. Supreme Court, it upheld the university's authority to allocate the mandatory fees to student organizations for the "purpose of facilitating the free and open exchange of ideas by, and among, its students." At the same time, the Court recognized that objecting students have a right to "certain safeguards with respect to the expressive activities which they are required to support" (529 U.S. at 229). The primary requirement that a university must meet to assure that its fee system facilitates "free and open exchange of ideas," and the primary safeguard for objecting students, is "viewpoint neutrality"—a concept that the Court had relied on in its earlier *Rosenberger* ruling (see Section 10.1.5 below) and that it expanded upon in *Southworth.* Thus, the *Southworth* case establishes the "viewpoint neutrality principle" as the primary criterion to use in evaluating the constitutionality of a public institution's mandatory fee system under the free speech clause.

Under the University of Wisconsin fee system challenged in *Southworth*, 20 percent of mandatory student fee collections went to registered student organizations (RSOs). The other 80 percent of student fees, not at issue in the case, were used for expenses such as student health services, intramural sports, and the maintenance and repair of student union facilities. Student fees were collected annually, and there was no opt-out provision by which students could decline to support certain RSOs and receive a pro rata refund of their fees. The collected fees were allocated to RSOs (of which there were more than six hundred at the time of the litigation) on the basis of applications from those RSOs requesting funding. Decisions on applications for funding were made by the student government, the Associated Students of Madison (ASM), through two of its committees, or by a student referendum in which the entire student body voted to fund or defund a particular RSO. Decisions to allocate funds were presented to the chancellor and the board of regents for final approval. RSOs generally received funding on a reimbursement basis, with reimbursement primarily paying for the organization's operating costs, the costs of sponsoring events, and travel expenses. According to university policy, reimbursements were not made for lobbying activities or for gifts or donations to other organizations; and RSOs with a primarily political mission could not be funded. The student plaintiffs in *Southworth* objected to the allocations to eighteen of the funded RSOs. These organizations included WISPIRG; the Lesbian, Gay Bisexual Campus Center; the UW Greens; Amnesty International; and La Colectiva Cultural de Aztlan.

Relying on *Abood v. Detroit Bd. of Education.*, 431 U.S. 209 (1977), and *Keller v. State Bar of California*, 496 U.S. 1 (1990), the U.S. District Court upheld the students' claim that the university's program violated their rights to free speech and association, and enjoined the board of regents from using its mandatory fee system to fund any RSO that engaged in ideological or political advocacy. The Seventh Circuit U.S. Court of Appeals affirmed in part, reversed in part, and vacated in part. Affirming the district court's reliance on *Abood* and *Keller*, the Seventh Circuit extended the analysis to include a three-part test articulated in *Lehnert v. Ferris Faculty Ass'n.*, 500 U.S. 507 (1991), a case concerning the expenditure of mandatory union dues in violation of the faculty members' First Amendment rights (see Section 4.5.3). Applying the *Lehnert* test, the appellate court determined that the educational benefits of the mandatory fee system did not justify the significant burden that the system placed on the free speech rights of the objecting students (*Southworth v. Grebe*, 151 F.3d 717, 732–33 (1998)). The U.S. Supreme Court then reversed the Seventh Circuit and remanded the case to the lower courts for further proceedings. Rather than applying the three-part test from the *Lehnert* case, the Court determined that the operation of the fee system was closely analogous to a public forum (see Section 9.5.2) and that the "standard of viewpoint neutrality found in the public forum cases provides the standard we find controlling."

Under the viewpoint neutrality standard, according to the U.S. Supreme Court, the university could allocate mandatory fee funds to RSOs via the student government and its committees so long as "viewpoint neutrality [is] the operational principle." But the university could not distribute these funds via a student referendum. "[I]t is unclear . . . what protection, if any, there is for viewpoint neutrality in [the referendum] process. . . . The whole theory of viewpoint neutrality is that minority views are treated with the same respect as are majority views" (529 U.S. at 235). The student referendum aspect of the program for funding speech and expressive activities thus "appears to be inconsistent with the viewpoint neutrality requirement" (529 U.S. at 230).

The university could include an "opt-out" or refund mechanism in its fee system if it wished. But it was not constitutionally obligated to do so. "The restriction could be so disruptive and expensive that the program to support extracurricular speech would be ineffective. The First Amendment does not require the University to put the program at risk" (529 U.S. at 232).

Because the plaintiffs and the university had stipulated early in the litigation that the student government and its committees operated in a viewpoint-neutral manner when allocating funds to RSOs, the Court did not need to make its own determination on this key issue. But the Court did remand the case to the court of appeals for "re-examin[ation] in light of the principles we have discussed," and the court of appeals in turn remanded the case to the district court. After remand, the student plaintiffs moved to void their stipulation that the mandatory fee funds were allocated on a viewpoint-neutral basis, and the district court granted the motion. That court did not reexamine the referendum process, however, since the university had eliminated this method of funding RSOs and the issue therefore was moot. The district court then reexamined the university's mandatory fee system to determine if it was viewpoint neutral, concluding that it was not because "the absence of express objective standards vests unfettered and unbridled discretion in the program decisionmakers . . ." (*Fry v. Board of Regents of Univ. of Wisconsin System*, 132 F. Supp. 2d 744 (W.D. Wis. 2000)). To allow the university time to revise its allocation procedures and policies to create "express objective standards" for making fee allocations, the district court deferred its judgment for two months.

The university administration, in conjunction with student government committees, then established criteria and procedures for students' use in allocating funds and granting reimbursements in a viewpoint-neutral manner. The student government bylaws were amended to include a provision entitled "Viewpoint Neutrality Compliance," which set procedures and guiding principles for student officers to follow and required student officers to take an oath to uphold the principle of viewpoint neutrality. An appellate process was also established by which an RSO could appeal a funding decision to the student judiciary and/or the chancellor and board of regents. This appellate process included procedural safeguards such as adequate and public notice and hearings on the record. While these changes to the mandatory fee system were substantial, the district court, upon further review, decided that the student government still retained too much discretion in allocating fees and enjoined the university from collecting fees from objecting students to support RSO expressive activities to which the students objected.

On appeal to the Seventh Circuit, the parties did not contest the referendum provision, since the university had deleted that method of funding from its fee allocation system. The appellate court did note in passing, however, that the "student referendum mechanism" was "constitutionally deficient" (307 F.3d at 594). The primary issue on appeal was "whether the unbridled discretion standard" that the district court relied on "is part of the constitutional requirement of viewpoint neutrality" (307 F.3d at 578). The appellate court sought to untangle the relationship between the viewpoint neutrality principle that the U.S. Supreme Court had applied in its *Southworth* decision and the "no unbridled discretion" principle that the Court had applied in earlier cases challenging governmental denials of a license or permit to speak in a public forum. It determined that the two standards were linked:

> While the Supreme Court has never expressly held that the prohibition on unbridled discretion is an element of viewpoint neutrality, we believe that conclusion inevitably flows from the Court's unbridled discretion cases. From the earliest unbridled discretion cases . . . , the Supreme Court has made clear that when a decisionmaker has unbridled discretion there are two risks: First, the risk of self-censorship, where the plaintiff may edit his own viewpoint or the content of his speech to avoid governmental censorship; and second, the risk that the decisionmaker will use its unduly broad discretion to favor or disfavor speech based on its viewpoint or content, and that without standards to guide the official's decision an as-applied challenge will be ineffective to ferret out viewpoint discrimination. Both of these risks threaten viewpoint neutrality [307 F.3d at 578–79].

The appellate court thus held that "the prohibition against unbridled discretion is a component [or a 'corollary'] of the viewpoint-neutrality requirement," and "the unbridled discretion standard appropriately applies to the University's mandatory fee system" (307 F.3d at 579–80).

Having established this framework for analysis, the appellate court then addressed the central issue in the case: "whether the University's mandatory fee system does in fact vest the student government with unbridled discretion" and thus fails the viewpoint neutrality requirement. In resolving this issue, the appellate court reviewed every aspect of the university's mandatory student fee allocation system, especially the various provisions the university had added to its policies after the district court had ruled, after trial, that the policies then in effect did not meet the constitutional requirements. In its thorough and detailed review of the university's revised policies (307 F.3d at 581–88), the appellate court considered the university's financial and administrative policies, as amended after the trial; the student government's bylaws pertaining to mandatory student fee allocations for RSOs, as amended; and the rules of the student government's finance committee, as amended. The court considered the principles embodied in these various documents, the criteria for allocating funds set forth in the documents, and the various procedures that they establish for applying for and challenging fund allocations. Grouping the various principles, criteria, and procedures together under the heading "Funding Standards," the court determined that they "greatly limit[ed] the discretion" of the student government and its committees in allocating the fees. The court took particular note of these features of the university's and student government's policies: (1) there were specific explicit statements requiring all persons involved in funding decisions to comply with the viewpoint neutrality requirement; (2) there was a requirement that every student involved in allocation decisions take an oath to support the viewpoint neutrality requirement, and there were provisions for removing from office any student who failed to do so; (3) there were "specific, narrowly drawn and clear criteria to guide the student government in their funding decisions"; (4) there were "detailed procedural requirements for the hearings" on funding applications; (5) there was a policy of full disclosure regarding all funding applications and the student government's decisions on these applications; and (6) there was a "comprehensive appeals process" by which any student organization that was denied funding, or any student who objected to a funding decision, could appeal the decision to the student council and then to the chancellor for the campus, whenever "it is alleged that the decision was based on an organization's extracurricular speech or expressive activities" (307 F.3d at 582). The court also highlighted "one particular aspect" of this appeal process:

> In reviewing funding decisions, the appeals procedures require the Student Council to compare the grant amounts [the student government committees] allocated to various RSOs to determine whether similar RSO's applications were treated equally. By comparing the funding decisions, the Student Council can determine whether the student government, while purporting to apply the Funding Standards in a viewpoint-neutral way, nonetheless treated similar RSOs with varying viewpoints differently. The Student Council can then rectify any differing treatment on appeal [307 F.3d at 588].

On the basis of this review, the court agreed with the university that the funding standards satisfied the constitutional requirements:

> In conclusion, in addition to expressly prohibiting viewpoint discrimination, requiring student officials to attest to their commitment to viewpoint neutrality, and providing for sanctions against student officials who engage in viewpoint discrimination, the Funding Standards provide narrowly drawn, detailed, and specific guidelines directing the SSFC [Student Service Finance Committee] and ASM Finance Committee's funding decisions as to all funding decisions other than travel grants. The SSFC and ASM Finance Committee's discretion is further limited by the procedural rules governing the funding and appeals process. While the Funding Standards grant a certain amount of discretion, that discretion is no greater than necessary to allow the student government to evaluate the funding requests. Accordingly, we conclude that these Funding Standards sufficiently bridled the SSFC and ASM Finance Committee's discretion to satisfy the First Amendment's mandate of viewpoint neutrality and the prohibition on granting decisionmakers unbridled discretion . . . [307 F.3d at 592].

The court identified two exceptions, however, to this broad ruling supporting the university's funding standards and also issued two cautions about the scope of its ruling. The first exception concerned the criteria used by the ASM finance committee, which was responsible for awarding three types of grants to RSOs: events grants, operations grants, and travel grants. At the time of the trial, the university had provided the court with the criteria for awarding the events grants and the operations grants but did not provide any criteria for the travel grants. Absent any clear and specific criteria, such as those for the events and operations grants, the travel grant portion of the mandatory fee allocation system gave unbridled discretion to the ASM finance committee that awarded the grants. The student government therefore could not award the travel grants until such time as it had implemented constitutionally suitable criteria.

The second exception to the court's broad approval concerned two of the criteria that the student government committees used to allocate funds: a criterion providing for consideration of "the length of time that an RSO has been in existence," and a criterion providing for consideration of "the amount of funding the RSO received in prior years." These criteria were not viewpoint neutral, said the court, for two reasons (see 307 F.3d at 593–94). *First,* to the extent that current funding decisions are based on the length of time an RSO has been in existence, or the amount of funding that the RSO has received in the past, these current decisions could depend in part on "viewpoint-based decisions of the past." *Second,* considering the length of time in existence or the amount of prior funding serves to favor "historically popular viewpoints" and to disadvantage nontraditional or minority viewpoints. Therefore, as to these two criteria, the court concluded that they "are related to the content or viewpoint of the applying RSO, as well as based on a prior system which lacks the constitutional safeguard of viewpoint neutrality."

The first of the court's two cautions concerns another criterion for awarding mandatory fees: a criterion permitting the funding committees to consider the number of students participating in or benefiting from the speech activities for which funding is sought. Although the court acknowledged that there are various content-neutral reasons for considering such information, it cautioned that such information could also permit the committees to "use the popularity of the speech as a factor in determining funding," thus providing an advantage to majority viewpoints at the expense of minority viewpoints. Since this criterion could be applied in permissible content-neutral ways, it was not "facially invalid," but the court warned that "improper consideration of the popularity of the speech may justify an as-applied challenge" in some circumstances (307 F.3d at 595).

The court's second caution also concerned possible "as-applied" challenges to the university's funding standards. The court held that, on their face, the funding standards satisfied viewpoint neutrality and were thus "facially" constitutional. But such a ruling does not necessarily validate all applications of the funding standards to particular situations. Thus the court cautioned, at various points in its opinion, that the funding standards might be applied to particular circumstances in ways that contravene the requirements of viewpoint neutrality; and that, in such situations, the funding standards would be subject to "as-applied" challenges either through the university's own internal appeal process or through the courts.

When the Supreme Court's *Southworth* decision is put together with the Seventh Circuit's further elaboration, and these cases are viewed against the backdrop provided by the earlier *Rosenberger* case (see subsection 10.1.5 below) and by the public forum cases (see Section 9.5.2), the result is a much clearer picture of this area of the law than has ever existed previously. This picture reveals the following guidelines that public institutions may use to help assure that their systems for allocating mandatory student activities fees to student organizations are constitutional under the First Amendment:

1. The fee allocation system should be designed and used to "facilitate a wide range of [student extracurricular] speech" and a "free and open exchange of ideas by, and among, [the institution's] students" (*Southworth*, 529 U.S. at 231, 229).

2. The fee allocation system, on paper and in operation, must comply with the "principle of viewpoint neutrality" (529 U.S. at 233–34) and the corollary principle of "no unbridled discretion" (307 F.3d at 575–81). These principles, at a minimum, require that the institution "may not prefer some [student] viewpoints over others" and must assure that "minority views are treated with the same respect as are majority views" (529 U.S. at 233, 235). As a safeguard for this required neutrality, the institution should have "specific, narrowly drawn, and clear criteria to guide the student government in their funding decisions" (307 F.3d at 588).

3. The institution should have an express written requirement that all mandatory student fee allocations to student organizations are subject to the viewpoint neutrality principle and that all student decision makers are bound to uphold this principle (307 F.3d at 581, 583). In conjunction with this requirement, the institution should implement various procedures to assure that the viewpoint neutrality principles will be met in practice. One procedural safeguard meriting particular attention is a requirement that the decision makers who allocate the funds, or those who review their decisions, must compare the amounts allocated to particular student organizations (307 F.3d at 588).

4. Institutions should be wary of using funding criteria that require or permit consideration of the number of prior years in which a student organization has received fee allocations, the amounts of funds an organization has received in the past, the size of the organization's membership, or the number of nonmembers who have attended or are expected to attend the organization's speech-related activities. If any such criteria are used, they must be carefully limited to content-neutral considerations (for example, considering the size of the organization's membership or the size of the audience for an event in order to estimate the expenses of setting up and maintaining the type of room or facility needed for the organization's meetings or events). Any such criteria should also be used in ways that do not give an advantage to

popular, traditional, or majoritarian viewpoints at the expense of controversial, nontraditional, or minority viewpoints (307 F.3d at 592–95).

5. A student referendum may not be used to make funding decisions regarding particular student groups—at least not when the referendum would "substitute[ ] majority determinations for viewpoint neutrality" and thus allow "majority views" to be "treated" with more "respect" than "minority views." A mandatory fee allocation, in other words, cannot "depend upon majoritarian consent" (529 U.S. at 235).

6. An institution may choose to include in its fee allocation system an opt-out provision or refund mechanism to protect objecting students, but the Constitution does not require the inclusion of such a mechanism (529 U.S. at 235).

7. An institution may choose to distinguish between the on-campus and off-campus expressive activities of student organizations in its fee allocation system, but it may do so only if it implements the distinction through "viewpoint neutral rules." The Constitution, however, does not require that the institution adopt any "territorial boundaries" for student speech activities or impose any "geographic or spatial restrictions" on student organizations' "entitlement" to a fee allocation (529 U.S. at 234). (For pre-*Southworth* cases about off-campus student speech, see *Carroll v. Blinken,* 957 F.2d 991 (2d Cir. 1992) and 42 F.3d 122 (2d Cir. 1994); and *Rounds v. Oregon State Board of Higher Education,* 166 F.3d 1032 (9th Cir. 1999).)

10.1.4. Principle of nondiscrimination. While the law prohibits administrators from imposing certain restrictions on student organizations (as subsections 10.1.1–10.1.3 above indicate), there are other restrictions that administrators may be required to impose. The primary example concerns discrimination, particularly on the basis of race or sex. Just as institutions are usually prohibited from discriminating on these grounds, their student organizations are usually prohibited from doing so as well. Thus, institutions generally have an obligation either to prohibit race and sex discrimination by student organizations or to withhold institutional support from those that do discriminate.

In public institutions, student organizations may be subject to constitutional equal protection principles under the federal Fourteenth Amendment or comparable state constitutional provisions if they act as agents of the institution or are otherwise controlled by or receive substantial encouragement from the institution (see generally Section 1.5.2). In *Joyner v. Whiting,* 477 F.2d 456 (4th Cir. 1973) (also discussed in Section 10.3.3), for example, a minority-oriented student newspaper allegedly had a segregationist editorial policy and had discriminated by race in staffing and in accepting advertising. Although the court prohibited the university president from permanently cutting off the paper's funds, because of the restraining effect of such a cut-off on free press, it did hold that the president could and must prohibit the discrimination in staffing and advertising: "The equal protection clause forbids racial discrimination in extracurricular activities of a state-supported institution . . . and freedom of the press furnishes no shield for discrimination" (477 F.2d at 463).

Uzzell v. Friday, 625 F.2d 1117 (4th Cir. 1980) (*en banc*), presents a more complex illustration of the equal protection clause's application and a possible affirmative action justification for some racial classifications. The case concerned certain rules of student organizations at the University of North Carolina. The Campus Governing Council, the legislative branch of the student government, was required under its constitution to have at least two minority students, two males, and two females among its eighteen members. The student Honor Court, under its rules, permitted defendants to demand that a majority of the judges hearing the case be of the same race (or the same sex) as the defendant. Eschewing the need for any extended analysis, the appellate court at first invalidated each of the provisions as race discrimination: "Without either reasonable basis or compelling interest, the composition of the council is formulated on the basis of race. This form of constituency blatantly fouls the letter and the spirit of both [Title VI] and the Fourteenth Amendment" (*Uzzell v. Friday,* 547 F.2d 801 (4th Cir. 1977)). (The sex discrimination aspects of the provisions were not challenged by the plaintiff students or addressed by the court.) In *Friday v. Uzzell,* 438 U.S. 912 (1978), the U.S. Supreme Court, seeing possible affirmative action issues underlying this use of racial considerations, vacated the appellate court's judgment and remanded the case for further consideration in light of the *Bakke* decision (discussed in Section 8.2.5).[5] The appeals court then reconsidered its earlier decision and, by a vote of 4 to 3, again invalidated the rules (*Uzzell v. Friday,* 591 F.2d 997 (4th Cir. 1979) (*en banc*)):

> The permeating defect in the organization of . . . the governing council is the imposition of an artificial racial structure upon this elective body that bars non-minority students from eligibility for appointment to the Council. This resort to race affronts *Bakke.* Although the regulation in question seeks to provide "protective representation," its effect is to establish a racial classification, as it relies exclusively on race to preclude non-minority students from enjoying opportunities and benefits available to others [591 F.2d at 998].

The minority, reading *Bakke* more liberally, argued that more facts were necessary before the court could ascertain whether the student government rules were invalid race discrimination, on the one hand, or valid affirmative action, on the other. They therefore asserted that the case should be returned to the district court for a full trial:

---

[5]For another example of race classifications that institutions may seek to justify by invoking affirmative action considerations, see Wendy Hernandez, "The Constitutionality of Racially Restrictive Organizations Within the University Setting," 21 *J. Coll. & Univ. Law* 429, 434–43 (1994); and Ben Gose, "A Place of Their Own," *Chron. Higher Educ.,* December 8, 1995, A33. These articles address the issue of minority student organizations (or living accommodations groups) that restrict membership (or entrance to living accommodations) on the basis of race or ethnicity. As noted in the next footnote below in this subsection, such issues would now be governed by the *Grutter* and *Gratz* cases rather than *Bakke.*

The present record simply does not permit a firm conclusion as to the extent of discrimination at the University of North Carolina and the need for and efficacy of the present regulations. The majority's condemnation of the regulations because they impinge upon the rights of others is simplistic. *Bakke* teaches that as a necessary remedial measure a victimized group may be preferred at the expense of other innocent persons. What cries out for determination in the instant case is whether such preferment is justified under the principles of *Bakke* [591 F.2d at 1001].

In June 1980, the Fourth Circuit recalled its 1979 decision because the *en banc* court that had heard the appeal was improperly constituted: a senior judge sat as a member of the panel—a violation of a federal statute (28 U.S.C. § 46) requiring that an *en banc* panel consist only of active circuit court judges. The new rehearing *en banc* placed the matter before the appeals court for the third time (*Uzzell v. Friday*, 625 F.2d 1117 (4th Cir. 1980) (*en banc*)). On this occasion the court ruled 5 to 3 to remand the case to the district court for a full development of the record and reconsideration in light of *Bakke*. In so ruling, the court expressly adopted the views of the dissenting judges in the 1979 decision. The majority indicated that race-conscious actions that impinge on one class of persons in order to ameliorate past discrimination against another class are not unlawful per se, and that "the university should have the opportunity to justify its regulations so that the district court can apply the *Bakke* test: is the classification necessary to the accomplishment of a constitutionally permissible purpose?"[6]

Federal civil rights laws (see Section 13.5 of this book) may require private as well as public institutions to ensure, as a condition of receiving federal funds, that student organizations do not discriminate. The Title VI regulations (see Section 13.5.2 of this book) contain several provisions broad enough to cover student organizations; in particular, 34 C.F.R. § 100.3(b)(1) prohibits institutions from discriminating by race, either "directly or through contractual or other arrangements," and 34 C.F.R. § 100.3(b)(4) prohibits institutions from discriminating by race in the provision of services or benefits that are offered "in or through a facility" constructed or operated in whole or part with federal funds. And the Title IX regulations (Section 13.5.3) prohibit institutions from "providing significant assistance" to any organization "which discriminates on the basis of sex in providing any aid, benefit, or service to students" (34 C.F.R. § 106.31(b)(6); see also § 106.6(c)). Title IX does not apply, however, to the membership practices of tax-exempt social fraternities and sororities (20 U.S.C. § 1681(a)6(A)). And more generally, under the Civil Rights Restoration Act (discussed in Section 13.5.7.4), all "programs" and "activities" of an institution

---

[6]Were similar issues to arise again in the future, the U.S. Supreme Court's decisions in *Grutter* and *Gratz*, the University of Michigan affirmative action cases discussed in Sections 8.2.5 and 8.3.4, would also become pertinent. Under these cases, strict scrutiny would still be the applicable standard of review. Under this standard, remedying the present effects of the institution's prior discrimination would be a compelling state interest, but considerable proof of the prior discrimination and its present effects would be required in order to rely on this justification.

receiving federal funds are subject to the nondiscrimination requirements of the civil rights statutes.

State statutes and regulations may also provide protection against discrimination by student organizations at both public and private institutions. In *Frank v. Ivy Club*, 576 A.2d 241 (N.J. 1990), for example, the court was asked to determine whether two private "eating clubs" affiliated with Princeton University, which at the time admitted only men to membership, were subject to a state law prohibiting nondiscrimination in places of public accommodation. The case began when Sally Frank, then an undergraduate at Princeton, filed a charge with the New Jersey Division on Civil Rights (the state's human rights agency), asserting that she was denied membership in the clubs on the basis of her gender, and that this denial constituted unlawful discrimination by a place of public accommodation. She claimed that the university was responsible for supervising the clubs and therefore was partially responsible for their discriminatory activities. The university (and the clubs) contended that the clubs were private organizations not formally affiliated with the university. The Division on Civil Rights determined that the clubs were places of public accommodation and thus subject to the nondiscrimination requirements of state law. It also ruled that the clubs enjoyed a "symbiotic relationship" with the university, since the university had assisted them in their business affairs, a majority of upper-division Princeton students took their meals at the clubs (relieving the university of the responsibility of providing meals for them), and the clubs would not have come into being without the existence of the university. From these findings, the Division on Civil Rights concluded that probable cause existed to believe that the clubs had unlawfully discriminated against Frank on the basis of her gender.

After several appeals to intermediate courts and other procedural wrangling, the New Jersey Supreme Court affirmed the Division on Civil Rights' jurisdiction over the case and accepted its findings and conclusions that the clubs must cease their discriminatory membership practices. The court reasoned that:

> [w]here a place of public accommodation [the university] and an organization that deems itself private [the clubs] share a symbiotic relationship, particularly where the allegedly "private" entity supplies an essential service which is not provided by the public accommodation, the servicing entity loses its private character and becomes subject to laws against discrimination [576 A.2d at 257].[7]

In light of such constitutional and regulatory requirements, it is clear that administrators cannot ignore alleged discrimination by student organizations. In some areas of concern, race and sex discrimination being the primary

---

[7]While the state court proceedings were in progress, one of the clubs filed a claim in federal court, asserting that the state civil rights agency's assertion of jurisdiction over its activities violated its freedom of association under the First Amendment of the U.S. Constitution. A federal appellate court affirmed a trial court's finding that the club's federal claims were not moot and could be litigated in federal court (*Ivy Club v. Edwards*, 943 F.2d 270 (3d Cir. 1991)).

examples, institutions' obligations to prohibit such discrimination are relatively clear. In other areas of concern, however, the law is either more sparse or less clear regarding the institution's obligations to prohibit discrimination. Religious discrimination and sexual orientation discrimination by student organizations are the primary contemporary examples. (See generally Burton Bollag, "Choosing Their Flock," *Chron. Higher Educ.*, January 28, 2005, A33.) The federal civil rights statutes (above), for instance, do not cover either of these types of discrimination, and federal constitutional law provides a lower standard of scrutiny for sexual orientation discrimination than for race or gender discrimination (see *Romer v. Evans*, 517 U.S. 620 (1996)).

Regarding religious discrimination, at least in public institutions, the First Amendment's free exercise clause actually provides a zone of protection for student organizations that have religious qualifications, based on sincere religious belief, for leadership positions, membership, or other prerogatives (see generally Section 1.6 of this book). The freedom of expressive association implicit in the First Amendment may also provide some protection for such student organizations (see *Boy Scouts of America v. Dale*, 530 U.S. 640 (2000)). Regarding sexual orientation discrimination, the free exercise clause may also provide some protection for student organizations that discriminate on the basis of sexual orientation if they do so based upon sincerely held religious beliefs; and the First Amendment freedom of association, as applied in the *Dale* case (above), may provide some protection to organizations discriminating by sexual orientation even when their policy is not based on religious belief. These developments do not mean that public institutions must forgo all regulation or oversight of religious or sexual orientation discrimination based on religious belief or expressive association, but they do mean that administrators should exercise particular care in this sensitive arena and involve counsel in all aspects of these matters. (For a review of litigation emerging in 2005, see Sara Lipka, "Arizona State U. Settles Lawsuit by Agreeing to Allow Christian Group to Bar Members on Sexual Grounds," *Chron. Higher Educ.*, September 16, 2005, A42; Elizabeth Farrell, "Federal Appeals Court Orders Illinois University to Recognize Christian Group, Pending Ruling," *Chron. Higher Educ.*, September 9, 2005, A36; and for periodically updated information on litigation, go to http://www.clsnet.org, and click on The Center.)

10.1.5. Religious activities. Numerous legal issues may arise concerning student organizations that engage in religious activities or have a religious purpose or a religious affiliation. The most significant issues usually arise under the free speech, free exercise, or establishment clauses of the First Amendment, or under parallel provisions of state constitutions, and are therefore of primary concern to public institutions. This subsection addresses constitutional problems concerning religious student organizations' use of campus facilities and receipt of student activities fee allocations. Subsection 10.1.4 above addresses student organizations' restrictive membership policies.

In *Widmar v. Vincent*, 454 U.S. 263 (1981), a case involving the University of Missouri-Kansas City (UMKC), the U.S. Supreme Court established important rights for student religious groups at public postsecondary institutions that seek to use the institution's facilities. In 1972, the Board of Curators of UMKC promulgated a regulation prohibiting the use of university buildings or grounds "for purposes of religious worship or religious teaching." In 1977, UMKC applied this regulation to a student religious group called Cornerstone. This group was "an organization of evangelical Christian students from various denominational backgrounds. . . . [It] held its on-campus meetings in classrooms and in the student center. These meetings were open to the public and attracted up to 125 students. A typical Cornerstone meeting included prayer, hymns, Bible commentary, and discussion of religious views and experiences" (454 U.S. at 265, n.2). When UMKC denied Cornerstone permission to continue meeting in university facilities, eleven members of the organization sued the university, alleging that it had abridged their rights to free exercise of religion and freedom of speech under the First Amendment.

For the Supreme Court, as for the lower courts, the threshold question was whether the case would be treated as a free speech case. In considering this question, Justice Powell's opinion for the Court (with Justice White dissenting) characterized the students' activities as "religious speech," which, like other speech, is protected by the free speech clause. The university, by making its facilities generally available to student organizations, had created a "forum" open to speech activities, which the Court described both as a "limited public forum" and an "open forum." The free speech clause therefore applied to the situation. This clause did not require UMKC to establish a forum; but once UMKC had done so, the clause required it to justify any exclusion of a student group from this forum because of the content of its activities:

> In order to justify discriminatory exclusion from a public forum based on the religious content of a group's intended speech, the university must satisfy the standard of review appropriate to content-based exclusions. It must show that its regulation is necessary to serve a compelling state interest and that it is narrowly drawn to achieve that end [454 U.S. at 269–70].

In attempting to justify its regulation under this standard, UMKC relied on the First Amendment's establishment clause and on the establishment clause in the Missouri state constitution. Its argument was that maintaining separation of church and state, as mandated by these clauses, was a "compelling state interest," which justified its no-religious-worship regulation under the free speech clause. Resorting to establishment clause jurisprudence, the Court rejected this argument. Although the Court agreed that maintaining separation of church and state was a compelling interest, it did not believe that an equal access policy violated the establishment clause. The Court relied on the three-part test of *Lemon v. Kurtzman,* 403 U.S. 602, 612–13 (1971): "First, the [governmental policy] must have a secular legislative purpose; second, its principal or primary effect must be one that neither advances nor inhibits religion . . . ; finally, the [policy] must not foster an excessive government entanglement with religion." Applying the test, the Court reasoned:

> In this case two prongs of the test are clearly met. Both the District Court and the Court of Appeals held that an open-forum policy, including nondiscrimination against religious speech, would have a secular purpose and would avoid entanglement with religion. But the District Court concluded, and the University argues here, that allowing religious groups to share the limited public forum would have the "primary effect" of advancing religion.
>
> The University's argument misconceives the nature of this case. The question is not whether the creation of a religious forum would violate the Establishment Clause. The University has opened its facilities for use by student groups, and the question is whether it can now exclude groups because of the content of their speech (see *Healy v. James,* 408 U.S. 169 . . . (1972)). In this context we are unpersuaded that the primary effect of the public forum, open to all forms of discourse, would be to advance religion.
>
> We are not oblivious to the range of an open forum's likely effects. It is possible—perhaps even foreseeable—that religious groups will benefit from access to University facilities. But this Court has explained that a religious organization's enjoyment of merely "incidental" benefits does not violate the prohibition against the "primary advancement" of religion [citations omitted].
>
> We are satisfied that any religious benefits of an open forum at UMKC would be "incidental" within the meaning of our cases. Two factors are especially relevant.
>
> First, an open forum in a public university does not confer any imprimatur of state approval on religious sects or practices. As the court of appeals quite aptly stated, such a policy "would no more commit the University . . . to religious goals" than it is "now committed to the goals of the Students for a Democratic Society, the Young Socialist Alliance," or any other group eligible to use its facilities (*Chess v. Widmar,* 635 F.2d at 1317).
>
> Second, the forum is available to a broad class of nonreligious as well as religious speakers; there are over 100 recognized student groups at UMKC. The provision of benefits to so broad a spectrum of groups is an important index of secular effect [citations omitted]. If the Establishment Clause barred the extension of general benefits to religious groups, "a church could not be protected by the police and fire departments, or have its public sidewalk kept in repair" (*Roemer v. Maryland Public Works Board,* 426 U.S. 736, 747 . . . (1976) (plurality opinion)). . . . At least in the absence of empirical evidence that religious groups will dominate UMKC's open forum, we agree with the Court of Appeals that the advancement of religion would not be the forum's "primary effect" [454 U.S. at 271–75].

With regard to the university's argument that its interest in enforcing the Missouri constitution's prohibition against public support for religious activities outweighed the students' free speech claim, the Court stated:

> Our cases have required the most exacting scrutiny in cases in which a state undertakes to regulate speech on the basis of its content (see, for example, *Carey v. Brown,* 447 U.S. 455 (1980); *Police Dept. v. Mosley,* 408 U.S. 92 . . . (1972)). On the other hand, the state interest asserted here—in achieving greater separation of church and State than is already ensured under the establishment clause of the Federal Constitution—is limited by the Free Exercise Clause and in this

case by the Free Speech Clause as well. In this constitutional context, we are unable to recognize the State's interest as sufficiently "compelling" to justify content-based discrimination against respondents' religious speech [454 U.S. at 276].

Since UMKC could not justify its content-based restriction on access to the forum it had created, the Court declared the university's regulation unconstitutional. The plaintiff students thereby obtained the right to have their religious group hold its meetings in campus facilities generally open to student groups. It follows that other student religious groups at other public postsecondary institutions have the same right to use campus facilities; institutions may not exclude them, whether by written policy or otherwise, on the basis of the religious content of their activities.[8]

Widmar has substantial relevance for public institutions, most of which have created forums similar to the forum at UMKC. The opinion falls far short, however, of requiring institutions to relinquish all authority over student religious groups. There are substantial limits to the opinion's reach:

1. *Widmar* does not require (nor does it permit) institutions to create forums especially for religious groups, or to give them any other preferential treatment. As the Court noted, "Because this case involves a forum already made generally available to student groups, it differs from those cases in which this Court has invalidated statutes permitting school facilities to be used for instruction by religious groups but not by others" (454 U.S. at 271, n.10; see also 454 U.S. at 273, n.13).

2. Nor does *Widmar* require institutions to create a forum for student groups generally, or to continue to maintain one, if they choose not to do so. The case applies only to situations where the institution has created and voluntarily continues to maintain a forum for student groups.

3. *Widmar* requires access only to facilities that are part of a forum created by the institution, not to any other facilities. Similarly, *Widmar* requires access only for students: "We have not held . . . that a campus must make all of its facilities equally available to students and nonstudents alike, or that a university must grant free access to all of its grounds or buildings" (454 U.S. at 268, n.5).

4. *Widmar* does not prohibit all regulation of student organizations' use of forum facilities; it prohibits only content-based restrictions on access. Thus, the Court noted that "a university's mission is education, and decisions of this Court have never denied a university's authority to impose reasonable regulations compatible with that mission upon the use of its campus and facilities" (454 U.S. at 268, n.5). In particular, according to the Court, the *Widmar* opinion "in

---

[8]In 1984, Congress passed and the President signed the Equal Access Act, Pub. L. No. 98-377, 98 Stat. 1302, giving limited statutory recognition to the principles underlying *Widmar.* By its terms, however, the Act extends these principles to, and applies only to, "public secondary school[s] . . . receiv[ing] federal financial assistance."

no way undermines the capacity of the university to establish reasonable time, place, and manner regulations" (454 U.S. at 276) for use of the forum. Such regulations must be imposed on all student groups, however, not just student religious organizations, and must be imposed without regard to the content of the group's speech activities (see *Heffron v. International Society for Krishna Consciousness,* 452 U.S. 640 (1981)). If a student religious group or other student group "violate[s] [such] reasonable campus rules or substantially interfere[s] with the opportunity of other students to obtain an education" (454 U.S. at 277), the institution may prohibit the group from using campus facilities for its activities.

5. *Widmar* does not rule out every possible content-based restriction on access to a forum. The Court's analysis quoted above makes clear that a content-based regulation would be constitutional under the First Amendment if it were "necessary to serve a compelling state interest and . . . narrowly drawn to achieve that end." As *Widmar* and other First Amendment cases demonstrate, this standard is exceedingly difficult to meet. But the *Widmar* opinion suggests at least two possibilities, the contours of which are left for further development should the occasion arise. First, the Court hints that, if there is "empirical evidence that religious groups will dominate . . . [the institution's] open forum" (454 U.S. at 275, also quoted above), the institution apparently may regulate access by these groups to the extent necessary to prevent domination. Second, if the student demand for use of forum facilities exceeds the supply, the institution may "make academic judgments as to how best to allocate scarce resources" (454 U.S. at 276). In making such academic judgments, the institution may apparently prefer the educational content of some group activities over others and allocate its facilities in accord with these academic preferences. Justice Stevens's opinion concurring in the Court's judgment contains an example for consideration:

> If two groups of twenty-five students requested the use of a room at a particular time—one to view Mickey Mouse cartoons and the other to rehearse an amateur performance of *Hamlet*—the First Amendment would not require that the room be reserved for the group that submitted its application first. . . . [A] university should be allowed to decide for itself whether a program that illuminates the genius of Walt Disney should be given precedence over one that may duplicate material adequately covered in the classroom. . . . A university legitimately may regard some subjects as more relevant to its educational mission than others. But the university, like the police officer, may not allow its agreement or disagreement with the viewpoint of a particular speaker to determine whether access to a forum will be granted [454 U.S. at 278–80].

For a different example of a content-based restriction—approved by one federal appellate court subsequent to *Widmar*—see *Chapman v. Thomas,* 743 F.2d 1056 (4th Cir. 1984). In this case, the court ruled that North Carolina State University could prohibit a student from door-to-door canvassing in dormitories to publicize campus Bible study meetings, even though it permitted candidates for top student government offices to campaign door to door.

A subsequent Supreme Court case, *Rosenberger v. Rector and Visitors of the University of Virginia*, 515 U.S. 819 (1995), concerns religious student organizations' eligibility for funding from mandatory student fee assessments. A student group, Wide Awake Productions (WAP), had been recognized by the university and was entitled to use university facilities just as other organizations did. But the university's guidelines for allocating mandatory student fees excluded certain types of organizations, including fraternities and sororities, political and religious organizations, and organizations whose membership policies were exclusionary. The guidelines also prohibited the funding of, among others, religious and political activities. WAP published a journal containing articles written from a religious perspective, and its constitution stated that the organization's purpose included the expression of religious views. The student council, which had been delegated the authority to disburse the funds from student fees, had denied funding to WAP, characterizing its publication of the journal as "religious activity."

The student members of WAP sued the university, alleging that the denial of funding violated their rights to freedom of speech, press, association, religious exercise, and equal protection under both the federal and state constitutions. The district court rejected all of the plaintiffs' arguments and granted the university's motion for summary judgment on all claims. The appellate court, focusing particularly on the free speech and establishment clause issues, upheld the district court in all respects.

The U.S. Supreme Court then reversed the judgments of the district and appellate courts. By a 5-to-4 vote, the majority held that (1) the university's refusal to provide Student Activities Fund (SAF) funds to Wide Awake Productions violated the students' First Amendment free speech rights; and (2) university funding for WAP would not violate the First Amendment's establishment clause, and the university therefore could not justify its violation of the free speech clause by asserting a need to adhere to the establishment clause. Justice Kennedy wrote the opinion for the majority of five; Justice O'Connor wrote an important concurring opinion; and Justice Souter wrote the opinion for the four dissenters.

The tension between the free speech and establishment clauses of the First Amendment is clearly illuminated by the sharply divergent majority and dissenting opinions. The majority opinion addresses *Rosenberger* from a free speech standpoint, and finds no establishment clause justification for infringing the rights of a student publication that reports the news from a religious perspective. On the other hand, the dissent characterizes the students' publication as an evangelical magazine directly financed by the state, and regards such funding to be a clear example of an establishment clause violation. Justice O'Connor's narrow concurring opinion, tailored specifically to the facts of the case, serves to limit the majority's holding and reduce the gulf between the majority and the dissent.

As the Court explained the situation, the university had established a mandatory student activities fee, the income from which supported a student activities fund used to subsidize a variety of student organizations. All recognized student groups had to achieve the status of a "Contracted Independent Organization" (CIO), after which some groups could then submit certain of its bills to the student council for payment from SAF funds. The eligible bills were those from "outside contractors" or "third-party contractors" that provided services or products to the student organization. Disbursement was made directly to the third party; no payments went directly to a student group. The university's SAF guidelines prohibited the use of SAF funds for, among others, religious activities, defined by the guidelines as an activity that "primarily promotes or manifests a particular belief in or about a deity or an ultimate reality." Wide Awake Productions was a CIO established to publish a campus magazine that "'offers a Christian perspective on both personal and community issues'" (515 U.S. at 826, quoting from the magazine's first issue). WAP applied for SAF funding—funding already provided to fifteen student "media groups"—to be used to pay the printer that printed its magazine. The university rejected the request on grounds that WAP's activities were religious.

Explicating the majority's free speech analysis, Justice Kennedy described the SAF as a forum "more in a metaphysical sense than in a spatial or geographic sense," but nonetheless determined that the SAF, as established and operated by the university, is a "limited public forum" for First Amendment purposes. Having opened the SAF to the university community, the university

> must respect the lawful boundaries it has itself set. [It] may not exclude speech where its distinction is not "reasonable in light of the purpose served by the forum" (citing *Cornelius v. NAACP Legal Defense & Education Fund,* 473 U.S. 788, 804–6 (1985)), nor may it discriminate against speech on the basis of its viewpoint (citing *Lamb's Chapel v. Center Moriches Union Free School District,* 508 U.S. 384, 392 (1993)) [515 U.S. 827–28].

The majority then determined that the university had denied funding to WAP because of WAP's perspective, or viewpoint, rather than because WAP dealt with the general subject matter of religion. Thus, although "it is something of an understatement to speak of religious thought and discussion as just a viewpoint," "viewpoint discrimination is the proper way to interpret the university's objection to Wide Awake":

> By the very terms of the SAF prohibition, the [u]niversity does not exclude religion as a subject matter but selects for disfavored treatment those student journalistic efforts with religious editorial viewpoints. Religion may be a vast area of inquiry, but it also provides, as it did here, a specific premise, a perspective, a standpoint from which a variety of subjects may be discussed and considered. The prohibited perspective, not the general subject matter, resulted in the refusal to make the third-party payments [to the printer], for the subjects discussed were otherwise within the approved category of publications [515 U.S. at 831].

Furthermore, the majority rejected the university's contention that "no viewpoint discrimination occurs because the Guidelines discriminate against an entire class of viewpoints." Because of the "complex and multifaceted nature of public discourse . . . [i]t is as objectionable to exclude both a theistic and an atheistic perspective on the debate as it is to exclude one, the other, or yet another political, economic, or social viewpoint" (515 U.S. at 831).

Having determined that the university had violated the students' free speech rights, the majority considered whether providing SAF funds to WAP would nevertheless violate the establishment clause. In order for a government regulation to survive an establishment clause challenge, it must be neutral toward religion (see Section 1.6 of this book). Relying on past decisions upholding governmental programs when "the government, following neutral criteria and evenhanded policies, extends benefits to recipients whose ideologies and viewpoints, including religious ones, are broad and diverse" (515 U.S. at 839), the Court held that the SAF is neutral toward religion:

> There is no suggestion that the university created [the SAF] to advance religion or adopted some ingenious device with the purpose of aiding a religious cause. The object of the SAF is to open a forum for speech and to support various student enterprises, including the publication of newspapers, in recognition of the diversity and creativity of student life. . . . The category of support here is for "student news, information, opinion, entertainment, or academic communications media groups," of which *Wide Awake* was 1 of 15 in the 1990 school year. WAP did not seek a subsidy because of its Christian editorial viewpoint; it sought funding as a student journal, which it was [515 U.S. at 840].

Thus, the WAP application for funding depended not on the religious editorial viewpoint of the publication, nor on WAP being a religious organization, but rather on the neutral factor of its status as a student journal. "Any benefit to religion is incidental to the government's provision of secular services for secular purposes on a religion-neutral basis" (515 U.S. at 843–44).

In completing its establishment clause analysis, the majority distinguished another line of cases forbidding the use of tax funds to support religious activities and rejected the contention that the mandatory student activities fee is a tax levied for the support of a church or religion. Unlike a tax, which the majority describes as an exaction to support the government and a revenue-raising device, the student activity fee is used for the limited purpose of funding student organizations consistent with the educational purposes of the university. No public funds would flow directly into WAP's coffers; instead, the university would pay printers (third-party contractors) to produce WAP's publications. This method of third-party payment, along with university-required disclaimers stating that the university is not responsible for or represented by the recipient organization, evidenced the attenuated relationship between the university and WAP. The majority found no difference in "logic or principle, and no difference of constitutional significance, between a school using its funds to operate a facility to which students have access [as in *Widmar*], and a school paying a third-party contractor to operate the facility on its behalf."

Justice O'Connor's concurring opinion carefully limits her analysis to the facts of the case, emphasizing that "[t]he nature of the dispute does not admit of any categorical answers, nor should any be inferred from the Court's decision today." Justice O'Connor based her concurrence on four specific considerations that ameliorate the establishment clause concerns that otherwise would arise from government funding of religious messages. *First,* at the insistence of the university, student organizations such as WAP are separate and distinct from the university. All groups that wish to be considered for SAF funding are required to sign a contract stating that the organization exists and operates independently of the university. Moreover, all publications, contracts, letters, or other written materials distributed by the group must bear a disclaimer acknowledging that, while members of the university faculty and student body may be associated with the group, the organization is independent of the "corporation which is the university and which is not responsible for the organizations' contracts, acts, or omissions." *Second,* no money is given directly to WAP. By paying a third-party vendor, in this case a printer that printed WAP's journal, the university is able to ensure that the funding that it has granted is being used to "further the University's purpose in maintaining a free and robust marketplace of ideas, from whatever perspective." This method of funding, according to the concurrence, is analogous to a school providing equal access to a generally available physical facility, like a printing press on campus. *Third,* because WAP does not exist "in a vacuum," it will not be mistakenly perceived to be university endorsed. This potential danger is greatly diminished by both the number and variety of other publications receiving SAF funding. O'Connor thus found it illogical to equate university funding of WAP with the endorsement of one particular viewpoint. And *fourth,* the "proceeds of the student fees in this case [may be distinguishable] from proceeds of the general assessments in support of religion that lie at the core of the prohibition against religious funding, . . . and from government funds generally":

> Unlike moneys dispensed from state or federal treasuries, the Student Activities Fund is collected from students who themselves administer the fund and select qualifying recipients only from among those who originally paid the fee. The government neither pays into nor draws out of this common pool, and a fee of this sort appears conducive to granting individual students proportional refunds.[9] The Student Activities Fund, then, represents not government resources, whether derived from tax revenue, sales of assets, or otherwise, but a fund that simply belongs to the students [515 U.S. at 851–52 (O'Connor, J., concurring)].

Although the first three of Justice O'Connor's distinctions were also relied on by Justice Kennedy, Justice O'Connor states her conclusions more narrowly than does Kennedy and limits her reasoning more tightly to the unique facts of the case. Justice O'Connor also adds the fourth consideration regarding the character of the student fee proceeds. Since Justice O'Connor provides the critical

---

[9][Author's footnote] This issue of proportional refunds for objecting students, or an "opt-out" system, was later addressed by the Court in *Board of Regents of the University of Wisconsin System v. Southworth,* 529 U.S. 217 (2000), discussed in subsection 10.1.3 above.

fifth vote that forms the 5-to-4 majority, her opinion carries unusual significance. To the extent that her establishment clause analysis is narrower than Justice Kennedy's, it is her opinion rather than his that apparently provides the current baseline for understanding the establishment clause restrictions on public institutions' funding of student religious groups.

The four dissenting Justices disagreed with both the majority's free speech clause analysis and its establishment clause analysis. Regarding the former, Justice Souter insisted that the university's refusal to fund WAP was not viewpoint discrimination but rather a "subject-matter distinction," an educational judgment not to fund student dialogue on the particular subject of religion regardless of the viewpoints expressed. Regarding the establishment issue, which he termed the "central question in this case," Justice Souter argued that, because "there is no warrant for distinguishing among public funding sources for purposes of applying the First Amendment's prohibition of religious establishment, . . . the university's refusal to support petitioners' religious activities is compelled by the Establishment Clause." Emphasizing that WAP's publications call on Christians "'to live, in word and deed, according to the faith they proclaim . . . and to consider what a personal relationship with Jesus Christ means'" (551 U.S. at 868, quoting from WAP's first issue), Justice Souter likens the paper to an "evangelist's mission station and pulpit" (515 U.S. at 868). He thus argues that the use of public (SAF) funds for this activity is a "direct subsidization of preaching the word" and a "direct funding of core religious activities by an arm of the State" (515 U.S. at 863).

The majority's reasoning in *Rosenberger* generally parallels the Court's earlier reasoning in *Widmar v. Vincent* (above) and generally affirms the free speech and establishment principles articulated in that case. More important, both Justice Kennedy's and Justice O'Connor's opinions extend student organizations' First Amendment rights beyond access to *facilities* (the issue in *Widmar*) to include access to *services*. The Kennedy and O'Connor opinions also refine the *Widmar* free speech analysis by distinguishing between *content*-based restrictions on speech (the issue in *Widmar*) and *viewpoint*-based restrictions (the issue as the Court framed it in *Rosenberger*). The latter type of restriction, sometimes called "viewpoint discrimination," is the most suspect of all speech restrictions and the type least likely to be tolerated by the courts (see generally Sections 9.6.2 & 10.1.3). *Widmar* appears to reserve a range of discretion for a higher educational institution to make academic judgments based on the educational *content* of a student organization's activities; *Rosenberger* appears to prohibit any such discretion when the institution's academic judgment is based on consideration of the student group's *viewpoints* (see 515 U.S. at 845).

Sec. 10.2. Fraternities and Sororities

10.2.1 Overview. Fraternal organizations have been part of campus life at many colleges and universities for more than a century. Some, such as Phi Beta Kappa, were founded to recognize academic achievement, while others have a predominantly social focus. Because of their strong ties to colleges and universities, whether because the houses occupied by members are on or near the college's property or because their members are students at the college, the consequences of the individual and group behavior of fraternity and sorority members can involve the college in legal problems.

The legal issues that affect nonfraternal student organizations (see Section 10.1) may also arise with respect to fraternities and sororities. But because fraternal organizations have their own unique histories and traditions, are related to national organizations that may influence their activities, and play a significant social role on many campuses, they may pose unique legal problems for the college with which they are affiliated.

Supporters of fraternal, or "Greek," organizations argue that members perform more service to the college and the community and make larger alumni contributions than nonmembers, and that fraternity houses provide room and board to undergraduate students whom the college would otherwise be required to accommodate. Critics of fraternal organizations argue that they foster "elitism, sexism, racism and in worst instances, criminal activity" (V. L. Brown, "College Fraternities and Sororities: Tort Liability and the Regulatory Authority of Public Institutions of Higher Education," 58 *West's Educ. Law Rptr.* (1990)). Institutions have responded to problems such as hazing, alcohol and drug abuse, sexual harassment and assault, and the death or serious injury of fraternity members in various ways—for instance, by regulating social activities, suspending or expelling individual fraternities, or abolishing the entire Greek system on campus.

Fraternities and sororities may be chapters of a national organization or may be independent organizations. The local chapters, whether or not they are tied to a national organization, may be either incorporated or unincorporated associations. If the fraternity or sorority provides a house for some of its members, it may be located on land owned by the colleges or it may be off campus. In either case, the college may own the fraternity house, or an alumni organization (sometimes called a "house corporation") may own the house and assume responsibility for its upkeep.

Litigation concerning fraternal organizations has increased sharply in the past decade. Institutional attempts to regulate, discipline, or ban fraternal organizations have met with stiff resistance, both on campus and in the courts. Students or other individuals injured as a result of fraternal organizations' activities, or the activities of individual members of fraternal organizations, have sought to hold colleges legally responsible for those injuries. And fraternal organizations themselves are facing increasing legal liability as citizens and courts have grown less tolerant of the problems of hazing and other forms of misconduct that continue to trouble U.S. college campuses.

10.2.2. Institutional recognition and regulation of fraternal organizations.

Recognition by a college is significant to fraternal organizations because many national fraternal organizations require such recognition as a condition of the local organization's continued affiliation with the national. The conditions under which recognition is awarded by the college are important because they may determine the college's power to regulate the conduct of the organization or its members.

Some colleges and universities require, as a condition of recognition of fraternal organizations, that each local fraternity sign a "relationship statement." These statements outline the college's regulations and elicit the organization's assurance that it will obtain insurance coverage, adhere to fire and building codes, and comply with the institution's policy on the serving of alcohol.[10] Some of these statements also require members to participate in alcohol awareness programs or community service. Some statements include restrictions on parties and noise, and extend the jurisdiction of the college's student conduct code and disciplinary system to acts that take place where students live, even if they live off campus.

On some campuses, institutional regulation of fraternal organizations extends to their membership practices. Traditionally, fraternities and sororities have limited their membership to one gender, and in the past many of these organizations prohibited membership for nonwhite and non-Christian individuals. In more recent years, however, several colleges and universities, including Middlebury, Bowdoin, and Trinity (Conn.) Colleges, have required fraternities and sororities to admit members of both sexes (see N. S. Horton, "Traditional Single-Sex Fraternities on College Campuses: Will They Survive in the 1990s?" 18 *J. Coll. & Univ. Law* 419 (1992)) and, in general, to avoid discriminatory practices. (See, for example, Eric Hoover, "Black Student Breaks Color Barrier in U. of Alabama's Fraternity System," *Chron. Higher Educ.*, November 9, 2001, A31.)

Other colleges have banned fraternities altogether. For example, Colby College, a private liberal arts college, withdrew recognition of all its fraternities and sororities in 1984 because administrators believed that fraternal activities were incompatible with its goals for student residential life. When a group of students continued some of the activities of a banned fraternity, despite numerous attempts by the college's administration to halt them, the president and college dean imposed discipline on the "fraternity" members, ranging from disciplinary probation to one-semester suspensions.

In *Phelps v. President and Trustees of Colby College*, 595 A.2d 403 (Maine 1991), the students sought to enjoin the discipline and the ban on fraternities under Maine's Civil Rights Act, 5 M.R.S.A. §§ 4681 *et seq.* (2003), and the state constitution's guarantees of free speech and the right to associate. Maine's Supreme Judicial Court rejected the students' claims. It held that the state law, directed against harassment and intimidation, did not apply to the actions of the college because the law "stopped short of authorizing Maine courts to mediate disputes between private parties exercising their respective rights of free expression and association" (595 A.2d at 407). The court also held that the actions of private entities, such as the college, were not subject to state constitutional restrictions.

Although private institutions are not subject to constitutional requirements, their attempts to discipline fraternal organizations and their members are still

---

[10]Cases and authorities are collected in R. A. Vinluan, Annot., "Regulations as to Fraternities and Similar Associations Connected with Educational Institution," 10 A.L.R.3d 389.

subject to challenge. In *In re Rensselaer Society of Engineers v. Rensselaer Polytechnic Institute*, 689 N.Y.S.2d 292 (N.Y. Ct. App. 1999), the Society of Engineers, a fraternity, brought a state administrative law claim against Rensselaer Polytechnic Institute (RPI), challenging the institution's decision to suspend the fraternity for several years for various violations of RPI's code of student conduct. The fraternity was already on disciplinary probation for earlier infractions of the code of conduct. Ruling that the institution's conduct was neither arbitrary nor capricious, the court said: "Judicial scrutiny of the determination of disciplinary matters between a university and its students, or student organizations, is limited to determining whether the university substantially adhered to its own published rules and guidelines for disciplinary proceedings" (689 N.Y.S.2d at 295). The institution's actions were eminently reasonable, said the court; it followed its "detailed" grievance procedure in both making and reviewing the challenged disciplinary decision, and afforded the fraternity three levels of administrative review.

But the decision of another private institution to suspend a fraternity was vacated by a state appellate court, and the university was ordered to provide additional procedural protections to the fraternity. In *Gamma Phi Chapter of Sigma Chi Fraternity v. University of Miami*, 718 So. 2d 910 (Fla. Ct. App. 1998), the fraternity had sought an injunction to prevent the university's enforcement of sanctions against it. The fraternity claimed that the procedure used by the university to impose sanctions, including the suspension of rushing, was based on an *ex parte* fact-finding process (a process that did not allow the fraternity an opportunity to participate or to speak in its own behalf). The appellate court enjoined the sanctions and ordered the university to provide a fair hearing. The vice president for student affairs then appointed a panel consisting of two students, two faculty members, and an attorney not employed by the university. The fraternity, however, sought a second injunction to prevent the panel from hearing the case, arguing that the Interfraternity Council had the responsibility to decide such matters. The court denied the second injunction, ruling that, until the university had acted and the fraternity had pursued all internal remedies, the court would not exercise jurisdiction.

Although some colleges have banned fraternities altogether, others have sought less drastic methods of controlling them. The attempt of Hamilton College to minimize the influence of fraternities on campus was stalled temporarily by an unusual use of the Sherman Act, which outlaws monopolies that are in restraint of trade (see Section 13.2.8). Hamilton College announced a policy, to become effective in the 1995–96 academic year, of requiring all students to live in college-owned facilities and to purchase college-sponsored meal plans. The college made this change, it said, to minimize the dominance of fraternities over the social life of the college and to encourage more women applicants. Four fraternities that owned their own fraternity houses, and that had previously received approximately $1 million in payment for housing and feeding their members, sought to enjoin the implementation of the new housing policy, arguing that it was an attempt by the college to exercise monopoly power over the market for student room and board. A trial court granted the college's motion to dismiss the lawsuit, stating that the provision of room and board to students was not "trade or commerce," and that there was no nexus between the college's conduct and interstate commerce. The trial court did not rule on the issue of whether the product market at issue was the market for room and board for Hamilton students (as the fraternities claimed), or the market for highly selective liberal arts colleges with which Hamilton competes for students (as the college had claimed).

The appellate court reversed the dismissal, stating that the fraternities had alleged sufficient facts that, if they could be proven, could constitute a Sherman Act violation (*Hamilton Chapter of Alpha Delta Phi v. Hamilton College,* 128 F.3d 59 (2d Cir. 1997)). The plaintiffs had claimed that the college's goal was to raise revenues by forcing students to purchase housing from the college, to raise its housing prices due to the lack of competition for housing, and to purchase the fraternity houses at below-market prices. Because Hamilton recruits students from throughout the United States, and because more than half of its room and board revenue was obtained from out-of-state students, there was clearly a nexus between Hamilton's housing policy and interstate commerce. Therefore, since antitrust jurisdiction was established, the appellate court reversed the lower court's judgment and remanded the case. On remand, the trial court ruled that the plaintiffs' characterization of the product market was incorrect, and awarded summary judgment to the college (106 F. Supp. 2d 406 (N.D.N.Y. 2000)).

Dartmouth College's decision to eliminate fraternities and sororities drew litigation not from students, but from alumni who had contributed to the college's fund-raising campaign. Seven alumni sued the Dartmouth Trustees after the trustees used funds raised in a capital campaign to restructure the college's residential life program, eliminating Greek organizations in the process. In *Brzica v. Trustees of Dartmouth College,* 791 A.2d 990 (N.H. 2002), the New Hampshire Supreme Court rejected the plaintiffs' claim that the trustees had a fiduciary duty to the alumni, and found that there was no evidence that the trustees had conspired to eliminate Greek organizations prior to the fund-raising campaign.

Public colleges and universities face possible constitutional obstacles to banning fraternities, including the First Amendment's guarantee of the right to associate (see Sections 9.5.1, 9.5.2, & 10.1). The U.S. Supreme Court, in *Roberts v. United States Jaycees,* 468 U.S. 609 (1983), and *Boy Scouts of America v. Dale,* 530 U.S. 640 (2000), established the parameters of constitutionally protected rights of association and provided the impetus for constitutional challenges to institutional attempts to suspend or eliminate fraternal organizations.

The U.S. Court of Appeals for the Third Circuit addressed the extent of a fraternity's constitutionally protected rights of association in *Pi Lambda Phi Fraternity v. University of Pittsburgh,* 229 F.3d 435 (3d Cir. 2000). The local and national fraternity challenged the university's decision to revoke the local chapter's status as a recognized student organization after a drug raid at the fraternity house yielded cocaine, heroin, opium, and Rohypnol (the "date rape" drug). Four chapter members were charged with possession of controlled substances. The university followed the recommendation of a student judiciary panel that determined that the chapter had violated the university's policy of holding fraternal organizations accountable "for actions of individual members and their guests." The local and national fraternities sued the university and several of its administrators under 42 U.S.C. § 1983 for violation of the chapter's First Amendment rights of intimate and expressive association. The trial court awarded summary judgment to the university, ruling that the fraternity's primary activities were social rather than either intimate or expressive, and thus unprotected by the First Amendment.

Although the appellate court affirmed the outcome, it performed a more extensive analysis of the fraternity's freedom of association claims. The local chapter did not meet the test of *Roberts* for intimate association, said the court, because of the large number of members (approximately eighty) and the fact that the chapter "is not particularly selective in whom it admits" (229 F.3d at 442). With respect to the expressive association claim, the court applied the three-step test created by the Supreme Court in *Dale*. *First,* the court ruled that the fraternity's purpose was not expressive because there was virtually no evidence that the chapter engaged in expressive activity (such as political advocacy or even extensive charitable activities). *Second,* the university's act to revoke the fraternity's charter had only an indirect or attenuated effect on its expressive activity. Furthermore, the reason for the university's "burden" on the fraternity's activities was punishing illegal drug activity, which was not a form of expression protected by the First Amendment. And *third,* the university's interest in enforcing its rules and regulations, and in preventing student use of drugs, outweighed any possible burden on the fraternity's expressive activity.

The court similarly rejected the fraternity's equal protection claim, ruling that the university's policy of holding fraternities accountable for the actions of their members and guests was virtually identical to a rule holding students living in residence halls responsible for the actions of their guests. And even if the university had treated fraternities differently from other student organizations, said the court, fraternities are not a suspect classification for constitutional purposes, and thus any differential treatment by a public university would be reviewed under the "rational basis" test, a relatively deferential standard for a public university to meet.

The unsuccessful legal challenges to the banning of fraternities stimulated congressional action. In the Higher Education Amendments of 1998 (Pub. L. No. 105-244), Congress added a nonbinding "sense of Congress" provision protecting the speech and association rights of students. The provision reads, in part:

> It is the sense of Congress that no student attending an institution of higher education on a full- or part-time basis should, on the basis of participation in protected speech or protected association, be excluded from participation in, be denied the benefits of, or be subjected to discrimination or official sanction under any education program, activity, or division of the institution directly or indirectly receiving financial assistance under this Act, whether or not such program, activity, or division is sponsored or officially sanctioned by the institution [20 U.S.C. § 1011a(a)].

The provision does allow institutions to regulate disruptive conduct and to take "action to prevent violation of State liquor laws, to discourage binge drinking and other alcohol abuse, to protect students from sexual harassment including assault and date rape, to prevent hazing, or to regulate unsanitary or unsafe conditions in any student residence" (20 U.S.C. § 1011a(b)(2)). The provision is not legally binding on colleges, and does not appear to have caused those institutions that have banned fraternal organizations to reinstate them.

Although a clear articulation of the college's expectations regarding the behavior of fraternity members may provide a deterrent to misconduct, some courts have viewed institutional attempts to regulate the conduct of fraternity members as an assumption of a duty to control their behavior, with a correlative obligation to exercise appropriate restraint over members' conduct. For example, in *Furek v. University of Delaware,* 594 A.2d 506 (Del. 1991), the state's supreme court ruled that the university could be found liable for injuries a student received during fraternity hazing, since the university's strict rules against hazing demonstrated that it had assumed a duty to protect students against hazing injuries. (See Section 10.2.3 below for further discussion of these liability issues.)

Because of the potential for greater liability when regulation is extensive (because a student, parent, or injured third party may claim that the college assumed a duty to regulate the conduct of the fraternity and its members), some institutions have opted for "recognition" statements such as those used to recognize other student organizations. Although this minimal approach may defeat a claim that the institution has assumed a duty to supervise the activities of fraternity members, it may limit the institution's authority to regulate the activities of the organization, although the institution can still discipline individual student members who violate its code of student conduct.

A study that examined tort liability issues related to fraternal organizations (E. D. Gulland & M. B. Powell, *Colleges, Fraternities and Sororities: A White Paper on Tort Liability Issues* (American Council on Education, 1989), at 14–15) recommends that recognition statements include the following provisions:

1. Description of the limited purpose of recognition (no endorsement, but access to institutional facilities);

2. Specification of the lack of principal-agent relationship between college and fraternity;

3. Acknowledgment that the fraternity is an independently chartered corporation existing under state laws;

4. Confirmation that the college assumes no responsibility for supervision, control, safety, security, or other services;

5. Restrictions on use of the college's name, tax identification number, or other representations that the fraternity is affiliated with the college;

6. Requirement that the fraternity furnish evidence that it carries insurance sufficient to cover its risks.

One area where institutional regulation of fraternal organizations is receiving judicial—and legislative—attention is the "ritual" of hazing, often included as part of pledging activities. If an institution promulgates a policy against hazing, it may be held legally liable if it does not enforce that policy vigorously. A case not involving fraternal organizations is nevertheless instructive on the potential for liability when hazing occurs. In a case brought by a former student injured by hazing, the Supreme Court of Vermont affirmed a sizable jury verdict against Norwich University, a paramilitary college that entrusts to upper-class students the responsibility to "indoctrinate and orient" first-year students, called "rooks." Although Norwich had adopted policies against hazing and had included precautions against hazing in its training for the upper-class "cadre," who were entrusted with the "indoctrination and orientation" responsibility, the former student alleged that hazing was commonplace and tolerated by the university's administration, and that it caused him both physical and financial injury.

In *Brueckner v. Norwich University*, 730 A.2d 1086 (Vt. 1999), the student, who withdrew from Norwich after enduring physical and psychological harassment, filed claims for assault and battery, negligent infliction of emotional distress, intentional infliction of emotional distress, and negligent supervision. A jury found Norwich liable on all counts and awarded the student $488,600 in compensatory damages and $1.75 million in punitive damages. On appeal, the state supreme court affirmed the liability verdicts, holding that cadre members were authorized by Norwich to indoctrinate and orient rooks, and Norwich was thus vicariously liable for the tortious acts of the cadre because these actions were within the "scope of their employment" (despite the fact that Norwich forbade such behavior). The court affirmed the compensatory damage award, but reversed the punitive damage award, stating that Norwich's behavior was negligent but did not rise to the standard of malice required by that state's case law on punitive damages. One justice dissented, arguing that Norwich's behavior had demonstrated indifference and its tolerance for hazing constituted reckless disregard for the safety of its students.

Although an institution may not wish explicitly to assume a duty to supervise the conduct of fraternity members, it does have the power to sanction fraternal organizations and their members if they violate institutional policies against hazing or other dangerous conduct. In *Psi Upsilon v. University of Pennsylvania*, 591 A.2d 755 (Pa. Super. Ct. 1991), a state appellate court refused to enjoin the university's imposition of sanctions against a fraternity whose members kidnapped and terrorized a nonmember as part of a hazing activity. The student filed criminal charges against the twenty students who participated in the prank, and the university held a hearing before imposing sanctions on the fraternity. After the hearing, the university withdrew its recognition of the fraternity for three years, took possession of the fraternity house without compensating the fraternity, and prohibited anyone who took part in the kidnapping from participating in a future reapplication for recognition.

In evaluating the university's authority to impose these sanctions, the court first examined whether the disciplinary procedures met legal requirements. Noting that the university was privately controlled, the court ruled that the students were entitled only to whatever procedural protections university policies had given them. The court then turned to the relationship statement that the fraternity had entered into with the university.

Characterizing the relationship statement as contractual, the court ruled that it gave ample notice to the members that they must assume collective responsibility for the activities of individual members, and that breaching the statement was sufficient grounds for sanctions. After reviewing several claims of unfairness in the conduct of the disciplinary proceeding, the court upheld the trial judge's denial of injunctive relief.

More than thirty states have passed laws outlawing hazing. Illinois's anti-hazing law (Ill. Rev. Stat. ch. 144, para. 221 (1989)) was upheld against a constitutional challenge in *People v. Anderson,* 591 N.E.2d 461 (Ill. 1992), as was Ohio's anti-hazing law in *Carpetta v. Pi Kappa Alpha Fraternity,* 100 Ohio Misc. 2d 42 (Ct. Common Pleas, Lucas Co. 1998). (See also Mass. Ann. Laws ch. 269, §§ 17–19 (Supp. 1987); Cal. Educ. Code § 32050 (West 1990); and Virginia Hazing, Civil and Criminal Liability, Va. Code Ann. § 18.2-56. Florida's anti-hazing law makes hazing a third-class felony, punishable by up to five years in prison (Fla. Stat. § 1006.63(2) (2005).) The Missouri anti-hazing statute survived a void for vagueness challenge. Where a student was convicted of hazing Kappa Alpha Psi pledges, resulting in the death of one of them, the Supreme Court of Missouri held that the anti-hazing statute was not void for vagueness, nor did it violate the equal protection clause, and the student was adequately informed of the charges against him (*State v. Allen,* 905 S.W.2d 874 (Mo. 1995)). And the Texas Court of Criminal Appeals upheld a Texas statute that requires individuals who are involved in or witness hazing to report it or face criminal sanctions, rejecting a claim that the law violated the Fifth Amendment's privilege against self-incrimination (*State v. Boyd,* 38 S.W.3d 155 (Tex. Crim. App. 2001)).

Although institutions may have the authority to sanction fraternities and their members for criminal conduct or violations of the campus conduct code, conduct that may be construed as antisocial but is not unlawful may be difficult to sanction. For example, some public institutions have undertaken to prohibit such fraternity activities as theme parties with ethnic or gender overtones or offensive speech. These proscriptions, however, may run afoul of the First Amendment's free speech guarantees. For example, George Mason University sanctioned Sigma Chi fraternity for holding an "ugly woman contest," a fundraising activity in which fraternity members dressed as caricatures of various types of women, including an offensive caricature of a black woman. (For a discussion of this case, see Section 9.6.) The fraternity sued the university under 42 U.S.C. § 1983 (see this book, Section 3.5), alleging a violation of its rights under the First and Fourteenth Amendments. In *Iota Xi Chapter of Sigma Chi Fraternity v. George Mason University,* 993 F.2d 386 (4th Cir. 1993), a federal appellate court affirmed an award of summary judgment to the fraternity on the grounds that the skit was "expressive entertainment" and "expressive conduct," both protected under First Amendment jurisprudence.

Although colleges are limited in their ability to sanction fraternities for offensive speech (or expressive conduct), they can hold individual student members to the same code of conduct expected of all students, particularly with regard to social activities and the use of alcohol. The complexity of balancing the need for a college to regulate fraternal organizations with its potential liability for their unlawful acts is the subject of the next subsection.

10.2.3. Institutional liability for the acts of fraternal organizations.

Despite the fact that fraternal organizations are separate legal entities, colleges and universities have faced legal liability from injured students, parents of students injured or killed as a result of fraternity activity, or victims of violence related to fraternity activities.[11] Because most claims are brought under state tort law theories, the response of the courts has not been completely consistent. The various decisions suggest, however, that colleges and universities can limit their liability in these situations but that fraternities and their members face increased liability, particularly for actions that courts view as intentional or reckless.

As discussed in Section 3.3, liability may attach if a judge or jury finds that the college owed an individual a duty of care, then breached that duty, and that the breach was the proximate cause of the injury. Because colleges are legally separate entities from fraternal organizations, the college owes fraternities, their members, and others only the ordinary duty of care to avoid injuring others. But in some cases courts have found either that a special relationship exists between the college and the injured student or that the college has assumed a duty to protect the student.

In *Furek v. University of Delaware,* 594 A.2d 506 (Del. 1991), the Delaware Supreme Court reversed a directed verdict for the university and ordered a new trial on the issue of liability in a lawsuit by a student injured during a hazing incident. The court noted the following factors in determining that a jury could hold the institution at least partially responsible for the injuries: (1) The university owned the land on which the fraternity house was located, although it did not own the house. The injury occurred in the house. (2) The university prohibited hazing and was aware of earlier hazing incidents by this fraternity. The court said that the likelihood of hazing was foreseeable, as was the likelihood of injury as a result of hazing.

While *Furek* may be an anomaly among the cases in which colleges are sued for negligence (see subsection 3.3.2.4), the opinion suggests some of the dangers of institutional attempts to regulate the conduct of fraternities or their members—for instance, by assuming duties of inspecting kitchens or houses, requiring that fraternities have faculty or staff advisers employed by the college, providing police or security services for off-campus houses, or assisting these organizations in dealing with local municipal authorities. Such actions may suggest to juries deliberating a student's negligence claim that the institution had assumed a duty of supervision (see Gulland & Powell, *Colleges, Fraternities and Sororities,* cited in Section 10.2.2).

---

[11]Cases and authorities are collected in Cheryl M. Bailey, Annot., "Tort Liability of College, University, or Fraternity or Sorority for Injury or Death of Member or Prospective Member by Hazing or Initiation Activity," 68 A.L.R.4th 228.

Colleges and universities have been codefendants with fraternities in several cases. In most of these cases, the institution has escaped liability. For example, in *Thomas v. Lamar University-Beaumont,* 830 S.W.2d 217 (Tex. Ct. App. 1992), the mother of a student who died as a result of pledge hazing sued both the fraternity and the university, which owned the track that was used during the hazing incident. The plaintiff asserted that the university had waived its sovereign immunity because it had failed to supervise those who used its track. The trial court determined that the university had no duty of supervision and awarded summary judgment for the university. The appellate court affirmed.

In *Estate of Hernandez v. Board of Regents,* 838 P.2d 1283 (Ariz. Ct. App. 1991), the personal representative of a man killed in an automobile accident caused by an intoxicated fraternity member sued the University of Arizona and the fraternity. The plaintiff asserted that the university was negligent in continuing to lease the fraternity house to the house corporation when it knew that the fraternity served alcohol to students who were under the legal drinking age of twenty-one.

The plaintiff cited the "Greek Relationship Statement," which required all fraternities to participate in an alcohol awareness educational program, as evidence of the university's assumption of a duty to supervise. The statement also required an upper-division student to be assigned to each fraternal organization to educate its members about responsible conduct relating to alcohol. Furthermore, the university employed a staff member who was responsible for administering its policies on the activities of fraternities and sororities. Despite these attempts to suggest that the university had assumed a duty to supervise the activities of fraternities, the court applied Arizona's social host law, which absolved both the fraternity and the university of liability and affirmed the trial court's award of summary judgment.

The Supreme Court of Arizona reversed the trial court's award of summary judgment to the defendant fraternity and the individual fraternity members and pledges (866 P.2d 1330 (Ariz. 1994)). The court said that the lower courts had misinterpreted Arizona's social host law. It did not immunize nonlicensees (social hosts, as compared with bar owners) who served individuals who were under the legal drinking age. The immunity, said the court, applies only to entities that are licensed to serve alcohol, not social hosts. Moreover, the court also ruled that state tort law provided a liability theory for one who provides alcohol to an underage individual who then drives a car, stating that "a minor is similar to an adult who has diminished judgment and capacity to control his alcohol consumption" (866 P.2d at 1341).

On remand, the trial court entered summary judgment in favor of the national fraternity and various individual members and pledges of the local chapter. The appellate court then reversed the summary judgments that had been granted the individual fraternity members and pledges, noting that a jury could find that each individual knew that alcohol would be served to minors, and that his contribution to the fund to purchase the alcohol made him a participant in an illegal venture. Even those pledges who had not yet contributed to the fund were participants in the illegal venture, said the appellate court (924

P.2d 1036 (Ariz. Ct. App. 1995)). Regarding the national fraternity, the appellate court stated:

> The national fraternity, having sponsored what amounts to a group of local drinking clubs, cannot disclaim responsibility for the risks of what it has sponsored. . . . That a duty exists in this circumstance was implicitly admitted by the act of the national fraternity in sending to local chapters instructions to abide by local laws and university regulations in serving alcohol at chapter functions. . . . The argument that the national fraternity had no power to control the activities of the local chapter or its members is belied by the much stricter alcohol policy adopted by the local chapter at the request of the national after the incident in this case [924 P.2d at 1038–39].

The court nevertheless affirmed summary judgment for the national fraternity on other grounds, including *respondeat superior* and landlord-tenant law.

The defendants appealed again, to the Arizona Supreme Court, which addressed only the arguments of the pledges. Reversing the intermediate appellate court's ruling with respect to the pledges, the Arizona Supreme Court reinstated the trial court's summary judgment on their behalf (*Hernandez-Wheeler v. Flavio,* 930 P.2d 1309 (Ariz. 1997)). The court noted that the pledges had no control over the arrangements for the party and did not contribute funds or purchase any alcohol, compared with the members of the fraternity who acted through a committee to purchase and distribute the alcohol to minors. The court therefore ruled as a matter of law that the pledges did not participate in the joint venture. The court left undisturbed the intermediate appellate court's rulings regarding the national fraternity and the individual members of the local chapter.

When the student's own behavior is a cause of the injury, the courts have typically refused to hold colleges or fraternities liable for damages. In *Whitlock v. University of Denver,* 744 P.2d 54 (Colo. 1987), the Colorado Supreme Court rejected a student's contention that the university had undertaken to regulate the use of a trampoline in the yard of a fraternity house, even though the university owned the land and had regulated other potentially dangerous activities in the past. Similarly, students injured in social events sponsored by fraternities have not prevailed when the injury was a result of the student's voluntary and intentional action. For example, in *Foster v. Purdue University,* 567 N.E.2d 865 (Ind. Ct. App. 1991), a student who became a quadriplegic after diving headfirst into a fraternity's "water slide" was unsuccessful in his suit against both the university and the fraternity of which he was a member. Similarly, in *Hughes v. Beta Upsilon Building Ass'n.,* 619 A.2d 525 (Maine 1993), a student who was paralyzed after diving into a muddy field on the fraternity's property at the University of Maine was unsuccessful because the court ruled that the Building Association, landlord for the local fraternity chapter, was not responsible for the chapter's activities.

When, however, the injury is a result of misconduct by *other* fraternity members, individual and organizational liability may attach. Particularly in cases where pledges have been forced to consume large amounts of alcohol as part of a hazing ritual, fraternities and their members have been held responsible for damages.[12] Because of the increasing tendency of plaintiffs to look to national fraternities for damages, several national fraternities have developed risk management information and training programs for local chapters. College administrators responsible for oversight of fraternal organizations should work with national fraternities to advance their mutual interest in minimizing dangerous activity, student injuries, and ensuing legal liability. Given the seriousness of injuries related to misconduct by fraternities and their members, administrators should examine their institutional regulations, their relationship or recognition statements, and their institutional code of student conduct to ascertain the extent of the college's potential liability. Educational programs regarding the responsible use of alcohol, swift disciplinary action for breaches of the code of student conduct, and monitoring (rather than regulation) of the activities of fraternal organizations may reduce the likelihood of harm to students or others and of liability for the college.

For example, a Louisiana appellate court upheld a jury award of liability against Louisiana Tech on the grounds of negligence, stemming from an injury incurred by a student who encountered hazing during the pledging process. In *Morrison v. Kappa Alpha Psi Fraternity*, 738 So. 2d 1105 (La. Ct. App. 1999), *appeal denied*, 749 So. 2d 634 (La. 1999), a student at Louisiana Tech had been beaten by the president of the local chapter of Kappa Alpha Psi during pledging activities. The student sustained serious head and neck injuries, and reported the assault to the campus police. After an investigation, both the university and the national chapter of the fraternity suspended the local chapter. The injured student sued the university, the national fraternity, the local chapter, and the assailant. A jury found the university, the national fraternity, and the assailant equally liable, and awarded $312,000 in compensatory damages. (The charges against the local chapter were dismissed on procedural grounds.) The jury found that the university owed the student a duty to protect him against the tortious actions of fellow students. The university appealed.

The appellate court affirmed the jury verdict, ruling that the university's own actions and its knowledge of previous hazing incidents by the local chapter created a special relationship between the injured student and the institution. A university official had received written and oral complaints about hazing by the local chapter, and a local judge had called the official to express his concerns about hazing by chapter members that his son had experienced. Although the

---

[12]In *Ballou v. Sigma Nu General Fraternity*, 352 S.E.2d 488 (S.C. Ct. App. 1986), a state appellate court found that the national fraternity owes a duty of care to initiates not to injure them; the court therefore held that fraternity responsible for damages related to a pledge's wrongful death from alcohol poisoning. A student who sustained serious neurological damage after forced intoxication was similarly successful in *Quinn v. Sigma Rho Chapter*, 507 N.E.2d 1193 (Ill. App. Ct. 1987), as was the father of a student who died after being forced to drink as part of an initiation ritual for the lacrosse team at Western Illinois University. In that case, the students were found liable as individuals (*Haben v. Anderson*, 597 N.E.2d 655 (Ill. App. Ct. 1993)). For a review of the potential liability of national fraternities for hazing injuries, see Note, "Alcohol and Hazing Risks in College Fraternities: Re-evaluating Vicarious and Custodial Liability of National Fraternities," 7 *Rev. Litig.* 191 (1988).

university cited the ruling of the Louisiana Supreme Court in *Pitre* (Section 3.3.2.1), which denied that the university had a duty to protect students against the dangers of sledding down a hillside, the court replied that "the pledging process to join a fraternal organization is not an activity which an adult college student would regard as hazardous." The court found that the university's prior knowledge of hazing activity and the potential dangers of hazing justified the creation of a special relationship, which thus imposed a duty on the university to monitor the chapter's behavior and to prevent further hazing incidents.

This ruling is directly contrary to a ruling by the Supreme Court of Idaho, which rejected the "special relationship" standard in *Coghlan v. Beta Theta Pi et al.,* 987 P.2d 300 (Idaho 1999). In *Coghlan,* a student at the University of Idaho sued three national fraternities whose local chapter parties she had attended, her own sorority, and the university for injuries she sustained when, after becoming intoxicated at fraternity parties, she returned to her sorority house and fell off a third-floor fire escape. She sought to hold the university liable under the "special relationship" doctrine, arguing that such a relationship created a duty to protect her from the risks associated with her own intoxication. The court rejected that claim, citing *Beach* and *Bradshaw* (Section 3.3.2). But the court was somewhat more sympathetic to the plaintiff's claim that the university had assumed a duty to the student because of its own behavior. The student argued that because two university employees were present at one of the fraternity parties and should have known that underage students were being served alcohol, the university had assumed a duty to protect her. Although the court declined to conclude as a matter of law that the university had assumed such a duty, it remanded the case for further litigation, overturning the trial court's dismissal of the action.

The majority rule, however, appears still to be that the college has no duty to protect an individual from injury resulting from a student's or fraternal organization's misconduct. For example, in *Lloyd v. Alpha Phi Alpha and Cornell University,* 1999 U.S. Dist. LEXIS 906 (N.D.N.Y., January 26, 1999), a student injured during hazing by a fraternity sued Cornell under three theories: negligent supervision and control, premises liability, and breach of implied contract. The court rejected all three claims. With respect to the negligent supervision claim, the court ruled that, despite the fact that Cornell published materials about the dangers of hazing and provided training to fraternities to help them improve the pledging process, it had not assumed a duty to supervise the student-plaintiff and prevent him from participating in the pledging process because "this involvement does not rise to the level of encouraging and monitoring pledge participation." The court rejected the plaintiff's premises liability claim because it found that Cornell had no knowledge that recent hazing activities had taken place in the fraternity house (which Cornell owned). The local chapter had been forbidden by the national fraternity from taking in new members, so Cornell was entitled to presume that no pledging, and thus no hazing, was occurring. And although Cornell required fraternities to have an advisor, that did not transform the advisor into an agent of Cornell. The court rejected the breach of contract claim because the university had not promised to protect students from hazing. In fact, because hazing was a violation of Cornell's code of student conduct, it was the obligation of students, not the university, to refrain from hazing. Although Cornell argued that the plaintiff had assumed the risk of injury by participating in hazing activities, a theory that would bar a negligence claim, the court explicitly rejected this reasoning, which the Alabama Supreme Court had used in *Jones v. Kappa Alpha Order, Inc.* (Section 10.2.4), saying that New York law differed from Alabama law in this regard.

In *Rothbard v. Colgate University*, 652 N.Y.S.2d 146 (N.Y. App. Div. 1997), a New York intermediate appeals court rejected a fraternity member's claim that the university should be held liable for injuries resulting from his fall, while intoxicated, from the portico outside his window. University rules prohibited students from both underage drinking and from standing on roofs or porticos. The fraternity member claimed that the university should have been aware that both policies were routinely violated at the fraternity house and that the university's failure to enforce its own rules caused his injuries. The court held that the inclusion of rules in the student handbook did not impose a duty upon the university to supervise the plaintiff and take affirmative steps to prevent him from violating the rules. Quite succinctly, the court held that an institution has no duty to shield students from their own dangerous activities.

Although, for the most part, colleges appear to be shielded from a duty to supervise students and fraternal organizations, they may face liability under landlord-tenant law. A recent ruling by the Supreme Court of Nebraska held that the university has a duty to students to protect them from foreseeable risks when those students live in campus housing. In *Knoll v. Board of Regents of the University of Nebraska*, 601 N.W.2d 757 (1999), the state supreme court did not discuss the special relationship theory, but rather, the duty of a landowner to an invitee. In this case, which is discussed more fully in Section 8.6.2, a pledge was injured as the result of a fraternity's hazing activities. The court's analysis focused primarily on the fact that the student was abducted on university property, that the university considered fraternity houses to be student housing units that were subject to regulation by the university, and that university policy required that the plaintiff live in a university housing unit. The court ruled that the university had notice of earlier hazing activities by members of other fraternities, and also had notice of several criminal incidents perpetrated by members of the fraternity that abducted the plaintiff. Therefore, said the court, the abduction and hazing of the plaintiff were foreseeable and created "a landowner-invitee duty to students to take reasonable steps to protect" them against such actions and the resultant harm. The court returned the case to the trial court for determination of whether the university breached its duty to act reasonably and whether the university's inaction was the proximate cause of the plaintiff's injury.[13]

---

[13]For a case in which a court rejected a student's attempt to hold both the university and the fraternity responsible for a sexual assault that occurred in an off-campus house rented by a group of fraternity members, but not leased or owned by either the fraternity or the university, see *Ostrander v. Duggan*, 341 F.3d 745 (8th Cir. 2003).

Given the volume of litigation by students and others who allege injuries as a result of the actions of local fraternities or their members, colleges and national fraternities—both of which have been found liable in several of these cases— should work to reduce the amount of underage drinking and to educate students about the dangers of hazing. (These and other suggestions are contained in Gregory E. Rutledge, "Hell Night Hath No Fury Like a Pledge Scorned . . . and Injured: Hazing Litigation in U.S. Colleges and Universities," 25 *J. Coll. & Univ. Law* 361 (1998).)

10.2.4. Liability of fraternal organizations or their members. Even if a college or university is not sued, fraternities and their members are facing litigation by students, the parents of students who died as a result of hazing incidents, or other individuals who were injured as a result of social events or hazing by members of fraternal organizations. The cases are fact sensitive, and often turn on whether the court views the excessive drinking or otherwise dangerous behavior as voluntary on the part of the injured student or coerced as part of a hazing ritual. Most of the cases involve excessive alcohol consumption, often by underage students.

The social host and alcohol control laws, which vary by state, cover some of the legal issues related to a fraternal organization's liability for injuries resulting from serving alcohol at a fraternity.[14] Where a first-year coed was sexually assaulted by an alumni member in a fraternity house after a homecoming party at Indiana University, the court held that the local fraternity chapter and the national fraternity had no duty to protect the invitee from sexual assault, nor was the local chapter liable under Indiana's Dram Shop Act (subsection 3.3.2.4). The court held that the attack was not foreseeable merely because alcohol was served to the alumni member, and that there was no actual evidence that the alumni member drank beer provided by the fraternity (*Motz v. Johnson*, 651 N.E.2d 1163 (Ind. App. 1995)). On appeal, the Indiana Supreme Court upheld the Dram Shop ruling for the fraternities, but reversed the trial court's summary judgment award on the issue of duty (*Delta Tau Delta v. Johnson*, 712 N.E.2d 968 (Ind. 1999)). The fraternity did have a duty to an invitee to exercise reasonable care for her protection, said the court. Because of similar assaults at the fraternity house in the two previous years, and because the national fraternity had sent educational information about the correlation between underage drinking at fraternities and assault, a jury could reasonably decide that the assault on the plaintiff was foreseeable, and thus summary judgment was inappropriate.

Cases in which injured parties attempt to hold fraternities liable seem to turn on whether the dangerous conduct (usually, but not always, excessive drinking) was voluntary or coerced. If the conduct occurred during hazing, a

---

[14]If fraternity members serve alcohol to underage guests, they may face criminal liability. Cases and authorities are collected at Milton Roberts, Annot., "Criminal Liability of Member or Agent of Private Club or Association, or of Owner or Lessor of Its Premises, for Violation of State or Local Liquor or Gambling Laws Thereon," 98 A.L.R.3d 694. For a summary of the *Hernandez* case, in which the Arizona Supreme Court interpreted its social host law to hold fraternity members who purchased alcohol for underage drinkers liable, see Section 10.2.3.

court may conclude that it was coerced. For example, in *Oja v. Grand Chapter of Theta Chi Fraternity, Inc.,* 684 N.Y.S.2d 344 (N.Y. Sup. Ct. App. Div. 1999), the parents of a student who died after consuming excessive amounts of alcohol during a hazing ritual sued the local chapter and several of its members. The appellate court affirmed the trial court's refusal to dismiss the parents' claims of negligence and violations of the anti-hazing statute. The court ruled that the plaintiffs had alleged facts that could support a finding that the deceased student's intoxication was not voluntary, and that the failure of the fraternity members to care for the student after he became intoxicated could also warrant a finding of liability.

In *Nisbet v. Bucher,* 949 S.W.2d 111 (Mo. Ct. App. 1997), parents of a student who died after a hazing ritual filed a wrongful death suit against the fraternities and another association, alleging that the students forced their son to consume alcohol, including a "heated preparation of grain alcohol and peas"; that they coerced him to drink until he became intoxicated and even after he became unconscious; and that they left him face down and unattended, delaying medical treatment for him. The appellate court rejected the defendants' argument that the student was the proximate cause of his own death, noting that participation in initiation activities was required for new members, and that the student was pressured to drink by the organization's members.

But not all courts view hazing as coerced behavior. In *Ex Parte Barran* (*Jones v. Kappa Alpha Order*), 730 So. 2d 203 (Ala. 1998), the Supreme Court of Alabama rejected a former Auburn University student's tort claims against a fraternity he had pledged. The student had claimed negligence, assault and battery, negligent supervision, conspiracy, and the tort of outrage. He had endured the hazing for an entire academic year and had been suspended at the end of his first year for poor academic performance. The court noted that the student submitted voluntarily to the hazing, that 20 to 40 percent of the pledge class had withdrawn from the fraternity because of the hazing, and that the student had lied to university officials and to his parents when asked whether he was being hazed. Because the student could have stopped the hazing by withdrawing from the fraternity, the court ruled that he assumed the risk of injury by remaining.

In *Kenner v. Kappa Alpha Psi Fraternity,* 808 A.2d 178 (Pa. Super. 2002), a student seriously injured when he was beaten during a hazing ritual sued both the national fraternity and the members of the local chapter who beat him. Although the trial court awarded summary judgment to the fraternity and its members, the state appellate court ruled that the case must go to trial. The appellate court found that the fraternity owed the student a duty to protect him from harm because the national fraternity knew that there had been earlier incidents of hazing by the local chapter. The national fraternity had a policy against hazing, which created a duty to protect initiates from that behavior. The court went on to rule that the fraternity had not breached its duty to the plaintiff because it had suspended the local chapter for two years for violations of the national fraternity's hazing policy, which the members understood was punishment for previous hazing incidents. But the court ruled that the fraternity's chapter advisor may have breached his individual duty to protect the plaintiff from injury because the advisor had not warned chapter members against hazing nor discussed the national fraternity's policy against hazing. Prohibition of hazing by another national fraternity resulted in a summary judgment in its favor in *Walker v. Phi Beta Sigma Fraternity*, 706 So. 2d 525 (La. Ct. App. 1997); the court ruled that the national was not in a position to control the day-to-day activities of its local chapters.

The Michigan Court of Appeals held that the Tau Kappa Epsilon national fraternity was not liable for a fatal accident involving alcohol supplied by the local chapter. In *Colangelo v. Theta Psi Chapter of Tau Kappa Epsilon*, 517 N.W.2d 289 (Mich. Ct. App. 1994), the court reasoned that the national fraternity had no duty to supervise the local chapter's daily activities, and that the national fraternity could not have foreseen that the local chapter would have a party that would result in intoxication and injury. The court further reasoned that the national fraternity was ill equipped to supervise the drinking and other activities carried on by local chapters, and that to impose a duty would result in fundamentally changing the role of national fraternities "from an instructor of the principles, rituals, and traditions of the fraternity to a central planning and policing authority" (517 N.W.2d at 292). A similar result, using similar reasoning, was reached in *Walker v. Phi Beta Sigma Fraternity*, 706 So. 2d 525 (La. Ct. App. 1997).

If a fraternal organization has undertaken to protect a pledge or member from harm, failure to do so may breach a duty. The Idaho Supreme Court reversed a summary judgment ruling for a sorority and remanded for trial on the issue of whether the sorority had assumed a duty to protect one of its new members. The plaintiff, a student at the University of Idaho, had fallen out of a third-story window of her sorority house after returning, highly intoxicated, from two fraternity parties at which alcohol was served. Because the sorority had encouraged the plaintiff, who was too young to drink legally, to attend the fraternity parties, had assigned an older sorority member as a "guardian angel" to supervise her at the party (but who refused to do so), and because sorority members had escorted the plaintiff home and left her, unattended and still intoxicated, a material issue of fact existed as to whether the sorority voluntarily assumed a duty of reasonable care to supervise and protect the plaintiff until she was no longer intoxicated (*Coghlan v. Beta Theta Pi Fraternity*, 987 P.2d 300 (Idaho 1999)).

Plaintiffs seeking to hold fraternal organizations liable for injuries to members have not been successful when the conduct was not coerced. For example, in *Prime v. Beta Gamma Chapter of Pi Kappa Alpha*, 47 P.3d 402 (Kan. 2002), the Kansas Supreme Court dismissed a negligence action against the local fraternity and several individual members. The plaintiff voluntarily drank the alcohol that led to his injuries, according to the court, and because he was not required to do so, liability did not attach. Similarly, the parents of a college junior who drowned in a river after drinking beer at a fraternity party were unsuccessful in holding the local and national fraternities responsible. In *Rocha v. Pi Kappa Alpha*, 69 S.W.3d 315 (Tex. Ct. App. 2002), the court ruled that the fraternities owed no duty to the deceased student; there was no evidence that the fraternity had planned the swimming trip, and simply because some of the individuals who participated in the swimming outing were fraternity members did not make the event a fraternity-sponsored social occasion. Nor, according to the Iowa Supreme Court, does a special relationship exist between a fraternity and one of its members if the misconduct (here, excessive drinking) was not part of an initiation ritual or hazing (*Garofalo v. Lambda Chi Alpha,* 616 N.W.2d 647 (Iowa 2000)).

In addition to being sued under negligence theories, a few fraternities have faced litigation brought on the grounds of premises liability. For example, in *Brakeman v. Theta Lambda Chapter of Pi Kappa Alpha,* 2002 Iowa App. LEXIS 1258 (Iowa Ct. App. 2002) (unpublished), a student who fell out of the upper window of a bar at which a fraternity was sponsoring a party sued the fraternity. The court of appeals reversed a jury verdict for the plaintiff, ruling that the fraternity did not have the requisite control of the premises to incur liability, as the staff of the bar were present during the party and had the responsibility to ensure that they served only those of legal age. Similarly, an attempt by a woman assaulted at an off-campus house rented by several fraternity members to hold the fraternity responsible under a premises liability theory failed because the fraternity did not own or control the premises (*Ostrander v. Duggan,* 341 F.3d 745 (8th Cir. 2003)).

The U.S. Department of Justice has determined that fraternity or sorority houses owned and operated by a college or university are covered by Title III of the Americans With Disabilities Act (see Section 13.2.11). (See Technical Assistance Letter #488 (May 2002), available at http://www.usdoj.gov/crt/foia/talindex.htm.) This would require a new fraternity or sorority house to be constructed in compliance with Title III access specifications and would also be relevant to renovation of such a building.

Sec. 10.3. The Student Press

10.3.1. General principles. In general, student newspapers and other student publications have the same rights and responsibilities as other student organizations on campus (see Section 10.1 above), and the student journalists have the same rights and responsibilities as other students.[15] The rights of student press organizations and their staffs (and contributors) will vary considerably, however, depending on whether the institution is public or private. This is because the key federal constitutional rights of freedom of the press and freedom of association protect the student press in its relations with public institutions; in private institutions these constitutional rights do not apply (see Section 1.5.2), and the student press' relationship with the institution is primarily a contractual relationship that may vary from institution to institution (see Section 8.1.3).[16]

---

[15]Regarding responsibilities, however, student journalists may be subject to ethical obligations that differ from those of other students. For examples and discussion, see Gary Pavela, "The Ethical Principles for College Journalists," *Synthesis, Law & Pol'y. Higher Educ.* Vol. 15, no. 2 (Fall 2003), pp. 1069–1070, 1088.

[16]If a student publication at a private institution is restricted by an outside governmental entity, however, it is protected by federal constitutional rights in much the same way as a student publication at a public institution would be protected. Examples would include a libel suit in which a private institution's student newspaper is a defendant subject to a court's jurisdiction (see Section 10.3.6 below) and a search of the office of a private institution's student newspaper by local police officers (see Section 11.5).

Sections 10.3.2 through 10.3.6 below focus primarily on the First Amendment free press rights of student publications at public institutions. Section 10.3.7 focuses on private institutions. Other First Amendment issues pertinent to student publications are discussed in Sections 8.1.4, 8.5.1, 9.5.6, and 9.6.

Fourth Amendment rights regarding searches and seizures may also become implicated in a public institution's relationship with student publications. In *Desyllas v. Bernstine,* 351 F.3d 934 (9th Cir. 2003), for example, the editor of a student newspaper claimed that the institution's public safety director and a campus police officer had violated his constitutional rights when they sought to recover some missing confidential student records that they believed were in the editor's possession. They had temporarily secured the newspaper office by locking the door with a "clam shell" lock; had allegedly detained the editor temporarily for questioning about the missing records; and had then convinced the editor to surrender the records. The court held that, under the circumstances (set out at length in the opinion), none of the actions—the locking of the office, the alleged detention of the editor, nor the recovery of the records—was an unlawful "seizure" under the Fourth Amendment. The court determined, moreover, that the First Amendment generally does not provide any additional protections from searches and seizures in such circumstances beyond what the Fourth Amendment already provides (see *Zurcher v. Stanford Daily,* 436 U.S. 547 (1978), discussed in Section 11.5), and that the student editor's position with the student newspaper did not accord him any greater rights under the Fourth Amendment than any other student would have in similar circumstances. (In circumstances in which a seizure directly "interfere[s] with the [newspaper's] publication of the news" (*Desyllas,* 351 F.3d at 942), however, the First Amendment would provide additional protections; see, for example, *Kincaid v. Gibson,* discussed in Section 10.3.3 below.)[17]

Freedom of the press is perhaps the most staunchly guarded of all First Amendment rights. The right to a free press protects student publications from virtually all encroachments on their editorial prerogatives by public institutions. In a series of forceful cases, courts have implemented this student press freedom, using First Amendment principles akin to those that would protect a big-city daily from government interference.[18]

The chief concern of the First Amendment's free press guarantee is censorship. Thus, whenever a public institution seeks to control or coercively influence the content of a student publication, it will have a legal problem

---

[17]For extensive resources on the rights of student journalists, see the Web site of the Student Press Law Center, available at http://www.splc.org.

[18]Cases are collected in Donald T. Kramer, Annot., "Validity, Under Federal Constitution, of Public School or State College Regulation of Student Newspapers, Magazines, or Other Publications—Federal Cases," 16 A.L.R. Fed. 182. The more recent cases in this line do suggest that an exception to the principle of broad protection may operate if the student publication is part of a course or other curriculum-related activity, or is otherwise characterized as a "non-public forum." See, for example, *Hosty v. Carter,* 412 F.3d 731 (7th Cir. 2005) (*en banc*), discussed in Section 10.3.3 below.

on its hands.[19] The problem will be exacerbated if the institution imposes a prior restraint on publication—that is, a prohibition imposed in advance of publication rather than a sanction imposed subsequently (see generally Section 9.5.4). Conversely, the institution's legal problems will be alleviated if the institution's regulations do not affect the message, ideas, or subject matter of the publication and do not permit prior restraints on publication. Such "neutral" regulations might involve, for example, the allocation of office space, procedures for payment of printing costs, or limitations on the time, place, or manner of distribution.

10.3.2. Mandatory student fee allocations to student publications.

Objecting students have no more right to challenge the allocation of mandatory student fees to student newspapers that express a particular viewpoint than they have to challenge such allocations to other student organizations expressing particular viewpoints. These issues are now controlled, at least for public institutions and their recognized student organizations that produce publications, by the principles established by the U.S. Supreme Court in *Board of Regents, University of Wisconsin v. Southworth,* discussed in Section 10.1.2 above. Long before *Southworth,* however, lower federal courts had protected student newspapers from losing their student fee allocations because they had editorial viewpoints with which other students disagreed.

In *Larson v. Board of Regents of the University of Nebraska,* 204 N.W.2d 568 (Neb. 1973), for example, the court rejected a student challenge to mandatory fee allocations for a student newspaper whose views the students opposed. The next year, in *Arrington v. Taylor,* 380 F. Supp. 1348 (M.D.N.C. 1974), *affirmed without published opinion,* 526 F.2d 587 (4th Cir. 1975), the court rejected a challenge to the University of North Carolina's use of mandatory fees to subsidize its campus newspaper, the *Daily Tar Heel.* Since the paper did not purport to speak for the entire student body and its existence did not inhibit students from expressing or supporting opposing viewpoints, the subsidy did not infringe First Amendment rights. Eight years later, the same court reconsidered and reaffirmed *Arrington* in *Kania v. Fordham,* 702 F.2d 475 (4th Cir. 1983); and in 1992 another U.S. Court of Appeals (citing *Kania*) reached the same result (*Hays County Guardian v. Supple,* 969 F.2d 111, 123 (5th Cir. 1992)).

Stanley v. Magrath, 719 F.2d 279 (8th Cir. 1983), provides another instructive example of a court rejecting an attempt to terminate a student newspaper's mandatory fee allocations. The University of Minnesota had changed the funding mechanism of one of its student newspapers by eliminating mandatory

---

[19]Legal problems may also arise if a public institution seeks to regulate the distribution, on campus, of newspapers published off campus and not recognized or supported by the institution. Students may claim First Amendment rights to obtain such newspapers. In *Hays County Guardian v. Supple,* 969 F.2d 111 (5th Cir. 1992), for example, the court invalidated restrictions on distribution of a free newspaper distributed throughout the county. Other problems may arise when public institutions prohibit the sale of publications on campus; see *Spartacus Youth League v. Board of Trustees of Illinois Industrial University,* 502 F. Supp. 789, 799–803, 805–6 (appendix) (N.D. Ill. 1980). These types of problems would now likely be resolved using principles developed by the U.S. Supreme Court in *City of Cincinnati v. Discovery Network,* 507 U.S. 410 (1993).

student fees and instead allowing students to elect individually whether or not a portion of their fees would go to the *Minnesota Daily.* Implementation of this refundable fee system came on the heels of intense criticism from students, faculty, religious groups, and the state legislature over a satirical "Humor Issue" of the paper. Although the university argued that the change in funding mechanism came in response to general student objections about having to fund the paper (which the court assumed, *arguendo,* would be a legitimate motive for the change in funding), the court pointed to evidence suggesting that, at least in part, the change was impermissibly in retaliation for the content of the Humor Issue. Holding that the school failed to carry its burden of showing that the permissible motive would have produced the same result, even in the absence of the impermissible retaliatory motive, the court struck down the funding change.

Shortly before its decision in the *Southworth* case, the U.S. Supreme Court decided *Rosenberger v. Rector and Visitors of University of Virginia,* 515 U.S. 819 (1995) (further discussed in Section 10.1.5 above), its first pronouncement on mandatory student fee allocations for student publications. The Court's reasoning in *Rosenberg* is consistent with the principles later developed in *Southworth.* But *Rosenberger* also went beyond the analysis in *Southworth,* and in the earlier lower court cases, in two important respects: (1) *Rosenberger* focuses specifically on viewpoint discrimination issues that may arise when a university or its student government decides to fund some student publications but not others; and (2) *Rosenberger* addresses the special situation that arises when a student publication has an editorial policy based on a religious perspective.

The plaintiffs in *Rosenberger* were students who published a magazine titled "Wide Awake: A Christian Perspective at the University of Virginia." As described by the U.S. Supreme Court:

> The paper's Christian viewpoint was evident from the first issue, in which its editors wrote that the journal "offers a Christian perspective on both personal and community issues, especially those relevant to college students at the University of Virginia." The editors committed the paper to a two-fold mission: "to challenge Christians to live, in word and deed, according to the faith they proclaim and to encourage students to consider what a personal relationship with Jesus Christ means." The first issue had articles about racism, crisis pregnancy, stress, prayer, C. S. Lewis' ideas about evil and free will, and reviews of religious music. In the next two issues, Wide Awake featured stories about homosexuality, Christian missionary work, and eating disorders, as well as music reviews and interviews with University professors. Each page of Wide Awake, and the end of each article or review, is marked by a cross. The advertisements carried in Wide Awake also reveal the Christian perspective of the journal. For the most part, the advertisers are churches, centers for Christian study, or Christian bookstores [515 U.S. at 826].

The university's guidelines for student fee allocations ("Guidelines") permitted "student news, information, opinion, entertainment, or academic communications media groups," among other groups, to apply for allocations that the university would then use to pay each group's bills from outside contractors that printed its publication. The Guidelines provided, however, that student groups could not use fee allocations to support "religious activity," defined as activity that "primarily promotes or manifests a particular belief in or about a deity or an ultimate reality." Fifteen student publications received funding, but the Wide Awake publication did not because the student council determined that it was a religious activity. Wide Awake's members challenged this denial as a violation of their free speech and press rights under the First Amendment.

The U.S. Supreme Court upheld Wide Awake's claim because the university's action was a kind of censorship based on the publication's viewpoint. The Court then addressed the additional considerations that arose in the case because Wide Awake published *religious* viewpoints rather than *secular* viewpoints based on politics or culture. Since Wide Awake sought to use public (university) funds to subsidize religious viewpoints, the First Amendment establishment clause also became a focus of the analysis. The Court, however, rejected the argument that funding Wide Awake would violate the establishment clause (see the discussion in Section 10.1.5 above). Concluding that the university funding would be "neutral toward religion," the Court emphasized that this funding was part of a broad program that "support[ed] various student enterprises, including the publication of newspapers, in recognition of the diversity and creativity of student life." The Court also emphasized that:

> [the university's Guidelines] have a separate classification for, and do not make third-party payments on behalf of, "religious organizations," which are those "whose purpose is to practice a devotion to an acknowledged ultimate reality or deity." The category of support here is for "student news, information, opinion, entertainment, or academic communications media groups," of which Wide Awake was 1 of 15 in the 1990 school year. WAP did not seek a subsidy because of its Christian editorial viewpoint; it sought funding as a student journal, which it was [515 U.S. at 840].

10.3.3. Permissible scope of institutional regulation. Three classic 1970s cases—the *Joyner, Bazaar,* and *Schiff* cases, discussed below—illustrate the strength and scope of First Amendment protection accorded the student press in public institutions. These cases also illustrate the different techniques by which an institution may seek to regulate a student newspaper, and they explain when and why such techniques may be considered unconstitutional censorship.

In *Joyner v. Whiting*, 477 F.2d 456 (4th Cir. 1973), the president of North Carolina Central University had permanently terminated university financial support for the campus newspaper. The president asserted that the newspaper had printed articles urging segregation and had advocated the maintenance of an all-black university. The court held that the president's action violated the student staff's First Amendment rights:

> It may well be that a college need not establish a campus newspaper, or, if a paper has been established, the college may permanently discontinue publication for reasons wholly unrelated to the First Amendment. But if a college has a

student newspaper, its publication cannot be suppressed because college officials dislike its editorial comment. . . .

The principles reaffirmed in *Healy* [see *Healy v. James,* discussed in Section 10.1 above] have been extensively applied to strike down every form of censorship of student publications at state-supported institutions. Censorship of constitutionally protected expression cannot be imposed by suspending the editors, suppressing circulation, requiring imprimatur of controversial articles, excising repugnant materials, withdrawing financial support, or asserting any other form of censorial oversight based on the institution's power of the purse [477 F.2d at 460].

The president also asserted, as grounds for terminating the paper's support, that the newspaper would employ only blacks and would not accept advertising from white-owned businesses. While such practices were not protected by the First Amendment and could be enjoined, the court held that the permanent cut-off of funds was an inappropriate remedy for such problems because of its broad effect on all future ability to publish.

In *Bazaar v. Fortune,* 476 F.2d 570, *rehearing,* 489 F.2d 225 (5th Cir. 1973), the University of Mississippi had halted publication of an issue of *Images,* a student literary magazine written and edited with the advice of a professor from the English department, because a university committee had found two stories objectionable on grounds of "taste." While the stories concerned interracial marriage and black pride, the university disclaimed objection on this basis and relied solely on the stories' inclusion of "earthy" language. The university argued that the stories would stir an adverse public reaction, and, since the magazine had a faculty adviser, their publication would reflect badly on the university. The court held that the involvement of a faculty adviser did not enlarge the university's authority over the magazine's content. The university's action violated the First Amendment because

speech cannot be stifled by the state merely because it would perhaps draw an adverse reaction from the majority of people, be they politicians or ordinary citizens, and newspapers. To come forth with such a rule would be to virtually read the First Amendment out of the Constitution and, thus, cost this nation one of its strongest tenets [476 F.2d at 579].

Schiff v. Williams, 519 F.2d 257 (5th Cir. 1975), concerned the firing of the editors of the *Atlantic Sun,* the student newspaper of Florida Atlantic University. The university's president based his action on the poor quality of the newspaper and on the editors' failure to respect university guidelines regarding the publication of the paper. The court characterized the president's action as a form of direct control over the paper's content and held that such action violated the First Amendment. Poor quality, even though it "could embarrass, and perhaps bring some element of disrepute to the school," was not a permissible basis on which to limit free speech. The university president in *Schiff* attempted to bolster his case by arguing that the student editors were employees of the state. The court did not give the point the attention it deserved. Presumably, if a public institution chose to operate its own publication (such as an alumni magazine) and hired a student editor, the institution could fire that student if the technical quality of his or her work was inadequate. The situation in *Schiff* did not fit this model, however, because the newspaper was not set up as the university's own publication. Rather, it was recognized by the university as a publication primarily by and for the student body, and the student editors were paid from a special student activities fee fund under the general control of the student government association.

While arrangements such as those in *Schiff* may insulate a student newspaper from university control, it might nevertheless be argued that a newspaper's receipt of mandatory student fee allocations, and its use of university facilities and equipment, could constitute state action (see Section 1.5.2), thus subjecting the student editors themselves to First Amendment restraints when dealing with other students and with outsiders. In *Mississippi Gay Alliance v. Goudelock,* 536 F.2d 1073 (5th Cir. 1976), however, the court rejected a state action argument (over a strong dissent) and upheld a student newspaper's refusal to print an ad for a gay counseling service. And in *Sinn v. The Daily Nebraskan,* 829 F.2d 662 (8th Cir. 1987), the court held that the newspaper was not engaged in state action when it refused to print sexual preferences in classified ads. In *Gay and Lesbian Students Ass'n. v. Gohn,* 850 F.3d 361 (8th Cir. 1988), however, the court distinguished *Sinn* and found state action in a situation where the student organization's activity was "not free from university control." Later, in *Leeds v. Meltz,* 85 F.3d 51 (2d Cir. 1996) (discussed further in Section 1.5.2), the court—like the courts in *Goudelock* and *Sinn*—refused to find that a student newspaper was engaged in state action when it rejected an advertisement submitted to the paper.

In a more recent and highly important case, *Kincaid v. Gibson,* 236 F.3d 342 (6th Cir. 2001) (*en banc*), the court reaffirmed the strong protections of these earlier cases and also confirmed that a confiscation of the printed copies of a student publication will often be considered a classic First Amendment violation. In addition, moving beyond the reasoning in the earlier cases, the court emphasized the importance of "public forum" analysis (see generally Section 9.5.2) in First Amendment cases about student publications.

Kincaid v. Gibson concerned a student yearbook, *The Thorobred,* published by students at Kentucky State University (KSU). KSU administrators had confiscated the yearbook covering the 1992–93 and the 1993–94 academic years when the printer delivered it to the university for distribution. The vice president for student affairs (Gibson) claimed that the yearbook was of poor quality and "inappropriate," citing, in particular, the failure to use the school colors on the cover, the lack of captions for many photos, the inappropriateness of the "destination unknown" theme, and the inclusion of current events unrelated to the school. The yearbook's student editor and another student sued the vice president, the president, and members of the board of trustees, claiming that the confiscation violated their First Amendment rights.

Relying in part on *Hazelwood School District v. Kuhlmeier,* 484 U.S. 260 (1988), a case about a high school newspaper, the federal district court granted the defendants' motion for summary judgment, holding that the yearbook was a "nonpublic forum" and that the university's action was consistent with the principles applicable to nonpublic forums. A three-judge panel of the Sixth Circuit upheld the district court's decision (191 F.3d 719 (6th Cir. 1999)); but on further review the full appellate court, sitting *en banc,* disagreed with the panel, reversed the district court, and ordered it to enter summary judgment for the students.

The *en banc* court applied the leading U.S. Supreme Court public forum cases but, unlike the district court and the three-judge panel, it determined that the yearbook was a "limited public forum." Specifically, the court noted that KSU had a written policy placing the yearbook under the management of the Student Publications Board (SPB) but lodging responsibility for the yearbook's content with the student editors. Although the SPB was to appoint a school employee to act as advisor of the publication, the policy provided that "[i]n order to meet the responsible standards of journalism, an advisor may require changes in the form of materials submitted by students, but such changes must deal only with the form or the time and manner of expressions rather than alteration of content." The written policy thus indicated to the court that the university's "intent" was "to create a limited public forum rather than reserve to itself the right to edit or determine [the yearbook's] content."

Following the teachings of the *Rosenberger* case (Section 10.3.2 above), the *en banc* court declined to follow the Court's decision in *Hazelwood,* the high school newspaper case. According to the court: "There can be no serious argument about the fact that, in its most basic form, the yearbook serves as a forum in which student editors present pictures, captions, and other written material, and that these materials constitute expression for purposes of the First Amendment." In particular, the yearbook was distinguishable from the newspaper in *Hazelwood* because it was not a "closely-monitored classroom activity in which an instructor assigns student editors a grade, or in which a university official edits content." Moreover, in a university setting, unlike a high school setting, the editors and readers of the yearbook "are likely to be young adults." Therefore, "there can be no justification for suppressing the yearbook on the grounds that it might be 'unsuitable for immature audiences'" (quoting *Hazelwood,* 484 U.S. at 271).

On the basis of these factors, the court concluded that the yearbook was a limited public forum open for student expression. In such a forum,

> the government may impose only reasonable time, place and manner regulations, and content-based regulations that are narrowly drawn to effectuate a compelling state interest. . . . In addition, as with all manner of fora, the government may not suppress expression on the basis that state officials oppose a speaker's view [236 F.3d at 354].

The court then found that "KSU officials ran afoul of these restrictions" when they confiscated the copies of *The Thorobred* without notification or explanation and refused to distribute them. Such action

is not a reasonable time, place, or manner regulation of expressive activity. . . .
Nor is it a narrowly crafted regulation designed to preserve a compelling state
interest. . . . [There was] no other student forum for recording words and pictures to reflect the experience of KSU students during the 1992 through 1994
school years. Indeed, the likelihood of the existence of any such alternative
forum at this late date, when virtually all of the students who were at KSU
in the early 1990s will have surely moved on, is extraordinarily slim. Accordingly,
the KSU officials' confiscation of the yearbooks violates the First Amendment,
and the university has no constitutionally valid reason to withhold distribution
of the 1992–94 *Thorobred* from KSU students from that era [236 F.3d at 354].

The *en banc* court especially emphasized that the university's confiscation
was based on the yearbook's content, and that "[c]onfiscation ranks with forced
government speech as amongst the purest forms of content alteration." According to the court:

> [T]he record makes clear that Gibson sought to regulate the content of the
> 1992–94 yearbook: in addition to complaining about the yearbook's color, lack
> of captions, and overall quality, Gibson withheld the yearbooks because she
> found the yearbook theme of "destination unknown" inappropriate. Gibson also
> disapproved of the inclusion of pictures of current events, and testified that
> "[t]here were a lot of pictures in the back of the book that . . . to me, looked like
> a *Life* magazine." . . . And after the yearbooks came back from the printer,
> Gibson complained to Cullen that "[s]everal persons have received the book,
> and are thoroughly disappointed at the quality and content." Thus, it is quite
> clear that Gibson attempted to regulate the content of *The Thorobred* once it
> was printed [236 F.3d at 354–55].

The court also determined that, even if the yearbook were a nonpublic
forum, rather than a limited public forum, the university's confiscation of the
yearbooks would still have violated the First Amendment. This was because
"suppression of the yearbook smacks of viewpoint discrimination as well," and
"government may not regulate even a nonpublic forum based upon the
speaker's viewpoint." According to the court, "[A]n editor's choice of theme, selection of particular pictures, and expression of opinions are clear examples of the
editor's viewpoint . . ." (236 F.3d at 356). (For further, detailed, discussion of
Kincaid v. Gibson, see Richard Peltz, "Censorship Tsunami Spares College
Media: To Protect Free Expression on Public Campuses, Lessons from the
'College *Hazelwood*' Case," 68 *Tenn. L. Rev.* 481 (2001).)

Thus *Kincaid,* like the earlier cases of *Joyner, Bazaar,* and *Schiff,* clearly
demonstrates the very substantial limits on administrators' authority to regulate the student press at public institutions. But these cases do not stand for the
proposition that *no* regulation is permissible. To the contrary, each case suggests
narrow grounds on which student publications can be subjected to some regulation. The *Joyner* case indicates that the student press can be prohibited from
racial discrimination in its staffing and advertising policies. *Stanley* suggests that
institutions may alter the funding mechanisms for student publications as long
as they do not do so for reasons associated with a publication's content. *Bazaar*

indicates that institutions may dissociate themselves from student publications to the extent of requiring or placing a disclaimer on the cover or format of the publication. (The court specifically approved the following disclaimer after it reheard the case: "This is not an official publication of the university.") *Schiff* suggests enigmatically that there may be "special circumstances" where administrators may regulate the press to prevent "significant disruption on the university campus or within its educational processes." And *Kincaid* indicates that institutions may impose content-neutral "time, place, and manner regulations" on the student press, and also suggests that institutions may regulate student publications that are part of a curricular activity or that are established to operate under the editorial control of the institution.

The latter points from *Kincaid* were further developed, and integrated with public forum analysis, in another highly important case decided by another U.S. Court of Appeals, also sitting *en banc*. *Hosty v. Carter,* 412 F.3d 731 (7th Cir. 2005 (*en banc*)), concerned the validity of a dean's alleged order to halt the printing of a subsidized student newspaper until she had reviewed and approved the issues. The *en banc* court used the U.S. Supreme Court's *Hazelwood* case as the "starting point" and the "framework" for its analysis. Following *Hazelwood,* the court held that, if a subsidized student newspaper falls within the category of a nonpublic forum, then it "may be open to reasonable regulation" by the institution, including content regulation imposed for "legitimate pedagogical reasons" (412 F.3d at 735, 737). The appellate court then remanded the case to the district court for further proceedings on the issue of whether the student newspaper was a nonpublic forum subject to such regulation or a public forum not subject to content regulation.

The clear lesson of the student publication cases, then, it not so much "Don't regulate" as it is "Don't censor." So long as administrators avoid censorship, there will be some room for them to regulate student publications; and, in general, they may regulate publications by student organizations or individual students in much the same way that they may regulate other expressive activities of student organizations (see Section 10.1 above) or students generally (see Section 9.5). Even content need not be totally beyond an administrator's concern. A disclaimer requirement can be imposed to avoid confusion about the publication's status within the institution. If the publication were a nonpublic forum, some content regulation for pedagogical purposes would be permissible. Advertising content in a publication may also be controlled to some extent, as discussed in subsection 10.3.4 below. Content that is obscene or libelous as defined by the U.S. Supreme Court may also be regulated, as subsections 10.3.5 and 10.3.6 below suggest. And as the *Rosenberger* case in subsection 10.3.2 above suggests, religious content may be regulated to an extent necessary to prevent establishment clause violations.

10.3.4. Advertising in student publications. In *Pittsburgh Press Co. v. Pittsburgh Commission on Human Relations,* 413 U.S. 376 (1973), the U.S. Supreme Court upheld a regulation prohibiting newspapers from publishing "help-wanted" advertisements in sex-designated columns. And in *Virginia State*

Bd. of Pharmacy v. Virginia Citizens Consumer Council, 425 U.S. 748 (1976), while invalidating a statutory ban on advertising prescription drug prices, the Court affirmed the state's authority to regulate false or misleading advertising and advertising that proposes illegal transactions. These foundational cases suggest that there is at least some narrow room within which public institutions may regulate advertising in student newspapers.

Issues regarding advertising in student newspapers are considered at length in *Lueth v. St. Clair County Community College,* 732 F. Supp. 1410 (E.D. Mich. 1990). The plaintiff, a former editor of the student newspaper, sued the college because it had prohibited the publication of ads for an off-campus nude-dancing club. Concluding that the advertising was "commercial speech" (Section 11.6.4.1) and that the student-run newspaper was a public forum (Section 9.5.2), the court applied the First Amendment standards for commercial speech set out in *Central Hudson Gas & Electric Corp. v. Public Service Commission,* 447 U.S. 557 (1980), as modified by *Board of Trustees of the State University of New York v. Fox,* 492 U.S. 469 (1989) (both discussed in Section 11.6.4.1). Although the college had substantial interests in not fostering underage drinking or the degradation of women, the court held the advertising prohibition unconstitutional because the college had no advertising guidelines or other limits on its authority that would ensure that its regulation of advertising was "narrowly tailored" to achieve its interests. (To similar effect, see *The Pitt News v. Pappert,* 379 F.3d 96 (3d Cir. 2004), in which the court held a state statute regulating alcohol beverage advertising to be unconstitutional as applied to a student newspaper.)

As the *Lueth* and *Pitt News* cases suggest, advertising of alcoholic beverages has been a particular concern for colleges and universities for many years. Advertising of tobacco products, unlawful drugs, and firearms may raise similar concerns. The validity of regulations limiting such advertising has become more doubtful since the U.S. Supreme Court's decisions in *44 Liquormart v. Rhode Island,* 517 U.S. 484 (1996), invalidating certain state restrictions on advertising of alcoholic beverages, and *Lorillard Tobacco Co. v. Reilly,* 533 U.S. 525 (2001), invalidating certain state restrictions on advertising of tobacco products. Relying on *Lorillard,* the court in *Khademi v. South Orange County Community College District,* 194 F. Supp. 2d 1011, 1028–29 (C.D. Cal. 2002), invalidated campus regulations that prohibited advertising for alcoholic beverages, tobacco products, or firearms. The court, however, did uphold a campus regulation prohibiting advertising of "illegal substances as identified by the Federal Government, and/or by the State of California," because it was limited to products made illegal by criminal law. As to tobacco, alcohol, and firearms advertising regulations, they were content-based regulations of speech that did not meet the standard of justification required by the case law. It was not enough that some of the community college district's students were underage and, therefore, prohibited by state law from purchasing these products. According to the court, "sixty-eight percent of the District's students are legally of age to buy alcohol, tobacco, and firearms products," and a complete ban on advertising these products would therefore not be narrowly tailored to effectuate the community college's legitimate interests (194 F. Supp. 2d at 1029, n.13).

10.3.5. Obscenity. It is clear that public institutions may discipline students or student organizations for having published obscene material. Public institutions may even halt the publication of such material if they do so under carefully constructed and conscientiously followed procedural safeguards. A leading case is *Antonelli v. Hammond,* 308 F. Supp. 1329 (D. Mass. 1970), which invalidated a system of prior review and approval by a faculty advisory board, because the system did not place the burden of proving obscenity on the board, or provide for a prompt review and internal appeal of the board's decisions, or provide for a prompt final judicial determination. *Baughman v. Freienmuth,* 478 F.2d 1345 (4th Cir. 1973), which sets out prior review requirements in the secondary school context, is also illustrative. Clearly, the constitutional requirements for prior review regarding obscenity are stringent, and the creation of a constitutionally acceptable system is a very difficult and delicate task. (For U.S. Supreme Court teaching on prior review, see *Southeastern Promotions, Ltd. v. Conrad,* 420 U.S. 546 (1975).)

Moreover, institutional authority extends only to material that is actually obscene, and the definition or identification of obscenity is, at best, an exceedingly difficult proposition. In a leading Supreme Court case, *Papish v. Board of Curators of the University of Missouri,* 410 U.S. 667 (1973), the plaintiff was a graduate student who had been expelled for violating a board of curators bylaw prohibiting distribution of newspapers "containing forms of indecent speech." The newspaper at issue had a political cartoon on its cover that "depicted policemen raping the Statue of Liberty and the Goddess of Justice. The caption under the cartoon read: 'With Liberty and Justice for All.'" The newspaper also "contained an article entitled 'M——F—— Acquitted,' which discussed the trial and acquittal on an assault charge of a New York City youth who was a member of an organization known as 'Up Against the Wall, M——F——.'" After being expelled, the student sued the university, alleging a violation of her First Amendment rights. The Court, in a *per curiam* opinion, ruled in favor of the student:

> We think [*Healy v. James,* Section 10.1.1 above] makes it clear that the mere dissemination of ideas—no matter how offensive to good taste—on a state university campus may not be shut off in the name alone of "conventions of decency." Other recent precedents of this Court make it equally clear that neither the political cartoon nor the headline story involved in this case can be labeled as constitutionally obscene or otherwise unprotected [410 U.S. at 670].

Obscenity, then, is not definable in terms of an institution's or an administrator's own personal conceptions of taste, decency, or propriety. Obscenity can be defined only in terms of the guidelines that courts have constructed to prevent the concept from being used to choke off controversial social or political dialogue. As the U.S. Supreme Court stated in the leading case, *Miller v. California,* 413 U.S. 15 (1973):

> We now confine the permissible scope of . . . regulation [of obscenity] to works which depict or describe sexual conduct. That conduct must be specifically

defined by the applicable state law, as written or authoritatively construed. A state offense must also be limited to works which, taken as a whole, appeal to the prurient interest in sex, which portray sexual conduct in a patently offensive way, and which, taken as a whole, do not have serious literary, artistic, political, or scientific value [413 U.S. at 24 (1973)].

Although these guidelines were devised for the general community, the Supreme Court made clear in *Papish* that "the First Amendment leaves no room for the operation of a dual standard in the academic community with respect to the content of speech." Administrators devising campus rules for public institutions are thus bound by the same obscenity guidelines that bind the legislators promulgating obscenity laws. Under these guidelines, the permissible scope of regulation is very narrow, and the drafting or application of rules is a technical exercise that administrators should undertake with the assistance of counsel, if at all.

10.3.6. Libel. As they may for obscenity, institutions may discipline students or organizations that publish libelous matter. Here again, however, the authority of public institutions extends only to matter that is libelous according to technical legal definitions. It is not sufficient that a particular statement be false or misleading. Common law and constitutional doctrines require that (1) the statement be false; (2) the publication serve to identify the particular person libeled; (3) the publication cause at least nominal injury to the person libeled, usually including but not limited to injury to reputation; and (4) the falsehood be attributable to some fault on the part of the person or organization publishing it. The degree of fault depends on the subject of the alleged libel. If the subject is a public official or what the courts call a "public figure," the statement must have been made with "actual malice"; that is, with knowledge of its falsity or with "reckless disregard" for its truth or falsity. In all other situations governed by the First Amendment, the statement need only have been made negligently. Courts make this distinction in order to give publishers extra breathing space when reporting on certain matters of high public interest.[20]

A decision of the Virginia Supreme Court illustrates that a false statement *of fact* is at the heart of a defamation claim. The claim in *Yeagle v. Collegiate Times*, 497 S.E.2d 136 (Va. 1998), arose from the student newspaper's publication of an article about a program facilitated by the plaintiff, a university administrator. Although otherwise complimentary of the administrator, the article included a large-print block quotation attributed to her and identifying her as "Director of Butt Licking." The court rejected the defamation claim because the expression "cannot reasonably be understood as stating an actual fact about [the plaintiff's] job title or her conduct, or that she committed a crime of moral

---

[20]The U.S. Supreme Court has developed these constitutional principles of libel law in a progression of decisions beginning with *New York Times v. Sullivan*, 376 U.S. 254 (1964). See also *Curtis Publishing Co. v. Butts*, 388 U.S. 130 (1967); *Associated Press v. Walker*, 389 U.S. 997 (1967); *Gertz v. Robert Welch, Inc.*, 418 U.S. 323 (1974); and *Time, Inc. v. Firestone*, 424 U.S. 448 (1976).

turpitude." Although the phrase "Director of Butt Licking" is "disgusting, offensive, and in extremely bad taste," in the circumstances of this case it was "no more than 'rhetorical hyperbole.'" The court further rejected the plaintiff's argument that "the phrase connotes a lack of integrity in the performance of her duties." Explaining that "inferences cannot extend the statements by innuendo, beyond what would be the ordinary and common acceptance of the statement," the court relied on the complimentary content of the article itself to find that there was no basis for the inference the plaintiff sought to draw.

An instructive illustration of the "public official" concept and the "actual malice" standard is provided by *Waterson v. Cleveland State University*, 639 N.E.2d 1236 (Ohio 1994). The plaintiff, then deputy chief of the campus police force at the defendant university, claimed that he had been defamed in an editorial published in the campus student newspaper and written by its then editor-in-chief, Quarles. The university claimed that the deputy chief was a "public official" within the meaning of the leading U.S. Supreme Court precedents and that he therefore could not prevail on a defamation claim unless he proved that Quarles or the university had acted with "actual malice" in publishing the editorial. The court accepted the university's argument and categorized the plaintiff as a public official:

> [T]he students and faculty of CSU [Cleveland State University] have a significant interest in the qualifications, performance and conduct of the officers of the CSU police department, as they rely on these officers for their campus security and are more likely to have day-to-day contact with them than with the officers of the greater Cleveland community. Further, the interest of the campus community in any individual officer's performance is likely to increase with the authority and influence of the officer. At the time the editorial in question was published, . . . plaintiff was second in command in the department, ranking only below the Chief of Police, and was responsible for the continued training of the approximately thirty officers on the force. Plaintiff thus was in a position to wield considerable influence over the rank and file members of the department and to set the tone within the department on issues such as the appropriate use of force and ethnic sensitivity. Finally, the CSU community is the principal audience of the publication in which the editorial in question appeared, precisely the audience with the greatest interest in the performance of CSU police officers, including plaintiff [639 N.E.2d at 1238–39].

The plaintiff (the deputy chief) then argued that, even if he was a public official, he had met his burden of proof of demonstrating "actual malice." Again, the court disagreed:

> [T]he focus of an actual-malice inquiry is on the conduct and state of mind of the defendant. *Herbert v. Lando*, 441 U.S. 153 (1979). To prevail, a plaintiff must show that the false statements were made with a "high degree of awareness of their probable falsity . . ." *Garrison v. Louisiana*, 379 U.S. 64, 74 (1964). . . . The record in this case reveals that plaintiff presented no evidence of who Quarles' sources for the editorial were, and hence no evidence of the reliability of those sources. Nor did plaintiff present any evidence as to what, if any, investigations Quarles undertook prior to publishing her editorial. In fact, plaintiff

presented no evidence whatsoever which would allow one to conclude that Quarles either knew that the allegations contained in her editorial were false or that
she entertained serious doubts as to their veracity [639 N.E.2d at 1239–140].

The appellate court therefore affirmed the trial court's order dismissing the
deputy chief's defamation claim.

Given the complexity of the libel concept, administrators should approach it
most cautiously. Because of the need to assess both injury and fault, as well as
identify the defamatory falsehood, libel may be even more difficult to combat
than obscenity. Suppression in advance of publication is particularly perilous,
since injury can only be speculated about at that point, and reliable facts concerning fault may not be attainable. Much of the material in campus publications, moreover, may involve public officials or public figures and thus be
protected by the higher-fault standard of actual malice.

Though these factors might reasonably lead administrators to forgo any regulation of libel, there is a countervailing consideration: institutions or administrators may occasionally be held liable in court for libelous statements in
student publications (see Sections 3.3.4). Such liability could exist where the
institution sponsors a publication (such as a paper operated by the journalism department as a training ground for its students), employs the editors of
the publication, establishes a formal committee to review the content of material in advance of publication, or otherwise exercises some control (constitutionally or unconstitutionally) over the publication's content. In any case,
liability would exist only for statements deemed libelous under the criteria set
out above.

Such potential liability, however, need not necessarily prompt increased surveillance of student publications. Increased surveillance would demand regulations that stay within constitutional limits yet are strong enough to weed out all
libel—an unlikely combination. And since institutional control of the publication is the predicate to the institution's liability, increased regulation increases
the likelihood of liability should a libel be published. Thus, administrators may
choose to handle liability problems by lessening rather than enlarging control.
The privately incorporated student newspaper operating independently of the
institution would be the clearest example of a no-control/no-liability situation.

The decision of the New York State Court of Claims in *Mazart v. State*, 441
N.Y.S.2d 600 (N.Y. Ct. Cl. 1981), not only illustrates the basic steps for establishing libel but also affirms that institutional control over the newspaper, or
lack thereof, is a key to establishing or avoiding institutional liability. The opinion also discusses the question of whether an institution can ever restrain in
advance the planned publication of libelous material.

The plaintiffs (claimants) in *Mazart* were two students at the State University of New York-Binghamton who were the targets of an allegedly libelous letter to the editor published in the student newspaper, the *Pipe Dream*. The letter
described a prank that it said had occurred in a male dormitory and characterized the act as prejudice against homosexuals. The plaintiffs' names appeared
at the end of the letter, although they had not in fact written it, and the body of
the letter identified them as "members of the gay community."

The court analyzed the case in three stages. *First,* applying accepted principles of libel law to the educational context in which the incident occurred, the court determined that this letter was libelous:

> Did the letter in the *Pipe Dream* expose claimants to hatred, contempt, or aversion, or induce an evil or unsavory opinion of them in the minds of a substantial number of the [university] community? The answer to the question is far from simple. . . . According to the chairman of the English Department at the University, . . . sexual orientation had no more bearing in the classroom than religious affiliation. The Assistant Vice President for Finance, Management, and Control of the University opined that the published letter had a "[v]ery low, very little affect" [*sic*] on the campus community.
>
> No doubt the impact of the published letter on the collective mind of the University was considerably less than it might have been had the letter been published in a conservative rural American village. Nonetheless, the court finds that an unsavory opinion of the claimants did settle in the minds of a substantial number of persons in the university community. . . . The question of homosexuality was a significant one on the university campus. . . . Both claimants testified that they were accosted by numerous fellow students after the event and queried about their sexual orientation, and the court finds their testimony, in this respect, credible. Deviant sexual intercourse and sodomy were crimes in the state of New York at the time the letter was published (Penal Law, §§ 130 and 130.38). Certainly those members of the University community who did not personally know the claimants would logically conclude that claimants were homosexual, since the letter identified them as being members of the "gay community." The court finds that a substantial number of the University community would naturally assume that the claimants engaged in homosexual acts from such identification [441 N.Y.S.2d at 603–4].

Second, the court considered the state's argument that, even if the letter was libelous, its publication was protected by a qualified privilege because the subject matter was of public concern. Again using commonly accepted libel principles, the court concluded that a privilege did not apply because

> the editors of the *Pipe Dream* acted in a grossly irresponsible manner by failing to give due consideration to the standards of information gathering and dissemination. It is obvious that authorship of a letter wherein the purported author appears to be libeled should be verified. Not only was the authorship of the letter herein not verified but it appears that the *Pipe Dream*, at least in November of 1977, had no procedures or guidelines with regard to the verification of the authorship of any letters to the editor [441 N.Y.S.2d at 604].

Third, the court held that, although the letter was libelous and not privileged, the university (and thus the state) was not liable for the unlawful acts of the student newspaper. In its analysis the court considered and rejected two theories of liability:

> (1) [that] the state, through the University, may be vicariously liable for the torts of the *Pipe Dream* and its editors on the theory of *respondeat superior* (that is, the University, as principal, might be liable for the torts of its agents, the student

paper and editors); and (2) [that] the state, through the University, may have been negligent in failing to provide guidelines to the *Pipe Dream* staff regarding libel generally, and specifically, regarding the need to review and verify letters to the editor [441 N.Y.S.2d at 600].

In rejecting the first theory, the court relied heavily on First Amendment principles:

> [T]he state could be held vicariously liable if the University and the *Pipe Dream* staff operated in some form of agency relationship. However, it is characteristic of the relationship of principal and agent that the principal has a right to control the conduct of the agent with respect to matters entrusted to him. While this control need not apply to every detail of an agent's conduct and can be found where there is merely a right held by the principal to make management and policy decisions affecting the agent, there can be no agency relationship where the alleged principal has no right of control over the alleged agent. . . .
>
> There are severe constitutional limitations on the exercise of any form of control by a state university over a student newspaper . . . (*Panarella v. Birenbaum,* 37 A.D.2d 987, 327 N.Y.S.2d 755, *affirmed,* 32 N.Y.2d 108, 343 N.Y.S.2d 333, 296 N.E.2d 238). . . . Censorship or prior restraint of constitutionally protected expression in student publications at State-supported institutions has been uniformly proscribed by the Courts. Such censorship or prior restraint cannot be imposed by suspending editors . . . , by suppressing circulation . . . , by requiring prior approval of controversial articles . . . , by excising or suppressing distasteful material . . . , or by withdrawing financial support . . . [441 N.Y.S.2d at 604–5 (most citations omitted)].[21]

Due to these strong constitutional protections for student newspapers at public institutions, the defendant university had no authority "to prevent the publication of the letter." A "policy of prior approval of items to be published in a student newspaper, even if directed only to restraining the publication of potentially libelous material . . . , would run afoul of [the First Amendment]" (citing *Near v. State of Minnesota,* 283 U.S. 697 (1931)). The court therefore ruled that the university did not have a right of control over the *Pipe Dream* sufficient to sustain an agency theory:

> The Court recognizes that the *Pipe Dream* and its staff may be incapable of compensating claimants for any damages flowing from the libel. But, in light of the university's eschewing control, editorial or otherwise, over the paper and the constitutionally imposed barriers to the exercise by the University of any editorial control over the newspaper, the Court must reluctantly conclude that the relationship of the university and the *Pipe Dream* is not such as would warrant the imposition of vicarious liability on the state for defamatory material appearing in the student newspaper (see "Tort Liability of a University for Libelous Material in Student Publications," 71 *Mich. L. Rev.* 1061) [441 N.Y.S.2d at 604–6; most citations omitted].

---

[21]For discussion of these principles and illustrative cases, see subsection 10.3.3 of this Section.

The court then also rejected the plaintiffs' second liability theory. Focusing particularly on the tort law concept of "duty" (see generally Section 3.3.1), the court ruled that the university and state were not negligent "for failing to provide to the student editors guidelines and procedures designed to avoid the publication of libelous material." The issue, the court said, was "whether there was a duty on the part of the University administration" to furnish such guidelines; and the "constitutional limitations on the actual exercise of editorial control by the university," noted above, did "not necessarily preclude the existence of [such] a duty." But the courts, as well as the New York state legislature, regard college students as young adults and not children, and the *Pipe Dream* editors, as young adults, are therefore presumed to have "that degree of maturity and common sense necessary to comprehend the normal procedures for information gathering and dissemination."

> The court must, therefore, find that the University had no duty to supply news gathering and dissemination guidelines to the *Pipe Dream* editors since they were presumed to already know those guidelines. Admittedly, it appears that the student editors of the *Pipe Dream* in 1977 either did not know or simply ignored commonsense verification guidelines with regard to the publication of the instant letter. But that was not the fault of the University. In either event, there was no duty on the part of the University. The editors' lack of knowledge of or failure to adhere to standards which are common knowledge (*Greenberg v. CBS, Inc.* [419 N.Y.S.2d 988 (N.Y. App. Div. 1979)],) and ordinarily followed by reasonable persons . . . was not reasonably foreseeable [441 N.Y.S.2d at 607].

The validity and importance of the *Mazart* case was reaffirmed in *McEvaddy v. City University of New York,* 633 N.Y.S.2d 4 (N.Y. App. Div. 1995). The *McEvaddy* court dismissed a defamation claim brought against City University of New York for an allegedly libelous article published in the student newspaper. Citing *Mazart,* the court held that "[t]he presence of a faculty advisor to the paper, whose advice is nonbinding, and the financing of the paper through student activity fees . . . , do not demonstrate such editorial control or influence over the paper by [the university] as to suggest an agency relationship." The New York Court of Appeals, the state's highest court, denied the claimant's motion for leave to appeal (664 N.E.2d 1258 (N.Y. 1996)). (For another, more recent, affirmation of the principles in *Mazart* and *McEvaddy,* see *Lewis v. St. Cloud State University,* 693 N.W.2d 466 (Minn. App. 2005).)

Mazart v. State is an extensively reasoned precedent in an area where there had been little precedent. The court's opinion, together with the later opinions in *McEvaddy* and *Lewis,* provide much useful guidance for administrators of public institutions. The reasoning in these opinions depends, however, on the particular circumstances concerning the campus setting in which the newspaper operated and the degree of control the institution exercised over the newspaper, and also, under *Mazart,* on the foreseeability of libelous actions by the student editors. Administrators will therefore want to consult with counsel before attempting to apply the principles of these cases to occurrences on their own campuses. Moreover, tort concepts of duty applicable to colleges and universities have been evolving since the *Mazart* case (see Robert Bickel & Peter Lake, *The Rights and Responsibilities of the Modern University: Who Assumes the Risk of College Life?* (Carolina Academic Press, 1999)), and counsel will want to take these developments into consideration as well when applying the duty principles from the *Mazart* case.

10.3.7. Obscenity and libel in private institutions.

Since the First Amendment does not apply to private institutions that are not engaged in state action (see Section 1.5.2), such institutions have a freer hand in regulating obscenity and libel. Yet private institutions should devise their regulatory role cautiously. Regulations broadly construing libel and obscenity based on lay concepts of those terms could stifle the flow of dialogue within the institution, while attempts to avoid this problem with narrow regulations may lead the institution into the same definitional complexities that public institutions face when seeking to comply with the First Amendment. Moreover, in devising their policies on obscenity and libel, private institutions will want to consider the potential impact of state law. Violation of state obscenity or libel law by student publications could subject the responsible students to damage actions, possibly to court injunctions, and even to criminal prosecutions, causing unwanted publicity for the institution. But if the institution regulates the student publications to prevent such problems, the institution could be held liable along with the students if it exercises sufficient control over the publication (see generally Sections 2.1.3 & 3.3.4).

Sec. 10.4. Athletics Teams and Clubs

10.4.1. General principles.

Athletics, as a subsystem of the postsecondary institution, is governed by the general principles set forth elsewhere in this chapter and this book. These principles, however, must be applied in light of the particular characteristics and problems of curricular, extracurricular, and intercollegiate athletic programs. A student athlete's eligibility for financial aid, for instance, would be viewed under the general principles in Section 8.3, but aid conditions related to the student's eligibility for or performance in intercollegiate athletics create a special focus for the problem (see subsection 10.4.5 below). The institution's tort liability for injuries to students would be subject to the general principles in Section 3.3, but the circumstances and risks of athletic participation provide a special focus for the problem (see subsection 10.4.9 below). Similarly, the due process principles in Section 9.4 may apply when a student athlete is disciplined, and the First Amendment principles in Section 9.5 may apply when student athletes engage in protest activities. But in each case the problem may have a special focus (see subsections 10.4.2 & 10.4.3 below). Moreover, as in many other areas of the law, there are various statutes that have special applications to athletics (see subsection 10.4.4 below).

Surrounding these special applications of the law to athletics, there are major legal and policy issues that pertain specifically to the status of "big-time" intercollegiate athletics within the higher education world. In addition to low graduation rates of athletes, the debate has focused on academic entrance requirements for student athletes; postsecondary institutions' recruiting practices; alleged doctoring or padding of high school and college transcripts to obtain or maintain athletic eligibility; drug use among athletes and mandatory drug testing (subsection 10.4.8 below); other misconduct by student athletes, such as sexual assaults, and institutional responses to the alleged misconduct; alleged exploitation of minority athletes; improper financial incentives and rewards or improper academic assistance for student athletes; and the authority and practices of the National Collegiate Athletic Association (NCAA) and athletic conferences (see Section 14.4) regarding such matters. The overarching concern prompted by these issues is one of integrity: the integrity of individual institutions' athletic programs, the integrity of academic standards at institutions emphasizing major intercollegiate competition, the integrity of higher education's mission in an era when athletics has assumed such a substantial role in the operation of the system. (For discussion of these issues, see John R. Thelin, *Games Colleges Play: Scandal and Reform in Intercollegiate Athletics* (John Hopkins University Press, 1996) (exploring evolution of intercollegiate athletics from 1910 to 1990); Andrew Zimbalist, *Unpaid Professionals: Commercialism and Conflict in Big-Time College Sports* (Princeton University Press, 1999) (exploring current problems, need for reform, and recommendations for the future); and Timothy Davis, "Racism in Athletics: Subtle Yet Persistent," 21 *U. Ark. Little Rock L. Rev.* 881 (1999) (exploring continuing problems of racism). For a study that reaches troubling conclusions about the effect of athletics on student and institutional academic performance, see James L. Shulman & William G. Bowen, *The Game of Life: College Sports and Educational Values* (Princeton University Press, 2001) (presenting numerous findings based on data from three databases). And for recommendations for reforming college athletics by two college presidents, see James J. Duderstadt, *Intercollegiate Athletics and the American University* (University of Michigan Press, 2000), and William G. Bowen & Sarah A. Levin, *Reclaiming the Game: College Sports and Educational Values* (Princeton University Press, 2003).)

good bibliography

10.4.2. Athletes' due process rights. If a student athlete is being disciplined for some infraction, the penalty may be suspension from the team. In such instances, the issue raised is whether the procedural protections accompanying suspension from school are also applicable to suspension from a team. For institutions engaging in state action (see Sections 1.5.2 & 14.4.2), the constitutional issue is whether the student athlete has a "property interest" or "liberty interest" in continued intercollegiate competition sufficient to make suspension or some other form of disqualification a deprivation of "liberty or property" within the meaning of the due process clause. Several courts have addressed this question. (Parallel "liberty or property" issues also arise in the context of faculty dismissals (Section 6.6.2) as well as student suspensions and dismissals (Section 9.4.2).)

In *Behagen v. Intercollegiate Conference of Faculty Representatives*, 346 F. Supp. 602 (D. Minn. 1972), a suit brought by University of Minnesota basketball players suspended from the team for participating in an altercation during a game, the court reasoned that participation in intercollegiate athletics has "the potential to bring [student athletes] great economic rewards" and is thus as important as continuing in school. The court therefore held that the students' interests in intercollegiate participation were protected by procedural due process and granted the suspended athletes the protections established in the *Dixon* case (Section 9.4.2). In *Regents of the University of Minnesota v. NCAA*, 422 F. Supp. 1158 (D. Minn. 1976), the same district court reaffirmed and further explained its analysis of student athletes' due process rights. The court reasoned that the opportunity to participate in intercollegiate competition is a property interest entitled to due process protection, not only because of the possible remunerative careers that result but also because such participation is an important part of the student athlete's educational experience.[22] The same court later used much the same analysis in *Hall v. University of Minnesota*, 530 F. Supp. 104 (D. Minn. 1982).

In contrast, the court in *Colorado Seminary v. NCAA*, 417 F. Supp. 885 (D. Colo. 1976), relying on an appellate court's opinion in a case involving high school athletes (*Albach v. Odle*, 531 F.2d 983 (10th Cir. 1976)), held that college athletes have no property or liberty interests in participating in intercollegiate sports, participating in postseason competition, or appearing on television. The appellate court affirmed (570 F.2d 320 (10th Cir. 1978)). (The trial court did suggest, however, that revocation of an athletic scholarship would infringe a student's property or liberty interests and therefore would require due process safeguards (see Section 10.4.5 below).) And in *Hawkins v. NCAA*, 652 F. Supp. 602, 609–11 (C.D. Ill. 1987), the court held that student athletes have no property interest in participating in postseason competition. Given the intense interest and frequently high stakes for college athletes, administrators at both public and private colleges should provide at least a minimal form of due process when barring college athletes from playing in games or postseason tournaments, and should provide notice and an opportunity for the student to be heard if a scholarship is to be rescinded.

Other forms of disqualification from competition may also implicate due process protections for students at public institutions of higher education. In *NCAA v. Yeo*, 114 S.W.3d 584 (Tex. App. 2003), *reversed*, 171 S.W.3d 863 (Tex. 2005), the Texas Supreme Court rejected a student athlete's claim that she possessed a "constitutionally protected interest" in participation in athletic events. The Texas Court of Appeals, applying state rather than federal constitutional due process guarantees, had found that a student athlete's athletic career was a protected interest requiring procedural due process protections when that student already had an "established athletic reputation" prior to her college matriculation. The due process claim stemmed from an athletic eligibility

---

[22]Although the appellate court reversed this decision, 560 F.2d 352 (8th Cir. 1977), it did so on other grounds and did not question the district court's due process analysis.

dispute at the University of Texas (UT)-Austin. The athlete in this dispute, Joscelin Yeo, is a world-class swimmer who had competed in two Olympic Games for her native country, Singapore. Yeo began her college career at University of California-Berkeley, and then transferred to the University of Texas-Austin when her coach accepted a position at Texas. National Collegiate Athletic Association regulations required that "a transferring student-athlete refrain from athletic competition for two full long-semesters." After completion of this one-year residency requirement at her new institution, Yeo could compete in swimming competitions.

Complications arose with the residency requirement when Yeo was training for the 2000 Olympic Games. Yeo had to obtain a waiver to take less than a full courseload while she was training for the Sydney Olympics, and UT-Austin's athletic department obtained a waiver from the NCAA allowing Yeo to be "eligible for practice, competition, and athletically related financial aid for the fall 2000 term *without being enrolled in any courses at Texas*" (114 S.W.3d at 589). When Yeo attempted to compete for the University of Texas in the 2000–2001 academic year, the NCAA determined that the Olympic waiver did not operate as a waiver of its two-semester residency requirement. After the NCAA made the residency determination, the UT athletic director declared the athlete ineligible to swim in competitions, without consulting Yeo or allowing an opportunity for hearing. After the athletic director's determination of ineligibility, Yeo's only option was to request reinstatement. However, Yeo was not informed of her ineligibility until nearly six months after the determination, when she was told that she had to miss four additional collegiate competitions in 2002. Additionally, no one provided Yeo with the determinations made by the NCAA or the guidelines for appealing its decisions. When Yeo finally learned that her status was in dispute, she participated in a hearing to decide her eligibility for an upcoming swim meet, but she was not told that the hearing was nonappealable. After Yeo was informed of her ineligibility status in the hearing, days before a major swimming tournament, UT-Austin recommended that she seek independent legal counsel. As a result, Yeo sued in district court to compete in the NCAA championship tournament. The court granted her a temporary restraining order to permit her to swim in the competition, and Yeo obtained a permanent injunction against declaring her ineligible from competition.

In reviewing Yeo's due process claim, the Texas Court of Appeals had first to determine whether Yeo's interest in competing in intercollegiate sports created either a property or liberty interest, and, if so, what protections were due. The court refused to determine whether a liberty or property interest was at stake, preferring to call the interest a "protected interest" without deciding whether it was liberty or property. The court analogized Yeo's circumstances to an injury of professional reputation, stating that "[r]eputation plays an important role in this calculation; when a person's good name, reputation, honor, or integrity is at stake because of what the government is doing to her, due process protections are more likely to apply" (114 S.W.3d at 596). The court found that Yeo's athletic reputation was a protected interest, since it was established prior to her college athletic career.

> [T]he protected interest of constitutional dimension presented by this case is not her right to participate in intercollegiate athletics generally, but rather the right to protect her reputation and good name that would be adversely affected by a declaration of ineligibility made without an opportunity to be heard. . . . We recognize that interference by the courts in athletic eligibility determinations, if unfettered, would impede the efficient administration of academic and extracurricular programs and undercut the credibility of athletic competition and academic preparedness. We reaffirm that there is no constitutionally protected interest in extracurricular participation per se [114 S.W.3d at 597].

After establishing that Yeo had a protected interest, the court then analyzed what process she was entitled to. The court found several procedural flaws in the UT athletic director's determination of Yeo's ineligibility. There was no record of the decision, Yeo was given no notice of the decision, and as a result, Yeo could not participate in the hearing. Even though UT was aware of the impact such a determination would make on her career, Yeo was not advised to retain counsel until much later, after the determination of athletic ineligibility. Moreover, UT did not even suggest to Yeo at the outset that she could have avoided the entire athletic eligibility dispute by obtaining a waiver to participate from the University of California-Berkeley. The court found further flaws in the school's actions after the determination of athletic ineligibility. When UT attempted to add additional meets to the spring swim schedule to comply with the residency requirement, UT again failed to notify Yeo until the eligibility process was almost complete. According to the court, UT's failure to notify again foreclosed Yeo's ability to meaningfully participate in the second eligibility determination and retain counsel. The court then stated that:

> [d]ue process generally involves a meaningful opportunity to be heard. It is not the NCAA reinstatement process that failed Yeo, but the fact that important decisions regarding her eligibility were made by UT-Austin without notice that a problem existed and with no opportunity for Yeo to advocate for her own position [114 S.W.3d at 600].

The court noted that a formal hearing was not necessary, but that UT should have given Yeo notice and an opportunity to communicate with officials informally prior to the final determination by the NCAA. According to the court, had the compliance staff notified Yeo of the eligibility problem in a timely way, and had they given her an opportunity to respond, she would have received the required due process protections.

The Texas Supreme Court rejected the reasoning and outcome of the appellate court. The state's high court refused to distinguish between nationally ranked student athletes and nonranked students. The court asserted: "The United States Supreme Court has stated, and we agree, that whether an interest is protected by due process depends not on its *weight* but on its *nature*" (citing *Board of Regents v. Roth,* discussed in Section 6.7.2). The court viewed an individual's interest in his or her good name as "the same no matter how good the reputation is." Citing a case it had decided twenty years earlier (*Spring*

Branch I.S.D. v. Stamos, 695 S.W.2d 556 (Tex. 1985)), the court reiterated that "students do not possess a constitutionally protected interest in their participation in extracurricular activities" (695 S.W.2d at 561). Furthermore, said the court, Yeo's assertion that her future financial opportunities were substantial was "too speculative" to implicate constitutional protections. Said the court: "While student-athletes remain amateurs, their future financial opportunities remain expectations" (171 S.W.3d at 870). Comparing Yeo's alleged liberty interest with that at issue in *University of Texas Medical School v. Than* (discussed in Section 9.4.3), the court said: "We decline to equate an interest in intercollegiate athletics with an interest in graduate education" (171 S.W.3d at 870).

10.4.3. Athletes' freedom of speech.
When student athletes are participants in a protest or demonstration, their First Amendment rights must be viewed in light of the institution's particular interest in maintaining order and discipline in its athletic programs. An athlete's protest that disrupts an athletic program would no more be protected by the First Amendment than any other student protest that disrupts institutional functions. While the case law regarding athletes' First Amendment rights is even more sparse than that regarding their due process rights, *Williams v. Eaton,* 468 F.2d 1079 (10th Cir. 1972), does specifically apply the *Tinker* case (Section 9.5.1) to a protest by intercollegiate football players. Black football players had been suspended from the team for insisting on wearing black armbands during a game to protest the alleged racial discrimination of the opposing church-related school. The court held that the athletes' protest was unprotected by the First Amendment because it would interfere with the religious freedom rights of the opposing players and their church-related institution. The *Williams* opinion is unusual in that it mixes considerations of free speech and freedom of religion. The court's analysis would have little relevance to situations where religious freedom is not involved. Since the court did not find that the athletes' protest was disruptive, it relied solely on the seldom-used "interference with the rights of others" branch of the *Tinker* case.

In *Marcum v. Dahl,* 658 F.2d 731 (10th Cir. 1981), the court considered a First Amendment challenge to an institution's nonrenewal of the scholarships of several student athletes. The plaintiffs, basketball players on the University of Oklahoma's women's team, had been involved during the season in a dispute with other players over who should be the team's head coach. At the end of the season, they had announced to the press that they would not play the next year if the current coach was retained. The plaintiffs argued that the institution had refused to renew their scholarships because of this statement to the press and that the statement was constitutionally protected. The trial court and then the appellate court disagreed. Analogizing the scholarship athletes to public employees for First Amendment purposes (see Sections 7.1 & 7.3), the appellate court held that (1) the dispute about the coach was not a matter of "general public concern" and the plaintiffs' press statement on this subject was therefore not protected by the First Amendment, and (2) the plaintiffs' participation in the dispute prior to the press statement, and the resultant disharmony, provided an independent basis for the scholarship nonrenewal.

Free speech issues may also arise when student athletes are the intended recipients of a message rather than the speakers. In such situations, the free speech rights at stake will be those of others—employees, other students, members of the general public—who wish to speak to athletes either individually or as a group. Sometimes the athlete's own First Amendment right to receive information could also be at issue.

In *Dambrot v. Central Michigan University*, 55 F.3d 1177 (6th Cir. 1995), the head basketball coach at Central Michigan University was terminated when it became widely publicized that he had used the word "nigger" in at least one instance when addressing basketball team members in the locker room. In terminating the coach, the university relied on the institution's discriminatory harassment policy. The coach and many of the team members sued the university, claiming that it had violated the coach's free speech rights. Dambrot argued that he was using the N-word in a positive manner, urging his players to be "fearless, mentally strong, and tough." Although the appellate court ruled that the university's discriminatory harassment policy was unconstitutionally overbroad and vague (see Section 9.6.2), it also held that the coach was not wrongfully terminated because his speech neither touched a matter of public concern nor implicated academic freedom.

In *Crue v. Aiken*, 370 F.3d 668 (7th Cir. 2004), the question was whether students and faculty members of the University of Illinois could speak with prospective student athletes being recruited for the university's athletic teams. The question arose because of a controversy concerning the university's athletic "mascot" or "symbol," called "Chief Illiniwek." To some, Chief Illiniwek was a respectful representation of the Illinois Nations of Native Americans, or the "fighting spirit," or "the strong, agile human body." To others, Chief Illiniwek was an offensive representation of the Illinois Nations, or a "mockery" or distortion of tribal customs, or the source of a "hostile environment" for Native American students (370 F.3d at 673–74).[23] The plaintiffs wished to speak with prospective athletes about this controversy and the negative implications of competing for a university that uses the Chief Illiniwek symbol. The chancellor issued a directive prohibiting students and employees from contacting prospective student athletes without the express approval of the athletics director. The federal district court held that the university's directive violated the free speech rights of university employees and students, and the U.S. Court of Appeals affirmed by a 2-to-1 vote. Neither court directly addressed the free speech rights of students apart from those of employees who were restrained by the directive, or the potential free speech rights of the prospective student athletes to "receive" the message.[24]

---

[23]For more on Chief Illiniwek, see 370 F.3d at 672–74; and for more on college athletic mascots, see 370 F.3d at 671–72. For a view of the continuing controversy over "Indian" mascots for athletic teams, including Chief Illiniwek, see Eric Wills, "Pride or Prejudice?" *Chron. Higher Educ.*, June 3, 2005, A29.

[24]A related issue in the case was whether the employees' and students' contacts with the student athlete recruits would violate NCAA rules. See 370 F.3d at 679–80 (majority) and 686–87 (dissent). For discussion of NCAA rule making and enforcement, see Section 14.4 of this book.

The most recent issue to arise concerning speech directed to (rather than the speech of) student athletes is one that involves the spectators at sporting events. The students in the student sections at intercollegiate basketball games, for instance, often have unique methods of communicating with the visiting team's athletes on the floor. In some situations, at some schools, the communicative activities of the student section have been considered by school officials, or by other spectators, to be profane or otherwise offensive.[25] The issue that then may arise is whether or not the university can limit the speech of students in the student section in ways that would not violate their First Amendment free speech rights. In Maryland, this issue was the subject of a memorandum from the State Attorney General's Office to the president of the University of Maryland (March 17, 2004), in which the attorney general's office concluded, without providing specific examples, that some regulation of student speech at university basketball games would be constitutionally permissible. In general, this delicate issue of student crowd speech at athletic events would be subject to the same five free speech principles, and the same suggestions for regulatory strategies, that are set out in Section 9.6.3 of this book concerning hate speech. There would likely be particular attention given to the problem of "captive audiences" that is mentioned in the fifth suggestion for regulating hate speech on campus. (For further legal and policy analysis of this problem, see Gary Pavela, "Incivility and Profanity at Athletic Events," Part 1 & Part 2, in *Synfax Weekly Report*, February 16, 2004, and February 23, 2004.)

Because issues concerning the free speech rights of persons wishing to address student athletes arise in such varied contexts, as the above examples indicate, and because there are substantial questions of strategy to consider along with the law, university administrators and counsel should be wary about drawing any fast and firm conclusions concerning problems that they may face. Instead, the analysis should depend on the specific context, including who the speaker is, where the speech takes place, the purpose of the speech, and its effect on others. If an institution chooses to regulate in this area, the cases make clear that the overbreadth and vagueness problem will be a major challenge for those drafting the regulations. In *Dambrot* (above), for example, even though the court upheld the termination of the coach, it invalidated the university's discriminatory harassment policy because it was overbroad and vague. (For a discussion of the tension between free speech and civility at athletics events, see Howard M. Wasserman, "Cheers, Profanity, and Free Speech," 31 *J. Coll. & Univ. Law* 377 (2005).)

10.4.4. Pertinent statutory law.

Similarly, state and federal statutory law has some special applications to an institution's athletes or athletic programs.

---

[25]The opposite situation can also arise if student-athletes seek to communicate with spectators at a game. In *State v. Hoshijo ex rel. White*, 76 P.3d 550 (Hawaii S. Ct. 2003), for example, a student manager of the basketball team directed an offensive comment to a spectator during a game. A key question in the case that followed was whether the student manager's speech was protected by the First Amendment. The court concluded that the speech constituted "fighting words" (see Section 9.6.2) and was therefore not protected.

Questions have arisen, for example, about the eligibility of injured intercollegiate athletes for workers' compensation (see Section 4.6.6). Laws in some states prohibit agents from entering representation agreements with student athletes (see, for example, Mich. Comp. Laws Ann. § 750.411e) or from entering into such an agreement without notifying the student's institution (see, for example, Fla. Stat. Ann. § 468.454).[26] State anti-hazing statutes may have applications to the activities of athletic teams and clubs (see, for example, Ill. Comp. Stat. Ann. § 720 ILCS 120/5). An earlier version of this law was upheld in *People v. Anderson*, 591 N.E.2d 461 (Ill. 1992), a prosecution brought against members of a university lacrosse club. Regarding federal law, the antitrust statutes may have some application to the institution's relations with its student athletes when those relations are governed by athletic association and conference rules (Section 14.4.3). And the Student Right-to-Know and Campus Security Act, discussed below, contains separate provisions dealing with low graduation rates of student athletes in certain sports.

The Student Right-to-Know Act (Title I of the Student Right-to-Know and Campus Security Act, 104 Stat. 2381–84 (1990)), ensures that potential student athletes will have access to data that will help them make informed choices when selecting an institution. Under the Act, an institution of higher education that participates in federal student aid programs and that awards "athletically related student aid" must annually provide the Department of Education with certain information about its student athletes. Athletically related student aid is defined as "any scholarship, grant, or other form of financial assistance the terms of which require the recipient to participate in a program of intercollegiate athletics at an institution of higher education in order to be eligible to receive such assistance" (104 Stat. 2384, 20 U.S.C. § 1092(e)(8)).

Institutions must report the following information, broken down by race and gender: (1) the number of students receiving athletically related student aid in basketball, football, baseball, cross country/track, and all other sports combined (20 U.S.C. § 1092(e)(1)(A)); (2) the completion or graduation rates of those students (20 U.S.C. § 1092(e)(1)(C)); and (3) the average completion or graduation rate for the four most recent classes (20 U.S.C. § 1092(e)(1)(E)). The same types of information must be collected on students in general (20 U.S.C. § 1092(e)(1)(B, D, & F)). In addition to reporting to the Department of Education, institutions must provide this information to potential student athletes and their parents, guidance counselors, and coaches (20 U.S.C. § 1092(e)(2)). Other students may receive the information upon request.[27] The Secretary of Education may waive the annual reporting requirements if, in his or her opinion, an institution of higher education is a member of an athletic association or conference that publishes data "substantially comparable" to the information specified in the Act (20 U.S.C. § 1092(e)(6)). Regulations implementing the Act are published at 34 C.F.R. Part 668.

---

[26]For a discussion of these laws, see Diane Sudia & Rob Remis, "Statutory Regulation of Agent Gifts to Athletes," 10 *Seton Hall J. Sports L.* 265 (2000).

[27]This information is in addition to other information institutions must provide to prospective and enrolled students under 20 U.S.C. § 1092. See Section 8.3.2, and see also Section 13.4.4.3.

In addition to the Student Right-to-Know Act, Congress also passed the Equity in Athletics Disclosure Act, 108 Stat. 3518, 3970, codified at 20 U.S.C. § 1092(g). This Act, like the earlier Student Right-to-Know Act, requires institutions annually to report certain data regarding their athletic programs to the U.S. Department of Education. Both Acts are implemented by regulations codified in 34 C.F.R. Part 668 (the Student Assistance General Provisions) under subpart D (Student Consumer Information Services). The particular focus of the Equity in Athletics Disclosure Act is 34 C.F.R. § 668.48, while the particular focus of the Student Right-to-Know Act is 34 C.F.R §§ 668.46 and 668.49.

The Equity in Athletics Disclosure Act applies to "each co-educational institution that participates in any [Title IV, HEA student aid] program . . . and has an intercollegiate athletic program" (20 U.S.C. § 1092(g)(1)). Such institutions must make a variety of athletic program statistics available to prospective and current students, and the public upon request, including the number of male and female undergraduate students; the number of participants on each varsity athletic team; the operating expenses of each team; the gender of each team's head coach; the full- or part-time status of each head coach; the number and gender of assistant coaches and graduate assistants; statistics on "athletically-related student aid," reported separately for men's and women's teams and male and female athletes; recruiting expenditures for men's and for women's teams; revenues from athletics for men's and women's teams; and average salaries for male coaches and for female coaches.

10.4.5. *Athletic scholarships.*

An athletic scholarship will usually be treated in the courts as a contract between the institution and the student. Typically the institution offers to pay the student's educational expenses in return for the student's promise to participate in a particular sport and maintain athletic eligibility by complying with university, conference, and NCAA regulations (see generally Section 14.4). Unlike other student-institutional contracts (see Section 8.1.3), the athletic scholarship contract may be a formal written agreement signed by the student and, if the student is underage, by a parent or guardian. Moreover, the terms of the athletic scholarship may be heavily influenced by athletic conference and NCAA rules regarding scholarships and athletic eligibility (see Section 14.4).

In NCAA member institutions, a letter-of-intent document is provided to prospective student athletes. The student athlete's signature on this document functions as a promise that the student will attend the institution and participate in intercollegiate athletics in exchange for the institution's promise to provide a scholarship or other financial assistance. Courts have generally not addressed the issue of whether the letter of intent, standing alone, is an enforceable contract that binds the institution and the student athlete to their respective commitments. Instead, courts have viewed the signing of a letter of intent as one among many factors to consider in determining whether a contractual relationship exists. Thus, although the letter of intent serves as additional evidence of a contractual relationship, it does not yet have independent legal status and, in effect, must be coupled with a financial aid offer in order to bind either party. (See generally Michael Cozzillio, "The Athletic Scholarship and the College National Letter of Intent: A Contract by Any Other Name," 35 *Wayne L. Rev.* 1275 (1989); and Robert N. Davis, "The Courts and Athletic Scholarships," 67 *Notre Dame L. Rev.* 163 (1991).)

Although it is possible for either the institution or the student to breach the scholarship contract and for either party to sue, as a practical matter the cases generally involve students who file suit after the institution terminates or withdraws the scholarship. Such institutional action may occur if the student becomes ineligible for intercollegiate competition, has fraudulently misrepresented information regarding his or her academic credentials or athletic eligibility, has engaged in serious misconduct warranting substantial disciplinary action, or has declined to participate in the sport for personal reasons. The following three cases illustrate how such issues arise and how courts resolve them.

In *Begley v. Corp. of Mercer University,* 367 F. Supp. 908 (E.D. Tenn. 1973), the university withdrew from its agreement to provide an athletic scholarship for Begley after realizing that a university assistant coach had miscalculated Begley's high school grade point average (GPA), and that his true GPA did not meet the NCAA's minimum requirements. Begley filed suit, asking the court to award money damages for the university's breach of contract. The court dismissed the suit, holding that the university was justified in not performing its part of the agreement, since the agreement also required Begley to abide by all NCAA rules and regulations. Because Begley, from the outset, did not have the minimum GPA, he was unable to perform his part of the agreement. Thus, the court based its decision on the fundamental principle of contract law that "'where one party is unable to perform his part of the contract, he cannot be entitled to the performance of the contract by the other party'" (quoting 17 Am. Jur. 2d at 791–92, *Contracts,* § 355). (For a more contemporary case involving issues of academic eligibility and the interpretation of NCAA rules, see *Williams v. University of Cincinnati,* 752 N.E.2d 367 (Ohio Ct. Claims 2001).)

In *Taylor v. Wake Forest University,* 191 S.E.2d 379 (N.C. Ct. App. 1972), the university terminated the student's scholarship after he refused to participate in the football program. Originally, the student had withdrawn from the team to concentrate on academics when his grades fell below the minimum that the university required for athletic participation. Even after he raised his GPA above the minimum, however, the student continued his refusal to participate. The student alleged that the university's termination of his athletic scholarship was a breach and asked the court to award money damages equal to the costs incurred in completing his degree. He argued that, in case of conflict between his educational achievement and his athletic involvement, the scholarship terms allowed him to curtail his participation in the football program in order to "assure reasonable academic progress." He also argued that he was to be the judge of "reasonable academic progress." The court rejected the student's argument and granted summary judgment for the university. According to the court, permitting the student to be his own judge of his academic progress would be a "strange construction of the contract." Further, by accepting the scholarship, the student was obligated to "maintain his athletic eligibility . . . both physically and scholastically. . . . When he refused to [participate] in the absence of any injury or excuse other than to devote more time to his studies, he was not complying with his contractual agreements."

In *Conard v. University of Washington,* 814 P.2d 1242 (Wash. Ct. App. 1991), after three years of providing financial aid, the university declined to renew the scholarships of two student athletes for a fourth year because of the students' "serious misconduct." Although the scholarship agreement stipulated a one-year award of aid that would be considered for renewal under certain conditions, the students argued that it was their expectation, and the university's practice, that the scholarship would be automatically renewed for at least four years. The appellate court did not accept the students' evidence to this effect because the agreement, by its "clear terms," lasted only one academic year and provided only for the *consideration* of renewal (see generally Section 1.4.2.3). The university's withdrawal of aid, therefore, was not a breach of the contract.

Due process issues may also arise if an institution terminates or withdraws an athletic scholarship. The contract itself may specify certain procedural steps that the institution must take before withdrawal or termination. Conference or NCAA rules may contain other procedural requirements. And for public institutions, the federal Constitution's Fourteenth Amendment (or comparable state constitutional provision) may sometimes superimpose other procedural obligations upon those contained in the contract and rules.

In the *Conard* case above, for example, the Washington Court of Appeals held that the students had a "legitimate claim of entitlement" to the renewal of their scholarships because each scholarship was "issued under the representation that it would be renewed subject to certain conditions," and because it was the university's practice to renew athletic scholarships for at least four years. Since this "entitlement" constituted a property interest under the Fourteenth Amendment, the court held that any deprivation of this entitlement "warrants the protection of due process" (see Section 10.4.2).

The Washington Supreme Court reversed the court of appeals on the due process issue (834 P.2d 17 (Wash. 1992)). The students' primary contention was that a "mutually explicit understanding" (see generally Section 6.7.2.1) had been created by "the language of their contracts and the common understanding, based upon the surrounding circumstances and the conduct of the parties." The court rejected this argument, stating that "the language of the offers and the NCAA regulations are not sufficiently certain to support a mutually explicit understanding, [and] the fact that scholarships are, in fact, normally renewed does not create a 'common law' of renewal, absent other consistent and supportive [university] policies or rules." Consequently, the court held that the students had no legitimate claim of entitlement to renewal of the scholarships, and that the university thus had no obligation to extend them due process protections prior to nonrenewal.

Occasionally student athletes have sued their institutions even when the institution has not terminated or withdrawn the athlete's scholarship. Such cases are likely to involve alleged exploitation or abuse of the athlete, and may present not only breach of contract issues paralleling those in the cases above but also more innovative tort law issues. The leading case, highly publicized in its day, is *Ross v. Creighton University,* 957 F.2d 410 (7th Cir. 1992). The plaintiff in this case had been awarded a basketball scholarship from Creighton even though his academic credentials were substantially below those of the average Creighton student. The plaintiff alleged that the university knew of his academic limitations but nevertheless lured him to Creighton with assurances that it would provide sufficient academic support so that he would "receive a meaningful education." While at Creighton, the plaintiff maintained a D average; and, on the advice of the athletic department, his curriculum consisted largely of courses such as "Theory of Basketball." After four years, he "had the overall language skills of a fourth grader and the reading skills of a seventh grader."

The plaintiff based his suit on three tort theories and a breach of contract theory. The trial court originally dismissed all four claims. The appellate court agreed with the trial court on the tort claims but reversed the trial court and allowed the plaintiff to proceed to trial on the breach of contract claim. The plaintiff's first tort claim was a claim of "educational malpractice" based on Creighton's not providing him with "a meaningful education [or] preparing him for employment after college." The court refused to recognize educational malpractice as a cause of action, listing four policy concerns supporting its decision: (1) the inability of a court to fashion "a satisfactory standard of care by which to evaluate" instruction, (2) its inability to determine the cause and nature of damage to the student, (3) the potential flood of litigation that would divert institutions' attention from their primary mission, and (4) the threat of involving courts in the oversight of daily institutional operations. The plaintiff's second claim was that Creighton had committed "negligent admission" because it owed a duty to "recruit and enroll only those students reasonably qualified to and able to academically perform at CREIGHTON." The court rejected this novel theory because of similar problems in identifying a standard of care by which to judge the institution's admissions decisions. The court also noted that, if institutions were subjected to such claims, they would admit only exceptional students, thus severely limiting the opportunities for marginal students. The plaintiff's last tort claim was negligent infliction of emotional distress. The court quickly rejected this claim because its rejection of the first two claims left no basis for proving that the defendant had been negligent in undertaking the actions that may have distressed the plaintiff.

Although the court rejected all the plaintiff's negligence claims, it did embrace his breach of contract claim. In order to discourage "any attempt to repackage an educational malpractice claim as a contract claim," however, the court required the plaintiff to

> do more than simply allege that the education was not good enough. Instead, he must point to an identifiable contractual promise that the defendant failed to honor. . . . [T]he essence of the plaintiff's complaint would not be that the institution failed to perform adequately a promised educational service, but rather that it failed to perform that service at all.

Judicial consideration of such a claim is therefore not an inquiry "into the nuances of educational processes and theories, but rather an objective assessment of whether the institution made a good faith effort to perform on its promise."

Following this approach, the court reviewed the plaintiff's allegations that the university failed (1) to provide adequate tutoring, (2) to require that the plaintiff attend tutoring sessions, (3) to allow the plaintiff to "red-shirt" for one year to concentrate on his studies, and (4) to afford the plaintiff a reasonable opportunity to take advantage of tutoring services. The court concluded that these allegations were sufficient to warrant further proceedings and therefore remanded the case to the trial court. (Soon thereafter, the parties settled the case.)

The court's disposition of the tort claims in *Ross* does not mean that student athletes can never succeed with such claims. In a similar case, *Jackson v. Drake University,* 778 F. Supp. 1490 (S.D. Iowa 1991), the court did recognize two tort claims—negligent misrepresentation and fraud—brought by a former student athlete. After rejecting an educational malpractice claim for reasons similar to those in *Ross,* the court allowed the plaintiff to proceed with his claims that "Drake did not exercise reasonable care in making representations [about its commitment to academic excellence] and had no intention of providing the support services it had promised." The court reasoned that the policy concerns "do not weigh as heavily in favor of precluding the claims for negligent misrepresentation and fraud as in the claim for [educational malpractice]."

But a student seeking to hold Clemson University responsible for the erroneous advice of an academic advisor, resulting in his ineligibility to play baseball under NCAA rules, was unsuccessful in his attempt to state claims of negligence, breach of fiduciary duty, and breach of contract. In *Hendricks v. Clemson University,* 578 S.E.2d 711 (S.C. 2003), a trial court had granted summary judgment to the university on the student's claims, but a state intermediate appellate court reversed, ruling that the case must proceed to trial. The state supreme court reinstated the summary judgment, ruling that no state law common law precedent could support the assumption by the university of a duty of care to advise the student accurately. Said the court: "We believe recognizing a duty flowing from advisors to students is not required by any precedent and would be unwise, considering the great potential for embroiling schools in litigation that such recognition would create" (578 S.E.2d at 715). In addition, said the court, it would not recognize, as a matter of first impression, a fiduciary relationship between the student and the advisor because such relationships are typically recognized between lawyers and clients, or for members of corporate boards of directors. And finally, according to the court, citing *Ross v. Creighton,* it would not allow the breach of contract claim to go forward because the plaintiff's claim involved an evaluation of the adequacy of the university's services, a claim specifically rejected by the court in *Ross.* Here, said the court, the university had not made any written promise to ensure the athletic eligibility of the student.

10.4.6. Sex discrimination.
The equitable treatment of male and female college athletes remains a major issue in athletics programs. Despite the fact that Title IX has been in existence for more than thirty years, conflict remains as to whether it has provided appropriate standards for equalizing opportunities for men and women to participate in college sports. Litigation under Title IX

has focused on two primary issues: providing equal access to resources for both men's and women's sports, and equal treatment of athletes of both genders. Equal access litigation involves allegedly inequitable resource allocation to women's sports and the elimination of men's teams by some institutions in order to comply with Title IX's proportionality requirements. Equal treatment cases typically involve challenges to individual treatment of female athletes, including the availability of scholarships, the compensation of coaches, and related issues.

Before the passage of Title IX (20 U.S.C. § 1681 *et seq.*) (see Section 13.5.3), the legal aspects of this controversy centered on the Fourteenth Amendment's equal protection clause. As in earlier admissions cases (Section 8.2.4.2), courts searched for an appropriate analysis by which to ascertain the constitutionality of sex-based classifications in athletics. Since the implementation in 1975 of the Title IX regulations (34 C.F.R. Part 106), the equal protection aspects of sex discrimination in high school and college athletics have played second fiddle to Title IX. Title IX applies to both public and private institutions receiving federal aid and thus has a broader reach than equal protection, which applies only to public institutions (see Section 1.5.2). Title IX also has several provisions on athletics that establish requirements more extensive than anything devised under the banner of equal protection. And Title IX is supported by enforcement mechanisms beyond those available for the equal protection clause (see Sections 13.5.8 & 13.5.9).

In addition to Title IX, state law (including state equal rights amendments) also has significant applications to college athletics.[28] In *Blair v. Washington State University,* 740 P.2d 1379 (Wash. 1987), for example, women athletes and coaches at Washington State University used the state's equal rights amendment and the state nondiscrimination law to challenge the institution's funding for women's athletic programs. The trial court had ruled against the university, saying that funding for women's athletic programs should be based on the percentage of women enrolled as undergraduates. In calculating the formula, however, the trial court had excluded football revenues. The Washington Supreme Court reversed on that point, declaring that the state's equal rights amendment "contains no exception for football." It remanded the case to the trial court for revision of the funding formula. (See "Comment: *Blair v. Washington State University:* Making State ERAs a Potent Remedy for Sex Discrimination in Athletics," 14 *J. Coll. & Univ. Law* 575 (1988).)

Although the regulations interpreting Title IX with regard to athletics became effective in 1975, they were not appreciably enforced at the postsecondary level until the late 1980s—partly because the U.S. Supreme Court, in *Grove City College v. Bell* (discussed in Section 13.5.7.3), had held that Title IX's non-discrimination provisions applied only to those programs that were direct recipients of federal aid. Congress reversed the result in *Grove City* in the Civil Rights

---

[28]The cases are collected in Jeffrey H. Ghent, Annot., "Application of State Law to Sex Discrimination in Sports," 66 A.L.R.3d 1262.

Restoration Act of 1987, making it clear that Title IX applies to all activities of colleges and universities that receive federal funds.

Section 106.41 of the Title IX regulations is the primary provision on athletics; it establishes various equal opportunity requirements applicable to "interscholastic, intercollegiate, club, or intramural athletics." Section 106.37(c) establishes equal opportunity requirements regarding the availability of athletic scholarships. Physical education classes are covered by Section 106.34, and extracurricular activities related to athletics, such as cheerleading and booster clubs, are covered generally under Section 106.31. The regulations impose nondiscrimination requirements on these activities whether or not they are directly subsidized by federal funds (see this book, Section 13.5.7.4), and they do not exempt revenue-generating sports, such as men's football or basketball, from the calculation of funds available for the institution's athletic programs.

One of the greatest controversies stirred by Title IX concerns the choice of sex-segregated versus unitary (integrated) athletic teams. The regulations develop a compromise approach to this issue, which roughly parallels the equal protection principles that emerged from the earlier court cases.[29] Under Section 106.41(b):

> [An institution] may operate or sponsor separate teams for members of each sex where selection for such teams is based upon competitive skill or the activity involved is a contact sport. However, where a recipient operates or sponsors a team in a particular sport for members of one sex but operates or sponsors no such team for members of the other sex, and athletic opportunities for members of that sex have previously been limited, members of the excluded sex must be allowed to try out for the team offered unless the sport involved is a contact sport. For the purposes of this part, contact sports include boxing, wrestling, rugby, ice hockey, football, basketball, and other sports the purpose or major activity of which involves bodily contact.

This regulation requires institutions to operate unitary teams only for noncontact sports where selection is not competitive. Otherwise, the institution may operate either unitary or separate teams and may even operate a team for one sex without having any team in the sport for the opposite sex, as long as the

---

[29]It is still somewhat an open question whether Title IX's athletic regulations fully comply with constitutional equal protection and due process requirements. There is some basis for arguing that the Title IX regulations do not fully meet the equal protection requirements that courts have constructed or will construct in this area (see W. Kaplin & S. Marmur, "Validity of the 'Separate but Equal' Policy of the Title IX Regulations on Athletics," a memorandum reprinted in 121 *Cong. Rec.* 1090, 94th Cong., 1st Sess. (1975)). One court has ruled on the question, holding Section 86.41(b) (now 106.41(b)) of the Title IX regulations unconstitutional as applied to exclude physically qualified girls from competing with boys in contact sports (*Yellow Springs Exempted Village School District v. Ohio High School Athletic Association*, 443 F. Supp. 753 (S.D. Ohio 1978)). On appeal, however, a U.S. Court of Appeals reversed the district court's ruling (647 F.2d 651 (6th Cir. 1981)). The appellate court held that, because of the posture of the case and the absence of evidence in the record, "we believe it inappropriate for this court to make any ruling on the matter at this time." The majority opinion and a concurring/dissenting opinion include extensive constitutional analysis of sex segregation in athletic teams.

institution's overall athletic program "effectively accommodate[s] the interests and abilities of members of both sexes" (34 C.F.R. § 106.41(c)(1)). In a non-contact sport, however, if an institution operates only one competitively selected team, it must be open to both sexes whenever the "athletic opportunities" of the traditionally excluded sex "have previously been limited" (34 C.F.R. § 106.41(b)).

Regardless of whether its teams are separate or unitary, the institution must "provide equal athletic opportunity for members of both sexes" (34 C.F.R. § 106.41(c)). While equality of opportunity does not require either equality of "aggregate expenditures for members of each sex" or equality of "expenditures for male and female teams," an institution's "failure to provide necessary funds for teams for one sex" is a relevant factor in determining compliance (34 C.F.R. § 106.41(c)). Postsecondary administrators grappling with this slippery equal opportunity concept will be helped by Section 106.41(c)'s list of ten nonexclusive factors by which to measure overall equality:

1. Whether the selection of sports and levels of competition effectively accommodate the interests and abilities of members of both sexes;

2. The provision of equipment and supplies;

3. Scheduling of games and practice time;

4. Travel and per diem allowance;

5. Opportunity to receive coaching and academic tutoring;

6. Assignment and compensation of coaches and tutors;

7. Provision of locker rooms and practice and competitive facilities;

8. Provision of medical and training facilities and services;

9. Provision of housing and dining facilities and services;

10. Publicity.

The equal opportunity focus of the regulations also applies to athletic scholarships. Institutions must "provide reasonable opportunities for such awards for members of each sex in proportion to the number of each sex participating in . . . intercollegiate athletics" (34 C.F.R. § 106.37(c)(1)). If the institution operates separate teams for each sex (as permitted in § 106.41), it may allocate athletic scholarships on the basis of sex to implement its separate-team philosophy, as long as the overall allocation achieves equal opportunity.

In 1979, after a period of substantial controversy, the Department of Health, Education and Welfare (now Department of Education) issued a lengthy "Policy Interpretation" of its Title IX regulations as they apply to intercollegiate athletics (44 Fed. Reg. 71413 (December 11, 1979)). This "Policy Interpretation," available on the Web site of the Office for Civil Rights (OCR) (http://www.ed. gov/about/offices/list/ocr/docs/t9interp.html), is still considered authoritative and is currently used by federal courts reviewing allegations of Title IX violations. It addresses each of the ten factors listed in Section 106.41(c) of the regulations, providing examples of information the Department of Education will use to determine whether an institution has complied with Title IX. For example, "opportunity to receive coaching and academic tutoring" would include the availability of full-time and part-time coaches for male and female athletes, the relative availability of graduate assistants, and the availability of tutors for male and female athletes. "Compensation of coaches" includes attention to the rates of compensation, conditions relating to contract renewal, nature of coaching duties performed, and working conditions of coaches for male and female teams (44 Fed. Reg. at 71416). Also on the OCR Web site is a "Clarification of Intercollegiate Athletics Policy Guidance: The Three-Part Test" (available at http://www.ed.gov/about/offices/list/ocr/docs/clarific.html). This Clarification was issued in January 1996.

The debate over Title IX intensified during 2002–2003 when a Commission on Opportunities in Athletics, appointed by then U.S. Secretary of Education Rod Paige, deliberated about the possibility of changing the way that Title IX was enforced. The commission's final report made various recommendations about the operation and enforcement of "three-prong test" and the Title IX athletics regulations (Secretary of Education's Commission on Opportunity in Athletics, *Open to All: Title IX at Thirty* (U.S. Dept. of Education, February 28, 2003). On July 11, 2003, the U.S. Department of Education issued a "Further Clarification of Intercollegiate Athletics Policy Guidance Regarding Title IX Compliance" (available at http://www.ed.gov/ocr/docs/clarific.html). The ultimate outcome of the commission's work and the Office of Civil Rights' response to it was to ratify the "three-prong test" for determining whether an institution's athletic program is complying with Title IX, a result that disappointed critics of the "proportionality" requirement that had apparently stimulated some institutions to drop certain men's varsity sports in order to reallocate funding to women's sports. In March 2005, the Office of Civil Rights issued an "Additional Clarification of Intercollegiate Athletics: Three-Part Test—Part Three" (available at http://www.ed.gov/print/about/offices/list/ocr/docs/title9guidanceadditional.html) that allows institutions to use a survey to measure student athletic interest. The NCAA and proponents of gender equity in college sports have criticized the new OCR policy. (For a thorough review and analysis of these "clarifications," see Catherine Pieronek, "An Analysis of the New Clarification of Intercollegiate Athletics Policy Regarding Part Three of the Three-Part Test for Compliance with the Effective Accommodation Guidelines of Title IX," 32 *J. Coll. & Univ. Law* 105 (2005).)

Most Title IX disputes have involved complaints to the Office for Civil Rights. In the past, this office has been criticized for its "lax" enforcement efforts and for permitting institutions to remain out of compliance with Title IX (*Gender Equity in Intercollegiate Athletics: The Inadequacy of Title IX Enforcement by the U.S. Office for Civil Rights* (Lyndon B. Johnson School of Public Affairs, University of Texas, 1993)). Perhaps partly for this reason, women athletes in recent years have chosen to litigate their claims in the courts.

Although the first major court challenge to an institution's funding for intercollegiate athletics ended with a settlement rather than a court order (*Haffer v. Temple University*, 678 F. Supp. 517 (E.D. Pa. 1987)), this case set the tone for subsequent litigation. In *Haffer,* a federal trial judge certified a class of "all current women students at Temple University who participate, or who are or have been deterred from participating because of sex discrimination[,] in Temple's intercollegiate athletic program." Although the case was settled, with the university agreeing to various changes in scholarships and support for women athletes, it encouraged women students at other colleges and universities to challenge the revenues allocated to women's and men's sports. (For discussion, see "Comment: *Haffer v. Temple University:* A Reawakening of Gender Discrimination in Intercollegiate Athletics," 16 *J. Coll. & Univ. Law* 137 (1989).)

The leading case to date on Title IX's application to alleged inequality in funding for women's intercollegiate sports is *Cohen v. Brown University,* 991 F.2d 888 (1st Cir. 1993). In that case, a U.S. Court of Appeals upheld a district court's preliminary injunction ordering Brown University to reinstate its women's gymnastics and women's volleyball programs to full varsity status pending the trial of a Title IX claim. Until 1971, Brown had been an all-male university. At that time it merged with a women's college and, over the next six years, upgraded the women's athletic program to include fourteen varsity teams. It later added one other such team. It thus had fifteen women's varsity teams as compared to sixteen men's varsity teams; the women had 36.7 percent of all the varsity athletic opportunities available at the university, and the men had 63.3 percent. (Brown's student population is approximately 48 percent women.) In 1991, however, the university cut four varsity teams: two men's teams (for a savings of $15,795) and two women's teams (for a savings of $62,028). These cuts disproportionately reduced the budgeted funds for women, but they did not significantly change the ratio of athletic opportunities, since women retained 36.6 percent of the available slots.

In upholding the district court's injunction, the appellate court first noted that an institution would not be found in violation of Title IX merely because there was a statistical disparity between the percentage of women and the percentage of men in its athletic programs. The court then focused on the ten factors listed in Section 106.41(c) of the Title IX regulations (see above) and noted that the district court based its injunction on the first of these factors: "Brown's failure effectively to accommodate the interests and abilities of female students in the selection and level of sports." To be in compliance with this factor, a university must satisfy at least one of three tests set out in the Title IX Policy Interpretation:

> (1) Whether intercollegiate level participation opportunities for male and female students are provided in numbers substantially proportionate to their respective enrollments; or
> (2) Where the members of one sex have been and are underrepresented among intercollegiate athletes, whether the institution can show a history and continuing practice of program expansion which is demonstrably responsive to the developing interest and abilities of the members of that sex; or
> (3) Where the members of one sex have been and are underrepresented among intercollegiate athletes, and the institution cannot show a continuing practice of program expansion such as that cited above, whether it can be

demonstrated that the interests and abilities of the members of that sex have been fully and effectively accommodated by the present program [44 Fed. Reg. at 71418].

The appellate court agreed with the district court that Brown clearly did not fall within the first option. Further, the district court did not abuse its discretion in deciding that, although the university had made a large number of improvements between 1971 and 1977, the lack of continuing expansion efforts precluded the university from satisfying the second option. Thus, since the university could not comply with either of the first two options, "it must comply with the third benchmark. To do so, the school must fully and effectively accommodate the underrepresented gender's interests and abilities, even if that requires it to give the underrepresented gender . . . what amounts to a larger slice of a shrinking athletic-opportunity pie." The appellate court then focused on the word "fully" in the third option, interpreting it literally to the effect that the underrepresented sex must be "fully" accommodated, not merely proportionately accommodated as in the first option. Since Brown's cuts in the women's athletic programs had created a demand for athletics opportunities for women that was not filled, women were not "fully" accommodated. Thus, since Brown could meet none of the three options specified in the Policy Interpretation, the court concluded that the university had likely violated Title IX, and it therefore affirmed the district court's entry of the preliminary injunction.[30]

Holding that the plaintiffs had made their required showing and that Brown had not, the court turned to the issue of remedy. Although the appellate court upheld the preliminary injunction, it noted the need to balance the institution's academic freedom with the need for an effective remedy for the Title IX violation. The appellate court stated that, since the lower court had not yet held a trial on the merits, its order that Brown maintain women's varsity volleyball and gymnastics teams pending trial was within its discretion. The appellate court noted, however, that a more appropriate posttrial remedy, assuming that a Title IX violation was established, would be for Brown to propose a program for compliance. In balancing academic freedom against Title IX's regulatory scheme, the court noted:

This litigation presents an array of complicated and important issues at a crossroads of the law that few courts have explored. The beacon by which we must steer is Congress's unmistakably clear mandate that educational institutions not use federal monies to perpetuate gender-based discrimination. At the same time, we must remain sensitive to the fact that suits of this genre implicate the discretion of universities to pursue their missions free from governmental interference and, in the bargain, to deploy increasingly scarce resources in the most advantageous way [991 F.2d at 907].

---

[30]The appellate court's opinion also contained an important discussion of the plaintiff's and defendant's burdens of proof in presenting and rebutting a Title IX athletics claim (991 F.2d at 902). See also *Roberts v. Colorado State Board of Agriculture*, 998 F.2d 824, 831–32 (10th Cir. 1993); and compare *Cook v. Colgate University*, 802 F. Supp. 737 (N.D.N.Y. 1992), *vacated on other grounds*, 992 F.2d 17 (2d Cir. 1993).

After the appellate court remanded the case to the district court, that court held a full trial on the merits, after which it ruled again in favor of the plaintiffs and ordered Brown to submit a plan for achieving full compliance with Title IX. When the district court found Brown's plan to be inadequate and entered its own order specifying that Brown must remedy its Title IX violation by elevating four women's teams to full varsity status, Brown appealed again. In late 1996, the First Circuit issued another ruling in what it called *"Cohen IV" (Cohen II* being its earlier 1993 ruling, and *Cohen* I and *Cohen* III being the district court rulings that preceded *Cohen* II and *Cohen* IV). By a 2-to-1 vote in *Cohen* IV, 101 F.3d 155 (1st Cir. 1996), the appellate court affirmed the district court's ruling that Brown was in violation of Title IX. The court explicitly relied upon, and refused to reconsider, its legal analysis from *Cohen* II. The *Cohen* II reasoning, as further explicated in *Cohen* IV, thus remains the law in the First Circuit and the leading example of how courts will apply Title IX to the claims of women athletes.

One of Brown's major arguments in *Cohen* IV was that women were less interested in participating in collegiate sports, and that the trial court's ruling required Brown to provide opportunities for women that went beyond their interests and abilities. The court viewed this argument "with great suspicion" and rejected it:

> Thus, there exists the danger that, rather than providing a true measure of women's interest in sports, statistical evidence purporting to reflect women's interest instead provides only a measure of the very discrimination that is and has been the basis for women's lack of opportunity to participate in sports. . . . [E]ven if it can be empirically demonstrated that, at a particular time, women have less interest in sports than do men, such evidence, standing alone, cannot justify providing fewer athletics opportunities for women than for men. Furthermore, such evidence is completely irrelevant where, as here, viable and successful women's varsity teams have been demoted or eliminated [101 F.3d at 179–80].

Regarding Brown's obligation to remedy its Title IX violation, however, the *Cohen* IV court overruled the district court, because that court "erred in substituting its own specific relief in place of Brown's statutorily permissible proposal to comply with Title IX by cutting men's teams until substantial proportionality was achieved." The appellate court "agree[d] with the district court that Brown's proposed plan fell short of a good faith effort to meet the requirements of Title IX as explicated by this court in *Cohen* II and as applied by the district court on remand." Nevertheless, it determined that cutting men's teams "is a permissible means of effectuating compliance with the statute," and that Brown should have the opportunity to submit another plan to the district court. This disposition, said the court, was driven by "our respect for academic freedom and reluctance to interject ourselves into the conduct of university affairs."[31]

---

[31]On remand from *Cohen* IV, the federal district court approved a settlement of the case. See Jim Naughton, "Settlement Approval in Brown Title IX Case," *Chron. Higher Educ.*, July 3, 1998, at A31. For cases reaching results similar to the *Cohen* case, see *Favia v. Indiana University of Pennsylvania*, 7 F.3d 332 (3d Cir. 1993); *Roberts v. Colorado State Board of Agriculture*, 998 F.2d 824 (10th Cir. 1993).

In *Pederson v. Louisiana State University,* 213 F.3d 858 (5th Cir. 2000), another federal appellate court ruled that the university had engaged in "systematic, intentional, differential treatment of women," and affirmed a trial court's ruling that the university had violated Title IX. The plaintiffs, representing a class of all women students at Louisiana State University (LSU) who wished to participate in varsity sports that were not provided by LSU, alleged that the university had

> den[ied] them equal opportunity to participate in intercollegiate athletics, equal opportunity to compete for and to receive athletic scholarships, and equal access to the benefits and services that LSU provides to its varsity intercollegiate athletes, and by discriminating against women in the provision of athletic scholarships and in the compensation paid coaches [213 F.3d at 864].

Because the record not only contained evidence of a lack of opportunities for women to play varsity soccer and fast-pitch softball (the sports in question) and substantial differences in the financial resources afforded women's sports compared with men's, but also included a multitude of sexist comments to the women athletes by university sports administrators and admissions that they would only add women's teams "if forced to," the appellate court ruled that the discrimination was intentional and "motivated by chauvinist notions" (213 F.3d at 882).

Both in *Cohen* and in *Pederson,* the courts appeared to serve warning on institutions that do not provide equivalent funding for men's and women's sports. And *Cohen,* in particular, demonstrates that, for institutions that have either a stringently limited athletic budget or one that must be cut, compliance with Title IX can occur only if the institution reduces opportunities for men's sports to the level available for women's sports. Both appellate opinions deferred to the institution's right to determine for itself how it will structure its athletic programs, but once the institution was out of Title IX compliance, these courts did not hesitate to order specific remedies. Financial problems do not exempt an institution from Title IX compliance.[32]

As noted above, individuals who believe that an institution is violating Title IX's requirements of equity in athletics have two choices: they may file a complaint with the Education Department's Office of Civil Rights, or they may file a lawsuit in federal court. The ruling of the U.S. Supreme Court in *Alexander v. Sandoval,* discussed in Sections 13.5.7.2 and 13.5.9 of this book, may complicate future litigation challenging the equity of athletics programs by gender. In *Alexander,* the Court ruled that there is no private right of action for disparate impact claims under Title VI (see Section 13.5.2 of this book). Because the language of Title IX is virtually identical to the language of Title VI, courts

---

[32]The cases are collected in Brian L. Porto, Annot., "Suits by Female College Athletes Against Colleges and Universities Claiming That Decisions to Discontinue Particular Sports or to Deny Varsity Status to Particular Sports Deprive Plaintiffs of Equal Educational Opportunities Required by Title IX (§§ 20 U.S.C.A. 1681–1688)," 129 A.L.R. Fed. 571.

have applied Title VI jurisprudence to claims brought under Title IX. Thus, the outcome in *Alexander* suggests that courts will reject the attempts of plaintiffs to bring disparate impact claims under Title IX. A federal district court has confirmed this interpretation of *Alexander* in *Barrett v. West Chester University*, 2003 U.S. Dist. LEXIS 21095 (E.D. Pa., November 12, 2003), but found that the university had intentionally discriminated against women students by eliminating the women's gymnastic team, by failing to provide equal coaching resources to male and female teams, and by paying coaches of women's teams less than coaches of men's teams. The court granted the plaintiffs' motion for an injunction, requiring the reinstatement of the women's gymnastic team. Had the plaintiffs been limited to a claim of disparate impact, rather than intentional discrimination, the court would have dismissed their claim.

Under *Alexander v. Sandoval*, therefore, plaintiffs may challenge discrimination in athletics in court only by asserting claims of intentional discrimination brought under § 901 of the Title IX *statute*, which has been interpreted to permit a private right of action. Should the Title IX regulations or ED policy interpretations be interpreted as prohibiting discriminatory actions that are unintentional, but which have a harsher impact on members of one gender, athletes with such disparate impact claims may assert them only in the institution's Title IX grievance process or in ED's administrative complaint process. In addition, under *Alexander*, plaintiffs will not be able to bring private causes of action claiming *intentional* violations of the Title IX regulations or the ED policy interpretations unless they can show that the cause of action is also grounded on the Title IX statute itself and not merely on the regulations and/or policy interpretation(s).

Although federal courts have analyzed cases involving equal access to athletics opportunities using one or more of the factors listed in the regulations (discussed above), the appellate courts are divided as to whether the burden of proof created by the U.S. Supreme Court in 1998 for plaintiffs suing under Title IX for sexual harassment should also be applied to Title IX litigation concerning athletics. In *Gebser v. Lago Vista Independent School District*, discussed in Section 9.3.4, the U.S. Supreme Court ruled that a plaintiff must prove that (1) the school had actual notice of the alleged discrimination, and (2) the school demonstrated "deliberate indifference" in its response to the student's claim. The U.S. Court of Appeals for the Fifth Circuit in *Pederson v. Louisiana State University*, discussed above, rejected the defendant's argument that the *Gebser* test should apply in a lawsuit regarding equal access to athletic opportunities, using instead the traditional three-part test from the OCR's Policy Interpretation.

The *Pederson* court reasoned that the institution itself had intentionally discriminated against the women athletes, so the *Gebser* framework, which addressed whether the school was on notice of discriminatory conduct by an employee, was not relevant. On the other hand, the U.S. Court of Appeals for the Eighth Circuit, in *Grandson v. University of Minnesota*, 272 F.3d 568 (8th Cir. 2001), *cert. denied*, 535 U.S. 1054 (2002), dismissed a Title IX lawsuit filed by a woman student seeking compensatory damages for the university's alleged failure to provide equitable funding for the women's soccer team, scholarships, and other resources. The court, applying the *Gebser* test, ruled that the plaintiff had not proved that a responsible university individual had "actual notice" of the alleged discrimination, and that the plaintiff's allegations of a funding disparity between men's and women's athletics was insufficient proof of intentional discrimination.

In addition to claims from women students that funding is inadequate, courts have also considered Title IX claims of men seeking reinstatement of men's teams that their institutions had cut. An early example of such a case is *Kelley v. Board of Trustees of University of Illinois*, 35 F.3d 265 (7th Cir. 1994), in which a federal appellate court upheld the university's discontinuance of the men's swimming team. The appellate court accorded deference to the Title IX regulations and the Policy Interpretation on intercollegiate athletics. Because the university had done its cutting of teams in accordance with the regulations and the interpretation, seeking to achieve proportionality between men's and women's athletic teams, the court affirmed the district court's grant of summary judgment for the university.

The same appellate court (the Seventh Circuit) later expanded upon its *Kelley* ruling in *Boulahanis v. Board of Regents*, 198 F.3d 633 (7th Cir. 1999). That case involved Illinois State University's decision to cut the men's soccer and wrestling teams in order to achieve compliance with Title IX. Reiterating its ruling in *Kelley*, the court rejected the plaintiffs' attempt to distinguish their case from *Kelley* by arguing that the university in *Kelley* cut its men's athletic teams for budgetary reasons while the university here did so for the sole purpose of Title IX compliance. The court quickly recognized that financial considerations cannot be "neatly separated" from Title IX considerations and that decisions regarding which athletic programs to retain are "based on a combination of financial and sex-based concerns that are not easily distinguished."[33]

Another leading case on men's teams is *Neal v. California State University*, 198 F.3d 763 (9th Cir. 1999). In that case, California State University at Bakersfield (CSUB), in the face of shrinking budgetary resources, was working to achieve compliance with Title IX under a consent decree entered in a previous Title IX suit. CSUB decided to limit the size of several of its male athletic teams. After it required the men's wrestling team to reduce its roster, the wrestlers brought suit under Title IX, and the federal district court enjoined the reduction. On appeal, the Ninth Circuit vacated the injunction and upheld the university's actions.

The wrestlers argued that the "substantially proportionate" requirement in the Policy Interpretation could be met by providing opportunities in proportion

---

[33]The *Boulahanis* court also had the opportunity to address an equal protection clause challenge to the Title IX regulations. Rejecting the argument that the regulations, if interpreted to permit elimination of men's teams, would violate equal protection, the court explained that the university's action met the standard of review applicable to gender discrimination under the equal protection clause: "[t]he elimination of sex-based discrimination in federally-funded educational institutions is an important government objective, and the actions of Illinois State University in eliminating the men's soccer and the men's wrestling programs were substantially related to that objective."

to the interest levels of each gender, rather than in proportion to the actual enrollment figures. Rejecting this argument, the court determined that such an interest-based interpretation of the Policy Interpretation "'limit[s] required program expansion for the underrepresented sex to the status quo level of relative interests'" (198 F.3d at 768, quoting *Cohen* IV (above), 101 F.3d at 174) and does so "'under circumstances where men's athletic teams have a considerable head start'" (198 F.3d at 768, quoting *Cohen* II, 991 F.2d at 900).

The appellate court also addressed the wrestlers' argument that Title IX does not permit cutting of men's teams as a means to remedy gender inequity in athletics, but provides only for increasing women's teams. In responding to this argument, the court relied on the decisions of other circuits, such as the Seventh Circuit's decision in *Kelley v. Board of Trustees* that had already approved of universities' cutting men's teams to comply with Title IX. The *Neal* court also asserted that the legislative history of Title IX indicates Congress was aware that compliance might sometimes be achieved only by cutting men's athletics.

Finally, the appellate court in *Neal* explained that the district court had erred in not deferring to the U.S. Department of Education's Policy Interpretation. Citing U.S. Supreme Court precedent, the court emphasized that "federal courts are to defer substantially to an agency's interpretation of its own regulations," unless that interpretation is plainly inconsistent with the statute or would raise "serious constitutional issues"—neither of which is the case with the Policy Interpretation.

Following *Boulahanis* and *Neal*, federal appellate courts rejected challenges to the elimination of varsity wrestling teams at the University of North Dakota (*Chalenor v. Univ. of N. Dakota*, 291 F.3d 1042 (8th Cir. 2002)), and Miami University (*Miami Wrestling Club v. Miami Univ.*, 302 F.3d 608 (6th Cir. 2002)). The National Wrestling Coaches Association brought a lawsuit against the U.S. Office for Civil Rights, challenging the 1996 "Clarification of Intercollegiate Athletics Policy Guidance: The Three Part Test" as well as the "Policy Interpretation" issued in 1979 (both of which are on the OCR's Web site, noted above). The district court dismissed the case on the grounds that the plaintiffs did not have standing to pursue that claim, and the appellate court affirmed. *National Wrestling Coaches Assoc. v. U.S. Department of Educ.*, 263 F. Supp. 2d 82 (D.D.C. 2003), *affirmed*, 366 F.3d 930 (D.C. Cir. 2004). According to the appellate court, even if the two documents challenged by the Coaches Association were revoked, the law would still permit an institution to eliminate the men's wrestling program in order to comply with Title IX's gender equity mandate.

The plaintiffs filed a motion for an *en banc* review by the appellate court. The panel, in a 2-to-1 decision, rejected the coaches' request for rehearing, stating that the coaches' real dispute was with the institutions that had cut wrestling, not with the Department of Education (383 F.3d 1047 (D.C. Cir. 2004)). Rejecting the coaches' argument that the U.S. Department of Education had "forced" colleges and universities to adopt policies with respect to proportionality that are unlawful under Title IX, the majority noted that the department's policy statements are not regulations, and that universities are not required to follow them. Because the plaintiffs had a "fully adequate" private cause of action against the institutions that dropped their wrestling teams, said the court, the coaches needed to look to the institutions for relief. As these cases suggest, male athletes are likely to have a much more difficult time contesting the cutting of men's teams than are female athletes in contesting the cutting of women's teams.

In addition to litigating the allocation of resources to men's and women's teams, individual athletes have occasionally used Title IX to gain a position on a varsity team. For example, in *Mercer v. Duke University*, 32 F. Supp. 2d 836 (M.D.N.C. 1998), *reversed*, 190 F.3d 643 (4th Cir. 1999), a student claimed that Duke University violated Title IX by excluding her from the university's inter-collegiate football team. The student had been an all-state place kicker while in high school in New York State. During the first year of college, she sought to join the football team as a walk-on. Although she attended tryouts and practiced with the team for two seasons, the head coach ultimately excluded her from the team. The plaintiff alleged in the lawsuit that the university treated her differently from male walk-on place kickers of lesser ability and failed to give her full and fair consideration for team membership because of her gender. The district court held that, even if the student's allegations were true, the university would nevertheless prevail. Relying on the "contact sport" exception in applicable Title IX regulations prohibiting different treatment in athletics based on gender (34 C.F.R. § 106.41), the court granted the university's motion to dismiss. According to the court, since "football is clearly a 'contact sport,' a straightforward reading of this regulation demands the holding that, as a matter of law, Duke University had no obligation to allow Mercer, or any female, onto its football team."

On appeal, the U.S. Court of Appeals read the applicable regulation differently from the district court and reinstated the case for further proceedings. The appellate court determined that, contrary to providing a "blanket exemption for contact sports," subsection (b) of the regulation (34 C.F.R. § 106.41(b)) merely "excepts contact sports from the tryout requirement," that is, the requirement that members of the excluded sex be allowed to try out for a single-sex team. But "once an institution has allowed a member of one sex to try out for a team operated . . . for the other sex in a contact sport," the institution is subject to "the general anti-discrimination provision" in subsection (a) of the applicable regulation (34 C.F.R. § 106.41(a)). The appellate court therefore held that once a university has allowed tryouts, it is "subject to Title IX and therefore prohibited from discriminating against [the person trying out] on the basis of his or her sex."

The Title IX controversy about dropping and adding men's and women's teams has extended to the area of athletic scholarships. The pertinent regulation is 34 C.F.R. § 106.37(c), as interpreted in 44 Fed. Reg. 71413, 71415–23. This regulation, somewhat like the regulation at issue in *Cohen* (34 C.F.R. § 106.41(c)), uses a proportionality test to determine whether benefits are equitably distributed between men and women. In 1998, the U.S. Department of Education's Office for Civil Rights issued a clarification of its requirements for scholarships. And litigation by male athletes whose teams (and scholarships) have been cut in order to comply with Title IX has been unavailing. (See, for example, *Harper v. Board of Regents, Illinois State University,* 35 F. Supp. 2d 1118 (C.D. Ill. 1999), *affirmed, Boulahanis et al. v. Board of Regents,* 198 F.3d 633 (7th Cir. 1999), in which the court awarded summary judgment to the university on grounds that elimination of men's teams and scholarships was not discriminatory; Title IX compliance was a legitimate nondiscriminatory reason for the action.)

10.4.7. Discrimination on the basis of disability.
Under Section 504 of the Rehabilitation Act of 1973 and its implementing regulations (see Section 13.5.4 of this book), institutions must afford disabled students an equal opportunity to participate in physical education, athletic, and recreational programs. Like Title IX, Section 504 applies to athletic activities even if they are not directly subsidized by federal funds (see Section 13.5.7.4). The Department of Education's regulations set forth the basic requirements at 34 C.F.R. § 104.47(a), requiring institutions to offer physical education courses and athletic activities on a nondiscriminatory basis to disabled students.

By these regulations, a student in a wheelchair could be eligible to participate in a regular archery program, for instance, or a deaf student on a regular wrestling team (34 C.F.R. Part 104 Appendix A), because they would retain full capacity to play those sports despite their disabilities. In these and other situations, however, questions may arise concerning whether the student's skill level would qualify him to participate in the program or allow him to succeed in the competition required for selection to intercollegiate teams.

Litigation involving challenges under Section 504 by disabled athletes has been infrequent, although there are several cases involving student challenges to NCAA eligibility rulings, which are discussed in Section 14.4.5. In an early case, *Wright v. Columbia University,* 520 F. Supp. 789 (E.D. Pa. 1981), the court relied on Section 504 to protect a disabled student's right to participate in intercollegiate football. The student had been blind in one eye since infancy; because of the potential danger to his "good" eye, the institution had denied him permission to participate. In issuing a temporary restraining order against the university, the court accepted (pending trial) the student's argument that the institution's decision was discriminatory within the meaning of Section 504 because the student was qualified to play football despite his disability and was capable of making his own decisions about "his health and well-being."

But another federal trial court sided with the university in its determination that participation by a student was potentially dangerous. In *Pahulu v. University of Kansas,* 897 F. Supp. 1387 (D. Kan. 1995), the plaintiff was a football player who had sustained a blow to the head during a scrimmage and consequently experienced tingling and numbness in his arms and legs. After the team physician and a consulting neurosurgeon diagnosed the symptoms as transient quadriplegia caused by a congenitally narrow cervical cord, they recommended that the student be disqualified from play for his senior year—even though he obtained the opinions of three other specialists who concluded he was fit to play. The student then sought a preliminary injunction, claiming that the university's decision violated Section 504. The court disagreed, holding that the plaintiff (1) was not disabled within the meaning of Section 504 and (2) was not "otherwise qualified" to play football even if he was disabled. As to (1), the court reasoned that the plaintiff's physical impairment did not "substantially limit" the "major life activity" of learning, since he still retained his athletic scholarship, continued to have the same access to educational opportunities and academic resources, and could participate in the football program in some other capacity. As to (2), the court reasoned that the plaintiff did not meet the "technical standards" of the football program because he had failed to obtain medical clearance, and that the university's position was reasonable and rational, albeit conservative.

Knapp v. Northwestern University, 101 F.3d 473 (7th Cir. 1996), uses reasoning similar to—but more fully developed than—that in *Pahulu* to deny relief to a basketball player who had been declared ineligible due to a heart problem. Applying the Section 504 definition of disability, the court ruled that (1) playing intercollegiate basketball is not itself a "major life activit[y]," nor is it an integral part of "learning," which the Section 504 regulations do acknowledge to be a major life activity; (2) the plaintiff's heart problem only precludes him from performing "a particular function" and does not otherwise "substantially limit" his major life activity of learning at the university; and (3) consequently, the plaintiff is not disabled within the meaning of Section 504 and cannot claim its protections. The court also ruled that the plaintiff could not claim Section 504 protection because he was not "otherwise qualified," since he could not meet the physical standards. In reaching this conclusion, the court deferred to the university's judgment regarding the substantiality of risk and the severity of harm to the plaintiff, stating that, as long as the university and its medical advisors used reasonable criteria to make the decisions, the court should not second-guess those judgments.

In addition to Section 504, the Americans With Disabilities Act (see Section 13.2.11) may also provide protections for student athletes subjected to discrimination on the basis of a disability in institutional athletic programs. Title II of the Act (public services) (42 U.S.C. §§ 12131–12134) would apply to students in public institutions, and Title III (public accommodations) (42 U.S.C. §§ 12181–12189) would apply to students in private institutions. (See generally C. Jones, "College Athletes: Illness or Injury and the Decision to Return to Play," 40 *Buffalo L. Rev.* 113, 189–97 (1992).)

In addition to the right of disabled students to participate in a particular sport, an emerging issue concerns whether academic eligibility requirements for student athletes may discriminate against learning-disabled athletes. The cases thus far have arisen primarily under the Americans With Disabilities Act rather than under Section 504. Although these cases have focused on eligibility requirements of the NCAA (especially the "core course requirement") (see Section 14.4.6.2) rather than separate requirements of individual institutions, many of the same legal issues would arise if a learning disabled athlete were to challenge his or her school's own eligibility requirements or were to challenge the school for following NCAA requirements. These issues would include whether the learning disability is a "disability" within the meaning of the ADA (see the

Tatum case, discussed in Section 14.4.6.2); whether the institution's academic eligibility requirements are discriminatory because, for instance, they "screen out or tend to screen out" learning disabled students under Title III of the ADA, § 12182(b)(2)(A)(i) (see the *Ganden* case, discussed in Section 14.4.6.2); whether the student's requested modifications to the eligibility requirements were "reasonable" or, to the contrary, would fundamentally alter the intercollegiate athletic program or the institution's academic mission as it interfaces with athletics (see *Ganden* and also the *Bowers* case in Section 14.4.6.2); and whether the institution has conducted a suitable individualized assessment of the student's need for modifications (see *Bowers* in Section 14.4.6.2).

An emerging issue, albeit one that has yet to see litigation, is whether either Section 504 or the ADA requires a university to provide separate athletic teams for students with disabilities, as is required by Title IX for women students. (For a discussion of this issue that includes a range of opinions by legal experts and proponents of athletics opportunities for students with disabilities, see Welch Suggs, "'Varsity' with an Asterisk: Disabled Students Are Making a Case for Equal Access to College Athletics Budgets," *Chron. Higher Educ.*, February 13, 2004, A35 (available at http://chronicle.com/weekly/v50/i23/23a03501.htm). For a critical analysis of the judicial rulings discussed above, see Adam A. Milani, "Can I Play? The Dilemma of the Disabled Athlete in Interscholastic Sports," 49 *Ala. L. Rev.* 817 (1998).)

10.4.8. Drug testing.

10.4.8. Drug testing. Drug testing of athletes has become a focus of controversy in both amateur and professional sports. Intercollegiate athletics is no exception. Legal issues may arise under the federal Constitution's Fourth Amendment search and seizure clause and its Fourteenth Amendment due process clause; under search and seizure, due process, or right to privacy clauses of state constitutions; under various state civil rights statutes; under state tort law (see generally Section 3.3.2); or under the institution's own regulations, including statements of students' rights. Public institutions may be subject to challenges based on any of these sources; private institutions generally are subject only to challenges based on tort law, their own regulations, civil rights statutes applicable to private action, and (in some states) state constitutional provisions limiting private as well as public action (see generally Section 1.5).

For public institutions, the primary concern is the Fourth Amendment of the federal Constitution, which protects individuals against unreasonable searches and seizures, and parallel state constitutional provisions that may provide similar (and sometimes greater) protections. In *Skinner v. Railway Labor Executives Ass'n.*, 489 U.S. 602, 619 (1989), the U.S. Supreme Court held that the collection of urine or blood for drug testing constitutes a search within the meaning of the Fourth Amendment, and that the validity of such a search is determined by balancing the legitimacy of the government's interest against the degree of intrusion upon the individual's privacy interest.

Drug-testing policies may provide for testing if there is a reasonable suspicion that a student may either have used drugs recently or may be currently impaired; or they may provide for random testing, where a reasonable suspicion of drug use is not an issue. The courts have examined both types of policies. Although policies that require a reasonable suspicion are more likely to be upheld than those involving random testing, they are still subject to the standards set forth in *Skinner.*

Derdeyn v. University of Colorado, 832 P.2d 1031 (Colo. Ct. App. 1991), *affirmed,* 863 P.2d 929 (Colo. 1993), provides an example of a university drug-testing program held to be unreasonable under the *Skinner* standard. The university initiated a program for testing its student athletes when it had a "reasonable suspicion" that they were using drugs. As a condition to participation in intercollegiate athletics, all athletes were asked to sign a form consenting to such tests. The university initiated the program "because of a desire to prepare its athletes for drug testing in NCAA sanctioned sporting events, a concern for athletes' health, an interest in promoting its image, and a desire to ensure fair competition" (832 P.2d at 1032). In a class action suit, student athletes challenged this program on several grounds. The Supreme Court of Colorado held that the program violated both the federal Constitution's Fourth Amendment and a similar provision of the Colorado constitution. Applying the *Skinner* test, the court determined that the drug-testing program was unconstitutional. In addition, the court held that the university's consent form was not sufficient to waive the athletes' constitutional rights. The university bore the burden of proof in showing that the waiver was signed voluntarily. Relying on the trial testimony of several athletes, which "revealed that, because of economic or other commitments the students had made to the University, [the students] were not faced with an unfettered choice in regard to signing the consent" (832 P.2d at 1035), the Colorado Supreme Court invalidated the university's program and prohibited its continuation.

The U.S. Supreme Court addressed the lawfulness of testing student athletes in K–12 settings twice since its *Skinner* ruling, and in both cases the Court upheld the testing program. *Vernonia School District 47J v. Acton,* 515 U.S. 646 (1995), involved a constitutional challenge to a public school district's *random* drug testing of student athletes. Seventh grader James Acton and his parents sued the school district after James had been barred from the school football team because he and his parents refused to sign a form consenting to random urinalysis drug testing. In an attempt to control a "sharp increase" in drug use among students, the district had implemented a policy requiring that all student athletes be tested at the beginning of each season for their sport, and that thereafter 10 percent of the athletes be chosen at random for testing each week of the season. In a 6-to-3 decision, the U.S. Supreme Court reversed the U.S. Court of Appeals for the Ninth Circuit (23 F. 3d 1514 (9th Cir. 1994)) and upheld the policy.

The majority opinion by Justice Scalia relied on *Skinner v. Railway Labor Executives Association* to conclude that the collection of urine samples from students is a search that must be analyzed under the reasonableness test. The majority then examined three factors to determine the reasonableness of the search: (1) "the nature of the privacy interest upon which the search . . . intrudes"; (2) "the character of the intrusion that is complained of"; and

(3) "the nature and immediacy of the governmental concern at issue . . . , and the efficacy of [the drug test in] meeting it." Regarding the first factor, the Court emphasized that "particularly with regard to medical examinations and procedures," student athletes have even less of an expectation of privacy than students in general due to the "communal" nature of locker rooms and the additional regulations to which student athletes are subject on matters such as preseason physicals, insurance coverage, and training rules.

Regarding the second factor, the Court stated that urinalysis drug testing is not a significant invasion of the student's privacy because the process for collecting urine samples is "nearly identical to those [conditions] typically encountered in restrooms"; the information revealed by the urinalysis (what drugs, if any, are present in the student's urine) is negligible; the test results are confidential and available only to specific personnel; and the results are not turned over to law enforcement officials. And regarding the third factor, the Court determined that the school district has an "important, indeed perhaps compelling," interest in deterring schoolchildren from drug use as well as a more particular interest in protecting athletes from physical harm that could result from competing in events under the influence of drugs; that there was evidence of a crisis of disciplinary actions and "rebellion . . . being fueled by alcohol and drug abuse," which underscored the immediacy of the district's concerns; and that the drug testing policy "effectively addressed" these concerns. The plaintiffs had argued that the district could fulfill its interests by testing when it had reason to suspect a particular athlete of drug use, and that this would be a less intrusive means of effectuating the interests. The Court rejected this proposal, explaining that it could be abused by teachers singling out misbehaving students, and it would stimulate litigation challenging such testing.

Although *Vernonia* is an elementary/secondary school case, its reasonableness test and the three factors for applying it will also likely guide analysis of Fourth Amendment challenges to drug testing of student athletes at colleges and universities. Some of the considerations relevant to application of the three factors would differ for higher education, however, so it is unclear whether the balance would tip in favor of drug-testing plans, as it did in *Vernonia*. The Court itself took pains to limit its holding to public elementary/secondary education, warning that its analysis might not "pass constitutional muster in other contexts."

(On remand in *Vernonia*, the Ninth Circuit ruled on the merits that the defendant's drug-testing program did not violate the Fourth Amendment or the Oregon constitution; 66 F.3d 217 (9th Cir. 1995).)

The Supreme Court issued another ruling in 2002, this time upholding a random drug-testing policy that covered any student who participated in extracurricular school activities, whether or not they involved athletics. In *Board of Education of Independent School District No. 92 v. Earls*, 536 U.S. 822 (2002), a 5-to-4 decision with a vigorous dissent, the Court, following the three-part test it had established in *Vernonia*, found the random drug-testing policy reasonable. *First*, said the Court, the students had a limited expectation of privacy, even though most nonathletic activities did not involve disrobing or regular physical examinations. The limited expectation of privacy, according to the Court, did not depend upon communal undress, but on the custodial responsibilities of the school for the children in its care. *Second,* the Court found the invasion of the students' privacy to be minimally intrusive, and virtually identical to that found lawful in *Vernonia.* And *third,* the Court found that the policy had a close relationship to the school district's interest in protecting the students' health and safety. There was evidence of some drug use by students who participated in extracurricular activities, although the Court stated that "a demonstrated drug abuse problem is not always necessary to the validity of a testing regime." The dissenting justices found the school district's testing program to be unreasonable because it targeted students "least likely to be at risk from illicit drugs and their damaging effects" (536 U.S. at 843).

Although most of the litigation involving drug-testing policies has involved federal constitutional claims, two cases decided prior to the Supreme Court's *Vernonia* opinion illustrate that state constitutions or civil rights laws provide avenues to challenge these policies. In *Hill v. NCAA,* 273 Cal. Rptr. 402 (Cal. Ct. App. 1990), *reversed,* 865 P.2d 633 (Cal. 1994), Stanford University student athletes challenged the university's implementation of the NCAA's required drug-testing program. The constitutional clause at issue was not a search and seizure clause as such but rather a right to privacy guarantee (Cal. Const. Art. I, § 1). Both the intermediate appellate court and the Supreme Court of California determined that this guarantee covered drug testing, an activity designed to gather and preserve private information about individuals. Further, both courts determined that the privacy clause limited the information-gathering activities of private as well as public entities, since the language revealed that privacy was an "inalienable right" that no one may violate. Although the private entity designated as the defendant in the *Hill* case was an athletic conference (the NCAA) rather than a private university, the courts' reasoning would apply to the latter as well.

In *Hill,* the intermediate appellate court's privacy analysis differed from the Fourth Amendment balancing test of *Skinner* because the court required the NCAA "to show a compelling interest before it can invade a fundamental privacy right"—a test that places a heavier burden of justification on the alleged violator than does the Fourth Amendment balancing test. The Supreme Court of California disagreed on this point, holding that the correct approach "requires that privacy interests be specifically identified and carefully compared with competing or countervailing privacy and nonprivacy interests in a 'balancing test'" (865 P.2d at 655). Under this approach, "[i]nvasion of a privacy interest is not a violation of the state constitutional right to privacy if the invasion is justified by a legitimate and important competing interest" (865 P.2d at 655–56), rather than a compelling interest, as the lower court had specified. Using this balancing test, the California Supreme Court concluded that "the NCAA's decision to enforce a ban on the use of drugs by means of a drug testing program is reasonably calculated to further its legitimate interest in maintaining the integrity of intercollegiate athletic competition" and therefore does not violate the California constitution's privacy guarantee.

In addition to its illustration of state privacy concepts, the *Hill* case also demonstrates the precarious position of institutions that are subject to NCAA or conference drug-testing requirements. As the intermediate appellate court indicated, Stanford, the institution that the *Hill* plaintiffs attended, was in a dilemma: "as an NCAA member institution, if it refused to enforce the consent provision, it could be sanctioned, but if it did enforce the program, either by requiring students to sign or withholding them from competition, it could be sued." To help resolve the dilemma, Stanford intervened in the litigation and sought its own declaratory and injunctive relief. These are the same issues and choices that other institutions will continue to face until the various legal issues concerning drug testing have finally been resolved.

In *Bally v. Northeastern University,* 532 N.E.2d 49 (Mass. 1989), a state civil rights law provided the basis for a challenge to a private institution's drug-testing program. The defendant, Northeastern University, required all students participating in intercollegiate athletics to sign an NCAA student athlete statement that includes a drug-testing consent form. The institution's program called for testing of each athlete once a year as well as other random testing throughout the school year. When a member of the cross-country and track teams refused to sign the consent form, the institution declared him ineligible. The student claimed that this action breached his contract with the institution and violated his rights under both the Massachusetts Civil Rights Act and a state right to privacy statute. A lower court granted summary judgment for Northeastern on the contract claim and for the student on the civil rights and privacy claims.

The Massachusetts Supreme Court reversed the lower court's judgment for the student. To prevail on the civil rights claim, according to the statute, the student had to prove that the institution had interfered with rights secured by the Constitution or laws of the United States or the Commonwealth and that such interference was by "threats, intimidation, or coercion." Although the court assumed *arguendo* that the drug-testing program interfered with the student's rights to be free from unreasonable searches and seizures and from invasions of reasonable expectations of privacy, it nevertheless denied his claim because he had made no showing of "threats, intimidation, or coercion." Similarly, the court denied the student's claim under the privacy statute because "[t]he majority of our opinions involving a claim of an invasion of privacy concern the public dissemination of information," and the student had made no showing of any public dissemination of the drug-testing results. In addition, because the student was not an employee, state case law precedents regarding employee privacy, on which the student had relied, did not apply.

Given the outcomes in *Vernonia* and *Earls,* students challenging random or for-cause drug testing policies in K–12 school districts have sought relief under state constitutions rather than the Fourth Amendment. The results have been mixed. For example, although the New Jersey Supreme Court upheld a random drug- and alcohol-testing program that covered all students participating in extracurricular activities under the state constitution in *Joye v. Hunterdon Central Regional High School Board of Education,* 826 A.2d 624 (N.J. 2003), the Pennsylvania Supreme Court struck a similar policy. In *Theodore v. Delaware*

Valley School District, 836 A.2d 76 (Pa. 2003), the state's high court pointed out that the state constitution's privacy protections went beyond those of the U.S. Constitution's Fourth Amendment. While the challenged random drug- and alcohol-screening policy at the Pennsylvania school district may have been permissible under the Fourth Amendment, said the court, the school district had not provided evidence of a drug problem at the high school sufficient to out-weigh the students' privacy rights under the Pennsylvania constitution. The court also rejected the school district's explanation that the policy had been extended to the plaintiffs, honor students whose extracurricular activities were only academic, because they were "role models" for other students, stating that this rationale did not justify the invasion of their privacy.

Since the courts have not spoken definitively with respect to higher educa-tion, it is not clear what drug-testing programs and procedures will be valid. In the meantime, institutions (and athletic conferences) that wish to engage in drug testing of student athletes may follow these minimum suggestions, which are likely to enhance their program's capacity to survive challenge under the various sources of law listed at the beginning of this Section:

1. Articulate *and document* both the strong institutional interests that would be compromised by student athletes' drug use and the institu-tion's basis for believing that such drug use is occurring in one or more of its athletic programs.

2. Limit drug testing to those athletic programs where drug use is occur-ring and is interfering with institutional interests.

3. Develop evenhanded and objective criteria for determining who will be tested and in what circumstances.

4. Specify the substances whose use is banned and for which athletes will be tested, limiting the named substances to those whose use would compromise important institutional interests.

5. Develop detailed and specific protocols for testing of individuals and lab analysis of specimens, limiting the monitoring of specimen collec-tion to that which is necessary to ensure the integrity of the collection process, and limiting the lab analyses to those necessary to detect the banned substances (rather than to discover other personal information about the athlete).

6. Develop procedures for protecting the confidentiality and accuracy of the testing process and the laboratory results.

7. Embody all the above considerations into a clear written policy that is made available to student athletes before they accept athletic scholar-ships or join a team.

10.4.9. Tort liability for athletic injuries. Tort law (see Sections 3.3 & 4.7.2) poses special problems for athletic programs and departments. Because of the physical nature of athletics and because athletic activities often require travel to other locations, the danger of injury to students and the possibilities for institutional liability are greater than those resulting from other institutional functions. In *Scott v. State,* 158 N.Y.S.2d 617 (N.Y. Ct. Cl. 1956), for instance, a student collided with a flagpole while chasing a fly ball during an intercollegiate baseball game; the student was awarded $12,000 in damages because the school had negligently maintained the playing field in a dangerous condition and the student had not assumed the risk of such danger.

Although most of the litigation involving injuries to student athletes has involved injuries sustained during either practice or competition, students have also attempted to hold their institution responsible for injuries resulting from assaults by students or fans from competing teams, or from hazing activities. Although students have not been uniformly successful in these lawsuits, the courts appear to be growing more sympathetic to their claims.

In considering whether student athletes may hold their institutions liable for injuries sustained in practice, competition, or hazing, courts have addressed whether the institution has a duty to protect the student from the type of harm that was encountered. The specific harm that occurred must have been reasonably foreseeable to the institution in order for a duty to arise. On the other hand, institutions have argued that the athlete assumes the risk of injury because sports, particularly contact sports, involve occasional injuries that are not unusual. The courts have traced a path between these two concepts.

One area of litigation focuses on whether a university can be held liable for its failure to prepare adequately for emergency medical situations. In *Kleinknecht v. Gettysburg College,* 989 F.2d 1360 (3d Cir. 1993), parents of a student athlete sued the college for the wrongful death of their son, who had died from a heart attack suffered during a practice session of the intercollegiate lacrosse team. The student had no medical history that would indicate any danger of such an occurrence. No trainers were present when he was stricken, and no plan prescribing steps to take in medical emergencies was in effect. Students and coaches reacted as quickly as they could to reach the nearest phone, more than 200 yards away, and call an ambulance. The parents sued the college for negligence (see generally Section 3.3.2), alleging that the college owed a duty to its student athletes to have measures in place to provide prompt medical attention in emergencies. They contended that the delay in securing an ambulance, caused by the college's failure to have an emergency plan in effect, resulted in their son's death. The federal district court, applying Pennsylvania law, granted summary judgment for the college, holding that the college owed no duty to the plaintiffs' son in the circumstances of this case and that, even if a duty were owed, the actions of the college's employees were reasonable and did not breach the duty.[34]

The appellate court reversed the district court's judgment and remanded the case for a jury trial, ruling that a special relationship existed between the student and the college because he was participating in a scheduled athletic

---

[34]The district court's opinion also contains an interesting discussion of the application of the state's Good Samaritan law to athletic injuries. See 786 F. Supp. 449, 457 (M.D. Pa. 1992).

practice supervised by college employees. Thus, the college had a duty of reasonable care. The court then delineated the specific demands that that duty placed on the college in the circumstances of this case. Since it was generally foreseeable that a life-threatening injury could occur during sports activities such as lacrosse, and given the magnitude of such a risk and its consequences, "the College owed a duty to Drew to have measures in place at the lacrosse team's practice . . . to provide prompt treatment in the event that he or any other members of the lacrosse team suffered a life-threatening injury." However, "the determination whether the College has breached this duty at all is a question of fact for the jury."

Similarly, a North Carolina appellate court found that a special relationship may have existed between the University of North Carolina and members of its junior varsity cheerleading squad sufficient to hold the university liable for negligence when a cheerleader was injured during practice. In *Davidson v. University of North Carolina at Chapel Hill,* 543 S.E.2d 920 (N.C. Ct. App. 2001), a cheerleader was injured while practicing a stunt without mats or other safety equipment. The university did not provide a coach for the junior varsity squad, and had provided no safety training for the students. It provided uniforms, transportation to away games, and access to university facilities and equipment. Although certain university administrators had expressed reservations about the safety of some of the cheerleaders' stunts, including the pyramid stunt on which the plaintiff was injured, no action had been taken to supervise the junior varsity squad or to limit its discretion in selecting stunts.

The appellate court ruled that the degree of control that the university exercised over the cheerleading squad created a special relationship that, in turn, created a duty of care on the part of the university. Relying on *Kleinknecht,* the court limited its ruling to the facts of the case, refusing to create a broader duty of care that would extend to the general activities of college students.[35]

Even when the institution does or may owe a duty to the student athlete in a particular case, the student athlete will have no cause of action against the institution if its breach of duty was not the cause of the harm suffered. In *Hanson v. Kynast,* 494 N.E.2d 1091 (Ohio 1986), for example, the court avoided the issue of whether the defendant university owed a duty to a student athlete to provide for a proper emergency plan, because the delay in treating the athlete, allegedly caused by the university's negligent failure to have such a plan, caused the athlete no further harm. The athlete had suffered a broken neck in a lacrosse game and was rendered a quadriplegic; the evidence made it clear that, even if medical help had arrived sooner, nothing could have been done to lessen the injuries. In other words, the full extent of these injuries had been determined before any alleged negligence by the university could have come into play.

---

[35]An emerging issue involving potential liability for colleges is the combination of performance-enhancing substances and extreme heat, which has led to the deaths of several college football players. For a discussion of this issue, and a call for the NCAA to ban all off-season "voluntary practices" that occur during warm summer months, see Sarah Lemons, "'Voluntary' Practices: The Last Gasp of Big-Time College Football and the NCAA," 5 *Vand. J. Ent. L. & Prac.* 12 (2003).

As the *Kleinknecht* court's reasoning suggests, the scope of the institution's duty to protect student athletes in emergencies and otherwise may depend on a number of factors, including whether the activity is intercollegiate (versus a club team) or an extracurricular activity, whether the particular activity was officially scheduled or sponsored, and perhaps whether the athlete was recruited or not. The institution's duty will also differ if the student athlete is a member of a visiting team rather than the institution's own team. In general, there is no special relationship such as that in *Kleinknecht* between the institution and a visiting athlete; there is only the relationship arising from the visiting student's status as an invitee of the institution (see generally Section 3.3.2.1). In *Fox v. Board of Supervisors of Louisiana State University and Agricultural and Mechanical College*, 576 So. 2d 978 (La. 1991), for example, a visiting rugby player from St. Olaf's club team was severely injured when he missed a tackle during a tournament held at Louisiana State University (LSU). The court determined that the injured player had no cause of action against LSU based on the institution's own actions or omissions. The only possible direct liability claim he could have had would have been based on a theory that the playing field onto which he had been invited was unsafe for play, a contention completely unsupported by the evidence.

In addition to the institution's liability for its own negligent acts, there are also issues concerning the institution's possible vicarious liability for the acts of its student athletes or its athletic clubs. In the *Fox* case above, the visiting athlete also claimed that the university was vicariously liable for negligent actions of its rugby club in holding a cocktail party the night before the tournament, in scheduling teams to play more than one game per day (the athlete was injured in his second match of the day), and in failing to ensure that visiting clubs were properly trained and coached. His theory was that these actions had resulted in fatigued athletes playing when they should not have, thus becoming more susceptible to injury. The appellate court held that LSU could not be vicariously liable for the actions of its rugby club. Although LSU provided its rugby team with some offices, finances, and supervision, and a playing field for the tournament, LSU offered such support to its rugby club (and other student clubs) only to enrich students' overall educational experience by providing increased opportunities for personal growth. The university did not recruit students for the club, and it did not control the club's activities. The club therefore was not an agent of the university and could not bind LSU by its actions.

In *Regan v. State*, 654 N.Y.S.2d 488 (N.Y. App. Div. 1997), the court addressed whether a student at a state college who suffered a broken neck while playing rugby, and was rendered a quadriplegic, had assumed the risk of such injury and was therefore barred from recovery against the state. The student had played and practiced with the college's Rugby Club for three years at the time of the incident. During those three years, the student had regularly practiced with student coaches on the same field where the injury occurred, and had witnessed prior rugby injuries. Relying on these factors, the court affirmed summary judgment in favor of the state, finding unpersuasive the plaintiff's contention that he was unaware of the inherent risk in playing rugby. Reaching a similar conclusion, the court in *Sicard v. University of Dayton,* 660 N.E.2d 1241, 1244 (Ohio Ct. App. 1995), noted that a player assumes the ordinary risks of playing a contact sport, but does not assume the risk of injuries that occur when rules are violated. Because of these assumed risks, according to the court in *Sicard,* injured athletes suing in tort must make a stronger showing of misconduct than persons injured in nonathletic contexts. The defendant's misconduct must amount to more than ordinary negligence and must rise to the level of "intentional" or "reckless" wrongdoing.

Using these principles, the court in *Sicard* reversed the trial court's summary judgment for the defendants—the university and an employee who was a "spotter" in the weight room and allegedly failed to perform this function for the athlete, which could have prevented his injury. The court remanded the case for trial because "[a] reasonable mind could . . . conclude that . . . [the spotter's] acts and omissions were reckless because they created an unreasonable risk of physical harm to Sicard, one substantially greater than that necessary to make his conduct merely negligent . . ." (660 N.E.2d at 1244).

The same conclusion was reached in *Hanson v. Kynast* (cited above), which concerned a university's vicarious liability for a student's actions. During an intercollegiate lacrosse game, Kynast body-checked and taunted a player on the opposing team. When Hanson (another opposing team player) grabbed Kynast, Kynast threw Hanson to the ground, breaking his neck. Hanson sued Kynast and Ashland University, the team for which Kynast was playing when the incident occurred. The court held that Ashland University, which Kynast attended, was not liable for his actions because he received no scholarship, joined the team voluntarily, used his own playing equipment, and was guided but not controlled by the coach. In essence, the court held that Kynast was operating as an individual, voluntarily playing on the team, not as an agent of the university. (See also *Townsend v. State,* 237 Cal. Rptr. 146 (Cal. Ct. App. 1987), in which the court, relying on state statutes, similarly refused to hold a university vicariously liable for a nonscholarship varsity basketball player's assault on another team's player.)

A similar result would also likely obtain when a student is injured in an informal recreational sports activity. In *Swanson v. Wabash College,* 504 N.E.2d 327 (Ind. Ct. App. 1987), for example, a student injured in a recreational basketball game sued the college for negligence. The court ruled that the college had no legal duty to supervise a recreational activity among adult students, and that the student who had organized the game was neither an agent nor an employee of the college, so *respondeat superior* liability did not attach.

An Arkansas case provides fair warning that institutions may incur tort liability not only due to athletic injuries, but also due to the administration of painkillers and other prescription drugs used for athletic injuries. In *Wallace v. Broyles,* 961 S.W.2d 712 (Ark. 1998), a varsity football player at the University of Arkansas shot and killed himself. His mother sued the university's director of athletics, the head athletic trainer, the football team physician, and various doctors, alleging that, after her son had sustained a severe shoulder injury during a football game, university personnel had supplied him with heavy doses of Darvocet, a "mind-altering drug" with "potentially dangerous side effects." The Darvocet allegedly caused the state of mind that precipitated the football player's suicide. The player's mother claimed that the defendants had been negligent in the way they stored and dispensed prescription drugs and in failing to keep adequate records of inventory or of athletes' use of prescription drugs; and that the athletic department's practices were inconsistent both with federal drug laws and with guidelines that the NCAA had issued to the university.

The Supreme Court of Arkansas reversed the trial court's grant of summary judgment for the defendants and let the case proceed to trial. The court emphasized that "to be negligent, the defendants here need not be shown to have foreseen the particular injury which occurred, but only that they reasonably could be said to have foreseen an appreciable risk of harm to others." On that basis, the court concluded that "the pleadings and evidentiary documents raise a fact issue concerning whether the defendants' acts or omissions were negligence in the circumstances described."

In contrast to their potential liability for injuries to their student athletes during practice or competition, institutions have been more successful in persuading courts that they should not be liable for assaults on their students by students or fans from visiting teams, or for assaults on visitors by their students. An example of the first category is *Blake v. University of Rochester,* 758 N.Y.S.2d 323 (N.Y. App. Div. 2003), in which a student playing in an intramural basketball game was assaulted by a player on the opposing team. Because no one on either team knew the player who assaulted Blake, Blake argued that the university's security was lax in that it allowed an intruder to gain access to the gymnasium where the game took place. The court rejected Blake's theory as speculative and dismissed the case.

Similarly, a player for a visiting team who was punched by a Boston University basketball player during a game was unable to persuade the Massachusetts Supreme Court to hold the university vicariously liable for his injury. In *Kavanagh v. Trustees of Boston University,* 795 N.E.2d 1170 (Mass. 2003), the court refused to recognize a special relationship between the university and a student from another institution. Furthermore, according to the court, the assault was not foreseeable, and therefore there was no duty to protect the visiting student.[36]

Hazing in college athletics is a common practice that is only recently receiving the type of attention that hazing by members of fraternal organizations has attracted during the past decade. (Hazing litigation involving fraternal

---

[36]But see *Avila v. Citrus Community College,* 4 Cal. Rptr. 3d 264 (Cal. App. 2003), in which a state appellate court refused to apply the "recreational immunity" provision of state law to a college baseball game because that doctrine was intended to apply to inherently dangerous activities such as skydiving or hang-gliding. The court remanded the case for trial. The California Supreme Court agreed to hear an appeal of the appellate court's ruling (81 P.3d 222 (Cal. 2003)), but no published opinion had been issued as of late 2005.

organizations is discussed in Section 10.2.4.) A national survey of 325,000 athletes participating in intercollegiate sports at more than 1,000 NCAA colleges was conducted by Alfred University in 1999. The survey found that more than three-quarters of the respondents reported that they had experienced some form of hazing as a precursor of joining a college sports team, and 20 percent of the respondents reported "unacceptable and potentially illegal hazing," including being kidnapped, beaten or tied up and abandoned, forced to commit crimes, and alcohol abuse (Nadine C. Hoover, "National Survey: Initiation Rites and Athletics for NCAA Sports Teams," August 20, 1999, available at http://www.alfred.edu/news/hazing.pdf).

Hazing of college athletes has attracted some recent litigation, but there have been no published court opinions. Kathleen Peay sued the University of Oklahoma for "physical and mental abuse" resulting from hazing activities required by the soccer team and its coach. The case was settled.[37] The University of Vermont was sued by a student hockey team member, Corey LaTulippe, who was required to endure a hazing ritual at the hands of his teammates. The university settled the lawsuit.[38] Given the existence of state laws against hazing, and the lack of any rational relationship between hazing that exposes a student to danger and the educational mission of the institution, it is likely that courts will expect institutions to prevent hazing, to make hazing a violation of the student code of conduct, and to hold students who engage in hazing activities strictly accountable for their actions, whether or not they result in physical or mental injury to students.

Selected Annotated Bibliography

Sec. 10.1 (Student Organizations)

Hernandez, Wendy. "The Constitutionality of Racially Restrictive Organizations Within the University Setting," 21 *J. Coll. & Univ. Law* 429 (1994). Discusses the prevalence of racially restrictive student organizations and reviews the laws and jurisprudence that affect the way a college may respond to a request for official recognition of such organizations. Offers recommendations for working with these organizations.

Paulsen, Michael. "A Funny Thing Happened on the Way to the Limited Public Forum: Unconstitutional Conditions on 'Equal Access' for Religious Speakers and Groups," 29 *U.C. Davis L. Rev.* 653 (1996). Part of a symposium entitled "Developments in Free Speech Doctrine: Charting the Nexus Between Speech and Religion, Abortion, and Equality." In light of *Rosenberger v. Rectors and Visitors of the University of Virginia,* examines the rejection of the premise that the establishment clause creates an exception to First Amendment free speech principles when the speech or speaker in question is of a religious nature.

---

[37]For a discussion of the facts of this case and its resolution, see Joshua A. Sussberg, Note, "Shattered Dreams: Hazing in College Athletics," 24 *Cardozo L. Rev.* 1421 (2003).

[38]This case is discussed in R. Brian Crow & Scott R. Rosner, "Institutional and Organizational Liability for Hazing in Intercollegiate and Professional Team Sports," 76 *St. John's L. Rev.* 87 (2002).

Sec. 10.2 (Fraternities and Sororities)

Curry, Susan J. "Hazing and the 'Rush' Toward Reform: Responses from Universities, Fraternities, State Legislatures, and the Courts," 16 *J. Coll. & Univ. Law* 93 (1989). Examines the various legal theories used against local and national fraternities, universities, and individual fraternity members to redress injury or death resulting from hazing. Also reviews the response of one university to the hazing death of a pledge and its revised regulation of fraternities. Two state anti-hazing laws are also discussed.

Fraternal Law Newsletter (subscription information available at http://www.manley-burke.com/fraternallaw.html). Designed for administrators, counsel, and national fraternal organizations; focuses on prevention of legal problems related to housing, alcohol abuse, hazing, and relationships between colleges and fraternal organizations. Tax issues are considered in some issues.

Gregory, Dennis E., et al. *The Administration of Fraternal Organizations on North American Campuses: A Pattern for a New Millennium* (College Administration Publications, 2003). Chapters include historical reviews of male, female, black, and emerging fraternal organizations; the role of national and North American fraternal associations; the oversight of fraternal organizations on campus; risk management issues; and developing responsible leaders for fraternal organizations.

Hauser, Gregory F. "Intimate Associations Under the Law: The Rights of Social Fraternities to Exist and to Be Free from Undue Interference by Host Institutions," 24 *J. Coll. & Univ. Law* 59 (1997). Argues that many attempts by public institutions to restrict the activities and policies of fraternal organizations are unconstitutional. Discusses the doctrine of "intimate association" in detail and its application to the activities of fraternal organizations.

Lewis, Darryll M. H. "The Criminalization of Fraternity, Non-Fraternity and Non-Collegiate Hazing," 51 *Miss. L.J.* 111 (1991). Describes state laws that make hazing and associated activities subject to criminal penalties.

MacLachlan, Jenna. "Dangerous Traditions: Hazing Rituals on Campus and University Liability," 26 *J. Coll. & Univ. Law* 511 (2000). Discusses litigation concerning institution of higher educations' potential liability for injuries and deaths resulting from hazing. Traces the development of the law from *in loco parentis* to the current tendency of courts to hold institutions legally responsible for injuries that are foreseeable, including injuries that result from hazing.

McBride, Scott Patrick. "Freedom of Association in the Public University Setting: How Broad Is the Right to Participate in Greek Life?" 23 *U. Dayton L. Rev.* 133 (1997). Reviews constitutional protections for freedom of association; discusses their application and their limitations for the activities of fraternal organizations.

Nuwer, Hank. *Wrongs of Passage: Fraternities, Sororities, Hazing, and Binge Drinking* (Indiana University Press, 1999). Reviews anti-hazing laws and discusses the social context in which hazing occurs. Recommends steps institutions can take to reduce hazing and to protect students from hazing.

Rutledge, Gregory E. "Hell Night Hath No Fury Like a Pledge Scorned . . . and Injured: Hazing Litigation in U.S. Colleges and Universities," 25 *J. Coll. & Univ. Law* 361 (1998). Discusses the definition, scope, and history of hazing, as well as reviewing litigation concerning hazing. Reviews theories of liability and defenses to liability claims. Suggests strategies for reducing hazing and related liability.

Walton, Spring J., Bassler, Stephen E., & Cunningham, Robert Briggs. "The High Cost of Partying: Social Host Liability for Fraternities and Colleges," 14 *Whittier L. Rev.* 659 (1993). Discusses the implications of state social host laws for local and national fraternities and for colleges and universities. Concludes that increased regulation of fraternities by colleges may prompt judicial imposition of a duty on colleges to prevent injuries related to fraternity social activity.

Sec. 10.3 *(The Student Press)*

Comment, "Student Editorial Discretion, the First Amendment, and Public Access to the Campus Press," 16 *U.C. Davis L. Rev.* 1089 (1983). Reviews the constitutional status of student newspapers under the First Amendment, analyzes the applicability of the state action doctrine to student newspapers on public campuses, and discusses the question of whether noncampus groups have any right to have material published in campus newspapers on public campuses.

Duscha, Julius, & Fischer, Thomas. *The Campus Press: Freedom and Responsibility* (American Association of State Colleges and Universities, 1973). A handbook that provides historical, philosophical, and legal information on college newspapers. Discusses case law that affects the campus press and illustrates the variety of ways the press may be organized on campus and the responsibilities the institution may have for its student publications.

Ingelhart, Louis E. *Student Publications: Legalities, Governance, and Operation* (Iowa State University Press, 1993). An overview of issues regarding publication of student newspapers, yearbooks, and magazines. Aimed primarily at administrators, the book discusses organizational, management, and funding issues as well as censorship and other potential legal problems associated with such publications.

Nichols, John E. "Vulgarity and Obscenity in the Student Press," 10 *J. Law & Educ.* 207 (1981). Examines the legal definitions of vulgarity and obscenity as they apply to higher education and secondary education and reviews the questions these concepts pose for the student press.

Note, "Tort Liability of a University for Libelous Material in Student Publications," 71 *Mich. L. Rev.* 1061 (1973). Provides the reader with a general understanding of libel law and discusses the various theories under which a university may be held liable for the torts of its student press. Author also recommends preventive measures to minimize university liability.

Student Press Law Center. *Law of the Student Press* (2d ed., Student Press Law Center, Inc., 1994). Surveys the legal rights and responsibilities of high school and college journalists. Contains extensive discussion of freedom of press and its limits in the education context, including discussion of defamation, invasion of privacy, obscenity, the "underground" press, and electronic media.

See Ugland entry in Selected Annotated Bibliography for Chapter 11, Section 11.6.

Sec. 10.4 *(Athletics Teams and Clubs)*

Association of Governing Boards. "Statement on Board Responsibilities for Intercollegiate Athletics" (Association of Governing Boards, March 28, 2004). Discusses the board's responsibility to provide oversight of intercollegiate athletics; presidential authority and the board's review of the use of that authority; fiscal responsibility; the welfare of student athletes, and related issues.

Berry, Robert C., & Wong, Glenn M. *Law and Business of the Sports Industries: Common Issues in Amateur and Professional Sports* (2d ed., Greenwood, 1993). The second volume of a comprehensive, two-volume overview of the law applicable to athletics. Most of the discussion either focuses on or has direct application to inter-collegiate sports. The twelve chapters cover such topics as "The Amateur Athlete," "Sex Discrimination in Athletics," "Application of Tort Law," "Drug Testing," and "Criminal Law and Its Relationship to Sports." Includes numerous descriptions or edited versions of leading cases, set off from and used to illustrate the textual analysis.

Brake, Deborah. "The Struggle for Sex Equality in Sport and the Theory Behind Title IX," 34 *U. Mich. J.L. Ref.* 13 (2000–2001). Discusses the interpretation of Title IX's equality standard used by the Office of Civil Rights and the courts; reviews the law's "participation test" and discusses its applications in litigation; and suggests that institutions need to provide greater equality of treatment to female athletes.

Burns, Beverly H. (ed.). *A Practical Guide to Title IX in Athletics: Law, Principles, and Practices* (2d ed., National Association of College and University Attorneys, 2000). Contains selected materials from various sources that illuminate the range of Title IX athletic issues facing colleges and universities. Special attention is given to equal opportunity regarding coaching contracts, access, and gender equity. Also available is an *In-House Legal Audit* that institutions can use to review their compliance with Title IX.

Davis, Timothy. "An Absence of Good Faith: Defining a University's Educational Obligation to Student Athletes," 28 *Houston L. Rev.* 743 (1991). Examines the relationship between the student athlete and the university, the potential exploitation of the student athlete, and the resulting compromise of academic integrity. Author argues that the good-faith doctrine of contract law should be used to define the university's obligation, so that the contract will be breached if the university "obstructs or fails to further the student-athlete's educational opportunity."

Davis, Timothy. "College Athletics: Testing the Boundaries of Contract and Tort," 29 *U.C. Davis L. Rev.* 971 (1996). Explores the tort and contract theories of liability by which institutions may become liable to student athletes, the "intersection" of these theories, and their potential expansion. Also criticizes the extent to which courts have deferred to institutional decision making regarding student athletes.

Davis, Timothy, Mathewson, Alfred, & Shropshire, Kenneth (eds.). *Sports and the Law: A Modern Anthology* (Carolina Academic Press, 1999). Provides a well-organized and carefully selected collection of excerpts from law review articles and other journal articles, books, and government and commission reports. Part III of the anthology (the longest of six parts) covers intercollegiate athletics, including topics such as disabled athletes, gender discrimination, due process, and antitrust issues. A separate Part IV covers tort liability, and Part V covers drug testing.

Freitas, Mark. "Applying the Rehabilitation Act and the Americans With Disabilities Act to Student-Athletes," 5 *Sports Law. J.* 139 (1998). Compares Section 504, ADA Title II, and ADA Title III in terms of their applicability to disabled student athletes. Elucidates each major step in the legal analysis under the three sources of law. Discusses the *Pahula* case, the *Knapp* case, and the *Bowers* case.

Jones, Cathy J. "College Athletes: Illness or Injury and the Decision to Return to Play," 40 *Buffalo L. Rev.* 113 (1992). Discusses the rights and liabilities in situations where a student athlete seeks to play or return to play after being diagnosed with a medical condition that could cause injury or death. Analyzes the rights of the athletes under the U.S. Constitution, Section 504 of the Rehabilitation Act of 1973, and the Americans With Disabilities Act of 1990. Suggests that athletes' autonomy must be respected and that "[l]iability on the part of the institution and its employees should be judged by a reasonableness standard."

McCaskey, Anthony S., & Biedzynski, Kenneth W. "A Guide to the Legal Liability of Coaches for a Sports Participant's Injuries," 6 *Seton Hall J. Sports L.* 7 (1996). Discusses negligence actions brought against coaches by injured athletes; reviews the legal duties of coaches and the defenses available to coaches in such litigation.

Mitten, Matthew. "Amateur Athletes with Handicaps or Physical Abnormalities: Who Makes the Participation Decision?" 71 *Neb. L. Rev.* 987 (1992). Discusses the circumstances under which athletes with disabilities may participate in competitive sports. Outlines the problem from the perspectives of the athletic associations, the athlete, the team physician, and university administrators. Traces the rights and obligations of the parties under state statutory law, federal constitutional law, and Section 504 of the Rehabilitation Act. Does not discuss the ramifications of the Americans With Disabilities Act.

Pieronek, Catherine. "Title IX and Intercollegiate Athletics in the Federal Appellate Courts: Myth vs. Reality," 27 *J. Coll. & Univ. Law* 447 (2000). Reviews the history of Title IX enforcement in collegiate athletics, and discusses current regulatory enforcement and litigation. Discusses the limitations of the Title IX jurisprudence and suggests areas where greater clarification is needed.

Pieronek, Catherine. "Title IX Beyond Thirty: A Review of Recent Developments," 30 *J. Coll. & Univ. Law* 75 (2003). Summarizes developments in Title IX jurisprudence since the article cited above. Reviews litigation involving high schools as well as colleges, including the litigation brought by the National Wrestling Coaches Association.

Ranney, James T. "The Constitutionality of Drug Testing of College Athletes: A Brandeis Brief for a Narrowly-Intrusive Approach," 16 *J. Coll. & Univ. Law* 397 (1990). Identifies the legal and policy issues that institutions should consider in developing a drug-testing program. Author concludes that the threat of "performance-enhancing drugs" justifies random warrantless searches, while the threat of "street drugs" only justifies searches based on reasonable suspicion or probable cause. Article also discusses procedural safeguards to guarantee the reliability of the testing and protect the athletes' due process rights.

Remis, Rob. "Analysis of Civil and Criminal Penalties in Athlete Agent Status and Support for the Imposition of Civil and Criminal Liability upon Athletes," 8 *Seton Hall J. Sport L.* 1 (1998). Discusses state laws regulating athletes and athlete agents; includes a list of such state laws, and argues that these laws should impose liability upon athletes as well as upon agents.

Symposium, "Gender & Sports: Setting a Course for College Athletics," 3 *Duke J. Gender L. & Pol'y.* 1–264 (1996). Provides various perspectives on Title IX's effect in combating unequal opportunity in the realm of intercollegiate athletics. Contains six articles: Brian Snow & William Thro, "Still on the Sidelines; Developing the

Non-Discrimination Paradigm Under Title IX"; Deborah Brake & Elizabeth Catlin, "The Path of Most Resistance: The Long Road Toward Gender Equity in Intercollegiate Athletics"; Mary Jo Kane, "Media Coverage of the Post Title IX Female Athlete: A Feminist Analysis of Sport, Gender, and Power"; Jeffrey Orleans, "An End to the Odyssey: Equal Athletic Opportunity for Women"; Mary Gray, "The Concept of Substantial Proportionality in Title IX Athletics Cases"; and John Weistart, "Can Gender Equity Find a Place in Commercialized College Sports?".

Symposium, "Race and Sports," 6 *Marquette Sports L.J.* 199–421 (1996). Provides various perspectives on racial and ethnic discrimination in athletics. Contains nine articles, including Timothy Davis, "African-American Student-Athletes: Marginalizing the NCC Regulatory Structure"; Alfred Mathewson, "Black Women, Gender Equity, and the Function at the Junction"; Phoebe Williams, "Performing in a Racially Hostile Environment"; Paul Anderson, "Racism in Sports: A Question of Ethics"; and Cathryn Claussen, "Ethnic Team Names and Logos—Is There a Legal Solution?".

Weistart, John C., & Lowell, Cym H. *The Law of Sports* (Michie, 1979, with 1985 supp.). A reference work, with comprehensive citations to authorities, treating the legal issues concerning sports. Of particular relevance to postsecondary institutions are the chapters on "Regulation of Amateur Athletics," "Public Regulation of Sports Activities," and "Liability for Injuries in Sports Activities."

Wong, Glenn M. *Essentials of Amateur Sports Law* (2d ed., Praeger, 1994). Provides background information and a quick reference guide on sports law issues. Covers contract and tort law problems, sex discrimination in athletics, broadcasting, trademark law, drug testing, and various matters regarding athletic associations and athletic eligibility. Also includes detailed descriptions of the NCAA; sample forms for athletic contracts, financial aid agreements, and releases of liability; and a glossary of legal and sports terms. Of particular interest to nonlawyers such as athletic directors, coaches, and student athletes.

PART FIVE

THE COLLEGE AND LOCAL, STATE, AND FEDERAL GOVERNMENTS

11

Local Governments and the Local Community

Sec. 11.1. General Principles

Postsecondary institutions are typically subject to the regulatory authority of one or more local government entities, such as cities, towns, or county governments. Some local government regulations, such as fire and safety codes, are relatively noncontroversial. Other regulations or proposed regulations may be highly controversial. Controversies have arisen, for instance, over local governments' attempts to regulate or prohibit genetic experimentation, nuclear weapons research or production, storage of radioactive materials, laboratory experiments using animals, stem cell or cloning research, and bioterrorism research involving biological agents. Other more common examples of local government actions that can become controversial include ordinances requiring permits for large-group gatherings at which alcohol will be served, ordinances restricting smoking in the workplace, rent control ordinances, ordinances prohibiting discrimination on the basis of sexual orientation, and ordinances requiring the provision of health insurance benefits for domestic partners. (For an example of the latter, see *University of Pittsburgh v. City of Pittsburgh, Commission on Human Relations*, No. G.D. 99-21287 (Pa. Ct. of Common Pleas, Allegheny County, April 20, 2000); and Robin Wilson, "Pitt's Bitter Battle over Benefits," *Chron. Higher Educ.*, June 4, 2004, A8.)

Local land use regulations and zoning board rulings are also frequently controversial, as Section 11.2 below illustrates. In addition, as Section 11.3 illustrates, local governments' exertion of tax powers may become controversial either when a postsecondary institution is taxed on the basis of activities it considers educational and charitable or when it is exempted and thus subject to criticism that the institution does not contribute its fair share to the local government's coffers. Sections 11.4 to 11.7 below present yet other examples of controversies that may arise between a local government and a postsecondary institution or its students, faculty members, or staff members.

In dealing with local government agencies and officials, postsecondary administrators should be aware of the scope of, and limits on, each local government's regulatory and taxing authority. A local government has only the authority delegated to it by state law. When a city or county has been delegated "home rule" powers, its authority will usually be broadly interpreted; otherwise, its authority will usually be narrowly construed. In determining whether a local government's action is within the scope of its authority, the first step is to determine whether the local government's action is within the scope of the authority delegated to it by the state. In addition to construing the terms of the delegation, the court must also determine whether the scope of the particular local government's authority is to be broadly or narrowly construed. If the local government action at issue falls outside the scope, it will be found to be *ultra vires,* that is, beyond the scope of authority and thus invalid.

In *Lexington-Fayette Urban County Board of Health v. Board of Trustees of the University of Kentucky,* 879 S.W.2d 485 (Ky. 1994), for example, Urban County Board of Health had sought to apply local health code regulations to the university's construction of a "spa pool" in a university sports facility. The parties agreed that the board of health had authority to enforce *state* regulations against the university; the issue was whether the state legislature had also delegated authority to the board to enforce *local* regulations. The Supreme Court of Kentucky distinguished between these two levels of regulation:

> We agree, and the University concedes, that the Board of Health is the enforcement agent for the Cabinet for Human Resources and has the authority to inspect and enforce state health laws and state health regulations against the University. However, we do not believe that when the legislature designated the Board of Health as the enforcement agent of the Cabinet for Human Resources that the legislature intended to grant the Board of Health authority to enforce local health laws or enact local regulations against state agencies . . . [879 S.W.2d at 485–86].

In the key part of its reasoning, the court interpreted the terms of the statute delegating authority to the board, using this rule of construction:

> "Statutes in derogation of sovereignty should be strictly construed in favor of the state, so that its sovereignty may be upheld and not narrowed or destroyed, and should not be permitted to divest the state or its government of any of its prerogatives, rights, or remedies, unless the intention of the legislature to effect this object is clearly expressed" [879 S.W.2d at 486, quoting *City of Bowling Green v. T. & E. Electrical Contractors,* 602 S.W.2d 434 (1980)].

Applying this rule, the court held that "the legislature has not made clear its intention to grant authority," and "has [not] granted specific authority," to the board to enforce local health regulations against state agencies. The board's application of such regulations to the university's construction of the spa pool was therefore invalid.

Where a local body is acting within the scope of its state-delegated authority, but the action arguably violates state interests or some other state law, the courts may use other methods to determine whether local or state laws will govern. For instance, courts have held that (1) a local government may not regulate matters that the state has otherwise "preempted" by its own regulation of the field; (2) a local government may not regulate matters that are protected by the state's sovereign immunity; and (3) a local government may not regulate state institutions when such regulations would intrude upon the state's "plenary powers" granted by the state's constitution. Usually the state will win such contests.[1]

Although these principles apply to regulation (and sometimes taxation) of both public and private institutions, public institutions are more likely than private institutions to escape a local government's net. Since public institutions are more closely tied to the state and are usually "arms" of the state (see Section 12.2), for instance, they are more likely in particular cases to have preemption defenses. Public institutions may also defend against local regulation by asserting sovereign immunity, defenses not available to private institutions.

When the public institution being regulated is a local community college, however, rather than a state college or university, somewhat different issues may arise. The community college may be considered a local political subdivision (community college district) rather than a state entity, and the question may be whether the community college is subject to the local laws of some other local government whose territory overlaps its own (see, for example, *Stearns v. Mariani*, 741 N.Y.S.2d 357 (N.Y. App. Div. 2002)). Or the community college may be established by a county government (pursuant to state law), and the question may be whether the college is an arm of the county government and whether county law or state law governs the college on some particular matter. *Atlantic Community College v. Civil Service Commission*, 279 A.2d 820 (N.J. 1971) (discussed in Section 11.2.1 below), illustrates some of these issues, as do *Appeal of Community College of Delaware County*, 254 A.2d 641 (Pa. 1969) (Section 11.2.2), and *People ex rel. Cooper v. Rancho Santiago College*, 277 Cal. Rptr. 69 (Cal. Ct. App. 1990) (Section 11.2.6).

The preemption doctrine governs situations in which the state government's regulatory activities overlap with those of a local government. For example, in the University of Pittsburgh dispute about domestic partner benefits discussed above, the Pittsburgh City Council enacted an ordinance prohibiting discrimination in employment on the basis of sexual orientation, and the city's Commission on Human Relations agreed to hear a case on whether the ordinance

---

[1]State laws may also be held invalid because they regulate matters of "purely local concern" that the state constitution reserves to local "home rule" governments, or because they constitute "local" or "special" legislation that is prohibited by the state constitution. In such a case, there is no conflict, and the local law may prevail. For examples of such an issue in a higher education case, see the two *City of Chicago* cases at the end of this Section.

prohibited employers from denying health insurance benefits to same-sex domestic partners. While the case was pending, the state legislature passed a statute exempting state colleges and universities from any municipal ordinance that required employers to provide health care benefits (53 Pa. Stat. Ann. § 2181). The university could then claim (in addition to any other arguments it had) that the new state law preempted the city council's nondiscrimination ordinance.

If a local government ordinance regulates the same kind of activity as a state law (as in the Pittsburgh situation), the institution being regulated may be bound only by the state law (as claimed in the Pittsburgh situation). Courts will resolve any apparent overlapping of state law and local ordinances by determining, on a case-by-case basis, whether state law has preempted the field and precluded local regulation. A rather unusual case concerning colleges and universities illustrates the application of these principles.[2] In *Board of Trustees v. City of Los Angeles*, 122 Cal. Rptr. 361 (Cal. Ct. App. 1975), a state university had leased one of its facilities to a circus and claimed that the municipal ordinance regulating circus operations was preempted by a state statute authorizing the board of regents to promulgate rules for the governance of state colleges. In rejecting this claim and upholding the ordinance, the court found as follows:

> The general statutory grant of authority ([Cal. Educ.] Code §§ 23604, 23604.1, 23751) to promulgate regulations for the governing of the state colleges and the general regulations promulgated pursuant to that authority (Cal. Admin. Code Title 5, § 4000 et seq.) contain no comprehensive state scheme for regulating the conduct of circuses or similar exhibitions with specific references to the safety, health, and sanitary problems attendant on such activities. Nor can the board point to any attempt by it to control the activities of its lessees for the purpose of protecting the public, the animals or the neighboring community.
>
> In the absence of the enforcement of the city's ordinance, there would be a void in regulating circuses and similar exhibitions when those activities were conducted on university property thereby creating a status for tenants of the u͏... hich would be preferential to tenants of other landowners. This p͏... status, under the circumstances, serves no governmental purpose. ... matter of Los Angeles Municipal Code section 53.50 has not been ... y the state [122 Cal. Rptr. at 365].

The state preemption doctrine (above) also has a counterpart in federal law. Under the federal preemption doctrine, courts may sometimes invalidate local government regulations because the federal government has preempted that particular subject of regulation. In *United States v. City of Philadelphia*, 798 F.2d 81 (3d Cir. 1986), for example, the court invalidated an order of the city's Human Relations Commission that required Temple University's law school to bar

---

[2]The Pennsylvania Court of Common Pleas case, discussed above, provides another illustration of preemption principles in the context of the *University of Pittsburgh* same-sex health benefits dispute.

military recruiters from its placement facilities because the military discriminated against homosexuals. By statute, Congress had prohibited the expenditure of defense funds at colleges or universities that did not permit military personnel to recruit on campus. The court held that the city commission's order conflicted with the congressional policy embodied in this legislation and was therefore preempted.

The sovereign immunity doctrine holds that state institutions, as arms of state government, cannot be regulated by a lesser governmental entity that has only the powers delegated to it by the state. In order to claim sovereign immunity, the public institution must be performing state "governmental" functions, not acting in a merely "proprietary" capacity. In *Board of Trustees v. City of Los Angeles,* above, the court rejected the board's sovereign immunity defense by using this distinction:

> In the case at bar, the board leases . . . [its facilities] as a revenue-producing activity. The activities which are conducted thereon by private operators have no relation to the governmental function of the university. "The state is acting in a proprietary capacity when it enters into activities . . . to amuse and entertain the public. The activities of [the board] do not differ from those of private enterprise in the entertainment industry" (*Guidi v. California,* 41 Cal. 2d 623, 627, 262 P.2d 3, 6). The doctrine of sovereign immunity cannot shield the university from local regulation in this case. Even less defensible is the university's attempt here to extend its immunity to private entrepreneurs who are involved in the local commercial market where their competitors are subject to local regulation. By the terms of the lease, the university specifically disavowed any governmental status for its lessee [122 Cal. Rptr. at 364].

In contrast, a sovereign immunity defense was successful in *Board of Regents of Universities and State College v. City of Tempe,* 356 P.2d 399 (Ariz. 1960). The board sought an injunction to prohibit the city from applying its local construction codes to the board. In granting the board's request, the court reasoned:

> The essential point is that the powers, duties, and responsibilities assigned and delegated to a state agency performing a governmental function must be exercised free of control and supervision by a municipality within whose corporate limits the state agency must act. The ultimate responsibility for higher education is reposed by our Constitution in the State. The legislature has empowered the Board of Regents to fulfill that responsibility subject only to the supervision of the legislature and the governor. It is inconsistent with this manifest Constitutional and legislative purpose to permit a municipality to exercise its own control over the Board's performance of these functions. A central, unified agency, responsible to State officials rather than to the officials of each municipality in which a university or college is located, is essential to the efficient and orderly administration of a system of higher education responsive to the needs of all the people of the State [356 P.2d at 406–7].

A similar result was reached in *Inspector of Buildings of Salem v. Salem State College,* 546 N.E.2d 388 (Mass. App. Ct. 1989). The inspector of buildings for a city had issued a stop-work order interrupting the construction of six dormito-ries at the defendant college because they did not adhere to local zoning require-ments regarding height and other dimensional criteria. The question for the court was whether the local zoning ordinance could apply to the college, and to the state college building authority, when they were engaged in governmen-tal functions. In answering "No" to this question, the court noted that gener-ally "the State and State instrumentalities are immune from municipal zoning regulations, unless a statute otherwise expressly provides the contrary." Ana-lyzing the state statute that delegated zoning powers to municipalities, as it applied to state building projects for state educational institutions, the court concluded that the statute's language did not constitute an "express and unmis-takable suspension of the usual State supremacy." The court therefore held that the college could continue the project without complying with the local zoning laws. The court noted, however, that the college did not have free rein to con-struct buildings without regard to air pollution, noise, growth, traffic, and other considerations, since it still must comply with state environmental requirements imposed on state instrumentalities.

Under the plenary powers doctrine, a state's laws creating and authorizing a state postsecondary institution may be considered so all-inclusive that they even prevail over a local government's home rule powers (see footnote 1 above). In two separate decisions, an appellate court in Illinois held that the state constitution delegated "plenary powers" to the board of trustees of a state university and that a city's constitutionally granted local home rule powers did not enable the city to enforce local ordinances against the state university without specific authorization by state statute. In *City of Chicago v. Board of Trustees of the University of Illinois*, 689 N.E.2d 125 (Ill. App. 1997), the court rejected the city's argument that its home rule powers authorized it to require the board to collect certain local taxes from university students and customers and remit them to the city. In a later case concerning the same par-ties, *Board of Trustees of the University of Illinois v. City of Chicago*, 740 N.E.2d 515 (Ill. App. 2000), the court rejected the city's argument that its home rule powers authorized it to inspect university buildings, to cite the university for violations, and to collect fees for proven violations of the city's building, fire safety, and health ordinances. The court held that the state legislature, acting under the Illinois constitution, had granted full "plenary powers" to the board to operate a statewide educational system. "The state has 'plenary power' over state-operated educational institutions, and any attempt by a home rule munic-ipality to impose burdens on those institutions, in the absence of state approval, is unauthorized" (740 N.E.2d at 518, quoting *City of Chicago*, 689 N.E.2d at 130). Consequently, the court refused to recognize any city author-ity to enforce tax collections or to monitor and cite the state university for violations of its fire, safety, and health ordinances.

College counsel and administrators will want to carefully consider of all of these principles concerning authority in determining whether particular local government regulations can be construed to apply to the college or university, and whether the college or university will be bound by such regulations.

Sec. 11.2. Zoning and Land Use Regulation

11.2.1. Overview. The zoning and other land use regulations of local governments can influence the operation of postsecondary institutions in many ways.[3] The institution's location, the size of its campus, its ability to expand its facilities, the density of its land development, the character of its buildings, the traffic and parking patterns of its campus—all can be affected by zoning laws. Zoning problems are not the typical daily fare of administrators; but when problems do arise, they can be critical to the institution's future development. Local land use laws can limit, and even prevent, an institution's building programs, its expansion of the campus area (see especially the *George Washington University* case in Section 11.2.4), its use of unneeded land for commercial real estate ventures, its development of branch campuses or additional facilities in other locations (see especially the *New York Institute of Technology* case in Section 11.2.4), or program changes that would increase the size and change the character of the student body (see especially the *Marjorie Webster Junior College* case in Section 11.2.4). Thus, administrators should be careful not to underestimate the formidable challenge that zoning and other land use laws can present in such circumstances. Since successful maneuvering through such laws necessitates many legal strategy choices and technical considerations, administrators should involve counsel at the beginning of any land use problem.

Local governments that have the authority to zone typically do so by enacting zoning ordinances, which are administered by a local zoning board. Ordinances may altogether exclude educational uses of property from certain zones (called "exclusionary zoning"). Where educational uses are permitted, the ordinances may impose general regulations, such as architectural and aesthetic standards, setback requirements, and height and bulk controls, which limit the way that educational property may be used (called "regulatory zoning"). Public postsecondary institutions are more protected from zoning, just as they are from other types of local regulation, than are private institutions, because public institutions often have sovereign immunity or the authority to preempt local law.

11.2.2. Public institutions and zoning regulations. The courts have employed three tests to determine whether a unit of government, such as a state university, is subject to another government's local zoning law. As summarized in *City of Temple Terrace v. Hillsborough Ass'n.*, 322 So. 2d 571 (Fla. Dist. Ct. App. 1975), *affirmed without opinion*, 332 So. 2d 610 (Fla. 1976), these tests are (1) the superior sovereign test, (2) the governmental/proprietary distinction,

---

[3]The relevant cases and authorities are collected in David J. Oliveiri, Annot., "Zoning Regulations as Applied to Colleges, Universities, or Similar Institutions for Higher Education," 64 A.L.R.3d 1138. See also Jeffrey F. Ghent, Annot., "What Constitutes 'School,' 'Educational Use,' or the Like Within Zoning Ordinances," 64 A.L.R.3d 1087.

and (3) the balancing test. The court's opinion summarizes the case law on the first two tests:

> One approach utilized by a number of courts is to rule in favor of the superior sovereign. Thus, where immunity from a local zoning ordinance is claimed by an agency occupying a superior position in the governmental hierarchy, it is presumed that immunity was intended in the absence of express statutory language to the contrary. . . . A second test frequently employed is to determine whether the institutional use proposed for the land is "governmental" or "proprietary" in nature. If the political unit is found to be performing a governmental function, it is immune from the conflicting zoning ordinance. . . . On the other hand, when the use is considered proprietary, the zoning ordinance prevails. . . . Where the power of eminent domain has been granted to the governmental unit seeking immunity from local zoning, some courts have concluded that this conclusively demonstrates the unit's superiority where its proposed use conflicts with zoning regulations. . . . Other cases are controlled by explicit statutory provisions dealing with the question of whether the operation of a particular governmental unit is subject to local zoning. . . .
>
> When the governmental unit which seeks to circumvent a zoning ordinance is an arm of the state, the application of any of the foregoing tests has generally resulted in a judgment permitting the proposed use. This has accounted for statements of horn-book law to the effect that a state agency authorized to carry out a function of the state is not bound by local zoning regulations [322 So. 2d at 576; citations omitted].

In applying these tests to postsecondary education, the court in *City of Newark v. University of Delaware*, 304 A.2d 347 (Del. Ch. 1973), used a traditional sovereign immunity analysis combining tests 1 and 2 to decide that, because the University of Delaware was a state agency and had the power of eminent domain, it was immune from local zoning law. Similarly, a Wisconsin appellate court upheld the decision of a county zoning board that the construction of a radio tower in conjunction with a student-run radio station at the University of Wisconsin-Madison was a "governmental use" because the radio station would be an "integral part" of the university's educational system (*Board of Regents of the University of Wisconsin v. Dane County Board of Adjustment*, 618 N.W.2d 537 (Ct. App. Wis. 2000), *review denied*, 629 N.W.2d 784 (Wis. 2001)).

Rutgers, The State University v. Piluso, 286 A.2d 697 (N.J. 1972), is the leading case on the third test—the balancing test. A balancing approach weighs the state's interest in providing immunity for the institution against the local interest in land use regulation. In determining the strength of the state's interest, the *Rutgers* court analyzed the implied legislative intent to confer immunity on the university. The court explained that a variety of factors should be considered to determine legislative intent:

> the nature and scope of the instrumentality seeking immunity, the kind of function or land use involved, the extent of the public interest to be served thereby, the effect local land use regulation would have upon the enterprise concerned, and the impact upon legitimate local interests. . . . In some instances one factor will

be more influential than another or may be so significant as to completely over-shadow all others. No one, such as the granting or withholding of the power of eminent domain, is to be thought of as ritualistically required or controlling. And there will undoubtedly be cases, as there have been in the past, where the broader public interest is so important that immunity must be granted even though the local interests may be great. The point is that there is no precise formula or set of criteria which will determine every case mechanically and automatically [286 A.2d at 702–3].

On the facts of the *Rutgers* case, the court decided that because the univer-sity was "performing an essential governmental function for the benefit of all the people of the state," the legislature must have intended to exempt it from local land use regulation. The court emphasized, however, that immunity is not absolute and may be conditioned by local needs. It cautioned the university against arbitrary action, and counseled it to consult with local authorities and to give "every consideration" to local concerns in order to minimize conflict. The court then held that, under the facts of the case, the local interests did not outweigh the university's claim of immunity.

State institutions may be in a stronger position to assert sovereign immunity successfully than are community colleges sponsored by local governments. In confrontations with a local zoning board, a state institution is clearly the supe-rior sovereign, whereas an institution of another local government may not be. Moreover, the legislature's intent regarding immunity may be clearer for state insti-tutions than for local ones. (For an example of a case where a community college was subjected to local zoning laws, see *Appeal of Community College of Delaware County,* 254 A.2d 641 (Pa. 1969).) Constitutionally autonomous state universities (see Section 12.2.2) would usually have the strongest claim to immunity. In *Regents of the University of California v. City of Santa Monica,* 143 Cal. Rptr. 276 (Cal. Ct. App. 1978), for example, the city had attempted to apply various require-ments in its zoning and building codes to a construction project undertaken within the city by the university. Relying on various provisions of the California constitution and statutes, and applying a variation of the superior sovereign test; the court held the university to be immune from such regulation.

The university's power of eminent domain does not depend upon whether the source of funds used to acquire the property is public or private. For exam-ple, in *Curators of University of Missouri v. Brown,* 809 S.W.2d 64 (Mo. Ct. App. 1991), the university sought to acquire through condemnation some property owned by Brown. The proposed use was to create a parking lot to serve the Scholars' Center, which was to be built on land that was privately owned but that would be devoted entirely to university purposes. The funds to purchase the condemned property were contributed by a private trust. The court of appeals found that the Scholars' Center would be part of the university, and ruled that the source of funding for the land the university was seeking to acquire did not transform the public use into a private one.

11.2.3. Private institutions and zoning regulations.

In seeking redress against a local government's zoning regulations, private postsecondary institutions may challenge the zoning board's interpretation and application of the zoning ordinance or may argue that the ordinance conflicts with the federal Constitution or some state law limiting the local government's zoning authority. Where those arguments are unavailing, the institution may seek an exception or a variance (Section 11.2.4), or an amendment to the zoning ordinance (Section 11.2.5).

The Constitution limits a local government's zoning power in several ways. The ordinance may not create classifications that burden certain groups of people, unless there is a rational public purpose for its doing so (see Section 11.2.7). And although a municipality may attempt to regulate the use of land through its zoning ordinances and their application, it may not deprive individuals of the use of their land in such a fashion as to constitute a "taking."

In *Nollan v. California Coastal Commission,* 483 U.S. 825 (1987), the U.S. Supreme Court distinguished between a governmental entity's power to limit the way that land is used and its power to so limit the landowner's rights that the limitation becomes a "taking" without compensation. The Coastal Commission had placed a condition on the permit issued to the owners of beachfront property so that they could rebuild their home—they must give the public access to the beach through their property, which was located between two public beaches. The Court considered the commission's purpose, which was to increase public access to the beach. The Court held that the required easement was a "taking" and that the commission must pay the plaintiffs for the easement. Similarly, in *Dolan v. City of Tigard,* 512 U.S. 374 (1994), the U.S. Supreme Court considered the city's requirement that, as a condition to improving its commercial property, the landowner dedicate certain portions to a public greenway and a bicycle pathway. The Court held these requirements to be an unconstitutional taking because the city had not demonstrated "a reasonable relationship" between the requirements and the adverse impact of the proposed development. For a recent U.S. Supreme Court case approving the use of eminent domain on economic grounds, see *Kelo v. City of New London,* 125 S. Ct. 2655 (2005).

Despite these constitutional limitations, however, constitutional challenges to governmental land use restrictions have seldom succeeded. For example, in *Northwestern University v. City of Evanston,* 2002 U.S. Dist. LEXIS 17104 (N.D. Ill., September 11, 2002), the university filed constitutional claims against Evanston when the city decided to designate part of the university's campus as a historic preservation district, which would have required the university to obtain permission before altering or demolishing any structures within the district. The university asked the city to exclude its property from the proposed historic preservation district, but the city refused. The university then sued Evanston, claiming denial of equal protection, substantive due process, and procedural due process, and alleging First Amendment violations. In reviewing the city's motion for summary judgment, the court ruled in the city's favor on all but one of the university's constitutional claims. The court held that the university's claim that the city's actions were motivated by animus against the university, an equal protection claim, raised questions of material fact that necessitated a trial. The parties later settled the litigation (Audrey Williams June, "Northwestern U. Settles Long Property Dispute with Illinois City," *Chron. Higher Educ.,* February 12, 2004, available at http://chronicle.com/daily/2004/02/2004021206n.htm).

Similarly, in *In the Matter of Canisius College v. City of Buffalo,* 629 N.Y.S.2d 886 (N.Y. App. Div. 1995), the college had planned to raze a former rectory and use the property for student parking. A preservation group applied for landmark status for the building, and the Buffalo Common Council approved landmark designation, despite a negative recommendation by the Preservation Board. The college challenged the council's action, asserting that it was arbitrary and capricious, lacked a rational basis, and was an unconstitutional taking of its property. The appellate court rejected the college's claims, asserting that the council's action had a reasonable basis in law and was neither arbitrary nor capricious. Furthermore, said the court, there was no evidence that designating the rectory as a landmark prevented the college from carrying out its charitable purposes. On the other hand, in a challenge to a zoning board decision by Northwestern College, the court ruled that, in the particular circumstances, the city's denial of a zoning variance to the college was arbitrary and discriminatory, thus violating constitutional equal protection principles (*Northwestern College v. City of Arden Hills,* 281 N.W.2d 865 (Minn. 1979)).

In several cases, educational institutions have challenged zoning ordinances that exclude educational uses of land in residential zones. In *Yanow v. Seven Oaks Park,* 94 A.2d 482 (N.J. 1953), a postsecondary religious training school challenged the reasonableness of an ordinance that excluded schools of higher or special education from residential zones where elementary and secondary schools were permitted. The court, determining that the former schools could be "reasonably placed in a separate classification" from the latter, upheld the exclusion. But in *Long Island University v. Tappan,* 113 N.Y.S.2d 795 (N.Y. App. Div. 1952), *affirmed summarily,* 114 N.E.2d 432 (N.Y. 1953), the institution won its battle against an exclusionary ordinance. After the university had obtained a certificate of occupancy from the local township, a nearby village annexed the tract of land where the university was located. The village then passed a zoning ordinance that would have prohibited the operation of the university. The court concluded:

> Insofar as the zoning ordinance seeks to prohibit entirely the use of plaintiff's lands in the village for the purposes for which it is chartered, the zoning ordinance is void and ineffectual, as beyond the power of the village board to enact and as bearing no reasonable relation to the promotion of the health, safety, morals, or general welfare of the community [113 N.Y.S.2d at 799].

Even when the zoning ordinance permits all or particular kinds of educational institutions to operate in a residential or other zone, the zoning board may not consider all the institution's uses of its land and buildings to be educational use.[4] The distinction is much the same as that drawn in local taxation law (see Section 11.3), where the tax status of an educational institution's property depends not only on the character of the institution but also on whether

---

[4]The relevant cases and authorities are collected in Jay M. Zitter, Annot., "What Constitutes Accessory or Incidental Use of Religious or Educational Property Within Zoning Ordinance," 11 A.L.R.4th 1084; and Phillip E. Hassman, Annot., "Eminent Domain: Right to Condemn Property Owned or Used by Private Educational, Charitable, or Religious Organization," 80 A.L.R.3d 833.

the particular property is being used for educational purposes. When there are no specific definitions or restrictions in the ordinance itself, courts tend to interpret phrases such as "educational use" broadly, to permit a wide range of uses. In *Scheuller v. Board of Adjustment,* 95 N.W.2d 731 (Iowa 1959), the court held that a seminary's dormitory building was an educational use under an ordinance that permitted educational uses but did not permit apartment houses or multiple dwellings. And in *Property Owners Ass'n. v. Board of Zoning Appeals,* 123 N.Y.S.2d 716 (N.Y. Sup. Ct. 1953), the court held that seating to be constructed adjacent to a college's athletic field was an educational use.

Where a zoning ordinance prohibits or narrowly restricts educational uses in a particular zone, an educational institution may be able to argue that its proposed use is a permissible noneducational use under some other part of the ordinance. In *Application of LaPorte,* 152 N.Y.S.2d 916 (N.Y. App. Div. 1956), *affirmed,* 141 N.E.2d 917 (N.Y. 1957), a college was allowed to construct a residence to accommodate more than sixty students because the residence came within the ordinance's authorization of single-family dwelling units. Since the city had not placed any limitations on the number of persons who could constitute a "family," the court ruled that this use complied with local laws.

Fraternity houses may be excluded from residential districts or may be a permissible educational or noneducational use, depending on the terms of the ordinance and the facts of the case.[5] In *City of Baltimore v. Poe,* 168 A.2d 193 (Md. 1961), a fraternity was permitted in a zone that excluded any "club, the chief activity of which is a service customarily carried on as a business." The court found that "the chief activities carried on at this fraternity house . . . have clearly been established to be social and educational functions for the benefit of the whole membership." But in *Theta Kappa, Inc. v. City of Terre Haute,* 226 N.E.2d 907 (Ind. Ct. App. 1967), the court found that a fraternity did not come within the term "dwelling" as defined by the zoning ordinance and was therefore not a permissible use in the residential district in which it was located.

Other problems concerning zoning ordinances arise not because the ordinances exclude a particular use of property but because they regulate the way in which the landholder implements the permitted use. The validity of such "regulatory zoning" also often depends on the interpretation and application of the ordinance and its consistency with state law. In *Franklin and Marshall College v. Zoning Hearing Board of the City of Lancaster,* 371 A.2d 557 (Pa. Commw. Ct. 1977), for example, the college sought to convert a single-family home it owned into a fraternity house. The fraternity house was a permissible use under the ordinance. The town opposed the conversion, however, arguing that it would violate other provisions of the zoning ordinance dealing with the adequacy of parking and the width of side yards. Applying these provisions, the court held that the proposed number of parking spaces was adequate but that the width of the side yard would have to be increased before the conversion would be allowed.

---

[5]The relevant cases and authorities are collected in R. A. Shapiro, Annot., "Application of Zoning Regulations to College Fraternities and Sororities," 25 A.L.R.3d 921.

In *Sisters of Holy Cross v. Brookline,* 198 N.E.2d 624 (Mass. 1964), a state statute was the focus of the dispute about regulatory zoning. A local zoning authority had attempted to apply construction requirements for single-family homes to the facilities of a private college. A state statute provided that "no ordinance or bylaw which prohibits or limits the use of land for any church or other religious purpose or for any educational purpose . . . shall be valid." The court rejected the town's claim that the statute did not cover ordinances regulating the dimensions of buildings: "We think that this bylaw, as applied to Holy Cross, 'limits the use' of its land and, therefore, we think such application valid." In contrast, the court in *Radcliffe College v. City of Cambridge,* 215 N.E.2d 892 (Mass. 1966), held that the same state statute did not conflict with a Cambridge zoning ordinance requiring the college to provide off-street parking for newly constructed facilities. The court ruled that providing for parking for students or employees was an "educational use" of the property, and thus did not limit the college's ability to use its land for educational purposes.

11.2.4. Special exceptions and variances. Particular educational or non-educational uses may be permitted as "conditional uses" in an otherwise restricted zone. In this situation, the institution must apply for a special exception to the zoning ordinance. An educational institution may seek a special exception by demonstrating that it satisfies the conditions imposed by the zoning board. If it cannot do so, it may challenge the conditions as being unreasonable or beyond the zoning board's authority under the ordinance or state law.

The plaintiff in *Marjorie Webster Junior College v. District of Columbia Board of Zoning Adjustment,* 309 A.2d 314 (D.C. 1973), had operated a girls' finishing school in a residential zone under a special exception granted by the zoning board. The discretion of the zoning board was limited by a regulation specifying that exceptions would be granted only where "in the judgment of the board such special exceptions will be in harmony with the general purpose and intent of the zoning regulations and maps and will not tend to affect adversely the use of neighboring property in accordance with said zoning regulations and maps." Another regulation specifically authorized exceptions for colleges and universities, but only if "such use is so located that it is not likely to become objectionable to neighboring property because of noise, traffic, number of students, or other objectionable conditions." The college was sold to new owners, who instituted new programs (mostly short-term continuing education programs) that altered the curriculum of the school and attracted a new clientele to the campus. After a citizens' group complained that this new use was outside the scope of the college's special exception, the college filed an amendment to the campus plan that the prior owners had filed in order to obtain the special exception. The zoning board rejected the amendment after extensive hearings, concluding that, under the applicable regulations, the new use of the college property would not be in harmony with the general purpose and intent of the zone and would adversely affect neighboring property by attracting large numbers of transient men and women to the campus and increasing vehicular traffic in the neighborhood. On appeal by the college, the court held that the zoning regulations contained adequate standards to control the board's discretion and that the board's decision was supported by sufficient evidence.

New York Institute of Technology v. LeBoutillier, 305 N.E.2d 754 (N.Y. 1973), took up a similar issue. A private college had entered an agreement with the local government regarding the use of the college's existing property. Subsequent to the agreement, the college acquired property not contiguous with the main campus, in a residential zone that permitted educational use by special exception. The college's application for a special exception was denied by the zoning board, and the court upheld the board's decision in an interesting opinion combining fact, policy, and law.

The court noted that the institute already owned more than 400 acres in the town, the main campus had substantial undeveloped land, and the buildings that it needed for a new teacher education program could be built on the main campus without violating the earlier agreement with the town to limit its expansion and enrollments. Although the institute had argued that renovating existing buildings on the new property was less costly than building new buildings on the main campus, the court, although acknowledging that "[t]here is force to the argument that these judgments should be made by college administrators, not zoning boards of appeal or courts . . . at some point, probably not definable with precision, a college's desire to expand, here by the path of least economic resistance, should yield to the legitimate interests of village residents" (305 N.E.2d at 758–59). The court noted that the town had been amenable to previous requests by the institute to expand while maintaining the residential character of the town, and that the latest request by the institute would have a negative impact on the town. (For a case with a similar outcome, see *Lafayette College v. Zoning Hearing Board of the City of Easton,* 588 A.2d 1323 (Pa. Commw. Ct. 1991).)

A series of lawsuits involving George Washington University suggests that local zoning boards may limit a private university's expansion plans and even dictate the mix of buildings that it constructs. The university is located in the Foggy Bottom area of Washington, D.C., in a neighborhood that is partly residential. District of Columbia zoning law permits university use in residential areas as a special exception which must be approved by the Board of Zoning Adjustment (BZA). After local community members challenged the university's planned construction of dormitories and academic buildings near its campus, the Board of Zoning Adjustment placed conditions on its approval of a special exception for the university's long-term campus improvement plan. Under these conditions, the university had to provide additional living quarters on campus for students by 2006; should the university fail to meet this requirement, the BZA would not issue any permit to the university to construct or occupy additional nonresidential buildings, either on or off campus.

The university challenged the rulings of the BZA in federal court, claiming that they were arbitrary and capricious, and violated the due process clause. It also claimed that the BZA's order violated the university's academic freedom by limiting its discretion to decide how to use campus space. Although the federal trial court agreed with some of the university's legal claims, the federal appellate court reversed those rulings of the trial court (*George Washington University v. District of Columbia*, 2002 U.S. Dist. LEXIS 26729 (D.D.C., April 12, 2002), *affirmed in part and reversed in part*, 318 F.3d 203 (D.C. Cir. 2003)). The appellate court held that the BZA's order was neither arbitrary nor capricious and was consistent with substantive due process. It also rejected the university's academic freedom claim, asserting that this issue was "wholly different" from the restrictions on speech in classic academic freedom cases. Furthermore, said the court, the university's claim that the District of Columbia's zoning regulations were facially discriminatory in violation of the Fifth Amendment's due process clause was unavailing. Because universities are not a specially protected class for equal protection purposes, ordinances may classify persons in any manner "rationally related to legitimate governmental objectives," and the BZA had met that standard.

The university also challenged the BZA's order in the District of Columbia's own courts. In *George Washington University v. District of Columbia Board of Zoning Adjustment*, 831 A.2d 921 (D.C. 2003), the D.C. Court of Appeals considered the university's claims that the BZA's order was arbitrary, capricious, and irrational, and that it violated the District of Columbia's Human Rights Act because it discriminated against students by placing limits on the university's ability to house them off campus in the Foggy Bottom neighborhood. The university also challenged the BZA's ruling that, should any portion of the board's condition that the university increase on-campus student housing be invalidated by a court, no application for a special exception or a permit to occupy or construct any nonresidential building on campus could be processed without the board's express authorization. The university argued that this provision chilled its right to seek judicial review of BZA orders. The D.C. court ruled that this BZA ruling intruded upon the separation of powers in an "arbitrary and unreasonable way," and it therefore remanded the issue to the board.

In most other respects, however, the D.C. court upheld the BZA's decisions. It ruled that the board's order that the university provide additional on-campus student housing was based upon sufficient evidence, and was neither arbitrary nor capricious. Furthermore, the BZA's threat to stop construction of nonresidential buildings on or off campus was also a permissible use of its powers because it provided an appropriate incentive for the university to comply with the BZA's order. It also ruled that the order did not violate the D.C. Human Rights Act because the zoning regulations' requirement that the interests of the neighbors be considered suggested that the BZA could balance their needs, and the impact of student housing in the neighborhood, against the university's and students' needs.

On the other hand, George Washington University was successful in other litigation brought by a neighborhood group challenging the BZA's approval of the university's plans to convert a hotel located in a residential district into a student residence hall. In *Watergate West v. District of Columbia Board of Zoning Adjustment*, 815 A.2d 762 (D.C. Ct. App. 2003), the BZA had granted the university a certificate of occupancy (as a dormitory) for the former hotel it had purchased. The objecting neighbors sought judicial review of the BZA's decision.

The court ruled for the BZA, stating that its decision was rational, and that converting a hotel to a dormitory did not reduce the amount of housing stock in the neighborhood.

In addition to these skirmishes with George Washington University, the District of Columbia Board of Zoning Adjustment also imposed a number of conditions on Georgetown University's campus plan. Georgetown challenged several of these conditions before the District of Columbia Court of Appeals as either unsupported by substantial evidence or beyond the authority and competence of the BZA. Georgetown University is also located in a residential neighborhood in the District of Columbia, and much of its campus is zoned for residential use. The university submitted its proposed campus plan to the Board of Zoning Adjustment in 2000. Responding in part to neighbors who objected to the conduct of Georgetown students living off campus, the BZA placed a number of conditions on Georgetown's campus plan. Among other conditions, the BZA required Georgetown to cap its enrollment at the level set in its 1990 campus plan, to seek BZA approval if it decided to change the composition of a disciplinary hearing board that dealt with off-campus infractions, and to operate a full-time "hotline" for complaints about student off-campus misconduct. Another condition required the university to "report a violation of the Code of Conduct to the parents or guardians of the violator to the extent permitted by law," and to investigate alleged violations of housing or sanitation regulations by students living off campus. Failure to comply with these requirements would be grounds for placing a moratorium on any nonresidential construction on campus and for the imposition of fines against the university.

In *President and Directors of Georgetown College v. District of Columbia Board of Zoning Adjustment*, 837 A.2d 58 (D.C. 2003), the D.C. Court of Appeals found many of these conditions "inappropriate and unreasonable," characterizing them as "micromanagement" of the university's disciplinary process and beyond the expertise of the zoning board. The court also stated that the requirement that enrollment be capped was not supported by substantial evidence. On the other hand, the court noted that imposing a moratorium on nonresidential development on campus, "if imposed for a meaningful violation" was not necessarily unreasonable. The court vacated the BZA's decision and remanded the case to the board to remove those conditions that the court had found to be arbitrary, capricious, and beyond the expertise of the board, and to formulate appropriate conditions for granting the exception to Georgetown that were consistent with applicable legal requirements.

If a proposed use by an educational institution does not conform to the general standards of the zone or to the terms of a special exception, the institution may seek a variance.

> A variance is an exercise of the power of the governmental authority to grant relief, in a proper case, from the liberal application of the terms of an ordinance. It is to be used where strict application of the ordinance would cause unnecessary and substantial hardship to the property holder peculiar to the property in question, without serving a warranted and corresponding benefit to the public interest [*Arcadia Development Corp. v. Bloomington*, 125 N.W.2d 846, 851 (Minn. 1964)].

Zoning boards may grant variances only in these narrow circumstances and only on the basis of standards created by state or local law. Variances that constitute substantial changes in the zoning plan or alter the boundaries of established zones may be considered in excess of the zoning board's authority. In *Ranney v. Instituto Pontificio Delle Maestre Filippini,* 119 A.2d 142 (N.J. 1955), the college had applied for a variance to expand its existing facilities, located in a restrictive residential zone. The zoning board granted the variance. The New Jersey Supreme Court reversed the board's decision, however, relying on a statutory provision that authorized variances only where there would be no "substantial detriment to the public good" and "the intent and purpose of the zone plan and zoning ordinance" would not be "substantially impair[ed]" (N.J. Stat. Ann. § 40:55-39(d)). The court found that the variance would inappropriately alter the character of the residential neighborhood in which the college was located. (For a contrasting opinion, upholding a college's variance request, see *Salve Regina College v. Zoning Board of Review of City of Newport,* 594 A.2d 878 (R.I. 1991).)

11.2.5. Amendment of zoning ordinances. If an educational institution's proposed use is prohibited within a zone, and the institution cannot obtain a special exception or a variance, it may petition the local government to amend the zoning ordinance. Unlike an exception or a variance, an amendment is designed to correct an intrinsic flaw in the zoning ordinance rather than to relieve individual hardship imposed by zoning requirements. An institution seeking an amendment should be prepared to demonstrate that the proposed change is in the public interest rather than just for its own private advantage.

Courts vary in the presumptions and standards they apply to zoning amendments. In some jurisdictions courts give amendments a presumption of reasonableness; in others they presume that the original ordinance was reasonable and require that any amendment be justified. Many courts require that an amendment conform to the comprehensive zoning plan. "Spot zoning," which reclassifies a small segment of land, is frequently overturned for nonconformance with a comprehensive plan.

Bidwell v. Zoning Board of Adjustment, 286 A.2d 471 (Pa. Commw. Ct. 1972), illustrates many of the important legal considerations regarding zoning amendments. An amendment reclassified a tract of land from single-family to multi-family residential and granted an exception to a college to allow the construction of a library, a lecture hall, and an off-street parking area. The court upheld the amendment, noting that public hearings concerning the proposed amendment had been held and that it furthered the municipality's general program of land utilization.

Another college prevailed in its fight against a local ordinance that prohibited the college from using buildings it owned in a historical district. The city of Schenectady, New York, amended its zoning ordinance to exclude educational organizations, among others, from using single-family dwellings in a special historic district. Union College, which owned seven properties in the historic district, petitioned the city to amend the ordinance and allow the college to use these properties for faculty or administrative offices or for residences for guests visiting the college. The city refused, and the college sought a declaratory judgment, arguing that the ordinance, as applied to the college, was unconstitutional.

The trial court, intermediate appellate court, and highest state court agreed with the college. In *Trustees of Union College v. Members of the Schenectady City Council*, 667 N.Y.S.2d 978 (Ct. App. 1997), the court ruled that the ordinance's complete exclusion of educational uses in the historic district was unconstitutional because it bore no substantial relation to the public health, safety, morals, or general welfare, and thus was beyond the zoning authority of the city. The court stated that the city should have weighed the requested educational use against competing interests rather than excluding completely the use of the property by the college.

Some states may have a statute that authorizes the state courts to invalidate certain provisions of, and thus in effect to amend, local zoning ordinances. *Trustees of Tufts College v. City of Medford*, 602 N.E.2d 1105 (Mass. App. Ct. 1992), illustrates the operation of such a statute. The parties could not agree on how the off-street parking provisions in the city's zoning ordinance would apply to three new buildings Tufts was constructing in the heart of its campus. Tufts brought suit under a Massachusetts law that invalidated local zoning ordinances that prohibited or restricted the use for educational purposes of land or buildings owned by a nonprofit educational institution (Mass. Gen. Laws ch. 40A, § 3). The trial court invalidated portions of the city ordinance's parking provisions. The appellate court determined that invalidation was unnecessary, however, and modified the trial court's judgment. Recognizing the incongruity of zoning requirements that assume that all property occurs in "lots," when a college's property may consist of a "green" surrounded by clusters of buildings, the appellate court accepted the city's concession that parking spaces in Tufts' new parking garage, located several blocks away, could "count" as off-street parking for the new buildings.

In at least one state, community colleges (as school districts) have yet another means for securing an amendment to a local zoning ordinance. California's Government Code, Section 53094, provides that a school district may declare a city zoning ordinance inapplicable to a proposed use of its own property unless the proposed use is for "nonclassroom facilities." In *People v. Rancho Santiago College*, 277 Cal. Rptr. 69 (Cal. Ct. App. 1990), the college had contracted with a community group to use the college's parking lot for a weekly "swap meet." The parking lot was zoned for "open space," and the city sued the college, arguing that the use of the parking lot for a "swap meet" was not permitted. The court rejected the college's assertion that it could exempt this use from the zoning ordinance, noting that both uses—as a parking lot and for a swap meet—were "nonclassroom facilities" under Section 53094 and thus were not exempt from the ordinance.

11.2.6. Rights of other property owners. In considering the various approaches to zoning problems addressed in subsections 11.2.2 to 11.2.5 above, postsecondary administrators should be aware that other property owners may challenge zoning decisions favorable to the institution or may intervene in disputes between the institution and the zoning board (see generally the *George Washington University* and *Georgetown University* cases in subsection 11.2.4 above). The procedures of the zoning board may require notice to local property owners and an opportunity for a hearing before certain zoning decisions are made. Thus, zoning problems may require administrators to "do battle" with the local community in a very real and direct way.

Landowners usually can challenge a zoning decision if they have suffered a special loss different from that suffered by the public generally. Adjacent landowners almost always are considered to have suffered such loss and thus to have "standing" (that is, a legal capacity) to challenge zoning decisions regarding the adjacent land. Property owners' associations may or may not have standing based on their special loss or that of their members, depending on the jurisdiction. In *Peirce Junior College v. Schumaker*, 333 A.2d 510 (Pa. Commw. Ct. 1975), neighboring landowners were denied permission to intervene in a local college's appeal of a zoning decision because they were not the owners or tenants of the property directly involved. But in *Citizens Ass'n. of Georgetown v. District of Columbia Board of Zoning Adjustment*, 365 A.2d 372 (D.C. 1976), a citizens' association from the neighboring area was successful in challenging and overturning, on procedural grounds, a special exception granted to Georgetown University.

In *Sharp v. Zoning Hearing Board of the Township of Radnor*, 628 A.2d 1223 (Pa. Commw. Ct. 1993), Villanova University had a tract of its land rezoned from residential to institutional use. The tract, which was to be developed for dormitories, was contiguous to existing dormitory and classroom buildings but had been in a residential zone. The university had negotiated with owners of adjacent property regarding setbacks, lighting, traffic, security measures, and other measures to reduce the impact of the university's building plans on its neighbors. One of the adjacent property owners challenged the rezoning in court, arguing that the ordinance was invalid because of procedural defects in its enactment and that the zoning board's action was unconstitutional "spot zoning." Quickly rejecting the first argument, the court turned to the constitutional claim. Asserting that "a zoning ordinance is presumed to be valid and constitutional, and the challenging party has the heavy burden of proving otherwise" (628 A.2d at 1227), the court upheld the board's decision. Since most of the land surrounding the rezoned tract was already used by the university for educational purposes, and since the university's need for additional on-campus student housing had a "substantial relation[ship] to the public health, safety, morals and general welfare," the zoning board's action could not be considered to be arbitrary and unreasonable spot zoning.

American University encountered similar objections from some of its neighbors when it proposed a new location for its law school and changes in the campus border. In *Glenbrook Road Ass'n. v. District of Columbia Board of Zoning Adjustment*, 605 A.2d 22 (D.C. 1992), two groups of neighbors challenged the zoning board's decision to grant the university's request. The court found that the zoning board had required the university to comply with several actions that would minimize the effect of the law school on the neighborhood, and had sufficiently taken into consideration the concerns of the neighbors during the hearing process.[6]

In *New York Botanical Garden v. Board of Standards and Appeals and Fordham University,* 671 N.Y.S.2d 423 (Ct. App. 1998), the Botanical Garden had objected to a decision of the New York Board of Standards and Appeals to allow Fordham University to build a radio broadcasting tower on its campus. The board had found that the operation of a radio station of the size and power that necessitated the new tower was clearly incidental to the educational mission of the university and, thus, a permitted use under the zoning laws. New York's highest court upheld the board's decision, affirming the rulings of both the trial court and the intermediate appellate court. The standard of review for the board's zoning decision, according to the court, was one of reasonableness, and the Botanical Garden had made no showing that the board's ruling was unreasonable or irrational. Indeed, commented the court, the Botanical Garden's objection to the tower appeared to be primarily on aesthetic grounds; there was no proof that the Botanical Garden would suffer economic harm, that the tower was dangerous, or that the tower would prompt an "undesirable change in the character of the neighborhood."

When St. Joseph's University decided to convert an existing apartment building, located in a residential zone, to a student dormitory, some neighbors sought review of the zoning board's approval of that plan. In *Greaton Properties v. Lower Merion Township,* 796 A.2d 1038 (Commw. Ct. Pa. 2002), the court ruled that the dormitory was not exclusively residential, but that it was an "integral part of the overall educational experience" and thus was not subject to the zoning code's spacing provisions. Furthermore, there was no showing that the dorm would be a detriment to the health or safety of the community. (For another similar case, see the *Watergate West* case in subsection 11.2.4 above.)

11.2.7. *Zoning off-campus housing.*

Zoning ordinances that prevent groups of college students from living together in residential areas may create particular problems for institutions that depend on housing opportunities in the community to help meet student housing needs.[7] Some communities have enacted ordinances that specify the number of unrelated individuals who may live in the same residential dwelling, and many of these ordinances have survived constitutional challenge. In *Village of Belle Terre v. Boraas,* 416 U.S. 1 (1974), for example, the U.S. Supreme Court rejected the argument that such a

---

[6]For other cases challenging the location of the law school, see *Spring Valley Wesley Heights Citizens Association v. District of Columbia Board of Zoning Adjustment,* 644 A.2d 434 (D.C. 1994); and *Duke v. The American University,* 675 A.2d 26 (D.C. 1996).

[7]Cases and authorities are collected in Vitauts M. Gulbis, Annot., "Validity of Ordinance Restricting Number of Unrelated Persons Who Can Live Together in Residential Zone," 12 A.L.R.4th 238; and James L. Rigelhaupt, Jr., Annot., "What Constitutes a 'Family' Within Meaning of Zoning Regulation or Restrictive Covenant," 71 A.L.R.3d 693.

restriction violates the residents' freedom of association rights. In other cases, however, courts have invalidated particular types of restrictions on student occupancy of residential dwellings.

In *Borough of Glassboro v. Vallorosi,* 568 A.2d 888 (N.J. 1990), the borough had sought an injunction against the leasing of a house in a residential district to ten unrelated male college students. The borough had recently amended its zoning ordinance to limit "use and occupancy" in the residential districts to "families" only. The ordinance defined "family" as "one or more persons occupying a dwelling unit as a single nonprofit housekeeping unit, who are living together as a stable and permanent living unit, being a traditional family unit or the functional equivalency [*sic*] thereof."

Tracking the ordinance's language, the court determined that the ten students constituted a "single housekeeping unit" that was a "stable and permanent living unit" (568 A.2d at 894). The court relied particularly on the fact that the students planned to live together for three years, and that they "ate together, shared household chores, and paid expenses from a common fund" (568 A.2d at 894). The court also cautioned that zoning ordinances are not the most appropriate means for dealing with problems of noise, traffic congestion, and disruptive behavior.

Another type of restriction on off-campus housing was invalidated in *Kirsch v. Prince Georges County,* 626 A.2d 372 (Md. 1993). Prince Georges County, Maryland, had enacted a "mini-dorm" ordinance that regulated the rental of residential property to students attending college. Homeowners and prospective student renters brought an equal protection claim against the county. The ordinance defined a "mini-dormitory" as "[a]n off-campus residence, located in a building that is, or was originally constructed as[,] a one-family, two-family, or three-family dwelling which houses at least three (3), but not more than five (5), individuals, *all or part of whom are unrelated to one another by blood, adoption or marriage and who are registered full-time or part-time students at an institution of higher learning*" (§ 27-107.1(a) (150.1), cited in 626 A.2d at 373–74; emphasis added). For each mini-dorm, the ordinance specified a certain square footage per person for bedrooms, one parking space per resident, and various other requirements. The ordinance also prohibited local zoning boards from granting variances for mini-dorms, from approving departures from the required number of parking spaces, and from permitting nonconforming existing uses.

The court determined that Maryland's constitution provides equal protection guarantees similar to those of the U.S. Constitution's Fourteenth Amendment. Relying on *City of Cleburne v. Cleburne Living Center,* 473 U.S. 432 (1985), as the source of a strengthened "rational basis" test to use for Fourteenth Amendment challenges to restrictive zoning laws, the court determined that this test was the appropriate one to evaluate whether the mini-dorm ordinance was "rationally related to a legitimate governmental purpose." The court then examined the purpose of the ordinance, which was to prevent or control "detrimental effects" upon neighbors (such as increased demands for parking, litter, and noise). The court was careful to distinguish the *Boraas* case (above), on which the county had relied in its defense of the ordinance:

> Unlike the zoning ordinance analyzed in *Boraas*, the Prince Georges County "mini-dorm" ordinance does not differentiate based on the nature of the use of the property, such as a fraternity house or a lodging house, but rather on the occupation of the persons who would dwell therein. Therefore, under the ordinance a landlord of a building . . . is permitted to rent the same for occupancy by three to five unrelated persons so long as they are not pursuing a higher education without incurring the burdens of complying with the arduous requirements of the ordinance [626 A.2d at 381].

Noting that the problems the ordinance sought to avoid would occur irrespective of whether the tenants were students, the court held that the ordinance "creat[ed] more strenuous zoning requirements for some [residential tenant classes] and less for others based solely on the occupation which the tenant pursues away from that residence," thus establishing an irrational classification forbidden by both the federal and the state constitutions.

In *College Area Renters and Landlord Association v. City of San Diego*, 50 Cal. Rptr. 2d 515 (Cal. App. 1996), a municipal ordinance regulated the number of individuals over age eighteen who could live in a non-owner-occupied residence in certain areas of the city, based upon the number of rooms and their square footage, the amount of parking per inhabitant, and the size of rooms that were not bedrooms. The ordinance did not apply to owner-occupied housing. An organization of renters and landlords challenged the law under the California constitution's equal protection clause, as well as under preemption (see Section 11.1 above) and constitutional right to privacy theories. The court, affirming a lower court's summary judgment for the plaintiffs, ruled that renters and homeowners were similarly situated with respect to the problems that the ordinance sought to ameliorate—noise, congestion, and littering—and thus the ordinance was an unconstitutional violation of equal protection because it irrationally distinguished between owners and renters. Although the court declined to reach the plaintiffs' other claims, it stated in *dicta* that there was a possible preemption problem because state occupancy standards were more lenient than those of the ordinance, and that the city should follow the statewide standards in dealing with the problem of overcrowding. The court also added, again in *dicta*, that the ordinance could trigger privacy concerns and, thus, should be upheld only if it served a compelling public need.

The federal Fair Housing Act may also provide a source of relief if students with disabilities wish to share an off-campus residence. A Fair Housing Act challenge to a zoning ordinance that restricts single-family homes to four individuals, unless the home's residents are "family" members, although unsuccessful, provides an example of challenges that might be successful under other circumstances. In *Elliott v. City of Athens*, 960 F.2d 975 (11th Cir. 1992), an organization that provided rehabilitation for individuals with alcoholism sought to use a single-family home as a group home, or "halfway house," for individuals completing their treatment. When the city denied the organization's application for an exemption from the zoning regulation, the organization sued the city and claimed that the restrictive definition of family (individuals related by blood, marriage, or adoption) discriminated against individuals with disabilities in violation of the Fair Housing Act, 42 U.S.C. §§ 3601 *et seq.* The court ruled for the city, noting that the Fair Housing Act contains an exemption, Section 3607(b)(1), for "reasonable local, state or federal restrictions regarding the maximum number of occupants permitted to occupy a dwelling." In this case, the organization wanted to house twelve men in the home. The court reasoned that the organization had not demonstrated that the occupancy restrictions were unreasonable, nor had it demonstrated why the law was a greater burden on individuals with disabilities than it was on students or other unrelated people.

Sec. 11.3. Local Government Taxation

11.3.1. General tax concepts. Local government taxation is one of the most traditional problems in postsecondary education law.[8] Although the basic concepts are more settled here than they are in many other areas, these concepts often prove difficult to apply in particular cases. Moreover, in an era of tight budgets, where local governments seek new revenue sources and postsecondary institutions attempt to minimize expenditures, the sensitivity of local tax questions has increased. Pressures to tax institutions' auxiliary services (Section 15.3.4.2) have grown, for instance, as have pressures for institutions to make payments "in lieu of taxes" to local governments. (See generally D. Kay, W. Brown, & D. Allee, *University and Local Government Fiscal Relations,* IHELG Monograph 89-2 (IHELG, University of Houston Law Center, 1989).)

The real property tax is the most common tax imposed by local governments on educational institutions. Sales taxes and admission taxes are also imposed in a number of jurisdictions. A local government's authority to tax is usually grounded in state enabling legislation, which delegates various types of taxing power to various types of local governments. Most local tax questions involving postsecondary institutions concern the interpretation of this state legislation, particularly its exemption provisions. A local government must implement its taxing power by local ordinance, and questions may also arise concerning the interpretation of these ordinances.

A public institution's defenses against local taxation may differ from those of a private institution. Public institutions may be shielded from local taxation by tax exemptions for state government contained in state constitutional provisions or statutes. Public institutions may also make sovereign immunity claims (see Section 11.1) against attempts by a local government to impose taxes or tax collection responsibilities on them. Private institutions, on the other hand,

---

[8]Another local government revenue-raising measure, to be distinguished from taxation, is the special assessment—a payment covering a proportionate share of the costs of a particular improvement that confers a "special benefit" on the property owners whose property is assessed. See generally Osborne Reynolds, *Local Government Law* § 99 (West, 1982). Special assessments are imposed less frequently than real estate taxes, and legal issues concerning assessments arise less frequently for colleges and universities than legal issues concerning taxation.

depend on state constitutional or statutory exemptions (or, occasionally, special legislation and charter provisions) that limit the local government's authority to tax. Although the provisions vary, most tax codes contain some form of tax exemption for religious, charitable, and educational organizations. These exemptions are usually "strictly construed to the end that such concession[s] will be neither enlarged nor extended beyond the plain meaning of the language employed" (*Cedars of Lebanon Hospital v. Los Angeles County*, 221 P.2d 31, 34 (Cal. 1950)). The party requesting the exemption has the burden of proving that the particular activity for which it seeks exemption is covered by the exemption provision. The strictness with which exemptions are construed depends on the state and the type of exemption involved.

Determinations on taxability and tax exemptions will depend not only on the particular property or function being taxed and the particular character of the institution, but also on the statutory and constitutional provisions, and judicial interpretations, that vary from state to state. A first and key step in tax planning, therefore, is to identify the particular provisions and exemptions that will apply to each property and function for which taxability is or could become an issue. The cases in subsections 11.3.2 to 11.3.3 below provide numerous examples.

11.3.2. Property taxes. Public colleges and universities are often exempt from local property taxation under state law exemptions for state property. As the *Southern University* case below illustrates, one of the threshold issues that may arise when courts apply these exemptions is whether the particular property that the government seeks to tax actually belongs to the institution and, therefore, to the state. Private nonprofit colleges and universities are also often exempt from local property taxation. Generally, as many of the cases below illustrate, the applicable state law provisions will exempt property of institutions organized for an educational purpose if the property at issue is used for that purpose (see, for example, *Berkshire School v. Town of Reading*, 781 A.2d 282 (Vt. 2001)). Sometimes such exemptions will extend to public institutions as well as private.[9] In the *Southern Illinois University* case below, for example, the court held that the property at issue was exempt not only as state property but also as property of an educational institution devoted to an educational use. In some states, private institutions may also obtain exemption from property taxation under an exemption for charities, or "public charities," as the *City of Washington* case below illustrates.

The states vary in the tests that they apply to implement the state property/"public use," "educational use," and "charitable use" exemptions. Some require that the property be used "exclusively" for educational or charitable purposes to qualify for an exemption. Others require only that the property be used "primarily" for such purposes. The cases below illustrate the variety of decisions reached under the different standards of "use" and

[9]Some of the cases are collected in William B. Johnson, Annot., "What Are Educational Institutions or Schools Within State Property Tax Exemption Provisions," 34 A.L.R.4th 698.

involving different types of institutional property and different types of ownership interests.

In *Southern Illinois University Foundation v. Booker,* 425 N.E.2d 465 (Ill. App. Ct. 1981), the county in which Southern Illinois University is located attempted to assess a property tax on low-cost housing that the university maintained for its married students. The housing consisted of apartments financed by the Federal Housing Administration and the Southern Illinois University Foundation. The foundation was the legal owner of the property. It is a nonprofit corporation whose purpose, under its bylaws, is "to buy, sell, lease, own, manage, convey, and mortgage real estate" and "in a manner specified by the Board of Trustees of Southern Illinois University, to act as the business agent of the said board in respect to . . . acquisition, management, and leasing of real property and buildings." The university claimed that the married students' apartments were state property and thus exempt from local government taxation. The county argued, however, that legal ownership vested in the foundation, not the university, thus making the exemption for state property inapplicable. In rejecting the county's argument, the court relied on the time-honored distinction between "legal title" and "equitable title":

> With respect to control and enjoyment of the benefits of the property, the stipulated facts show that the University, not the Foundation, in fact controls the property and has the right to enjoy the benefits of it in the manner of an owner in fee simple absolute. The Foundation acquired title to the property from the university solely as a convenience to the University with regard to long-term financing. The property is used to house students of the University. The facilities are controlled, operated, and maintained by the University. From funds derived from the operation of the property, the University pays annually as rent the amount of the Foundation's mortgage payment and, as agent of the Foundation, transmits that sum to the Federal National Mortgage Association. Furthermore, when the mortgage is eventually retired, the university will receive title to the improved property with no further payment whatsoever required as consideration for the transfer. The Foundation holds but naked legal title to property plainly controlled and enjoyed by the University and, hence, the State. Although the Foundation is a corporate entity legally distinct from that of the University, the function of the one is expressly "to promote the interests and welfare" of the other, and some of the highest officers of the University are required, under the bylaws of the Foundation, to serve in some of the highest positions of the Foundation. Thus, a further reality of the ownership of this property is the identification to a certain extent between the holder of bare legal title and the State as holder of the entire equitable interest. In this case, then, not only does the Foundation hold but naked legal title to property controlled and enjoyed by the State, but a certain identity exists as well between the holder of naked legal title and the State. For these reasons we hold the property exempt from taxation as property belonging to the State [425 N.E.2d at 471].

In a similar case involving a real property *ad valorem* tax, *In re Appalachian Student Housing Corp.,* 598 S.E.2d 701 (N.C. App. 2004), the court held that a student apartment complex at a state university was exempt as state property, even though a separate nonprofit corporation held legal title and operated the complex.

Appeal of University of Pittsburgh, 180 A.2d 760 (Pa. 1962), is a leading case concerning the exemption of houses provided by postsecondary institutions for their presidents or chancellors.[10] The court allowed an exemption under a lenient standard of use:

> The head of such an institution, whether he be called president or chancellor, represents to the public eye the "image" of the institution. Both an educator and an administrator of the tremendous "business" which any university or college now is, he must also be the official representative to host those who, for one reason or the other, find the university or college a place of interest and, if he is to assume the full scope and responsibility of his duties to the university or college, he must be universal in his contacts. Many years ago the Supreme Court of Massachusetts in *Amherst College v. Assessors,* . . . 79 N.E. 248, stated: "At the same time the usage and customs of the college impose upon the president certain social obligations. . . . The scope, observations, and usage of the character mentioned are not matters of express requirement or exaction. They are, however, required of a president in the use of the house, and noncompliance with them unquestionably would subject him to unfavorable comment from the trustees and others, or, at least, be regarded as a failure on his part to discharge the obligations and hospitality associated with his official position." . . . The residence of the head of a university or college necessarily renders a real function, tangibly and intangibly, in the life of the institution. While its utility to the purposes and objectives of the institution is incapable of exact measurement and evaluation, it is nonetheless real and valuable [180 A.2d at 763].

Another court, citing the *University of Pittsburgh* case and using the same lenient test, denied an exemption for the house of a president emeritus. The court made a finding of fact that the house was not actually used for institutional purposes:

> [The court in the *Pittsburgh* case] held that a president's or chancellor's residence could enjoy tax exemption where the record showed that the majority of the events for which the residence was utilized bore a direct relationship to the proper functioning of the University of Pittsburgh and served its aims and objectives. In this appeal the record does not support the test laid down in [that case]. This record reflects that the president emeritus is retained on a consultative basis in development and public relations. The residence provided the president emeritus by the Trustees appears to properly afford him an appropriate dwelling house commensurate with his past worthy service to Albright College. The record does not support, as in the case of the chancellor's residence of the University of Pittsburgh, that the residence in fact was used for the general purposes of Albright College [*In re Albright College,* 249 A.2d 833, 835 (Pa. Super. Ct. 1968)].

---

[10]Cases on housing for institutional personnel are collected in Maurice T. Brunner, Annot., "Tax Exemption of Property of Educational Body as Extending to Property Used by Personnel as Living Quarters," 55 A.L.R.3d 485.

In *Cook County Collector v. National College of Education*, 354 N.E.2d 507 (Ill. App. Ct. 1976), the court affirmed the trial court's denial of an exemption for the college president's house. The institution had introduced extensive evidence of the institutional use of the president's house. The vice president for business affairs testified that the house, "although used as the residence of the president, . . . is used as well for a number of educational, fund-raising, business, alumni, and social activities of the College," citing many examples. The court held, however, that the evidence did not satisfy the more stringent use test applied in that jurisdiction. The court emphasized that "[o]n cross-examination [the vice president] stated that classes are not held in the home; that access to the home is by invitation only; and that the primary use of the premises is to house the president and his family." Based on such facts, the appellate court agreed with the trial court "that the primary use of the president's mansion was residential and its school use was only incidental." More recently, a Texas court reached the same result in a similar case, denying a tax exemption for a college president's house under a strictly construed "exclusive use" statute (*Bexar Appraisal Dist. v. Incarnate Word College*, 824 S.W.2d 295 (Tex. App. 1992)).

Cases dealing with faculty and staff housing illustrate a similar split of opinions, depending on the facts of the case and the tests applied. In *MacMurray College v. Wright*, 230 N.E.2d 846 (Ill. 1967), for example, the court, applying a "primary use" test, denied tax exemptions for MacMurray College and Rockford College:

> The colleges have failed to demonstrate clearly that the faculty and staff housing was primarily used for purposes which were reasonably necessary for the carrying out of the schools' educational purposes. The record does not show that any of the faculty or staff members of either college were required, because of their educational duties, to live in these residences, or that they were required to or did perform any of their professional duties there. Also, though both records before us contain general statements that there were associations between the concerned faculty and students outside the classroom, there was no specific proof presented, aside from one isolated example, to show that student, academic, faculty, administrative, or any other type of college-connected activities were ever actually conducted at home by any member of the faculty or staff of either of the colleges [230 N.E.2d at 850].

The same result was reached by the California Supreme Court in a case involving the taxability of the leasehold interests of faculty and staff members who owned homes situated on land they leased from their employer, a state university that owned the land. In *Connolly v. County of Orange*, 824 P.2d 663 (Cal. 1992), a faculty member, supported by the university and the university housing corporation, sought exemption under a state constitutional provision applicable to "property used exclusively for . . . state colleges, and state universities" (Cal. Const. Art. XIII, § 3(d)). The state university's own ownership interest in the property was tax exempt under another constitutional provision (§ 3(a)), which exempted property owned by the state. In an elaborate opinion, the court held that, although the leasehold interest in the land could qualify as property under Section 3(d), land that is the site for a private residence is not "used exclusively" for the state university's purposes, and the leasehold interest in the land is therefore not exempt from taxation.

Student dormitories present a clearer case. They are usually exempt from property taxation, even if the institution charges students rent. Other types of student housing, however, may present additional complexities. In *Southern Illinois University Foundation v. Booker*, 425 N.E.2d 465 (Ill. App. Ct. 1981) (discussed earlier in this Section), the court considered whether apartments for married students were exempt from taxation. The question was whether this housing was more like dormitory housing for single students, which is generally considered an exempt educational use in Illinois, or like faculty and staff housing, which is generally not considered an exempt educational use in Illinois. Making ample use of the facts, the court chose the former:

> Without belaboring the point, we think that married students, for purposes of the comparison with faculty members, are first and foremost students. They are, therefore, more nearly analogous to single students, whose dormitory housing, as we have said, has long enjoyed tax-exempt status in Illinois. Married students seeking an education seem analogous to faculty members, for purposes of this comparison, only insofar as faculty members are often married and raising families. Faculty members, however, have usually completed their educations and are obviously employed, whereas students, by their very nature, have not completed their educations and are, if not unemployed, generally living on quite limited incomes. If a student cannot both attend school and afford to support his or her family in private housing, family obligations being what they are, the student cannot attend school, at least in the absence of low-cost family housing of the kind in issue here. Similarly, if a student cannot find available private housing for his or her family in a community crowded by students seeking housing not provided by the educational institution itself, the student cannot attend school. Therefore, we consider married student housing as necessary to the education of a married student as single-student housing is to a single student. Since the use of dormitory housing, serving essentially single students, is deemed primarily educational rather than residential, the use of family housing for married students should likewise be deemed primarily educational, and such property should enjoy tax-exempt status [425 N.E.2d at 474].

Similarly, courts may or may not accord sorority and fraternity houses the same tax treatment as student dormitories. If the institution itself owns the property, it must prove that the property is used for the educational or charitable purposes of the institution. In *Alford v. Emory University*, 116 S.E.2d 596 (Ga. 1960), for example, the court held that fraternity houses operated by the university as part of its residential program were entitled to a tax exemption:

> Under the evidence in this case, these fraternity buildings were built by the university; they are regulated and supervised by the university; they are located in the heart of the campus, upon property owned by the university, required to be so located and to be occupied only by students of the university; adopted as a part of the dormitory and feeding system of the college, and an integral part of

the operation of the college. In our opinion these fraternity houses are buildings erected for and used as a college, and not used for the purpose of making either private or corporate income or profit for the university, and our law says that they shall be exempt from taxes [116 S.E.2d at 601].

More recently, *Alford* was followed in *Johnson v. Southern Greek Housing Corp.,* 307 S.E.2d 491 (Ga. 1983). Georgia Southern College, part of the University of Georgia System, organized the Southern Greek Housing Corporation in order to provide the college's fraternities and sororities with housing close to campus. The corporation, not the college, held title to the property on which the fraternity houses were to be built. The Georgia Supreme Court concluded that the fraternity and sorority houses would be "'buildings erected for and used as a college' [quoting *Alford*] and that such buildings [would be] used for the operation of an educational institution." The court held that, even though the property was owned by a corporation and not the college, the fact that the corporation "performs an educational function in conjunction with and under the auspices of" the college sufficed to bring the case within *Alford.*

In contrast, the court in *Cornell University v. Board of Assessors,* 260 N.Y.S.2d 197 (N.Y. App. Div. 1965), focused on the social uses of university-owned fraternity houses to deny an exemption under an "exclusive use" test:

> It is true, of course, that the fraternities perform the essential functions of housing and feeding students, but it is clear that, in each case, the use of the premises is also devoted, in substantial part, to the social and other personal objectives of a privately organized, self-perpetuating club, controlled by graduate as well as student members. The burden of demonstrating these objectives to be educational purposes was not sustained and thus . . . [the lower court] properly found that the premises were not used "exclusively" for educational purposes, within the intendment of the exemption statute [260 N.Y.S.2d at 199].

But in a later case, *University of Rochester v. Wagner,* 408 N.Y.S.2d 157 (N.Y. App. Div. 1978), *affirmed summarily,* 392 N.E.2d 569 (N.Y. 1979), the court qualified the *Cornell University* holding. The University of Rochester owned nine fraternity houses for which it sought tax-exempt status. Unlike the *Cornell* case, where the houses served "social and other personal objectives" (but somewhat like the *Alford* case), the University of Rochester houses had become integrated into the university's housing program: the university controlled the houses' "exterior grounds, walkways, and access points"; the houses' dining programs were part of the university's dining program; the university periodically "review[ed] the health and viability" of the houses; and the university occasionally assigned nonfraternity members to live in the houses. Applying the "exclusive use" test, and analogizing these fraternity houses to dormitories, the courts granted the university's application for tax exemption:

> Like dormitories, the fraternity houses here serve the primary function of housing and feeding students while they attend the University and complete the required curriculum. This use has been held to be in furtherance of the

University's educational purposes. Moreover, the social intercourse and recreational activities that take place in the fraternity houses are similar both in quantity and quality to that which occurs in the dormitories. This social activity, although incidental to the primary use of the facilities, is essential to the personal, social and moral development of the student and should not be found to change the character of the property from one whose use is reasonably incident to and in furtherance of the University's exempt purposes to a use which is not. For the same reasons that dormitories have traditionally been held tax exempt, we see no reason why under the facts of this case the fraternity houses should not be accorded similar treatment [408 N.Y.S.2d at 164–65].

If an independently incorporated fraternity or sorority seeks its own property tax exemption, it must demonstrate an educational or charitable purpose independent of the university and prove that the property is used for that purpose. Greek letter and other social fraternities usually do not qualify for exemptions. In *Alpha Gamma Zeta House Association v. Clay County Board of Equalization*, 583 N.W.2d 167 (S.D. 1998), for example, tax exemptions were sought by various "house corporations" that owned real estate used as a primary residence for fraternity or sorority members who were students at the University of South Dakota (USD). Each house was located off campus "on property in which USD does not have any ownership interest." Each house corporation rented the real property to an affiliated fraternity or sorority chapter. Each chapter was recognized by USD as a student organization, and the members living in each house were required to comply with the university's housing policies and student code of conduct.

The house corporations sought a charitable exemption available to "benevolent organization(s)" under state law (S.D. Stat. Ann. Tit. 10, ch. 4, § 9.2). The statute required that the organization's property be "used exclusively for benevolent purposes," thus adopting an exclusive use test. The court held that the house corporations could not meet this test:

> The House Corporations argue that the purpose of their corporations is to provide lodging for their respective fraternities and sororities and a convenient method of ownership of real property. They assert that all of the benevolent and charitable functions of the chapters should be attributed to the corporations, who associate only for "fraternal purposes." In *South Dakota Sigma Chapter House Ass'n v. Clay County*, 65 S.D. 559, 567, 276 N.W. 258, 263 (1937) we recognized the close ties of the householding corporation to the fraternity, but stated that "notwithstanding its intimate relation to and its solicitude for the chapter," the house corporation may not be characterized by the purposes and practices of the chapter. The House Corporations may be a convenient "legal fiction" standing in for the Greek Chapters themselves, but this does not mandate commensurate legal treatment [583 N.W.2d at 169].

Similarly, in *Kappa Alpha Educational Foundation, Inc. v. Holliday*, 226 A.2d 825 (Del. 1967), the court found that a fraternity house was being held as an investment by the corporation that owned it and therefore did not qualify for exemption.

Professional fraternities may be somewhat more successful in establishing the educational purpose and use of their property in order to qualify for exemption. In *City of Memphis v. Alpha Beta Welfare Ass'n.,* 126 S.W.2d 323 (Tenn. 1939), for example, the Supreme Court of Tennessee upheld a district court's finding of fact that a medical fraternity's house was used exclusively for educational purposes:

> It is shown in proof that the student members of the Fraternity by reason of being housed together receive medical, ethical, and cultural instruction that they otherwise would not get. The acquisition of the property in order that the students might be housed together was but the means to the end that the purpose of the Phi Chi Medical Fraternity to promote the welfare of medical students morally and scientifically might be more effectively carried out [126 S.W.2d at 326].

Moreover, even if a campus sorority or fraternity does not qualify for an educational exemption, it may qualify in some jurisdictions under a statutory exemption for certain social organizations. In *Gamma Phi Chapter of Sigma Chi Building Fund Corp. v. Dade County,* 199 So. 2d 717 (Fla. 1967), the court held that the property of a national college fraternity was eligible for a statutory exemption designed for fraternal lodges.[11] (The exemption was denied on a technicality, however, because the fraternity missed the filing date.)

Athletic and recreational facilities owned by an educational institution may be exempt if the institution can prove that the facilities are used for educational purposes. Facilities with capacities far in excess of the institution's potential use may be subject to judicial scrutiny. In *Trustees of Rutgers University v. Piscataway Township in Middlesex County,* 46 A.2d 56 (N.J. 1946), for example, the court held that a stadium with a seating capacity of twenty thousand owned by an institution with a student body of seventeen hundred was not entitled to a property tax exemption.

Facilities for the arts (performance centers, art galleries, and so forth) present similar issues. The case of *City of Fayetteville v. Phillips,* 899 S.W.2d 57 (Ark. 1995), provides an instructive example of an "exclusive use" test's application to *public* arts facilities as well as the special usage issues that can arise when a college or university creates or affiliates with another entity. The case concerned the Walton Art Center, which the University of Arkansas owned jointly with the city of Fayetteville. The Art Center challenged the county assessor's determination that it was subject to real property taxation, relying on a provision of the Arkansas constitution that exempts "public property used exclusively for public purposes." The issue was whether the center was used "exclusively" for public purposes, since it was occasionally rented out to private groups for their own private use. The Supreme Court of Arkansas held that the rental of the center was a private use and could not be converted to a public

---

[11]The relevant cases on sorority and fraternity houses are collected in F. M. English, Annot., "Exemption from Taxation of College Fraternity or Sorority House," 66 A.L.R.2d 904.

use merely by applying the rental profits to other university or city public purposes. The focus was on the actual use of the property, not the use of the income derived from the property. Nor was the rental use sufficiently "incidental" to public uses as to be irrelevant.

In reaching its decision to uphold the county's tax assessment, the court emphasized that, under Arkansas law, "a taxpayer must establish an entitlement to an exemption beyond a reasonable doubt," and a "presumption operates in favor of the taxing power," and then proceeded to construe the public purpose exemption very strictly. The case thus stands in sharp contrast to other cases, such as the *Illini Media Company* case below, in which the courts flexibly construe exemption statutes.

Dining facilities that are located on the property of an educational institution and whose purpose is to serve the college community rather than to generate a profit have long been recognized as part of the educational program and there-fore entitled to a property tax exemption.[12] In *People ex rel. Goodman v. University of Illinois Foundation*, 58 N.E.2d 33 (Ill. 1944), the court upheld an exemption for dining halls (as well as dormitory and recreational facilities) even though the university derived incidental income by charging for the services. Dining facilities may be tax exempt even if the institution contracts with a private caterer to provide food services. In *Blair Academy v. Blairstown*, 232 A.2d 178 (N.J. Super Ct. App. Div. 1967), the court held:

> The use of a catering system to feed the students and faculty of this boarding school cannot be regarded as a commercial activity or business venture of the school. Blair pays for this catering service an annual charge of $376 per person. It has been found expedient by the management of the school to have such a private caterer, in lieu of providing its own personnel to furnish this necessary service. The practice has been carried on for at least ten years. Nor do we find material as affecting Blair's nonprofit status that the catering system uses Blair's kitchen equipment and facilities in its performance, or that some of the caterer's employees were permitted by the school to occupy quarters at the school, rent-free [232 A.2d at 181–82].

Exemptions of various other kinds of institutional property also depend on the particular use of the property and the particular test applied in the jurisdiction. In *Princeton University Press v. Borough of Princeton*, 172 A.2d 420 (N.J. 1961), a university press was denied exemption under an "exclusive use" test.

> There is no question that the petitioner has been organized exclusively for the mental and moral improvements of men, women and children. The Press's publication of outstanding scholarly works, which the trade houses would not be apt to publish because of insufficient financial returns, carries out not only the purposes for which it was organized but also performs a valuable public

---

[12]Cases on dining facilities are collected in D. E. Buckner, Annot., "Property Used as Dining Rooms or Restaurants as Within Tax Exemptions Extended to Property of Religious, Educational, Charitable, or Hospital Organizations," 72 A.L.R.2d 521.

service. It cannot be likewise concluded, however, that the property is *exclusively used* for the mental and moral improvement of men, women and children as required by the statute. A substantial portion of the Press's activity consists of printing work taken in for the purpose of offsetting the losses incurred in the publication of scholarly books. Such printing, which includes work done for educational and nonprofit organizations other than Princeton University, is undertaken for the purpose of making a profit. Hence, in this sense the printing takes on the nature of a commercial enterprise and, therefore, it cannot be said that the property is *exclusively used* for the statutory purpose [172 A.2d at 424; emphasis added].

But in *District of Columbia v. Catholic Education Press,* 199 F.2d 176 (D.C. Cir. 1952), a university press was granted an exemption:

> [T]he Catholic Education Press does not stand alone. It is a publishing arm of the [Catholic University of America]. It is an integral part of it. It has no separate life except bare technical corporate existence. It is not a private independent corporation, but to all intents and purposes it is a facility of the University. . . .
>
> If the Catholic University of America, in its own name, should engage in activities identical with those of its subsidiary, the Catholic Education Press, we suppose its right to exemption from taxation on the personal property used in such activities would not be questioned. We see no reason for denying the exemption to the University merely because it chooses to do the work through a separate nonprofit corporation [199 F.2d at 178–79].

In *City of Ann Arbor v. University Cellar,* 258 N.W.2d 1 (Mich. 1977), the issue was the application of a local personal property tax to the inventory of a campus bookstore at the University of Michigan. The statute provided an exemption for property "belonging to" the state or to an incorporated educational institution. The bookstore, the University Cellar, was a nonprofit corporation whose creation had been authorized by the university's board of regents. The majority of the corporation's board of directors, however, were appointed by the student government. The court determined that the directors did not represent the board of regents or the university administration and that the regents did not control the operation of the bookstore. Distinguishing the *Catholic Education Press* case, where the separately incorporated entity was essentially the alter ego of the university, the court denied the exemption because the property could not be said to "belong to" the university.

As the *University Cellar* case demonstrates, some of the most important tax exemption issues that arise concern the property of separate entities that the institution establishes or with which it affiliates (see Sections 3.6.3 & 15.3.4.2). The cases about fraternities, housing or facilities corporations, and university presses also illustrate this problem. Two other, more recent, illustrations come from a case concerning the property of a nonprofit media corporation created by a state university, and a case concerning the property of an athletic conference whose members were universities.

The first case, *Illini Media Company v. Department of Revenue,* 664 N.E.2d 706 (Ill. App. Ct. 1996), involved three parcels of land owned by the Illini Media

Company, a nonprofit corporation established by the University of Illinois. Pursuant to its corporate purposes, the company operates a campus radio station and publishes the campus newspaper, the university yearbook, and a technical journal. The company's board of directors is composed of university students and faculty members, and its activities are subject to the authority of the university chancellor. Illini Media sought a tax exemption under a state statute exempting property that is used for "college, theological, seminary, university, or other educational purposes . . ." (35 ILCS 205-19.1, formerly Ill. Rev. Stat. ch. 120, par. 500.1). The State Department of Revenue denied the tax exemption, but the Illinois appellate court reversed. The court first affirmed that an activity need not be a "school in a traditional sense," nor need it involve classroom instruction, in order to be exempt from property taxation under the statute. The court then declared that the company's general purpose is "educational development," and that educational development is an educational purpose within the meaning of the statute. It was also important to the court that the company's corporate charter stated that the company was engaged in educational purposes, that the company had close ties to the university, that both faculty and students were involved in company management, and that the corporation employed students from the university. (This case provides a good illustration of how to read a statute broadly or flexibly in order to achieve exempt status.)

In the second case, *In re Atlantic Coast Conference,* 434 S.E.2d 865 (N.C. Ct. App. 1993), the county in which the Atlantic Coast Conference (ACC) maintained its headquarters denied the ACC's request for an exemption from property taxes for the building it used as administrative offices. Reviewing the county's decision, the Court of Appeals of North Carolina examined "the four separate and distinct requirements" of the statute that must be met before an exemption will be granted: (1) the property is owned by an educational institution, (2) the owner is organized and operated as a nonprofit entity, (3) the property must be used for activities incident to the operation of an educational institution, and (4) the property is used by the owner only for educational purposes (N.C. Gen. Stat. § 105-278.4). The court found that, since the ACC was an unincorporated association whose only members were institutions that were themselves exempt from property taxes, the first element was satisfied. The third element was satisfied because "athletic activities are a natural part of the education process," and "in collegiate athletics, the negotiation of network contracts and management of broadcasts [functions of the ACC for which it used its building] are . . . necessarily incidental to the operation of educational institutions. . . ." The fourth element was also satisfied because the ACC's main activities, negotiating TV contracts and managing tournaments, both "qualify as 'educational.'" The court, however, could not determine whether the second element (a nonprofit entity) was met. Because neither the member institutions nor the ACC had disclosed adequate financial information for the court's review, the court remanded the case to the lower court for a ruling on the second element. The Supreme Court of North Carolina affirmed without opinion (441 S.E.2d 550 (N.C. 1994)).

Similar tax exemption problems may also arise when a postsecondary institution enters a lease arrangement with a separate entity. If the institution leases some of its property to another entity, the property may or may not retain its exempt status. In such cases, exemption again depends on the use of the property and the exemption tests applied in the jurisdiction,[13] and particular consideration may be given to the extent to which the institution controls the property in the hands of the separate entity. Parallel tax exemption problems may also be encountered when an institution leases property *from* (rather than *to*) another entity. *Wheaton College v. Department of Revenue*, 508 N.E.2d 1136 (Ill. App. Ct. 1987) (although a case involving the state rather than a local government), is illustrative. The college had entered a thirty-year lease for an apartment building that it used for student housing—concededly a tax-exempt purpose. The question was whether the college had sufficient indicia of ownership to be considered the property's owner for tax purposes. Although recognizing that "ownership of real estate is a broad concept and can apply to one other than the record titleholder" (508 N.E.2d at 1137), the court held that the college was not the actual owner of the property and was not entitled to the tax exemption. The court found that the "leasing arrangement in question was undertaken primarily for the benefit" of the lessor rather than the college, and "the tax and other advantages of the transaction inured" to the lessors' benefit (508 N.E.2d at 1138). Moreover, "although the lease gives [the college] several incidents of ownership, including the right to remove existing structures and the right to sublease the property, it does not give others, such as the right to alienate fully the property" (508 N.E.2d at 1138).

If institutional property (or that of a separate entity) is denied an exemption and subjected to property taxation, the institution (or the separate entity) must then deal with the problem of valuation. After a property tax assessor makes the initial assessment, the institution or an affiliated entity may challenge the assessment through procedures established by the local government. The assessment of property used for educational purposes may be difficult because of the absence of comparable market values. In *Dartmouth Corp. of Alpha Delta v. Town of Hanover*, 332 A.2d 390 (N.H. 1975), an independent fraternity challenged the assessment of its property. To arrive at an evaluation, the town had compared the fraternity property to dormitory facilities. The court upheld the assessor's estimate, reasoning that "in view of the functional similarity between fraternities and dormitories and considering that the college regulates the rents of both types of facilities, it was not unlawful for the board to consider the income and costs of the fraternity buildings if used as dormitories in ascertaining their assessed value."

If an institution cannot obtain or maintain a property tax exemption, it is limited to challenging the periodic valuation assessments of its property, as in the *Dartmouth Corp.* case above. The far better approach, from the institution's

---

[13]Cases dealing with leased property are collected in Maurice T. Brunner, Annot., "Property Tax: Exemption of Property Leased by and Used for Purposes of Otherwise Tax-Exempt Body," 55 A.L.R.3d 430.

perspective, is to establish and maintain the conditions necessary for a tax exemption. The case of *City of Washington v. Board of Assessment Appeals of Washington County*, 704 A.2d 120 (Pa. 1997), provides useful suggestions for institutions in this regard, and also indicates for challengers the avenues they may have to travel to challenge an institution's exemption. The city of Washington had challenged the tax-exempt status of Washington and Jefferson College (W&J), a private, nonsectarian, liberal arts college in Pennsylvania. The Supreme Court of Pennsylvania applied Pennsylvania's five-prong test for determining whether an entity could qualify for tax exemption as a "purely public charity" under the state constitution and the applicable statute (72 Pa. Stat. § 5020-204(a)(3)):

> The test requires that the entity (1) advance a charitable purpose; (2) donate or render gratuitously a substantial portion of its services; (3) benefit a substantial and indefinite class of persons who are legitimate subjects of charity; (4) relieve the government of some of its burden; and (5) operate entirely free from private profit motive [704 A.2d at 122].

Working through the prongs in order, the court reasoned as follows: (1) "W&J provides education for youths . . . and thereby serves a charitable purpose." (2) The college makes extensive use of scholarships, grants, and contributions from its endowment to provide W&J students with approximately one-half of their education without charge, and did so even when W&J suffered operating losses from 1991 through 1994. In light of Pennsylvania precedent that charities need not provide wholly gratuitous services, W&J's "level of assistance is well above what [the court has] deemed adequate to qualify as a purely public charity." (3) Through its admission and financial aid policies, "W&J makes education attainable for innumerable youths who would not otherwise be able to afford it. . . . The vast majority of the aid that W&J provides is directed to the financially needy . . . , [and] the admissions policies at W&J do not discriminate against applicants who will need such grants." (4) "W&J, like other independent colleges and universities, relieves the load placed on the state-owned system of college and universities." And (5) W&J's continued use of scholarships, grants, and endowment funds in lieu of significant tuition increases to compensate for operating losses was favorable evidence of the college's lack of profit motive. Further, W&J's trustees serve without compensation, and any operating surplus W&J generated would be reinvested in the college. Thus, the court concluded, W&J satisfied all five elements of the test, and could properly maintain a tax exemption as a purely public charity.

Although the institution was victorious, the case nevertheless raises important issues for other colleges and universities to consider in light of increasing fiscal pressures on cash-strapped local governments. Local government leaders are often hesitant to raise their constituents' taxes and may, instead, seek to increase tax revenues by challenging the tax exemptions of an independent college or university located in the community. (This problem is described, and options for managing it are suggested, in Brian C. Mitchell, "Private Colleges Should Stay on Guard Against Challenges to Their Tax-Exempt Status," *Chron.*

Higher Educ., December 12, 1997, B6.) The *City of Washington* court's analysis of Washington and Jefferson's charitable characteristics, and the guidance it provides, should be a help to other institutions needing to defend themselves, either in the political process or in court, against tax-exempt challenges.

11.3.3. Sales, admission, and amusement taxes.

A local government may have authority to impose a sales tax on the sales or purchases of educational institutions. The institution may claim a specific exemption based on a particular provision of the sales tax ordinance or a general exemption provided by a state statute or the state constitution. The language of the provision may limit the exemption to sales by an educational institution, or to purchases by an educational institution, or may cover both. The institution's eligibility for exemption from these taxes, as from property taxes, depends on the language of the provision creating the exemption, as interpreted by the courts, and on particular factual circumstances concerning the institution and the sales transactions.[14]

New York University v. Taylor, 296 N.Y.S. 848 (N.Y. App. Div. 1937), *affirmed without opinion,* 12 N.E.2d 606 (N.Y. 1938), arose after the comptroller of the City of New York tried to impose a sales tax on both the sales and the purchases of a nonprofit educational institution. The law in effect at that time provided that "receipts from sales or services . . . by or to semipublic institutions . . . shall not be subject to tax hereunder." Semipublic institutions were defined as "those charitable and religious institutions which are supported wholly or in part by public subscriptions or endowment and are not organized or operated for profit." The court made a finding of fact that the university was a "semipublic institution" within the meaning of the statute and therefore was not subject to taxation on its sales or purchases.

Sales by an educational institution may be exempt even if some of the institution's activities generate a profit. The exemption will depend on the use of the profits and the language of the exemption. In *YMCA of Philadelphia v. City of Philadelphia,* 11 A.2d 529 (Pa. Super. Ct. 1940), the court held that the sale was not subject to taxation under an ordinance that exempted sales by or to semipublic institutions:

> [C]ertainly, the ordinance contemplated a departure by such institutions from the activities of a public charity, which, in its narrowest sense, sells nothing and is supported wholly by public subscriptions and contributions or endowment; and may be said to recognize that many institutions organized for charitable purposes and supported in part by public subscriptions or endowment, do engage in certain incidental activities, of a commercial nature, the proceeds of which, and any profits derived therefrom, are devoted to the general charitable work of the institution and applied to no alien or selfish purpose [11 A.2d at 531].

---

[14]The relevant cases on sales taxes, as well as "use" taxes sometimes levied in place of sales taxes, are collected in Roland F. Chase, Annot., "Exemption of Charitable or Educational Organization from Sales or Use Tax," 53 A.L.R.3d 748.

City of Boulder v. Regents of the University of Colorado, 501 P.2d 123 (Colo. 1972), concerned the city's attempt to impose an admission tax on various events, including intercollegiate football games, held on the University of Colorado's campus. The trial court held that the city could not impose tax collection responsibilities on the university because its board of regents, as an entity established by the state constitution, had exclusive control of the university's funding and fiscal operations. The Supreme Court of Colorado upheld this part of the trial court's ruling, quoting the trial court's opinion with approval:

"In the instant case the city is attempting to impose duties on the Board of Regents which would necessarily interfere with the Regents' control of the University. The Constitution establishes a statewide Board of Regents and vests control in the Board of Regents. The Board of Regents has Exclusive control and direction of all funds of, and appropriations to, the University. . . . Thus, the City of Boulder cannot force the Regents to apply any funds toward the collection of the tax in question. Even if the City claims that sufficient funds would be generated by the tax to compensate the Regents for collection expense and, arguably, such funds could be paid to the Regents by the City, the Regents are still vested with the 'general supervision' of the University. The University would necessarily be required to expend both money and manpower for the collection, identification, and payment of such funds to the City. This interferes with the financial conduct of the University and the allocation of its manpower for its statewide educational duties. . . .

"Thus, since the Constitution has established a state-wide University at Boulder and vested general supervisory control in a state-wide Board of Regents and management in control of the state, a city, even though a home rule city, has no power to interfere with the management or supervision of the activities of the University of Colorado. If the City of Boulder was allowed to impose duties on the University, such duties would necessarily interfere with the functions of the state institution. There is no authority to permit the City of Boulder to force a state institution to collect such a local tax. Consequently, the City of Boulder cannot require the Board of Regents of the University of Colorado to become involuntary collectors of the City of Boulder's Admission Tax" [501 P.2d at 125, quoting the trial court].

The court also held, over two dissents, that the admission tax was itself invalid as applied to various university functions:

When academic departments of the University, or others acting under the auspices of the University, sponsor lectures, dissertations, art exhibitions, concerts, and dramatic performances, whether or not an admission fee is charged, these functions become a part of the educational process. This educational process is not merely for the enrolled students of the University, but it is a part of the educational process for those members of the public attending the events. In our view the home rule authority of a city does not permit it to tax a person's acquisition of education furnished by the State. We hold that the tax is invalid when applied to University lectures, dissertations, art exhibitions, concerts, and dramatic performances [501 P.2d at 126].

With respect to football games, however, the Colorado court affirmed the tax's validity because the university had not made "a showing that football is so related to the educational process that its devotees may not be taxed by a home rule city." This latter ruling is "probably academic," the court acknowledged, since under sovereign immunity the university could not be required to collect the tax, even if it were valid.[15] Subsequently, another court reached much the same result, but on different reasoning, in *City of Morgantown v. West Virginia Board of Regents,* 354 S.E.2d 616 (W. Va. 1987). At issue was an amusement tax that the city attempted to apply to ticket sales for university entertainment and athletic events. Under the authorizing statute, only amusements conducted "for private gain" could be taxed. Determining that the university's ticket receipts were "public moneys" and that the university did not conduct these events for private profit, the court held the tax to be contrary to the statute and invalid.

Sec. 11.4. Student Voting in the Community

11.4.1. Registering to vote.
Every citizen over the age of eighteen does not necessarily have the right to vote. All potential voters must register with the board of elections of their legal residence in order to exercise their right. Determining the legal residence of students attending residential institutions has created major controversies. Some small communities near colleges and universities, fearful of the impact of the student vote, have tried to limit student registration, while students eager to participate in local affairs and to avoid the inconveniences of absentee voting have pushed for local registration.

The trend of the cases has been to overturn statutes and election board practices that impede student registration, and sometimes to overturn state statutes that authorize such practices.[16] In *Jolicoeur v. Mihaly,* 488 P.2d 1 (Cal. 1971), the court considered a statute that created an almost conclusive presumption that an unmarried minor's residence was his or her parents' home. The court held that this statute violated the equal protection clause and the Twenty-Sixth Amendment:

> Sophisticated legal arguments regarding a minor's presumed residence cannot blind us to the real burden placed on the right to vote and associated rights of political expression by requiring minor voters residing apart from their parents to vote in their parents' district. . . .
>
> An unmarried minor must be subject to the same requirements in proving the location of his domicile as is any other voter. Fears of the way minors may vote or of their impermanency in the community may not be used to justify special presumptions—conclusive or otherwise—that they are not bona fide residents of

---

[15]Relevant cases on admission taxes are collected in Kenneth J. Rampino, Annot., "Validity of Municipal Admission Tax for College Football Games or Other College Sponsored Events," 60 A.L.R.3d 1027.

[16]Cases are collected at Donald T. Kramer, Annot., "Validity, Under Federal Constitution, of State Residency Requirements for Voting in Elections," 31 L. Ed. 2d 861.

the community in which they live. . . . It is clear that respondents have abridged petitioners' right to vote in precisely one of the ways that Congress sought to avoid—by singling minor voters out for special treatment and effectively making many of them vote by absentee ballot. . . .

Respondents' policy would clearly frustrate youthful willingness to accomplish change at the local level through the political system. Whether a youth lives in Quincy, Berkeley, or Orange County, he will not be brought into the bosom of the political system by being told that he may not have a voice in the community in which he lives, but must instead vote wherever his parents live or may move to. Surely as well, such a system would give any group of voters less incentive "in devising responsible programs" in the town in which they live [488 P.2d at 4, 7].

Another court invalidated a Michigan statute that created a rebuttable presumption that students are not voting residents of the district where their institution is located. The statute was implemented through elaborate procedures applicable only to students. The court held that the statute infringed the right to vote in violation of the equal protection clause (*Wilkins v. Bentley,* 189 N.W.2d 423 (Mich. 1971)). And in *United States v. State of Texas,* 445 F. Supp. 1245 (S.D. Tex. 1978), a three-judge federal court enjoined the voting registrar of Waller County from applying a burdensome presumption of nonresident to unmarried dormitory students at Prairie View A&M University. The U.S. Supreme Court summarily affirmed the lower court's decision without issuing any written opinion (*Symm v. United States,* 439 U.S. 1105 (1979)).

In contrast, courts have upheld statutory provisions making attendance at a local college or university irrelevant as a factor in determining a student's residence. In *Whittingham v. Board of Elections,* 320 F. Supp. 889 (N.D.N.Y. 1970), a special three-judge court upheld a "gain or loss provision" of the New York constitution. This provision, found in many state constitutions and statutes, requires a student to prove residency by indicia other than student status. The *Whittingham* case was followed by *Gorenberg v. Onondaga County Board of Elections,* 328 N.Y.S.2d 198 (N.Y. App. Div. 1972), *modified,* 286 N.E.2d 247 (N.Y. 1972), upholding the New York State voting statute specifying criteria for determining residence, including dependency, employment, marital status, age, and location of property.

A series of New York cases illustrates and refines the principles developed in these earlier cases. In *Auerbach v. Rettaliata,* 765 F.2d 350 (2d Cir. 1985), students from two State University of New York (SUNY) campuses challenged the constitutionality of the New York voting residency statute, a virtually identical successor to the statute upheld in *Gorenberg.* The students claimed that the statute—by authorizing county voting registrars to consider factors such as students' financial independence and the residence of their parents—imposed unduly heavy burdens on their eligibility to vote. The court upheld the *facial* validity of the statute because it did not establish any "presumption against student residency." As interpreted by the court, the statute merely specified criteria that could demonstrate "physical presence and intention to remain for the time at least." Although these criteria would require "classes of likely transients" to demonstrate more than physical presence in the county, such treatment was permissible under the equal protection clause.

The *Auerbach* court did caution, however, that even though the New York statute was constitutional on its face, courts would nevertheless intervene in residency determinations if election officials administered the law in a manner that discriminated against students. In *Williams v. Salerno,* 792 F.2d 323 (2d Cir. 1986), the same U.S. Court of Appeals had occasion to put that caution into practice. Students from another SUNY campus challenged an election board's ruling that a dormitory could not be considered a voting residence under the New York voter residency statute, thus prohibiting college dormitory residents from registering. Building on *Auerbach,* the court agreed that the state election law would allow election boards to make more searching inquiries about the residence of students and other presumably transient groups, as long as the boards did not apply more rigorous substantive requirements regarding residency to these groups than they did to other voters. But the court nevertheless invalidated the election board's action under the equal protection clause because it did impose a more rigorous requirement on dormitory students that barred them from voting regardless of the presence of other circumstances that could demonstrate an intent to remain.

Similarly, in *Levy v. Scranton,* 780 F. Supp. 897 (N.D.N.Y. 1991), another court in a suit brought by students at Skidmore College used *Auerbach* and *Williams v. Salerno* to invalidate a county board of elections policy under which the board disqualified students from voting if they had an on-campus residence. The court enjoined the board from denying the right to vote solely on this basis. At the same time, however, the court reconsidered and upheld the validity of the New York statute itself.

Some general rules for constitutionally sound determinations of student residency emerge from these cases. The mere fact that the student lives in campus housing is not sufficient grounds to deny residency. On the other hand, mere presence as a student is not itself sufficient to establish voting residency. Rather, election boards can require not only physical presence but also manifestation of an intent to establish residency in the community. Present intent to establish residency is probably sufficient. Students who intend to leave the community after graduation do not have such intent. Students who are uncertain about their postgraduate plans, but consider the community to be their home for the time being, probably do have such intent. A statute that required proof of intent to remain indefinitely in the community after graduation was held a denial of equal protection in *Whatley v. Clark,* 482 F.2d 1230 (5th Cir. 1973).

Uncertainties concerning future plans and the difficulties of proving intent complicate the application of these general rules. To address these complexities, election boards may use a range of criteria for determining whether a student intends to establish residence. Such criteria may include vacation activity, the location of property owned by the student, the choice of banks and other services, membership in community groups, location of employment, and the declaration of residence for other purposes, such as tax payment and automobile registration. Election officials must be careful to apply such criteria evenhandedly to all voter registrants and, if more searching inquiries are made of some registrants, to apply the same level of inquiry to all potential transient groups.

In 1998, Congress amended the Higher Education Act, adding subsection 23 to 20 U.S.C. § 1094(a) (Pub. L. No. 105-244, 112 Stat. 1751, October 7, 1998). This subsection provides that all institutions, as a condition of receiving federal student aid funds, must "make a good faith effort to distribute a mail voter registration form, requested and received from the State, to each student enrolled in a degree or certificate program and physically in attendance at the institution, and to make such forms widely available to students at the institution." This provision applies to elections for federal office and for the governor of the state. During the fall of 2004, just prior to the presidential election, a survey found that most colleges and universities who responded to the survey had not fully complied with the law's requirements (Elizabeth F. Farrell & Eric Hoover, "Many Colleges Fall Short on Registering Student Voters," *Chron. Higher Educ.,* September 17, 2004, A1).

11.4.2. Scheduling elections.

11.4.2. Scheduling elections. A case that deals with the timing of an election in a district with a substantial student population is *Walgren v. Board of Selectmen of the Town of Amherst,* 519 F.2d 1364 (1st Cir. 1975). Walgren, a student at the University of Massachusetts, had asked the selectmen of Amherst, Massachusetts, to change the date of the town's primary election, which had been scheduled for January 19, a date that fell during the university's winter recess. After several votes and attempted changes of the date, the selectmen decided to keep the primary election on its original date. The election was held, and Walgren sued on behalf of his fellow students to set aside the election, alleging violations of the Twenty-Sixth Amendment (which lowered the voting age to eighteen) and the equal protection clause.

The lower court refused to set aside the election. Although disagreeing with the lower court's finding that the burden on students' and faculty members' right to vote was insignificant, the appellate court relied on the good-faith efforts of the selectmen to schedule an appropriate date:

> In short, we would be disturbed if, given time to explore alternatives and given alternatives which would satisfy all reasonable town objectives, a town continued to insist on elections during vacations or recess, secure in the conviction that returning to town and absentee voting would be considered insignificant burdens.
>
> The critical element which in our view serves to sustain the 1973 election is the foreshortened time frame within which the selectmen were forced to face up to and resolve a problem which was then novel. . . .
>
> We would add that, under the circumstances of this case, even if we had found the burden impermissible, we would have looked upon the novelty and complexity of the issue, the shortness of time, and the good-faith efforts of the defendants as sufficient justification for refusing to order a new election at this late date [519 F.2d at 1368].

The special facts of the case and the narrowness of the court's holding limit *Walgren's* authority as precedent. But *Walgren* does suggest that, under some circumstances, an election deliberately scheduled so as to disenfranchise an identifiable segment of the student electorate can be successfully challenged.

11.4.3. Canvassing and registration on campus. The regulation of voter canvassing and registration on campus is the voting issue most likely to require the direct involvement of college and university administrators. Any regulation must accommodate the First Amendment rights of the canvassers; the First Amendment rights of the students, faculty, and staff who may be potential listeners; the privacy interests of those who may not wish to be canvassed; the requirements of local election law; and the institution's interests in order and safety. Not all of these considerations have been explored in litigation.[17]

Although not in the higher education context, the U.S. Supreme Court addressed the constitutionality of restrictions on canvassing in *Watchtower Bible & Tract Society of New York, Inc. v. Village of Stratton*, 536 U.S. 150 (2002), ruling that a town ordinance that required a permit for both commercial and noncommercial canvassing violated the First Amendment. The Court noted that not only was religious exercise burdened by the requirement of a permit, but political activity was impermissibly burdened as well. Holding that the permit requirement was overbroad in its application to noncommercial speech, the Court said: "It is offensive—not only to the values protected by the First Amendment, but to the very notion of a free society—that in the context of everyday public discourse a citizen must first inform the government of her desire to speak to her neighbors and then obtain a permit to do so" (536 U.S. at 165–66). The Court noted that a permit requirement properly tailored to the town's stated interests—the prevention of fraud and protecting the privacy of its residents— might avoid First Amendment pitfalls if it were limited to commercial activity, although there were "less intrusive and more effective measures" available to further the town's goals, such as "No Solicitation" signs.

James v. Nelson, 349 F. Supp. 1061 (N.D. Ill. 1972), illustrates a First Amendment challenge to a campus canvassing regulation. Northern Illinois University had for some time prohibited all canvassing in student living areas. After receiving requests to modify this prohibition, the university proposed a new regulation, which would have permitted canvassing under specified conditions. Before the new regulation could go into effect, however, it had to be adopted in a referendum by two-thirds of the students in each dormitory, after which individual floors could implement it by a two-thirds vote. The court held that this referendum requirement unconstitutionally infringed the freedom of association and freedom of speech rights of the students who wished to canvas or be canvassed. The basis for the *James* decision is difficult to discern. The court emphasized that the proposed canvassing regulation was not "in any way unreasonable or beyond the powers of the university administration to impose in the interests of good order and the safety and comfort of the student body." If the proposed regulation could thus be constitutionally implemented by the university itself, it is

---

[17]Cases are collected in John H. Derrick, Annot., "Validity of College or University Regulation of Political or Voter Registration Activity in Student Housing Facilities," 39 A.L.R.4th 1137.

not clear why a referendum to approve the university's proposed regulation would infringe students' constitutional rights. (But see also the *Southworth* litigation in Section 10.1.3 for more on student referenda.) The court's implicit ruling in *James* may therefore be that the university's blanket prohibition on canvassing was an infringement of First Amendment rights, and a requirement that this prohibition could be removed only by a two-thirds vote of the students in each dormitory and each floor was also an infringement on the rights of those students who would desire a liberalized canvassing policy.

National Movement for the Student Vote v. Regents of the University of California, 123 Cal. Rptr. 141 (Cal. Ct. App. 1975), was decided on statutory grounds. A local statute permitted registrars to register voters at their residence. University policy, uniformly enforced, did not allow canvassing in student living areas. Registrars were permitted to canvas in public areas of the campus and in the lobbies of the dormitories. The court held that the privacy interest of the students limited the registrars' right to canvas to reasonable times and places and that the limitations imposed by the university were reasonable and in compliance with the law. In determining reasonableness, the court emphasized the following facts:

> There was evidence and findings to the effect that dining and other facilities of the dormitories are on the main floor; the private rooms of the students are on the upper floors; the rooms do not contain kitchen, washing, or toilet facilities; each student must walk from his or her room to restroom facilities in the halls of the upper floors in order to bathe or use the toilet facilities; defendants, in order to "recognize and enhance the privacy" of the students and to minimize assaults upon them and thefts of their property, have maintained a policy and regulations prohibiting solicitation, distribution of materials, and recruitment of students in the upper-floor rooms; students in the upper rooms complained to university officials about persons coming to their rooms and canvassing them and seeking their registrations; defendants permitted signs regarding the election to be posted throughout the dormitories and permitted deputy registrars to maintain tables and stands in the main lobby of each dormitory for registration of students; students in each dormitory had to pass through the main lobby thereof in order to go to and from their rooms; a sign encouraging registration to vote was at each table, and students registered to vote at the tables [123 Cal. Rptr. at 146].

Though the *National Movement v. Regents* decision is based on a statute, the court's language suggests that it would use similar principles and factors in considering the constitutionality of a public institution's canvassing regulations under the First Amendment. In a later case, *Harrell v. Southern Illinois University*, 457 N.E.2d 971 (Ill. App. Ct. 1983), the court did use similar reasoning in upholding, against a First Amendment challenge, a university policy that prohibited political candidates from canvassing dormitory rooms except during designated hours in the weeks preceding elections. The court also indicated that the First Amendment (as well as that state's election law) would permit similar restrictions on canvassing by voter registrars. Thus, although public institutions may not completely prohibit voter canvassing on campus, they may impose reasonable restrictions on the "time, place, and manner" of canvassing in dormitories and other such "private" locations on campus. (See also Section 11.6.4.3.)

11.4.4. Reapportionment. A series of U.S. Supreme Court decisions in the early 1960s established that "the fundamental principle of representative government in this country is one of equal representation for equal numbers of people, without regard to race, sex, economic status, or place of residence within a state" (*Reynolds v. Sims,* 377 U.S. 533, 560–61 (1964)). This "one person, one vote" standard was extended to local government elections in *Avery v. Midland County,* 390 U.S. 474 (1968), and *Hadley v. Junior College District,* 397 U.S. 50 (1970):

> Whenever a state or local government decides to select persons by popular election to perform governmental functions, the equal protection clause of the Fourteenth Amendment requires that each qualified voter must be given an equal opportunity to participate in that election, and when members of an elective body are chosen from separate districts, each district must be established on a basis that will insure, as far as is practicable, that equal numbers of voters can vote for proportionately equal numbers of officials [*Hadley,* 397 U.S. at 56].

Consistent with this basic constitutional requirement, local and state governments must periodically "reapportion" the populations of election districts and redraw their boundaries accordingly. If the election districts containing the largest percentages of student voters were to include more voters per elected official than other districts, thus diluting the voting strength of district voters (malapportionment), students or other voters could claim a violation of "one person, one vote" principles. Even if the districts with concentrations of student voters have populations substantially equal to those of other districts, students could still raise an equal protection challenge if the district lines were drawn in a way that minimized their voting strength (gerrymandering). Case law indicates, however, that both types of claims would be difficult to sustain. Beginning with *Abate v. Mundt,* 403 U.S. 182 (1971) (local elections), and *Mahan v. Howell,* 410 U.S. 315 (1973) (state elections), the U.S. Supreme Court has accepted various justifications for departing from strict population equality among districts, thus making it harder for plaintiffs to prevail on malapportionment claims. And in *Gaffney v. Cummings,* 412 U.S. 735 (1973), and later cases, the Court has flagged its reluctance to scrutinize gerrymandering that is undertaken to balance or maintain the voting strengths of political groups within the jurisdiction. (But compare *Shaw v. Reno,* 509 U.S. 630 (1993); *Easley v. Cromartie,* 532 U.S. 234 (2001) (racial gerrymandering).)

In re House Bill 2620, 595 P.2d 334 (Kan. 1979), illustrates the difficulty of prevailing on such malapportionment claims.[18] The student senate of the

---

[18]Although few reported cases deal with student challenges to reapportionment, dilution of minority voting power as a result of inclusion or exclusion of student populations in redistricting has been challenged by other plaintiffs. See, for example, *Fauley v. Forrest County, Mississippi,* 814 F. Supp. 1327 (S.D. Miss. 1993).

University of Kansas (and others) filed suit objecting to the reapportionment of two state legislative districts covering the city of Lawrence. Prior to reapportionment, the three voting precincts with the most concentrated student vote ("L," "K," and "O") were located in one legislative district. The reapportionment plan placed two of these precincts in one district and the third in a separate district. The students contended that this redistricting was done in order to split the student vote, thus diluting student voting power. The Kansas Supreme Court disagreed, holding that the redistricting did not invidiously discriminate against students:

> There are presently 22,228 students enrolled in the University of Kansas. It is stated [that] a large portion of the students hold similar political beliefs, and those living in precincts identified as "L," "K," and "O" form a cohesive homogeneous unit that cannot be separated without discrimination. . . . In 1978 there were 5,138 "census persons" residing in these three precincts, and 3,156 voters were registered on October 27, 1978. Even assuming that all registered voters in these three precincts were students, which is highly questionable, the three precincts involved would represent no more than 14.2 percent of the students in the university.
>
> Other factors militate against a solid cohesive student body. The students come from different family and political backgrounds and from different localities. Many students vote in their home districts. It is extremely doubtful that all would be of one party. Considering modern trends in higher education, each student is trained for independent thinking. Unanimity among a student body seems unlikely. Keeping all these factors in mind, we cannot say that removing precincts K and O from District 44 and placing them in the newly constituted District 46 was done for the purpose of canceling the voting strength of the 22,228 students attending the University of Kansas. We are not convinced that invidious discrimination resulted [595 P.2d at 343–44].

Students had somewhat more success challenging the reapportionment decisions of the city of Bowling Green, Ohio. In *Regensburger v. City of Bowling Green, Ohio,* 278 F.3d 588 (6th Cir. 2002), a group of individuals, including students at Bowling Green State University, sued the city, alleging that its reapportionment plan violated their rights under the equal protection clause. The city council consisted of three at-large members and one member elected from each of the city's four wards. The plaintiffs argued that Ward 1, the ward that contained most of the college students, contained more than twice the number of residents as each of the other three wards, thus diluting their votes. A magistrate judge found that the city's plan deviated from absolute population equality by more than 66 percent, which exceeded constitutional limits, and ordered the city to redesign its reapportionment plan within constitutional guidelines. The appellate court affirmed the findings of the magistrate judge.

Sec. 11.5. Relations with Local Police

Since the academic community is part of the surrounding community, it will generally be within the geographical jurisdiction of one or more local (town, village, city, county) police forces. The circumstances under which local police may and will come onto the campus, and their authority once on campus, are thus of concern to every administrator. The role of local police on campus depends on a mixture of considerations: the state and local law of the jurisdiction, federal constitutional limitations on police powers, the adequacy of the institution's own security services, and the terms of any explicit or implicit understanding between local police and campus authorities.

If the institution has its own uniformed security officers, administrators must decide what working relationships these officers will have with local police. This decision will depend partly on the extent of the security officers' authority, especially regarding arrests, searches, and seizures—authority that should also be carefully delineated (see generally Section 8.6.1). Similarly, administrators must understand the relationship between arrest and prosecution in local courts, on the one hand, and campus disciplinary proceedings on the other (see Section 9.1). Although administrators cannot make crime an internal affair by hiding evidence of crime from local police, they may be able to assist local law enforcement officials in determining prosecution priorities. Campus and local officials may also be able to cooperate in determining whether a campus proceeding should be stayed pending the outcome of a court proceeding, or vice versa.

The powers of local police are circumscribed by various federal constitutional provisions, particularly the Fourth Amendment strictures on arrests, searches, and seizures. These provisions limit local police authority on both public and private campuses. Under the Fourth Amendment, local police usually must obtain a warrant before arresting or searching a member of the academic community or searching or seizing any private property on the campus (see Section 8.4.2). On a private institution's campus, nearly all the property may be private, and local police may need a warrant or the consent of whoever effectively controls the property before entering most areas of the campus. On a public institution's campus, it is more difficult to determine which property would be considered public and which private, and thus more difficult to determine when local police must have a warrant or consent prior to entry. In general, for both public and private institutions, police will need a warrant or consent before entering any area in which members of the academic community have a "reasonable expectation of privacy" (see generally *Katz v. United States,* 389 U.S. 347 (1967)). The constitutional rules and concepts are especially complex in this area, however; and administrators should consult counsel whenever questions arise concerning the authority of local police on campus.

In *People v. Dickson,* 154 Cal. Rptr. 116 (Cal. Ct. App. 1979), the court considered the validity of a warrantless search of a chemistry laboratory conducted by local police and campus security officers at the Bakersfield campus of California State University. The search uncovered samples of an illegal drug and materials used in its manufacture—evidence that led to the arrest and conviction of the defendant, a chemistry professor who used the laboratory. The court upheld the search and the conviction because, under the facts of the case (particularly facts indicating ready access to the laboratory by many persons, including campus police), the professor had no "objectively reasonable expectation of privacy" in his laboratory.

Under a similar rationale, the court in *Commonwealth v. Tau Kappa Epsilon,* 560 A.2d 786 (Pa. Super. Ct. 1989), rejected the argument that undercover police were required to obtain a search warrant before they entered a fraternity party. Two undercover officers, recent graduates of Pennsylvania State University, had entered parties at eleven fraternities and observed the serving of beer to minors. When fraternities were convicted of serving beer to minors, they appealed the convictions, arguing that the police officers' warrantless entry violated the Fourth Amendment. The court disagreed:

> Security was so lax as to be virtually nonexistent; a person could enter and be furnished beverages almost at will. Under these circumstances, the fraternities could be found to have consented to the entry of [the police] and to have surrendered any reasonable expectation of privacy with respect to the events occurring in their houses [560 A.2d at 791].[19]

That these particular searches were upheld even though the officers did not procure a warrant, however, does not mean that local police forces may routinely dispense with the practice of obtaining warrants. In circumstances where the person has a reasonable expectation of privacy that would be invaded by the search, procuring a warrant or the consent of the person to be searched will generally be required.

In 1980, Congress enacted legislation that limits police search and seizure activities on college campuses. The legislation, the Privacy Protection Act of 1980 (42 U.S.C. § 2000aa *et seq.*), was passed in part to counter the U.S. Supreme Court's decision in *Zurcher v. Stanford Daily,* 436 U.S. 547 (1978). In *Zurcher,* the Palo Alto, California, Police Department had obtained a warrant to search the files of the *Stanford Daily,* a student newspaper, for photographs of participants in a demonstration during which several police officers had been assaulted. The lower court found probable cause to believe that the *Stanford Daily*'s files did contain such photographs, but no probable cause to believe that the newspaper itself was engaged in any wrongdoing. The U.S. Supreme Court held that the *Stanford Daily,* even though an innocent third party and even though engaged in publication activities, had no First or Fourth Amendment rights to assert against the search warrant.

The Privacy Protection Act's coverage is not confined to newspapers, the subject of the *Zurcher* case. As its legislative history makes clear, the Act also protects scholars and other persons engaged in "public communication"—that is, the "flow of information to the public" (see S. Rep. No. 874, 96th Cong., 2d Sess., in 4 *U.S. Code Cong. & Admin. News* 3950, 3956 (1980)).

Section 101(a) of the Act pertains to the "work product materials" of individuals intending "to disseminate to the public a newspaper, book, broadcast,

---

[19]The court's decision was subsequently reversed by the Pennsylvania Supreme Court, but on other grounds not involving the constitutionality of the search (609 A.2d 791 (Pa. 1992)).

or other similar form of public communication." The section prohibits the searching for or seizure of the work product of such individuals by any "government officer or employee [acting] in connection with the investigation or prosecution of a criminal offense." There are several exceptions, however, to the general prohibition in Section 101(a). Search and seizure of work product material is permitted (1) where "there is probable cause to believe that the person possessing such materials has committed or is committing the criminal offense to which the materials relate" and this offense does not consist of "the receipt, possession, communication, or withholding of such materials"; (2) where there is probable cause to believe that the possessor has committed or is committing an offense consisting "of the receipt, possession, or communication of information relating to the national defense, classified information, or restricted data" prohibited under specified provisions of national security laws; and (3) where "there is reason to believe that the immediate seizure of such materials is necessary to prevent the death of, or serious bodily injury to, a human being."

Section 101(b) of the Act covers "documentary materials, other than work product materials." This section prohibits search and seizure of such materials in the same way that Section 101(a) prohibits search and seizure of work product. The same exceptions to the general prohibition also apply. There are two additional exceptions unique to Section 101(b), under which search and seizure of documentary materials is permitted if:

(3) there is reason to believe that the giving of notice pursuant to a subpoena duces tecum would result in the destruction, alteration, or concealment of such materials; or

(4) such materials have not been produced in response to a court order directing compliance with a subpoena duces tecum, and—

  (A) all appellate remedies have been exhausted; or

  (B) there is reason to believe that the delay in an investigation or trial occasioned by further proceedings relating to the subpoena would threaten the interests of justice.

Section 106 of the Act authorizes a civil suit for damages for any person subjected to a search or seizure that is illegal under Section 101(a) or 101(b).

The Act's language and legislative history clearly indicate that the Act applies to local and state, as well as federal, government officers and employees. It thus limits the authority of city, town, and county police officers both on campus and in off-campus investigations of campus scholars or journalists. The Act limits police officers and other government officials, however, only when they are investigating criminal, as opposed to civil, offenses. Scholars and journalists thus are not protected, for example, from the seizure of property to satisfy outstanding tax debts or from the regulatory inspections or compliance reviews conducted by government agencies administering civil laws. Moreover, the Act's legislative history makes clear that traditional subpoena powers and limitations are untouched by the Act (see S. Rep. No. 874, 96th Cong., 2d Sess., in 4 *U.S. Code Cong. & Admin. News* 3950, 3956–60

(1980)). (Subpoenas of scholarly information are discussed in Section 7.7.3 of this book.)

Different problems arise when local police enter a campus not to make an arrest or conduct a search but to engage in surveillance of members of the campus community. In *White v. Davis*, 533 P.2d 222 (Cal. 1975), a history professor at UCLA sued the Los Angeles police chief to enjoin the use of undercover police agents for generalized surveillance in the university. Unidentified police agents had registered at the university and compiled dossiers on students and professors based on information obtained during classes and public meetings. The California Supreme Court held that the surveillance was a *prima facie* violation of students' and faculty members' First Amendment freedoms of speech, assembly, and association, as well as a violation of the "right-to-privacy" provision of the California constitution. Such police actions could be justifiable only if they were necessary to accomplish a compelling state interest. The court returned the case to the trial court to determine whether the police could prove such a justification.

The California Supreme Court's opinion differentiates the First Amendment surveillance problem from the more traditional Fourth Amendment search and seizure problem:

> The most familiar limitations on police investigatory and surveillance activities, of course, find embodiment in the Fourth Amendment of the federal Constitution and article I, section 13 (formerly art. I, § 19) of the California constitution. On numerous occasions in the past, these provisions have been applied to preclude specific ongoing police investigatory practices. Thus, for example, the court in *Wirin v. Parker*, 48 Cal. 2d 890, 313 P.2d 844, prohibited the police practice of conducting warrantless surveillance of private residences by means of concealed microphones. . . .
>
> Unlike these past cases involving the limits on police surveillance prescribed by the constitutional "search-and-seizure" provisions, the instant case presents the more unusual question of the limits placed upon police investigatory activities by the guarantees of freedom of speech (U.S. Const. 1st and 14th Amends.; Cal. Const., art. I, § 2). As discussed below, this issue is not entirely novel; to our knowledge, however, the present case represents the first instance in which a court has confronted the issue in relation to ongoing police surveillance of a university community.
>
> Our analysis of the limits imposed by the First Amendment upon police surveillance activities must begin with the recognition that with respect to First Amendment freedoms "the Constitution's protection is not limited to direct interference with fundamental rights" (*Healy v. James* (1972) 408 U.S. 169, 183 . . .). Thus, although police surveillance of university classrooms and organizations' meetings may not constitute a direct prohibition of speech or association, such surveillance may still run afoul of the constitutional guarantee if the effect of such activity is to chill constitutionally protected activity. . . .
>
> As a practical matter, the presence in a university classroom of undercover officers taking notes to be preserved in police dossiers must inevitably inhibit the exercise of free speech both by professors and students [533 P.2d at 228–29].

The court also emphasized the special danger that police surveillance poses for academic freedom:

> The threat to First Amendment freedoms posed by any covert intelligence gathering network is considerably exacerbated when, as in the instant case, the police surveillance activities focus upon university classrooms and their environs. As the United States Supreme Court has recognized time and again: "The vigilant protection of constitutional freedoms is nowhere more vital than in the community of American schools" (*Shelton v. Tucker,* 364 U.S. 479, 487 . . . (1960)).
>
> The police investigatory conduct at issue unquestionably poses . . . [a] debilitating . . . threat to academic freedom. . . . According to the allegations of the complaint, which for purposes of this appeal must be accepted as true, the Los Angeles Police Department has established a network of undercover agents which keeps regular check on discussions occurring in various university classes. Because the identity of such police officers is unknown, no professor or student can be confident that whatever opinion he may express in class will not find its way into a police file. . . . The crucible of new thought is the university classroom; the campus is the sacred ground of free discussion. Once we expose the teacher or the student to possible future prosecution for the ideas he may express, we forfeit the security that nourishes change and advancement. The censorship of totalitarian regimes that so often condemns developments in art, science, and politics is but a step removed from the inchoate surveillance of free discussion in the university; such intrusion stifles creativity and to a large degree shackles democracy [533 P.2d at 229–31].

The principles of *White v. Davis* would apply equally to local police surveillance at private institutions. As an agency of government, the police are prohibited from violating any person's freedom of expression or right to privacy under the federal and state constitutions, whether on a public campus or a private one.[20]

Sec. 11.6. Community Access to the College's Campus

11.6.1. Public versus private institutions.
Postsecondary institutions have often been the locations for many types of events that attract people from the surrounding community and sometimes from other parts of the state, country, or world. Because of their capacity for large audiences and the sheer numbers of students and faculty and staff members on campus every day, postsecondary institutions provide an excellent forum for lectures, conferences,

---

[20]The right-to-privacy reasoning used in *White v. Davis* would apply only to states that recognize an individual right to privacy similar to that created under the California constitution. The applicability of the case's First Amendment reasoning may be limited to states whose courts would grant professors or students standing to raise claims of illegal surveillance. The *White* plaintiffs obtained standing under a California "taxpayer standing" statute. They apparently would not have succeeded in the federal court, since the U.S. Supreme Court has held, in *Laird v. Tatum,* 408 U.S. 1 (1972), that government surveillance, standing alone, does not cause the type of specific harm necessary to establish federal court standing.

and exhibits, as well as leafleting, posting of notices, circulation of petitions, and other kinds of information exchanges. In addition, cultural, entertainment, and sporting events attract large numbers of outside persons. The potential commercial market presented by concentrations of student consumers may also attract entrepreneurs to the campus, and the potential labor pool that these students represent may attract employment recruiters. Whether public or private, postsecondary institutions have considerable authority to determine how and when their property will be used for such events and activities and to regulate access by outside persons. (Regarding private institutions, see *Commonwealth of Pennsylvania v. Downing*, 511 A.2d 792 (Pa. 1986).) Although a public institution's authority is more limited than that of a private institution, as explained below, the case of *State v. Schmid*, 423 A.2d 615 (N.J. 1980) (discussed in Section 11.6.3 below), indicates that state constitutions (or state statutes) may sometimes limit private as well as public institutions, and thus may diminish the distinction in some states between their respective authority to deny access to outsiders seeking to engage in expressive activities.

Both private and public institutions customarily have ownership or leasehold interests in their campuses and buildings—interests protected by the property law of the state. Subject to this statutory and common law, both types of institutions have authority to regulate how and by whom their property is used.[21] Typically, an institution's authority to regulate use by its students and faculty members is limited by the contractual commitments it has made to these groups (see Sections 6.2 & 8.1.3). Thus, for instance, students may have contractual rights to the reasonable use of dormitory rooms and the public areas of residence halls or of campus libraries and study rooms; and faculty members may have contractual rights to the reasonable use of office space, classrooms, laboratories, and studios. For the outside community, however, such contractual rights usually do not exist.

A public institution's authority to regulate the use of its property is further limited by the federal Constitution, in particular the First Amendment, which may provide rights of access to institutional property not only to students and faculty (see, for example, Sections 9.5.3 & 9.5.4) but also to the outside community (see, for example, *Lamb's Chapel v. Center Moriches Union Free School District*, 508 U.S. 384 (1993)). As the *Lamb's Chapel* case illustrates, the "public forum doctrine" (Section 9.5.2) is especially important in determining the extent to which particular institutional property is open to outsiders for First Amendment expressive activities. Although the public forum doctrine provides First Amendment access rights for outsiders in some circumstances, it also provides substantial leeway for public institutions to limit outsiders' access to the campus for expressive purposes (see, for example, *Bourgault v. Yudof*, 316 F.

---

[21]But institutions are also subject to the tort law of the state when the use of their property leads to injuries to outsiders. For illustrative cases concerning negligence, see *Hayden v. University of Notre Dame*, 716 N.E.2d 603 (Ind. Ct. App. 1999); *Rothstein v. City University of New York*, 562 N.Y.S.2d 340 (N.Y. Ct. Claims 1990), *affirmed*, 599 N.Y.S.2d 39 (N.Y. App. Div. 1993); *Bearman v. University of Notre Dame*, 453 N.E.2d 119 (Ind. Ct. App. 1983); and see generally Section 3.3.2.1 of this book.

Supp. 2d 411 (N.D. Tex. 2004), *affirmed without opinion,* 2005 WL 3332907, December 8, 2005). Various cases in subsections 11.6.3 and 11.6.4 below illustrate these roles of the public forum doctrine. Although the doctrine does not apply generally to private institutions, it would apply to the extent that public streets or sidewalks traverse or border a private institution's campus. In this circumstance, the public forum doctrine would prohibit—or at least would require that the government prohibit—the private institution from regulating outsiders' access to the public streets and sidewalks because they are "traditional public forums" (see Section 9.5.2).

A public institution's authority over access to its property may also be limited or channeled by state statutes and regulations specifically applicable to state educational institutions or their property. Like constitutional limitations, statutory and regulatory limits may provide access rights to outsiders as well as to students and faculty. Subsections 11.6.2 and 11.6.3 below provide examples of such statutes and regulations. As the trespass cases in subsection 11.6.3 illustrate, these state laws may themselves become subject to constitutional challenge under the First Amendment or the due process clause.

Subsections 11.6.2 to 11.6.4 explore various statutes, regulations, and constitutional considerations that affect outsiders' access to the property of postsecondary institutions.

11.6.2. Exclusion of speakers and events.

11.6.2. Exclusion of speakers and events. Administrators may seek to exclude particular speakers or events from campus in order to prevent disruption of campus activities, to avoid hate mongering and other offensive speech (see Robert O'Neil, "Hateful Messages That Force Free Speech to the Limit," *Chron. Higher Educ.,* February 16, 1994, A52), or to protect against other perceived harms. Such actions inevitably precipitate clashes between the administration and the students or faculty members who wish to invite the speaker or sponsor the event, or between the administration and the prospective speakers and participants. These clashes have sometimes resulted in litigation. The rights at issue may be those of the prospective outside speaker (the right to speak) or those of the students and faculty members wishing to hear the speaker (the "right to receive" information). When the institution excluding the speaker or event is a public institution, these rights can be asserted as First Amendment free speech rights. (See generally Sections 7.1.1, 7.1.4, 8.1.4, 9.5, & 9.6 of this book.) Occasionally the rights of outsiders who wish to hear the speaker or attend the event may also become involved. In *Brown v. Board of Regents of the University of Nebraska,* 640 F. Supp. 674 (D. Neb. 1986), for example, a university had cancelled a controversial film that was scheduled to be shown in an on-campus theater open to the public. Outsiders who wished to view the film sued the university and prevailed when the court recognized their First Amendment "right to receive information."

Under the First Amendment, administrators of public institutions may reasonably regulate the time, place, and manner of speeches and other communicative activities engaged in by outside persons. Problems arise when these basic rules of order are expanded to include regulations under which speakers or events can be banned because of the content of the speech or the political affiliations or persuasions of the participants.[22] Such regulations are particularly susceptible to judicial invalidation because they are prior restraints on speech (see Section 9.5.4). *Stacy v. Williams*, 306 F. Supp. 963 (N.D. Miss. 1969), is an illustrative example. The Board of Trustees for the Institutions of Higher Learning of the State of Mississippi promulgated rules providing, in part, that "all speakers invited to the campus of any of the state institutions of higher learning must first be investigated and approved by the head of the institution involved and when invited the names of such speakers must be filed with the Executive Secretary of the Board of Trustees." The regulations were amended several times to prohibit "speakers who will do violence to the academic atmosphere," "persons in disrepute from whence they come," persons "charged with crime or other moral wrongs," any person "who advocates a philosophy of the overthrow of the United States," and any person "who has been announced as a political candidate or any person who wishes to speak on behalf of a political candidate." In addition, political or sectarian meetings sponsored by any outside organization were prohibited.

When the board, under the authority of these regulations, prevented political activists Aaron Henry and Charles Evers from speaking on any Mississippi state campus, students joined faculty members and other persons as plaintiffs in an action to invalidate the regulations. A special three-judge court struck down the regulations because they created a prior restraint on the students' and faculty members' First Amendment right to hear speakers. Not all speaker bans, however, are unconstitutional under the court's reasoning. When the speech "presents a 'clear and present danger' of resulting in serious substantive evil," a ban would not violate the First Amendment:

> For purpose of illustration, we have no doubt that the college or university authority may deny an invitation to a guest speaker requested by a campus group if it reasonably appears that such person would, in the course of his speech, advocate (1) violent overthrow of the government of the United States, the state of Mississippi, or any political subdivision thereof; (2) willful destruction or seizure of the institution's buildings or other property; (3) disruption or impairment, by force, of the institution's regularly scheduled classes or other educational functions; (4) physical harm, coercion, intimidation or other invasion of lawful rights of the institution's officials, faculty members, or students; or (5) other campus disorder of violent nature. In drafting a regulation so providing, it must be made clear that the "advocacy" prohibited must be of the kind which prepares the group addressed for imminent action and steels it to such action, as opposed to the abstract espousal of the moral propriety of a course of action by resort to force; and there must be not only advocacy to action but also a reasonable apprehension of imminent danger to the essential functions and purposes of the institution, including the safety of its property and the protection of its officials, faculty members, and students [306 F. Supp. at 973–74].

---

[22]Cases are collected in Jeffrey F. Ghent, Annot., "Validity, Under Federal Constitution, of Regulation for Off-Campus Speakers at State Colleges and Universities—Federal Cases," 5 A.L.R. Fed. 841.

The court in *Stacy v. Williams* also promulgated a set of "Uniform Regulations for Off-Campus Speakers," which, in its view, complied with the First Amendment (306 F. Supp. at 979–80). These regulations provide that all speaker requests come from a recognized student or faculty group, thus precluding any outsider's insistence on using the campus as a forum. This approach accords with the court's basis for invalidating the regulations: the rights of students or faculty members to hear a speaker. In *Molpus v. Fortune*, 432 F.2d 916 (5th Cir. 1970), the appellate court applied the *Stacy v. Williams* regulations to an administrator's refusal to permit a student group to invite a student speaker from another campus in the state. The court invalidated the administrator's action, holding that the university could not show that the speaker would create a clear and present danger to campus operations.

Besides meeting a "clear and present danger" test—or more precisely, an incitement test (as established by *Brandenburg v. Ohio*, 395 U.S. 444 (1969), and relied on by the court in *Brooks v. Auburn University*, below)—speaker ban regulations must use language that is sufficiently clear and precise to be understood by the average reader. Ambiguous or vague regulations run the risk of being struck down, under the First and Fourteenth Amendments, as "void for vagueness" (see generally Sections 9.1.3, 9.2.2, & 9.5.3 of this book). In *Dickson v. Sitterson*, 280 F. Supp. 486 (M.D.N.C. 1968), a special three-judge court relied on this ground to invalidate state statutes and University of North Carolina regulations governing the use of university facilities by any speaker who is a "known member of the Communist party," is "known to advocate the overthrow of the Constitution of the United States or the State of North Carolina," or has "pleaded the Fifth Amendment" in response to questions relating to the Communist Party or other subversive organizations.

The absence of rules can be just as risky as poorly drafted ones, since either situation leaves administrators and affected persons with insufficient guidance. *Brooks v. Auburn University*, 412 F.2d 1171 (5th Cir. 1969), is illustrative. A student organization, the Human Rights Forum, had requested that the Reverend William Sloan Coffin speak on campus. After the request was approved by the Public Affairs Seminar Board, the president of Auburn overruled the decision because the Reverend Coffin was "a convicted felon and because he might advocate breaking the law." Students and faculty members filed suit contesting the president's action, and the U.S. Court of Appeals upheld their First Amendment claim:

> Attributing the highest good faith to Dr. Philpott in his action, it nevertheless is clear under the prior restraint doctrine that the right of the faculty and students to hear a speaker, selected as was the speaker here, cannot be left to the discretion of the university president on a pick and choose basis. As stated, Auburn had no rules or regulations as to who might or might not speak and thus no question of a compliance with or a departure from such rules or regulations is presented. This left the matter as a pure First Amendment question; hence the basis for prior restraint. Such a situation of no rules or regulations may be equated with a licensing system to speak or hear and this has been long prohibited.

It is strenuously urged on behalf of Auburn that the president was authorized in any event to bar a convicted felon or one advocating lawlessness from the campus. This again depends upon the right of the faculty and students to hear. We do not hold that Dr. Philpott could not bar a speaker under any circumstances. Here there was no claim that the Reverend Coffin's appearance would lead to violence or disorder or that the university would be otherwise disrupted. There is no claim that Dr. Philpott could not regulate the time or place of the speech or the manner in which it was to be delivered. The most recent statement of the applicable rule by the Supreme Court, perhaps its outer limits, is contained in the case of *Brandenburg v. Ohio,* [395 U.S. 444]: . . . "[T]he constitutional guarantees of free speech and free press do not permit a State to forbid or proscribe advocacy of the use of force or of law violation except where such advocacy is directed to inciting or producing imminent lawless action and is likely to incite or produce such action." . . . There was no claim that the Coffin speech would fall into the category of this exception [412 F.2d at 1172–73].

A quite different type of "speaker ban" was at issue in *DeBauche v. Trani,* 191 F. 3d 499 (4th Cir. 1999). The context was a state political campaign in which a public university provided facilities for a candidate's debate held on (and broadcast from) the campus. The debaters were the Democratic and Republican candidates for governor of Virginia; the Reform Party candidate was excluded from the debate. She sued various parties, including the university and the university president, in effect claiming she had been banned from speaking in the debate, in violation of her First Amendment rights to free speech. The court framed the free speech issue as "whether a candidate debate held by a state entity was a 'public forum' such that viewpoint discrimination would be restricted by the Constitution." (See generally the *Rosenberger* case, Section 10.1.5, on public forum and viewpoint discrimination.) The Fourth Circuit avoided any thorough analysis of this issue on the merits by accepting the university's and president's arguments for Eleventh Amendment immunity (see Section 3.5 of this book) and Section 1983 qualified immunity (see Section 4.7.4 of this book). But the court did provide some guidance by stating that the leading precedent to apply is *Arkansas Educational Television Commission v. Forbes,* 523 U.S. 666 (1998), in which the U.S. Supreme Court used the First Amendment public forum doctrine (see generally Section 9.5.2) and the "nonpublic forum" category to invalidate a public broadcaster's decision to exclude a minor party candidate from a televised debate. The Court in *Forbes* also made clear that government entities could still exclude candidates from political campaign debates if the exclusion is a "reasonable, viewpoint-neutral exercise of journalistic discretion" (523 U.S. at 683, quoted in *DeBauche,* 191 F.3d at 506). If the debates were not broadcast or otherwise transmitted by the media, the same guideline would apparently apply, except that the institution's academic or administrative discretion would be substituted for "journalistic discretion."

In contrast to the speaker cases, the case of *Reproductive Rights Network v. President of the University of Massachusetts,* 699 N.E.2d 829 (Mass. App. Ct. 1998), concerns administrators' attempts to exclude an event, rather than a particular speaker, from the campus. The case illustrates how a public institution's authority to regulate use of its property (here a campus building and meeting rooms) may be limited by the First Amendment, and also illustrates how access claims and free speech claims of outsiders may be strengthened when students or faculty members make property use requests on their behalf.

In the *Reproductive Rights Network* case, several outside organizations advocating pro-choice and gay rights positions, along with various faculty members and graduate students at the University of Massachusetts at Boston, had sought to use a campus classroom for two meetings called for the purpose of planning a demonstration to be held at a cathedral in Boston. A faculty member reserved the room for the meetings, and the public was invited to attend. Before the second meeting could be held, however, university officials closed and evacuated the building, locked it, and posted campus police officers as security guards. When the plaintiffs filed suit challenging this action, the trial court issued, and the appellate court affirmed, an injunction against university officials. According to these courts, the officials' actions were in response to the content of the planned meeting and the organizations' advocacy of particular positions. Moreover, the university's room reservation policy did not include any standards to limit administrators' discretion to determine when room use could be denied. The university's action, therefore, violated the First Amendment's free speech clause and the comparable provision of the Massachusetts state constitution.

Under cases such as those above, regulations concerning outside speakers and events present sensitive legal issues for public institutions, and sensitive policy issues for both public and private institutions. If such regulations are determined to be necessary, they should be drafted with extreme care and with the aid of counsel. The cases clearly permit public institutions to enforce reasonable regulations of "the time or place of the speech or the manner in which it . . . [is] delivered," as the *Brooks* opinion notes. But excluding a speech or event because of its content is permissible only in the narrowest of circumstances, as the *Stacy* and *Brooks* cases indicate; and regulating speech or an event because of viewpoint is virtually never permissible, as the *DeBauche* and *Reproductive Rights Network* cases indicate. The regulations promulgated by the court in *Stacy* provide useful guidance in drafting legally sound regulations. The five First Amendment principles set out in Section 9.6.2 of this book, and the regulatory strategies set out in Section 9.6.3, may also be helpful to administrators and counsel drafting speaker and event regulations.

11.6.3. Trespass statutes and ordinances, and related campus regulations. States and local governments often have trespass or unlawful entry laws that limit the use of a postsecondary institution's grounds and facilities by outsiders. (See, for example, Cal. Penal Code §§ 626.2, 626.4, 626.6, & 626.7; Mass. Gen. Laws, chap. 266, §§ 120, 121A, & 123.) Such statutes or ordinances typically provide that offenders are subject to ejection from the property and that violation of an order to leave, made by an authorized person, is punishable as a criminal misdemeanor and/or is subject to damage awards and injunctive relief in a civil suit. Counsel for institutions should carefully examine these laws, and the court decisions interpreting them, to

determine each law's particular coverage. Some laws may cover all types of property; others may cover only educational institutions. Some laws may cover all postsecondary institutions, public or private; others may apply only to public or only to private institutions. Some laws may be broad enough to restrict members of the campus community under some circumstances; others may be applicable only to outsiders. There may also be technical differences among statutes and ordinances in their standards for determining what acts will be considered a trespass or when an institution's actions will constitute implied consent to entry. (See generally *People v. Leonard*, 465 N.E.2d 831 (N.Y. 1984), concerning the applicability of state trespass law to the exclusion of outsiders via a *persona non grata* letter.) There may also be differences concerning when the alleged trespasser has a "privilege" to be on the institution's property. The issue of "privilege" is often shaped by consideration of the public forum doctrine (see Section 9.5.2). If the alleged trespasser sought access to the campus property for expressive purposes, and if the property were considered to be a traditional public forum or a designated forum open to outsiders, the speaker will generally be considered to have a "privilege" to be on the property, and the trespass law cannot lawfully be used to exclude or eject the speaker from the forum property (see *State of Ohio v. Spingola*, 736 N.E.2d 48 (Ohio 1999)). When a trespass law is invoked, there may also be questions of whether or when local police or campus security officers have probable cause to arrest the alleged trespasser. The presence of such probable cause may be a defense to claims of false arrest, false imprisonment, or other torts that the alleged trespasser may later assert against the institution or the arresting officer. (See *Orin v. Barclay*, 272 F.3d 1207, 1218–19 (majority) & 1219–20 (concurrence) (9th Cir. 2001).)

A number of reported cases have dealt with the federal and state constitutional limitations on a state or local government's authority to apply trespass laws or related regulations to the campus setting.[23] *Braxton v. Municipal Court*, 514 P.2d 697 (Cal. 1973), is an early, instructive example. Several individuals had demonstrated on the San Francisco State campus against the publication of campus newspaper articles that they considered "racist and chauvinistic." A college employee notified the protestors that they were temporarily barred from campus. When they disobeyed this order, they were arrested and charged under Section 626.4 of the California Penal Code. This statute authorized "the chief administrative officer of a campus or other facility of a community college, state college, or state university or his designate" to temporarily bar a person from the campus if there was "reasonable cause to believe that such person has willfully disrupted the orderly operation of such campus or facility." The protestors argued that the state trespass statute was unconstitutional for reasons of overbreadth and vagueness (see Sections 9.2.2, 9.5.3, & 9.6.2 of this book).

---

[23]Cases are collected in Jeffrey F. Ghent, Annot., "Validity and Construction of Statute or Ordinance Forbidding Unauthorized Persons to Enter upon or Remain in School Building or Premises," 50 A.L.R.3d 340.

The California Supreme Court rejected the protestors' argument, but did so only after narrowly construing the statute to avoid constitutional problems. Regarding overbreadth, the court reasoned:

> Without a narrowing construction, section 626.4 would suffer First Amendment overbreadth. For example, reasoned appeals for a student strike to protest the escalation of a war, or the firing of the football coach, might "disrupt" the "orderly operation" of a campus; so, too, might calls for the dismissal of the college president or for a cafeteria boycott to protest employment policies or the use of nonunion products. Yet neither the "content" of speech nor freedom of association can be restricted merely because such expression or association disrupts the tranquillity of a campus or offends the tastes of school administrators or the public. Protest may disrupt the placidity of the vacant mind just as a stone dropped in a still pool may disturb the tranquillity of the surface waters, but the courts have never held that such "disruption" falls outside the boundaries of the First Amendment. . . .
>
> Without a narrowing construction, section 626.4 would also suffer overbreadth by unnecessarily restricting conduct enmeshed with First Amendment activities. Although conduct entwined with speech may be regulated if it is completely incompatible with the peaceful functioning of the campus, section 626.4 on its face fails to distinguish between protected activity such as peaceful picketing or assembly and unprotected conduct that is violent, physically obstructive, or otherwise coercive. . . .
>
> In order to avoid the constitutional overbreadth that a literal construction of section 626.4 would entail, we interpret the statute to prohibit only incitement to violence or conduct physically incompatible with the peaceful functioning of the campus. We agree with the Attorney General in his statement: "The word 'disrupt' is commonly understood to mean a physical or forcible interference, interruption, or obstruction. In the campus context, disrupt means a *physical* or *forcible* interference with normal college activities."
>
> The disruption must also constitute "a substantial and material threat" to the orderly operation of the campus or facility (*Tinker v. Des Moines School District*, 393 U.S. 503, 514 (1969)). The words "substantial and material" appear in the portion of the statute which authorizes reinstatement of permission to come onto the campus (Penal Code § 626.4(c)). Accordingly, we read those words as expressing the legislature's intent as to the whole function of the statute; we thus construe section 626.4 to permit exclusion from the campus only of one whose conduct or words are such as to constitute, or incite to, a substantial and material physical disruption incompatible with the peaceful functioning of the academic institution and of those upon its campus. Such a substantial and material disruption creates an emergency situation justifying the statute's provision for summary, but temporary, exclusion [514 P.2d at 701, 703–5].

The court then also rejected the vagueness claim:

> Petitioners point out that even though the test of substantial and material physical disruption by acts of incitement of violence constitutes an acceptable constitutional standard for preventing overbroad applications of the statute in specific cases, the enactment still fails to provide the precision normally required

in criminal legislation. Thus, for example, persons subject to summary banishment must guess at *what* must be disrupted (i.e., classes or the attendance lines for athletic events), and *how* the disruption must take place (by picketing or by a single zealous shout in a classroom or by a sustained sit-in barring use of a classroom for several days).

Our examination of the legislative history and purposes of section 626.4 reveals, however, that the Legislature intended to authorize the extraordinary remedy of summary banishment only when the person excluded has committed acts illegal under other statutes; since these statutes provide ascertainable standards for persons seeking to avoid the embrace of section 626.4, the instant enactment is not void for vagueness [514 P.2d at 705].

In comparison with *Braxton,* the court in *Grody v. State,* 278 N.E.2d 280 (Ind. 1972), did invalidate a state trespass law due to its overbreadth. The law provided that "[i]t shall be a misdemeanor for any person to refuse to leave the premises of any institution established for the purpose of the education of students enrolled therein when so requested, regardless of the reason, by the duly constituted officials of any such institution" (Ind. Code Ann. § 10-4533). As the court read the law:

This statute attempts to grant to some undefined school "official" the power to order cessation of *any* kind of activity whatsoever, by *any* person whatsoever, and the official does not need to have any special reason for the order. The official's power extends to teachers, employees, students, and visitors and is in no way confined to suppressing activities that are interfering with the orderly use of the premises. This statute empowers the official to order any person off the premises because he does not approve of his looks, his opinions, his behavior, no matter how peaceful, or *for no reason at all.* Since there are no limitations on the reason for such an order, the official can request a person to leave the premises solely because the person is engaging in expressive conduct even though that conduct may be clearly protected by the First Amendment. If the person chooses to continue the First Amendment activity, he can be prosecuted for a crime under § 10-4533. This statute is clearly overbroad [278 N.E.2d at 282–83].

The court therefore held the trespass law to be facially invalid under the free speech clause.

Even if a trespass statute or ordinance does not contain the First Amendment flaws identified in *Braxton* and *Grody,* it may be challenged as a violation of Fourteenth Amendment procedural due process. The court in *Braxton* (above), 514 P.2d at 700, ruled in favor of the plaintiffs' due process arguments, as did the courts in *Dunkel v. Elkins,* 325 F. Supp. 1235 (D. Md. 1971), and *Watson v. Board of Regents of the University of Colorado,* 512 P.2d 1162, 1165 (Colo. 1973). In *Watson,* for example, the plaintiff was a consultant to the University of Colorado Black Student Alliance, with substantial ties to the campus. The university had rejected his application for admission. Believing that a particular admissions committee member had made the decision to reject him, the plaintiff threatened his safety. The university president then notified the plaintiff in writing that he would no longer be allowed on campus. Nevertheless, the plaintiff returned to campus and was arrested for trespass. Relying on *Dunkel v. Elkins,* the court agreed that the exclusion violated procedural due process:

> Where students have been subjected to disciplinary action by university officials, courts have recognized that procedural due process requires—prior to imposition of the disciplinary action—adequate notice of the charges, reasonable opportunity to prepare to meet the charges, an orderly administrative hearing adapted to the nature of the case, and a fair and impartial decision. . . . The same protection must be afforded nonstudents who may be permanently denied access to university functions and facilities.
>
> As part of a valid Regent's regulation of this type, in addition to providing for a hearing, there should be a provision for the person or persons who will act as adjudicator(s).
>
> In the present posture of this matter we should not attempt to "spell out" all proper elements of such a regulation. This task should be undertaken first by the regents. We should say, however, that when a genuine emergency appears to exist and it is impractical for university officials to grant a prior hearing, the right of nonstudents to access to the university may be suspended without a prior hearing, so long as a hearing is thereafter provided with reasonable promptness [512 P.2d at 1165].

The court in *Watson,* however, appears to overstate the case for procedural due process when it equates an outsider's rights with those of students. The Fourteenth Amendment requires a hearing or other procedural protections only when the government has violated "property interests" or "liberty interests" (see generally Sections 6.6.1, 6.6.2, & 9.4.2). If a student is ejected from the campus, the ejection will usually infringe a property or liberty interest of the student; that is not necessarily the case, however, if a nonstudent is ejected. For example, in a more recent case, *Souders v. Lucero,* 196 F.3d 1040 (9th Cir. 1999), the court rejected an outsider's claim to procedural due process protections.

The plaintiff in *Souders* was an alumnus of Oregon State University (OSU) who had been excluded from campus, based on several complaints that he was stalking female students. The women had pursued a procedure provided by the university's Security Services and had obtained "Trespass on Campus Exclusion Orders." When Souders appeared on the campus in violation of the orders, he was arrested by a campus security officer. Souders brought a Section 1983 action alleging that the university's exclusion order deprived him of constitutionally protected liberty and property interests and violated Fourteenth Amendment procedural due process. His reasoning, apparently, was that the campus was a "public forum" under the First Amendment (see generally Section 9.4.2), and he therefore had a constitutionally protected interest in being there. But the court (citing *Widmar v. Vincent,* 454 U.S. 263, at 267, n.5, & 278) determined that a university campus, even when open to the general public, is not the same as traditional fora such as streets or parks. Thus, according to the court:

> Souders' argument—that he has a right to be on the OSU campus, regardless of his conduct, because he is a member of the general public and the campus is open to the public—goes too far. This cannot be the case. Whatever right he has to be on campus must be balanced against the right of the University to exclude

him. The University may preserve such tranquility as the facilities' central purpose requires. See Laurence H. Tribe, *American Constitutional Law* 690 (1980). Not only must a university have the power to foster an atmosphere and conditions in which its educational mission can be carried out, it also has a duty to protect its students by imposing reasonable regulations on the conduct of those who come onto campus [196 F.3d at 1045].

The public forum argument having failed, the court concluded that "Souders has not established a constitutionally protected interest in having access to the University" and that, absent such an interest, "we need not decide whether the procedures employed in this case were adequate to afford . . . due process protection. . . ."

Postsecondary institutions may also have their own regulations that prohibit entry of outsiders into campus buildings or certain outside areas of the campus, or that provide for ejecting or banning outsiders from the campus in certain circumstances. For public institutions, such regulations are subject to the same federal constitutional restrictions as the state trespass statutes discussed above. In addition, if the institution's regulation were facially unconstitutional, or if the institution were to apply its regulation in an unconstitutional manner in a particular case, it would be impermissible for the institution to invoke a state trespass law or local ordinance to enforce its regulation. *Orin v. Barclay,* 272 F.3d 1207 (9th Cir. 2001), illustrates these principles.

In *Orin v. Barclay,* the court considered the constitutionality of a speech regulation prohibiting protestors from engaging in religious worship or instruction. The issue arose when members of the anti-abortion group Positively Pro-Life approached the interim dean of Olympic Community College (OCC), Richard Barclay, and asked for a permit to stage an event on the school's main quad. Barclay declined to grant the protestors a permit, but gave them permission to hold a demonstration provided they did not (1) breach the peace or cause a disturbance; (2) interfere with campus activities or access to school buildings; or (3) engage in religious worship or instruction. With the dean's permission, the protestors began their anti-abortion demonstration. After "four factious hours," the protestors were asked to leave the campus. They refused, and at least one protestor, Benjamin Orin, was arrested for criminal trespass and failure to disperse. Orin subsequently sued Barclay, among others, under 42 U.S.C. § 1983 for violating his First Amendment rights, and the district court granted the defendants' motions for summary judgment.

The appellate court focused on the conditions that Barclay had imposed on the anti-abortion group's protest. The first two conditions—that the protestors not breach the peace or interfere with campus activities or access to school buildings—were permissible content-neutral regulations. "The first two conditions survive constitutional scrutiny because they do not distinguish among speakers based on the content of their message and they are narrowly tailored to achieve OCC's pedagogical purpose" (272 F.3d at 1215). However, the third condition, that the protestors refrain from religious worship or instruction, violated the First Amendment. The court held that Barclay had created a public forum by granting the protestors permission to demonstrate. Consequently, he could not constitutionally limit the content of the protestors' speech by permitting secular, but prohibiting religious, speech. As the court explained:

> The third condition imposed by Barclay constitutes a content-based regula-
> tion that we may uphold only if it "is necessary to serve a compelling state inter-
> est and . . . is narrowly drawn to achieve that end." Barclay informed Orin that
> this condition was required by the Establishment Clause in order to maintain the
> separation of Church and State. The Supreme Court has ruled, however, that the
> First Amendment does not require public institutions to exclude religious speech
> from fora held open to secular speakers. In fact, it prohibits them from doing so.
> In [*Widmar v. Vincent,* 454 U.S. 263 (1981)] . . . , [t]he Court [held] that
> allowing religious organizations the same access to school facilities enjoyed by
> secular organizations did not violate the Establishment Clause. Since the govern-
> mental interest that purported to justify regulation was based on a misunder-
> standing of the Establishment Clause, the Court struck the regulation down as a
> content-based regulation of First Amendment rights of assembly, free exercise,
> and free speech that was not narrowly tailored to serve a compelling govern-
> mental interest.
> Barclay's "no religion" condition runs squarely afoul of *Widmar.* Having per-
> mitted Orin to conduct a demonstration on campus, Barclay could not, consis-
> tent with the First Amendment's free speech and free exercise clauses, limit his
> demonstration to secular content [272 F.2d at 1215–16].

The court therefore reversed the district court's grant of summary judgment to the defendants, and held that, based on the facts then in the record, the dean had violated the plaintiff's First Amendment rights and could become liable to the plaintiff in damages under Section 1983.

Other access cases concerning institutional regulations suggest, as *Orin v. Barclay* does, that the most contentious issues are likely to be First Amendment issues, especially free speech issues, and that the analysis will often turn on public forum considerations (see Section 9.5.2) and on the distinction between content-based and content-neutral regulations of speech. The public forum analysis applicable to outsiders' rights may differ from that for students' or fac-ulty members' rights because institutions may establish limited forums (desig-nated limited forums) that provide access for the campus community but not for outsiders. Overbreadth and vagueness analysis (as in the *Braxton* and *Grady* cases above) may also be pertinent in cases challenging institutional regulations.

In *Giebel v. Sylvester,* 244 F.3d 1182 (9th Cir. 2001), the court used forum analysis and viewpoint discrimination analysis in *protecting* an outsider who had posted notices on university bulletin boards. In *Mason v. Wolf,* 356 F. Supp. 2d 1147 (D. Colo. 2005), the court used forum analysis and time, place, and manner analysis in protecting an outside group seeking to have a demonstra-tion on campus. In contrast, in *State v. Spingola,* above, the court used public forum analysis, content-neutral analysis, and vagueness analysis in *rejecting* the free speech claim of an outside preacher. The court in *Bourgault v. Yudof,* 316 F. Supp. 2d 411 (N.D. Tex. 2004), *affirmed without opinion,* 2005 WL 3332907 (December 8, 2005), used forum analysis and viewpoint discrimination analy-sis in *rejecting* a traveling evangelist's free speech challenge to University of

Texas System rules that provided no access to outsiders. And in *ACLU Student Chapter v. Mote,* 321 F. Supp. 2d 670 (D. Md. 2004), the court used forum analysis in upholding the validity of a campus policy that allowed limited access to outsiders.

Most of the litigation concerning trespass laws and campus access regulations, such as the cases above, has involved public institutions and has probed federal constitutional limits on states and public postsecondary institutions. The debate was extended to private institutions, however, by the litigation in *State v. Schmid,* 423 A.2d 615 (N.J. 1980), sometimes known as the *Princeton University* case.

In this case, a nonstudent and member of the United States Labor Party, Chris Schmid, was arrested and convicted of trespass for attempting to distribute political materials on the campus of Princeton University. Princeton's regulations required nonstudents and non-university-affiliated organizations to obtain permission to distribute materials on campus. No such requirement applied to students or campus organizations. The regulations did not include any provisions indicating when permission would be granted or what times, manners, or places of expression were appropriate. Schmid claimed that the regulations violated his rights to freedom of expression under both the federal Constitution and the New Jersey state constitution.

First addressing the federal constitutional claim under the First Amendment, the court acknowledged that the "state action" requirement (see Section 1.5.2), a predicate to the application of the First Amendment, "is not readily met in the case of a private educational institution." Extensively analyzing the various theories of state action and their applicability to the case, the court held that Princeton's exclusion of Schmid did not constitute state action under any of the theories.

Although, in the absence of a state action finding, the federal First Amendment could not apply to Schmid's claim, the court did not find itself similarly constrained in applying the state constitution. Addressing Schmid's state constitutional claim, the court determined that the state constitutional provisions protecting freedom of expression (even though similar to the First Amendment provision) could be construed more expansively than the First Amendment so as to reach Princeton's actions. The court reaffirmed that state constitutions are independent sources of individual rights; that state constitutional protections may surpass the protections of the federal Constitution; and that this greater expansiveness could exist even if the state provision is identical to the federal provision, since state constitutional rights are not intended to be merely mirror images of federal rights (see Section 1.4.2.1).

In determining whether the more expansive state constitutional provision protected Schmid against the trespass claim, the court balanced the "legitimate interests in private property with individual freedoms of speech and assembly":

> The state constitutional equipoise between expressional rights and property rights must be . . . gauged on a scale measuring the nature and extent of the public's use of such property. Thus, even as against the exercise of important

rights of speech, assembly, petition, and the like, private property itself remains protected under due process standards from untoward interferences with or confiscatory restrictions upon its reasonable use. . . .

On the other hand, it is also clear that private property may be subjected by the state, within constitutional bounds, to reasonable restrictions upon its use in order to serve the public welfare. . . .

We are thus constrained to achieve the optimal balance between the protections to be accorded private property and those to be given to expressional freedoms exercised upon such property [423 A.2d at 629].

To strike the required balance, the court announced a "test" encompassing several "elements" and other "considerations":

We now hold that, under the state constitution, the test to be applied to ascertain the parameters of the rights of speech and assembly upon privately owned property and the extent to which such property reasonably can be restricted to accommodate these rights involves several elements. This standard must take into account (1) the nature, purposes, and primary use of such private property, generally, its "normal" use, (2) the extent and nature of the public's invitation to use that property, and (3) the purpose of the expressional activity undertaken upon such property in relation to both the private and public use of the property. This is a multifaceted test which must be applied to ascertain whether in a given case owners of private property may be required to permit, subject to suitable restrictions, the reasonable exercise by individuals of the constitutional freedoms of speech and assembly.

Even when an owner of private property is constitutionally obligated under such a standard to honor speech and assembly rights of others, private property rights themselves must nonetheless be protected. The owner of such private property, therefore, is entitled to fashion reasonable rules to control the mode, opportunity, and site for the individual exercise of expressional rights upon his property. It is at this level of analysis—assessing the reasonableness of such restrictions—that weight may be given to whether there exist convenient and feasible alternative means to individuals to engage in substantially the same expressional activity. While the presence of such alternatives will not eliminate the constitutional duty, it may lighten the obligations upon the private property owner to accommodate the expressional rights of others and may also serve to condition the content of any regulations governing the time, place, and manner for the exercise of such expressional rights [423 A.2d at 630].

Applying each of the three elements in its test to the particular facts concerning Princeton's campus and Schmid's activity on it, the court concluded that Schmid did have state constitutional speech and assembly rights that Princeton was obligated to honor:

The application of the appropriate standard in this case must commence with an examination of the primary use of the private property, namely, the campus and facilities of Princeton University. Princeton University itself has furnished the answer to this inquiry [in its university regulations] in expansively expressing its overriding educational goals, viz:

> The central purposes of a university are the pursuit of truth, the discovery of new knowledge through scholarship and research, the teaching and general development of students, and the transmission of knowledge and learning to society at large. Free inquiry and free expression within the academic community are indispensable to the achievement of these goals. The freedom to teach and to learn depends upon the creation of appropriate conditions and opportunities on the campus as a whole as well as in classrooms and lecture halls. All members of the academic community share the responsibility for securing and sustaining the general conditions conducive to this freedom. . . .
>
> Free speech and peaceable assembly are basic requirements of the university as a center for free inquiry and the search for knowledge and insight.

No one questions that Princeton University has honored this grand ideal and has in fact dedicated its facilities and property to achieve the educational goals expounded in this compelling statement.

In examining next the extent and nature of a public invitation to use its property, we note that a public presence within Princeton University is entirely consonant with the university's expressed educational mission. Princeton University, as a private institution of higher education, clearly seeks to encourage both a wide and continuous exchange of opinions and ideas and to foster a policy of openness and freedom with respect to the use of its facilities. The commitment of its property, facilities, and resources to educational purposes contemplates substantial public involvement and participation in the academic life of the university. The university itself has endorsed the educational value of an open campus and the full exposure of the college community to the "outside world"—that is, the public at large. Princeton University has indeed invited such public uses of its resources in fulfillment of its broader educational ideas and objectives.

The further question is whether the expressional activities undertaken by the defendant in this case are discordant in any sense with both the private and public uses of the campus and facilities of the university. There is nothing in the record to suggest that Schmid was evicted because the purpose of his activities, distributing political literature, offended the university's educational policies. The reasonable and normal inference thus to be extracted from the record in the instant case is that defendant's attempt to disseminate political material was not incompatible with either Princeton University's professed educational goals or the university's overall use of its property for educational purposes. Further, there is no indication that, even under the terms of the university's own regulations, Schmid's activities . . . directly or demonstrably "disrupt[ed] the regular and essential operations of the university" or that, in either the time, the place, or the manner of Schmid's distribution of the political materials, he "significantly infringed on the rights of others" or caused any interference or inconvenience with respect to the normal use of university property and the normal routine and activities of the college community [423 A.2d at 630–31].

Princeton, however, invoked the other considerations included in the court's test. It argued that, to protect its private property rights as an owner and its academic freedom as a higher education institution, it had to require that outsiders have permission to enter its campus and that its regulations reasonably implemented this necessary requirement. The court did not disagree with the first premise of Princeton's argument, but it did disagree that Princeton's regulations were a reasonable means of protecting its interests:

> In addressing this argument, we must give substantial deference to the importance of institutional integrity and independence. Private educational institutions perform an essential social function and have a fundamental responsibility to assure the academic and general well-being of their communities of students, teachers, and related personnel. At a minimum, these needs, implicating academic freedom and development, justify an educational institution in controlling those who seek to enter its domain. The singular need to achieve essential educational goals and regulate activities that impact upon these efforts has been acknowledged even with respect to public educational institutions (see, for example, *Healy v. James,* 408 U.S. at 180 . . . *Tinker v. Des Moines Indep. Community School Dist.,* 393 U.S. 503, 513–14 . . . (1969)). Hence, private colleges and universities must be accorded a generous measure of autonomy and self-governance if they are to fulfill their paramount role as vehicles of education and enlightenment.
>
> In this case, however, the university regulations that were applied to Schmid . . . contained no standards, aside from the requirement for invitation and permission, for governing the actual exercise of expressional freedom. Indeed, there were no standards extant regulating the granting or withholding of such authorization, nor did the regulations deal adequately with the time, place, or manner for individuals to exercise their rights of speech and assembly. Regulations thus devoid of reasonable standards designed to protect both the legitimate interests of the university as an institution of higher education and the individual exercise of expressional freedom cannot constitutionally be invoked to prohibit the otherwise noninjurious and reasonable exercise of such freedoms. . . .
>
> In these circumstances, given the absence of adequate reasonable regulations, the required accommodation of Schmid's expressional and associational rights, otherwise reasonably exercised, would not constitute an unconstitutional abridgment of Princeton University's property rights. . . . It follows that, in the absence of a reasonable regulatory scheme, Princeton University did in fact violate defendant's state constitutional rights of expression in evicting him and securing his arrest for distributing political literature upon its campus [423 A.2d at 632–33].

The court thus reversed Schmid's conviction for trespass.

Princeton sought U.S. Supreme Court review of the New Jersey court's decision. The university argued that the court's interpretation of *state* constitutional law violated its rights under *federal* law. Specifically, it claimed a First Amendment right to institutional academic freedom (see Section 7.1.6)[24] and a

---

[24]The arguments for and against the existence of a private institution's institutional academic freedom right are well developed in the briefs of the parties and the *amici curiae*. Lawyers facing this important issue may still want to consult these briefs and the resources they cite. See particularly the Brief Amicus Curiae of the American Association of University Professors, filed August 20, 1981, in *Princeton University and State of New Jersey v. Chris Schmid,* No. 80-1576, U.S. Supreme Court, October Term 1980.

Fifth Amendment right to protect its property from infringement by government (here the New Jersey court). In a *per curiam* opinion, the Supreme Court declined to address the merits of Princeton's arguments, declaring the appeal moot (see this volume, Section 1.4.2.3) because Princeton had changed its regulations since the time of Schmid's conviction (*Princeton University and State of New Jersey v. Schmid*, 455 U.S. 100 (1982)). Although the Supreme Court therefore dismissed the appeal, the dismissal had no negative effect on the New Jersey court's opinion, which stands as authoritative law for that state.

The New Jersey Supreme Court's reasoning was subsequently approved and followed by the Pennsylvania Supreme Court in *Pennsylvania v. Tate*, 432 A.2d 1382 (Pa. 1981), in which the defendants had been arrested for trespassing at Muhlenberg College, a private institution, when they distributed leaflets on campus announcing a community-sponsored lecture by the then FBI director. In a later case, however, *Western Pennsylvania Socialist Workers 1982 Campaign*, 515 A.2d 1331 (1986), the Pennsylvania Supreme Court apparently limited its *Tate* ruling to situations in which the private institution has opened up the contested portion of its property for a use comparable to that of a public forum (515 A.2d at 1338). A few other states also have case law suggesting that their state constitution includes some narrow protections for certain speakers seeking to use private property (see the discussion in *New Jersey Coalition Against War in the Middle East v. J.M.B. Realty Corp.*, 650 A.2d 757, 769–70 (N.J. 1994)).

State v. Schmid is a landmark case—the first to impose constitutional limitations on the authority of private institutions to exclude outsiders from their campuses. *Schmid* does not, however, create a new nationwide rule. The applicability of its analysis to private campuses in states other than New Jersey will vary, depending on the particular type of speech at issue, the particular individual rights clause in a state's constitution that is invoked, the existing precedents construing the clause's application to private entities, and the receptivity of a state's judges to the New Jersey court's view of the nature and use of private campuses. Even in New Jersey, the *Schmid* precedent does not create the same access rights to all private campuses; as *Schmid* emphasizes, the degree of access required depends on the primary use for which the institution dedicates its campus property and the scope of the public invitation to use that particular property. Nor does *Schmid* prohibit private institutions from regulating the activity of outsiders to whom they must permit entry. Indeed, the new regulations adopted by Princeton after Schmid's arrest were cited favorably by the New Jersey court. Although they were not at issue in the case, since they were not the basis of the trespass charge, the court noted that "these current amended regulations exemplify the approaches open to private educational entities seeking to protect their institutional integrity while at the same time recognizing individual rights of speech and assembly and accommodating the public whose presence nurtures academic inquiry and growth."

The revised Princeton regulations, which are set out in full in the court's opinion (423 A.2d at 617–18, n.2), thus provide substantial guidance for private institutions that may be subject to state law such as New Jersey's or that as a matter of educational policy desire to open their campus to outsiders in some circumstances. In addition to consulting these regulations, administrators of private institutions who are dealing with access of outsiders should consult counsel concerning their own state constitution's rights clauses, the applicability of state trespass laws, and their institution's status under them.

11.6.4. Soliciting and canvassing

11.6.4.1. Overview. The university campus may be an attractive marketplace not only for speakers, pamphleteers, and canvassers conveying social, political, or religious messages, but also for companies selling merchandise to college students (see C. Shea, "Businesses Cash in on a Wide-Open Bazaar of Frenzied Consumers: The College Campus," *Chron. Higher Educ.*, June 16, 1993, A33). Whether the enterprising outsider wishes to develop a market for ideas or for commodities, the public institution's authority to restrict contact with its students is limited by the First Amendment. As in other circumstances, because of the First Amendment's applicability, a public institution's authority to regulate soliciting and canvassing is more limited than that of a private institution.

Historically, litigation and discussion of free speech have focused on rights attending the communication of political or social thought. Although the U.S. Supreme Court's opinion in *Virginia State Board of Pharmacy v. Virginia Citizens Consumer Council*, 425 U.S. 748 (1976), made clear that the protection of the First Amendment likewise extends to purely "commercial speech," even when the communication is simply "I will sell you X at Y price," the degree of protection afforded commercial speech remains somewhat less than that afforded noncommercial speech.

The Supreme Court has consistently approved time, place, and manner restrictions on speech where they (1) are not based on the speech's "content or subject matter," (2) "serve a significant governmental interest," and (3) "leave open ample alternative channels for communication of the information" (*Heffron v. International Society for Krishna Consciousness*, 452 U.S. 640 (1981); see also *Clark v. Community for Creative Non-Violence*, discussed in Section 9.5.3). Within these guidelines public institutions may subject both noncommercial and commercial speech to reasonable regulation of the time, place, and manner of delivery.[25] In addition, public institutions may regulate the content of commercial speech in some ways that would not be permissible for other types of speech.

Because public institutions have somewhat more leeway to regulate commercial speech and because, in general, courts require restrictions on speech to be "narrowly tailored" to the institution's interest, administrators and counsel may decide to regulate outsiders' commercial speech separately from its

---

[25]Cases are collected in Donald M. Zupanec, Annot., "Validity of Regulation of College or University Denying or Restricting Right of Student to Receive Visitors in Dormitory," 78 A.L.R.3d 1109.

regulation of outsiders' noncommercial speech. In *Watchtower Bible & Tract Society v. Stratton, Ohio,* 536 U.S. 150 (2002), for instance, the Court invalidated a broad village ordinance requiring all door-to-door canvassers, regardless of their cause or purpose, to register with the mayor and carry a permit. This regulation, said the Court, was not "narrowly tailored" to the village's "important interests" in preventing fraud, deterring crime, or protecting residents' privacy. The Court explained, however, that had the ordinance applied "only to commercial activities and the solicitation of funds," it "arguably . . . would have been tailored to the Village's interest in protecting the privacy of its residents and preventing fraud," and therefore have been valid.

11.6.4.2. Commercial solicitation. Several court decisions involving American Future Systems, Inc., a corporation specializing in the sale of china and crystal, address the regulation of commercial speech by a public university. In *American Future Systems v. Pennsylvania State University,* 618 F.2d 252 (3d Cir. 1980) (*American Future Systems I*), the plaintiff corporation challenged the defendant university's regulations on commercial activities in campus residence halls. The regulations in question barred "the conducting of any business enterprise for profit" in student residence halls except where an individual student invites the salesperson to his or her room for the purpose of conducting business only with that student. No rules prevented businesses from placing advertisements in student newspapers or on student radio, or from making sales attempts by telephone or mail.

American Future Systems (AFS) scheduled a number of sales demonstrations in Penn State residence halls in the fall of 1977. When Penn State officials attempted to stop the sales demonstrations, AFS argued that such action violated its First Amendment "commercial speech" rights. At this point, Penn State informed AFS "that it would be permitted to conduct the demonstration portion of its show if no attempts were made to sell merchandise to the students during the presentation" (618 F.2d at 254). Claiming that the sales transactions were essential to its presentation, AFS ceased its activity and commenced its lawsuit. AFS based its argument on the *Virginia State Board of Pharmacy* case (cited in Section 11.6.4.1):

> Plaintiff AFS is correct that in *Virginia Pharmacy Board* the Supreme Court ruled that commercial speech is entitled to some level of protection by the First Amendment (425 U.S. at 770 . . .). This holding, by itself, does not resolve the issue presented by this case, however. The statutory scheme discussed in *Virginia Pharmacy Board* effectively suppressed all dissemination of price information throughout the state. The case at hand presents a dramatically different fact situation, implicating many different concerns.
>
> Penn State argues that it can restrict the use of its residence halls to purposes which further the educational function of the institution. It urges that transacting sales with groups of students in the dormitories does not further the educational goals of the university and, therefore, can be lawfully prohibited. It emphasizes that AFS seeks a ruling that its sales and demonstrations be permitted in the residence halls, areas which are not open to the general public. In light of all the facts of this case, we believe Penn State is correct [618 F.2d at 255].

In reaching its conclusion, the court inquired whether Penn State had established a "public forum" for free speech activity (see *Widmar v. Vincent*, Section 10.1.5 of this book) in the residence halls:

> When the state restricts speech in some way, the court must look to the special interests of the government in regulating speech in the particular location. The focus of the court's inquiry must be whether there is a basic incompatibility between the communication and the primary activity of an area (*Grayned v. City of Rockford*, 408 U.S. 104, 116 . . . (1972)). . . .
>
> As discussed above, members of the general public do not have unrestricted access to Penn State residence halls. "No Trespassing" signs are posted near the entrances to all the residence halls. Although nonresidents of the halls may enter the lobbies, they may not proceed freely to the private living areas. We believe that these facts demonstrate that the arena at issue here, the residence halls at Penn State, does not constitute a "public forum" under the First Amendment [618 F.2d at 256].

The court then inquired whether, despite the absence of a public forum, AFS could still claim First Amendment protection for solicitation and sales activities occurring in the residence halls. According to the court, such a claim depends on whether the activity impinges on the primary business for which the area in question is used:

> We recognize that the absence of a "public forum" from this case does not end our inquiry, however. There are some "non-public-forum" areas where the communication does not significantly impinge upon the primary business carried on there. Penn State asserts that the AFS group sales do impinge significantly on the primary activities of a college dormitory. Penn State argues that its residence halls are "exclusively dedicated to providing a living environment which is conducive to activities associated with being a student and succeeding academically." It contends that group sales activities within the residence halls would disrupt the proper study atmosphere and the privacy of the students. It reiterates that there is no history of allowing group commercial transactions to take place in the dormitories. We conclude that Penn State has articulated legitimate interests which support its ban on group sales activity in the dormitories. We also conclude that these interests are furthered by the proscription against commercial transactions [618 F.2d at 256–57].

Completing its analysis, the court addressed and rejected a final argument made by AFS: that Penn State cannot distinguish between commercial and noncommercial speech in making rules for its residence halls and that, since Penn State permits political and other noncommercial group activities, it must permit commercial activities as well. The court replied:

> In a case decided two years after *Virginia Pharmacy Board,* the Supreme Court explicitly rejected plaintiff's view that commercial and noncommercial speech must be treated exactly alike. "We have not discarded the 'common-sense' distinction between speech proposing a commercial transaction, which

occurs in an area traditionally subject to government regulation, and other varieties of speech. . . . To require a parity of constitutional protection for commercial and noncommercial speech alike could invite dilution, simply by a leveling process, of the force of the Amendment's guarantee with respect to the latter kind of speech. Rather than subject the First Amendment to such a devitalization, we instead have afforded commercial speech a limited measure of protection, commensurate with its subordinate position in the scale of First Amendment values, while allowing modes of regulation that might be impermissible in the realm of noncommercial expression." *Ohralick v. Ohio State Bar Association*, 436 U.S. 447, 455–56 (1978). . . .

Here Penn State has not totally suppressed the speech of plaintiff. It has restricted that speech somewhat, however. Although AFS sales representatives are allowed into the residence halls to present demonstrations to groups of students, they cannot consummate sales at these gatherings. Even that restriction is removed if the sales representative is invited to the hall by an individual student who decides to purchase the merchandise marketed by AFS.

As noted above, Penn State has advanced reasonable objectives to support its ban on group commercial activity in the residence halls. Further, it has emphasized that traditionally there has been an absence of such activity in the halls. This places commercial speech in a quite different category from activities historically associated with college life, such as political meetings or football rallies. We cannot say that the record in this case reveals any arbitrary, capricious, or invidious distinction between commercial and noncommercial speech. We therefore conclude that AFS is incorrect in its assertion that the Penn State policy violates the First Amendment because it treats noncommercial speech differently from commercial speech [618 F.2d at 257–59].

Having determined that AFS's activities were commercial speech entitled to First Amendment protection, but that Penn State's regulations complied with First Amendment requirements applicable to such speech, the court in *American Future Systems I* upheld the regulations and affirmed the lower court's judgment for Penn State.

Soon, however, a second generation of litigation was born. In accordance with its understanding of the appellate court's opinion in the first lawsuit, AFS requested Penn State to allow group demonstrations that would not include consummation of sales and would take place only in residence hall common areas. AFS provided the university with a copy of its "script" for these demonstrations, a series of seventy-six cue cards. Penn State responded that AFS could use certain cue cards with information the university considered to have "educational value" but not cue cards with "price guarantee and payment plan information," which the university considered "an outright group commercial solicitation." AFS sued again, along with several Penn State students, arguing that Penn State's censorship of its cue cards violated its right to commercial speech and contradicted the court's opinion in *American Future Systems I*. After losing again in the trial court, AFS finally gained a victory when the appellate court ruled in its favor (*American Future Systems v. Pennsylvania State University*, 688 F.2d 907 (3d Cir. 1982) (*American Future Systems II*)).

The appellate court carefully distinguished this litigation from the prior litigation in *American Future Systems I* and identified the new issue presented:

> It is important at the outset to clarify which issues are not before us. Although AFS construes our decision in *American Future Systems I* as having established its constitutional free speech right to conduct demonstrations of a commercial product in common areas within the university's residence halls, we do not read that opinion so broadly. Penn State has not sought to bar all commercial activity from its residence halls. It has limited what ostensibly appears to be such a ban through its definition of "commercial," which excludes student contact with a peddler "if the contact was invited by the individual student involved." Therefore, we need not decide whether a state university may properly ban all commercial activity in its residence halls. Similarly, AFS does not challenge the distinction which the earlier opinion made between an actual consummation or completion of the "commercial transaction" and a group demonstration of AFS's products (618 F.2d at 258–59). Instead, it seeks only to conduct the demonstration in the common areas without censorship of the contents of that demonstration.
>
> Finally, although the university has conceded that portions of the demonstration may have some educational value, and it and the district court sought to draw the line between those portions of the demonstration which they deem educational and those portions which they deem commercial, it is unmistakable that the demonstration is geared to the sales of the products and represents commercial speech. Thus, the only issue is whether Penn State may censor the content of AFS's commercial speech conducted in the dormitory common rooms, where AFS has been permitted by the university to conduct its sales demonstration [688 F.2d at 912].

In resolving this issue, the court applied the "four-step analysis" for ascertaining the validity of commercial speech regulations that the U.S. Supreme Court had established in *Central Hudson Gas & Electric Corp. v. Public Service Commission*, 447 U.S. 557 (1980):

> For commercial speech to come within [the First Amendment], it at least must concern lawful activity and not be misleading. Next, we ask whether the asserted governmental interest is substantial. If both inquiries yield positive answers, we must determine whether the regulation directly advances the government interest asserted, and whether it is not more extensive than is necessary to serve that interest [447 U.S. at 566, quoted in *American Future Systems*, 688 F.2d at 913].

Applying this test, the court determined that Penn State's prohibition of AFS's demonstration violated AFS's First Amendment rights:

> In the instant situation, there has been no allegation that AFS's commercial speech activities are fraudulent, misleading, or otherwise unlawful. . . .
>
> We, therefore, must first determine whether the university has advanced a substantial government interest to be achieved by the restrictions at issue. The only interest advanced by Penn State for precluding information on the price of

the company's products and the nature of the contract it enters into with purchasers is that asserted in the prior action before this court—that is, its interest in maintaining the proper study atmosphere in its dormitories and in protecting the privacy of the students residing in those facilities. Restrictions on the contents of the demonstration as distinguished from the conduct of the demonstration cannot further these interests. The Supreme Court cases provide ample precedent for the proposition that price information has value. . . . The university does not contend that the mere act of convening a group in the common areas of the residence halls is inimical to the study atmosphere, since its policy permits such group activity. We conclude that Penn State has failed to show a substantial state interest, much less a plausible explanation, for its policy differentiating between the nature of the information contained in the AFS demonstration [688 F.2d at 913].

The court therefore reversed the lower court's entry of summary judgment for Penn State and remanded the case for trial.

Several students were also plaintiffs in *American Future Systems II*. They claimed that the university had violated their First Amendment rights to make purchases in group settings in the residence hall common areas and to host and participate in sales demonstrations in the private rooms of residence halls. The students argued that these rights are not aspects of commercial speech, as AFS's rights are, but are noncommercial speech, as well as freedom of association and due process, rights that deserve higher protection. The appellate court determined that the lower court's record was not sufficiently developed on these points and remanded the students' claims to the lower court for further consideration—thus leaving these arguments unresolved.

In further proceedings, after remand to the trial court, the plaintiff students and American Future Systems, Inc., obtained a preliminary injunction against Penn State's ban on group sales demonstrations in individual students' rooms (*American Future Systems v. Pennsylvania State University*, 553 F. Supp. 1268 (M.D. Pa. 1982)); and subsequently the court entered a permanent injunction against this policy (*American Future Systems v. Pennsylvania State University*, 568 F. Supp. 666 (M.D. Pa. 1983)). The court emphasized the students' own rights to receive information and, from that perspective, did not consider the speech at issue to be subject to the lower standards applicable to commercial speech. On appeal by the university, however, the U.S. Court of Appeals for the Third Circuit disagreed, considering the speech to be commercial and overruling the district court (*American Future Systems, Inc. v. Pennsylvania State University*, 752 F.2d 854 (3d Cir. 1985) (*American Future Systems III*)).

The appellate court decided that a state university's substantial interest as a property owner and educator in preserving dormitories for their intended study-oriented use, and in preventing them from becoming "rent-free merchandise marts," was sufficient to overcome both the commercial vendor's free speech rights to make group sales presentations in students' dormitory rooms and the students' free speech rights to join with others to hear and discuss this information. In applying the *Central Hudson* standards (above), the court found that, although the sales activities involved were lawful, the state university's substantial interests justified a narrowly drawn regulation prohibiting group demonstrations in students' dormitory rooms.

Subsequent to *American Future Systems III,* students on another campus brought a similar issue to court in another case involving American Future Systems' group demonstrations. The subject of this suit was the defendant's regulation prohibiting "private commercial enterprises" from operating on State University of New York (SUNY) campuses or facilities. The defendant had used this resolution to bar AFS from holding group demonstrations in students' dormitory rooms. This case made it to the U.S. Supreme Court in *Board of Trustees of the State University of New York v. Fox,* 492 U.S. 469 (1989). The Court used the occasion to restate the last part of the *Central Hudson* test ("whether [the regulation] is not more extensive than necessary to serve [the government] interest"); as restated, it now requires only that the regulation be "narrowly tailored" to achieve the government's interest, or that there be a "reasonable fit" between the regulation and the government interest. This restatement makes the standard governing commercial speech more lenient, allowing courts to be more deferential to institutional interests when campus commercial activities are at issue. The Court remanded the case to the lower courts for reconsideration in accordance with this more deferential test. The Court also remanded the question whether the university's regulation was unconstitutionally overbroad on its face because it applied to and limited noncommercial speech (that is, more highly protected speech) as well as commercial speech.[26]

The three appellate court opinions in the complex *American Future Systems* litigation, supplemented by the Supreme Court's decision in the *Fox* case, yield considerable guidance for administrators concerned with commercial activity in public institutions. A public institution clearly has considerable authority to place restrictions on outsiders' access to its campus for such purposes. The institution may reasonably restrict the "time, place, and manner" of commercial activity—for instance, by limiting the places where group demonstrations may be held in residence halls, prohibiting the consummation of sales during group demonstrations, or prohibiting commercial solicitations in libraries or classrooms. The institution may also regulate the content of commercial activity to ensure that it is not fraudulent or misleading and does not propose illegal transactions. Other content restrictions—namely, restrictions that directly advance a substantial institutional interest and are narrowly tailored to achieve that interest—are also permissible.

Administrators cannot comfortably assume, however, that this authority is broad enough to validate every regulation of commercial activity. Regulations that censor or sharply curtail all dissemination of commercial information may

---

[26]On remand, the district court dismissed the case as moot (see the discussion of mootness in subsection 2.2.2.2), since the plaintiff students were no longer residing in the dormitory or at the university and AFS had dropped out of the suit (764 F. Supp. 747 (N.D.N.Y. 1991)). The district court also refused to allow the plaintiffs to amend the complaint to add currently enrolled students (148 F.R.D. 474 (N.D.N.Y. 1993)). The appellate court affirmed the trial court's dismissal of the case on mootness grounds in *Fox v. Board of Trustees of State Univ. of New York,* 42 F.3d 135 (2d Cir. 1994).

infringe the First Amendment. *American Future Systems II* is a leading example. (See also *44 Liquormart, Inc. v. Rhode Island,* 517 U.S. 484, 489–95, 514–16 (1996).) Similarly, a regulation prohibiting all in-person, one-on-one contacts with students, even when the representative does not attempt to close a deal or when the student has initiated the contact, may be invalid. In some locations, moreover, the institution's interest in regulating may be sufficiently weak that it cannot justify bans or sharp restrictions at these locations. Possible examples include orderly solicitations in the common areas of student unions or other less private or less studious places on campus; solicitations of an individual student conducted in the student's own room by prior arrangement; and solicitations at the request of student organizations in locations customarily used by such organizations, when such solicitations involve no deceptive practices and propose no illegal or hazardous activity.

It is also clear from U.S. Supreme Court precedents (see, for example, *Consolidated Edison Co. v. Public Service Commission,* 447 U.S. 530 (1980)), that not all speech activity of commercial entrepreneurs is "commercial" speech. Activity whose purpose is not to propose or close a commercial transaction— for example, an educational seminar or a statement on political, economic, or other issues of public interest—may fall within First Amendment protections higher than those accorded commercial speech. Administrators should also be guided by this distinction when regulating, since their authority to limit access to campus and their authority to restrict the content of what is said will be narrower when entrepreneurs wish to engage in "public-interest" rather than "commercial" speech. While this distinction may become blurred when an entrepreneur combines both types of speech in the same activity, there are discussions in both *American Future Systems III* (752 F.2d at 862) and *Fox* (492 U.S. at 481) that will provide guidance in this circumstance.

11.6.4.3. Noncommercial solicitation. As discussed in subsections 11.6.4.1 and 11.6.4.2 above, noncommercial speech is afforded somewhat greater protection under the First Amendment than commercial speech. Consequently, a public institution's authority to regulate political canvassing, charitable solicitations, public opinion polling, petition drives, and other types of noncommercial speech is more limited than its authority to regulate commercial sales and solicitations. (For discussion of the related topic of voter canvassing and registration, see Section 11.4.3 above.)

In *Brush v. Pennsylvania State University,* 414 A.2d 48 (Pa. 1980), students at Penn State challenged university restrictions on canvassing in residence halls. The regulations permitted canvassing (defined as "any attempt to influence student opinion, gain support, or promote a particular cause or interest") by registered individuals in the living areas of a dormitory if the residents of that building had voted in favor of open canvassing. A majority vote to ban canvassing precluded access to living areas by canvassers unless they were specifically invited in advance by a resident. All canvassers remained free, however, to reach students by mail or telephone and to contact residents in the dining halls, lobbies, and conference rooms of each dormitory.

The Supreme Court of Pennsylvania upheld these regulations. It determined that the university had substantial interests in protecting the privacy of its students, preventing breaches of security, and promoting quiet study conditions. The regulations reasonably restricted the time, place, and manner of speech in furtherance of these government interests. Additionally, insofar as the regulations did not eliminate effective alternatives to canvassing inside the living areas, the university had afforded canvassers ample opportunity to reach hall residents.

On the basis of *Brush,* public institutions may apparently implement content-neutral regulations excluding canvassers from the actual living quarters of student residence facilities, at least absent a specific invitation, in advance, to visit a particular student resident. Student residents' participation, by referenda, in canvassing decisions is also apparently permissible if the decisions would still remain content-neutral. (See also Section 11.4.3.) Similar restrictions applied to student lounges, dining halls, student unions, and other less private areas, however, may present more difficult issues concerning the rights of the speakers and of the potential listeners who are not in favor of the restriction, especially if the property at issue is a public forum (see generally Sections 9.5.2 & 9.5.6). No-canvassing rules imposed on student living areas with separate living units, such as married students' garden apartments or townhouses, may also be unconstitutional; in such circumstances the institution's interests in security and study conditions may be weaker, and the students' (or student families') interest in controlling their individual living space is greater. (See generally *Watchtower Bible & Tract Society v. Stratton, Ohio,* 536 U.S. 150 (2002); *Village of Schaumburg v. Citizens for Better Environment,* 444 U.S. 620 (1980).)

Whether rules such as Penn State's would be valid if imposed by the administration without any participation by the student residents was not directly addressed in *Brush.* But given the strong institutional interests in security and in preserving conditions appropriate for study, it is likely that narrowly drawn, content-neutral no-canvassing rules limited to living areas of dormitories and other similar spaces would be constitutional even without approval by student vote. In *Chapman v. Thomas,* 743 F.2d 1056 (4th Cir. 1984), the court upheld such a restriction, calling the dormitory living area a "nonpublic forum" (see Section 9.5.2 of this book) for which the institution may prohibit or selectively regulate access. For the same reason, no-canvassing rules would probably be constitutional, even without student vote, as applied to study halls, library stacks and reading rooms, laboratories, and similar restricted areas.

A later case, *Glover v. Cole,* 762 F.2d 1197 (4th Cir. 1985), provides further support for the validity of such content-neutral restrictions on noncommercial solicitation and also illustrates a different type of regulation that may be constitutionally employed to restrict such activity. The plaintiffs, members of a socialist political party, had sought to solicit donations and sell political publications on campus. The president of West Virginia State College (the defendant in the case) had prohibited this activity by invoking a systemwide policy prohibiting sales and fund-raising activities anywhere on campus by groups that were not sponsored by the students. The court determined that the plaintiffs' activities were "political advocacy" rather than commercial speech and thus highly protected by the First Amendment. Nevertheless, the regulation was valid because it was a content-neutral regulation of the *manner* of speech in a "limited public forum" and met the constitutional standards applicable to such regulations (see Sections 9.5.2 & 9.5.3):

> There has been no direct infringement on Glover's and Measel's expressive activity, simply a prohibition against sales and fund raising on campus. Since the campus area is generally open for all debate and expressive conduct, we do not find that first amendment interests seriously are damaged by the administration's decision to limit the use of its property through uniform application of a sensible "manner" restriction. Plaintiffs' activities may be at the core of the first amendment, but the college has a right to preserve the campus for its intended purpose and to protect college students from the pressures of solicitation. In so ruling, we note that plaintiffs have more than ample alternative channels available to tap the student market for fund raising. The literature itself sets out in plain English requests for donations for the cause. Anyone interested enough to peruse the material learns that the preparation of the materials costs something and that the group is in need of financial (as well as moral and political) support. In addition, if the campus is plaintiffs' key market, they can organize a student group or obtain a student sponsor to raise funds on campus [762 F.2d at 1203].

The features noted by the court are important to the validity of all campus regulations of noncommercial solicitation. First of all, the regulation was narrow—limited to sales and fund-raising—and left other "more than ample" channels for on-campus expression open to outsiders such as the plaintiffs. In addition, the regulation applied neutrally and uniformly to all outside groups, without reference to the beliefs of the group or the viewpoints its members would express on campus.[27] Finally, the university could demonstrate that the regulation was tailored to the protection of significant institutional interests that would be impeded if outsiders could raise funds and sell items on campus. Campus regulation of noncommercial solicitation will not always be supported by such interests. In *Hays County Guardian v. Supple,* 969 F.2d 111 (5th Cir. 1992), for example, Southwest Texas State University had a regulation prohibiting the in-person distribution on campus of free newspapers containing advertisements. The plaintiffs—the publishers of a free newspaper distributed countywide, joined by university students—challenged the regulation's application. The court

---

[27]In more recent First Amendment free speech cases, the U.S. Supreme Court has increasingly relied on this principle of viewpoint neutrality to strike down government regulations that serve to discriminate against individuals or groups on the basis of viewpoint. See, for example, *R.A.V. v. St. Paul* in Section 9.6.2, *Rosenberger v. Rectors & Visitors of University of Virginia* in Section 10.3.2, and *Board of Regents of University of Wisconsin System v. Southworth* in Section 10.1.3. The application of this viewpoint-neutrality principle to regulations limiting the access of outsiders to public education facilities is well illustrated by *Lamb's Chapel v. Center Moriches Union Free School District,* 508 U.S. 384 (1993), and *Good News Club v. Milford Central School,* 533 U.S. 98 (2001).

invalidated the regulation because the university did not demonstrate any significant interest that the regulation was "narrowly tailored" to protect (see generally *Watchtower Bible & Tract,* discussed in subsections 11.4.3 and 11.6.4.1 above).

Sec. 11.7. Community Activities of Faculty Members and Students

Besides being part of the academic community, faculty members and students are also private citizens, whose private lives may involve them in the broader local community. Thus, a postsecondary institution may be concerned not only with its authority over matters arising when the community comes onto the campus, as in Section 11.6, but also with its authority over matters arising when the campus goes out into the community.

Generally, an institution has much less authority over the activities of a student or a faculty member when those activities take place in the community rather than on the campus. The faculty-institution contract (Section 6.1) and the student-institution contract (Section 8.1.3) may have little or no application to the off-campus activities that faculty or students engage in as private citizens. In some cases, moreover, these contracts may affirmatively protect faculty members or students from institutional interference in their private lives. An exception to these general principles may apply for faculty members (or staff members), however, when their outside activities may conflict with their duties and responsibilities to the institution. Many institutions, for example, have conflict of interest policies that may prohibit faculty members from simultaneously holding a position (particularly a full-time or tenured position) at another college or university. Similarly, an exception may apply for students when their outside activities may cause harm to the institution.

In an important 1989 opinion, for example, Maryland's Attorney General ruled that, when an institution can demonstrate that a student's off-campus activities are "detrimental to the interests of the institution," it may have the authority to discipline the student for such misconduct, subject (for public institutions) "to the fundamental constitutional safeguards that apply to all disciplinary actions by educational officials" (74 *Opinions of the Attorney General* 147 (Maryland) (1989), Opinion No. 89-002).[28]

In public institutions, faculty members and students also have constitutional rights that protect them from undue institutional interference in their private lives (see especially Sections 7.5 (faculty) and 9.1.3 (students)). In relation to First Amendment rights, a landmark teacher case, *Pickering v. Board of Education,* 391

---

[28]The cases are collected in Dale Agthe, Annot., "Misconduct of College or University Student Off Campus as Grounds for Expulsion, Suspension, or Other Disciplinary Action," 28 A.L.R.4th 463. For related discussion of the potential criminal liability of students engaging in off-campus protests, see Sheldon R. Shapiro, Annot., "Participation of Students in Demonstration on or Near Campus as Warranting Imposition of Criminal Liability for Breach of Peace, Disorderly Conduct, Trespass, Unlawful Assembly, or Similar Offense," 32 A.L.R.3d 551.

U.S. 563 (1968) (see Section 7.1.1), created substantial protection for teachers against being disciplined for expressing themselves in the community on issues of public concern. A U.S. Court of Appeals case, *Pickings v. Bruce,* 430 F.2d 595 (8th Cir. 1970), established similar protections for students. In *Pickings,* Southern State College had placed SURE (Students United for Rights and Equality), an officially recognized campus group, on probation for writing a letter to a local church criticizing its racial policies. SURE members claimed that the college's action deprived them of their First Amendment rights. In holding for the students, the court made this general statement concerning campus involvement in the community:

> Students and teachers retain their rights to freedom of speech, expression, and association while attending or teaching at a college or university. They have a right to express their views individually or collectively with respect to matters of concern to a college or to a larger community. They are [not] required to limit their expression of views to the campus or to confine their opinions to matters that affect the academic community only. It follows that here the administrators had no right to prohibit SURE from expressing its views on integration to the College View Baptist Church or to impose sanctions on its members or advisors for expressing these views. Such statements may well increase the tensions within the college and between the college and the community, but this fact cannot serve to restrict freedom of expression [430 F.2d at 598, citing *Tinker v. Des Moines Community School Dist.,* 393 U.S. at 508–9].

Similarly, in *Thomas v. Granville Board of Education,* 607 F.2d 1043 (2d Cir. 1979)), the court protected the publication activities of students in the community. This case is discussed in Section 9.1.3 of this book.

Student and faculty activities in the community may occasion not only disputes with the institution, but also disputes with community members and local or state government officials. The cases below provide a variety of examples.

In *Lawrence Bicentennial Commission v. Appleton, Wisconsin,* 409 F. Supp. 1319 (E.D. Wis. 1976), a college student organization sought to rent a local high school gymnasium for a public lecture by Angela Davis, then a college professor and a member of the Communist Party of the United States. The school board refused to rent the gym for this purpose, citing a regulation prohibiting the use of school facilities by outsiders for partisan political purposes. The student organization then filed suit against the city, the school district, and the members of the board of education, challenging the defendants' refusal to rent the gymnasium. The federal district court held that the refusal was an unconstitutional content-based restriction on speech and issued a preliminary injunction ordering the defendants to rent the facilities to the student organization.

In *Woodbridge Terrace Associates v. Lake,* a faculty member's service as an expert witness for a county housing coalition resulted in a defamation claim against the professor by the owner of an apartment complex. The housing coalition's study of racial steering in apartment rentals had led to litigation against the apartment complex. The federal district court ruled that the professor's expert witness report was protected from defamation claims and dismissed those charges as well as additional charges that the professor had unlawfully interfered with the apartment complex's operations (R. Rudolph, "Judge Rejects Suit Against Prof Who Found Racial Bias in Apartment Rentals," *Newark Star Ledger*, September 19, 1989, at 22).

In *Little v. City of North Miami*, 805 F.2d 962 (11th Cir. 1986), a University of Florida law school professor had represented environmental groups, on a *pro bono* basis, in litigation against the state of Florida and the city of North Miami. The City Council of North Miami passed a resolution censuring the professor for "improper use of public funds to represent private parties in litigation against the State and against the interests of the City of North Miami" (805 F.2d at 964). Copies of the resolution were sent to the president, regents, law school dean, Dade County legislators, and others, and an investigation of Little's activities ensued. Little sued the city under Section 1983 (see Section 3.5 of this book), claiming First Amendment and due process violations, and asserting that his reputation and his relationship with the university had been damaged and that he had suffered emotional distress. After the trial court dismissed all the constitutional claims, the appellate court reversed and held that the city council's actions violated Little's First Amendment rights: "[A] municipality . . . may not retaliate against an individual because of that person's legitimate use of the courts" (805 F.2d at 968). The court also permitted Little's due process claim to go forward: "We see no reason why an attorney is not entitled to property or liberty interests in his or her business (professional) reputation/goodwill when the same rights have been extended to other businesses" (805 F.2d at 969).

Another case concerning *pro bono* legal representation, *Southern Christian Leadership Conference v. Supreme Court*, 252 F.3d 781 (5th Cir. 2001), *affirming* 61 F. Supp. 2d 499 (E.D. La. 1999), involved state court rules restricting law school legal clinics' representation of low-income clients. Students and faculty supervisors in an environmental law clinic at Tulane University's law school had represented local citizens and community associations that sought to prevent a chemical company from locating near poor, largely minority, neighborhoods. The chemical company eventually located in another state, to the consternation of local business and political leaders and state officials concerned about economic development. Business groups then persuaded the Louisiana Supreme Court to investigate the situation and review its student practice rules. The supreme court amended the rules, tightening the low-income requirements that individuals and associations must meet to be eligible for clinic services, and prohibiting students from representing any clients that they or other clinic-affiliated individuals had solicited. Students, faculty members, and various community organizations sued the court, claiming that the amended rule (Rule XX) violated their constitutional rights of free speech and association—in particular by "burdening their ability to associate and advocate for expression of collective views." The federal district court and the federal appellate court each rejected these arguments and upheld both of the restrictions on student representation. According to the appellate court, "Rather than stamping out or suppressing private speech, the [Louisiana Supreme Court]—the highest judicial body in Louisiana exercising its undisputed power and responsibility—had reduced this support by an across-the-board, wholly prospective and viewpoint-neutral general rule" (252 F.3d at 795). In supporting its conclusion, the federal appellate court noted that the amended Rule XX "imposes no restrictions on the kind of representations the clinics can engage in or on the arguments that can be made on behalf of a clinic client"; that the Rule restricted only the representation of clients by students, and did not restrict the faculty clinic supervisors who were members of the state bar; and that any allegations of retaliation against the Tulane clinic for its involvement in the chemical plant case, or of other improper political motivations, would concern only the actions of the business groups and state officials and could not be attributed to the state supreme court. Had any of those circumstances been involved in the plaintiff's case, other First Amendment issues could have been present that could have changed the appellate court's reasoning, and perhaps its result.

Outside activities of public college and university employees may also occasion disputes under state laws or regulations that restrict certain outside activities of public employees. Conflict of interest regulations provide one example (see above, this Section, and see also Section 15.4.7). Another example is provided by state regulations or constitutional provisions that prohibit state employees, or faculty members specifically, from serving concurrently in the state legislature. (See, for example, *State ex rel. Spire v. Conway,* 472 N.W.2d 403 (Neb. 1991); but see 26 *Opinions of the Attorney General* (Kansas) (March 2, 1992), Opinion No. 92-31).) Laws that prohibit state employees from serving as advocates before state agencies may also catch faculty or staff in their web, although a New Jersey court extricated a faculty member from the provisions of such a law in the case of *In re Determination of Executive Commission on Ethical Standards,* 561 A.2d 542 (N.J. 1989), discussed in Section 12.5.1.

The case of *Hoover v. Morales,* 164 F.3d 221 (5th Cir. 1998), provides a highly instructive illustration of a situation where state law limited certain outside activities of faculty members. Both a Texas state law and a policy of Texas A&M University were at issue in the case. Both the law and the policy prohibited faculty members from serving as consultants or expert witnesses against the state, the reason being that such activity would put the faculty member in conflict with the interests of the state that employs him or her. The law and policy were challenged by the Texas Faculty Association, as well as by various professors who had been retained or who had volunteered *pro bono* to testify against the state in various cases. One plaintiff, for instance, was serving as an expert witness for various tobacco companies in the state's lawsuit against them; and another plaintiff served as *pro bono* counsel to a neighborhood association opposing the issuance of a state permit to construct an incinerator. The plaintiffs argued that the law and policy violated their free speech rights under the First Amendment.

The court first determined that the speech prohibited by the law and the policy did not fall under the lesser protections accorded commercial speech. Rather, much of the speech that the law and policy suppressed could be considered "public concern" speech, subject to the *Pickering* analysis applicable to the speech of public employees and enjoying greater protection (see Section 7.1.1).

Testimony on the health consequences of cigarette smoking, for instance, would involve matters of "public concern." Accordingly, since the law and policy "can be expected to curtail speech on a wide variety of matters of public concern," the state and the university bore a heavy burden of justifying the full range of these restrictions. The court concluded that the defendants could not do so. While the state's interest in promoting the efficiency of the public services it provides (as articulated in *Pickering*) could serve to justify some applications of the law and policy, the law and policy could also be used to silence employees whose testimony would not disrupt the state's interests. "[T]he notion that the State may silence the testimony of State employees simply because that testimony is contrary to the interests of the State in litigation or otherwise, is antithetical to the protection extended by the First Amendment" (164 F.3d at 226). The law and the policy, therefore, were unconstitutionally overbroad.

In addition, the court also held that the law and policy at issue were unconstitutional as content-based restrictions on free speech. Testimony on behalf of the state would be permitted, for instance, while only testimony against the state would be prohibited. To support this analysis, the court quoted *Regan v. Time, Inc.,* 468 U.S. 641, 648–49 (1984), in which the U.S. Supreme Court stated that "regulations which permit the Government to discriminate on the basis of the content of the message cannot be tolerated under the First Amendment."[29]

Caution must be exercised in interpreting the *Hoover* case and applying it to other situations. The opinion does not require that institutions refrain from any limitation whatsoever on the consultant and expert witness activities of their faculty members. Many content-neutral limitations would be permissible under *Hoover.* The institution could limit outside faculty activities that created a conflict of interest for the faculty member (see Section 15.4.7). Some content-based limitations would also be permissible, pursuant to narrowly drafted policies, when the university can demonstrate that particular consulting or expert witness activities would sufficiently disrupt state interests to prevail under the *Pickering/Connick* balancing test. Public institutions' constitutional leeway in using such "disruption" rationales was apparently expanded by the U.S. Supreme Court's decision in *Waters v. Churchill,* 511 U.S. 661 (1994) (see Sections 7.1.1 & 7.5.2 of this book). (For guidance, see Diane Krejsa, "*Hoover v. Morales:* Commentary and Analysis," in *Synfax Weekly Report,* February 22, 1999, at 819–21.)

In yet another variant of campus-community conflict, community members on occasion have sued a college because it restricted faculty members or students from interacting with the community in certain ways. For example, in *Pyeatte v. Board of Regents of the University of Oklahoma,* 102 F. Supp. 407 (W.D. Okla. 1951), *affirmed per curiam,* 342 U.S. 936 (1952), a group of boarding house owners in Norman, Oklahoma (site of the University of Oklahoma), sued the state board of regents when it promulgated a rule requiring all unmarried

---

[29]It would be more precise to articulate the Texas law and policy's restrictions as "viewpoint based" rather than "content based." The flaw would then be one of "viewpoint discrimination," and the more appropriate U.S. Supreme Court cases to cite would be those listed in footnote 27 above.

students to live in university dormitories if space was available. The plaintiffs asserted that the rule limited their right to contract with the university to provide student housing and thus violated the Fourteenth Amendment's equal protection clause. The courts viewed the rule as clearly within the regents' power to pass for the benefit of the university's students.

Selected Annotated Bibliography

Sec. 11.1 (General Principles)

Reynolds, Osborne M. *Handbook of Local Government Law* (West, 1982, plus periodic pocket part). A comprehensive, well-documented review of local government law. Divided into twenty-two chapters, including "Limits on State Control of Municipalities," "Relationship of Municipalities to Federal Government," "Powers of Municipalities," "Finances of Local Government," "Local Control of the Use of Property," and "Local Regulation of Trade, Business, and Other Enterprises."

Sec. 11.2 (Zoning and Land Use Regulation)

Frug, Jerry. "Surveying Law and Borders: The Geography of Community," 48 *Stan. L. Rev.* 1047 (1996). Criticizes current zoning policy that isolates individuals by wealth and education, and perpetuates ghettos, segregation, and urban isolation. This policy tends to discourage interaction among individuals of different races, opinions, values, and cultures.

Juergensmeyer, Julian C., & Roberts, Thomas E. *Land Use Planning and Development Regulation Law* (West, 2003). A thorough survey of land use law. Discusses zoning, the planning process, building and housing codes, and other land use issues. Includes discussion of constitutional limitations on land use law, and the interplay between land use regulation and environmental regulation.

Pearlman, Kenneth. "Zoning and the First Amendment," 16 *Urb. Law.* 217 (1984). Examines the power of local government to zone land and reviews U.S. Supreme Court decisions on zoning, particularly with regard to commercial activity.

"Special Project: The Private Use of Public Power: The Private University and the Power of Eminent Domain," 27 *Vanderbilt L. Rev.* 681 (1974). A lengthy study of eminent domain as a land use planning technique to benefit private universities. Emphasis is on the use of eminent domain in conjunction with federal urban renewal programs. A case study involving Nashville, Tennessee, is included.

Tracy, JoAnn. "Comment: Single-Family Zoning Ordinances: The Constitutionality of Suburban Barriers Against Nontraditional Households," 31 *St. Louis U. L.J.* 1023 (1987). Reviews decisions of the Supreme Court and other courts on the definition of "family" for zoning purposes. Discusses Fourteenth Amendment implications of restrictions on relationships between residents, and suggests alternatives to marriage, blood, or adoption for limiting the number of occupants of single-family homes.

Sec. 11.3 (Local Government Taxation)

Ginsberg, William R. "The Real Property Tax Exemption of Nonprofit Organizations: A Perspective," 53 *Temple L.Q.* 291 (1980). An overview of the issues involved in granting tax-exempt status to nonprofit organizations. Discusses the judicial and statutory tests used to determine exempt status, the theoretical foundations for property tax exemption, and the problems unique to educational and religious uses of property. Includes numerous citations to state constitutional and statutory provisions on property tax exemption.

See Colombo entry in Selected Annotated Bibliography for Chapter 13, Section 13.3.

Sec. 11.4 (Student Voting in the Community)

Ostrow, Ashira Pelman. Note, "Dual Resident Voting: Traditional Disenfranchisement and Prospects for Change," 102 *Columbia L. Rev.* 1954 (2002). Argues that prohibiting individuals with two residences from voting in local elections in both localities violates the equal protection clause. Discusses a mechanism for ensuring that the rights of property owners and local residents are protected.

Sec. 11.5 (Relations with Local Police)

Bickel, Robert. "The Relationship Between the University and Local Law Enforcement Agencies in Their Response to the Problem of Drug Abuse on the Campus," in D. Parker Young (ed.), *Higher Education: The Law and Campus Issues* (Institute of Higher Education, University of Georgia, 1973), 17–27. A practical discussion of the general principles of search and seizure, double jeopardy, and confidentiality in the campus drug abuse context; also discusses the necessity of administrators' having the advice of counsel.

Cowen, Lindsay. "The Campus and the Community: Problems of Dual Jurisdiction," in D. Parker Young (ed.), *Proceedings of a Conference on Higher Education: The Law and Student Protest* (Institute of Higher Education, University of Georgia, 1970), 28–32. A brief discussion of the policy considerations governing the division of authority between the institution and local law enforcement agencies.

Ferdico, John N. *Criminal Procedure for the Criminal Justice Professional* (9th ed., West, 2004). An introductory text on police procedures and criminal court procedure, including arrests, searches, confessions, and identifications, with special emphasis on U.S. Supreme Court cases.

Kalaidjian, Ed. "Problems of Dual Jurisdiction of Campus and Community," in G. Holmes (ed.), *Student Protest and the Law* (Institute of Continuing Legal Education, University of Michigan, 1969), 131–48. Addresses issues arising out of concurrent criminal and disciplinary proceedings and police entry onto campus.

Note, "Privacy Protection Act of 1980: Curbing Unrestricted Third-Party Searches in the Wake of *Zurcher v. Stanford Daily*," 14 *U. Mich. J.L. Reform* 519 (1981). Reviews the constitutional law implications of the *Zurcher* case and analyzes the various provisions of the Act passed by Congress in response to *Zurcher*.

Sklansky, David. "The Private Police," 46 *UCLA L. Rev.* 1165 (1999). Examines the changing dynamics between public and private police work occasioned by the growth of "private policing" and the phenomenon of "police privatization." Indicates that the number of persons doing private police work is now greater than the number doing police work for local, state, and federal governments. Explores the challenges these trends create for the law, and suggests a reexamination of the state action doctrine and public/private distinction as it applies to police and security functions.

Sec. 11.6 (Community Access to the College's Campus)

"Comment: The University and the Public: The Right of Access by Nonstudents to University Property," 54 *Cal. L. Rev.* 132 (1966). Discusses the appropriateness and constitutionality of using state trespass laws to limit the public's access to state university and college campuses. California's criminal trespass law designed for state colleges and universities (Cal. Penal Code § 602–7 (West 1965), since amended and recodified as Cal. Penal Code § 626.6 (West 1988)) is highlighted.

Finkin, Matthew. "On 'Institutional' Academic Freedom," 61 *Tex. L. Rev.* 817 (1983). Considers the collapse of the distinction between institutional autonomy and academic freedom and applies this discussion to *State v. Schmid,* the *Princeton University* case. Further described in Finkin entry in Selected Annotated Bibliography for Chapter 1, Section 1.2.

Ugland, Erik. "Hawkers, Thieves and Lonely Pamphleteers: Distributing Publications in the University Marketplace," 20 *J. Coll. & Univ. Law* 935 (1996). Analyzes First Amendment issues that arise when college and university administrators seek to restrict distribution of, and access to, publications on campus. Covers full range of distribution activities and types of publications, and includes consideration of the distribution activities of off-campus publishers from small, alternative press efforts to large major newspapers. Contains a special section on newspaper theft on campus. Addresses educational policy issues, as well as legal issues, and offers suggestions for administrators.

Sec. 11.7 (Community Activities of Faculty Members and Students)

McKay, R. "The Student as Private Citizen," 45 *Denver L.J.* 558 (1968). With three responding commentaries by other authors, provides a legal and policy overview of students' status as private citizens of the larger community.

12

The College and
the State Government

Sec. 12.1. Overview

Unlike the federal government (see Section 13.1) and local governments (Section 11.1), state governments have general rather than limited powers and can claim all power that is not denied them by the federal Constitution or their own state constitutions, or that has not been preempted by federal law. Thus, the states have the greatest reservoir of legal authority over postsecondary education, although the extent to which this source is tapped varies substantially from state to state.

In states that do assert substantial authority over postsecondary education, questions may arise about the division of authority between the legislative and the executive branches. In *Inter-Faculty Organization v. Carlson,* 478 N.W.2d 192 (Minn. 1991), for example, the Minnesota Supreme Court invalidated a governor's line item vetoes of certain expenditure estimates in the legislature's higher education funding bill, because the action went beyond the governor's veto authority, which extended only to identifiable amounts dedicated to specific purposes. Similar questions may concern the division of authority among other state boards or officials that have functions regarding higher education (see Section 12.2 below).

Questions may also be raised about the state's legal authority, in relation to the federal government's, under federal spending or regulatory programs. In *Shapp v. Sloan,* 391 A.2d 595 (Pa. 1978), for instance, the specific questions were (1) whether, under Pennsylvania state law, the state legislature or the governor was legally entrusted with control over federal funds made available to the state; and (2) whether, under federal law, state legislative control of federal funds was consistent with the supremacy clause of the U.S. Constitution and the provisions of the funding statutes. In a lengthy opinion addressing an array of legal complexities, the Pennsylvania Supreme Court held that the legislature had control of the federal funds under state law and that such control had not been exercised inconsistently with federal law.

The states' functions in matters concerning postsecondary education include operating public systems, regulating and funding private institutions and programs, statewide planning and coordinating, supporting assessment and accountability initiatives, and providing scholarships and other financial aid for students (see, for example, Sections 1.6.3 & 8.3.7). These functions are performed through myriad agencies, such as boards of regents; departments of education or higher education; statewide planning or coordinating boards; institutional licensure boards or commissions; construction financing authorities; and state approval agencies (SAAs) that operate under contract to the federal Veterans Administration to approve courses for which veterans' benefits may be expended. In addition, various professional and occupational licensure boards indirectly regulate postsecondary education by evaluating programs of study and establishing educational prerequisites for taking licensure examinations.[1]

Various other state agencies whose primary function is not education—such as workers' compensation boards, labor relations boards, ethics boards, civil rights enforcement agencies, and environmental quality agencies—may also regulate postsecondary education as part of a broader class of covered institutions, corporations, or government agencies (see, for example, Sections 12.5.2–12.5.5 below). And in some circumstances, states may regulate some particular aspect of postsecondary education through the processes of the criminal law rather than through state regulatory agencies. Various examples of such legislation are discussed in Section 12.5.1 below.

In addition, states exert authority or influence over postsecondary institutions' own borrowing and financing activities. For instance, states may facilitate institutions' borrowing for capital development projects by issuing tax-exempt government bonds. In Virginia, for example, under the Education Facilities Authority Act (Va. Code §§ 23–30.39 et seq.; see also Va. Const. Art. VIII, § 11), the Virginia College Building Authority issues revenue bonds to finance construction projects for nonprofit higher education institutions in the state.[2] States may also influence institutional financing by regulating charitable solicitations by institutions and their fund-raising firms (see generally New York University School of Law, Program on Philanthropy and the Law, "Fundraising into the 1990s: State Regulation of Charitable Solicitation After *Riley*," 24 *U.S.F. L. Rev.* 571 (1990)). Moreover, a state can either encourage or deter various financial activities (and affect institutions' after-tax bottom line) through its system of taxation. Private institutions, or institutional property and activities within the

---

[1]Under federal law (20 U.S.C. § 1099a(a)), each state, acting through one or more of the agencies and boards listed in this paragraph, must assist the U.S. Secretary of Education with a program to ensure the "integrity" of federal student aid programs.

[2]In *Virginia College Building Authority v. Barry Lynn*, 538 S.E.2d 682 (Va. 2000), the Virginia Supreme Court construed and applied the Virginia statute and upheld the issuance of bonds to finance building projects of a private religious university. Regarding the church-state issues implicated in such arrangements, see generally Section 1.6.3 of this book.

state, usually are presumed subject to taxation under the state's various tax statutes unless a specific statutory or constitutional provision grants an exemption. *In re Middlebury College Sales and Use Tax*, 400 A.2d 965 (Vt. 1979), is illustrative. Although the Vermont statute granted general tax-exempt status to private institutions meeting federal standards for tax exemption under the Internal Revenue Code (see Section 13.3.2 of this book), the statute contained an exception for institutional "activities which are mainly commercial enterprises." Middlebury College operated a golf course and a skiing complex, the facilities of which were used for its physical education program and other college purposes. The facilities were also open to the public upon payment of rates comparable to those charged by commercial establishments. When the state sought to tax the college's purchases of equipment and supplies for the facilities, the college claimed that its purchases were tax exempt under the Vermont statute. The court rejected Middlebury's claim, holding that the college had failed to meet its burden of proving that the golfing and skiing activities were not "mainly commercial enterprises." (For other examples of state tax laws applied to higher educational institutions, see Sections 3.6.3 and 15.3.4.2; and see also *Wheaton College v. Department of Revenue*, 508 N.E.2d 1136 (Ill. App. Ct. 1987), discussed in Section 11.3.2.)

In addition to performing these planning, regulatory, and fiscal functions through their agencies and boards, the states are also the source of eminent domain (condemnation) powers by which private property may be taken for public use. The scope of these powers, and the extent of compensation required for particular takings, may be at issue either when the state seeks to take land owned by a private postsecondary institution or when a state postsecondary institution or board seeks to take land owned by a private party. In *Curators of the University of Missouri v. Brown*, 809 S.W.2d 64 (Mo. Ct. App. 1991), for instance, the university successfully brought a condemnation action to obtain Brown's land to use as a parking lot for a Scholars' Center that operated as part of the university but was privately owned. On the other hand, in *Regents of University of Minnesota v. Chicago and North Western Transportation Co.*, 552 N.W.2d 578 (Minn. App. 1996), the university was not successful in a condemnation action. The regents challenged the trial court's dismissal of its petition to acquire a thirty-acre tract of land, owned by the defendant railway company, located near the university's East Bank campus. The appellate court affirmed the trial court's ruling that the university had not shown the requisite necessity for taking the property by means of eminent domain. According to the appellate court:

> First, the record indicates that the University has not included this property on its master plan for its anticipated development of the Twin Cities campus. Second, although the University claims to have at least three potential uses for the land, the uses are mutually exclusive, and the Board of Regents has not yet approved a single project for the property. Finally, because of soil contamination problems, it is undisputed that the University could not currently use the property for any of its proposed uses. The parties have not yet agreed on a remediation plan; decontamination of the property will require from approximately two to seven years to complete [552 N.W.2d at 580].

Thus, the university's purposes were speculative, and while the university "may well have the right to purchase this property, . . . it cannot acquire it for speculative future use (stockpiling) by condemnation."

Finally, the states, through their court systems, are the source of the common law (see Section 1.4.2.4) that provides the basis for the legal relationships between institutions and their students, faculties, and staff, and also provides general legal context for many of the transactions and disputes in which institutions may become involved. Common law contract principles, for example, may constrain an institution's freedom to terminate the employment of its personnel (see Section 4.3); tort law principles may shape the institution's responsibilities for its students' safety and well-being (see Sections 3.3.2.1–3.3.2.6); and contract law, tort law, and property law principles may guide the institution's business relationships with outside parties (see Sections 15.2, 15.3, & 15.4.2).

Given the considerable, and growing, state involvement in the affairs of higher educational institutions that is suggested by this discussion and is illustrated by Sections 12.2 through 12.5 below, postsecondary administrators have increasingly bumped against state agencies and state legal requirements in the course of their daily institutional duties. Administrators should therefore stay abreast of pertinent state agency processes, state programs, and state legal requirements affecting the operations of their institutions, and also of the oversight activities and legislative initiatives of the state legislature's education committees. Administrators should also encourage their legal counsel or their government relations office to monitor the growing body of state statutory law and administrative regulations, and to keep key institutional personnel apprised of developments that may potentially impact on the institution. Legal counsel should also be prepared to obtain the services of specialized legal experts when addressing certain complex matters of state law, such as the issuance of bonds.

In addition, presidents, key administrators, and legal counsel (especially for public institutions) should follow, and be prepared to participate in, the vigorous and wide-ranging debates on higher education policy that are now occurring in various states. Prime topics concern structural changes in state governance of higher education (see generally Section 1.3.3), state financing of higher education, and strategies for serving underserved population groups. (For representative commentary, see Ronald G. Ehrenberg & Michael J. Rizzo, "Financial Forces and the Future of American Higher Education," *Academe*, July–August 2004, 28; Peter Schmidt, "A Public Vision for Public Colleges," *Chron. Higher Educ.*, June 11, 2004, A16; Judd Slivka, "University Aims for 2-Tier System," *Arizona Republic*, May 23, 2004; Amy Argetsinger, "3 Public Universities Try to Ease Va.'s Reins," *Washington Post*, January 12, 2004, p. B1; Sara Hebel "To Ease Budget Crunch, Public Universities Seek Freedom from State Concerns," *Chron. Higher Educ.*, June 20, 2003, A19.)

Sec. 12.2. State Provision of Public Postsecondary Education

12.2.1. Overview. Public postsecondary education systems vary in type and organization from state to state. Such systems may be established by the

state constitution, by legislative acts, or by a combination of the two, and may encompass a variety of institutions—from the large state university to smaller state colleges or teachers colleges, to community colleges, technical schools, and vocational schools.

Every state has at least one designated body that bears statewide responsibility for at least some aspects of its public postsecondary system.[3] These bodies are known by such titles as Board of Higher Education, Commission on Higher Education, Board of Regents, Regents, Board of Educational Finance, or Board of Governors. Most such boards are involved in some phase of planning, program review and approval, and budget development for the institutions under their control or within their sphere of influence. Other responsibilities—such as the development of databases and management information systems or the establishment of new degree-granting institutions—might also be imposed. Depending on their functions, boards are classifiable into two groups: governing and coordinating. Governing boards are legally responsible for the management and operation of the institutions under their control. Coordinating boards have the lesser responsibilities that their name implies. Most governing boards work directly with the institutions for which they are responsible. Coordinating boards may or may not do so. Although community colleges are closely tied to their locales, most come within the jurisdiction of some state board or agency.

The legal status of the institutions in the public postsecondary system varies from state to state and may vary as well from institution to institution within the same state. Typically, institutions established directly by a state constitution have more authority than institutions established by statute and, correspondingly, have more autonomy from the state governing board and the state legislature. In dealing with problems of legal authority, therefore, one must distinguish between "statutory" and "constitutional" institutions and, within these basic categories, carefully examine the terms of the provisions granting authority to each particular institution. (See Valerie L. Brown, "A Comparative Analysis of College Autonomy in Selected States," 60 *West's Educ. Law Rptr.* 299 (1990).)

State constitutional and statutory provisions may also grant certain authority over institutions to the state governing board or some other state agency or official. It is thus also important to examine the terms of any such provisions that are part of the law of the particular state. The relevant statutes and constitutional clauses do not always project clear answers, however, to the questions that may arise concerning the division of authority among the individual institution, the statewide governing or coordinating body, the legislature, the governor, and other state agencies (such as a civil service commission or a budget office) or officials (such as a commissioner of education). Because of the uncertainties, courts often have had to determine who holds the ultimate authority to make various critical decisions regarding public postsecondary education.

---

[3]The information in this paragraph is drawn heavily from Richard M. Millard, *State Boards of Higher Education,* ERIC Higher Education Research Report no. 4 (American Association for Higher Education, 1976).

Disputes over the division of authority among the state, a statewide govern-ing or coordinating body, the legislature, or other entities typically arise in one of two contexts: the creation or dissolution of an institution, and the manage-ment and control of the affairs of a public institution. Although public institu-tions created by a state constitution, such as the flagship universities of California and Michigan, can be dissolved only by an amendment to the state constitution and are insulated from legislative control because of their consti-tutional status, public institutions created by legislative action (a statute) can also be dissolved by the legislature and are subject to legislative control. In some states, however, the allocation of authority is less clear. For example, in South Dakota, the state constitution created the statewide governing board for public colleges and universities (the board of regents), but the state colleges and uni-versities were created by statute. In *Kanaly v. State of South Dakota,* 368 N.W.2d 819 (S.D. 1985), taxpayers challenged the state legislature's decision to close the University of South Dakota-Springfield and transfer its campus and facilities to the state prison system. The state's supreme court ruled that the decision to change the use of these assets was clearly within the legislature's power. How-ever, under the terms of a perpetual trust the legislature had established to fund state universities, the prison system had to reimburse the trust for the value of the land and buildings.

The court distinguished between the power to manage and control a state college (given by the state constitution to the board of regents) and the "power of the purse" (a legislative power). The state constitution, said the court, did not create the board of regents as "a fourth branch of government independent of any legislative policies." Previous decisions by the South Dakota Supreme Court had established that the board of regents did not have the power to change the character of an institution, to determine state educational policy, or to appropriate funding for the institutions (368 N.W.2d at 825). "The legislature has the power to create schools, to fund them as it has the power of the purse, and to establish state educational policy and this necessarily includes the power to close a school if efficiency and economy so direct" (368 N.W.2d at 825). Transferring the property upon which the university was located to the state prison system was not the same, said the court, as transferring control of the institution itself from the regents to the prison system.

In situations where a state governing or coordinating board has the author-ity to establish or dissolve a college, a court's powers to review the criteria by which such a decision is made are limited. For example, a group of citizens formed a nonprofit corporation and asked the State of Missouri to approve the corporation's application to form a community college. In *State ex rel. Lake of the Ozarks Community College Steering Committee v. Coordinating Board for Higher Education,* 802 S.W.2d 533 (Mo. Ct. App. 1991), the steering committee of the corporation sued the state coordinating board for rejecting its application. The court dismissed the lawsuit as moot because the board had considered the petition and, having rejected it, had acted within its authority. The court noted that it was not proper in this instance for a court to define the standards by which the board evaluated the application.

Litigated issues related to the management and control of colleges and universities are numerous. They include academic matters, such as the registration of doctoral programs (see *Moore v. Board of Regents of the University of the State of New York,* discussed in Section 12.2.2 below), as well as resource allocation matters, such as the approval of budget amendments and appropriation of funds for the university system (see *Board of Regents of Higher Education v. Judge,* 543 P.2d 1323 (Mont. 1975)).

Part of the state's power to provide postsecondary education is the power to appoint trustees or regents. When a governor and a state legislature are in conflict, such appointments may be adversely affected. In *Tucker v. Watkins,* 737 So. 2d 443 (Ala. 1999), for example, two Alabama State University trustees had been appointed by the former governor of Alabama, but had not been confirmed by the state senate before it recessed. The subsequent governor removed the trustees from their positions and appointed two other trustees in their place. The state supreme court upheld the ruling of a state trial court that the removal was contrary to state law, and that only the state senate could revoke the appointments. In a similar case regarding the appointment of trustees to the board of Auburn University, the state supreme court ruled that trustees appointed by a former governor could remain on the board until their replacements were approved by the state senate (*James v. Langford,* 695 So. 2d 1164 (Ala. 1997)).

12.2.2. Statutorily based institutions.

A public institution established by state statute is usually characterized, for legal purposes, by terms such as "state agency," "public corporation," or state "political subdivision." Such institutions, particularly institutions considered "state agencies," are often subject to an array of state legislation applicable to state-created entities. A state agency, for example, is usually subject to the state's administrative procedure act and other requirements of state administrative law. State agencies, and sometimes other statutory institutions, may also be able to assert the legal defenses available to the state, such as sovereign immunity. In *Board of Trustees of Howard Community College v. John K. Ruff, Inc.,* 366 A.2d 360 (Md. 1976), for instance, the court's holding that the board of a regional community college was a state agency enabled the board to assert sovereign immunity as a defense against a suit for breach of contract.

The case of *Moore v. Board of Regents of the University of the State of New York,* 390 N.Y.S.2d 582 (N.Y. Sup. Ct. 1977), *affirmed,* 397 N.Y.S.2d 449 (N.Y. App. Div. 1977), *affirmed,* 407 N.Y.S.2d 452 (N.Y. 1978), illustrates the problem of dividing authority between a statutory institution and other entities claiming some authority over it. The trustees and chancellor of the State University of New York (SUNY), together with several professors and doctoral students in the affected departments, sought a declaratory judgment that the university trustees were responsible under the law for providing the standards and regulations for the organization and operation of university programs, courses, and curricula in accordance with the state's master plan. The defendants were the state board of regents and the state commissioner of education. The case concerned the commissioner's deregistration of the doctoral programs in history and English at the State University of New York at Albany. In statements for the news media, each of the opposing litigants foresaw an ominous impact from a decision for the other side: if the commissioner and the state board won, the institution would continue to be subjected to "unprecedented intervention"; if the trustees won, the university would be placed beyond public accountability (*Chron. Higher Educ.*, March 8, 1976, A3).

After analyzing the state's constitution, education law, and administrative regulations, the trial court concluded that the commissioner, acting for the board of regents, which was established by the state constitution, had the authority to make the decision. In reaching this conclusion, the court noted that the New York constitution had created the board of regents with jurisdiction over all institutions of higher education in the state. The regents were given the power to charter colleges and universities, and had, in fact, registered programs within such colleges since 1787. Furthermore, said the court, the legislature created the State University of New York in 1948 as a corporation within the State Education Department, and made it subject to the authority of the board of regents. A 1961 statute gave the Board of Trustees of the State University of New York the authority to administer the university's internal affairs, but included no language to suggest that SUNY was not "subject to the same requirements imposed by the regents and commissioner on private institutions of higher education in this state" (390 N.Y.S.2d at 586).

This decision was affirmed by the Appellate Division of the New York Supreme Court (an intermediate appellate court) and subsequently by the New York Court of Appeals. In affirming, however, the New York Court of Appeals cautioned that the broad "policy-making" and "rule-making" power of the regents "is not unbridled and is not an all-encompassing power permitting the regents' intervention in the day-to-day operations of the institutions of higher education in New York."

A case involving Texas A&M University illustrates the reach of regulation by the state over a statutory university. Texas A&M entered an affiliation agreement with South Texas College of Law, a private institution, in which the two institutions agreed that A&M would appoint some of the law college's board of directors, would appoint a member of the law college's admissions committee, and would have an active role in tenure decisions and in the hiring of the law college's dean and president. Texas A&M had no law school, and had not received permission from the Texas Higher Education Coordinating Board to create one. The coordinating board learned of this agreement and informed both institutions that the agreement could not be implemented until the board had added law to A&M's academic mission. Both institutions sought a declaratory judgment from a state court concerning the validity of the affiliation agreement.

In *South Texas College of Law v. Texas Higher Education Coordinating Board*, 40 S.W.3d 130 (Tex. App. 2000), a state appellate court affirmed the trial court's award of summary judgment to the coordinating board. The court held that the agreement would extend A&M's academic programs, and because the coordinating board had not approved either a law school or a program in law for

A&M, the affiliation agreement infringed upon the coordinating board's statutory authority to determine which degree programs a public university should offer. The colleges appealed to the Texas Supreme Court, which refused to hear the case.

Although state law defines the relationship between statutorily based institutions and relevant state agencies, clashes between these institutions and the state may also raise issues of federal law. Furthermore, third parties may also occasionally be able to use federal civil rights law to intervene in disputes between state boards and statutorily based institutions. For example, in *United States v. State of Alabama,* 791 F.2d 1450 (11th Cir. 1986), Alabama State University and several faculty, students, and citizens suing as individuals attempted to use Section 1983 (see Section 3.5 of this book) and Title VI (see Section 13.5.2 of this book) to reverse the state board of education's decertification of teacher education programs at that institution. The plaintiffs claimed that the state board's actions were in retaliation for the plaintiffs' involvement in desegregation litigation against the board. Although the appellate court ruled that the institution had no standing to sue the state board (because the university was a creation of the state), the individual plaintiffs could proceed against individual members of the board of education under federal civil rights law.

(For a discussion of an apparent trend toward decentralizing trustee authority to the local college level, see Peter Schmidt, "Weakening the Grip of Multicampus Boards," *Chron. Higher Educ.,* March 23, 2001, A24.)

12.2.3. *Constitutionally based institutions.* A public institution established by the state's constitution is usually characterized, for legal purposes, as a "public trust," an "autonomous university," a "constitutional university," or a "constitutional body corporate." Such institutions enjoy considerable freedom from state legislative control and generally are not subject to state administrative law. Such institutions also may not be able to assert all the defenses to suit that the state may assert. If the institution is considered a public trust, its trustees must fulfill the special fiduciary duties of public trustees and administer the trust for the educational benefit of the public.

The case of *Regents of the University of Michigan v. State of Michigan,* 235 N.W.2d 1 (Mich. 1975), illustrates both the greater autonomy of constitutional (as opposed to statutory) institutions and the differing divisions of authority that are likely between the institution and other entities claiming authority over it. The University of Michigan, Michigan State University, and Wayne State University, all "constitutional" universities, challenged the constitutionality of various provisions in legislative appropriation acts that allegedly infringed on their autonomy. The court affirmed that, although the legislature could impose conditions on its appropriations to the institutions, it could not do so in a way that would "interfere with the management and control of those institutions." Thus, any particular condition in an appropriation act will be held unconstitutional if it constitutes an interference with institutional autonomy. Since most of the provisions challenged were no longer in effect and the controversy was therefore moot, the court refused to determine whether or not they constituted an interference. But the court did consider the challenge to a provision that prohibited the institutions from contracting for the construction of any "self-liquidating project" (a project that would ultimately pay for itself) without first submitting to the legislature schedules for liquidation of the debt incurred for construction and operation of the project. The court upheld this provision because it did not give the legislature power over construction decisions, but merely required that a report be made.

The institutions also challenged the State Board of Education's authority over higher education. The State Board of Education argued that it had the authority to approve program changes or new construction at the universities. Relying on the express terms of a constitutional provision setting out the board's powers and their relationship to powers of individual institutions, the court held that the State Board of Education's authority over the institutions was advisory only. The institutions were required only to inform the board of program changes, so that it could "knowledgeably carry out its advisory duties." Thus, although the state could impose some requirements on the plaintiff universities to accommodate the authority given other state agencies or branches of government, constitutionally created institutions retain exclusive authority to manage and control their own operations.

Similarly, in *San Francisco Labor Council v. Regents of the University of California*, 608 P.2d 277 (Cal. 1980), the court gave substantial protection to a constitutionally based institution's autonomy. The plaintiff labor council argued that the regents had failed to comply with a requirement set forth in the State Education Code, namely, that the board of regents, in setting salaries, must take account of prevailing minimum and maximum salaries in various localities. The board asserted that the state constitution exempted it from the Education Code's mandate. The California Supreme Court agreed with the board. The state constitutional provision at issue (as quoted by the court) reads:

> The University of California shall constitute a public trust, to be administered by the existing corporation known as "The Regents of the University of California," with full powers of organization and government, subject only to such legislative control as may be necessary to insure the security of its funds and compliance with the terms of the endowments of the university and such competitive bidding procedures as may be made applicable to the university by statute for the letting of construction contracts, sales of real property, and purchasing of materials, goods, and services [Cal. Const. Art. IX, § 9].

The court discussed the autonomy that the board enjoyed under this constitutional provision, pointing out that the state constitution gives the regents "broad powers to organize and govern the university and limits the legislature's power to regulate either the university or the regents," compared with the legislature's direct authority over state agencies. In addition, said the court, the regents have rule-making power over the university, and have "virtually exclusive" power to "operate, control, and administer the university" (608 P.2d at 278).

On the other hand, the court noted, the regents are not completely independent of control by the legislature. The legislature retained the power to appropriate funds for the university, the legislature's general police powers that apply to private persons and corporations also apply to the university, and the legislature could subject the university to laws regulating "matters of statewide concern not involving internal university affairs" (608 P.2d at 278, 279). The court then held that the Education Code provision relied on by the plaintiff did not fit any of these three areas where the legislature could intervene and thus did not bind the board of regents. (For another case with similar facts and a similar outcome, see *Board of Regents of the University of Oklahoma v. Baker,* 638 P.2d 464 (Okla. 1981).)

In *Regents of the University of Michigan v. State,* 419 N.W.2d 773 (Mich. Ct. App. 1988), the University of Michigan was once again required to assert its constitutional autonomy against state attempts to regulate its operations. The Michigan legislature passed a law prohibiting any public educational institution from "making or maintaining . . . an investment in an organization operating in the Republic of South Africa." Although the University of Michigan had nearly completed its divestiture of South African–related assets, it challenged the law as violating its constitutional autonomy to make its own decisions about its resources. The state appellate court agreed, and the state appealed. The Michigan Supreme Court affirmed the lower courts (453 N.W.2d 656 (Mich. 1990)), despite the state's argument that the issue was moot because the university had divested its South African–related stocks voluntarily. (For an analysis of the issues in the case, written by the university's counsel, see R. K. Daane, "*Regents of the University of Michigan v. State of Michigan:* South African Divestiture and Constitutional Autonomy," 15 *J. Coll. & Univ. Law* 313 (1989).)

Similarly, in *Board of Regents of Oklahoma State University v. Oklahoma Merit Protection Commission,* 19 P.3d 865 (Okla. 2001), the Supreme Court of Oklahoma ruled that the Oklahoma Merit Protection Commission, a state agency that adjudicated grievances by state employees against public employers, had no authority over grievances of employees of Oklahoma State University. The court declared that Article 6 § 31a, Article 13-A, and Article 13-B of the Oklahoma constitution granted the board of regents "exclusive authority to manage the affairs of institutions," and that the legislature was "powerless to create a body to take over the responsibility" (19 P.3d at 866).

But statutes of general application that regulate the employment relationship between public employers and their employees have usually (but not always) been applied to constitutionally based institutions. For example, the University of Colorado asserted that its constitutional status exempted it from the application of the state's Civil Rights Act. In *Colorado Civil Rights Commission v. Regents of the University of Colorado,* 759 P.2d 726 (Colo. 1988), the university claimed that the state Civil Rights Commission lacked jurisdiction over a challenge to the university's decision to deny tenure to a Hispanic professor. Although the university argued that previous state supreme court decisions had required the legislature to "explicitly refer to the Regents in defining the term 'employer' for purposes of discriminatory employment practices" (759 P.2d at 733), the court found an implied legislative intent to include the regents within the term "employer" in the state's antidiscrimination statute.

The court noted that the Colorado constitution provided that colleges and universities "shall be subject to the control of the state, under the provisions of the constitution and such laws and regulations as the general assembly may provide" (Colo. Const. Art. VIII, § 5(1)). The constitution gives to the governing boards of the state colleges and universities, "whether established by constitution or by law," the power of general supervision over these institutions "unless otherwise provided by law" (Art. VIII, § 5(2)). This language, said the court, "clearly contemplates a limited power of 'general supervision' only" (759 P.2d at 730). The enactment by the Colorado legislature of the nondiscrimination law, and its creation of a Civil Rights Commission to investigate discrimination claims against employers, constituted such a law that limited the authority of the university's governing board. (See also *Regents of the University of Michigan v. Michigan Employment Relations Commission,* 204 N.W.2d 218 (Mich. 1973), where the court held that the University of Michigan is a public employer subject to the state's Public Employment Relations Act.)

But a different result was reached in a Minnesota case in which the court was asked to determine whether the state's Veterans Preference Act applied to non-faculty employment decisions of the University of Minnesota, a constitutionally based university. In *Winberg v. University of Minnesota,* 485 N.W.2d 325 (Minn. Ct. App. 1992), a state appellate court recognized the university's autonomy but ruled that limits could be placed on that autonomy by the legislature, given the university's acceptance of public funds. The Minnesota Supreme Court reversed (499 N.W.2d 799 (Minn. 1993)), holding that the Veterans Preference Act did not apply to the university's employment decisions because the university was not a "political subdivision" of the state. Only if the legislature had specifically referred to the university in the text of the law would it have bound the university, said the court. Having resolved the dispute through statutory interpretation, the court declined to address the constitutional issues raised by the university.

Sec. 12.3. State Chartering and Licensure of Private Postsecondary Institutions

12.3.1. Scope of state authority.
The authority of states to regulate private postsecondary education is not as broad as their authority over their own public institutions (see Section 1.5.1). Nevertheless, under their police powers, states do have extensive regulatory authority that they have implemented through statutes and administrative regulations. This authority has generally been upheld by the courts. In the leading case of *Shelton College v. State Board of Education,* 226 A.2d 612 (N.J. 1967), for instance, the court reviewed the authority of New Jersey to license degree-granting institutions and approve the basis and conditions on which they grant degrees. The State Board of Education had refused to approve the granting of degrees by the plaintiff college, and the college challenged the board's authority on a variety of grounds. In an informative opinion, the New Jersey Supreme Court rejected all the challenges and broadly upheld the board's decision and the validity of the statute under which the board had acted.

Similarly, in *Warder v. Board of Regents of the University of the State of New York,* 423 N.E.2d 352 (N.Y. 1981), the court rejected state administrative law and constitutional due process challenges to New York's authority to charter post-secondary institutions. The Unification Theological Seminary, a subdivision of the Unification Church (the church of Reverend Sun Myung Moon), sought to incorporate in New York and offer a master's degree in religious education. It applied for a provisional charter. In reviewing the application, the state education department subjected the seminary to an unprecedented lengthy and intensive investigation. The department had been concerned about charges of brainwashing and deceptive practices directed against the Unification Church. The department's investigation did not substantiate these charges but did uncover evidence suggesting other deficiencies. Ultimately, the department determined that the seminary had misrepresented itself as having degree-granting status, had refused to provide financial statements, and had not enforced its admissions policies.

The New York Court of Appeals held that, despite the singular treatment the seminary had received, the education department had a rational basis for its decision to deny the charter:

> Petitioners do not and cannot dispute that the board validly could deny a provisional charter to an institution that engaged in "brainwashing" and deception. That the broad investigation revealed no evidence of such practices does not mean that it was improperly undertaken in the first instance. The board cannot now be faulted because it discharged its responsibility for ensuring ethical educational programs of quality and in the process discovered serious deficiencies in the conduct of the academic program [423 N.E.2d at 357].

The seminary also charged that the legislature's grant of authority to the education department was vague and overbroad, and that the department had reviewed the seminary in a discriminatory and biased manner. Dispensing with the latter argument, the court found that the record did not contain evidence of discrimination or bias. Also rejecting the former argument, the court held that the New York statutes constituted a lawful delegation of authority to the state's board of regents:

> The board of regents is charged with broad policy-making responsibility for the state's educational system (Education Law § 207) and is specifically empowered to charter institutions of higher education (Education Law §§ 216, 217). In the meaningful discharge of those functions and to "encourage and promote education" (Education Law § 201), the regents ensure that acceptable academic standards are maintained in the programs offered (see *Moore v. Board of Regents of University of the State of New York*, . . . 378 N.E.2d 1022 [1978]). Thus, before an institution may be admitted to the academic community with degree-granting status, it must meet established standards (see 8 NYCRR [New York Code, Rules and Regulations] 3.21, 3.22, 52.1, 52.2); its purposes must be, "in whole or in part, of educational or cultural value deemed worthy of recognition and encouragement" (Education Law § 216). Given the broad responsibility of the board of regents for the quality of education provided in this state, it must be given wide latitude to investigate and evaluate institutions seeking to operate within the system [423 N.E.2d at 357].

Authority over private postsecondary institutions is exercised, in varying degrees depending on the state, in two basic ways. The first is incorporation or chartering, a function performed by all states. In some states postsecondary institutions are subject to the nonprofit corporation laws applicable to all nonprofit corporations; in others postsecondary institutions come under corporation statutes designed particularly for charitable institutions; and in a few states there are special statutes for incorporating educational institutions. Proprietary (profit-making) schools often fall under general business corporation laws. The states also have laws applicable to "foreign" corporations (that is, those chartered in another state), under which states may "register" or "qualify" out-of-state institutions that seek to do business in their jurisdiction.

The second method for regulating private postsecondary institutions is licensure.[4] Imposed as a condition to offering education programs in the state or to granting degrees or using a collegiate name, licensure is a more substantial form of regulation than chartering. (An overview of the kinds of provisions that are or can be included in state licensing systems, as well as some of the policy choices involved, can be found in *Model State Legislation: Report of the Task Force on Model State Legislation for Approval of Postsecondary Educational Institutions and Authorization to Grant Degrees,* Report no. 39 (Education Commission of the States, June 1973).)

There are three different approaches to licensure:

First, a state can license on the basis of *minimum standards.* The state may choose to specify, for example, that all degree-granting institutions have a board, administration, and faculty of certain characteristics, an organized curriculum with stipulated features, a library of given size, and facilities defined as adequate to the instruction offered. Among states pursuing this approach, the debate centers on what and in what detail the state should prescribe—some want higher levels of prescription to assure "quality," others want to allow room for "innovation."

A second approach follows models developed in contemporary regional accreditation and stresses *realization of objectives.* Here the focus is less on a set of standards applicable to all than on encouragement for institutions to set their own goals and realize them as fully as possible. The role of the visiting team is not to inspect on the basis of predetermined criteria but to analyze the institution on its own terms and suggest new paths to improvement. This help-oriented model is especially strong in the eastern states with large numbers of well-established institutions; in some cases, a combined state-regional team will be formed to make a single visit and joint recommendation.

A third model would take an *honest practice* approach. The essence of it is that one inspects to verify that an institution is run with integrity and fulfills basic claims made to the public. The honesty and probity of institutional officers,

---

[4]Under federal law, 20 U.S.C. § 1099a (also discussed in footnote 1 above), each state must provide to the U.S. Secretary of Education, on request, information regarding its "process of licensing or other authorization for institutions of higher education to operate within the State" (1099a(a)(1)), and must "notify the Secretary promptly" whenever it "revokes" any such license or authorization (1099a(a)(2)).

integrity of the faculty, solvency of the balance sheet, accuracy of the catalogue, adequacy of student records, equity of refund policies—these and related matters would be the subject of investigation. If an institution had an occupation-related program, employment records of graduates would be examined. It is unclear whether any state follows this model in its pure form, though it is increasingly advocated, and aspects of it do appear in state criteria. A claimed advantage is that, since it does not specify curricular components or assess their strengths and weaknesses (as the other two models might), an "honest practice" approach avoids undue state "control" of education [*Approaches to State Licensing of Private Degree-Granting Institutions* (Postsecondary Education Convening Authority, George Washington University, 1975), 17–19].

Almost all states have some form of licensing laws applicable to proprietary institutions, and the trend is toward increasingly stringent regulation of the proprietary sector (see, for example, M. C. Cage, "Plan Would Increase State Regulation of For-Profit Schools," *Chron. Higher Educ.*, August 14, 1994, A17). Some states apply special requirements to non-degree-granting proprietary schools that are more extensive than the requirements for degree-granting institutions. In *New York Ass'n. of Career Schools v. State Education Department*, 749 F. Supp. 1264 (S.D.N.Y. 1990), the court upheld the New York regulations on non-degree-granting schools as against an equal protection clause attack.

Regarding licensure of nonprofit institutions, in contrast, there is considerable variance among the states in the application and strength of state laws and in their enforcement. Often, by statutory mandate or the administrative practice of the licensing agency, regionally accredited institutions (see Section 14.3.1 of this book) are exempted from all or most licensing requirements for nonprofit schools.

In addition to chartering and licensure, some states also have a third way of exerting authority over private postsecondary institutions: through the award of financial aid to such institutions or their students. By establishing criteria for institutional eligibility and reviewing institutions that choose to apply, states may impose additional requirements, beyond those in corporation or licensure laws, on institutions that are willing and able to come into compliance and thus receive the aid. A New York case concerning New York's "Bundy Aid" program, *In the Matter of Excelsior College v. New York State Education Department*, 761 N.Y.S.2d 700 (N.Y. App. Div. 2003), provides a contemporary, but stark, illustration of this point. Excelsior College is chartered by the state board of regents and is authorized to confer degrees. But, as the court emphasized, "the degrees . . . are awarded by [the college] based upon examinations it administers and an 'assessment' of the applicant's aggregate lifetime learning experiences," and the college "'does not offer an instructional program'" of its own. The college was therefore ineligible for state aid because the Bundy Law (N.Y. Education Law, § 6401) provides aid only to institutions of "higher education," which the court construed to mean institutions that provide an instructional program for their students.

State corporation laws ordinarily do not pose significant problems for postsecondary institutions, since their requirements can usually be met easily and

The College and the State Government

routinely. Although licensing laws contain more substantial requirements, even in the more rigorous states these laws present few problems for established institutions, either because the institutions are exempted by accreditation or because their established character makes compliance easy. For these institutions, problems with licensing laws are more likely to arise if they establish new programs in other states and must therefore comply with the various licensing laws of those other states (see Section 12.4 below). The story is quite different for new institutions, especially if they have innovative (nontraditional) structures, programs, or delivery systems, or if they operate across state lines (Section 12.4). For these institutions, licensing laws can be quite burdensome because they may not be adapted to the particular characteristics of nontraditional education or receptive to out-of-state institutions.

When an institution does encounter problems with state licensing laws, administrators may have several possible legal arguments to raise, which generally stem from state administrative law or the due process clauses of state constitutions or the federal Constitution. Administrators should insist that the licensing agency proceed according to written standards and procedures, that it make them available to the institution, and that it scrupulously follow its own standards and procedures. If any standard or procedure appears to be outside the authority delegated to the licensing agency by state statute, it may be questioned before the licensing agency and challenged in court. Occasionally, even if standards and procedures are within the agency's delegated authority, the authorizing statute itself may be challenged as an unlawful delegation of legislative power. In *Packer Collegiate Institute v. University of the State of New York,* 81 N.E.2d 80 (N.Y. 1948), the court invalidated New York's licensing legislation because "the legislature has not only failed to set out standards or tests by which the qualifications of the schools might be measured, but has not specified, even in most general terms, what the subject matter of the regulations is to be." In *State v. Williams,* 117 S.E.2d 444 (N.C. 1960), the court used similar reasoning to invalidate a North Carolina law. However, a much more hospitable approach to legislative delegations of authority is found in more recent cases, such as *Shelton College* and *Warder,* both discussed earlier in this Section, where the courts upheld state laws against charges that they were unlawful delegations of authority.

Perhaps the soundest legal argument for an institution involved with a state licensing agency is that the agency must follow the procedures in the state's administrative procedure act (where applicable) or the constitutional requirements of procedural due process. *Blackwell College of Business v. Attorney General,* 454 F.2d 928 (D.C. Cir. 1971), a case involving a federal agency function analogous to licensing, provides a good illustration. The case involved the withdrawal by the Immigration and Naturalization Service (INS) of Blackwell College's status as a school approved for attendance by nonimmigrant alien students under Section 1101(a)(15)(F) of the Immigration and Nationality Act. The INS had not afforded the college a hearing on the withdrawal of its approved status, but only an interview with agency officials and an opportunity to examine agency records concerning the withdrawal. The appellate court found that "the proceedings . . . were formless and uncharted" and did not meet the require-ments of either the federal Administrative Procedure Act or constitutional due process. Invalidating the INS withdrawal of approval because of this lack of pro-cedural due process, the court established guidelines for future government proceedings concerning the withdrawal of a school's license or approved status:

> The notice of intention to withdraw approval . . . should specify in reason-able detail the particular instances of failure to . . . [comply with agency require-ments]. The documentary evidence the school is permitted to submit . . . can then be directed to the specific grounds alleged. In addition, if requested, the school should be granted a hearing before an official other than the one upon whose investigation the [agency] has relied for initiating its withdrawal proceed-ings. If the evidence against the school is based upon authentic records, findings may be based thereon, unless the purport of the evidence is denied, in which event the school may be required to support its denial by authentic records or live testimony. If, however, the data presented in support of noncompliance [are] hearsay evidence, the college, if it denies the truth of the evidence, shall have opportunity, if it so desires, to confront and cross-examine the person or persons who supplied the evidence, unless the particular hearsay evidence is appropriate for consideration under some accepted exception to the hearsay rule. In all the proceedings the school, of course, shall be entitled to representa-tion and participation by counsel. The factual decision of the [agency] shall be based on a record thus compiled; and the record shall be preserved in a manner to enable review of the decision. . . . We should add that we do not mean that each and every procedural item discussed constitutes by itself a prerequisite of procedural due process. Rather our conclusion of unfairness relates to the total-ity of the procedure. . . . The ultimate requirement is a procedure that permits a meaningful opportunity to test and offer facts, present perspective, and invoke official discretion [454 F.2d at 936].

The case of *Ramos v. California Committee of Bar Examiners,* 857 F. Supp. 702 (N.D. Cal. 1994), like the *Blackwell College of Business* case, was a procedural due process challenge to a government decision concerning the recognition of educa-tional institutions. But, unlike *Blackwell, Ramos* involved a *denial* rather than a *withdrawal* of recognition. The court addressed a threshold due process issue that may present difficulties in denial cases, but generally not in withdrawal or termi-nation cases: whether the government action deprived the institution of a "prop-erty interest" or "liberty interest" (see generally Section 6.6.2). The plaintiff in *Ramos* had been denied registration as a law school in the state of California. Focusing on property interests, the court considered whether "the statutory and regulatory provisions pertaining to the availability of registration" created any "right or entitlement" for applicants for state registration. Because the answer was "No," the plaintiff had no property interest at stake and therefore no basis for a due process claim.

The *Ramos* opinion also indicates that, even if the plaintiff did have a prop-erty interest at stake, the due process claim would still fail because the bar exam-iners committee had provided all the procedure the Fourteenth Amendment would then require. In particular, the committee had provided the plaintiff with registration forms, had provided the opportunity for a hearing, and had notified the plaintiff of the hearing date. Moreover, the committee's findings apparently were supported by "substantial evidence," and its conclusions were not "arbitrary" (or at least the plaintiff did not contend to the contrary).

Although state incorporation and licensing laws are often sleeping dogs, they can bite hard when awakened. Institutional administrators and counsel—especially in new, expanding, or innovating institutions—should remain aware of the potential impact of these laws and of the legal arguments available to the institution if problems do arise.

12.3.2. Chartering and licensure of religious institutions.

In some respects, religiously affiliated and other religious institutions stand on the same footing as private secular institutions with respect to state chartering and licensure. In the *Warder* case (Section 12.3.1), for example, a religious seminary encountered the same kinds of problems that a secular institution might have encountered and raised the same kinds of legal issues that a secular institution might have raised. In other respects, however, the problems encountered and issues raised by religious institutions may be unique to their religious mission and status. The predominant consideration in such situations is likely to be whether the religious institution may invoke the freedom of religion guarantees in the federal Constitution or the state constitution—thus obtaining a shield against state regulation not available to secular institutions. The following two cases are illustrative.

In the first case, *New Jersey Board of Higher Education v. Shelton College*, 448 A.2d 988 (N.J. 1982) (*Shelton II*),[5] the New Jersey Supreme Court held that a state law requiring a license to grant degrees applied to religious as well as nonreligious private colleges. The court also held that application of the law to Shelton, a small fundamentalist Presbyterian college, did not violate either the free exercise clause or the establishment clause of the First Amendment (see Section 1.6.2). The college had begun offering instruction leading to the baccalaureate degree without first obtaining a state license. The state sought to enjoin Shelton from engaging in this activity within the state, and the New Jersey court granted the state's request.

While acknowledging that the state's licensing scheme imposed some burdens on Shelton's free exercise rights, the court found that the state had an overriding interest in regulating education and maintaining minimum academic standards. Given the strength of the state's interest in regulating and the absence of less restrictive means for fulfilling this interest, the state's interest outweighed the college's religious interests:

> Legislation that impedes the exercise of religion may be constitutional if there exists no less restrictive means of achieving some overriding state interest. . . .
>
> The legislation at issue here advances the state's interest in ensuring educational standards and maintaining the integrity of the baccalaureate degree. . . .

---

[5]The court referred to this litigation as *Shelton II* to distinguish it from *Shelton I* (*Shelton College v. State Board of Education,* discussed in Section 12.3.1).

That maintenance of minimum educational standards in all schools constitutes a substantial state interest is now beyond question. . . .

[Moreover,] the First Amendment does not require the provision of religious exemptions where accommodation would significantly interfere with the attainment of an overriding state interest. . . .

Here, accommodation of defendants' religious beliefs would entail a complete exemption from state regulation. . . . Such accommodation would cut to the heart of the legislation and severely impede the achievement of important state goals. Furthermore, if an exemption were created here, Shelton College would receive an advantage at the expense of those educational institutions that have submitted to state regulation. Such a development would undermine the integrity of the baccalaureate degree, erode respect for the state higher education scheme, and encourage others to seek exemptions. Thus, the uniform application of these licensing requirements is essential to the achievement of the state's interests. . . .

In sum, although defendants' freedom of religion may suffer some indirect burden from this legislation, the constitutional balance nonetheless favors the state interest in uniform application of these higher education laws [448 A.2d at 995–97].

Nor did the state regulations result in any "excessive entanglement" with religion or otherwise infringe the establishment clause. Instead, the New Jersey law on its face created a religiously neutral regulatory scheme:

The allegation of excessive entanglement rests on speculation about the manner in which these statutes and regulations might be applied. Although one could imagine an unconstitutional application of this regulatory scheme, we are confident that the board of higher education will pursue the least restrictive means to achieve the state's overriding concerns. Of course, should the board exercise its discretion in a manner that unnecessarily intrudes into Shelton's religious affairs, the college would then be free to challenge the constitutionality of such action [448 A.2d at 998].

In a similar case decided the same month as *Shelton II,* the Supreme Court of Tennessee upheld that state's authority to regulate degree granting by religious colleges. In *State ex rel. McLemore v. Clarksville School of Theology,* 636 S.W.2d 706 (Tenn. 1982), the school had also been offering instruction leading to a degree without obtaining a state license. When the state sought to enjoin it from offering degrees, the school argued that application of the state law would infringe its freedom of religion under the First Amendment.

The court agreed with the state's contention that the award of degrees is a purely secular activity and that the state's licensing requirement therefore did not interfere with the school's religious freedoms:

The school is inhibited in no way by the Act as far as religion is concerned, the Act only proscribing the issuance of educational credentials by those institutions failing to meet the minimum requirements. The court holds, therefore, that applying the Act to defendant school does not violate the free exercise of religion clause of the Constitution, state or federal. . . .

If the Act placed a burden upon the free exercise of religion by the defendants or posed a threat of entanglement between the affairs of the church and the state, the state would be required to show that "some compelling state interest" justified the burden and that there exists no less restrictive or entangling alternative (*Sherbert v. Verner*, 374 U.S. 398 . . . (1963); *Wisconsin v. Yoder*, 406 U.S. 205 . . . (1972)).

We conclude, however, that this Act places neither a direct nor [an] indirect burden upon the free exercise of religion by the defendants nor threatens an entanglement between the affairs of church and state. . . .

The Act does not regulate the beliefs, practices, or teachings of any institution; it merely sets forth minimum standards which must be met in order for an institution to be authorized to issue degrees. Moreover, the evidence shows that the granting of degrees is a purely secular activity. It is only this activity that brings the school under the regulation of the Act [636 S.W.2d at 708–9].

The court emphasized that the licensing statute did not interfere with the content of the school's teaching or with the act of teaching itself. But when the school sought to provide educational credentials as an end product of that teaching, it was properly subject to the state's authority to regulate a secular activity intimately related to the public welfare:

The fact remains that the state is merely regulating the awarding of educational degrees. The supposed predicament of the school is not a result of the state's regulation of its religious function of training ministers but of its preeminent role of *awarding degrees*[,] which is, as conceded by its president and founder, a purely secular activity [636 S.W.2d at 711].

The Tennessee court thus rejected the school's First Amendment claims because the state regulation did not burden any religious activity of the school. In contrast, the New Jersey court recognized that the state regulation burdened Shelton College's religious activities; nonetheless, the court rejected the school's First Amendment claims because the state's educational interests were sufficiently strong to justify the burden. By these varying paths, both cases broadly uphold state licensing authority over religiously affiliated degree-granting institutions.[6] (For a dissenting view on the issues involved, see Russell Kirk, "Shelton College and State Licensing of Religious Schools: An Educator's View of the Interface Between the Establishment and Free Exercise Clauses," 44 *Law & Contemp. Probs.* 169 (1981).)

In a later case, *HEB Ministries, Inc. v. Texas Higher Education Coordinating Board*, 114 S.W.3d 617 (Tex. App. 2003), a Texas appellate court relied on more

---

[6]Later U.S. Supreme Court cases on the free exercise and establishment clauses suggest that the analysis of cases like *Shelton II* and *Clarkesville School of Theology* may be somewhat different now, and that it may be easier for states to prevail against a religious institution's First Amendment challenges to a state licensing system (see generally Section 1.6.2). In particular, the case of *Employment Division v. Smith*, 494 U.S. 872 (1990) (discussed in Section 1.6.2), would allow for a lower standard of review under the federal free exercise clause when the licensing scheme is "generally applicable" and religiously "neutral." This approach may not always be available under state constitutions, however, which may require a stricter review similar to that in *Shelton II*.

recent caselaw to reach a result similar to that in the *Shelton II* and *Clarksville* cases. The plaintiff, which operated a theological seminary, challenged the state statute (Tex. Educ. Code Ann. §§ 61.301–.319) and administrative regulations under which Texas requires private institutions to obtain a certificate of authority from the state in order to award postsecondary degrees. The plaintiff based its challenges on the First Amendment's establishment clause, free exercise clause, and free speech clause, and on the parallel clauses in the state constitution. The appellate court rejected all of these challenges. In rejecting the establishment clause claims, the court applied the *Lemon* test (see Section 1.6.3 of this book) and cited the *Shelton II* case with approval. In rejecting the free exercise claims, the court relied on *Employment Division v. Smith* (see footnote 6 above), a U.S. Supreme Court case decided some years after the *Shelton II* and *Clarksville* cases, to hold that the Texas statute and regulations were religiously neutral within the meaning of *Smith* and that the state's secular interests justified any minimal burden that the certificate of authority requirement may place on the plaintiff's operations.

Sec. 12.4. State Regulation of Out-of-State Institutions and Programs

Postsecondary institutions have increasingly departed from the traditional mold of a campus-based organization existing at a fixed location within a single state. Both established and new institutions, public as well as private, may have branch campuses; off-campus programs; experiential learning programs; computer and Internet-based programs; and other innovative systems for delivering education to a wider audience. These developments have given institutions a presence in states other than the home states where they are incorporated, thus sometimes subjecting them to the regulatory jurisdiction of other (perhaps multiple) states.

For these multistate institutions, whether public or private, legal problems may increase both in number and in complexity.[7] Not only must the institution meet the widely differing and possibly conflicting legal requirements of various states, but it must also be prepared to contend with laws or administrative practices that may not be suited to or hospitable to either out-of-state or nontraditional programs. Institutional administrators contemplating the development of any program that will cross state lines should be sensitive to this added legal burden and to the legal arguments that may be used to lighten it.

A multistate institution may seek to apply the legal arguments in Section 12.3 to states that prohibit or limit the operation of the institution's programs within their borders; these legal arguments apply to all state regulation, whether it concerns out-of-state institutions or not. Out-of-state institutions may also raise particular questions concerning the state's authority over out-of-state, as opposed

---

[7]Some of the background material in the first part of this Section is drawn from prior work of one of the authors, included in Chapter Nine of *Nova University's Three National Doctoral Degree Programs* (Nova/N.Y.I.T. Press, 1977), and in Section 4.3 of *Legal and Other Constraints to the Development of External Degree Programs* (report under Grant NE-G-00-3-0208, National Institute of Education, January 1975).

to in-state, institutions. Is the state licensing agency authorized under state law to license out-of-state schools that award degrees under the authority of their home states? Is the licensing agency authorized to apply standards to an out-of-state school that are higher than or different from the standards it applies to in-state schools? And, most intriguing, may the agency's authority be challenged under provisions of the federal or state constitution—in particular, the commerce clause or the First Amendment of the federal Constitution?

The commerce clause (U.S. Const., Art. I, Sec. 8, cl. 3), in addition to being a rich lode of power for the federal government (see Section 13.1.4), also limits the authority of states to use their regulatory powers in ways that interfere with the free movement of goods and people across state lines. As the U.S. Supreme Court has emphasized, "[T]he very purpose of the commerce clause was to create an area of free trade among the several states. . . . By its own force [the clause] created an area of trade free from interference by the states" (*Great A&P Tea Co. v. Cottrell*, 424 U.S. 366 (1976)). The term "commerce" has been broadly construed by the courts. It includes both business and nonbusiness, profit and nonprofit activities. It encompasses the movement of goods or people, the communication of information or ideas, the provision of services that cross state lines, and all component parts of such transactions. As far back as 1910, in *International Textbook Co. v. Pigg*, 217 U.S. 91, the Supreme Court held that interstate educational activities were included in the category of commerce and that, therefore, an out-of-state correspondence school could not constitutionally be subjected to Kansas's foreign corporation requirements.[8]

What protection, then, might the commerce clause yield for multistate institutions? The zone of protection has been clearly identified in one circumstance: when the state subjects an out-of-state program to requirements that are different from and harsher than those applied to in-state (domestic) programs. Such differentiation is clearly unconstitutional. For one hundred years, it has been settled that states may not discriminate against interstate commerce, or goods or services from other states, in favor of their own intrastate commerce, goods, and services (see, for example, *Philadelphia v. New Jersey*, 437 U.S. 617 (1978)).

An Oregon case, *City University v. Oregon Office of Educational Policy & Planning*, 870 P.2d 222 (Or. 1994), *affirmed on other grounds*, 885 P.2d 701 (Or. 1994), illustrates this principle of nondiscrimination. The court used the federal commerce clause, and the nondiscrimination principle derived from it, to invalidate an Oregon statutory provision. The plaintiff was a regionally accredited private university incorporated in the state of Washington that had a branch campus in Oregon. Oregon law (Ore. Rev. Stat. § 348.835) required degree-granting institutions (including the plaintiff) to submit their degree requirements to the state for approval. Section 2(c) of the statute excepted regionally accredited *Oregon* schools from this requirement (emphasis added). The intermediate

---

[8]Lawyers will want to compare the *Pigg* case with *Eli Lilly and Co. v. Sav-On Drugs*, 366 U.S. 276 (1961), where the Supreme Court distinguished between the intrastate and interstate activities of a foreign corporation engaged in interstate commerce and permitted the state to regulate the corporation's intrastate activities. See generally C. R. McCorkle, Annot., "Regulation and Licensing of Correspondence Schools and Their Canvassers or Solicitors," 92 A.L.R.2d 522.

appellate court, affirming the trial court, ruled that this provision discriminates on its face against accredited out-of-state schools and thus against interstate commerce. Since the defendant could not justify the distinction between in-state and out-of-state accredited schools, the court held Section 2(c) to be unconstitutional. (On a further appeal, regarding the appropriate remedy, the state conceded the invalidity of Section 2(c), and did not contest the intermediate appellate court's holding of unconstitutionality.)

Beyond the principle of nondiscrimination or evenhandedness, the commerce clause's umbrella of protection against state regulation becomes more uncertain and more dependent on the facts of each particular case. Although a state may evenhandedly regulate the in-state or "localized" activities of out-of-state institutions, a potential commerce clause problem arises when the state regulation burdens the institution's ability to participate in interstate commerce. To resolve such problems, the courts engage in a delicate balancing process, attempting to preserve the authority of states to protect their governmental interests while protecting the principle of free trade and intercourse among the states. After a long period of feeling its way, the Supreme Court in 1970 finally agreed unanimously on this general approach, called the *"Pike* test":

> Where the statute regulates evenhandedly to effectuate a legitimate local public interest, and its effects on interstate commerce are only incidental, it will be upheld unless the burden imposed on such commerce is clearly excessive in relation to the putative local benefits. If a legitimate local purpose is found, then the question becomes one of degree. And the extent of the burden that will be tolerated will, of course, depend on the nature of the local interest involved, and on whether it could be promoted as well with a lesser impact on interstate activities [*Pike v. Bruce Church,* 397 U.S. 137, 142 (1970)].

Under this test the state's interest must be "legitimate"—a label that courts have sometimes refused to apply to parochial or protectionist interests prompted by a state's desire to isolate itself from the national economy. In one famous case, which arose after a state had refused to license an out-of-state business because the in-state market was already adequately served, the Court said that the state's decision was "imposed for the avowed purpose and with the practical effect of curtailing the volume of interstate commerce to aid local economic interests" and held that "the state may not promote its own economic advantages by curtailment or burdening of interstate commerce" (*H. P. Hood & Sons v. DuMond,* 336 U.S. 525 (1949)). On the other hand, under the *Pike* test, state interests in safety, fair dealing, accountability, or institutional competence would be legitimate interests to be accorded considerable weight. States clearly may regulate the localized activities of out-of-state institutions—along with those of in-state institutions—in order to promote such legitimate interests. In doing so, however, states must regulate sensitively, minimizing the impact on the institutions' interstate activities and ensuring that each regulation actually does further the interest asserted.

Commerce clause issues, or other constitutional or statutory issues concerning state authority, are most likely to arise in situations in which a state denies entry to an out-of-state program or places such burdensome restrictions on its entry that it is excluded in practical effect. A state might, for instance, deny entry to an out-of-state program by using academic standards higher than those applied to in-state programs. A state might impose a "need requirement" to which in-state programs are not subjected. Or a state might institute a need requirement that is applicable to both out-of-state and in-state programs but serves to freeze and preserve a market dominated by in-state schools. A state might also deny entry for lack of approval by a regional or statewide coordinating council dominated by in-state institutions. The relevant legal principles point to the possible vulnerability of state authority in each instance.

In *Nova University v. Board of Governors of the University of North Carolina*, 267 S.E.2d 596 (N.C. Ct. App. 1980), *affirmed*, 287 S.E.2d 872 (N.C. 1982), the North Carolina courts issued the first published court opinions exploring the legal questions raised in this Section. By a 4-to-2 vote, the state's supreme court held that the state did not have the authority to regulate out-of-state institutions that operate educational programs in North Carolina but award degrees under the auspices of their home states. The plaintiff, Nova University, was licensed to award degrees under Florida law but organized small-group "cluster" programs in other states, including North Carolina. Successful participants received graduate degrees awarded in Florida. The Board of Governors of the University of North Carolina (pursuant to North Carolina General Statute 116-15, which authorized it to license degree-conferring institutions) claimed that Nova's curriculum was deficient and sought to deny the institution authority to operate its cluster programs in the state. The board claimed that the statute that authorized it to license degree conferrals included, by implication, the power to license teaching as well.

In rejecting the board's argument, the court acknowledged the important constitutional questions that the board's position would raise: "Were we . . . to interpret G.S. 116-15 as the Board suggests, serious constitutional questions arising under the First Amendment and the interstate commerce and Fourteenth Amendment due process clauses of the United States Constitution and the law of the land clause of the North Carolina constitution would arise." Looking to the language of General Statute 116-15, the court determined that it could reasonably be interpreted, and should be interpreted, to avoid these constitutional issues:

> All that Nova does in North Carolina is teach. Teaching and academic freedom are "special concern[s]" of the First Amendment to the United States Constitution (*Keyishian v. Board of Regents of New York*, 385 U.S. 589, 603 . . . (1967)); and the freedom to engage in teaching by individuals and private institutions comes within those liberties protected by the Fourteenth Amendment to the United States Constitution. . . .
>
> To say that it is conducting a "degree program" which is somehow different from or more than mere teaching, as the Board would have it, is nothing more than the Board's euphemization. Teaching is teaching and learning is learning, notwithstanding what reward might follow either process. The Board's argument that the power to license teaching is necessarily implied from the power to license degree conferrals simply fails to appreciate the large difference, in terms

of the state's power to regulate, between the two kinds of activities. The Board accuses Nova of trying to accomplish an "end run" around the statute. In truth, the Board, if we adopted its position, would be guilty of an "end run" around the statutory limits on its licensing authority. . . .

Here the legislature has clearly authorized the Board to license only degree conferrals, not teaching. Because of the statute's clear language limiting the Board's authority to license only degree conferrals and not separately to license the teaching which may lead to the conferral, the statute is simply not reasonably susceptible to a construction which would give the board the power to license such teaching [287 S.E.2d at 878, 881–82].

In a follow-up case, *Nova University v. Educational Institution Licensure Commission*, 483 A.2d 1172 (D.C. 1984), the same university challenged a District of Columbia statute that required all educational institutions seeking to operate in D.C. to obtain a license—even if they did not confer degrees in D.C. In upholding the statute, the court addressed the First Amendment issue outlined but not disposed of in the first *Nova* case. Nova argued that D.C.'s licensing was unconstitutional under the First Amendment, since it was a regulation of teaching and learning activities that were "pure speech." The court held that, even if Nova were engaged in free speech activities, the First Amendment does not immunize such institutions from all state regulation of business conduct determined to be adverse to the public interest. To determine whether the D.C. statute unduly restrained First Amendment activities, the court considered the purpose of the statute. Here the D.C. statute's sole purpose was to ensure that educational institutions in the District of Columbia meet minimal academic standards, regardless of the message being conveyed through their teaching. Since this important interest is content neutral (regarding content neutrality, see Sections 9.5.3, 9.5.6, & 9.6.2 of this book), and since Nova and other out-of-state schools were not being singled out (local schools being subject to the same regulation), the statute was constitutional.

Thus, the courts in the *Nova University* cases not only analyzed the state statutory issues but also outlined the sensitive constitutional issues that may loom on the horizon whenever state licensing authority is broadly construed. In contrast to other recent cases, which broadly construe state licensing authority over in-state institutions (see Section 12.3 above), the first *Nova* case more narrowly construes state authority over out-of-state schools. Moreover, although a more broadly and explicitly worded statute like that in the District of Columbia could resolve the statutory issue in the first *Nova* case, such broader statutes may still be subjected to federal and state constitutional limitations such as those suggested by both *Nova* courts. Although the First Amendment argument in the second *Nova* case did not succeed, the result could be different for a statute that was not applied to out-of-state schools in a content-neutral and evenhanded fashion; or that regulated institutions' programs more than needed to maintain minimal academic standards, prevent fraud, or serve some other obviously legitimate state interest. Moreover, interstate commerce and other constitutional issues may arise, as the first *Nova* court indicated. The *Nova* cases therefore confirm that the legal principles in this Section do provide substantial ammunition to out-of-state institutions, making it likely that they can hit the mark in some cases where state regulation stifles the development of legitimate interstate postsecondary programs.

The *Nova* cases, however, concerned an institution with a *physical* presence in other jurisdictions. In contrast, and in light of developments in distance learning, both established and newly formed postsecondary institutions extend their presence in other states by technological means. For the most part, state authority over such programs, for which the institution has no physical presence in the state, is subject to the same legal principles as are set out above in this Section. The free speech and press clauses of the First Amendment and parallel state constitutional provisions, however, are likely to be of particular importance. The cases in which the U.S. Supreme Court has protected speech in cyberspace—cases that are set out in Section 13.2.12 of this book—are therefore also particularly important in situations in which a state has regulated distance education.

The federal commerce clause may also have particular applications to distance learning. A New York case provides an example and suggests the need for states to move most cautiously when attempting to regulate Internet-based instructional activities of postsecondary institutions. The court's reasoning in *American Libraries Association v. Pataki,* 969 F. Supp. 160 (S.D.N.Y. 1997), appears to have relevance for both the regulation of out-of-state institutions whose Internet instruction reaches in-state residents, and the regulation of in-state institutions (see Section 12.3.1 above) whose Internet instruction reaches residents of other states. In either context, state regulations could apparently be subject to analysis and possible invalidation under the federal Constitution's commerce clause.

The *American Libraries Association* case concerned a New York law that prohibited the use of computers to disseminate obscene material to minors. The court issued a preliminary injunction against the law's enforcement because of the burden the law imposed on interstate communications. The court's reasoning emphasized the unique characteristics of communication over the Internet:

> The unique nature of the Internet highlights the likelihood that a single actor might be subject to haphazard, uncoordinated, and even outright inconsistent regulation by states. . . . Typically, states' jurisdictional limits are related to geography; geography, however, is a virtually meaningless construct on the Internet. The menace of inconsistent state regulation invites analysis under the Commerce Clause of the Constitution . . . [969 F. Supp. at 168].

As distance education programs become more technologically and educationally sophisticated, and their quality and economic efficiency increases, thus spurring expansion of the interstate market for such services, the constitutional and regulatory problems discussed in this Section will continue to grow in importance. Institutions that plan to be continuing participants in this market will want carefully to track current and future developments—legal, policy, technological, and educational.

Sec. 12.5. Other State Regulatory Laws Affecting Postsecondary Education Programs

12.5.1. Overview. Aside from the body of state law specifically designed to govern the establishment and licensure of colleges and universities, discussed in Sections 12.2 through 12.4, public and private postsecondary institutions are subject to a variety of other state statutes and regulations, most of which are not specifically tailored to educational operations. Many of these laws concern the institution's role as an employer or, in the case of public institutions, as a government agency. Subsections 12.5.2 to 12.5.5 below provide examples of the kinds of legal disputes that may arise under such laws.

In some regulatory areas, especially with regard to private institutions, federal legislation has "preempted the field" (see Section 13.1.1), leaving little or no room for state law. Private sector collective bargaining is a major example (see Section 4.5.2.1). In other areas, where there is little or no federal legislation, state legislation is primary. Major examples include public sector collective bargaining laws (see Section 4.5.2.3); workers' compensation laws; deceptive practices laws (for nonprofit entities); and open meeting laws, administrative procedure acts, ethics codes, civil service laws, and contract and competitive bidding procedures applicable to state agencies. In yet other areas, federal and state governments may share regulatory responsibilities, with some overlap and coordination of federal and state laws. Fair employment laws, environmental protection laws, unfair trade laws, unemployment compensation laws, and laws on solicitation of funds by charitable organizations are major examples. In this latter area, federal law will prevail over state law in case of conflict if the subject being regulated is within the federal government's constitutional powers.

As this discussion suggests, state regulatory laws of general application may restrict the autonomy of public, and in many instances private, colleges and universities in various important respects. There are many examples in addition to those in the preceding paragraph and in subsections 12.5.2 to 12.5.5 below, and their numbers are increasing over time. Traditional examples include social host laws and other beverage control laws (sometimes applicable to campus social events), landlord-tenant laws (sometimes applicable to residence halls and other student or faculty housing), traffic safety laws (applicable to public roads traversing or bordering the campus); and regulations (and state common law) concerning the discharge of employees (see, for example, Mont. Code Ann. Sec. 39-2-901 *et seq.;* and see generally Section 4.3.2 of this book).

Of the newer examples, one of the most important is nondiscrimination laws. Each state has its own nondiscrimination laws, whose protections may be broader than or different from those of federal civil rights laws.[9] State law on sexual harassment, for instance, may provide different standards than those developed

---

[9]Some of the cases and authorities are collected in Phillip E. Hassman, Annot., "Construction and Application of State Equal Rights Amendments Forbidding Determination of Rights Based on Sex," 90 A.L.R.3d 158.

under federal legislation.[10] States may also have laws or executive orders that prohibit discrimination on the basis of sexual orientation in employment (see Section 5.3.7), education, or public accommodations, a type of discrimination not covered by federal statutes. (For discussion of a conflict between a Connecticut sexual orientation law and the federal "Solomon Amendment" regarding military recruiting on college campuses, see Section 13.4.4 of this book.)

Other newer examples of laws of general application include toxic waste laws[11] (applicable, for instance, to laboratories); state whistleblower statutes (and common law protections) that prohibit retaliation against employees who "reasonably believe" that their employer or its agents have violated a law or tolerated an unsafe condition (see Section 4.6.8 of this book);[12] and conflict-of-interest laws that restrict some activities of public employees. In *In re Executive Commission on Ethical Standards*, 561 A.2d 542 (N.J. 1989), for example, the New Jersey Supreme Court considered whether a state ethics law (N.J. Stat. Ann. §§ 52:13D-12 to -27) applied to a Rutgers University law school professor in his conduct of a clinical program. The professor represented clients before the state's Council on Affordable Housing. The court ruled that the law's purpose was to prohibit state legislators from appearing before state agencies as advocates; and that the state legislature never intended the law to apply to professors in this situation.

In addition to such laws of general application, state legislatures have enacted laws that focus directly on activities on college campuses, including academic activities. Several states, for example, have laws requiring fluency in English for all instructors, including teaching assistants (see Section 5.3.2). One such statute is Pennsylvania's English Fluency in Higher Education Act (24 Pa. Cons. Stat. Ann. §§ 6801–6806 (2004)). New York and California have passed "truth-in-testing" laws that require disclosure of the questions and answers for standardized tests used to make admission decisions (see Section 13.2.5.8.5. Other state laws affecting admissions decisions include a Texas law that prohibits graduate or professional programs at state institutions from using scores on standardized tests as the sole admission criterion (Tex. Educ. Code § 51.842 (b)). A different kind of example, from 2005, comes from New Jersey, where the legislature enacted a law on smoking on college campuses, in particular requiring the governing boards or responsible administrators of both public and private institutions to prohibit smoking "in any portion of a building used as a student dormitory . . ." (N.J. Stat., c.320, C.26:3D-17, August 22, 2005).

---

[10]Cases and authorities are collected in Carol Shultz Vento, Annot., "When Is Work Environment Intimidating, Hostile or Offensive, so as to Constitute Sexual Harassment Under State Law?" 93 A.L.R.5th 47.

[11]Cases and authorities are collected in William B. Johnson, Annot., "Validity, Construction, and Application of State Hazardous Waste Regulations," 86 A.L.R.4th 401.

[12]Private as well as public institutions may be subject to state whistleblower laws. Pennsylvania's Whistleblower Law, 43 P.S. § 1421 *et seq.*, provides a remedy for at-will employees of organizations that receive funding from the state or one of its political subdivisions. In *Riggio v. Burns*, 711 A.2d 497 (Pa. Super. 1998) (*en banc*), *appeal denied*, 739 A.2d 161 (Pa. 1999), the court allowed a whistleblower claim against the Medical College of Pennsylvania, a private medical school, because it had received more than $4 million from the state legislature.

The states have also enacted criminal legislation prohibiting various types of acts that specifically involve postsecondary education. Some states, for instance, make it a crime to sell term papers or theses to students who will use them as course work (see, for example, Md. Code, Education, § 26-201; and compare §§ 66400–66402 of the California Education Code (civil penalties)). Some states have made it a crime to confer academic degrees or use the name university without the formal approval of the state (see, for example, N.Y. Educ. Law, § 224(1)(a)); or to buy or sell an academic diploma or degree or obtain one by fraud (see, for example, N.Y. Educ. Law, § 224(2)); or to make or use a forged or counterfeited transcript or diploma (see, for example, Md. Code, Education, § 26-301); or to misrepresent oneself as having a diploma for a particular profession (see, for example, Mass. Gen. Laws Ann., Ch. 112, § 52). (See generally Joan Van Tol, "Detecting and Punishing the Use of Fraudulent Academic Credentials: A Play in Two Acts, 30 *Santa Clara L. Rev.* 791 (1990).)

Addressing other concerns, many states have passed legislation criminalizing vandalism against research facilities that use animals (see, for example, New York's Agriculture and Markets Law, which forbids unlawful tampering with animal research (N.Y.C.L.S. Agr. & M. § 378)). A Texas law (§ 4.30(a)&(b)(2) of the Texas Education Code) makes it a misdemeanor to engage in disruptive activity on a university campus. The constitutionality of this law was upheld in *Arnold v. State,* 853 S.W.2d 543 (Tex. Ct. App. 1993). Other state laws make hazing a crime, defining hazing specifically with reference to student organizations (see, for example, Mass. Stat. Ann. Ch. 269, §§ 17–19; Cal. Educ. Code, § 32050); and see generally Section 10.2.3 of this book). Yet other statutes impose certain reporting requirements on student athletes' agents (see, for example, Fla. Stat. Ann. §§ 468.454 & .456; Mich. Comp. Laws Ann. § 750.411e; and 18 Pa. Cons. Stat. Ann. § 7107); and Nev. Rev. Stat. § 398.482. and some of these statutes impose criminal penalties (see, for example, S.C. Code Ann. § 59-102-30).

Other statutes are civil laws that have a particular relationship to criminal law. Some states, for example, have laws that suspend or exclude students from state-funded financial aid for a period of time if they are convicted of participating in riots (Ohio Rev. Code Ann. 3333.38 (2004); Colorado Rev. Stat. 23-5-124 (2004)). A California law requires individuals convicted of sex crimes to register with campus police if they study or work at a public college or university (Cal. Penal Code § 290(a)(1)(A) (2004)). Various state laws also require institutions to disclose campus crime statistics (see, for example, 24 Pa. Cons. Stat. Ann. § 2502; Wis. Stat. § 36.11(22)).

The power of the purse has motivated legislatures in some states to demand increased faculty productivity. In Ohio, for example, the legislature enacted Ohio Revised Code Section 3345.45, which mandates an increase in teaching time for faculty at public colleges. Litigation related to this statute is discussed in Section 4.5.3 of this book. (This and other state legislative efforts to regulate faculty activities in public higher education are discussed in an American Association of University Professors (AAUP) Report of Committee C, "The Politics of Intervention: External Regulation of Academic Activities and Workloads in Public Higher Education," *Academe,* January–February 1996, 46–52.)

As the faculty workload legislation suggests, some state laws could have implications for academic freedom. A New Jersey statute, passed during the Desert Storm conflict of the early 1990s, provides an example. The statute required instructors to give final grades to any student who was called to active duty, as long as the student had completed at least eight weeks of course work. A professor at Montclair State University refused to give a student, who had been called to active duty partway through the semester, the grade to which the state law said he was entitled. The student sued the professor and the university. The consequences for the professor are discussed in Section 2.5.3.2. The constitutionality of the law itself was not challenged (*Chasin v. Montclair State University*, 732 A.2d 457 (N.J. 1999)).

State laws attempting to restrict faculty or student use of state-owned computers or Internet access connections may also have implications for academic freedom at public institutions. These problems are discussed in Sections 7.3 and 8.5 of this book. And since the start of the new century, legislative initiatives concerning the "intellectual diversity" of faculties and alleged political bias in the classroom have been considered by legislative committees and legislatures in various states, a few of which had passed legislative resolutions at the time this book went to press. The academic freedom implications of these initiatives are discussed in Sections 7.1.5 and 8.1.5 of this book.

Given the plethora of state laws, both general and specific, that apply to colleges, administrators and counsel will want to monitor legislative and judicial developments in their state just as carefully as they do those at the federal level.

12.5.2. Open meetings and public disclosure.

Open meetings laws provide a particularly good illustration of the controversy and litigation that can be occasioned when a general state law is applied to the particular circumstances of postsecondary education. In an era of skepticism about public officials and institutions, public postsecondary administrators must be especially sensitive to laws whose purpose is to promote openness and accountability in government. As state entities, public postsecondary institutions are often subject to open meetings laws and similar legislation, and the growing body of legal actions under such laws indicates that the public intends to make sure that public institutions comply. These laws typically require that meetings of decision-making bodies of public agencies be open to the public, that the agendas of these meetings be provided in advance, and that matters not on the agenda not be discussed. In *Sandoval v. Board of Regents of the University and Community College System of Nevada*, 67 P.3d 902 (Nev. 2003), the court rejected claims by the regents that forbidding them to stray from the published agenda violated their First Amendment rights.

Every state in the United States has enacted open public meetings laws,[13] and these laws have often changed the way that boards and committees at public institutions conduct their business. Two primary issues have sparked litigation

---

[13]For a list of these statutes, see Stephen Schaeffer, Comment, "Sunshine in Cyberspace? Electronic Deliberation and Open Meetings Laws," 48 *St. Louis L.J.* 755 (2004).

concerning these laws: which bodies or groups are subject to the law, and under what circumstances are they subject to the law. Because the provisions of open public meetings acts differ by state, the cases below are discussed for illustrative purposes only. Legal counsel and administrators should review the relevant rulings under their own state's law. (For a review of the interplay between these laws and the attorney-client privilege, see Roderick K. Daane, "Open Meetings Acts and the Attorney's 'Privilege' to Meet Privately with the School Board," 20 *Coll. L. Dig.* 193 (March 1, 1990).)

Meetings of the full board of trustees of a public college or university are usually subject to open public meetings laws. Litigation has focused instead on whether meetings of board committees must be conducted in public, and whether communications among board members by telephone or fax, culminating in a decision, constitute a "meeting" for purposes of open public meetings laws. In *Del Papa v. Board of Regents of University and Community College System of Nevada,* 956 P.2d 770 (Nev. 1998), the Nevada Supreme Court ruled that individual telephone calls and faxes between board members that culminated in a statement issued by the board violated the state's open public meeting law, although the court refused to enjoin the board, viewing the violation as a one-time event. The Alabama Supreme Court addressed the question of whether meetings of board committees at which less than a quorum of board members were present were subject to the state's Sunshine Law. The court ruled that they were not (*Auburn University v. Advertiser Co.,* 867 So. 2d 293 (Ala. 2003)).

In New York, a state appellate court reversed a ruling by a trial court that meetings of a community college senate are subject to that state's Open Meetings Law (*Perez v. City University of New York,* 753 N.Y.S.2d 641 (N.Y. Sup. Ct. 2002), *reversed,* 780 N.Y.S.2d 325 (N.Y. App. Div. 2004)). The appellate court was then reversed by the state's highest court (2005 N.Y. LEXIS 3211 (N.Y., November 17, 2005)). The appellate court had reasoned that the university's board of trustees had not delegated decision-making authority to the senate; that, although the senate appointed members to board committees that did have final decision-making authority on some issues, the senate itself was not empowered to make the ultimate decisions on any of those issues; and that the senate and its executive committee therefore were not subject to either New York's open meetings law or the freedom of information law. But the state's highest court disagreed, ruling that the senate is the only legislative body on campus authorized to send proposals to the board of trustees on "all college matters," and thus that the senate was exercising "a quintessentially governmental function" which brought it under the open meetings law.

Other state courts have ruled that open meetings laws apply to meetings of committees as well as to those of the governing board. For example, in *Arkansas Gazette Co. v. Pickens,* 522 S.W.2d 350 (Ark. 1975), a newspaper and one of its reporters argued that committees of the University of Arkansas Board of Trustees, and not just the full board itself, were subject to the Arkansas Freedom of Information Act. The reporter had been excluded from a committee meeting on a proposed rule change that would have allowed students of legal age to possess and consume intoxicating beverages in university-controlled facilities at the Fayetteville campus. The Arkansas Supreme Court could find no difference between the business of the board of trustees and that of its committees, and applied the open meetings law to both.

Similar results obtained in *Wood v. Marston,* 442 So. 2d 934 (Fla. 1983) with respect to the search committee for a new dean of the law school at the University of Florida, and in *University of Alaska v. Geistauts,* 666 P.2d 424 (Alaska 1983), which applied the state's open meetings law to the meetings of a tenure committee at the University of Alaska. Although there was an exception in the Alaska open meetings statute for meetings in which the performance of individuals was discussed, the affected individual had the right to request a public meeting. The plaintiff in *Geistauts,* a disappointed candidate for tenure, had not been given that choice. The court held that the statutory exception applied. It then further held, however, that the tenure committee had failed to notify the plaintiff of the committee's meetings and that this failure deprived him of his statutory right to request that the meetings be open. The court therefore concluded that the committee's decision denying tenure was void and ordered that the plaintiff be reinstated for an additional year with the option to reapply for tenure and be considered by the then-current tenure committee. Left undiscussed by the Alaska court is the impact of the statute and decision on third parties whose opinions of the applicant may be sought, perhaps with a tacit or express understanding of confidentiality, in the course of the tenure review. (For a contrary result in a different state, see *Donahue v. State,* 474 N.W.2d 537 (Iowa 1991).)

Courts have also addressed whether committees of students, administrators, or other institutional staff are subject to open meetings laws. Again, the answer depends upon the wording of the statute and on prior state court interpretations of the statute. For example, in *Associated Press v. Crofts,* 89 P.3d 971 (Mont. 2004), the Montana Supreme Court determined that a "Policy Committee" made up of the presidents and chancellors of the University of Montana system was subject to the state's open meeting law. The Policy Committee discussed issues related to changes in policy for the system, tuition and fee changes, budgeting issues, contractual issues, employee salaries, and legislative initiatives. The court weighed seven factors in reaching its decision: (1) whether the committee's members are public employees acting in their official capacity; (2) whether the meetings are paid for with public funds; (3) the frequency of the meetings; (4) whether the committee deliberates rather than simply gathers facts and reports; (5) whether the deliberations concern matters of policy rather than merely ministerial or administrative functions; (6) whether the committee's members have executive authority and experience; and (7) the results of the meetings. The court ruled that the significance of the issues that the Policy Committee addressed and its role in providing advice to the state's commissioner of higher education brought the committee within the scope of the open public meetings act.

Litigation has also addressed whether the meetings of private entities that are created to assist or support public institutions are subject to state open meetings laws. For example, in *Hopf v. Topcorp, Inc.,* 628 N.E.2d 311 (Ill. App. Ct. 1993), two private for-profit corporations had been created by Northwestern University and the city of Evanston in order to acquire land and develop a research park. Several citizens petitioned the court to declare these corporations to be public bodies, and thus subject to the open meetings law. The court ruled that these corporations were not subject to the open meetings law because they were not "subsidiary bodies" of the city, nor was the city able to influence their decisions. But in *Board of Regents of the Regency University System v. Reynard*, 686 N.E.2d 1222 (Ill. Ct. App. 1997), an appellate court in the same state determined that the Athletic Council of Illinois State University is a public body and is subject to the state's open meeting law. The broad scope of responsibility afforded the council, as well as the significant issues on which it provided advice to the president, persuaded the court that it met the "public body" definition in the Illinois open meeting statute and freedom of information act. This case is discussed further in Section 3.6.4.

Probably the most hotly contested issue with regard to open public meetings laws is whether the public (primarily the press) has the right to attend meetings at which candidates for the institution's presidency are interviewed, and the right to know the identity of presidential candidates. Litigation results have differed sharply. For example, in *Federated Publications v. Board of Trustees of Michigan State University*, 594 N.W.2d 491 (Mich. 1999), the Michigan Supreme Court rejected a newspaper's claim that the university had violated the state's Open Meetings Act by holding private meetings at which the search committee interviewed and discussed presidential candidates. The court stated that, because Michigan State University was created by the state's constitution, the legislature lacked the authority to regulate the management and control of university operations. The court said that the law applied to formal sessions of the governing board, but not to meetings of committees created by the board. Similarly, the Supreme Court of Nevada ruled that, because community college presidents are not public officers, the process for selecting a community college president in that state was not subject to the open meetings law (*Community College System of Nevada v. DR Partners*, 18 P.3d 1042 (Nev. 2001)).

On the other hand, the fact that the University of Minnesota was created by the state constitution did not prevent the Minnesota Supreme Court from ruling that the state's Open Meeting Law and its Data Practices Act both applied to the university's search for a new president (*Star Tribune Co. v. University of Minnesota Board of Regents*, 683 N.W.2d 274 (Minn. 2004)). The search committee appointed by the trustees had conducted the search in private in order to avoid losing candidates who did not want their candidacies to be revealed early in the search process. The trustees agreed to meet privately with the top candidates and conferred privately prior to conducting public interviews of the finalists. The trustees selected the interim president for the permanent position. Several newspapers sued the university, seeking the names of other candidates for the presidency. The trial court ruled that the regents had violated the state laws, and the appellate court concurred.

Using a theory similar to that which was used successfully in the case against Michigan State University, the university argued that because it enjoyed constitutional status, the legislature did not have the power to "interfere" with its management and operation. Furthermore, the university reminded the court, it had ruled in *University of Minnesota v. Chase,* 220 N.W. 951 (Minn. 1928), that a law requiring all state agencies to seek state approval before spending funds or entering contracts did not apply to the university because of its constitutional status. The Minnesota Supreme Court, however, said that *Chase* did not apply to the open meetings act because its intrusion on university autonomy was much more limited than that of the state law at issue in *Chase.* The open meetings law did not intrude on the "internal management of the university," according to the court, and affected the presidential search process "only in its interface with the outside world," by providing information to the taxpayers who fund the university.

The legislative intent and clear meaning of the statutory language of open meetings laws has great significance for the outcome of challenges under these laws. For example, the question of whether meetings of a university's animal use committees (see Section 13.2.3.3) are "public meetings" has been answered differently in several states. In *Animal Legal Defense Fund v. Institutional Animal Care and Use Committee of the University of Vermont,* 616 A.2d 224 (Vt. 1992), the Vermont Supreme Court determined that the animal use committee was a university committee and thus fell under the state law's ambit. But in *In re American Society for the Prevention of Cruelty to Animals, et al. v. Board of Trustees of the State University of New York,* 568 N.Y.S.2d 631 (N.Y. App. Div. 1991), a New York appellate court ruled that the animal use committee was not a "public body" for purposes of the state law because the committee performed a federal function under federal law. The result was affirmed by the state's highest court (582 N.Y.S.2d 983 (N.Y. 1992)).

The applicability of state open meeting laws to student disciplinary hearings has been at issue in other cases. In *Red & Black Publishing Co. v. Board of Regents,* 427 S.E.2d 257 (Ga. 1993), Georgia's highest court ruled that the proceedings of the University of Georgia's student disciplinary board were subject to that state's open meetings and open records laws. The university's student newspaper had sought access to the Student Organization Court's records and proceedings regarding hazing charges against two fraternities. Although the law provided that meetings of the "governing body" of any state agency must be open to the public, the law also covered the meetings of committees created by the governing body at which official action is taken. The court found that the judicial board was a vehicle through which the university took official action in that it enforced the university's code of student conduct. Thus, the court ruled that the university must permit members of the public, including the media, to attend the disciplinary board's hearings.

In contrast, the Supreme Court of Vermont rejected the attempt of a newspaper to obtain student disciplinary records and access to disciplinary hearings. In *Caledonian-Record Publishing Co. v. Vermont State Colleges,* 833 A.2d 1273 (Vt. 2003), the court ruled that an exception in the state public records law for "student records" blocked access to disciplinary records and that, although the state's Open Meeting Law did not contain such an exemption, allowing the public to attend student disciplinary hearings would make meaningless the exemption in the Public Records Act that protects the records of such hearings from disclosure.

12.5.3. Open records laws. Individuals and groups seeking information

about a public college or university's activities are making increasing use of
state open public records laws. These laws typically contain exceptions for certain kinds of records, and may also exempt from disclosure those records that
are required by other laws, both state and federal, to remain confidential (see
Section 9.7.2 for a discussion of the interplay between the Family Educational
Rights and Privacy Act (FERPA) and state open public records laws). The presumption, however, in applying these laws to requests for information, is that
the public should have access to information created or maintained by a public agency, and unless the information is covered by a statutory exception to disclosure, there typically must be strong public policy reason for a court to agree
to shield a "public record" from disclosure.

The courts have addressed two primary issues with respect to the application of open public records laws to colleges and universities. First is the issue
of whether the institution or organization from which the record is sought is
subject to the law. If the answer is in the affirmative, then the second issue
is whether the records sought are either exempt by statute or should be shielded
from disclosure for some public policy reason—for example, attorney-client privilege or crime victim privacy.

The first issue may have an easy answer if the entity is a public college or
university that holds the records itself. But if the entity is, for example, a separately chartered foundation that exists to support the operations of a public college or university, the issue will be more complicated. In *State ex rel. Toledo
Blade Co. v. University of Toledo Foundation,* 602 N.E.2d 1159 (Ohio 1992),
Ohio's Supreme Court determined that the state's public records disclosure
statute covered the foundation as a "public office." The plaintiff newspaper had
sought the names of donors to the foundation, and the court ruled that these
names must be disclosed. Similarly, the Supreme Court of South Carolina held
that the state's freedom of information act compelled the Carolina Research and
Development Foundation, which acquires and develops real estate for the University of South Carolina, to disclose its records. In *Weston v. Carolina Research
and Development Foundation,* 401 S.E.2d 161 (S.C. 1991), the court ruled that,
because the foundation received part of its funding from public monies, it met
the definition of "public body" in the state freedom of information act.

But in *State ex rel. Guste v. Nicholls College Foundation,* 592 So. 2d 419 (La.
Ct. App. 1991) (further discussed in Section 3.6.4), the court found that the
foundation, a private nonprofit corporation linked to a state college, was not a
public body (although the court said that the state had the authority to inspect
records of *public* funds received by the foundation). Similarly, the court in *Hopf
v. Topcorp,* discussed in Section 12.5.2 above, ruled that a private, for-profit corporation created by the city of Evanston and Northwestern University was not
subject to the open public records law.

Is a private college or university subject to a state's open public records law?
If one component of an otherwise private institution is publicly funded, as is
the case with some of the schools within Cornell University, then that component may be subject to open records laws. In *Alderson v. New York State College*

of Agriculture and Life Sciences, 749 N.Y.S.2d 581 (N.Y. App. Div. 2002), *affirmed and modified,* 4 N.Y.3d 225 (N.Y. 2005), the plaintiff sought financial information on a proposed agricultural park and on research on genetically modified organisms from the College of Agriculture. The appellate court ruled that the legislation that created the "statutory colleges" (those that are state supported) "bears significant indicia of a public function subject to state oversight." Therefore, the court ruled that the financial information sought by the plaintiff fell within the "more public aspects of the statutory colleges," and thus was subject to the state's freedom of information law. The state's highest court affirmed the appellate court's reasoning, but limited the financial information subject to the freedom of information law to documents accounting for the expenditure of state funds.

A contrasting view of the New York law's application to Cornell's "statutory colleges" is provided by *Stoll v. New York State College of Veterinary Medicine at Cornell University,* 701 N.Y.S.2d 316 (N.Y. 1999). In *Stoll,* New York's highest court rejected a claim that Cornell's disciplinary records are subject to the state's freedom of information act. The attorney for a professor accused of sexual harassment had filed a freedom of information act request for all of Cornell's records related to complaints brought under the university's campus code of conduct. The court ruled that the "statutory colleges" at Cornell were not state agencies, even though those units that receive state funding are subject to certain oversight by the SUNY Board of Trustees. The legislature had vested Cornell's administration (part of the private entity Cornell University) with the power to impose and maintain discipline at the statutory colleges, and this delegation of authority meant that the university's actions relating to campus discipline were those of a private, not a public, entity.

In a case against Mercer University (a private institution), a state trial court addressed whether records related to sexual assaults on campus compiled by the university's campus police were subject to the Georgia Open Records Act. A former student at Mercer, the victim of an alleged rape, had sued the university. The plaintiff's attorney requested the records, citing the state open records law. Records sought included incident reports, log books, crime logs, radio dispatch logs, and contact person reports prepared by the university's police department. The university refused to produce the records, saying that it was not subject to the open records law. The law firm sought a temporary restraining order against the university, and made two arguments. First, the law firm argued, the Mercer University Police Department (MUPD) was a "public agency" as defined by the Georgia Open Records Act (O.C.G.A. § 50-18-79 *et seq.*) because its police offers had law enforcement powers under state law. Alternatively, the law firm argued that the MUPD, although a private entity, maintained public records on behalf of a public office or agency, which are also required to be disclosed under Section 50-18-79(b) of the state law. The university asserted that its campus police officers received their authority from the university's governing board, not from the state, quoting Section 20-8-2 of the Georgia code, which provides that campus police "shall have the same law enforcement powers" as other state police officers "when authorized by the governing body or authority of such educational facility." With respect to the second argument, the university responded that the campus police records were maintained on behalf of the university, not the public, and thus they were not public records.

The trial court sided with the law firm, but the appellate court reversed in *Corporation of Mercer University v. Barrett & Farahany, LLP,* 610 S.E.2d 138 (Ga. Ct. App. 2005). The court ruled that Mercer University was not a public agency, and that the legislature had not intended that private entities be covered by the Open Records Act. The court also ruled that MUPD documents were not public records, but were maintained solely on behalf of the university. (For information on a similar lawsuit, seeking access to campus police records under Massachusetts' open public records law, see Eric Hoover, "Harvard's Student Newspaper Sues for Access to Police Records," *Chron. Higher Educ.,* July 30, 2003, available at http://chronicle.com/daily/2003/07/2003073003n.htm; and Brad Wolverton, "Harvard U. Can Withhold Campus-Police Records from Student Newspaper, Court Rules," *Chron. Higher Educ.,* January 16, 2006, available at http://chronicle.com/daily/2006/01/20060111604n.htm.)

In *Red & Black Publishing Co. v. Board of Regents* (discussed in Section 12.5.2), the Georgia Supreme Court also ruled that the state's open records law applied to the records of the student disciplinary board. Although the university argued that releasing the records would violate the federal Family Educational Rights and Privacy Act (FERPA), the state's high court disagreed. (For subsequent changes in the FERPA regulations, permitting disclosure of disciplinary records in certain circumstances, see Section 9.7.1 of this book; and for discussion of several cases involving press access to student disciplinary proceedings, see Section 9.7.2.) In contrast to the breadth of the Georgia court's interpretation of its open records law, Connecticut's Supreme Court, in *University of Connecticut v. Freedom of Information Commission,* 585 A.2d 690 (Conn. 1991), ruled that Connecticut's open records law did not require disclosure of names of students who worked for the university's police force.

Inquiries related to college athletics have also spawned litigation over the application of state open records laws. For example, in *University of Kentucky v. Courier-Journal,* 830 S.W.2d 373 (Ky. 1992), the University of Kentucky was required to disclose its response to a National Collegiate Athletic Association (NCAA) investigation of alleged rules violations. Although the university argued that appendices to the report, including documents and transcripts of interviews, came within the law's exception for "preliminary materials," the court disagreed, ruling that the entire report was a public document. And in *Milwaukee Journal v. Board of Regents of the University of Wisconsin System,* 472 N.W.2d 607 (Wis. Ct. App. 1991), the court ruled that the University of Wisconsin must disclose the names of applicants for the positions of football coach and athletic director.

Similarly, contracts negotiated by athletics coaches at public universities have caught the interest of the media. In *Cremins v. Atlanta Journal,* 405 S.E.2d 675 (Ga. 1991), the *Atlanta Journal* succeeded in gaining information about the outside income of some university coaches. But in *University System of Maryland v. The Baltimore Sun Co.,* 847 A.2d 427 (Md. 2004), the state's highest court distinguished between disclosure of coaches' employment contracts with the state university and their contracts with third parties (for commercial endorsements, for example). The court ordered an *in camera* review of the contracts in order to determine whether the contracts with third parties were sufficiently related to their university contracts so as to make payments under contracts with third parties part of their official compensation from the university (and thus subject to disclosure).

In some states, curriculum materials at a public institution may be considered a "public record" subject to inspection by the public. In *Russo v. Nassau County Community College,* 603 N.Y.S.2d 294 (N.Y. 1993), an individual filed a request under the state's freedom of information act for class materials used in a college sex education course. Although a state appellate court denied the request, stating that the materials were not "records" under the law's definition, the state's high court reversed and granted access to the materials.

Many other cases deal with the second of the two primary issues set out at the beginning of this subsection—whether there is a statutory exemption or a strong public policy reason for protecting from disclosure certain records that otherwise would be covered by the open records act. State open records laws typically do not require the individual or group requesting disclosure of certain information to demonstrate a particular need for the information. Thus, if the information is covered by the law, and no statutory exemption applies, it must usually be disclosed to anyone for any purpose. Individuals have therefore been able to use these laws for commercial purposes. In *Lieber v. Board of Trustees of Southern Illinois University,* 680 N.E.2d 374 (Ill. 1997), for example, the state supreme court ruled that the university had violated the Illinois Freedom of Information Act by refusing to provide the names and addresses of admitted students to the owner of a private, for-profit residence hall. The court held that the commercial nature of the use to which the information would be put did not serve to exempt the institution from disclosing the information.

Several other commercial cases involve private individuals or groups operating a bookstore near the campus of a public college or university who seek the book lists for courses to be taught at the college. In *Mohawk Book Co. v. State University of New York,* 732 N.Y.S.2d 272 (N.Y. App. Div. 2001), the court ruled that book lists, even though compiled by faculty members rather than compiled centrally by the university, were public records and subject to disclosure. But in *Dynamic Student Services v. State System of Higher Education,* 697 A.2d 239 (Pa. 1997), the Pennsylvania Supreme Court ruled that Millersville University and West Chester University did not have to provide the names of professors, courses, or the number of students enrolled in courses to an entity that sought to purchase used textbooks from students at the universities. At each university, the bookstore was not part of the university and received the course and text information directly from the faculty; the university itself did not create or maintain these records. For that reason, said the court, the universities did not have to provide information that they did not possess.

In other types of cases, there may be a basis to claim that interests in personal privacy provide a strong public policy reason for protecting certain records from disclosure. This argument has arisen, for instance, in cases where organizations opposed to affirmative action in admissions have requested admissions data from selective public universities and colleges under state open public records acts. The information requested has included grades and standardized test scores of applicants, and of admitted students, by racial and ethnic categories. For example, in *Osborn v. Board of Regents of the University of Wisconsin System,* 647 N.W.2d 158 (Wis. 2002), the Center for Equal Opportunity made open record requests under Wisconsin's law for data on applicants to undergraduate campuses, as well as to the University of Wisconsin Law School and Medical School. The university produced some of the requested records, but refused to provide information in students' application records. After the Center filed a mandamus action, the trial court ruled that the university must provide all requested records, even those containing personally identifiable information. Both parties appealed to the state appellate court, which reversed the trial court's order, stating that the records of individuals who had matriculated and those who had not were protected by the Family Educational Rights and Privacy Act (FERPA) (see Section 9.7.1 of this book). It also affirmed the lower court's decision that the university need not create new records in order to comply with the request.

The Wisconsin Supreme Court then reversed the appellate court's decision, concluding that the plaintiffs had not requested personally identifiable information, which eliminated the conflict with FERPA. The court balanced the public policy interests involved in disclosure with the university's concerns for privacy, and ruled that there was "no overriding public policy interest in keeping the requested records confidential." It also ruled that the university must redact certain records, and that the university could charge the plaintiffs a fee for the "actual, necessary, and direct cost of complying with these open record requests." (For a review of open records requests and related information requests in other states by groups opposing affirmative action, see Peter Schmidt, "Advocacy Groups Pressure Colleges to Disclose Affirmative-Action Policies," *Chron. Higher Educ.,* April 2, 2004, A26.)

State open records laws are being interpreted to cover a wide array of other information. For example, in *Keddie v. Rutgers, The State University,* 689 A.2d 702 (N.J. 1997), the Supreme Court of New Jersey ruled that bills for the services of outside counsel, and documents related to these services, are public records, and must be disclosed to the faculty union upon request. In *State ex rel. James v. Ohio State University,* 637 N.E.2d 911 (Ohio 1994), the Supreme Court of Ohio ruled that a professor's tenure file, including letters from evaluators and their identities, is subject to disclosure under that state's Public Records Act. The *James* case is discussed in Section 7.7.1. And in *An Unincorporated Operating Division of Indiana Newspapers v. Trustees of Indiana University,* 787 N.E.2d 893 (Ind. Ct. App. 2003), a newspaper had sought investigative materials concerning the behavior of a basketball coach who was eventually fired. Both the police and the trustees had conducted investigations of the coach's behavior. The court exempted the police investigation from disclosure because of a "law enforcement privilege," but said that the portions of the trustees' investigation that did not contain personally identifiable information about students must be produced.

In another case involving personal privacy, *Marder v. Board of Regents of the University of Wisconsin System,* 596 N.W.2d 502 (Wis. Ct. App. 1999), the university was asked by a newspaper and radio station to provide copies of employment records and investigatory files compiled in response to a sexual harassment claim against a faculty member. The university agreed to provide the materials, and the faculty member sued the university. The court ruled that personnel records are not exempt from disclosure under Wisconsin's Open Records Law, and that the public had a "substantial interest in student-faculty relations at our state universities" that outweighed the faculty member's privacy concerns.

State open records laws may be applied as well to e-mail sent to or from state employees. To cover this eventuality, colleges may wish to develop and distribute policies on the use of e-mail that advise employees of the potential for disclosure of what may appear to be private communications. (For a discussion of the application of open records laws to e-mail messages by faculty or students, and several examples of the legal and practical problems that incautious use of e-mail may create, see Andrea L. Foster, "Your E-Mail Message to a Colleague Could Be Tomorrow's Headline," *Chron. Higher Educ.,* June 21, 2002, A31.)

As the cases in this subsection demonstrate, the general problem created by open records statutes and similar laws is how to balance the public's right to know against an individual's right to privacy or an institution's legitimate need for confidentiality. Administrators and counsel must consider the complex interplay of all these interests. Sometimes the legislation provides guidelines or rules for striking this balance. Even in the absence of such provisions, some courts have narrowly construed open records laws to avoid intrusion on compelling interests of privacy or confidentiality. The trend, however, appears to be in the direction of openness and public access, even when the institution considers the information sensitive or private.

12.5.4. *State administrative procedure laws.*

State administrative law is another area of state law that has had an impact on the campus. Like the federal government, many states have statutes requiring that state agencies follow prescribed procedures when formulating binding rules. State boards and state institutions of higher education may be considered state agencies subject to these rule-making statutes. In *Florida State University v. Dann,* 400 So. 2d 1304 (Fla. Dist. Ct. App. 1980), for instance, several faculty members challenged university procedures used to determine merit raises and other salary increases. The faculty members argued that the university had not conformed to the state rule-making statute when it created the salary increase procedures. The court agreed and invalidated the procedures.

Similarly, in *Board of Trustees v. Department of Administrative Services,* 429 N.E.2d 428 (Ohio 1981), laid-off employees of Ohio State University argued that they were entitled to reinstatement and other relief because their layoffs were executed under improperly issued rules. The court agreed. It considered the university's rules to be state agency rules subject to the state's Administrative Procedure Act (APA). This Act required public notice of rule making, filing of rules with the executive and legislative branches of government, a public hearing on proposed rules, and notification of persons who would be especially affected by the rules. The university had failed to follow these procedures. Moreover, it had erroneously issued the rules under the aegis of its board of trustees. The applicable statutory provision grants such rule-making authority to the personnel departments of state universities, not the boards of trustees.

And in *McGrath v. University of Alaska,* 813 P.2d 1370 (Alaska 1991), the Alaska Supreme Court reviewed the claim of state university faculty that the state's Administrative Procedure Act applied to faculty grievance proceedings at the university. The university had promulgated its own policies regarding grievance proceedings; however, the court ruled that the APA superseded the university's policies.

State courts may interpret the state's administrative procedure act to require progressive discipline prior to the termination of a tenured faculty member, whose expectation of continued employment establishes a constitutionally protected property interest in his job (see Section 6.6.2). For example, in *Trimble v. West Virginia Board of Directors, Southern West Virginia Community and Technical College,* 549 S.E.2d 294 (W. Va. 2001), a tenured professor who had been terminated for "insubordination" challenged that decision. West Virginia's Administrative Procedure Act, Chapter 29A, Article 5, Section 4(g) gives the state's courts jurisdiction to review the determination of a state agency (in this case, the college's "Board of Directors"). The court ruled that the college's decision to terminate him without having first afforded him progressive discipline violated his constitutional right to due process. The professor, who led the faculty union, had refused to administer student course evaluations, as all faculty members were required to do. Because he had an otherwise good work record and had received good annual evaluations in prior years, the court ruled that termination was too harsh a penalty and that progressive discipline should have been used.

A faculty member whose contract was not renewed attempted to avoid a review under administrative law, preferring instead to file a breach of contract action in court. In *Gaskill v. Ft. Hays State University,* 70 P.3d 693 (Kan. Ct. App. 2003), the court dismissed the claim, concluding that the Kansas Act for Judicial Review and Civil Enforcement of Agency Actions (Kan. Stat. Ann. §§ 77-601 *et seq.*) was the professor's exclusive remedy for his claim of wrongful nonrenewal of his contract. The court noted that the defendant institution was listed in Kansas law (Kan. Stat. Ann. § 76-711(a)) as a state educational institution subject to the Kansas Act for Judicial Review, and thus affirmed the trial court's finding that it lacked jurisdiction to hear the case.

Although administrative procedure act protections typically extend to personnel decisions (such as hiring, promotion, tenure, discipline, and termination), work assignments and other "managerial prerogatives" may not be included within these regulations. For example, in *Johnson v. Southern University,* 803 So. 2d 1140 (La. Ct. App. 1st Cir. 2002), the court ruled that a professor could not challenge his teaching assignments under Louisiana's Administrative Procedure Act because teaching assignments were not reviewable under this law. The decision to assign him only multisectioned classes did not deprive him of a property or liberty interest, said the court.

On the other hand, administrative procedure acts may provide for judicial review in situations in which an individual might otherwise be required to follow the more limited review by an administrative law judge. For example, in Tennessee, a state statute, Tenn. Code Ann. § 49-8-304, provides that individuals challenging a negative tenure decision are entitled to a *de novo* judicial review rather than the more limited review provided for by the Administrative Procedures Act for other types of challenges to agency decisions. In *Stephens v. Roane State Community College*, 2003 Tenn. App. LEXIS 567 (Tenn. Ct. App., August 12, 2003), the court ruled for a second time in a case involving the plaintiff's six-month suspension for sexual harassment of a student. His first judicial hearing had been a limited one under the more general APA standard, and he had been found guilty of the harassment charge; on remand, the trial judge reviewed the entire record and concluded that the suspension was justified. The appellate court ruled that the trial court's determination was supported by clear and convincing evidence.

Faculty members who challenge denial of tenure, nonreappointment, or termination may find their freedom to litigate these decisions in court circumscribed somewhat by state administrative procedure acts. This is the teaching of the *Gaskill* case, above. Other cases presenting these issues are discussed in Section 6.7.4.

12.5.5. *Laws regulating medical services and medical research.*
State laws and court decisions regarding hospitals, clinics, and health care professionals are of particular concern to universities that have a university-affiliated hospital or health care clinical programs that utilize hospitals or clinics as training sites. Some of these laws and decisions also have important applications to campus medical clinics and campus health services for students. The applicable requirements are usually found in state statutes and administrative regulations, but these laws must often be interpreted in light of state common law principles or principles of state or federal constitutional law.

All states have licensing laws for certain health care facilities, and some also have certificate-of-need requirements for the construction of new facilities (see, for example, *Tulsa Area Hospital Council v. Oral Roberts University*, 626 P.2d 316 (Okla. 1981)). All states also have licensing laws for various health care practitioners, as well as unauthorized practice laws. Informed consent laws regarding medical treatment are another common example. Many states also have labor relations laws governing unionization of personnel in public hospitals, and some of these laws also cover medical residents (see Sections 4.5.2.3 & 4.5.3 of this book).

More recent and controversial examples include laws on the disposal of medical and infectious waste (for example, Cal. Health & Safety Code § 7054.4); on human medical experimentation (for example, Cal. Health & Safety Code, ch. 1.3); on anatomical gifts (see Marjorie Shields, Annot., "Validity and Application of Uniform Anatomical Gift Act," 6 A.L.R.6th 365; on living wills and durable medical powers-of-attorney;[14] on hospitals' authority to regulate use of certain procedures, such as abortion or sterilization (for example, Md. Code Ann., Health—General § 20-214(b), applied in *St. Agnes Hospital v. Riddick*, 668 F. Supp. 478 (D. Md. 1987)); on hospitals' duty to refuse to perform certain services, such as abortion (for example, Ark. Const. Amend. 68, § 1, applied in *Unborn Child Amendment Committee v. Ward*, 943 S.W.2d 591 (Ark. 1997)); on regulating certain controversial research, such as genetic or fetal research (for example, Ill. Rev. Stat. ch. 38, para. 81-26, applied in the *Lifchez* case below); on AIDS testing (for example, 35 Pa. Stat. Ann. § 7602 *et seq.*, applied in *In re Milton S. Hershey Medical Center of the Pennsylvania State University*, 634 A.2d 159 (Pa. 1993)); and on health professionals' obligations to treat AIDS patients (for example, the Minnesota Human Rights Act (Minn. Stat. Ann. § 363 A.01 *et seq.*), applied in *State by Beaulieu v. Clausen*, 491 N.W.2d 662 (Minn. Ct. App. 1992)).

A line of U.S. Supreme Court cases on the constitutional right to privacy provides examples of how state laws on medical services may be limited by federal constitutional law. In *Cruzan v. Director, Missouri Department of Health*, 497 U.S. 261 (1990), Missouri law required that a comatose patient's desire to withdraw life-sustaining medical treatment be proven by clear and convincing evidence. Although the U.S. Supreme Court upheld the constitutionality of this requirement, it also recognized that the states' regulatory authority in this area is limited because, under the Fourteenth Amendment's due process clause, persons have "a constitutionally protected liberty interest in refusing unwanted medical treatment." In a later case, *Washington v. Glucksberg*, 521 U.S. 702 (1997), a Washington state law prohibited any person, including a physician, from assisting another (including a terminally ill patient) in terminating his or her life. The Court upheld this law under the due process clause.[15] In *Planned Parenthood of Southeastern Pennsylvania v. Casey*, 505 U.S. 833 (1992), a Pennsylvania law on abortions included informed consent requirements, a husband notification requirement, and reporting requirements for facilities that perform abortions. The Court upheld the first and third of these restrictions, rejecting arguments that they unduly burdened the right to choose abortion. Regarding the husband notification requirement, however, the Court held that it did unduly burden choice and therefore violated the due process clause.

Other important cases illustrate constitutional issues raised by laws that restrict medical research. In *Lifchez v. Hartigan*, 735 F. Supp. 1361 (N.D. Ill. 1990), for example, physicians challenged an Illinois statute providing that "[n]o person shall sell or experiment upon a fetus produced by the fertilization of a human ovum by a human sperm unless such experimentation is therapeutic to the fetus thereby produced" (Ill. Rev. Stat. ch. 38, para. 81-26, § 6(7)). The court held that the statute was unconstitutionally vague and that it invaded the woman's constitutional freedom to choose procedures such as embryo transfer. Similarly, in *Forbes*

---

[14]Federal law requires that Medicare and Medicaid providers inform patients of these state laws (see 42 U.S.C. § 1396a(w)(1) & 42 U.S.C. § 1395c(f)(1)).

[15]At the same time, the Court also upheld a similar New York law under the equal protection clause (*Vacco v. Quill*, 521 U.S. 793 (1997)).

v. Woods, 71 F. Supp. 2d 1015 (D. Ariz. 1999), *affirmed, Forbes v. Napolitano,* 236 F.3d 1009 (9th Cir. 2000), the trial and appellate courts invalidated Arizona statutes that made it a crime to engage in experimentation or investigation using fetal tissue (Ariz. Rev. Stat. §§ 36–2302, 32–1401(25)(x), & 32–1854(45)). In *Moore v. Regents of the University of California,* 793 P.2d 479 (Cal. 1990), the plaintiff claimed that California property law accorded him ownership rights over the cells from his diseased spleen that researchers had used, and that he was therefore entitled to a share of the profits reaped from the research. Overruling an intermediate appellate court's decision, the California Supreme Court held that California law did not create any such property right for the plaintiff but did create fiduciary duties and informed consent requirements obligating the physician to inform the patient of any personal or economic interest that the physician might have in using the patient's tissue. And in *Brotherton v. Cleveland,* 923 F.2d 477 (6th Cir. 1991), the court held that a wife had a constitutionally protected property interest in her deceased husband's body under Ohio law, and that the Fourteenth Amendment's due process clause therefore limited the authority of state employees to use body parts for organ transplants or research without the wife's prior consent. *Brotherton v. Cleveland* was relied upon in *Whaley v. County of Tuscola,* 58 F.3d 1111 (6th Cir. 1995), in which the court held that relatives had a property interest in the deceased's body parts under Michigan law that was protected by the due process clause; and that the defendant's removal of the deceased's eyeballs and corneas without the relatives' consent was therefore a violation of procedural due process. (For another, similar, case in which the court also relies on state common law, see *Newman v. Sathyavaglswaran,* 287 F.3d 786 (9th Cir. 2002).)

In addition, a New York court and a Maryland court have provided important examples of legal problems that may arise regarding human subject research. In *T.D. v. New York State Office of Mental Health,* 650 N.Y.S.2d 173 (N.Y. App. Div. 1996), a case brought by medical patients incapable of giving their own informed consent, the court invalidated state regulations of human subject research. According to the court, analysis of such regulations—and human subject research regulations generally—

> necessarily requires a balancing of this State's responsibility to protect individuals who, because of mental illness, age, birth defect, other disease or some combination of these factors, are incapable of speaking for themselves, from needless pain, indignity and abuse, against its worthwhile goal of fostering the development of better methods to diagnose, treat and otherwise care for these same individuals through cooperation with the medical community and private industry [650 N.Y.S.2d at 176].

The court held that the state's regulations did not suitably strike this balance, since they did not adequately safeguard the constitutional and common law rights of the patients:

> The provisions concerning the assessment of a potential subject's capacity do not adequately protect the common law privacy and due process rights of potential subjects. The regulations do not identify or set out specific or even minimum

qualifications for the individual or individuals who initially assess a potential subject's capacity, and do not contain a specific protocol for how the assessment is to be carried out. Further, there are no provisions requiring any notice to the patient that his or her capacity to provide or withhold consent for a particular study is being questioned. Consequently, there is no provision for review of a determination of lack of capacity at the patient's request [650 N.Y.S.2d at 189].

In addition, the court held that the New York State Office of Mental Health "lacked the authority to promulgate the challenged regulations governing human subject research as such authority is given exclusively to the Commissioner of the Department of Health pursuant to Article 24-A of the Public Health Law."

In a subsequent case, *Grimes v. Kennedy Krieger Institute, Inc.*, 782 A.2d 807 (Md. 2001), the highest court of Maryland dealt specifically with human subject research involving children. The state did not have an applicable statute or administrative regulation, but the court used common law principles of tort and contract to limit researchers' use of children as human subjects. *Grimes* is further discussed below and also in Section 15.4.2.

As *Grimes* indicates, state tort law (see generally Section 3.3.1) is also very important in the health care context.[16] Malpractice law (setting professional standards of care for health care workers), the law on releases and waivers (see Section 2.5.3.3), products liability law (regarding the safety of drugs and medical equipment), and the tort of battery (covering physical, and sometimes emotional, harm from invasive medical procedures performed without informed consent) are all pertinent, as well as the duty of care that negligence law establishes for researchers using human subjects in their research. In *Grimes v. Kennedy Krieger Institute* (above), for example, the court established the circumstances in which researchers owe a duty of care to children who are human subjects in research projects; and in addition the court limited the circumstances in which researchers may seek, and parents may grant, informed consent for the participation of children. And in *Mink v. University of Chicago*, 460 F. Supp. 713 (N.D. Ill. 1978), the court held that the women plaintiffs had a cause of action for battery against the university and the drug manufacturer for administering a drug as part of a medical experiment without their knowledge or consent; that the plaintiffs did not have a products liability claim against the manufacturer absent evidence of physical injury; and that the plaintiffs would have a claim for failure to notify of the drug's risks only if they had been physically injured. (Compare *Miller ex rel. Miller v. HCA, Inc.*, 118 S.W.3d 758 (Tex. 2003), in which the Texas Supreme Court ruled for the defendants in another type of battery case involving the birth of a premature infant.)

---

[16]For a sampling of the many types of cases that may arise, see Thomas M. Fleming, Annot., "Hospital's Liability for Injury Resulting from Failure to Have Sufficient Number of Nurses on Duty," 2 A.L.R.5th 286; David B. Harrison, Annot., "Application of Rule of Strict Liability in Tort to Person or Entity Rendering Medical Services," 100 A.L.R.3d 1205; Marc L. Carmichael, Annot., "Liability of Hospital or Medical Practitioner Under Doctrine of Strict Liability in Tort, or Breach of Warranty, for Harm Caused by Drug, Medical Instrument, or Similar Device Used in Treating Patient," 54 A.L.R.3d 258; A. M. Swarthout, Annot., "Validity and Construction of Contract Exempting Hospital or Doctor from Liability for Negligence to Patient," 6 A.L.R.3d 704.

Tort liability issues may be especially complex in health care cases because of the numbers of parties potentially involved: the university; the medical center or hospital, which may be an entity separate from the university (see Section 3.6); physicians, who may or may not be employees or agents of the university; nurses, laboratory technicians, and other allied health personnel; and outside parties such as laboratories, drug and equipment manufacturers, and drug and equipment suppliers. (See, for example, *Jaar v. University of Miami*, 474 So. 2d 239 (Fla. Dist. Ct. App. 1985).) When the defendants are governmental entities or their employees, issues concerning sovereign or "official" immunity and waiver of immunity may also be involved. (See, for example, *Texas Tech University Health Sciences Center v. Mendoza*, 2003 WL 1359549, 2003 Tex. App. LEXIS 2370 (March 20, 2003); and *Crannan v. Maxwell*, 1999 WL 1065051 (Ala. 1999).)

Selected Annotated Bibliography

Sec. 12.1 (Overview)

Schwartz, Bernard. *Administrative Law* (3d ed., Little, Brown, 1991). A comprehensive overview of the principles of administrative law. Although the book does not focus on education, its analyses can be applied to state postsecondary systems (to the extent that they are considered state agencies), to state agencies that charter or license private institutions, and to other state agencies whose regulatory authority extends to postsecondary institutions.

Sec. 12.2 (State Provision of Public Postsecondary Education)

Beckham, Joseph. "Reasonable Independence for Public Higher Education: Legal Implications of Constitutionally Autonomous Status," 7 *J. Law & Educ.* 177 (1978). Author argues for a constitutional grant of "limited autonomy" to "the state's higher education system" in order to "insure reasonable autonomy on selected issues of college and university governance." Article also discusses related issues, such as the constitutionality of legislative attempts to transfer power from an autonomous system, the effect "legislation relating to statewide concerns" has on an autonomous system, and the distinction between "appropriations and expenditures."

Crockett, Richard B. "Constitutional Autonomy and the North Dakota State Board of Higher Education," 54 *N.D. L. Rev.* 529 (1978). A study of the autonomy granted to North Dakota's public institutions of higher education by amendment to the state constitution. Examines judicial decisions both in North Dakota and in neighboring jurisdictions. Author concludes that "a grant of autonomy is significant and the constitutional authority of a governing board to control, manage, administer, or supervise the institutions under its jurisdiction may not be invoked or interfered with by a state legislature."

Feller, Irwin. *Universities and State Governments: A Study in Policy Analysis* (Praeger, 1986). Describes the role of universities in the shaping of public policy at the state level during the 1970s. The author—at various times a faculty member, member of a governor's staff, and researcher—discusses the ways in which policy research is used by lawmakers at the state level and the overall relationship of universities to state government.

Heller, Donald E. (ed.). *The States and Public Higher Education Policy: Affordability, Access, and Accountability* (Johns Hopkins University Press, 2000). A collection of essays by fourteen scholars assembled to address key issues regarding the states' role in setting and implementing higher education policy. Includes analysis of the structure of state systems and governing boards, and the role of pubic trustees.

Hines, Edward R. *Higher Education and State Governments: Renewed Partnership, Cooperation, or Competition?* ASHE-ERIC Higher Education Report no. 5 (Association for the Study of Higher Education, 1988). Examines state leadership in higher education (governing boards, coordinating boards, legislators, and lobbyists), state financial support for higher education in transition (including tuition pricing and student financial aid), current state/campus policy issues (such as academic program review and outcomes assessment), and the policy implications of state regulatory actions.

Horowitz, Harold W. "The Autonomy of the University of California Under the State Constitution," 25 *UCLA L. Rev.* 23 (1977). Discusses the state constitutional provisions that grant the University of California "constitutional" rather than "statutory" legal status. Analyzes judicial decisions interpreting the relative position of the board of regents under the state constitution vis-à-vis other branches of state government, and proposes a theory that would limit legislative interference with the governance of the university.

McGuinness, Aimes, & Paulson, Christine. *State Postsecondary Education Structures Handbook* (Education Commission of the States, 1991). Describes the structure, governance, and coordination of higher education in every state. Also includes recent trends and summaries of state boards and agencies.

Millard, Richard M. *State Boards of Higher Education,* ASHE-ERIC Higher Education Research Report no. 4 (American Association for Higher Education, 1976). Examines the history, structure, functions, and future directions of state governing and coordinating boards for higher education. Includes state-by-state tables and a bibliography.

Schaefer, Hugh. "The Legal Status of the Montana University System Under the New Montana Constitution," 35 *Mont. L. Rev.* 189 (1974). Compares and analyzes the new and old Montana constitutional provisions and discusses comparable provisions in other state constitutions. Considers the impact of such provisions on the state institution's relationships with other branches of state government.

Shekleton, James F. "The Road Not Taken: The Curious Jurisprudence Touching upon the Constitutional Status of the South Dakota Board of Regents," 39 *S.D. L. Rev.* 312 (1994). Reviews the constitutional powers given the state's governing board and analyzes the division of authority between that board and the state legislature to create, abolish, govern, and control the state's public colleges and universities.

Sec. 12.3 (State Chartering and Licensure of Private Postsecondary Institutions)

Committee on Nonprofit Corporations. *Guidebook for Directors of Nonprofit Corporations* (2d ed., American Bar Association, 2002). This Guidebook apprises directors and trustees of nonprofit corporations of a range of legal and governance issues that arise under state corporation law and federal and state tax laws. Topics addressed include the roles of the board of directors, the duties and rights of directors, director liability, and risk management.

Dutile, Fernand, & Gaffney, Edward. *State and Campus: State Regulation of Religiously Affiliated Higher Education* (University of Notre Dame Press, 1984). Explores the relationship between state governments and church-related colleges and universities. Reviews the various types of state regulations and their validity under federal and state constitutions.

Jung, Steven, et al. *The Final Technical Report: A Study of State Oversight in Postsecondary Education* (American Institutes for Research, 1977). An extensive report done by AIR under contract with the U.S. Office of Education. Compiles and assesses statutes and administrative regulations under which state agencies regulate postsecondary institutions. Includes studies of consumer protection incidents reported by state officials. Office (now Department) of Education reference: HEW, USOE, Contract No. 300-76-0377. AIR reference: AIR-59400-1277-FR.

Millard, Richard M. "Postsecondary Education and 'The Best Interests of the People of the States,'" 50 *J. Higher Educ.* 121 (1979). Discusses the status of licensing in the fifty states and other developments with respect to licensing.

Oleck, Howard. *Nonprofit Corporations, Organizations, and Associations* (6th ed., Prentice-Hall, 1994). A comprehensive survey of all types of nonprofit and tax-exempt institutions, foundations, and corporations. Has numerous chapters covering hundreds of subjects. Issues addressed include formation and dissolution of nonprofit entities, organization, tax exemptions, and lobbying. Also includes model forms.

O'Neill, Joseph P., & Barnett, Samuel. *Colleges and Corporate Change: Merger, Bankruptcy and Closure* (Conference of Small Colleges, 1981). A handbook primarily for trustees and administrators but also useful to attorneys. Chapters include "Indicators of Institutional Health," "Options for Collegiate Corporate Change," "Merger," and "Dissolution of the College Corporation." Discusses procedures for amending the college charter, disposition of assets, placement of faculty, and reorganization under federal bankruptcy law. Also includes state-by-state summary of laws and regulations governing collegiate corporate changes and state-by-state summary of regulations regarding institutional responsibility for student records.

Postsecondary Education Convening Authority. *Approaches to State Licensing of Private Degree-Granting Institutions*, Institute for Educational Leadership Report no. 8 (George Washington University, 1975). A report on the first conference of state officials who license private degree-granting institutions. Explores the concepts of chartering and licensing, the status of licensing in the fifty states, and the policy and legal problems facing licensing officials. Makes recommendations for the future.

Stewart, David, & Spille, Henry. *Diploma Mills: Degrees of Fraud* (American Council on Education/Macmillan, 1989). Addresses the problem of the sale of phony diplomas. Analyzes the businesses that engage in such activities, the lax state laws under which these businesses are licensed and allowed to sell the degrees, and the role of the federal government in alleviating the problem. Includes an appendix listing relevant state laws. Authors call for strengthening of the current laws that allow fraudulent degree-granting businesses to operate, and propose other steps to alleviate the problem.

Sec. 12.4 (State Regulation of Out-of-State Institutions and Programs)

Hughes, Earl, et al. *Nova University's Three National Doctoral Degree Programs* (Nova University, 1977). A Ford Foundation–funded case study on the development of multistate education programs. Chapter Nine (by Fred Nelson & William Kaplin) provides a discussion of "Legal and Political Constraints on Nova University's External Degree Programs."

Sec. 12.5 (Other State Regulatory Laws Affecting Postsecondary Education Programs)

Bakaly, Charles, & Grossman, Joel. *Modern Law of Employment Contracts: Formation, Operation and Remedies for Breach* (Harcourt Brace Jovanovich, 1983, and periodic supp.). A practical handbook on the legal relationship between employer and nonunionized employee. Topics include application of state contract law principles to employment contracts, issues regarding employee handbooks and employment manuals, wrongful discharge and the employment-at-will doctrine, and internal dispute resolution mechanisms for employment disputes. Also includes appendices with state-by-state review of wrongful discharge law, sample provisions for employee handbooks, and sample employment contract provisions.

Brown, Kimberly, Fishman, Phillip, & Jones, Nancy. *Legal and Policy Issues in the Language Proficiency Assessment of International Teaching Assistants* (Institute for Higher Education Law and Governance, University of Houston, 1990). Reviews the laws of eleven states that require English proficiency and discusses various legal theories that could be used to attack the application of these laws. An appendix includes the text of the laws.

Cleveland, Harlan. *The Costs and Benefits of Openness: Sunshine Laws and Higher Education* (Association of Governing Boards of Universities and Colleges, 1985). A research report that reviews state open meeting laws and the court decisions and state attorney general opinions construing these laws. Compares the various state laws, using a list of twenty-three characteristics relating to openness. Author analyzes the costs and benefits of openness under these laws, concluding that the costs generally outweigh the benefits. Report includes an appendix of attorney general opinions and a bibliography. Reprinted in 12 *J. Coll. & Univ. Law* 127 (1985).

Davis, Charles N. "Scaling the Ivory Tower: State Public Records Laws and University Presidential Searches," 21 *J. Coll. & Univ. Law* 353 (1994). Examines the decisions of state courts and state laws relating to presidential searches. Suggests guidelines for search committees, the press, and the candidates for determining the scope of these laws.

Greer, Darryl G. *"Truth-in-Testing Legislation": An Analysis of Political and Legal Consequences, and Prospects* (Institute for Higher Education Law and Governance, University of Houston, 1983). Reviews the history and origins of testing legislation and discusses in depth two laws—those of California and New York—that mandate disclosure of standardized test questions and answers. An evaluation of the educational, legal, and political consequences of the laws is provided.

Hopkins, Bruce. *The Law of Fundraising* (3d ed., Wiley, 2002). Describes and analyzes governmental systems for regulating fundraising by nonprofit organizations. Presents state-by-state summary of laws on charitable solicitations; analyzes legal issues raised by government regulation of fund-raising; explores federal IRS oversight of tax-exempt organizations and the activities of private agencies as part of the overall regulatory scheme; and offers advice on how to comply with existing rules. Supplemented annually.

Madsen, Helen H. "New State Legislation on Informing Workers About Hazardous Substances in the Workplace: Will It Impact on University Teaching and Research?" 9 *J. Coll. & Univ. Law* 325 (1982–83). Reviews the legal situation in states that have enacted "laws giving employees the right to obtain basic information about hazardous substances with which they work." Provides an overview of some major issues involved in this area of regulation, contrasting different states' responses (or lack of response) to these issues. Also discusses factors that could improve state regulation of hazardous substances in the higher education context.

Remis, Rob. "Analysis of Civil and Criminal Penalties in Athletic Agent Statutes and Support for the Imposition of Civil and Criminal Liability upon Athletes," 8 *Seton Hall J. Sport L.* 1 (1998). Reviews state laws that impose civil penalties or damages on athletes' agents, but not on athletes, for violations of the law's provisions. Argues that athletes should also be subject to these laws. Reviews civil and criminal proceedings under these laws, and provides appendices in which the athlete agent statutes are summarized.

Rich, Ben A. "Malpractice Issues in the Academic Medical Center," 13 *J. Coll. & Univ. Law* 149 (1986). Considers the "standards of care applicable to health care practitioners," and the "special problems of patient care delivery" in academic medical centers, as well as the "special status of public academic medical centers and their employees." Gives special attention to problems of informed consent and to legal relations between universities and affiliated medical institutions.

See Bell & Majestic entry in Selected Annotated Bibliography for Chapter 13, Section 13.2.

See Dutile & Gaffney entry for Section 12.3.

13

The College and the Federal Government

Sec. 13.1. Federal Constitutional Powers over Education

13.1.1. Overview. The federal government is a government of limited powers; it has only those powers that are expressly conferred by the U.S. Constitution or can reasonably be implied from those conferred. The remaining powers are, under the Tenth Amendment, "reserved to the states respectively, or to the People." Although the Constitution does not mention education, let alone delegate power over it to the federal government, it does not follow that the Tenth Amendment reserves all authority over education to the states or the people (see *Case v. Bowles,* 327 U.S. 92 (1946)). Many federal constitutional powers— particularly the spending power, the taxing power, the commerce power, and the civil rights enforcement powers (see subsections 13.1.2 through 13.1.5 below)— are broad enough to extend to many matters concerning education. Whenever an education activity falls within the scope of one of these federal powers, the federal government has authority over it.

When Congress passes a law pursuant to its federal constitutional powers, and the law is within the scope of these powers, it will "preempt" or supersede any state and local laws that impinge on the effectuation of the federal law.[1] The application of this federal "preemption doctrine" to postsecondary education is illustrated by *United States v. City of Philadelphia,* 798 F.2d 81 (3d Cir. 1986), discussed briefly in Section 11.1 of this book. Noting that the federal military recruiting laws and policies at issue in that case were within the scope of

---

[1]For summaries of preemption law and examples, see *Hillsborough County v. Automated Medical Laboratories,* 471 U.S. 707, 712–13 (1985); and *Pacific Gas & Electric Co. v. State Energy Resources Conservation & Development Comm'n.,* 461 U.S. 190, 203–4 (1983).

Congress's constitutional powers to raise and support armies, the court held that they preempted a local civil rights ordinance prohibiting discrimination against homosexuals. In addition, when Congress passes a federal law pursuant to its constitutional powers, it sometimes may abrogate the states' Eleventh Amendment immunity from suit and permit private individuals to enforce the law by suing the states for money damages (see subsection 13.1.6 below).

In a number of cases since the early 1990s, the U.S. Supreme Court has emphasized principles of federalism and the limits that they place on federal power. In so doing, the Court has created new protections against federal authority for the states and state agencies. In *Printz v. United States*, 521 U.S. 898 (1997), for example, the Court relied on a principle of state sovereignty. The question was whether Congress could compel state officers (in this case sheriffs) "to execute Federal Laws." The Court answered this question in the negative, thus invalidating provisions of the federal Brady Handgun Violence Prevention Act that commanded state and local law enforcement officers to conduct background checks on prospective handgun purchasers. According to the Court, these provisions of the federal Brady law violated state sovereignty protections: "[I]t is the whole *object* of the law to direct the functioning of the state executive, and hence to compromise the structural framework of dual sovereignty. . . . It is the very *principle* of separate state sovereignty that such a law offends. . . ." Tying its holding in *Printz* to an earlier holding in the case of *New York v. United States*, 505 U.S. 144 (1992), the Court concluded:

> We held in *New York* that Congress cannot compel the States to enact or enforce a federal regulatory program. Today we hold that Congress cannot circumvent that prohibition by conscripting the States' officers directly. The Federal Government may neither issue directives requiring the States to address particular problems, nor command the States' officers, or those of their political subdivisions, to administer or enforce a Federal regulatory program [521 U.S. at 944].

Similarly, in *Seminole Tribe v. Florida* (1996), in several successor cases relying on *Seminole Tribe*, in *Alden v. Maine* (1999), and in *Federal Maritime Comm'n. v. South Carolina Ports Authority* (2002), the Court again cited state sovereignty principles in providing states a broad immunity from private plaintiffs' suits raising federal claims in federal and state courts and before federal administrative agencies. (These cases are discussed in Section 13.1.6 below.) In 1997 in *City of Boerne v. Flores*, in several successor cases relying on *Boerne*, and in 2000 in *United States v. Morrison*, the Court narrowed Congress's authority to regulate the states under its civil rights enforcement powers. (These cases are discussed in Section 13.1.5 below.) And in 1995 in *United States v. Lopez*, and in 2000 in *United States v. Morrison*, the Court limited Congress's commerce power not only over the states but, more particularly, over private individuals and institutions. (These cases are discussed in Section 13.1.4 below.) All of these cases were controversial. The extent of the controversy, and the contested nature of the law in this arena, are illustrated by the Court's voting patterns in these cases; *Printz, Seminole Tribe, Alden, South Carolina Ports Authority, City of*

Boerne, Morrison, and *Lopez,* and most of the cases followir   re all decided by 5-to-4 votes.

13.1.2. Spending power. Contemporary federal involvement in education stems primarily from Congress's power under Article I, Section 8, Clause 1 to spend its funds for the "general welfare of the United States." (See generally A. Rosenthal, "Conditional Federal Spending and the Constitution," 39 *Stan. L. Rev.* 1103 (1987).) The spending power is the basis of the federal aid-to-education programs and "cross-cutting" requirements discussed in Section 13.4 below, the student aid programs discussed in Section 8.3.2, the civil rights requirements discussed in Section 13.5 below, and the Family Educational Rights and Privacy Act (FERPA) requirements discussed in Section 9.7.1. The placement of conditions on grants for postsecondary education has been an accepted practice at least since the Morrill Acts (see Section 13.4.1 of this book) and the case of *Wyoming ex rel. Wyoming Agricultural College v. Irvin,* 206 U.S. 278 (1907)). The constitutional validity of such conditions has also been clear at least since the late 1930s, when the U.S. Supreme Court broadly construed the spending power in the course of upholding innovative New Deal spending programs (see *Steward Machine Co. v. Davis,* 301 U.S. 548 (1937)). Thereafter, the courts have been willing to uphold virtually any spending program that Congress believes will further the general welfare (see, for example, *Helvering v. Davis,* 301 U.S. 619 (1937)) and any condition on spending, whether imposed on governmental or private entities, that is "germane" to (or related to) the activities and objectives for which the federal government is expending the funds (see *South Dakota v. Dole,* 483 U.S. 203, 208, n.3 (majority opinion), & 213–16 (dissenting opinion)). The spending power, however, does not give the federal government a roving commission to regulate postsecondary education. What leverage the federal government exerts through the spending power arises from its establishment of the purposes and conditions for its expenditure of funds. Although fund recipients may be under considerable financial pressure to accept the funds, and although they are subject to all the federal requirements of the program if they accept the funds, they can avoid the requirements by declining the funds.

In a 1981 case, *Pennhurst State School and Hospital v. Halderman,* 451 U.S. 1 (1981), the Court made its most important pronouncement on the spending power since the New Deal cases of the 1930s. The plaintiff, a mentally retarded resident of a special school and hospital operated by the State of Pennsylvania, claimed that she had a right to "appropriate treatment"—a right derived in part from conditions that the federal government had attached to certain grants received by the school. The Court rejected the plaintiff's claim, asserting that Congress had not conditioned the grants on the state's willingness to guarantee appropriate treatment and that the language about treatment in the grant statute "represent[s] general statements of federal policy, not newly created legal duties." In reaching its decision, the Court adopted an interpretation of the spending power that emphasizes Congress's responsibility to speak clearly if it seeks to create "entitlements" or "rights" that state entities (and apparently private sector grantees as well) must recognize as a condition to receiving federal money:

> [O]ur cases have long recognized that Congress may fix the terms on which it shall disburse federal money to the states. . . . However, legislation enacted pursuant to the spending power is much in the nature of a contract: in return for federal funds, the states agree to comply with federally imposed conditions. The legitimacy of Congress's power to legislate under the spending power thus rests on whether the state voluntarily and knowingly accepts the terms of the "contract" (see *Steward Machine Co. v. Davis*, 301 U.S. 548, 585–98 . . . (1937)). There can, of course, be no knowing acceptance if a state is unaware of the conditions or is unable to ascertain what is expected of it. Accordingly, if Congress intends to impose a condition on the grant of federal moneys, it must do so unambiguously. . . . By insisting that Congress speak with a clear voice, we enable the states to exercise their choice knowingly, cognizant of the consequences of their participation [451 U.S. at 17; see also 451 U.S. at 24–25].

Although this interpretation clearly benefits states in their dealings with the federal government, it does not create new substantive limits on the number or type of conditions that Congress may impose under the spending power. Instead, *Pennhurst* limits the circumstances in which courts may recognize, and federal agencies may enforce, grant conditions upon grantees. If Congress and the federal agencies fit within these circumstances by defining their conditions clearly before they award grants, they may impose such conditions to the same extent after *Pennhurst* as they could before. The best contemporary guide to the extent of this power of conditional spending is *South Dakota v. Dole* (above).

While the spending power has been an important source of congressional authority throughout the history of higher education, and particularly since the 1950s (see Section 13.4.1), the power has taken on added importance since the closing years of the twentieth century. In a line of cases beginning with *United States v. Lopez,* 514 U.S. 549 (1995), the U.S. Supreme Court cut back on the scope of Congress's commerce power (see subsection 13.1.4 below). These developments have created an impetus for Congress and interest groups to seek other sources of power to accomplish objectives that can no longer be accomplished under the commerce power, and for courts and litigants to consider other sources of power that might be used to uphold legislation that can no longer be upheld under the commerce power. (See Lynn Baker, "Constitutional Federal Spending After Lopez," 95 *Columbia L. Rev.* 1911 (1995).) Similarly, in a related set of developments, the Supreme Court has prohibited Congress from using the commerce clause to abrogate state sovereign immunity from suit and limited Congress's authority to do so under its Fourteenth Amendment enforcement power (see subsections 13.1.5 & 13.1.6 below). These developments have also created an impetus to seek other sources of power by which states' assertions of sovereign immunity may be nullified or avoided. For both sets of developments, the federal spending power has been the chief power to be tapped as an alternative. In *College Savings Bank v. Florida Prepaid Postsecondary*

Education Expense Board, 527 U.S. 666 (1999), the Court emphasized that "Congress may, in the exercise of its spending power, condition its grant of funds to the States upon their taking certain actions that Congress could not require them to take, and that acceptance of the funds entails an agreement to the actions" (527 U.S. at 686). Using the spending power in this way, Congress may not only impose conditions on recipients (including states) that it could once, but can no longer, impose under the commerce power; it may also condition a state's receipt of federal funds upon its waiver of its immunity from suit on particular federal claims (see, for example, *Litman v. George Mason University,* 186 F.3d 544, 551–53, 554–57 (4th Cir. 1999); and see generally subsection 13.1.6 below). Any such conditions, of course, must be stated with the clarity required by the *Pennhurst State School* case above.

13.1.3. *Taxing power.* The federal taxing power also comes from Article I, Section 8, clause 1, which authorizes Congress "to lay and collect taxes" in order to raise the money it spends for the general welfare, and from the Sixteenth Amendment, which specifically authorizes Congress to impose an income tax. The tax power is the basis for the laws discussed in Section 13.3. Though the purpose of the tax power is to raise revenue rather than to regulate as such, the power has been broadly construed to permit tax measures with substantial regulatory effects. The application of the tax power to postsecondary education, including in some cases public postsecondary education, was upheld in *Allen v. Regents of the University System of Georgia,* 304 U.S. 439 (1938), which concerned an admissions tax that the federal government had levied on state college football games. The tax power may be somewhat greater over private than over public institutions, however, since public institutions may sometimes enjoy a constitutional immunity from federal taxation of their sovereign functions (see *South Carolina v. Baker,* 485 U.S. 505 (1988)), and the federal tax laws often treat public and private institutions differently (see Section 13.3.2 below).

13.1.4. *Commerce power.* The federal commerce power stems from Article I, Section 8, Clause 3 of the Constitution, which authorizes Congress to "regulate commerce with foreign nations, and among the several states. . . ." This is the primary federal regulatory power that has been applied to postsecondary education and is the basis for most of the laws discussed in Section 13.2 below. The commerce power has been broadly construed to permit the regulation of activities that are in or that "affect" interstate or foreign commerce. As the U.S. Supreme Court has often acknowledged, "Congress's power under the commerce clause is very broad. Even activity that is purely intrastate in character may be regulated by Congress, where the activity, combined with like conduct by others similarly situated, affects commerce among the states or with foreign nations" (*Fry v. United States,* 421 U.S. 542, 547 (1975)).

In a series of opinions in the late 1970s and early 1980s, the U.S. Supreme Court did attempt to limit Congress's use of the commerce power as a basis for regulating state and local governments. The key case was *National League of Cities v. Usery*, 426 U.S. 833 (1976). By a 5-to-4 vote, the Court relied on the Tenth Amendment to invalidate federal wage and hour laws as applied to state and local government employees, reasoning that "their application will significantly alter or displace the states' abilities to structure employer-employee relationships . . . in areas of traditional governmental functions." The Court premised this decision on a general principle that "Congress may not exercise . . . [the commerce] power so as to force directly upon the states its choices as to how essential decisions regarding the conduct of integral governmental functions are to be made." In subsequent years, however, lower courts and the Supreme Court itself struggled to understand and apply *National League*'s enigmatic distinctions between "traditional" and "nontraditional," and "integral" and "noninte-gral," government functions. Finally, in *Garcia v. San Antonio Metropolitan Transit Authority*, 469 U.S. 528 (1985), by a 5-to-4 vote, the Court overruled *National League:*

> We therefore now reject, as unsound in principle and unworkable in prac-tice, a rule of state immunity from federal regulation that turns on a judicial appraisal of whether a particular governmental function is "integral" or "traditional." . . .
>
> [T]he principal and basic limit on the federal commerce power is that inherent in all congressional action—the built-in constraints that our system provides through state participation in federal governmental action. The political process ensures that laws that unduly burden the states will not be promulgated. . . .
>
> [T]he model of democratic decision making [that] the Court [identified in *National League*] underestimated, in our view, the solicitude of the national political process for the continued vitality of the states. Attempts by other courts since then to draw guidance from this model have proved it both impracticable and doctrinally barren. In sum, in *National League of Cities* the Court tried to repair what did not need repair [469 U.S. at 546–47, 556–57].

In the 1990s, the U.S. Supreme Court made another attempt—analytically distinct from the *National League* line of cases in the 1970s and 1980s—to limit Congress's commerce power. The key case is *United States v. Lopez,* 514 U.S. 549 (1995), in which the Court invalidated the Gun-Free School Zones Act, a federal statute making it a crime to possess a firearm on or within 1,000 feet of school grounds. The statute exceeded the scope of the commerce power because Congress had not required prosecutors to prove that the defendant's actions had some "nexus" to interstate commerce, nor had Congress made findings or produced evidence that gun possession on or near school grounds "substantially affects" interstate commerce. Regarding the second point, the Court emphasized that "education" is an area "where States historically have been sovereign," thus making it especially important that Congress develop findings or evidence to justify federal involvement under the commerce power. The commerce power does not extend to the regulation of all "activities that adversely affect the learning environment," and the Court will not presume (absent congressional findings or evidence) that all such activities adversely affect interstate commerce:

> We do not doubt that Congress has authority under the Commerce Clause to regulate numerous commercial activities that substantially affect interstate commerce and also affect the educational process. That authority, though broad, does not include the authority to regulate each and every aspect of local schools [514 U.S. at 565–66].

United States v. Lopez was confirmed and extended in *United States v. Morrison,* 529 U.S. 598 (2000), affirming *Brzonkala v. Virginia Polytechnic Institute and State University,* 169 F.3d 820 (4th Cir. 1999) (*en banc*). The issue was whether the federal Violence Against Women Act (42 U.S.C. § 13981) was a valid exercise of Congress's commerce power. The U.S. Supreme Court struck down the Act as beyond the scope of congressional power. Relying heavily on *United States v. Lopez,* the Court majority held that Congress had not demonstrated that the violent acts targeted by the statute had a substantial adverse effect on interstate commerce. The Court majority also extended *Lopez* by limiting the types of congressional findings that will justify resort to the commerce power. Unlike the *Lopez* case, in passing the Violence Against Women Act, Congress had made numerous findings regarding adverse effects on interstate commerce (something it had not done for the firearms statute in *Lopez*). Nevertheless, the Court considered these findings to be based on a "but-for causal chain" that was too "attenuated" and too focused on "noneconomic" conduct to justify the Act under the commerce clause.

Thus *Lopez* and *Morrison,* taken together, indicate that the courts are now less deferential to Congress than they previously were in commerce clause cases, that the Supreme Court has developed (or is in the process of developing) judicially enforceable limits on the scope of the commerce power, and that these limits apply to Congress's regulation of education. A later case, however, *Gonzales v. Raich,* 125 S. Ct. 2195 (2005), limits the reach of *Lopez* and *Morrison* by indicating that they apply to Congress's regulation of intrastate noneconomic activity (like gun possession on school grounds) under statutes that directly target such activity (like the Gun-Free School Zones Act), but do not apply to Congress's regulation of intrastate noneconomic activity under broader statutes that "directly regulate[ ] economic, commercial activity" and include coverage of the intrastate noneconomic activity only as a means (among others) of making the broader economic regulation effective.

In addition to *Lopez* and *Morrison,* the Court has limited the reach of the commerce power in another way, having particular application to the state agencies and instrumentalities. In 1996, in *Seminole Tribe v. Florida,* the Court held that Congress cannot use the commerce power to abrogate the states' immunity from private suits in federal court, thus removing a major means for enforcing commerce clause regulations of the type authorized in *Garcia v. Metropolitan Transit Authority* (above). Then, in *Alden v. Maine,* the Court held that states also have an immunity from private suits on federal law claims brought in the state's own courts, and that Congress cannot use the commerce power to abrogate this immunity; and in *Federal Maritime Comm'n. v. South Carolina Ports Authority*, the Court held that states are immune from private claims brought against them in adjudicatory proceedings of federal administrative agencies, and that Congress cannot use the commerce power to abrogate this immunity. (These cases are discussed in Section 13.1.6 below.) As a result of these cases, even though Congress may still regulate the states (and state colleges and universities) under the commerce power, it may not provide for the enforcement of commerce clause regulations against the states through lawsuits by the individuals whom such regulations protect. If a state were to violate the Fair Labor Standards Act (FLSA), for example, by denying state employees certain rights regarding wages and hours (see Section 4.6.2 of this book), these employees can no longer sue the state for damages in order to enforce their rights.

13.1.5. Civil rights enforcement powers. The civil rights enforcement powers are the fourth major federal power source applicable to education. These powers derive from the enforcement clauses of various constitutional amendments, particularly the Fourteenth Amendment (due process and equal protection), whose fifth Section provides that "the Congress shall have power to enforce, by appropriate legislation, the provisions of this article." In *Katzenbach v. Morgan*, 384 U.S. 641 (1966), the U.S. Supreme Court held that Section 5 of the Fourteenth Amendment empowers Congress to "exercise its discretion in determining whether and what legislation is needed to secure the [Amendment's] guarantees," as long as the legislation is "adapted to carry out the objects the . . . [Amendment has] in view" and is not otherwise prohibited by the Constitution.

The civil rights enforcement powers are the basis for many of the federal employment discrimination laws (see Section 5.2 of this book) insofar as they apply to state and local government entities. In *Fitzpatrick v. Bitzer*, 427 U.S. 445 (1976), for instance, the Court upheld the 1972 extension of the Title VII employment discrimination law to state and local governments as an appropriate exercise of the Fourteenth Amendment (Section 5) enforcement power. This power is also the basis for the generic federal civil rights law known as Section 1983 (see Sections 3.5 & 4.7.4 of this book). As interpreted in *United States v. Morrison*, 529 U.S. 598 (2000), however, the Fourteenth Amendment enforcement power authorizes Congress to regulate only states and local governments, and not the private sector; Congress therefore cannot use Section 5 of the Fourteenth Amendment to create civil remedies against private entities or individuals that are not engaged in state action.[2]

---

[2]The plaintiff in *Morrison* was a female college student who sued two male students who she alleged had raped her. The plaintiff claimed that the two students' actions violated Congress's Violence Against Women Act, 42 U.S.C. § 13981, which provided a civil remedy against private individuals for their acts of gender-motivated violence. Since the enforcement power extended only to state and local governments, and could not be used by Congress to regulate private conduct, the Court invalidated the statute.

In contrast, the Thirteenth Amendment enforcement power, which empowers Congress to eradicate "badges" and "incidents" of slavery, extends to both the private and the public sector, as the U.S. Supreme Court affirmed in *Jones v. Alfred H. Mayer Co.*, 392 U.S. 409 (1968), and *Runyon v. McCrary,* 427 U.S. 160 (1976), both discussed in Section 8.2.4.1).[3]

In *City of Boerne v. Flores*, 521 U.S. 507 (1997) (see Section 1.6.2), the U.S. Supreme Court clarified the limits on Congress's enforcement power under Section 5 of the Fourteenth Amendment and thus alleviated some of the uncertainty that had existed regarding this power. In particular, the Court emphasized that:

> Congress' power under § 5 . . . extends only to "enforc[ing]" the provisions of the Fourteenth Amendment. The Court has described this power as "remedial," *South Carolina v. Katzenbach,* [383 U.S.] at 326. The design of the Amendment and the text of § 5 are inconsistent with the suggestion that Congress has the power to decree the substance of the Fourteenth Amendment's restrictions on the States. Legislation which alters the meaning of [rights incorporated into the due process clause] cannot be said to be enforcing the Clause. Congress does not enforce a constitutional right by changing what the right is. It has been given the power "to enforce," not the power to determine what constitutes a constitutional violation. Were it not so, what Congress would be enforcing would no longer be, in any meaningful sense, the "provisions of [the Fourteenth Amendment]" [521 U.S. at 519].

The Court has reaffirmed and applied *Boerne* in several important cases involving postsecondary education. In the two *College Savings Bank* cases (see Section 13.1.6 below and Sections 13.2.6 & 13.2.7), the Court invalidated applications of two federal laws to the states because these laws did not remedy or deter violations of property rights under the Fourteenth Amendment's due process clause. Similarly, in *Kimel v. Florida Board of Regents,* 528 U.S. 62 (2000), by a 5-to-4 vote, the Court invalidated the Age Discrimination in Employment Act (see Section 5.2.6 of this book) insofar as it authorizes private damages actions against the states, and specifically against state colleges and universities. After noting that age discrimination is not a "suspect" classification under the Fourteenth Amendment's equal protection clause and receives only a minimal "rational basis" review, the Court determined that:

> Judged against the backdrop of our equal protection jurisprudence, it is clear that the ADEA is "so out of proportion to a supposed remedial or preventive object that it cannot be understood as responsive to, or designed to prevent, unconstitutional behavior." *City of Boerne,* 521 U.S. at 532. The Act, through its broad restriction on the use of age as a discriminating factor, prohibits substantially more state employment decisions and practices than would likely be held unconstitutional under the applicable equal protection, rational basis standard [528 U.S. at 64].

---

[3]For a review of enforcement issues under Section 1981 and the Thirteenth Amendment, see "Developments in the Law—Section 1981," 15 *Harv. Civil Rights—Civil Liberties L. Rev.* 29 (1981).

And in another 5-to-4 decision, *Board of Trustees of the University of Alabama v. Garrett,* 531 U.S. 356 (2001), the Court relied on *Kimel* to invalidate Congress's application of Title I of the Americans With Disabilities Act (42 U.S.C. §§ 12111–12117) to the states. Noting that disability discrimination, like age discrimination, as in *Kimel,* receives only a "rational basis" review under the equal protection clause, the Court held that Congress had not identified "a pattern of [disability] discrimination by the States which violates the Fourteenth Amendment." "[T]he remedy imposed by Congress [was therefore not] congruent and proportional to the targeted violation." Under these circumstances, "to uphold the Act's application to the State would allow Congress to rewrite the Fourteenth Amendment law laid down by this Court. . . . Section 5 does not so broadly enlarge congressional authority" (531 U.S. at 374). In other words, according to the majority, upholding Congress's action would have accorded Congress a substantive (rather than a remedial) power under Section 5—a result that the line of cases subsequent to *Katzenbach v. Morgan* had rejected. The holding was the product of a 5-to-4 vote, with Justices Breyer, Stevens, Souter, and Ginsburg dissenting. (The Court remanded the case to the district court, at which point the plaintiff advanced a different claim; this claim is discussed in subsection 13.1.6 below.)

Two later cases, however, have softened the hard edges of these developments limiting the scope of Congress's authority to impose civil rights requirements on the states. In *Nevada Dept. of Human Resources v. Hibbs,* 538 U.S. 721 (2003), the Court upheld Congress's use of its enforcement power to apply the Family and Medical Leave Act (FMLA) (29 U.S.C. § 2611 *et seq.*) to the states. The six-Justice majority, in an opinion by Chief Justice Rehnquist, noted that "[w]hen it enacted the FMLA, Congress had before it significant evidence of a long and extensive history of sex discrimination with respect to the administration of leave benefits by the States" (*Id.* at 730), and that "the FMLA is narrowly targeted at the fault line between work and family—precisely where sex-based overgeneralization has been and remains strongest . . . (*Id.* at 738). The Court also distinguished *Kimel* and *Garrett* because age discrimination (as in *Kimel*) and disability discrimination (as in *Garrett*) are subject only to rational basis scrutiny under the equal protection clause, while gender discrimination (as in this case) is subject to heightened judicial scrutiny. Since the heightened scrutiny makes it more difficult for the states to justify gender classifications, compared to age and disability classifications that are subject only to rational basis scrutiny, "it was easier for Congress" to demonstrate the "pattern of state constitutional violations" that Section 5 requires (*Id.* at 722). Congress's evidence was "weighty enough to justify enactment of [the FMLA as] prophylactic § 5 legislation," and the "narrowly targeted" provisions of the FMLA are "congruent and proportional to [their] remedial object," as required by *City of Boerne* (*Id.* at 740). The FMLA was thus a constitutional exercise of Congress's Section 5 power and could be enforced against the states.

In the second case, *Tennessee v. Lane,* 541 U.S. 509 (2004), the Court upheld a particular application of Congress's Section 5 enforcement power to the states under Title II of the Americans With Disabilities Act (as opposed to Title I, as in

Garrett). The application of Title II that was at issue in *Lane* concerned Congress's enforcement of the Fourteenth Amendment's due process clause rather than the equal protection clause, as in *Garrett*. The *Lane* decision is the first Section 5 case to focus on a particular application of a federal statute to a state entity, rather than on a facial challenge to an entire statute (or title of a statute) regulating the states; it is also the first decision to make clear that particular applications of a statute may be upheld as within the scope of Congress's enforcement power even if other applications of the same statute are not upheld. The importance of these aspects of *Lane* are illustrated by the subsequent case of *Constantine v. The Rectors & Visitors of George Mason University*, 411 F.3d 474 (4th Cir. 2005). In that case, the court, relying on *Lane*, considered the validity of ADA Title II as applied to "the class of cases implicating the right to be free from irrational disability discrimination in public higher education." Reviewing Title II's legislative history and the Court's statements in *Lane*, the U.S. Court of Appeals held that this application of Title II is within the scope of Congress's Section 5 power, and that the plaintiff student could proceed with her claim that the defendant, a public university and its law school, had irrationally discriminated against her on grounds of disability. (To the same effect, see *Association for Disabled Americans v. Florida International University*, 405 F.3d 954 (11th Cir. 2005).)

The Court's decisions from *Boerne* to *Lane* emphasize and clarify that Congress's Fourteenth Amendment, Section 5, power may be used only to *remedy* actual violations, or to *deter* potential violations, of the Fourteenth Amendment's equal protection and due process clauses; in other words, legislation must be either remedial or "reasonably prophylactic" (see, for example, *Lane*, above, at 1988) to fit within the scope of Section 5. Congress must have "identified a history and pattern of unconstitutional [actions] by the States," and must have included sufficient documentation of such actions in the legislative record to support its determination that the legislation was needed to remedy or deter these equal protection or due process violations (*Garrett*, 531 U.S. at 368; see also *Kimel*, 528 U.S. at 90). The remedy that Congress creates in its legislation must also be "congruent" with and "proportional" to the pattern of violations that Congress has identified in the legislative record and targeted in the legislation (*Kimel*, 528 U.S. at 81–83; *Garrett*, 531 U.S. at 374). Parallel restrictions would apparently apply to Congress's exercise of its enforcement powers under the Thirteenth and Fifteenth Amendments.

13.1.6. State sovereign immunity from suit.

13.1.6. State sovereign immunity from suit. In many situations, effective exertion of Congress's powers and enforcement of federal law may depend on the capacity of the courts to enforce the law directly against the states, state government agencies, and state institutions. Traditionally, states have argued that the Eleventh Amendment protects them from attempts to enforce federal law against them in federal courts (see generally Section 3.5; and see also Brian Snow & William Thro, "The Significance of Blackstone's Understanding of Sovereign Immunity for America's Institutions of Higher Education," 28 *J. Coll. & Univ. Law* 97, 110–25 (2001)). This amendment limits the judicial power of the federal courts under Article III of the U.S. Constitution. As the U.S. Supreme

Court explained in *Pennhurst State School and Hospital v. Halderman,* 465 U.S. 89, 98 (1984), the Eleventh Amendment affirms "that the fundamental principle of sovereign immunity limits the grant of judicial authority in Article III." The immunity from suit therefore extends to federal court suits brought against states and state agencies by their own citizens (*Hans v. Louisiana,* 134 U.S. 1 (1890)), or by persons in other states. The immunity does not extend to local governments such as cities, counties, and school districts, however (*Lincoln County v. Luning,* 133 U.S. 529, 530 (1890)), or to other "political subdivision(s)" of the state that are not "arm(s) of the state," for Eleventh Amendment purposes (*Lake County Estates v. Tahoe Regional Planning Agency,* 440 U.S. 391, 401–2 (1979)). In more recent cases, the U.S. Supreme Court has extended state sovereign immunity to suits filed against the state by private parties in *state* court and in certain federal *administrative agency* proceedings (see the *Alden* and *Federal Maritime Commission* cases, discussed below).

Although it is clear that states, including state colleges and universities, may waive their immunity and consent to suit, there must be exceedingly clear evidence of a waiver before a court will recognize it (see *Atascadero State Hospital v. Scanlon,* 473 U.S. 234, 238–41, 247 (1985)). If the waiver is to be effective in federal courts, the courts will require an "unequivocal waiver specifically applicable to federal court jurisdiction" (473 U.S. at 241). Arguments for implied waiver or implied consent based on implications from a relevant text (for example, a state statute), or from background facts and circumstances, will not be accepted unless the implication is exceedingly clear (see *Cowan v. University of Louisville School of Medicine,* 900 F.2d 936, 941 (6th Cir. 1990)). Thus, the inclusion of a provision in a state institution's charter or enabling legislation, authorizing the institution to "sue and be sued," is generally not sufficient to constitute a waiver of sovereign immunity (see, for example, *Power v. Summers,* 226 F.3d 815, 818–19 (7th Cir. 2000)). But if a state institution is sued in state court and voluntarily removes the case to federal court, this action generally will be considered to constitute a waiver of immunity and consent to be sued in the federal court. In *Lapides v. Board of Regents of the University System of Georgia,* 535 U.S. 613 (2002), for example, a professor's suit alleging Section 1983 and tort law claims had been removed to federal court upon the motion of the defendant state university. When the university then moved to dismiss the suit in federal court on grounds of sovereign immunity, the district court held that the university had waived its immunity. After the court of appeals reversed, the U.S. Supreme Court sided with the district court and the professor, holding that the university's removal request constituted a waiver of its immunity because it necessarily implied that the university was submitting itself to the jurisdiction of the federal court.

Before 1996, state sovereign immunity was usually not a major impediment to the enforcement of federal laws against the states, and their state colleges and universities, because Congress could usually "abrogate" or cancel this state immunity if it chose to do. Congress's authority to abrogate has been greatly restricted, however, by a series of U.S. Supreme Court cases, beginning with *Seminole Tribe v. Florida,* 517 U.S. 44 (1996), which overruled *Pennsylvania v.*

Union Gas, 491 U.S. 1 (1989). By a 5-to-4 vote, the Court in *Seminole Tribe* declared that "[e]ven when the Constitution vests in Congress complete law-making authority over a particular area [for example, interstate commerce], the Eleventh Amendment prevents congressional authorization of suits by private parties against unconsenting States." The Court also acknowledged, however, that this principle does not apply to Congress's power to enforce the Fourteenth Amendment because—according to earlier cases other than *Union Gas*—that amendment permits Congress to authorize private suits against unconsenting states that have allegedly violated its provisions. (See especially *Fitzpatrick v. Bitzer,* 427 U.S. 445 (1976); and *Atascadero State Hospital v. Scanlon,* 473 U.S. 234 (1985).) The dissenters in *Seminole Tribe* complained that the majority's decision "prevents Congress from providing a federal [judicial] forum for a broad range of actions against States, from those sounding in copyright and patent law, to those concerning bankruptcy, environmental law, and the regulation of our vast national economy."

After *Seminole Tribe,* Congress can abrogate state sovereign immunity and authorize suits against state institutions only if (1) Congress has clearly indicated its intention to abrogate state immunity (see *Atascadero State Hospital* above, 473 U.S. at 242); and (2) the statute authorizing the particular suit is within the scope of Congress's Fourteenth Amendment enforcement power (or, apparently, its Thirteenth or Fifteenth Amendment enforcement powers).[4] In numerous cases since *Seminole Tribe,* both in the U.S. Supreme Court and in the lower courts, these two considerations have framed the sovereign immunity analysis. In *Kimel v. Florida Board of Regents,* 528 U.S. 62 (2000), for instance, the Court stated that "[t]o determine whether [immunity has been abrogated], we must resolve two predicate questions: first, whether Congress unequivocally expressed its intent to abrogate that immunity; and second, if it did, whether Congress acted pursuant to a valid grant of constitutional authority" (528 U.S. at 73). Analysis of the second of these questions is now guided by another of the Court's post-*Seminole* decisions, *City of Boerne v. Flores,* 521 U.S. 507 (1997) (discussed in Section 13.1.5 above), which restricted the scope of Congress's regulatory authority under Section 5 of the Fourteenth Amendment. Thus, not only has the Court strengthened state immunity in *Seminole Tribe* by prohibiting Congress from using the commerce clause to abrogate immunity, but at almost the same time the Court has also strengthened state immunity in *Boerne* by narrowing the scope of the only other clause giving Congress substantial authority to abrogate immunity, thus limiting the occasions in which this clause (Section 5) may serve as a tool of abrogation. The combination of events makes it extremely difficult for private plaintiffs to enforce federal laws directly against the states, including state colleges and universities and state postsecondary education agencies.

---

[4]In a subsequent case, *Tennessee v. Lane,* 541 U.S. 509 (2004), the Court refined the second part of this analysis to allow for abrogation when the *particular application* of the statute involved in the suit is within the scope of Congress's Section 5 power. See the discussion of *Lane* below in this Section and in Section 13.1.5 above.

In *Florida Prepaid Postsecondary Education Expense Board v. College Savings Bank* (discussed in Section 13.2.6), for instance, the Court (again by a 5-to-4 vote) held that a 1992 federal patent infringement law was not within the scope of Congress's power under Section 5 of the Fourteenth Amendment and therefore could not be enforced in federal court against a Florida state education agency. In *College Savings Bank v. Florida Prepaid Postsecondary Education Expense Board,* discussed in Section 13.2.7, the Court held (by another 5-to-4 vote) that a federal false advertising law was not within the scope of Congress's Section 5 power and therefore could not be enforced in federal court against the same Florida education agency. In *Kimel v. Florida Board of Regents* (discussed above in this Section and in Section 13.1.5 above), by another split vote, the Court held that the federal Age Discrimination in Employment Act (Section 5.2.6 of this book) "does contain a clear statement of Congress's intent to abrogate the states' immunity," but that "the abrogation exceeded Congress's authority under § 5 of the Fourteenth Amendment" (528 U.S. at 67). The plaintiffs—faculty members and librarians—therefore could not pursue their age discrimination claims against state universities in Florida and Alabama. And in yet another 5-to-4 decision, *Board of Trustees of the University of Alabama v. Garrett,* 531 U.S. 356 (2001), the Court majority relied on *Kimel* in holding that Congress did not have authority, under Section 5 of the Fourteenth Amendment, to abrogate the state's sovereign immunity from private party claims for damages brought under Title I of the Americans With Disabilities Act (ADA) (Section 5.2.5 of this book). The Court therefore dismissed the ADA claim of a former director of nursing at the university's hospital who was demoted to a lower-paying position after missing a substantial amount of work due to treatment for breast cancer.

All these post-*Seminole* cases focus on the Eleventh Amendment, which prohibits suits against the states in *federal* court. Suits in *state* courts to enforce federal law against state agencies were thus considered to be an option for prospective plaintiffs both before and after *Seminole Tribe* (see, for example, Section 3.5). That option was drastically limited in a U.S. Supreme Court case, *Alden v. Maine,* 527 U.S. 706 (1999), which imported state sovereign immunity protections into the state court arena. Thus, at the same time that the Court has been using the Eleventh Amendment to strengthen the states' sovereign immunity from federal court suits, it has begun to use other constitutional principles to strengthen state sovereign immunity in state courts.

Alden concerned the federal Fair Labor Standards Act (see Section 4.6.2 of this book), in particular the provisions authorizing state employees to enforce their FLSA rights against the states in their own courts (29 U.S.C. § 216(b) & § 203(x)). Claiming a violation of the FLSA overtime pay provisions, employees of the State of Maine filed suit against the state in state court. (They had originally sued the state in federal court but refiled in state court after the federal court held the state immune from suit in federal court.) The state courts also held the state immune from suit on grounds of sovereign immunity, and the U.S. Supreme Court affirmed by a 5-to-4 vote. Although the Eleventh Amendment does not itself apply to suits in state court and thus could not itself provide the basis for the Court's decision, the Court determined that sovereign immunity, in a broader sense, "derives not from the Eleventh Amendment but from the structure of the original Constitution itself" and that the "scope of the states' immunity from suit is demarcated not by the text of the Amendment alone but by fundamental postulates implicit in the constitutional design" (527 U.S. at 729).

The *Alden* plaintiffs nevertheless relied on FLSA provisions permitting suits against states (above) as a clear congressional abrogation of state sovereign immunity. Echoing *Seminole Tribe,* the Court ruled that Congress had no authority under the commerce clause, or its other powers under Article I of the Constitution, to abrogate state sovereign immunity in state courts. The Court therefore affirmed the state courts' dismissal of the case because Maine could successfully assert a sovereign immunity defense against its employees' attempts to enforce federally created FLSA rights. (Three years later, the Court extended its *Alden* reasoning to provide states sovereign immunity from private parties' federal law claims filed in adjudicative proceedings before federal administrative agencies (*Federal Maritime Comm'n. v. South Carolina Ports Authority,* 535 U.S. 743 (2002)).)

Taken together, the cases from *Seminole Tribe* to *Alden* and *Federal Maritime Comm'n.* provide state colleges and universities with strong protection against liability for violations of federally created rights. But these cases should not be construed as an invitation to be less than vigilant about compliance with federal laws, or to be in any measure insensitive to the federal rights of students, faculty, and other members of the academic community. Legally speaking, that would be unwise, because, even after these recent cases, avenues are still open for enforcing federal rights against the states. Congress can still use Section 5 of the Fourteenth Amendment to abrogate state immunity from various federal civil rights claims (see, for example, *Nevada Dept. of Human Resources v. Hibbs,* discussed in Section 13.1.5; and see also *Okruhlik v. University of Arkansas ex rel. May,* 255 F.3d 615 (8th Cir. 2001); *Lesage v. University of Texas,* 158 F.3d 213, 216–19 (5th Cir 1998)). Courts may hold that *particular applications* of a civil rights statute are within the scope of Congress's Section 5 power (even though other applications of the same statute are not) and that the state's sovereign immunity is thus abrogated as to those particular applications (see *Tennessee v. Lane* and *Constantine v. The Rectors & Visitors of George Mason University* in subsection 13.1.5 above). Moreover, private suits for prospective injunctive relief may still be brought against a state institution's officers and administrators using the *Ex Parte Young* exception (see *Garrett,* above, 531 U.S. at 374, n.9; and see generally Section 3.5 of this book);[5] and they may also be sued for damages in their *personal* (or *individual*) capacities in some circumstances. It has also long

---

[5]But see *Idaho v. Coeur d'Alene Tribe of Idaho,* 521 U.S. 261 (1997), in which the Court majority suggested a reconsideration and limitation of *Ex Parte Young* in light of *Seminole Tribe* (see 521 U.S. at 267–70). See also *Seminole Tribe,* 517 U.S. at 74, where the Court indicated that *Ex Parte Young* would not apply in situations where Congress had created a "detailed remedial scheme" for enforcement of the federal right at issue.

been established that state sovereign immunity does not prevent the federal government itself from suing the states for damages and other relief for federal law violations. The Court in *Seminole Tribe* distinguished such suits from those in which a private party is the plaintiff: "[T]he Federal Government can bring suit in federal court against a State . . . (517 U.S. at 71, n.14, citing *United States v. Texas,* 143 U.S. 621, 644–45 (1892)). Similarly, in *Alden,* the Court emphasized that "[i]n ratifying the Constitution, the States consented to suits brought by . . . the Federal Government" (527 U.S. at 755; see also *Garrett,* 531 U.S. at 374, n.9).[6]

In addition to these avenues for enforcing federal law against the states, Congress also apparently has authority under its spending power (subsection 13.1.2 above) to require that state institutions waive their immunity from certain private suits as a condition of their participation in federal grant programs (see generally the discussion of abrogation and waiver in Section 13.5.9). The litigation in the *Garrett* case, above, illustrates this point and its significance. After the U.S. Supreme Court held that the plaintiff nurse's ADA claim was barred by state sovereign immunity, she returned to the federal district court to pursue a similar disability discrimination claim under Section 504 of the Rehabilitation Act (see Sections 5.2.5 & 13.5.4 of this book), which she had pleaded in the original court suit (989 F. Supp. 1409 (N.D. Ala. 1998)). After the district court granted summary judgment for the state (223 F. Supp. 2d 1244 (N.D. Ala. 2002)), finding that Section 504 did not abrogate the state's sovereign immunity and had not established a waiver of such immunity, the circuit court reversed, focusing on the plaintiff's waiver argument (*Garrett v. University of Alabama at Birmingham Board of Trustees,* 344 F.3d 1288 (11th Cir. 2003)). The court asserted that waiver is different from abrogation, and that the spending power allowed Congress to condition "the receipt of federal funds on a waiver of Eleventh Amendment immunity to claims under section 504 of the Rehabilitation Act. By continuing to accept federal funds, the [university has] waived [its] immunity." The plaintiff was therefore able to proceed against the state university under Section 504, using the waiver theory, even though she could not bring a similar claim under the ADA due to Congress's lack of authority to abrogate. Similarly, in *Litman v. George Mason University,* 186 F.3d 544 (4th Cir. 1999), discussed in Section 13.5.9, the court used the waiver argument to reject the sovereign immunity defense of a university in a Title IX action. (See also *Pace v. Bogalusa City School Board,* 403 F.3d 272, 277–287 (5th Cir. 2005) (*en banc*).) The result in these cases is supported by the Court's statement in *Alden* that, under the spending power, "the Federal Government lack[s] [neither] the authority or means to seek the States' voluntary consent to private suits" (527 U.S. at 755).

Because these various avenues for enforcing federal rights against the states remain open, the legal consequences of noncompliance should continue to propel state institutions toward a healthy respect for federal rights that

---

[6]This distinction between the federal government and private plaintiffs has also become critically important in cases brought against state institutions under the federal False Claims Act; see Section 13.2.15 of this book.

counterbalances the obvious temptation to broadly limit liability by invoking sovereign immunity. As a matter of policy, if not law, institutions should not emphasize the use of immunity claims to protect themselves from federal legal liability, rather than maintaining an ongoing legal planning process (see Section 2.4.2) that assures legal compliance. As even the *Alden* Court noted, there should be "a sense of justice" that mitigates the "rights of sovereign immunity" (527 U.S. 755).

Sec. 13.2. Federal Regulation of Postsecondary Education

13.2.1. Overview. Despite the attempts of institutions and their national associations to limit the impact of federal regulations and federal funding conditions on postsecondary education, the federal presence on campus continues to expand. Although higher education has experienced some successes, particularly in the area of autonomy over "who may teach, what may be taught, how it shall be taught, and who may be admitted to study" (*Sweezy v. New Hampshire*; see Section 7.1.4), federal regulation affects even the academic core of a college or university. Although mandated self-regulation is still used in some areas of federal regulation, such as restrictions on the use of human subjects or research on animals, self-regulatory actions by institutions have been criticized as insufficient or self-serving. And while the federal government has relied on the private accrediting agencies to help ensure the integrity of certain federal aid programs, these agencies' standards and practices have been periodically criticized by federal officials, and federal regulation of the accrediting process has increased over time (see Section 14.3.3).

In the following subsections of this Section, the regulatory issues with the broadest application to postsecondary education have been selected for analysis. In addition to those discussed, other federal statutes and regulations may also become important in particular circumstances. The federal bankruptcy law (11 U.S.C. § 101 *et seq.*), for instance, is important when a student loan recipient declares bankruptcy (see Section 8.3.8.1) and when an institution encounters severe financial distress. The Military Selective Service Act (50 U.S.C. § 451 *et seq.*) is important when the federal government seeks to prohibit individuals who have not registered from receiving federal student aid (see Section 8.3.2).

The Lobbying Disclosure Act of 1995 (2 U.S.C. § 1601 *et seq.*) requires the disclosure of efforts by paid lobbyists to affect decisions by the executive and legislative branches of the federal government. An organization that spends at least $20,000 every six months and has at least one employee who spends more than 20 percent of his or her time in lobbying activities, as defined in the Act, must be listed on a registration form; reports must be filed with Congress every six months.

The National Voter Registration Act, 42 U.S.C. § 1973gg5(a)(2)(B), commonly known as the "motor voter" law, requires states to designate as voter registration agencies all offices that are primarily engaged in providing services to persons with disabilities. A federal appellate court has ruled that the offices at two public universities in Virginia that provide services to disabled students are subject to this law. The case, *National Coalition for Students with Disabilities Education and Legal Defense Fund v. Allen,* is discussed in Section 8.7 of this book.

Corporate accounting scandals of the early twenty-first century prompted Congress to enact the Sarbanes-Oxley Act (15 U.S.C. § 7201 *et seq.*), which applies to publicly traded organizations. Although most of its provisions do not apply directly to colleges and universities, the law nevertheless raises significant issues concerning governance of organizations, transparency in accounting for financial matters, and the responsibilities of top executives. As such, the law has importance as guidance for trustees and senior administrators of colleges and universities. (For an analysis of the Sarbanes-Oxley Act and suggested "best practices" for academic organizations, see "The Sarbanes-Oxley Act of 2002: Recommendations for Higher Education," National Association of College and University Business Officers Advisory Report 2003-3 (2003).)

The CAN-SPAM Act of 2003 ("Controlling the Assault of Non-Solicited Pornography and Marketing Act of 2003"), 15 U.S.C. § 7701 *et seq.,* is important for institutions that use broadcast e-mail to contact alumni, potential students, or other audiences. Regulations implementing the law are found at 16 C.F.R. Part 316. The law imposes limitations on the use of unsolicited e-mail that is sent for a commercial purpose, and provides for penalties for its violation. Non-profit organizations are not exempt from this law.

The laws mentioned briefly above have important consequences for post-secondary institutions' ability to manage their affairs efficiently and to exchange information. The arena of federal regulation has expanded even more in areas related to terrorism and technology. The subsections below can only hint at the scope and complexity of regulation in these and other areas. The assistance of expert counsel is recommended when issues arise for institutions in these areas.

13.2.2. Immigration laws. Many citizens of other countries come to the United States to study, teach, lecture, or do research at American higher education institutions. The conditions under which such foreign nationals may enter and remain in the United States are governed by a complex set of federal statutes codified in Title 8 of the *United States Code* and by regulations promulgated and administered primarily by the U.S. Department of State and the Department of Homeland Security (DHS). The Department of Labor is involved when a nonresident applies for an H1-B visa, which allows the foreign national to work in the United States (discussed in Section 4.6.5 of this book). The statutes and regulations establish numerous categories and subcategories for aliens entering the United States, with differing eligibility requirements and conditions of stay attaching to each.

After the terrorist attacks of September 11, 2001, Congress amended the immigration laws to place further restrictions on entry of noncitizens into the United States, and also reorganized the federal agencies that administer immigration laws. A foreign national who is employed at a college or university is now subject to laws enforced by the Department of Homeland Security (available at http://www.dhs.gov). Within the DHS, the U.S. Citizenship and Immigration Services (http://www.uscis.gov), Immigration and Customs Enforcement (http://www.ice.gov), and the Customs and Border Protection Bureau (http://www.Customs.treas.gov) enforce various aspects of U.S. immigration law.

Under the Immigration and Nationality Act and its various amendments (codified at 8 U.S.C. § 1101 *et seq.*), aliens may enter the United States either as immigrants or as nonimmigrants. Immigrants are admitted for permanent residence in the country (resident aliens). Nonimmigrants are admitted only for limited time periods to engage in narrowly defined types of activities (nonresident aliens). Eligibility for the immigrant class is subject to various numerical limitations and various priorities or preferences for certain categories of aliens (8 U.S.C. §§ 1151–1159). The nonimmigrant class is subdivided into eighteen specific categories (A through R) which define, and thus serve to limit, eligibility for nonimmigrant status.

Of particular importance to postsecondary institutions are the "H" category (see Section 4.6.5) for aliens who will be employed in the United States, the "F" and "M" categories for students (see Section 8.7.4), and the "J" category for exchange visitors. This subsection discusses the application of immigration laws and regulations to individuals who are not employees or students of the institution, such as international visitors. Requirements for hiring noncitizens, on either a permanent or temporary basis, are discussed in Section 4.6.5 of this book, and requirements for enrolling and monitoring foreign students are discussed in Section 8.7.4.

Beginning with the Iranian crisis in 1979–80, when the federal government imposed new restrictions on students from Iran, and continuing through the aftermath of the terrorist attacks of September 11, 2001, higher education institutions have been directly and increasingly affected by immigration law. Institutions are required to know and document the immigration status of each foreign national whom they enroll as a student, hire as an employee, or invite to the campus as a temporary guest, and to help these foreign nationals adapt to this country and maintain their legal status for the term of their stay. To fulfill these responsibilities, administrators and counsel will need a sound grasp of the federal laws and regulations governing immigration. (For an overview of the effect of immigration law on both faculty and staff, see Laura W. Khatcheressian, *Immigration Law: Faculty and Staff Issues* (National Association of College and University Attorneys, 2004).)

One provision of the statute, 8 U.S.C. § 1182(e), establishes the conditions under which an alien who has been an exchange visitor may remain in the United States, or return to the United States after returning to his or her country of nationality, for purposes of employment.[7] Three nonimmigrant categories are particularly important: "exchange visitor" (8 U.S.C. § 1101(a)(15)(J)), "temporary visitor" (8 U.S.C. § 1101(a)(15)(B)), and "temporary worker" in a

---

[7]The statute defines various categories of exchange visitors who must have returned to their homeland or last foreign residence, and been physically present there for at least two years after departing the United States, to be eligible for a visa or permanent residence. See Russell G. Donaldson, Annot., "Foreign Residence Requirement for Educational (Exchange) Visitors Under § 212(e) of Immigration and Nationality Act [8 U.S.C. § 1182(e)]," 48 A.L.R. Fed. 509.

"specialty occupation" (8 U.S.C. § 1101(a)(15)(H)). For the first and third, but not the second, of these categories, the statute also provides that the "alien spouse and minor children" of the alien may qualify for admission "if accompanying him or following to join him."

The first category, the exchange visitor or "J" category, includes any alien (and the family of any alien):

> who is a bona fide student, scholar, trainee, teacher, professor, research assistant, specialist, or leader in a field of specialized knowledge or skill, or other person of similar description, who is coming temporarily to the United States as a participant in a program designated by the Director of the United States Information Agency, for the purpose of teaching, instructing or lecturing, studying, observing, conducting research, consulting, demonstrating special skills, or receiving training [8 U.S.C. § 1101(a)(15)(J)].

This statutory definition is broad enough to include some types of employees as well. The second or "B" category is for aliens "visiting the United States temporarily for business or temporarily for pleasure," except those "coming for the purpose of study or of performing skilled or unskilled labor or as a representative of foreign press, radio, film, or other foreign information media coming to engage in such vocation" (8 U.S.C. § 1101(a)(15)(B)). Visitors for business are B-1's, and visitors for pleasure are B-2's.

The Department of State regulates the exchange visitor program. Regulations implementing the program are codified in 22 C.F.R. Part 62. Obligations of sponsors of exchange visitors appear at 22 C.F.R. § 62.9. Exchange visitors, who are typically professors or research scholars, must also demonstrate that they intend to return to their home country. The college or university must also maintain current data on its exchange visitors in the Student and Exchange Visitors Information System (SEVIS). J-1 visas may be granted for periods between three weeks and three years. Regulations governing visits by professors and research scholars may be found at 22 C.F.R. § 62.20.

Three additional categories have relevance for higher education institutions. The "O" visa is for nonimmigrant visitors who have extraordinary ability in the areas of arts, sciences, education, business, or athletics and are to be employed for a specific project or event such as an academic-year appointment or a lecture tour (8 U.S.C. § 1101(a)(15)(O); 8 C.F.R. § 214.2(o)). The "P" visa is for performing artists and athletes at an internationally recognized level of performance who seek to enter the United States as nonimmigrant visitors to perform, teach, or coach (8 U.S.C. § 1101(a)(15)(P); 8 C.F.R. § 214.2(p)). The "Q" visa is designated for international cultural exchange visitors

> coming temporarily (for a period not to exceed fifteen months) to the United States as a participant in an international cultural exchange program approved by the Attorney General for the purpose of providing practical training, employment, and the sharing of the history, culture, and traditions of the country of the alien's nationality [8 U.S.C. §1101(a)(15)(Q); 8 C.F.R. §214.2(q)].

A personal interview is required for all applicants for nonimmigrant visas, which has greatly lengthened the time needed to obtain a visa, and has resulted in the denial of visas to some international applicants. The requirement of maintaining current data in SEVIS, the additional documentation required for international applicants, and the stricter standards for obtaining H1-B visas (for employment of faculty or staff) have affected offices serving international students and faculty, creating both administrative burdens and heightened potential legal liability.

Various federal income tax issues may arise concerning colleges' and universities' payments to students, employees, and visitors who are nonresident aliens (see Section 13.3.1).

Federal law provides that aliens may be denied visas on a variety of grounds, such as health conditions, prior criminal behavior, or participation in terrorist activities. 8 U.S.C. § 1182 details these categories of exclusion, and contains language of relevance to potential visitors to U.S. colleges or universities. Section 1182(a)(3)(C) permits exclusion of aliens whom "the Secretary of State has reasonable ground to believe would have potentially serious adverse foreign policy consequences for the United States." There are, however, two important exceptions to this exclusion. One is for foreign officials (§ 1182(a)(3)(C)(ii)). The other is for aliens whose "past, current, or expected beliefs, statements, or associations" might otherwise raise foreign policy concerns but are "lawful within the United States" (§ 1182(A)(3)(C)(iii)), unless the Secretary of State "personally determines that the alien's admission would compromise a compelling United States foreign policy interest."

The ideology-based exclusions were the subject of a U.S. Supreme Court case involving higher education. *Kleindienst v. Mandel*, 408 U.S. 753 (1976), concerned a Belgian citizen, Mandel, whose writings involved Marxist economics and revolution. He had been invited to present a lecture at Stanford University, among other institutions. The American Consulate in Brussels denied him a visa on the basis of two provisions in Section 1182 (since repealed) concerning writings on communism and totalitarianism. Mandel brought suit, and was joined in the litigation by several professors at the institutions that had invited Mandel to speak. The Court held that Congress had plenary authority to enact legislation excluding aliens with certain political affiliations and beliefs, and that Mandel had no constitutional right to enter the United States. And although the Court agreed that the other plaintiffs had First Amendment rights to receive information from Mandel, their First Amendment rights were subordinate to the right of Congress to exclude certain aliens and the right of the executive branch to exercise the discretion provided to it in the immigration law. The case demonstrates the plenary power of Congress in the area of immigration, and its ability to overcome the constitutional rights of U.S. citizens to receive information.

Administrators should be aware that the federal government's treatment of visitors, as well as other foreign nationals within or seeking to enter the United States, may depend on contemporary trends in U.S. foreign policy. At various times in the past decades, Congress has either broadened or tightened immigration laws (with corresponding changes in federal regulations) for individuals from certain countries. Given the complexity and volatility of the regulation of the entry of foreign nationals, there is no substitute for experienced legal counsel and well-trained staff to manage these matters.

13.2.3. Regulation of research

13.2.3.1. Overview. Federal agencies that fund academic research have developed a complex system for overseeing this research on campus, assuring that there are appropriate financial controls on spending under research grants and contracts, and reviewing research proposals to ensure the safety of the subjects of the research, whether they are human or animal. Federal regulations also prescribe the manner in which research misconduct must be investigated and the timing and content of reports that investigatory committees make to the funding agency. (These regulations are discussed in subsection 13.2.3.4 below.) Other regulations prescribe conflict of interest guidelines (see the discussion in subsection 15.4.7). In addition, statutes and regulations cover various aspects of scientific research that may have national security implications. (These laws are discussed in subsection 13.2.4 below.)

The regulations of several federal agencies that fund research require that each institution that receives federal research funding establish an Institutional Review Board (IRB) to approve research that involves humans as subjects. Requirements for IRBs with respect to research involving human subjects are discussed in Section 13.2.3.2. A similar committee, the Institutional Animal Care and Use Committee (IACUC), must be established at institutions that receive federal funding for research involving animals. Regulations for conducting research using animals are discussed in Section 13.2.3.3. Although not all academic research is funded by the federal government, most colleges and universities use the federally mandated system for reviewing research proposals and investigating research misconduct for all human subject and animal research conducted by faculty, staff, or students.[8]

13.2.3.2. Laws governing research on human subjects. Federal law regulates scientific and medical research, especially research on human subjects and genetic engineering. This body of law has been a focal point for the ongoing debate concerning the federal regulatory presence on the campuses. A number of interrelated policy issues have been implicated in the debate: the academic freedom of researchers, the burden and efficiency of federal "paperwork," the standards and methods for protecting safety and privacy of human subjects, and the interplay of legal and ethical standards.

Regulations on human subjects and related research are promulgated by various federal agencies. Regulations promulgated by the Department of Health

---

[8]For a case not involving federal regulation, but discussing the legal liability faced by a university for intentional infliction of emotional distress, libel per se, negligent and fraudulent misrepresentation, and punitive damages claims resulting from a research project that falsely claimed that several restaurants had served tainted food, see *164 Mulberry Street Corp. v. Columbia Univ.,* 771 N.Y.S.2d 16 (N.Y. Sup. App. Div. 2004). The research project had apparently not been reviewed by the university's Institutional Review Board.

and Human Services are codified at 45 C.F.R. Part 46. Similar regulations pro-mulgated by the Food and Drug Administration (FDA) are codified at 21 C.F.R. Parts 50 and 56. FDA regulations cover research on any product under its regu-latory purview, whether or not that research is federally funded. Other federal agencies require that researchers receiving funds from their agencies follow cer-tain guidelines with regard to the protection of human subjects.

The unit of HHS with the responsibility for enforcing regulations protecting human subjects is the Office for Human Research Protections (OHRP). Infor-mation and guidance concerning regulatory matters under the purview of OHRP may be found at http://www.hhs.gov/ohrp. The primary unit of the FDA with responsibility for enforcing regulations protecting human subjects (especially those involving clinical trials of drugs) is the Office for Good Clinical Practice Staff, although other FDA units perform inspections and monitor IRB actions. That office's Web site, containing information and resources, is available at http://www.fda.gov/oc/gcp/default.htm.

The primary regulatory approach of these agencies is to require that institu-tions receiving research funding evaluate the research projects proposed for funding, using both their own staff and external individuals, to ensure that human research subjects are protected from harm. The regulations require insti-tutions to set up review panels (Institutional Review Boards) and to determine when informed consent must be obtained from the research subjects and what information must be provided to them. The regulations also require these indi-viduals to receive training, to follow written guidelines, and to act within the scope of the regulations' policies for the protections of human subjects.

The HHS and FDA regulations require that IRBs perform the following responsibilities:

1. Ensure that risks to human subjects are minimized (45 C.F.R. § 46.111(a)(1) and 21 C.F.R. § 56.111(a)(1));

2. Determine that risks to subjects are reasonable in relation to antici-pated benefits, if any, to subjects (45 C.F.R. § 46.111(a)(2) and 21 C.F.R. § 56.111(a)(2));

3. Determine that methods for selecting subjects are equitable (45 C.F.R. § 46.111(a)(3) and 21 C.F.R. § 56.111(a)(3));

4. Ensure that informed consent will be sought from each prospective subject (45 C.F.R. § 46.111(a)(4) and 21 C.F.R. § 56.111(a)(4));

5. Ensure that the possibility of coercion or undue influence over subjects is minimized (45 C.F.R. § 46.116 and 21 C.F.R. § 50.20)).

The regulations also give the IRB the authority to require that additional information be given to subjects when such information "would meaningfully add to protection of the rights and welfare of subjects" (45 C.F.R. § 46.109(b) and 21 C.F.R. § 56.109(b)).

The FDA regulations apply to clinical investigations regulated by the FDA under the Federal Food, Drug and Cosmetic Act (21 U.S.C. § 301 *et seq.*) and to clinical investigations that support applications for research or marketing permits regulated by the FDA. If an institution fails to comply with the FDA regulations, the agency may impose any of a number of sanctions. It may "(1) withhold approval of new studies . . . that are conducted at the institution" or reviewed by its institutional review board; "(2) direct that no new subjects be added to ongoing studies subject to [the FDA rules]; (3) terminate ongoing studies subject to [the FDA rules] where doing so would not endanger the subjects"; and "(4) when the apparent noncompliance creates a significant threat to the rights and welfare of human subjects," the agency may "notify the relevant State and Federal regulatory agencies and other parties with a direct interest" in the FDA's actions (21 C.F.R. § 56.120). If the institution's "IRB has refused or repeatedly failed to comply with" the FDA regulations and "the noncompliance adversely affects the rights or welfare of the subjects of a clinical investigation," the FDA commissioner may, when he or she deems it appropriate, disqualify the IRB or the parent institution from participation in FDA-governed research. Further, the FDA

> will [refuse to] approve an application for a research permit for a clinical investigation that is to be under the review of a disqualified IRB or that is to be conducted at a disqualified institution, and it may refuse to consider in support of a marketing permit the data from a clinical investigation that was reviewed by a disqualified IRB [or] conducted at a disqualified institution [21 C.F.R. § 56.121(d)].

The commissioner may reinstate a disqualified IRB or institution upon its submission of a written plan for corrective action and adequate assurances that it will comply with FDA regulations (21 C.F.R. § 56.123).

The Department of Health and Human Services and several other federal agencies have issued common final rules regarding the protection of human subjects ("Federal Policy for the Protection of Human Subjects," 56 Fed. Reg. 28003 (June 18, 1991)), but each agency has retained control over the enforcement of these regulations for its own grantees. The FDA did not adopt the Federal Policy, given the FDA's broader mandate to regulate all research involving human subjects.

The following federal agencies have adopted the joint final rules:

Department of Agriculture (7 C.F.R. Part 1c)

Department of Energy (10 C.F.R. Part 745)

National Aeronautics and Space Administration (14 C.F.R. Part 1230)

Department of Commerce (15 C.F.R. Part 27)

Consumer Product Safety Commission (16 C.F.R. Part 1028)

International Development Cooperation Agency, Agency for International Development (22 C.F.R. Part 225)

Department of Housing and Urban Development (24 C.F.R. Part 60)

Department of Justice (28 C.F.R. Part 46)

Department of Defense (32 C.F.R. Part 219)

Department of Education (34 C.F.R. Part 97)

Department of Veterans Affairs (38 C.F.R. Part 16)

Environmental Protection Agency (40 C.F.R. Part 26)

Department of Health and Human Services (45 C.F.R. Part 46)

National Science Foundation (45 C.F.R. Part 690)

Department of Transportation (49 C.F.R. Part 11)

Subsections of each agency's regulations are numbered identically for each provision (for example, the "Definitions" section under Department of Health and Human services regulations is 45 C.F.R. § 46.102, and the same section under Department of Housing and Urban Development regulations is 24 C.F.R. § 60.102).

The regulations, except for specifically enumerated exemptions set out below (or authorized by a department or agency head and published in the *Federal Register*), apply to all research involving human subjects conducted by these agencies or research funded in whole or part by a grant, contract, cooperative agreement, or fellowship from one of these agencies. Under Section .103(b)[9] of the regulations,

> [d]epartments or agencies will conduct or support research covered by this policy only if the institution has an assurance approved as provided in this section, and only if the institution has certified to the department or agency head that the research has been reviewed and approved by an IRB [institutional review board] provided for in the assurance, and will be subject to continuing review by the IRB.

The joint regulations do not provide elaborate sanctions for noncompliance, as do other agency regulations, but only general provisions on fund termination (§§ .122 & .123).

As noted above, both the FDA and the joint federal agency regulations specify that an IRB must review research proposals involving the use of human subjects before the research is conducted. IRBs are fairly recent phenomena; until the early 1960s, only a small minority of research facilities had such committees. As now conceived by the federal agencies, the IRB is designed to ameliorate the tension that exists between institutional autonomy and federal supervision of research. Under these regulations, the IRB must have at least five members with backgrounds sufficiently varied to supervise completely the common research activities conducted by the

---

[9]As noted in the previous paragraph, regulations pertaining to human subjects are identical for fifteen agencies. In this discussion of various subsections of the joint regulations, the chapter of the *Code of Federal Regulations* would correspond to the agency that provided the research funds, but the section number for each agency's human subjects regulations is identical. For the Department of Agriculture, for example, the section noted here would read "7 C.F.R. § 1c.103(b)."

particular institution. Since the IRB must "ascertain the acceptability of proposed research in terms of institutional commitments and regulations, applicable law, and standards of professional conduct and practice" (§ .107), the IRB must include members knowledgeable in these areas. No IRB may consist entirely of members of the same sex or the same profession. The IRB must also include at least one member whose primary expertise is nonscientific, such as an attorney, an ethicist, or a member of the clergy. Each IRB must have "at least one member who is not otherwise affiliated with the institution" and who is not a member of a family immediately affiliated with the institution. And no IRB may have a member participate in the IRB's initial or continuing review of any project "in which the member has a conflicting interest, except to provide information requested by the IRB" (§ .107).

The IRB has the duty, under the regulations, "to approve, require modifications in (to secure approval), or to disapprove" all research conducted under the regulations (§ .109(a)). The IRB must also monitor the information provided subjects to ensure informed consent (§ .109(b)). In addition, the IRB must conduct follow-up reviews of research it has approved "at intervals appropriate to the degree of risk, but not less than once per year" (§ .109(e)). The institution may also review research already approved by an IRB and may either approve or disapprove such research, but an institution may not approve research disapproved by the IRB (§ .112). If research is being conducted in violation of IRB requirements or if subjects have been seriously and unexpectedly harmed, the IRB may suspend or terminate the research (§ .113). The FDA regulations governing IRB responsibilities and functions are similar to the joint regulations on these points (see 21 C.F.R. §§ 56.108–56.112).

Informed consent, a doctrine arising from the law of torts, concerns the information that must be provided about the research to the human subject. The regulations are fairly typical in what they establish as the basic elements of informed consent:

(1) A statement that the study involves research, an explanation of the purposes of the research and the expected duration of the subject's participation, a description of the procedures to be followed, and identification of any procedures which are experimental;

(2) A description of any reasonably foreseeable risks or discomforts to the subject;

(3) A description of any benefits to the subject or to others which may reasonably be expected from the research;

(4) A disclosure of appropriate alternative procedures or courses of treatment, if any, that might be advantageous to the subject;

(5) A statement describing the extent, if any, to which confidentiality of records identifying the subject will be maintained;

(6) For research involving more than minimal risk, an explanation as to whether any compensation [will be given] and an explanation as to whether any medical treatments are available if injury occurs and, if so, what they consist of, or where further information may be obtained;

(7) An explanation of whom to contact for answers to pertinent questions about the research and research subjects' rights, and whom to contact in the event of a research-related injury to the subject; and

(8) A statement that participation is voluntary, refusal to participate will involve no penalty or loss of benefits to which the subject is otherwise entitled, and the subject may discontinue participation at any time without penalty or loss of benefits to which the subject is otherwise entitled [§ .116(a)(1)–(8)].

The regulations also require that, in "appropriate" circumstances (a concept the regulations do not define), additional elements of informed consent must be met, as outlined in § .116(b)(1)–(6). The FDA regulations contain the same informed consent requirements (21 C.F.R. § 50.25(a) & (b)).

The FDA informed consent regulations create an exception to the requirement that research subjects provide an informed consent. The exception applies in emergency situations in which the subject is unable to consent (for example, because he or she is unconscious). The investigator and a physician who is not participating in the research must both certify all of the following:

(1) The human subject is confronted by a life-threatening situation necessitating the use of the [experimental substance].

(2) Informed consent cannot be obtained from the subject because of an inability to communicate with, or obtain legally effective consent from, the subject.

(3) Time is not sufficient to obtain consent from the subject's legal representative.

(4) There is available no alternative method of approved or generally recognized therapy that provides an equal or greater likelihood of saving the life of the subject.

The documentation described above must then be submitted to the IRB. The revised rules may be found at 21 C.F.R. § 50.23.

The joint regulations also contain requirements for documenting informed consent. Unlike their FDA counterparts, the joint regulations set out several circumstances in which the IRB may either alter the elements of informed consent or waive the informed consent requirement (see § .116(c)(1) & (2), and compare 21 C.F.R. § 50.25).

The joint regulations contain several broad exemptions for specific areas of research (§ .101(b)(1)–(5)). The department or agency head has final authority to determine whether a particular activity is covered by the joint regulations (§ .101(c)). The department or agency head may also "require that specific research activities . . . conducted by [the department or agency], but not otherwise covered by this policy, comply with some or all of the requirements of this policy" (§ .101 (d)). And the department or agency head may "waive the applicability of this policy to specific research activities otherwise covered by this policy" (§ .101(i)).

Both the Office for Human Research Protections (OHRP, which is part of HHS) and the FDA have issued proposed rules regarding the registration of IRBs. The proposed OHRP rules will add a subpart F to 45 C.F.R. Part 46 that specifies how IRBs are to register with the Office for Human Research Protections, what information must be provided, how the IRB can register, and how IRB information may be revised. The required information includes the name, gender, contact information, and professional credentials of each member of the IRB, the number of full-time staff supporting the IRB's work, and the number of active protocols undergoing initial and continuing review. The OHRP proposed regulations are found at 69 Fed. Reg. 40584–40590. The FDA's proposed regulations, which will amend 21 C.F.R. Part 56, apply to IRBs that review clinical investigations regulated by the FDA, and are similar to the OHRP proposed regulations. They can be found at 69 Fed. Reg. 40556–40562.

In 2004, the Office of Public Health and Science of the Department of Health and Human Services issued a final guidance entitled "Financial Relationships and Interests in Research Involving Human Subjects: Guidance for Human Subjects Protection" (69 Fed. Reg. 26393–26397, May 12, 2004). The guidance provides suggested questions for IRBs to ask during their deliberations about proposed research projects that may involve financial conflicts of interests (such as whether the research is funded by a private company that is also a business partner with the principal investigator, or whether the principal investigator has received payments from the sponsor of the proposed research). (For a summary of the regulations and guidance, as well as a discussion of the areas of financial conflicts of interest that are of particular concern to institutions and funding agencies, see Lance Shea, *Managing Financial Conflicts of Interest in Human Subjects Research,* available at http://www.nacua.org.)

(For general discussion of informed consent and the role of IRBs, see Robert J. Katerberg, "Institutional Review Boards, Research on Children, and Informed Consent of Parents: Walking the Tightrope Between Encouraging Vital Experimentation and Protecting Subjects' Rights," 24 *J. Coll. & Univ. Law* 545 (1998).)[10]

Federally funded research using recombinant DNA is regulated differently from other federally funded research. Research projects are proposed to the National Institutes of Health (NIH) Recombinant DNA Advisory Committee. This committee recommends either approval or rejection, and the proposed action is published in the *Federal Register.* NIH "Guidelines for Research Involving Recombinant DNA Molecules" are revised several times a year, focusing on how such research may be conducted, and are published on the Web site of the Centers for Disease Control at http://www.cdc.gov. Because of the volatility of this

---

[10]A former student dismissed on academic grounds attempted to argue that a private institution, Boston University, was a "state actor" because of the involvement of the Institutional Review Board in the research that graduate students conduct on human subjects. In *Missert v. Trustees of Boston University,* 73 F. Supp. 2d 68 (D. Mass. 1999), *affirmed,* 248 F.3d 1127 (1st Cir. 2000), a federal district court dismissed the student's state and federal constitutional claims, ruling that because the IRB had not been involved in the decision to dismiss the student, no state action had occurred. This case is discussed further in Section 1.5.2.

regulatory area, the only safe prediction is that frequent and substantial change can be expected, and that expert assistance is advisable.

As reflected in the various regulatory actions discussed above, the law of human subject research is complex and rapidly evolving. The impact of this law on individual campuses will vary considerably, depending on their own research programs. Postsecondary administrators responsible for research will want to stay abreast of their institution's research emphases and issues of concern. In consultation with counsel, administrators should also keep abreast of changes in federal regulations and engage in a continuing process of extracting from the various sets of regulations the particular legal requirements applicable to their institution's research programs, particularly with respect to institutional review boards. Given the recent growth and volatility of legal developments and the sensitivity of some current areas of research emphasis, institutions that do not have a particular office or committee to oversee research may wish to reconsider their organizational structure.

13.2.3.3. Laws governing animal research. Although all states have statutes forbidding cruelty to animals, and antivivisection movements have been active in certain states for more than a century, federal legislation to protect animals was not enacted until 1966. Activity by both scholars and animal rights activists has focused government, press, and scholarly attention on the issue of using animals in scientific research. Entire scholarly journals (for example, the *International Journal of the Study of Animal Problems,* founded in 1979) are devoted to this issue.

✓ /1966

The Animal Welfare Act (AWA) (7 U.S.C. § 2131 *et seq.*) governs the treatment of animals used for research (whether or not it is federally funded) in or substantially affecting interstate or foreign commerce. The law "insure[s] that animals intended for use in research facilities or for exhibition purposes or for use as pets are provided humane care and treatment." Amended in 1970, 1976, and 1985, the law covers "any live or dead dog, cat, or monkey, guinea pig, hamster, or such warm-blooded animal as the Secretary may determine is being used, or is intended for use, for research, testing, experimentation, or exhibition purposes, or as a pet" (§ 2132(g)). Although the regulations promulgated under this law did not originally include rats, mice, and birds, a federal judge ruled that the exclusion of these animals was arbitrary and capricious (*Animal Legal Defense Fund v. Madigan,* 781 F. Supp. 797 (D.D.C. 1992)). A federal appellate court overturned this ruling on procedural grounds (23 F.3d 496 (D.C. Cir. 1994)). Section 2132(g) of the AWA was amended in 2002 to specifically exclude rats, birds, and mice bred for research purposes (Pub. L. No. 107-171, Title X, Subtitle D, § 10301, 116 Stat. 491, May 13, 2002).

use of Commerce clause Constitutional I seul

The AWA is enforced by the Animal and Plant Health Inspection Service of the U.S. Department of Agriculture (whose regulations are codified at 9 C.F.R. ch. 1, subch. A, Parts 1, 2, and 3). The regulations, amended and substantially strengthened in 1991, require an institution, whether or not it receives federal funds, to appoint an Institutional Animal Care and Use Committee (IACUC), which operates in a manner similar to the IRBs that are used to review the use of human subjects in research. The IACUC must include at least one doctor of veterinary medicine, at least one member who is not affiliated (and who has no family members affiliated) with the institution, and no more than three members from the same administrative unit. The regulations are silent on whether, or how, a member of the IACUC may be removed.

The IACUC is required to

(1) Review, once every six months, the research facility's program for humane care and use of animals. . . . (2) Inspect, at least once every six months, all of the research facility's animal facilities, including animal study areas. . . . (3) Prepare reports of its evaluations conducted as required by paragraphs (1) and (2) of this section, and submit the reports to the Institutional Official of the research facility.

The IACUC must also investigate public or employee complaints regarding the care and use of animals; it must review and approve, require modifications in, or withhold approval of proposed changes in the use or care of animals; and it may also suspend activity involving animals (9 C.F.R. § 2.31(c)).

In order to conduct research using animals or to modify an approved research proposal, the researcher must submit the following information to the IACUC:

(1) Identification of the species and the approximate number of animals to be used;

(2) A rationale for involving animals, and for the appropriateness of the species and numbers of animals to be used;

(3) A complete description of the proposed use of the animals;

(4) A description of procedures designed to assure that discomfort and pain to animals will be limited to that which is unavoidable for the conduct of scientifically valuable research, including provision for the use of analgesic, anesthetic, and tranquilizing drugs where indicated and appropriate to minimize discomfort and pain to animals; and

(5) A description of any euthanasia method to be used [9 C.F.R. § 2.31(e)].

In addition to the elements required to be present in the proposal, the regulations charge the IACUC with the responsibility of determining whether a research project meets a number of requirements, including minimizing discomfort or pain to the animals, a discussion of why alternatives to painful procedures are not available, and a statement that animals will be housed appropriately and will be cared for by trained and qualified individuals (9 C.F.R. § 2.31(d)). The regulations also specify the procedures to be used if surgery is performed.

The training of laboratory personnel is detailed in the regulations, as are the responsibilities of the attending veterinarian and record-keeping requirements. The regulations further detail how handling, housing, exercise, transportation, and socialization of the animals should be carried out. Institutions must develop written plans for providing exercise for dogs and improving the psychological well-being of primates (9 C.F.R. ch. 1, subch. A, Part 3). Penalties for violating the AWA include civil and criminal sanctions, civil money penalties, imprisonment for not more than one year, and/or a fine of $2,500 or less. Termination of federal funds, if relevant, is also provided for.

The Agriculture Department's regulations have been criticized by animal rights activists as providing insufficient protection for laboratory animals and as contrary to congressional intent. In early 1993, a federal trial judge agreed, ruling that the regulations implementing the 1985 Animal Welfare Act were too lax and gave too much authority to colleges and universities to regulate researchers' use and treatment of animals (*Animal Legal Defense Fund v. Madigan,* 781 F. Supp. 797 (D.D.C. 1992), *vacated and remanded sub nom Animal Legal Defense Fund v. Espy,* 23 F.3d 496 (D.C. Cir. 1994)). This ruling was overturned in 1994 because the appellate court ruled that the fund did not have the legal right to sue the government.

The Public Health Service (PHS) policy governing the use and treatment of animals in federally funded research has provisions similar to many of those in the AWA. The PHS policy covers all vertebrates, including rats and mice, and requires institutions to follow the guidelines in the "Guide for the Care and Use of Laboratory Animals" (1996), prepared by the Institute of Laboratory Animal Resources, Commission on Life Sciences of the National Research Council. The guidelines include a section on "institutional policies and responsibilities" regarding the IACUC, housing and caring for animals, staff training and safety, and other issues. They may be found at http://oacu.od.nih.gov/regs/guide/guidex.htm.

Animal rights activists have had little success in using the AWA to challenge the use or treatment of animals at particular research locations. For example, a federal appellate court held that the AWA does not provide a private right of action for individuals or organizations, nor does it authorize the court to name them guardians of certain animals taken from a medical research institute (*International Primate Protection League v. Institute for Behavioral Research, Inc.,* 799 F.2d 934 (4th Cir. 1988)). In *People for the Ethical Treatment of Animals (PETA) v. Institutional Animal Care and Use Committee,* 817 P.2d 1299 (Or. 1991), the Oregon Supreme Court ruled that the animal rights group lacked standing to seek judicial review of an IACUC's approval of a University of Oregon professor's research proposal involving the auditory systems of barn owls. The court said that the public's interest in the treatment of animals was represented by the IACUC, and that the plaintiffs had no personal stake in the outcome of the litigation. (For a discussion of the merits of amending the Animal Welfare Act to provide for a private cause of action, see Cass R. Sunstein, "A Tribute to Kenneth L. Karst: Standing for Animals (With Notes on Animal Rights)," 47 *UCLA L. Rev.* 1333 (2000).)

A federal trial court ruled that an academic researcher's grant application was subject to disclosure under the federal Freedom of Information Act (FOIA) (5 U.S.C. § 552). In *Physicians Committee for Responsible Medicine v. National Institutes of Health,* 2004 U.S. Dist. LEXIS 12464 (D.D.C., June 29, 2004), an animal rights group sought an unredacted copy of a professor's grant proposal, which had been funded by NIH. The agency argued that the requested material was exempt under FOIA's exemption for trade secrets, commercial information, or interagency memoranda (5 U.S.C. § 552(b)(4) & (5)). The court ruled that, because the professor was a noncommercial research scientist, the design of his research was not a trade secret, so exemption 4 did not apply. The court rejected the professor's and agency's assertions that disclosure would limit his ability to publish his work as "conclusory and generalized allegations" that did not establish "substantial competitive harm." With respect to exemption 5, the court ruled that the professor was not a consultant to the government, nor was the proposal part of the agency's deliberative process, and thus exemption 5 did not protect the proposal from disclosure. The court awarded summary judgment to the plaintiffs, and ordered certain portions of the proposal released to them.

Animal rights groups have also used state open meetings laws (see Section 12.5.2) to seek access to the deliberations of IACUCs. In *Medlock v. Board of Trustees of the University of Massachusetts*, 580 N.E.2d 387 (Mass. App. Ct. 1991), plaintiffs argued that Massachusetts' open meetings law required the IACUC to hold public meetings. The court ruled that the state law applied only to the university's board of trustees and that the IACUC did not "consider or discuss public policy matters in order to arrive at a decision on any public business" (580 N.E.2d at 392). A similar result, with different reasoning, occurred in *In re American Society for the Prevention of Cruelty to Animals, et al. v. Board of Trustees of the State University of New York*, 582 N.Y.S.2d 983 (N.Y. 1992), where the state's highest court ruled that the powers of the IACUC derived solely from federal law and thus that the committee was not a "public body" for purposes of New York's open meetings law. But the Supreme Court of Vermont determined, in *Animal Legal Defense Fund v. Institutional Animal Care and Use Committee of the University of Vermont*, 616 A.2d 224 (Vt. 1992), that the university's IACUC was a public body under the state's open meetings law, and was also subject to the state's Public Records Act.

In *In re: Citizens for Alternatives to Animal Labs, Inc. v. Board of Trustees of the State University of New York*, 703 N.E.2d 1218 (N.Y. 1998), an animal rights group sought records related to the source of animals used by research laboratories at a State University of New York (SUNY) campus. New York's highest court ruled that SUNY's Health Science Center at Brooklyn was an "agency" for purposes of the state Freedom of Information Law (FOIL), stating that the purpose of the FOIL was broad disclosure of the activities of government agencies.

Some laboratories that use animals and related research facilities have sustained damage, allegedly at the hands of animal rights activists. In 1992, Congress passed legislation that made destruction of or serious damage to animal research facilities a federal crime. The Animal Enterprise Protection Act of 1992 (Pub. L. No. 102-346, 106 Stat. 928) amends Title 18 of the *United States Code* by adding Section 43, directed at persons who cross state lines to disrupt or inflict serious damage on an animal enterprise. "Animal enterprise" is defined as a "commercial or academic enterprise that uses animals for food or fiber production, agriculture, research, or testing." "Serious damage" is defined as stealing, damaging, or causing property loss exceeding $10,000; causing serious bodily injury to another individual; or causing an individual's death. Penalties include fines, imprisonment, or both, and restitution is required.

13.2.3.4. Research misconduct. Academic norms have long viewed research misconduct, such as the falsification of data or the use of another's work without attribution, as a major failing in an individual—a failing that can lead to termination of a faculty member's tenure, expulsion of a student, or dismissal of a staff member. Federal agencies that fund research have become more active in the oversight of institutions' responses to allegations of misconduct in research, and have prescribed standards and procedures that they expect institutions to use in investigating and responding to such allegations. The federal government's general policy, to be implemented by all federal agencies that fund research, is contained in the Federal Research Misconduct Policy promulgated by the Office of Science and Technology Policy and published at 65 Fed. Reg. 76260–76264 (December 6, 2000).

The Department of Health and Human Services, the National Science Foundation (NSF), and the National Aeronautics and Space Administration (NASA) have issued regulations that establish procedures to be used when either the institution or the agency receives a report of alleged research misconduct. The regulations allow for an investigation by the institution, by the agency, or both. They also detail the possible sanctions that the agency may levy should research misconduct be established, and provide opportunity for an appeal of the finding and the sanctions. Regulations issued by the National Science Foundation are codified at 45 C.F.R. Part 689, and became effective in 2002. NASA's regulations are codified at 14 C.F.R. Part 1275, and became effective in 2004.

The Department of Health and Human Service issued proposed regulations, published at 69 Fed. Reg. 20778–20803 (April 16, 2004), that are designed to replace the previous regulations, which were codified at 42 C.F.R. Part 50, and which were issued in 1989. The new rules will be codified at 42 C.F.R. Part 93, and implement Section 493 of the Public Health Act (42 U.S.C. § 289b). That law established the Office of Research Integrity (ORI) within the Department of Health and Human Services and requires each institution receiving a grant from the Public Health Service to submit

(1) assurances that it has established an administrative process to review reports of research misconduct in connection with biomedical and behavioral research conducted at or sponsored by such entity;

(2) an agreement that the entity will report to the Director any investigation of alleged research misconduct in connection with projects for which funds have been made available under this Act that appears substantial; and

(3) an agreement that the entity will comply with regulations issued under this section [42 U.S.C. § 289b(b)].

The law also charges the HHS with developing protections for whistleblowers who make allegations of misconduct in research funded by the Public Health Service.

The proposed HHS regulations are substantially more detailed than the regulations of either the National Science Foundation or NASA. The HHS definition of research misconduct, which tracks NSF's definition, includes fabrication of data or results, falsification of results (including manipulating research materials or equipment to obtain false results), and plagiarism; it does not include "honest error or differences of opinion" (42 C.F.R. § 93.103). In order to make a finding of research misconduct, a three-part test must be met:

(a) there [was] a significant departure from accepted practices of the relevant research community; and

(b) the misconduct [was] committed intentionally, knowingly, or recklessly; and

(c) the allegation [has been] proven by a preponderance of the evidence [42 C.F.R. § 93.104].

This three-part test is identical to the test in the NSF regulations (45 C.F.R. § 689.2(c)).

The proposed HHS regulations include a series of definitions, including definitions of "research" and "research record" (42 C.F.R. §§ 93.224 & 93.226, respectively). They specify that, when an allegation of research misconduct is made, the institution must conduct an inquiry in order to "conduct an initial review of the evidence to determine whether to conduct an investigation" (42 C.F.R. § 93.307). Should the inquiry conclude that an investigation is warranted, it must be begun within thirty days of that determination (42 C.F.R. § 93.310). Due process protections for the individual(s) accused of research misconduct are included in the regulations throughout the inquiry and investigation processes. Time limits for the conduct of the inquiry and the investigation are also included (42 C.F.R. §§ 93.308 & 93.311, respectively). The proposed regulations also specify what type of information must be included in the investigation report (42 C.F.R. § 93.313) and the type of information that must be transmitted to the Office of Research Integrity at the conclusion of the investigation (42 C.F.R. § 93.315). Responsibilities of HHS are also detailed in the regulations, including provisions for HHS to take enforcement actions against institutions that HHS finds have not maintained appropriate policies and practices with respect to research integrity (42 C.F.R. § 93.413).

The Web site of the Office of Research Integrity, available at http://ori.dhhs. gov/html/publications/guidelines.asp, contains a list of resources for administrators and faculty, including the *ORI Introduction to the Responsible Conduct of Research* (2004) and the *ORI Handbook for Institutional Research Integrity Officers* (n.d.).

13.2.4. USA PATRIOT Act and related laws.

13.2.4. USA PATRIOT Act and related laws. Congress passed the "Uniting and Strengthening America by Providing Appropriate Tools Required to Intercept and Obstruct Terrorism (USA PATRIOT Act) of 2001" in October 2001 as a response to the terrorist attacks of September 11, 2001. The law, Pub. L. No. 107-56, 115 Stat. 272, is codified in scattered sections of the *United States Code* and affects numerous activities of colleges and universities, including scientific research, the record-keeping policies of academic libraries, the monitoring of international students' immigration status, the release of information about students, and operation of the campus's computer systems. A discussion of the application of the USA PATRIOT Act with respect to computer systems is found in Section 13.2.12.2 of this book. The effect of the USA PATRIOT Act on FERPA is discussed in Section 9.7.1. (For a general review of the effects of the USA PATRIOT Act on colleges and universities, see David Lombard Harrison, "Higher Education Issues After the USA PATRIOT Act," available at http://www.nacua.org.)

Section 416 of the law amends and expands the Illegal Immigration Reform and Immigrant Responsibility Act (8 U.S.C. § 1372(a)) to provide for the collection of information on nonimmigrant foreign students and exchange visitors who are nationals of countries that are on a list developed by the U.S. Attorney General. This information system (SEVIS) is more fully discussed in Section 8.7.4 of this book. This provision of the law also exempts informat___ ___S from the requirements of FERPA.

Section 817 of the law amends Title 18, chapter 10 ___ to create criminal sanctions for the use and p___ agents and toxins. The law provides for fir___ years for "restricted persons" who "ship o or foreign commerce, or possess in or affect. any biological agent or toxin, or receive any been shipped or transported in interstate or fol agent or toxin is listed as a select agent" under t. is not otherwise exempted from these provisions. any individual who:

(A) is under indictment for a crime punishable by im. exceeding 1 year;

(B) has been convicted in any court of a crime punisha for a term exceeding 1 year;

(C) is a fugitive from justice;

(D) is an unlawful user of any controlled substance (as defi___ ___ection 102 of the Controlled Substances Act (21 U.S.C. § 802));

(E) is an alien illegally or unlawfully in the United States;

(F) has been adjudicated as a mental defective or has been committed to any mental institution;

(G) is an alien (other than an alien lawfully admitted for permanent residence) who is a national of a country as to which the Secretary of State, pursuant to section 6(j) of the Export Administration Act of 1979 (50 U.S.C. App. 2405(j)), section 620A of chapter 1 of part M of the Foreign Assistance Act of 1961 (22 U.S.C. 2371), or section 40(d) of chapter 3 of the Arms Export Control Act (22 U.S.C. 2780(d)), has made a determination (that remains in effect) that such country has repeatedly provided support for acts of international terrorism; or

(H) has been discharged from the Armed Services of the United States under dishonorable conditions (18 U.S.C. § 175b(d)(2)).

Individuals who possess or use select agents must register with the Public Health Service under the provisions of 42 U.S.C. § 262a; penalties for transfer of these substances to an unregistered person include fines and/or imprisonment for up to five years. The law also provides for up to ten years imprisonment for an individual who "knowingly" possesses a biological agent, toxin, or "delivery system" of a type or quantity that "is not reasonably justified by a prophylactic, protective, bona fide research, or other peaceful purpose" (18 U.S.C. § 175(b)).

These provisions have the potential to conflict with institutional policies on employee privacy, background checks, and risk assessment policies. (For an in-depth discussion of the effect on colleges and universities of the bioterrorism provisions of the USA PATRIOT Act (and of the Public Health Security and Bioterrorism Preparedness and Response Act of 2002), see Jamie Lewis Keith, "The War on Terrorism Affects the Academy: Principal Post-September 11, 2001 Federal Anti-Terrorism Statutes, Regulations and Policies That Apply to College and Universities," 30 *J. Coll. & Univ. Law* 239 (2004).)

The USA PATRIOT Act also amends several federal laws concerning surveillance. Some of the statutes so amended are the federal law restricting wiretaps (18 U.S.C. § 2510 *et seq.*);[11] the Foreign Intelligence Surveillance Act (50 U.S.C. § 1801 *et seq.*); and the Cable Act (47 U.S.C. § 551 (which regulates privacy of individuals subscribing to cable service)), among others.

The law also permits government officials to require colleges to provide stored voice mail messages without the authorization typically required by the wiretap statutes, and expands the list of information that telephone and Internet access providers must disclose if required by an administrative subpoena, including local and long distance telephone call records, and sources of payment (including credit card and bank account numbers). It also permits the Federal Bureau of Investigation (FBI) to obtain a court order for business records that are believed to be relevant to a terrorism or intelligence investigation.

This latter provision, "Access to Certain Business Records for Foreign Intelligence Purposes" (50 U.S.C. § 1861) is of particular concern to librarians and scholars. The law provides that the FBI may apply for an *ex parte* order from a judge or federal magistrate if the agency specifies that "the records concerned are sought for an authorized investigation conducted in accordance with subsection (a)(2) to obtain foreign intelligence information not concerning a United States person or to protect against international terrorism or clandestine intelligence activities") (50 U.S.C. § 1861(b)(2)). Furthermore, the law prohibits any individual receiving such a request for records from disclosing that the FBI has sought or obtained these records (50 U.S.C. § 1861(d)). (For a review and discussion of the effects of the USA PATRIOT Act on libraries and their patrons, and suggestions for policy and practice in light of this law, see Lee S. Strickland, Mary Minow, & Tomas Lipinski, "Patriot in the Library: Management

---

[11]These amendments "sunseted" at the end of 2005. Congress voted to extend the Act in March 2006.

Approaches When Demands for Information Are Received from Law Enforcement and Intelligence Agents," 30 *J. Coll. & Univ. Law* 363 (2004).)

Title III of the USA PATRIOT Act, known as the International Money Laundering Abatement and Anti-Terrorism Financing Act of 2001 (codified in scattered Sections of titles 12, 15, 18, 21, 22, 28, and 31 of the *United States Code*), amends banking laws to prohibit banks and other financial institutions from participating in money laundering of funds used to support terrorism. This portion of the USA PATRIOT Act amends the Bank Secrecy Act of 1970 (codified in scattered Sections of Title 31), to which college and university credit unions have been subject since its enactment. The law expands the definition of a "financial institution" that is subject to the record-keeping and reporting requirements of the Bank Secrecy Act, including travel agencies and offices that cash and process checks, traveler's checks, and money orders, or that operate credit card systems. A college or university's financial aid office, campus credit union, and other offices in which financial transactions are accomplished may be subject to the requirements of the Bank Secrecy Act. (For a discussion of the additional requirements under the amendments to the Bank Secrecy Act, see Cynthia J. Larose, "International Money Laundering Abatement and Anti-Terrorism Financing Act of 2001," 30 *J. Coll. & Univ. Law* 417 (2004).)

Another law, The Public Health Security and Bioterrorism Preparedness and Response Act of 2002 (BPARA), codified at 42 U.S.C. § 262a, imposes controls on research using certain biological materials and limits the ability of foreign nationals to participate in or have access to such research unless they are given permission by the U.S. Attorney General. The regulations implementing this law are found at 42 C.F.R. Part 73, 7 C.F.R. Part 331, and 9 C.F.R. Part 121. The law provides that all persons possessing, using, or transferring such agents or toxins must notify the U.S. Department of Health and Human Services. In addition, persons possessing, using, or transferring agents or toxins that could harm animals or plants must notify the U.S. Department of Agriculture (USDA). Universities whose faculty or staff members use these substances in research must register with HHS and report the names of all persons who use or who request access to these substances. The university must wait until it has either received permission from HHS to provide the substance(s) to the requesting individual, or has been informed that the individual requesting the substance is on a list compiled by the Attorney General of the United States of "restricted persons" under the USA PATRIOT Act. In that case, access to the substance(s) must be denied.

This legislation has significant implications for faculty, staff, and students involved in biochemical research. Faculty and administrators involved in such research need to familiarize themselves with the laws' and regulations' requirements and ensure compliance. Policies may have to be revised to comply with this legislation, and the impact of the investigation and reporting requirements on noncitizen employees and graduate students is not only severe, but will create delays in their ability to participate in research that is subject to these requirements.

The Centers for Disease Control and Prevention (CDC) is responsible for providing guidance to HHS, and the Animal and Plant Health Inspection Service provides guidance to the USDA in implementing this law. Further information is provided on the CDC's Web site at http://www.cdc.gov/od/ohs/lrsat/faq.htm. Guidelines for complying with this statute are published at 67 Fed. Reg. 51058–64.

Export control regulations are another concern for colleges and universities in the post-9/11 world. Although these regulations were in place well before September 11, 2001, the federal government is applying them in new ways to attempt to limit the ability of potential terrorists to benefit from substances or information supplied by individuals in the United States. An example of such regulations is the Department of State's International Traffic in Arms Regulations (ITAR) (15 C.F.R. §§ 120–130. These regulations implement the Arms Export Control Act (22 U.S.C. § 2278), which regulates the export of technology and research results that could have military applications. Another example is the Department of Commerce's Export Administration Regulations (EAR) (15 C.F.R. §§ 730–774), which interpret the Export Administration Act of 1979 (50 U.S.C. §§ 2401–2420). EAR controls the exports of technology or materials that have commercial applications, but which could also have military applications. Under both the Arms Export Control Act and the Export Administration Act, "fundamental research" conducted by colleges and universities has, in the past, been exempt from export control regulations, even if the faculty and staff members involved in the research were foreign nationals. Now, however, if foreign nationals are involved in U.S.-based research that may fall within the ambit of the export control regulations, the institution may have to obtain an export license from the relevant agency. In addition, the Treasury Department's Office of Foreign Assets Control (31 C.F.R. § 500) regulates the transfers and travel to certain countries of individuals who may be involved in terrorism, drug trafficking, or other illegal activities. (For a summary of export controls legislation and enforcement, see Jamie Lewis Keith, "The War on Terrorism Affects the Academy: Principal Post-September 11, 2001 Federal Anti-Terrorism Statutes, Regulations and Policies That Apply to Colleges and Universities," 30 *J. Coll. & Univ. Law* 239 (2004). And for developments during 2004 with respect to export controls regulation and related federal regulation, see Jamie Lewis Keith, "Recent Developments in Export Controls," Outline for Annual Conference of National Association of College and University Attorneys, June 2004, available at http://web.mit. edu/srcounsel.)

13.2.5. Copyright law[12]

13.2.5.1. Overview. Congress is authorized in Article I, Section 8, Clause 8 of the U.S. Constitution to create the Copyright Act "to promote the progress of science and useful arts, by securing for limited times to authors and inventors the exclusive right to their respective writings and discoveries." This purpose, simply stated, is to increase knowledge. Every one of the more than 230 Sections of the Act (17 U.S.C. § 101 *et seq.*) should contribute to the achievement

---

[12]This Section was updated and expanded by Georgia Harper, Senior Attorney and Manager, Intellectual Property Section, Office of General Counsel, the University of Texas System.

of this purpose, and, in fact, many recent statutory amendments and court opinions are controversial because it is not clear whether or to what extent they do so or, on the contrary, whether they undermine the achievement of those goals. Until recently, copyright law merited little attention within the academy, but the rapid integration of digital technologies into American life has increased the relevance of this body of law and made necessary a broader understanding of its basis, how it works, and the role it plays in the controversies that are shaping how faculty and students will use technology and information in the future.

In a broad attempt to keep the law up to date and "bring it into the twenty-first century" after its complete overhaul in the mid-1970s, there was considerable activity in the late 1980s and 1990s: Congress passed amendments affecting state sovereign immunity, artists' moral rights, the fair use of unpublished manuscripts, penalties (including criminal sanctions for significant infringements), the term of copyright protection, digital archiving in university libraries, special procedures to protect works on the Internet, and legal status for technological protections of copyrighted works, among other things. Courts tried cases involving, among other issues, the commercial preparation of coursepacks, making research copies of journal articles, Internet service provider liability limitations, authorship and ownership of creative works, states' sovereign immunity for claims for damages in federal courts, and whether copyright protects the exact photographic reproduction of a two-dimensional artwork in the public domain.

By 2000, most legislative and court battles were pitched around digital themes: legislative efforts slowed down somewhat, but included continuing efforts to eliminate state sovereign immunity as a bar to suits for money damages, refine the scope of educational performance rights to encourage the use of digital technologies in distance education, protect databases and incorporate copy prohibition technology in all computing devices. While Congress appeared to be moving somewhat slowly, activity in the courts went on unabated. There were challenges to what seems to be perpetual term extension for existing works, to the technological protection of works without regard to the statutory limitations on copyright owners' rights contained in the Copyright Act (that is, anti-circumvention), and to the use of peer-to-peer file-sharing technology to share music and other works more freely, among others.

Certain core issues have emerged for universities: fair use; performance rights; ownership; vicarious liability; the implications of the shift from acquiring books to licensing digital databases of information; and anti-circumvention. Of interest to state universities is the explosive issue of Eleventh Amendment immunity from damage awards for infringement. These and other issues are discussed below.

13.2.5.2. The fair use doctrine. Section 107 of the Act states that "the fair use of a copyrighted work . . . for purposes such as criticism, comment, news reporting, teaching (including multiple copies for classroom use), scholarship, or research is not an infringement of copyright." The section lists four factors that one must consider in determining whether a particular use is fair:

(1) the purpose and character of the use, including whether such use is of a commercial nature or is for nonprofit educational purposes; (2) the nature of the

copyrighted work; (3) the amount and substantiality of the portion used in relation to the copyrighted work as a whole; and (4) the effect of the use upon the potential market for or value of the copyrighted work.

13.2.5.2.1. GUIDELINES. Application of these rather vague standards to individual cases is left to the courts. Some guidance on their meaning may be found, however, in a document included in the legislative history of the revised Copyright Act: the Agreement on Guidelines for Classroom Copying in Not-for-Profit Educational Institutions (in H.R. Rep. No. 94-1476, 94th Cong., 2d Sess. (1976), available at http://www.copyright.gov/circs/circ21.pdf). A second document in the legislative history, the Guidelines for the Proviso of Subsection 108(g)(2) (the "Contu Guidelines") (Conf. Rep. No. 94-1733, 94th Cong., 2d Sess. (1976)), also available at http://www.copyright.gov/circs/circ21.pdf, provides comparable guidance on the provision within Section 108 dealing with copying for purposes of interlibrary lending. Although the Guidelines for Classroom Copying were adopted by thirty-eight educational organizations and the publishing industry to set minimum standards of educational fair use under Section 107 of the Act, the Association of American Law Schools and the American Association of University Professors (AAUP) did not endorse the provisions and described them as too restrictive in the university setting (H.R. Rep. No. 94-1476, pp. 65–74). The Guidelines establish limits for "Single Copying for Teaching" (for example, a chapter from a book may be copied for the individual teacher's use in scholarly research, class preparation, or teaching) as well as for "Multiple Copies for Classroom Use" (for example, one copy per pupil in one course may be made, provided that the copying meets several tests; these tests, set out in the House Report, concern the brevity of the excerpt to be copied, the spontaneity of the use, and the cumulative effect of multiple copying in classes within the institution).

During the mid-1990s, the Conference on Fair Use produced additional guidelines covering synchronous distance education, image archives, and multimedia works; however, there was insufficient consensus on these documents to confer upon them the status enjoyed by the Guidelines for Classroom Copying and the Contu Guidelines for copying for interlibrary lending by libraries. Nevertheless, these guidelines are useful starting points for evaluating educational uses: if a use fits within them, the user need go no further to determine whether the use is fair. On the other hand, if a use does not fit within them, the user still has recourse to the statute.

For example, guidelines for the fair use of copyrighted material used to create CD-ROMS and other multimedia projects were approved by the Consortium of College and University Media Centers and several copyright owner groups. The Guidelines limit the amount of a work of music or other copyrighted material that can be used in multimedia projects created by professors and students. The Guidelines permit the resulting works to be used for distance learning, so long as their access is limited to enrolled students (Goldie Blumenstyk, "Educators and Publishers Reach Agreement on 'Fair Use' Guidelines for CD-ROMS," *Chron. Higher Educ.,* October 25, 1996, at A28). These and other guidelines are available at http://www.utsystem.edu/ogc/intellectualproperty/copypol2.htm.

The fair use doctrine applies to all works that are protected by the copyright laws, including works posted on the Internet and materials used in distance education courses, whether transmitted in real time via interactive video or presented in an asynchronous format, such as an online course. According to an expert on computer technology and copyright law, "[T]he more you can make the online classroom resemble a traditional classroom—limiting access through the use of passwords for registered students, posting materials for only a short time, including statements about copyright restrictions, and so forth— the stronger your fair use argument will be" (Steven J. McDonald, *Synfax Weekly Report,* February 8, 1999, 813. This article also includes a brief summary of the Digital Millennium Copyright Act (see discussion in Section 13.2.5.5 below) and applications of the fair use doctrine to distance learning courses.)

13.2.5.2.2. COURSEPACKS. The Guidelines for Classroom Copying were cited by a federal appeals court in the first higher education copyright case resulting in a judicial opinion, *Basic Books v. Kinko's Graphics Corp.,* 758 F. Supp. 1522 (S.D.N.Y. 1991). A group of publishers brought a copyright infringement action against a chain of copying shops for copying excerpts from their books without permission, compiling those excerpts into packets ("coursepacks"), and selling them to college students. Kinko's argued that its actions fit within the fair use doctrine of Section 107 of the Copyright Act. The trial judge wrote: "The search for a coherent, predictable interpretation applicable to all cases remains elusive. This is so particularly because any common law interpretation proceeds on a case-by-case basis" (758 F. Supp at 1530). Using the four factors in the statute, as well as the Guidelines for Classroom Copying, the court ruled that (1) Kinko's was merely repackaging the material for its own commercial purposes; (2) the material in the books was factual (which would suggest a broader scope of fair use); (3) Kinko's had copied a substantial proportion of each work; and (4) Kinko's copying reduced the market for textbooks. Furthermore, the court ruled that for an entire compilation to avoid violating the Act, each item in the compilation must pass the fair use test. The judge awarded the plaintiffs $510,000 in statutory damages plus legal fees. Kinko's decided not to appeal the decision, and settled the case in October 1991 for $1.875 million in combined damages and legal fees.

More recently, the Sixth Circuit added to our understanding of the fair use doctrine in the context of preparing commercial coursepacks. In *Princeton University Press v. Michigan Document Services, Inc.,* 99 F.3d 1381 (6th Cir. 1996), the full appellate court, in an 8-to-5 opinion, reversed an appellate panel's finding that the copying at issue constituted fair use. Michigan Document Services (MDS) is a commercial copying service that creates coursepacks and sells them to students at the University of Michigan. Although other copy shops near the university had paid copyright fees and royalties, MDS did not, and stated this policy in its advertising. Despite the earlier holding in *Basic Books v. Kinko's Graphics Corp.,* the owner of MDS had been advised by his attorney that the opinion was "flawed"; he believed that production of coursepacks was protected under the fair use doctrine. Although the trial court found that the copying was not protected under the fair use doctrine, an appellate panel reversed; however, the full court sided with the trial court in most respects.

The full court analyzed the copying under the four elements of the fair use test and found that, because MDS profited from the sale of coursepacks, the purpose of the copying was commercial; furthermore, the loss of copyright permission fees diminished the value of the books to their owners. In response to the defendant's argument that under the fourth factor the court should look only at the effect on actual sales of the books, rather than the diminished revenue from copyright fees, the court stated that there was a strong market for copyright permission fees, and that the reduction in such fees should be considered in an analysis of the market impact of the alleged infringement.

With respect to the remaining factors, the court ruled that the copied material was creative and that the excerpts were lengthy (8,000 words and longer), given the 1,000-word "safe harbor" established in the Guidelines for Classroom Copying.

Although the trial court had ruled that MDS's behavior had been a willful violation of the Copyright Act, and thus supported enhanced damages, the full appellate court stated that the fair use doctrine was "one of the most unsettled areas of the law," and thus the defendant's belief that his interpretation of the fair use doctrine was correct was not so unreasonable that the violation could be termed willful.

Further, five judges joined a dissenting opinion that noted that the fair use doctrine permits the making of "multiple copies for classroom use," which these judges believed applied to the copying by MDS. Characterizing the majority's opinion as a narrow reading of the fair use doctrine, they predicted that costs would increase and student access to publications would be limited as a result of this ruling. The U.S. Supreme Court denied review (520 U.S. 1156 (1997)).

Today, most colleges and universities obtain permission to make coursepacks, even in their own internal copy shops, especially for repeated use of the same article by the same faculty member for the same course. Permission for most materials can be efficiently handled through the Copyright Clearance Center (CCC). The CCC "manages rights relating to over 1.75 million works and represents more than 9,600 publishers and hundreds of thousands of authors and other creators, directly or through their representatives." (See http://www.copyright.com for more information. For a discussion of the fair use doctrine in the higher education classroom, see R. Kasunic, "Fair Use and the Educator's Right to Photocopy Copyrighted Material for Classroom Use," 19 *J. Coll. & Univ. Law* 271 (1993).)

13.2.5.2.3. RESEARCH COPIES. The existence of the CCC may undercut a fair use argument in cases involving the kinds of materials it licenses. In *American Geophysical Union v. Texaco, Inc.*, 802 F. Supp. 1 (S.D.N.Y. 1992), a federal trial judge found that Texaco had infringed the copyrights of several scientific journals by making multiple copies of scientific articles for its scientists and researchers to keep in their files. The judge noted that Texaco could have obtained a license that permits copying of the journals licensed by the CCC, and found that Texaco's failure to take advantage of that license weighed against fair use in consideration of the fourth factor. The court also acknowledged, however, that to avoid using circular reasoning in the analysis of the fourth factor (that is, assuming the use is unfair and would therefore result in lost permission fees in the process of trying to determine whether it is fair), the availability of a license might not have weighed against fair use were the results of the evaluation of the first three factors to have shown the use to be likely a fair use. In this case, however, the court found that two of the first three factors also weighed in favor of getting permission, so it took the lost revenues into account.

The result in *American Geophysical Union v. Texaco* was affirmed by the court of appeals at 60 F.3d 913 (2d Cir. 1994). Although the court of appeals subsequently amended its earlier opinion to distinguish between institutional researchers, such as Texaco, and individual scientists or professors (1994 U.S. App. LEXIS 36735 (2d Cir., December 23, 1994)), some copyright experts believe that the opinion may require universities to enter licensing agreements with publishers to avoid infringement (Goldie Blumenstyk, "Court's Revisions in Copyright Case Add to Confusion for Scholars," *Chron. Higher Educ.,* August 11, 1995, at A14). Others believe that the distinction drawn between Texaco researchers and university professors admits that the results would be different were internal university research copying analyzed.

13.2.5.2.4. Use of Author's Own Work. Even the authors of published articles must seek permission from their publishers to copy their own articles unless they retain their copyrights or reserve the right to make copies in their publishing agreements.

13.2.5.2.5. Use of Unpublished Material. The copyright laws cover unpublished as well as published material. Although the unauthorized use of unpublished material would ordinarily result in liability for the researcher, the college or university could also face vicarious liability if the research were funded by an external grant made to the institution or if the faculty member is otherwise performing the research within the scope of his or her employment.

A pair of cases in the late 1980s interpreted the scope of fair use in publishing unpublished materials so narrowly as to nearly bar any use of such materials (*New Era Publications International v. Henry Holt and Co.,* 873 F.2d 576 (2d Cir. 1989); *Salinger v. Random House,* 811 F.2d 90 (2d Cir. 1987)).

Legal scholars so criticized this pair of decisions that Congress reacted by passing the Copyright Amendments Act in late 1992 (Pub. L. No. 102-492, 106 Stat. 3145). The law amends the fair use doctrine by adding: "The fact that a work is unpublished shall not itself bar a finding of fair use if such finding is made upon consideration of all the above factors." This restored the balance inherent within the fair use statute as it applies to unpublished works.

13.2.5.2.6. Fair Use of Other Types of Expression. For a useful summary of the fair use doctrine and the application of copyright law to videotapes, software, images, performances, and music, as well as written material, see Georgia Harper, "A Guide to Copyright Issues in Higher Education" (National Association of College and University Attorneys, 2005, available at http://www. nacua.org/publications/pamphlets/copyright2000.html). Faculty may wish to consult "Using Software: A Guide to the Ethical and Legal Use of Software for Members of the Academic Community" (1987) (available at http://www.cni.org/ docs/EDUCOM.html).

Those who use thumbnail images as indices in the online environment received long-awaited guidance in the Ninth Circuit's opinion in *Kelly v. Arriba Soft Corporation*, 280 F. 3d 934 (9th Cir. 2002), *amended by* 336 F.3d 811 (9th Cir. 2003). Kelly is a well-known photographer who publishes images on his Web site. Arriba Soft, which has since changed its name to Ditto.com, is a search engine that searches for images, rather than text, and displays search results in the form of a "list" of thumbnail copies of the original images that meet the search criteria. Kelly complained that this use, and the subsequent displays of the images in full size outside the original Web site environment where they were located, was an infringement. Although the trial court found both uses to be fair use, the Ninth Circuit agreed only with respect to the thumbnails.

This is very good news to university image archive managers who use thumbnail images to provide students, faculty, and staff a way to access images for educational purposes. While it was believed that such use was fair, it is encouraging to know now that an appellate court agrees.

Finally, for the tens of millions of users of peer-to-peer file-sharing technologies who transfer music and other media files among themselves, there is bad news about fair use. In *A&M Records v. Napster*, 239 F.3d 1004 (9th Cir. 2001), the court rejected the defendant's defenses, including the claim that its users made fair uses of plaintiffs' recordings. Napster operated a Web site that permitted users of its software to establish direct peer-to-peer connections to download files stored on the peer machines and make files stored on the user's machine available to others for download. Napster provided a current directory of the locations of requested files on peer machines that were connected to the network at a given time. Thus, Napster did not actually make or transfer copies of music files, but it facilitated their transfer through its own computer network. Napster argued that its users' activities were fair use and its activities could not be contributory infringement if there were substantial non-infringing uses of its software system. This argument is based on the Supreme Court's decision in the *Sony* case decided in 1984 (*Sony Corp. of America v. Universal City Studios, Inc.*, 464 U.S. 417 (1984)). The *Sony* court had determined that the manufacturers of videocassette recorders were not vicariously liable for the infringements of their customers because the recorders had substantial non-infringing uses, namely, timeshifting of television programming. The court found that taping a broadcast television program off the air to view it later was a fair use. The Napster court rejected the "substantial non-infringing use" argument in this new context. In assessing whether Napster's customers' uses would qualify as fair use, it determined under the first factor that the purpose and character of the use was repeated and exploitative, aimed at avoiding purchases; under the second factor, that the works were creative; under the third factor, that whole works were copied and distributed; and under the fourth factor, that the copies reduced CD sales and raised barriers to plaintiffs' entry into the digital download market, thus harming the value of the copyrighted works to their owners. Overall, all four factors weighed against fair use. (See below for a discussion of this and other cases with respect to Internet service provider liability.)

Several years later, in a different case with slightly different facts, a court determined that there is a valid defense to contributory infringement in the file-sharing context (*MGM Studios, Inc. v. Grokster, Ltd.*, 380 F.3d 1154 (9th Cir. 2004)). Grokster and Streamcast Networks disseminate Grokster and Morpheus software, respectively, popular programs that have filled the void created by Napster's demise. Their networks work differently from Napster's: at no time is any hardware or software over which the companies have any control involved in the activities of potential infringers. Once the companies have distributed their software, their control over what happens with it is over. Thus, the court determined that Grokster could not contribute to customer infringements because contributory liability only attached if the companies had specific knowledge of infringement at a time when they could do something about it and failed to act on the information. This inability to control what people do with their software also provided the companies a defense against vicarious liability, which only applies where the company has a right and ability to supervise and control customer activity.

The plaintiffs in this case appealed the decision to the U.S. Supreme Court, and approached Congress as well with proposed legislation that would overturn the *Sony* rule on which the *Grokster* decision was based. The Supreme Court vacated the appellate court's decision (125 S. Ct. 2764 (2005)), ruling that the case must be tried. The Court distinguished *Sony*, noting that the facts in this case were significantly different. These distributors could be liable for a particular type of contributory infringement, labeled "inducement," because they promoted the software as a device for infringing copyright. Furthermore, said the Court, the distributors clearly expressed their intent to target former users of Napster, and made no attempt to develop filtering mechanisms that would prohibit unauthorized file sharing. Finally, the Court noted, most of the profits that would accrue to the distributors would be from activities that infringed copyright.

13.2.5.2.7. FAIR USE SUMMARY. Given many courts' strict interpretations of the fair use doctrine and the opportunities provided by computer networks and other technology for violation of the copyright laws, it may be surprising that publishers have not pursued colleges and universities more aggressively; however, university responses to good-faith efforts by publishers to address these issues by promptly responding to allegations of infringement and by providing education and compliance training may explain why so few complaints against universities make it to the courthouse. This attitude has not prevailed with respect to the direct infringers themselves. The Recording Industry Association of America (RIAA) began in 2003 to sue its customers directly. (See Section 13.2.5.5 below, on Liability for Infringement, for more on these cases.)

In light of developments in copyright law, postsecondary institutions should thoroughly review their policies and practices on photocopying and digitizing supplementary reading materials, the use of others' works in the creation of online courses and multimedia works, and the copying and distribution of computer software. Institutions are now required to provide faculty and staff with accurate information on the use of copyrighted material, including text, unpublished material, computer software, images, and music, in order to take advantage of certain limits on their liability. The institution's policy and educational materials should be published online for staff and students as well as faculty members, and a notice apprising users of the policy's existence and location should be posted at campus photocopying and computer facilities. (Visit "The Copyright Crash Course," a comprehensive Web site devoted to a large variety of copyright matters, developed by Georgia Harper of the University of Texas System, at http://www.utsystem.edu/ogc/intellectualproperty/cprtindex.htm#top. It offers good information on copyright that is comprehensible to nonlawyers. Other Web sites providing useful information on copyright to colleges and their employees and students include the Copyright Management Center at Indiana University-Purdue University Indiana, at http://copyright.iupui. edu, and "Ten Big Myths About Copyright Explained," by Brad Templeton, at http://www.templetons.com/brad//copymyths.html.)

13.2.5.3. Performance rights. In addition to fair use, the Copyright Act provides educators with rights to show (perform or play) and display others' works in the classroom and to a limited extent, in distance education. Section 110(1), authorizing displays and performances for face-to-face teaching, and Section 110(2), authorizing more limited rights to transmit works to distant learners, were intended to authorize the performances and displays of others' works that were common in classrooms and in distance education at the time the statute was written (1976).

When Congress enacted the Digital Millennium Copyright Act in 1998 (discussed in Section 13.2.5.5 below), it instructed the U.S. Copyright Office to study how best to facilitate the use of digital technologies in distance education and to report back with recommendations within six months. The "Report on Copyright and Digital Distance Education" was released on May 19, 1999. It can be found at http://www.copyright.gov/disted.

The report discussed the nature of distance education, the technologies used, and the different positions of educational institutions and copyright owners on whether Section 110(2) should be broadened in order to provide additional protection for providers of distance learning. The report recommended amending Section 110 of the Copyright Act to ensure, among other things, that it would apply to digital distribution, and to ensure that permitted performances and displays would be available only in a setting of "mediated instruction" in order to prevent multiple or unprotected uses of the otherwise lawfully used copyrighted material. It also recommended expanding the categories of materials covered by Section 110(2) to close the gap between what educators may show in their classrooms and what they may show via transmissions to distant learners, among other things.

The report's recommendations were introduced as the TEACH Act and signed into law in November 2002. It may still be necessary for educators to rely on fair use to bridge the gap between what is authorized for face-to-face teaching and the expanded but still significantly smaller scope of performances and displays authorized for distance education. Nevertheless, the TEACH Act has broadened what distance educators may perform to include the following:

1. Transmitting performances of all of a non-dramatic literary or musical work [this is a very slim category because (1) the definition of a literary work excludes audiovisual works, and (2) nondramatic works are limited to those that do not "tell a story," so to speak; thus, examples might include a poetry or short story reading and performances of all music other than opera, music videos, and the like];

2. Transmitting reasonable and limited portions of any other performance [this category includes all audiovisual works such as films and videos of all types, and the dramatic musical works excluded above];

3. Transmitting displays of any work in amounts comparable to typical face-to-face displays [this category would include still images of all kinds].

There are several explicit exclusions, however. Section 110(2) only applies to accredited nonprofit educational institutions. The rights granted do not extend to the use of works primarily produced or marketed for the digital distance education market, works the instructor knows or has reason to believe were not lawfully made or acquired, or textbooks, coursepacks, and other materials typically purchased by students individually. This last exclusion results from the definition of "mediated instructional activities," a key concept within the expanded Section 110(2) meant to limit it to the kinds of materials an instructor would actually incorporate into a classtime lecture.

Further affecting the exercise of these rights is a series of limits regarding the circumstances under which the permitted uses may be made:

1. The performance or display must be:
   a. A regular part of systematic mediated instructional activity;
   b. Made by, at the direction of, or under the supervision of the instructor;
   c. Directly related and of material assistance to the teaching content; and
   d. For and technologically limited to students enrolled in the class.

2. The institution must:
   a. Have policies and provide information about and give notice that the materials used may be protected by copyright;
   b. Apply technological measures that reasonably prevent recipients from retaining the works beyond the class session and further distributing them; and
   c. Not interfere with technological measures taken by copyright owners that prevent retention and distribution.

Finally, new Section 112(f) (ephemeral recordings) permits those authorized to perform and display works under Section 110 to digitize analog works and duplicate digital works in order to make authorized displays and performances so long as:

1. Such copies are retained only by the institution and used only for the activities authorized by Section 110; and

2. No digital version of the work is available free from technological protections that would prevent the uses authorized in Section 110.

13.2.5.4. The "work made for hire" doctrine. Although the Copyright Act's work made for hire doctrine has seldom been applied in the higher education context, the issues associated with ownership and use of works created by university employees are raising awareness of the implications of this law for the university community. The work made for hire doctrine is an exception to the Act's presumption that the creator of a work is its author and holds its copyright. In a work made for hire, the employer is considered the "author" and owns the copyright unless the parties enter a written agreement that gives the copyright to the employee. A work is "made for hire" if (1) it is created by an employee within the scope of his or her employment, or (2) if not created within an employment relationship, it is part of a larger work (such as a motion picture, a compilation, a text, or an atlas) and the parties agree in writing that it is made for hire. Thus, there are two "arms" of the work for hire statute, that is, two ways a person or entity may be the author and owner of a work created by someone else.

In *Community for Creative Non-Violence v. Reid,* 490 U.S. 730 (1989), the Supreme Court was asked to decide who owned the copyright in a statue commissioned by Community for Creative Non-Violence (CCNV), an organization devoted to helping homeless people. The Court decided that the work made for hire doctrine did not apply to Reid because he was neither an employee of CCNV nor was there a contract between him and CCNV that satisfied the rigorous requirements of the contractual arm of the work for hire statute.

The case is significant because it rejected approaches to the Act's interpretation used by federal appellate courts, which had ruled that a work was made for hire if an employer exercised control over its production (see, for example, *Siegel v. National Periodical Publications, Inc.,* 508 F.2d 909 (2d Cir. 1974)). The Reid Court stated that the controlling issue for the employer arm of the statute is whether the author is an "employee," listing the factors relevant to such a determination; but, because the Court found that Reid was an independent contractor and not an employee, it did not go on to explain how to determine whether work is "within the scope of employment." Some clarification of this would have been helpful.

Brown University became a defendant in a lawsuit regarding whether statements in its Intellectual Property Policy were sufficient to overcome the presumption that works created by an employee within the scope of employment belong to the university (*Forasté v. Brown University,* 248 F. Supp. 2d 71 (D.C.R.I. 2003)). Forasté was undisputedly an employee, and taking photographs was clearly within his scope of employment, but Brown's intellectual property policy gave ownership of copyrighted works to their authors. The statute, however, requires a written agreement, signed by both employer and employee, to rebut the presumption of employer ownership (17 U.S.C. § 201(b)). The Court determined that an intellectual property policy was inadequate to rebut this presumption.

As it is likely that many universities have policies that grant ownership of certain copyrighted works to their authors (scholarly texts, articles, and literary, artistic, and musical works in the author's field of expertise), this case strongly suggests that more is required to effectuate the intentions that policies embody. Employment contracts *signed by both parties* that refer to the policies may better survive judicial scrutiny.

The mushrooming of distance learning, in both synchronous and asynchronous formats, has stimulated concern among some faculty about their right to participate in decisions concerning distance learning, and in the ownership and use of online courses. Although the former issue may involve principles of contract law or academic custom and usage (see Section 1.4.3.3 of this book), the latter issue is controlled in the first instance by copyright law. Traditionally, educational institutions do not claim ownership of faculty writings and publications (such as books, lecture notes, or research reports). Without application of the work for hire doctrine, copyright would have to be transferred from the faculty member to the institution in order for the institution to be the owner of the copyright. No such transfer is required, however, if the work is made for hire. In the development of online distance learning courses, institutions may argue that because the faculty member has made extensive use of institutional resources (computer hardware and software, technical experts and advisors, institutional licenses to use certain software packages, and so forth) that go far beyond what a faculty member uses in conducting research or writing a book or article, the materials produced should be considered within the scope of employment. Some institutions are developing policies that state that the institution is the owner of any online course that a faculty member develops and teaches, but that the faculty member will receive a royalty each time the course is taught or that the faculty member has the right to make use of the course at another institution upon terminating employment. Faculty members are concerned that in some cases where the institution owns a work, the faculty member may not have control over whether the course is repeated, updated, or taught by some other individual. These are issues that can easily be addressed in a policy statement. Even though the law takes an "all or nothing" approach to ownership (either the creator owns it or the employer owns it, completely), universities need not leave it at that, but can provide the non-owner with rights to use course materials, based on academic norms as well as practicalities.

A special committee of the AAUP has developed statements on distance education and on copyright, as well as suggested guidelines and sample language for policies and contracts. The Association's "Statement on Distance Education, Statement on Copyright, Suggestions and Guidelines: Sample Language for Institutional Policies and Contract Language for Distance Education and for Ownership of Intellectual Property" may be found at http://www.aaup.org/spcintro.htm.

13.2.5.4.1. COPYRIGHT AND COAUTHORSHIP. On occasion, coauthors (or former coauthors) become involved in copyright disputes when one bases a new publication on earlier, coauthored material. In *Weismann v. Freeman,* 868 F.2d 1313 (2d Cir. 1989), *cert. denied,* 493 U.S. 883 (1989), a former research assistant sued her medical school professor, with whom she had researched and coauthored many scholarly works on nuclear medicine, when the professor put his name on a subsequent work she alone had authored. Because the work (a syllabus reviewing the state of scientific knowledge on a medical issue) was based in large part on work the two had coauthored, the professor believed that he was a coauthor of the subsequent work as well. He also claimed that his use of the material was a fair use.

The former assistant, now a professor herself, argued that the work in question contained new material and was solely her work for copyright purposes. The appellate court ruled that joint authorship in prior existing works did not make the defendant a joint author in a derivative work: "[W]hen the work has been prepared in different versions, each version constitutes a separate work"; Section 103(b), according to the court, gives copyright protection to new portions of the derivative work but not to preexisting portions (868 F.2d at 1317). The court added: "The joint authorship of the underlying work does not confer any property right in the new work, save those rights which the co-author . . . of the previous works retains in the material used as part of the compilation of the derivative work" (868 F.2d at 1319), and, "To support a copyright, a derivative work must be more than trivial, and the protection afforded a derivative work must reflect the degree to which the derivative work relies on preexisting material, without diminishing the scope of the latter's copyright protection" (868 F.2d at 1321). The court also rejected the defendant's fair use defense, noting in its discussion of the fourth factor (impact on the value of a work) that professional advancement in academe depends, in large part, on publication, and even if the plaintiff had no money damages, the defendant's appropriation of her work could "impair [her] scholarly recognition" (868 F.2d at 1325–26).

13.2.5.5. Liability for infringement. Infringement is similar to a strict-liability tort. Ignorance of the law is no excuse, although it may affect the amount of damages awarded. The penalties are stiff; nevertheless, copyright owners have sought many increases in the penalties for infringement over the last decade and Congress has obliged them.

Advances in computer technology and the spread of digital copies prompted Congress to enact amendments entitled "Criminal Penalties for Copyright Infringement" (Pub. L. No. 102-561, 106 Stat. 4233) in 1992. These amendments to the criminal code make certain types of copyright infringement a felony (18 U.S.C. § 2319(b)). They provide that willful violations of 18 U.S.C. § 2319(a) shall result in imprisonment for not more than five years or fines in the amount set forth in the criminal law, or both, if the offense consists of reproduction or distribution or both during any 180-day period of at least ten copies or records of one or more copyrighted works with a retail value of over $2,500. Stiffer penalties are prescribed for second and subsequent violations. In 1997, Congress enacted the "No Electronic Theft Act" (the "NET Act," Pub. L. No. 105-147, 111 Stat. 2678), which, among other things, closed a loophole in the law that prevented criminal prosecution of willful infringing distributions over the Internet if the infringer did not profit financially. The NET Act provided a definition of financial gain in 17 U.S.C. § 101 that includes receipt of anything of value, including other copyrighted works, and made it a criminal violation to distribute works valued at more than $1,000 over a 180-day period without permission.

Congress further reacted to the concerns of publishers, Internet service providers, and the music and entertainment industries by passing the Digital Millennium Copyright Act (DMCA), Pub. L. No. 105-304, 112 Stat. 2860 (October 28, 1998), affecting institutions, faculty, and students. The DMCA was passed to implement the World Intellectual Property Organization Copyright Treaty and the Performances and Phonograms Treaty, as well as to deal with issues of potential liability for Internet service providers (ISPs) and other matters. This law provides a potential "safe harbor" for ISPs whose subscribers use the ISP's network to transmit or post copyrighted material without legal authorization (for example, where the use does not constitute fair use) or without having received permission to do so from the copyright holder. The law states that an ISP can limit its own liability for infringements caused by its subscribers if the ISP designates an agent to receive notices of alleged infringements, removes allegedly infringing posted material quickly, and notifies the individual who posted the material that it has been removed. The law also protects ISPs from liability for removing material if, in fact, no infringement occurred.

Regarding materials posted on the ISP's servers, for the most part the law only protects university ISPs from liability for the infringements of students. Most faculty and staff who place materials online do so as employees. If the alleged infringer is an employee of the institution that owns or is the ISP, the institution will likely be vicariously liable. The law gives university ISPs a narrow exception from vicarious liability for infringements by faculty or graduate student employees who post materials online, but only for those materials not required or recommended for courses taught at the institution within the past three years, so long as the alleged infringer was not the subject of more than two good-faith infringement notices during that same period of time, and so long as the institution provides its employees with accurate information about and promotes compliance with copyright laws.

Regarding materials that merely pass through the provider's network, such as materials traded or stored over peer-to-peer networks, university ISPs enjoy very broad protection so long as they are not involved in the selection or routing of the infringing materials.

Many cases refine the scope of the ISP liability limitations. In the *Napster* case, described above in the discussion of fair use, the court rejected Napster's claim that its activities were protected by the ISP safe harbors. The court indicated that if ISPs wish to take advantage of limits on their liability for files stored on their computers, they should take action when they have actual knowledge of infringement, know facts from which it can be inferred, or receive notice sufficient to identify works alleged to infringe. They also must have policies in place that require copyright compliance and provide for termination of accounts of repeat infringers. The court's admonitions in this regard simply state the statutory requirements, which Napster failed to follow.

Three recent cases discuss in more detail the adequacy of ISPs' policies of terminating the accounts of repeat infringers (*Ellison v. Robertson,* 357 F.3d 1072 (9th Cir. 2004); *Perfect 10, Inc. v. Cybernet Ventures, Inc.,* 213 F. Supp. 2d 1146 (C.D. Cal. 2002); *In re Aimster Copyright Litigation,* 334 F.3d 643 (7th Cir. 2003)). In *Ellison,* Harlan Ellison sued (among others) America Online (AOL) because it offered its subscribers a Usenet newsgroup to which one subscriber uploaded Ellison's literary works without his permission. In *Perfect 10,* the defendant, Cybernet, operated an adult verification service that provided authorization to adult customers to access participating adult content Web sites. Perfect 10 alleged that some of the participating sites contained photos from Perfect 10's site.

The *Ellison* court initially found that AOL needed only to provide a realistic threat of termination and considered AOL's policy adequate even though it had never terminated an account for repeat infringement. Two years later, however, the Ninth Circuit reversed the lower court's grant of summary judgment. It was troubled by the fact that AOL did not have an adequate notification system in that it had changed its e-mail address for complaints, waited months to register the new address with the copyright office, and provided no forwarding function for e-mails continuing to go to the old address. The *Perfect 10* court also found a defendant's efforts unavailing, concluding that it was not likely that Cybernet would be able to satisfy the termination policy requirement without evidence that it had actually terminated accounts under appropriate circumstances, such as but not limited to where it had knowledge of blatant, repeated infringement.

In re Aimster goes even further. In this case, the defendant had a policy and informed users of it, but it was impossible for it ever to know that its users were infringing because the Aimster software encrypted all information traveling among users of its private networks. The court found that "by teaching its users how to encrypt their unlawful distribution of copyrighted materials [it] disabled itself from doing anything to prevent it" (334 F.3d at 655). The court affirmed the lower court's finding that Aimster did not qualify for ISP protection.

The statute also requires that ISPs designate an agent to receive notices of infringement in order to be eligible for the limitations on its liability contained in Section 512(c). Thus, an ISP cannot claim the safe harbors for infringements that occur before it registers its agent (*CoStar Group Inc. v. LoopNet, Inc.,* 164 F. Supp. 2d 688 (D. Md. 2001), *affirmed,* 373 F.3d 544 (4th Cir. 2004)); however, an agent need not be a person, but can be a department or office (*Hendrickson v. eBay Inc.,* 165 F. Supp. 2d 1082 (C.D. Cal. 2001), discussed below).

On the issue of what kind of a notice is sufficient, *ALS Scan, Inc. v. RemarQ Communities, Inc.,* 239 F.3d 619 (4th Cir. 2001), indicates that all that is required of the copyright owner is "substantial" compliance with the law's notice provisions. RemarQ, the defendant ISP, declined to stop carrying two newsgroups posted on its servers and identified by the plaintiff as containing "virtually all Federally Copyrighted images," but agreed to take down images identified with "sufficient specificity." The plaintiff sued, and the district court granted the defendant's motion to dismiss on the grounds that the notice was not sufficient under Section 512; it did not include a representative list of the infringing works and did not provide sufficient detail to allow the works to be located and disabled. The Fourth Circuit reversed on the grounds that the statute only requires "substantial" compliance with the notice provisions, and that by directing the ISP to the newsgroups, the plaintiff supplied the equivalent of a representative list.

On the other hand, *Arista Records, Inc. v. MP3Board, Inc.,* 2002 U.S. Dist. LEXIS 16165 (S.D.N.Y., August 28, 2002), tells us that "citation to a handful of performers does not constitute a representative list of infringing material." In this case, the plaintiff's first two notices to the ISP noted merely that the defendant's site contained links to infringing files on the Internet by artists it represented, naming ten artists. The third notice was different: it included, in addition to the general allegation, printouts of screen shots of defendant's pages with asterisks by 662 links to files the plaintiff alleged were infringing. The court found that the third notice complied with the requirements of the statute.

Hendrickson v. eBay Inc., 165 F. Supp. 2d 1082 (C.D. Cal. 2001), indicates that a simple cease and desist letter that does not enable the ISP to distinguish pirated from legitimate copies of a DVD is not adequate to identify the allegedly infringing material. eBay received a cease and desist letter from Robert Hendrickson regarding copies of a DVD entitled *Manson.* Hendrickson did not specifically identify the allegedly infringing copies, nor did he comply with other requirements of the statute: he did not state under oath that the information he provided was accurate, that he was authorized to act on behalf of the owner, or that the use was not authorized. When eBay requested additional information, he refused to provide it and instituted suit instead. The court had little trouble finding that eBay's response was appropriate under the circumstances. It also confirmed that an inadequate notice cannot be used to establish actual or constructive knowledge, nor can having policies that block access or that require the service provider to terminate the accounts of repeat infringers be used to show ability to control, an element of vicarious liability. *Hendrickson v. Amazon.com, Inc.,* 298 F. Supp. 2d 914 (C.D. Cal. 2003), involved the timing of notifications. The court found that a notice sent in January advising Amazon.com that "all copies of Manson on DVD infringe [Hendrickson's] copyright" was inadequate to require Amazon.com to remove material posted by a user ten months later.

Verizon Internet Services, Inc., battled the Recording Industry Association of America several times in 2003 regarding whether the subpoena power contained in Section 512(h) applies to ISPs availing themselves of the protections contained in the conduit provisions of Section 512(a) (those that apply to peer-to-peer transfers), and if it does, whether Section 512(h) as so construed is constitutional. The district court twice ruled against Verizon, and the court of appeals refused to permit Verizon to delay its compliance with the subpoenas while the appeal on the merits went forward (*In re Verizon Internet Services, Inc.*, 240 F. Supp. 2d 24, 257 F. Supp. 2d 244 (D.D.C. 2003), *stay vacated by* 2003 U.S. App. LEXIS 11250 (D.C. Cir., June 4, 2003)). Verizon argued initially that the subpoena power, which allows copyright owners to obtain a subpoena requesting identifying information about subscribers in any U.S. district court, only applied when an ISP's subscribers were accused of placing infringing materials on the ISP's servers (§ 512(c)). The court found that the subpoena provision applied to all four safe harbors, referencing the legislative history of the Act that indicated that in exchange for limitations on their liability, ISPs agreed to assist copyright owners in identifying and dealing with infringers.

The court also rejected Verizon's secondary constitutional argument, finding that Congress had authority to authorize court clerks to issue subpoenas in the absence of a pending case or controversy, pointing to other examples such as criminal warrants and wiretapping applications, among others. It also found that subscribers had no right to anonymously infringe copyrights and that safeguards within the Act were sufficient to prevent encroachment on protected anonymous speech, disposing of Verizon's First Amendment claim. In December 2003, the court of appeals reversed the lower court, finding that Section 512(h) did not authorize subpoenas against ISPs who were only transmitting files that resided on subscribers' machines (*Recording Industry Assn. of America, Inc. v. Verizon Internet Services, Inc.*, 351 F.3d 1229 (D.C. Cir. 2003), *cert. denied*, 125 S. Ct. 309 (2004).

In an unexpected and surprising turn of events in spring 2003, the RIAA sued four university students directly, without first sending the universities a notice under the DMCA. The cases alleged that the students were operating file-sharing networks using institutional resources. All four cases settled within one month. With this easy victory and the subpoena power established by the lower court in *Verizon*, the RIAA embarked on an ambitious campaign to sue individuals directly, serving subpoenas on thousands of ISPs and later filing hundreds of lawsuits. When the District of Columbia Circuit ruled that the Section 512(h) subpoena process could not be used to learn the names of subscribers who were utilizing their ISP's network (conduit) services only and not storing files on the network servers, RIAA began to file "John Doe" lawsuits against individuals. This activity continues.

In addition to the DMCA, Congress most recently passed the Digital Theft Deterrence and Copyright Damages Improvement Act of 1999 (Pub. L. No. 106-160, 113 Stat. 1774 (December 9, 1999)), which amends 17 U.S.C. § 504(c) by providing for enhanced statutory damages for certain copyright violations.

13.2.5.6. Licensing. As college and university libraries license more extensive amounts of their collections from digital database providers, copyright law, the backdrop against which owners' and users' rights are balanced in the analog world, risks becoming irrelevant: contract law, not copyright, controls the terms of access and use in a license agreement. Problems emerge when licenses do not permit the typical uses of digital materials that users have come to expect they may make of the same materials in analog form. For example, library patrons are entitled to request, and libraries are authorized to provide, copies of works that are out of print, or copies of portions of more recent works (17 U.S.C. § 108(d) & (e)). Patrons are permitted to make their own fair use copies of items in library collections, such as copies of journal articles for personal use, research, or scholarship (17 U.S.C. § 107). Faculty members may supply photocopies to library reserve rooms in accordance with fair use (*Id.*). These and other typical university uses are protected by the Copyright Act; however, unless it is carefully negotiated, a database contract may contain specific or general prohibitions that prevent such university, library, and patron activities.

13.2.5.7. Sovereign immunity. Following several appellate court rulings in the late 1980s that the Eleventh Amendment to the U.S. Constitution prohibited the application of the Copyright Act's damages provisions to state agencies, Congress passed the Copyright Remedy Clarification Act in 1990 (Pub. L. No. 101-553, 104 Stat. 2749) to allow copyright holders to collect damages from public colleges and universities. Only six years later, however, this law's constitutionality became questionable when the U.S. Supreme Court ruled in a series of cases beginning with *Seminole Tribe of Florida v. Florida,* 517 U.S. 44 (1996) (discussed in Section 13.1.6) that state agencies in those states that had not waived sovereign immunity against federal court litigation could not be sued by private parties and that sovereign immunity protected them from suits for money damages in federal court for patent infringement (discussed in Section 13.2.6) and trademark infringement (discussed in Section 13.2.7) (*College Savings Bank v. Florida Prepaid Postsecondary Education Expense Board,* 527 U.S. 627(1999)).

The issue arose with respect to copyright claims in *Chavez v. Arte Publico Press,* 180 F.3d 674 (5th Cir. 1999). After the Supreme Court's *Seminole* decision, but prior to its decisions in *Florida Prepaid* and *College Savings Bank,* a panel of the Fifth Circuit Court of Appeals ruled that plaintiff Denise Chavez's claims of copyright infringement were barred by the Eleventh Amendment. The full court vacated the earlier opinion (59 F.3d 539) and granted a rehearing (178 F.3d 281), after which it reached the same conclusion, this time basing its decision on the two Supreme Court cases decided in the interim.

Arte Publico Press is part of the University of Houston, a Texas state university. The Press became involved in a contract dispute with one of its authors, Denise Chavez. When her contract claims failed because of the state's immunity under state law, she raised federal claims to which the state's immunity would not apply. The University of Houston contended that its Eleventh Amendment immunity protected it from Chavez's copyright and trademark claims for damages. The Fifth Circuit agreed, stating that the Eleventh Amendment denies Congress the power to create a cause of action in federal court against a state for damages for violations of federal copyright or trademark laws, except under special circumstances, which were not met in this case: Congress could not legally act under Article I of the Constitution (where Congress is authorized to enact the copyright and patent laws), nor under subsection 5 of the Fourteenth Amendment (where Congress is given the power to enforce against the states the Fourteenth Amendment's prohibition on taking property without compensation or denying anyone due process under the law). Without proper authority for its actions, Congress's enactment of the Copyright Remedy Clarification Act was unconstitutional.

Thus, *Seminole* and its progeny indicate that public colleges and universities that are protected by the sovereign immunity doctrine (discussed in Section 13.1.6, this book) are immune from this litigation. This fact has motivated additional congressional effort to force states to waive their immunity. Bills to do so are regularly introduced; however, none has passed as of the printing of this book. Administrators should consult counsel for further developments in this regard.

While the *Seminole* line of cases appears to afford a measure of relief to public colleges and universities against copyright infringement litigation for money damages in federal courts, these institutions and their faculty and staff still face some types of liability for copyright infringement, and private institutions do not share the immunity of public colleges. For example, a copyright holder can file a motion in federal court for injunctive relief against an alleged infringer. Institutions or individuals who have entered licensing agreements with copyright holders (an increasingly common requirement to access software and databases) can be sued for breach of contract in either state or federal court. Furthermore, individual employees of public colleges and universities may be sued under federal copyright law; they do not enjoy the sovereign immunity protection afforded to their institutions if they are acting outside the scope of the copyright statutes.

13.2.5.8. Other copyright issues. Both the courts and Congress have addressed many other issues of interest to universities. Below are some of the more significant developments.

13.2.5.8.1. SCOPE OF COPYRIGHT PROTECTION. The scope of copyright protection has been interpreted in a case of interest to scholars who use copyrighted compilations of material that is in the public domain, such as the decisions of state and federal courts. In *Matthew Bender and Co., Inc. v. West Publishing Co.,* 158 F.3d 693 (2d Cir. 1998), *cert. denied,* 526 U.S. 1154 (1999), a federal appellate court ruled that the plaintiffs, Matthew Bender and Hyperlaw, could include "star pagination" used by West's versions of published court opinions in the plaintiffs' CD-ROM versions of these court opinions. The court ruled that the only material inserted by West that the plaintiffs wished to use was the page breaks in the otherwise uncopyrighted judicial opinions. The court ruled that page breaks were not protected by the copyright law. Although compilations of uncopyrighted materials may be protected under the copyright laws, said the court, the protection extends only to original creative material contributed by the author of the compilation. "Because the internal pagination of West's case reporters does not entail even a modicum of creativity," the court ruled that these items were not "original contributions" by West and thus were not protected (158 F.3d at 699).

A federal trial court addressed the issue of whether photographic reproductions of art in the public domain have the requisite originality to qualify for copyright protection. In *Bridgeman Art Library, Ltd. v. Corel Corporation*, 36 F. Supp. 2d 191 (S.D.N.Y. 1998), the plaintiffs attempted to secure copyright protection for color photographs of public domain paintings. The court ruled that because the photographs were copies of the paintings, they were not "creative" and therefore were not entitled to copyright protection. This ruling confirms the ability of college and university image archives to use photographic reproductions of art that is in the public domain.

13.2.5.8.2. MUSIC. In addition to its chapter on ISP liability limitations, the DMCA contained other chapters relevant to universities. Among them were provisions affecting music. Although institutions may pay blanket royalty fees for all copyrighted music in the American Society of Authors, Publishers and Composers/Broadcast Music, Inc. (ASCAP/BMI) repertory that is publicly performed at their institutions, these fees do not cover copying or distribution of music or streaming radio broadcasts over the Web ("Webcasting"). As digital audio transmissions are now protected by law, Webcasting must be licensed. In May 2003, college Webcasters negotiated fees with the recording industry that are low enough that most college radio stations will be able to pay them. The fees are based on the enrollment at the university and the number of listeners logged on the Webcast over the course of a month. Noncommercial university radio stations with fewer than 10,000 students paid a blanket fee of $250 for 2004. A station at a college with more than 10,000 students paid $500 for that year. If listeners exceed 146,000 hours' worth of music per month, the station pays two-hundredths of a cent per song per listener above the limit. Most stations do not expect to exceed the limit. For 2003 and 2004, any station that paid did not have to track and provide information on each song played. Left for later determination is the difficult issue of whether the stations will be required to track such information starting in 2005. Information on this licensing process is available at http://www.riaa.com/issues/music/webcasting.asp.

13.2.5.8.3. ANTI-CIRCUMVENTION. The DMCA also prohibits the circumvention of copyright protection systems that control access to digital material that is copyrighted. This law is quite controversial because, with few exceptions as discussed below, the reason a person might circumvent a technology is irrelevant to the determination of whether circumvention violates the law. In other words, it is illegal to circumvent a technology protecting a work, even if one's purpose is to make an authorized use of the work, for example, to make a fair use of it, to make an archival copy for a library, to make an adapted copy for a handicapped person, to lend a work, or to access parts of it that are in the public domain or not protected by copyright at all (facts and ideas). All of these examples are uses protected by the Copyright Act, but they do not provide one any authority to circumvent technologies protecting works. This restriction appears to create an unlimited right rather than the original intent of Congress to create limited rights for limited times (Pub. L. No. 105-304, 112 Stat. 2860, codified at 17 U.S.C. § 1201 *et seq.*).

Although the law contains several exemptions, such as an exemption for libraries, archives, and educational institutions to gain access to a copyrighted work in order to make a good-faith determination about acquiring a copy of that work, the exceptions are of little or no value to universities for two reasons: (1) the devices that would be needed to exercise the rights to circumvent are made illegal by the statute; and (2) the rights themselves are generally so narrow as to be useless as a practical matter. For example, one may easily obtain permission to try a product before buying it, making the right to circumvent a protective technology for that purpose of little value.

The constitutionality of this law has been challenged on the grounds that it bans more speech than is necessary to achieve the government's goals by interfering with fair uses and restricting access to the public domain (*Universal City Studios, Inc. v. Reimerdes*, 111 F. Supp. 2d 294 (S.D.N.Y 2000), *affirmed sub nom Universal City Studios, Inc. v. Corley*, 273 F.3d 429 (2d Cir. 2001); *Felton v. Recording Industry Association of America*, 63 PTCS 115 (D.N.J. 2001); *U.S. v. Elcom, Ltd.*, 203 F. Supp. 2d 1111 (N.D. Cal. 2002)). So far, no challenge has succeeded. Further, Congress included a provision calling for triennial rule making by the Library of Congress. The Library of Congress is authorized to establish classes of works to which the anti-circumvention provisions will not apply (for the three years until the next rule making) where the provisions are shown to have adversely affected the public's ability to make non-infringing uses of particular classes of copyrighted works. Even though the Library of Congress has interpreted its authority to exempt classes of works very narrowly, this mechanism may nevertheless be deemed adequate to protect First Amendment values. For example, on October 27, 2003, the Library of Congress exempted literary works distributed as e-books whose access controls disabled read-aloud and screen-reader functions if the e-book publisher offered no e-book edition permitting such adaptive uses. This rule accommodates anti-circumvention to the needs of the blind by permitting adaptive uses as permitted in 17 U.S.C. § 121 even if the work in question is technologically protected.

13.2.5.8.4. TERM EXTENSION. The Sonny Bono Copyright Term Extension Act (CTEA) extends copyright protection for an additional twenty years for all works currently subject to protection by copyright law. It contains provisions that permit libraries to make certain scholarly, preservation, and research uses of works during their final twenty years of copyright protection so long as the work is not being commercially exploited, as specifically defined in the statute. The exemption does not apply to any subsequent uses by users other than such library or archives (§ 104, Pub. L. No. 105-298, codified at 17 U.S.C. § 108(h)). CTEA has also been unsuccessfully challenged as unconstitutional. In *Eldred v. Ashcroft*, 537 U.S. 186 (2003), the Supreme Court determined that Congress did have the authority under Article I of the Constitution to extend the term of existing copyrights, that a term of life plus seventy years is "a limited time" as required by the Constitution, and that the fair use provision and the idea/expression distinction (copyright only protects expression, not ideas) adequately protected rights of free speech, blunting any complaint on First Amendment grounds. Petitioners were various individuals and businesses that relied upon the public domain for their livelihood and who had suffered direct financial loss as a result of CTEA's delay for twenty years of the entry of hundreds of thousands of works into the public domain. The case has far-reaching implications regarding Congress's power to modify the law.

13.2.5.8.5. COPYRIGHT AND STANDARDIZED TESTS. One further issue in copyright law of interest to colleges and universities, and most particularly to testing agencies, is whether states can require disclosure of test questions, answers, and other copyrighted information under "truth-in-testing" laws. New York's Standardized Testing Act (N.Y. Educ. Law §§ 340–348) requires developers of standardized tests to disclose to test takers and to the public test questions, answers, answer sheets, and related research reports. In *Ass'n. of American Medical Colleges v. Carey,* 728 F. Supp. 873 (N.D.N.Y. 1990), the Association of American Medical Colleges (AAMC), which develops the Medical College Admissions Test, sought a declaratory judgment that the Copyright Act preempted such disclosure. A federal trial court issued a permanent injunction barring enforcement of Sections 341, 341(a), and 342 of the law. The state argued that two of the Copyright Act's exemptions permitted disclosure of the test materials (the "fair use" exemption and the "archives" exemption). The U.S. Court of Appeals for the Second Circuit vacated the permanent injunction and reversed and remanded the case for trial, stating that genuine issues of fact were unresolved concerning the effect of disclosure of test questions and answers on reuse of the test (the fourth, or "market impact," test under the fair use doctrine) (*Assn. of American Medical Colleges v. Cuomo,* 928 F.2d 519 (2d Cir. 1991)).

In *College Entrance Examination Board v. Pataki,* 889 F. Supp. 554 (N.D.N.Y. 1995), the board argued that the New York Standardized Testing Act was preempted by the Copyright Act. The court ruled that the board had established a *prima facie* case of copyright infringement sufficient to support the entry of a preliminary injunction; however, in order to partially implement the policy goals of the New York law, the court fashioned a compromise requiring the board to disclose several Scholastic Aptitude Tests (SATs), Graduate Record Exams (GREs), and Tests of English as a Foreign Language until the litigation was resolved on the merits (893 F. Supp. 152 (N.D.N.Y. 1995)). No further proceedings have been reported.

13.2.6. Patent law[13]

13.2.6.1. Overview. The basis for all patent law (as well as copyright law) is Article I, Section 8, Clause 8 of the Constitution, which authorizes Congress "to promote the progress of science and useful arts, by securing for limited times to authors and inventors the exclusive right to their respective writings and discoveries." The patent laws, contained in Title 35 of the *United States Code,* are critical to the research mission of higher education. They establish the means by and the extent to which institutions or their faculty members, laboratory staffs, students, or external funding sources may protect and exploit the products of research, and they tell us what inventions or discoveries may be patented, who may hold the patents, and what arrangements may be made for licensing them.

---

[13]This Section was updated and expanded by Georgia Harper, Senior Attorney and Manager, Intellectual Property Section, Office of General Counsel, the University of Texas System.

Behind these legal issues, however, lurk serious policy questions: What degree and type of protection will allow researchers to share information without fear that their discoveries will be "stolen" by others? As among the institution and its faculty, staff, and students, and government or industry sponsors of university research, who should hold the patents or license rights for patentable research products? The complexity of new research in fields such as biotechnology, nanotechnology, and computer sciences, growing research relationships between industry and academia, substantial government support for university research, and the development of university research consortia underscore the importance of both the legal and policy questions.

13.2.6.2. Patentability. Section 101 of the Patent Act provides: "Whoever invents or discovers any new and useful process, machine, manufacture, or composition of matter, or any new and useful improvement thereof, may obtain a patent therefor, subject to the conditions and requirements of this title" (35 U.S.C. § 101).

An invention must also be "novel" (§ 102) and "nonobvious" (§ 103). The patent holder has the right to exclude others from using the invention from the date the patent issues until twenty years after the date the application was filed.

The U.S. Supreme Court has explained what kinds of processes, inventions, or discoveries Congress intended to protect as follows:

> In choosing such expansive terms as "manufacture" and "composition of matter," modified by the comprehensive "any," Congress plainly contemplated that the patent laws would be given wide scope. . . .
>
> This is not to suggest that Section 101 has no limits or that it embraces every discovery. The laws of nature, physical phenomena, and abstract ideas have been held not patentable (see *Parker v. Flook*, 437 U.S. 584 (1978)). . . . Thus, a new mineral discovered in the earth or a new plant found in the wild is not patentable subject matter. Likewise, Einstein could not patent his celebrated law that $E = mc^2$; nor could Newton have patented the law of gravity. Such discoveries are "manifestations of . . . nature, free to all men and reserved exclusively to none" [*Funk Brothers Seed Co. v. Kalo Inoculant Co.*, 333 U.S. 127, 130 (1948), quoted in *Diamond v. Chakrabarty*, 447 U.S. 303, 309 (1980)].

The scope of potentially patentable items has expanded geometrically with our increasing sophistication in biotechnology and genetics. Two U.S. Supreme Court cases decided in 1980 and 1981 laid the foundation for current interpretations of what is patentable and demonstrate how difficult it is to determine what products of modern research are "patentable subject matter" under 35 U.S.C. § 101. The first of these cases, *Diamond v. Chakrabarty,* concerned a microbiologist with General Electric who sought to patent a strain of bacteria he developed by genetic manipulation of a naturally occurring bacterium. The new organism broke down multiple components of crude oil, a property possessed by no bacterium in its natural state, and was an important discovery in the control of oil spills. The patent examiner rejected the application on the grounds that microorganisms are "products of nature" and, as living things, are not patentable subject matter. Chakrabarty, on the other hand, argued that his microorganism constituted a "manufacture" or "composition of matter" within 35 U.S.C. § 101.

In a 5-to-4 decision, the Court agreed with Chakrabarty, concluding that his microorganism was patentable because it was not a previously unknown natural phenomenon but a non-naturally occurring manufacture—a product of human ingenuity. Rejecting the argument that patent law distinguishes between animate and inanimate things and encompasses only the latter, the Court found the relevant distinction to be between products of nature, whether living or not, and man-made inventions.

In the second case, *Diamond v. Diehr,* 450 U.S. 175 (1981), Diehr sought a patent on a method for molding uncured synthetic rubber into cured products. He developed a computer program that continuously recalculated the cure time based on information from sensors inside the mold and opened the mold at the right time to ensure a perfect cure. The Court concluded by a narrow 5-to-4 margin that the invention qualified as a "process" under Section 101 rather than a "mathematical formula" and that the involvement of a computer did not affect patentability. The dissenters, in contrast, concluded that the invention made "no contribution to the art that is not entirely dependent upon the utilization of a computer in a familiar process" and was therefore unpatentable under *Gottschalk v. Benson,* 409 U.S. 63 (1971), and *Parker v. Flook,* 437 U.S. 584 (1978), which held that computer programs for solving mathematical problems were not patentable.

Another controversy involves the patentability of business methods. Until recently, business methods were generally protected by keeping them secret. If secrecy were not possible, competitors were free to emulate each others' business methods. *State Street Bank & Trust Co. v. Signature Financial Group, Inc.,* 149 F.3d 1368 (1998), *cert. denied,* 535 U.S. 1093 (1999), changed this. *State Street Bank* upheld a patent on a software program that was used to make mutual fund asset allocation calculations. Soon, patent applications on business methods soared. Unfortunately, these patents present unique problems: since secrecy was the dominant method for protecting business methods until *State Street Bank,* published "prior art" (information that is already known and thus not patentable) is difficult if not impossible to uncover. Thus, patents issue on methods of doing business that may be quite obvious and not at all new—to everyone but the patent examiner. The business community and even the patent bar wants improvement in this process, and we may expect legislative guidance as well as changes at the U.S. Patent and Trademark Office in response.

As the range of patentable subject matter broadens, so, too, does the debate about the propriety of issuing patents on certain discoveries. For example, the U.S. Patent and Trademark Office routinely issues patents on computer software today, even though software is already protected by federal copyright law and state trade secret laws. Patent infringement proceedings are a much stronger disincentive than the remedies available under the Copyright Act. Experts in software design, however, worry that software patents will "slow the rate of development and limit opportunities for the individual and collaborative genius that created much of the best software in the past" (B. Kahin, "Software

Patents: Franchising the Information Infrastructure," *Change,* May/June 1989, at 24; but see Ronald J. Mann, "The Myth of the Software Patent Thicket: An Empirical Investigation of the Relationship Between Intellectual Property and Innovation in Software Firms," The University of Texas School of Law, Law and Economics Working Paper No. 022, February 2004, available at http://papers. ssrn.com/sol3/papers.cfm?abstract_id = 510103).

The decision of the Patent and Trademark Office to consider non-naturally occurring, nonhuman multicellular organisms, including animals, to be patentable subject matter within the scope of 35 U.S.C. § 101 is even more controversial. Although animal rights groups mounted both procedural and substantive challenges to this interpretive notice, the federal courts dismissed their case for lack of standing (*Animal Legal Defense Fund v. Quigg,* 710 F. Supp. 728 (N.D. Cal. 1989), *affirmed,* 932 F.2d 920 (Fed. Cir. 1991)). The first animal patent issued in 1988, protecting a genetically altered mouse with genes sensitive to cancer. In 2002, however, the same mouse was rejected as unpatentable subject matter by Canada's Supreme Court (*Harvard College v. Canada,* 2002 SCC 76, available at www.lexum.umontreal.ca/csc-scc/en/pub/2002/vol4/html/ 2002scr4_0045.html).

Some commentators have suggested that a "research exemption" should be added to the law to permit scientists to experiment without fear of patent infringement proceedings. Many universities place severe restrictions on how patented cell material, processes, and genetically altered animals may be used because biotechnical research has become such a high-stakes game. (For an assessment of policy issues related to these patents, see R. Merges, "Intellectual Property in Higher Life Forms: The Patent System and Controversial Technologies," 47 *Maryland L. Rev.* 1051 (1988).)

Patents have been awarded for discoveries made under the human genome project; every element of that sophisticated gene-mapping program might eventually be patented, although experts doubt that patents would extend to human beings because of constitutional limitations (see Human Genome Project Information, available at http://www.ornl.gov/sci/techresources/Human_Genome/ elsi/patents.shtml).

13.2.6.3. Ownership of patents. The level of patenting activity and the potential for high profits and even higher penalties make it essential that institu   employees, and funding sources clearly identify who will apply f   patents resulting from university research. Fortunately, the patent   s considerable guidance on these two issues when research is federally funded. Chapter 18, entitled "Patent Rights in Inventions Made with Federal Assistance," contains thirteen provisions applicable to colleges and universities. Sections 200 to 212 embody the "Bayh-Dole Act" or simply, "Bayh-Dole," as it is commonly called, after the congressional sponsors of the bill that added the chapter to the Patent Act.

The goals of Bayh-Dole were to "promote the utilization of inventions arising from federally supported research or development"; "promote collaboration between commercial concerns and nonprofit organizations, including universities"; and "ensure that inventions made by nonprofit organizations . . . are used in a manner to promote free competition and enterprise" (35 U.S.C. § 200). The Act achieves these goals by establishing uniform policy for licensing patentable inventions discovered in the course of federally funded research applicable to any contract, grant, or cooperative agreement between a federal agency and a nonprofit organization, even if the federal agency only partly funds the research (35 U.S.C. § 201).

Colleges and universities may obtain title to inventions made with the assistance of federal funding (35 U.S.C. § 202). Although the funding agency may refuse to grant title, in practice this is rarely, if ever, done (35 U.S.C. § 202(a)(i)–(iii)).

If the fund recipient obtains title, the funding agency receives a nonexclusive royalty-free license on behalf of the United States (35 U.S.C. § 202(c)(4)). In addition, the Act reserves "march-in" rights to federal agencies to ensure adequate utilization of inventions where the fund recipient has not fully exercised its right to use the patented invention (35 U.S.C. § 203). Other provisions deal with assignment and licensing of patent rights by the fund recipient (35 U.S.C. § 202(c)(7) & (f)) and withholding information about patentable inventions from third parties filing Freedom of Information Act requests (35 U.S.C. §§ 202(e)(5) & 205).

When research is privately funded, ownership and licensing rights are generally controlled by the funding agreement. Institutions typically agree not to disclose research results until patent applications are filed, and to provide the research sponsors with an opportunity to review research results.

While *inventorship* is determined in accordance with federal patent laws, state property law governs *ownership* of a patented invention or discovery, since a patent is considered personal property. Ownership of a patented (or patentable) discovery created by an individual in the course of employment would depend on the factual circumstances surrounding the invention and the nature of the employment relationship. In the absence of language in an employment contract requiring assignment of ownership of any patentable discoveries to the employer, the employee generally would be the owner, but the employer might retain "shop rights" (the right to the royalty-free use of the patented invention or discovery for its business purposes).

The law today is quite settled that universities may claim ownership of patents where there has been a knowing and voluntary waiver by the faculty inventor, such as signing an agreement to abide by institutional policies or an agreement to assign inventions.

A case decided by a New York state appellate court illustrates the waiver method of clarifying the relative rights of the institution, the faculty member, and other employees. In *Yeshiva University v. Greenberg*, 644 N.Y.S.2d 313 (S. Ct. N.Y. App. Div. 1996), Greenberg and Yeshiva University disagreed about the ownership of an antibody Greenberg developed while employed in a laboratory at the university's medical school. The antibody was potentially useful in diagnosing and treating patients with Alzheimer's disease. Greenberg asserted that she had the right to patent, sell, or license her discovery, but the university filed a motion for a preliminary injunction to prevent Greenberg from doing so.

Greenberg had agreed in writing to abide by the university's patent policy, which gave the university the right to seek a patent on the discovery. The court found that the patent policy reserved all rights in the discovery to the university, and affirmed the trial court's preliminary injunction against Greenberg.

Unfortunately, in many circumstances, there is no signed agreement. A separate line of cases discussed in detail in Section 15.4.3 has established that institutions may bind not only employee inventors but even university graduate students to assign inventions to the institution even in the absence of a signed agreement (*University Patents, Inc. v. Kligman et al.,* 762 F. Supp. 1212 (E.D. Pa. 1991); *E. I. DuPont de Nemours and Co. v. Okuley,* 2000 U.S. Dist. Lexis 21385 (S.D. Ohio, December 21, 2000); *Chou v. University of Chicago and Arch Development Corp.,* 254 F.3d 1347 (Fed. Cir. 2001); *University of West Virginia Board of Trustees v. Van Voorhies,* 278 F.3d 1288 (Fed. Cir. 2002)). Generally, the policy must clearly require assignment of all inventions by all persons likely to be inventors, and the inventor must have known about the policy.

13.2.6.4. Infringement lawsuits. A patent owner may bring infringement proceedings against unauthorized use or manufacture of the patented item or use of a patented process, among other things. Remedies include (1) lost profits or a reasonable royalty, with interest and costs (35 U.S.C. § 284); (2) treble damages, if infringement is willful; and (3) in exceptional cases, reasonable attorney's fees (35 U.S.C. § 285). The federal courts hear infringement proceedings and the U.S. Court of Appeals for the Federal Circuit, a special court designed to create a uniform body of federal patent law, hears all appeals.

Persons and entities deprived of rightful ownership of an invention by fraud or deception may also bring an infringement lawsuit. The *Cyanimid* case described in Section 15.4.3 provides useful guidance for institutions in this regard.

13.2.6.5. Sovereign immunity. Although the U.S. Congress amended the patent laws in 1992 to permit suits against states for infringing patent rights (the Patent and Plant Variety Protection Remedy Clarification Act of 1992), the U.S. Supreme Court ruled that the amendment was an unconstitutional abrogation of states' sovereign immunity. *Florida Prepaid Postsecondary Education Expense Board v. College Savings Bank,* 527 U.S. 627 (1999), involved a private bank located in New Jersey and the state of Florida. The bank patented a methodology that guaranteed investors in its certificates of deposit sufficient funds to cover future college tuition costs. Florida created a competing product that allegedly infringed the bank's patent.

Although the bank argued that Congress abrogated sovereign immunity under the authority of the Fourteenth Amendment's due process clause (Section 5 of the amendment), the Court disagreed in a 5-to-4 decision written by Justice Rehnquist. The Court found no pattern of widespread violations by states of the patent laws, and no indication that state courts could not provide an appropriate remedy if a state were charged with infringement. The Court agreed that a patent could be considered property, and that infringement of it could jeopardize a property right, but it ruled that patent infringement by a state would not violate the Constitution unless the state provided either no remedy or an inadequate remedy for that infringement. Since Congress produced no findings on the adequacy of state law remedies for patent infringement, the Court was not willing to assume they were inadequate.

The four dissenting Justices were skeptical about the willingness of states to provide adequate remedies for their own violations of the patent rights of others, and in a pointed reference to public research universities, noted that since states had taken advantage of the protections of federal patent law on numerous occasions, they should be regarded as having waived their sovereign immunity with respect to patent infringement lawsuits.

Waiver appears to be the more popular approach for subsequent congressional attempts to pass legislation that would subject states to suit in federal court now that a long series of cases has firmly established that abrogation theories are not likely to succeed. To date, none of these bills has passed, but administrators should confer with university counsel for developments in this area.

(For a discussion of the application of *Seminole Tribe* to patents (anticipating the ruling in *Florida Prepaid*) and a criticism of the application of Eleventh Amendment immunity to states in patent cases, see Carlos Manuel Vazquez, "What Is Eleventh Amendment Immunity," 106 *Yale L.J.* 1683 (1997). For a discussion of the importance of the Eleventh Amendment to the federalist system of government, see William Thro, "Why You Cannot Sue State U: A Guide to Sovereign Immunity," available at the National Association of College and University Attorneys publication Web site: http://www.nacua.org/publications/spring2002.pdf.)

13.2.7. Trademark law. A trademark, trade name, or service mark is a symbol of a product (or, in the cases of colleges and universities, of an institution) that identifies that product, service, or institution to the general public. Princeton University's tiger, Yale's bulldog, and Wisconsin's badger are symbols of the institutions (and, of course, their athletic teams). Trademark law confers a property right on the user of the symbol. Any other entity that uses a similar mark— if that mark could confuse the general public (or the consumer) about the entity the mark represents or about the maker of the product symbolized by the mark or name—may be subject to legal action for trademark infringement.

Trademark is governed by federal, state, and common law. The Trademark Act of 1946 (known as the Lanham Act), 15 U.S.C. § 1051 *et seq.,* as amended, regulates the registration of trademarks and establishes the rights of the trademark holder and the remedies for infringement. Many states also have statutes similar to the Lanham Act, and the common law of unfair competition (discussed briefly in Section 13.2.8) is also used to challenge unauthorized use of trademarks.

The U.S. Department of Commerce's Office of Patent and Trademark records all federal registrations of trademarks, including those that have expired or been abandoned or canceled. Registration provides constructive notice on a national level to all potential infringers that this mark belongs to another. It also allows the mark to become "incontestable" after five years of continuous use, which confers the right to exclusive use of the trademark. Most state laws provide for registration of trademarks or service marks that are not used in interstate commerce, and thus would not qualify for Lanham Act protection.

Although the Lanham Act specifies how a trademark may be registered, and registration is generally recommended, it is not required in order to bring a trademark infringement action under the Lanham Act or state law. A federal cause of action for trademark infringement is created by 15 U.S.C. § 1114, which permits a cause of action when a mark is registered and an individual reproduces or copies it without the registrant's consent, and uses it in interstate commerce in connection with a sale, where such use is likely to cause confusion or mistake, or to deceive. The plaintiff must demonstrate that its use of the trademarked symbol preceded the use by the alleged infringer. The plaintiff typically seeks a preliminary injunction and temporary restraining order. Under similar state laws, the trademark holder may also state a cause of action for trademark dilution (the diminution in value of the "good will" attached to the trademark by unauthorized use and application to inferior products or services, or the blurring of the product's identity) or misappropriation (appropriation of another's time and/or economic investment and resulting injury to the trademark holder).

Remedies under both federal and state laws include injunctive relief and other equitable remedies, such as product recalls, destruction of the infringing materials, halting of advertising, or a requirement that the trademark infringer disclose the unauthorized trademark use in an advertisement. Monetary relief is available under federal law in the form of lost profits, royalties, or even treble damages. Attorney's fees are available in "exceptional cases" under Section 1117 of the Lanham Act. Punitive damages are not available under the Lanham Act, but may be available under some state laws.

Not all names or symbols may be registered with the U.S. Office of Patent and Trademark. The courts have developed four categories, in increasing degrees of protection:

1. Generic names, such as "aspirin," "tea" or "cola" cannot be a trademark.

2. Descriptive marks are protected only if they have a secondary meaning (such as Georgia Bulldog) and the public recognizes the mark as naming a specific product or entity.

3. Suggestive names, such as Coppertone and Sure, are protected if they suggest a characteristic of the product.

4. Distinctive names—fabricated words such as Exxon or words whose meaning has no direct connection to the product, such as Ivory soap or Apple computers—are protected [Robert Lattinville, "Logo Cops: The Law and Business of Collegiate Licensing," 5 *Kan. J.L. & Pub. Pol'y.* 81 (1996)].

Amendments to the Lanham Act by the Trademark Law Revision Act of 1988 resulted in extensive changes designed to bring U.S. trademark law closer to the law of other industrialized nations. Current law now permits registration of a trademark before it is actually used, as long as the trademark owner demonstrates a bona fide intent to use the trademark and then uses the trademark within six months to two years after registration. The term of trademark registration was reduced from twenty to ten years (at which time it may be renewed), and various definitions in the law were clarified and conformed to judicial precedent. Significant requirements for registration are also included in the law, and counsel inexperienced in trademark practice should seek expert advice before embarking on registration of licensing of trademarks.

Another section of the Lanham Act may be of interest to administrators and counsel because it provides similar protection to trademark protection without requiring registration. Section 1125(a) of the Lanham Act provides that a person who uses in commerce "any word, term, name, symbol, or device, or any combination thereof, or any false designation of origin, false or misleading description of fact, or false or misleading representation of fact" that can cause confusion or mistake, or that may deceive, either with respect to its origin or its quality, may be liable to the injured party (15 U.S.C. § 1125(a)).

Section 1125(a) "evolved into something of a federal law of unfair competition, encompassing the infringement of unregistered marks, names, and trade dress" (R. S. Brown & R. C. Denicola, *Cases on Copyright: Unfair Competition and Related Topics* (5th ed., Foundation Press, 1990), at 531). Cases under Section 1125 are brought in federal court.

Trademark issues related to higher education typically involve an action by the college or university to prevent (or stop) an unrelated business or organization from using the name of the institution or a picture of its symbol. In order to avoid the appropriation of the institution's name or symbol for the sale of unlicensed products, institutions develop a licensing program for the college's symbols for clothing, souvenirs, and related items, for which the college receives a royalty.[14] Technically, these are "educational service marks" because the mark identifies a service—higher education—rather than a consumer product. Because the trademark laws provide protection to the trademark as a symbol of the product's integrity, a licensor must monitor the quality of the goods to which the trademark is attached in order to protect its rights in the mark.

Given the popularity of intercollegiate sports, institutions have been required to initiate trademark infringement litigation for the unlawful appropriation of the name or the likeness of the institution's symbol. For example, in *Board of Governors of the University of North Carolina v. Helpingstine*, 714 F. Supp. 167 (M.D.N.C. 1989), the university filed a trademark infringement action against the owner of a local T-shirt shop who had imprinted clothing with the name and symbols of the university. The university had created a licensing program in 1982, and had registered four trademarks with the U.S. Patent Office. Despite

---

[14]For analysis of cases relating to trademark protection for symbols or logos, see Martin J. McMahon, Annot., "Design of Recreational Object as Valid Trademark," 82 A.L.R. Fed. 9; and Marjorie A. Shields, Annot., "What Constitutes 'Famous Mark' for Purposes of Federal Trademark Dilution Act (15 U.S.C. §1125(c)) Which Provides Remedies for Dilution of Famous Marks," 165 A.L.R. Fed. 625.

the university's offer to grant the owner of the T-shirt store a license to sell authorized products bearing the university's name and symbol, the owner had refused, and had sold unlicensed apparel since 1983. The defendant argued that the university had abandoned its right to its name and symbols because it had allowed uncontrolled use of them for many years prior to 1982. The court, in awarding summary judgment to the university, rejected the abandonment theory, ruling that the university had used its name and symbols continuously, and simply the fact that the university had not previously prosecuted trademark infringers did not mean that it had abandoned its rights to its name and symbol.

Similarly, in *University Book Store v. Board of Regents of the University of Wisconsin System*, 1994 TTAB LEXIS 8 (Trademark Trial and Appeal Board, 1994), the Trademark Trial and Appeal Board explained that the 1988 amendments changed the definition of "abandonment" of a trademark to state that abandonment only occurs when a mark loses its significance as a mark. The practical result of this amendment is to remove the requirement that some courts had imposed on applicants who seek to register a trademark that the applicants prove that they acted to oppose unauthorized use of the mark as soon as they were aware of that unauthorized use. As a result of this and similar cases (see, for example, *Board of Trustees of the University of Arkansas v. Professional Therapy Services*, 873 F. Supp. 1280 (W.D. Ark. 1995)), as well as the 1988 amendments, colleges are meeting with greater success in protecting their names, insignia, and other marks.

In *White v. Board of Regents of the University of Nebraska*, 614 N.W.2d 330 (Neb. 2000), the University of Nebraska found itself on the receiving end of a trademark infringement lawsuit brought by a local businessman, White, who had registered the trade name "Husker Authentics" and produced merchandise with the university's name and symbol. When the university attempted to register the same name with the state, its application was rejected because White had already registered it. The university opened a store selling "Husker Authentic" merchandise, and White filed an action in state court to enjoin the university from using the registered name. The supreme court affirmed the cancellation of White's registration, and ruled that the university had a common law right to the name "Husker Authentics" because it had been used on correspondence and in a merchandise catalog that the university had approved for marketing its logo clothing.

Licensing of the university's name and symbols is important for colleges and universities because it gives them control of the quality and identity of businesses that use these marks, and also serves as an important source of income for the institution. (For advice on creating and enforcing a licensing program, see Scott Bearby & Bruce Siegal, "From the Stadium Parking Lot to the Information Superhighway: How to Protect Your Trademarks from Infringement," 28 *J. Coll. & Univ. Law* 633 (2002).)

In addition to opposing the manufacture and sale of unlicensed merchandise, colleges and universities have also filed infringement proceedings against businesses that use the same or similar names. For example, in *The Pennsylvania State University v. University Orthopedics*, 706 A.2d 863 (Pa. Super. Ct. 1998),

Penn State University sought to enjoin University Orthopedics (UO), a medical practice unrelated to the university, from using "University" in its name. Penn State filed a federal trademark law claim, a state breach of contract claim, an unfair competition claim under common law, and a claim under Pennsylvania's anti-dilution law.

Several years earlier, Penn State and UO had entered an agreement under which the university agreed not to sue UO for trademark infringement if UO promised to include a disclaimer in all its advertisements and literature that it was not affiliated with Penn State. Two years later, Penn State argued that UO was not including the disclaimer in many of its materials, and that the public confused the university's own network of health care facilities with University Orthopedics, citing numerous examples of UO patients mistakenly calling the university health care centers. A trial court awarded summary judgment to UO, stating that the word "university" is a generic term, unprotected by trademark law.

The appellate court reversed and remanded the case for trial. Although the appellate court agreed with the trial court that "university" is a generic term, that determination was not the end of the analysis. A party may claim unfair competition because of the use of a generic name if "a company's use of the competitor's generic name confuses the public into mistakenly purchasing its product in the belief it is the product of the competitor." UO's occasional omission of the disclaimer from its materials, its practice of distributing advertisements at Penn State sporting events, and the patients' confusion about the two organizations raised issues of material fact to be determined at trial. Furthermore, said the court, the university might be able to establish its other claims, given the evidence of consumer confusion and UO's apparent breach of its earlier agreement with the university.

On the other hand, Columbia University was unable to persuade a federal trial court that "Columbia Healthcare Corporation" was either infringing on its trademark or diluting its value. In *Trustees of Columbia University v. Columbia/HCA Healthcare Corp.*, 964 F. Supp. 733 (S.D.N.Y. 1997), the court ruled that Columbia did not have exclusive use of its mark under federal trademark law because it had not registered that name in connection with medical or health care services. The court also rejected Columbia's assertion that the use of its name for a health care provider would cause confusion. But in a case where the infringing user provided the same services as a university, the court enjoined the use of the university's name. In *Temple University v. Tsokas,* 1989 U.S. Dist. LEXIS 19682 (E.D. Pa., September 11, 1989), the university argued that the dentist who used the name "Temple Dental Laboratories" created confusion with Temple's own dental school. The court agreed, noting that the fact that the infringing business was located near the university campus also created confusion. The fact that businesses such as restaurants and jewelry stores also used the university's name was not relevant, according to the court, because the university did not provide those services.

In *University of Florida v. KPB, Inc.,* 89 F.3d 773 (11th Cir. 1996), the court rejected the University of Florida's trademark claims against a company that provides "class notes" for university students. A-Plus Notes, a private corporation, hires students to attend lectures and take notes, and then markets those notes to students at the University of Florida. In its lawsuit against A-Plus notes, the university claimed that A-Plus's use of the university's course numbering system to market its "study guides" violated the Lanham Act because this use constituted false representation of the origin of the information and deceptive advertising. The federal district court awarded summary judgment to A-Plus on the Lanham Act claim, and the university appealed.

The appellate court examined the various types of unfair competition that the Lanham Act forbids. The law prohibits unfair trade practices that make false representations as to the origins or descriptions of certain products. In this case, the university was asserting that A-Plus's use of the university's course numbering system was deceptive and confused the purchasers as to the origin of the materials (in other words, the purchasers might believe that the "study guides" were produced by the university rather than by A-Plus). The university characterized its course numbering system as a service mark, which is a word or symbol used by a person (here, the university) to identify and distinguish a service that it provides (here, college courses). In order to satisfy the elements of a Lanham Act claim, said the court, the university had to prove that its service mark was distinctive, that it was primarily nonfunctional, and that the defendant's service mark was confusingly similar. Since the "marks" that the university was attempting to protect were numbers, locations of classes, and the times that classes met, the court determined that this information was functional. The university, thus, could not establish all three elements of the claim, and the appellate court affirmed the district court's summary judgment award for A-Plus.

The Internet has provided a fertile ground for trademark infringement, as individuals and companies have registered Internet addresses or domain names that use an institution's name or symbol, and then have insisted that the institution purchase from the domain name holder the right to use the institution's own name on the Internet. In order to prevent such "cybersquatting," Congress passed the Anticybersquatting Consumer Protection Act (ACPA), Pub. L. No. 106-113, § 3002, 113 Stat. 1501, 1537 (1999), codified at 15 U.S.C. § 1125(d). The victim of such cybersquatting can file an action in federal court, alleging that the registration of the domain name was done in bad faith. There is no requirement that the plaintiff demonstrate that the cybersquatter has used the domain name in a way that infringes the plaintiff's trademark. The law provides for civil liability if the defendant "has a bad faith intent to profit from that mark . . . [and] registers, traffics in, or uses a domain name that . . . is identical or confusingly similar" to the plaintiff's registered mark. The defendant's offer to sell the domain name to the owner of the trademark is one statutory factor that the court may use to determine bad faith. Plaintiffs may be awarded either actual damages or up to $100,000 per domain name. (For a discussion of the use of ACPA by Harvard University to halt the use of the domain name "notHarvard.com" in one case, and the registration of sixty-five domain names including the words "Harvard" or "Radcliffe," see Alayne E. Manas, "NOTE & COMMENT: Harvard as a Model in Trademark and Domain Name Protection,"

29 *Rutgers Computer & Tech. L.J.* 475 (2003). See also Aaron L. Melville, "New Cybersquatting Law Brings Mixed Reactions from Trademark Owners," 6 *B.U. J. Sci. & Tech. L.* 13 (2000).)

The U.S. Supreme Court's foray into the area of federalism versus states' rights has reached trademark law. The Court invalidated a provision of the Trademark Remedy Clarification Act (TRCA), Pub. Law No. 102-542, 106 Stat. 3567 (1992), that amended Section 43(a) of the Lanham Act to provide that states could be sued under that law for using false descriptions or making false representations in commerce (15 U.S.C. § 1125(a)), and that also provided that Eleventh Amendment immunity defenses would not be effective (15 U.S.C. § 1122). The College Savings Bank, a private bank that marketed certificates of deposit to finance college tuition, sued the state of Florida for patent infringement when the state developed a very similar program (see Section 13.2.6 of this book). The bank also sued Florida for an infringement of its trademark under the Lanham Act, accusing the state of making misstatements about Florida's tuition savings plan. The state argued that it had not waived sovereign immunity, and also that the TRCA was not a valid exercise of congressional authority to waive a state's immunity from suit in federal court. The trial and appellate courts agreed with Florida, and the bank appealed to the Supreme Court.

In a 5-to-4 decision, whose majority opinion was written by Justice Scalia, the Supreme Court affirmed the rulings of the lower courts in *College Savings Bank v. Florida Prepaid Postsecondary Education Expense Board,* 527 U. S. 666 (1999). The bank had argued that the TRCA had been enacted not only under the commerce clause (which, the Court had ruled earlier in *Seminole Tribe,* would not provide the basis for a valid abrogation of sovereign immunity; see Section 13.1.6), but also under Section 5 of the Fourteenth Amendment (which would provide a valid basis for abrogation). The Court rejected the Fourteenth Amendment argument, stating that the bank's interests in this dispute were not property rights under the Fourteenth Amendment's due process clause and, thus, Section 5 could not authorize the TRCA. Said the Court: "[T]he hallmark of a protected property interest is the right to exclude others" (527 U.S. at 673). The false advertising provisions of Section 43(a) of the Lanham Act were unrelated to any right to exclude. The Court distinguished trademark infringement actions from actions brought under Section 43(a), stating that, because a trademark was a property right, infringement could implicate constitutional issues, but false advertising claims did not. Nor had the state waived sovereign immunity by entering the prepaid college savings market.

The Court did not address whether states were protected against enforcement of other provisions of the Lanham Act by Eleventh Amendment immunity. The discussion of possible constitutional claims for trademark infringement is *dicta,* and is speculative rather than dispositive of the issue.

The key to protecting the institution's trademarks and service marks is vigilance. The institution should assign at least one individual the responsibility to monitor the use of the institution's name and symbols: on the Internet, on clothing and other merchandise, and in the local or regional community. License agreements should be carefully drafted to require the institution's approval prior to the sale or distribution of merchandise using the institution's name or symbol. Preventing the unauthorized use of the trademark is critical to success in trademark infringement or unfair competition litigation. Records of the activities taken to protect the trademark are also critical to success in this arena. Registration does not ensure trademark protection—it is only the beginning of the process.

13.2.8. Antitrust law. There are three primary federal antitrust laws, each focusing on different types of anticompetitive conduct. The Sherman Act (15 U.S.C. § 1 *et seq.*), the basic antitrust statute, prohibits "every contract, combination . . . , or conspiracy, in restraint of trade or commerce." The Clayton Act, as amended by the Robinson-Patman Act (15 U.S.C. § 12 *et seq.*), supplements the Sherman Act with special provisions on price discrimination, exclusive dealing arrangements, and mergers. The Federal Trade Commission (FTC) Act (15 U.S.C. § 41 *et seq.*), which is discussed separately in Section 13.2.9, prohibits "unfair methods of competition." These three statutes are enforceable by federal agencies: the Sherman and Clayton Acts by the Antitrust Division of the U.S. Department of Justice; the Clayton Act and the FTC Act by the Federal Trade Commission. The Sherman and Clayton Acts may also be enforced directly by private parties, who may bring "treble-damage" suits against alleged violators in federal court; if victorious, such private plaintiffs will be awarded three times the actual damages the violation caused them. Postsecondary institutions, whose activities have been ruled to be in interstate commerce, are subject to these laws, and could thus find themselves defendants in antitrust suits brought by either government or private parties, as well as plaintiffs bringing their own treble-damage actions.

The constitutions of twenty states include antitrust provisions, and most states have statutes of general application that parallel, in most respects, the Sherman and Clayton Acts. Plaintiffs often combine state and federal claims in their federal court actions; the long history of common law remedies against monopolies and unfair business practices makes federal preemption of state antitrust laws unlikely. (For an analysis of state antitrust law, see *State Antitrust Practice and Statutes (Third),* ABA Section on Antitrust Law (2004), available at http://www.abanet.org.)

The courts use three standards, in descending order of severity, to determine whether the actions of an organization (or group) violate the antitrust laws. *First,* the "*per se*" rule applies to activities, such as price fixing, bid rigging, group boycotts, or dividing markets in order to compete, that are examples of activities that are *per se* illegal under both federal and state antitrust laws. *Second,* the "rule of reason" examines all of the circumstances surrounding the allegedly anticompetitive act(s), using a balancing test to determine whether the benefits of the action outweigh the limitation to competition. For example, an allegedly anticompetitive action that provided significant benefits to students might enable a college to prevail under the rule of reason. And *third,* the "quick look" test evaluates restraints on competition in special markets, such as educational services. In these cases, the defendant college must provide a "sound procompetitive justification" for the limitation on competition. This test is described further in *U.S. v. Brown University,* discussed below. (For a review of antitrust law's applications to higher education, see Eliot G. Disner & Kenneth H. Abbe, "You Can't Always Get What You Want: A Primer on Antitrust Traps for the Unwary," National Association of College and University Attorneys Conference Outline (1999), available from http://www.nacua.org.)

In the past, it was thought that the antitrust laws had little, if any, application to colleges and universities. Being institutions whose mission was higher education, they were said to be engaged in the "liberal arts and learned professions" rather than in "trade or commerce" subject to antitrust liability (see generally *Atlantic Cleaners and Dyers v. United States,* 286 U.S. 427, 435–36 (1932)). Moreover, public institutions were considered immune from antitrust liability under the "state action" exemption developed in *Parker v. Brown,* 317 U.S. 341 (1943).[15] Postsecondary institutions, however, can no longer rest comfortably with this easy view of the law. Restrictions in the scope of both the "liberal arts and learned professions" exemption and the state action exemption have greatly increased the risk that particular institutions and institutional practices will be subjected to antitrust scrutiny.

The first chink in postsecondary education's armor was made in *Marjorie Webster Junior College v. Middle States Assn. of Colleges and Secondary Schools,* 432 F.2d 650 (D.C. Cir. 1970), discussed in Section 14.3.2.1. Although the court in that case affirmed the applicability of the "liberal arts and learned professions" exemption, it made clear that antitrust laws could nevertheless be applied to the "commercial aspects" of higher education and that educational institutions and associations could be subjected to antitrust liability if they acted with "a commercial motive." Then, in 1975, the U.S. Supreme Court went beyond the *Marjorie Webster* reasoning in establishing that "the nature of an occupation, standing alone, does not provide sanctuary from the Sherman Act" (*Goldfarb v. Virginia State Bar,* 421 U.S. 773 (1975)). The *Goldfarb* opinion refuted the existence of any blanket "learned professions" or (apparently) "liberal arts" exemption. The Court did caution, however, in its often-quoted footnote 17 (421 U.S. at 788–89, n.17), that the "public service aspect" or other unique aspects of particular professional activities may require that they "be treated differently" than typical business activities. Finally, in *National Society of Professional Engineers v. United States,* 435 U.S. 679 (1978), the Supreme Court reaffirmed its rejection of a blanket "learned professions" exemption and emphasized that footnote 17 in *Goldfarb* should not be read as fashioning any broad new defense for professions. According to *Professional Engineers,* the learned professions (and presumably the liberal arts) cannot defend against antitrust claims by

---

[15]This state action concept is a term of art with its own special meaning under the federal antitrust statutes and has no relation to the state action doctrine used in constitutional interpretation and discussed in Section 1.5.2. Cases and authorities are collected at John E. Theuman, Annot., "Applicability of 'State Action' Doctrine Granting Immunity from Federal Antitrust Laws for Activities of, or Directed by, State Governments—Supreme Court Cases," 119 L. Ed. 2d 641.

relying on an ethical position "that competition itself is unreasonable." And in *Jefferson County Pharmaceutical Assn. v. Abbott Laboratories*, 460 U.S. 150 (1983), the Court, in the special context of a Robinson-Patman Act price discrimination claim, held that the Act applies to a state university's purchases "for the purpose of competing against private enterprise in the retail market" but assumed, without deciding, that the Act would not apply to the state university's purchases "for consumption in traditional governmental functions."

Another Supreme Court case expands postsecondary education's exposure to antitrust liability in yet another way. In *American Society of Mechanical Engineers v. Hydrolevel Corp.*, 456 U.S. 556 (1982), the Court held that nonprofit organizations may be held liable under the antitrust laws not only for the actions of their officers and employees but also for the actions of unpaid volunteers with apparent authority (see Section 3.1) to act for the organization. As applied to postsecondary education, this decision could apparently subject institutions to antitrust liability for anticompetitive acts of volunteer groups—such as alumni councils, booster clubs, recruitment committees, and student organizations—if these acts are carried out with apparent authority.

In response to several U.S. Supreme Court cases in the 1970s and 1980s that refused to extend the antitrust immunity enjoyed by states to municipalities, Congress passed the Local Government Antitrust Act of 1984, which is codified at 15 U.S.C. §§ 34–36. The law provides that no damages, interest on damages, costs, or attorney's fees may be recovered under the Clayton Act "in any claim against a person based on any official action directed by a local government, or official or employee thereof acting in an official capacity" (15 U.S.C. § 36(a)). "Local government" is defined as "a city, county, parish, town, township, village, or any other general function governmental unit established by State law" as well as a school district (15 U.S.C. § 33(1)). As a result, community colleges that are agencies of municipal or county governments will share the same antitrust immunity as state-controlled institutions. Hospitals that are controlled by municipalities or counties (as well as hospitals that are part of state-controlled universities) would also be immune from antitrust liability for their "government functions," but not when acting in a commercial context. This legislation could be important for an institution in its capacity as a landlord or if the institution entered a joint venture with a municipality to build a mixed-use project that included student housing.

Another area of antitrust immunity protects lobbying by higher education organizations and the institutions they represent. The U.S. Supreme Court ruled in *Eastern Railroad Presidents Conference v. Noerr Motor Freight*, 365 U.S. 127 (1961), that an attempt to influence the passage of laws or decisions of the executive branch of the government does not violate the Sherman Act, even if the purpose is anticompetitive and would otherwise violate the Sherman Act. The Court reasoned that where the restraint is the result of valid governmental action, as opposed to private action, those urging the government action enjoy absolute immunity (under the First Amendment) from antitrust liability.

Despite these limitations on antitrust liability, both public and private colleges may face antitrust liability in a variety of areas. Financial aid price fixing, the subject of a case against the "Overlap Group," is discussed below. Antitrust law has also been used to challenge a college's campus housing policy (*Hack v. President and Fellows of Yale College*, 16 F. Supp. 2d 183 (D. Conn. 1998); and *Hamilton Chapter of Alpha Delta Phi v. Hamilton College*, 128 F.3d 59 (2d Cir. 1997), discussed in Section 8.4.1), and the regulation of intercollegiate athletics (see Section 14.4.3). When the college acts as a purchaser or seller, it is acting in a commercial context and may face antitrust liability (see Section 15.3.3). The actions of accrediting associations have been attacked under antitrust law (see Section 14.3.2.4).

The most serious antitrust issue facing private higher education in recent years is the decision by the U.S. Department of Justice to investigate the practices of the "Overlap Group," a loose confederation of twenty-three northeastern colleges that, since 1956, have met annually to compare financial aid offers made to applicants. The members of the group adjusted their financial aid awards to students accepted at more than one of the colleges in the Overlap Group so that the cost to the student was approximately the same, no matter which institution the student attended. In addition to the Justice Department's investigation, a student from Wesleyan University initiated a class action antitrust lawsuit against the Ivy League members of the Overlap Group and two other institutions. The financial stakes were high in this case, for prevailing parties could be awarded treble damages. Eight Ivy League institutions entered a consent decree with the U.S. Department of Justice (*United States v. Brown University et al.*, Civil Action No. 91-CV-3274 (E.D. Pa., May 22, 1991)), in which they agreed to stop sharing financial aid information, but the Massachusetts Institute of Technology (MIT) refused to sign the consent decree and chose to defend the Justice Department's antitrust action in court. In September 1992, a federal trial judge ruled that MIT's participation in the Overlap Group violated federal antitrust law (*United States v. Brown University*, 805 F. Supp. 288 (E.D. Pa. 1992)). The judge conceded that some educational functions might be exempt from antitrust legislation, but he also held that any function that was "commercial in nature" was not exempt. To MIT's argument that providing financial aid was "charitable," rather than commercial, activity, the judge replied: "M.I.T.'s attempt to disassociate the Overlap process from the commercial aspects of higher education is pure sophistry. . . . The court can conceive of few aspects of higher education that are more commercial than the price charged to students" (805 F. Supp. at 289).

Although the judge believed that the Overlap process constituted price fixing *per se*, "in light of the Supreme Court's repeated counsel against presumptive invalidation of restraints involving professional associations," the judge evaluated the Overlap Group's conduct under the rule of reason.[16]

---

[16]Under the rule of reason, a court makes a factual determination of whether the restraint promotes competition through regulation or whether it suppresses competition. Relevant issues are the history of the restraint, the problem the restraint was designed to solve, the reason for selecting the remedy, and the purpose to be attained. See *Chicago Board of Trade v. United States*, 246 U.S. 231 (1918).

No reasonable person could conclude that the Ivy Overlap Agreements did not suppress competition. . . . [T]he member schools created a horizontal restraint which interfered with the natural functioning of the marketplace by eliminating students' ability to consider price differences when choosing a school and by depriving students of the ability to receive financial incentives which competition between those schools may have generated. Indeed, the member institutions formed the Ivy Overlap Group for the very purpose of eliminating economic competition for students [805 F. Supp. at 302].

On appeal, the Third Circuit upheld the trial court's determination that tuition policies were not exempt from antitrust law, but it remanded the case for further consideration of the university's argument that the benefits of information sharing could be achieved only through the anticompetitive practices with which the Overlap Group was charged (*United States v. Brown University,* 5 F.3d 658 (3d Cir. 1993)). The court, in a 2-to-1 opinion, explained:

We note the unfortunate fact that financial aid resources are limited even at the Ivy League schools. A trade-off may need to be made between providing some financial aid to a large number of the most needy students or allowing the free market to bestow the limited financial aid on the very few most talented who may not need financial aid to attain their academic goals. Under such circumstances, if this trade-off is proven to be worthy in terms of obtaining a more diverse student body (or other legitimate institutional goals), the limitation on the choices of the most talented students might not be so egregious as to trigger [an antitrust violation] [5 F.3d at 677].

In December 1993, MIT and the U.S. Department of Justice announced a settlement of the case. The settlement permits MIT, and the other colleges that are members of the Overlap Group, to share applicants' financial data, through a computer network, on the assets, income, number of family members, and other relevant information for individuals accepted at more than one college in the Overlap Group. Although the amount of financial aid offered to these students may not be shared, the settlement permits the group to develop general guidelines for calculating financial aid awards, and will permit auditors to report imbalances in awards to other institutions (W. Honan, "MIT Wins Right to Share Financial Aid Data in Antitrust Accord," *New York Times,* December 23, 1993, p. A13).

The outcome of *U.S. v. Brown University* stimulated an amendment to the Sherman Act in 1994. In the "Improving America's Schools Act of 1994," a statutory note was added to 15 U.S.C. § 1 that essentially codifies the settlement agreement. Entitled "Application of Antitrust Laws to Award of Need-Based Educational Aid," the note permits institutions of higher education to collaborate on financial aid award amounts, provided that they award such financial aid on a need-blind basis. The note originally expired in 1997; it was extended until 2001, and in that year, Congress passed the "Need–Based Educational Aid Act of 2001" (Pub. L. No. 107-72, 115 Stat. 648), which extends the exemption until September 30, 2008.

(For an analysis of the application of antitrust law to higher education, and a discussion of *U.S. v. Brown University*, see Jeffrey C. Sun & Philip T. K. Daniel, "The Sherman Act Antitrust Provisions and Collegiate Action: Should There Be a Continued Exception for the Business of the University?" 25 *J. Coll. & Univ. Law* 451 (1999); and for a critique of the court opinions in *U.S. v. Brown University*, see Julie L. Seitz, Comment, "Consideration of Noneconomic Procompetitive Justifications in the MIT Antitrust Case," 44 *Emory L.J.* 395 (1995). For other issues related to financial aid and tuition packages, see Section 8.3.)

The national system of computerized medical residency matching was challenged using antitrust and constitutional theories. The plaintiffs, a class of current and former medical residents, alleged that the national matching system, which places residents in medical school or hospital residency programs, violated the Sherman Act because it "displace[s] competition in the recruitment, hiring, employment, and compensation of resident physicians" and depresses compensation for residents by removing competition. Early in 2004, the trial court refused to dismiss certain of the claims (*Jung v. Association of American Medical Colleges*, 300 F. Supp. 2d 119 (D.D.C. 2004)).

In response, Congress enacted, as part of the Pension Funding Equity Act of 2004 (Pub. L. No. 108-218, 118 Stat. 596 (2004)), a provision exempting medical residency matching programs from antitrust liability. The provision, "Confirmation of Antitrust Status of Graduate Medical Resident Matching Programs," codified as 15 U.S.C. § 37b, states that: "It shall not be unlawful under the antitrust laws to sponsor, conduct, or participate in a graduate medical education residency matching program, or to agree to sponsor, conduct, or participate in such a program." Furthermore, the law makes evidence of any such conduct inadmissible in federal court to support any antitrust claim, and makes the amendment retroactive, applying to any cases or claims pending on the date of its enactment (April 10, 2004). However, the amendment makes it clear that "any agreement on the part of 2 or more graduate medical education programs to fix the amount of the stipend or other benefits received by students participating in such programs" is not protected by this exemption.

The plaintiffs in the *Jung* case returned to court, arguing that the new legislation violated their constitutional rights to due process, equal protection, and access to courts. The court, in a second opinion, 339 F. Supp. 2d 26 (D.D.C. 2004), ruled that the new legislation did not create a due process violation, and that Congress's purpose in enacting the legislation was a rational use of its power, so the access to courts claims failed as well. And because medical residents were not a suspect class for constitutional purposes, the plaintiffs' equal protection claims were dismissed.

Universities with hospitals also face antitrust claims, but those in the public sector may be protected from antitrust liability by Eleventh Amendment sovereign immunity (see Section 13.1.6). In *Neo Gen Screening, Inc. v. University of Massachusetts*, 187 F.3d 24 (1st Cir. 1999), a federal appellate court affirmed the dismissal of an antitrust case against the university and its medical center by a private entity that performed testing on newborn babies. The court upheld the district court's ruling that the university, in conducting the screening program, was acting as an "agency or arm" of the state and was therefore covered by the Eleventh Amendment. Furthermore, said the court, because the state Department of Public Health had contracted with the university medical center to conduct the testing, the university shared the state's immunity from antitrust liability because it was engaging in state action.

Similarly, in *Daniel v. American Board of Emergency Medicine, et al.*, 988 F. Supp. 127 (W.D.N.Y. 1996), a federal trial judge dismissed antitrust claims against several hospitals affiliated with public universities, including the University of California at Los Angeles and Irvine, the University of Massachusetts, and the University of Arizona, but denied motions to dismiss by some hospitals affiliated with private colleges, such as Johns Hopkins Hospital and Loma Linda University Medical Center. The plaintiffs were challenging a change in the American Board of Emergency Medicine's (ABEM) policy that would no longer permit an alternate route to certification as an emergency room physician, claiming that previously certified emergency doctors and the ABEM were conspiring to limit entry into the profession. The hospitals affiliated with public entities claimed they were immune from suit, while the private hospitals claimed that the court lacked personal jurisdiction over them. Regarding the former hospitals, the court noted that, because they were affiliated with public universities, and because public higher education is a purpose of state government for each of the states sponsoring these hospitals, the hospitals were protected by the state's Eleventh Amendment immunity. Alternatively, said the court, these public hospitals were engaging in state action and, for that reason, were immune from liability under the federal antitrust laws. In addition, two hospitals owned by municipalities were found to be immune under the Local Government Antitrust Act. But the court rejected the jurisdictional defense of the hospitals affiliated with private universities, finding that the defendants that were domestic corporations were subject to personal jurisdiction under Section 12 of the Clayton Act.

Universities with hospitals may also face antitrust liability when peer review committees determine which doctors and other health care professionals may have hospital practice privileges. This is a complicated area of the law, and counsel to institutions with hospitals may wish to consult *Antitrust Health Care Handbook* (3d ed., American Bar Association, Section on Antitrust Law, 2004).

As a result of these various developments, administrators and counsel should accord antitrust considerations an important place in their legal planning.[17] At the same time they plan to avoid antitrust liability, administrators and counsel should also consider the protections that antitrust law may provide them against the anticompetitive acts of others. In *NCAA v. Board of Regents of the University*

---

[17]In one situation, nonprofit postsecondary institutions are still, by express statutory provision, excluded from antitrust liability for alleged price discrimination: "Nothing in [the Robinson-Patman Act] shall apply to purchases of their supplies for their own use by schools, colleges, universities, public libraries, churches, hospitals, and charitable institutions not operated for profit" (15 U.S.C. § 13c) (see this book, Section 15.3.3). See also Section 13.2.9 regarding the limited application of the Federal Trade Commission Act to postsecondary institutions.

of Oklahoma, 468 U.S. 85 (1984) (discussed in Section 14.4.4), for instance, two institutions used the antitrust laws to secure the right to negotiate their own deals for television broadcasting of their sports events. Antitrust law, then, has two sides to its coin; while one side may restrain the institution's policy choices, the other side may free it from restraints imposed by others.

13.2.9. *Federal Trade Commission Act.*

The Federal Trade Commission Act (15 U.S.C. § 41 *et seq.*) prohibits covered entities from "using unfair methods of competition in or affecting commerce and unfair or deceptive acts or practices in or affecting commerce" (§ 45(a)(1)). The Act defines the entities it covers as "any company, trust, . . . or association, incorporated or unincorporated, which is organized to carry on business for its own profit or for that of its members" (15 U.S.C. § 44). This language clearly covers proprietary postsecondary institutions, thus subjecting them to the Act's prohibitions. Public institutions, on the other hand, are not covered. Nor, in most situations, could private nonprofit institutions be covered. In a leading precedent regarding nonprofit entities, *Community Blood Bank of Kansas City Area v. FTC,* 405 F.2d 1011 (8th Cir. 1969), the court refused to subject a blood bank to FTC jurisdiction, reasoning in part that the organization was "not organized for the profit of members or shareholders [and] [a]ny profit realized in [its] operations is devoted exclusively to the charitable purposes of the corporation."

The Supreme Court has held, however, that the Act's definition of covered entities is broad enough to include a nonprofit entity if it is engaging in activities designed to benefit other, profit-making, entities economically. In *California Dental Association v. Federal Trade Commission,* 526 U.S. 756 (1999), the Court held that, because the dental association "provided substantial economic benefits to its for-profit members," it was subject to the Act. And in the *Community Blood Bank* case, above, the court suggested that "trade associations" organized for the "pecuniary profits" of their members would be a classic example of nonprofit entities covered by the Act. Although the principles of these cases would usually not apply to private, nonprofit postsecondary institutions, an institution's activities could apparently come within these principles if the institution entered into a profit-making business venture with another entity. A real estate syndicate, for example, or a research joint venture with industry might fall within the Act's definition, thus subjecting the institution's activities within that relationship to FTC jurisdiction.

The FTC's primary activity regarding proprietary postsecondary institutions has been its attempts to regulate certain practices of proprietary vocational and home-study schools. In 1998, the FTC issued "Guides for Private Vocational and Distance Education Schools" (16 C.F.R. Part 254), covering programs of instruction that "purport[ ] to prepare or qualify individuals for employment in any occupation or trade, or in work requiring mechanical, technical, artistic, business, or clerical skills, or that is for the purpose of enabling a person to improve his appearance, social aptitude, personality, or other attributes" (§ 254.0(a)). Excluded, however, are "institutions of higher education offering at least a 2-year program of accredited college level studies generally acceptable for credit toward a bachelor's degree."

Proprietary schools have been faced with another potential source of problems under the FTC Act. In some cases proprietary schools have recruited students, assisted them in obtaining federally guaranteed student loans, and then declared bankruptcy, leaving the students without an education but with a loan to repay. In several of these cases, the proprietary schools have had close relationships with one or more banks that provide federally guaranteed student loans to the proprietary schools' students. The FTC's "Holder Rule" allows the purchaser or borrower to hold a related lender responsible for the seller's misconduct (16 C.F.R. § 433.2(d)) and requires that such language appear in the loan document. Two federal courts have ruled that the Holder Rule does not provide a federal remedy for recipients of federally guaranteed student loans (*Jackson v. Culinary School of Washington,* 788 F. Supp. 1233 (D.D.C. 1992), *affirmed on other grounds,* 27 F.3d 573 (D.C. Cir. 1994);[18] *Veal v. First American Savings Bank,* 914 F.2d 909 (7th Cir. 1990)). However, the FTC has issued a letter stating that the rule does apply (J. DeParle, "Indebted Students Gain in Battle on Fraudulent Trade Schools," *New York Times,* August 4, 1991, at p. 32). If the Holder Rule does apply and the required language is not in loan documents, students whose loans have been obtained through the now defunct proprietary school may be able to avoid repaying the loan. (For discussion of these issues, see C. Mansfield, "The Federal Trade Commission Holder Rule and Its Applicability to Student Loans—Reallocating the Risk of Proprietary School Failure," 26 *Wake Forest L. Rev.* 635 (1991). And for an argument that the Department of Education should increase its monitoring of the practices of proprietary schools, see Patrick F. Linehan, Note, "Dreams Protected: A New Approach to Policing Proprietary Schools' Misrepresentations," 89 *Georgetown L.J.* 753 (2001).)

Congress has reversed an interpretation by the FTC of the Fair Credit Reporting Act (FCRA) (15 U.S.C. § 1681 *et seq.*) that had required employers using third parties to conduct investigations of employee misconduct to comply with the FCRA's requirements for disclosing information to the "consumer" (the subject of the investigation) (see Section 4.8). In the "Fair and Accurate Credit Transactions Act of 2003," Pub. L. No. 108-159, 117 Stat. 1953 (2003), Congress amended the earlier definition of "consumer report" to exclude such investigatory reports, provided that the report is disclosed only to the employer or relevant government officials, and that if adverse action is taken against the employee as a result of the report, the employer must give a summary of the report to the employee (15 U.S.C. § 1681a(x)).

13.2.10. Environmental laws. A complex web of federal and state laws regulates landowners and disposers of waste that may pollute water, soil, or

---

[18]The U.S. Supreme Court (515 U.S. 1139 (1995)) vacated and remanded the case to the appellate court, ordering it to reconsider its ruling in light of *Wilton v. Seven Falls Company,* 515 U.S. 277 (1995), a case involving the propriety of federal courts entertaining actions for declaratory judgment when a parallel state proceeding was under way. The appellate court, at 59 F.3d 254, remanded the case to the trial court. There were no further proceedings.

air. Institutions of higher education fall into both of these categories and thus are subject to the strict regulation and the heavy civil and criminal penalties provided by these laws.[19] Although most environmental laws have been in effect for twenty-five years or more, enforcement activities against colleges and universities have escalated in recent years, and many institutions have been fined for violations ranging from storage of laboratory chemicals to disposing of certain toxic materials without a permit.[20] Compliance with environmental laws is particularly difficult for colleges and universities because the sites at which regulated materials are located or activities using such materials take place are typically spread throughout the campus (science laboratories, maintenance storage areas, hospitals, art rooms, campus heating plants, and so forth). Furthermore, a wide array of individuals, including students, laboratory staff, faculty, maintenance workers, and even patients may be involved with the handling and disposal of materials that are regulated under these laws.

Most of the federal environmental protection laws are enforced by the Environmental Protection Agency (EPA). The two laws of major importance to institutions of higher education are the Resource Conservation and Recovery Act of 1976 (RCRA) and the Comprehensive Environmental Response, Compensation, and Liability Act of 1980 (CERCLA, also known as the Superfund Law). The Toxic Substances Control Act (TSCA) is also important to most colleges and universities, and most must also comply with the Clean Air Act and the Clean Water Act. The handling, storage, and disposal of radioactive materials are regulated by the Nuclear Regulatory Commission; the Occupational Safety and Health Administration (OSHA) regulates the communication of information about hazardous substances to workers (see Section 4.6.1, this book). The Emergency Planning and Community Right-to-Know Act (EPCRA, 42 U.S.C. §§ 11001–11050, also known as Title III of the Superfund Amendments and Reauthorization Act (SARA)) requires institutions to disclose all chemicals that they use or store. Other laws regulate the use and disposal of asbestos, PCBs (polycholorinated biphenyls), lead paint, and other potentially harmful substances.

The Resource Conservation and Recovery Act of 1976 (RCRA) (42 U.S.C. § 6901 *et seq.*) regulates the generation, transportation, storage, and disposal of

---

[19]Pertinent summaries of case law on environmental regulation include John F. Wagner, Jr., Annot., "Validity and Construction of § 106(a) and (b)(1) of Comprehensive Environmental Response, Compensation, and Liability Act (42 U.S.C. § 9606(a) and (b)(1)), Authorizing Equitable Abatement Actions and Administrative Orders and Prescribing Fines for Noncompliance with Such Orders," 87 A.L.R. Fed. 217; Annot., "Governmental Recovery of Cost of Hazardous Waste Removal Under Comprehensive Environmental Response, Compensation, and Liability Act (42 U.S.C. § 9601 et seq.)," 70 A.L.R. Fed. 329; and Carol A. Crocca, Annot., "Liability Insurance Coverage for Violations of Antipollution Laws," 87 A.L.R.4th 444.

[20]See, for example, Jeffrey Brainard, "Kent State U. Agrees to Settlement for Smokestack Violations," *Chron. Higher Educ.*, May 7, 2003, available at http://chronicle.com/daily/2003/05/200305073n.htm. See also Jeffrey Selingo, "Long Island U. Settles with EPA over Hazardous Waste," *Chron. Higher Educ.*, June 18, 2004, available at http://chronicle.com/weekly/v50/i41/41a02301.htm.

hazardous waste.[21] The law defines which "hazardous waste" is regulated, and excludes some substances, such as household products and specified industrial wastes. The law covers products intended to be recycled as well as those that are discarded, and specifies record-keeping requirements for tracking the waste from the time it is obtained until the time it is discarded. Generators, transporters, and owners of storage and disposal sites are covered by RCRA. Penalties include administrative compliance orders and revocation of RCRA permits; civil penalties of up to $25,000 per day per violation and criminal penalties of two to five years' imprisonment and fines of up to $50,000 per day per violation; and, for "knowing endangerment," imprisonment of up to fifteen years and fines of up to $250,000 for individuals and $1 million for corporations (42 U.S.C. § 6928). Under RCRA, improper disposal of a hazardous substance by an employee or a student could result in criminal penalties.

Other federal environmental laws, such as CERCLA and the Clean Water and Clean Air Acts, contain similar civil and criminal penalties. Furthermore, federal judges are interpreting the laws' *scienter* (knowledge) requirements for individual liability to permit juries to infer that a corporate officer, depending on his or her position in the organization, would know about the violation. (For a discussion of these issues, see R. Marzulla & B. Kappel, "Nowhere to Run, Nowhere to Hide: Criminal Liability for Violations of Environmental Statutes in the 1990s," 16 *Columbia J. Envtl. L.* 201 (1991).) Most insurers do not include coverage for toxic waste cleanup or liability in their directors' and officers' policies, potentially leaving corporations and their officers and directors personally liable. (See Comment, "Whistling Past the Waste Site: Directors' and Officers' Personal Liability for Environmental Decisions and the Role of Liability Insurance Coverage," 140 *U. Pa. L. Rev.* 241 (1991), which, among other issues, discusses retroactive liability of officers and directors for disposal that was not unlawful prior to CERCLA.)

The Comprehensive Environmental Response, Compensation, and Liability Act of 1980 (CERCLA) (42 U.S.C. § 9601 *et seq.*) and its amendments (Superfund Amendments and Reauthorization Act) govern the cleanup of hazardous waste sites. Under CERCLA, the generator of toxic material, the transporter of the material, and the owner of the dump site have joint and several liability for cleanup costs. Institutions face potential liability under CERCLA when property that they own is contaminated, whether or not the institution generated the hazardous waste or even knew that it was on the site. They may also share the legal responsibility with others for cleanup of a contaminated site if they generated any of the waste that was dumped at the site.[22] The only way that a property owner may be able to avoid CERCLA liability is by establishing a "due

---

[21]Cases and authorities are collected in William B. Johnson, Annot., "Liability Under § 7003 of Resource Conservation and Recovery Act (RCRA) (42 U.S.C.S. § 6973) Pertaining to Imminent Danger from Solid or Hazardous Waste," 115 A.L.R. Fed. 491.

[22]For an example of a concerted response by approximately one hundred colleges and universities involved in the Maxey Flats (Ky.) Superfund cleanup, see "Maxey Flats Superfund Proceeding Settled," 77 *Educ. Record* 53 (1996).

diligence" defense: that it did not know, nor did it have reason to know, that the property was contaminated. To establish this defense, the purchaser of property must demonstrate that an investigation was made to determine whether the property was contaminated, and possibly that extensive testing was conducted. Such precautions are particularly important in cases where the property was formerly an industrial site. (For an overview of this subject, see P. Marcotte, "Toxic Blackacre: Unprecedented Liability for Landowners," *A.B.A. J.*, November 1, 1987, 67–70.)

CERCLA contains provisions for actions against "potentially responsible parties" to recover cleanup costs, even if the cleanup is not mandated by a government agency (42 U.S.C. § 9607(a)(B)). Thus, institutions of higher education could take advantage of this provision if they purchase contaminated property, or they could be liable for contamination of property they no longer own, even if they did not cause the contamination. (For a general overview of CERCLA and RCRA, see John S. Applegate, *Environmental Law—RECRA and CERCLA: The Management of Hazardous Waste* (West, 2004).)

Other federal laws that regulate the actions of most colleges and universities include the Clean Air Act (42 U.S.C. § 7401 *et seq.*, and § 7551 *et seq.*), which regulates emissions of substances into the air. Emission sites on campuses may include laboratories, boilers, incinerators, and print shops. The Clean Water Act (33 U.S.C. § 1251 *et seq.*) prohibits the discharge of any pollutant into navigable waters, unless the EPA has issued a permit for such discharge. The law also prohibits the discharge of pollutants into storm sewers through such actions as landscape irrigation, air conditioning condensation, lawn watering, or swimming pool discharge. This law also regulates the treatment of wetlands. The Toxic Substances Control Act (15 U.S.C. § 2601 *et seq.*) regulates the use and disposal of "chemical substances which present an unreasonable risk of injury to health or the environment" (§ 2601(b)(2)), including PCBs and asbestos; it also imposes record-keeping and labeling requirements. Underground storage tanks and the land-based disposal of certain hazardous substances are regulated by the Hazardous and Solid Waste Amendments of 1984 (42 U.S.C. § 6924 *et seq.*).

Most of the federal environmental laws allow individuals to bring claims against anyone alleged to be violating these laws, as well as against the Administrator of the EPA for failure to enforce these laws (see, for example, the Federal Water Pollution Control Act (the Clean Water Act), 33 U.S.C. § 1365; the Resource Conservation and Recovery Act (RCRA), 42 U.S.C. § 7002; and the Comprehensive Environmental Response, Compensation, and Liability Act (CERCLA), 42 U.S.C. § 9659). For example, in *Adair v. Troy State University of Montgomery*, 892 F. Supp. 1401 (M.D. Ala. 1995), workers engaged in renovating a building at the university alleged that asbestos was released during the renovation in violation of the Clean Air Act. The Act specifically provides that "any person" may bring a cause of action against anyone alleged to have violated the emission standards of the Act (42 U.S.C. § 7604a). The court ruled that the sixty-day notice provision in the law (42 U.S.C. § 7604(b)) did not apply in this case because the violation had already occurred. The court ruled that the plaintiffs could sue for past violations of the Act if the plaintiff could demonstrate that the violations were repeated.

Public institutions, however, may be able to avoid liability from litigation under the federal environmental laws by employees. In *Rhode Island Department of Environmental Management v. United States*, 304 F.3d 31 (1st Cir. 2002), three employees of the Rhode Island Department of Environmental Management, a state agency, sued their employer under the "whistleblower" provision of the Solid Waste Disposal Act (SWDA) (42 U.S.C. § 6971(a)), alleging that they had been retaliated against after reporting what they believed were violations of the SWDA. The SWDA provides that any individual who believes he or she has been retaliated against for complaining of actions made unlawful under the Act may request a review of the adverse employment action by the Secretary of Labor (29 C.F.R. Part 24). A similar administrative review provision is included in several other environmental statutes (see 15 U.S.C. § 2622 (Toxic Substances Control Act); 33 U.S.C. § 1367 (Water Pollution Control Act); 42 U.S.C. § 300j-9 (Safe Drinking Water Act); 42 U.S.C. § 5851 (Energy Reorganization Act); 42 U.S.C. § 7622 (Clean Air Act); and 42 U.S.C. § 9610 (Comprehensive Environmental Response, Compensation, and Liability Act). The court ruled that nothing in the SWDA abrogated the state's sovereign immunity (see Section 13.1.6, this book), but that if the Secretary of Labor intervened in the proceeding, then sovereign immunity would not protect the state defendant.

Many states have passed environmental laws that are even more restrictive than federal law. Administrators and counsel should secure expert advice on compliance with both sets of laws, particularly in situations where the laws differ or cannot be complied with simultaneously.

Faced with the myriad laws and the severe penalties they carry, colleges and universities should consider, if they have not already done so, adding one or more individuals with expertise in environmental regulation to their administrative staff. Training for students, staff, and faculty who work with substances regulated by these laws must be conducted in order to make these users aware of regulatory requirements and the potential for institutional and individual liability. Institutional counsel should consider the wisdom of an environmental compliance audit, both to ascertain the institution's compliance with these laws and to demonstrate the institution's good faith should a violation be alleged. (For guidance on conducting such audits, see J. Moorman & L. Kirsch, "Environmental Compliance Assessments: Why Do Them, How to Do Them, and How Not to Do Them," 26 *Wake Forest L. Rev.* 97 (1991), as well as M. E. Kris & G. L. Vannelli, "Today's Criminal Environmental Enforcement Program: Why You May Be Vulnerable and Why You Should Guard Against Prosecution Through an Environmental Audit," 16 *Columbia J. Envtl. L.* 227 (1991).)

The Web site of the EPA contains important information on the laws and compliance issues. In addition, the EPA has created a "Colleges and Universities Sector Partnership," which is described at http://www.epa.gov/sectors/colleges/index.html. The partnership is developing "outreach tools, training resources, and support" to assist colleges in managing compliance with environmental laws. The American Council on Education and the National

Association of College and University Business Officers, among other organizations, are working with the EPA. (For additional information and links to additional resources, see Sheldon E. Steinbach, "Why Your College May Run Afoul of Environmental Laws, and What to Do Next," *Chron. Higher Educ.*, June 25, 2004, available at http://chronicle.com/weekly/v50/i42/42b01402.htm. See also the resources included in the Selected Annotated Bibliography.)

13.2.11. Americans with Disabilities Act.
The Americans With Disabilities Act of 1990 (ADA) (Pub. L. No. 101-336, codified at 42 U.S.C. § 12101 *et seq.*) provides broad protections for individuals with disabilities in five areas: employment (see Section 5.2.5), public accommodations (see Section 8.2.4.3, this book), state and local government services, transportation, and telecommunications. Similar in intent to Section 504 of the Rehabilitation Act (see Section 13.5.4), the ADA provides broader protection, since a larger number of entities are subject to it (they need not be recipients of federal funds) and a larger number of activities are encompassed by it.[23]

The law protects an "individual with a disability." "Disability" is defined as "a physical or mental impairment that substantially limits one or more major life activities" of the individual; "a record of such impairment; or being regarded as having such impairment" (42 U.S.C. § 12102). This definition, while covering current disabilities, also would prohibit discrimination against an individual based on a past disability that no longer exists, or a perceived disability that does not, in fact, exist. The definition of "impairment" includes contagious diseases, learning disabilities, HIV (whether symptomatic or asymptomatic), drug addiction, and alcoholism (36 C.F.R. § 104), although the employment provisions exclude current abusers of controlled substances from the law's protections.

Title I of the ADA covers employment, and is discussed in Section 5.2.5. Title II requires nondiscrimination on the part of state and local government, a category that specifically includes state colleges and universities. Title II provides that "no qualified individual with a disability shall, by reason of such disability[,] be excluded from participation in or be denied the benefits of the services, programs, or activities of a public entity, or be subjected to discrimination by any such entity" (42 U.S.C. § 12132). For purposes of Title II, an individual with a disability is "qualified" when "with or without reasonable modification to rules, policies, or practices, the removal of architectural, communication, or transportation barriers, or the provision of auxiliary aids and services, [the individual] meets the essential eligibility requirements for the receipt of services or his participation in programs or activities provided by a public entity" (42 U.S.C. § 12131). Title II also incorporates the provisions of Titles I and III (public accommodations), making them applicable to public institutions.

---

[23]Cases and authorities are collected at Ann K. Wooster, Annot., "When Does a Public Entity Discriminate Against Disabled Individuals in Provision of Services, Programs, or Activities Under the Americans With Disabilities Act, 42 U.S.C.A. § 12132," 163 A.L.R. Fed. 339; and John A. Bourdeau, Annot., "Validity, Construction, and Application of § 302 of Americans With Disabilities Act (42 U.S.C.A. § 12182), Prohibiting Discrimination on Basis of Disability by Owners or Operators of Places of Public Accommodation," 136 A.L.R. Fed. 1.

The U.S. Department of Justice has the responsibility for providing technical assistance for, and for enforcing, Titles II and III of the ADA. Regulations interpreting Title II appear at 28 C.F.R. Part 35.

Title III extends the nondiscrimination provisions to places of public accommodation, whose definition includes colleges and universities, whether public or private, if they "affect commerce" (42 U.S.C. § 12181). Title III focuses on ten areas of institutional activity:

1. Eligibility criteria for the services provided by colleges and universities (28 C.F.R. §36.301).

2. Modifications in policies, practices, or procedures (such as rules and regulations for parking or the policies of libraries) (28 C.F.R. § 36.302).

3. Auxiliary aids and services (such as interpreters or assistive technology) (28 C.F.R. § 36.303).

4. Removal of architectural barriers (28 C.F.R. § 36.304).

5. Alternatives to barrier removal (if removal is not readily achievable) (28 C.F.R. § 36.305).

6. Personal devices and services, which the law does not require the public accommodation to provide (28 C.F.R. § 36.306).

7. Conditions under which the public accommodation must provide accessible or special goods upon request (28 C.F.R. § 36.307).

8. Accessible seating in assembly areas (28 C.F.R. § 36.308).

9. Accessibility to and alternatives for examinations and courses that reflect the individual's ability rather than the individual's impairment (28 C.F.R. § 36.309).

10. Accessible transportation (28 C.F.R. § 36.310).

Title III imposes a wide range of requirements on colleges and universities, from admissions policies to residence hall and classroom accessibility to the actions of individual faculty (who may, for instance, be required to modify examinations or to use special technology in the classroom). Issues involving the admission or accommodation of students are discussed in this book in Sections 8.2.4.3 and 9.3.5, respectively. The regulations also affect the college's planning for public performances, such as plays, concerts, or athletic events, and provide detailed guidelines for making buildings accessible during their renovation or construction. The implications of the ADA for a college's responsibility to provide auxiliary aids and services is discussed in Section 8.7. Public telephones must also be made accessible to individuals with disabilities, including those with hearing impairments. (For an overview of some of the implications of the ADA for institutions of higher education, see F. Thrasher, "The Impact of Titles II and III of the Americans With Disabilities Act of 1990 on Academic and Student Services at Colleges, Universities, and Proprietary Schools," 22 *Coll. L. Dig.* 257 (June 18, 1992).)

The Supreme Court's activity in enlarging the arena of state sovereign immunity has included attention to the ADA. In *Board of Trustees of University of Alabama v. Garrett,* discussed in Section 5.2.5 of this book, the Supreme Court ruled that Congress had not abrogated the immunity of states under Title I of the ADA, and thus state agencies could not be sued in federal court for money damages for alleged employment discrimination. The Court's *Garrett* ruling has been applied to claims against public universities brought under Title II of the Act (see, for example, *Robinson v. University of Akron School of Law,* 307 F.3d 409 (6th Cir. 2002)). The Court, however, refused to apply the reasoning of *Garrett* to a case brought under Title II of the ADA by a disabled individual with paraplegia who was unable to gain physical access to a courthouse. In *Tennessee v. Lane,* 541 U.S. 509 (2004), the Court reviewed the legislative history of the ADA, noting the "pervasive unequal treatment of persons with disabilities in the administration of state services and programs, including systematic deprivations of fundamental rights" (541 U.S. at 524). Because the plaintiff had framed the ADA violation as an infringement on his constitutional access to the courts, the Supreme Court ruled that Title II, "as it applies to the class of cases implicating the fundamental right of access to the courts, constitutes a valid exercise of Congress' §5 authority to enforce the guarantees of the Fourteenth Amendment." The narrow basis upon which the Court decided this case does not answer the question of whether Congress validly abrogated state sovereign immunity in Titles II or III under circumstances not involving access to courts.

In *Barnes v. Gorman,* 536 U.S. 181 (2002), the high Court ruled that courts may not award punitive damages in private suits brought under Section 202 of the ADA and Section 504 of the Rehabilitation Act. Although the Court acknowledged that Title II of the ADA could be enforced through a private cause of action, it ruled that Title II's remedies are "coextensive" with those of Title VI of the Civil Rights Act of 1964 (discussed in this book, Section 13.5.2). Because punitive damages are not available in private causes of action brought under Title VI, said the court, they are similarly unavailable under Title II of the ADA.

The case involving the Professional Golfers Association (PGA) and Casey Martin may be of interest to athletics administrators because of its language concerning the scope of the reasonable accommodation requirement. In *PGA Tour, Inc. v. Martin,* 532 U.S. 661 (2001), the plaintiff, Casey Martin, met the eligibility criteria for playing professional golf on PGA events. Because he had a documented disability that made walking the golf course very difficult, he asked for permission to use a motorized golf cart during tournaments, although tournament rules required participants to walk the course. The PGA denied his request. Martin sued the PGA, and the Supreme Court ruled that PGA tournaments were a "public accommodation" because Section 12181 of the ADA specifically included golf courses as public accommodations. Because the tour was subject to the ADA, the Court addressed the issue of whether allowing a player to use a motorized cart would be an undue hardship for the tour. Under Rehabilitation Act and ADA jurisprudence, an accommodation is an undue hardship if it fundamentally alters the nature of the program or activity (see this book, Section 9.3.5.4). The Court found that allowing Martin the use of a golf cart would not fundamentally alter the nature of the tournament because it did not give a disabled player any advantage over players without disabilities, nor did it alter the nature of the game itself.

A final rule to implement both the ADA and the Architectural Barriers Act (42 U.S.C. § 4151 *et seq.*) has been published. The "ADA Accessibility Guidelines for Buildings and Facilities; Architectural Barriers Act (ABA) Guidelines" were published at 69 Fed. Reg. No. 141 (July 23, 2004), and are codified at 36 C.F.R. Parts 1190 and 1191.

13.2.12. Laws regulating computer network communications

13.2.12.1. Overview. Under the Communications Act of 1934, as amended by the Telecommunications Act of 1996 (110 Stat. 56), the federal government is the primary regulator of radio, television, and telephone communications. As new communication technologies have evolved, the federal government has also included them within its regulatory reach. The newest focus of regulatory activity and legal and policy concerns is computer technology and the Internet.[24]

As the subsections below indicate, the applications of federal laws to computer networks are expanding rapidly, and the laws are complex and technical. These developments carry multiple messages for higher educational administrators and counsel. *First,* administrators and counsel should be vigilant in ascertaining when the First Amendment (or other constitutional rights) may protect the institution or its faculty members, staff, or students from excesses of government regulation. *Second* (assuming valid statutes), administrators and counsel should be sensitive to the increased risks of liability that federal statutes may present for the institution and the members of its campus community when third parties claim harm resulting from the use of the institution's computer networks. *Third,* administrators and counsel should assure that their institution has well-drafted computer use policies that comply with federal (and state) law, that fill in gaps not covered by federal (or state) law, and—equally important—that clearly specify the rights and responsibilities of computer users as determined by campus policy makers (see also Section 8.5.2 of this book). *Fourth,* administrators and counsel should consider the role that *external* federal (and state) law enforcement agencies should play in the institution's own strategies for dealing with computer misuse. Most institutions, of course, will have their own internal computer policies and other regulations—for example, student disciplinary codes—that can be used to combat computer misuse. But when the misuse may be a crime, institutional interests regarding computer abuse may sometimes be better served by seeking the assistance of external law enforcement authorities in addition to or in lieu of processing the matter internally. (The strategy and policy issues here are similar to those the institution faces when it confronts problems such as drug abuse or sexual assaults.)

---

[24]State governments have also initiated various attempts to regulate computer technology and the Internet. For examples of such legislation and resultant judicial challenges, see Section 7.3 (the *Urofsky* case from Virginia), Section 8.5.1 (the *Miller* case from Georgia), and Section 12.4 (the *American Libraries Association* case from New York; and see also Amy Keane, Annot., Validity of State Statutes and Administrative Regulations Regulating Internet Communications Under the Commerce Clause and the First Amendment of the Federal Constitution," 98 A.L.R. 5th 167.

13.2.12.2. Computer statutes. The first major federal legislation regarding computers was enacted in 1986. In that year, Congress passed the Computer Fraud and Abuse Act of 1986 (18 U.S.C. § 1030) and the Electronic Communications Privacy Act of 1986 (18 U.S.C. § 2510 *et seq.* & § 2701 *et seq.*). The former act, substantially amended in 1996 (Pub. L. No. 104-294, §§ 201 & 204), is a computer crime statute. It prohibits various types of unauthorized access to "protected computer(s)" (computers used by or for government or a "financial institution," or computers used in interstate or foreign commerce), and also prohibits unauthorized communication of various types of information obtained through unauthorized access to a computer. (See Scott Charney & Kent Alexander, "Computer Crime," 45 *Emory L.J.* 931, 950–53 (1996).) The unauthorized access provisions of the Computer Fraud and Abuse Act (specifically 18 U.S.C. § 1030(a)(5)(A)) were the basis for the prosecution of Robert Morris, the Cornell University graduate student in computer science who, in 1988, experimentally introduced a "worm" into the Internet that caused various computers at educational institutions and military installations to crash. Morris's conviction was upheld in *United States v. Morris,* 928 F.2d 504 (2d Cir. 1991). The Act was further amended in 2001 by the USA PATRIOT Act (Pub. L. No. 107-56, 115 Stat. 272) (see below in this subsection) to criminalize knowing transmission of malicious code, such as a virus, over a computer network (18 U.S.C. § 1030 (a)(5)(A)(i)) and unauthorized access to a protected network (18 U.S.C. § 1030(a)(5)(A)(ii)–(iii)).

The latter act, the Electronic Communications Privacy Act (ECPA), creates limited privacy rights for computer users. Title I of the ECPA generally prohibits interception of communications, disclosure of intercepted communications, and use of the contents of intercepted communications (18 U.S.C. § 2511(1)(a), (c), (d)). Title II generally prohibits unauthorized access to, and alteration or disclosure of, stored computer communications (18 U.S.C. §§ 2701(a), 2702(a)). These prohibitions apply to colleges and universities as systems operators as well as to individual faculty, students, and staff members. There are various important exceptions, however, that permit system operators to intercept or disclose in certain circumstances (18 U.S.C. §§ 2511(2), 2701(c)). Under Section 2511(2)(a)(i), for instance, certain operators may intercept when it is necessary to view the content in order to forward the message; and under Section 2511(2)(a)(ii) an operator may disclose information to federal agents in certain circumstances pursuant to an appropriate court order or written certification.

ECPA's Title I provisions concerning "interception" and its Title II provisions concerning access to communications in "electronic storage" were both helpfully examined in *Fraser v. Nationwide Mutual Ins. Co.,* 352 F.3d 107 (3d. Cir. 2004), a case in which the court rejected an employee's challenge to his employer's search of his e-mail stored on the employer's central file server. In particular, the court of appeals used an exception to Title II contained in 18 U.S.C. § 2701(c)(1) to hold that Title II does not protect an employee from the employer's access to his stored e-mail when the employer is the service provider and the e-mail is stored on its own system (352 F.3d at 115). The ECPA Title I provisions on intentional disclosure of intercepted communications, particularly

Section 2511(1)(c), were also examined in *Bartnicki v. Vopper,* 532 U.S. 514 (2001), in which the Supreme Court held the "privacy concerns" protected by Title I must sometimes "give way" to the First Amendment "interest in publishing matters of public importance."

The ECPA was significantly modified by the USA PATRIOT Act of 2001 (Pub. L. No. 107-56, 115 Stat. 272.[25] Prior to the PATRIOT Act, the ECPA required the government to obtain an administrative subpoena before seizing transactional records (such as Internet addressing records) of computer communications service subscribers. The ECPA also required government to obtain a warrant supported by probable cause before seizing e-mail stored "for one-hundred eighty days or less." Section 210 of the PATRIOT Act broadens the information available by administrative subpoena to include more subscriber information than previously permitted (see 18 U.S.C. § 2703), including access to e-mail older than six months. (Information that a computer communications provider now "shall disclose" to a government entity is listed in 18 U.S.C. § 2703(c).) Section 217 of the PATRIOT Act permits "a person acting under color of law to intercept the . . . electronic communications of a computer trespasser" if the person is authorized to do so by the owner of the "protected computer," is "lawfully engaged in an investigation," and "has reasonable grounds to believe that the contents of the computer trespasser's communications will be relevant to the investigation," and if the "interception does not acquire communications other than those transmitted to or from the computer trespasser" (18 U.S.C. § 2511(2)(i)). Section 217 of the PATRIOT Act further permits a person acting under color of law to intercept an "electronic communication" if "one of the parties to the communication has given prior consent" to the communication, and permits the owner of a protected computer to authorize such interception (18 U.S.C. § 2511(2)(c)). Section 212 of the PATRIOT Act permits, but does not require, an Internet service provider to disclose subscriber records, not including the content of the messages, "if the provider reasonably believes that an emergency involving immediate danger of death or serious injury to any person justifies disclosure of the information" (18 U.S.C. § 2702 (c)(4)), or if disclosure is necessary to the "protection of the rights or property of the provider of that service" (18 U.S.C. § 2702(c)(3)).[26]

More recently, the Cyber Security Enhancement Act of 2002 (enacted as one title of the Homeland Security Act of 2002), Pub. L. No. 107-296, § 225(d), 116 Stat. 2135, 2157 (2002)), relaxed the ECPA provisions in 18 U.S.C. § 2702(b)

---

[25]For a more thorough examination of the impact of the USA PATRIOT Act amendments on law enforcement and intelligence surveillance activities pertinent to higher education, see Lee S. Strickland, Mary Minow, & Tomas Lipinski, "PATRIOT in the Library: Management Approaches When Demands for Information Are Received from Law Enforcement and Intelligence Agents," 30 *J. Coll. & Univ. Law* 363 (2004); Nancy Tribbensee, "Privacy and Security in Higher Education Computing Environments After the USA PATRIOT Act," 30 *J. Coll. & Univ. Law* 337 (2004); and David Harrison, "The USA PATRIOT Act: A New Way of Thinking, An Old Way of Reacting, Higher Education Responds," 5 *N.C. J.L. & Tech.* 177 (2004).

[26]The amendments from Section 212 of the USA PATRIOT Act expired on December 31, 2005 (Pub. L. No. 107-56, 115 Stat. 272 § 224). In early March 2006, Congress voted to extend the Act.

concerning when a provider of an electronic communication service may "divulge the contents of a communication" to a "government entity." Such disclosure may now be made upon "a good faith belief that an emergency involving danger of death or serious physical injury to any person requires disclosure without delay" (18 U.S.C. § 2702 (b)(8)).

When enacted in 1986, ECPA required communications service providers to disclose subscriber information to the FBI upon receipt of a so-called National Security Letter (NSL) from the FBI certifying that the information is relevant to a "counterintelligence investigation" and that there is "specific and articulable . . . reason to believe" the target of the request is a "foreign power or agent of a foreign power" (18 U.S.C. § 2709 (b) (1988)). Section 505(a) of the USA PATRIOT Act replaced this requirement with a more relaxed requirement that the information sought is "relevant to an authorized investigation to protect against international terrorism or clandestine intelligence activities . . ." (18 U.S.C. § 2709(b) (2005)). In addition, Section 2709(c) of ECPA states that "[n]o wire or electronic communication service provider, or officer, employee, or agent thereof, shall disclose to any person that the Federal Bureau of Investigation has sought or obtained access to information or records under this section." In *Doe v. Ashcroft*, 334 F. Supp. 2d 471 (S.D.N.Y. 2004), a federal district court held, in a lengthy opinion, that the National Security Letter authority in Section 2709 violates the Fourth Amendment because it effectively bars or substantially deters any judicial challenge to the propriety of an NSL request. The court also held that Section 2709(c) violates the First Amendment because its "permanent ban on disclosure . . . operates as an unconstitutional prior restraint on speech . . ." (334 F. Supp. 2d at 475).

In the years after 1986, Congress also passed legislation to restrict obscenity, pornography, and "indecent" speech in computer communications—especially with respect to communications accessible to children. The first major statute of this type was the Communications Decency Act of 1996 (CDA), enacted as Title V of the Telecommunications Act of 1996 (110 Stat. 56). The CDA amended Title 47, Section 223 of the *United States Code* to add a new Section 223(a)(1)(B), called the "indecency" provision, and a new Section 223(d), called the "patently offensive" provision. The indecency provision applied criminal penalties to anyone who "knowingly" used the Internet to transmit any "communication *which is obscene or indecent,* knowing that the recipient of the communication is *under 18 years of age* . . ." (emphasis added). The "patently offensive" provision applied criminal penalties to anyone who "knowingly" used "an interactive computer service" to send to or display for a person "*under 18 years of age*" any "communication *that, in context, depicts or describes, in terms patently offensive as measured by contemporary community standards,* sexual or excretory activities or organs . . ." (emphasis added). These provisions were challenged in court and invalidated first by a three-judge U.S. district court and then by the U.S. Supreme Court in *Reno v. American Civil Liberties Union* (discussed below). (Section 223(a)(1)(B)'s application to "obscenity" was not challenged in this case.)

Other provisions of the CDA, § 223(a)(1)(A)(ii) and § 223(a)(2), imposed criminal penalties for the transmission over the Internet of "obscene, lewd, lascivious, filthy, or indecent" communications that are intended to "annoy, abuse, threaten, or harass another person." These sections apply regardless of the age of the recipient. The courts construed these sections to apply only to obscene communications that meet the U.S. Supreme Court's definition of obscenity; and so construed, their constitutionality was upheld. (See *Apollo Media Corp. v. Reno*, 19 F. Supp. 2d 1081 (N.D. Cal. 1998), *affirmed summarily*, 526 U.S. 1061 (1999).)

In 2003, in response to the court cases above, Congress amended all of these CDA Sections to apply only to communications that are "obscene" or "are child pornography" (Pub. L. No. 108-21, §§ 603(1)(A), 603(1)(B), & 603(2)). These amendments apparently resolve the constitutional issues concerning the prior sections, since the U.S. Supreme Court permits regulation of both "obscenity" and "child pornography," as the Court has narrowly defined those terms. (Regarding obscenity, see *Apollo Media Corp.* above; and regarding child pornography, see *New York v. Ferber*, 458 U.S. 747 (1982).)

Sections 223(a)(1)(B), 223(d), 223(a)(1)(A), and 223(a)(2), as now amended, apply not only to persons who transmit the prohibited communications but also to any person who "knowingly permits" computer facilities "under [the person's] control to be used for" the prohibited communications (47 U.S.C. § 223(a)(2) & (d)(2)). There are several affirmative defenses (47 U.S.C. § 223(e)), including a defense that partially absolves employers from the prohibited actions of their employees and agents (47 U.S.C. § 223(e)(4)).

Another computer statute that regulated obscene and pornographic speech (and that also ran into difficulties in the courts), is the Child Pornography Prevention Act of 1996 (CPPA), 18 U.S.C. § 2251 *et seq.*, which extended existing prohibitions against child pornography to cover virtual images of children created with computer technology. In *Ashcroft v. Free Speech Coalition*, 535 U.S. 234 (2002), the U.S. Supreme Court struck down this provision of the CPPA. The Court explained that the virtual images of minors covered by the statute did not fall within the Court's definition of obscenity; and since they did not involve "real children," they did not fall within the Court's definition of child pornography. The statutory provision therefore prohibited "a substantial amount of lawful speech" without adequate justifications and was "overbroad and unconstitutional" (535 U.S. at 256).

In 1998, after *Reno v. American Civil Liberties Union* but well before the 2003 amendments to the CDA (above), Congress sought to remedy the legal shortcomings of Sections 223(a)(1)(B) and 223(d) in a manner that would still permit regulation of "indecent" and "patently offensive" computer speech. The statute, the Child Online Protection Act (COPA), 112 Stat. 2681–2736, 47 U.S.C. § 231, provides criminal penalties for any knowing "communication *for commercial purposes* that is available to any minor and that includes any material that is harmful to minors" (47 U.S.C. § 231(a)(1)) (emphasis added). The "commercial purposes" limitation was not part of the CDA. COPA also provides that "material that is harmful to minors" is to be identified, in part, with reference to "contemporary community standards" (47 U.S.C. § 231(e)(6)(A)), a phrase that was used in the CDA.

COPA, like the CDA, was challenged on First Amendment grounds once it went into effect. In *American Civil Liberties Union v. Reno*, 31 F. Supp. 2d 473 (E.D. Pa. 1999), the district court rejected the argument that COPA regulated only "commercial speech" subject to a lower level of scrutiny from the courts and issued a preliminary injunction prohibiting the federal government from enforcing COPA. Aspects of this ruling led to two U.S. Supreme Court decisions, *Ashcroft v. ACLU*, 535 U.S. 564 (2002), and *Ashcroft v. ACLU*, 542 U.S. 656 (2004), as a result of which the district court's injunction was upheld pending a full trial on the merits. As this book went to press, the preliminary injunction against COPA's enforcement remained in effect.

Another section of the CDA that was not at issue either in *Reno v. American Civil Liberties Union* or in *Apollo Media Corp. v. Reno* is Section 509, which added a new Section 230 to 47 U.S.C. Rather than imposing any criminal penalties on computer transmissions, this section provides protection for "provider(s)" of "interactive computer service(s)" against certain types of liability regarding computer communications (47 U.S.C. § 230(c)), including liability for "good faith" uses of software to filter or block "material that the provider . . . considers to be obscene, lewd, lascivious, filthy, excessively violent, harassing, or otherwise objectionable" (47 U.S.C. § 230(c)(2)(A)). Section 230 is further discussed in Section 8.5.2 of this book.

Other computer statutes of interest to colleges and universities include the Digital Millennium Copyright Act (DMCA), 17 U.S.C. § 1201 *et seq.,* enacted in 1998, which protects copyright holders from certain infringements via the Internet and establishes various rules regarding the liability of Internet service providers, and which is discussed in subsection 13.2.5 above and in Section 8.5.2 of this book; the Anti-Cybersquatting Consumer Protection Act, codified in various sections of Title 15, U.S.C., enacted in 1999, which protects trademark holders and others from persons who traffic in domain names, and which is discussed in Section 13.2.7 of this book; the Children's Online Privacy Protection Act of 1998, 15 U.S.C. §§ 6501–6506, which prohibits the online collection or disclosure of private information from children under thirteen; and the TEACH Act, codified in various sections of Title 17, U.S.C., enacted in 2002, which addresses copyright issues concerning distance education via computer technology, and which is discussed in subsection 13.2.5 above.

Issues concerning computer statutes are increasingly being resolved by the courts, as the cases above suggest. The leading case to date—the one that provides the most extensive discussion and the best guidance on how the First Amendment applies to, and limits government's authority to regulate, the content of computer communications—is *Reno v. American Civil Liberties Union*, 521 U.S. 844 (1997), *affirming* 929 F. Supp. 824 (E. D. Pa. 1996), in which the U.S. Supreme Court struck down two provisions of the Communications Decency Act. The plaintiffs argued that the two provisions, Section 223(a)(1)(B) and Section 223(d) (see above), were unconstitutional under the First Amendment because they were "overbroad" and "vague." Seven of the nine Justices agreed that these provisions were unconstitutional, and the other two Justices agreed that they were unconstitutional in most of their applications. Justice Stevens wrote the majority opinion for the seven Justices; Justice O'Connor wrote a concurring and dissenting opinion for the other two.

The Court majority relied primarily on the First Amendment "overbreadth" arguments and did not directly rule on "vagueness" issues. The Court did, however, "discuss the vagueness of the CDA because of its relevance to the First Amendment overbreadth inquiry. . . ." Reasoning that the challenged provisions of the CDA were content-based restrictions on speech that, due to their overbreadth, created "an unacceptably heavy burden on protected speech," the Court held these provisions to be facially overbroad. Regarding Section 223(a)(1)(B), the Court invalidated the "indecency" provision but not the "obscenity" provision, which was not challenged and remains valid because, as the Court noted, "obscene speech . . . can be banned totally because it enjoys no First Amendment protection."[27]

The Court left no doubt about its view of the capacities and importance of cyberspace as a communication medium. At various points, the Court described the Internet as a "vast democratic for[um]"; a "new marketplace of ideas"; a "unique and wholly new medium of worldwide human communication" (agreeing with the district court); and a "dynamic, multifaceted category of communication 'providing' relatively unlimited low-cost capacity for communication of all kinds." The World Wide Web itself, according to the Court, is "comparable, from the readers' viewpoint, to both a vast library, including millions of readily available and indexed publications, and a sprawling mall offering goods and services;" and "from the publishers' point of view, it constitutes a vast platform from which to address and hear from a world-wide audience of millions of readers, viewers, researchers, and buyers." Moreover, the Internet:

> includes not only traditional print and news services, but also audio, video, and still images, as well as interactive, real-time dialogue. Through the use of chat rooms, any person with a phone line can become a town crier with a voice that resonates farther than it could from any soap box. Through the use of Web pages, mail exploders, and newsgroups, the same individual can become a pamphleteer [521 U.S. at 896–97].[28]

The Court was also clear about the substantial burdens that the CDA placed on cyberspace communications. "[T]he CDA is a content-based blanket restriction on speech." There are "many ambiguities concerning the scope of its coverage" because the statute does not define the term "indecent" or the term "patently offensive." "Given the vague contours of the coverage of the statute, it

---

[27]Obscenity law may need to be modified, however, if it is to have any sensible application to obscene materials transmitted in cyberspace (or perhaps may ultimately need to be abandoned as to cyberspace because it can have no sensible application there). See, for example, Randolph Sergent, "The 'Hamlet' Fallacy: Computer Networks and the Geographic Roots of Obscenity Regulation," 23 *Hastings Const. L.Q.* 671 (1996); but compare *Ashcroft v. ACLU*, 535 U.S. 564 (2002) (*Ashcroft I*), discussed briefly above in this subsection.

[28][Author's footnote] This does not mean, however, that courts would treat the entire Internet as a "public forum" for First Amendment purposes. See *United States v. American Library Association*, 539 U.S. 194 (2003).

unquestionably silences some speakers whose messages would be entitled to constitutional protection. . . . In order to deny minors access to potentially harmful speech, the CDA effectively suppresses a large amount of speech that adults have a constitutional right to receive and to address to one another."

Nor did the defenses provided in the statute (§ 223(e)(5)) alleviate the statute's burden on cyberspace communication. These defenses depend upon the use of technology to screen communications or to identify users. According to the Court, either the "proposed screening software does not currently exist," or "it is not economically feasible for most noncommercial speakers to employ" the identification or verification technology that is currently available. Thus, "[g]iven that the risk of criminal sanctions 'hovers over each content provider, like the proverbial sword of Damocles' [quoting the district court], the District Court correctly refused to rely on unproven future technology to save the statute.[29] The Government thus failed to prove that the proffered defense would significantly reduce the heavy burden on adult speech produced by the prohibition on offensive displays" (551 U.S. at 880–81).

In language particularly important to educational institutions, the Court specifically recognized that the CDA would burden not only adult speech in general, but, more specifically, speech that is used to convey academic or instructional content. The CDA omits any requirement that the covered speech lack "serious literary, artistic, political, or scientific value" (indeed, Congress had "rejected amendments that would have limited the proscribed materials to those lacking redeeming value" (551 U.S. at 871, n.37)); and therefore, the CDA covers "large amounts of nonpornographic material with serious educational or other value." Thus, for instance, the speech covered by the statute could "extend to discussions about prison rape or safe sexual practices, artistic images that include nude subjects, and arguably the card catalogue of the Carnegie Library."

It is settled constitutional law that a regulation burdening the content of speech, as the CDA did, is subject to strict judicial scrutiny—a standard of review requiring the government to demonstrate that its regulation is supported by a "compelling" government interest and that there are no "less restrictive alternatives" by which the government could effectuate its interest. In *Reno,* the Court refused to craft any exception to these standards for the new medium of cyberspace and emphatically subjected the statute to "the most stringent review." According to the Court, the medium of cyberspace could not be analogized to the broadcast media and treated more leniently under the law, nor is there any other "basis for qualifying the level of First Amendment scrutiny that should be applied to this medium."

Applying strict scrutiny review to the two challenged CDA provisions, the Court in *Reno* acknowledged that the federal government had a compelling

---

[29][Author's footnote] For later U.S. Supreme Court analysis regarding the constitutionality of government regulations that permit or require the use of "filtering" or "blocking" technology, see *United States v. American Library Association,* 539 U.S. 194 (2003); and see generally Patrick Garry, "The Flip Side of the First Amendment: A Right to Filter," 2004 *Mich. St. L. Rev.* 57.

interest in protecting children from indecency. But neither provision, in the view of the Court, was drafted with sufficient specificity or "narrow tailoring" to survive the "less restrictive alternative" portion of the test:

> We are persuaded that the CDA lacks the precision that the First Amendment requires when a statute regulates the content of speech. . . . [The CDA's] burden on adult speech is unacceptable if less restrictive alternatives would be at least as effective in achieving the legitimate purpose that the statute was enacted to serve. . . .
>
> The breadth of this content-based restriction of speech imposes an especially heavy burden on the Government to explain why a less restrictive provision would not be as effective as the CDA. It has not done so. . . . [T]he CDA is not narrowly tailored if the requirement has any meaning at all. . . .
>
> In *Sable* [*Communications v. FCC*], 492 U.S. at 127, we remarked that the speech restriction at issue there amounted to "burn[ing] the house to roast the pig." The CDA, casting a far darker shadow over free speech, threatens to torch a large segment of the Internet community [551 U.S. at 874, 878, 882].[30]

The government also argued that "in addition to its interest in protecting children," it has a compelling interest in "fostering the growth of the Internet" that "provides an independent basis for upholding the constitutionality of the CDA." The Court quickly and strongly rejected this alternative argument:

> We find this argument singularly unpersuasive. . . . As a matter of constitutional tradition, in the absence of evidence to the contrary, we presume that governmental regulation of the content of speech is more likely to interfere with the free exchange of ideas than to encourage it. The interest in encouraging freedom of expression in a democratic society outweighs any theoretical but unproven benefit of censorship [521 U.S. at 885].

In her concurring/dissenting opinion, Justice O'Connor attempted to soften the impact of the Court's opinion by preserving some room in which the government may constitutionally implement content restrictions on cyberspace speech. In particular, Justice O'Connor advocated a theory of "cyberspace zoning" similar to the theory advocated by the government. But Justice O'Connor's argument depends entirely on future technological advances. She admitted that the technology needed to make "adults only" zones and other zones feasible in cyberspace did not yet exist.[31] If and when it does come into being in a form economically accessible to all, Justice O'Connor would then permit the kind of

---

[30][Author's footnote] For further, extensive analysis of the "least restrictive alternative" test, as applied to cyberspace speech, see *Ashcroft v. ACLU*, 542 U.S. 656 (2004) (*Ashcroft II*), discussed briefly above in this subsection.

[31]Since *Reno*, Congress has amended child abuse statutes to impose penalties for use of a "misleading domain name" with "intent to deceive a person into viewing . . . obscenity," and has created the "Dot Kids" second-level domain to provide material suitable for "any person under 13 years of age." Both of these statutes, which move toward something like Internet zoning, are discussed in Sec. 13.2.12.3, below.

regulation represented by the CDA. According to Justice O'Connor, "[T]he prospects for the eventual zoning of the Internet appear promising," and "our precedent indicates that the creation of such zones can be constitutionally sound."

Overall, neither the Court's reasoning nor its use of precedent in *Reno* is surprising. The Court's decision is clearly the correct one, although the forecast in Justice O'Connor's opinion is also worth taking to heart. What is somewhat surprising, and noteworthy, is the degree of consensus the Court achieved. In an era when the Court is frequently divided, the near consensus in *Reno* indicates that the constitutional question was not a close one and that the government's position had little support in precedent.

The good news in *Reno* for both public and private educational institutions is that they and their campus communities are free from the burden of a statute that the Court admitted would have prohibited much communication having educational value. More broadly, *Reno* provides a solid First Amendment foundation upon which public and private institutions can defend themselves from other governmental attempts to regulate the content of their cyberspace speech and that of their faculty and students. Conversely, the no-so-good news for some public institutions is that they are also bound by the principles espoused by the Court in *Reno* and, therefore, will be prohibited from regulating cyberspace communications on their own campuses in much the same way that Congress and the state legislatures are prohibited from doing so under *Reno* (see Section 8.5.1). Private institutions, of course, will not be subject to these same limitations, since the First Amendment binds only the public sector (see Section 1.5.2).

13.2.12.3. General statutes. In addition to federal statutes focusing predominantly on computer communications (subsection 13.2.12.2 above), there are various regulatory and spending statutes that do not focus on computers or cyberspace but nevertheless may have some applications to computer communications or stored computer data. A sex discrimination law that covers sexual harassment, such as Title VII (see Section 5.2.1 of this book) or Title IX (see Section 13.5.3 of this book), for example, would apply to e-mails that constitute such harassment. A research misconduct law (see Section 13.2.3.4 above) would apply to misconduct that involves the use of computers. In short, cyberspace and the users of cyberspace are not freed from the coverage of generally applicable laws merely because the statute does not specifically mention computers or computer communications. (The First Amendment, however, does establish limits on such statutes' applications to computer communications, just as it does with statutes that specifically focus on computers (see subsection 13.2.12.2 above).)

In addition, some general statutes have been specifically extended to computers by congressional amendment, administrative regulation, or judicial interpretation. The federal obscenity statute that prohibits the sale or distribution of obscene material in interstate commerce (18 U.S.C. § 1465), for instance, has been amended to cover obscene communications using interactive computer services (Pub. L. No. 104-104, Title V, § 507, 110 Stat. 56, 137; see *United States v. Thomas,* 74 F.3d 701 (6th Cir. 1996); and see generally Donald Stepka, "Obscenity On-Line: A Transactional Approach to Computer Transfers of Potentially Obscene Material," 82 *Cornell L. Rev.* 905 (1997)). The federal child pornography laws, 18 U.S.C. §§ 2251, 2252, 2252A, and 2256, have also been amended to proscribe computer transmissions of materials that sexually exploit minors (see Pub. L. No. 100-690, Title VII, § 7511, 102 Stat. 4485; Pub. L. No. 104-208, Title I, § 121(3)(a), 110 Stat. 3009–3028). In *Ashcroft v. Free Speech Coalition* (discussed in subsection 13.2.12.2 above), however, the U.S. Supreme Court invalidated portions of these amendments that extended to "virtual" pornography created by computer simulation and not involving actual children). Similarly, a 2003 amendment (Pub. L. No. 108-21) to a child abuse law, 18 U.S.C. § 2252B, Pub. L. No. 108-21, Title V, § 521(a), extended its coverage to include the knowing use of "a misleading domain name on the Internet with the intent to deceive a person into viewing material constituting obscenity," or "the intent to deceive a minor into viewing material that is harmful to minors on the Internet" (18 U.S.C. § 2252B(b)).

The federal copyright law (Section 13.2.5 of this book) has been amended to provide criminal penalties for distribution of software that infringes the copyright holder's interests (Pub. L. No. 102-307 and Pub. L. No. 102-561, 106 Stat. 4233, amending 18 U.S.C. § 2319(b), (c)(1), & (c)(2)). It has also been amended to increase protections against criminal copyright infringements that occur over the Internet (Pub. L. No. 105-147, 111 Stat. 2678, the No Electronic Theft Act). (The Digital Millennium Copyright Act, another and more comprehensive amendment, is discussed in subsection 13.2.12.2 above.)

In addition, the USA PATRIOT Act of 2001 (also discussed in subsection 13.2.12.2 above) expands the federal crime of terrorism (18 U.S.C. § 2332b) to include computer network intrusions and dissemination of malicious code (18 U.S.C. § 1030(a)(1) & (a)(5)(B)(ii) & (v)) and "destruction of communication lines, stations or systems" (18 U.S.C. § 1362). The Arms Export Control Act and the Export Administration Act (Section 13.2.4 of this book) have been extended by regulation to cover encryption software used to maintain the secrecy of computer communications (see the International Traffic in Arms Regulations (ITAR), 22 C.F.R. § 121.1, Category XIII(b)(1), and the Export Administration Regulations (EAR), 15 C.F.R. §§ 738.2(d)(2), 772, & 774 supp. I). (Courts have warned, however, that encryption software may be considered expression for purposes of the First Amendment, thus raising constitutional issues concerning the EAR's (and other similar federal regulations') applicability to such software; see, for example, *Junger v. Daly,* 209 F.3d 481 (6th Cir. 2000).) The Fraud by Wire, Radio, or Television Communications Act (18 U.S.C. § 1343) has also been interpreted by the courts to cover some computer network communications; see *United States v. Seidlitz,* 589 F.2d 152 (4th Cir. 1978); and *United States v. Riggs,* 739 F. Supp. 414, 420 (N.D. Ill. 1990). And a federal statute that prohibits communications containing threats to kidnap or injure another person (18 U.S.C. § 875(c)) has been applied by the courts to computer communications (see the *Baker* and *Morales* cases below).

Among the most interesting cases to date concerning these various statutes are the cases concerning the applicability of 18 U.S.C. § 875(c) (above) to threats conveyed by computer communication. In *United States v. Alkhabaz aka Jake Baker,* 104 F.3d 1492 (6th Cir. 1997), *affirming (on other grounds)* 890 F. Supp. 1375 (E.D. Mich. 1995), a U.S. Court of Appeals considered the applicability of 18 U.S.C. § 875(c) to a former University of Michigan student who had sent e-mail messages over the Internet. The student, Mr. Baker, had exchanged e-mail messages with a Mr. Gonda expressing an interest in the rape and torture of women and girls. In addition, Baker had posted various fictional stories involving the "abduction, rape, torture, mutilation, and murder of women and young girls." One of these stories had a character with the same name as one of Baker's classmates at the University of Michigan. Baker was indicted and charged with exchanging e-mail messages that threatened to injure (or, in one instance, to kidnap) another person in violation of 18 U.S.C. § 875(c).

The federal district court had agreed that the statute applies to computer communications: "While new technology such as the Internet may complicate analysis and may sometimes require new or modified laws, it does not in this instance qualitatively change the analysis under the statute or under the First Amendment" (890 F. Supp. at 1390). Nevertheless, the court dismissed the indictment against Baker because the e-mail messages sent and received by Baker and Gonda were "pure speech" that is "constitutionally protected" under the First Amendment. Although threats are excepted from the Amendment's protection, the district court determined that the e-mail messages did not constitute "true threats." The district court made clear that "statements expressing musings, considerations of what it would be like to kidnap or injure someone, desires to kidnap or injure someone, however unsavory, are not constitutionally actionable . . . absent some expression of an intent to commit the injury or kidnaping." In addition, while the statement need not identify a specific individual as its target, it must be sufficiently specific as to its potential target or targets to render the statement more than hypothetical" (890 F. Supp. at 1386). Applying these standards to Baker, the court found that his messages communicating a desire to kidnap or injure young girls, and detailing a method for abducting of a female student in his dormitory, merely expressed his desire to commit these acts, not an actual intention to act on those desires. As a result, the district court held that the statements in the defendant's private e-mail messages to Gonda did not meet the First Amendment "true threat" requirement.

While the district court decision focused heavily on First Amendment analysis, the court of appeals, in upholding the decision, focused on the interpretation of the statute under which Baker was indicted. Title 18, Section 875(c) states:

> Whoever transmits in interstate or foreign commerce any communication containing any threat to kidnap any person or any threat to injure the person of another, shall be fined under this title or imprisoned not more than five years, or both.

According to the appellate court, "to constitute a 'communication containing any threat,' under Section 875 (c), a communication must be such that a reasonable person (1) would take the statement as a serious expression of an intention to inflict bodily harm . . . , and (2) would perceive such expression as being communicated to effect some change or achieve some goal through intimidation."

In applying this standard to the facts of the case, the appellate court determined that the messages sent and received by Baker did not constitute a "communication containing any threat" under Section 875(c). The court reasoned that, "even if a reasonable person would take the communications between Baker and Gonda as serious expressions of an intention to inflict bodily harm, no reasonable person would perceive such communications as being conveyed to effect some change or achieve some goal through intimidation." "Although it may offend our sensibilities," the court remarked, "a communication objectively indicating a serious expression of an intention to inflict bodily harm cannot constitute a threat unless the communication is also conveyed for the purpose of furthering some goal through the use of intimidation." Since the indictment failed to meet the requirements of Section 875(c) as it interpreted them, the appellate court declined to address the First Amendment issue. (In contrast, a dissenting judge argued that "by publishing his sadistic Jane Doe story on the Internet, Baker could reasonably foresee that his threats to harm Jane Doe would ultimately be communicated to her (as they were), and would cause her fear and intimidation, which in fact ultimately occurred.")

In contrast to *Baker*, another U.S. Court of Appeals found the requirements of Section 875(c) satisfied in *U.S. v. Morales*, 272 F.3d 284 (5th Cir. 2001). The defendant Morales, an eighteen-year-old high school student, had made statements about killing students at his high school in Houston, Texas. The statements were communicated in a chatroom on the Internet. One of the participants, a resident of Washington, subsequently alerted the principal at Morales's high school, who increased security measures at the school. Police investigators traced the statements to Morales, who admitted making the statements, but claimed he was only joking and pretending to be the ghost of one of the assailants from the Columbine High School shooting. Nevertheless, a jury convicted Morales of violating Section 875(c). The appellate court, in affirming Morales's conviction, asserted that "a communication is a threat under Section 875(c) if 'in its context [it] would have a reasonable tendency to create apprehension that its originator will act according to its tenor'" and if the statement was made "voluntarily and intentionally, and not because of mistake or accident." Section 875(c) required only proof that the statement was made; the threshold for a communication to be evaluated as a threat was therefore fairly low. The evidence in the record, in particular Morales's own admissions, was sufficient to meet this requirement. In addition, the appellate court required that the statement, in context, must have a "reasonable tendency to create apprehension that its originator will act according to its tenor"—a requirement designed to assure that the threat amounted to a "true threat" and was thus not subject to First Amendment protection. The evidence indicated that Morales repeated his threat several times during the chatroom conversation and that he gave no indication that he was joking. Furthermore, because Morales admitted that he was seeking to tie his statements to the Columbine High School shootings, his remarks could not be "divorced from the reality of that tragedy." Even though Morales's chatroom statements did not correctly identify the Columbine assailant that Morales attempted to represent, the court nevertheless found that the general context in which he made his remarks was sufficient to permit a reasonable juror to find that Morales's statements were a "true threat" covered by Section 875(c).

As a comparison of *Baker* and *Morales* indicates, the "threat" language of 18 U.S.C. § 875(c) has created interpretive difficulties for the courts that are not yet resolved. This statutory language has also raised issues of whether computer communications considered to be within the scope of Section 875(c) may nevertheless sometimes be protected by the First Amendment's free speech clause; the district court's opinion in *Baker* illustrates this concern.

13.2.13. Medicare. Medicare is a two-part program through which the federal government provides a form of health insurance for individuals age sixty-five and over, younger individuals with disabilities, and people with permanent kidney failure (end-stage renal disease). Part A covers inpatient hospital services, skilled nursing facilities, home health services, and hospice care. Part B covers part of the costs of physician services, outpatient hospital services, medical equipment and supplies, and some other health services and supplies. Hospitals and other health care facilities that have contracts with and that treat individuals covered by Medicare must seek reimbursement from the federal government for the care received by Medicare patients. The federal rules governing Part A reimbursement, especially for teaching hospitals, are highly technical and intricate, and are of particular interest to institutions with medical schools and affiliated teaching hospitals and medical centers.

Generally, Part A pays hospitals and similar providers for services prospectively in a predetermined amount on a per-discharge basis, under a diagnosis-related grouping system. This "prospective payment system" is based on what the federal government determines under a complex formula to be the "reasonable costs" of providing the care. Part B pays for medical services on the basis of "reasonable charges" or maximum allowable amounts set by Medicare.

Under Part A, a Medicare service provider enters into an agreement with the Secretary of Health and Human Services ("Secretary") to receive reimbursement for the "reasonable cost" of services provided to Medicare recipients (42 U.S.C. §§ 1395cc, 1395ww). Although the patient may be required by Medicare to pay copayments or deductibles, the provider agrees not to charge the patient otherwise "for items or services for which such individual is entitled to have payment made under [Medicare]" (42 U.S.C. § 1395cc(a)(1)(A)). Under 42 U.S.C. §1395cc(a)(F)(i), in-patient hospitals must agree to:

> maintain an agreement with a professional standards review organization . . . or with a utilization and quality control peer review organization . . . [that will] review the validity of diagnostic information provided by such hospital, the completeness, adequacy and quality of care provided, the appropriateness of admissions and discharges, and the appropriateness of care provided for which

additional payments are sought under section 1393ww(d)(5) [a provision on hospital stays that exceed the "mean length of stay"].

From Medicare's inception, reimbursements have been an important means of support for graduate medical education (GME), that is, the clinical internship and residency programs for doctors who have received their M.D. degrees. Hospital costs associated with GME include the salaries of residents and interns and costs of recruiting and maintaining an experienced teaching staff. Under the "related organization principle," costs incurred by an affiliated medical school in connection with the GME program may also be allowable. The regulations provide that "costs applicable to services, facilities, and supplies furnished to the provider by organizations related to the provider by common ownership or control are includable in the allowable cost of the provider at the cost to the related organization" (42 C.F.R. § 413.17(a)).

Teaching hospitals are reimbursed by Medicare for their direct and indirect GME costs (42 C.F.R. § 412.2(f)(2), (7); see 42 C.F.R. § 413.75, *et seq.,* regarding direct GME costs of certain approved residency programs and 42 C.F.R. § 12.105 regarding indirect GME). Certain other costs of approved nursing and allied health education activities are also paid by Medicare (42 C.F.R. § 413.85). Medicare will not pay for "costs incurred for research purposes, over and above usual patient care . . ." (42 C.F.R. § 413.90(a)).

In order to receive reimbursement, a provider must file a reimbursement claim with an intermediary fiscal agent ("intermediary"). An intermediary, often a private insurance company, acts under contract with the Secretary and is responsible for reviewing the provider claims and making initial reimbursement determinations (42 U.S.C. § 1395h). Intermediaries may also subcontract with auditing or other firms to assist in the determination of which costs of graduate medical education are reimbursable under the current version of Medicare regulations. A provider may contest denial of reimbursement by requesting a hearing before the Provider Reimbursement Review Board (PRRB), a board within the Department of Health and Human Services that has exclusive jurisdiction over Medicare reimbursement claims (42 U.S.C. § 1395oo). The Secretary may, on his or her own motion, review the decision of the PRRB. In addition, providers have the right "to obtain judicial review of any action of the fiscal intermediary which involves a question of law or regulations relevant to the matters in controversy where the [PRRB] determines (on its own motion or at the request of a provider of services . . .) that it is without authority to decide the question" (42 U.S.C. § 1395oo(f)(1)). The civil action must be initiated within sixty days of the adverse determination.

In addition, the services of staff physicians at teaching hospitals who render services to Medicare recipients may also be eligible for reimbursement. According to the statute:

> [P]ayment under this part [Part A] shall be made to such fund as designated by the organized medical staff of the hospital in which such services were furnished or, if such services were furnished in such hospital by the faculty of a medical school, to such fund as may be designated by such faculty, but only

if—(1) such hospital has an agreement with the Secretary under section 1395cc of this title, and (2) the Secretary has received written assurance that (A) such payment will be used by such fund solely for the improvement of care of hospital patients or for educational or charitable purposes and (B) the individuals who were furnished such services or any other persons will not be charged for such services (or if charged, provision will be made for return of any moneys incorrectly collected) [42 U.S.C. § 1395f(g)].

The regulations also provide that Medicare will not reimburse a hospital for direct GME expenses that have previously been covered by "community support," which includes "all non-Medicare sources of funding (other than payments made for furnishing services to individual patients), including State and local government appropriations" (42 C.F.R. § 413.81(a)(1); see the definition of "community support" at 42 C.F.R. § 413.75).[32] The intent of this provision is to avoid the shifting of costs that would otherwise be paid by the hospital or other sources to Medicare.

Reimbursement for the costs of graduate medical education has been the subject of several lawsuits by academic medical centers over the past decade. Because the law and regulations have changed several times during this period, the cases are discussed briefly as an indicator of the standards used by the courts to analyze challenges, either to the regulations themselves or to the government's interpretation and application of these regulations.

An earlier version of the GME reimbursement regulation was at issue in a case decided by the U.S. Supreme Court: *Thomas Jefferson University v. Shalala,* 512 U.S. 504 (1994). In 1985, Thomas Jefferson University Hospital hired an independent accounting firm to review and calculate the hospital's GME costs, particularly in light of the 1984 amendments to the Medicare statute, and to refine its "cost allocation techniques." On the advice of the accounting firm, the hospital submitted to the intermediary a reimbursement claim for $8.8 million, $2.9 million of which represented previously unclaimed direct and indirect administrative costs associated with the hospital's residency program. Previously, the hospital had claimed and received reimbursement for three categories of salary-related GME costs: (1) salaries paid by the hospital to medical college faculty for services rendered to the hospital's Medicare patients; (2) salaries paid by the hospital to residents and interns; and (3) funds transferred internally from the hospital to the medical college as payment for faculty time devoted to the hospital's GME program. It was not until after the accounting firm review that the hospital sought reimbursement for non-salary-related GME costs, such as the cost of administering the hospital's GME program.

The intermediary denied the hospital's claim as to all non-salary-related GME costs. At the hospital's request, the PRRB reviewed and reversed the

---

[32]"Community support means funding that is provided by the community and generally includes all non-Medicare sources of funding (other than payments made for furnishing services to individual patients), including State and local government appropriations. Community support does not include grants, gifts, and endowments of the kind that are not to be offset in accordance with section 1134 of the Act."

intermediary's decision. The Secretary intervened on her own motion and reinstated the decision of the intermediary, basing her decision on the anti-redistribution principle: "[s]ince the non-salary GME costs here in issue were borne in prior years by the Medical College, . . . reimbursement of these costs would constitute an impermissible 'redistribution of costs' under § 413.85(c) [of the regulations]" (512 U.S. at 511). Furthermore, the Secretary reasoned that the hospital's failure to claim the costs in years past indicated "community support" for the costs of the program under Section 413.85(c).

Following general principles of administrative law, the Court in *Thomas Jefferson* deferred to the Secretary's interpretation of the regulations, determining that it was neither "plainly erroneous nor inconsistent with the regulation" (512 U.S. at 513). By a 5-to-4 vote, the Supreme Court upheld the Secretary's decision to deny reimbursement to the hospital. Interestingly, the Secretary did not assert that the types of nonsalary costs for which the hospital sought reimbursement were unallowable, but rather that the hospital's timing and procedure for seeking reimbursement made these costs unallowable. Had the hospital claimed the nonsalary administrative costs from the beginning (it is not clear from the record why the hospital did not do so), Medicare apparently would have reimbursed these costs.

(For a review of the *Thomas Jefferson* decision and its implications, along with background on the Medicare statute and regulations, see Kellyann Horger, "Medicare Reimbursement to Provider University Hospitals for Graduate Medical Education Expenses in Light of *Thomas Jefferson University v. Shalala,*" 23 *J. Coll. & Univ. Law* 122 (1996); and Paul Koster, "*Thomas Jefferson University v. Shalala*: Dollars or Sense? The Illogical Restriction of Medicare's Funding of Graduate Medical Education," 12 *J. Contemp. Health L. & Pol'y.* 269 (1995).)

The second U.S. Supreme Court case, *Regions Hospital v. Shalala*, 522 U.S. 448 (1998),[33] resolved other technical issues concerning federal audits of GME costs, in particular audits under the so-called reaudit rule (42 C.F.R. § 413.86(e)), which was later removed and replaced with Subpart F (42 C.F.R. §§ 413.75–413.83). As a result of such a reaudit, Regions Hospital's cost basis for annual GME cost reimbursements was lowered by almost $4 million, thus substantially reducing its "per resident amount" used to compute reimbursements. The hospital (a teaching hospital) challenged the validity of the reaudit rule, arguing that it was invalid because it operated retroactively and because it was not authorized by the terms of Congress's GME Amendment. In an opinion filled with technical statutory interpretation, the Court rejected these arguments and upheld the reaudit rule as a "reasonable interpretation" of the GME Amendment that was within the Secretary's discretion.

In *University of Iowa Hospitals and Clinics v. Shalala*, 180 F.3d 943 (8th Cir. 1999), a teaching hospital challenged the Secretary's calculation of Medicare reimbursement for graduate medical education. The trial court upheld the Secretary's determinations in total and granted her motion for summary

---

[33]In the courts below, the case was styled *St. Paul-Ramsey Medical Center v. Shalala* (see 91 F.3d 57 (8th Cir. 1996)). The hospital changed its name after it was granted Supreme Court review.

judgment. The appellate court agreed with all but one ruling, reversing the summary judgment award on the issue of the documentation of the use of office space. The Secretary had rejected the hospital's claim for reimbursement of the costs of teaching physicians' office space because the hospital did not have contemporaneous documentation of that usage. The court ruled that the rule had been applied retroactively and was not enforceable. Another challenge to the same rule, however, was rejected in *Presbyterian Medical Center of the University of Pennsylvania Health System v. Shalala,* 170 F.3d 1146 (D.C. Cir. 1999).

Another teaching hospital successfully challenged the calculation of GME reimbursement by the intermediary. In *Mercy Catholic Medical Center v. Thompson,* 380 F.3d 142 (3d Cir. 2004), during a reaudit, the hospital had challenged the intermediary's calculations of the hospital's GME costs (classifying them instead as operating costs, which would not be reimbursable as GME costs). The PRRB upheld the intermediary's recommendations. The interpretation of former 42 C.F.R. § 413.86 (now 42 C.F.R. §§ 413.75–413.83) was at issue. The court agreed with the hospital, ruling that the PRRB should have considered the documentation provided during the reaudit process and thus should have reclassified the costs as requested by the hospital.

Increasingly, the federal False Claims Act (FCA) (Section 13.2.15 of this book) is used to enforce Medicare requirements. Private individuals have brought FCA suits, on behalf of the federal government, against health care providers alleging Medicare fraud. (See, for example, *U.S. ex rel. Thompson v. Columbia/HCA Healthcare,* 20 F. Supp. 2d 1017 (S.D. Tex. 1998).) In addition, the civil Monetary Penalty Act (CMPA), codified at 42 U.S.C. § 1320a-7a in the Medicare legislation, provides for monetary penalties and "assessment[s] . . . in lieu of damages" as administrative remedies against persons and organizations that file improper reimbursement claims or engage in other forms of Medicare abuse. (See Pamela Bucy, "Civil Prosecution of Health Care Fraud," 30 *Wake Forest L. Rev.* 693, 737–45 (1995).) Penalties and assessments are levied in proceedings before the Secretary of Health and Human Services, who may also "make a determination . . . to exclude the person [or organization] from participation in Medicare." (See Bucy, above, 30 *Wake Forest L. Rev.* at 720–37.)

On a more global scale, the federal government, through the U.S. Department of Justice (including its U.S. Attorneys' regional offices) and the Office of the Inspector General at the U.S. Department of Health and Human Services, has been conducting investigations and "national enforcement initiatives" on Medicare billing and other forms of Medicare abuse. The threat of a False Claims Act lawsuit is the underlying basis for these investigatory efforts. (For a review of issues related to the investigation of claims of fraud or the misuse of Medicare funds, see Christopher M. Patti, "Managing the Difficult Research Misconduct Case," June 2004, available at http://www.nacua.org.)

13.2.14. Health Insurance Portability and Accountability Act.

This law (the Health Insurance Portability and Accountability Act (HIPAA), Pub. L. No. 104-191, 110 Stat. 1936 (1996), codified in various sections of Titles 18, 29, and 42 of the *United States Code*) has important implications for colleges and universities if they provide health insurance to employees, provide health care to staff or the general public, or transmit personally identifiable health information electronically. Although the law's primary purpose is to assist individuals who were moving from one employer to another to obtain health insurance, it also covers the privacy of an individual's health care information. The law's Privacy Rule creates compliance, training, and data protection issues (and potential liability) for many colleges and universities.[34] The Office of Civil Rights, part of the Department of Health and Human Services, enforces the law. Regulations related to HIPAA are found at 45 C.F.R. Parts 160 and 164. Although HIPAA preempts state laws that conflict with its provisions, state privacy laws that are more protective of individuals' health care information are not preempted by HIPAA. (For a partial summary of relevant state privacy laws, see http://www.healthprivacy.org/resources/statereports/contents.html.)

HIPAA specifically excludes from the definition of personal health information "education records" covered by the Family Educational Rights and Privacy Act (FERPA) (see Section 9.7.1), or education records that are exempt from FERPA under 20 U.S.C. § 1232g(a)(4)(b)(iv) (records made by a doctor, psychiatrist, or other health care provider that are "made, maintained, or used only in connection with the provision of treatment to the student"). For this reason, student health records are not covered by HIPAA, but by FERPA.

Universities with medical schools are covered by HIPAA, as well as those colleges that treat staff at campus health centers, provide counseling for staff, and who use electronic transactions for billing, determining health plan eligibility of employees, or health plan enrollment and disenrollment (45 C.F.R. § 160.103). The regulations define "covered entities" as health plans, health care clearinghouses, and health care providers who transmit "any health information in electronic form in connection with a transaction covered by" the regulations (45 C.F.R. § 160.103).

HIPAA applies to organizations that meet its definition of "covered entity." Organizations that contract with institutions to provide employer-sponsored health plans may be considered to be "covered entities" under HIPAA (45 C.F.R. § 164.501). Such plans include medical insurance plans, dental plans, vision care plans, employee assistance plans, and flexible medical spending accounts. The definition does not include workers' compensation plans, disability insurance, or plans that are self-administered and include fewer than fifty participants. The health plan is the covered entity, and any "outside" individuals or organizations that provide services to the "covered entity" and with which the plan shares information are defined as "business associates" of the "covered entity" and must enter into agreements with respect to the privacy of information that is exchanged (45 C.F.R. §§ 164.502(e), 164.504(e)). Sample business associate contract language can be found at http://www.hhs.gov/ocr/hipaa/contractprov.html.

---

[34]Cases and authorities are collected at Deborah F. Buckman, Annot., "Validity, Construction, and Application of Health Insurance Portability and Accountability Act of 1966 (HIPAA) and Regulations Promulgated Thereunder," 194 A.L.R. Fed. 133.

Institutions that provide health care services, which are defined as any "care, services or supplies related to the health of an individual" (45 C.F.R. § 160.103), must comply with HIPAA. The regulations define health care services as:

> (1) Preventive, diagnostic, therapeutic, rehabilitative, maintenance, or palliative care, and counseling, service, assessment, or procedure with respect to the physical or mental condition, or functional status, of an individual or that affects the structure or function of the body; and (2) Sale or dispensing of a drug, device, equipment, or other item in accordance with a prescription.

Therefore, health centers or counseling centers for staff could be included in the definition, if they transmit personally identifiable health information electronically. Athletic training operations involving medication or physical therapy for student athletes are covered by FERPA.

The regulations allow an institution to decide whether the entire institution will be the "covered entity," or whether it will be a "hybrid entity," in which case only those units that actually meet the definition of providing "health care" will be covered (45 C.F.R. § 164.504(a)–(c)). If the institution chooses to be a "hybrid entity," then release of health information to units that are not involved in HIPAA-related activities will be treated like a "disclosure" to a separate organization. (For a discussion of the policy issues related to deciding whether or not to use the "hybrid entity" provision, as well as a thorough overview of HIPAA and its implications for colleges and universities, see Pietrina Scaraglino, "Complying With HIPAA: A Guide for the University and Its Counsel," 29 *J. Coll. & Univ. Law* 525 (2003).)

HIPAA requires the covered entity to appoint an individual who will develop, supervise, and update privacy policies. It also requires that an individual be designated to receive complaints and to provide information upon request (45 C.F.R. § 164.530(a)(1)). The covered entity must also provide training concerning the Privacy Rule to all employees who work with personal health information or other information covered by HIPAA, to all new employees with such responsibilities, and whenever a "material change" in the covered entity's policies and procedures occurs (45 C.F.R. § 164.530(b)). It must also adopt a procedure for individuals to make complaints about the covered entity's policies and procedures or its compliance with HIPAA regulations (45 C.F.R. § 164.530(d)(1)).

Record-keeping requirements include accounting for disclosures of personal health information, except for those disclosures for which the individual has signed a written authorization and in certain other circumstances. The record of disclosure must be made available to the individual who requests it about him- or herself. Records of disclosures must be maintained for six years. Special provisions are included for disclosures of information for research purposes.

The HIPAA requirements are lengthy, and there is no substitute for careful review of the regulations, reading Department of Health and Human Services guidance documents (including sample contract language), and consulting experienced counsel. Many resources exist to assist administrators and counsel with HIPAA compliance. A good beginning, in addition to the Scaraglino article cited above, is the "Summary of the HIPAA Privacy Rule," available from the Office for Civil Rights at http://www.hhs.gov/privacysummary.pdf. Another helpful resource is Gerald W. Woods, "HIPAA Privacy Rule Primer for the College or University Administrator," available at www.acenet.edu/washington/legalupdate.

The impact of HIPAA is particularly important for research using personal health information, clinical trials, medical school education, and other health-related research and training programs. For example, researchers who may not otherwise be subject to HIPAA nevertheless may be affected by it if they must acquire protected health information from a covered entity. Individual students, staff, and faculty, as well as the institution, may face civil and criminal penalties under HIPAA for unlawful disclosure of personal health information. Individuals who believe their rights under HIPAA have been violated may file complaints with the "covered entity" or with the Office for Civil Rights, Department of Health and Human Services. The law provides for both civil and criminal penalties, including imprisonment (42 U.S.C. § 1320d-6). (For resources on the application of HIPAA to academic research, see *Protecting Personal Health Information in Research: Understanding the HIPAA Privacy Rule*, available at http://privacyruleandresearch.nih.gov/pr_02.asp. For a variety of resources on HIPAA compliance, see http://www.hhs.gov/ocr/hipaa.)

13.2.15. False Claims Act and other fraud statutes.

In addition to enforcement actions that may be brought against the recipients of federal funds, and criminal prosecutions for fraudulent actions involving federal funds, the federal government may bring civil suits under statutes such as the False Claims Act (FCA). Such actions may be brought against institutions or their employees who have engaged in fraudulent activities relating to federal grant or contract funds. When such suits arise from allegations initially made by an employee of the institution that is the subject of the suit (or when an employee makes such allegations even if they are not followed by any lawsuit), the employee will often be protected from retaliation by a federal or state "whistleblower" statute (see Section 4.6.8 of this book).

There has been considerable litigation in recent years under the False Claims Act, 31 U.S.C. § 3729 *et seq.* Not only does the FCA authorize the federal government to bring an action against those who defraud the government, it also authorizes private persons, under a *"qui tam"* provision, to bring suit on behalf of the United States against a "person" who has allegedly made a false monetary claim or false statement to the United States. The successful private plaintiff who proves a violation of the Act may receive between 25 and 30 percent of the damages assessed against the defendant (31 U.S.C. § 3730). The private plaintiff's share may be limited to 10 percent if action is based on publicly disclosed information and to 15 to 25 percent if the government intervenes in the action. The statute provides for civil penalties of not less than $5,500 nor more than $11,000 (see 28 C.F.R. § 85.3 for periodic inflationary adjustments to the penalties), plus three times the amount of damages actually sustained by the federal government. If the U.S. Department of Justice decides to join the litigation, the amount that plaintiffs can recover drops, but the government bears most of the cost of the litigation. In addition to a portion of the damages, the successful *qui tam* plaintiff may receive reasonable attorney's fees as well.

Various legal issues have arisen, especially the issue of whether *public* institutions may be sued under the Act. Following recent trends regarding sovereign immunity (see Section 13.1.6 of this book), various state government agencies, including state colleges and universities, have argued that they are immune under the Eleventh Amendment from False Claims Act suits or, alternatively, that they are not "persons" within the meaning of the FCA and therefore are not covered by it.

Although the federal appellate courts were originally split as to whether states and their agencies were "persons" subject to the False Claims Act, the U.S. Supreme Court settled this issue in *Vermont Agency of Natural Resources v. United States ex rel. Stevens,* 529 U.S. 765 (2000). A division of the Vermont Agency of Natural Resources (VANR) had allegedly required its employees to submit false timesheets that reflected the time that the Agency had submitted to the federal Environmental Protection Agency rather than actual hours the employees had worked. A VANR employee brought suit against the state of Vermont and the VANR under the False Claims Act. The state defended the suit by arguing that the FCA did not impose liability on the states, and furthermore, that such claims against the state would be barred by the Eleventh Amendment. The plaintiff countered by arguing that the statute gives no indication that a state is an improper defendant and that, since the claim is brought on behalf of the federal government, to whom the Eleventh Amendment does not apply, there can be no defense of state sovereign immunity, even if the United States does not intervene in the particular case. The Supreme Court ruled that the False Claims Act's use of "person" did not include states for the purposes of *qui tam* liability. The Court did not address the issue of whether the federal government could sue a state or one of its agencies under the False Claims Act.

The anti-retaliation provisions of the FCA have given rise to attempts to hold individual supervisors liable for alleged FCA violations. In *Yesudian ex rel. United States v. Howard University,* 270 F.3d 969 (D.C. Cir. 2001), the court ruled that only the employer would be liable for FCA violations. (For an overview of the False Claims Act and the litigation process under this statute, see Anna Mae Walsh Burke, "Qui Tam: Blowing the Whistle for Uncle Sam," 21 *Nova L. Rev.* 869 (1997).)

The federal government may fight fraud and abuse in federal spending programs not only by using the False Claims Act, but also by using the Program Fraud Civil Remedies Act of 1986 (PFCRA) (31 U.S.C. §§ 3801–3812), an administrative analogue to the False Claims Act. The PFCRA provides for civil monetary penalties and "assessment(s) in lieu of damages" (31 U.S.C. § 3802) that may be imposed in administrative proceedings of the federal agency operating the spending program in which the alleged fraud occurs (31 U.S.C. § 3803). (A separate but similar statute applicable to Medicare claims is discussed in Section 13.2.13.) The PFCRA does not raise the issue about coverage of the states that is being litigated under the False Claims Act (see above), since the Act expressly omits states from the definition of "persons" subject to the Act (31 U.S.C. § 3801(a)(6)).

Another statute under which the federal government may bring criminal prosecutions against institutions and their employees is 20 U.S.C. § 1097(a), which provides fines and imprisonment for "[a]ny person who knowingly and willfully embezzles, misapplies, steals, or obtains by fraud, false statement, or forgery any funds, assets, or property provided or insured under" the federal student assistance programs. The U.S. Supreme Court case of *Bates v. United States*, 522 U.S. 23 (1997), concerned the application of Section 1097(a) to a technical school's treasurer who had been indicted for allegedly misapplying federally guaranteed loan funds (see this book, Section 8.3.2). The federal district court had dismissed the indictment because it did not allege an intent to injure or defraud the United States. In reversing and reinstating the prosecution, the U.S. Supreme Court held that, although proof of intentional conversion of student aid funds was required, "specific intent to injure or defraud someone, whether the United States or another, is not an element of the misapplication of funds proscribed by § 1097(a)."

Sec. 13.3. *Federal Taxation of Postsecondary Education*[35]

13.3.1. Introduction and overview. Colleges and universities have a substantial stake in the federal tax system. They are subject to numerous filing, reporting, disclosure, withholding, and payment requirements imposed on them by a complex array of Internal Revenue Code provisions and regulations[36] implemented pursuant to Congress's taxing power (see Section 13.1.3). Four categories of federal taxes are of particular importance: (1) income taxes (I.R.C. §§ 1–1563); (2) estate and gift taxes (I.R.C. §§ 2001–2704); (3) employment taxes (including Social Security and Medicare taxes under the Federal Insurance Contributions Act (FICA) and unemployment taxes under the Federal Unemployment Tax Act (FUTA)) (I.R.C. §§ 3101–3501); and (4) excise taxes (I.R.C. §§ 4001–5000). Institutions have large potential financial exposure if they fail to comply with these various federal tax requirements.

Perhaps the most important aspect of the tax laws for colleges and universities is the institutions' tax-exempt status. The tax rules regarding tax-exempt status are discussed below in subsection 13.3.2. The benefits and requirements that tax-exempt status entails for colleges and universities are discussed below in subsections 13.3.3 (the "intermediate sanctions" penalty regime for violations of tax-exempt status requirements) and 13.3.6 (taxes on business income that is unrelated to an organization's tax-exempt purpose).

---

[35]This Section was reorganized and drafted primarily by Randolph M. Goodman, partner at Wilmer, Cutler, Pickering, Hale and Dorr, LLP, Washington, D.C., and Patrick T. Gutierrez, an associate at Wilmer, Cutler, Pickering, Hale and Dorr, LLP.

[36]The Internal Revenue Code ("I.R.C." or the "Code") is Title 26 of the *United States Code.* All statutory Sections cited below are from the Code, unless otherwise indicated. The regulations implementing the Code are in Volume 26 of the *Code of Federal Regulations* and are cited as "Treas. Reg."

In addition to the responsibilities and burdens of tax-exempt status, colleges and universities have many other substantial tax and tax-compliance concerns. For example, they must withhold income and FICA taxes from wages paid to their employees, including students whom they employ, and they must follow detailed rules on taxability, withholding, and reporting for scholarships and fellowships they award to students (see subsection 13.3.4 below for special rules regarding students).

The tax rules may also affect a college or university indirectly. For example, donors to colleges and universities may deduct their gifts from their personal income taxes. This provides a strong incentive to donors and a large source of revenue to institutions, both private and public. Gifts come from many sources (from individuals, corporations, foundations, and trusts) and in many forms (for example, cash, securities, real estate, and intellectual property). The basic rules for charitable contributions are discussed in subsection 13.3.5 below.

Moreover, as colleges and universities become more sophisticated in their corporate structuring and commercialization efforts, these activities add additional levels of tax considerations. Subsection 13.3.7 below discusses some of the considerations involved with related entities and commercialization.

Since federal tax law in general is complex and technical, and the consequences of noncompliance can be substantial, expert advice and support services are essential for most colleges and universities. Ready access to accountants, compensation consultants, and other tax professionals, and to the institution's counsel or outside tax counsel, will all be important.

Moreover, the Internal Revenue Service (the IRS or the Service) and state taxing authorities have become increasingly attentive to tax compliance by colleges and universities. The Service has issued detailed audit guidelines to its agents, discussed in subsection 13.3.8 below, and has been conducting comprehensive tax audits on colleges and universities throughout the country.[37] Congress has likewise become more attentive to tax issues regarding tax-exempt organizations, and in some cases colleges and universities in particular, in areas such as charitable giving, corporate sponsorship, compensation practices, and employee benefit plans.

Today, colleges and universities are often big, and increasingly sophisticated, businesses that employ a large and diverse group of employees and have

---

[37]The IRS also publishes various types of guidance to aid in interpreting the Code and the Treasury regulations. The IRS may issue revenue rulings (stating an IRS position on how the law is applied to a specific set of facts), revenue procedures (providing guidance on procedures to follow in certain situations), technical advice memoranda (publishing guidance furnished by the IRS's Chief Counsel's office in response to an internal IRS request for an interpretation on a technical issue), and Treasury Decisions (providing public pronouncement by the Department of Treasury used for publishing proposed regulations for comment and for issuing temporary and final regulations). On occasion, when the law is unclear and the institution is in need of guidance for some major undertaking with potential tax consequences, counsel may need to obtain a "private letter ruling" from the IRS, which will state the IRS's position on the requestor's particular set of facts (as opposed to a revenue ruling, which involves a generic set of facts). See, for example, H. Massler, "How to Get and Use IRS Private Letter Rulings," 33 *Practical Lawyer* 11 (1987); Rev. Proc. 2005-1, 2005-1 I.R.B. 1 (providing current guidance on how to apply for letter rulings).

operations that range far beyond the traditional campus setting. They have payroll and accounts payable functions requiring internal expertise. They provide pension benefits, health benefits, and other welfare benefits for their employees, often guided by special tax rules that apply exclusively to nonprofits or, in some cases, exclusively to colleges and universities. They also have large numbers of foreign faculty, scholars, researchers, and students that are subject to special tax rules, including rules imposed by tax treaties that have been entered into between the United States and other countries (see Donna E. Kepley & Bertrand M. Harding, Jr., *Nonresident Alien Tax Compliance: A Guide for Institutions Making Payments to Foreign Students, Scholars, Employees, and Other International Visitors* (Artic International, 1996)). They conduct activities in other states and countries, requiring that they pay careful attention to the separate tax laws of these other jurisdictions.

A discussion of all the innumerable tax and tax-related considerations that colleges and universities might face is beyond the scope of this text; only the most important and pervasive aspects of tax law are addressed below. Other examples of important tax concerns include: the taxability of prizes and awards for scientific, educational, artistic, or literary achievements (see I.R.C. § 74); the availability of tax credits for sponsoring university research (see I.R.C. § 41); the taxability of employer-provided educational benefits for employees and their spouses and dependents (see I.R.C. § 127); qualification requirements for employer-sponsored retirement or pension plans (see Randolph M. Goodman, *Retirement and Benefit Planning—Strategy and Design for Businesses and Tax-Exempt Organizations* (Butterworth Legal Publishers, 1994)); and the taxability of grants and fellowships awarded to U.S. and foreign students and scholars (see I.R.C. §§ 117, 871).[38]

13.3.2. Tax-exempt status. Private, nonprofit colleges and universities receive their tax exemptions under I.R.C. Section 501(c)(3). They must apply for exemptions with the IRS by filing federal Form 1023—Application for Recognition of Exemption Under 501(c)(3) of the Internal Revenue Code.[39] Public colleges and universities are automatically exempt from federal income taxes under Section 115, which exempts income of states and their political subdivisions, including public colleges and universities. Some public colleges and universities

---

[38]For a more detailed discussion of various tax issues facing nonprofit organizations in general, see Frances R. Hill & Barbara L. Kirschten, *Federal and State Taxation of Exempt Organizations* (Warren, Gorham & Lamont, 1994).

[39]In most cases, colleges and universities routinely receive their tax exemptions. However, in *Bob Jones University v. United States*, 461 U.S. 574 (1983), the U.S. Supreme Court upheld the Internal Revenue Service's denial of tax-exempt status for Bob Jones University as well as a second plaintiff, Goldsboro Christian Academy, based on their racially discriminatory policies. Bob Jones University prohibited students from interracial dating or marriage, and Goldsboro denied admission to most blacks. The Court determined that "[r]acially discriminatory educational institutions cannot be viewed as conferring a public benefit" within the common law concept of "charity" or "within the congressional intent" underlying both Section 50(c)(3) and Section 170, the provision authorizing deductions for charitable contributions (461 U.S. at 595–96).

have still applied, successfully, for tax exemption under Section 501(c)(3). Although this "extra" status is not required, these public institutions have obtained it largely for symbolic reasons (for example, because Section 501(c)(3) status would be more understandable to potential donors).

A college or university's tax-exempt status provides a number of key advantages that are central to financial stability and accomplishment of long-term objectives. *First,* the institution is exempt from income taxes on its receipts from tuition and, in general, on its endowment earnings (for example, interest, dividends, royalties, and capital gains). An important exception is "unrelated business income taxes," which require private and public institutions to pay income taxes on net income when they conduct an unrelated trade or business (such as selling golf club memberships to the public for a university-owned golf facility) or when they make certain debt-financed investments. These rules are discussed in subsection 13.3.6 below. Another important exception is income from research. These rules are discussed in Section 15.4.4 of this book.

Second, donors to tax-exempt colleges and universities may deduct their gifts from their income taxes. The basic rules for charitable contributions are discussed in subsection 13.3.5 below.

Third, tax-exempt colleges and universities may finance their facilities using not only gifts, internal resources, or regular borrowings from banks or other financial institutions, but also using tax-exempt bonds, which enable colleges and universities to obtain financing at below-market rates. Tax-exempt bonds are typically issued on behalf of private universities by state agencies that assist state educational institutions with facilities financing (see, for example, Section 1.6.3 of this book). These state agencies may also issue tax-exempt bonds for public universities, although it is possible for public universities to issue such bonds directly. Once a tax-exempt bond is issued, the holders of the bonds (which may be institutions, such as banks or insurance companies, or private investors) may exclude the "interest" that is received from their taxable income. Section 103 of the Code excludes from gross income the interest on state or local bonds, even if the bonds are being issued on behalf of another entity such as a college or university. This exclusion provides a very substantial tax benefit to the bondholders, who would otherwise have to pay tax on the interest. This benefit to bondholders allows the issuer to offer a lesser rate of interest than would be offered if the interest were taxable to the holders—that is, holders are willing to accept a lesser interest rate return, often by several percentage points, because their return is tax free. Likewise, of course, universities enjoy the advantage of paying below-market interest, which can reduce substantially the cost of financing academic facilities. Tax-exempt bonds are increasingly the subject of IRS audit activity. The rules regarding them are very complex, and there is a perceived potential for inappropriate use of funds, such as through arbitrage or by private use of the financed facilities.

Fourth, tax-exempt status permits colleges and universities to seek funding from sources that are usually made available only to tax-exempt organizations. These include federal grants and contracts for research or other purposes, as well as funding from private foundations and other charitable organizations.

Fifth, tax-exempt status carries with it a series of other benefits, including exemptions from state property and sales taxes, postal privileges, and some special exemptions and rules that apply in various federal and state statutory schemes, such as the securities and pension laws.

The benefits of tax-exemption for colleges and universities come with responsibilities and burdens. Institutional administrators will need to be aware of, and ensure institutional compliance with, the various filing requirements and public disclosure requirements (see, for example, I.R.C. § 6033(a)(1), and I.R.C. § 6104(e)), that are applicable to colleges and universities, both at the federal and state levels. For example, private institutions must file federal Form 990 on an annual basis, which discloses a great amount of information about their activities, including the compensation paid to officers, trustees, and the five most highly compensated employees. Private and public institutions must properly acknowledge gifts from donors (see I.R.C. § 170(f) for substantiation requirements for contributions of $250 or more). Private institutions must conduct their activities in ways that avoid private inurement and excess benefits or compensation to their key insiders, under threat of losing tax-exempt status or facing intermediate sanctions (see subsection 13.3.3 below). Private and public institutions must monitor their activities to track "unrelated business income" (see subsection 13.3.6 below) and must follow complex operating and reporting rules for tax-exempt bond financing.

13.3.3. Tax-exempt status and intermediate sanctions.

For private colleges and universities, one of the main requirements for tax exemption under Section 501(c)(3) is that "no part of the net earnings of [the organization] inures to the benefit of any private shareholder or individual." This is commonly referred to as the "private inurement test" and is meant to ensure that trustees, officers, and other insiders do not improperly benefit from an organization's tax-exempt status. A college or university that violates the private inurement test is subject to revocation of its tax-exempt status.[40]

Prior to the Taxpayers' Bill of Rights 2 (Pub. L. No. 104-168, signed on July 30, 1996), the IRS did not have a penalty or enforcement mechanism for violations of the private inurement prohibition by public charities, short of revoking the public charity's tax-exempt status. From the point of view of the Service, the threat of revocation of an organization's tax-exempt status was an unwieldy tool for enforcement, impractical for properly addressing other than the most serious violations. From the point of view of the exempt organization, actual revocation of tax-exempt status was an extreme and often unreasonable response that would cripple the organization's operations. In situations in which it deemed revocation inappropriate, the Service was left with negotiating individual closing agreements (settlement agreements) with exempt organizations that had

---

[40]There is also another doctrine known as the "private benefit" doctrine, under which providing excess benefits to any person or entity, whether an insider or not, can be grounds for loss of tax-exempt status. In general, this doctrine is applied to major abuses, whereas the private inurement test can, theoretically, apply even to very small abuses.

engaged in private inurement transactions, allowing the organization to maintain its exempt status while addressing the areas of concern raised by the Service. Such individual agreements were an excessive drain on the Service's time and resources. Moreover, enforcement through individual agreements not only risked unfair and inconsistent application of the law, but these inherently private agreements also did not provide any public guidance upon which other organizations could model their actions.

Another failing of the prior law was that it provided for penalties against the public charity and not against the private individuals who improperly benefited from the violation. Even in situations in which private individuals may have been responsible for the violation, such as through improper use of their authority or influence, it was the public charity that was the most at risk by the revocation of its tax-exempt status.

In the Taxpayers' Bill of Rights 2, Congress sought to address this lack of a proper enforcement mechanism by adding Section 4958—commonly referred to as the "intermediate sanctions"—to the Code. Intermediate sanctions provide for an excise tax (essentially a penalty) upon a disqualified person (and not the public charity) for engaging in an excess benefit transaction.[41] Section 4958 defines a "disqualified person" generally as (1) a person who at any time during the five years preceding the transaction is in a position to exercise substantial influence over the exempt organization, such as a director, president, treasurer, or similar officer; (2) a member of such a person's family; or (3) an entity that is 35 percent controlled by such a person. An "excess benefit" is defined generally as non-fair market value transactions and certain "revenue sharing" transactions that result in private inurement. The excise tax is equal to 25 percent of the excess benefit. An additional tax equal to *200 percent* of the excess benefit is imposed on the disqualified person if the excess benefit transaction is not corrected within a certain period, thus ensuring that the disqualified person does not benefit from the transaction. In addition to the tax on the disqualified person, Section 4958 also imposes a tax equal to 10 percent of the excess benefit on an organizational manager (such as an officer, director, or trustee) who knowingly approves such a transaction. Accordingly, in contrast to prior law, under intermediate sanctions it is the individuals who are responsible for, or who benefit from, the improper transaction who are penalized and not the public charity.

Intermediate sanctions constituted a dramatic change in the legal landscape for public charities. The Service recognized the scope of the change and the importance of involving the affected taxpayers in drafting regulations to flesh

---

[41] *The Committee to Save Adelphi v. Diamandopoulos* (New York Board of Regents 1997) represents an alternative approach for dealing with private inurement issues. The case was a private action brought not against a nonprofit institution itself but against the individual trustees of the school for breach of duty regarding, among other things, the excessive salary and benefits of the school president (including an $82,000 Mercedes and reimbursed expenses such as cognac at $150 a glass). In the action brought before the New York Board of Regents, the governing body for educational institutions in New York, the board removed eighteen of the nineteen trustees of Adelphi University.

out the new rules, a lengthy process that took nearly three and a half years. Final regulations for the intermediate sanctions were issued on January 22, 2002. The regulations provide examples of disqualified persons. In respect to universities, a disqualified person would include voting members of the governing board (that is, the board of trustees or regents), the chief executive officer or chief operating officers (that is, president or chancellor), and the treasurer and chief financial officers. Beyond providing the necessary details to implement Section 4958, the final regulations also provide for a procedure for a public charity to establish a rebuttable presumption of reasonableness for its transactions that involve compensation of a disqualified person. If the public charity follows the proper steps in approving and documenting the approval, the compensation is presumed to be reasonable and the burden shifts to the Service to prove that it is not. This presumption provides a significant procedural benefit in the case of an IRS challenge, and thus is considered a best practices standard.

13.3.4. Tax rules regarding students.
Colleges and universities must be aware of their obligations under the complex tax rules applicable to students, including their obligations to withhold taxes on student wages. Students themselves also often have independent tax reporting and payment obligations regarding amounts they receive as scholarships or fellowships, as well as amounts received as wages if they perform services for their university employers.

Section 117(a) provides that gross income does not include any amount received as a "qualified scholarship" by degree candidates at educational organizations. A qualified scholarship is an amount given as a scholarship or fellowship grant if the amount is used for "qualified tuition and related expenses." These qualified expenses include tuition and required fees for enrollment or attendance, as well as books, supplies, equipment, and fees required for courses of instruction. Notably, expenses for room and board are not included. Under an important exception, qualified scholarships do not include payments by the college or university for teaching, research, or other services that the student performs as a condition for receiving the scholarship.[42]

This statutory tax scheme provides, in effect, three types of treatment for amounts paid or credited to students by universities. *First,* if the payment is a "qualified scholarship" used for qualified expenses, it is completely excludable from the student's income. *Second,* if the payment is not a qualified scholarship, but no services are performed by the student, the payment is taxable to the student as nonwage income. This treatment applies, for example, to the portion of scholarships covering room and board—that is, amounts of the scholarship that exceeded qualified expenses. This treatment also applies to fellowships given to nondegree students, for example, postdoctoral fellows, where there are no services

---

[42]In *Bingler v. Johnson*, 394 U.S. 741 (1969), the U.S. Supreme Court established the requirement that a grantor must have a lack of self-interest in making a payment in order for the payment to be considered a scholarship pursuant to Section 117. The requirement of disinterest distinguishes a scholarship from bargained-for-consideration, such as a promise to work for the grantor.

performed for the university. *Third,* when students perform services for the university, the amounts paid to the students for the services are taxable as wages. This rule applies whether the work by the students is directly related to their education (such as teaching or research assistantships) or is unrelated (such as working in the cafeteria or library as part of a student work-study award).

It is important to allocate properly the amounts paid to students in order to determine the correct reporting and withholding treatment. Generally, amounts paid as qualified scholarships or as nonqualifying scholarships and fellowships for research do not need to be reported on Form 1099 or other tax forms that the institution provides to students. While students must include as income on their personal tax returns any amounts that exceed qualified expenses under a qualified scholarship, this reporting obligation is the students' responsibility. Often, the college or university will provide students with adequate information to permit accurate reporting, and some universities issue Form 1099 for the portion of scholarships or fellowships that are taxable even if they are not required to do so.

A key issue when wages are paid to students is the university's obligations to withhold Federal Insurance Contributions Act (FICA) employment taxes (which serve to fund both Social Security and Medicare). These withholding issues have tended to be an important item for review during IRS audits (see subsection 13.3.8 below). Amounts paid to certain students are exempted from FICA taxes by various statutory provisions. For example, Section 3121(b)(13) exempts income earned by student nurses "in the employ of a hospital or a nurses' training school," provided the individual "is enrolled and is regularly attending classes." For foreign students and scholars, Section 3121(b)(19) provides that "service which is performed by a nonresident alien individual for the period he is temporarily present in the United States" under certain categories of nonimmigrant status, such as a bona fide student, scholar, trainee, teacher, professor, or research assistant (see Section 8.7.4 of this book) is exempted from FICA if the services are performed to carry out the purposes of the visa status.

A broader FICA exemption for students is provided by Section 3121(b)(10), which states that income earned from "services performed in the employ of a school, college, or university," or a related Section 509(a)(3) supporting organization,[43] is not wages subject to FICA taxes "if such service is performed by a student who is enrolled and regularly attending classes at such school, college, or university." There has been an extended series of rulings and guidance over the years from the IRS on the student FICA exemption (see, for example, Revenue Procedure 98-16, 1998-5 I.R.B. 19; Technical Advice Memorandum 9332005 (May 3, 1993); Revenue Ruling 78-17, 1978-1 C.B. 306). On December 21, 2004, the Service issued final regulations that provide additional guidance (Treasury Decision 9167, 69 Fed. Reg. 76404–01), and also issued Revenue Procedure 2005-11, 2005-2 I.R.B. 307, which provides new safe harbor standards superceding those established in the prior

---

[43]A 509(a)(3) supporting organization is a separate tax-exempt organization that is affiliated with and operated for the benefit of a college or university. Supporting organizations are often used as special purpose vehicles, for example, university presses or fund-raising foundations.

guidance under Revenue Procedure 98-16. The new final regulations clarify the definitions of "school, college, or university" and "classes," as used in Section 3121(b)(10), and provide factors to be considered in determining whether the person performing the employment services should be treated as a student, as opposed to a regular employee, for purposes of the exemption. One factor, for example, is whether the person is a career employee, or is entitled to certain employment benefits.

Similar exemption issues may also arise under the Federal Unemployment Tax Act (FUTA) with respect to colleges' and universities' obligation to contribute to the federal, or a state, unemployment compensation fund.[44] There are exemptions for FUTA regarding contributions on behalf of student workers that mirror the withholding exemptions for FICA. For example, Section 3306(c)(10)(B) provides an exemption regarding wages paid to students; Section 3306(c)(13) provides an exemption regarding student nurses and medical interns; and Section 3306(c)(19) provides an exemption for nonresident aliens who are bona fide students or scholars.

There are various other tax issues, and available tax benefits, that affect students. Among the most pertinent are the following:

- Section 117(d) governs the tax status of qualified tuition reduction plans for employees and their dependents. In general, this section excludes from gross income the amount of any tuition reduction for employees or their dependents who are taking undergraduate courses either at the institution where they are employed or at another college or university that grants a tuition reduction to employees of that institution. To maintain this tax-free treatment, however, the institution must award tuition reduction assistance in a way that does not discriminate in favor of highly compensated employees.

- Section 117(d) also has special rules for tuition reduction for teaching and research assistants, authorizing graduate students engaged in teaching and research to exclude from gross income a reduction in tuition that is not compensation for their teaching and research.

- Section 529 governs "qualified state tuition programs" (QSTPs), which are prepaid tuition programs or contribution programs sponsored by the states. Section 529 exempts QSTPs from federal taxation except for any unrelated business income they may generate. It also governs the tax treatment of contributions to a QSTP and of payments to beneficiaries from a QSTP.

- Section 108(f) provides an exclusion from income for the forgiveness of student loans where forgiveness is contingent upon the person agreeing

---

[44]The purpose of the Federal Unemployment Tax Act is to generate revenues that may be used for unemployment benefits for qualifying employees who are temporarily out of work. The federal government and the states share responsibility for the Act's operation. The Act provides a very narrow exemption for some church-related postsecondary institutions (see § 3309(b)(1), and *St. Martin Evangelical Lutheran Church v. South Dakota*, 451 U.S. 772 (1981)).

to public service work (for instance, providing medical services in rural or isolated areas where there is a shortage).

- Section 135 provides that, for certain taxpayers and their dependents, the proceeds from redemption of U.S. Savings Bonds are not taxable if they are used for "qualified higher education expenses."

- Section 221 provides for deductions for interest paid on "qualified education loans."

- Section 222 provides deductions for "qualified tuition and related expenses."

- Section 25A establishes tuition tax credits—the HOPE Scholarship Credit and the Lifetime Learning Credit—that are intended to be a widely available type of indirect financial aid for students. The tuition credits, however, also impose substantial reporting requirements on colleges and universities, which must file information returns with the IRS and issue payee statements to students who receive one of the tuition credits (see I.R.C. § 6050S).

13.3.5. *Gifts and contributions.* The tax laws have an enormous impact on the ability of colleges and universities to attract gifts from alumni and other donors who wish to support higher educational institutions or specific institutional programs or activities.

The tax rules that apply to gifts made to Section 501(c)(3) public charities likewise apply generally to colleges and universities, whether private or public institutions. The rules for donors' charitable deductions are set forth in Section 170. An individual donor is permitted to take a deduction not to exceed 50 percent of the individual's "contribution base" for the year with respect to contributions to eight listed types of organizations, including "an educational organization that normally maintains a regular faculty and curriculum and normally has a regularly enrolled body of pupils or students in attendance at the place where the educational activities are regularly carried on" (see I.R.C. § 170(b)(1)(A)(ii)). Charitable deductions by a corporation are generally limited to 10 percent of taxable income. There are many intricate rules that apply to charitable gifts, including limits on contributions of capital gain property, valuation and substantiation requirements, and carryovers and carrybacks of excess contributions in a year.

In addition, there are rules that allow unlimited charitable deductions for estate and gift tax purposes (see I.R.C. §§ 2055, 2522).[45]

Charitable contributions to colleges and universities take many forms, including cash, securities, real estate, oil and gas property interests, insurance policies and proceeds, limited liability company and partnership interests, retirement plan assets and Individual Retirement Accounts, intellectual property, art, and

---

[45]*The Harvard Manual on Tax Aspects of Charitable Giving* (8th ed., Harvard University Planned Giving Office, 1999), by David M. Donaldson & Carolyn M. Osteen, provides an excellent discussion of the various rules and requirements, as well as other insights on charitable giving to colleges and universities.

books. Colleges and universities are often wary of taking certain kinds of gifts for reasons such as environmental liabilities from real property, or exposure to unrelated business income taxes for S corporation, limited liability company (LLC), or partnership interests.

Donors often make charitable contributions directly (for example, by check, credit card, transfer of title, or actual delivery) as straightforward transfers or, in some cases, as bargain sales. Major donors also frequently use techniques that accomplish their own individual and estate planning needs, and that sometimes provide them with income generated from the funds donated for a period of years or for their lives and the lives of their spouses or beneficiaries. Examples of the latter include gift annuities, pooled income funds, pledges, and charitable lead trusts, charitable remainder annuity trusts, and unitrusts. (See David M. Donaldson & Carolyn M. Osteen, *The Harvard Manual on Tax Aspects of Charitable Giving* (8th ed., Harvard University Planned Giving Office, 1999); and BNA Tax Management Portfolios 521–2d, *Charitable Contributions: Income Tax Aspects,* by Barbara L. Kirschten & Carla Neeley Freitag, which provide excellent discussions of various methods used for charitable contributions.) Many gifts are also restricted to a particular use—for example, an endowed chair—or are subject to subsequent donor advice regarding their use.

A detailed explanation of the tax rules on giving is well beyond the scope of this book. However, some special charitable rules that primarily or exclusively affect colleges and universities have received particular attention in recent years. For example, one subsection of Section 170 limits the deduction available to donors for amounts contributed to a university in exchange for the right to purchase school athletic tickets. The American Jobs Creation Act of 2004 revised another subsection of Section 170 to limit the amount that can be immediately deducted for donations of patent or other intellectual property (other than certain copyrights), but provides for future deductions for the next twelve years based on the "qualified donee income" resulting from the donated intellectual property (see I.R.C. § 170(m), as amended by the American Jobs Creation Act of 2004, Pub. L. No. 108-311, § 882, signed on October 22, 2004). In the gift tax area, the Code provides for an exclusion from gift tax for prepaid tuition (see I.R.C. § 2503(e)). One of the more unique rules is the exclusion from income available to "officers or employees of the Federal Government" who assign income that they are entitled to receive to a charity—for instance, a Senator who has a speaking honorarium paid to a college instead of himself or herself (see I.R.C. § 7701(k)).

13.3.6. The unrelated business income tax.

Income that a public or private college or university generates from unrelated business activities, regularly carried on, is subject to the unrelated business income tax, often referred to as UBIT.[46] Under I.R.C. §§ 511–514, this income is subject to UBIT

---

[46]The unrelated business income tax explicitly applies not only to private colleges and universities that are exempt under Section 501(c)(3), but also to public colleges and universities (see I.R.C. § 512(a)(2)).

if the activities are conducted directly or through partnerships (including an LLC that is treated as a partnership) in which the institution is a member (see I.R.C. § 512(c)).

UBIT applies when the institution or partnership receives income from providing services or selling goods unless these activities are within the exempt purposes of the organization—for example, teaching and research, but typically excluding product and clinical testing. (See I.R.C. § 513(a); Treas. Reg. § 1.513-1(a), (d); see also I.R.C. § 512(b)(7), (8), (9) with respect to income derived from research activities.) Services that are arguably related to the institution's exempt purposes, such as management and administrative services, must be carefully analyzed to determine whether they have become "unrelated" under developing IRS interpretations (see, for example, Tech. Adv. Mem. 9711002 (April 21, 1995); IRS Private Letter Ruling 9617031 (January 26, 1996)). Rents from equipment or personal property are also generally taxable unless the personal property is rented with real property, and the rent attributable to the personal property is incidental to the total rent paid (see I.R.C. § 512(b)(3)). The mere fact that the revenues from such activities subsidize the exempt organization is not a sufficient basis for avoiding UBIT (see I.R.C. § 513(a)).

There are important statutory exemptions from UBIT. One of the most important is the exemption for a trade or business that is conducted "by the organization primarily for the convenience of its members, students, patients, officers, or employees" (see I.R.C. § 513(a)(2)).[47] This exemption covers a number of basic activities of a college or university, such as a laundry the institution operates for the purpose of laundering dormitory linens and the clothing of students, officers, or employees; or vending machines located in dormitories and other campus buildings. Sales of textbooks by a campus bookstore are directly related to a school's educational purpose and thus not subject to UBIT, but the exemption would also allow a bookstore to sell noneducational related supplies, such as toiletries, snacks, and beverages.

Another important exemption from UBIT is passive investment income. Thus, dividends, interest, royalties, rents from real property, and gains or losses from the sale or disposition of property that is not inventory or property held primarily for sale in a trade or business, are not generally subject to UBIT (see I.R.C. § 512(b)).[48] On the other hand, some categories of income that include passive income may be taxable in limited circumstances. Payments from controlled entities (more than 50 percent ownership

---

[47]By statute, UBIT also does not apply to income from a trade or business where "substantially all the work in carrying on [the] trade or business is performed for the organization without compensation" (see I.R.C. § 513(a)(1)), or to income from the "selling of merchandise substantially all of which has been received by the organization as gifts or contributions" (see I.R.C. § 513(a)(3)).

[48]Section 512(b) also provides rules for measuring the amount of income; for example, royalties may be measured by production or by gross or net receipts (see I.R.C. § 512(b)(2); Treas. Reg. § 512(b)-1(b)), while rents may be measured by gross, but not by net, revenue from the property (see I.R.C. § 512(b)(3)).

in a corporation or partnership, and including exempt and nonexempt organizations) are considered unrelated income if the controlled entity claims the payment as a deduction in computing its own taxes, for example, interest payments on a debt, royalties, or real property rentals (see I.R.C. § 512(b)(13)). The proportionate share of income generated by an S corporation (that is, a small business corporation that elects pass-through treatment for income of the corporation) is also taxable to the exempt organization even if it is passive income (see I.R.C. § 512(e)), as is gain on the sale of S corporation stock.

There is another category of UBIT—unrelated debt-financed income under Section 514—that applies the tax to income generated from debt-financed property owned by the exempt organization directly or indirectly through an interest in a partnership or LLC. There are certain exceptions, such as an exemption for property used in research or in performing exempt functions (see I.R.C. § 514(b)(1)(A), (C)). Debt-financed property is property with respect to which there is acquisition indebtedness, such as a mortgage or an equity indebtedness incurred to improve the property. If property is only partially debt financed, then a pro rata share of the income is subject to UBIT. There is a special exemption from UBIT for real property if the property is subject to indebtedness incurred to acquire or improve the property (see I.R.C. § 514(c)(9)).

When a college or university receives unrelated business income, it must file a federal UBIT tax return, as well as a tax return in any state in which it is doing business (see I.R.C. § 6033; Treas. Reg. § 1.6033-2(a)(2); Federal Form 990T and instructions).[49]

UBIT is imposed on the net income from unrelated business activities, meaning that the exempt organization may claim appropriate deductions that are directly connected to the gross income from unrelated business activities (see I.R.C. § 512(a)(1)). Also, net losses from one taxable activity may be used to offset net income from other taxable activities. However, losses from exempt activities may not offset taxable income (see IRS Private Letter Ruling 8532009 (April 29, 1985); see also I.R.C. § 512(b)(6) regarding the allowance of net operating loss deductions in computing UBIT).

Institutions must maintain careful records that permit the identification of taxable and exempt income, as well as related expenses. Some organizations have faced taxation on gross unrelated business income due to the failure to account properly (or maintain proper records) for expenses that are directly attributable to taxable, as opposed to exempt, income. A common problem, for example, concerns segregating the costs attributable to exempt royalty income from the costs attributable to taxable sales or services. Provisions for proper accounting and record keeping are necessary in any joint venture that may produce both exempt and taxable income. Similarly, institutions need to consider

---

[49]If the unrelated business income is received from a pass-through entity, such as a partnership or LLC, then state returns need to be filed by the exempt organization in any state where the pass-through entity is doing business.

whether a revenue stream that is typically exempt from UBIT, such as royalties, can become subject to UBIT because there are additional services performed as part of the arrangement.[50]

The fact that a particular investment opportunity may result in unrelated business income should not in itself counsel rejection. Exempt status is not placed at risk where unrelated activities are not substantial in relation to overall exempt function activities. UBIT arising from a potential revenue stream should, of course, be taken into account in valuing a particular business opportunity.

13.3.7. Related entities and commercialization.

Colleges and universities have become increasingly complex legal enterprises. Many institutions exist as single legal entities (or as an arm of a state or local government). It has become common, however, for colleges and universities to have various parts of their operations conducted through other entities (see generally Section 3.6 of this book). Academic medical centers and affiliated or controlled hospitals, for instance, are often separately incorporated from their "parent" universities. In addition, there may be a host of other entities that are affiliated with or controlled by college or universities. These include supporting organizations, related foundations, and nonprofit affiliates whose boards of directors are appointed in whole or part by the university. Often colleges and universities also own substantial, controlling, or sole interests in for-profit entities. These for-profit entities may be corporations, S corporations, partnerships, or LLCs.

The reasons for conducting activities through separate entities vary widely with the particular facts. Most of the time, the reasons are not tax related (except, notably, when a for-profit activity is so large that it could endanger the institution's tax-exempt status). Common reasons are to achieve limited liability, to have a separate management or governance structure, to have focused financial accountability, to commercialize an invention or other intellectual property, or to allow different forms of compensation than the university typically uses (for example, equity-based compensation in a for-profit subsidiary). University presses, technology transfer operations, investment operations, spin-offs of commercial entities, and foreign ventures are frequently, but certainly not universally or exclusively, considered as appropriate activities to place in a separate entity.

---

[50]In a series of highly publicized cases, organizations have been successful in challenging the imposition of UBIT on royalties received from affinity card arrangements, where the IRS had argued that additional services "tainted" the royalty stream. See *Sierra Club v. Commissioner*, T.C. Memo 1999-86; *Sierra Club v. Commissioner*, 86 F.3d 1526 (9th Cir. 1996); *Mississippi State Alumni Association, Inc. v. Commissioner*, T.C. Memo 1997-397; *Oregon State University Alumni Association v. Commissioner*, T.C. Memo 1996-34; *Alumni Association of the University of Oregon v. Commissioner*, T.C. Memo 1996-63. See generally *Texas Farm Bureau v. Commissioner*, 53 F.3d 120 (5th Cir. 1995); Tech. Adv. Mem. 9440001 (June 17, 1994). To the extent that any significant services performed are otherwise exempt from UBIT, such as education or research, or are performed under a separate and distinct arrangement, such as for administrative or marketing services unrelated to the royalties, there should presumably be no tainting of royalties for UBIT purposes.

Tax considerations become important in deciding what type of entity the college or university should use to accomplish its purposes. A separate tax-exempt affiliate will need to apply for and obtain Section 501(c)(3) status (see subsection 13.3.2 above). A for-profit corporation pays taxes on its net income, so a college or university would not want to conduct activities through this type of entity that it could otherwise conduct directly on a tax-free basis. Examples would be nondegree education and research. A college or university that is a partner in a partnership, or a member of a limited liability company, will be treated as receiving directly its share of the income, deductions, and losses of that entity for tax purposes. This could result in unrelated business income tax exposure to the college or university, depending on the nature of the activities conducted by the partnership or LLC. Separate entities will also frequently require separate payrolls, with the attendant tax reporting and withholding obligations, as well as separate benefit programs. The separate entity may not be eligible to provide certain types of benefits, such as a Section 403(b) retirement program, if the entity is not itself tax exempt under Section 501(c)(3); and it will not be able to provide tuition reduction benefits if it does not qualify as an educational organization (see subsection 13.3.4 above).

There may be additional tax consequences to consider if the separate entity is dissolved, sold, or its assets are distributed to its parent. The unrelated business income tax rules (see I.R.C. § 512(b)(13)) provide that payments from controlled entities (more than 50 percent ownership in a corporation or partnership, and including exempt and nonexempt organizations) are considered unrelated income if the controlled entity claims the payment as a deduction in computing its own taxes (for example, a deduction for interest on a debt, royalties, or real property rentals). The general rule is that a sale of stock by a Section 501(c)(3) organization is exempt from unrelated business income taxes. The sale of partnership and limited liability company interests may have greater complexity, particularly where the partnership or LLC has debt that could result in unrelated business income taxes on the sale based on treatment as debt-financed property taxable under Section 514.

The IRS has instructed its agents to examine affiliates as part of its audit process (see subsection 13.3.8 below). While there are many issues that may arise, one area that is drawing increased attention is ensuring that multiple entities are not used as a means to pay excessive compensation.

13.3.8. IRS audit guidelines.
The IRS has increased its audit activities regarding colleges and universities. This development is not surprising given the size of many institutions, the expanding scope of their operations, and the complexity of the laws affecting them. In the early 1990s, the IRS recognized that both its agents and the colleges and universities themselves would benefit from guidelines for audits. After receiving comments from the public on a proposed version, the IRS released "Final Examination Guidelines for Colleges and Universities," Announcement 94-112 (August 25, 1994), commonly called the "IRS Guidelines." They "are intended to provide a framework which agents may follow in conducting the examination." They also serve as a roadmap and a

primer for colleges and universities on the various tax issues the IRS is likely to pursue in an audit and on the various document requests it is likely to make.

The IRS Guidelines identify various documents that an examiner may want to review during an audit. These include traditional documents such as financial statements and minutes of board of trustees' meetings, as well as more college-specific documents such as accreditation reports, student newspapers, and athletic coaches' financial disclosures to the NCAA.

The IRS Guidelines also identify specific issues that an examiner will want to review during the course of the audit. The following are examples of some of these issues:

- *Employment taxes.* Colleges and universities typically have a large number of employees, so there are a number of basic tax issues that would apply to any large employer, such as ensuring proper reporting. More specific to colleges and universities are issues such as the student FICA/FUTA exemptions discussed in subsection 13.3.4 above. Colleges and universities also often have independent contractor tax issues, specifically whether they have properly classified someone as an independent contractor as opposed to an employee (see generally Section 4.2 of this book).

- *Services performed by nonresident aliens.* When foreign students or scholars perform compensated services for their university, federal tax issues may arise (see above), as well as special issues concerning tax treaties.

- *Fringe benefits.* In addition to exploring traditional fringe benefit issues, such as qualifications for a cafeteria plan, IRS examiners are advised to focus on numerous college and university issues such as the provision of automobiles, parking, flights on school aircraft, personal transportation for postseason athletics, awards, prizes, free or discounted tickets to school functions, subsidized dining rooms, meals, insurance, housing allowances, club memberships, use of athletic facilities, tuition assistance, and other educational assistance. There are a number of school-specific exemptions for colleges and universities in the Internal Revenue Code, such as the Section 119(d) exclusion for qualified campus lodging and the Section 117(d) qualified tuition reduction rules.

- *Retirement or pension plans and other deferred compensation arrangements.* In addition to standard qualification issues that must be reviewed for qualified retirement plans, there are also plans that are specific to 501(c)(3) entities or public schools, such as Section 403(b) retirement plan or eligible deferred compensation plans under Section 457.

- *Contributions.* Universities and colleges, like other tax-exempt organizations, receive large amounts of money from contributions. The IRS Guidelines advise examiners to review traditional issues such as the provision of receipts, appraisals, or benefits to the donor (*quid pro quo* contributions), and reporting requirements such as Form 8283 for gifts in excess of $5,000 and Form 8282 (Donee Information Return) for property that is disposed of by the donee within two years of the donation. Examiners also review the terms and management of endowment funds and other restricted donations. In addition, there are university-specific and college-specific issues, such as donations made for the right to purchase athletic tickets or for naming rights, as with a building. (See generally subsection 13.3.5 above.)

- *Financing activities.* In regard to financing activities, examiners are advised to review interest rates and terms of loan agreements, compared to rates that were available on the market, to determine (among other things) if there was an improper benefit conveyed. If the college or university raises funds through the issuance of tax-exempt bonds, there will also be numerous issues that a tax-exempt bond specialist will need to review.

- *Research and contracts.* The IRS Guidelines advise examiners to review the funding of research, whether it is through research contracts, joint ventures, spin-off companies, commercial licenses, clinical trial agreements, or other means. In addition to the potential UBIT issues, there may be issues with accounting for the sharing of royalties with the faculty inventors and even non-tax issues such as conflicts of interest. (See Randolph M. Goodman & Linda A. Arnsbarger, "Trading Technology for Equity: A Guide to Participating in Start-Up Companies, Joint Ventures and Affiliates" (Matthew Bender, 1999) (reprinted from the Proceedings of the New York University 27th Conference on Tax Planning for 501(c)(3) Organizations).)

- *Scholarships and fellowships.* As discussed in subsection 13.3.4, there are special rules for the award of scholarships and fellowships. The guidelines advise the examiner to confirm the proper application of these rules and the reporting of the amounts of awards.

- *Legislative and political activities and expenses.* Tax-exempt status under Section 501(c)(3) requires that "no substantial part of the activities of [the college or university] is carrying on propaganda, or otherwise attempting, to influence legislation." Moreover, the college and university must "not participate in, or intervene in (including the publishing or distributing of statements), any political campaign on behalf of (or in opposition to) any candidate for public office" (see I.R.C. § 501(c)(3)). Because a private school's tax exemption is tied to this restriction, the examiner must look into this matter, especially since the restriction has been interpreted to permit some on-campus activities (for example, open debates, or certain activities for a course on campaigning) (see IRS Guidelines § 342.(12); Rev. Rul. 72-512, 1972-2 C.B. 246).

- *University bookstores.* Nearly all colleges and universities have a bookstore, a large part of whose sales are exempted from UBIT. As discussed in subsection 13.3.6, institutions are able to sell supplies and other items that are necessary for the courses that the institution offers, since the courses and thus the supplies are substantially related to the institution's tax-exempt purposes. Sales of other materials that further the intellectual life of the campus community—for example, books, tapes, records, and computer hardware and software—are also exempt from UBIT. In addition, proceeds from items sold primarily for the convenience of the student or employee—such as toiletries, wearing apparel, candy, and cigarettes are also exempt. The exemption, however, is not a blanket exemption; it is limited, for example, to sales to students, officers, and employees of the institution.

- *Other UBIT issues.* The guidelines also advise examiners to review various other UBIT issues. One example concerns income from the rental of university facilities for purposes unrelated to the school, such as the rental of an auditorium for a private party. Another example concerns income from auxiliary enterprises that many colleges and universities operate, such as hotels, motels, and parking lots (see Section 15.3.4.1).

- *Related entities.* As discussed in subsection 13.3.7 above, subsidiaries and other affiliated entities are becoming more common among colleges and universities. Examiners are therefore advised to review carefully the interactions between the various entities for issues such as improper accounting, improper reporting, and private inurement.

Sec. 13.4. Federal Aid-to-Education Programs

13.4.1. Functions and history. The federal government's major function regarding postsecondary education is to establish national priorities and objectives for federal spending on education and to provide funds in accordance with those decisions. To implement its priorities and objectives, the federal government attaches a wide and varied range of conditions to the funds it makes available under its spending power (Section 13.1.2) and enforces these conditions against postsecondary institutions and against faculty members, students, and other individual recipients of federal aid. Some of these conditions are specific to the program for which funds are given. Other "cross-cutting" conditions apply across a range of programs; they are discussed in Section 13.4.4 below. The nondiscrimination requirements discussed in Section 13.5 are also major examples of cross-cutting conditions. Cumulatively, such conditions have exerted a substantial influence on postsecondary institutions, and have sometimes resulted in institutional cries of economic coercion and federal control. There have periodically also been charges that the federal government provides insufficient funds for higher education or that its priorities are misguided. In light of such criticisms, the federal role in funding postsecondary education has for many years been a major political and policy issue. The particular national goals to be achieved through funding and fund conditions, the adjustment of priorities, and the delivery and compliance mechanisms best suited to achieving these goals will likely remain subjects of debate for the foreseeable future.

Federal spending for postsecondary education has a long history. Shortly after the founding of the United States, the federal government began endowing public higher education institutions with public lands. In 1862, Congress passed the first Morrill Act, providing grants of land or land scrip to the states for the support of agricultural and mechanical colleges, for which it later provided continuing appropriations. The second Morrill Act, providing money grants for instruction in various branches of higher education, was passed in 1890. In 1944, Congress enacted the first GI Bill, which was followed in later years by successive programs providing funds to veterans to further their education. The National Defense Education Act, passed in 1958 after Congress was spurred by Russia's launching of *Sputnik,* included a large-scale program of low-interest loans for students in institutions of higher education. The Higher Education Facilities Act of 1963 authorized grants and low-interest loans to public and private nonprofit institutions of higher education for constructing and improving various educational facilities. Then, in 1965, Congress finally jumped broadly into supporting higher education with the passage of the Higher Education Act of 1965 (20 U.S.C. § 1001 *et seq.*). The Act's various titles authorized federal support for a range of postsecondary education activities, including community educational services; resources, training, and research for college libraries and personnel; strengthening of developing institutions; and student financial aid programs (see Section 8.3.2). The Act has been frequently amended since 1965 and continues to be the primary authorizing legislation for federal higher education spending.

13.4.2. Distinction between federal aid and federal procurement.

Funds provided under the Higher Education Act and other aid programs should be sharply distinguished from funds provided under federal procurement programs. Many federal agencies, such as the U.S. Department of Defense, enter into procurement contracts with postsecondary institutions or consortia, the primary purpose of which is to obtain research or other services that meet the government's own needs. True aid-to-education programs, in contrast, directly serve the needs of institutions, their students and faculty, or the education community in general, rather than the government's own needs for goods or services. The two systems—assistance and procurement—operate independently of one another, with different statutory bases and different regulations, and often with different agency officials in charge. Guidelines for differentiating the two systems are set out in Chapter 63 of Subtitle V of 41 U.S.C.: "Using Procurement Contracts and Grant and Cooperative Agreements."

The bases of the federal procurement system are Title III of the Federal Property and Administrative Services Act of 1949 (41 U.S.C. § 251 *et seq.*), the Office of Federal Procurement Policy Act of 1974 (41 U.S.C. § 401 *et seq.*), the Armed Services Procurement Act (10 U.S.C. § 2301 *et seq.*), the Federal Acquisition Regulation (FAR) (48 C.F.R. ch. 1); and other miscellaneous public contract provisions (found particularly in 41 C.F.R. chs. 50–61). These sources establish uniform policies and procedures that individual agencies implement and supplement with regulations specific to their own procurement activities. The individual agency regulations are set out in 48 C.F.R. Chapters 2–49.

Federal procurement law permits federal agencies to exercise more substantial control over the details of procurement contracts than is typical with grants and other forms of federal aid; many standard clauses that must be used in procurement contracts are prescribed by federal regulations (see 48 C.F.R. §§ 16.1–16.7). Unlike assistance, moreover, procurement contracts "shall terminate . . . , whether for default or convenience, only when it is in the government's interest" (48 C.F.R. § 49.101(b) (1992)). Government contractors found guilty of fraud, embezzlement, antitrust violations, or other criminal or civil offenses impugning business integrity may be debarred or suspended for a specified time from obtaining other government contracts (48 C.F.R. §§ 3.104–3.111 (1992)). Contractors may appeal disputes concerning their government contracts to agency Boards of Contract Appeals, established pursuant to the Contract Disputes Act (41 U.S.C. § 601 *et seq.*), or may bypass this appeals process and bring an action directly in the U.S. Court of Federal Claims (41 U.S.C. § 609(a)(1)).

Other important federal laws also establish requirements applicable to the federal procurement system. Executive Orders 11246 and 11375 (Section 5.2.8 of this book), for instance, establish affirmative action requirements for federal government contractors. Similarly, the Davis-Bacon Act (40 U.S.C. § 276a *et seq.*), as implemented by Department of Labor regulations (29 C.F.R. Part 5), establishes rate-of-pay requirements for employees working under federal construction contracts. The Service Contract Labor Standards Act (41 U.S.C. § 351 *et seq.*) and its implementing regulations (29 C.F.R. Part 4) establish comparable requirements for employees working under federal service contracts.

Although laws such as these are designed for the procurement system rather than the federal aid system, they are often extended to federal aid recipients who enter procurement contracts as a means of accomplishing part of their work under a federal grant, loan, or cooperative agreement. (See, for example, 20 U.S.C. § 1232b (application of Davis-Bacon Act to procurement contracts of Department of Education (ED) aid recipients); 48 C.F.R. § 22.300 *et seq.* (application of Davis-Bacon Act, Executive Orders 11246 and 11375, and Contract Work Hours and Safety Standards Act (40 U.S.C. § 327 *et seq.*), to procurement contracts of ED aid recipients); 29 C.F.R. § 5.2(h) and 41 C.F.R. § 60-1.1 (application of Davis-Bacon Act and Executive Order 11246 to procurement contracts of other federal aid recipients).)

The Department of Defense, the General Services Administration, and the National Aeronautics and Space Administration have proposed a series of amendments to the Federal Acquisition Regulation. The proposed rule is published at 64 Fed. Reg. 37360–37361 (July 9, 1999). One section of the proposed rule, which would amend 48 CFR § 9.104-1(d), apparently supports the disqualification of a prospective federal contractor for "lack of compliance with tax laws, or substantial noncompliance with labor laws, employment laws, environmental laws, anti-trust laws or consumer protection laws. . . ."

13.4.3. Legal structure of aid programs. Federal aid for postsecondary education is disbursed by a number of federal agencies. The five most important are the U.S. Department of Education, the U.S. Department of Health and Human Services, the National Foundation on the Arts and Humanities

(comprised of the National Endowment for the Humanities, the National Endowment for the Arts, and the Institute of Museum Services), the National Science Foundation, and (at least with respect to student aid) the Department of Veterans Affairs.

Federal aid to postsecondary education is dispensed in a variety of ways. Depending on the program involved, federal agencies may award grants or make loans directly to individual students; guarantee loans made to individual students by third parties; award grants directly to faculty members; make grants or loans to postsecondary institutions; enter "cooperative agreements" (as opposed to procurement contracts) with postsecondary institutions; or award grants, make loans, or enter agreements with state agencies, which in turn provide aid to institutions or their students or faculty. Whether an institution is eligible to receive federal aid, either directly from the federal agency or a state agency or indirectly through its student recipients, depends on the requirements of the particular aid program. Typically, however, the institution must be accredited by a recognized accrediting agency or demonstrate compliance with one of the few statutorily prescribed substitutes for accreditation (see Section 14.3).

The "rules of the game" regarding eligibility, application procedures, the selection of recipients, allowable expenditures, conditions on spending, records and reports requirements, compliance reviews, and other federal aid requirements are set out in a variety of sources. Postsecondary administrators will want to be familiar with these sources in order to maximize their institution's ability to obtain and effectively utilize federal money. Legal counsel will want to be familiar with these sources in order to protect their institution from challenges to its eligibility or to its compliance with applicable requirements.

The starting point is the statute that authorizes the particular federal aid program, along with the statute's legislative history. Occasionally, the appropriations legislation funding the program for a particular fiscal year will also contain requirements applicable to the expenditure of the appropriated funds. The next source, adding specificity to the statutory base, is the regulations for the program. These regulations, which are published in the *Federal Register* (Fed. Reg.) and then codified in the *Code of Federal Regulations* (C.F.R.), are the primary source of the administering agency's program requirements. Title 34 of the *Code of Federal Regulations* is the Education title, the location of the U.S. Department of Education's regulations.

Published regulations have the force of law and bind the government, the aid recipients, and all the outside parties. In addition, agencies may supplement their regulations with program manuals, program guidelines, policy guidance or memoranda, agency interpretations, and "Dear Colleague" letters. These materials generally do not have the status of law; although they may sometimes be binding on recipients who had actual notice of them before receiving federal funds, more often they are treated as agency suggestions that do not bind anyone (see 5 U.S.C. § 552(a)(1); 20 U.S.C. § 1232). Additional requirements or suggestions may be found in the grant award documents or agreements under which the agency dispenses the aid, or in agency grant and contract manuals that establish general agency policy.

Yet other rules of the game are in executive branch directives or congressional legislation applicable to a range of federal agencies or their contractors or grantees. The circulars of the executive branch's Office of Management and Budget (OMB), for instance, set government-wide policy on matters such as allowable costs, indirect cost rates, and audit requirements. These circulars are available from OMB's home page at http://www.whitehouse.gov/omb/circulars. One of the most important of these circulars is OMB Circular A-21, titled "Cost Principles for Educational Institutions."

Another circular of particular importance to higher education is OMB Circular A-110, "Uniform Administration Requirements for Grants and Agreements with Institutions of Higher Education, Hospitals, and Other Non-Profit Organizations." This circular seeks to standardize the administration of federal grants in the various executive branch administrative agencies. A revision to OMB Circular A-110, published at 64 Fed. Reg. 54926 (October 8, 1999), clarifies an institution's obligation to respond to federal Freedom of Information Act (FOIA) requests for research data gathered under federal research grants. The revisions require that such data be made available only after publication in a journal or upon citation or use by an agency official as part of an agency action that has the force and effect of law. Accordingly, FOIA requesters may not obtain any preliminary part of researchers' work or any physical object associated with the research. Nor, under this revision, may requesters obtain research material that contains trade secrets, commercial information, or certain other confidential matter such as personal medical information.

An example of legislation that sets general requirements is the Single Audit Act of 1984, as amended, codified at 31 U.S.C. § 7501 *et seq.,* which establishes uniform requirements for audits of state and local governments and non-profit organizations that receive federal financial assistance or federal "cost-reimbursement contracts" from federal agencies. This Act has been implemented by the OMB via OMB Circular A-133, "Audits of States, Local Governments, and Non-Profit Organizations."

Another example of general legislation is the Byrd Amendment (31 U.S.C. § 1352), which limits the use of federal funds for lobbying activities. This provision provides in part that:

(a)(1) None of the funds appropriated by any Act may be expended by the recipient of a Federal contract, grant, loan, or cooperative agreement to pay any person for influencing or attempting to influence an officer or employee of any agency, a Member of Congress, an officer or employee of Congress, or an employee of a Member of Congress in connection with any Federal action described in paragraph (2) of this subsection.

   (2) The prohibition in paragraph (1) of this subsection applies with respect to the following Federal actions:

     (A) The awarding of any Federal contract.

     (B) The making of any Federal grant.

     (C) The making of any Federal loan.

     (D) The entering into of any cooperative agreement.

     (E) The extension, continuation, renewal, amendment, or modification of any Federal contract, grant, loan, or cooperative agreement.

Applicants for federal assistance must certify that they are and will remain in compliance with this requirement, and they must also disclose certain lobbying activities paid for with nonfederal funds. The Office of Management and Budget promulgated Interim Final Guidance for implementing the Byrd Amendment in December 1989 (54 Fed. Reg. 52306–52311 (December 20, 1989)). The OMB guidance required that the executive departments and agencies promulgate two sets of common rules to implement the amendment: one set for procurement contracts to appear in the Federal Acquisition Regulation; and one set for nonprocurement contracts, grants, loans, cooperative agreements, loan insurance commitments, and loan guarantee commitments. Both the Department of Defense and the Department of Education have issued final regulations implementing the Byrd Amendment (32 C.F.R. § 28.100 *et seq.,* and 34 C.F.R. § 82.100 *et seq.*).

There is also a federal statute, the General Education Provisions Act (GEPA) (20 U.S.C. § 1221 *et seq.*), that applies specifically and only to the U.S. Department of Education. The Act establishes numerous organizational, administrative, and other requirements applicable to ED spending programs. For instance, the Act establishes procedures that ED must follow when proposing program regulations (20 U.S.C. § 1232). The GEPA provisions on enforcement of conditions attached to federal funds do not apply, however, to Higher Education Act programs (20 U.S.C. § 1234i(2)). To supplement GEPA, the Department of Education has promulgated extensive general regulations published at 34 C.F.R. Parts 74–81. These "Education Department General Administrative Regulations" (EDGAR) establish uniform policies for all ED grant programs. The applicability of Part 74 of these regulations to higher education institutions is specified at 34 C.F.R. §§ 74.1(a), 74.4(b), and 81.2. Running to well over 100 pages in the *Code of Federal Regulations,* EDGAR tells you almost everything you wanted to know but were afraid to ask about the legal requirements for obtaining and administering ED grants.

Other funding agencies also have general regulations that set certain conditions applicable to a range of their aid programs. Several agencies, for example, have promulgated regulations on research misconduct. These regulations are discussed in Section 13.2.3.4 of this book. Similarly, some agencies have promulgated "rules of the game" on financial conflicts of interest. These provisions are discussed in Section 15.4.7 of this book.

13.4.4. *"Cross-cutting" aid conditions.* In addition to the programmatic and fiscal requirements discussed in Section 13.4.2 above, various statutes and agency regulations establish requirements that are not specific to any particular aid program but, rather, implement broader federal policy objectives that "cut across" a range of programs or agencies. The civil rights statutes and regulations discussed in Section 13.5 are a prominent example. Others are the requirements concerning the privacy of student records (discussed in Section 9.7.1) and campus security (discussed in Section 8.6). Other leading examples are discussed in Sections 13.4.4.1 through 13.4.4.3 below. The growth and increasing variety of these "cross-cutting" requirements mark what is perhaps the most significant contemporary trend regarding federal involvement in postsecondary education.

Concern over student alcohol and drug use has stimulated Congress to enact cross-cutting provisions that impose additional reporting and compliance requirements on the recipients of federal funds. In 1998, Congress enacted the "Collegiate Initiative to Reduce Binge Drinking and Illegal Alcohol Consumption" as Section 119 of the Higher Education Amendments of 1998, which includes mandates for federally funded colleges and universities (112 Stat. 1596, codified at 20 U.S.C. § 1011i). This provision conditions federal funding on a requirement that an institution has "implemented a program to prevent the use of illicit drugs and the abuse of alcohol by students and employees . . ." (20 U.S.C. § 1011i(a)). The standards that each program must meet are set out in the legislation. The institution must disseminate certain information to students and employees annually and to the U.S. Department of Education and the public on request. In conjunction with these requirements, there is also a system of grants and contracts for the development of innovative drug and alcohol abuse programs on campus (20 U.S.C. § 1011i(e)).

In addition, in yet another section of the 1998 Higher Education Amendments, Congress took more drastic action concerning campus drug abuse. Section 483(f)(1), codified at 20 U.S.C. § 1091(r), bars students who have been convicted of certain drug-related offenses from receiving federal financial assistance. This law is discussed further in Section 8.3.2.

Congress has also passed various federal funding restrictions designed to prevent institutional interference with Reserve Officer Training Corps (ROTC) programs and with military recruiting on campus. These restrictions are often popularly referred to as the "Solomon Amendment," after the congressman who originally introduced them. The law, codified at 10 U.S.C. § 983, provides that institutions of higher education or their "subelements" that prevent ROTC access or military recruiting on campus will be denied grants and contracts from the Departments of Defense, Homeland Security, Transportation, Education, Health and Human Services, Labor, and certain "Related Agencies" (10 U.S.C. § 983(d)). Federal student financial aid funds are exempt from this legislation (Pub. L. No. 106-79, 113 Stat. 1212, 1260 (1999)). If the institution has no such restrictions, but one or more of its "subelements" prevent military recruiting, the "subelement" loses federal funding from all of the federal agencies listed above, while the institution loses only funds from the Department of Defense (32 C.F.R. § 216.3(b)(1)). Such funds may not be provided to any college or university (or one or more subelements) that has, as determined by the Secretary of Defense, "a policy or practice" that either prohibits the military from "obtaining, for military recruiting purposes, entry to campuses, access to students on campuses, or access to directory information on students (student recruiting information)" or prohibits the military from "maintaining, establishing, or efficiently operating a unit of the Senior ROTC at the covered school," or prevents a student from enrolling in an ROTC unit at another college or university (32 C.F.R. §§ 216.3 & 216.4). Exceptions to the funding limitations are found at 32 C.F.R. § 216.4.

Law school faculty, students, and law student organizations filed several legal challenges to the Solomon Amendment. In *Forum for Academic and Institutional*

Rights (FAIR), Inc. v. Rumsfeld, 291 F. Supp. 2d 269 (D.N.J. 2003), *reversed and remanded,* 390 F.3d 219 (3d Cir. 2004), a coalition of law schools, law faculty, and student associations challenged the constitutionality of the Solomon Amendment in federal court. The plaintiffs claimed that the Solomon Amendment conditioned federal funding on the law schools' giving up their First Amendment freedom of speech and expressive association rights by requiring that the schools admit military recruiters to campus. The plaintiffs also claimed that the law discriminated on the basis of viewpoint because it required the law schools to espouse a pro-military recruiting message, punishing those schools (by making them ineligible for federal grants and contracts) that found the military's position on homosexuality "morally objectionable." Finally, the plaintiffs alleged that the statute was unconstitutionally vague in that it allowed the military "unbridled discretion" in determining which institutions to target for noncompliance. The plaintiffs sought a preliminary injunction to halt the enforcement of the law.

The U.S. government filed a motion to dismiss, arguing that the association of law schools lacked standing to bring the lawsuit because their parent universities were the appropriate parties to the litigation. The federal trial judge disagreed, ruling that because the law schools had the autonomy to develop their own nondiscrimination policies, which the Solomon Amendment required them to suspend in order to allow military recruitment at the law schools, they had demonstrated a "concrete injury fairly traceable to the Solomon Amendment," which was "the government-induced abandonment of the schools' nondiscrimination" (291 F. Supp. 2d at 286). Similarly, the court determined that the law student associations and the association of law professors also had standing to challenge the law.

The court rejected the plaintiffs' motion for a preliminary injunction, however, ruling that the Solomon Amendment did not violate the Constitution. Despite the fact that the statute requires law schools to offer "affirmative assistance" to military recruiters, said the court, it did not restrict either speech or academic freedom of students or faculty, nor did it limit the plaintiffs' ability to openly and publicly disagree with the military's policy on homosexuals. Because the recruiters' presence did not significantly intrude on the ability of the plaintiffs to express their views, and because the forbidden behavior and its potential consequences were very clear in the language of the statute, said the court, the plaintiffs did not have a strong probability of prevailing on the merits, and thus the preliminary injunction motion was denied.

A three-judge panel of the U.S. Court of Appeals for the Third Circuit, in a 2-to-1 decision, reversed the district court and remanded the case for the entry of a permanent injunction against the enforcement of the Solomon Amendment. With respect to the plaintiffs' claim that the Solomon Amendment violated their First Amendment right of expressive activity, the court, relying on *Boy Scouts of America v. Dale,* 530 U.S. 640 (2000) (discussed in Section 10.1 of this book), applied strict scrutiny (discussed in Section 8.2.5 of this book). Under *Dale,* said the court, the group claiming a violation of its right of expressive association must demonstrate (1) that it is an expressive association, (2) that the state action being challenged "significantly affects the group's ability to advocate its viewpoint," and (3) that the state's interest "justifies the burden it imposes on the group's expressive association" in that the state's interest is compelling and is narrowly tailored to achieve that interest. The court concluded that law schools are "highly" expressive organizations, and that the Solomon Amendment placed a substantial burden on the law school's expressive associational rights under the deferential standard articulated in *Dale*. Furthermore, said the court, the law's provisions to deny federal funding to institutions or "subelements" was not narrowly tailored, as there was no evidence that on-campus recruiting was the most effective mechanism for attracting talented lawyers to military service.

With respect to the plaintiffs' claim that the Solomon Amendment was a form of compelled speech, the court ruled that the law required the law schools to "propagate, accommodate, and subsidize" the military's recruiting message. Providing services to help military recruiters schedule appointments, communicating with students about the presence of military recruiters at the law school, and providing resources to assist the military in arranging for its campus visits constitute compelled speech, said the court, and the recently added provision that military recruiters must be given the same quality of access to students as that given to other types of employers did not even allow the law school to disclaim the military's policies on homosexuals. Given the requirements of the law, said the court, it conflicted with the First Amendment's prohibition on compelled speech.

Although the court stated firmly that the Solomon Amendment should be analyzed under the strict scrutiny test because of its burdens on expressive association, the court briefly considered whether the law would survive the intermediate scrutiny test of *United States v. O'Brien*, 391 U.S. 367 (1968), which is applied to governmental regulations that only incidentally burden expressive conduct rather than burdening speech. While disavowing the *O'Brien* test as inappropriate in this case, the court concluded that the Solomon Amendment was likely to impair expressive conduct as well. Because the United States had not presented evidence that enforcement of the Solomon Amendment had enhanced on-campus recruiting, there was no showing of an important governmental interest at stake, a necessity to a finding that a law survives the *O'Brien* test. In fact, said the court, it was equally plausible that stricter enforcement of the Solomon Amendment actually hampered military recruiting because of the strong negative reaction on campus to the military's policies with respect to homosexuals.

The U.S. government sought review by the U.S. Supreme Court, which ruled unanimously (8-0) that the Solomon Amendment does not violate the First Amendment (*Rumsfeld v. FAIR*, 126 S. Ct. 1297). Chief Justice Roberts, for the Court, rejected the appellate court's reasoning in full, ruling that the Solomon Amendment neither requires the law schools to endorse the military's policies nor prohibits the law schools from criticizing them, and thus does not regulate or compel speech. Nor, said the Court, does the Solomon Amendment regulate expressive conduct, in that the conduct required of the law schools by the Solomon Amendment is not "inherently expressive." Said the Court: "If combining speech and conduct were enough to create expressive conduct, a regulated party could always transform conduct into 'speech' simply by talking about it" (2006 U.S. LEXIS 2025 at *34). And finally, the Court rejected the appellate court's ruling that the Solomon Amendment violated the law schools' freedom of expressive association, noting that the law merely required law school employees to interact with military recruiters, not to offer them membership (unlike the state law requiring the Boy Scouts to allow gay scoutmasters to join, as discussed in the *Dale* case, cited above). The Court concluded with this observation:

> Students and faculty are free to associate to voice their disapproval of the military's message; nothing about the statute affects the composition of the group by making group membership less desirable. The Solomon Amendment therefore does not violate a law school's First Amendment rights. A military recruiter's mere presence on campus does not violate a law school's right to associate, regardless of how repugnant the law school considers the recruiter's message [2006 U.S. LEXIS 2025 at *39–40].

State colleges and universities in Connecticut found themselves caught between the Solomon Amendment and the state's nondiscrimination law that prohibited discrimination on the basis of sexual orientation. In 1996, the Connecticut Supreme Court ruled that the state's nondiscrimination law precluded state colleges and universities from allowing military recruiters on campus (*Gay Law Students v. Board of Trustees*, 673 A.2d 484 (Conn. 1996)). The Department of Defense threatened to cut off federal funding to the state university in response to the court ruling. In 1997, the Connecticut legislature enacted Conn. Gen. Stat. § 10a-149c, which states that each public college and university "shall provide access to directory information and on-campus recruiting opportunities to representatives of the armed forces . . . to the extent necessary under federal law to prevent the loss of federal funds . . ." (§ 10a-149c(a)).

As an additional condition for obtaining federal funding, colleges and universities in states that are not covered by certain parts of the National Voter Registration Act (see Section 13.2.1) are required to encourage students to register to vote. Section 489(b) of the Higher Education Amendments of 1998, Pub. L. No. 105-244, 112 Stat. 1581, 1750, codified at 20 U.S.C. § 1094(a)(23). This section requires that institutions "make a good faith effort to distribute a mail voter registration form, requested and received from the State, to each student enrolled in a degree or certificate program and physically in attendance at the institution, and to make such forms widely available to students at the institution."

13.4.4.1. Drug-Free Workplace Act of 1988. The Drug-Free Workplace Act of 1988 (41 U.S.C. § 701 *et seq.*) applies to institutions of higher education that contract with a federal agency to provide services or property worth at least the amount of the "simplified acquisition threshold" (currently $100,000 (41 U.S.C. § 403(11))) or that receive a grant from a federal agency for any amount.[51] To

---

[51]In addition to the requirements of the Drug-Free Workplace Act, some higher education institutions that contract with the Department of Defense will also be subject to that department's separate Drug-Free Workplace regulations, which are found at 32 C.F.R. Part 26.

qualify for such a contract or grant, an applicant institution must certify to the contracting or granting agency that it will undertake various activities to provide a drug-free workplace. Grantees' activities must include:

(A) publishing a statement notifying employees that the unlawful manufacture, distribution, dispensation, possession, or use of a controlled substance is prohibited in the grantee's workplace and specifying the actions that will be taken against employees for violations of such prohibition;

(B) establishing a drug-free awareness program to inform employees about—
   (i) the dangers of drug abuse in the workplace;
   (ii) the grantee's policy of maintaining a drug-free workplace;
   (iii) any available drug counseling, rehabilitation, and employee assistance programs; and
   (iv) the penalties that may be imposed upon employees for drug abuse violations;

(C) making it a requirement that each employee to be engaged in the performance of such grant be given a copy of the statement required by subparagraph (A);

(D) notifying the employee in the statement required by subparagraph (A), that as a condition of employment on such grant, the employee will—
   (i) abide by the terms of the statement; and
   (ii) notify the employer of any criminal drug statute conviction for a violation occurring in the workplace no later than 5 days after such conviction;

(E) notifying the granting agency within 10 days after receiving notice of a conviction under subparagraph (D)(ii) from an employee or otherwise receiving actual notice of such conviction;

(F) imposing a sanction on, or requiring the satisfactory participation in a drug abuse assistance or rehabilitation program by, any employee who is so convicted, as required by section 7033 of this title; and

(G) making a good faith effort to continue to maintain a drug-free workplace through implementation of subparagraphs (A), (B), (C), (D), (E), and (F) [41 U.S.C. § 702(a)(1)].

Section 706(2) of the Act defines "employee" as any employee of the grantee or contractor "directly engaged in the performance of work pursuant to the provisions of the grant or contract."

The Act also applies to individuals who receive a grant from a federal agency or who contract with a federal agency for any amount. Such individuals must certify that they "will not engage in the unlawful manufacture, distribution, dispensation, possession, or use of a controlled substance" in conducting grant activities or performing the contract (41 U.S.C. §§ 701(a)(2) & 702(a)(2)). Recipients of Pell Grants (see Section 8.3.2) are not considered to be individual grantees for purposes of this Section (20 U.S.C. § 1070a(i)).

Under Sections 701(b)(1) and 702(b)(1), contracts and grants (including contracts and grants to individuals) are "subject to suspension of payments . . . or termination . . . or both" and contractors and grantees are "subject to suspension or debarment" if they make a false certification, or violate their certification, or if so many of their employees have been convicted under criminal drug statutes for violations occurring in the workplace as to indicate the contractor's or grantee's failure to "make a good faith effort to provide a drug-free workplace."

The final regulations for grantees, entitled "Government-Wide Requirements for Drug-Free Workplace (Grants)" (55 Fed. Reg. 21681 (May 25, 1990)), are in the form of a common rule that was codified in various sections of the *Code of Federal Regulations* in the form adopted by each individual agency. The Department of Education regulations, for example, are codified in 34 C.F.R. Part 84. The regulations for contractors are in a separate final rule amending the Federal Acquisition Regulation, codified at 48 C.F.R. subpart 23.5.

The final grantee regulations include helpful advice in the form of public comments on the previous interim final rule, followed by the agencies' responses (55 Fed. Reg. at 21683–21688). The responses indicate, among other things, that the Act does not require grantees to have alcohol and drug abuse programs, nor does the Act require drug testing (at 21684–85). There are also responses prepared by the U.S. Department of Education that address several matters, including the certifications required under the various student financial aid programs (at 21688).

(See generally Larry White, *Complying with "Drug-Free Workplace" Laws on College and University Campuses* (National Association of College and University Attorneys, 1989).)

13.4.4.2. Drug-Free Schools and Communities Act Amendments. The Drug-Free Schools and Communities Act Amendments of 1989 (103 Stat. 1928) require institutions receiving federal financial assistance to establish drug and alcohol programs for both students and employees. Specifically, the Act, now codified at 20 U.S.C. § 7101, was incorporated into the Higher Education Act in 2002 (Pub. L. No. 107-110, § 401). Regulations implementing the law are codified at 34 C.F.R. Part 86, and require institutions to distribute the following materials annually to all students and employees:

(1) standards of conduct that clearly prohibit, at a minimum, the unlawful possession, use, or distribution of illicit drugs and alcohol by students and employees on its property or as a part of any of its activities;

(2) a description of the applicable legal sanctions under local, State, or Federal law for the unlawful possession or distribution of illicit drugs and alcohol;

(3) a description of the health risks associated with the use of illicit drugs and the abuse of alcohol;

(4) a description of any drug or alcohol counseling, treatment, or rehabilitation or re-entry programs that are available to employees or students; and

(5) a clear statement that the institution will impose sanctions on students and employees (consistent with local, State, and Federal law), and a description of those sanctions, up to and including expulsion or termination of employment and referral for prosecution, for violations of the standards of conduct required by paragraph (a)(1) [34 C.F.R. § 86.100].

In addition, institutions must biennially review their programs to determine their effectiveness, to implement changes if needed, and to ensure that the required sanctions are being carried out. Upon request, institutions must provide to the Secretary of Education or to the public a copy of all materials they are required to distribute to students and employees and a copy of the report from the biennial review.

The statute does not require institutions to conduct drug tests or to identify students or employees who abuse alcohol. However, if an institution has notice that a student or an employee has violated one of the standards of conduct promulgated under the statute, it must enforce its published sanctions. The statute also does not require institutions to operate treatment programs; institutions must, however, notify students of counseling and treatment programs that are available to them.

In enforcing the standards of conduct and sanctions required by the statute, institutions should, of course, comply with the requirements of constitutional due process (Sections 6.6.2 & 9.4.2; see also Section 1.5.2) as well as the record-keeping requirements of FERPA (Section 9.7.1).

13.4.4.3. Student Right-to-Know Act. The Student Right-to-Know Act (Title I of the Student-Right-to-Know and Campus Security Act) (104 Stat. 2381–2384 (1990)) amended Section 485 of the Higher Education Act (20 U.S.C. § 1092) to impose information-sharing requirements on higher education institutions that participate in federal student aid programs. Section 103 (20 U.S.C. § 1092(a)(1)(L)) requires such institutions to compile and disclose "the completion or graduation rate of certificate-or-degree-seeking, full-time students" entering the institutions. Disclosure must be made both to current students and to prospective students. Section 104 of the Act (20 U.S.C. § 1092(e)) includes additional compilation and disclosure requirements applicable to those institutions that are "attended by students receiving athletically related student aid"; these requirements are discussed in Section 10.4.1 of this book.

13.4.5. Enforcing compliance with aid conditions. The federal government has several methods for enforcing compliance with its various aid requirements. The responsible agency may periodically audit the institution's expenditures of federal money (see, for example, 20 U.S.C. § 1094(c)(1)(A)) and may take an "audit exception" for funds not spent in compliance with program requirements (see, for example, 20 U.S.C. § 1094(c)(1)(A) & (c)(5)–(7)). The institution then owes the federal government the amount specified in the audit exception. In addition to audit exceptions, the agency may suspend or terminate the institution's funding under the program or programs in which noncompliance is found (see 34 C.F.R. §§ 74.61, 75.901, & 75.903). Special provisions have been developed for the "limitation, suspension, or termination" of an institution's eligibility to participate in the Department of Education's major student aid programs (20 U.S.C. § 1094(c)(1)(D), (c)(1)(F), & (c)(3)(A); 34 C.F.R. §§ 668.85–668.98); see also 34 C.F.R. § 682.713 (disqualifications in FFEL programs) and 34 C.F.R. §§ 668.185–668.198) (loan default rate proceedings)). Agencies are sometimes also authorized to impose civil monetary penalties on institutions that fail to comply with program requirements. Under Title IV of the Higher Education Act, for example, the U.S. Department of Education may impose a civil monetary penalty on institutions that have violated any program requirements in Title IV or its implementing regulations, or have "engaged in substantial misrepresentation of the nature of its educational program, its financial charges, or the employability of its graduates" (20 U.S.C. § 1094(c)(1)(F) & (c)(3)(B); 34 C.F.R. §§ 668.84 & 668.92). And under the Clery Act (Campus Security Act), 20 U.S.C. § 1092(f), the department may impose civil penalties on any institution that has "substantially misrepresented the number, location, or nature of the crimes required to be reported . . ." (20 U.S.C. § 1092(f)(13)). The procedures to be used are those in 20 U.S.C. § 1094(c)(3)(B) (above).

Federal funding agencies also apparently have implied authority to sue fund recipients in court to enforce compliance with grant and contract conditions, although agencies seldom exercise this power. In *United States v. Frazer*, 297 F. Supp. 319 (M.D. Ala. 1968), a suit against the administrators of the Alabama state welfare system, the court held that the United States had standing to sue to enforce welfare grant requirements that personnel for federally financed programs be hired on a merit basis. In *United States v. Institute of Computer Technology*, 403 F. Supp. 922 (E.D. Mich. 1975), the court permitted the United States to sue a school that had allegedly breached a contract with the U.S. Office of Education, under which the school disbursed funds for the Basic Educational Opportunity Grant program. In *United States v. Duffy*, 879 F.2d 192 (6th Cir. 1989), and other similar cases, courts have permitted the federal government to sue recipients of health professions scholarships for breach of contract for failing to perform their required service commitments. And in *United States of America v. Miami University*, 294 F.3d 797 (6th Cir. 2002), the court permitted the United States, on behalf of the U.S. Secretary of Education, to sue two universities to enforce compliance with the nondisclosure provisions of the Federal Education Rights and Privacy Act (FERPA) (see Section 9.7.1 of this book). According to the court: "Even in the absence of statutory authority, the United States has the inherent power to sue to enforce conditions imposed on the recipients of federal grants" (*Id.* at 808, citing U.S. Supreme Court cases).

The federal government may also bring both civil suits and criminal prosecutions under the False Claims Act, 31 U.S.C.A. § 3729, against institutions or institutional employees who have engaged in fraudulent activities relating to federal grant or contract funds (see S. D. Gordon, "The Liability of Colleges and Universities for Fraud, Waste, and Abuse in Federally Funded Grants and Projects," 75 *West's Educ. Law Rptr.* 13 (August 13, 1992). In addition, the federal government may fight fraud and abuse in federal spending programs by using the Program Fraud Civil Remedies Act of 1986 (PFCRA), Pub. L. No. 99-509, codified as 31 U.S.C. §§ 3801–3812, which is an administrative analogue to the False Claims Act. The PFCRA provides for civil monetary penalties and "assessment(s) in lieu of damages" (31 U.S.C. § 3802) that may be imposed in administrative proceedings of the federal agency operating the spending program in which the alleged fraud occurs (31 U.S.C. § 3803). The PRCRA expressly omits states from the definition of "persons" subject to the Act (31 U.S.C. § 3801 (a)(6)). (The False Claims Act and the PFCRA are further discussed in Section 13.2.15 of this book; a separate but similar statute applicable to Medicare claims is discussed in Section 13.2.13.) When such suits and claims arise from allegations initially made by an employee of the institution that is the subject of the complaint (or when an employee makes such allegations even if they are not followed by any lawsuit or administrative hearing), the employee will often be protected from retaliation by the False Claims Act or a state "whistleblower" statute (see P. Burling & K. A. Mathews, *Responding to Whistleblowers: An Analysis of Whistleblower Protection Acts and Their Consequences* (National Association of College and University Attorneys (1992)).

In addition to the False Claims Act, another statute under which the federal government may bring criminal prosecutions against institutions and their employees is 20 U.S.C. § 1097(a), which provides fines and imprisonment for "[a]ny person who knowingly and willfully embezzles, misapplies, steals, obtains by fraud, false statement, or forgery, or fails to refund any funds, assets, or property provided or insured under" the federal student assistance programs. The case of *Bates v. United States,* 522 U.S. 23 (1997), concerned the application of Section 1097(a) to a technical school's treasurer who had been indicted for allegedly misapplying Guaranteed Student Loan Program funds. The federal district court had dismissed the indictment because it did not allege an intent to injure or defraud the United States. In reversing and reinstating the prosecution, the U.S. Supreme Court held that, although proof of intentional conversion of student aid funds was required, "specific intent to injure or defraud someone, whether the United States or another, is not an element of the misapplication of funds proscribed by § 1097(a)."

In some circumstances private parties may also be able to sue institutions to enforce federal grant or contract conditions. For example, courts permit persons harmed by institutional noncompliance to bring an implied "private cause of action" to enforce the nondiscrimination requirements imposed on federal aid recipients under the civil rights spending statutes (see Section 13.5.9 of this book). For other types of requirements, however, courts have been less willing to permit such causes of action. In *Gonzaga University v. Doe,* 536 U.S. 273 (2002), for example, the U.S. Supreme Court rejected an implied private cause of action to enforce the Family Educational Rights and Privacy Act (FERPA) (discussed in Section 9.7.1 of this book). According to the Court, it will recognize such causes of action only when the federal statute "create(s) new individual rights." The "text and structure of [the] statute" must clearly and unambiguously indicate "that Congress intends to create" such rights before a court will permit private plaintiffs to enforce the statute by implied causes of action. FERPA did not meet this test. Similarly, courts usually have not permitted plaintiffs to use private causes of action to enforce the Higher Education Act (HEA) (see Section 13.4.1 of this book). In *L'ggrke v. Benkula,* 966 F.2d 1346 (10th Cir. 1992), and *Slovinec v. DePaul University,* 332 F.3d 1068 (7th Cir. 2003), for example, federal appellate courts held that student borrowers do not have any implied private cause of action against postsecondary institutions that allegedly have violated the HEA. And in *McCulloch v. PNC Bank, Inc.,* 298 F.3d 1217 (11th

Cir. 2002), another federal appellate court held that parents of college-bound students do not have any private cause of action against student loan marketers and lenders for alleged violations of HEA requirements.

In other circumstances, some federal statutes may create an express private cause of action by which private parties may sue institutions in their own name, or in the name of the federal government. The False Claims Act (discussed above), for example, authorizes not only suits by the federal government but also *"qui tam"* suits—suits by a private individual or "informer" on behalf of himself and the United States. State colleges and universities, however, are not subject to *qui tam* suits under the False Claims Act (see *Vermont Agency of Natural Resources v. United States ex. rel. Stevens*, 529 U.S. 765 (2000)). *Qui tam* suits under the False Claims Act are further discussed in Section 13.2.15 of this book.

In addition to all these means of enforcement, Executive Order 12549 requires that departments and agencies in the executive branch participate in a government-wide system for debarment and suspension of eligibility for nonprocurement federal assistance. The Office of Management and Budget has promulgated debarment and suspension guidelines, as provided in Section 6 of the Executive Order, and individual agencies have promulgated their own agency regulations implementing the executive order and the OMB guidelines. The Department of Education's regulations are published at 34 C.F.R. Part 85. These regulations apply to any person "against whom the Department . . . has initiated a debarment or suspension action," as well as any person "who has been, is, or may reasonably be expected to be a participant" in transactions under Federal nonprocurement programs (§ 85.105). The covered transactions are set out in §§ 85.200–85.220. Section 85.811 contains special provisions concerning the effect of debarment or suspension on an educational institution's participation in student aid programs under Title IV of the Higher Education Act.

13.4.6. Protecting institutional interests in disputes with funding agencies.

Given the number and complexity of the conditions attached to federal spending programs, and the federal government's substantial enforcement powers, postsecondary institutions will want to keep attuned to all the procedural rights, legal arguments, and negotiating leverage they may have if a dispute with a federal funding agency arises.[52] The institution's legal position and negotiating strength, and the available avenues for settling disputes, will depend in large part on the applicable "rules of the game" (see subsection 13.4.3 above) for the program and agency involved. They will also depend on whether the institution is applying to receive aid or participate in a funding program, being subjected to a compliance review, being threatened with an audit exception, or being threatened with a fund cut-off or termination of program participation. Typically, applicants have fewer procedural rights than recipients do; and

---

[52]This Section deals primarily with "adjudicative" types of disputes. For discussion of rulemaking, see Section 13.6.1 below.

recipients subject to a fund cut-off or termination of program participation typically have the greatest array of procedural rights.

Under the various statutes and regulations applicable to federal aid programs, fund recipients usually must be given notice and an opportunity for a hearing prior to any termination of funding (see, for example, 20 U.S.C. § 1094(c)(1)(D) & (c)(2)(A)) or any termination (or suspension or limitation) of program participation (see 20 U.S.C. § 1094(b) & (c)(1)(F), and *Continental Training Services, Inc., v. Cavazos,* 893 F.2d 877, 881–89 (7th Cir. 1990)). Hearings may also be required before finalization of audit exceptions taken by federal auditors (see, for example, 20 U.S.C. § 1094(b)). If the applicable statutes and regulations do not specify notice and hearing requirements prior to termination or suspension of federal funding, or prior to recoupment of funds by audit exception, fund recipients may assert the Fifth Amendment due process clause as a source of procedural rights. The argument would be that the recipient of the funds has a property or liberty interest in retention of the funds and benefits, and that the funding agency cannot infringe this interest without first according the recipient basic procedural safeguards (see *Continental Training Services, Inc. v. Cavazos,* 893 F.2d 877, 892–94 (1990)). In addition to such formal dispute resolution procedures, federal funding agencies may also have various informal mechanisms—for example, mediation—for the settlement of disputes. (See Section 13.6.1 below for discussion of these mechanisms.)

Postsecondary institutions have two basic types of legal arguments that they may use in formal or informal agency proceedings to challenge an agency action: procedural arguments and substantive arguments. Using procedural arguments, an institution may assert that the dispute resolution procedures that the agency is using are inconsistent with an applicable statute, an agency regulation, or (alternatively) the procedures courts have required under the Fifth Amendment due process clause. In addition, an institution may occasionally be able to argue that the rule the agency is enforcing was not promulgated in compliance with applicable rule-making procedures. Using substantive arguments, an institution may assert that the agency is acting beyond the scope of its authority, that the agency has incorrectly interpreted the statutory provision or agency regulation at issue, or that the agency has incorrectly applied the statute or regulation to the facts of the case.

In addition to these various ways that institutions may represent their interests within an agency's administrative processes, institutions may also be able to obtain judicial review of federal funding agency decisions that affect them adversely. Questions about the availability of judicial review arise when an institution is unsuccessful defending itself in the administrative process and seeks to have an unfavorable administrative decision reversed by a court, or when an institution seeks to bypass the available administrative process by going directly to court. Judicial review questions may also arise when no administrative review process is available, and the only potential forum for contesting an adverse administrative action is a court.

Whether or not judicial review is available to an institution will depend on the judicial review provisions in the statutes that establish the particular federal funding program at issue or that otherwise govern the operations of the funding agency that has made the adverse decision. Absent any such statutory provisions, the availability of judicial review will be governed by 28 U.S.C. § 1331, which grants the federal courts jurisdiction over, among others, suits against federal administrative agencies and their officers and employees (see *Califano v. Sanders*, 430 U.S. 99, 104–7 (1977)). Generally, some form of judicial review will be available to institutions that are subjected to a termination of funding or other penalty, or are otherwise adversely affected by a federal funding agency action. (See, for example, *Atlanta College of Medical & Dental Careers, Inc. v. Riley*, 987 F.2d 821 (D.C. Cir. 1993).) Judicial review may also sometimes be available to higher education associations whose members are adversely affected by agency action (see, for example, *California Cosmetology Coalition v. Riley*, 110 F.3d 1454 (9th Cir. 1997)). Often, however: (1) the "exhaustion" of administrative remedies will be a prerequisite to judicial review; or (2) the availability of judicial remedies against other parties may preclude suit against the agency; or (3) the plaintiff may be precluded from suing by a technical doctrine such as the "standing" doctrine or "ripeness" doctrine; or (4) there will be limits on the types of judicial relief that a court may order.

The first type of problem is illustrated by *Career Education v. Department of Education*, 6 F.3d 817 (D.C. Cir. 1993). In this case, a proprietary postsecondary school claimed that the department had failed to act on the school's reeligibility application for HEA federal student loan programs. The school sued the department and asked the court to order the department to act. The court dismissed the case because the school had administrative remedies available to it which it had failed to exhaust, and there was no basis for concluding that pursuit of these remedies would ultimately be unfair or futile for the school. And in *American Association of Cosmetology Schools v. Riley*, 170 F.3d 1250 (9th Cir. 1999), the plaintiff challenged the validity of the departmental appeals process for schools facing termination from certain Title IV, HEA, student loan programs. The court dismissed the association's suit because individual schools could raise these issues through the administrative processes available to them. According to this court, the departmental appeals process affects different schools in different ways and thus, "as a practical matter," a court would need to have "a complete administrative record to review." Moreover, after resorting to the available administrative process for challenging a departmental termination decision, an individual school could then go to court to "raise precisely the same systemic flaws [the plaintiff association] raises here."

Regarding the second type of problem, if suit is brought against an agency under the federal Administrative Procedure Act (APA), 5 U.S.C. § 704 *et seq.*, the court may dismiss the challenge because there is some other "adequate [judicial] remedy" for contesting the agency action. In *National Wrestling Coaches Association v. Department of Education*, 366 F.3d 930, 945–47

(D.C. Cir. 2004), for instance, the court rejected a challenge to the department's Title IX policy interpretations on intercollegiate athletics programs, reasoning that the "availability of a private cause of action under Title IX directly against the universities themselves constitutes an adequate remedy that precludes judicial review under § 704" (366 F.3d at 933–34).[53]

Regarding the third type of problem (technical doctrines precluding suit), plaintiffs must, in general, demonstrate that they have been, or imminently will be, adversely affected by the agency action being challenged and that they have a "personal stake" in the dispute (see generally Section 2.2.2.2). The "standing" doctrine is the most likely source of such problems for plaintiffs. The doctrine is particularly likely to become an issue when the challenge is brought by an association or other third party rather than by the postsecondary institution itself. In the *National Wrestling Coaches* case (above), for example, the court also dismissed the case because the plaintiff association could not meet the applicable tests for standing (366 F.3d at 936–45).

Regarding the fourth type of problem (limits on judicial relief), there sometimes will be a statutory provision limiting the types of relief that are available in suits against the federal funding agency. For example, the Higher Education Act expressly provides that, with respect to Title IV of the Act, the Secretary of Education may "sue and be sued" in state and federal courts, but that injunctive relief may not be granted against the Secretary (20 U.S.C. § 1082(a)(2)). In *Thomas v. Bennett*, 856 F.2d 1165 (8th Cir. 1988), the court acknowledged that Section 1082(a)(2) prohibited the plaintiff from obtaining an injunction against the Secretary of Education, but also made clear that this Section did not prohibit the entry of a declaratory judgment against the Secretary. In *American Association of Cosmetology Schools v. Riley*, 170 F.3d 1250 (9th Cir. 1999), the court generally recognized this distinction between injunctive and declaratory relief under Section 1082(a)(2), but then added that Section 1082(a)(2) does prohibit courts from entering declaratory judgments that "would have the same coercive effect as an injunction." Characterizing the requested declaratory relief as "plainly coercive," the court concluded that such relief was barred by Section 1082(a)(2). These rules barring injunctive relief and its equivalent in Title IV actions, however, may not apply to an "across-the-board" or "facial" challenge to the validity of departmental regulations (see *California Cosmetology Coalition v. Riley*, 110 F.3d 1454 (9th Cir. 1997); and see generally *American Association of Cosmetology Schools*, above, 170 F.3d at 1257 (Reinhardt, J., dissenting)).

Equally as important as questions concerning the availability of judicial review are questions about the types of challenges on the merits that higher education institutions (or associations of institutions) may bring to court. (See generally Philip Lacovara, "How Far Can the Federal Camel Slip Under the Academic Tent?" 4 *J. Coll. & Univ. Law* 223, 229–39 (1977).) As with internal

---

[53]The universities that the court had in mind are those that have eliminated their men's varsity wrestling programs, presumably in order to comply with the department's Title IX policy interpretations. For discussion of implied private causes of action under Title IX, see Section 13.5.9 of this book.

agency proceedings, judicial challenges may be either procedural or substantive (see above). Substantive challenges generally pose greater difficulties for institutions. Such challenges are usually based either on federal administrative law or on federal constitutional law.

Using federal administrative law, an institution may challenge: (1) the facial validity of an agency rule or regulation that has adversely affected the institution; (2) an agency's interpretation of one of its rules or of a provision of the federal funding statute at issue; or (3) a particular result that an agency reaches or decision that it makes regarding the institution (see generally 5 U.S.C. § 706 (APA)).

The first type of challenge usually arises when a condition on federal aid is created by an agency rule or regulation rather than by the funding statute itself. Such a rule or regulation may sometimes be challenged on its face on grounds that it is *ultra vires*—that is, beyond the bounds of the authority delegated to the agency under the funding statute or other pertinent statutes. In *Gay Men's Health Crisis v. Sullivan*, 792 F. Supp. 278 (S.D.N.Y. 1992), for example, the plaintiff challenged grant conditions of the Centers for Disease Control (CDC) on grounds that they went beyond the statutory authority under which CDC operated the grant program. This program provided grants for the development and use of AIDS educational materials. In the authorizing legislation, Congress included a condition that "any informational materials used are not obscene" (42 U.S.C. § 300ee(d)). CDC's grant terms for the program, however, provided that the materials used must not be "offensive." CDC argued that Congress's standard was merely a floor or minimum and did not prevent CDC from adopting a higher standard. The court disagreed:

> Congress . . . addressed the precise issue addressed by the CDC grant terms, i.e., the funding of potentially "offensive" materials, and expressly limited the funding restriction to "obscene" materials. Thus, in enacting section 300ee Congress did not merely apply additional restrictions to supplement those promulgated by the CDC, but rather clearly articulated its own standard for limitations on the content of HIV prevention materials, which can only be plausibly construed as inconsistent with the [CDC's] "offensiveness" standard.
>
> Because Congress has directly spoken on the precise issue in question by enacting an "obscenity" standard, and has made its intent clear both in the language of the statute and in its legislative history, "that is the end of the matter." . . . Accordingly, the court finds that the CDC has exceeded its statutory authority, and the [CDC grant terms] are without effect [792 F. Supp. at 292; citations omitted].

(For another example of a successful *ultra vires* challenge, see *California Cosmetology Coalition v. Riley,* 110 F.3d 1454 (9th Cir. 1997).)

The second type of administrative law challenge arises when an agency has issued an interpretation of a statutory provision (or agency regulation) and an institution claims that the agency's interpretation is incorrect. Under the standard of review for such challenges, a court will uphold the agency's interpretation if it is not "arbitrary, capricious, or manifestly contrary to the statute" that the agency is implementing (*Chevron U.S.A. v. Natural Resources Defense*

Council, 467 U.S. 837, 844 (1984); but see also *Christensen v. Harris County,* 529 U.S. 576 (2000)). This type of challenge is very difficult to mount because courts usually accord considerable deference (called *"Chevron* deference") to the agency's interpretations, especially interpretations of the statute that are embodied in formal agency regulations and the agency's interpretations of its own regulations. In *Chalenor v. University of North Dakota,* 291 F.3d 1042 (8th Cir. 2002), for instance, the court rejected a challenge to the U.S. Department of Education's interpretation of Title IX's applicability to intercollegiate athletics (see Section 10.4.6 of this book). Finding that the interpretation was "reasonable," the court deferred to ED's judgment. But in *Mercy Catholic Medical Center v. Thompson,* 380 F.3d 142 (3d Cir. 2004), the court held that a written interpretation of the Secretary of Health and Human Services was arbitrary and capricious. Finding the interpretation was "plainly inconsistent" with language of the regulation being interpreted, the court declined to defer to the Secretary's judgment. (To the same effect, see *Continental Training Services, Inc., v. Cavazos,* 893 F.2d 877, 884–86 (7th Cir. 1990).) For further discussion of judicial deference to administrative agency interpretations, see Section 13.6.1 below.

The third type of administrative law challenge may arise if an institution has grounds for arguing that, under the facts and circumstances of the case, a particular result that the agency reached was unreasonable or irrational. When such a claim is based on the Administrative Procedure Act, the pertinent provision is 5 U.S.C. § 706(2)(A), which provides that "the reviewing court shall" invalidate an agency action if it is "arbitrary, capricious, an abuse of discretion, or otherwise not in accordance with law." (See generally *Motor Vehicle Manufacturers Association v. State Farm Mutual Automobile Insurance Co.,* 463 U.S. 29 (1983).)

In addition to the administrative law challenges suggested above, federal constitutional law challenges may also be available to institutions (or associations of institutions) in some circumstances. In particular, constitutional law may be used to challenge the substantive validity of a particular condition that Congress or a federal agency has attached to the expenditure of federal funds. Because the federal government's constitutional power to tax and spend is so broad (see Sections 13.1.1 & 13.1.2), such substantive challenges are difficult and speculative. But they also provide an arena ripe for creative arguments by institutions and higher education associations, and their legal counsel. The following cases are illustrative.

In *Rust v. Sullivan,* 500 U.S. 173 (1991), the Supreme Court considered the constitutionality of regulations promulgated by the U.S. Department of Health and Human Services to implement Title X of the Public Health Service Act, which provides federal funding for family-planning services. The Act states that "[n]one of the funds appropriated under this subchapter shall be used in programs where abortion is a method of family planning" (42 U.S.C. § 300a-6). The implementing regulations then in effect created three basic conditions that fund recipients must meet: (1) the funded project "may not provide counseling concerning the use of abortion as a method of family planning or provide referral for abortion as a method of family planning"; (2) the funded project may not engage in activities that "encourage, promote or advocate abortion as a method of family planning"; and (3) the funded project must be "physically and financially separate" from any abortion-related activities that the fund recipient may engage in (53 Fed. Reg. 2922, 2945 (February 2, 1998), §§ 59.8(a)(1), 59.9, & 59.10(a)). Doctors from Title X clinics challenged the validity of the regulations on the ground that they violated their First Amendment free speech rights.

The doctors first argued that the regulations constituted a form of "viewpoint discrimination" because recipients who remained silent about or opposed abortion could retain their funding but recipients who advocated abortion could not. The Supreme Court rejected this argument:

> The Government can, without violating the Constitution, selectively fund a program to encourage certain activities it believes to be in the public interest, without at the same time funding an alternate program which seeks to deal with the problem in another way. In so doing, the Government has not discriminated on the basis of viewpoint; it has merely chosen to fund one activity to the exclusion of the other [500 U.S. at 192].

The doctors also argued that the regulations unconstitutionally conditioned the receipt of a benefit (Title X funding) on the grantee's relinquishment of a constitutional right (freedom of speech regarding abortion-related matters). The Court rejected this argument as well and thus upheld the regulations:

> [H]ere the government is not denying a benefit to anyone, but is instead simply insisting that public funds be spent for the purposes for which they were authorized. The Secretary's regulations do not force the Title X grantee to give up abortion-related speech; they merely require that the grantee keep such activities separate and distinct from Title X activities. Title X expressly distinguishes between a Title X *grantee* and a Title X *project*. The grantee, which normally is a health care organization, may receive funds from a variety of sources for a variety of purposes. . . . The grantee receives Title X funds, however, for the specific and limited purpose of establishing and operating a Title X project. . . . The regulations govern the scope of the Title X *project's* activities, and leave the grantee unfettered in its other activities. The Title X *grantee* can continue to perform abortions, provide abortion-related services, and engage in abortion advocacy; it simply is required to conduct those activities through programs that are separate and independent from the project that receives Title X funds. . . .
>
> In contrast, our "unconstitutional conditions" cases involve situations in which the Government has placed a condition on the *recipient* of the subsidy rather than on a particular program or service, thus effectively prohibiting the recipient from engaging in the protected conduct outside the scope of the federally funded program [500 U.S. at 196; citations omitted].

Despite the Court's strong statements in *Rust*, it is still possible in some circumstances to argue that particular aid conditions violate constitutional individual rights principles. *Rust* itself apparently establishes that the government's funding conditions may not substantially restrict the grantee's freedom of speech in a *nonproject* context. Furthermore, *Rust* contains cautionary language emphasizing that special sensitivities arise whenever funding conditions arguably restrict speech in an academic setting:

> This is not to suggest that funding by the Government, even when coupled with the freedom of the fund recipients to speak outside the scope of the Government-funded project, is invariably sufficient to justify Government control over the content of expression. For example, this Court has . . . recognized that the university is a traditional sphere of free expression so funda- mental to the functioning of our society that the Government's ability to control speech within that sphere by means of conditions attached to the expenditure of Government funds is restricted by the vagueness and overbreadth doctrines of the First Amendment [500 U.S. at 199–200].

These limitations on the scope of *Rust* have been influential in several subsequent cases.

Board of Trustees of the Leland Stanford Junior University v. Sullivan, 773 F. Supp. 472 (D.D.C. 1991), directly presented questions concerning a federal fund- ing agency's restrictions on speech in an academic context. The National Institutes of Health (NIH) had issued a notice of its intention to award two contracts of $1.5 million each to universities to do research on an artificial heart device. Stanford submitted a proposal in response to this notice, in which it objected to a "Confi- dentiality of Information Clause" that NIH intended to insert into the contract (see Section 7.7.3 for further discussion of this clause and this case). Stanford and NIH entered a contract contingent on the resolution of this objection (and several oth- ers). When the parties could reach no resolution, NIH withdrew the contract from Stanford and awarded it to St. Louis University Medical Center.

Stanford sued, arguing that the confidentiality clause was an unconstitutional prior restraint (see generally Sections 9.5.4 & 10.3.3 of this book) on the free speech of its researchers. The district court agreed with the university and ordered that the contract, minus the clause, be reawarded to Stanford. The court relied on *Rust* for the proposition that, although the government may place cer- tain free speech restrictions upon project activities that receive federal funding, it may not so restrict other activities of the grantee. Distinguishing the situation before it from that in *Rust,* the court reasoned:

> The regulations at issue in the instant case broadly bind the grantee and not merely the artificial heart project. Dr. Oyer and the other individuals working for Stanford on the project are prohibited by defendants' regulations from dis- cussing preliminary findings of that project without permission. Unlike the health professionals in *Rust,* the Stanford researchers lack the option of speaking regarding artificial heart research on their own time, or in circumstances where their speech is paid for by Stanford University or some other private donor, or not paid for by anyone at all. . . .
>
> The regulation at issue here is not tailored to reach only the particular *pro- gram* that is in receipt of government funds; it broadly forbids the *recipients* of the funds from engaging in publishing activity related to artificial heart research at any time, under any auspices, and wholly apart from the particular program that is being aided [773 F. Supp. at 476; footnotes omitted].

The court was also favorably impressed by *Rust*'s language emphasizing the university's special role in society and the need for special care to avoid government conditions that are vague or overbroad (see generally Section 6.6.1). Relying on this language, the court concluded:

> The regulations permit the contracting officer to prevent Stanford from issuing "preliminary invalidated findings" that "could create erroneous conclusions which might threaten public health or safety if acted upon," or that might have "adverse effects on . . . the Federal agency." 48 C.F.R. § 352.224–70. In the view of this Court, these standards are impermissibly vague. . . .
>
> There is the related problem of the chilling effect of these vague and overbroad conditions. . . . [N]o prudent grantee is likely to publish that which the contracting officer has not cleared even if the reason for the refusal to clear appears to be wholly invalid. In sum, this case fits snugly in the "free expression at a university" category that *Rust* carved out of its general ruling . . . [773 F. Supp. at 477–78].

(See also *Gay Men's Health Crisis v. Sullivan,* 792 F. Supp. 278, 292–304 (S.D.N.Y. 1992), another post-*Rust* case in which a court invalidated federal grant conditions—this time those of the Centers for Disease Control—on grounds of vagueness and overbreadth.)

The U.S. Supreme Court clarified the scope and limits of the *Rust* case in its later decision in *Rosenberger v. Rector and Visitors of the University of Virginia* (Section 10.1.5 of this book). The Court drew a distinction in *Rosenberger* between situations (like *Rust*) in which the government is a speaker and "enlists private entities to convey its own [favored] message"; and situations (like *Rosenberger*) in which the government subsidizes "private speakers who convey their own messages" and are not the government's agents:

> [W]hen the State is the speaker, it may make content-based choices. When the University determines the content of the education it provides, it is the University speaking, and we have permitted the government to regulate the content of what is or is not expressed when it is the speaker or when it enlists private entities to convey its own message. In the same vein, in *Rust v. Sullivan, supra,* we upheld the government's prohibition on abortion-related advice applicable to recipients of federal funds for family planning counseling. There, the government did not create a program to encourage private speech but instead used private speakers to transmit specific information pertaining to its own program. We recognized that when the government appropriates public funds to promote a particular policy of its own it is entitled to say what it wishes. 500 U.S. at 194. When the government disburses public funds to private entities to convey a governmental message, it may take legitimate and appropriate steps to ensure that its message is neither garbled nor distorted by the grantee. See *id.,* at 196–200.
>
> It does not follow, however, and we did not suggest in *Widmar,* that viewpoint-based restrictions are proper when the University does not itself speak or subsidize transmittal of a message it favors but instead expends funds to encourage a diversity of views from private speakers. A holding that the

University may not discriminate based on the viewpoint of private persons whose speech it facilitates does not restrict the University's own speech, which is controlled by different principles [515 U.S. at 833–34].

In a subsequent case, *National Endowment for the Arts v. Finley*, 524 U.S. 569 (1998), the U.S. Supreme Court upheld the facial constitutionality of the "decency and respect" clause in legislation governing the grant-making process of the National Endowment for the Arts (NEA), expressly rejecting the plaintiffs' arguments that the "decency and respect" provision is overbroad and vague. Key to the Court's overbreadth analysis was its conviction that the provision played only a modest role in the NEA's decisions on grant applications. The language was only "advisory," according to the Court; it "admonishes the NEA merely to take 'decency and respect' into consideration" in assessing artistic merit and "imposes no categorical requirement." Thus, "the provision does not introduce considerations that, in practice, would effectively preclude or punish the expression of particular views." Moreover, the provision was contained in government funding legislation rather than in a criminal or regulatory statute:

> Any content-based considerations that may be taken into account in the grant-making process are a consequence of the nature of arts funding. The NEA has limited resources, and it must deny the majority of the grant applications that it receives, including many that propose "artistically excellent" projects. . . . The "very assumption" of the NEA is that grants will be awarded according to the "artistic worth of competing applications," and absolute neutrality is simply "inconceivable." *Advocates for the Arts v. Thomson*, 532 F. 2d 792, 795–796 (1st Cir.), cert. denied, 429 U.S. 894 (1976) [524 U.S. at 585–86].

The Court also relied on its distinction between subsidies and direct regulations to reject the plaintiffs' void-for-vagueness challenge to the "decency and respect" provision. The language is "undeniably opaque," the Court admitted, and "could raise substantial vagueness concerns" if used in a regulatory or criminal statute. But the Court did not believe similar concerns would arise in "the context of selective subsidies" where "it is not always feasible for Congress to legislate with clarity." Thus, "*when the Government is acting as patron rather than as sovereign,* the consequences of imprecision are not constitutionally severe" (emphasis added).

In reaching its result in *Finley*, the Supreme Court distinguished *Rosenberger*:

> We held [in *Rosenberger*] that by subsidizing the Student Activities Fund, the University had created a limited public forum, from which it impermissibly excluded all publications with religious editorial viewpoints. [*Rosenberger*, 515 U.S.] at 837. Although the scarcity of NEA funding does not distinguish this case from *Rosenberger*, . . . the competitive process according to which the grants are allocated does. In the context of arts funding, in contrast to many other subsidies, the Government does not indiscriminately "encourage a diversity of views from private speakers," Id. at 834. The NEA's mandate is to make aesthetic

judgments, and the inherently content-based "excellence" threshold for NEA support sets it apart from the subsidy at issue in *Rosenberger*—which was available to all student organizations that were "'related to the educational purpose of the University,'" Id. at 824—and from comparably objective decisions on allocating public benefits . . . [524 U.S. at 586].

Although the result in *Finley* is clearly unfavorable to individual and institutional grant applicants, the Court's opinion is actually quite narrow. First, the Court had to go to great lengths to dilute the force of the "decency and respect" provision. (Justice Scalia, in a concurring opinion, asserted that the NEA had "distorted" the provision and the Court had "gutted" it.) The constitutionality of a more direct or specific provision that affected speech would presumably not be controlled by the Court's opinion. Second, the Court carefully noted that it was determining only the *facial* constitutionality of the provision:

> Respondents do not allege discrimination in any particular funding decision. (In fact, after filing suit to challenge § 954(d)(1), two of the individual respondents received NEA grants. . . .) Thus, we have no occasion here to address an as-applied challenge in a situation where the denial of a grant may be shown to be the product of invidious viewpoint discrimination. If the NEA were to leverage its power to award subsidies on the basis of subjective criteria into a penalty on disfavored viewpoints, then we would confront a different case. We have stated that, even in the provision of subsidies, the Government may not "ai[m] at the suppression of dangerous ideas," *Regan v. Taxation with Representation,* 461 U.S. 540, 550 (1983) (internal quotation marks omitted), and if a subsidy were "manipulated" to have a "coercive effect," then relief could be appropriate. See *Arkansas Writers' Project, Inc. v. Ragland,* 481 U.S. 221, 237 (1987) (Scalia, J., dissenting); see also *Leathers v. Medlock,* 499 U.S. 439, 447 (1991) ("[D]ifferential taxation of First Amendment speakers is constitutionally suspect when it threatens to suppress the expression of particular ideas or viewpoints"). In addition, as the NEA itself concedes, a more pressing constitutional question would arise if government funding resulted in the imposition of a disproportionate burden calculated to drive "certain ideas or viewpoints from the marketplace." *Simon & Schuster, Inc. v. Members of N.Y. State Crime Victims Bd.,* 502 U.S. 105, 116 (1991). . . . Unless and until § 954(d)(1) is applied in a manner that raises concern about the suppression of disfavored viewpoints, however, we uphold the constitutionality of the provision [524 U.S. at 586–87].

The Court thus leaves an open channel for *as applied* challenges of funding criteria that affect speech, even if the criteria on their face are as diluted as those in *Finley.*

In another post-*Rust* case, *Board of County Commissioners v. Umbehr,* 518 U.S. 668 (1996), the U.S. Supreme Court indicated what analysis would apply to a situation in which government seeks to regulate the content of a grantee or contractor's private speech that is not within the scope of the activities government has funded. In particular, *Umbehr* addresses the situation where government officials terminate or refuse to renew a contract or grant because they disagree with or take offense at views expressed by the contractor or grantee. The Court ruled in *Umbehr* that contractors and grantees have First Amendment protections in such circumstances that are comparable to those of public employees (see Section 7.1.1 of this book). Thus, if a government agency or official were to penalize a contractor or grantee for speech on matters "of public concern" (*Connick v. Myers*, 461 U.S. 138 (1983)), the government could not rely on *Rust* or *Finley*, and the contractor or grantee would often be protected.

Sec. 13.5. Civil Rights Compliance

13.5.1. General considerations. Postsecondary institutions receiving assistance under federal aid programs are obligated to follow not only the programmatic and technical requirements of each program under which aid is received (see Section 13.4 above) but also various civil rights requirements that apply generally to federal aid programs. These requirements are a major focus of federal spending policy, importing substantial social goals into education policy and making equality of educational opportunity a clear national priority in education. As conditions on spending, the civil rights requirements represent an exercise of Congress's spending power (see Section 13.1.1), implemented by delegating authority to the various federal departments and agencies that administer federal aid programs. There has often been controversy, however, concerning the specifics of implementing and enforcing such civil rights requirements. Some argue that the federal role is too great, and others say that it is too small; some argue that the federal government proceeds too quickly, and others insist that it is too slow; some argue that the compliance process is too cumbersome and costly for the affected institutions; others argue that such effects are inevitable for any system that is to be genuinely effective. Despite the controversy, it is clear that these federal civil rights efforts, over time, have provided a major force for social change in America.

Four different federal statutes prohibit discrimination in educational programs receiving federal financial assistance. Title VI of the Civil Rights Act of 1964 prohibits discrimination on the basis of race, color, or national origin. Title IX of the Education Amendments of 1972 prohibits discrimination on the basis of sex. Section 504 of the Rehabilitation Act of 1973, as amended in 1974, prohibits discrimination against individuals with disabilities. The Age Discrimination Act of 1975 prohibits discrimination on the basis of age. Title IX is specifically limited to educational programs receiving federal financial assistance, while Title VI, Section 504, and the Age Discrimination Act apply to all programs receiving such assistance.

Each statute delegates enforcement responsibilities to each of the federal agencies disbursing federal financial assistance. Postsecondary institutions may thus be subject to the civil rights regulations of several federal agencies, the most important one being the Department of Education (ED), created in 1979. At that time, ED assumed the functions of the former Department of Health, Education, and Welfare's (HEW) Office for Civil Rights with respect to all educational programs transferred from the U.S. Office of Education that was a constituent part of HEW. ED has its own Office for Civil Rights (OCR) under an assistant secretary for civil rights. The HEW civil rights regulations, formerly published in Volume 45 of the *Code of Federal Regulations* (C.F.R.), were redesignated as ED regulations and republished in 34 C.F.R. Parts 100–106. These administrative regulations, as amended over time, have considerably fleshed out the meaning of the statutes. ED's Office for Civil Rights has also published "policy interpretations" and "guidance" regarding the statutes and regulations in the *Federal Register*. Judicial decisions contribute additional interpretive gloss on major points and resolve major controversies, but the administrative regulations and OCR interpretations remain the initial, and usually the primary, source for understanding the civil rights requirements.

Although the nondiscrimination language of the four statutes is similar, each statute protects a different group of beneficiaries, and an act that constitutes discrimination against one group does not necessarily constitute discrimination if directed against another group. "Separate but equal" treatment of the sexes is sometimes permissible under Title IX, for instance, but such treatment of the races is never permissible under Title VI. Similarly, the enforcement mechanisms for the four statutes are similar, but they are not identical. There may be private causes of action for damages under Title VI, Title IX, and Section 504, for instance, but under the Age Discrimination Act only equitable relief is available (see subsection 13.5.9 below).

Over the years, various issues have arisen concerning the scope and coverage of the civil rights statutes (see subsection 13.5.7 below). During their time in the limelight, these issues have become the focus of various U.S. Supreme Court cases as well as a legislative battle in Congress that led to a major new piece of legislation, the Civil Rights Restoration Act of 1987 (see subsection 13.5.7.4 below). As the volume of the litigation has increased, it has become apparent that the similarities of statutory language among the four civil rights statutes give rise to similar scope and coverage issues. Answers to an issue under one statute will thus provide guidance in answering comparable issues under another statute, and the answers will often be the same from one statute to another. There are some critical differences, however, in the statutory language and implementing regulations for each statute. For example, as explained in subsection 13.5.7.1 below, Title VI and the Age Discrimination Act have provisions limiting their applicability to employment discrimination, whereas Title IX and Section 504 do not. Each statute also has its own unique legislative history, which sometimes affects interpretation of the statute in a way that may have no parallel for the other statutes. Title IX's legislative history on coverage of athletics is an example. Therefore, to gain a fine-tuned view of particular developments, administrators and counsel should approach each statute and each scope and coverage issue separately, taking account of both their similarities to and their differences from the other statutes and other issues.

13.5.2. Title VI. Title VI of the Civil Rights Act of 1964 (42 U.S.C. § 2000d) declares:

> No person in the United States shall, on the ground of race, color, or national origin, be excluded from participation in, be denied the benefits of, or be subjected to discrimination under any program or activity receiving federal financial assistance.

Courts have generally held that Title VI incorporates the same standards for identifying unlawful racial discrimination as have been developed under the Fourteenth Amendment's equal protection clause (see the discussion of the *Bakke* case in Section 8.2.5, and see generally Section 8.2.4.1). But courts have also held that the Department of Education and other federal agencies implementing Title VI may impose nondiscrimination requirements on recipients beyond those developed under the equal protection clause (see *Guardians Assn. v. Civil Service Commission of the City of New York,* 463 U.S. 582 (1983), discussed in Section 13.5.7.2).

The Education Department's regulations, found at 34 C.F.R. § 100.3(b), provide the basic, and most specific, reference point for determining what actions are unlawful under Title VI. The regulations prohibit a recipient of federal funds from denying, or providing a different quality of service, financial aid, or other benefit of the institution's programs, on the basis of race, color, or national origin. The regulations also prohibit institutions from treating individuals differently with respect to satisfying admission, enrollment, eligibility, membership, or other requirements, as well as denying individuals the opportunity to participate in programs or on planning or advisory committees on the basis of race, color, or national origin.

To supplement these regulations, the Department of Education has also developed criteria, as discussed below, that deal specifically with the problem of desegregating statewide systems of postsecondary education.

The dismantling of the formerly *de jure* segregated systems of higher education has given rise to considerable litigation over more than three decades. Although most of the litigation has attacked continued segregation in the higher education system of one state, the lengthiest lawsuit involved the alleged failure of the federal government to enforce Title VI in ten states. This litigation—begun in 1970 as *Adams v. Richardson,* continuing with various Education Department secretaries as defendant until it became *Adams v. Bell* in the 1980s, and culminating as *Women's Equity Action League v. Cavazos* in 1990—focused on the responsibilities of the Department of Health, Education and Welfare, and later the Education Department, to enforce Title VI, rather than examining the standards applicable to state higher education officials. The U.S. District Court ordered HEW to initiate enforcement proceedings against these states (*Adams v. Richardson,* 356 F. Supp. 92 (D.D.C. 1973)), and the U.S. Court of Appeals affirmed the decision (480 F.2d 1159 (D.C. Cir. 1973)). (See the further discussion of the case in Section 13.5.8.) In subsequent proceedings, the district judge ordered HEW to revoke its acceptance of desegregation plans submitted by several states after the 1973 court opinions and to devise criteria for reviewing new desegregation plans to be submitted by the states that were the subject of the case (see *Adams v. Califano,* 430 F. Supp. 118 (D.D.C. 1977)). Finally, in 1990, the U.S. Court of Appeals for the D.C. Circuit ruled that no private right of action against government enforcement agencies existed under Title VI, and dismissed the case for lack of jurisdiction (*Women's Equity Action League v. Cavazos,* 906 F.2d 742 (D.C. Cir. 1990)).

After developing the criteria (42 Fed. Reg. 40780 (August 11, 1977)), HEW revised and republished them (43 Fed. Reg. 6658 (February 15, 1978)) as criteria applicable to all states having a history of *de jure* segregation in public higher education.[54] These "Revised Criteria Specifying the Ingredients of Acceptable Plans to Desegregate State Systems of Public Higher Education" require the affected states to take various affirmative steps, such as enhancing the quality of black state-supported colleges and universities, placing new "high-demand" programs on traditionally black campuses, eliminating unnecessary program duplication between black and white institutions, increasing the percentage of black academic employees in the system, and increasing the enrollment of blacks at traditionally white public colleges.

Litigation alleging continued *de jure* segregation by state higher education officials resulted in federal appellate court opinions in four states; the U.S. Supreme Court ruled in one of these cases. Despite the amount of litigation, and the many years of litigation, settlement, or conciliation attempts, the standards imposed by the equal protection clause of the Fourteenth Amendment and by Title VI are still unclear. These cases—brought by private plaintiffs, with the United States acting as intervenor—were brought under both the equal protection clause (by the private plaintiffs and the United States) and Title VI (by the United States); judicial analysis generally used the equal protection clause standard. Although the U.S. Supreme Court's opinion in *United States v. Fordice,* 505 U.S. 717 (1992), is controlling, appellate court rulings in prior cases demonstrate the complexities of this issue and illustrate the remaining disputes over the responsibilities of the states with histories of *de jure* segregation.

Fordice and other related federal court opinions must be read in the context of Supreme Court precedent in cases related to desegregating the public elementary and secondary schools. It is clear under the Fourteenth Amendment's equal protection clause that, in the absence of a "compelling" state interest (see Section 8.2.5 of this book), no public institution may treat students differently on the basis of race. The leading case, of course, is *Brown v. Board of Education,* 347 U.S. 483 (1954). Though *Brown* concerned elementary and secondary schools, the precedent clearly applies to postsecondary education as well, as the Supreme Court affirmed in *Florida ex rel. Hawkins v. Board of Control,* 350 U.S. 413 (1956).

Cases involving postsecondary education have generally considered racial segregation within a state postsecondary system rather than within a single institution. One case, for instance, *Alabama State Teachers Assn. v. Alabama Public School and College Authority,* 289 F. Supp. 784 (D. Ala. 1968), *affirmed without majority opinion,* 393 U.S. 400 (1969), concerned the state's establishment of a branch of a predominantly white institution in a city already served by a predominantly black institution. The court rejected the plaintiff's argument that this action unconstitutionally perpetuated segregation in the

---

[54]Counsel concerned about the legal status of these criteria, and the extent to which they bind ED and the states, should consult *Adams v. Bell,* 711 F.2d 161, 165–66 (majority opinion), 206–7 (dissent) (D.C. Cir. 1983).

state system, holding that states do not have an affirmative duty to dismantle segregated higher education (as opposed to elementary and secondary education). This interpretation of the equal protection clause is clearly questionable after *Fordice*. Another case, *Norris v. State Council of Higher Education*, 327 F. Supp. 1368 (E.D. Va. 1971), *affirmed without opinion*, 404 U.S. 907 (1971), concerned a state plan to expand a predominantly white two-year institution into a four-year institution in an area where a predominantly black four-year institution already existed. In contrast to the Alabama case, the court overturned the action because it impeded desegregation in the state system.

The crux of the legal debate in the higher education desegregation cases has been whether the equal protection clause and Title VI require the state to do no more than enact race-neutral policies (the "effort" test), or whether the state must go beyond race neutrality to ensure that any remaining vestige of the formerly segregated system (for example, racially identifiable institutions or concentrations of minority students in less prestigious or less well-funded institutions) is removed. Unlike elementary and secondary students, college students select the institution they wish to attend (assuming they meet the admission standards); and the remedies used in elementary and secondary school desegregation, such as busing and race-conscious assignment practices, are unavailable to colleges and universities. But just how the courts should weigh the "student choice" argument against the clear mandate of the Fourteenth Amendment was sharply debated by several federal courts prior to *Fordice*.

In *Geier v. University of Tennessee*, 597 F.2d 1056 (6th Cir. 1979), *cert. denied*, 444 U.S. 886 (1979), the court ordered the merger of two Tennessee universities, despite the state's claim that the racial imbalances at the schools were created by the students' exercise of free choice. The state had proposed expanding its programming at predominantly white University of Tennessee-Nashville; this action, the plaintiffs argued, would negatively affect the ability of Tennessee A&I State University, a predominantly black institution in Nashville, to desegregate its faculty and student body. Applying the reasoning of *Brown* and other elementary/secondary cases, the court ruled that the state's adoption of an "open admissions" policy had not effectively dismantled the state's dual system of higher education, and ordered state officials to submit a plan for desegregating public higher education in Tennessee. In a separate decision, *Richardson v. Blanton*, 597 F.2d 1078 (6th Cir. 1979), the same court upheld the district court's approval of the state's desegregation plan.

The court found that open admissions and the cessation of discrimination were not enough to meet the state's constitutional obligation in this situation, "where segregation was once required by state law and 'egregious' conditions of segregation continued to exist in public higher education in the Nashville area. What was required, the [district] court found, was affirmative action to remove these vestiges" (597 F.2d at 1065). Furthermore, the Sixth Circuit rejected the state's argument that elementary/secondary desegregation precedent, most specifically *Green v. County School Board*, 391 U.S. 430 (1968), did not apply to higher education.[55]

Desegregation cases brought in Mississippi and Louisiana, both within the jurisdiction of the U.S. Court of Appeals for the Fifth Circuit, show the complexities of these issues and the sharply differing interpretations of the equal protection clause and Title VI. These cases proceeded through the judicial system at the same time; and, considered together, they illustrate the significance of the U.S. Supreme Court's pronouncements in *Fordice*.

The case that culminated in the Supreme Court's *Fordice* opinion began in 1975, when Jake Ayers and other private plaintiffs sued the governor of Mississippi and other state officials for maintaining the vestiges of a *de jure* segregated system. Although HEW had begun Title VI enforcement proceedings against Mississippi in 1969, it had rejected both desegregation plans submitted by the state, and this private litigation ensued. The United States intervened, and the parties attempted to conciliate the dispute for twelve years. They were unable to do so, and the trial ensued in 1987.

Mississippi had designated three categories of public higher education institutions: comprehensive universities (three historically white, none historically black); one urban institution (black); and four regional institutions (two white, two black). Admission standards differed both among categories and within categories, with the lowest admission standards at the historically black regional institutions. The plaintiffs argued, among other things, that the state's admission standards, institutional classification and mission designations, duplication of programs, faculty and staff hiring and assignments, and funding perpetuated the prior segregated system of higher education; among other data, they cited the concentration of black students at the black institutions (more than 95 percent of the students at each of the three black institutions were black, whereas blacks comprised fewer than 10 percent of the students at the three white universities and 13 percent at both white regional institutions). The state asserted that the existence of racially identifiable universities was permissible, since students could choose which institution to attend, and that the state's higher education policies and practices were race neutral in intent.

Although the district court acknowledged that the state had an affirmative duty to desegregate its higher education system, it rejected the *Green* precedent as inapplicable to higher education systems and followed the Court's ruling in *Bazemore*, described above. The district court said that the proper inquiry was

---

[55]Subsequent to *Geier I*, the Sixth Circuit ruled that the consent decree's requirement to develop an affirmative action program for seventy-five black preprofessional students was lawful, and that *Bazemore v. Friday*, 478 U.S. 385 (1986), did not apply to education (*Geier v. Alexander*, 801 F.2d 799 (6th Cir. 1986) (*Geier II*)). For a discussion of the court's analysis of the affirmative action provisions of the consent decree, see Section 8.2.5 of this book. In 1994, the State of Tennessee moved to vacate the 1984 settlement approved in *Geier II*, relying on the Supreme Court's decision in *Fordice*. The trial court did not rule on this motion, and the parties eventually reached a new settlement, culminating in a consent decree (*Geier v. Sundquist*, 128 F. Supp. 2d 519 (M.D. Tenn. 2001)). For a discussion of *Geier* and the 2001 settlement, see Deon D. Owensby, Comment, "Affirmative Action and Desegregating Tennessee's Higher-Education System: The *Geier* Case in Perspective," 69 *Tenn. L. Rev.* 701 (2002).

whether state higher education policies and practices were racially neutral, not whether there was racial balance in the various sectors of public higher education. Applying this standard to the state's actions, and relying on the voluntariness of student choice under *Bazemore,* the court found no violation of law.

A three-judge panel of the U.S. Court of Appeals for the Fifth Circuit initially did not view *Bazemore* as controlling, and overruled the district court. Because the plaintiffs in *Ayers* had alleged *de jure* segregation (*Bazemore* involved *de facto* segregation), the court ruled that the correct standard was that of *Geier v. Alexander.* The panel cited lower admission standards for predominantly black institutions, the small number of black faculty at white colleges, program duplication at nearby black and white institutions, and continued underfunding of black institutions as evidence of an illegal dual system (*Ayers v. Allain,* 893 F.2d 732 (5th Cir. 1990)). The state petitioned the Fifth Circuit for a rehearing *en banc,* which was granted. The *en banc* court reversed the panel, reinstating the decision of the district court (914 F.2d 676 (5th Cir. 1990)).

The *en banc* court relied on a case decided two decades earlier, *Alabama State Teachers Assn. v. Alabama Public School and College Authority,* 289 F. Supp. 784 (M.D. Ala. 1968), *affirmed per curiam,* 393 U.S. 400 (1969), which held that the scope of the state's duty to dismantle a racially dual system of higher education differed from, and was less strict than, its duty to desegregate public elementary and secondary school systems. The *en banc* court said that *Green* did not apply to the desegregation of higher education and that the standard articulated in *Bazemore* should have been applied in this case. Furthermore, it saw no conflict between *Green* and *Bazemore,* stating that *Green* had not outlawed all "freedom-of-choice" desegregation plans outside elementary and secondary education. The opinion in *Geier,* on which the earlier panel opinion had relied, received sharp criticism as an overreading of *Bazemore.*

Despite its conclusion that the state's conduct did not violate the equal protection clause (and, without specifically addressing it, Title VI), the court did find some present effects of the former *de jure* segregation. The majority concluded that the inequalities in racial composition were a result of the different historical missions of the three sectors of public higher education, but that current state policies provided equal educational opportunity irrespective of race.

The *en banc* majority interpreted the legal standard to require affirmative efforts, but not to mandate equivalent funding, admission standards, enrollment patterns, or program allocation. The plaintiffs appealed the *en banc* court's ruling to the U.S. Supreme Court.

At the same time, similar litigation was in progress in Louisiana. In 1974, the U.S. Department of Justice sued the state of Louisiana under both the equal protection clause and Title VI, asserting that the state had established and maintained a racially segregated higher education system. The Justice Department cited duplicate programs at contiguous black and white institutions and the existence of three systems of public higher education as examples of continuing racial segregation. After seven years of pretrial conferences, the parties agreed to a consent decree, which was approved by a district court judge in 1981. Six years later, the United States charged that the state had not implemented the consent decree and that almost all of the state's institutions of higher education were still racially identifiable. The state argued that its good-faith efforts to desegregate higher education were sufficient.

In *United States v. Louisiana,* 692 F. Supp. 642 (E.D. La. 1988), a federal district judge granted summary judgment for the United States, agreeing that the state's actions had been insufficient to dismantle the segregated system. In later opinions (718 F. Supp. 499 (E.D. La. 1989), 718 F. Supp. 525 (E.D. La. 1989)), the judge ordered Louisiana to merge its three systems of public higher education, create a community college system, and reduce unwarranted duplicate programs, especially in legal education. Appeals to the Supreme Court followed from all parties,[56] but the U.S. Supreme Court denied review for want of jurisdiction (*Louisiana, ex rel. Guste v. United States,* 493 U.S. 1013 (1990)).

Despite the flurry of appeals, the district court continued to seek a remedy in this case. It adopted the report of a special master, which recommended that a single governing board be created, that the board classify each institution by mission, and that the graduate programs at the state's comprehensive institutions be evaluated for possible termination. The court also ordered the state to abolish its open admissions policy and to use new admissions criteria consisting of a combination of high school grades, rank, courses, recommendations, extracurricular activities, and essays in addition to test scores (751 F. Supp. 621 (E.D. La. 1990)). After the Fifth Circuit's *en banc* opinion in *Ayers v. Allain* was issued, however, the district court judge vacated his earlier summary judgment, stating that although he disagreed with the Fifth Circuit's ruling, he had no choice but to follow it (*United States v. Louisiana,* 751 F. Supp. 606 (E.D. La. 1990)). The Governor of Louisiana appealed this ruling, but the judge stayed both the appeal and the remedies he had ordered, pending the Supreme Court's opinion in *Ayers v. Allain,* now titled *United States v. Fordice.*[57]

The U.S. Supreme Court was faced with the issue addressed in *Geier:* Which Supreme Court precedents control equal protection and Title VI jurisprudence

---

[56]For a description of the litigation history of this case, see Note, "Realizing the Dream: *U.S. v. State of Louisiana,*" 50 *La. L. Rev.* 583 (1990).

[57]In proceedings subsequent to the Supreme Court's opinion in *Fordice,* the legal skirmishes in Louisiana continued. After *Fordice* was announced, the Fifth Circuit vacated the district court's summary judgment for the state and remanded the case for further proceedings in light of *Fordice.* The district court then ordered the parties to show cause why the 1988 liability determination and remedy should not be reinstated. It also reinstated its earlier liability finding and entered a new remedial order at 811 F. Supp. 1151 (E.D. La. 1993). By the end of 1993, the U.S. Court of Appeals for the Fifth Circuit had overturned a district court's order to create a single higher education system for the state's public colleges, to create new admissions criteria for state colleges, to create a community college system, and to eliminate duplicative programs in adjacent racially identifiable state institutions (*United States v. Louisiana,* 9 F.3d 1159 (5th Cir. 1993)). The case was remanded to the trial court for resolution of disputed facts and determination of whether program duplication violated *Fordice.* The Department of Justice and a federal judge approved a plan that would increase spending at several historically black institutions, and create one governing board for the state's public colleges rather than four, but would not result in the merger of any institutions ("Court Backs College Plan in Louisiana," *New York Times,* October 15, 1994, p. A24; "The Country's Only Historically Black Public-College System Would Be Split Up . . . ," *Chron. Higher Educ.,* February 2, 1996, A26).

in higher education desegregation—*Bazemore* or *Green*? In *United States v. Fordice*, 505 U.S. 717(1992), the Court reversed the decision of the Fifth Circuit's *en banc* majority, sharply criticizing the court's reasoning and the legal standard it had applied. First, the Court refused to choose between the two precedents. Justice White, writing for the eight-Justice majority, rejected the Fifth Circuit's argument that *Bazemore* limited *Green* to segregation in elementary/secondary education.

The Court also criticized the lower courts for their interpretation of the *Alabama State Teachers Association* case: "Respondents are incorrect to suppose that *ASTA* validates policies traceable to the *de jure* system regardless of whether or not they are educationally justifiable or can be practicably altered to reduce their segregative effects" (505 U.S. at 730).

White's opinion articulated a standard that appears to be much closer to *Green* than to *Bazemore*, despite his insistence that *Bazemore* can be read to require the outcome in *Fordice*. He rejected the lower courts' assertion that a state's adoption of race-neutral policies was sufficient to cure the constitutional wrongs of a dual system.

> . . . In a system based on choice, student attendance is determined not simply by admission policies, but also by many other factors. Although some of these factors clearly cannot be attributed to State policies, many can be. Thus, even after a State dismantles its segregative *admissions* policy, there may still be state action that is traceable to the State's prior *de jure* segregation and that continues to foster segregation. . . . If policies traceable to the *de jure* system are still in force and have discriminatory effects, those policies too must be reformed to the extent practicable and consistent with sound educational practices [505 U.S. at 729].

The Court asserted that "there are several surviving aspects of Mississippi's prior dual system which are constitutionally suspect" (at 733). Although it refused to list all these elements, it discussed four policies that, in particular, appeared to perpetuate the effects of prior *de jure* discrimination: admission policies (for discussion of this portion of the case, see Section 8.2.4.1), the duplication of programs at nearby white and black colleges, the state's "mission classification," and the fact that Mississippi operates eight public institutions. For each category, the court noted the foundations of state policy in previous *de jure* segregation and a failure to alter that policy when *de jure* segregation officially ended. Furthermore, the Court took the lower courts to task for their failure to consider that state policies in each of these areas had influenced student access to higher education and had perpetuated segregation.

The Court emphasized that it was not calling for racial quotas; in its view, the fact "that an institution is predominantly white or black does not in itself make out a constitutional violation" (at 743). It also refused the plaintiffs' invitation to order the state to provide equal funding for the three traditionally black institutions. The Court remanded the case so that the lower court could determine whether the state had "met its affirmative obligation to dismantle its prior dual system" under the standards of the equal protection clause and Title VI.

Although they joined the Court's opinion, two Justices provided concurring opinions, articulating concerns they believed were not adequately addressed in the majority opinion. Justice O'Connor reminded the Court that only in the most "narrow" of circumstances should a state be permitted to "maintain a policy or practice traceable to *de jure* segregation that has segregative effects" (at 744). O'Connor wrote: "Where the State can accomplish legitimate educational objectives through less segregative means, the courts may infer lack of good faith." Even if the state could demonstrate that "maintenance of certain remnants of its prior system is essential to accomplish its legitimate goals," O'Connor added, "it still must prove that it has counteracted and minimized the segregative impact of such policies to the extent possible" (505 U.S. at 744–45). O'Connor's approach would appear to preclude a state from arguing that certain policies that had continued segregative impacts were justified by "sound educational policy."

Justice Thomas's concurrence articulates a concern expressed by many proponents of historically black colleges, who worry that the Court's opinion might result in the destruction of black colleges.[58] Because the black colleges could be considered "vestiges of a segregated system" and thus vulnerable under the Court's interpretation of the equal protection clause and Title VI, Thomas wanted to stress that the *Fordice* ruling did *not* require the dismantling of traditionally black colleges. Thomas wrote:

> Today, we hold that "[i]f policies traceable to the *de jure* system are still in force and have discriminatory effects, those policies too must be reformed to the extent practicable and consistent with sound educational policies." . . . In particular, because [this statement] does not compel the elimination of all observed racial imbalance, it portends neither the destruction of historically black colleges nor the severing of those institutions from their distinctive histories and traditions [505 U.S. at 745].

The majority opinion, Thomas noted, focused on the state's policies, not on the racial imbalances they had caused. He suggested that, as a result of the ruling in this case, district courts "will spend their time determining whether such policies have been adequately justified—a far narrower, more manageable task than that imposed under *Green*" (505 U.S. at 746). Thomas emphasized the majority opinion's use of "sound educational practices" as a touchstone for determining whether a state's actions are justifiable:

> In particular, we do not foreclose the possibility that there exists "sound educational justification" for maintaining historically black colleges *as such.* . . .
> I think it indisputable that these institutions have succeeded in part because of their distinctive histories and traditions. . . . Obviously, a State cannot maintain such traditions by closing particular institutions, historically white or

---

[58]The unique issues facing historically black colleges with regard to desegregation are discussed later in this Section.

historically black, to particular racial groups. . . . Although I agree that a State is not constitutionally *required to* maintain its historically black institutions as such . . . I do not understand our opinion to hold that a State is *forbidden* from doing so. It would be ironic, to say the least, if the institutions that sustained blacks during segregation were themselves destroyed in an effort to combat its vestiges [505 U.S. at 747–49; emphasis in original].

Thomas's concurrence articulates the concerns of some of the parties in the Louisiana and Mississippi cases—namely, that desegregation remedies would fundamentally change or even destroy the distinctive character of historically black colleges, instead of raising their funding to the level enjoyed by the public white institutions in those states (see P. Applebome, "Epilogue to Integration Fight at South's Public Universities," *New York Times,* May 29, 1992, pp. A1, A21).

Justice Scalia wrote a blistering dissent, criticizing the "effectively unsustainable burden the Court imposes on Mississippi, and all States that formerly operated segregated universities" and stating unequivocally that *Green* "has no proper application in the context of higher education, provides no genuine guidance to States and lower courts, and is as likely to subvert as to promote the interests of those citizens on whose behalf the present suit was brought" (505 U.S. at 750–51).

In Scalia's view, the Court's tests for ascertaining compliance with *Brown* were confusing and vague. He questioned how one would measure whether policies that perpetuate segregation have been eliminated to the extent "practicable" and consistent with "sound educational" practices (at 750). According to Scalia, "*Bazemore*'s standard for dismantling a dual system ought to control here: discontinuation of discriminatory practices and adoption of a neutral admissions policy. . . . Only one aspect of an historically segregated university system need be eliminated: discriminatory admissions standards" (at 757, 758). In this regard, Scalia agreed with the majority opinion that the state's sole reliance on standardized admission tests appeared to have a racially exclusionary purpose and was not evidence of a neutral admissions process.

Scalia then argued that the majority opinion would harm traditionally black colleges, because it did not require equal funding of black and white institutions. Equal funding, he noted, would encourage students to attend their own-race institutions without "paying a penalty in the quality of education" (at 759).

What the Court's test is designed to achieve is the elimination of predominantly black institutions. . . . There is nothing unconstitutional about a "black" school in the sense, not of a school that blacks *must* attend and that whites *cannot,* but of a school that, as a consequence of private choice in residence or in school selection, contains, and has long contained, a large black majority [at 760].

Despite Scalia's criticism, the opinion makes it clear that, although many elementary/secondary school desegregation remedies are unavailable to higher education, *Green* controls a district court judge's analysis of whether a state has eliminated the vestiges of a *de jure* segregated system of higher education.

On remand, the U.S. Court of Appeals for the Fifth Circuit reversed the prior ruling of the district court and remanded for further proceedings (*Ayers v. Fordice*, 970 F. 2d 1378 (5th Cir. 1992)). The ruling of the district court (879 F. Supp. 1419 (N.D. Miss. 1995)) considers a wide range of issues including admission standards, collegiate missions and the duplication of academic programs, racial identifiability of the campuses, the campus climate, and how the institution's and state's policies and practices interacted to perpetuate segregation. The court rejected the defendants' proposal that the state merge two pairs of historically white and historically black colleges, ordering them to consider other alternatives to ascertain if they would be more successful in reducing racial identifiability of the campuses.

The court found that the admissions standards proposed by the state were discriminatory, and that use of scores on the American College Test (ACT) as the sole criterion for admission was also discriminatory, but that the use of ACT scores for awarding scholarships was not discriminatory. The court approved the defendants' proposal for uniform admission standards for all Mississippi colleges and universities, rejecting the plaintiffs' argument that some of the colleges should have open admissions policies until greater racial balance was achieved. Regarding institutional missions, the court ruled that the limited missions allocated to the historically black institutions were a vestige of segregation, and ordered a study of program duplication, commenting that not all duplication necessarily resulted in segregation. The judge also ruled that funding should not be completely tied to institutional mission, given that mission assignments were made during the period of segregation.

The U.S. Department of Justice appealed the district court's decision. In April 1997, the U.S. Court of Appeals for the Fifth Circuit upheld part of the district court's findings, reversed another part, and remanded for further proceedings (111 F.3d 1183 (5th Cir. 1997)). The appellate court held that the financial aid policies of the historically white colleges perpetuated prior discrimination on the basis of race, but that the uniform admissions standards proposed by the state were appropriate. The court also directed the district court to amend the remedial decree to require the state to submit proposals for increasing the enrollment of white students at several historically black institutions. The U.S. Supreme Court denied review (522 U.S. 1084).[59]

---

[59]After several more rulings by the district court on funding issues and an attempt by some of the private parties to opt out of the class (which was denied by the trial court and affirmed on appeal), a settlement was reached that set uniform admission policies for the state colleges and provided for additional funding for the historically black colleges in order that they might attract white students. Upon receiving assurances from the state legislature that it would provide $500 million in funding over the next seventeen years to enhance current and create new academic programs at the historically black state institutions, as well as funding for remedial summer programs for underprepared students, the trial and appellate courts approved the settlement (*Ayers v. Thompson*, 358 F.3d 356 (5th Cir. 2004)). The plaintiffs appealed to the U.S. Supreme Court, which denied review (543 U.S. 951 (2004)), ending nearly thirty years of litigation. See Sara Hebel, "Supreme Court Clears Way for Settlement of College-Desegregation Case," *Chron. Higher Educ.*, October 29, 2004, A26.

The cases pending in Louisiana, as well as in Alabama, at the time of the *Fordice* ruling were influenced by it. For example, in *Knight v. Alabama,* 787 F. Supp. 1030 (N.D. Ala. 1991), a case that began in 1983, the plaintiffs, a group of black citizens that had joined the Justice Department's litigation, had argued that the state's allocation of "missions" to predominantly white and black public colleges perpetuated racial segregation because the black colleges received few funds for research or graduate education. They also argued that the white colleges' refusal to teach subjects related to race, such as black culture or history, had a discriminatory effect on black students.

A trial court had found, prior to *Fordice,* that the public system of higher education perpetuated earlier *de jure* segregation, but it had ruled against the plaintiffs on the curriculum issue. Both parties appealed. The state argued that its policies were race neutral and that public universities had a constitutionally protected right of academic freedom to determine what programs and courses would be offered to students, and the plaintiffs took issue with the academic freedom defense. A federal appellate court affirmed the trial court in part (14 F.3d 1534 (11th Cir. 1994)), and applied *Fordice*'s teachings to the actions of the state. The court held that, simply because the state could demonstrate legitimate, race-neutral reasons for continuing its past practice of limiting the types of programs and degrees offered by historically black colleges, it was not excused from its obligation to redress the continuing segregative effects of such a policy. But the appellate court differed with the trial court on the curriculum issue, stating that the First Amendment did not limit the court's power to order white colleges and universities to modify their programs and curricula to redress the continuing effects of prior discrimination. The court remanded the case to the trial court to determine whether the state's allocation of research missions to predominantly white colleges perpetuates segregation, and, if so, to determine "whether such effects can be remedied in a manner that is practicable and educationally sound" (14 F.3d at 1556). The trial court entered a remedial decree, to be in effect until 2005, creating trust funds to promote "educational excellence" for two historically black colleges and scholarship funds to be used by historically black institutions to attract white students, and ordering other actions by the state to strengthen the historically black institutions (see 900 F. Supp. 272 (N.D. Ala. 1995)).

(For analysis of the Mississippi and Alabama cases post-*Fordice,* see Scott L. Sroka, "Discrimination Against Students in Higher Education: A Review of the 1995 Judicial Decisions," 23 *J. Coll. & Univ. Law* 431 (1997). For a discussion of the implications of *Fordice* for historically black colleges and universities, see Kenneth S. Tollett, Sr., "The Fate of Minority-Based Institutions After *Fordice*: An Essay," 13 *Rev. Litig.* 447 (1994).)

The *Fordice* opinion has been criticized by individuals of all races and political affiliations as insufficiently clear to provide appropriate guidance to states as they attempt to apply its outcome to desegregation of the still racially identifiable public institutions in many states. (For a discussion of some of the unresolved issues, see S. Jaschik, "Whither Desegregation?" *Chron. Higher Educ.,* January 26, 1991, A33.)

As the history of the past three decades of Title VI litigation makes clear, the desegregation of higher education is very much an unfinished business. Its completion poses knotty legal, policy, and administrative enforcement problems and requires a sensitive appreciation of the differing missions and histories of traditionally black and traditionally white institutions. The challenge is for lawyers, administrators, government officials, and the judiciary to work together to fashion solutions that will be consonant with the law's requirement to desegregate but will increase rather than limit the opportunities available to minority students and faculty.

13.5.3. Title IX. The central provision of Title IX of the Education Amendments of 1972 (20 U.S.C. § 1681 *et seq.*) declares:

> (a) No person in the United States shall, on the basis of sex, be excluded from participation in, be denied the benefits of, or be subjected to discrimination under any education program or activity receiving federal financial assistance. . . .

Unlike Title VI, Title IX has various exceptions to its prohibition on sex discrimination. It does "not apply to an educational institution which is controlled by a religious organization if the application of this subsection would not be consistent with the religious tenets of such organization" (20 U.S.C. § 1681 (a)(3)). It does "not apply to an educational institution whose primary purpose is the training of individuals for the military services of the United States, or the merchant marine" (20 U.S.C. § 1681(a)(4)). There are also several exceptions concerning admissions (20 U.S.C. § 1681(a)(1), (2), (5)). In addition, Title IX excludes from its coverage the membership practices of tax-exempt social fraternities and sororities (20 U.S.C. § 1681(a)(6)(A)); the membership practices of the YMCA, YWCA, Girl Scouts, Boy Scouts, Campfire Girls, and other tax-exempt, traditionally single-sex "youth service organizations" (20 U.S.C. § 1681(a)(6)(B)); American Legion, Boys State, Boys Nation, Girls State, and Girls Nation activities (20 U.S.C. § 1681(a)(7)); and father-son and mother-daughter activities if provided on a reasonably comparable basis for students of both sexes (20 U.S.C. § 1681(a)(8)).

The Department of Education's regulations implementing Title IX (34 C.F.R. Part 106) specify in much greater detail the types of acts that are considered to be prohibited sex discrimination. Educational institutions may not discriminate on the basis of sex in admissions and recruitment, with exceptions for certain institutions as noted above (see Section 8.2.4.2 of this book). Institutions may not discriminate in awarding financial assistance (see Section 8.3.3 of this book), in athletic programs (see Section 10.4.6), or in the employment of faculty and staff members (see Sections 5.2.3 & 13.5.7.1). Section 106.32 of the Title IX regulations prohibits sex discrimination in housing accommodations with respect to fees, services, or benefits, but does not prohibit separate housing by sex (see Section 8.4.1 of this book). Section 106.33 of the regulations requires that separate facilities for toilets, locker rooms, and shower rooms be comparable. Section 106.34 prohibits sex discrimination in student access to course offerings. Sections 106.36 and 106.38 require that counseling services and employment placement services be offered to students in such a way that there is no discrimination on the basis of sex. Section 106.39 prohibits sex discrimination in health and insurance benefits and services (see Section 8.7.2 of this book). Section 106.40 prohibits certain discrimination on the basis of "parental, family, or marital status" or on the basis of pregnancy or childbirth. In addition to these regulations, the Department of Education has published guidelines and interpretive advice on certain, particularly difficult, applications of Title IX. The most important of these documents are *Sexual Harassment Guidance: Harassment of Students by School Employees, Other Students, or Third Parties,* which is discussed in Sections 8.1.5 and 9.3.4 of this book; and the Policy Interpretation on intercollegiate athletics, which is discussed in Section 10.4.6.

Litigation brought under Title IX has primarily addressed alleged sex discrimination in the funding and support of women's athletics (see Section 10.4.6 of this book), the employment of women faculty and athletics coaches (male or female) (see Section 5.3.3), and sexual harassment of students by faculty members (see Section 9.3.4) or by other students (see Section 8.1.5). In *Franklin v. Gwinnett County Public Schools,* 503 U.S. 60 (1992), discussed in subsection 13.5.9 below, the U.S. Supreme Court ruled unanimously that private parties who are victims of sex discrimination may bring "private causes of action" for money damages to enforce their nondiscrimination rights under Title IX. As a result of this 1992 ruling, which resolved a long-standing split among the lower courts, an increasing number of both students and faculty have used Title IX to sue postsecondary institutions. The availability of a money damages remedy under Title IX is particularly important to students, for whom typical equitable remedies, such as back pay and orders requiring the institution to refrain from future discriminatory conduct, are of little use because students are usually due no pay and are likely to have graduated or left school before the litigation has been completed. The Court's ruling in *Franklin* thus has great significance for colleges and universities because it increases the incentives for students, faculty members, and staff members to challenge sex discrimination in court. (See generally E. J. Vargyas, "*Franklin v. Gwinnett County Public Schools* and Its Impact on Title IX Enforcement," 19 *J. Coll. & Univ. Law* 373 (1993).) It also may persuade individuals considering litigation over alleged employment discrimination to use Title IX instead of Title VII, since Title IX has no caps on damage awards and no detailed procedural prerequisites, as Title VII does (see Section 5.2.1 of this book). Courts are split, however, on whether the availability of express private causes of actions for employment discrimination under Title VII precludes the use of Title IX for the same purpose (see Section 5.2.3 of this book).

As litigation has progressed after *Franklin,* courts have emphasized the distinction between institutional liability and individual (or personal) liability under Title IX. Title IX imposes liability only on the institution (the college, university, or college or university system as an entity) and not on its officers, administrators, faculty members, or staff members as individuals. This is because individual officers and employees are not themselves "education programs or activities" within the meaning of Title IX and usually are not themselves the recipients of the "federal financial assistance." In *Soper v. Hoben*, 195 F.3d 845 (6th Cir. 1999), for instance, the court enumerated cases—including *Franklin* but particularly *Davis v. Monroe County Board of Education*, 526 U.S. 629 at 639–40 (see Section 8.1.5)—supporting the view that individuals cannot be sued in their individual capacities under Title IX.

Courts have seldom addressed whether institutional employees can be sued in their official, rather than individual, capacities under Title IX. In *Doe v. Lance*, 1996 WL 663159, 1996 U.S. Dist. LEXIS 16836 (N.D. Ind. 1996), the court seemed willing to permit a Title IX suit against a school superintendent in her official capacity, but held that such a suit against the superintendent was the same as a suit against the school district itself. Because the school district was already a party to the lawsuit, the court dismissed the claim against the superintendent in her official capacity because it afforded the plaintiff "no additional avenue of relief."

Sex discrimination that is actionable under Title IX may also be actionable under the federal civil rights statute known as Section 1983 (see Sections 3.5 & 4.7.4 of this book) if the discrimination amounts to a "deprivation" of rights "secured by the [federal] Constitution." The Fourteenth Amendment's equal protection clause would be the basis for this type of claim. The advantage for victims of discrimination is that they may sue the individuals responsible for the discrimination under Section 1983, which they cannot do under Title IX. Section 1983 claims, however, may be brought only against individuals who are acting "under color of law," such as faculty and staff members at public institutions.

Although defendants have sometimes asserted that Title IX "subsumes" or "precludes" Section 1983 claims covering the same discriminatory acts, it is clear that courts will reject such arguments, at least when the Section 1983 equal protection claim is asserted against individuals rather than the institution itself. In *Crawford v. Davis*, 109 F.3d 1281 (8th Cir. 1997), for instance, the court emphatically recognized that Title IX "in no way restricts a plaintiff's ability to seek redress under § 1983 for the violation of independently existing constitutional rights," such as equal protection rights. And in *Delgado v. Stegall*, 367 F.3d 668 (7th Cir. 2004), the court reached the same result as to a student's Section 1983 claim against the alleged harasser (a professor), while adding nuance to the analysis.

13.5.4. *Section 504.* Section 504 of the Rehabilitation Act of 1973, as amended (29 U.S.C. § 794), states:

> No otherwise qualified individual with a disability in the United States . . .
> shall, solely by reason of his disability, be excluded from the participation in, be
> denied the benefits of, or be subjected to discrimination under any program or
> activity receiving federal financial assistance.

The Department of Education's regulations on Section 504 (34 C.F.R. Part 104) contain specific provisions that establish standards for postsecondary institutions to follow in their dealings with "qualified" students and applicants with disabilities, "qualified" employees and applicants for employment, and members of the public with disabilities who are seeking to take advantage of institutional programs and activities open to the public. A "qualified individual with a disability" is "any person who (i) has a physical or mental impairment which substantially limits one or more major life activities, (ii) has a record of such an impairment, or (iii) is regarded as having such an impairment" (34 C.F.R. § 104.3(j)). In the context of postsecondary and vocational education services, a "qualified" person with a disability is someone who "meets the academic and technical standards requisite to admission or participation in the recipient's education program or activity" (34 C.F.R. § 104.3(l)(3)). Whether an individual with a disability is "qualified" in other situations depends on different criteria. In the context of employment, a qualified individual with a disability is one who, "with reasonable accommodation, can perform the essential functions of the job in question" (34 C.F.R. § 104.3(l)(1)). With regard to other services, a qualified individual with a disability is someone who "meets the essential eligibility requirements for the receipt of such services" (34 C.F.R. § 104.3(l)(4)).[60]

Although the Section 504 regulations resemble those for Title VI and Title IX in the types of programs and activities considered, they differ in some of the means used for achieving nondiscrimination. The reason for these differences is that "different or special treatment of handicapped persons, because of their handicaps, may be necessary in a number of contexts in order to ensure equal opportunity" (42 Fed. Reg. 22676 (May 4, 1977)). Institutions receiving federal funds may not discriminate on the basis of disability in admission and recruitment of students (see this book, Section 8.2.4.3); in providing financial assistance (Section 8.3.3); in athletic programs (Section 10.4.7); in housing accommodations (Section 8.4.1); or in the employment of faculty and staff members (Section 5.2.5) or students (see 34 C.F.R. § 104.46(c)). The regulations also prohibit discrimination on the basis of disability in a number of other programs and activities of postsecondary institutions.

Section 104.43 requires nondiscriminatory "treatment" of students in general. Besides prohibiting discrimination in the institution's own programs and activities, this section requires that, when an institution places students in an educational program or activity not wholly under its control, the institution "shall assure itself that the other education program or activity, as a whole,

---

[60]Cases and authorities are collected in Francis M. Dougherty, Annot., "Who Is 'Individual with Handicaps' Under Rehabilitation Act of 1973 (29 U.S.C.S. §§ 701 et seq.)," 97 A.L.R. Fed. 40; Colleen Courtade, Annot., "Who Is 'Qualified' Handicapped Person Protected from Employment Discrimination Under Rehabilitation Act of 1973 (29 U.S.C.S. §§ 701 et seq.) and Regulations Promulgated Thereunder," 80 A.L.R. Fed. 830; James Lockhart, Annot., "Who Is Recipient of, and What Constitutes Program or Activity Receiving Federal Financial Assistance for Purposes of § 504 of Rehabilitation Act (29 U.S.C.A. § 794), Which Prohibits Any Program or Activity Receiving Financial Assistance from Discriminating on Basis of Disability," 160 A.L.R. Fed. 297; James Lockhart, Annot., "What Constitutes Federal Financial Assistance for Purposes of § 504 of Rehabilitation Act (29 U.S.C.A. § 794), Which Prohibits Any Program or Activity Receiving Federal Financial Assistance from Discriminating on Basis of Disability," 147 A.L.R. Fed. 205.

provides an equal opportunity for the participation of qualified handicapped persons." In a student teaching program, for example, the "as a whole" concept allows the institution to make use of a particular external activity even though it discriminates, provided that the institution's entire student teaching program, taken as a whole, offers student teachers with disabilities "the same range and quality of choice in student-teaching assignments afforded nonhandicapped students" (42 Fed. Reg. at 22692 (comment 30)). Furthermore, the institution must operate its programs and activities in "the most integrated setting appropriate"; that is, by integrating disabled persons with nondisabled persons to the maximum extent appropriate (34 C.F.R. § 104.43(d)).

The Education Department's regulations recognize that certain academic adjustment may be necessary to protect against discrimination on the basis of disability. However, those academic requirements that the institution "can demonstrate are essential to the program of instruction being pursued by such student or to any directly related licensing requirement" need not be adjusted. Adjustments that do not affect the academic integrity of a program, such as changes in the length of time to earn a degree or the modification of certain course requirements, are examples of adjustments that may be required by the regulations. The regulations also limit the institution's right to prohibit tape recorders or service animals if a disabled student needs these accommodations to participate in the educational program. The regulations also discuss the modification of examination formats and the provision of "auxiliary aids" such as taped texts or readers (34 C.F.R. § 104.44).

Section 104.47(b) provides that counseling and placement services be offered on the same basis to disabled and nondisabled students. The institution is specifically charged with ensuring that job counseling is not more restrictive for disabled students. Under Section 104.47(c), an institution that supplies significant assistance to student social organizations must determine that these organizations do not discriminate against disabled students in their membership practices.

The institution's programs or activities—"when viewed in their entirety"— must be physically accessible to students with disabilities, and the institution's facilities must be usable by them. The regulations applicable to existing facilities differ from those applied to new construction; existing facilities need not be modified in their entirety if other methods of accessibility can be used (34 C.F.R. § 104.22). All new construction must be readily accessible when it is completed.[61]

---

[61]A final rule to implement both the ADA and the Architectural Barriers Act (42 U.S.C. § 4151 et seq.) has been published. The "ADA Accessibility Guidelines for Buildings and Facilities; Architectural Barriers Act (ABA) Guidelines" were published at 69 Fed. Reg. No. 141 (July 23, 2004), and are codified at 36 C.F.R. Parts 1190 and 1191. Under 26 U.S.C. § 190, recipients who pay federal income tax are eligible to claim a tax deduction of up to $15,000 for architectural and transportation modifications made to improve accessibility for handicapped persons. See also 42 U.S.C. § 4151 et seq. (Architectural Barriers Act of 1968) and 29 U.S.C. § 792 (the Act's federal Compliance Board) for further requirements applicable to buildings constructed, altered, or leased with federal aid funds.

In *Southeastern Community College v. Davis*, 442 U.S. 397 (1979), set forth in Section 8.2.4.3 of this book, the U.S. Supreme Court added some important interpretive gloss to the regulation on academic adjustments and assistance for disabled students (34 C.F.R. § 104.44). The Court quoted but did not question the validity of the regulation's requirement that an institution provide "auxiliary aids"—such as interpreters, taped texts, or braille materials—for students with sensory impairments. It made very clear, however, that the law does not require "major" or "substantial" modifications in an institution's curriculum or academic standards to accommodate disabled students. To require such modifications, the Court said, would be to read into Section 504 an "affirmative action obligation" not warranted by its "language, purpose, [or] history." Moreover, if the regulations were to be interpreted to impose such obligation, they would to that extent be invalid.

The Court acknowledged, however, that the line between discrimination and a lawful refusal to take affirmative action is not always clear. Thus, in some instances programmatic changes may be required where they would not fundamentally alter the program itself. In determining where this line is to be drawn, the Court would apparently extend considerable deference to postsecondary institutions' legitimate educational judgments respecting academic standards and course requirements. While *Davis* thus limits postsecondary institutions' legal obligation to modify their academic programs to accommodate disabled students, the opinion does not limit an institution's obligation to make its facilities physically accessible to qualified students with disabilities, as required by the regulations (34 C.F.R. § 104.22)—even when doing so involves major expense. In *Davis*, the Court found that, because of her hearing disability, the plaintiff was not "otherwise qualified" for admission to the nursing program. When a person with a disability is qualified and has been admitted, however, Section 104.22 requires that facilities as a whole be "readily accessible" to that person.

The U.S. Supreme Court spoke a second time on the significance of Section 504—this time with regard to whether individuals with contagious diseases are protected by Section 504. In *School Board of Nassau County v. Arline*, 480 U.S. 273 (1987), the Court held that a teacher with tuberculosis was protected by Section 504 and that her employer was required to determine whether a reasonable accommodation could be made for her. Subsequent to *Arline*, Congress, in amendments to Section 504 (42 U.S.C. § 706 (8)(D)), and the Equal Employment Opportunity Commission (EEOC), in regulations interpreting the employment provisions of the Americans With Disabilities Act (ADA) (29 C.F.R. § 1630.2(r)), provided other statutory protections for students and staff with contagious diseases. (For a discussion of the relevant legal principles under Section 504 in a case where a university dismissed a dental student suffering from AIDS, see *Doe v. Washington University*, 780 F. Supp. 628 (E.D. Mo. 1991).)

The availability of compensatory damages under Section 504 was addressed in *Tanberg v. Weld County Sheriff*, 787 F. Supp. 970 (D. Colo. 1992). Citing *Franklin v. Gwinnett County Public Schools* (Section 13.5.9), the federal trial judge ruled that a plaintiff who proves intentional discrimination under Section 504 can be entitled to compensatory damages.

The significance of *Davis* may be limited for an additional reason, in that the Americans With Disabilities Act affords broader rights of access and accommodation to students, employees, and, in some cases, the general public than contemplated by *Davis*. The employment provisions of the Americans With Disabilities Act are discussed in Section 5.2.5, while its public accommodations and other provisions are discussed in Section 13.2.11. Remedies are broader than those provided for by Section 504, and apply to all colleges and universities, whether or not they receive federal funds. (For a comparison of Section 504 and the ADA with regard to access to colleges and universities for students with disabilities, see H. Kaufman, *Access to Institutions of Higher Education for Students with Disabilities* (National Association of College and University Attorneys, 2005). See also Note, "Americans With Disabilities Act of 1990: Significant Overlap with Section 504 for Colleges and Universities," 18 *J. Coll. & Univ. Law* 389 (1992).)

The U.S. Supreme Court has ruled that the federal government may not be sued for damages for violating Section 504 because Congress did not explicitly waive the federal government's sovereign immunity. In *Lane v. Pena,* 518 U.S. 187 (1996) a student at the U.S. Merchant Marine Academy was dismissed after he was diagnosed with diabetes during his first year at the academy. The Merchant Marine Academy is administered by a unit of the U.S. Department of Transportation. Although the trial court initially ordered him reinstated and awarded him damages, it vacated the damages award when a higher court stated, in a different case, that plaintiffs could not be awarded damages against the federal government for claims under Section 504. The appellate court affirmed summarily, and Lane appealed to the U.S. Supreme Court. In a 7-to-2 decision written by Justice O'Connor, the Court ruled that Congress had not "unequivocally expressed" its intent to waive federal sovereign immunity. Examining both the language of the statute and its legislative history, the Court declined to read into the statute a waiver that had not been clearly articulated by Congress.

As with Title IX (see Section 13.5.3 of this book), Section 504 apparently imposes liability only on institutions as such and not on individual officers or employees of the institution. In *Coddington v. Adelphi University,* 45 F. Supp. 2d 211 (E.D.N.Y. 1999), a suit by a former nursing student alleging discrimination based on learning disabilities, the district court dismissed four individual defendants—the former university president, the current president, the nursing school dean, and an associate professor of law—and let the case proceed only against the university itself. In an earlier case, however, the court in *Lee v. Trustees of Dartmouth College,* 958 F. Supp. 37 (D.N.H. 1997), did indicate that a "person who discriminates in violation of [Section 504] may be personally liable if he or she is in a position to accept or reject federal funds" (958 F. Supp. at 45).

Despite the broader reach of the ADA, Section 504 remains an important source of rights for students, employees, and visitors to the campus. For public institutions that now cannot be sued in federal court under the ADA (see Section 13.2.11 of this book), Section 504 may become a more significant source of remedies for plaintiffs who seek damages from these institutions.

13.5.5. Age Discrimination Act. The Age Discrimination Act of 1975 (42 U.S.C. § 6101 *et seq.*) contains a general prohibition on age discrimination in federally funded programs and activities. Under the Age Discrimination Act's original statement-of-purpose clause, the prohibition applied only to "unreasonable" discrimination—a limitation not found in the Title VI, Title IX, or Section 504 civil rights statutes (see Sections 13.5.2–13.5.4). Congress postponed the Act's effective date, however, and directed the U.S. Commission on Civil Rights to study age discrimination in federally assisted programs. After considering the commission's report, submitted in January 1978, Congress amended the Age Discrimination Act in October 1978 (Pub. L. No. 95-478) to strike the word "unreasonable" from the statement-of-purpose clause, thus removing a critical restriction on the Act's scope.

Regulations interpreting the Age Discrimination Act are codified in 45 C.F.R. Part 90, and "state general, government-wide rules" for implementing this law (45 C.F.R. § 90.2(a)). Every federal agency administering federal aid programs must implement its own specific regulations consistent with the general regulations. The law does not cover age discrimination in employment, which is prohibited by the Age Discrimination in Employment Act (ADEA; see Section 5.2.6, this book).

The general regulations, together with the extensive commentary that accompanies them (44 Fed. Reg. 33768–33775, 33780–33787), provide a detailed explanation of the Age Discrimination Act. The regulations are divided into several subparts. Subpart A explains the purpose and coverage of the Act and regulations and defines some of the regulatory terminology. Subpart B of the regulations explains the law's prohibition against age discrimination in programs covered by the Act. It also lists the exceptions to this prohibition. Exceptions involve using age as a proxy for some other qualification where age and that qualification are closely linked (for example, being at least age eighteen if a program requires that the student be at or beyond the age of majority).

Although the regulations and commentary add considerable particularity to the brief provisions of the Act, the full import of the Act for postsecondary institutions can be ascertained only by a study of the specific regulations that agencies have promulgated or will promulgate to fulfill the mandate of the general regulations. The Department of Health and Human Services' (HHS) specific regulations, for example, are codified in 45 C.F.R. Part 91.

The Education Department published final rules to interpret the Age Discrimination Act as it applies to the department's financial assistance programs (most notably, the student financial assistance programs) at 34 C.F.R. Part 110. The Education Department's regulations track the general regulations in many respects, and require institutions to provide the same type of assurance of compliance that they must provide under Titles IV and IX and Section 504. The regulations establish a procedure for filing a complaint with the department under the Age Discrimination Act (34 C.F.R. § 110.31), provide for mediation of disputes under the Act by the Federal Mediation and Conciliation Service (34 C.F.R. § 110.32), and describe the department's investigation process if mediation fails to resolve the complaint (34 C.F.R. § 110.33). Penalties for violations of the Act, including termination of funding or debarment from future funding, are contained at 34 C.F.R. § 110.35. A person filing a complaint under the Act must exhaust the administrative remedies provided by the regulations before filing a civil complaint in court (34 C.F.R. § 110.39).

Postsecondary administrators and counsel should consult both the specific and the general agency regulations, in conjunction with the Act itself, when reviewing institutional policies or practices that employ explicit or implicit age distinctions.

A federal appellate court was asked to examine the circumstances under which a plaintiff using the Age Discrimination Act would be considered to have exhausted the administrative remedies that must be pursued before filing civil lawsuit. In *Williams v. Trevecca Nazarene College*, 1998 U.S. App. LEXIS 20546 (6th Cir. 1998) (unpublished), a student dismissed from a physician assistant program on academic grounds challenged the college's refusal to readmit him under the Age Discrimination Act. The plaintiff claimed that younger students who had been dismissed were readmitted despite their poor academic performance.

The plaintiff first had filed a complaint with the Office for Civil Rights. OCR regulations require that complaints go through a mediation process for sixty days before the agency begins an investigation. But, about a month after filing the OCR claim, the plaintiff filed an action in state court against the college (although he did not include an age discrimination claim). OCR then dismissed his complaint because he had filed the lawsuit instead of pursuing mediation. The OCR's letter informed the plaintiff that he could refile his claim within sixty days of the termination of legal proceedings. The litigation was dismissed, and the plaintiff refiled his claim with OCR, which refused to accept it. When the plaintiff then filed an Age Discrimination Act suit in federal district court, the court dismissed his claim for failure to exhaust administrative remedies.

The appellate court reversed the trial court's dismissal, ruling that the plaintiff had done "all that he had to do" under Section 6104(f) of the Age Discrimination Act. OCR's refusal to reopen the complaint, said the court, was an error, and the plaintiff should be regarded as having exhausted his administrative remedies such that the federal court now had jurisdiction to hear his age discrimination claim. The case was remanded for trial.

Faculty and administrators who develop admissions or grading policies that have the potential to exclude or disfavor older applicants or students should ensure that these policies have a firm foundation in the institution's mission and the needs of its academic programs. For example, Georgetown University's policy of not admitting applicants who had already earned a bachelor's degree was challenged as having a discriminatory effect on older applicants. The Education Department's Office for Civil Rights ruled that, although Georgetown's policy clearly impacted more negatively on older applicants than those who had just completed secondary school, the university's justification—that the normal operation of its regular undergraduate admission program is to offer a postsecondary educational opportunity to students who have not yet had that opportunity—fell within the exception to the Age Discrimination Act in 34 C.F.R. § 110.13 (OCR Compliant #11-98-2025, July 13, 1998). The university's ability to articulate a non-age-related justification for its policy was important to the successful outcome of this complaint.

13.5.6. Affirmative action.

Affirmative action poses a special problem under the federal civil rights statutes. The Department of Education's Title VI regulations, for example, both require and permit affirmative action under certain circumstances:

(i) In administering a program regarding which the recipient has previously discriminated against persons on the ground of race, color, or national origin, the recipient must take affirmative action to overcome the effects of prior discrimination.

(ii) Even in the absence of such prior discrimination, a recipient in administering a program may take affirmative action to overcome the effects of conditions which resulted in limiting participation by persons of a particular race, color, or national origin [34 C.F.R. § 100.3(b)(6)].

Similarly, the Title IX regulations require and permit affirmative action to alleviate sex discrimination (34 C.F.R. § 106.3). However, the Title IX regulations use the phrase "remedial action" rather than "affirmative action" to describe the institution's obligation to overcome the effects of its own prior discrimination (34 C.F.R. § 106.3(a))—a phrase also used in the Section 504 regulations (34 C.F.R. § 104.6(a)). The Section 504 regulations also use the phrase "voluntary action" rather than "affirmative action" to denote the institution's discretion to correct conditions that resulted in limited participation by disabled persons (34 C.F.R. § 104.6(b)). But none of the regulations define "affirmative action," "remedial action," or "voluntary action," or set out particular requirements for permissible or required actions.

One federal district court has ruled in a Title VI case that "affirmative action" may sometimes itself constitute a Title VI violation. In *Flanagan v. President and Directors of Georgetown College,* 417 F. Supp. 377 (D.D.C. 1976), the issue was that Georgetown Law Center had allocated 60 percent of its scholarship funds to minority students, who constituted only 11 percent of the class. The university claimed that the program was permissible under Section 100.3(b)(6)(ii) of the Title VI regulations. The court disagreed, holding that the scholarship program was not administered on a "racially neutral basis" and was "reverse discrimination on the basis of race, which cannot be justified by a claim of affirmative action." Subsequently, in *Regents of University of California v. Bakke,* 438 U.S. 265 (1978) (see Section 8.2.5), the first U.S. Supreme Court case on affirmative action under Title VI, a 5-to-4 majority of the Court agreed that Title VI did not require complete racial neutrality in affirmative action. But no majority of Justices could agree on the extent to which Title VI and its regulations permit racial or ethnic preferences to be used as one part of an affirmative action program.

In 2004, the U.S. Supreme Court ruled in two cases involving the University of Michigan that affirmative action in admissions was permissible under Title VI (and the equal protection clause) if the admissions program could survive strict scrutiny. The two cases are discussed in Section 8.2.5 of this book.

Like the Title VI, Title IX, and Section 504 regulations, the HHS general regulations under the Age Discrimination Act of 1975 (see subsection 13.5.5 of this book) also include a provision on affirmative action. A recipient of federal funds may take action to remedy prior discrimination or to overcome prior limits in accessibility of these programs to older individuals. Furthermore, programs that provide special benefits to the elderly or to children are permissible as voluntary affirmative action as long as they do not exclude other eligible individuals (45 C.F.R. § 90.49). Like the Title IX and Section 504 regulations, this regulation specifies that "remedial action" is permitted only when the recipient has discriminated in the past against the class of persons whom the regulations protect. In addition, the Age Discrimination Act regulation contains a unique provision (subsection (c)of Section 90.49) that, under certain circumstances, brings the provision of special benefits to two age groups—the elderly and children—under the protective umbrella of "voluntary affirmative action." The Act's regulations do not include explanatory commentary on Section 90.49. Nor, in common with the other civil rights regulations, do they define "remedial action" or "affirmative action" or (except for subsection (c)) the scope of permissible action.

Thus, the federal regulations give postsecondary administrators little guidance concerning the affirmative or remedial actions that they must take to maintain compliance, or that they may take without jeopardizing compliance. Insufficient guidance, however, is not a justification for avoiding affirmative action when it is required by the regulations, nor should it deter administrators from taking voluntary action when it is their institution's policy to do so. Rather, administrators should proceed carefully, seeking the assistance of legal counsel and keeping abreast of the developing case law and agency policy interpretations on affirmative action. (See also Sections 5.4, 6.5, 8.2.5, & 8.3.4 of this book.)

13.5.7. Scope and coverage problems

13.5.7.1. Coverage of employment discrimination. One question concerning the scope and coverage of the civil rights statutes is whether they prohibit discrimination not only against students but also against employees. Both Title VI and the Age Discrimination Act contain provisions that permit coverage of discrimination against employees only when a "primary objective" of the federal aid is "to provide employment" (42 U.S.C. § 2000d-3; 42 U.S.C. § 6103(c)). Title IX and Section 504 do not contain any such express limitation. Consistent with the apparent open-endedness of the latter two statutes, both the Title IX and the Section 504 regulations have provisions comprehensively covering discrimination against employees (see Sections 5.2.3 & 5.2.5 of this book), while the Title VI and the Age Discrimination Act regulations cover employment discrimination only in narrow circumstances (34 C.F.R. §§ 100.2 & 100.3(c); 45 C.F.R. § 90.3(b)(2)).

The first major U.S. Supreme Court case on scope and coverage issues—
North Haven Board of Education v. Bell, 456 U.S. 512 (1982)—concerned
employment. *North Haven* was a Title IX case. The plaintiffs, two school boards
in Connecticut, challenged the validity of subpart E of the Department of Health,
Education and Welfare's (HEW) (now ED) Title IX regulations, which prohibits
federal fund recipients from discriminating against their employees on the basis
of sex. Looking to the wording of Title IX, the statute's legislative history, and
the statute's "postenactment history" in Congress and at HEW, the Court (with
three dissenters) rejected the challenge and upheld the subpart E regulations:

> Our starting point in determining the scope of Title IX is, of course, the statu-
> tory language. . . . Section 901(a)'s broad directive that "no person" may be
> discriminated against on the basis of gender appears, on its face, to include
> employees as well as students. Under that provision, employees, like other
> "persons," may not be "excluded from participation in," "denied the benefits
> of," or "subjected to discrimination under" education programs receiving federal
> financial support. . . . Because Section 901(a) neither expressly nor impliedly
> excludes employees from its reach, we should interpret the provision as covering
> and protecting these "persons" unless other considerations counsel to the
> contrary. After all, Congress easily could have substituted "student" or
> "beneficiary" for the word "person" if it had wished to restrict the scope
> of Section 901(a) [456 U.S. at 520–21].

The U.S. Supreme Court has also upheld Section 504's applicability to discrimination against employees. In *Consolidated Rail Corp. v. Darrone,* 465 U.S.
624 (1984), a locomotive engineer had been dismissed after having had his left
hand and forearm amputated as a result of an accident. When the engineer
claimed that he was fit for work and had been discriminated against because
of his disability, the employer argued that Darrone was not protected by
Section 504. That law, argued the railroad, applies to employment discrimination "only if the primary objective of the federal aid that [the employer] receives
is to promote employment." In other words, unless the employee was paid with
federal funds, the railroad argued, Section 504 did not apply. The Court rejected
this argument:

> It is clear that Section 504 itself contains no such limitation . . . ; rather, that
> section prohibits discrimination against the handicapped under "*any* program or
> activity receiving Federal financial assistance." And it is unquestionable that the
> section was intended to reach employment discrimination. Indeed, enhancing
> employment of the handicapped was so much the focus of the 1973 legislation
> that Congress the next year felt it necessary to amend the statute to clarify
> whether Section 504 was intended to prohibit other types of discrimination as
> well (see § 111(a), Pub. L. 93-516, 88 Stat. 1617, 1619 (1974)). Thus, the
> language of Section 504 suggests that its bar on employment discrimination
> should not be limited to programs that receive federal aid the primary purpose
> of which is to promote employment.
>
> The legislative history, executive interpretation, and purpose of the 1973
> enactment all are consistent with this construction [465 U.S. at 632–33].

These Supreme Court rulings on Title IX's and Section 504's applicability to employment discrimination do not end the matter. Once this coverage is affirmed, the next question is how the two statutes and their employment regulations may be enforced: by private causes of action in court (see subsection 13.5.9 below) or only by administrative enforcement (see subsection 13.5.8 below). Regarding Title IX, the Court has not answered this question, and the lower courts are split on whether a victim of sex discrimination in employment may bring a Title IX private cause of action in court. The courts answering in the negative argue that the availability of private causes of action for employment discrimination under Title VII precludes them from being maintained under Title IX (see Section 5.2.3 of this book, and see also *Duello v. Board of Regents of the University of Wisconsin System,* 583 N.W.2d 863 (Wis. Ct. App. 1998)). Regarding Section 504, the U.S. Supreme Court did permit a private cause of action for employment discrimination in the *Darrone* case (above). But *Darrone* was decided before passage of the Americans With Disabilities Act of 1990. Since Title I of this Act, covering employment discrimination, is structurally similar to Title VII, it is possible that some courts will determine that the Americans With Disabilities Act now serves to preclude private causes of action for employment discrimination under Section 504 in the same way that (according to some lower courts) Title VII precludes such causes of action under Title IX.

13.5.7.2. Coverage of unintentional discriminatory acts. None of the four civil rights statutes explicitly states whether they prohibit actions whose effects are discriminatory (that is, actions that have a disproportionate or disparate impact on the class of persons protected) or whether such actions are prohibited only if taken with a discriminatory intent or motive. The regulations for Title VI and the Age Discrimination Act, however, contain provisions that apparently prohibit actions with discriminatory effects, even if those actions are not intentionally discriminatory (34 C.F.R. § 100.3(b)(2); 45 C.F.R. § 90.12); and the Section 504 regulations prohibit actions that have the effect of subjecting a qualified individual to discrimination on the basis of disability (34 C.F.R. § 104.4(b)(4) & (5)). Title IX's regulations prohibit testing or evaluation of skill that has a discriminatory effect on the basis of sex (34 C.F.R. §§ 106.21(b)(2) & 106.34), and prohibit the use of "any rule concerning a student's actual or potential parental, family, or marital status" that would have the effect of discriminating on the basis of sex (34 C.F.R. § 106.40). The Title IX regulations also prohibit certain employment practices with discriminatory effects (34 C.F.R. § 106.51(a)(3)). In addition, some of the Title IX regulations on intercollegiate athletics programs could be construed to cover unintentional actions with discriminatory effects, especially as those regulations are interpreted in the 1979 Policy Interpretation (see Section 10.4.6).

In a leading U.S. Supreme Court case, *Guardians Ass'n. v. Civil Service Commission of the City of New York,* 463 U.S. 582 (1983), the Court could not agree on the legal status of disparate impact cases under Title VI. The Justices issued six opinions in the case, none of which commanded a majority and which, according to Justice Powell, "further confuse rather than guide." The Court's basic difficulty was reconciling *Lau v. Nichols,* 414 U.S. 563 (1974), which held that the Department of Health, Education and Welfare's (now the Department of Education's) Title VI regulations validly prohibit actions with discriminatory effects, with *Regents of the University of California v. Bakke,* 438 U.S. 265 (1978), which indicated that Title VI reaches no further than the Fourteenth Amendment's equal protection clause, which prohibits only intentional discrimination.

Although the Court could not agree on the import of these two cases, or on the analysis to adopt in the case before it, one can extract some meaning from *Guardians* by pooling the views expressed in the various opinions. A majority of the Justices did hold that the discriminatory intent requirement is a necessary component of the Title VI statute. A different majority, however, held that, even though the *statute* embodies an intent test, the ED *regulations* that adopt an effects test are nevertheless valid. In his opinion, Justice White tallied the differing views of the Justices on these points (463 U.S. at 584, n.2 & 607, n.27). He then rationalized these seemingly contradictory conclusions by explaining that "the language of Title VI on its face is ambiguous; the word 'discrimination' is inherently so." The statute should therefore be amenable to a broader construction by ED, "at least to the extent of permitting, if not requiring, regulations that reach" discriminatory effects (463 U.S. at 592; see also 463 U.S. at 643–45 (opinion of Justice Stevens)).

The result of this confusing mélange of opinions is to validate the Education Department's regulations extending Title VI coverage to actions with discriminatory effects. At the same time, however, the *Guardians* opinions suggest that, if the department were to change its regulations so as to require proof of discriminatory intent, such a change would also be valid. Any such change, though, would in turn be subject to invalidation by Congress, which could amend the Title VI statute (or other statutes under which the issue arose) to replace its intent standard with an effects test. Such legislation would apparently be constitutional (see Sections 13.1.2 and 13.1.5 of this book; and see *City of Rome v. United States,* 446 U.S. 156 (1980)).

In *Alexander v. Choate,* 469 U.S. 287 (1985), the Court also considered the discriminatory intent issue under Section 504. After reviewing the various opinions in the *Guardians* case on Title VI, the Court determined that that case does not control the intent issue under Section 504 because Section 504 raises considerations different from those raised by Title VI. In particular:

> Discrimination against the handicapped was perceived by Congress to be most often the product, not of invidious animus, but rather of thoughtlessness and indifference—of benign neglect. . . . Federal agencies and commentators on the plight of the handicapped similarly have found that discrimination against the handicapped is primarily the result of apathetic attitudes rather than affirmative animus.
>
> In addition, much of the conduct that Congress sought to alter in passing the Rehabilitation Act would be difficult if not impossible to reach were the Act construed to proscribe only conduct fueled by a discriminatory intent. For example, elimination of architectural barriers was one of the central aims

of the Act (see, for example, S. Rep. No. 93-318, p. 4 (1973), U.S. Code Cong. & Admin. News 1973, pp. 2076, 2080), yet such barriers were clearly not erected with the aim or intent of excluding the handicapped [469 U.S. at 295–97].

Although these considerations suggest that discriminatory intent is not a requirement under Section 504, the Court also noted some countervailing considerations:

> At the same time, the position urged by respondents—that we interpret Section 504 to reach all action disparately affecting the handicapped—is also troubling. Because the handicapped typically are not similarly situated to the nonhandicapped, respondents' position would in essence require each recipient of federal funds first to evaluate the effect on the handicapped of every proposed action that might touch the interests of the handicapped, and then to consider alternatives for achieving the same objectives with less severe disadvantage to the handicapped. The formalization and policing of this process could lead to a wholly unwieldy administrative and adjudicative burden [469 U.S. at 298].

Faced with these difficulties, the Court declined to hold that one group of considerations would always have priority over the other: "While we reject the boundless notion that all disparate-impact showings constitute prima facie cases under Section 504, we assume without deciding that Section 504 reaches at least some conduct that has an unjustifiable disparate impact upon the handicapped." Thus "splitting the difference," the Court left for another day the specification of what types of Section 504 claims will not require evidence of a discriminatory intent.

A related, but different, issue is whether private plaintiffs (the victims of discrimination) may bring private causes of action in court to enforce ED's (or other agencies') disparate impact regulations, rather than relying solely on the administrative complaint process. (See subsection 13.5.9 below on private causes of action and subsection 13.5.8 on administrative enforcement.) If disparate impact regulations are valid under the four civil rights statutes, it necessarily follows that they may be enforced through the administrative processes of the agencies that promulgate the regulations. It does not automatically follow, however, that disparate impact regulations may be enforced through the implied private cause of action that, under *Cannon* and *Franklin* (subsection 13.5.9 below), may be used to enforce the statues themselves. The Court's *Lau v. Nichols* ruling in 1974 did permit a private cause of action to enforce Title VI impact regulations, but the status of *Lau* became unclear after *Bakke. Guardians* then validated the Title VI impact regulations, and a bare majority of the Justices seemed willing to permit their enforcement by private causes of action. Most lower courts took this position as well. But in *Alexander v. Sandoval,* 532 U.S. 275 (2001), in an opinion by Justice Scalia, the Court reconsidered these cases and ruled directly on the issue of private causes of action to enforce Title VI's impact regulations. The Court majority assumed, for purposes of the case, that the Title VI impact regulations are valid, and it acknowledged that five Justices in *Guardians* had taken that position. But in a hotly contested 5-to-4 decision, the Court prohibited private causes of action to enforce these regulations. Since there is no private cause of action to enforce the disparate impact regulations, and since private causes of action to enforce the Title VI statute itself require a showing of discriminatory intent, it follows from *Sandoval* that victims of race discrimination may not sue fund recipients under Title VI for actions that have discriminatory effects but are not intentionally discriminatory. The same conclusion apparently applies to Title IX, since the courts have treated the two statutes in much the same way, and probably also to the Age Discrimination Act. Section 504 is different, however, since the Section 504 statute does not require proof of discriminatory intent for all claims of statutory violations (see *Alexander v. Choate*, above).

13.5.7.3. Scope of the phrase "receiving federal financial assistance." Each of the four civil rights statutes prohibits discrimination in (1) "a program or activity" that is (2) "receiving federal financial assistance." Uncertainties about the definitions of these two terms, and their interrelation, have created substantial questions about the scope of the civil rights statutes. Most of these questions have not been resolved. The "program or activity" issues are discussed in subsection 13.5.7.4 below; the "receiving . . . assistance" (or "recipient") issues are discussed in this subsection.

The statutes do not define the phrase "receiving federal financial assistance." But the Education Department's regulations for each statute do contain a definition of "federal financial assistance" and a definition of "recipient" (the derivative of the statutory phrase "receiving"). Under the Title IX regulations, for instance:

> "Federal financial assistance" means any of the following, when authorized or extended under a law administered by the department:
> (1) A grant or loan of federal financial assistance, including funds made available for:
>   (i) The acquisition, construction, renovation, restoration, or repair of a building or facility or any portion thereof; and
>   (ii) Scholarships, loans, grants, wages, or other funds extended to any entity for payment to or on behalf of students admitted to that entity, or extended directly to such students for payment to that entity.
> (2) A grant of federal real or personal property or any interest therein, including surplus property, and the proceeds of the sale or transfer of such property, if the federal share of the fair market value of the property is not, upon such sale or transfer, properly accounted for to the Federal government.
> (3) Provision of the services of Federal personnel.
> (4) Sale or lease of Federal property or any interest therein at nominal consideration, or at consideration reduced for the purpose of assisting the recipient or in recognition of public interest to be served thereby, or permission to use federal property or any interest therein without consideration.
> (5) Any other contract, agreement, or arrangement which has as one of its purposes the provision of assistance to any education program or activity, except a contract of insurance or guaranty [34 C.F.R. § 106.2(g)].

And:

> "Recipient" means any public or private agency, institution, or organization, or other entity, or any other person, to whom Federal financial assistance is extended directly or through another recipient and which operates an educational program or activity which receives or benefits from such assistance, including any subunit, successor, assignee, or transferee thereof [34 C.F.R. § 106.2(h)].

These definitions, however, left several questions open.

The leading case addressing the meaning of "receiving federal financial assistance," and raising the most notable issue, is *Grove City College v. Bell*, 465 U.S. 555 (1984), a Title IX case. The college, a private liberal arts institution, received no direct federal or state financial assistance. Many of the college's students, however, did receive Basic Educational Opportunity Grants (now Pell Grants), which they used to defray their educational costs at the college. The Education Department determined that Grove City was a recipient of "federal financial assistance" under 34 C.F.R. § 106.2(g)(1) and advised the college to execute an Assurance of Compliance (a form certifying that the college will comply with Title IX) as required by 34 C.F.R. § 106.4. The college refused, arguing that the indirect aid received by its students did not constitute federal financial assistance to the college.

The U.S. Supreme Court unanimously held that the student aid constituted aid to the college and that, if the college did not execute an Assurance of Compliance, the Education Department could terminate the student aid:

> The linchpin of Grove City's argument that none of its programs receives any federal assistance is a perceived distinction between direct and indirect aid, a distinction that finds no support in the text of Section 901(a). Nothing in Section 901(a) suggests that Congress elevated form over substance by making the application of the nondiscrimination principle dependent on the manner in which a program or activity receives federal assistance. There is no basis in the statute for the view that only institutions that themselves apply for federal aid or receive checks directly from the federal government are subject to regulation (*Bob Jones University v. Johnson*, 396 F. Supp. 597, 601–04 (D.S.C. 1974), *affirmed*, 529 F.2d 514 (4th Cir. 1975) [reaching a similar conclusion under Title VI regarding veterans' education benefits]). As the Court of Appeals observed, "by its all-inclusive terminology [Section 901(a)] appears to encompass *all* forms of federal aid to education, direct or indirect" (687 F.2d at 691 (emphasis in original)) [465 U.S. at 564].[62]

In a later case, *United States Department of Transportation v. Paralyzed Veterans of America*, 477 U.S. 597 (1986), the Court clarified the meaning of

---

[62][Author's footnote] Another part of the *Grove City* case is discussed in subsection 13.5.7.4 below. That part (concerning the "program or activity" issue) was later overridden legislatively by Congress. The part of *Grove City* discussed in this subsection (the "receiving . . . assistance" issue) is still good law in all respects.

"recipient" under Section 504 by addressing the difference between a recipient and a "beneficiary" of federal funds. The Court rejected the argument that a beneficiary of federal funding granted to another entity can be considered an indirect recipient of the funds. *Paralyzed Veterans* was followed and applied to Title IX in *Smith v. NCAA,* 525 U.S. 459 (1999) (discussed in Section 14.4.6), in which the Court asserted that economic benefit alone does not make an entity a "recipient" of Title IX funds, and that an entity must actually "receive" the funds, "directly or through an intermediary," in order to be a recipient under Title IX.

13.5.7.4. Scope of the phrase "program or activity."

The civil rights spending statutes proscribe discrimination in a "program or activity" that is "receiving" federal aid. Prior to 1988, when Congress passed the Civil Rights Restoration Act (discussed below), it was not clear whether the entire institution was considered a "program or activity" for purposes of the civil rights statutes, or whether only the particular "programs" or "activities" that received the funding were subject to the statutes. The Title VI regulations did contain a comprehensive definition of "program," including within it the concept of "activity" (34 C.F.R. § 100.13(g)), that was of some help; but the Title IX, Section 504, and Age Discrimination Act regulations had only sketchy references to these terms (34 C.F.R. § 106.31(a); 34 C.F.R. § 104.43(a); 45 C.F.R. § 90.3(a)).

Numerous questions about the "program or activity" concept had arisen in litigation prior to 1988. The most controversial was the question of how to apply this concept to indirect or student-based aid, such as Pell Grants or veterans' education benefits. Did the entire institution "receive" this aid, thus binding the entire institution to nondiscrimination requirements whenever its students used federal student aid to defray the costs of their education? Or was only the institution's financial aid office, or some lesser portion of the institution, considered to be the "program" that "received" the student aid and was thus bound by the nondiscrimination requirements? Another set of questions related to both indirect student-based aid and direct (or earmarked) institution-based aid, such as construction grants. If a program or an activity in an institution did not directly receive federal funds but benefited from the receipt of funds by other institutional programs or activities, was it subject to nondiscrimination requirements? (See *Haffer v. Temple University,* 688 F.2d 14 (3d Cir. 1982), applying the "benefit theory" for extending the scope of a civil rights statute.) Or if a program or an activity did not directly receive federal funds but engaged in discriminatory practices that "infected" programs or activities that did directly receive funds, was it subject to nondiscrimination requirements? (See *Iron Arrow Honor Society v. Heckler,* 702 F.2d 549 (5th Cir. 1983), *vacated as moot,* 464 U.S. 67 (1983), adopting the "infection theory" for extending the scope of a civil rights statute.)

In *Grove City College v. Bell,* 465 U.S. 555 (1984), discussed in subsection 13.5.7.3, the Court also addressed the definition of "program or activity." Having unanimously agreed that the students' receipt of Basic Educational Opportunity Grants (BEOGs) constituted "federal financial assistance" for the college, the Justices then faced the problem of identifying the "program" that received this assistance and was therefore subject to Title IX. With three of the Justices dissenting, the Court held that the program was not the entire institution (as the lower court had determined) but only the college's financial aid program: "We conclude that the receipt of BEOGs by some of Grove City's students does not trigger institution-wide coverage under Title IX. In purpose and effect, BEOGs represent federal financial assistance to the college's own financial aid program, and it is that program that may properly be regulated under Title IX" (465 U.S. at 574).

The *Grove City* analysis of the "program or activity" issue proved to be highly controversial. Members of Congress criticized the analysis as being inconsistent with congressional intent. Civil rights groups and other interested parties criticized the decision's narrowing effect on federal enforcement of civil rights—not only under Title IX but also under the other three civil rights statutes using the same "program or activity" language, and not only for federal aid to education but for other types of federal assistance as well. Several bills were introduced in Congress to overturn the *Grove City* decision. In 1987, Congress passed the Civil Rights Restoration Act (CRRA) of 1987 (Pub. L. No. 100-259, 102 Stat. 28). When President Reagan vetoed the legislation, Congress voted to override the veto, and the Act became effective on March 22, 1988.

The CRRA amends all four civil rights spending statutes (Title VI, Title IX, Section 504, and the Age Discrimination Act) by defining "program or activity" as "all the operations of . . . a college, university, or other postsecondary institution . . . any part of which is extended federal financial assistance" (20 U.S.C. § 1687). This language clearly indicates that postsecondary institutions will be covered in their entirety by these laws if any part of their operations is extended federal aid.[63] (For analysis of the effect of the CRRA on colleges and universities, see R. Hendrickson, B. Lee, F. Loomis, & S. Olswang, "The Impact of the Civil Rights Restoration Act on Higher Education," 60 *West's Educ. Law Rptr.* 671 (1990).)

Other cases, before and after passage of the CRRA, have addressed additional aspects of the "program or activity" definition that are unique to Title IX. Unlike the other three statutes, Title IX covers only "education" programs and activities. Questions have thus arisen concerning whether the particular program or activity at issue is an "education" program or activity, whether a particular activity (for example, an off-campus activity) is an activity *of the educational institution* (the college or university), and whether another entity's program or

---

[63]This does not mean, however, that all of the institution's funds would be subject to termination if any part of the institution's operations were out of compliance with Title IX. Each statute has a separate provision, called a "pinpoint provision," that more narrowly limits the scope of any fund cut-off. Title IX's pinpoint provision (Section 902, codified at 20 U.S.C. § 1682), requires that any fund termination by a federal agency "be limited in its effect to the particular program, or part thereof, in which . . . noncompliance has been . . . found." Title VI has a similar provision (42 U.S.C. § 2000d-1). Section 504 incorporates the "remedies, procedures, and rights" available under Title VI, thus apparently including the same pinpoint provision (29 U.S.C. § 794a(2)). The Age Discrimination Act's pinpoint provision (42 (U.S.C. § 6104(b)), as developed in the general regulations (45 C.F.R. § 90.47(b)), is the most exacting of all, since it appears to prohibit the agency from using the infection theory (see text above) to expand the scope of the fund cut-off.

activity may be considered an "education" program or activity for purposes of Title IX.

In *Preyer v. Dartmouth College,* 968 F. Supp. 20 (D.N.H. 1997), for example, the plaintiff alleged that, as a result of sex discrimination, she had not been extended a permanent employment offer with Dartmouth College Dining Services. The U.S. District Court explained that, in order to give effect to the word "education" that precedes the phrase "program or activity" in Title IX, the statute applied only to the institution's programs or activities "that are educational in nature or bear some relation to the educational goals of the institution." The court then analogized to an earlier decision in which another federal district court determined that the building and grounds department of Harvard University is not an education program or activity for purposes of Title IX. In *Walters v. President & Fellows of Harvard College,* 601 F. Supp. 867 (D. Mass 1985), the plaintiff alleged that she had been forced to leave her job with the building and grounds department because of sexual harassment and intimidation. The *Walters* court determined that the building and grounds department did not have a sufficiently direct relation to the "delivery of educational services" and that including such custodial services under the definition of "education program or activity" would unnecessarily "strain" the language of Title IX. Although the *Walters* case was decided before the Civil Rights Restoration Act of 1987 had broadened the "program or activity" definition, the *Preyer* court was nevertheless quick to follow *Walters.* It held that Dartmouth College Dining Services was not an "education" program or activity and therefore dismissed the plaintiff's Title IX complaint. This reasoning seems inconsistent with Congress's intentions in passing the CRRA (see *Lam v. Curators of University of Missouri,* 122 F.3d 654, 656 (8th Cir. 1997)) and would create the incongruous result that all operations of a college or university (including dining services and buildings and grounds services) would now be covered by Title VI, Section 504, and the Age Discrimination Act, but only some operations (excluding dining services and buildings and grounds) would be covered by Title IX.

In a second case, *Lam v. Curators of University of Missouri* (above), the court considered a sexual harassment claim based on events that occurred at an off-campus, private dental office. The plaintiff (Lam) was a student in the university's dental program. The alleged harasser (Kim) was a clinical instructor in the dental program and was also the operator of the private dental office where he allegedly made sexual advances to the student. These advances allegedly occurred on two occasions when the instructor hired the student to assist him in his private dental practice. The student argued that, due to Kim's dual relationship with the university's dental program and the private dental office, the off-campus dental practice was sufficiently connected to the university to be considered a university program or activity. The court rejected this argument and emphasized four considerations that supported its conclusion:

> Kim conferred no benefit to the Dental School by operating a separate, competing dental clinic. Correspondingly, the university exercised no control over

the conduct of business at Kim's office. The University did not provide staff, funding, or any other support. There was no University requirement of private clinical work for students like Lam [122 F. 3d at 656].

In another case involving alleged harassment of a student engaged in an off-campus activity, *O'Connor v. Davis*, 126 F.3d 112 (2d Cir. 1997), the court considered whether a student assigned by her college to intern at a state hospital for mentally disabled persons could sue the hospital under Title IX. The student argued that, even if the hospital was not itself an "education" program, the college's operation of its education program could be "imputed" to the hospital. Even though the college had required the student to complete an internship (unlike the college in the *Lam* case), the court rejected the student's argument:

> [T]he fact that Marymount operates an "education program" may not be imputed to Rockland simply because O'Connor was a student at the former while she performed volunteer work with the latter. Factors that could lead to a different conclusion simply are not present here: the two entities have no institutional affiliation; there is no written agreement binding the two entities in any way; no staff are shared; no funds are circulated between them; and, indeed, Marymount students had previously volunteered at Rockland on only a few occasions. The only hint of a connection between Marymount and Rockland lies in the fact that (1) Marymount contacted Rockland for the purpose of placing O'Connor in an internship, and (2) Marymount appears to base its evaluation of its students' performance during their internships in part on an evaluation prepared by the person who supervised the student on-site. . . . Such connections are insufficient to establish Rockland as an agent or arm of Marymount for Title IX purposes [126 F.3d at 118–19].

Had the student in *O'Connor* sued the college rather than the hospital (as the student did in *Lam*), she would probably have avoided this result because the internship would likely have been considered part of the college's educational program. But in such a situation, it would be questionable whether the college could be held liable in money damages for the actions of the alleged harasser, a psychiatrist on staff at the hospital (see Section 9.3.4).

13.5.7.5. Coverage of retaliatory acts. The thrust of a retaliation claim is that the defendant has taken some kind adverse action against the plaintiff because the plaintiff has complained about or otherwise opposed the defendant's alleged violation of some statutory or constitutional duty of nondiscrimination. In some circumstances (for example, those concerning employment discrimination; see Section 5.2.3 of this book), a retaliation claim may be as important to a plaintiff as the discrimination claim itself. Indeed, a plaintiff may often maintain a retaliation claim even if he or she was not the victim of the alleged discrimination.

None of the four civil rights spending statutes contains a provision prohibiting retaliation against an individual who complains that a federal fund recipient has violated the statute's antidiscrimination provision. The U.S. Department of Education's regulations for each of these statutes, however, do include a retaliation provision. The Title VI regulations provide:

> No recipient or other person shall intimidate, threaten, coerce, or discriminate against any individual for the purpose of interfering with any right or privilege secured by section 601 of the Act or this part, or because he has made a complaint, testified, assisted, or participated in any manner in an investigation, proceeding or hearing under this part [34 C.F.R. § 100.7(e)].

The Title IX regulations include the same provision (34 C.F.R. § 106.71), as do the Section 504 regulations (34 C.F.R. § 104.61). The provision in the Age Discrimination Act regulations is somewhat different:

> [A] recipient may not engage in acts of intimidation or retaliation against any person who: (a) Attempts to assert a right protected by the Act or these regulations; or (b) Cooperates in any mediation, investigation, hearing, or other part of ED's investigation, conciliation, and enforcement process [34 C.F.R. § 110.34; see also 45 C.F.R. § 91.45].

It is clear that these retaliation regulations may be enforced by the U.S. Department of Education through its administrative processes. But it is a separate question whether they may be enforced in court through private causes of action (see subsection 13.5.9 below) brought by the victims of retaliation. This question became particularly important and complicated as a result of the U.S. Supreme Court's decision in *Alexander v. Sandoval,* 532 U.S. 275 (2001) (Section 13.5.9 below), a Title VI case. The essential holding of *Sandoval*—which applies as well to the other three statutes—is that courts may consider only the "text and structure" of the Title VI statute when determining whether a plaintiff may bring a private cause of action to enforce the statute; and agency regulations not based directly on the statute may not provide the basis for a private cause of action.

Under *Sandoval,* therefore, the retaliation regulations above could not be enforced in court by a private cause of action unless Congress had intended that acts of retaliation would be considered discrimination prohibited by the statutes themselves. After *Sandoval,* the lower courts differed on whether Congress's intent could be so construed. (Compare *Peters v. Jenney,* 327 F.3d 307 (4th Cir. 2003), permitting a private cause of action for retaliation, with *Litman v. George Mason University,* 156 F. Supp. 2d 579 (E.D. Va. 2001), prohibiting such a cause of action.) In 2005, however, the U.S. Supreme Court resolved this issue in favor of private causes of action in a Title IX case, *Jackson v. Birmingham Board of Education,* 125 S. Ct. 1497 (2005), whose reasoning will likely apply to all four civil rights statutes.

The plaintiff in *Jackson* was a teacher and the former coach of the girls' basketball team at a public high school. He alleged that he was removed as the coach because he had complained to his supervisors about unequal treatment of the girl's basketball team regarding funding, equipment, and facilities; and he claimed that this removal constituted retaliation violative of

Title IX. The federal district court and the U.S. Court of Appeals both determined that the coach's complaint failed to state a claim under Title IX, but by a 5-to-4 vote, the U.S. Supreme Court reversed and remanded the case for further proceedings.

According to Justice O'Connor's majority opinion in *Jackson*:

> Retaliation against a person because that person has complained of sex discrimination is another form of intentional sex discrimination encompassed by Title IX's private cause of action. Retaliation is, by definition, an intentional act. It is a form of "discrimination" because the complainant is being subjected to differential treatment. . . . Moreover, retaliation is discrimination "on the basis of sex" because it is an intentional response to the nature of the complaint: an allegation of sex discrimination [125 S. Ct. at 1504].

Sandoval did not affect this conclusion because the Court in *Jackson* did not rely directly on the Department of Education's Title IX *regulation* on retaliation (see above) but relied instead on the Title IX *statute*. As Justice O'Connor explained: "In step with *Sandoval,* we hold that Title IX's private right of action encompasses suits for retaliation, because retaliation falls within the statute's prohibition of intentional discrimination. . . ."

The Court in *Jackson* also made clear that "the victim of the retaliation" need not also have been "the victim of discrimination that is the subject of the original complaint." Even if Jackson had complained only about discrimination against members of the girls' basketball team, and not about discrimination against him as coach, he could still maintain a cause of action for retaliation. Thus, whenever a plaintiff can show that he or she had complained about or opposed sex discrimination by a federal fund recipient and that the recipient had taken adverse action against him or her because of this complaint or opposition, the statutory requirements for a retaliation claim are met—regardless of whether the plaintiff was also the target of the original discrimination. The claim is against the institution itself, as with other private causes of action under the four civil rights statutes, and money damages is a permissible remedy in such cases (see Section 13.5.9 below).

13.5.7.6. Coverage of extraterritorial acts of discrimination. Another coverage issue concerns the applicability of the Civil Rights spending statutes to discrimination that occurs in a foreign country. In other words, does or to what extent do these statutes have "extraterritorial" application? When examining questions of whether laws apply extraterritorially, courts have historically employed a presumption against extraterritorial application. (See *EEOC v. Arabian American Oil Co., 499* U.S. 244 (1991); *Foley Bros. v. Filardo,* 336 U.S. 281 (1941); see also Arlene Kanter, "The Presumption Against Extraterritoriality as Applied to Disability Discrimination Laws: Where Does It Leave Students with Disabilities Studying Abroad?" 14 *Stan. L. & Pol'y. Rev.* 291, 292 (2003).) The courts, however, have not applied this presumption to the federal civil rights spending statutes. On the one hand, these statutes do protect only persons "in the United States" from discrimination (see, for example, Title VI, 42 U.S.C.

§ 2000d)—language that seems to preclude extraterritorial application. On the other hand, however, these statutes explicitly apply to "all the operations" of a college or university receiving federal financial assistance (see, for example, Title IX, 20 U.S.C. § 1687; and see generally subsection 13.5.7.4 above).

In *King v. Board of Control of Eastern Michigan University,* 221 F. Supp. 2d 783 (2002), the leading case thus far, the question was whether the protections of the Title IX statute applied to six female students participating in their university's study abroad program in South Africa. The students alleged that they were sexually harassed by males also participating in the program. They alleged that an assistant to the program director had joined in the sexual harassment and that the program director had done nothing to stop the harassment, even though one of the students had notified him of it, and he had also been present on several occasions when the female students had been sexually harassed. Ultimately, the female students left the program and returned to the States.

The university emphasized the phrase "No person in the United States" in Title IX, reasoning that the phrase illustrates the congressional intent to apply the statute only "within the borders of the United States." The court rejected this argument, stating that "study abroad programs are operations of the university which are explicitly covered by Title IX and which *necessarily* require students to leave U.S. territory in order to pursue their educations." Moreover:

> Equality of opportunity in study abroad programs, unquestionably mandated by Title IX, requires extraterritorial application of Title IX. Holding otherwise could clearly create discrimination within the United States. That is, allowing sex discrimination to occur unremedied in study abroad programs could close those educational opportunities to female students by requiring them to submit to sexual harassment in order to participate. This is exactly the situation that Title IX was meant to remedy: female students should not have to submit to sexual harassment as the price of educational opportunity [221 F. Supp. 2d at 790].

The court in *King* also examined "the broad language of Title IX itself, including the limited number of exceptions to Title IX's broad reach," as well as the legislative history and the implementing regulations, concluding that they all confirmed Congress's intent that Title IX applied "to every single program of a university or college, including study abroad programs." The court therefore ruled that Title IX's provisions did apply extraterritorially, and protected the plaintiff students from discrimination in the study abroad program in South Africa.

Two years before the *King* case, a federal district court in Oregon issued a similar ruling in a similar case involving Section 504. In *Bird v. Lewis & Clark College,* 104 F. Supp. 2d 1271 (D. Ore. 2000), a paraplegic student argued that the college did not provide her with appropriate accommodations while she participated in the college's study abroad program in Australia. In an unpublished pretrial Order Ruling on Extraterritoriality (October 13, 1999), the federal district court ruled that Section 504 did have extraterritorial application. "Rejecting the college's argument in support of the application of the presumption against extraterritoriality, the court stated that if Section 504 [was] not applied extraterritorially, 'students in overseas programs would become the proverbial "floating sanctuaries from authority" not unlike stateless vessels on the high seas.' And even a stateless vessel . . . 'may be subject to United States jurisdiction where defendants are all citizens or resident aliens of the United States'" (Kanter, above, 14 *Stan. L. & Pol'y. Rev.* at 308, quoting Order Ruling on Extraterritoriality). On the merits of the claim, however, the federal district court denied the student equitable relief under Section 504 because, viewing the program and her experience in its entirety, she was not denied accommodations in the Australia program solely because of her disability.[64]

In contrast to *King* and *Bird,* the case of *Wolff v. South Colonie Central School District,* 534 F. Supp. 758 (1982), involved a class trip abroad rather than a study abroad program. (The case also involved a high school rather than a college, but the court's reasoning would apparently apply to colleges as well.) The student-plaintiff had a congenital limb deficiency that limited her mobility. The school denied her permission to participate in a class trip to Spain after determining that there would be a substantial degree of physical risk to her safety. When the student brought suit under Section 504, the court determined that Section 504 did apply extraterritorially to the trip to Spain:

> The trip to Spain can be considered an activity or program receiving Federal financial assistance within the meaning of the Act since, although the students pay for a substantial portion of the expenses of the trip, regular salaried teachers will be attending as chaperones while school is in session, the School District has sponsored and planned the program, and students will be under the supervision of teacher and School District personnel during this trip [534 F. Supp. at 761].

On the merits, however, the court rejected the student's claim under the Rehabilitation Act even though it found that Section 504 had extraterritorial application. The claim failed, the court determined, because the student was not "otherwise qualified" to participate in the program within the meaning of Section 504.

Taken together, *King, Bird,* and *Wolff* suggest that the four civil rights spending statutes will apply extraterritorially whenever the victim of the discrimination is a participant in or applicant for a "program or activity" offered abroad by an American college or university receiving federal funds. In addition, the victim of the discrimination must apparently be a continuing student or employee at an American campus of an American college or university (even though engaged in study abroad at the time of the alleged discrimination) in order to be considered a person "in the United States" as required by each of the four nondiscrimination statutes (see *King,* above, 104 F.Supp.2d at 791).

13.5.8. Administrative enforcement. Compliance with each of the four civil rights spending statutes is enforced through a complex system of

---

[64]The district court did, however, find for Bird on her claim for breach of fiduciary duty. On appeal, the U.S. Court of Appeals affirmed the district court's rulings in the case without explicitly addressing the issue of extraterritoriality (303 F.3d 1015 (9th Cir. 2002)).

procedures and mechanisms administered by the federal agencies that provide financial assistance.

Administrative enforcement of these statutes has always been important for higher educational institutions and aggrieved members of the academic community, but it has taken on added importance since the mid-1990s as courts have increasingly imposed limits on the use of private lawsuits to enforce the four civil rights statutes and the spending statutes providing aid to higher education. In *Alexander v. Sandoval,* 532 U.S. 275 (2001), for example, the U.S. Supreme Court disallowed private lawsuits to enforce Title VI regulations that prohibit actions with discriminatory "effects" (see subsections 13.5.7.2 above and 13.5.9 below)—a ruling that apparently applies to the Title IX regulations as well, and may also apply to some suits to enforce Section 504 regulations. In *Gebser v. Lago Vista Independent School District,* 524 U.S. 274 (1998), and *Davis v. Monroe County Board of Education,* 526 U.S. 629 (1999), the Court imposed strict limits on the availability of money damages suits to challenge sexual harassment under Title IX (see Sections 8.1.5 & 9.3.4 of this book). These rulings would also apparently limit harassment claims for money damages under Title VI and Section 504 and have some limiting effect as well on other types of discrimination claims under these statutes. In the *Women's Equity Action League* case below in this subsection and the *Wrestling Coaches Association* case in subsection 14.1, courts used the technical doctrine of "standing" to dismiss cases under Title VI and Title IX. In the *Marlow* and *Salvador* cases below in this subsection, the courts used administrative law doctrines to dismiss cases under Section 504. And in the line of cases from *City of Boerne* to *Garrett* (see Section 13.1.5), the U.S. Supreme Court rejected private damages suits against the states under the Age Discrimination in Employment Act and Title I of the Americans With Disabilities Act—rulings that some courts have also applied to suits under Title IX and Section 504 (see Section 13.1.6, and compare the discussion of abrogation and waiver in Section 13.5.9).

Other examples of judicial limits on private lawsuits can be found in cases where the courts have declined to recognize private causes of action to enforce the student aid program requirements of the Higher Education Act. These cases are discussed in Section 13.4.5. Similarly, in *Gonzaga University v. Doe,* 536 U.S. 273 (2002) (Section 9.7.1), the U.S. Supreme Court disallowed private causes of action to enforce the Family Educational Rights and Privacy Act (FERPA) and regulations. And in other cases, courts have used administrative law doctrines to forestall institutions and aggrieved parties from suing the U.S. Department of Education. (See, for example, the *Career Education* case and the *American Association of Cosmetology Schools* case in subsection 13.4.6.)

The less available the judicial forum becomes, either for suits against institutions or for suits against the U.S. Department of Education or other federal agencies, the more likely it is that complaints and disputes will be processed through the department's administrative mechanisms (and those of other agencies). For these reasons, postsecondary administrators and counsel should take special care to develop a sound understanding of this administrative process, so that they can effectively represent their institution's interests should compliance issues arise about nondiscrimination (or other matters regarding the federal aid programs).

The first of the civil rights spending statutes, Title VI, delegates enforcement responsibility to the various federal funding agencies. Under Executive Order 12250, 45 Fed. Reg. 72995 (1980), the U.S. Attorney General is responsible for coordinating agency enforcement efforts. The Attorney General has implemented enforcement regulations (28 C.F.R. Part 42) as well as "Guidelines for the Enforcement of Title VI" (28 C.F.R. § 50.3), which impose various requirements on agencies responsible for enforcement. Each agency, for instance, must issue guidelines or regulations on Title VI for all programs under which it provides federal financial assistance (28 C.F.R. § 42.404). These regulations and guidelines must be available to the public (28 C.F.R. § 42.405). The Justice Department's regulations require the agencies to collect sufficient data, on such items as the racial composition of the population eligible for the program and the location of facilities, to determine compliance (28 C.F.R. § 42.406). All Title VI compliance decisions must be made by or be subject to the review of the agency's civil rights office. Programs found to be complying must be reviewed periodically to ensure continued compliance. A finding of probable noncompliance must be reported to the Assistant Attorney General (28 C.F.R. § 42.407). Each agency must establish complaint procedures and publish them in its guidelines. All Title VI complaints must be logged in the agency records (28 C.F.R. § 42.408). If a finding of probable noncompliance is made, enforcement procedures shall be instituted after a "reasonable period" of negotiation. If negotiations continue for more than sixty days after the finding of noncompliance, the agency must notify the Assistant Attorney General (28 C.F.R. § 42.411). If several agencies provide federal financial assistance to a substantial number of the same recipients for similar or related purposes, the agencies must coordinate Title VI enforcement efforts. The agencies shall designate one agency as the lead agency for Title VI compliance (28 C.F.R. § 42.413). Each agency must develop a written enforcement plan, specifying priorities, timetables, and procedures, which shall be available to the public (28 C.F.R. § 42.415).

Under the Title VI regulations of the Department of Education, fund recipients must file assurances with ED that their programs comply with Title VI (34 C.F.R. § 100.4) and must submit "timely, complete and accurate compliance reports at such times, and in such form and containing such information, as the responsible Department official or his designee may determine to be necessary to enable him to ascertain whether the recipient has complied or is complying" with Title VI (34 C.F.R. § 100.6(b)). ED may make periodic compliance reviews and must accept and respond to individual complaints from persons who believe that they are victims of discrimination (34 C.F.R. § 100.7). If an investigation reveals a violation that cannot be resolved by negotiation and voluntary compliance (34 C.F.R. § 100.7(d)), ED may refer the case to the Justice Department for prosecution (see this volume, Section 13.5.9) or commence administrative proceedings for fund termination (34 C.F.R. § 100.8). Any termination of funds must be "limited in its effect to the particular program, or part thereof, in which . . . noncompliance has been . . . found" (42 U.S.C. § 2000d-1; 34 C.F.R. § 100.8(c)). The regulations specify the procedural safeguards that must be observed in the fund termination proceedings: notice, the right to counsel, a written decision, an appeal to a reviewing authority, and a discretionary appeal to the Secretary of Education (34 C.F.R. §§ 100.9 & 100.10).

Title IX enforcement, like that for Title VI, is coordinated by the Attorney General under Executive Order 12250. Title IX also includes the same limit as Title VI on the scope of fund termination (20 U.S.C. § 1682) and utilizes the same procedures for fund termination (34 C.F.R. § 106.71). An institution subject to Title IX must appoint at least one employee to coordinate its compliance efforts and must establish a grievance procedure for handling gender discrimination complaints within the institution (34 C.F.R. § 106.8).

Section 504 is also subject to Executive Order 12250, and funding agencies' enforcement efforts are thus also coordinated by the Attorney General. The Attorney General's coordination regulations, setting forth enforcement responsibilities of federal agencies for nondiscrimination on the basis of disability, are published in 28 C.F.R. Part 41. The Section 504 statute also establishes an Interagency Coordinating Council for Section 504 enforcement, the membership of which includes, among others, the Attorney General and the Secretary of Education (29 U.S.C. § 794c). The Department of Education's Section 504 regulations for its own programs impose compliance responsibilities similar to those under Title IX. However, recipients with fewer than fifteen employees need not conform to certain requirements: (1) having a copy of the remedial plan available for inspection (34 C.F.R. § 104.6(c)(2)); (2) appointing an agency employee to coordinate the compliance effort (34 C.F.R. § 104.7(a)); and (3) establishing a grievance procedure for handling discrimination complaints (34 C.F.R. § 104.7(b)). Most postsecondary educational institutions are not excepted from these requirements, since most have more than the minimum number of employees. Section 504 also adopts the Title VI procedural regulations concerning fund terminations.

Under the Age Discrimination Act, federal funding agencies must propose implementing regulations and submit them to the Secretary of Health and Human Services for review; all such agency regulations must be consistent with HHS's "general regulations" (42 U.S.C. § 6103(a)(4); 45 C.F.R. § 90.31). Each agency must hold "compliance reviews" and other investigations to determine adherence to the Act's requirements (45 C.F.R. § 90.44(a)). Each agency must also follow specified procedures when undertaking to terminate a recipient's funding (45 C.F.R. § 90.47). Termination of funds is limited to the "particular program or activity, or part of such program or activity, with respect to which [a] finding [of discrimination] has been made," and may not be based "in whole or in part on any finding with respect to any program or activity which does not receive Federal financial assistance" (42 U.S.C. § 6104(b)). The Act contains a number of substantive exceptions to coverage, more expansive than the exceptions to the other civil rights statutes (see subsection 13.5.5 above).

The federal courts exercise a limited review of federal agencies' enforcement efforts. If a federal agency terminates an institution's funding, the institution may appeal that decision to the courts once it has exhausted administrative review procedures within the agency.[65] In addition, if a federal agency abuses its enforcement authority during enforcement proceedings and before a final decision, an affected educational institution may also seek injunctive relief from such improper enforcement efforts.

In *Mandel v. U.S. Department of Health, Education and Welfare,* 411 F. Supp. 542 (D. Md. 1976), the State of Maryland brought suit after the Department of Health, Education, and Welfare (HEW) had commenced fund termination proceedings against the state, alleging Title VI violations in its system of higher education. The state sought judicial intervention, claiming that HEW had not in good faith sought voluntary compliance. Maryland complained that HEW delayed review of the state's original desegregation plan, prematurely cut off negotiations, did not provide guidelines on how to effect desegregation, and refused to rule either on the importance of statistics in assessing compliance or on the future of traditionally black educational institutions. The court found that HEW did not seek voluntary compliance in good faith. Maryland also complained that HEW failed to "pinpoint" which of the state's programs violated Title VI. The court held that HEW must pinpoint the offending programs before enforcement proceedings are begun:

> [I]n . . . the State system . . . there are multitudinal programs receiving federal financing which, due to the non-programmatic approach assumed, are being condemned by defendants en masse. . . . [In the state system] there is federal funding to programs within twenty-eight institutions of higher education ranging from a unique cancer research center to the student work study program. To compel all of these programs, regardless of whether or not each is discriminatory, to prepare a defense and endure protracted enforcement proceedings is wasteful, counterproductive, and probably inimical to the interests of the very persons Title VI was enacted to protect. It is far more equitable, and more consistent with Congressional intent, to require program delineation prior to enforcement hearings than to include all programs in enforcement proceedings [411 F. Supp. at 558].

The U.S. Court of Appeals for the Fourth Circuit subsequently modified the lower court's ruling to allow HEW to take a systemic approach if it first adopted systemwide guidelines and gave Maryland time to comply voluntarily (*Mayor and City Council of Baltimore v. Mathews,* 562 F.2d 914 (4th Cir. 1977)). A rehearing was scheduled, however, because one judge had died before the court's opinion was issued. On rehearing, three appellate judges voted to affirm

---

[65]Such judicial review is expressly authorized by the Title VI and Title IX statutes (see 42 U.S.C. § 2000d-2; 20 U.S.C. § 1683). The Section 504 statute incorporates the remedies available under Title VI, thus apparently authorizing judicial review to the same extent authorized by Title VI (29 U.S.C. § 794(a)(c)). The Age Discrimination Act also specifically authorizes judicial review of administrative agency actions, but in terms somewhat different from those in Title VI and Title IX (42 U.S.C. § 6105).

the lower court and three voted to reverse, and the equally divided vote had the effect of automatically affirming the lower court (571 F.2d 1273 (4th Cir. 1978)).

Different questions are presented when judicial review of federal agency enforcement is sought not by postsecondary institutions but by the victims of the institutions' alleged discrimination. Such victims may seek judicial orders requiring a federal agency to fulfill its statutory duty to enforce the civil rights statutes; or, on a smaller scale, an alleged victim may challenge in court an agency's failure or refusal to act on a complaint that he or she had filed with an agency responsible for enforcing the civil rights statutes. The case law indicates that courts will not be receptive to such requests for judicial intervention in administrative enforcement activities—at least not unless Congress itself authorizes victims to seek such redress from the courts.

In *Adams v. Richardson*, 356 F. Supp. 92 (D.D.C. 1973), *judgment modified by* 480 F.2d 1159 (D.C. Cir. 1973), some victims of unlawful discrimination sought judicial intervention to compel enforcement of Title VI. The plaintiffs accused HEW of failure to enforce Title VI in the southern states. In the part of the case dealing with higher education, HEW had found the higher education systems of ten states out of compliance with Title VI and had requested each state to submit a desegregation plan within four months. Three years later, after the lawsuit had been filed and the court was ready to rule, five states still had not submitted any plan and five had submitted plans that did not remedy the violations. HEW had not commenced administrative enforcement efforts or referred the cases to the Justice Department for prosecution. The district court ordered HEW to commence enforcement proceedings:

> The time permitted by Title VI of the Civil Rights Act of 1964 to delay the commencement of enforcement proceedings against the ten states for the purpose of securing voluntary compliance has long since passed. The continuation of HEW financial assistance to the segregated systems of higher education in the ten states violates the rights of plaintiffs and others similarly situated protected by Title VI of the Civil Rights Act of 1964. Having once determined that a state system of higher education is in violation of Title VI, and having failed during a substantial period of time to achieve voluntary compliance, defendants have a duty to commence enforcement proceedings [356 F. Supp. at 94].

The appellate court agreed with the district court's conclusion but expressed more sympathy for HEW's enforcement problem, in particular its need to "carefully assess the significance of a variety of new factors as it moves into an unaccustomed area" of enforcement. The appellate court therefore modified the terms of the district court's injunction, so that HEW would be given more time to initiate enforcement proceedings.

After the appellate court's decision, the district court maintained jurisdiction over the case in order to supervise compliance with its injunction. The judge issued a number of other decisions after 1973, some of which were reviewed by the appellate court. In April 1977, the district court revoked HEW's approval of several states' higher education desegregation plans and ordered HEW to devise criteria (see Section 13.5.2) by which it would evaluate new plans to be submitted by these states. In March 1983, the court entered another order requiring HEW (by then ED) to obtain new plans from five states that had defaulted on plans previously accepted by HEW. This order established time limits by which ED was required to initiate formal enforcement proceedings against these states, and several others whose plans had never been approved, if they had not submitted new acceptable plans. The order also required ED to report systematically to the plaintiffs on enforcement activities regarding the states subject to the suit.

On the government's appeal of the district court's 1983 order, the appellate court remanded the case to the district court for a determination of whether the plaintiffs continued to have the legal "standing" necessary to maintain the lawsuit and justify judicial enforcement of the order (*Women's Equity Action League v. Bell* and *Adams v. Bell,* 743 F.2d 42 (D.C. Cir. 1984)). In 1987, the district court dismissed the case, ruling that the plaintiffs lacked standing to pursue the litigation (*Adams v. Bennett,* 675 F. Supp. 668 (D.D.C. 1987)). The district judge reasoned that ED's Office for Civil Rights had not caused the segregation that the plaintiffs were subjected to, and that the degree to which ED's continued monitoring of state acts would redress this segregation was "speculative."

Although initially the appellate court reversed the district court, ordering additional hearings on what remedies should be granted to desegregate the dual systems, in 1990 it decided to dismiss the case, by then titled *Women's Equity Action League v. Cavazos* (906 F.2d 742 (D.C. Cir. 1990)). In the opinion, Judge Ruth Bader Ginsburg said that "Congress has not explicitly or implicitly authorized the grand scale action plaintiffs delineate" and called the plaintiffs' action an attempt to make the trial court a "nationwide overseer or pacer of procedures government agencies use to enforce civil rights prescriptions controlling educational institutions that receive federal funds" (906 F.2d at 744). If suits directly against a discriminating entity (for which a private right of action does exist under Title VI; see Section 13.5.9) are adequate to redress injuries, "'federal courts will not oversee the overseer'" (906 F.2d at 748, quoting *Coker v. Sullivan,* 902 F.2d 84, 89 (D.C. Cir. 1990)). The court further stated:

> Suits directly against the discriminating entities may be more arduous, and less effective in providing systemic relief, than continuing judicial oversight of federal government enforcement. But under our precedent, situation-specific litigation affords an adequate, even if imperfect, remedy. So far as we can tell, the suit targeting specific discriminatory acts of fund recipients is the only court remedy Congress has authorized for private parties, situated as plaintiffs currently are [906 F.2d at 751].

Only if Congress creates such a private right of action, said the court, may plaintiffs file claims directly against the government agency charged with enforcing the law.

Two other cases have reached similar results in situations where an individual victim has challenged an agency's enforcement activities. In *Marlow v. United States Department of Education,* 820 F.2d 581 (2d Cir. 1987), the court dismissed a lawsuit challenging ED's decision to take no action on an administrative complaint the plaintiff had filed under Section 504. The court held that there is no statutory or implied right of action against the federal funding agency for individual complainants who seek only judicial review of the agency's disposition of a particular complaint. And in *Salvador v. Bennett*, 800 F.2d 97 (7th Cir. 1986), the court held that an individual complainant cannot enjoin ED from continuing to fund the institution against which the individual had filed a Section 504 complaint.

13.5.9. Other enforcement remedies. Compliance reviews, administrative negotiations, and fund terminations are not the only means federal agencies have for enforcing the federal civil rights statutes. In some cases the responsible federal agency may also go to court to enforce the civil rights obligations that recipients (including postsecondary institutions) have assumed by accepting federal funds. Title VI, for instance, authorizes agencies to enforce compliance not only by fund termination but also by "any other means authorized by law" (42 U.S.C. § 2000d-1). The Title VI regulations of the U.S. Department of Education explain that "such other means may include, but are not limited to, (1) a reference to the Department of Justice with a recommendation that appropriate proceedings be brought to enforce any rights of the United States under any law of the United States . . . , or any assurance or other contractual undertaking, and (2) any applicable proceeding under State or local law" (34 C.F.R. § 100.9(a)). ED may not pursue these alternatives, however, "until (1) the responsible Department official has determined that compliance cannot be secured by voluntary means, (2) the recipient or other person has been notified of its failure to comply and of the action to be taken to effect compliance, and (3) the expiration of at least ten days from the mailing of such notice to the recipient or other person" (34 C.F.R. § 100.8(d)).

Similar enforcement alternatives and procedural limitations apply to enforcement of Title IX, Section 504, and the Age Discrimination Act. ED's Title IX and Section 504 regulations incorporate the enforcement regulations for Title VI (see 34 C.F.R. § 106.71; 34 C.F.R. § 104.61). The Title IX statute also contains the same "other means authorized by law" language found in Title VI (see 20 U.S.C. § 1682), and the Section 504 statute incorporates the remedies and procedures available under Title VI (29 U.S.C. § 794a(a)). The Age Discrimination Act has its own enforcement scheme, set out in the statute (42 U.S.C. § 6104) and the general regulations (45 C.F.R. §§ 90.41–90.50).

Besides court suits by administrative agencies enforcing the civil rights statutes, educational institutions may also be subject to private lawsuits brought by individuals who claim that their rights under the civil rights statutes and regulations have been violated. In legal terminology, the issue is whether the civil rights statutes afford these victims of discrimination a "private cause of action" against the institution that is allegedly discriminating. Sometimes statutes provide explicitly for such private causes of action. That is the case with the Age Discrimination Act, which authorizes private suits in federal district courts by "any interested person" alleging that a fund recipient has violated the Act (42 U.S.C. § 6104(e)). But Title VI, Title IX, and Section 504 are silent on this question; the issue, therefore, is whether courts will recognize an "implied private cause of action" to enforce these statutes.

The basic requisites for an implied private cause of action are outlined in *Cort v. Ash,* 422 U.S. 66 (1975):

> In determining whether a private remedy is implicit in a statute not expressly providing one, several factors are relevant. First, is the plaintiff one of the class for whose *especial* benefit the statute was enacted—that is, does the statute create a federal right in favor of the plaintiff? Second, is there any indication of legislative intent, explicit or implicit, either to create such a remedy or to deny one? Third, is it consistent with the underlying purposes of the legislative scheme to imply such a remedy for the plaintiff? And finally, is the cause of action one traditionally relegated to state law, in an area basically the concern of the States, so that it would be inappropriate to infer a cause of action based solely on federal law? [422 U.S. at 78; citations omitted].

If an individual can meet these requirements, three related issues may then arise: whether the individual must "exhaust" any available "administrative remedies" before bringing a private suit; whether the individual may obtain monetary damages, in addition to or instead of injunctive relief, if successful in the private suit; and whether the individual may obtain attorney's fees from the defendant if successful in the suit.

For many years courts and commentators disagreed on whether Title VI, Title IX, and Section 504 could be enforced by private causes of action. Developments since the late 1970s, however, have established a strong basis for private causes of action under all three statutes. The case of *Cannon v. University of Chicago,* 441 U.S. 677 (1979), arising under Title IX, is illustrative.

The plaintiff in *Cannon* had been denied admission to the medical schools of the University of Chicago and Northwestern University. She sued both institutions, claiming that they had rejected her applications because of her sex and that such action violated Title IX. The U.S. Court of Appeals for the Seventh Circuit held that individuals cannot institute private suits to enforce Title IX. The U.S. Supreme Court reversed. While acknowledging that the statute does not expressly authorize a private cause of action, the Court held that one can be implied into the statute under the principles of *Cort v. Ash.* In applying the four considerations specified in that case, the Court in *Cannon* concluded: "Not only the words and history of Title IX, but also its subject matter and underlying purposes, counsel application of a cause of action in favor of private victims of discrimination."

The discussion of the third consideration in *Cort*—whether a private cause of action would frustrate the statute's underlying purposes—is particularly illuminating. The Court identified two purposes of Title IX: to avoid the use of federal funds to support sex discrimination and to give individual citizens effective protection against such practices. While the first purpose is served by the statutory procedure for fund termination (see subsection 13.5.8 above), the Court determined that a private remedy would be appropriate to effect a second purpose:

> [Termination] is . . . severe and often may not provide an appropriate means of accomplishing the second purpose if merely an isolated violation has

occurred. In that situation, the violation might be remedied more efficiently by an order requiring an institution to accept an applicant who had been improperly excluded. Moreover, in that kind of situation it makes little sense to impose on an individual whose only interest is in obtaining a benefit for herself, or on HEW [now ED], the burden of demonstrating that an institution's practices are so pervasively discriminatory that a complete cutoff of federal funding is appropriate. The award of individual relief to a private litigant who has prosecuted her own suit is not only sensible but is also fully consistent with—and in some cases even necessary to—ordinary enforcement of the statute [441 U.S. at 705–6].

In a statement of particular interest to postsecondary administrators, the Court in *Cannon* also addressed and rejected the universities' argument that private suits would unduly interfere with their institutional autonomy:

> Respondents' principal argument against implying a cause of action under Title IX is that it is unwise to subject admissions decisions of universities to judicial scrutiny at the behest of disappointed applicants on a case-by-case basis. They argue that this kind of litigation is burdensome and inevitably will have an adverse effect on the independence of members of university committees.
>
> This argument is not original to this litigation. It was forcefully advanced in both 1964 and 1972 by the congressional opponents of Title VI and Title IX, and squarely rejected by the congressional majorities that passed the two statutes. In short, respondents' principal contention is not a legal argument at all; it addresses a policy issue that Congress has already resolved.
>
> History has borne out the judgment of Congress. Although victims of discrimination on the basis of race, religion, or national origin have had private Title VI remedies available at least since 1965, respondents have not come forward with any demonstration that Title VI litigation has been so costly or voluminous that either the academic community or the courts have been unduly burdened. Nothing but speculation supports the argument that university administrators will be so concerned about the risk of litigation that they will fail to discharge their important responsibilities in an independent and professional manner [441 U.S. at 709–10].[66]

Subsequently, in the case of *Guardians Ass'n. v. Civil Service Commission of the City of New York,* 463 U.S. 582 (1983), the Supreme Court affirmed the availability of implied private causes of action under Title VI. The Court issued no majority opinion, however, so the case's teaching on the issue is limited and can be gleaned only from tallying the views of those Justices who accepted private causes of action under Title VI. A year after *Guardians,* and relying in part on that case, the Supreme Court also held that individuals may bring private

---

[66]The courts are divided on whether the Title IX implied private cause of action recognized in the *Cannon* case is available to plaintiffs claiming gender discrimination in employment. When the plaintiff is an employee or prospective employee, rather than a student or prospective student, some courts have reasoned that the Title IX private cause of action is not available because Title VII (see Section 5.2.1 of this book) provides an express private cause of action and suitable remedies for gender discrimination in employment, thus making a Title IX cause of action unnecessary. For further discussion, see Section 5.2.3.

lawsuits to enforce Section 504 (*Consolidated Rail Corp. v. Darrone,* 465 U.S. 624 (1984))—a conclusion that the Court later affirmed and further explicated in *Barnes v. Gorman,* 536 U.S. 181, 185–89 (2002).

Courts usually have not required plaintiffs to exhaust administrative remedies before filing a private cause of action under the civil rights statutes. In the *Cannon* case, for instance, the U.S. Supreme Court noted that it had "never withheld a private remedy where the statute explicitly confers a benefit on a class of persons . . . [but] does not assure those persons the ability to activate and participate in the administrative process contemplated by the statute." Title IX not only contains no such mechanism, according to the Court, but even HEW's (now ED's) procedures do not permit the complainant to participate in the administrative proceedings. Moreover, even if HEW were to find an institution to be in violation of Title IX, the resulting compliance agreement need not necessarily include relief for the particular complainant. Accordingly, the Court concluded that individuals may institute suits to enforce Title IX without exhausting administrative remedies (441 U.S. at 706–8, n.41). Similarly, relying on *Cannon,* federal appeals courts have held that exhaustion is not required under Title VI (see, for example, *Neighborhood Action Coalition v. City of* Canton, 882 F.2d 1012 (6th Cir. 1989) or under Section 504 (see, for example, *Pushkin v. Regents of the University of Colorado,* 658 F.2d 1372, 1380–83 (10th Cir. 1981)). The exception to this trend is the Age Discrimination Act, for which Congress itself has provided an exhaustion requirement. The provision of that statute authorizing private causes of action (see above) also prohibits bringing such suits "if administrative remedies have not been exhausted" (42 U.S.C. § 6104(e)(2)(B)). Section 6104(f) and the general ADA regulations (45 C.F.R. § 90.50) indicate when such exhaustion shall be deemed to have occurred.

Authorization of private causes of action, even when exhaustion has occurred or is not required, does not necessarily mean that a complainant may obtain every kind of remedy ordinarily available in civil lawsuits. *Cannon* did not itself resolve the remedies question, and in the wake of *Cannon,* a number of lower courts ruled that private causes of action under Title IX were limited to injunctive relief and that money damages were not available (see, for example, *Lieberman v. University of Chicago,* 660 F.2d 1185 (7th Cir. 1981)). In the *Guardians Ass'n.* case (above) however, a majority of the Justices asserted that they would permit a damages remedy under Title VI when the plaintiff could prove that the defendant had discriminated *intentionally* (463 U.S. at 607 n.27; see also subsection 13.5.7.2 above). And in *Darrone,* although the Court declined to determine "the extent to which money damages are available" in a Section 504 case, it did authorize back-pay awards for employees who were victims of intentional discrimination.

In 1992, the Supreme Court alleviated much of the remaining uncertainty concerning remedies under the civil rights statutes. In *Franklin v. Gwinnett County Public Schools,* 503 U.S. 60 (1992), a student brought an action under Title IX seeking compensatory damages for alleged intentional sex discrimination—particularly, sexual harassment by a coach/teacher at her high school and the school administration's failure to protect her from this harassment despite having knowledge of it.[67] The school district had agreed to close its investigation in return for the teacher's resignation. Although the U.S. Department of Education had investigated and determined that the school district had violated the student's Title IX rights, the department terminated the investigation after the school and the school district came into compliance with Title IX. The student then filed her cause of action for damages, which was rejected by the lower courts.

Reversing, the Supreme Court identified several bases for holding that money damages is a permissible remedy under Title IX. In particular, it relied on the firmly established principle that, once a cause of action exists, courts may use all appropriate remedies to enforce the plaintiff's rights unless Congress has expressly indicated otherwise; and on Congress's passage, subsequent to *Cannon,* of the Civil Rights Remedies Equalization Amendment of 1986 (42 U.S.C. § 2000d-7), discussed later in this subsection) and the Civil Rights Restoration Act of 1987 (see subsection 13.5.7.4 above), which the Court regarded as implicit congressional acknowledgments that private remedies, including money damages, are available under Title IX. Although confessing that the multiple opinions in *Guardians Association* had made it difficult to determine the Court's viewpoint on damage remedies, the Court in *Gwinnett* confirmed that "a clear majority [in *Guardians Association*] expressed the view that damages were available under Title VI in an action seeking remedies for an intentional violation, and no Justice challenged the traditional presumption in favor of a federal court's power to award appropriate relief in a cognizable cause of action." (See generally E. Vargyas, "*Franklin v. Gwinnett County Public Schools* and Its Impact on Title IX Enforcement," 19 *J. Coll. & Univ. Law* 373 (1993).)

The *Franklin* case, permitting compensatory damages under Title IX, also serves to reinforce the availability of such damages under Title VI—as the Court indicated by its reliance on the prior *Guardians Ass'n.* case. The *Franklin* reasoning apparently applied to Section 504 as well as the Court confirmed in *Barnes v. Gorman,* 536 U.S. 181 (2002). The *Franklin* analysis does not extend to the Age Discrimination Act, however, since that statute's express authorization for private causes of action is limited to suits "to enjoin a violation of this Act" (42 U.S.C. § 6104(e)), thus indicating that only injunctive relief (and not money damages) is available.

Nine years after *Franklin,* in *Alexander v. Sandoval,* 532 U.S. 275 (2001), the Court reaffirmed (consistent with *Guardians* and *Franklin*) that private causes of action for money damages are available to enforce Title VI. At the same time, however, the Court imposed a major new limitation on private causes of action by rejecting the particular cause of action asserted in that case. The plaintiffs had based their claim on a Title VI "disparate impact" regulation (34 C.F.R. § 100.3(b)(2)) that did not require proof of discriminatory intent (see subsection 13.5.7.2 above). Section 601 of Title VI prohibits only intentional sex discrimination, the

---

[67]Two later U.S. Supreme Court cases provided further clarification on the Title IX private cause of action for sexual harassment authorized by the *Franklin* case. These two cases—*Gebser v. Lago Vista Independent School District,* 524 U.S. 274 (1998), and *Davis v. Monroe County Board of Education,* 526 U.S. 629 (1999)—are discussed fully in Sections 9.3.4 and 8.1.5.

Court asserted, and Section 602, which authorizes federal agencies to promulgate regulations implementing Section 601, did not itself create any new rights. Regulations issued under Section 602, therefore, could not be used as a basis for private causes of action for unintentional, or "disparate impact," discrimination, since such discrimination was beyond the scope of Section 601. (The Court split severely on this point, with four dissenting Justices adamantly asserting the contrary view.) While the majority's ruling in *Sandoval* substantially restricts the availability of private causes of action, the majority did not go so far as to rule that Title VI regulations can never be enforced by a private cause of action. Specifically, the majority's ruling is that a regulation may be enforced by a private cause of action only if it prohibits *intentional* sex discrimination that is within the general prohibition of Section 601. This ruling would presumably apply to Title IX as well; but its applicability to Section 504 may be problematic because it is not clear that that statute prohibits only intentional discrimination (see *Alexander v. Choate* in subsection 13.5.7.2 above).

Under *Franklin*, it was unclear whether damages awards under Title IX were limited to compensatory damages or could also include *punitive* damages. The law was unclear on this point for Title VI and Section 504 as well. But the Court later resolved the issue in *Barnes v. Gorman*, 536 U.S. 181 (2002). In this Section 504 case, the Court reasoned that Section 504 remedies "are coextensive with the remedies available in a private cause of action brought under Title VI" (see 29 U.S.C. § 794a(a)(2)); that under Title VI, the federal government's relationship with fund recipients is analogous to a contractual relationship (see Section 13.1.1 of this book); that "punitive damages, unlike compensatory damages and injunctions, are generally not available for breach of contract"; that punitive damages are therefore not available under Title VI; and that "it follows that they may not be awarded in suits brought under . . . § 504" (536 U.S. at 185–89). The same reasoning would apply to Title IX, the other spending statute permitting compensatory damages, since it is also patterned after Title VI.

An additional complexity may arise when a private cause of action for money damages is brought against a state college or university. Such institutions are often considered arms of the state and, as such, may claim sovereign immunity from private suits alleging violations of federal law (see Section 13.1.6). In *Atascadero State Hospital v. Scanlon*, 473 U.S. 234 (1985), the U.S. Supreme Court highlighted this point by holding that, in enacting Section 504, Congress did not abrogate the states' Eleventh Amendment sovereign immunity. Subsequently, however, Congress enacted the Civil Rights Remedies Equalization Amendment of 1986 (100 Stat. 1845, 42 U.S.C. § 2000d-7). This statute specifically declares that states are not immune under the Eleventh Amendment from federal court suits alleging violations of Section 504, Title IX, Title VI, the Age Discrimination Act, or any other federal statute prohibiting discrimination by recipients of federal financial assistance.

Nevertheless, in the wake of the U.S. Supreme Court's decision in the *Seminole Tribe* case (see Section 13.1.6), sovereign immunity issues have frequently arisen in money damages suits brought against state colleges and universities under these statutes. Before *Seminole Tribe*, it was generally accepted that the

Civil Rights Remedies Equalization Amendment constituted an abrogation of state sovereign immunity. But after *Seminole Tribe* and related Supreme Court cases, state institutions have argued that Congress has no power to abrogate state immunity under the nondiscrimination statutes. Alternatively, state institutions have argued that Congress has no power to require that states waive their immunity as a condition to participating in a federal funding program or that, even if Congress has this power, the Equalization Amendment does not establish such a waiver. Most cases thus far have involved Title IX or Title VI, and the results suggest that these arguments are not likely to succeed under either of these statutes.

In *Crawford v. Davis,* 109 F.3d 1281 (8th Cir. 1997), for example, a student at the University of Central Arkansas filed a Title IX sexual harassment claim. Relying on *Seminole Tribe,* the university contended that Congress had passed Title IX under its spending power rather than its enforcement power under Section 5 of the Fourteenth Amendment; and that Congress had no authority under the spending clause to abrogate the university's sovereign immunity. The court disagreed, holding that Title IX was within the scope of Congress's Fourteenth Amendment enforcement power, since the Fourteenth Amendment's equal protection clause has often been used to proscribe gender discrimination—as, for example, the U.S. Supreme Court did in the Virginia Military Institute (VMI) case, *United States v. Commonwealth of Virginia* (see Section 8.2.4.2). The court in *Crawford* was not concerned with whether Congress "had the specific intent to legislate pursuant to" Section 5 of the Fourteenth Amendment, but only with whether Congress "could have enacted Title IX pursuant to" Section 5. Therefore, since Title IX did fit within Section 5, under which Congress has power to abrogate, and since the Equalization Amendment clearly indicates a congressional intent to abrogate, the court rejected the university's immunity defense. (*Crawford* was approved and followed by another federal circuit in *Doe v. University of Illinois,* 138 F.3d 653 (7th Cir. 1998), and 200 F.3d 499 (7th Cir. 1999).)

The reasoning and results in Title VI cases thus far have been similar to the Title IX cases. In *Lesage v. State of Texas,* 158 F.3d 213 (5th Cir. 1998), for instance, the appellate court determined that Title VI paralleled the Fourteenth Amendment's equal protection clause, prohibiting "precisely that which the Constitution prohibits in virtually all possible applications"; and that the Equalization Amendment, which abrogated state immunity under Title VI, was also within the scope of Congress's power under Section 5 of the Fourteenth Amendment (158 F.3d at 215–17).[68] And in *Fuller v. Rayburn,* 161 F.3d 516 (8th Cir. 1998), another appellate court concluded that the university could not assert a sovereign immunity defense against a student's Title VI claim because Congress, by enacting the Equalization Amendment, had validly abrogated state immunity under Title VI.

---

[68]*Lesage* was reversed in part, on other grounds, in *Texas v. Lesage,* 528 U.S. 18 (1999) (see Section 8.2.5 of this book).

Even if a court were to determine that Congress had *not* validly abrogated state immunity under Title IX or Title VI, it is likely that these suits could proceed on an alternative basis. In *Doe v. University of Illinois* (above), the court identified this alternative: "that the University affirmatively waived its Eleventh Amendment immunity by choosing to accept federal funds under Title IX" (138 F.3d at 660). The *Doe* court did not rule on this waiver argument (a spending power argument) because it had already determined that Congress had validly abrogated immunity under its Fourteenth Amendment, Section 5 power. But the U.S. Supreme Court has been receptive to this waiver argument (see *Atascadero State Hospital v. Scanlon*, 473 U.S. 234, 238–40, 246–47 (1985), and *Alden v. Maine*, 527 U.S.706, 755 (1999)), and some lower courts have also accepted it. In *Litman v. George Mason University*, 186 F.3d 544 (4th Cir. 1999), for example, a female student who had been expelled filed a Title IX suit against the university, and the university asserted sovereign immunity. Using a spending power analysis, the court concluded that the Equalization Amendment (above) constituted "a clear, unambiguous, and unequivocal condition of waiver of Eleventh Amendment immunity"; and that "when a condition under the Spending Clause includes an unambiguous waiver of Eleventh Amendment immunity, the condition is constitutionally permissible as long as it rests on the state's voluntary and knowing acceptance of it" (186 F.3d at 554–55). The court therefore ruled that the university had "waived its Eleventh Amendment immunity" by accepting federal funds that were unambiguously conditioned on the recipient's waiver of its immunity. (See also *Pederson v. Louisiana State University*, 213 F.3d 858 (5th Cir. 2000).)

The waiver argument, as a spending power argument, has also been held to apply to Section 504 (see *Garrett v. University of Alabama*, discussed in Section 13.1.6) and would apparently apply to Title VI and the Age Discrimination Act as well, since all these statutes fit within Congress's spending power, and the Equalization Amendment applies to them all. But the applicability of the abrogation argument (the Fourteenth Amendment, Section 5 argument) to Section 504 and ADA cases is more problematic. Race discrimination claims and gender discrimination claims are clearly subject to heightened scrutiny under the Fourteenth Amendment's equal protection clause. They therefore clearly fall within the scope of Congress's Section 5 power to enforce the Fourteenth Amendment, which Congress may use to abrogate state immunity. Disability discrimination and age discrimination, in contrast, do not usually receive heightened scrutiny under the equal protection clause and are therefore much harder to fit within the scope of Congress's enforcement power under the Fourteenth Amendment (see Section 13.1.4 of this book). Thus, if state colleges and universities are subjected to private causes of action under Section 504 and the ADA, it will apparently be waiver arguments, not abrogation arguments, that will achieve this result.

The final issue regarding private causes of action concerns attorney's fees (see generally Section 2.2.4.4). When a plaintiff successfully invokes one of the civil rights statutes against an institution, the institution may be liable for the plaintiff's attorney's fees. Under the Civil Rights Attorney's Fees Awards Act of 1976 (42 U.S.C. § 1988), courts have discretion to award "a reasonable attorney's fee" to "the prevailing party" in actions under Title IX, Title VI, and several other civil rights statutes.[69] Although this Act does not apply to Section 504 suits or Age Discrimination Act suits, the omission is inconsequential, because both Section 504 and the ADA have their own comparable provisions authorizing the award of attorney's fees (29 U.S.C. § 794a(b); 42 U.S.C. § 6104(e)(1)).

Sec. 13.6. Dealing with the Federal Government

13.6.1. Handling federal rule making and regulations. Administrative agencies write regulations both to implement legislation and to formalize their own housekeeping functions. To prepare such regulations, agencies typically engage in a process of rule making, which includes an opportunity for the public to comment on regulatory proposals. Information on particular agencies' rule-making activities is published in the *Federal Register.* Final regulations (along with summaries of public comment on proposed drafts) are also published in the *Federal Register,* and these regulations are then codified in the *Code of Federal Regulations.*

Postsecondary administrators have long complained that the multitude of federal regulations applying to the programs and practices of postsecondary institutions creates financial and administrative burdens for their institutions. These burdens can be decreased as postsecondary administrators and legal counsel take more active roles in the process by which the federal government makes and enforces rules. The following suggestions outline a strategy for active involvement that an institution may undertake by itself, in conjunction with other similarly situated institutions, or through educational associations (see Section 14.1) to which it belongs. (See generally C. Saunders, "Regulating the Regulators," *Chron. Higher Educ.,* March 22, 1976, A32, which includes suggestions similar to some of those below.)

1. Appoint someone to be responsible for monitoring federal agency Web sites, the *Federal Register,* and other publications for announcements and information on regulatory proposals and regulations that will affect postsecondary education. Each agency periodically prepares an agenda of all regulations it expects to propose, promulgate, or review in the near future, and publishes this agenda in the *Federal Register.* The *Federal Register* also publishes "Notice(s) of Intent" to publish rules (NOIs) (sometimes called "Advance Notice(s) of Proposed Rulemaking" (ANPRs)) and "Notice(s) of Proposed Rulemaking" (NPRMs), the latter of which are drafts of proposed regulations along with invitations for comments from interested parties. Notices of the establishment of a *committee* to negotiate rule making on a subject or proposed rule are also

---

[69]The cases are collected in Ralph V. Seep, Annot., "What Persons or Entities May Be Liable to Pay Attorney's Fees Awarded Under Civil Rights Attorney's Fees Awards Act of 1976 (42 U.S.C.S. § 1988)," 106 A.L.R Fed. 636; Francis M. Dougherty, Annot., "Propriety of Amount of Attorneys' Fees Awarded to Prevailing Parties Under Civil Rights Attorney's Fees Award Act of 1976 (42 U.S.C.A. § 1988)," 118 A.L.R. Fed. 1.

published in the *Federal Register*. If further information on a particular rule-making process or a particular regulatory proposal would be useful, have institutional personnel ask the agency for the pertinent information. Some agencies may have policies that make draft regulations or summaries available for review before the proposed form is published.

2. File comments and deliver testimony in response to NOIs and NPRMs when the rules would have a likely impact on institutional operations. Support these comments with specific explanations and data showing how the proposed regulations would have a negative impact on the institution. Have legal counsel review the proposed rules for legal and interpretive problems, and include legal questions or objections with your comments when appropriate. Consider filing comments in conjunction with other institutions that would be similarly affected by the proposed regulations. In addition, when negotiated rule making is provided, participate in the negotiation process if your institution is eligible to do so.

3. Keep federal agencies informed of your views on and experiences with particular federal regulations. Compile data concerning the regulations' impact on your institution and present these data to the responsible agency. Continue to communicate complaints and difficulties with final regulations to the responsible agency, even if the regulations were promulgated months or years ago. In addition, determine whether any federal advisory committee has been appointed for the agency or the issues that are of concern to your institution. (The Federal Advisory Committee Act, 5 U.S.C. Appx. § 10, regulates the formation and operation of such committees.) If so, also keep the committee informed of your views and experience regarding particular regulations.

4. When the institution desires guidance concerning ambiguities or gaps in particular regulations, consider submitting questions to the administering agency. Make the questions specific and, if the institution has a particular viewpoint on how the ambiguity or gap should be resolved, forcefully argue that view. Legal counsel should be involved in this process. Once questions are submitted, press the agency for answers.

5. Be concerned not only with the substance of regulations but also with the adequacy of the rule-making and rule-enforcing procedures. Be prepared to object whenever institutions are given insufficient notice of an agency's plans to make rules, too few opportunities to participate in rule making, or inadequate opportunities to criticize or receive guidance on already implemented regulations. (For example, see *Student Loan Marketing Association v. Riley*, 104 F.3d 397 (D.C. Cir. 1997), which provides an example of a successful challenge to an agency's interpretation of a statute that was effectuated by sending two interpretive letters rather than by promulgating a regulation.)

6. Develop an effective process for institutional self-regulation. With other institutions, develop criteria and data to use in determining the circumstances in which self-regulation is more effective than government regulation (see A. Blumrosen, "Six Conditions for Meaningful Self-Regulation," 69 *A.B.A. J.* 1264 (1983)). Use a record of institutional success at self-regulation, combined with developed rationales for self-regulation, to argue in selected situations that government regulation is unnecessary.

7. When an agency passes a particular regulation that your institution (and presumably others) believes will have an ill-advised impact on higher education interests, consider obtaining a review of the regulation's legality. Section 13.4.6 of this book examines legal defects that may exist and legal challenges that may be made. One of the most important considerations is whether the regulation is *"ultra vires"*—that is, whether, in promulgating the regulation, the agency has exceeded the scope of authority Congress has delegated to it. Such issues may be the basis for a court challenge of agency regulations. In *Bowen v. American Hospital Ass'n.,* 476 U.S. 610 (1986), for example, the U.S. Supreme Court invalidated Department of Health and Human Services regulations on the protection of disabled infants because they were beyond the agency's scope of authority under Section 504 of the Rehabilitation Act. *California Cosmetology Coalition v. Riley,* 110 F.3d 1454 (9th Cir. 1997), provides another instructive example of a successful challenge to a federal regulation (a Department of Education regulation implementing federal loan programs) on grounds that it is *ultra vires.* Such legal issues may also be raised during the rule-making process itself, to bolster policy reasons for opposing particular regulations. (For a discussion of various strategies for contesting the application of a federal agency's regulation, see subsection 13.4.6).

Several pieces of legislation enacted since the early 1980s provide assistance for postsecondary institutions that do involve themselves in the federal regulatory process. One statute, the Regulatory Flexibility Act (5 U.S.C. § 601 *et seq.*), added Chapter VI to the federal Administrative Procedure Act. Another statute, the Negotiated Rulemaking Act of 1990 (5 U.S.C. § 561 *et seq.*), added subchapter III to the Administrative Procedure Act. A third statute, the Equal Access to Justice Act (28 U.S.C. § 2412), amended Chapter V of the Administrative Procedure Act.

The Regulatory Flexibility Act benefits three types of "small entities," each of which is defined in Section 601: the "small business," the "small organization," and the "small governmental jurisdiction." The Act's purpose is "to establish as a principle of regulatory issuance that [federal administrative] agencies shall endeavor . . . to fit regulatory and informational requirements to the scale of the businesses, organizations, and governmental jurisdictions subject to regulation" (96 Stat. 1164 § 2(b)). To implement this principle, the Act provides that (1) in October and April of every year, agencies must publish a "regulatory flexibility agenda," which describes and explains any forthcoming regulations that are "likely to have a significant economic impact on a substantial number of small entities" (5 U.S.C. § 602); (2) agencies proposing new regulations must provide, for public comment, an "initial regulatory flexibility analysis" containing a description of "the impact of the proposed rule on small entities" and a description of "alternatives to the proposed rule" that would lessen its economic impact on small entities (§ 603); (3) agencies promulgating final regulations must issue a "final regulatory flexibility analysis" containing a summary of comments on the initial analysis and, where regulatory alternatives were rejected, an explanation of why they were rejected (§ 604); (4) for any regulation "which will have a significant economic impact on a substantial number of small entities," agencies must "assure that small entities have been given an opportunity to participate in the rulemaking" (§ 609); and (5) agencies must periodically review and, where appropriate, revise their regulations with an eye to reducing their economic impact on small entities (§ 610).

The key issue for postsecondary institutions under the Regulatory Flexibility Act is one of definition: To what extent will postsecondary institutions be considered to be within the definition for one of the three groups of "small entities" protected by the Act? The first definition, for the "small business" (§ 601(3)), is unlikely to apply, except to some proprietary institutions. The second definition, for the "small organization" (§ 601(4)), will apply to many, but not necessarily all, private nonprofit institutions. And the third definition, for the "small governmental jurisdiction" (§ 601(5)), will apparently apply to some, but relatively few, public institutions—primarily community colleges. Thus, not every postsecondary institution will be within the Act's protected classes.[70]

The second statute, the Negotiated Rulemaking Act of 1990 (104 Stat. 4969 (1990), codified at 5 U.S.C. § 561 et seq.), was enacted to encourage agencies to use negotiations among interested parties as part of their rule-making process. Through an agency-established committee (5 U.S.C. § 565), agencies may informally negotiate a proposed rule that accommodates the varying interests of groups participating in the process and represents a consensus on the subject for which the committee was established. The rationale is that greater involvement and face-to-face discussion of opposing viewpoints will yield a proposed rule that may be formally adopted and enforced more quickly than would occur under more formal rule-making procedures (5 U.S.C. § 561 note).

The third statute, the Equal Access to Justice Act, was originally promulgated in 1980 (Pub. L. No. 96-481, 94 Stat. 2321 (1980)), and then was amended and permanently renewed in 1985 (Pub. L. No. 99-80, 99 Stat. 183 (1985)). (See Comment, "Institutionalizing an Experiment: The Extension of the Equal Access to Justice Act—Questions Remaining, Questions Resolved," 14 Fla. St. L. Rev. 925 (1987).) By authorizing courts to award attorney's fees and other expenses to certain parties that prevail in a civil action brought against or by a federal administrative agency, this Act assists institutions that must litigate with the federal government over procedural defects in rule making, substantive defects in regulations that were not resolved during the rule-making process, or interpretive issues regarding the application of regulations. If an institution prevails in such litigation, it may receive attorney's fees unless the agency shows that its position in the suit was "substantially justified" (28 U.S.C. § 2412(d)(1)(A)). Like the Regulatory Flexibility Act, this Act's application to postsecondary education is limited by its definitions: apparently, to be a "party" eligible for attorney's fees, a postsecondary institution must have no more than five hundred employees and, unless it is a 501(c)(3) organization (see this book, Section 13.3.1), must have a net worth of not more than $7 million (28 U.S.C.

---

[70]Institutions falling outside the definitions in the Regulatory Flexibility Act, and covered institutions seeking additional leverage in the administrative process, will be aided by the rule-making protections in Executive Order 12866, discussed later in this Section.

§ 2412(d)(2)(B)).[71] Moreover, state colleges and universities do not appear to be within the definition of "party," which includes a "unit of local government" but makes no reference to state-level agencies and entities. Individual agencies must publish their own regulations implementing the Act; the Department of Education's regulations, for example, are in 34 C.F.R. Part 21.

Another development that helps postsecondary institutions cope with the federal regulatory process is Executive Order 12866, issued by President Clinton on September 30, 1993 (58 Fed. Reg. 51725). The Executive Order sets out twelve principles of regulation for federal administrative agencies, including the requirement that each agency "shall identify and assess available alternatives to direct regulation" (§ 1(b)(3)); "shall assess both the costs and the benefits of the intended regulation" (§ 1(b)(6)); and "shall seek views of appropriate state, local, and tribal officials before imposing regulatory requirements" on those entities (§ 1(b)(9)). The order also establishes a number of procedural requirements—for example, requiring each agency periodically to "prepare an agenda of all regulations under development or review" (§ 4(b) and (c)), periodically to "review its existing significant regulations to determine whether any such regulations should be modified or eliminated so as to make the agency's regulatory program more effective [and] less burdensome" (§ 5(a)), and to "provide the public with meaningful participation in the regulatory process" and "afford the public a meaningful opportunity to comment" on any proposed regulation (§ 6(a)(1)). In addition, the order addresses various structural matters. For example, it assigns to the Office of Information and Regulatory Affairs (OIRA) within the Office of Management and Budget (§ 2(b)) various responsibilities for monitoring the regulatory processes of each agency (see, for example, § 4(e)), and it requires that each agency appoint a regulatory policy officer "to foster the development of effective, innovative, and least burdensome regulations and to further the principles" in Section 1(b) of the order (§ 6(a)(2)).

The Administrative Dispute Resolution Act of 1996 (Pub. L. No. 104-320, 110 Stat. 3870), amending the Administrative Dispute Resolution Act of 1990 (Pub. L. No. 101-552, 104 Stat. 2736), authorizes the use of alternative methods of dispute resolution to resolve conflicts with federal agencies that arise under an "administrative program." Under the Act, which is codified at 5 U.S.C. §§ 571–573, an "administrative program" is defined as "a Federal function which involves protection of the public interest and the determination of rights, privileges, and obligations of private persons through rule making, adjudication, licensing, or investigation" (5 U.S.C. § 571(2)). The alternative dispute resolution methods encouraged by the Act are "conciliation, facilitation, mediation, factfinding, minitrials, arbitration, and use of ombuds" (5 U.S.C. § 571(3)). The Act facilitates the use of such alternative dispute resolution techniques and provides for their availability when the parties agree to their use; they are voluntary and are intended to supplement rather than replace other agency dispute resolution techniques (5 U.S.C. §§ 572(a) & (c)).

---

[71]Cases are collected in Ralph V. Seep, Annot., "Who Is a Party Entitled to Recover Attorney's Fees Under Equal Access to Justice Act (28 U.S.C.S. § 2412(d))," 107 A.L.R. Fed. 827.

*13.6.2. **Obtaining information.*** Information will often be an indispensable key to a postsecondary institution's ability to deal effectively with the federal government, in rule-making processes or otherwise. Critical information sometimes will be within the control of the institution—for example, information about its own operations and the effect of federal programs on these operations. At other times, critical information will be under the government's control—for example, data collected by the government itself or information on competing policy considerations being weighed internally by an agency as it formulates regulatory proposals. When the latter type of information is needed, it may sometimes be obtained during the course of a rule-making proceeding (see Section 13.6.1 above). In addition, the following legislation may help institutional administrators and legal counsel: the Freedom of Information Act (FOIA) Amendments of 1974; the Privacy Act of 1974; the Government in the Sunshine Act of 1976; and the Government Printing Office Electronic Information Access Enhancement Act of 1993 (Pub. L. No. 103-40, 107 Stat. 112 (1993)), an Act facilitating electronic access to government data. Executive Orders 12866 and 12356 and successor government orders may also be of help.

The Freedom of Information Act Amendments (5 U.S.C. § 552) afford the public access to information from federal government files that is not specifically exempted from disclosure by the legislation.[72] Nine categories of information are exempted from disclosure under Section 552(b), the most relevant to postsecondary institutions being national security information, federal agencies' internal personnel rules and practices, interagency or intra-agency memoranda or letters that would not be available except in litigation, and investigatory files compiled for law enforcement purposes.

The FOIA is useful when an institution believes that the government holds information that would be helpful in a certain situation but informal requests have not yielded the necessary materials. By making an FOIA request, an institution can obtain agency information that may help the institution understand agency policy initiatives; or document a claim, process a grievance, or prepare a lawsuit against the government or some third party; or determine what information the government has that it could use against the institution—for example, in a threatened fund termination proceeding. Specific procedures to follow in requesting such information are set out in the statute and in each agency's own policies on FOIA requests. Persons or institutions whose requests are denied by the agency may file a suit against the agency in a U.S. district court. The burden of proof is on the agency to support its reasons for denial. Guidelines for making a Freedom of Information Act request to the U.S. Education Department are on its Web site, available at http://www.ed.gov/policy/gen/leg/foia/foiatoc.html.

The Privacy Act (codified in part at 5 U.S.C. § 552a) is discussed in Section 9.7.3 of this book with regard to student records. The point to be made here

---

[72]For analysis and discussion of when information may be considered to be "agency records" accessible under the Freedom of Information Act, see *Kissinger v. Reporters Committee for Freedom of the Press*, 445 U.S. 136 (1980); and *Forsham v. Harris*, 445 U.S. 169 (1980).

is that someone who requests certain information under the FOIA may find an obstacle in the Privacy Act. The FOIA itself exempts "personnel and medical files and similar files the disclosure of which would constitute a clearly unwarranted invasion of personal privacy" (5 U.S.C. § 552(b)(6)). The Privacy Act provides an even broader protection for information whose release would infringe privacy interests. While the Act thus may foil someone who requests information, it may also protect a postsecondary institution and its employees and students when the federal government has information concerning them in its files. (For a discussion of the implications of technological advances on the FOIA and Privacy Acts, see Julianne M. Sullivan, Comment, "Will the Privacy Act of 1974 Still Hold Up in 2004?: How Advancing Technology Has Created a Need for Change in the 'System of Records' Analysis," 39 *Cal. W. L. Rev.* 295 (2003).)

Individual agencies each publish their own regulations implementing the Privacy Act. The Department of Education's regulations are published in 34 C.F.R. § 5b.1 *et seq.*

The Government in the Sunshine Act (5 U.S.C. § 552b) assures the public that "meetings of multimember federal agencies shall be open with the exception of discussions of several narrowly defined areas" (H.R. Rep. No. 880, 94th Cong., 2d Sess. (1976), at 2, reprinted in 3 *U.S. Code Cong. & Admin. News* 2184 (1976)). Institutions can individually or collectively make use of this Act by sending a representative to observe and report on agency decision making that is expected to have a substantial impact on their operations.

Executive Order 12866 (also discussed in Section 13.6.1 above) requires agencies to do various cost-benefit assessments of proposed regulations and to make this information available to the public after the regulations are published (§ 6(1)(3)(E)(i)). The order also provides that OIRA (see Section 13.6.1 above) will "maintain a publicly available log" containing information about the status of regulatory actions and the oral and written communications received from outsiders regarding regulatory matters (§ 6(b)(4)(C)). And Executive Order 12958 (60 Fed. Reg. 19825, April 17, 1995) specifies the procedures and the schedule for classifying and declassifying government documents related to national security.

Selected Annotated Bibliography

General

Gaffney, Edward M., & Moots, Philip R. *Government and Campus: Federal Regulation of Religiously Affiliated Higher Education* (University of Notre Dame Press, 1982). Analyzes various aspects of federal regulation of religiously affiliated colleges and universities. Chapters treat religious preference in employment; student admissions and discipline policies; restrictions on the use of federal funds; accommodation to the needs of disabled persons, including reformed alcoholics and drug abusers; tax problems; labor law problems; and sexual segregation of on- and off-campus student housing. Each chapter offers recommendations for regulatory changes that would reduce church-state tension. See also these authors' earlier work, *Church and Campus*, listed in the Selected Annotated Bibliography for Chapter 1, Section 1.6).

Sec. 13.1 (Federal Constitutional Powers over Education)

Hartley, Roger. "Enforcing Federal Civil Rights Against Public Entities After *Garrett*," 28 *J. Coll. & Univ. Law* 41 (2001). Author evaluates the U.S. Supreme Court's current posture with respect to abrogation of state sovereign immunity through Section 5 of the Fourteenth Amendment, a posture the author describes as a "federalism revival." After a basic overview of state sovereign immunity, the Eleventh Amendment, and the abrogation doctrine, the author explores the *Garrett* case and its implications for redressing disability-based discrimination. Author also includes discussion of whether Congress can "purchase" a "waiver" of state sovereign immunity as a condition of federal funding, focusing on Section 504 of the Rehabilitation Act.

Kaplin, William. *American Constitutional Law: An Overview, Analysis, and Integration* (Carolina Academic Press, 2004). Chapter 6 covers "Congressional Powers and Federalism" and addresses, among other issues, the commerce power (Sec. C), the taxing and spending powers (Sec. D), the civil rights enforcement powers (Sec. E), and state immunity from federal legislation (Sec. G). Chapter 5, Section E, covers state sovereign immunity from suit in federal courts. Chapter 14, Sections C and D, includes additional analysis of the civil rights enforcement powers and their interrelation with state sovereign immunity, particularly with regard to the problem of congressional "abrogation" of state immunity.

Merico-Stephens, Ana Maria. "*United States v. Morrison* and the Emperor's New Clothes," 27 J. *Coll. & Univ. Law* 735(2001). Three-part article. Part I provides a brief history of the Supreme Court's treatment of the commerce clause up to *United States v. Lopez.* Part II examines the Court's refusal in *U.S. v. Morrison* to uphold the constitutionality of the Violence Against Women Act under either the commerce clause or, alternatively, Section 5 of the Fourteenth Amendment. Part III considers the ramifications of the Court's rejection of the government's arguments in *Morrison* and contemplates the impact that the "new federalism" now being developed by the Supreme Court may have on congressional power in the future.

Sec. 13.2 (Federal Regulation of Postsecondary Education)

Baharlias, Andrew D. "Yes, I Think the Yankees Might Sue If We Named Our Popcorn 'Yankees Toffee Crunch.' A Comprehensive Look at Trademark Infringement Defenses in the Context of the Professional and Collegiate Sports Industry," 8 *Seton Hall J. Sports L.* 99 (1998). The staff counsel for the New York Yankees reviews case law involving both professional sports teams and collegiate teams, explores the defense of trademark abandonment, and suggests future directions that such litigation may take.

Bartow, Ann. "Educational Fair Use in Copyright: Reclaiming the Right to Photocopy Freely," 60 *U. Pitt. L. Rev.* 149 (1998). Discusses routine violations of copyright law by faculty; the impact of litigation by publishers on the development of the fair use doctrine, and the impact of the "Agreement on Guidelines for Classroom Copying in Not for Profit Educational Institutions."

Beh, Hazel Glenn. "The Role of Institutional Review Boards in Protecting Human Subjects: Are We Really Ready to Fix a Broken System?" 26 *Law & Psychol. Rev.* 1 (2002). Discusses federal court opinions critical of institutional review board actions; describes federal requirements for institutional review boards and instances in which they have allowed ethical lapses; proposes reforms for institutional review boards and researchers.

Bell, Sheila, & Majestic, Martin. "Protection and Enforcement of College and University Trademarks," 10 *J. Coll. & Univ. Law* 63 (1983–84). Reviews issues of trademark law in the higher education setting. Describes and differentiates the trademark protection available under federal statutes, state statutes, and common law; explains the procedures to be followed in registering for state, federal, or international protection; and discusses the licensing of trademarks and the administrative and judicial remedies available for trademark violations.

Benbow, Shannon. Note, "Conflict + Interest: Financial Incentives and Informed Consent in Human Subjects Research," 17 *Notre Dame J.L. Ethics & Pub. Pol'y.* 181 (2003). Discusses patient protection and financial incentives in medical research; addresses informed consent and the role of Institutional Review Boards in reviewing informed consent provisions. Recommends changes in both the law and in the processes used by medical researchers.

Bennett, Barbara. *e-Health Business and Transactional Law* (Bureau of National Affairs, 2002). A reference work that discusses the regulation of fraud and abuse in health care; proprietary rights in technology and information; contracting principles for electronic health transactions; Internet pharmacies and FDA regulation of electronic health, antitrust issues; international and comparative issues in e-health; and legal ethics related to e-health.

Biagioli, Mario. "Rights or Rewards? Changing Contexts and Definitions of Scientific Authorship," 27 *J. Coll. & Univ. Law* 83 (2000). Discusses the meaning of "authorship" and the increasing practice of multiple authorship related to large collaborative research projects. Reviews two frameworks for the definition of scientific authorship and provides suggestions for giving credit and recognizing responsibility for the work.

Bienstock, Robert Eisig. "Anti-Bioterrorism Research Post-9/11 Legislation: The USA PATRIOT Act and Beyond," 30 *J. Coll. & Univ. Law* 465 (2004). Discusses the implications of the USA PATRIOT Act and the Bioterrorism Preparedness and Response Act. Identifies the key provisions of these statutes that affect university-based research, and provides a detailed discussion of their implementing regulations. Provides recommendations for compliance with the provisions involving "select agents" and other substances regulated by these acts.

Boswell, Donna A., & Barefoot, Bartley L. *HIPAA and Research* (National Association of College & University Attorneys, 2005). Provides a general overview of the HIPAA Privacy Rule and its research-related provisions. Discusses authorization and waiver of authorization, protected health information review for living and deceased subjects, minimum disclosure requirements, and other relevant issues.

Byman, Abigail, & Geller, Randolph. (eds.). *Intellectual Property Issues in Higher Education: A Legal Compendium* (National Association of College and University Attorneys (NACUA), 2001). Focuses on copyright, patent, trademark, and other laws regulating intellectual property. Includes journal articles, policies, and NACUA workshop outlines related to distance learning, software, the Internet, and research data. Provides an annotated list of Web sites, court opinions, policy papers, and other materials.

Carter, Stephen L. "The Trouble With Trademark," 99 *Yale L.J.* 759 (1990). A critical analysis of contemporary trademark law as deviating from common law. Author argues that common law actions for unfair competition are more appropriate than laws that give the trademark holder nationwide exclusive use of the mark.

Chadd, Charles M., & Satinover, Terry. *Avoiding Liability for Hazardous Waste: RCRA, CERCLA, and Related Corporate Law Issues* (Bureau of National Affairs, 1991). An overview of federal laws and their interpretive regulations regarding the manage- ment of hazardous waste and the cleanup of contaminated sites. Also included are guidelines from the Environmental Protection Agency and a glossary.

Chase, Marcelle P. "Animal Rights: An Interdisciplinary, Selective Bibliography," 82 *Law Libr. J.* 359 (1990). An annotated comprehensive list of publications on animal rights and research.

Chastain, Garvin, & Landrum, R. Eric. *Protecting Human Subjects: Departmental Subject Pools and Institutional Review Boards* (American Psychological Association, 1999). Discusses the use of students as research subjects, as well as more general issues concerning institutional review boards and faculty research using human subjects.

Childress, James, et al. (eds.). *Biolaw: A Legal and Ethical Reporter on Medicine, Health Care, and Bioengineering* (University Publications of America, 1986, and periodic supp. through 1999). A collection of chapters by eminent legal scholars on a variety of issues intersecting law and medicine. Topics discussed include the health care system, public health law, reproductive issues (including the effect of new technology in reproduction), genetic screening, mental health treatment, human experimentation, animal experimentation, death and dying, and artificial and transplanted organs.

Colecchia, Theresa J. *Legal Issues in Sponsored Research Programs: From Contracting to Compliance* (National Association of College and University Attorneys, 2005). Compendium of articles, checklists, form agreements, and sample policies on grants and contracts, the responsible conduct of research, research in the interna- tional setting, and other relevant subjects.

Crews, Kenneth D. *Copyright, Fair Use, and the Challenge for Universities: Promoting the Progress of Higher Education* (University of Chicago Press, 1993). Provides back- ground on copyright law and discusses the fair use doctrine. Includes a survey of copyright policies at ninety-eight research universities and describes how universi- ties have responded to legislation and litigation related to copyright. Guidelines for the development of institutional copyright policy are provided, and the *Basic Books v. Kinko's Graphics* case is discussed.

Crews, Kenneth D. "Distance Education and Copyright Law: The Limits and Meaning of Copyright Policy," 27 *J. Coll. & Univ. Law* 15 (2000). Reviews the relevance of copyright law and policy to distance education, suggesting that reforms are needed.

Curry, Judith L. (ed.). *Technology Transfer Issues for Colleges and Universities: A Legal Compendium.* (National Association of College and University Attorneys, 2005). Provides sample policies, agreements, forms, and licenses, as well as articles on technology transfer administration, intellectual property licensing, tax considera- tions, and other relevant topics.

"Developments in the Law—Toxic Waste Litigation," 99 *Harvard L. Rev.* 1462 (1986). An overview of toxic waste litigation and regulation through the mid–1980s.

Elias, Stephen. *Patent, Copyright & Trademark* (7th ed., Nolo, 2004). Provides defini- tions of patent, copyright, trademark, and trade secret law. Discusses recent devel- opments in intellectual property law, particularly that related to the Internet.

Elias, Stephen, & Goldoftas, Lisa. *Patent, Copyright and Trademark: A Desk Reference to Intellectual Property Law* (3d ed., Nolo, 1999). Includes an overview of patent, copyright, trademark, and trade secret law. Explains the scope of each area of the law, defines terms, and provides examples. Also includes sample nondisclosure agreements.

Flygare, Thomas J. *What to Do When the Department of Labor Comes to Campus: Wage and Hour Law in Higher Education* (National Association of College and University Attorneys, 1999). Provides guidelines for colleges in responding to Department of Labor investigations of alleged pay infractions. Includes a case study that illustrates basic FLSA principles, examines the exemptions from overtime requirements, discusses how to calculate work time and overtime compensation.

Gasaway, Laura N. "Impasse: Distance Learning and Copyright Law," 62 *Ohio St. L.J.* 783 (2001). Discusses the use of copyrighted material for instructional purposes in a distance learning format, the lawfulness of distributing copyrighted material to students enrolled in distance education courses, and providing library services to individuals involved in distance education.

Gindin, Susan E. "Lost and Found in Cyberspace: Informational Privacy in the Age of the Internet," 34 *San Diego L. Rev.* 1153 (1997). Discusses the various ways in which personal privacy may be invaded electronically, the various ways users and systems operators can protect against privacy invasions, and the legal rights of individuals whose privacy has been invaded. Includes analysis of the Electronic Communications Privacy Act, the Computer Fraud and Abuse Act, and other federal (and state) statutes protecting privacy interests.

Goldberg, Daniel. "Research Fraud: A Sui Generis Problem Demands a Sui Generis Solution (Plus a Little Due Process)," 20 *T.M. Cooley L. Rev.* 27 (2003). Criticizes the effectiveness of the False Claims Act to remedy fraud; also criticizes the federal Office of Research Integrity. Provides suggestions for reducing research fraud.

Hajian, Tamar, Sizer, Judith R., & Ambash, Joseph W. *Record Keeping and Reporting Requirements for Independent and Public Colleges and Universities* (National Association of College and University Attorneys, 1998). Summarizes relevant federal laws governing record keeping, reporting requirements, and retention of records for both public and private colleges. Covers student and employee records, student financial aid, grants and sponsored research, law enforcement, licensure and accreditation, and other miscellaneous records. Includes diskette for downloading materials, as well as "hotlinks" to URL citations for laws and regulations.

Harper, Georgia K. *Copyright Issues in Higher Education, 2005 Edition* (National Association of College and University Attorneys, 2005). Describes the basic concepts of copyright, including what are and are not protected works, what constitutes fair use, the application of the law to academia, institutional liability for copyright infringement by employees and students, and the numerous issues relating to authorship and ownership. Includes URLs for more than fifty additional sites, all relating to some aspect of copyright.

Harper, Georgia. "Developing a Comprehensive Copyright Policy to Facilitate Online Learning," 27 *J. Coll. & Univ. Law* 5 (2000). Reviews the special copyright issues related to online learning, and discusses the need for a copyright policy that recognizes these special issues. Reviews the concept of fair use and its restrictions in the context of online learning. Provides an appendix with links to helpful Internet resources.

Harrington, Peter J. "Faculty Conflicts of Interest in an Age of Academic Entrepreneurialism: An Analysis of the Problem, the Law and Selected University Policies," 27 *J. Coll. & Univ. Law* 775 (2001). Discusses conflicts of interest in financial, professional, familial, and other areas. Focuses primarily on conflicts related to industry-sponsored research and faculty consulting.

Hovenkamp, Herbert. *Federal Antitrust Policy: The Law of Competition and Its Practice* (West, 1999). Reviews all aspects of federal antitrust law; discusses relevant litigation and policy issues.

Kaufman, Hattie E. *Access to Institutions of Higher Education for Students with Disabilities* (National Association of College and University Attorneys, 1998). Discusses the impact of disability discrimination laws and regulations on admissions, accommodations in academic programs, auxiliary aids, financial aid, housing, physical accessibility, and transportation systems. Provides checklists of actions for administrators to take to ensure compliance and avoid liability.

Kelch, Thomas G. "Animal Experimentation and the First Amendment," 22 *W. New Eng. L. Rev.* 467 (2001). An opponent of the use of animals in scientific research argues that the First Amendment provides no special protection for scientific research, and argues for restrictions on animal experimentation.

Kirby, Wendy T. "Federal Antitrust Issues Affecting Institutions of Higher Education: An Overview," 11 *J. Coll. & Univ. Law* 345 (1984). A review of general antitrust law principles that apply to colleges and universities. Analyzes the potential antitrust liability of undergraduate institutions in the areas of commercial activities, athletics, accreditation, and joint ventures with private industry; and lists the "exemptions" or "immunities" that may be available to protect institutions threatened with antitrust liability. Includes a bibliography of secondary sources on antitrust law's application to higher education.

Lape, Laura G. "Ownership of Copyrightable Works of University Professors: The Interplay Between the Copyright Act and University Copyright Policies," 37 *Villanova L. Rev.* 223 (1992). Discusses attempts by universities to control the copyrightable works of professors. Analyzes cases about works made for hire, discusses the effectiveness of university copyright policies, and examines copyright policies at seventy research universities. Includes recommendations about how copyright ownership questions between professors and their institutions should be resolved.

Lazarus, Richard J. "The Greening of America and the Graying of United States Environmental Law: Reflections on Environmental Law's First Three Decades in the United States," 20 *Va. Envtl. L.J.* 75 (2001). Reviews the historical development of environmental law and policy, discusses current environmental policy, and predicts the future development of environmental law. Discusses several areas of continuing controversy, as well as the impact of international trade and development on U.S. environmental law and policy.

Levine, Robert J. *Ethics and Regulation of Clinical Research* (2d ed., Yale University Press, 1986). Focuses on the ethics of research for administrators, members of institutional review boards, and researchers themselves. Discusses federal regulations, ethical analyses, and specific research projects that use humans as research subjects.

Loundy, David J. "A Primer on Trademark Law and Internet Addresses," 15 *J. Marshall J. Computer & Info. L.* 465 (1997). Examines trademark law as applied to a variety of Internet addressing issues, including domain names and e-mail addresses. Analyzes several recent court opinions relevant to this issue.

McCarthy, J. Thomas, Schechter, Roger E., & Franklyn, David J. *McCarthy's Desk Encyclopedia of Intellectual Property* (3d ed., Bureau of National Affairs, 2004). A reference guide for lawyers and administrators who work regularly with intellectual property issues. Defines terms from patent, trademark, copyright, trade secret, entertainment, and computer law. Entries are annotated with cases and statutes, regulations, treaties, and bibliographical citations. Includes all recent federal copyright amendments and new legislation.

McSherry, Corynne. *Who Owns Academic Work?* (Harvard University Press, 2001). Reviews a range of legal issues faced by institutions of higher education regarding the ownership of intellectual property produced by employees and students. Copyright and patent issues are discussed, as well as the role of the Internet in ownership disputes.

Paradis, Laurence. "Developments in Disability Rights: Title II of the Americans With Disabilities Act and Section 504 of the Rehabilitation Act: Making Programs, Services, and Activities Accessible to All," 14 *Stan. L. & Pol'y. Rev.* 389 (2003). Examines the effectiveness of Section 504 and the ADA with respect to discrimination against individuals with disabilities who participate in government-funded programs. Reviews judicial interpretation of these laws' requirements, particularly with respect to access to programs, the definitions of "fundamental alteration," "undue burden," and qualification standards for program participation. Also discusses sovereign immunity challenges to the application of these laws to public organizations.

Patry, William F. *Copyright Law and Practice* (2d ed., Bureau of National Affairs, 1994, with 2000 cumulative supplement). A standard reference on copyright law. Thoroughly treats provisions of domestic copyright law, analyzing both the 1909 and the 1976 Copyright Acts. Includes appendices containing texts of the 1909 and 1976 Acts, Copyright Office regulations, and leading international conventions on copyrights.

Richmond, Douglas R. "Antitrust and Higher Education: An Overview," 61 *Mo. L. Rev.* 417 (1993). A review of antitrust theory, with special emphasis on the price-fixing charges against several Ivy League schools.

Rothstein, Laura F. *Disabilities and the Law* (2d. ed., Shepard's/McGraw-Hill, 1997, with annual supplements). A reference guide designed for lawyers, educators, and medical professionals. Includes chapters on the Americans With Disabilities Act, the Rehabilitation Act, and federal and state laws related to disability discrimination, among others. The chapter on higher education discusses admissions, programs and services (including academic modifications and auxiliary services), athletics, health insurance, physical facilities, confidentiality requirements, learning-disabled students, and mentally impaired students.

Rothstein, Laura. "Disability Law and Higher Education: A Road Map for Where We've Been and Where We May Be Heading," 63 *Maryland L. Rev.* 122 (2004). Provides an overview of court decisions and agency opinions, and reviews relevant Supreme Court decisions, assessing their impact on higher education policy. Predicts the direction of future national policy related to disability discrimination in higher education.

Sermersheim, Michael D. *Environmental Law: Selected Issues for Higher Education Managers and Counsel* (National Association of College and University Attorneys, 2001).

Discusses selected environmental laws and regulations, provides suggested compliance standards used by institutions, as well as sample institutional policies. Includes appendices and lists of references.

Shea, Lance, Robinson, Frederick, & Parkin, Lara. *Managing Financial Conflicts of Interest in Human Subjects Research* (National Association of College and University Attorneys, 2004). Discusses the range of financial interests that may pose conflicts for academic researchers and/or their sponsors, reviews federal regulations and guidance related to these interests, and provides suggestions for managing conflicts of interests.

Skitol, Robert A. "The Shifting Sands of Antitrust Policy: Where It Has Been, Where It Is Now, Where It Will Be in Its Third Century," 9 *Cornell J.L. & Pub. Pol'y.* 239 (1999). Provides commentary on the evolution of antitrust policy; argues that recent changes have improved enforcement, but that many inconsistencies and unanswered questions remain.

Stim, Richard. *Getting Permission: How to License and Clear Copyrighted Materials Online and Off* (2d ed., Nolo, 2004). Discusses fair use, what is meant by the "public domain," and other matters of significance for faculty and other non-attorneys. Includes agreement forms in paper and CD-ROM format.

Symposium, "The Future of Medicare, Post Great Society and Post Plus-Choice: Legal and Policy Issues," 60 *Wash. & Lee L. Rev.* 1137 (2003). Special issue devoted to Medicare, including Jonathan Oberlander, "The Politics of Medicare Reform"; Marilyn Moon, "Modernizing Medicare's Benefit Structure"; Mark V. Pauly, "What if Technology Never Stops Improving? Medicare's Future Under Continuous Cost Increases"; Thomas H. Stanton, "The Administration of Medicare: A Neglected Issue"; Robert A. Berenson, "Paying for Quality and Doing It Right"; Eleanor D. Kinney, "Medicare Coverage Decision-Making and Appeal Procedures: Can Process Meet the Challenge of New Medical Technology?"

Symposium, "Legal Regulation of the Internet," 28 *Conn. L. Rev. 953* (1996). Provides various insights and analyses on the development and regulation of online technology. Contains six articles: M. Ethan Katsh, "Dispute Resolution in Cyberspace"; Julie Cohen, "A Right to Read Anonymously: A Closer Look at 'Copyright Management'"; Mark Lemley, "Antitrust and the Internet Standardization Problem"; Dan Burk, "Federalism in Cyberspace"; Bruce Stanford & Michael Lorenger, "Teaching an Old Dog New Tricks: The First Amendment in an Online World"; and Robert Charles & Jacob Zamansky, "Liability for Online Libel after *Stratton Oakmont v. Prodigy Services, Co.*"

Tribbensee, Nancy. "Privacy and Security in Higher Education Computing Environments After the USA PATRIOT Act," 30 *J. Coll. & Univ. Law* 337 (2004). Examines the implications of the USA PATRIOT Act for the privacy and security of information stored on campus computer systems. Discusses changes to electronic surveillance law and the implications of the USA PATRIOT Act for constitutional interests. Provides suggestions for improving the security of campus computer systems.

Wallach, Paul G., Davidson, Jeffery J., Atlas, Mark, & Meade, Kenneth R. *Environmental Requirements for Colleges and Universities* (American Council on Education, 1989). Summarizes eleven areas of federal environmental law, including RCRA, CERCLA, the Clean Water Act, the Hazard Communication Standard, the Toxic Substances Control Act, asbestos issues, underground storage tanks, the Clean Air Act, and the Safe Drinking Water Act.

Yale-Loehr, Stephen (ed.). *Understanding the Immigration Act of 1990* (Federal Publications, 1991). A descriptive and analytical review of the 1990 legislation and its comprehensive overhaul of U.S. immigration law. Each of the thirteen chapters is aimed at a major aspect of the new law. Chapters 3 (employment-based immigrants), 5 (F-1 nonimmigrants), and 6 (H-1B nonimmigrants) will be particularly helpful to higher education institutions. Also includes the full text of the 1990 Act.

See Selected Annotated Bibliographies for Chapter Four, Section 4.6, for references on federal regulation of employment generally, and Chapter Five, Section 5.2, for references on federal regulation of employment discrimination.

Sec. 13.3 (*Federal Taxation of Postsecondary Education*)

Ashford, Deborah, & Frank, Robert. *Lobbying and the Law: A Guide to Federal Tax Law Limitations on Legislative and Political Activities by Nonprofit Organizations* (2d ed., Hogan & Hartson/Frank & Company, 1990). Covers participation in political campaigns, direct and grass-roots lobbying, mass media communications, and activities excluded from the definition of lobbying. An appendix includes an overview of the lobbying laws of every state.

Bittker, Boris, & Rahdert, George K. "The Exemption of Nonprofit Organizations from Federal Income Taxation," 85 *Yale L.J.* 299 (1976). An overview of issues regarding the federal tax status of nonprofit entities. Discusses the unrelated business income tax, the taxation of capital gains and investment income of private foundations, and the tax status of organizations that engage in political activity. Also contains sections on the exemption of educational institutions and on appropriate methods by which to measure the income of nonprofit entities.

Colombo, John D. "Why Is Harvard Tax-Exempt? (and Other Mysteries of Tax Exemption for Private Educational Institutions)," 35 *Ariz. L. Rev.* 841 (1993). Examines federal and state exemptions for private educational institutions. Discusses the rationales presented to justify tax exemption for charitable institutions in general, including the donative theory that would limit exemption to those entities receiving a certain percentage of revenues from donations. Also discusses both the expansive definition of "education" and the manner in which the IRS and state taxing authorities circumscribe this definition. Includes five tables, setting out the total charitable donations received by various types of postsecondary institutions.

Harding, Bertrand M., Jr. "Federal Tax Issues Raised by International Study Abroad Programs," 27 *J. Coll. & Univ. Law* 207 (2000). Examines the domestic and foreign tax implications of study abroad programs administered by American colleges and universities. Author suggests how programs can be structured to minimize adverse tax consequences and provides an overview of the personal income tax consequences for employees who participate in a study abroad program outside of the United States, including implications for American employees who elect to file for a "foreign earned income exclusion."

Harding, Bertrand M., Jr. *The Tax Law of Colleges and Universities* (Wiley, 1997). Provides a comprehensive examination of the tax problems and issues faced by colleges and universities. Topics covered include unrelated business income, employment taxes, IRS audits, and other related topics. Outlines tax planning and compliance aspects of managing the institution's business.

Harding, Bertrand, Jr., & Peterson, Norm. *U.S. Taxation of International Students and Scholars: A Manual for Advisers and Administrators* (rev. ed., National Association for Foreign Student Affairs, 1993). Practical advice on the taxability of scholarships, fellowships, living allowances, and travel grants for foreign students and scholars, as well as the withholding and reporting requirements imposed on their institutions.

Hopkins, Bruce. *The Law of Tax-Exempt Organizations* (7th ed., Wiley, 1998, and periodic supp.). A reference volume, for managers and administrators as well as counsel, that examines the pertinent federal law affecting the different types of nonprofit organizations, including colleges and universities. Emphasis is on how to obtain and maintain tax-exempt status. Contains citations to Internal Revenue Code provisions, Treasury Department revenue rulings, and court decisions.

Hopkins, Bruce. *The Nonprofit Counsel* (Wiley). A monthly newsletter that analyzes current developments in Congress, the Treasury Department, the IRS, and the courts regarding taxation of nonprofit organizations and related issues. See also entry in Selected Annotated Bibliography for Section 12.3.

Jones, Darryll K. "Tax Exemption Issues Facing Academic Health Centers in the Managed Care Environment," 24 *J. Coll. & Univ. Law* 261 (1997). Discusses and analyzes the tax statutes, regulations, IRS interpretations, and case law "applicable to operating strategies employed by academic health centers adapting to the managed care environment." Operating strategies discussed include "primary care physician recruitment, primary care practice acquisitions, joint operating agreements, joint ventures and tax-exempt health maintenance organizations."

Kaplan, Richard L. "Intercollegiate Athletics and the Unrelated Business Income Tax," 80 *Columbia L. Rev.* 1430 (1980). Reviews the unrelated business income tax as it affects the postsecondary institution's athletic program. Author argues that many schools' intercollegiate athletic programs have taken on the appearance of business activities unrelated to the institution's educational mission, and thus may be liable to taxation. Article also includes broader discussion of the unrelated business income tax in the higher education context.

Kelly, Marci. "Financing Higher Education: Federal Income-Tax Consequences," 17 *J. Coll. & Univ. Law* 307 (1991). Discusses federal tax law as it applies to the financing of education through scholarships, prizes, loans, and student employment. Provides guidance for administrators in counseling students, structuring new financial aid programs, and administering existing programs.

National Association of College and University Business Officers. *A Guide to Federal Tax Issues for Colleges and Universities* (NACUBO, 1999). In thirteen chapters, discusses numerous tax topics, from basic to highly complex, including UBIT, public access to the institution's tax forms, and preparing for IRS audits. Updated monthly and quarterly.

Roady, Celia & others (eds.). *A Guide to Federal Tax Issues for Colleges and Universities* (National Association of College and University Business Officers). A looseleaf binder updated quarterly and written by various tax experts specifically for college and university "business officers, auditors, and attorneys." Provides analysis and guidance on a wide range of tax subjects. Includes "checklists, flow charts, and forms." A monthly newsletter (by Bertrand Harding) is also available.

Symposium, "Federal Taxation and Charitable Organizations," 39 *Law & Contemp. Probs.* 1–262 (1975). A sophisticated collection of articles on federal tax policy and law concerning charitable organizations. Includes J. H. Levi on "Financing

Education and the Effects of the Tax Law," which discusses the impact of the Internal Revenue Code's charitable deduction provisions on postsecondary institutions; and J. F. Kirkwood & D. S. Mundel on "The Role of Tax Policy in Federal Support for Higher Education," which examines federal tax policy regarding higher education and compares tax programs with spending and regulatory programs.

Vance, Deborah. *U.S. Federal Income Tax Guide for International Students and Scholars* (rev. ed., National Association for Foreign Student Affairs, 1994). Provides a layperson's guide to U.S. taxation and filing requirements for foreign students and scholars.

Sec. 13.4 (Federal Aid-to-Education Programs)

Advisory Commission on Intergovernmental Relations. *The Evolution of a Problematic Partnership: The Feds and Higher Education* (Advisory Commission on Intergovernmental Relations, 1981). Examines the history and growth of the federal government's involvement in higher education. Chapters include "The Scope of Federal Involvement in Higher Education," "The Evolution of a Federal Role: 1787–1958," "Beginnings of a New Federal Role in Higher Education: The National Defense Education Act," "A Direct Federal Role Established: The Higher Education Acts of 1963 and 1965," "Equal Opportunity Preeminent: The 1972 Higher Education Amendments," and "A Growing Regulatory Presence." Contains various figures, graphs, and tables charting major developments in the relationship between the federal government and higher education.

Arriola, Elvia. "Democracy and Dissent: Challenging the Solomon Amendment as a Cultural Threat to Academic Freedom and Civil Rights," 24 *St. Louis U. Pub. L. Rev.* 149 (2005). Describes the litigation challenging the Solomon Amendment; provides historical context for the clash between First Amendment concerns and military priorities; and discusses the role of the First Amendment in the debate over gay marriage and its relationship to the tension between academic freedom and military priorities.

Lacovara, Philip. "How Far Can the Federal Camel Slip Under the Academic Tent?" 4 *J. Coll. & Univ. Law* 233 (1977). A constitutional analysis, in the postsecondary education context, of the federal government's spending power and potential First Amendment and due process limitations on that power. Outdated in its case law, but a good source for the foundational principles.

Olivas, Michael. *The Tribally Controlled Community College Assistance Act of 1978: The Failure of Federal Indian Higher Education Policy,* IHELG Monograph 82-1 (Institute for Higher Education Law and Governance, University of Houston, 1982). An analysis of the Act's design flaws, the bureaucratic delays in its implementation, and the impoverished condition of the tribal colleges that are the Act's intended beneficiaries. Includes recommendations for improving the Act and its administration. Another version of this paper is published in 9 *Am. Indian L. Rev.* 219 (1981).

O'Neil, Robert M. "Artists, Grants and Rights: The NEA Controversy Revisited," 9 *N.Y.L. Sch. J. Hum. Rts.* 85 (1991). Considers the viability of constitutional challenges to restrictions on the use of grant funds administered by the National Endowment for the Arts (NEA). Reviews the First Amendment's applicability to NEA grants, discusses the Helms amendment and congressional changes that followed, and analyzes recent cases challenging NEA grant restrictions on First Amendment grounds.

O'Neil, Robert M. "God and Government at Yale: The Limits of Federal Regulation of Higher Education," 44 *U. Cincinnati L. Rev.* 525 (1975). An analysis of constitutional and nonconstitutional issues regarding the extent of federal authority to regulate higher education. Outdated in its case law, but another good source for the foundational principles.

Palmer, Carolyn, & Gehring, Donald (eds.). *A Handbook for Complying with the Program and Review Requirements of the 1989 Amendments to the Drug-Free Schools and Communities Act* (College Administration Publications, 1992). A how-to manual for college administrators who are setting up or reviewing on-campus drug and alcohol programs in accordance with federal law. The handbook also provides a guide, supplemented by a comprehensive appendix, to federal and private funding sources, research and studies on the subject, organizations concerned with drug-free education, and model standards and guidelines.

Wallick, Robert D., & Chamblee, Daryl A. "Bridling the Trojan Horse: Rights and Remedies of Colleges and Universities Under Federal Grant-Type Assistance Programs," 4 *J. Coll. & Univ. Law* 241 (1977). Discusses legal and policy aspects of federal assistance to postsecondary institutions. Suggests steps that legal counsel might take to protect the interests of institutions in grant programs.

Whitehead, Kenneth D. *Catholic Colleges and Federal Funding* (Ignatius Press, 1988). Examines the question whether religiously affiliated colleges and universities must safeguard "academic freedom" and have "institutional autonomy" in order to be eligible for federal aid. Discusses eligibility requirements (such as accreditation), accrediting agencies' policies, the current understanding of academic freedom and the role of the AAUP, and parallel issues regarding state (rather than federal) aid for religiously affiliated institutions. Written by the then deputy assistant secretary for higher education programs in the U.S. Department of Education.

See the Constance Cook and the Michael Parsons entries in bibliography for Chapter 14, Section 14.1.

Sec. 13.5 (Civil Rights Compliance)

Baxter, Felix V. "The Affirmative Duty to Desegregate Institutions of Higher Education—Defining the Role of the Traditionally Black College," 11 *J. Law & Educ.* 1 (1982). Provides "an analytical framework to assess, in a consistent fashion, the role which [black] institutions should play in a unitary system." Reviews various legal strategies to deflect the "very real threat to black efforts to desegregate state systems of higher education."

Bell, Derrick A., Jr. "Black Colleges and the Desegregation Dilemma," 28 *Emory L.J.* 949 (1979). Reviews the development of desegregation law and its impact on black colleges. Author argues that black colleges continue to provide a special service to black Americans and that litigation and legislation should be tailored to accommodate and promote this service.

Brown-Scott, Wendy. "Race Consciousness in Higher Education: Does 'Sound Educational Policy' Support the Continued Existence of Historically Black Colleges?" 43 *Emory L.J.* 1 (1994). Discusses the pedagogic and cultural significance of historically black institutions (HBIs), traces why HBIs developed, and explains their still important role in the United States. Argues that requiring racial balance or race-neutral remedies does not constitute "sound educational policy" under the *Fordice* standard, and that racial identifiability is not per se harmful for colleges or their students.

Fossey, Richard (ed.). *Race, the Courts, and Equal Education: The Limits of the Law* (AMS Press, 1998). Contains chapters on desegregation litigation both K–12 and higher education. Includes discussion of the post-*Fordice* legal environment, race-based financial aid, and a consideration of affirmative action.

Neiger, Jan Alan. "Actual Knowledge Under *Gebser v. Lago Vista*: Evidence of the Court's Deliberate Indifference or an Appropriate Response for Finding Institutional Liability?" 26 *J. Coll. & Univ. Law* 1 (1999). Provides a comprehensive review and analysis of Title IX's application to sexual harassment, with a particular focus on the *Gebser* case. Traces Title IX developments from their origin in Title VII law, to the *Franklin* case, to the conflicts among the lower federal courts, to OCR's "Sexual Harassment Guidance," to *Gebser*, and finally to the lower federal courts' initial attempts to apply the *Gebser* liability standards. Author is generally supportive of the majority's opinion in *Gebser*.

O'Brien, Molly. "Discriminatory Effects: Desegregation Litigation in Higher Education in Georgia," 8 *Wm. & Mary Bill Rts. J.* 1 (1999). Reviews the history of racial segregation and desegregation in Georgia's system of public higher education, including the establishment of dual systems of higher education, litigation by both black and white plaintiffs to change funding and enrollment patterns in Georgia public colleges and universities, and argues that the "affirmative duty" concept articulated in *Fordice* is inadequate to foster desegregation and imperils traditionally black colleges and universities.

Preer, Jean. "Lawyers v. Educators: Changing Perceptions of Desegregation in Public Higher Education," 1 *N.C. Central L.J.* 74 (1979), reprinted in 53 *J. Higher Educ.* 119 (1982). Examines the tension between lawyers' and educators' perceptions of desegregation in public universities and colleges. Discusses three historical examples: the Morrill Act of 1890, "the reactions of civil rights lawyers and educators to the regional educational compact of the 1940s," and the "legal and educational paradoxes" of *Adams v. Richardson* (see Sections 13.5.2 & 13.5.8 of this book). Author concludes that "both lawyers and educators need to expand their vision." An extended version of these themes appears in Jean Preer, *Lawyers v. Educators: Black Colleges and Desegregation in Public Higher Education* (Greenwood, 1982), especially rich in historical materials.

Rothstein, Laura. "Reflections on Disability Discrimination Policy—25 Years," 22 *U. Ark. L. Rev.* 147 (2000). Traces the development of disability policy over the last quarter of the twentieth century, analyzing the roles of the courts, the enforcement agencies, and Congress. Responds to claims that disability policy limits the efficient function of the workplace or the educational arena.

Rutherford, Lisa, & Jewett, Cynthia. *What to Do When the U.S. Office of Civil Rights Comes to Campus* (National Association of College and University Attorneys, 2005). Describes the enforcement process of the Office of Civil Rights, from the filing of a complaint through the investigation and resolution of the complaint. Provides advice on how administrators and counsel should respond to a complaint, how to prepare for an investigation, OCR's authority to review documents and interview witnesses, and issues to consider in reaching a resolution of the complaint.

Shuck, Peter H. "The Graying of Civil Rights Law: The Age Discrimination Act of 1975," 89 *Yale L.J.* 27 (1979). A theoretical study of the Age Discrimination Act.

Article is divided into four parts: "The ADA and the Analogy to Title VI"; "The Political Context and Legislative History of the ADA"; "Interpreting the ADA: Reading Shadows on Walls" (which presents a detailed explication of the statute's ambiguities and built-in exceptions); and "The Process, Substance, and Form of Age Discrimination Policy." Author is critical of the ADA and furnishes a trenchant analysis of its inherent difficulties.

Sum, Paul E., Light, Steven Andrew, & King, Ronald F. "Race, Reform, and Desegregation in Mississippi Higher Education: Historically Black Institutions after *United States v. Fordice,*" 29 *Law & Soc. Inquiry* 403 (2004). Beginning with the requirements of *Fordice,* the authors discuss the difficulties that states have in implementing desegregation. Criticizes the precept that the "success" of desegregation rests on increasing the proportions of white students in historically black institutions, given their findings concerning the resistance of white students to attend historically black institutions.

Tollett, Kenneth S., Sr. "The Fate of Minority-Based Institutions After *Fordice*: An Essay," 13 *Rev. Litig.* 447 (1994). Discusses seven significant functions of historically black colleges and argues that their continued existence is consistent with Supreme Court rulings.

Ware, Leland. "The Most Visible Vestige: Black Colleges After *Fordice,*" 35 *B.C. L. Rev.* 633 (1994). Examines whether there is a continuing justification for publicly funded black colleges, and whether the operation of these colleges as racially distinct institutions can be justified in light of the principles of *Fordice* and *Brown v. Board of Education.*

Wegner, Judith W. "The Antidiscrimination Model Reconsidered: Ensuring Equal Opportunity Without Respect to Handicap Under Section 504 of the Rehabilitation Act of 1973," 69 *Cornell L. Rev.* 401 (1984). Author compares Section 504 to other antidiscrimination measures and "discusses the extent to which traditional antidiscrimination principles . . . must be reshaped" to protect people with disabilities from discriminatory practices. Also discusses coverage and enforcement issues and analyzes the elements of the plaintiff's *prima facie* case and the defendant's defenses in situations where a disabled individual challenges an exclusion from participation in a program, the denial of benefits of a program, or unequal treatment within a program. Includes a section analyzing the U.S. Supreme Court's decision in *Southeastern Community College v. Davis.*

Williams, John B., IV (ed.). *Desegregating America's Colleges and Universities: Title VI Regulation of Higher Education* (Teachers College Press, 1987). Offers a range of policy proposals aimed at increasing the proportion of blacks among college students and faculty. Authors—including Barbara Newell, Larry Leslie, James Blackwood, Charles Willie, and Edgar Epps—discuss trends in black enrollment and degree attainment at the undergraduate and graduate levels, financial inequities in previously segregated systems of public postsecondary education, achievement of black and white students in predominantly white and predominantly black institutions, and the future of Title VI enforcement. The book is intended for administrators, faculty, policy makers, and researchers.

Williams, John B. *Race Discrimination in Public Higher Education: Interpreting Federal Civil Rights Enforcement, 1964–1996* (Praeger, 1997). Traces the history of resistance to desegregation by public systems of higher education in the South. Examines the history of desegregation litigation in Georgia, Louisiana, Alabama, and

Mississippi, including an analysis of the implementation of the U.S. Supreme Court's *Fordice* ruling.

Wilson, Reginald (ed.). *Race and Equity in Higher Education* (American Council on Education, 1983). Contains five essays produced by the American Council on Education-Aspen Institute Seminar on the Desegregation of Higher Education. Essays (by J. Egerton, J. E. Blackwell, J. L. Prestage, P. R. Dimond, and A. L. Berrian) examine the history and politics of higher education desegregation, provide data on demographic changes in recent decades, analyze constitutional standards and remedies, evaluate desegregation plans of states involved in *Adams v. Richardson* litigation (see Sections 13.5.2 & 13.5.8), and propose new policies and agendas.

Sec. 13.6 (Dealing with the Federal Government)

Administrative Conference of the United States. *Federal Administrative Procedure Sourcebook: Statutes and Related Materials* (2d ed., Office of the Chairman, Administrative Conference, 1992). A handy guide that collects together materials on the Administrative Procedure Act, Equal Access to Justice Act, Federal Advisory Committee Act, Freedom of Information Act, Negotiated Rulemaking Act, Privacy Act, Regulatory Flexibility Act, and other legislation regarding the administrative process. Includes texts of the Acts, legislative histories, an overview of each Act, agency regulations and Executive Orders, citations and bibliographies, and materials on judicial review of federal agency decisions.

Brademus, John. *The Politics of Education* (University of Oklahoma Press, 1987). Discusses the federal role in education, the legislative process with reference to education, contemporary themes and concerns regarding education policy, and the relationship between education and democracy. Written "from a highly personal perspective" by a former congressman who became president of a large private university after leaving Congress.

Clune, William, III. *The Deregulation Critique of the Federal Role in Education,* Project Report no. 82-A11 (Institute for Research on Educational Finance and Governance, Stanford University, 1982). Analyzes the theoretical basis for deregulation, the criticisms of then current federal regulatory efforts, and the benefits and disadvantages of deregulation.

Foerstel, Herbert N. *Freedom of Information and the Right to Know* (Greenwood, 1999). Reviews the history of the FOIA; discusses the operation of the law and its impact on the functioning of the federal government.

Hajian, Tamara, Sizer, Judith R., & Ambash, Joseph W. *Record Keeping and Reporting Requirements for Independent and Public Colleges and Universities* (National Association of College and University Attorneys, 1998). Summarizes relevant federal laws governing record keeping, reporting requirements, and retention of records, including student and employee records, student financial aid, grants and sponsored research, law enforcement, licensure and accreditation, and other records required by the federal government. Available in hard copy or electronic form.

Lisman, Natasha. "Freedom of Scientific Research: A Frontier Issue in First Amendment Law," 35 *Boston Bar J.* 4 (November–December 1991). Author argues "that the development of scientific knowledge is among the vital interests protected by the First Amendment, and that the very nature of the process by which science creates and advances scientific knowledge dictates that the First Amendment protections apply not only to the scientific expression but also to scientific experimentation."

Mintz, Benjamin, & Miller, Nancy. *A Guide to Federal Agency Rulemaking* (2d ed., Office of the Chairman, Administrative Conference of the United States, 1991). Provides comprehensive explanation and analysis of federal agency rule-making processes, including judicial review of rule making. Includes discussion of the Administrative Flexibility Act, the Negotiated Rulemaking Act of 1990, and the Paperwork Reduction Act.

Steadman, John M., Schwartz, David, & Jacoby, Sidney B. *Litigation with the Federal Government* (3d ed. by Urban Lester & Michael Noone, American Law Institute/American Bar Association, 1994). An overview and analysis of how to sue the federal government and handle the problems encountered in such suits. Includes extensive discussion of the Federal Tort Claims Act, the Tucker Act (for certain claims based on a federal statute or regulation or on an express or implied contract), the Contract Disputes Act of 1978, and the Equal Access to Justice Act. Also discusses the process of settling cases against the federal government and the remnants of the sovereign immunity doctrine that still pose some barriers to suing the federal government.

Youngers, Jane, & Norris, Julie T. *Managing Federal Grants* (National Council of University Research Administrators and National Association of College and University Business Officers, n.d., includes monthly newsletters and quarterly updates). A thorough reference guide that covers all steps in the grant process from pre-solicitation, application, and agency review through administering the grant, intellectual property issues, and closing out the grant. Available by subscription.

See the Lacovara, O'Neil ("God and Government"), and Wallick & Chamblee entries in Bibliography for Section 13.4.

PART SIX

THE COLLEGE AND EXTERNAL PRIVATE ENTITIES

14

The College and the Education Associations

Sec. 14.1. Overview of the Education Associations

The myriad of associations related, either wholly or in part, to postsecondary education exemplifies the diversity of missions, structure, and program mix of American colleges and universities. From the American Council on Education (ACE), which monitors and informs college presidents about a variety of issues affecting colleges and universities generally, to the League for Innovation in the Community Colleges, a small group that promotes new technology in community colleges, these associations perform numerous functions on behalf of all, some, or a few specialized institutions. The Web site of the U.S. Department of Education (ED) contains a searchable "Education Resources Information Directory" listing nearly three thousand organizations, related to either K–12 or postsecondary education, that is updated at least annually (available at http://wdcrobcolp01.ed.gov/Programs/EROD/). Although many of the associations are located in Washington, D.C., others are located in various cities throughout the United States. Education associations exist at the state level as well, particularly those whose members are institutions or boards of trustees.

Several education associations have institutions as members, and focus on monitoring and lobbying for (or against) federal legislation and regulatory changes that affect postsecondary education. Those institutional-membership organizations are the American Council on Education (htpp://www.acenet. org), the American Association of Community Colleges (http://www.aacc.nche. edu), the American Association of State Colleges and Universities (http://www. aascu.org), the Association of American Universities (http://www.aau.edu), the National Association of State Universities and Land-Grant Colleges (http://www.nasulgc.org), and the National Association of Independent Colleges and Universities (http://www.naicu.edu).

Other education associations, such as the American Association of University Professors (AAUP) (http://www.aaup.org) and the National Association of Student Personnel Administrators (NASPA) (http://www.naspa.org), have individuals as members, and focus, at least in part, on the professional development of their members and the advancement of the profession. The "National Academies," consisting of the National Academy of Sciences (http://www.nas.edu), the National Research Council (http://www.nationalacademies.org/nrc), the National Academy of Engineering (http://www.nae.edu), and the Institute of Medicine (http://www.iom.edu), are private, nonprofit institutions that "provide science, technology and health policy advice under a congressional charter," according to their Web site. Membership in the National Academies is by election by current members. The American Council of Learned Societies (http://www.acls.org) provides funding for research in the humanities and social sciences, and the American Association for the Advancement of Science advances the interests of science and publishes a journal, books, newsletters, and reports.

Regardless of whether their members are institutions or individuals, most of these organizations fulfill multiple purposes. Many, particularly those located in the nation's capital, engage in lobbying activities, attempting to influence congressional action or the regulatory activities of executive branch agencies. Their representatives may advise congressional staff in drafting legislation and ascertaining its impact on postsecondary education; they may also appear before congressional committees or assist congressional staff in inviting others to appear. They may attend agency meetings and hearings on draft regulations, to make drafting suggestions and to explain the implications of these regulations for postsecondary education. The state-level equivalents of the education associations perform similar activities with regard to state legislation and regulations. (For a discussion of the lobbying activities and influence of the education associations, see Chapters Five and Six of the Cook entry in the Selected Annotated Bibliography for this Section.) Many associations develop statements of policy on good professional practice and other matters for their constituencies. The statements promulgated by the American Association of University Professors, for instance, have had a substantial impact on the status of faculty on many campuses and on the judicial interpretation of "national custom and usage" in faculty employment relations (see Section 14.5).

Education and training, and information sharing, are significant activities of the education associations as well. Most have annual conferences, and many produce publications to inform and update their constituencies. Many serve an important monitoring function for their members, particularly with regard to new legislative, administrative, and judicial developments. In addition, most agencies have Web sites on which they post recent developments in the law and regulatory activities, standards of good practice, publications, and other important materials.

Many associations have special interests or expertise regarding the legal issues in this book, and are excellent sources of legal information and law-related conferences and workshops. The American Council on Education, for example, prepares important analyses and alerts on current legal issues, especially those concerning congressional legislation and legislative proposals. The National Association of Student Personnel Administrators prepares a monthly "Legal Issues Update" that is sent electronically to NASPA members. The Association for Student Judicial Affairs (http://asja.tamu.edu) has an annual national conference, regional gatherings, and a summer institute at which legal issues of interest to personnel responsible for campus judicial affairs are discussed. And the National Association of College and University Attorneys (NACUA) (http://www.nacua.org) provides a comprehensive array of services for member institutions and the attorneys who represent them, as well as for other "associate" members.

Some of the associations also act as *amici curiae,* or "friends of the court," in litigation affecting the interests of their members. When ongoing litigation affects the interests of postsecondary education generally, or a large group of institutions, many of the education organizations often will band together to submit an *amicus* brief, particularly if the case is before the U.S. Supreme Court. The associations have, on occasion, also provided expert witnesses to explain academic custom and practice, or to interpret the academic community's "general understanding" of important concepts such as tenure and academic freedom.

In addition, some associations perform the critical function of accrediting institutions or particular academic programs within institutions. The U.S. Department of Education relies on these private, nonprofit accrediting actions as a basis for certifying an institution's eligibility to participate in federal aid programs (see Section 14.3.3). The accrediting associations also play a significant role in the higher education community's self-regulation.

In their roles as monitors, quasi-regulators, or accreditors of higher education institutions, the education associations may make decisions that precipitate litigation against them by a college or university. For example, on many occasions a college or university has sued the National Collegiate Athletic Association (NCAA, http://www.ncaa.org) over its regulation of college athletics (see Section 14.4). Institutions have also sued accrediting associations to challenge a withdrawal, threatened withdrawal, or denial of accreditation (see Section 14.3.2).

The Council for the Advancement of Standards (CAS), founded in 1979, is a consortium of thirty-one higher education organizations. CAS was created to establish, disseminate, and advocate professional standards and guidelines for higher education programs and services. Member organizations are listed on CAS's homepage (available at http://www.cas.edu). The organization has developed standards and guidelines for professional practice in student affairs as well as other institutional functions; these standards and guidelines are useful for institutional self-assessment and accountability purposes.

The education associations are a source of information, assistance, and practical advice for colleges and universities, and for members of the academic community, particularly with regard to federal regulation and with regard to professional and ethical practices. They provide services and expertise that few institutions have the resources to provide for themselves, and a network of colleagues with similar interests and concerns.[1]

Sec. 14.2. Applicable Legal Principles

The various education associations described in Section 14.1 are private rather than governmental entities. Being private, they are not created by and do not owe their existence directly to state and federal constitutions and authorizing legislation, as do federal, state, and local government agencies. Rather, they are created by the actions of private individuals or groups, and their legal status is shaped by state corporation law and the common law of "voluntary associations." These associations thus have whatever powers are set forth in their articles of incorporation or association and in the accompanying bylaws and rules. These powers are exercised through organizational structures and enforced through private sanctions, which are specified in the articles, bylaws, and rules. Some education associations are membership organizations that exercise power through their members (either institutions or individuals), or that extend particular prerogatives to and impose particular responsibilities on members. In such situations the articles, bylaws, and rules will also establish the qualifications for obtaining and maintaining membership.

Education associations may also develop various kinds of working relationships with one another. In such cases, memoranda of understanding, consortium agreements, and other such documents may also become part of the basic governing law for the signatory associations. These documents will often have the legal status of contracts and will therefore be interpreted and enforced, as necessary, according to the common law of contract.

State and federal law restricts the powers of private associations in a number of important ways. State corporation law may restrict the structures and procedures through which an association may operate. The common law of

---

[1] A partial listing of education associations and their Web sites, in addition to those mentioned in the text of this section, include American Association of Collegiate Registrars and Admissions Officers, http://www.aacrao.org; American College Counseling Association, http://www.collegecounseling.org; American College Personnel Association, http://www.acpa.nche.edu; Association of American Colleges and Universities, http://www.aacu-edu.org; Association of American Medical Colleges, http://www.aamc.org; Association of Catholic Colleges and Universities, http://www.accunet.org; Association of College and University Housing Officers—International, http://www.acuho.ohio-state.edu; Association of Community College Trustees, http://www.acct.org; University Risk Management and Insurance Association, http://www.urmia.org; Association of Governing Boards of Universities and Colleges, http://www.agb.org; Association of Jesuit Colleges and Universities, http://www.ajcunet.edu; College and University Professional Association for Human Resources, http://www.cupahr.org; Council for Opportunity in Education, http://www.trioprograms.org.

voluntary associations may superimpose upon the association's own standards and procedures a general obligation to act reasonably and fairly, especially toward its members, and may also require that the association follow its own rules; judicial review may be available to persons or organizations harmed by an association's failure to do so (see Sections 14.3.2.2 & 14.4.5 below).[2] Federal and state antitrust law may restrict associational activities that have anticompetitive or monopolistic effects (see Sections 14.3.2.4 & 14.4.4 below). Other statutes may occasionally impose special requirements on certain associations (see, for example, Sections 14.3.3 & 14.4.6 below). In the past, state and federal constitutional provisions protecting individual rights have also been applied to limit the authority of some private associations; under current trends, however, these provisions will seldom apply to private education associations like those that are the focus of this chapter (see Sections 14.3.2.3 & 14.4.2 below; and compare Section 1.5.2).

Many of the suits against education associations have been brought by institutions or individuals who were rejected or terminated as members or who were sanctioned by an association. These cases have been a testing ground for the development of legal restrictions on the powers of private associations. Such suits are usually brought by institutions seeking to assert their rights as members or prospective members of the association (see, for example, the cases in Section 14.3.2). But suits are also occasionally brought *against* an institution when it sponsors a chapter of, or is otherwise affiliated with, an education association in which a student, faculty member, or staff member seeks to attain or maintain membership.

In *Blatt v. University of Southern California*, 85 Cal. Rptr. 601 (Cal. Ct. App. 1970), for instance, the plaintiff was a law student who was rejected for membership in his school's chapter of the Order of the Coif, a national legal honorary society. The student challenged his rejection on grounds that he had fulfilled all the prerequisites for membership in the society. He also asserted that the denial of membership would affect his financial and professional status—that is, his ability to obtain a higher-paying job and to attain the respect and prestige that membership affords. Holding that denial of membership in such an organization is not subject to judicial review unless the denial actually prevents the individual from attaining employment in a particular occupation or from practicing a specialty, the court rejected the plaintiff's request for an order compelling his admission:

> Membership in the Order does not give a member the right to practice the profession of law. It does not signify qualification for any specialized field of practice. It has no direct bearing on the number or type of clients that the attorney-member might have or on the income he will make in his professional practice. It does not affect his basic right to earn a living. We hold that in the

---

[2]For an extended analysis of common law principles and judicial review in an analogous area of concern, see William Kaplin, "Professional Power and Judicial Review: The Health Professions," 44 *Geo. Wash. L. Rev.* 710, 716–50 (1976).

absence of allegations of sufficient facts of arbitrary or discriminatory action, membership in the Order is an honor best determined by those in the academic field without judicial interference. Plaintiff's allegations of arbitrary or discriminatory action on the part of the election committee are insufficient to state a cause of action. No justiciable issue has been presented [85 Cal. Rptr. at 606].

The court also determined that, under the society's rules, the fulfillment of membership prerequisites does not entitle an individual to membership but only to a consideration of his or her application. According to the court, "The complaint alleges that [the plaintiff's] name was on the eligible list and did receive consideration by the election committee under the general standards set forth in the Order's constitution. This is all that the individual defendants promised. The facts pleaded do not support the alleged conclusion that there was a breach of contract."

Occasionally, an educational association may itself seek to bring suit. The suit could be against a member or chapter of the association, or against another association with which it has a contractual relationship. But more likely, and increasingly, associations as plaintiffs seek to sue an agency of government. An accrediting association whose federal recognition has been suspended or terminated, for example, may sue the U.S. Secretary of Education (see Section 14.3.3). In some situations, an association may sue a government agency on behalf of its members who are regulated or funded (or whose institutions are regulated or funded) by the agency. The association's "standing to sue" will be an issue in some of these cases. In *National Wrestling Coaches Association v. Department of Education*, 366 F.3d 930 (D.C. Cir. 2004), for instance, the court held that the plaintiff associations did not have standing to challenge the department's implementation of its Title IX Policy Interpretation on intercollegiate athletes (see Section 10.4.6 of this book) on behalf of coaches, athletes, and alumni whose institutions had eliminated their men's varsity wrestling teams.

Sec. 14.3. The College and the Accrediting Agencies

14.3.1. Overview of accrediting agencies. Among the associations with which postsecondary administrators must deal, the ones most concerned with the educational missions of institutions and programs are the educational accrediting agencies. Educational accreditation, conducted by private associations rather than by a ministry of education or other government agency, is a development unique to the United States. As the system has evolved, the private accrediting agencies have assumed an important role in the development and maintenance of standards for postsecondary education and have gained considerable influence over individual institutions and programs seeking to obtain or preserve the accreditation that only these agencies may bestow.

There are two types of accreditation: institutional (or "regional") accreditation and program (or "specialized") accreditation. Institutional accreditation applies to the entire institution and all its programs, departments, and schools; program accreditation applies to a particular school, department, or program within the institution, such as a school of medicine or law, a department of chemistry, or a program in medical technology. Program accreditation may also apply to an entire institution if it is a free-standing, specialized institution, such as a business school or technical school, whose curriculum is all in the same program area.

Institutional accreditation is granted by six regional agencies—membership associations composed of the accredited institutions in each region. Since each regional agency covers a separate, defined part of the country, each institution is subject to the jurisdiction of only one such agency. Program accreditation is granted by a multitude of proliferating "specialized" (or "professional" or "occupational") accrediting agencies, which may or may not be membership associations and are often sponsored by the particular profession or occupation whose educational programs are being accredited. The jurisdiction of these specialized agencies is nationwide.

From 1975 until 1993, a private organization, the Council on Postsecondary Accreditation (COPA), operated a nongovernmental recognition process for both regional and specialized agencies and served as their representative at the national level. The organization disbanded effective December 31, 1993. A successor organization to COPA, the Council for Higher Education Accreditation (CHEA), began operations in 1996 through the initiative of a group of college presidents. See generally Harland Bloland (ed.), *Creating the Council for Higher Education Accreditation* (Greenwood, 2001). CHEA oversees both institutional (regional) and program (specialized) accreditation. (Its purposes and structure, and the challenges it faces, are reviewed in Beth McMurtrie, "Assessing the Group That Assesses Accreditation," *Chron. Higher Educ.,* November 12, 1999, A41.)

Being private, accrediting agencies owe their existence and legal status to state corporation law and to the common law of "voluntary" (or private) associations (see Section 14.2). Their powers are enforced through private sanctions embodied in their articles, bylaws, and rules, the primary sanctions being the withdrawal and denial of accreditation. The force of these private sanctions is greatly enhanced, however, by the extensive public and private reliance on accrediting agencies' decisions.

The federal government relies in part on these agencies to identify the institutions and programs eligible for a wide range of aid-to-education programs, particularly those administered by the U.S. Department of Education (see Section 14.3.3). The states demonstrate their reliance on the agencies' assessments when they exempt accredited institutions or programs from various licensing or other regulatory requirements (see Section 12.3). Some states also use accreditation to determine students' or institutions' eligibility under their own state funding programs (see, for example, Fla. Stat. Ann. §§ 240.4022 & 240.605); and the state approving agencies operating under contract with the Department of Veterans Affairs depend on accreditation in approving courses for veterans' programs (38 U.S.C. § 3675(a)(2)). State professional and occupational licensing boards rely on the accrediting agencies by making graduation from an accredited school or program a prerequisite to obtaining a license to practice in the state (see, for example, Cal. Bus. & Prof. Code § 1260)). Some states also rely on an institution's accredited status in granting tax exemptions (see, for example, Idaho Code § 63-3029A and Ind. Code § 6-3-3-5(d)).

Private professional societies may use professional accreditation in determining who is eligible for membership. Students, parents, and guidance counselors may employ accreditation as one criterion in choosing a school. And postsecondary institutions themselves often rely on accreditation in determining the acceptability of transfer credits, and in determining what academic credentials will qualify persons to apply for particular academic positions. In *Merwine v. Board of Trustees for State Institutions of Higher Learning*, 754 F.2d 631 (5th Cir. 1985), for example, the court upheld the defendant's requirement that applicants for certain faculty librarian positions must hold a master's degree from a program accredited by the American Library Association.

Because of this extensive public and private reliance on accrediting agencies, postsecondary administrators usually consider it necessary to maintain both institutional and program accreditation even if they disagree with an association's standards or evaluation procedures. Consequently, administrators and counsel must be prepared to maintain working relationships with a multitude of agencies and should understand the legal limits on the agencies' powers, the legal or professional leverage an institution might apply if an agency threatens denial or withdrawal of accreditation, and the legal and practical consequences to the institution and its students if the institution or one of its programs loses (or voluntarily relinquishes) its accreditation. These matters are discussed in subsection 14.3.4 below.

Despite the clear importance of accreditation and the long-term continuing existence of accrediting agencies, the role of accrediting agencies over the years has sometimes been controversial and often been misunderstood. There has been frequent, sometimes intense debate about accreditation among college presidents, federal and state evaluation officials, Congress, accreditation agency officials, and officials of other higher education associations. Much of this debate since the early 1990s has concerned accrediting agencies' relationships with the federal government—especially the agencies' role in monitoring institutional integrity regarding federal student aid programs (see below and see also subsection 14.3.3).

In the Higher Education Amendments of 1992, Congress added a new Part H to Title IV of the Higher Education Act (Pub. L. No. 102-325, § 499, 106 Stat. at 634). This new part, for the first time, established statutory criteria that the Secretary of Education must follow in reviewing and "recognizing" accrediting agencies whose decisions the Secretary uses in certifying institutions' eligibility to participate in the Title IV student aid programs. Specifically, these criteria required that recognized agencies, when reviewing an institution's accreditation, were to consider its default rates for Title IV student loan programs, and were also to assist state agencies in reviewing institutions that have the potential for misusing Title IV funds (106 Stat. 640). In the Higher Education Amendments of 1998, however, Congress eased the criteria concerning agencies' Title IV compliance responsibilities and largely relinquished the 1992 Amendments' new cooperative role between the states and the accrediting agencies regarding institutional misuse of student aid funds—a role that had been codified in 20 U.S.C. § 1099a-3. Congress omitted Section 1099a-3 from Title IV, Part H ("Program Integrity") (see Pub. L. No. 105-244, § 491, 112 Stat. 1581, 1758–1759 (October 7, 1998)). This change from 1992 to 1998 resulted from an intense controversy regarding Section 1099a-3 and the U.S. Department of Education's proposed implementing regulations for that section. The controversy centered on the 1992 legislation's requirement (since repealed) that each state have a State Postsecondary Review Entity (SPRE), which was to contract with accrediting agencies in reviewing institutions' courses and programs. (See generally Constance Cook, *Lobbying for Higher Education: How Colleges and Universities Influence Federal Policy* (Johns Hopkins University Press, 1998), 44–51, 173–75.)

Debate in modern times has also sometimes focused on particular, existing or proposed, functions of accrediting agencies—for example, monitoring academic abuses on the part of student athletes; overseeing programs that accredited institutions sponsor in foreign countries or on branch campuses in the United States; and monitoring nondiscrimination and academic freedom in religiously affiliated institutions and other institutions. The need for, and the composition and functions of, private umbrella groups to oversee the accreditation systems (such as the former Council on Postsecondary Accreditation) has also periodically been debated. Other issues continuing into the twenty-first century include the accreditation of new "virtual" or "online" institutions (see, for example, Florence Olsen, "'Virtual' Institutions Challenge Accreditors to Devise New Ways of Measuring Quality," *Chron. Higher Educ.*, August 6, 1999, A29); the evaluation of distance education courses and other technological teaching innovations within established institutions (see, for example, Judith Eaton, *Distance Learning: Academic and Political Challenges for Higher Education Accreditation* (Monograph no. 1, Council for Higher Education Accreditation, 2001)); accreditation standards concerning use of part-time faculty members (see, for example, Courtney Leatherman, "Do Accreditors Look the Other Way When Colleges Rely on Part-Timers?" *Chron. Higher Educ.*, November 7, 1997, A12); the accreditation of teacher education programs, a new version of a traditional issue (see, for example, Julianne Basinger, "Fight Intensifies over Accreditation of Teacher-Education Programs," *Chron. Higher Educ.*, October 9, 1998, A12); the accreditation of medical residency training programs, especially with respect to duty hour rules for residents (see, for example, Richard Minicucci & John Bolton, "Accreditation of Medical Residency Training Programs in the Aftermath of the New Duty Hour Rules" (2004), a conference outline presented at the annual national conference of the National Association of College and University Attorneys); and accrediting standards to promote racial, ethnic, and cultural diversity at accredited institutions (see, for example, Katherine Mangan, "Law Schools May Get Diversity Rule," *Chron. Higher Educ.*, February 24, 2006, at A37).

Moreover, in the first years of the new century, issues concerning the U.S. Secretary of Education's criteria for recognizing accrediting agencies (see subsection 14.3.3 below) heated up again, as they had in the early 1990s. A major focus of this debate has been on whether Congress or the Secretary should do more to require that accrediting agencies use specific, concrete measures of the quality of student learning, in particular "output" rather than "input" measures. (See Jon Wergin, "Taking Responsibility for Student Learning: The Role of Accreditation," *Change*, January/February 2005, 30–33; James Ratcliff, Edward Lubinescu, & Maureen Gaffney (eds.), *How Accreditation Influences Assessment*, New Directions for Higher Education no. 113 (Jossey-Bass, 2001).)

14.3.2. Accreditation and the courts

14.3.2.1. Formative developments. The first reported case involving the powers of accrediting agencies arose in 1938, after the North Central Association of Colleges and Secondary Schools had threatened to withdraw the accreditation of North Dakota's State Agricultural College. The state's governor sought an injunction against North Central. Using traditional legal analysis, the court denied the governor's request, reasoning that "[i]n the absence of fraud, collusion, arbitrariness, or breach of contract, . . . the decisions of such voluntary associations must be accepted in litigation before the court as conclusive" (*North Dakota v. North Central Ass'n. of Colleges and Secondary Schools*, 23 F. Supp. 694 (E.D. Ill.), *affirmed*, 99 F.2d 697 (7th Cir. 1938)).[3]

Another case did not arise until 1967, when Parsons College sued the North Central Association. The association had placed the college on probation in 1963 and removed it in 1965 with the stipulation that the college's accreditation status be reviewed within three years. In 1967, the association conducted a two-day site visit of the college, after which the visiting team issued a report noting that some improvements "had not been realized" and that "other deficiencies persisted." After a meeting at which the college made statements and answered questions, the executive board recommended that Parsons be dropped from membership,

---

[3]Like the *North Central* case, most of the other cases in Section 14.3.2 involve litigation between institutions and accrediting agencies. Litigation concerning accreditation can also arise between institutions and their students, however, if the students consider themselves harmed by institutional actions or inactions that prompt a denial or withdrawal of accreditation. See *Behrend v. State*, 379 N.E.2d 617 (Ohio 1977); and compare *Lidecker v. Kendall College*, 550 N.E.2d 1121 (Ill. Ct. App. 1st Dist. 1990)). Cases may also be brought by students who consider themselves harmed by an institution's alleged misrepresentation of its accreditation status. See *Craig v. Forest Institute of Professional Psychology*, 713 So.2d 967 (Ala. 1997); *Malone v. Academy of Court Reporting*, 582 N.E.2d 54 (Ohio App. 10th Dist. 1990); and compare *Lidecker v. Kendall College* (above), and *Galdikas v. Fagan*, 342 F.3d 684 (7th Cir. 2003).

and the association's full membership voted to accept this recommendation. The college then appealed to the board of directors, which sustained the association's decision on the basis that the college was not "providing an adequate educational program for its students, especially those of limited ability."

When the college sought to enjoin the association from implementing its disaccreditation decision, the federal district court denied its request (*Parsons College v. North Central Ass'n. of Colleges and Secondary Schools,* 271 F. Supp. 65 (N.D. Ill. 1967)). Reflecting traditional judicial reluctance to examine the internal affairs of private associations, the court determined that the association was not bound by the federal Constitution's due process requirements, that the association had followed its own rules in withdrawing the college's accreditation, and that it had not acted arbitrarily or violated "rudimentary due process."

Shortly after *Parsons College,* another federal court tangled with accreditation issues in the *Marjorie Webster Junior College* case. The college, a proprietary (for-profit) institution, had applied to the Middle States Association for accreditation, and the association had refused to consider the application because the college was not a nonprofit organization. After a lengthy trial, the lower court held that the nonprofit criterion was invalid under the federal antitrust laws, the "developing common law regarding exclusion from membership in private associations," and the federal Constitution's due process clause (*Marjorie Webster Junior College v. Middle States Ass'n. of Colleges and Secondary Schools,* 302 F. Supp. 459 (D.D.C. 1969)). The lower court ordered the association to consider the college's application and to accredit the college "if it shall otherwise qualify" for accreditation under Middle States' standards. The appellate court reversed, finding that in the circumstances of the case the association's reason for refusing to consider the application (the proprietary character of the college) was valid (432 F.2d 650 (D.C. Cir. 1970)).

A later case, the *Marlboro Corporation* case, concerned the Emery School, a private proprietary business school operated by the Marlboro Corporation. The litigation arose from the school's efforts to have its accreditation renewed by the Accrediting Commission of the Association of Independent Colleges and Schools. During the reapplication process, an inspection team visited the school and filed a substantially negative evaluation, to which the school responded in writing. The commission ordered a temporary extension of the school's accreditation and requested the school to submit evidence of compliance with association criteria in twelve specified areas of weakness. Rather than complying, the school submitted a progress report that admitted its deficiencies and indicated its plans to correct them. Refusing to accept a letter of intent as evidence of the correction of deficiencies, the commission denied accreditation. When the school appealed, the commission held a short hearing at which the school presented its case and responded to questions, after which the commission reaffirmed its refusal to renew Emery's accreditation.

The lower court denied the school's request for an injunction requiring the association to grant accreditation, and the appellate court affirmed (*Marlboro Corp. v. Ass'n. of Independent Colleges and Schools,* 556 F.2d 78 (1st Cir. 1977)). The school contended that the association had violated its rights to due process under the Constitution and under common law principles and that the denial of accreditation deprived it of rights protected by the recognition criteria of the U.S. Commissioner (now Secretary) of Education (see subsection 14.3.3 below). The appellate court held that none of the school's procedural rights had been violated; that the commission's decision was not "arbitrary and capricious," because "the irregularities in Emery's financial statement alone . . . justified the commission's decision"; and that the Commissioner of Education's criteria were not violated by the association's internal appeal procedure.[4] (The *Marlboro* court's suggestion that the Secretary's recognition criteria are enforceable in court in such a lawsuit has not been followed by later courts; see subsection 4.3.3 below.)

The *Parsons College, Marjorie Webster,* and *Marlboro Corporation* cases form the foundation for the contemporary law on judicial review of accrediting decisions. Together, the cases make clear that the courts will impose some constraints on accrediting agencies in their dealings with postsecondary institutions. Though the accrediting agencies ultimately won all three cases, each court opinion suggests some limits on the authority to deny or withdraw accreditation. It is equally clear, however, that the courts still view accrediting agencies with a restrained eye and do not subject them to the full panoply of controls that state and federal governments impose on their own agencies. Though the law on accreditation is not sufficiently developed or unitary to permit a precise description of all the rights postsecondary institutions have in dealing with accrediting agencies,[5] the foundational cases, supplemented by later developments, do provide valuable guidance, as discussed below and in subsection 14.3.2.2.

Another important, and more recent, guideline on accreditation litigation has come from Congress. In the Higher Education Amendments of 1992 (see Section 14.3.3), Congress provided that, in order for the Secretary of Education to recognize its accreditation, an institution must agree to submit any accreditation disputes with accrediting agencies to arbitration before filing suit in court (20 U.S.C. § 1099b(e)); and that any such suits "involving the denial, withdrawal, or termination of accreditation" must be filed in the appropriate federal district court (20 U.S.C. § 1099b(f)). In *Chicago School of Automatic Transmissions v. Accreditation Alliance of Career Schools and Colleges,* 44 F.3d 447

---

[4]The procedures and standards of this same accrediting commission were also at issue in *Rockland Institute v. Ass'n. of Independent Colleges and Schools,* 412 F. Supp. 1015 (C.D. Cal. 1976). In relying on both *Parsons College* and *Marjorie Webster* to reject Rockland's challenge to its disaccreditation, the court ruled that the accrediting commission followed its own rules, that the rules provided sufficient procedural due process, and that the commission's evaluative standards were neither vague nor unreasonable.

[5]For further description of such rights in a related area of the law, which can be used to predict available rights in accreditation, see Kaplin, "Professional Power and Judicial Review: The Health Professions," in footnote 2 above in this Chapter.

(7th Cir. 1994), the appellate court relied on these statutory provisions in rejecting the school's claim against the accrediting agency. The court's analysis serves
to give added importance to federal law in the review of accrediting agency decisions, and to diminish the importance of state law in some cases.

The *Chicago School* case commenced after the defendant accrediting agency
refused to renew the plaintiff's accreditation because the school had failed to
provide prompt refunds of tuition money to withdrawing students. The school
claimed that the agency's action violated the agency's own rules and therefore
constituted a breach of contract under Illinois state law. The agency argued, to
the contrary, that the case should be reviewed under principles of federal administrative law and the federal Administrative Procedure Act. The court agreed
with the agency's perspective on the case:

> Accreditation serves a federal function, and two years ago (shortly after the
> commencement of this action under the diversity jurisdiction), Congress pro-
> vided for exclusive federal jurisdiction of any suit by a school or college protest-
> ing the denial or withdrawal of accreditation by [a recognized accrediting
> agency]. Congress did not specify a source of law for these suits, but it is hard to
> see how state law could govern when federal jurisdiction is *exclusive.* . . . [I]t is
> all but impossible to see how federal courts could apply state law to the actions
> of accrediting agencies when state courts have been silenced by the provision
> for exclusive jurisdiction. If a grant of federal jurisdiction sometimes justifies
> creation of federal common law, *see Textile Workers v. Lincoln Mills,* 353 U.S.
> 448 (1957) . . . , a grant of exclusive federal jurisdiction necessarily implies the
> application of federal law [44 F.3d at 449].

Similarly, the court asserted that the federal courts, when shaping a federal
law of accreditation, should not derive its principles from the contract law or
other common law of the states:

> [A]ccrediting bodies are not engaged in commercial transactions for which
> state-law contract principles are natural matches. The "contract" the School
> wants to enforce is not a bargained-for exchange but a set of rules developed by
> an entity with many of the attributes of an administrative agency. [Moreover,]
> [a]lthough the law of every state contains a set of rules for the conduct of volun-
> tary associations, distinct from the law of contracts, this too is not quite the
> right match; the School did not apply to "join" the Alliance. It wanted a key that
> would unlock the Federal Treasury. An accrediting agency is a proxy for the fed-
> eral department whose spigot it opens and closes [44 F.3d at 449].

Following this reasoning, the court concluded "that principles of federal administrative law supply the right perspective for review of accrediting agencies' decisions. Section 1099b(f) cements the case for the application of federal law."

Using rudimentary administrative law principles, the court then determined
that the defendant agency had not violated its own procedural rules in refusing
to renew the plaintiff school's accreditation. Alternatively, in response to one of the
school's arguments, the court also noted that if the defendant had departed from

one of its rules, "it was a harmless departure" that would not "lead to the whopping damages the School requests. . . ."

The court's decision in *Chicago School* should not affect federal antitrust law claims (see subsection 14.3.2.4 below), federal constitutional law claims involving "state action" (see subsection 14.3.2.3), or federal bankruptcy law claims (see subsection 14.3.2.6). Moreover, the court's opinion, like the federal statute upon which it relies (20 U.S.C. § 1099b(f)), applies only to disputes concerning the denial, withdrawal, or termination of accreditation. Thus, state law should continue to govern defamation claims such as those in *Avins v. White* (see subsection 14.3.2.5) and other tort claims such as those in *Keams v. Tempe Technical Institute* (see subsection 14.3.2.5). There are also some other state common law claims that are beyond the purview of the *Chicago School* case and 20 U.S.C. Section 1099b(f), as discussed in subsection 14.3.2.2 below.

14.3.2.2. State common law and "federal common law." [6] At the very least, it is clear under state common law that courts will require an accrediting agency to follow its own rules in withdrawing accreditation (as in *Parsons College*) or refusing to renew accreditation (as in *Marlboro Corporation*). In *Parsons,* the court decided that the "law applicable to determine the propriety of the expulsion of a member from a private association is the law which he agreed to when he voluntarily chose to join the association, that is, the rules of the association itself." The court then found that the college had neither charged nor proved that the association had violated these rules. It is less clear whether courts will require an agency to follow its own rules in considering an initial application for accreditation. There is no accreditation case on this point, and some judicial pronouncements in related areas suggest that the right to be judged by the rules accrues only after the applicant has been admitted to membership or otherwise approved by the association. The better view, however, is that an applicant can also require that the agency follow its own rules.

Beyond requiring that accrediting agencies follow their own rules, the courts may also hold agencies to a variously stated standard of fairness in their dealings with members and applicants. The old *North Central Association* case, for example, highlights "fraud" and "collusion" as circumstances that would invalidate agency actions. The *North Central* case and the *Parsons* case both highlight "arbitrariness," and *Parsons* also emphasizes the failure to provide "rudimentary due process." The *Marjorie Webster* case speaks of reasonableness, evenhandedness, and consistency with "public policy" as standards; the appellate court agreed with the lower court that, under a developing exception to the general rule of judicial nonintervention in private associations' affairs, an association possessing virtual monopolistic control in an area of public concern

---

[6]The role of the state common law principles set out in this Section, as they apply to judicial review of decisions to deny or withdraw accreditation, must now be considered in light of the *Chicago School of Automatic Transmissions* case discussed in subsection 14.3.2.1 above. Even though that case, and others following it, indicate that "federal common law" now controls challenges to denials, withdrawals, and terminations of accreditation, the federal common law principles that courts have articulated appear to parallel the state common law principles developed in this subsection.

must exercise its power reasonably, "with an even hand, and not in conflict with the public policy of the jurisdiction."

The primary "fairness" requirement seems to be that the agency must provide institutions with procedural due process before denying, withdrawing, or refusing to renew their accreditation. The institution appears to have a right to receive notice that its accreditation is being questioned, to know why, and to be heard on the question. *Parsons College* provides useful analysis of the extent of these protections.

In *Parsons,* the college argued that the association's action should be invalidated, even though consistent with its own rules, if the action was "contrary to rudimentary due process or grounded in arbitrariness." Without admitting that such a legal standard applied to accrediting agencies, the court did analyze the association's action under this common law standard. The court defined rudimentary due process to include (1) an adequate opportunity to be heard, (2) a notice of the proceedings, (3) a notice of the specific charges, (4) sufficiently definite standards of evaluation, and (5) substantively adequate reasons for the decision. After reviewing the entire process by which the association reached its disaccreditation decision, the court concluded that "the college has failed to establish a violation of the commands of any of the several rules." The court found that the college had been afforded the opportunity to speak and be heard at almost every stage of the proceedings and that the opportunity afforded was adequate for the type of proceeding involved:

> The nature of the hearing, if required by rudimentary due process, may properly be adjusted to the nature of the issue to be decided. In this case, the issue was not innocence but excellence. Procedures appropriate to decide whether a specific act of plain misconduct was committed are not suited to an expert evaluation of educational quality. . . .

* * * *

> Here, no trial-type hearing, with confrontation, cross-examination, and assistance of counsel, would have been suited to the resolution of the issues to be decided. The question was not principally a matter of historical fact, but rather of the application of a standard of quality in a field of recognized expertise [271 F. Supp. at 72–73].

The court further found that the college had ample notice of the proceedings because "after a long history of questionable status, the visit of the examining team was adequate notice without more." The requirement of specific charges was satisfied by the examining team's report given to the college. The court found that this report, "supplemented by the evidence produced by the college itself, contained all the information on which all subsequent decisions were made. No fuller disclosure could have been made." Finally, the court found that the evaluative standards of the association were sufficiently definite to inform the school of what was expected of it. Disagreeing with the college's claim that the standards were "so vague as to be unintelligible to men of ordinary intelligence," the court reasoned as follows:

> The standards of accreditation are not guides for the layman but for professionals in the field of education. Definiteness may prove, in another view, to be arbitrariness. The Association was entitled to make a conscious choice in favor of flexible standards to accommodate variation in purpose and character among its constituent institutions, and to avoid forcing all into a rigid and uniform mold [271 F. Supp. at 73].

In contrast to the procedural aspects of accrediting activities, an agency's substantive decisions and standards will receive very limited review. Courts are familiar with problems of procedural fairness, and are well equipped to resolve them, but they do not have experience and expertise in evaluating educational quality. The *Parsons* court used this distinction in determining that the accrediting agency had not violated the last of the five due process rules set out above:

> In this field, the courts are traditionally even more hesitant to intervene. The public benefits of accreditation, dispensing information and exposing misrepresentation, would not be enhanced by judicial intrusion. Evaluation by the peers of the college, enabled by experience to make comparative judgments, will best serve the paramount interest in the highest practicable standards in higher education. The price for such benefits is inevitably some injury to those who do not meet the measure, and some risk of conservatism produced by appraisals against a standard of what has already proven valuable in education [271 F. Supp. at 74].

The appellate court in *Marjorie Webster* also relied on the distinction between procedural and substantive decisions. To this court, the scope of judicial review depends on the amount of "deference" that courts should accord accrediting agencies, and this deference varies "both with the subject matter at issue and with the degree of harm resulting from the association's action." Since the issue in *Marjorie Webster* concerned the accrediting agency's "substantive standards" rather than "the fairness of the procedures by which the challenged determination was reached," the court accorded "substantial deference" to the agency and its judgments "regarding the ends that it serves and the means most appropriate to those ends." The court then considered the agency's nonprofit criterion, which was based on the assumption that the profit motive is inconsistent with educational quality. The lower court had determined that this assumption "is not supported by the evidence and is unwarranted." But the appellate court, in light of the substantial deference it accorded the agency's substantive judgments, held that it had not "been shown to be unreasonable for [the association] to conclude that the desire for personal profit might influence educational goals in subtle ways difficult to detect but destructive, in the long run, of that atmosphere of academic inquiry which . . . [the association's] standards for accreditation seek to foster."

The more recent case of *Wilfred Academy et al. v. Southern Ass'n. of Colleges and Schools,* 738 F. Supp. 200 (S.D. Tex. 1990), *reversed and vacated,* 957 F.2d 210 (5th Cir. 1992), illustrates the complexities that may arise when state common law concepts of fairness, developed in the above cases, are applied to accrediting agency decisions. Six cosmetology schools challenged the decision of the Southern Association of Colleges and Schools (SACS), a regional accrediting agency, and COEI (Commission on Occupation Education Institutions), an independent branch of SACS, to withdraw their accreditation. The district court held that, although it would give "great deference to the expertise of the accrediting agency," such agencies nevertheless have an implied "duty of good faith and fair dealing" that arises from the "special relationship of trust and confidence" between an agency and its member schools. This special relationship "results from the tremendous disparity of bargaining power in favor of the accrediting agency and from the fact that loss of accreditation can deprive a school of the opportunity to participate in governmental programs, such as federal financial aid." The duty of good faith and fair dealing is breached whenever an accrediting agency violates fundamental "fairness," which in turn requires that accrediting decisions be "reasonable," not "arbitrary," and "supported by substantial evidence." Applying these standards, the district court determined that, in processing their charges against the plaintiff schools, the defendants had violated fundamental fairness in various ways. In addition, the district court determined that the defendants failed to present "substantial evidence" that the plaintiffs had violated any of the defendants' accreditation standards. The court enjoined the defendants from implementing their decision to withdraw the plaintiffs' accreditation.

On appeal, the Fifth Circuit determined that the district court's fact findings "wholly disregard the deference due to the association's accrediting decisions" and that "[s]ubstantial evidence supports COEI's decision to withdraw accreditation. . . ." Considering the judicial role in cases like this, and focusing primarily on judicial review of an agency's *substantive* judgments, the appellate court commented:

> Federal courts have consistently limited their review of decisions of accrediting associations to whether the decisions were "arbitrary and unreasonable" and whether they were supported by "substantial evidence." See, e.g., *Medical Institute of Minnesota v. National Ass'n. of Trade and Technical Sch.,* 817 F.2d 1310, 1314 (8th Cir. 1987); *Rockland Inst. v. Association of Indep. Colleges and Sch.,* 412 F. Supp. 1015, 1016 (C.D. Cal. 1976). . . .
>
> In reviewing an accrediting association's decision to withdraw a member's accreditation, the courts have accorded the association's determination great deference. *Medical Inst. of Minnesota,* 817 F.2d at 1314; *Marjorie Webster Junior College, Inc. v. Middle States Ass'n. of Colleges and Secondary Sch.,* 432 F.2d 650, 657 (D.C. Cir. 1970). Courts give accrediting associations such deference because of the professional judgment these associations must necessarily employ in making accreditation decisions. In considering the substance of accrediting agencies' rules, courts have recognized that "[t]he standards of accreditation are not guides for the layman but for professionals in the field of education." *Parsons*

College v. North Cent. Ass'n. of Colleges and Secondary Sch., 271 F. Supp. 65, 73 (N.D. Ill. 1967). Consequently, courts are not free to conduct a *de novo* review or to substitute their judgment for the professional judgment of the educators involved in the accreditation process. *Medical Inst. of Minnesota,* 817 F.2d at 1315; *Rockland Inst.,* 412 F. Supp. at 1019). Instead, courts focus primarily on whether the accrediting body's internal rules provide a fair and impartial procedure and whether it has followed its rules in reaching its decision [957 F.2d at 214].

Congress's limitation of judicial review in the 1992 HEA Amendments (see 20 U.S.C. § 1099b(f)), as construed in the *Chicago School* case (see subsection 14.3.2.1), has had an important impact on the use of state common law in subsequent accreditation cases. It has not always precluded state common law cases from getting to court, however, nor has it always prevented arguments supported by state common law from being aired in court. State common law, for example, apparently still continues to apply to accreditation issues that do not arise in the context of a challenge to a "denial, withdrawal, or termination of accreditation," as prescribed by Section 1099b(f). In *Auburn University v. The Southern Ass'n. of Colleges and Schools,* 2002 WL 32375008 (N.D. Ga. 2002)), Auburn, a member institution of the accrediting association, challenged certain aspects of a process that the association was using to investigate some "accreditation-related" circumstances regarding Auburn. The court determined that "Auburn is not challenging the 'denial, withdrawal, or termination of accreditation' [20 U.S.C. § 1099b(f)]" but rather "is challenging the manner in which the accrediting agency is conducting an investigation into matters of accreditation" (*Auburn University,* pp. 15–16). Section 1099b(f) and the federal common law principles courts have read into it therefore did not apply to Auburn's claim, and the court instead applied state "common law of due process," citing cases such as *Parsons College, Marlboro Corporation,* and *Medical Institute of Minnesota* (*Auburn University,* pp. 6–7). And in *Foundation for Interior Design Education Research v. Savannah College of Art and Design,* 39 F. Supp. 2d 889 (W.D. Mich. 1998), *affirmed,* 244 F.3d 521 (6th Cir. 2001), the Foundation, an accrediting agency that had denied accreditation to the college, "was not at any relevant time [recognized] by the Secretary of Education" (244 F.3d at 528). The district and appellate courts therefore found Section 1099b(f) to be inapplicable and held that state law controls, citing much the same case law as did the court in the *Auburn University* case.

Moreover, and perhaps most important, when the federal law perspective of the court in *Chicago School of Automatic Transmissions* does apply, in most cases it should not substantially alter the reasoning or result in accreditation cases. It is true that the *Chicago School* case has been followed in later cases, and that the federal administrative law principles referenced in that case have become a kind of "federal common law" or federal "common law of due process" applicable to judicial review of accreditation decisions. (See, for example, *Thomas M. Cooley Law School v. American Bar Association,* 376 F. Supp. 2d 758 (W.D. Mich. 2005); *Western State University of Southern California v. American Bar Association,* 301 F. Supp. 2d 1129 (C.D. Cal. 2004).) But the courts' reasoning in the later cases, as in *Chicago School,* strongly suggests that the developing federal common law principles of judicial review are very similar to the state common law principles that were developed in the earlier cases beginning with *Parsons College.* It is likely, therefore, that counsel and courts, for the foreseeable future, will continue to consult and to cite state common law cases and judicial review principles when litigating and deciding federal common law cases covered by the grant of jurisdiction in Section 1099b(f). It should follow, then, at least for the foreseeable future, that the reasoning used and results reached in the federal common law cases will be similar to those in the state common law cases.

The court in *Chicago School,* however, did note one potentially significant major difference between federal common law and state common law:

> If this were a contract dispute, we would have to make an independent judgment about the meaning of . . . the [accrediting agency's rules and] internal operating procedures. In administrative law, however, the first question is how the agency understands its own rules—for an agency possessed of the ability to adopt and amend rules also may interpret them, even if the interpretation chosen is not the one that most impresses an outside observer [44 F.3d at 450].

But this difference may not be nearly as substantial as the court suggests, since there is already ample precedent in the state common law cases for courts deferring to accrediting agencies' interpretive judgments about their own rules, as the cases above indicate (see, for example the *Foundation for Interior Design* case, above, 244 F.3d at 527–28).

14.3.2.3. The U.S. Constitution. A number of cases have considered whether accrediting agency decisions are "state action" subject to the federal Constitution (see Section 1.5.2). The court in *Parsons College* rejected the college's claim that the association must comply with the due process requirements of the federal Constitution, reasoning that "the Association stands on the same footing as any private corporation" and is not subject to "the constitutional limits applicable to government" (see Section 1.5.2). The lower court in the *Marlboro Corporation* case (416 F. Supp. 958, 959 (D. Mass. 1976)) also rejected the state action argument. On the other hand, the lower court in *Marjorie Webster* accepted the state action argument; and the appellate courts in *Marjorie Webster* and in *Marlboro Corporation* assumed, without deciding, that the accrediting agency was engaged in state action.

The appeals court in *Marjorie Webster,* in holding that the association's nonprofit criterion was not unreasonable and therefore was valid, in fact engaged in a constitutional due process analysis. The lower court had found that the association's accreditation activities were "quasi-governmental" and thus could be considered "state action" subject to federal constitutional restraints. The appeals court then "assume[d] without deciding" that state action did exist. Thus, unlike the court in *Parsons College,* which specifically rejected the state action argument, the lower court in *Marjorie Webster* accepted the argument, and the appellate court left the question unanswered.

The appellate court in *Marlboro Corporation* considered whether the accrediting commission's procedures should be scrutinized under common law due process standards or under the more exacting standards of the U.S. Constitution's due process clause. The lower court had held that the Constitution did not apply because the commission's action was not "state action." The court of appeals, however, found it unnecessary to decide this "close question," since, "even assuming that constitutional due process applies," none of the Emery School's procedural rights had been violated. To reach this conclusion, the appellate court did review the commission's procedures under the constitutional standard, stating that under either "constitutional or common law standards . . . procedural fairness is a flexible concept" to be considered case by case. The court held that "due process did not . . . require a full-blown adversary hearing in this context." It noted that the commission's inquiry concerned a routine reapplication for accreditation and was "broadly evaluative" rather than an accusatory inquiry with specific charges. "Emery was given ample opportunity to present its position by written submission and to argue it orally," and more formalized proceedings would have imposed too heavy a burden on the commission.

The court then considered Emery's claim that the decision to deny accreditation was tainted by bias because the chairman of the accrediting commission was the president of a school in direct competition with Emery. While it emphasized that a "decision by an impartial tribunal is an element of due process under any standard," the court found that the chairman took no part in the discussion or vote on Emery's application and in fact did not chair, or participate in, the December hearing. Recognizing the "local realities"—the prolonged evaluation process, the large number of people participating in the decision at various levels, and the commission's general practice of allowing interested commissioners to remain present without participating—the court viewed the question as "troublesome" but concluded that "Emery has [not] shown sufficient actual or apparent impropriety."

In more recent cases, the weight of authority has shifted against state action findings. In *Medical Institute of Minnesota v. National Ass'n. of Trade and Technical Schools*, 817 F.2d 1310 (8th Cir. 1987), for example, the court rejected the school's claim that the accrediting agency's decision denying reaccreditation was state (or federal) action subject to federal constitutional constraints. The school's argument relied heavily on the rationale of the district court in the *Marjorie Webster* case, but the *Medical Institute* court determined that this rationale has been undermined by two cases decided by the U.S. Supreme Court in 1982: *Rendell-Baker v. Kohn* and *Blum v. Yaretsky* (see Section 1.5.2). In *St. Agnes Hospital v. Riddick*, 668 F. Supp. 478 (D. Md. 1987), and 748 F. Supp. 319 (D. Md. 1990), however, a federal district court distinguished the *Medical Institute* case and held that the Accreditation Council for Graduate Medical Education (ACGME) (of which defendant Riddick was chairman) had engaged in state action when it withdrew accreditation from the plaintiff's residency program in obstetrics and gynecology. The court relied on state regulations requiring that applicants for medical licensure must have at least one year of postgraduate clinical training in a program that meets "standards equivalent to those established by" ACGME. Under this regulatory scheme, according to the court, the state had delegated its authority to ACGME, and there was a direct "nexus" (see Section 1.5.2) between this delegation and the accreditation action challenged by the plaintiff.

In a similar case against ACGME, a different federal district court reached the same result, but the appellate court reversed (*McKeesport Hospital v. Accreditation Council for Graduate Medical Education*, 24 F.3d 519 (3d Cir. 1994)). Relying on the Supreme Court's decisions in *Rendell-Baker* and *Blum* and its later decision in *NCAA v. Tarkanian* (see Section 14.4.2), and following the *Medical Institute* case, the appellate court concluded that ACGME had not engaged in state action when it withdrew accreditation from the plaintiff's general surgery residency program. According to the two-judge majority:

> The district court concluded that the Board delegated its duties to the ACGME, thereby rendering the ACGME's actions fairly attributable to the state. We cannot agree. . . . [U]nder the [Pennsylvania Medical Practice] Act the state Board remains ultimately responsible for approving medical training facilities in Pennsylvania. Cf. *Tarkanian*, 488 U.S. at 195–98. . . . Merely because the state Board deems its obligation met by following the ACGME's accreditation decisions does not imbue the ACGME with the authority of the state nor does it shift the responsibility from the state Board to the ACGME. The Board remains the state actor. . . .

> * * * *

> The district court also found the connection between the state Board and the ACGME sufficient to turn the latter into a state actor. We must disagree. Sometimes, a state and an ostensibly private entity are so interdependent that state action will be found from their symbiotic relationship alone. . . . The ACGME's relationship to the state is clearly distinguishable. The ACGME is self-governed and financed, and its standards are independently set; the state Board simply recognizes and relies upon its expertise.

> Alternatively, a connection between the state and a specific decision of a private entity may render that decision chargeable to the state. . . . Under this approach, however, state action will be found only "when [the state] has exercised coercive power or has provided such significant encouragement, either overt or covert, that the [private decision] must in law be deemed that of the State[;] mere approval of or acquiescence in" the decision is not enough. *Blum*, 457 U.S. at 1004. . . . The required state coercion or encouragement of the ACGME's actions is not present here.

> . . . The Board . . . does not control or regulate the ACGME's standard-setting or decision-making processes. Although it recognizes them, state law does not dictate or influence those actions. Rather, the ACGME's decisions are "judgments made by private parties according to . . . standards that are not established by the State." *Blum*, 457 U.S. at 1008 [24 F.3d at 524–25].

A third judge disagreed with the majority's reasoning but concurred in the result because, in his view, ACGME had provided the plaintiff all the due process that the federal Constitution would require. In a separate opinion—whose analysis may be more sound than the majority's—this judge distinguished the *Medical Institute* case and relied on *Riddick* in concluding that ACGME's action was state action (24 F.3d at 526–29; Becker, J., concurring).

In more recent cases, courts have continued to reject state action arguments. In a 2004 case, for example, *Western State University of Southern California v. American Bar Association* (discussed in subsection 14.3.2.2 above), the court relied on the *Medical Institute* case and the *McKeesport* case (above), as well as a footnote on state action in the *Chicago School* case (see subsection 14.3.2.1 above, and see particularly 44 F.3d at 449, n.1). And in *Thomas M. Cooley Law School v. American Bar Association*, 376 F. Supp. 2d 758 (W.D. Mich. 2005), a court again relied on these same cases to reject the law school's state action argument.

Although Supreme Court cases such as *Rendell-Baker* have narrowed the state action concept, while *NCAA v. Tarkanian* (Section 14.4.2 below) has limited its application to membership associations, and although a trend against state action findings continues in the lower courts, there still appears to be grounds for judicial state action determinations in some accreditation cases. The most likely situation still appears to be that where a government agency has delegated authority to an accrediting agency, as perceived by the *Riddick* court and the dissenting judge in *McKeesport Hospital*. Similarly, it is possible that, for accrediting agencies recognized by the U.S. Secretary of Education, the more formalized relationship between accrediting agencies and the Secretary created by the 1992 and 1998 reauthorizations of the Higher Education Act, and the agencies' responsibilities in helping the Secretary to assure institutional compliance with the requirements of the federal student aid programs (see subsections 14.3.1 above and 14.3.3 below) could in some cases provide a basis for a state action finding. The U.S. Supreme Court's decision in *Brentwood Academy v. Tennessee Secondary School Athletic Association*, 531 U.S. 288 (2001), using an "entwinement" theory to hold that the association there was engaged in state action, might be used in some cases to support such a state action argument. (For a discussion of these points, see *Auburn University v. The Southern Ass'n. of Colleges and Schools*, 2002 WL 32375008 (N.D. Ga. 2002), pp. 7–9.)

14.3.2.4. Antitrust law. Federal or state antitrust law may sometimes also protect postsecondary institutions from certain accrediting actions that interfere with an institution's ability to compete with other institutions.

In responding to the plaintiff's antitrust claims in *Marjorie Webster* (subsections 14.3.2.2 & 14.3.2.3 above), the appellate court held that the "proscriptions of the Sherman Act were 'tailored . . . for the business world' [*Eastern Railroad Presidents Conference v. Noerr Motor Freight*, 365 U.S. 127, 141 (1961)], not for the noncommercial aspects of the liberal arts and the learned professions." The court also noted that, since the "process of accreditation is an activity distinct from the sphere of commerce," going "rather to the heart of the concept of education," an accreditation decision would violate the Act only if undertaken with "an intent or purpose to affect the commercial aspects of the profession." Since no such "commercial motive" had been shown, the association's action did not constitute a combination or conspiracy in restraint of the college's trade.

Subsequently, the antitrust approach was broadened and strengthened by the U.S. Supreme Court's decision in *Goldfarb v. Virginia State Bar*, 421 U.S. 773 (1975), the first case in which the Court clearly approved the applicability of federal antitrust law (see Section 13.2.8 of this book) to professional associations. The application of these laws to accreditation was further strengthened by two Supreme Court cases following *Goldfarb*. In *National Society of Professional Engineers v. United States*, 435 U.S. 679 (1978), the Court reaffirmed its *Goldfarb* determination that the standard-setting activities of nonprofit professional associations are subject to scrutiny under antitrust laws. The Court then invalidated the society's ethical canon prohibiting members of the society from submitting competitive bids for engineering services. In *American Society of Mechanical Engineers v. Hydrolevel Corp.*, 456 U.S. 556 (1982), the Court again subjected a nonprofit professional association to antitrust liability arising from its standard-setting activities. Going beyond *Goldfarb* and *National Society of Professional Engineers*, the Court held that a professional organization can be liable for the anticompetitive acts of its members and other agents, including unpaid volunteers, if the agents had "apparent authority" to act (see Section 3.2). The characteristics of the American Society of Mechanical Engineers (ASME) that subjected it to antitrust liability are similar to those that could be attributed to accrediting agencies:

> ASME contends it should not bear the risk of loss for antitrust violations committed by its agents acting with apparent authority because it is a nonprofit organization, not a business seeking profit. But it is beyond debate that nonprofit organizations can be held liable under the antitrust laws. Although ASME may not operate for profit, it does derive benefits from its codes, including the fees the Society receives for its code-related publications and services, the prestige the codes bring to the Society, the influence they permit ASME to wield, and the aid the standards provide the profession of mechanical engineering. Since the antitrust violation in this case could not have occurred without ASME's codes and ASME's method of administering them, it is not unfitting that ASME will be liable for the damages arising from that violation (see W. Prosser, *Law of Torts* 459 (4th ed. 1971); W. Seavey, *Law of Agency* § 83 (1964)). Furthermore . . . ASME is in the best position to take precautions that will prevent future antitrust violations. Thus, the fact that ASME is a nonprofit organization does not weaken the force of the antitrust and agency principles that indicate that ASME should be liable for Hydrolevel's antitrust injuries [456 U.S. at 576].

(See Charles Chambers, "Implications of the *Hydrolevel* Decision for Postsecondary Accrediting Associations," 7 *Accreditation*, no. 2 (Council on Postsecondary Accreditation, Summer 1982)).

As these decisions clearly indicate, federal antitrust law can be a meaningful source of rights for postsecondary institutions, as well as their students and faculty, if they are harmed by accrediting activities that can be characterized as anticompetitive. Such rights may be asserted not only against decisions to deny, terminate, or condition an institution's accreditation, as in *Marjorie Webster*, but also against other activities undertaken by accrediting agencies or their agents in the process of fashioning and applying standards.

However, although antitrust laws clearly *apply* to such activities, that does
not mean that such activities, or any substantial portion of them, will *violate*
antitrust laws. In *Zavaletta v. American Bar Ass'n.* 721 F. Supp. 96 (E.D. Va.
1989), for example, students at an unaccredited law school sued the American
Bar Association (ABA), claiming that its accrediting activities constituted an
unreasonable restraint of trade under the Sherman Antitrust Act. The court did
not dispute that the Act applied to the ABA's accrediting activities, but it nevertheless held that these "activities impose no restraint on trade, unreasonable
or otherwise." Rather, according to the court, "the ABA merely expresses its
educated opinion . . . about the quality of the school's program"—an expression protected by the First Amendment. Although the ABA communicates these
opinions to state courts that control bar admissions, the resulting restraint on
an unaccredited law school is caused by the independent actions of state courts
in determining who may sit for the bar exam, not by the ABA's accreditation
activities as such.

In *Massachusetts School of Law at Andover, Inc. v. American Bar Association,*
107 F.3d 1026 (3d Cir. 1997), another court considered the applicability of
antitrust law to accreditation, again in the context of legal education. The Massachusetts School of Law (MSL) alleged that the American Bar Association had
conspired to monopolize legal education, law school accreditation, and the
licensing of lawyers, in violation of the Sherman Act.[7] Specifically, MSL alleged
that the ABA established and enforced anticompetitive criteria in making accreditation decisions, that application of these criteria to MSL resulted in the denial
of its application for provisional accreditation, and that this denial put MSL "at
a competitive disadvantage in recruiting students because graduates of unaccredited schools cannot take the bar examination in most states," which in turn
caused the school "to suffer a 'loss of prestige' and direct economic damage in
the form of declining enrollments and tuition revenue." Regarding the ABA's
accreditation criteria, MSL alleged they created an anticompetitive effect by:

> [1] fixing the price of faculty salaries; [2] requiring reduced teaching hours and
> non-teaching duties; [3] requiring paid sabbaticals; [4] forcing the hiring of
> more professors in order to lower student/faculty ratios; [5] limiting the use of
> adjunct professors; [6] prohibiting the use of required or for-credit bar review
> courses; [7] forcing schools to limit the number of hours the students could
> work; [8] prohibiting ABA-accredited schools from accepting credit transfers
> from unaccredited schools and from enrolling graduates of unaccredited schools

---

[7]Some of the same issues raised in this litigation were also investigated by the Antitrust Division
of the U.S. Department of Justice (DOJ). The Massachusetts School of Law filed its suit against
the ABA in federal district court in 1993. This school and several other law schools also complained to DOJ. In 1994, DOJ began an investigation of the ABA's accreditation practices that led,
in 1995, to the filing of a Sherman Act lawsuit against the ABA and a settlement of the case by
the parties by way of a "Final Judgment without trial or adjudication" (*United States of America
v. American Bar Association,* 934 F. Supp. 435 (D.D.C. 1996)). In the Final Judgment, the ABA
agreed to change various accrediting practices, which DOJ alleged to have anticompetitive effects,
but the Judgment specifically provided that it was not "evidence or admission by any party with
respect to any issue of fact or law."

in graduate programs; [9] requiring more expensive and elaborate physical and library facilities; and [10] requiring schools to use the LSAT [Law School Admissions Test] [107 F.3d at 1031–32].

The appellate court held federal antitrust laws to be generally applicable to accrediting activities, but it did not find the ABA's enforcement of accreditation standards to be in violation of the antitrust laws. The court thus affirmed the trial court's grant of summary judgment to the ABA. In rejecting MSL's assertion that it suffered a competitive disadvantage in recruitment because graduates of MSL were prohibited from taking the bar examination in most states, the appellate court relied on the U.S. Supreme Court's decision in *Parker v. Brown* (see Section 13.2.8) to shield the ABA from liability. "[E]very state retains final authority to set all the bar admission rules," said the court, and since the alleged injury is the result of state action, it falls within *Parker*'s state immunity doctrine. "Without state action, the ABA's accreditation decisions would not affect state bar admissions requirements" (107 F.3d at 1036). Since the state determines that graduation from an ABA-accredited school is required to sit for the state bar examination, the ABA merely "assist[s] [the states] in their decision-making processes" and cannot be held liable for any competitive disadvantage MSL may suffer in recruiting students.

The court then addressed the "stigmatic effect [MSL has allegedly suffered] in the marketplace [as the result] of the denial of accreditation." MSL claimed that "the ABA has conducted a campaign to convey the idea that . . . [it] is the most, or only, competent organization to judge law schools." Relying on the *Noerr* case (above), the court held that the ABA's annual communication of its accreditation decisions to states was sufficient "petitioning activity" to grant the ABA immunity from any stigmatic effect its accreditation decision may have had on MSL. Any stigmatic injury suffered by MSL was merely incidental to the competitive disadvantage it suffered as a result of individual state requirements that individuals graduate from an ABA-accredited school prior to sitting for the bar examination.[8]

In a later case, *Foundation for Interior Design Education Research v. Savannah College of Art and Design*, 244 F.3d 521 (6th Cir. 2001), another U.S. Court of Appeals also applied federal antitrust law to accreditation but dismissed the college's antitrust claims. Affirming the district court's decision, the court of appeals ruled that the college "did not allege that the [accrediting agency] has market power in the relevant market . . . [and] did not allege that it has suffered an antitrust injury" (244 F.3d at 529–32).

14.3.2.5. Defamation law and other tort theories. The first application of defamation law (see Section 3.3.4) to accrediting agencies and officials occurred

---

[8]In a subsequent action, *Massachusetts School of Law at Andover v. American Bar Association, et al.*, 142 F.3d 26 (1st Cir. 1998), the plaintiff law school filed numerous additional claims against the ABA, the Association of American Law Schools (AALS), and various other defendants, alleging unfair competition, fraud and deceit, tortious misrepresentations, and breach of contract. The court of appeals, following the district court, dismissed all the claims on procedural and jurisdictional grounds or for failure to state a cognizable cause of action.

in *Avins v. White*, 627 F.2d 637 (3d Cir. 1980). The plaintiff was a school official who alleged that he had been defamed by an accrediting official in the
course of a site inspection. The case arose from the efforts of the Delaware Law
School (DLS) to gain provisional American Bar Association accreditation. After
a series of accreditation inspections of DLS, the then dean of DLS (Avins) sued
the ABA consultant (White) who had participated in two of the inspections. The
dean alleged three counts of defamation. The first two counts were based on
statements in the reports of the inspection team; the third was based on remarks
that the consultant had made to the dean at a luncheon meeting while they
were in the presence of a third party (a Judge DiBona). The dean prevailed at
a trial in federal district court, and the jury awarded him $50,000 in compen-
satory damages.

On appeal, the U.S. Court of Appeals for the Third Circuit considered each
of the three defamation counts separately. Regarding the first two counts, the
court held that the statements in the inspection team's reports could not be considered to have defamed the dean. The statements in the first report, according
to the court, were not based on fact but were expressions of "pure opinion."
Such expressions cannot be defamatory, because "ideas themselves," unlike
their underlying facts, "cannot be false." The statements in the second report,
according to the court, referred to the school rather than to the dean personally
and therefore could not have defamed him. Thus, instead of submitting the first
two counts to the jury, the district judge should have ruled the statements non-
defamatory as a matter of law. The appellate court therefore reversed the district court's judgment on the first two counts.

The third count presented different problems. The appellate court ruled that
the luncheon remarks cited in this count "may have been potentially defamatory." The consultant argued, however, that because of his role in the accreditation process, he possessed a "qualified privilege" to make the luncheon
remarks, which addressed matters regarding the accreditation inspection.
Neither the appellate court nor the dean disputed that the consultant could possess such a qualified privilege. The issue, rather, was whether the consultant
had abused the privilege by making his remarks in the presence of the third
party (Judge DiBona), who was not an official of the law school. The appellate
court held that this issue was one for the jury, that the district judge had properly instructed the jury on when it could consider the qualified privilege to be
abused, and that "the jury quite properly could have rejected the defense." The
appellate court could not determine whether the jury had actually found
the luncheon remarks to be defamatory, however, since the district judge had
submitted all three defamation counts to the jury as a package; it was "therefore impossible to determine if the jury had based its verdict on all three
allegedly defamatory statements or whether the verdict was based on only
one or two of the incidents." Because of this technical complexity, the appellate
court also reversed the district court's judgment on the third count and
remanded the case to the district court for a new trial on that count only.

One critical issue then remained: the "standard of proof" the dean had to
meet in order to sustain a defamation claim against the consultant. Although

the issue applied to all three counts, the appellate court needed to address it only with respect to the third count, which it was remanding for a new trial. The consultant argued that the dean was a "public figure" for purposes of this lawsuit and therefore had to meet a higher standard of proof than that required for ordinary defamation plaintiffs.[9] The district court had rejected this argument. The appellate court overruled the district court, determining that the dean was a public figure within the meaning of the applicable Supreme Court precedents:

> The [U.S. Supreme] Court in *Gertz* [*v. Robert Welch, Inc.,* 418 U.S. 323 (1974)] gave a description of who may be a public figure:
>
>> For the most part, those who attain [public-figure] status have assumed roles of especial prominence in the affairs of society. Some occupy positions of such persuasive power and influence that they are deemed public figures for all purposes. More commonly, those classed as public figures have thrust themselves to the forefront of particular controversies in order to influence the resolution of the issues involved. In either event, they invite attention and comment.
>
> The *Gertz* test envisions basically two types of public figures: (1) those who are public figures for all purposes; and (2) those who are public figures only in the context of a particular public controversy. . . .
>
> We have no difficulty in concluding that Avins is not a public figure for all purposes under the first part of the *Gertz* test. Although Avins was apparently well known in legal academic circles, we do not believe he possessed the fame and notoriety in the public eye necessary to make him a public figure for all purposes. This leaves the question whether Avins is a public figure in the limited context of the DLS accreditation struggle. We must accordingly consider whether (1) the DLS accreditation struggle was a public controversy and (2) if so, whether Avins voluntarily injected himself into that controversy.
>
> Although DLS was formed and operated as a purely private law school, its success or failure was of importance to the Delaware State Bar as well as to any individual interested in attending an accredited law school in Delaware. It is the only law school in the State of Delaware. Accreditation of DLS would create a new source of attorneys who could qualify to take the Delaware Bar examinations and be admitted to practice in the state. Furthermore, a majority of DLS students were from out of state. Thus, DLS accreditation would also affect the interests of students from a variety of locales and admission to state bars outside of Delaware.
>
> Further, there is evidence in the record that mass meetings were held and that individuals from other states concerned about DLS visited the school. The local news media, as well as the Delaware Bar Association publicized the events

---

[9]In a series of cases beginning with *New York Times v. Sullivan,* 376 U.S. 254 (1964), the U.S. Supreme Court has formulated a "public-figure" doctrine in order to ensure that certain speakers' free speech rights would not be unduly chilled by the fear of defamation suits. To prevail on a defamation claim, a public figure must prove "actual malice" on the part of the defendant—that is, that the defendant had made the statement with a knowledge of its falsity or with a reckless disregard for the truth. (See the discussion of defamation in subsections 3.3.4 and 4.7.2.3.)

surrounding DLS's formation and struggle for accreditation. . . . We therefore hold that DLS's accreditation was a legitimate public controversy within the meaning of *Gertz.*

. . . We have no difficulty in concluding that Avins voluntarily injected himself into the controversy surrounding DLS's accreditation. As creator, chief architect, and the first dean of DLS, Avins spearheaded its drive toward accreditation. Indeed, the first major hurdle which Avins had to surmount in behalf of DLS was accreditation. The record reveals that from the outset Avins, as dean, was actively involved in every facet of the accreditation struggle. He, in fact, invited the first three accreditation teams to inspect DLS and he personally presented DLS's case before the Council and Accreditation Committee. . . . It was Avins who as dean of DLS officially requested, invited, and affirmatively invoked the accreditation process of the American Bar Association. We therefore conclude that Avins played an affirmative and aggressive role in the accreditation process and that he was a public figure for that limited purpose [627 F.2d at 646–48].

The court justified this extension of the public figure doctrine to the accreditation context by relying on the nature of the accreditation process itself:

We believe the importance of the accreditation process underscores the need for extension of the *New York Times* [*v. Sullivan*] privilege to a private individual criticizing a public figure in the course of commenting on matters germane to accreditation. An accreditation evaluation by its nature is critical; the applicant school invites critical comments in seeking accreditation. In order to succeed, individuals involved in the accreditation process need to be assured that they may frankly and openly discuss accreditation matters. White, in criticizing Avins at the luncheon, was expressing a candid view of Avins' conduct during the accreditation process. To require an individual like White to insure the accuracy of his comments on accreditation matters would undoubtedly lead to self-censorship, which will jeopardize the efficacy and integrity of the accreditation process itself. Since the public is vitally affected by accreditation of educational institutions, we believe that self-censorship in the accreditation process would detrimentally affect an area of significant social importance [627 F.2d at 648–49].

Avins v. White thus provides additional insight into how courts view the accreditation process. The case affirms the societal importance of the process and underscores the need for courts to provide enough legal running room for accreditation to accomplish its societal purposes. More specifically, the case illustrates the steps administrators and counsel should take and the issues they will encounter in analyzing defamation claims in the accreditation context. The plaintiff's initial victory at trial suggests that defamation law can be a very real source of legal protection for institutions and their officials, and of legal liability for accrediting agencies and their officials. But the appellate court's reversal provides a mellowing effect: defamation law will not be applied so strictly that it discourages the candid criticism necessary to accreditation's success; and, when the institutional official allegedly defamed is a "public figure," defamation law will provide a remedy against accrediting agencies only in cases of malicious misconduct.

In another type of tort case, *Keams v. Tempe Technical Institute,* 39 F.3d 222 (9th Cir. 1994), the appellate court considered a negligence claim against an accrediting agency and addressed a new issue concerning the judicial role in accreditation cases: whether the Higher Education Act preempts state tort claims by students against accrediting agencies. (Only the accrediting associations were defendants for purposes of this appeal.) The trial court had ruled that the Higher Education Act did preempt such claims against the agencies, and also ruled that the Act did not provide for a private right of action by students against accrediting agencies. The appellate court reversed, finding no evidence in the Higher Education Act of a congressional intent to preempt state tort claims. Indeed, said the court, since it is difficult for the U.S. Secretary of Education to police the accreditors, and since the accrediting agencies and the schools they accredit had a commonality of interests, the students' "interest in honest and effective accreditation may be more effectively vindicated by private tort suits in state court" (39 F.3d at 227). The students could therefore proceed with their negligence action against the accrediting agencies.

The *Keams* case thus adds additional tort claims, beyond defamation, to the list of common law claims that may be asserted against accrediting agencies, thereby expanding the bases upon which courts may review accrediting agency decisions. In a later proceeding, however, the trial judge dismissed the students' negligence claims on the merits, ruling that state law had not recognized a duty of care that would create liability under the facts alleged by the students, and the appellate court affirmed (*Keams v. Tempe Technical Institute,* 110 F.3d 44 (9th Cir. 1997)).

14.3.2.6. Bankruptcy law. On occasion, an accredited institution may file for bankruptcy. Such an action does not protect the institution from an accrediting agency that is seeking to withdraw the institution's accreditation. The federal Bankruptcy Code (see Section 8.3.8.1 of this book), as amended by the Omnibus Reconciliation Act of 1990 (104 Stat. 1388), makes clear that the "accreditation status . . . of the debtor as an educational institution" is not considered to be property subject to the bankruptcy laws (11 U.S.C. § 541(b)(3)); and that the automatic stay provision, which prohibits others from obtaining possession or control of the debtor's property, does not apply to "any action by an accrediting agency regarding the accreditation status of the debtor as an educational institution" (11 U.S.C. § 362(b)(14)).

These Bankruptcy Code amendments adopt and give nationwide application to the holding in *In re Nasson College,* 80 Bankr. Rptr. 600 (D. Maine 1988), in which a college in bankruptcy sought an injunction ordering the New England Association of Schools and Colleges to restore its accreditation. The college had filed for bankruptcy and then ceased to offer educational programs, after which the accrediting agency had terminated the college's accreditation. The college argued that its accreditation was property included in the bankruptcy estate and that the agency's action therefore violated the Bankruptcy Code's automatic stay provision (11 U.S.C. § 362(a)(3)). The court rejected the college's argument, ruling that accreditation is not property but "[a] status . . . held in the nature of a trust for the [accrediting agency] and the public" (80 Bankr. Rptr. at 604).[10] (For another similar case, see *In re Draughon Training Institute,* 119 Bankr. Rptr. 927 (W.D. La. 1990).)

Given the thrust of the Bankruptcy Code amendments and the *In re Nasson College* case, it is apparently also clear that a debtor institution cannot protect its accreditation by resort to the "executory contract" provision of the Bankruptcy Code (11 U.S.C. § 365), which allows debtors to continue performance under certain of its contracts. In the case of *In re Statewide Oilfield Construction, Inc., d/b/a Golden State School,* 134 Bankr. Rptr. 399 (E.D. Cal. 1991), the bankruptcy court held that the bankruptcy amendments quoted above preclude a debtor from claiming that its accredited status constitutes an executory contract with the accrediting agency and an asset protected by 11 U.S.C. § 365. (See M. Pelesh, "Accreditation and Bankruptcy: The Death of Executory Contract," 71 *West's Educ. Law Rptr.* 975 (March 12, 1992).) The *Golden State* litigation apparently closes the last possible door through which an accredited institution might have used bankruptcy laws as a shield to protect its accreditation during difficult financial times.

14.3.3. Accreditation and the U.S. Department of Education.

The Department of Education (ED) plays an important and sometimes controversial role in the accrediting process. The federal aid-to-education statutes generally specify accreditation or "preaccreditation" by "a nationally recognized accrediting agency or association" as a prerequisite to eligibility for the institution and its students (see 20 U.S.C. § 1001(a)(5); 42 U.S.C. § 296(6)). These provisions authorize the Secretary of Education to "publish a list of nationally recognized accrediting agencies or associations that the Secretary determines . . . to be reliable authority as to the quality of education or training offered" (20 U.S.C. § 1001(c)). A National Advisory Committee on Institutional Quality and Integrity, established by statute, assists the Secretary with this responsibility (20 U.S.C. § 1011(c)). (The Committee was scheduled to go out of existence on September 30, 2004; its future apparently depends on the bills to reauthorize the Higher Education Act that were still pending in Congress as this book went to press.) Most postsecondary institutions and programs attain eligibility for federal funds by obtaining accreditation or preaccreditation from one of the agencies recognized by the Secretary.

For many years after passage of the Higher Education Act, the Secretary of Health, Education and Welfare (HEW), and then the Secretary of Education, promulgated and published criteria for determining whether to recognize particular accrediting agencies. It was not until 1992, with passage of the 1992

---

[10]The college also argued that the termination of accreditation violated Section 525(a) of the Bankruptcy Code, which prohibits "governmental unit(s)" from discriminating against debtors in bankruptcy. The court rejected this argument as well, holding that the defendant was not a "governmental unit" for purposes of Section 525(a) and that the termination occurred because the college had ceased offering programs, not because it had become a debtor in bankruptcy.

Amendments to the HEA, that Congress involved itself in the establishment of recognition criteria and procedures to be used by the Secretary (see subsection 14.3.1 above). These amendments established a list of requirements that accrediting agencies must comply with in order to be recognized and that the Secretary must include in the criteria for recognition.

In the Higher Education Amendments of 1998, Congress again addressed the statutory standards and procedures that the Secretary of Education must follow in recognizing accrediting agencies. These newer amendments (Pub. L. No. 105-244, Title IV, § 492, 112 Stat. 1622 at 1759–61, codified at 20 U.S.C. § 1099b), made several changes in the criteria that the Secretary must use. As amended in 1998, Section 1099b now specifies, for example, that the Secretary must have criteria that: require accrediting agencies to promulgate and enforce standards that assess institutions' compliance with their program responsibilities under the federal student aid programs (20 U.S.C. § 1099b(a)(5)(J)); require agencies to promulgate and enforce standards regarding nine other listed areas of institutional operations (20 U.S.C. § 1099b(a)(5)); require accrediting agencies to evaluate the quality of institutions' "distance education courses or programs" (20 U.S.C. § 1099b(a)(4)); assure that agencies follow "due process" procedures "throughout the accrediting process" (20 U.S.C. § 1099b(a)(6)); require most accrediting agencies to be "separate and independent, both administratively and financially of any related, associated, or affiliated trade association or membership organization" (20 U.S.C. § 1099b(a)(3)(A)); and require agencies to make various types of information available to the Secretary, to state licensing agencies, or to the public (20 U.S.C. § 1099b(a)(7), (a)(8), (c)(5), & (c)(6)).[11] (Most such matters had already been addressed in recognition criteria that the Secretary had adopted administratively prior to passage of the 1992 legislation.)

In 1999, using a negotiated rule-making process, the Secretary proposed regulations to implement the 1998 Amendments and to otherwise revise and reorder the department's recognition process (64 Fed. Reg. 34466–85 (June 25, 1999)). Several months later, the Secretary published the final version of these regulations (64 Fed. Reg. 56612–26 (October 20, 1999)). The new regulations, like the previous ones, are codified at 34 C.F.R. Part 602. Extensive and important departmental commentary on these regulations is included with both the proposed regulations and the final regulations.

Although accreditation or preaccreditation by a recognized agency is the predominant means for obtaining eligibility to participate in federal aid programs, alternative means for attaining eligibility under certain programs are sometimes provided. Approval by a state agency recognized by the Secretary, for example, is an alternative available under student financial aid programs for nursing

---

[11]Most of these matters, and others discussed in the rest of this subsection, could become involved in the congressional debates over the reauthorization of the Higher Education Act; and some of these matters could be affected by passage of the reauthorization act that was pending in Congress as this book went to press. Amendments to the due process requirements, for example, have been proposed (see H.R. 4795, 109th Cong., 2d Sess., introduced February 16, 2006).

education (42 U.S.C. § 296(6)); and state approval alternatives also exist for veterans' educational benefit programs (38 U.S.C. § 3452).

The Secretary of Education periodically publishes in the *Federal Register* a list of nationally recognized accrediting agencies and associations; the Secretary also publishes a list of recognized state agencies that approve public vocational education programs (34 C.F.R. Part 603) and a list of recognized state agencies for approval of nursing education (see 42 U.S.C. § 296(6)). The Secretary's criteria and procedures for recognition of accrediting agencies are also published in the *Federal Register* and codified in the *Code of Federal Regulations* (34 C.F.R. Parts 602 & 603). Periodically, the Secretary also publishes a pamphlet containing a current list of recognized agencies, the criteria and procedures for listing, and background information on accreditation.[12] The listing process and other aspects of institutional eligibility for federal aid are administered within the Department of Education by the Accrediting Agency Evaluation Branch, part of the Higher Education Management Services Directorate of the Office of Postsecondary Education.

To be included in the list of nationally recognized agencies, an agency must apply to the Secretary for recognition and must meet the Secretary's criteria for recognition. Agencies are reevaluated and their listings renewed or terminated at least once every five years (34 C.F.R. §§ 602.35(b)(1)(ii) & 602.36(c)). The criteria for recognition, as authorized by 20 U.S.C. § 1099b (see above), concern such matters as the agency's organization and membership, its administrative and fiscal capacities, its experience and its national acceptance by pertinent constituencies, its standards for reviewing institutional programs and functions, the procedures it follows in making accreditation decisions, and other operating processes (34 C.F.R. §§ 602.13–602.26). The criteria for recognition also cover matters concerning the agency's role in ensuring institutional compliance with the requirements of the federal student aid programs authorized by Title IV of the Higher Education Act (34 C.F.R. §§ 602.1, 602.10, 602.22(c), 602.24, & 602.27(e)–(f); see also 20 U.S.C. § 1099b(a)(5)(J)).

Although the statutory provisions and regulations discussed in this subsection give the Secretary of Education substantial influence over the accrediting process, the Secretary has no direct authority to regulate unwilling accrediting agencies. Agencies must apply for recognition before coming under the Secretary's jurisdiction. Moreover, recognition only gives the Secretary authority to ensure the agency's continued compliance with the criteria; it does not give him or her authority to overrule the agency's accrediting decisions on particular institutions or programs. (See, however, 34 C.F.R. § 602.28, setting out limits on a recognized agency's authority to accredit or preaccredit institutions and programs; and 34 C.F.R. § 602.31(b)(2), (3), on the Secretary's review of complaints against an agency during consideration of an application for recognition.)

Postsecondary administrators responsible for academic programs will find it beneficial to understand the relationship between the agencies and the

---

[12]U.S. Department of Education, "Accreditation in the United States," available at http://www.ed.gov/admins/finaid/accred./accreditation.html.

Department of Education. The requirements in the Secretary's criteria for recognition affect institutions in two ways: they are the source of additional standards that the agencies impose on institutions through the accreditation process, and they are a source of procedural and other protections that redound to the benefit of institutions and programs when an agency is investigating them or considering a denial or termination of accreditation. The criteria require, for example, that an accrediting agency follows specified processes in its accrediting activities (34 C.F.R. § 602.18); that an agency has "clear and effective controls" against conflicts of interest on the part of its evaluators and decision makers (34 C.F.R. §§ 602.14(b) & 602.15(a)(6)); that an agency applies its standards consistently and without bias (34 C.F.R. § 602.18(a), (b)); that an agency's policy and decision-making bodies include public representatives (34 C.F.R. §§ 602.14(b)(2) & 602.15(a)(5)); that an agency reviews and follows up on any complaint filed against it (34 C.F.R. § 602.23(c)(3)); and that all of an agency's procedures "satisfy due process requirements" (34 C.F.R. § 602.25). Because recognition is vitally important to an accrediting agency's influence and credibility in the postsecondary world, agencies will be disinclined to jeopardize their recognition by violating the Secretary's criteria in their dealings with institutions. Institutional administrators therefore have considerable leverage to insist that accrediting agencies comply with these criteria.

Although an institution may complain to the Secretary about an agency's violation of the recognition criteria (see 34 C.F.R. § 602.31(b)(2), (3)), it is unlikely that the Secretary's criteria are enforceable in the court through suits by individual institutions against accrediting agencies. The prevailing judicial view is that government regulations are to be enforced by the government agency that promulgated them, unless a contrary intention appears from the regulations and the statute that authorized the regulations (see generally the "private cause of action" cases in Sections 13.4.6 and 13.5.9). Since there is no indication that the Secretary's criteria are to be privately enforceable, the courts would likely leave problems concerning compliance with these criteria to the Secretary. Similarly, it is unlikely that 20 U.S.C. Section 1099b(f), passed in 1992 (see subsections 14.3.2.1 & 14.3.2.2 above), serves to create a private cause of action to enforce the statutory requirements that Section 1099b applies to accrediting agencies. In *Thomas M. Cooley Law School v. American Bar Association*, 376 F. Supp. 2d 758 (W.D. Mich. 2005), for example, the court rejected the law school's claim that the defendant had violated several of the requirements in Section 1099b, concluding that "there is no case law support for the proposition that [Section 1099b(f)] expressly or impliedly creates a private right of action in favor of an institution of higher education against an accrediting agency." The developing case law on this point is not definitive, however. In the *Auburn University* case (subsection 14.3.2.2 above), for instance, the court suggested in *dicta* that Section 1099b(f) "is susceptible of an interpretation" that would allow a private cause of action to enforce the requirements in the rest of Section 1099b (2002 WL 3237500 at p. 16); and in *Western State University of Southern California v. American Bar Ass'n*, 301 F. Supp. 2d 1129(C.D. Cal. 2004), the court suggested in *dicta* that, if Section 1099b(f) did not create a private right of action, this provision "might be superfluous."

Even if the recognition criteria are not privately enforceable, however, that does not mean they would be irrelevant in any suit by an institution against an accrediting agency. Since the judicial standards applying to accrediting agencies are not fully developed (see subsection 14.3.2.2 above), courts may look to the Secretary's criteria, especially in federal common law cases (subsection 14.3.2.2), as evidence of accepted practice in accreditation or as a model to consult in formulating a remedy for an agency's violation of legal standards.

When the Secretary applies the criteria to grant or deny recognition to a particular agency (see 34 C.F.R. §§ 602.34–602.45), a different question about the role of courts arises: On what grounds, and at whose request, may a court review the Secretary's recognition decisions? The case of *Sherman College of Straight Chiropractic v. U.S. Commissioner of Education*, 493 F. Supp. 976 (D.D.C. 1980), is illustrative. The plaintiffs were two chiropractic schools that were not accredited by the Council on Chiropractic Education (CCE), the recognized professional accrediting agency for chiropractic schools. The plaintiffs espoused a chiropractic philosophy divergent from that represented by CCE and the schools it had accredited: the plaintiffs adhered to a limited view regarding diagnosis, called the "straight doctrine," whereas CCE took a broader view of diagnosis as an essential part of chiropractic practice. When the Commissioner (who would now be the Secretary) renewed CCE's status as a nationally recognized accrediting agency, the plaintiffs challenged his action in court.

Using federal administrative law principles, the court determined that the Commissioner's renewal of CCE's recognition was a final agency action subject to judicial review. The court also determined that the plaintiffs, as parties aggrieved by the Commissioner's action, had standing to challenge it. On the merits, however, the court rejected the plaintiffs' claim that the Commissioner's decision was arbitrary and capricious, or an abuse of discretion. The court provided various reasons having to do with the nature and scope of the Commissioner's (now Secretary's) recognition authority and with the nature of accreditation, concluding that "the commissioner acted correctly in deciding the only issue [he] could legitimately determine: that CCE is a 'reliable authority' under the statute" (493 F. Supp. at 981).

The *Sherman College* case thus indicates that the Secretary of Education's decisions to grant or refuse recognition to petitioning accrediting agencies, or to renew or not renew such recognition, are reviewable in the federal courts. The Secretary has similarly concluded that accrediting agencies may sue in court to challenge decisions "to limit, suspend, or terminate" recognition (34 C.F.R. § 602.45). It is possible that the Secretary's recognition decisions may also be challenged by individual institutions, and by students and faculty members, if they suffer some concrete injury attributable to the decision. The availability of judicial review, however, does not mean that courts are likely to overturn the Secretary's decisions. As the *Sherman College* case illustrates, courts will accord the Secretary considerable latitude in applying the recognition criteria and will not expect the Secretary to take sides in disputes over educational philosophies, professional doctrine, or other matters outside the scope of the recognition criteria.

14.3.4. Dealing with accrediting agencies.
As a general proposition, institutional officials and counsel should not regard accrediting agencies as adversaries. Accreditation usually depends on mutual assistance and cooperation, and the dynamic between institution and agency can be very constructive. Institutions and programs that are willing to cooperate and expend the necessary effort usually can obtain and keep accreditation without serious threat of loss. But serious differences can and do arise, particularly with institutions that are innovating with curricula, the use of resources, or delivery systems. Such institutions may not fit neatly into accrediting standards or may otherwise be difficult for accrediting agencies to evaluate. Similarly, institutions that establish branch campuses, operate in more than one state (see Section 12.4), offer programs in foreign countries, contract for the delivery of educational services with nonaccredited outside organizations, or sponsor off-campus or "external" degree programs may pose particular problems for accrediting agencies.[13] So may institutions that are organized as proprietary entities, as illustrated by the *Marjorie Webster* case (Section 14.3.2.1; and see generally Kevin Kinser, *A Profile of Regionally-Accredited For-Profit Institutions of Higher Education* (University of Houston Law Center, IHELG Monograph 04-08, (2004)), or institutions in financial crisis, as illustrated by the cases in Section 14.3.2.6. Controversies may also arise, as they prominently did in the early 1990s, over accrediting standards regarding the cultural diversity of faculty and students. When these or other circumstances involve the institution in accreditation problems, they can be critical matters because of accreditation's importance to the institution. Administrators should then be prepared to deal, perhaps in an adversarial way at times, with the resulting conflicts between the institution and the agency. (For other more general suggestions, see Section 14.6 below.)

Whether a postsecondary institution is dealing with an accrediting agency in a cooperative or an adversarial manner, administrators should have complete information from the agency about its organization and operation. According to the Secretary of Education's criteria (subsection 14.3.3), an accrediting agency recognized by the Department of Education must provide, in clear written form, its standards and procedures for granting, suspending, and terminating accreditation and preaccreditation, as well as various types of other information covering its operations and its personnel. The accrediting agency must also provide written notice of its accrediting decisions regarding particular institutions or programs and, for negative decisions, must provide a brief statement of reasons (34 C.F.R. § 602.26). In addition, the agency must provide notice of any proposed changes in its standards to its "relevant constituencies" and to "other parties who have made their interest known"; must provide opportunity to comment

---

[13]See generally E. Kuhns & S. V. Martorana, *Toward Academic Quality Off-Campus: Monitoring Requirements of Institutional Accrediting Bodies and the States for Off-Campus, Military Base, and Study Abroad Programs* (Council on Postsecondary Accreditation, 1984).

on any such proposed changes; and must "take into account" all comments that are submitted in a timely fashion (34 C.F.R. § 602.21(c)). Most important for an administrator is the information on the agency's evaluative standards and its procedures for making accrediting decisions. A full understanding of the standards and procedures can be critical to representing the institution or program effectively before the agency or in court. Administrators should insist on receiving all this information (see 34 C.F.R. § 602.23) and should also insist, as the court cases discussed in Section 14.3.2.2 make clear, that the agency consistently follows its own rules in dealing with the institution.

If an institution's dispute with an accrediting agency does become sufficiently adversarial to result in litigation, institutional counsel and administrators can find substantial guidance on the applicable law in subsection 14.3.2 above. It will also be important to understand the effect of 20 U.S.C. Section 1099b(f) on the jurisdiction of courts to hear accreditation cases; this matter is discussed in subsections 14.3.2.1 and 14.3.2.2 above. In addition, questions may arise concerning whether an institution may litigate, in court, claims that an accrediting agency has violated the Secretary of Education's criteria for recognition in its dealings with the institution. This matter is discussed in subsection 14.3.3 above.

Sec. 14.4. Athletic Associations and Conferences

14.4.1. Overview. Various associations and conferences have a hand in regulating intercollegiate athletics. Most institutions with intercollegiate programs are members of both a national association (for example, the National Collegiate Athletic Association (NCAA)) and a conference (for example, the Atlantic Coast Conference (ACC)).

The NCAA (http://www.ncaa.org) is the largest and most influential of the athletic associations. It is an unincorporated association with a membership of more than one thousand public and private colleges and universities that are divided into three divisions. The association has a constitution that sets forth its fundamental law, and it has enacted extensive bylaws that govern its operations. (The constitution and bylaws, and the NCAA manuals (see below), are available on the NCAA's Web site under "legislation and governance.") To preserve the amateur nature of college athletics and the fairness of competition, the NCAA includes in its bylaws complex rules regarding recruiting, academic eligibility, other eligibility requirements, and the like. There are different rules for each of the three divisions, compiled into an *NCAA Manual* for each division, which is updated periodically. Regarding eligibility, for instance, the *NCAA Manual* for Division I has requirements on minimum grade point average (GPA) and Scholastic Aptitude Test (SAT) or American College Testing (ACT) scores for incoming freshman student athletes; requirements regarding satisfactory academic progress for student athletes; restrictions on transfers from one school to another; rules on "redshirting" and longevity as a player; limitations on financial aid, compensation, and employment; and limitations regarding professional contracts and players' agents (see generally G. Wong, *Essentials of Amateur Sports*

Law (2d ed., Praeger, 1994), 239–84). To enforce its rules, the NCAA has an enforcement program that includes compliance audits, self-reporting, investigations, and official inquiries, culminating in a range of penalties that the NCAA can impose against its member institutions but not directly against the institutions' employees. The various conferences affiliated with the NCAA may also have their own rules and enforcement processes, so long as they meet the minimum requirements of the NCAA.

Legal issues often arise as a result of the rule-making and enforcement activities of the various athletic associations and conferences. Individual institutions have become involved in such legal issues in two ways. First, coaches and student athletes penalized for violating conference or association rules have sued their institutions as well as the conference or association to contest the enforcement of these rules. Second, institutions themselves have sued conferences or associations over their rules, policies, or decisions. The majority of such disputes have involved the NCAA, since it is the primary regulator of intercollegiate athletics in the United States. The resulting litigation frequently presents a difficult threshold problem of determining what legal principles should apply to resolution of the dispute.

As the developments in the subsections below demonstrate, institutions of higher education do have legal weapons to use in disputes with the NCAA and other athletic associations or conferences. State common law clearly applies to such disputes (subsection 14.4.5). Antitrust law also has some applicability (subsection 14.4.4), as does federal civil rights law (subsection 14.4.6).

Federal constitutional rights may still have some application in a narrow range of cases (subsection 14.4.2). And some role may still be found for state regulatory statutes more narrowly crafted than those discussed in subsection 14.4.3. Administrators and counsel should be aware, however, that these weapons are two-edged: student athletes may also use them against the institution when the institution and the athletic association are jointly engaged in enforcing athletic rules against the student.

14.4.2. Federal constitutional constraints.

In a series of cases, courts have considered whether the NCAA, as an institutional membership association for both public and private colleges and universities, is engaged in "state action" (see Section 1.5.2) and thus is subject to the constraints of the U.S. Constitution, such as due process and equal protection. In an early leading case, *Parish v. NCAA*, 506 F.2d 1028 (5th Cir. 1975), for example, several basketball players at Centenary College, later joined by the college, challenged the constitutionality of an NCAA academic requirement then known as the "1.600 rule." Using first the "government contacts" theory and then the "public function" theory (both are explained in Section 1.5.2), the court held that the NCAA was engaged in state action. It then proceeded to examine the NCAA's rule under constitutional due process and equal protection principles, holding the rule valid in both respects.

Subsequent to the decision in *Parish* and other similar decisions in NCAA cases, the U.S. Supreme Court issued several opinions that narrowed the circumstances under which courts will find state action (see especially *Rendell-Baker v. Kohn*, discussed in Section 1.5.2). In *Arlosoroff v. NCAA*, 746 F.2d 1019 (4th Cir. 1984), the court relied on these Supreme Court opinions to reach a result contrary to the *Parish* line of cases. The plaintiff was a varsity tennis player at Duke University (a private institution) whom the NCAA had declared ineligible for further competition because he had participated in amateur competition for several years before enrolling at Duke. He claimed that the bylaw under which the NCAA had acted was invalid under the due process and equal protection clauses. Determining that the NCAA's promulgation and enforcement of the bylaw did not fit within either the government contacts or the public function theory, the court held that the NCAA was not engaged in state action and therefore was not subject to constitutional constraints.

In 1988, the U.S. Supreme Court came down on the *Arlosoroff* side of the debate in a 5-to-4 split decision in *NCAA v. Tarkanian*, 488 U.S. 179 (1988). The NCAA had opened an official inquiry in 1976 into the basketball program at the University of Nevada, Las Vegas (UNLV). UNLV conducted its own investigation into the NCAA's allegations and reported its findings to the NCAA's Committee on Infractions. After a hearing, the committee found that UNLV had committed thirty-eight infractions, ten of which directly involved its highly successful, towel-chewing basketball coach, Jerry Tarkanian, including a finding that he had failed to cooperate fully with the NCAA investigation. As a result, the NCAA placed UNLV's basketball team on a two-year probation and ordered UNLV to show cause why further penalties should not be imposed "unless UNLV severed all ties during the probation between its intercollegiate program and Tarkanian." Reluctantly, after holding a hearing, UNLV suspended Tarkanian in 1977. Tarkanian then sued both the university and the NCAA, alleging that they had deprived him of his property interest in the position of basketball coach without first affording him procedural due process protections. The trial court agreed and granted the coach injunctive relief and attorney's fees. The Nevada Supreme Court upheld the trial court's ruling, agreeing that Tarkanian's constitutional due process rights had been violated. This court regarded the NCAA's regulatory activities as state action because "many NCAA member institutions were either public or government supported" and because the NCAA had participated in the dismissal of a public employee, traditionally a function reserved to the state (*Tarkanian v. NCAA*, 741 P.2d 1345 (Nev. 1987)).

The U.S. Supreme Court, analyzing the NCAA's role and its relationship with UNLV and the state, disagreed with the Nevada courts and held that the NCAA was not a state actor. The Court noted that UNLV, clearly a state actor, had actually suspended Tarkanian, and that the issue therefore was "whether UNLV's actions in compliance with the NCAA rules and recommendations turned the NCAA's conduct into state action." Defining "state action" as action engaged in by those "'who carry a badge of authority of a State and represent it in some capacity, whether they act in accordance with their authority or misuse it'" (488 U.S. at 191; quoting *Monroe v. Pape*, 365 U.S. 167, 172 (1961)), the Court concluded that "the source of the legislation adopted by the NCAA is not Nevada but the collective membership, speaking through an organization that is independent of any particular State." It further noted that the majority of the NCAA's membership consisted of private institutions (488 U.S. at 193, n.13).

The Court also rejected arguments that the NCAA was a state actor because UNLV had delegated its state power to the NCAA. While such a delegation of power could serve to transform a private party into a state actor, no such delegation had occurred. Tarkanian was suspended by UNLV, not by the NCAA; the NCAA could only enforce sanctions against the institution as a whole, not against specific employees. Moreover, UNLV could have taken other paths of action, albeit unpleasant ones, in lieu of suspending the coach: it could have withdrawn from the NCAA or accepted additional sanctions while still remaining a member. Further, although UNLV, as a representative of the State of Nevada, did contribute to the development of NCAA policy, in reality it was the full membership of the organization that promulgated the rules leading to Tarkanian's suspension, not the State of Nevada.

The Court also found that UNLV had not delegated state investigatory authority to the NCAA. Moreover, UNLV had not formed a partnership with the NCAA simply because it decided to adhere to the NCAA's recommendation regarding Tarkanian. The interests of UNLV and the NCAA were in fact hostile to one another:

> During the several years that the NCAA investigated the alleged violations, the NCAA and UNLV acted much more like adversaries than like partners engaged in a dispassionate search for the truth. The NCAA cannot be regarded as an agent of UNLV for purposes of that proceeding. It is more correctly characterized as an agent of its remaining members which, as competitors of UNLV, had an interest in the effective and evenhanded enforcement of the NCAA's recruitment standards [488 U.S. at 196].

Disagreeing with the U.S. Supreme Court majority, the four dissenting Justices argued that UNLV and the NCAA had acted jointly in disciplining Tarkanian; that the NCAA, which had no subpoena power and no direct power to sanction Tarkanian, could have acted only through the state; and that the NCAA was therefore engaged in state action.

The *Tarkanian* case does not foreclose all possibilities for finding that an athletic association or conference is engaged in state action. As the Supreme Court itself recognized, state action may be present "if the membership consist[s] entirely of institutions located within the same State, many of them public institutions created by [that State]" (488 U.S. at 193, n.13). Even if the member institutions were not all located in the same state, state action might exist if the conference were composed entirely of state institutions. For example, in *Stanley v. Big Eight Conference*, 463 F. Supp. 920 (D. Mo. 1978), a case preceding *Tarkanian*, the court applied the Fourteenth Amendment's due process clause to the defendant conference because all its members were state universities. Even if a conference or association were like the NCAA, with both public and private members located in different states, courts might distinguish *Tarkanian* and find state action in a particular case where there was clear evidence that the conference or association and a state institution member had genuinely mutual interests and were acting jointly to take adverse action against a particular student or coach. Finally, even if there were no basis for finding that a particular conference is engaged in state action, courts would still be able to find an individual *state institution* to be engaged in state action (see Section 1.5.2) when it directed the enforcement of conference or association rules, and suit could therefore be brought against the institution rather than the conference or association. In *Spath v. NCAA*, 728 F.2d 25 (1st Cir. 1984), for example, the court held that the University of Lowell, also a defendant, was a state actor even if the NCAA was not and therefore proceeded to the merits of the plaintiff's equal protection and due process claims. (See also *Barbay v. NCAA and Louisiana State University*, 1987 WL 5619 (E.D. La. 1987).)

Moreover, even if federal state action arguments will not work and the federal Constitution therefore does not apply, athletic associations and conferences may occasionally be suable under state constitutions for violations of state constitutional rights (see generally Section 1.4.2.1). In *Hill v. NCAA*, 865 P.2d 633 (Cal. 1994) (Section 10.4.8 of this book), for example, the California Supreme Court held that the right to privacy guarantee of the California constitution could be applied to the NCAA even though it is a private organization.

14.4.3. State statutes regulating athletic associations' enforcement activities.
Partially in response to the *Tarkanian* litigation and NCAA investigations in other states, and to protect in-state institutions as well as their athletic personnel and student athletes, a number of states passed or considered "due process" statutes (see Fla. Stat. §§ 240.5339–240.5349 (1991); 110 ILCS § 25/1 *et seq.*(1991); Nev. Rev. Stat. § 398.155 et *seq.* (1991)). Such statutes require athletic associations to extend certain due process protections to those accused in any enforcement proceeding. The Nevada statute, for example, requires that the accused be given the opportunity to confront all witnesses, that an impartial entity be empaneled to adjudicate the proceeding, and that all proceedings be made public. These statutes may be enforced through injunctions issued by the state's courts or by damage suits against the association by institutions harmed by association action (see, for example, Nev. Rev. Stat. § 398.245). (See generally Comment, "Home Court Advantage: Florida Joins States Mandating Due Process in NCAA Proceedings," 20 *Fla. St. L. Rev.* 871, 889–900 (1993).) Some of these statutes have been repealed or invalidated by the courts (see, for example, the *Miller* case below). In such circumstances, however, a statute providing for suits by institutions against athletic associations may still remain (see, for example, Fla. Stat. § 468.4562; Nev. Rev. Stat. § 398.490).

In *NCAA v. Miller, Governor, State of Nevada*, 795 F. Supp. 1476 (D. Nev. 1992), *affirmed*, 10 F.3d 633 (9th Cir. 1993), the NCAA challenged the Nevada statute cited above. The lower court held the statute unconstitutional as both an invalid restraint on interstate commerce and an invalid interference with the NCAA's contract with its members. First, the court found that the NCAA and its member institutions are heavily involved in interstate commerce through their athletic programs, and that the statute restrained that commerce by curtailing the NCAA's capacity to establish uniform rules for all of its members throughout the United States, thus violating the federal Constitution's commerce clause (Article I, Section 8, Clause 3). Second, the court agreed that Nevada's statute "substantially impair[ed] existing contractual relations between itself and the Nevada member institutions[,] in violation of the Contracts Clause of Article I, Section 10 of the United States Constitution." Since the Nevada law would give Nevada schools an unfair advantage over other schools, it would undermine the basic purpose of the NCAA's agreement with its members and destroy the NCAA's goal of administering a uniform system for all its members.

In affirming, the appellate court focused only on the commerce clause problem. (See generally Section 12.4 of this book regarding the commerce clause.) The court held that the statute directly regulated interstate commerce:

> It is clear that the Statute is directed at interstate commerce and only interstate commerce. By its terms, it regulates only interstate organizations, *i.e.*, national collegiate athletic associations which have member institutions in 40 or more states. Nev. Rev. Stat. 398.055. Moreover, courts have consistently held that the NCAA, which seems to be the only organization regulated by the Statute, is engaged in interstate commerce in numerous ways. It markets interstate intercollegiate athletic competition, . . . [it] schedules events that call for transportation of teams across state lines and it governs nationwide amateur athlete recruiting and controls bids for lucrative national and regional television broadcasting of college athletics [10 F.3d at 638].

According to the court, the statute would "have a profound effect" on the NCAA's interstate activities. Since the NCAA must apply its enforcement procedures "even-handedly and uniformly on a national basis" in order to maintain integrity in accomplishing its goals, it would have to apply Nevada's procedures in every other state as well. Thus, "the practical effect of [Nevada's] regulation is to control conduct beyond the boundaries of the State." Moreover, since other states had enacted or might enact procedural statutes that differed from Nevada's, the NCAA would be subjected to the potentially conflicting requirements of various states. In both respects, the Nevada statute created an unconstitutional restraint on interstate commerce.

The *Miller* case was relied on in *NCAA v. Roberts*, 1994 WL 750585 (N.D. Fla. 1994), a case in which the court used the commerce clause to invalidate the Florida statute cited above.

The *Miller* and *Roberts* cases, however, should not be interpreted as casting doubt on all state statutes that regulate athletic associations and conferences. Not all statutes will have a substantial adverse effect on the association's activities in *other* states, and thus not all state statutes will work to restrain interstate commerce or to impair an association's contractual relations with its members. Various other types of regulatory statutes, and even some types of due process statutes, could be distinguishable from *Miller* in this respect. With such statutes, however, other legal issues may arise. In *Kneeland v. NCAA*, 850 F.2d 224 (5th Cir. 1988), for instance, the court refused to apply the Texas Open

Records Act to the NCAA and the Southwest Athletic Conference, because they could not be considered governmental bodies subject to the Act.

14.4.4. Antitrust laws. Federal and state antitrust laws will apply to athletic associations and conferences in some circumstances. Such laws may be used to challenge the membership rules of the associations and conferences, their eligibility rules for student athletes, and other joint or concerted activities of the members that allegedly have anticompetitive or monopolistic effects. (See generally Section 13.2.8 of this book.) Most cases thus far have been brought against the NCAA, either by a member institution or by a student athlete. Member institutions could also become defendants in such lawsuits, however, since they are the parties that would be engaging in the joint or concerted activity under auspices of the conference or association.

The leading case, *NCAA v. Board of Regents of the University of Oklahoma*, 468 U.S. 85 (1984), concerned an NCAA plan for regulating the televising of college football games by its member institutions. The U.S. Supreme Court held that the NCAA's enforcement of the plan violated Section 1 of the Sherman Antitrust Act (15 U.S.C. § 1) and was therefore invalid. In its salient features, the challenged television plan was mandatory for all NCAA members; it limited the total number of games a member institution could have televised; it fixed prices at which each institution could sell the broadcast rights to its games; and it prohibited member institutions from selling the broadcast rights to their games unless those games were included in the NCAA's television package agreed upon with the networks. The plan was challenged by schools desiring to negotiate their own television contracts free from the set prices and output limitations imposed on them by the NCAA plan.

Although acknowledging from the outset that the NCAA plan was "perhaps the paradigm of an unreasonable restraint of trade," the Court held that it was not a per se violation of the Sherman Act. The Court reasoned that in the "industry" of college football such "restraints on competition are essential if the product is to be available at all" (468 U.S. at 99). In order to ensure the integrity of intercollegiate athletic competition, participating schools must act jointly through the NCAA. Through its regulatory activities in this field, the NCAA enables institutions to preserve "the character of college football" and thus "enables a product to be marketed which might otherwise be unavailable" (468 U.S. at 102). The Court thus found that, by maintaining the existence of college football in its traditional form, as opposed to allowing it to die out or become professionalized, the NCAA's actions as a whole "widen consumer choice—not only the choices available to sports fans but also those available to athletes—and hence can be viewed as procompetitive" (468 U.S. at 102).

Having rejected a rule of per se invalidity, the Court then analyzed the case under the "rule of reason," considering both the plan's anticompetitive impact and its procompetitive impact. In a lengthy discussion, the Court found that the NCAA television plan restricted individual institutions from negotiating their own television contracts and had a significant adverse impact on member institutions' ability to compete openly in the sports broadcasting market. The Court also found that the NCAA wields market power in this market. The Court then turned to the NCAA's alleged justifications for the plan, to determine whether they should take precedence over the plan's anticompetitive impact.

The NCAA argued that, if individual institutions were permitted to negotiate their own television contracts, the market could become saturated, and the prices that networks would pay for college football games would decrease as a result. The Court disagreed with this premise, noting that the NCAA's television plan was not "necessary to enable the NCAA to penetrate the market through an attractive package sale. Since broadcasting rights to college football constitute a unique product for which there is no ready substitute, there is no need for collective action in order to enable the product to compete against its nonexistent competitors" (468 U.S. at 115). The NCAA also argued that, if there was too much college football on television, fewer people would attend live games, thereby decreasing ticket sales, and its television plan was therefore needed to protect gate attendance. The Court rejected this argument as well, because such protection—through collective action—of what was presumed to be an inferior product was itself "inconsistent with the basic policy of the Sherman [Antitrust] Act" (468 U.S. at 116).

Under the rule of reason, therefore, the Court held that the NCAA's enforcement of its television plan was a clear restraint of trade in violation of Section 1 of the Sherman Act.[14] (See B. Gregory & J. C. Busey, "Alternative Broadcasting Arrangements After *NCAA*," 61 *Indiana L.J.* 65 (1985).)

A later case involving a different type of competitive effects problem, *Law v. National Collegiate Athletic Association*, 902 F. Supp. 1394 (D. Kan. 1995), *affirmed*, 134 F.3d 1010 (10th Cir. 1998), provides another dramatic example of antitrust law's application to athletic associations and conferences. Using Section 1 of the Sherman Act, the district court and then the court of appeals invalidated the NCAA's "REC Rule" that established a category of "restricted earnings coaches" (RECs) for Division I men's sports (except football) and capped these coaches' salaries at $16,000 per year. The courts' decisions paved the way for a jury award of money damages to a plaintiff class of 2,000–3,000 coaches and, ultimately, a $54.5 million settlement in the case that was paid in part by the NCAA directly and in part by individual Division I schools. (See Welch Suggs, "NCAA Approves Plan to Finance Settlement with Coaches," *Chron. Higher Educ.*, April 30, 1999.)

The district and appellate courts in *Law* used rule-of-reason analysis similar to that used in many of the cases above, in particular the *University of Oklahoma* case in the U.S. Supreme Court. Affirming the district court's determination that no dispute of material fact existed between the parties, the appellate court first explained that the coaches had to demonstrate that, by imposing the

---

[14]Subsequent to the *University of Oklahoma* decision, the Federal Trade Commission (FTC) challenged the television broadcasting arrangements of the College Football Association, whose members had been plaintiffs in the *University of Oklahoma* case. An FTC administrative law judge dismissed the FTC's antitrust case on jurisdictional grounds (*In re College Football Ass'n. and Capital Cities/ABC, Inc.*, Docket No. 9242 (July 29, 1991)). See generally Section 13.2.9.

REC salary cap, "the NCAA (1) participated in an agreement that (2) unreasonably restrained trade in the relevant market." The NCAA did not contest the first point in this analysis, since it was evident "that the REC rule resulted from an agreement among its members." Turning to the second part of the analysis, the court noted that the salary cap constituted the type of horizontal price fixing that would ordinarily be struck down as invalid per se under the Sherman Act. Because some horizontal agreements among member schools are necessary in order for competitive collegiate basketball to exist, however, the court used the more flexible rule of reason to determine the salary cap's legality.

The court's rule-of-reason analysis consisted of two main steps. The first step "requires a determination of whether the challenged restraint has a substantially adverse effect on competition" (anticompetitive effect). The second step requires "an evaluation of whether the procompetitive virtues of the alleged wrongful conduct justify the otherwise anticompetitive impacts" (procompetitive effect). For the first step, plaintiffs may show anticompetitive effects either indirectly by showing "that the defendant possessed the requisite market power within a defined market" or directly "by showing actual anticompetitive effects, such as control over output or price." Since the coaches were able to demonstrate that the NCAA exerted direct control over the salaries of assistant coaches, the court did not need to examine the NCAA's market power or the proper delineation of the relevant market controlled by the NCAA. (This type of analysis is referred to as "quick look rule of reason.")

For the second step of the rule-of-reason analysis, the NCAA offered several "procompetitive justifications." The NCAA argued that the salary cap would help retain positions for younger, less experienced coaches so that they might gain experience at the collegiate level. It also argued that the salary cap would help level the playing field between teams, so that no team would have the benefit of a greater number of experienced coaches than another team. The court rejected those arguments on two grounds. First, the court noted that, although there may be social value in protecting positions for young coaches, such a result may not be considered unless it has a positive impact on competition. Second, the court explained that the NCAA did not present evidence that the salary caps would actually help level the playing field among teams. The NCAA also argued that, without the salary cap, certain teams would always emerge as the winners and, consequently, NCAA competition could disappear altogether. Again, the court rejected the argument, citing the NCAA's lack of evidence to support it.

Without any demonstrated procompetitive effects to justify the salary cap, the appellate court upheld the district court's grant of summary judgment for the plaintiffs.

Various other antitrust cases involve athletic eligibility rules. In *McCormack v. NCAA*, 845 F.2d 1338 (5th Cir. 1988), for example, the court considered the legality of NCAA rules restricting compensation for student athletes. The court used rule-of-reason analysis as articulated in the *University of Oklahoma* case but held that the eligibility rules, unlike the TV rules in *University of Oklahoma*, did not violate the rule of reason. In the *McCormack* case, alumni, football players, and cheerleaders of Southern Methodist University (SMU) sued the NCAA after it had suspended and imposed sanctions on the school's football program for violating the restrictions on student-athlete compensation. Assuming without deciding that the football players had standing to sue, the court upheld the dismissal of the plaintiffs' antitrust claim. It found that, under the rule of reason, the NCAA's eligibility rules were a reasonable means of promoting the amateurism of college football. Unlike the regulations regarding the television plan in the *University of Oklahoma* case, the court found that "[i]t is reasonable to assume that most of the regulatory controls of the NCAA are justifiable means of fostering competition among amateur athletic teams and intercollegiate athletics" (845 F.2d at 1344).

Other important cases have also upheld NCAA eligibility requirements against antitrust challenges, employing a variety of reasoning. In two similar cases, football players with one year of intercollegiate eligibility remaining entered themselves in the professional football draft and used the services of an agent. Neither of the players was drafted, and each then attempted to rejoin his college—despite NCAA "no-draft" rules, which at that time prohibited players who had entered the draft or obtained an agent from returning to play. When the NCAA refused to let them play, each player sued the NCAA and their schools, challenging the no-draft rule as well as the no-agent rule under the Sherman Act.

In one of these two cases, *Banks v. NCAA*, 746 F. Supp. 850 (N.D. Ind. 1990), *affirmed*, 977 F.2d 1081 (7th Cir. 1992), the player (Banks) filed suit under Section 1 of the Sherman Act (15 U.S.C. § 1). Although acknowledging that the rule of reason was the appropriate standard for the case, the district court nevertheless rejected Banks's request for injunctive relief, because he had alleged no anticompetitive effect of the NCAA's rules even though there was clear evidence of a procompetitive effect of upholding the amateur nature of college football. The appellate court affirmed:

> Banks' allegation that the no-draft rule restrains trade is absurd. None of the NCAA rules affecting college football eligibility restrain trade in the market for college players because the NCAA does not exist as a minor league training ground for future NFL players but rather to provide an opportunity for competition among amateur students pursuing a collegiate education. . . . [T]he regulations of the NCAA are designed to preserve the honesty and integrity of intercollegiate athletics and foster fair competition among the participating amateur college students [977 F.2d at 1089–90; footnotes and citations omitted].

In the second of these two cases, *Gaines v. NCAA*, 746 F. Supp. 738 (M.D. Tenn. 1990), the student football player filed suit under Section 2 of the Sherman Act (15 U.S.C. § 2) and sought an injunction against the NCAA and Vanderbilt University to reinstate his eligibility to play football. Unlike the court in *Banks*, the *Gaines* court accepted the NCAA's argument that its eligibility rules "are not subject to antitrust analysis because they are not designed to generate profits in a commercial activity but to preserve amateurism by assuring that the recruitment of student athletes does not become a commercial activity." The court distinguished the *University of Oklahoma* case by stressing that the rules involved there had commercial objectives (generation of broadcasting profits), whereas the no-draft and no-agent rules did not. The court also held that, even if the antitrust laws did apply to the NCAA's rules, these rules did not violate Section 2 of the Sherman Act, because the NCAA's no-agent and no-draft rules were justified by legitimate business reasons. (See generally Note, "An End Run Around the Sherman Act? *Banks v. NCAA* and *Gaines v. NCAA*," 19 *J. Coll. & Univ. Law* 295 (1993).)

In *Hairston v. Pacific 10 Conference*, 101 F.3d 1315 (9th Cir. 1996), football players at the University of Washington challenged a Pac-10 decision placing the football team on probation and levying sanctions against it for recruiting violations. As in the *Banks* case, the challenge was based on Section 1 of the Sherman Act, and the argument was that the conference's sanctions constituted an unreasonable restraint of trade. The court, employing the "rule-of-reason" analysis, rejected the plaintiffs' argument. The conference had submitted evidence "showing that there are significant pro-competitive effects of punishing football programs that violate the Pac-10s amateurism rules," and the plaintiffs had not produced any evidence that "the Pac-10s pro-competitive objectives could be achieved in a substantially less restrictive manner."

In *Smith v. NCAA*, 139 F.3d 180 (3d Cir. 1998) (also discussed in subsection 14.4.6.1 below), Renee Smith, a volleyball player for two years at her undergraduate institution, challenged the NCAA's "Postbaccalaureate Bylaw" that prevented her from playing intercollegiate volleyball at either of her two postgraduate institutions. As in the *Hairston* case and the *Banks* case (above), the challenge was based on Section 1 of the Sherman Act.

Smith alleged that the NCAA's enforcement of the Postbaccalaureate Bylaw violated Section 1 "because the bylaw unreasonably restrains trade and has an adverse anticompetitive effect." The NCAA argued (as in the *Gaines* case, above) that the Sherman Act applies only to a defendant's commercial or business activities, and that enforcement of the bylaw was not such an activity. The court thus focused on the NCAA's activities—rather than on the plaintiff's injuries—and posed the question "whether antitrust laws apply only to the alleged infringer's commercial activities." The court answered in the affirmative:

> [T]he eligibility rules are not related to the NCAA's commercial or business activities. Rather than intending to provide the NCAA with a commercial advantage, the eligibility rules primarily seek to ensure fair competition in intercollegiate athletics. Based upon the Supreme Court's recognition that the Sherman Act primarily was intended to prevent unreasonable restraints in "business and commercial transactions," *Apex [Hosiery Co. v. Leader]*, 310 U.S. at 493, 60 S. Ct. at 992 [(1940)], and therefore has only limited applicability to organizations which have principally noncommercial objectives . . . , we find that the Sherman Act does not apply to the NCAA's promulgation of eligibility requirements [139 F.3d at 185–86].

In addition, the court asserted that "even if the NCAA's actions in establishing eligibility requirements were subject to the Sherman Act," it would still dismiss the plaintiff's claim:

> The NCAA's eligibility requirements are not "plainly anticompetitive," *National Soc. of Professional Engineers v. United States*, 435 U.S. 679, 692 (1978), and therefore are not per se unreasonable, see *National Collegiate Athletic Ass'n. v. Board of Regents*, 468 U.S. at 101. . . . ; McCormack, 845 F.2d at 1343-44. . . . Consequently, if the eligibility requirements were subject to the Sherman Act, we would analyze them under the rule of reason [139 F.3d at 186].

Agreeing with the *McCormack, Banks,* and *Gaines* cases, which upheld NCAA eligibility rules under the rule of reason, the court held that "the bylaw at issue here is a reasonable restraint which furthers the NCAA's goal of fair competition and the survival of intercollegiate athletics and is thus procompetitive. . . ."

In a similar case, *Tanaka v. University of Southern California*, 252 F. 3d 1059 (9th Cir. 2001), in which the Pac-10 and the NCAA were also defendants, the court rejected an antitrust challenge to a rule governing intraconference transfers. The court declined to rule on whether the intraconference transfer rule "involve[s] commercial activity" and, if not, whether it is "immune from Sherman Act scrutiny." Then, citing the *University of Oklahoma* and the *Hairston* cases (above), the court determined that, if the Sherman Act did apply, rule-of-reason analysis would apply and the plaintiff would lose because she had "failed to identify an appropriately defined product market" or to "allege that the transfer rule has had significant anticompetitive effects within a relevant market." In addition, the court ruled that the plaintiff's case failed because she had alleged "nothing more than a personal injury to herself, not an injury to a definable market;" and explained that "'[i]t is the impact upon competitive conditions in a definable market which distinguishes the antitrust violation from the ordinary business tort'" (252 F.3d at 1064, quoting *McGlinchy v. Shell Chem. Co.*, 845 F.2d 802, 812–13 (9th Cir. 1988)).

These antitrust cases, beginning with *University of Oklahoma*, clearly establish that the NCAA and other athletic associations and conferences are subject to antitrust laws, at least when their actions have some commercial purpose or impact. But their rules, even when they have anticompetitive effects, will generally not be considered per se violations of the Sherman Antitrust Act. They may be upheld under Section 1 if they are reasonable and their procompetitive impact offsets their anticompetitive impact, and they can be upheld under Section 2 if they have legitimate business justifications.

14.4.5. *Common law principles.* Even if the courts refrain from applying the Constitution to most activities of athletic associations and conferences, and even if state statutes and antitrust laws have only a narrow range of applications, associations and conferences are still limited in an important way by another relevant body of legal principles: the common law of "voluntary private associations."[15] Primarily, these principles would require the NCAA and other conferences and associations to adhere to their own rules and procedures, fairly and in good faith, in their relations with their member institutions. *California State University, Hayward v. NCAA*, 121 Cal. Rptr. 85 (Cal. Ct. App. 1975), for instance, arose after the NCAA had declared the university's athletic teams indefinitely ineligible for postseason play. The university argued that the NCAA's decision was contrary to the NCAA's own constitution and bylaws. The appellate court affirmed the trial court's issuance of a preliminary injunction against the NCAA, holding the following principle applicable to the NCAA:

> Courts will intervene in the internal affairs of associations where the action by the association is in violation of its own bylaws or constitution. "It is true that courts will not interfere with the disciplining or expelling of members of such associations where the action is taken in good faith and in accordance its adopted laws or rules. But if the decision of the [association] is contrary to its laws or rules, [or] it is not authorized by the by-laws of the association, a court may review the ruling of the [association] and direct the reinstatement of the member" [quoting another case] [121 Cal. Rptr. at 88, 89].

The case then went back to the lower court for a trial on the merits. The lower court again held in favor of the university and made its injunction against the NCAA permanent. In a second appeal, under the name *Trustees of State Colleges and Universities v. NCAA*, 147 Cal. Rptr. 187 (Cal. Ct. App. 1978), the state appellate court again affirmed the lower court, holding that the NCAA had not complied with its constitution and bylaws in imposing a penalty on the institution. The appellate court also held that, even if the institution had violated NCAA rules, under the facts of the case the NCAA was estopped from imposing a penalty on the institution. (The *Hayward* case is extensively discussed in J. D. Dickerson & M. Chapman, "Contract Law, Due Process, and the NCAA," 5 *J. Coll. & Univ. Law* 197 (1978–79).)

Hairston v. Pac-10 Conference, a case also discussed in subsection 14.4.4 above, adds another issue to the state common law analysis. The plaintiff football players argued that the Pac-10's sanctions violated the conference's constitution, bylaws, and articles. In order to make such an argument, the plaintiffs had to show not only that the Pac-10's documents created a contract between the conference and its member institutions, but also that "the players were third-party beneficiaries of this contract." The federal appellate court did not challenge the first premise, but it did reject the second premise because the plaintiffs "have not demonstrated that the parties [the university and the conference] intended to create direct legal obligations between themselves and the students." The case is therefore distinguishable from, and an interesting contrast to,

---

[15]This same body of common law also applies to private accrediting associations, as discussed in Section 14.3.2.1 & .2. Regarding the application of voluntary private association law to the NCAA, see Note, "Judicial Review of Disputes Between Athletes and the National Collegiate Athletic Association," 24 *Stan. L. Rev.* 903, 909–16 (1972).

the case of *California State University, Hayward v. NCAA* (above), which was a suit brought by the institution itself rather than by its student-athletes and, therefore, required no third-party beneficiary arguments.

The case of *Phillip v. Fairfield University & The National Collegiate Athletic Association*, 118 F.3d 131 (2d Cir. 1997), also involved a third-party beneficiary issue. The plaintiff, Phillip, a freshman at Fairfield University, had been declared academically ineligible to play basketball by the NCAA. Phillip and Fairfield sought a waiver of the academic requirements, but the NCAA denied a waiver. Phillip claimed in court that the NCAA had previously granted waivers in similar cases and that its refusal to do so here was a breach of a contractual duty of good faith and fair dealing. The district court agreed and granted Phillip a preliminary injunction, but the appellate court reversed. According to that court, the district court had not demonstrated that the NCAA owed any such contractual duty to Phillip, either as a party to or third-party beneficiary of a contract with the NCAA. Moreover, even if the NCAA did owe Phillip a duty of good faith, the duty would be breached (under Connecticut law) only if the plaintiff can show that the defendant acted with a "dishonest purpose" or "sinister motive." A showing of "arbitrary enforcement of one's own rules," standing alone, which the district court had accepted, is not sufficient. The appellate court therefore remanded the case to the district court for further proceedings.

14.4.6. Federal civil rights statutes

14.4.6.1. The civil rights spending statutes. In *National Collegiate Athletic Association v. Smith*, 525 U.S. 459 (1999), a student athlete argued that the NCAA had violated the federal Title IX statute (see Section 13.5.3 of this book) when it refused to waive its postbaccalaureate bylaw that precluded her from further participation in intercollegiate volleyball. In particular, the plaintiff contended that the NCAA granted more waivers from the bylaw to men than to women and that the refusal in her case therefore excluded her from intercollegiate competition based upon her sex.

The threshold issue was whether the NCAA was subject to Title IX because it was a "recipient" of federal funds within the meaning of the Title IX statute (see Section 13.5.7.3 of this book). The plaintiff alleged that the NCAA's member institutions receive federal funds, that the NCAA receives dues payments from these member institutions, and that the NCAA is therefore an indirect recipient of federal funding. In considering these allegations, the appellate court (*Smith v. NCAA*, 139 F.3d 180 (3d Cir. 1998), also discussed in subsection 14.4.4 above) had analogized to *Grove City College v. Bell*, 465 U.S. 555 (1984) (Section 13.5.7.3 of this book), which held that the college was a "recipient" of federal funds under Title IX even though it received the funds indirectly from students who had received federal financial aid awards. Given the holding in *Grove City*, and "given the breadth of the language of the Title IX regulation defining recipient" (34 C.F.R. § 106.2(h)), said the appellate court, the plaintiff's allegations "if proven, would subject the NCAA to the requirements of Title IX."

On further appeal, the U.S. Supreme Court reversed the appellate court's decision, holding that the NCAA is not subject to the provisions of Title IX merely because it receives federal funds indirectly through its member institutions in the form of membership dues. Distinguishing its earlier decision in *Grove City,* the Court noted that no part of the federal funds granted to NCAA member institutions were specifically earmarked for payment of NCAA dues. Furthermore, the Court relied on its decision in *U.S. Department of Transportation v. Paralyzed Veterans of America,* 477 U.S. 597 (1986), in which it rejected the argument that a party benefiting from federal funds, even though it is not a recipient as such, must comply with statutes governing federal fund recipients. Since the NCAA was not the recipient of the federal funds—being a beneficiary rather than a recipient—it was not governed by Title IX. Similarly, the Court addressed the applicability to the NCAA of the U.S. Department of Education regulation defining a "recipient" for purposes of Title IX. The Court determined that, read in its entirety, the language limits "recipients" to entities "to whom Federal financial assistance is extended directly or through another recipient," and that this language did not cover mere beneficiaries. Thus, "entities that receive federal assistance, whether directly or through an intermediary, are recipients within the meaning of Title IX; entities that only benefit economically from federal assistance are not" (525 U.S. at 468).

Although the Court thus rejected the plaintiff's arguments for applying Title IX, the final segment of the Court's opinion described other theories under which the NCAA could possibly be classified as a federal funds recipient and consequently subjected to Title IX. The majority noted both the theory that the NCAA receives direct federal funding for its National Youth Sports Program (NYSP), and the theory that "when a recipient cedes controlling authority over a federally funded program to another entity, the controlling entity is covered by Title IX, regardless of whether it is itself a recipient." Since these issues were not properly raised by the appeal, the Court did not rule on the viability of these alternative theories.

In *Cureton v. NCAA,* 198 F.3d 107 (3d Cir. 1999) (*Cureton I*), *reversing* 37 F. Supp. 2d 687 (E.D. Pa. 1999), the court wrestled with the issues left open by the U.S. Supreme Court's decision in *Smith.* While *Cureton* arose under Title VI (see Section 13.5.2 of this book) rather than Title IX as in *Smith,* it is apparent from the Court's opinion in Smith that analysis the NCAA's status under the civil rights spending statutes will be comparable under all four statutes. In *Cureton,* therefore, and presumably in other cases under any of the statutes, the two conceptual issues that frame the analysis are the same as in *Smith:* (1) whether the NCAA is a "program or activity," and (2) whether the NCAA is "receiving Federal financial assistance."

Cureton concerned a challenge by two African American athletes to the NCAA's Proposition 16, setting academic requirements for initial eligibility for intercollegiate Division I competition. The plaintiffs argued that the SAT score portion of Proposition 16 had a "disparate impact" on African American student athletes and therefore violated the Title VI regulations. (See Section 13.5.7.2 regarding disparate impact and Title VI.) The NCAA's first defense to the suit was that it is not subject to Title VI. The district court held that the NCAA was subject to Title VI and that the plaintiffs had established their disparate impact claim. Regarding the first point, the district court adopted two theories to support its application of Title VI to the NCAA: that the NCAA was an "indirect recipient" of federal funds because (1) it effectively controlled funds the government had granted to the National Youth Sport Program, an affiliate organization of the NCAA; and (2) it had "controlling authority" over its member schools, which were direct recipients of federal funds.

By a 2-to-1 vote, the court of appeals reversed the district court, disagreeing with both of its coverage theories. Regarding the first theory, the appellate court determined that, even if the NCAA did "receive" the NYSP grant funds, Title VI would apply only to discrimination in the specific *program or activity* that received the funds. That program or activity was the NYSP, which was not the focus of the plaintiffs' complaint. "It therefore inexorably follows," said the court, "that, to the extent this action is predicated on the NCAA's receiving Federal financial assistance by reason of grants to the [NYSP], it must fail as the Fund's programs and activities are not at issue in this case" (198 F.3d at 115). Regarding the second coverage theory, the court of appeals majority flatly rejected it, prompting a lengthy dissent from the panel's third member. The majority noted that, under the Supreme Court's decision in *NCAA v. Smith* (above), "the controlling authority argument can be sustained, if at all, only on some basis beyond the NCAA's mere receipt of dues"; and the plaintiffs had not demonstrated any other basis:

> [T]he ultimate decision as to which freshmen an institution will permit to participate in varsity intercollegiate athletics and which applicants will be awarded athletic scholarships belongs to the member schools. The fact that the institutions make these decisions cognizant of NCAA sanctions does not mean that the NCAA controls them, because they have the option, albeit unpalatable, of risking sanctions, or voluntarily withdrawing from the NCAA. . . . We emphasize that the NCAA members have not ceded controlling authority to the NCAA by giving it the power to enforce its eligibility rules directly against students [198 F.3d at 117–18].

In another case decided before *Smith* or *Cureton,* the court considered the applicability of Section 504 (Section 13.5.4 of this book) to the NCAA. In *Bowers v. NCAA,* 9 F. Supp. 2d 460 (D.N.J. 1998), a student who had taken special education classes as a result of a learning disability was recruited to play football by several colleges and universities. Because the NCAA would not certify his special education classes as "core courses," Bowers was unable to satisfy the NCAA's academic eligibility requirements. He brought suit under Section 504, as well as the federal Americans With Disabilities Act (ADA) and a New Jersey state nondiscrimination law. (The ADA aspects of *Bowers* are discussed below in subsection 14.4.6.2 below.) The *Bowers* court focused on the NCAA's National Youth Sports Program Fund (as had the district court in *Cureton*) and acknowledged that it was, in fact, a direct recipient of federal funds. Although the NCAA attempted to disassociate itself from the fund, the court held that the relationship between the NCAA and the fund was to be determined at trial. The court therefore denied the NCAA's motion for summary judgment on the Section 504 claim. The court's opinion does not directly address the "program or activity" issue later raised with respect to the NYSP by the *Cureton* appellate court.

Additional issues arose in the wake of the Third Circuit's decision in *Cureton I* (above). In further proceedings in that case, and in another related case, the same court considered what type of discrimination claims may be brought against the NCAA if it is subjected to the civil rights spending statutes. After being reversed by the Third Circuit, the district court in *Cureton I* entered summary judgment for the NCAA. The plaintiffs then moved to amend the summary judgment order and amend their complaint to allege a claim of intentional discrimination. When the district court denied the motion, they appealed again to the Third Circuit. In *Cureton v. NCAA (Cureton II)*, 252 F.3d 267 (3d Cir. 2001), the appellate court affirmed the district court's denial of the plaintiff's motion, holding that the district court had not abused its discretion. The appellate court also noted that in *Alexander v. Sandoval*, 532 U.S. 275 (2001) (see Section 13.5.7.2 of this book), decided just before *Cureton II*, the U.S. Supreme Court had ruled that plaintiffs could not bring disparate impact (unintentional discrimination) claims under Title VI.

Two months after the appellate court's decision in *Cureton II*, the district court judge who had decided *Cureton I* and *Cureton II* dismissed another case, similar to the *Cureton* case, except that the African American student athletes claimed that the NCAA had engaged in *intentional* race discrimination through its adoption and implementation of Proposition 16 (*Pryor v. NCAA*, 153 F. Supp. 2d 710 (E.D. Pa. 2001)). On appeal (288 F.3d 548 (3d Cir. 2002)), the Third Circuit reversed the district court's decision, holding that the students had stated a valid claim of *intentional* race discrimination under Title VI and Section 1981 (42 U.S.C. § 1981; see Sections 5.2.4 & 8.2.4.1 of this book).

The alleged disparate impact of Proposition 16 on minority athletes, combined with allegations of the NCAA's purposeful consideration of race, provided the basis for the plaintiff's claim of intentional discrimination. Relying on the U.S. Supreme Court's decision in the *Feeney* case (see Section 5.2.7), the plaintiffs claimed that the "NCAA adopted Proposition 16 'because of' its alleged adverse impact on African American athletes." The NCAA countered that their data forecast an increase in graduation rates among student athletes, particularly African American student athletes, if Proposition 16 was implemented; and that this benefit to student athletes should justify the consideration of race in creating and implementing the athletic eligibility requirements. The Third Circuit sided with the plaintiffs. (At the same time it confirmed, as had the panel in *Cureton II*, that the Supreme Court's decision in *Sandoval* precluded the plaintiffs from bringing a disparate impact claim under the Title VI statute or regulations.) The appellate court in *Pryor* then determined that, on remand, if the plaintiffs could prove that the NCAA had intentionally discriminated against African American student athletes, the NCAA would then need to prove that its actions survived the strict scrutiny standard of review. "Laudable" or "beneficial" goals standing alone, the court warned, would not be an adequate defense to an intentional discrimination claim. "[C]onsiderations of race, well-intentioned or not, can still subject a decision-maker to liability for purposeful discrimination" under Title VI and Section 1981 (288 F.3d at 560–61).

14.4.6.2. The Americans with Disabilities Act. In addition to the decisions on the civil rights spending statutes, various courts have examined whether the NCAA is subject to the requirements of Title III of the Americans With Disabilities Act (ADA) (Section 13.2.11 of this book). The primary issue is whether the NCAA "operates a place of public accommodation" within the meaning of Title III (42 U.S.C. § 12182(a)).

A line of federal district court decisions suggests an affirmative answer to this question. In *Ganden v. NCAA,* 1996 WL 680000 (N.D. Ill. 1996), for example, the plaintiff Ganden was a swimmer who was denied NCAA academic eligibility to compete for Michigan State University (MSU) on its swim team. He had been diagnosed in the second grade with a learning disability that affected his reading and writing. During his high school years, he followed a specially developed curriculum addressing his educational weaknesses. Ganden filed suit against the NCAA, alleging that its denial of eligibility was disability discrimination violating Title III of the ADA. He sought a preliminary injunction permitting him to compete with the MSU swim team during his freshman year. In order to state a viable Title III claim, a plaintiff such as Ganden must allege as a threshold matter that the defendant falls within the statute's "public accommodation" category. The court considered two approaches for determining whether the NCAA did so. First, if the NCAA is itself a "place of public accommodation," it is subject to the provisions of Title III. Alternatively, if the NCAA "operates" a place of public accommodation, it is subject to Title III.

To reach a membership organization such as the NCAA under the first theory, said the *Ganden* court, the organization must meet the two requirements set out in *Welsh v. Boy Scouts of America,* 993 F.2d 1267, 1270 (7th Cir. 1993): "(1) the organization is affiliated with a particular facility, and (2) membership in (or certification by) that organization acts as a necessary predicate to use of the facility." Using this analysis, the court found that the NCAA does have such a connection to the athletic facilities of its member institutions: "It is evident that the NCAA . . . has a connection to a number of public accommodations; the athletic facilities of its member institutions. . . . NCAA events occur in stadiums or arenas, open to the public, with a significant number of competitors, support staff and fans" (1996 WL at 10). Moreover, said the court, the NCAA exercises control over its members' athletic facilities and students' access to these facilities. Therefore, Ganden could likely demonstrate that NCAA membership functions as a predicate to use of the facility.

Regarding the second theory, the court found that Ganden could also likely show that the NCAA "operates" a place of public accommodation because "the member institutions may have delegated to the NCAA a more significant degree of control over the management of the competitions and use of its facilities." There was thus a reasonable likelihood that the NCAA operates the MSU swimming facilities for the purposes of Title III. The court emphasized that it was irrelevant whether MSU actually owned and also "operated" the facilities at issue; even if this were true, "the NCAA may also 'operate' those facilities for purposes of Title III."

Three additional cases provide further insight into the NCAA's status as a place of public accommodation. A federal district court in Missouri addressed the issue in *Tatum v. National Collegiate Athletic Association*, 992 F. Supp. 1114 (E.D. Mo. 1998), a case brought by a freshman basketball player at Saint Louis University. Largely adopting the analysis of the *Ganden* court, the court in *Tatum* gave additional detail to the argument that the NCAA operates a place of public accommodation. Citing several NCAA bylaws that demonstrate its control over facilities of member institutions, the court determined that these bylaws:

> permit member institutions to reserve athletic training facilities for student-athletes only; direct under what guidelines a student-athlete may voluntarily choose to use the athletic training facilities; regulate the number of days a student-athlete may practice in the athletic training facilities; control what equipment may be used while the student-athlete uses the athletic training facilities; control the type of "conditioning activities" the student athlete may use; control the conditions surrounding when a student-athlete may seek advice or instruction from a coach; and regulate under what conditions individuals not enrolled in the school may use the athletic training facilities. . . . [Also], the NCAA exerts significant control over the operation of stadiums and auditoriums including: regulating ticket prices; controlling the types of beverages and goods that vendors may sell; regulating profits which may be earned from concession sales; controlling which press members may broadcast from the stadiums; and controlling which institutions are allowed to play in the stadiums [citation omitted]. Additionally, with regard to championship events and tournaments, plaintiff has shown that the NCAA actually leases athletic facilities [992 F. Supp. at 1120].

Embracing similar reasoning, another federal district court in New Jersey rejected the NCAA's motion for summary judgment in *Bowers v. National Collegiate Athletic Association*, 9 F. Supp. 2d 460 (D.N.J. 1998). Much like the *Ganden* and *Tatum* cases, *Bowers* involved a student who, as a result of a learning disability, had received special education throughout his primary and secondary education. He played football during high school and was recruited by numerous colleges and universities. Due to the NCAA's refusal to recognize his special education classes as "core courses," Bowers was unable to satisfy the NCAA's academic eligibility requirements.

Unlike the *Ganden* and *Tatum* courts, however, the *Bowers* court found that the NCAA is not itself a place of public accommodation. Citing an earlier decision, the court held "that a public accommodation within the meaning of 42 U.S.C. § 12181(7) is a physical place" (citing *Ford v. Schering-Plough*, 1998 WL 258386 (3d Cir. 1998)). As a result of *Schering-Plough*, the court explained, the *Welsh* test as used in *Ganden* and *Tatum* "has now been repudiated in this Circuit." Since the NCAA is not itself a physical place, it could not be deemed a place of public accommodation.

Although the NCAA was not itself a place of public accommodation, the *Bowers* court determined that mere operation of a place of public accommodation was sufficient to bring the NCAA within the scope of Title III. Then, investigating Bowers's allegations in his complaint, the court concluded that they "adequately allege that the NCAA at least operates the place or places of public accommodation of which Bowers was allegedly denied enjoyment," and that the NCAA operated these public accommodations "in such a way that the NCAA manages, regulates, or controls discriminatory conditions of that place or places . . . (9 F. Supp. 2d at 487).

In a later case, *Matthews v. National Collegiate Athletic Association,* 179 F. Supp. 2d 1209 (E.D. Wash. 2001), another federal district court looked favorably upon the ADA Title III claim of a learning-disabled student athlete. The plaintiff had been denied a waiver of the NCAA's "75/25 Rule," which requires athletes to earn at least 75 percent of their required academic credits in the regular school year, and not the summer. The court discussed and agreed with much of the reasoning in *Ganden, Tatum,* and *Bowers,* and concluded that the NCAA was subject to ADA Title III because it operated places of public accommodation. The court in *Matthews,* like the courts in *Tatum* and *Bowers,* focused particularly on the NCAA's control over access to athletic facilities; but unlike the earlier courts, it emphasized that both access for spectators and access for the athletes were pertinent: "the ADA applies not only to entities governing spectators' access to a sports facility but also to those entities governing athletes' access to the competition itself." For this proposition, the court cited the U.S. Supreme Court's decision in *PGA Tour, Inc. v. Martin,* 532 U.S. 661 (2001), holding that the PGA Tour is a place of public accommodation that must make reasonable accommodations for disabled golfers in PGA tournaments.

In each of these cases—*Ganden, Tatum, Bowers,* and *Matthews*—the courts were able to develop bases for bringing the NCAA under the requirements of Title III of the ADA. Emphasizing the NCAA's control of member institutions and their athletic programs and facilities through NCAA regulations, the courts each found sufficient allegations or evidence of control to support the classification of the NCAA as an operator of a place of public accommodation under the ADA.

In addition to the courts' discussions respecting the NCAA's fit within the public accommodations category, *Ganden, Tatum, Bowers,* and *Matthews* provide useful analysis of the alleged discriminatory character of NCAA academic eligibility requirements as applied to learning disabled athletes. In *Ganden,* for instance, the plaintiff alleged that "(1) the NCAA relied upon an eligibility criterion that 'screened' him out on the basis of his disability as prohibited under section 12182 (b)(2)(A)(i) [of the ADA;] and (2) the NCAA refused to make reasonable modifications to its eligibility requirements that discriminated against him on the basis of his disability as required under section 12182 (b)(2)(A)(ii)." In order to meet the NCAA's academic eligibility requirements for Division I schools, students must take "at least thirteen high school 'core courses'" and attain a GPA in those courses as determined by the student's performance on a standardized test; "the higher the test score, the lower the required GPA."

Because Ganden suffered from a learning disability, he took several remedial courses, which were not certifiable as "core courses" under the NCAA's requirements. Thus, Ganden argued that the "core course" requirement screened him out on the basis of his disability. The court was receptive to his argument that he had been discriminatorily screened out: "Because the NCAA's definition of 'core course' explicitly excludes special education, compensatory and remedial courses, this definition provides at least a prima facie case of disparate impact on learning disabled students."

The court in *Ganden* then addressed the requirement that a covered entity must make reasonable modifications to its policies that deny full access to disabled individuals, unless it can demonstrate that those modifications would "fundamentally alter" the entity's mission. Ganden suggested several modifications that he believed would not work such a fundamental alteration, including (1) a modification of the NCAA's "core course" requirement so that it would include two additional courses taken by Ganden; (2) a modified GPA requirement that took account of Ganden's improving academic record and other indications of his ability to succeed in college; and (3) a more open process for obtaining waivers of NCAA rules that would allow students and counselors direct participation in the process. The NCAA argued that it had already provided adequate modifications to Ganden, including a variation of its "core course" requirement and a lengthy discussion of a potential waiver. In considering these arguments, the court assessed the "purpose" and "reasonableness" of the NCAA academic eligibility requirements and waiver process and the effect that Ganden's proposed modifications would have on the NCAA's pursuit of its objectives. In this context, the modifications that the NCAA had already provided to Ganden were sufficient, in the court's view, to preclude Ganden's motion for preliminary injunction.

Similarly, in *Matthews* (above), the court indicated that a waiver of the 75/25 Rule would be a reasonable accommodation for that particular student athlete. The court drew its guidelines for this inquiry in part from *Bowers* and *Ganden* (along with a later case, *Cole v. National Collegiate Athletic Association,* 120 F. Supp. 2d 1060 (N.D. Ga. 2000)), and in part from the subsequent U.S. Supreme Court decision in *PGA Tour, Inc. v. Martin* (above).

In contrast to *Ganden* and *Matthews,* the *Bowers* court did not suggest that the NCAA had provided sufficient modifications to its eligibility requirements. Specifically, the court questioned the sufficiency of the NCAA waiver process because of its timing (9 F. Supp. 2d at 476–77, 490). Generally, the waiver process could only be initiated after a student had graduated from high school— a time long after college recruiting has concluded, and a time when the student no longer has any means to correct insufficiencies in his or her academic record. Also, the waiver procedure may be completed so late that, even if the student is granted a waiver, he or she may have missed the opportunity to compete in the fall athletic season.

In response to complaints such as those that led to the litigation between student athletes and the NCAA, the U.S. Department of Justice (DOJ) initiated an investigation of the NCAA's academic eligibility requirements. The investigation resulted in a complaint filed by the DOJ against the NCAA in the U.S. District Court for the District of Columbia, and an agreement between DOJ and the NCAA was embodied in a consent decree issued by that court in May 1998. (The complaint and the consent decree may be found at http://www.usdoj. gov/crt/ada/ncaacomp.htm.) Although the consent decree does not itself settle other pending litigation against the NCAA or preclude later litigation on similar issues, it does provide a basis for resolving or preventing problems such as those raised in *Ganden, Tatum, Bowers,* and *Matthews.* Under the decree, for instance, the NCAA was to certify as "core courses" classes designed for students with learning disabilities when these classes "are substantially comparable, quantitatively and qualitatively, to similar core course offerings in that academic discipline." The NCAA also was to adopt specific practices for granting initial eligibility waivers to learning disabled students. Although the decree provides that "the NCAA voluntarily agrees that any further legislative action by the NCAA will comply with Title III of the ADA," the parties also acknowledged that "the NCAA does not waive its position that it is not a place of public accommodation and therefore Title III of the ADA does not apply to it, nor does the NCAA admit liability under the ADA." The decree remained in effect until May 1, 2003.

Sec. 14.5. The American Association of University Professors

The American Association of University Professors (AAUP) is an organization of college and university faculty, librarians with faculty status, and graduate students. Administrators may be associate members but may not vote on AAUP policies. Since its inception in 1915, the AAUP has focused on developing "standards for sound academic practice" and affording faculty the protections of these standards. The organization was formed by a group of faculty, headed by John Dewey, in reaction to criticisms of the university from external and internal sources.[16] Early members were concerned about protecting academic freedom, developing a code of ethics, and creating agreed-upon standards for promotion through the faculty ranks. They also had a strong interest in strengthening and ensuring the faculty's role in institutional governance. Committees were established, most of which still exist today, on academic freedom and tenure (Committee A), appointment and promotion (Committee B), recruitment of faculty (Committee C), and a variety of other issues of concern to faculty, such as pensions and salaries.

The AAUP has led the movement to develop principles and standards that regulate faculty employment relationships. By the end of its founding year, 1915, the association issued a seminal declaration on academic freedom. In 1934, the AAUP and the Association of American Colleges (whose members were primarily liberal arts colleges) began developing what culminated in the "1940 Statement of Principles on Academic Freedom and Tenure," which more than 150 educational organizations have endorsed. Among the many other policy statements and

---

[16]This discussion relies on W. P. Metzger's "Origins of the Association," 51 *AAUP Bulletin* 229 (1965).

committee reports developed since the 1940 Statement are statements on procedural standards for the dismissal of faculty; recommended institutional regulations on academic freedom and tenure (including the standards for terminating faculty appointments on the grounds of financial exigency); and statements on discrimination, academic governance, and collective bargaining.

Committees deliberate about issues of significance to the academic community (such as the disclosure of confidential peer evaluations to candidates for promotion and tenure). The draft report circulates and then is presented to the membership for its comments. Administrators and other national organizations frequently provide comments as well. A revised version of the policy is then published and may be adopted by the association's governing body. Thus, by the time the policies and standards are published in final form, the academic community has been heavily involved in developing and refining them. The major policies, standards, and reports are collected in *AAUP Policy Documents and Reports* (9th ed., 2001), which is known as the "Redbook." According to two scholars long involved in the work of the AAUP:

> The policy documents of the American Association of University Professors may be used in any of three ways. First, they offer guidance to all components of the academic community either for the development of institutional policy or for the resolution of concrete issues as they arise. Second, some documents, like the *Recommended Institutional Regulations on Academic Freedom and Tenure* (RIR), are fashioned in a form that is explicitly adaptable as official institutional policy, and they formalize particular advice the AAUP staff gives in recurring situations. . . . [Third,] parties to lawsuits—both administrators and faculty—have begun to invoke AAUP standards to buttress their cases, either because these standards express academic custom generally or because they serve as an aid to the interpretation of institutional regulations or policies that derive from AAUP sources [R. S. Brown, Jr., & M. W. Finkin, "The Usefulness of AAUP Policy Statements," 59 *Educ. Record* 30 (1978)].

Many colleges and universities have incorporated the 1940 Statement into their policies and procedures, or into their collective bargaining agreements with faculty unions. Some institutions have incorporated other policy statements as well. If a college has explicitly incorporated an AAUP policy statement as institutional policy, the provisions of that statement are contractually binding on the institution (see Section 7.1.3 of this book). Even if the college has not formally incorporated the policy statement, it may have acted in conformance with its provisions over a long period of years; in such instances the policy statement may be regarded as binding under a theory of implied contract (see Section 6.2.2). Finally, in some cases (for instance, *Greene v. Howard University,* discussed in Section 6.2.3), courts have looked to AAUP policy statements as authoritative sources of academic custom and usage (see Section 1.4.3.3). Examples of the use of AAUP standards in litigation involving faculty status may be found in Sections 6.6.2 and 6.8.2. Thus, in various ways faculty members, institutions, and courts use AAUP standards and policies as guides to interpreting college policies, regulations, and faculty handbooks:

> The absence of detailed individual contracts, which are not common in the academic world, makes such documents the chief source of guidance toward the rights and duties of all parties. When regulations use terms customary in the academic world like "tenure," it is helpful to look to the academic community's understanding about what the term means, which to a large extent is found in the 1940 *Statement* and the commentary upon it [Introduction to *AAUP Policy Documents and Reports*, at xii].

Although its concerns are myriad, the AAUP historically has been most active in the area of the protection of faculty members' academic freedom and tenure rights (see Section 7.1.3 of this book). In fact, the AAUP's first investigation of academic freedom violations occurred in 1915, the year of its founding, when seventeen members of the University of Utah faculty resigned, protesting the discharge of several faculty members. As word of the new organization's existence spread, faculty at other institutions sought the AAUP's assistance, and thirteen cases of allegedly unjust dismissals were referred to the organization in the first year of its existence.[17] The organization reviews approximately two thousand inquiries each year on specific problems related to AAUP standards (J. Kurland, "Implementing AAUP Standards," 66 *Academe*, 1980, 414).

Approximately half of these inquiries are resolved with a single response; the other half involve a formal complaint by a faculty member against one or more administrators or against faculty colleagues. In these cases, the AAUP staff provide assistance in settling the dispute, and in some instances a group of AAUP members may investigate the complaint by visiting the institution and talking with the parties involved. Reports of the investigation of certain cases are published periodically in the AAUP's journal, *Academe*. If the membership believes that alleged violations of its principles of academic freedom or governance are sufficiently egregious and the institution is apparently not amenable to resolving these violations to the satisfaction of the membership, the membership may vote to sanction the institution's administration. As of late 2005, forty-five colleges and universities were on the list of censured administrations, including two that have been on the list since the 1960s and six that have been on the list since the 1970s. (For a history of the "censure list" and its use to protect academic freedom, see Jonathan Knight, "The AAUP's Censure List," 89 *Academe*, January–February 2003, 44.)

An area of AAUP activity that has created some controversy both outside and within the organization is its role in faculty collective bargaining. Discussions concerning a possible role for the AAUP in this regard began in the mid-1960s,

---

[17]For an account of the investigation of the University of Utah incidents and related historical information, see W. P. Metzger, "The First Investigation," 47 *AAUP Bulletin* 206 (1961).

when faculty at several large public colleges and universities began to organize into unions. Between that time and 1971, vigorous debates over the propriety of the association's serving as a bargaining agent occurred, and in 1971 the association's council adopted the following position:

> The Association will pursue collective bargaining as a major additional way of realizing the Association's goals in higher education, and will allocate such resources and staff as are necessary for the vigorous selective development of this activity beyond present levels ["Council Position on Collective Bargaining," 58 *AAUP Bulletin* 46 (1972)].

Local AAUP chapters thus joined local chapters of the National Education Association and the American Federation of Teachers in competing to represent the collective interests of faculty at various colleges and universities. The national association provides advice, assistance with contract negotiation if necessary, and other assistance to the local chapters, which act as the "union" for collective bargaining purposes. (For discussion of the activities of these three associations in the early days of faculty bargaining, see J. W. Garbarino, *Faculty Bargaining: Change and Conflict* (McGraw-Hill, 1975).)

A final area of AAUP activity is in the monitoring of legislation and litigation involving faculty status and academic freedom issues. The AAUP has provided *amicus* briefs in many significant cases, including *University of Pennsylvania v. EEOC* (discussed in Section 7.7.2); *Regents of the University of Michigan v. Ewing* (discussed in Section 9.3.2); *Board of Regents v. Roth* and *Perry v. Sindermann* (discussed in Section 6.7.2.1); and cases in Section 7.1.4. Although the association has a small Washington-based professional staff, much of its work depends on the talent and energy of its volunteer members, whose efforts have provided the academic community with significant guidance on standards and norms.

Sec. 14.6. Dealing with the Education Associations

Since educational associations can provide many benefits for institutions and their officers and personnel (see Section 14.1 above), postsecondary administrators should be knowledgeable about the various associations and their roles within academia. Armed with this knowledge, administrators should be able to make appropriate decisions about the institution's associational memberships and support of association goals, and about the institution's means for helping its personnel join and participate in associations that support their own job functions. In addition, administrators should have particular familiarity with those associations whose work most closely parallels their own, and should reserve time for their own participation in these associations.

Administrators who need specific information about a particular association's organization and operation may find it in the association's bylaws, rules, standards, and official statements, as well as in charters or articles of incorporation or association. Associations may make such documents available on their Web sites (see Section 14.1 above and footnote 1 in that section), or otherwise upon request, at least for members. Administrators can insist that, in its dealings with the institution, the association scrupulously follow the policies set out in these sources. The institution may have a legally enforceable claim against the association if it fails to do so, at least if the association is a membership association and the institution is a member. (See Sections 14.2, 14.3.2.2, & 14.4.5 above.)

If an institution's relationship with an association should become potentially adverse, institutional administrators should be sure that they have copies of the association's evaluative standards or criteria, the procedures that it follows in making adverse decisions about an institution, and the procedures that institutions can follow in appealing adverse decisions. A full understanding of the standards and procedures can be critical to effective representation of the institution before the association. In particular, administrators should take advantage of all dispute resolution mechanisms and all procedural rights, such as notice and hearing, that association rules provide in situations where institutional interests are in jeopardy. If associational rules are unclear or do not provide sufficient procedural safeguards, administrators will want to seek clarifications or additional safeguards from the association. Good communications between institutional administrators and counsel will be important, so that sensitive decisions can be made about whether or when the institution should assume an adversarial posture with the association, and whether or when counsel should become the institution's spokesperson with the association.

If the institution is subjected to an adverse association decision that appears to violate the association's own rules or the legal requirements developed in court cases, the first recourse usually is to exhaust all the association's internal appeals processes. Simultaneously, institutional administrators and counsel may want to negotiate with the association about ways that the institution can alleviate the association's concerns or comply with its rulings without undue burden on the institution. If negotiations and internal appeals fail to achieve a resolution satisfactory to the institution, outside recourse to the courts may be possible (see generally Section 2.2.6). But court actions should be a last resort, pursued only in exceptional circumstances and only when reasonable prospects for resolution within the association have ended.

Thus, the process for resolving disputes with education associations parallels the process for most other legal issues in this book. Courts may have a presence, but in the end it is usually in the best interests of academia for institutions and private educational associations to develop the capacity for constructive internal resolution of disputes. As long as affected parties have meaningful access to the internal process, and the process works fairly, courts and government agencies should allow it ample breathing space to permit educational expertise to operate. It should be a central goal of postsecondary institutions and educational associations to facilitate such constructive accommodations in the interests of all participants in the postsecondary community.

Selected Annotated Bibliography

Sec. 14.1 (Overview of the Education Associations)

Bloland, Harland. *Associations in Action: The Washington, D.C. Higher Education Community,* ASHE-ERIC Higher Education Report no. 2 (Association for the Study of Higher Education, 1985). Reviews the historical and political development of the associations that represent various higher education constituencies. Focuses on the activities and developing sophistication of the associations between 1960 and the mid-1980s.

Cook, Constance Ewing. *Lobbying for Higher Education: How Colleges and Universities Influence Federal Policy* (Vanderbilt University Press, 1998). Presents a history of lobbying by higher education associations, discusses differences in priorities and strategies in lobbying among institutions, describes the various lobbying techniques, and provides guidance for college presidents. Examines the effect of the proliferation of higher education associations on lobbying, and summarizes the benefits and limitations of lobbying by associations. Portions of the book are based on a survey of college and university presidents.

Hawkins, Hugh. *Banding Together: The Rise of National Associations in American Higher Education, 1887–1950* (Johns Hopkins University Press, 1992). Traces the history of four national higher education associations: the Association of American Colleges, the Association of American Universities, the American Council on Education, and the National Association of State Universities and Land-Grant Colleges. Discusses their transformation from organizations of scholar-administrators to lobbyists and shapers of post–World War II American higher education.

Parsons, Michael. *Power and Politics: Federal Higher Education Policymaking in the 1990s* (State University of New York Press, 1997). Reviews the events leading to the 1992 reauthorization of the Higher Education Act. Discusses direct loans, national service, and the effect of the Republican majority in Congress on federal student aid policy.

Washington Information Directory (Congressional Quarterly, published biannually). A section on "Education and Culture" lists relevant associations located in the metropolitan Washington, D.C., area.

Sec. 14.2 (Applicable Legal Principles)

Developments in the Law, "Judicial Control of Actions of Private Associations," 76 *Harvard L. Rev.* 983 (1963). A classical and comprehensive treatment of the legal status of private voluntary associations, with extensive citation of American case law to 1963 and its British predecessors.

See Oleck entry in Selected Annotated Bibliography for Section 12.3.

Sec. 14.3 (The College and the Accrediting Agencies)

Finkin, Matthew. "Federal Reliance and Voluntary Accreditation: The Power to Recognize as the Power to Regulate," 2 *J. Law & Educ.* 339 (1973). An overview of the accreditation process and the role of the federal government in that process. Emphasizes the evolution—through the various federal aid-to-education statutes—of the relationship between private accrediting agencies and the U.S. Office of

Education, and the legal basis for the Office (now Department) of Education's recognition function. Author later published a sequel to this article (*Federal Reliance on Educational Accreditation: The Scope of Administrative Discretion* (Council on Postsecondary Accreditation (1978)). Article and sequel are primarily of historical interest, given later legal developments such as the 1992 and 1998 Amendments to the Higher Education Act.

Finkin, Matthew W. "The Unfolding Tendency in the Federal Relationship to Private Accreditation in Higher Education," 57 *Law & Contemp. Probs.* 89 (1994). Reviews the origins and the structure of higher education accreditation. Critiques the connection between accrediting agencies and the federal government, the legislation creating this connection, and the ongoing controversy regarding this connection. The author expresses concern regarding the further development of the relationship between accrediting agencies and the federal government as it impacts on higher education institutions.

Fisk, Robert S., & Duryea, E. D. *Academic Collective Bargaining and Regional Accreditation* (Council on Postsecondary Accreditation, 1977). A COPA Occasional Paper. Analyzes the potential impact of collective bargaining on regional accreditation and on the relationship between the institution and the agency that accredits it. Provides helpful perspective for administrators who must deal with accrediting agencies in circumstances where their faculty is unionized.

Heilbron, Louis H. *Confidentiality and Accreditation* (Council on Postsecondary Accreditation, 1976). Another COPA Occasional Paper. Examines various issues concerning the confidentiality of an accrediting agency's records and other agency information regarding individual institutions. Discusses the kinds of information the accrediting agency may collect, the institution's right to obtain such information, and the accrediting agency's right to maintain the confidentiality of such information by denying claims of federal or state agencies, courts, or other third parties seeking the disclosure.

Kaplin, William A. "Judicial Review of Accreditation: The *Parsons College* Case," 40 *J. Higher Educ.* 543 (1969). Analyzes the *Parsons College* case and evaluates its impact on accreditation and the courts.

Kaplin, William A. "The *Marjorie Webster* Decisions on Accreditation," 52 *Educ. Record* 219 (1971). Analyzes the antitrust law, common law, and constitutional law aspects of the *Marjorie Webster* case and evaluates its impact on accreditation.

Kaplin, William A. *Respective Roles of Federal Government, State Governments, and Private Accrediting Agencies in the Governance of Postsecondary Education* (Council on Postsecondary Accreditation, 1975). Another COPA Occasional Paper. Examines the current and potential future roles of federal and state governments and the accrediting agencies, particularly with regard to determining eligibility for federal funding under U.S. Office (now Department) of Education programs. Useful background for understanding the Higher Education Amendments of 1992 and 1998 as they affect accreditation.

Martin, Jeffrey C. "Recent Developments Concerning Accrediting Agencies in Postsecondary Education," 57 *Law & Contemp. Probs.* 121 (1994). Reviews recent controversies regarding accreditation, including the use of accrediting standards to impose racial and gender diversity requirements on institutions, the accreditation of proprietary schools, and the federal government's role in recognizing accrediting agencies.

Project on Nontraditional Education Final Reports (Council on Postsecondary Accreditation, 1978). Product of a project sponsored by COPA and funded by the W. K. Kellogg Foundation. Discusses problems encountered in accrediting innovative or nontraditional programs and institutions. The four-volume set includes a summary report by project director Grover Andrews (Vol. 1) and nine individual reports (Vols. 2–4), including the following: J. Harris, "Institutional Accreditation and Nontraditional Undergraduate Educational Institutions and Programs" (Rpt. No. 3); P. Dressel, "Problems and Principles in the Recognition or Accreditation of Graduate Education" (Rpt. No. 4); and J. Harris, "Critical Characteristics of an Accreditable Institution, Basic Purposes of Accreditation, and Nontraditional Forms of Most Concern" (Rpt. No. 5).

Selden, William K., & Porter, Harry V. *Accreditation: Its Purposes and Uses* (Council on Postsecondary Accreditation, 1977). Another COPA Occasional Paper. Explains the historical derivation of private accreditation, the purposes and uses of accreditation, and pressures on the accreditation system.

Symposium, "Accreditation," 50 *J. Higher Educ.*, issue 2 (March–April 1979). Provides various perspectives on the accreditation system, its prospects, and its problems. Contains eleven articles, including Margaret Conway, "The Commissioner's Authority to List Accrediting Agencies and Associations: Necessary for an Eligibility Issue"; J. Hall, "Regional Accreditation and Nontraditional Colleges: A President's Point of View"; Jerry Miller & L. Boswell, "Accreditation, Assessment, and the Credentialing of Educational Accomplishment"; John Profit, "The Federal Connection for Accreditation"; W. Trout, "Regional Accreditation, Evaluative Criteria and Quality Assurance"; and Kenneth E. Young, "New Pressures on Accreditation." Symposium is now primarily of historical interest.

Tayler, C. William, & Hylden, Thomas. "Judicial Review of Accrediting Agency Actions: *Marlboro Corporation d/b/a The Emery School v. The Association of Independent Colleges and Schools*," 4 *J. Coll. & Univ. Law* 199 (1978). Analyzes the *Emery School* case in the context of the developing law of educational accreditation. Discusses the scope of judicial review and the legal standards courts will apply in accreditation cases.

Young, Kenneth E., Chambers, Charles M., Kells, H. R., & Associates. *Understanding Accreditation: Contemporary Perspectives on Issues and Practices in Evaluating Educational Quality* (Jossey-Bass, 1983). A sourcebook on the history, purposes, problems, and prospects of postsecondary accreditation. Includes eighteen chapters by fourteen different authors, a substantial prologue and epilogue tying the chapters together, an appendix with various COPA documents, a glossary of terms, and an extensive bibliography.

Sec. 14.4 (Athletic Associations and Conferences)

Connell, Mary Ann, Harris, Robin Green, & Ledbetter, Beverly E. *What to Do When the NCAA Comes Calling* (National Association of College and University Attorneys, 2005). Monograph discussing the components of an NCAA investigation, the types of violations that the NCAA may investigate, the types of documents the NCAA will use, the expectations it will have for the institution's response, and the institution's appeal rights. Also answers frequently asked questions and provides a checklist for the investigation process.

Heller, Greg. "Preparing for the Storm: The Representation of a University Accused of Violating the NCAA Regulations," 7 *Marquette Sports L.J.* 295 (1996). Reviews the various steps in the NCAA's enforcement process and provides practical guidance on the attorney's role in defending a university subjected to this process. Includes recent examples of NCAA enforcement actions and a hypothetical enforcement problem with suggestions for handling it. Author's research included interviews with university athletic administrators, NCAA staff, and sports law attorneys.

Meyers, D. Kent, & Horowitz, Ira. "Private Enforcement of the Antitrust Laws Works Occasionally: *Board of Regents of the University of Oklahoma v. NCAA*, A Case in Point," 48 *Okla. L. Rev.* 669 (1995). A retrospective on the *University of Oklahoma* case prepared a decade after the U.S. Supreme Court's decision by an attorney for the plaintiffs and one of the expert witnesses in the case. Reviews the issues in the litigation and explains the impact of the decision on "the universities, the television networks, the advertisers, and the viewing public."

Symposium, "NCAA Institutional Controls and Mechanisms and the Student-Athlete," 1995 *Wis. L. Rev.* 545 (1995). Examines individual institutions' mechanisms for governing intercollegiate athletics, and considers measures to increase the efficiency and fairness of institutional control of student athletes. Includes the following articles: Peter C. Carstensen & Paul Olszowka, "Antitrust Law, Student-Athletes, and the NCAA: Limiting the Scope and Conduct of Private Economic Regulation"; Timothy Davis, "A Model of Institutional Governance for Intercollegiate Athletics"; B. Glenn George, "Who Plays and Who Pays: Defining Equality in Intercollegiate Athletics"; and David A. Skeel, Jr., "Some Corporate and Securities Perspectives on Student-Athletes and the NCAA."

Weistart, John C. "Antitrust Issues in the Regulation of College Sports," 5 *J. Coll. & Univ. Law* 77 (1979). A systematic treatment of antitrust law's particular applications to intercollegiate athletics. Reviews issues facing the NCAA regional conferences and particular schools.

Weistart, John C. "Legal Accountability and the NCAA," 10 *J. Coll. & Univ. Law* 167 (1983–84). An essay exploring the unique status and role of the NCAA in intercollegiate athletics. Reviews structural deficiencies, such as the NCAA's alleged failure to accommodate the interests of student athletes in its governance structure; and suggests that the NCAA should be considered to have a fiduciary relationship to its member institutions. Also examines the role of judicial supervision of NCAA activities and its effect on the NCAA's regulatory objectives.

Young, Sherry. "The NCAA Enforcement Program and Due Process: The Case for Internal Reform," 43 *Syracuse L. Rev.* 747 (1992). Outlines complaints about NCAA rules enforcement, traces case law challenging NCAA procedures, explains and critiques the current enforcement program, and calls for further amendment of the NCAA's enforcement procedures.

See Wong entry in Selected Annotated Bibliography for Chapter 10, Section 10.4.

Sec. 14.5 *(The American Association of University Professors)*

American Association of University Professors. "Council Position on Collective Bargaining," 58 *AAUP Bulletin* 46 (1972). A report by the association's Collective Bargaining Council. Describes the rationale for the association's decision to act as a collective bargaining representative for college faculty, the issues addressed by the council in reaching this decision, and the supporting and dissenting opinions of AAUP leaders.

American Association of University Professors. "Seventy-Five Years: A Retrospective on the Occasion of the Seventy-Fifth Annual Meeting," 75 *Academe* 4 (1989). Special issue devoted to the history of the AAUP. Includes articles and reproductions of documents about the association's history and the development of its policies on academic freedom and tenure, as well as on collective bargaining and governance. Also examines the AAUP's work on the status of women, the economic status of the profession, the McCarthy era, and the association's activity in filling *amicus* briefs in cases of significance to higher education.

Hutcheson, Philo A. *A Professional Professoriate: Unionization, Bureaucratization, and the AAUP* (Vanderbilt University Press, 2000). Traces the history of the American Association of University Professors with particular emphasis on the expansion of higher education post–World War II, and describes how it changed in response to the increasing complexity of higher education governance.

Metzger, Walter P. "Origins of the Association: An Anniversary Address," 51 *AAUP Bulletin* 229 (1965). Discusses the context for and development of the AAUP and describes early efforts of the association in the areas of academic freedom, tenure, institutional governance, and other issues of concern to faculty and administrators.

See *AAUP Policy Documents and Reports* ("Redbook") and Furniss entries in Selected Annotated Bibliography for Chapter 6, Section 6.1.

15

The College and the Business/Industrial Community

Sec. 15.1. The Contract Context for College Business Transactions

15.1.1. Overview. Entry into the world of business and industry exposes higher education institutions to a substantial dose of commercial law. Since most commercial arrangements are embodied in contracts that define the core rights and responsibilities of the contracting parties, contract law is the foundation on which the institution's business relationships are built. This Section discusses the basics of contract law as they apply to relationships between the institution and the business world. While the discussion is addressed primarily to nonlawyers, it includes numerous illustrations, citations, and reminders that should be of use to counsel; it also provides a common ground upon which counsel can join with administrators to engage in business planning. Other Sections of this chapter discuss additional applications of contract law, designed as much for counsel as for administrators, as well as applications of other bodies of law (for example, tort law, real estate law, intellectual property law, and tax law) that are particularly important to institutions' activities in the world of business and industry.

15.1.2. Types of contracts and contract terms. A contract is a promise, or a performance or forbearance, given in exchange for some type of compensation. The three basic elements of a contract are the offer; the acceptance; and the compensation, legally referred to as "consideration." A contract may involve goods, services, real estate, or any combination thereof. A contract may be either written or oral. Virtually all states have a "statute of frauds," however, providing that certain types of contracts (for example, contracts for the sale of real property) must be in writing in order to be enforceable. A written contract may be either a standard form contract or an instrument specifically designed to meet individual circumstances. While contracts typically are viewed as an exchange (for example, money for goods), they also can take the form of cooperative arrangements such as affiliation agreements or joint venture agreements.

The types of clauses contained in a contract depend on the purposes of the contract, the interests of the parties, and the scope and complexity of the transaction. Most commercial contracts include clauses specifying the scope and duration of the contract; price, payment, or profit-sharing arrangements; delivery, installation, or implementation requirements; and definitions of contract terms. Most commercial contracts also include general clauses containing representations of authority to contract and to perform; warranties of products or performance; limitations on liability (indemnification or hold-harmless clauses); provisions for termination, renewal, or amendment; definitions of breach or default; remedies for breach; dispute resolution techniques (for example, arbitration); and a "choice of law," that is, a selection of a body of state law that will govern the transaction. Some contracts also may include special clauses containing representations that a party has complied with applicable law; has clear title to certain property; holds necessary licenses, bonds, or insurance coverages; or has certain copyright or patent rights. Overall, the parties can include any provisions they agree on that are not prohibited by state or federal law. They are, by a process of "private ordering," creating the private law that will govern their relationship.

Prior to 1954 state common law (see Section 1.4.2.4) governed all contracts. From 1954 to 1967, every state except Louisiana adopted some form of the Uniform Commercial Code (U.C.C.). The U.C.C. now governs contracts for the sale of goods, except for certain issues (for example, defenses) that the U.C.C. does not address. These issues are still governed by the common law (see U.C.C. § 1-103), as are domestic contracts that do not involve the sale of goods. For international transactions between parties in the United States and parties in certain other countries, the United Nations Convention on Contracts for the International Sale of Goods (15 U.S.C.A. Appendix (West Supp. 1993)) will govern the contract if the contract does not otherwise specify the applicable law.

For the most part, the U.C.C. is consistent with the common law of contract. Departures from the common law are contained primarily in Article 2, dealing with the sale of goods, and in Article 9, dealing with the assignment of contract rights. (See generally J. D. Calamari & J. M. Perillo, *The Law of Contracts* (3d ed., West, 1987).) When the U.C.C. does depart from the common law, the effect is that the rules applicable to the sale of goods will differ from those for the sale of labor, services, or land. Thus, it is important to know whether a particular contract is for the sale of goods, and thus subject to the U.C.C., or for the sale of services, labor, or land, and subject to the common law (see Section 15.2.2).

The starting point for making this distinction is the U.C.C.'s definition of "goods"—that is, "all things (including specifically manufactured goods) which are movable at the time of identification to the contract for sale" (U.C.C. § 2-105). This definition will sometimes be difficult to apply. In *Advent Systems*

Ltd. v. Unysis Corp., 925 F.2d 670 (3d Cir. 1991), for instance, a computer software producer sued a computer manufacturer for breach of contract. The plaintiff argued that the U.C.C. should not control the case because "the 'software' referred to in the agreement as a 'product' was not a 'good' but intellectual property outside the ambit of the [U.C.C.]." The court rejected the argument:

> [A] computer program may be copyrightable as intellectual property [but this] does not alter the fact that once in the form of a floppy disc or other medium, the program is tangible, movable and available in the marketplace. The fact that some programs may be tailored for specific purposes need not alter their status as "goods" because the code definition includes "specifically manufactured goods."

15.1.3. *Elements of the contract.* An "offer" is the offeror's expression of a present intent to be bound to particular terms, subject to the offeree's acceptance of those terms in an appropriate manner. The offer sets out the basic terms of the contract, although the terms are subject to negotiation and those ultimately agreed on need not have been expressed in the initial offer. The scope of the offer is determined by an objective standard that focuses on what the offeree should reasonably have understood from the offeror's communication rather than on the subjective meaning the offeror or offeree may have attached to the communication. In *Board of Governors of Wayne State University v. Building Systems Housing Corp.,* 233 N.W.2d 195 (Mich. Ct. App. 1975), for example, university officers believed that they had accepted the defendant's bid (offer) and thus formed a contract. According to the court, however, the university had made a conditional acceptance that functioned as a counteroffer. The conditional nature of the acceptance was evidenced by the university's statement (in a letter) that formal documents would be drawn after the Department of Housing and Urban Development (HUD) had approved the contract award and financing bonds had been sold. The court reasoned that this statement interjected additional terms that transformed the university's attempted acceptance into a counteroffer, since the defendant's bid did not contain any "promise to abide by the conditions of HUD approval and the sale of financing bonds."

In general, an offer remains open for the time specified in the offer, and that time begins to run when the offer is received. An acceptance after the time specified becomes a new offer. If no time is specified, the offer will lapse in a reasonable time. In the case of option contracts not governed by the U.C.C., legally sufficient consideration usually must be given in exchange for any promise to keep an offer open for a certain period of time. See *Board of Control of Eastern Michigan University v. Burgess,* 206 N.W.2d 256 (Mich. Ct. App. 1973) (court refused to enforce an option contract, although agreement stated that consideration had been received, where one party had, in fact, received no such consideration). Under U.C.C. § 2-205, however, consideration is not needed if a "merchant" offers to buy or sell goods and "gives assurance" that the offer is "open for a specified period." In *City University of New York v. Finalco, Inc.,* 514 N.Y.S.2d 244 (N.Y. App. Div. 1987), Finalco had stated in a bid to City University for a used IBM computer that "this offer is valid through the close of business, December 18, 1978." The court held that the offer was irrevocable, even with no consideration, and that Finalco was thus obligated to purchase the computer when the university accepted its bid on December 18.

The offeror may specify the manner by which the offer is to be accepted. The parties are bound when the offeree has appropriately communicated its return promise to the offeror or begun performances in the manner specified. In *Finalco,* for instance, the parties became bound when the university sent the letter to Finalco accepting its bid. The parties were bound at this point, despite their "manifested . . . intention to adopt a formal written agreement," because the letter and Finalco's bid included sufficient evidence of mutual assent between the parties "prior to the execution of the writing."

To be effective, an acceptance must be unequivocal, and under common law its terms must match the terms of the offer. As in the *Building Systems Housing* case, above, a proposed acceptance that conditions the offeree's consent to terms not in the original offer is a counteroffer; the original offeror then has the power to form the contract by accepting the counteroffer. Under the U.C.C., however, an acceptance may be effective despite some differences between its terms and those specified in the offer (U.C.C. § 2-207).

Generally, consideration is the price to be paid or the benefit to be extended by one party for the other party's promise. Consideration transforms the arrangement into a type of bargained exchange. *St. Norbert College Foundation v. McCormick,* 260 N.W.2d 776 (Wis. 1978), illustrates the application of this concept. McCormick had initially approached the college, indicating that he wished to make two gifts for its benefit. To maximize his own tax advantages, McCormick proposed to make two stock transfers to, and to enter two buy-sell agreements with, the college. In the second of these agreements, McCormick agreed to transfer to the college seven thousand shares of Procter & Gamble stock, worth approximately $500,000, in return for an annual annuity of $5,000 for life. McCormick thereafter revoked this agreement, contending that it was not enforceable because it lacked adequate consideration. The court disagreed:

> [T]he presence of consideration is clear from the document. Defendant agreed to sell the stock. Plaintiff agreed to pay the stipulated price—$5,000 per year for life to the defendant. It is not the amount of consideration that determines the validity of a contract. . . . "[I]nadequacy of consideration alone is not a fatal defect" [260 N.W.2d at 780, quoting *Rust v. Fitzhugh,* 112 N.W. 508, 511 (Wis. 1907)].

Related to consideration, and a kind of modern alternative to it, is the doctrine of promissory estoppel. Under this doctrine, if (1) a promise or assurance is made that could reasonably be expected to induce some particular action by the person to whom the promise is addressed, (2) the person does take action in reliance on the promise or assurance, and (3) an injustice would otherwise occur, the courts will enforce the promise as a contract even though there was no consideration for it (see *Restatement (Second) of Contracts* § 90 (1979); see also § 87(2), recognizing judicial enforcement of some offers even without a promise). The trend is toward a low threshold for find-ing a promise and an emphasis on the "reliance interest" of the person addressed. In *Howard University v. Good Food Services, Inc.,* 608 A.2d 116 (D.C. 1992), for example, the university had contracted with an outside ser-vice, Good Food Services (GFS) to provide meals campuswide. Although it was not required to do so by the contract, GFS listed the university as an additional insured on its insurance certificates each year for a four-year period, pursuant to the university's annual requests that it do so. Two years after GFS terminated this practice without notifying the university, a GFS employee was injured in a university kitchen and brought suit against the university. Among other defenses, the university asserted promissory estop-pel against GFS for failing to maintain the university as an insured, a prac-tice that the university claimed to have relied on to its detriment. In analyzing the university's defense, the court stated: "[T]o make out a claim of promis-sory estoppel, the following questions must be answered in the affirmative: First, was there a promise? Second, should the promisor have expected the promisee to rely on the promise? [Finally], did the promisee so rely to [its] detriment?" Although the court recognized that the university had grounds to assert promissory estoppel under this test, it nevertheless rejected the university's defense for procedural reasons.

15.1.4. Breach of contract and remedies for breach. Either party may breach a contract by failing to perform as it has promised. In case of breach, and in the absence of a viable defense, a court may award damages as well as other remedies.

If the promise to perform is a conditional one, there can be no breach until all the conditions have been fulfilled or excused. In *Pioneer Roofing Co. v. Mar-dian Construction Co.,* 733 P.2d 652 (Ariz. Ct. App. 1986), the court considered a defendant's claim that contract conditions had been excused because of an emergency and because of a waiver by the other party. The case concerned the obligation of the Arizona Board of Regents to pay for unanticipated extra work performed and materials purchased by a subcontractor for a sports facility on the Northern Arizona University campus. According to the contract, no addi-tional work that would increase the "Contract Sum" could be undertaken, except in an emergency, until the general contractor informed the architect about the additional work. The contract also required that the architect provide authorization "in advance and in writing" to the contractor before the extra work was initiated. Both conditions had to be met before the university would be obligated to pay claims for extra work. In defending itself against a claim for payment, the board of regents contended that neither condition had been met. The court rejected the board's defense. It held that the first condition did not apply, since the extra work, the reroofing of the structure, "was in response to an emergency that endangered the property"; and that the second condition had been waived by the architect's representative, who gave go-ahead instructions at a meeting where the emergency was discussed. (See also *Bellevue College v. Greater Omaha Realty Co.,* 348 N.W.2d 837 (Neb. 1984), where the plaintiff college successfully enforced a contract—despite an unfulfilled condition—because the failure to fulfill the condition was solely the fault of the defendant.)

Lack of performance also will not constitute a breach if there has been a rescission or release of the contract. When neither party has performed its promises, the parties may agree mutually to rescind their contract as long as no third party's rights are affected. If only one of the parties has performed its promise, a mutual rescission must be accompanied by some consideration (see Section 15.1.3) given by the nonperforming party to the party that has performed. Similarly, if one party releases the other from its contractual obligation to perform, some consideration from the nonperforming party may be required if the release is to be valid. The U.C.C. permits written release of an obligation without consideration, however, as do state statutes in some states.

Occasionally, a court may also rescind a contract for good cause. In *Boise Junior College District v. Mattefs Construction Co.*, 450 P.2d 604 (Idaho 1969), for instance, the court determined that a construction contractor was "entitled to the equitable relief of rescission" because it had made a "material" mistake in failing to include the glass subcontractor's bid when compiling subcontractors' bids in order to calculate its own bid. The court indicated that, among pertinent considerations, "enforcement of a contract pursuant to the terms of the erroneous bid would be unconscionable; the mistake did not result from [the contractor's] violation of a positive legal duty or from culpable negligence; the [other] party . . . will not be prejudiced except by the loss of his bargain; and prompt notice of the error [was] given."

If a condition to performance has occurred or has been excused, *and* if the promise still has not been fulfilled or otherwise discharged, then a breach exists, for which a court will award damages, and perhaps other remedies as well, as discussed below.

Because contracts are made in a bargained exchange, in which the parties presumably contemplate their resultant duties and liabilities, judicial remedies for breach of contract are limited to those that fulfill the reasonable expectations of the parties. American courts prefer money damages over "specific performance" (that is, an order to the breaching party to perform). Money damages may be "nominal" or "compensatory." Compensatory damages may be computed in one of three ways. "Expectation" damages are calculated to place the nonbreaching party as nearly as possible in the position it would have been in had the breaching party performed; "reliance" damages are calculated to return the nonbreaching party to its original position, as if it had never entered the contract; and "restitution" damages are calculated to return or restore to the nonbreaching party the dollar value of any benefit it had conferred on the breaching party. (See generally Calamari & Perillo, *The Law of Contracts* (cited in Section 15.1.1), Chaps. 14–16.) The nonbreaching party may choose which type of calculation to use and has the burden of proving the existence of damages and calculating their amount with reasonable certainty. The nonbreaching party must also "mitigate" its damages and may not recover for loss that could have been avoided or mitigated with reasonable effort. The nonbreaching party also may not recover damages that were not foreseeable to the breaching party.

In order to avoid complicated court proceedings on proof of damages, the parties may insert a "liquidated damages" clause into the contract at formation. Liquidated damages represent an agreed-upon estimate of the actual damages that would likely be incurred in case of breach. The U.C.C., for instance, permits the enforcement of liquidated damages clauses when "the amount is reasonable in the light of anticipated or actual harm caused by the breach, the difficulties of proof of loss, and the inconvenience or infeasibility of otherwise obtaining an adequate remedy" (§ 2-718(1)).

15.1.5. Arbitration. Arbitration is a process by which contracting parties may resolve a dispute by asking a neutral third party to examine the claims and render a decision. The parties can agree in advance to have contract disputes resolved through arbitration by including an arbitration clause in the contract at formation. Without such a clause, the parties can still agree to arbitrate a particular dispute after it has arisen. In either case, the parties may specify whether the decision is binding on the parties or only advisory.

In comparison to protracted court litigation, arbitration (like mediation) offers a much quicker resolution at a much lower cost (see generally Section 2.3). Arbitration is an informal process that decreases the adversarial character of the dispute and increases the likelihood of a mutually beneficial outcome. The arbitrator is not bound by judicial precedents or rules of law and is thus free to resolve the dispute in an equitable manner. In addition, since the parties choose the arbitrator, they can ensure that he or she is familiar with the business context and proficient in the issues to be resolved.

Most states as well as the federal government have statutes that promote the use and enforceability of arbitration agreements.[1] The federal statute, the Federal Arbitration Act (FAA) (9 U.S.C. § 1 *et seq.*), applies to written arbitration agreements involving interstate commerce or maritime transactions and provides that such agreements are "valid, irrevocable, and enforceable." Federal and state courts, upon the request of a party, must stay any litigation on a covered transaction that is also the subject of pending arbitration. The federal district courts also are empowered to compel arbitration when a party fails, neglects, or refuses to submit a dispute to arbitration. The FAA also limits judicial review of arbitrators' decisions. Either party may petition a court to confirm an arbitrator's decision, and the court must confirm the decision unless there are demonstrated grounds for vacating or modifying it. A decision may be vacated only if it was influenced by fraud, corruption, or misconduct, and it may be modified only if it goes beyond the scope of the issues presented by the parties or contains a material miscalculation.

In *Volt Information Sciences v. Board of Trustees of Leland Stanford Junior University*, 489 U.S. 468 (1989), the U.S. Supreme Court considered the relationship

---

[1]Most of the state statutes are based on the Uniform Arbitration Act (7 U.L.A. (Uniform Laws Annotated) 1 (Supp. 1991)). A number of states now also have statutes governing international arbitrations; see G. Walker, "Trends in State Legislation Governing International Arbitrations," 17 *N.C. J. Int'l. L. & Com. Reg.* 419 (1992).

between the Federal Arbitration Act (FAA) and state law. Volt and Stanford had entered into a construction contract. The contract included an arbitration clause as well as a "choice-of-law" clause providing that the contract would be governed by California law. When a dispute arose over compensation for additional work done by Volt, Volt demanded arbitration while Stanford filed a breach of contract suit in California Superior Court against Volt and also sought indemnity from two other contractors not subject to the arbitration agreement.

Under the FAA, the court would have been required to compel enforcement of the private arbitration contract clause and to stay the litigation until the arbitration process was complete. However, a California statute—the California Arbitration Act—allows "a court to stay arbitration pending the resolution of related litigation," and Stanford invoked this statute because its suit included the indemnity claims against two other contractors. The Supreme Court held that the FAA does not preempt the California statute (see generally Section 13.1.1 of this book), and that, under the contract's choice-of-law clause, the California law should apply: "[T]he federal policy [under the Federal Arbitration Act] is simply to ensure the enforceability, according to their terms, of private agreements to arbitrate. . . . Where, as here, the parties have agreed to abide by state arbitration rules, enforcing those rules according to the terms of the agreement is fully consistent with the FAA's goals, even if the result is that arbitration is stayed when the Act would otherwise permit it to go forward."

University of Alaska v. Modern Construction, Inc., 522 P.2d 1132 (Alaska 1974), provides another perspective on arbitration. The university contracted with Modern to build a Campus Activity Center. The contract provided that "[a]ll claims, disputes and other matters in question arising out of, or relating to, the Contract or the breach thereof" would be submitted to arbitration. The contract also contained elaborate procedures for approval of design changes and accompanying adjustments in the contract price (called "Change Orders"). After completing the project, Modern presented the university with a bill for "impact charges" attributable to several change orders. When the university refused to pay, Modern demanded arbitration. The university cooperated but recorded an objection that Modern's claims were beyond the scope of the contract and thus not arbitrable under the arbitration clause. The panel of arbitrators awarded Modern approximately 40 percent of its claim. Modern then asked the court to confirm the arbitration award, and the university simultaneously asked the court to vacate it. The court stated that, although the contract was ambiguous about whether the dispute was arbitrable, it would "allow ambiguous contract terms to be constructed in favor of arbitrability where such construction is not obviously contrary to the parties' intent, especially where, as here, the party contesting arbitrability drafted the contract." Thus, since "the arbitrators' decision on the arbitrability of Modern's claims for 'impact damages' due to delays was not based on an unreasonable interpretation of the contract," the Supreme Court of Alaska confirmed the arbitration award.

Sec. 15.2. The College as Purchaser

15.2.1. Purchase of goods. One of the most common commercial transactions of colleges and universities is the purchase of "goods"—that is, personal property generally categorizable as equipment, materials, or supplies. Computer equipment and software, for instance, would constitute goods whose acquisition commonly involves institutions in complex commercial transactions (see generally M. Bandman, "Balancing the Risks in Computer Contracts," 92 *Com. L.J.* 384 (1987)). Purchases of goods are effectuated by means of contracts providing for the transfer of title to (or a lease interest in) the goods from seller to purchaser in return for a monetary payment or other consideration. When payment is made over time, the parties may also execute and file documents giving the seller a security interest in the goods. Contracts for the sale of goods are typically governed by state contract and commercial law, in particular Article 2 (sales) and Article 9 (security interests) of the Uniform Commercial Code (U.C.C.) (see Section 15.1.2 of this book).

For public institutions, the state's procurement law, embodied in statutory provisions and administrative regulations, usually will establish further requirements regarding purchasing, or a state higher education system may adopt procurement regulations of its own.[2] For example, public institutions may be required to purchase certain products or services from a "procurement list" (see, for example, Ohio Rev. Code Ann. § 4115.34) or to use competitive bidding for certain purchases (see, for example, Tex. Rev. Civ. Stat. Ann. art. 601b). Public institutions may also be subject to a variety of special provisions, in procurement laws or otherwise, that require or authorize "purchase preferences" for particular products or sellers that would benefit the state's own residents.[3] Some states, for instance, accord purchase preferences to recycled paper products (for example, Cal. Pub. Cont. Code § 10860; Neb. Rev. Stat. § 81-15). Other states accord purchase preferences to designated small businesses (for example, Md. Code Ann., State Fin. & Proc. § 14-207(c); Minn. Stat. Ann. § 137.35). Iowa has a statute that requires state governing bodies (including state universities) to purchase coal "mined or produced within the state by producers who are, at the time such coal is purchased or produced, complying with all the workers' compensation and mining laws of the state" (Iowa Code Ann. § 73.6); and California has a statute that requires community colleges to give food purchase preferences to produce that is grown, or food that is processed, in the United States (Cal. Pub. Cont. Code § 3410).

In addition, some states have conflict of interest statutes that would apply to purchase transactions involving state higher education institutions and their

---

[2]Constitutionally based public institutions (Section 12.2.2) may be exempt from some or all state procurement statutes and may have authority to promulgate their own procurement rules and policies.

[3]The cases and authorities are collected in Gavin L. Phillips, Annot., "Validity, Construction, and Effect of State and Local Laws Requiring Governmental Units to Give 'Purchase Preference' to Goods Manufactured or Services Rendered in the State," 84 A.L.R.4th 419.

suppliers (for example, La. Rev. Stat. Ann. §§ 42.1111C(2)(d), 1112B(2) & (3), and 1113(B)). In *In Re Beychok*, 495 So. 2d 1278 (La. 1986), the Supreme Court of Louisiana interpreted these statutes to prohibit Louisiana State University from entering purchase contracts with members of its governing board or their firms. The court held that Beychok, a member of the university's governing board and the chief executive officer and majority stockholder of a baking company, had violated the statutes when his firm entered into a supply contract with the university. Beychok defended on the grounds that the university had awarded the contract through the use of sealed competitive bids. The court rejected the defense, however, because the statutes "protect against both actual and perceived conflicts of interest" and thus "do not require that there be actual corruption on the part of the public servant or actual loss by the state."

There is also some federal law that applies to institutional transactions for the sale of goods—in particular, federal antitrust law (see Section 13.2.8). The Robinson-Patman Act (15 U.S.C. § 13 *et seq.*), for instance, prohibits sellers from engaging in certain types of discriminatory pricing practices and prohibits purchasers from knowingly inducing or receiving discriminatory prices arising from such prohibited pricing practices. In *Jefferson County Pharmaceutical Ass'n., Inc. v. Abbott Laboratories,* 460 U.S. 150 (1983), the U.S. Supreme Court considered the Act's applicability to purchases by public higher education institutions. The case concerned purchases of pharmaceutical products by two pharmacies at the University of Alabama Medical Center. The plaintiff claimed that Abbott Laboratories and the university had violated the Act by entering transactions in which the pharmacies purchased products at lower prices than those charged to the plaintiff's member pharmacies. The university defended on the ground that the Act did not apply to purchases by state governmental entities. Because the university pharmacies had purchased the products at issue for *resale* in competition with private enterprises, the Court did not address the Act's application to state purchases "for *use* in traditional governmental functions"; the sole issue was whether the Act applied to purchases for resale. The Court answered this question affirmatively, since it could find no evidence that Congress intended to accord states the means to compete unfairly with commercial businesses by exempting them from the Act.

When the question concerns an institution's purchases for its own use, the Robinson-Patman Act expressly provides some protection for both public and private institutions. Section 13c (15 U.S.C. § 13c) exempts colleges, universities, and other listed entities from the Act with respect to "purchases of their supplies for their own use."[4] The exemption also extends to the sellers who enter into such transactions with colleges and universities. In *Logan Lanes v. Brunswick Corp.,* 378 F.2d 212 (9th Cir. 1967), the court broadly construed the scope of this exemption. At issue was the defendant's sale of bowling alleys and related equipment to a state board for use in the state university's student

---

[4]The cases are collected in J. M. Purver, Annot., "Construction and Application of Provision in Robinson-Patman Act (15 U.S.C. § 13c) Exempting Nonprofit Institutions from Price Discrimination Provisions of the Act," 3 A.L.R. Fed 996.

union. The alleys were used for a fee by the general public, as well as the university community, and were operated in competition with the plaintiff. The plaintiff challenged the sale, complaining that the defendant had charged it a higher price for alleys and equipment than the price it charged to the state board. The court held that the transaction fell within the Section 13c exemption. The alleys and equipment were "supplies," within the meaning of Section 13c, because that term includes "anything needed to meet the institution's needs," including nonconsumable items that constitute capital expenditures. The alleys and equipment were also for the university's "own use" within the meaning of Section 13c, even though they were also used by the public, since "the primary purpose of the purchases . . . was to fulfill the needs of the university in providing bowling facilities for its students, faculty and staff."

To avoid legal challenges and liability arising from purchasing activities, and to meet the institution's ongoing needs for goods, institutional purchasing officers and legal counsel will need to be thoroughly familiar with Article 2 of the U.C.C. and to identify all other state and federal laws potentially applicable to particular transactions. Careful negotiation and drafting of contract terms is necessary, as is effective assertion of legal rights should the seller perform inadequately. Among the most important protections for institutions are those available from warranties, which may be invoked to enforce the purchaser's interest in the quality and suitability of goods.

In most states Article 2 of the U.C.C. is the source of warranty law regarding the sale of goods. When a sales transaction involves both goods and services (for example, the purchase of carpet that the seller installs), U.C.C. warranty law will apply to the service as well as the goods provided by a particular supplier if the service is only incidental to the sale of the goods (see Section 15.2.2 of this book). Warranties may be either "express" or "implied." Section 2-313 of the U.C.C. governs express warranties. If a seller makes representations about product quality or performance by asserting facts, making promises, or providing a description, sample, or model of the goods, the goods must comply with these representations. In *Brooklyn Law School v. Raybon, Inc.*, 540 N.Y.S.2d 404 (N.Y. Sup. Ct. 1989), *reversed on other grounds*, 572 N.Y.S.2d 312 (N.Y. App. Div. 1991), for example, the school sued Raybon and twenty-six other defendants who had sold it asbestos products and installed them in the school facilities. The school alleged that the defendants made representations about the safety and fitness of the asbestos materials in advertisements directed at the general public, and that the school relied on these representations in purchasing the asbestos products. The trial court held that these allegations stated an express warranty claim, and it denied the defendant's motion to dismiss this claim. *In dictum,* the court suggested that any defendants whose primary function was to install the asbestos materials might not be subject to the express warranty claim, because the installation was a service incidental to the sale; but the court did not decide this potential issue, since none of the defendants had alleged that they primarily provided a service.

Implied warranties are governed by Sections 2-314 and 2-315 of the U.C.C. Section 2-314 recognizes an implied warranty that goods are "merchantable"—that is, suitable for the ordinary purpose for which such goods are used—if the seller is a "merchant" who deals in goods of that kind. Section 2-315 recognizes an implied warranty of "fitness for a particular purpose" when the seller knows the purchaser's purpose for wanting the goods and the purchaser relies on the seller's expertise to provide goods suitable for the purpose. *Western Waterproofing Co., Inc. v. Lindenwood Colleges*, 662 S.W.2d 288 (Mo. Ct. App. 1983), concerned an alleged breach of implied warranty. Lindenwood had contracted with Western Waterproofing Company (WWC) to install a soccer/football field in the college stadium. The field was used by Lindenwood's soccer team and was also leased to the St. Louis Cardinals football team for training camp. When the Cardinals used the field, parts of it "were torn up and holes and divots developed." In later use similar damage occurred, and pools of standing water formed on the field. Lindenwood claimed that WWC had "breached an implied warranty that the field was fit for its intended use." WWC argued that Lindenwood's implied warranty claim was barred, because Lindenwood was contributorily negligent for misusing the field by overwatering. The court rejected WWC's argument, holding that contributory negligence can be a defense to an implied warranty claim only if the purchaser's misuse is the "proximate cause of the alleged breach" of warranty. Thus, the court confirmed an arbitration award in Lindenwood's favor because the "principal cause of the field's deficiencies were in the design of the field itself and not Lindenwood's misuse of the field."

Sellers may disclaim (and thus avoid) warranties by inserting disclaimers into sales contracts. Purchasers may also disclaim (and thus lose) warranty protection in some circumstances by their own inaction. (Section 2-316(1) of the U.C.C. governs the disclaimer of express warranties; Section 2-316(2) governs the disclaimer of implied warranties.) When a warranty has not been disclaimed, there are nevertheless several defenses a seller may assert against a breach of warranty claim, including the complex "lack of privity" defense. To take full advantage of warranty law, administrators and purchasing officers will want to seek the assistance of counsel in dealing with these matters.

In addition to warranty and other breach of contract claims, institutions may also sometimes protect themselves by asserting claims for tortious performance of contract obligations. In *Board of Regents of the University of Washington v. Frederick & Nelson*, 579 P.2d 346 (Wash. 1978), for example, the university purchased furniture for a laboratory from Frederick & Nelson (F&N), the supplier. When the furniture did not meet the contract specifications, the manufacturer agreed to refinish the furniture on the university's premises. The university subsequently sustained fire damage at the site, apparently as a result of spontaneous combustion of oily rags that the manufacturer had left on the premises. The court held that, since F&N had allowed the manufacturer to perform F&N's contractual duty to bring the furniture up to specifications, F&N was liable to the university for the manufacturer's negligent performance of these duties, which resulted in the fire. See also *University Systems of New Hampshire v. United States Gypsum Co.*, 756 F. Supp. 640 (D.N.H. 1991) (asbestos case presenting numerous tort claims).

In *Regents of the University of Minnesota v. Chief Industries, Inc.*, 106 F.3d 1409 (8th Cir. 1997), a products liability case, the court addressed the issue of the money damages a university may seek in court when it has suffered economic loss due to a defect in goods it has purchased. The university had decided to purchase a new grain dryer for its agricultural research facilities. Before purchasing the equipment, the manager of the research facility consulted with an expert in the university's Department of Agricultural Engineering, Dr. Harold Cloud, who was regarded as "the expert, probably, in the United States on drying." Cloud was actively involved in assisting with the specifications for the new dryer. Several years after the purchase, a defect in a solenoid valve in the dryer caused it to overheat and start a fire that spread to another nearby building. The university then brought a products liability claim and other tort claims against Chief Industries, Inc., the manufacturer of the dryer, and Parker-Hannafin, Inc., the manufacturer of the solenoid component, seeking damages for its economic losses resulting from the fire. The district court granted summary judgment to the defendants, holding that the university was a "merchant in goods of the kind" and could not recover in tort for economic losses.

On appeal, the Eighth Circuit looked to Minnesota's version of the Uniform Commercial Code to determine whether the university's tort action was viable. The statute provides, in part, that "economic loss that arises from a sale of goods between parties *who are each merchants in goods of the kind* is not recoverable in tort" (Minn. Stat. § 604.10; emphasis added). The legislation further provides (adapted from UCC § 2-104) that:

> "Merchant" means a person who deals in goods of the kind or otherwise by his occupation holds himself out as having knowledge or skill peculiar to the practices or goods involved in the transaction or to whom such knowledge or skill may be attributed by his employment of an agent or broker or other intermediary who by his occupation holds himself out as having such knowledge or skill. [Minn. Stat. § 336.2-104(1), adapted from UCC § 2-104].

The court determined that, under this statute, the university itself was a "merchant in goods of the kind" because it was able to rely on its agricultural engineering expert, who specialized in drying. The court held that the university did not actually have to be a "dealer" of grain dryers to fit the statutory definition of a "merchant." It could be classified as a merchant simply because it had and could use its expert's knowledge of the goods to assist it in the transaction. Accordingly, the university was barred from bringing a tort action by § 604.10 and § 336.2-104(1), which limit merchants to contract remedies—remedies much narrower than tort remedies—for recovery of economic loss.

The opinion of the court garnered a strong dissent. The dissenting judge questioned both the way in which the majority had interpreted the statute and the way in which it had characterized Cloud's expertise.

15.2.2. Purchase of services. Institutions commonly contract for the purchase of services as well as goods. Sometimes the same contract will cover both services and goods, as when the seller of equipment agrees to install, provide maintenance for, or train personnel in the use of the equipment. At other times the institution will contract with one party to purchase goods and contract with other parties for services related to the goods. The acquisition and operation of computer systems, for example, will customarily involve purchases of both goods (hardware and software) and services (installation of hardware, implementation of systems, periodic maintenance, and so forth).

Services may also be unrelated to and purchased independently of goods. Examples include accounting services, legal services, services of consultants, payroll services, and custodial services. Such services are often performed by corporations or individuals that have the legal status of "independent contractors" rather than by being performed by employees. Generally the activities of an independent contractor are not subject to the same level of control by the employer as are the activities of an employee; therefore, the independent contractor generally has more discretion regarding methods and equipment for the job, and may also work for many different employers during the same day or week. An independent contractor may or may not be an agent of the institution (see Section 4.2.1) in performing particular contractual duties. Since an institution could be liable in contract, and occasionally in tort, for the acts of a contractor acting as its agent, close attention must be given to contractual provisions that characterize the contractor's status and authority to act for the institution (see Section 3.4), and that allocate the risk of loss from any unlawful acts of the contractor (see Section 2.5.3).

The use of outside independent contractors to provide services for the institution or for members of the campus community—often called "outsourcing" or "contracting out"—has become increasingly popular and widespread. This is particularly true with services for students. Food services is one common example, as illustrated by the *ABL Management, Inc.,* case discussed below in this subsection. Student housing is another example. (See generally Martin Van Der Werf, "Colleges Turn to Private Companies to Build and Run Student Housing," *Chron. Higher Educ.,* June 11, 1999, A37.) Not only are housing management responsibilities being outsourced, but also responsibilities for building and financing of student housing. The arrangements raise various potential issues of law and policy. There may be issues, for instance, of whether the institution has authority to enter such an arrangement (compare the janitorial services cases below); whether to use a captive or affiliated organization (see Section 3.6) as part of the arrangements; whether the construction process will be subject to state competitive bidding laws imposed upon public institutions (see subsection 15.2.4 below); and whether and how the institution can insulate itself from liability for student injuries and other harms occurring in the housing complex (see generally Sections 3.3.2.1 & 8.6.2).

Another example is outsourcing the management of college bookstores. These arrangements raise some of the same issues as student housing outsourcing, as well as issues concerning the responsiveness of outside entrepreneurs to the needs of students and faculty members. (See John Pulley, "Whose Bookstore Is It, Anyway?" *Chron. Higher Educ.,* February 4, 2000, A41.) Yet another example is outsourcing of janitorial services and building management services. Some of the issues concerning such arrangements are discussed in the cases below on janitorial services.

The purchase of services, like the purchase of goods, is effectuated by contractual agreements governed by the contract law of the state. Unlike the purchase of goods, however, the purchase of services as such is not subject to
Article 2 of the U.C.C. Even when the same transaction involves both goods and
services—for example, a contract for the acquisition of a computer system—the
U.C.C. will not apply to the service unless the goods are the dominant component of the transaction and the services are merely incidental to their sale.
(See, for example, *Ames Contracting Co., Inc. v. City University of New York*,
466 N.Y.S.2d 182, 184–85 (N.Y. Ct. Cl. 1983), *reversed on other grounds*, 485
N.Y.S.2d 259 (N.Y. App. Div. 1985).) Since Article 2 of the U.C.C. usually will
not apply to the purchase of services, U.C.C. warranties (Section 15.2.1) usually will not protect the institution if the purchased services are unsatisfactory.
Instead, the institution's legal recourse is a breach of contract claim (Section
15.1.4), supplemented by a tortious performance claim (Section 15.2.1) and,
when professional services are involved, a malpractice law claim.

For public institutions, state procurement law, purchase preference regulations, and conflict of interest regulations (see subsection 15.2.1 above) may
apply to the purchase of services as well as goods. Moreover, "prevailing
wage" statutes may sometimes apply to the purchase of contractors' services.
Such statutes require contractors working on certain public works projects
(including those at state universities and colleges) to pay laborers the "prevailing wage" in the locality. Applicability of the statute typically depends on
two factors: first, whether the project is considered a "public work"; second,
whether the particular type of work to be performed falls into one of the
statutorily defined categories (for example, construction, demolition, repair,
alteration) for which the prevailing wage must be paid.[5] In *Sarkisian Bros.,
Inc. v. Hartnett*, 568 N.Y.S.2d 190 (N.Y. App. Div. 1991), the state commissioner of labor found that a contractor renovating a state university classroom
building into a hotel/conference center had violated the state's prevailing
wage statute. The contractor appealed the commissioner's determination,
arguing that the renovation was not a public work but, rather, a "private venture for profit." The court disagreed and upheld the commissioner's decision.
To support its conclusion, the court cited a number of factors—including the
reservation of 75 percent of the facility's space for the use of the state university system and its affiliates—that "tend to demonstrate the public use,
public access, public ownership and public enjoyment characteristics of the
project and [to] support [the commissioner's] determination, which is neither irrational nor unreasonable."

Another pertinent type of state law that can become involved in disputes
about services, and that public institutions may seek to use as an alternative to
purchasing services, is a property leasing law. The case of *ABL Management,
Inc. v. Board of Supervisors of Southern University and Agricultural & Mechanical College*, 773 So. 2d 131 (La. 2000), illustrates such a law's application to

---

[5]The cases and statutes are collected in Annot., "What Projects Involve Work Subject to State
Statutes Requiring Payment of Prevailing Wages on Public Works Projects," 10 A.L.R.5th 337.

outsourcing food services and also illustrates a potential conflict between leasing laws and state procurement laws.

The Louisiana Procurement Code (La. Rev. Stat. Ann. §§ 39:1551–1755), which was at issue in the *ABL Management* case, requires public entities (including state universities) to follow requirements for selecting the lowest bidder when "buying, purchasing, renting, leasing, or otherwise obtaining any supplies, services, or major repairs" (La. Rev. Stat. Ann. § 39:1556). The Louisiana law on "Leases of College and University Properties" (La. Rev. Stat. Ann. § 17:3361), in contrast, authorizes state universities to "grant leases" of their property under terms obligating the private lessee "to construct improvements on the leased premises which will further the educational, scientific, research, or public services functions" of the university (La. Rev. Stat. Ann. § 17:3361 (A)(5)).

In 1987, under the latter statute, Southern University and Agricultural & Mechanical College (Southern) leased space in which to operate dining services for its Baton Rouge campus to Aramark, Inc. ABL Management, Inc., and D'Wiley's Services, Inc. (ABL), which had sought but did not receive the lease, filed a protest with the state's Division of Administrative Law, asserting that Southern's award of the lease violated the "lowest bidder" requirement of the Procurement Code. ABL argued that "the acquisition of food services was a procurement subject to" the Procurement Code. In response, Southern argued that "the lease did not constitute a procurement and that its award . . . was made pursuant to [the Leases law]." A lower state court recognized Southern's authority to award the lease under the Leases law but "held that the food services portion of the proposal could only be awarded in conformity with the Louisiana Procurement Code" (*ABL v. Board,* 752 So. 2d 384, 388 (La. App. 2000)).

The Supreme Court of Louisiana reversed, emphasizing that procurement subject to the Procurement Code "involves an *expenditure* of state funds," and that Southern, "[i]nstead of expending funds for this service, [had] contracted to receive lease payments and benefit from capital improvements that the lessee would provide." Under the Leases law, the court explained, a "private entity that leases a public college or university facility [must] provide a service that furthers at least one of the essential functions of the institution of higher learning" and must also "provide capital improvements" to the facility "without the involvement of funds from the public fisc." The court rejected ABL's argument that student payments to Southern for meal plans were converted into public funds when collected by Southern for remittance to the lessee under the lease. Southern merely collected the payments on behalf of the lessee, as the parties had "*agreed in the lease*" (emphasis in original), and "[s]uch a legal relationship does not convert student money to public funds." The court also rejected the proposition that the lease was partially subject to the Procurement Code and partially subject to the Leases law, since it could lead to the "absurd" possibility that the lessee would be unable to use the leased property due to the Procurement Code's requirement that the "service" component of the food contract be mechanically awarded to another, lower-bidding, entity.

In addition, other state laws may limit the authority of public institutions to purchase certain services from outsiders—services such as accounting or payroll services, legal services, consulting services, food services, janitorial or grounds-keeping work, and other building management services. State civil service laws, for instance, may expressly or implicitly require state agencies to use only civil service employees to perform such work, unless certain special circumstances exist (see, for example, Minn. Stat. § 16B.17 (1992); Cal. Govt. Code § 19130). Delegations of authority in the state constitution or state statutes may also impose such limits on state universities or colleges (see Cal. Const. art. IX, § 6; *California School Employees Ass'n. v. Sunnyvale Elementary School District of Santa Clara County,* 111 Cal. Rptr. 433 (Cal. Ct. App. 1973); and Cal. Govt. Code § 19130). Other state statutes or regulations, dealing specifically with contracts for special services, may also apply to and limit state educational institutions' authority to outsource or "contract out" for services (see, for example, Cal. Gov. Code § 53060).

A series of cases concerning contracts for janitorial services illustrate how such "contracting out" limits may affect public higher education institutions. In the first of these cases, *State ex rel. Sigall v. Aetna Cleaning Contractors of Cleveland, Inc.,* 345 N.E.2d 61 (Ohio 1976), the Ohio Supreme Court held that Kent State University could lawfully contract with an independent contractor to perform janitorial services that could also be performed by state civil service employees. The university had been unable to maintain a full complement of janitorial workers, despite regular recruiting from a state employment office, and had therefore contracted out for such services—admittedly at lower cost than the wages that civil service employees would have received for the same work. In the taxpayer's suit challenging this contract, the plaintiff alleged that Ohio's constitution and related state statutes required the school to use only civil service employees for such work. Determining that "no statutory provision exists which prohibits the contracting out of the custodial services at issue herein," and that the contracting out would not undermine the state's civil service system, the Ohio Supreme Court rejected the challenge:

> In the absence of proof of an intent to thwart the purposes of the civil service system, the board of trustees of a state university may lawfully contract to have an independent contractor perform services which might also be performed by civil service employees [345 N.E.2d at 65].

In contrast, the court in *Washington Federation of State Employees, AFL-CIO Council 28 v. Spokane Community College,* 585 P.2d 474 (Wash. 1978), held that the college had violated the policy underlying the civil service system—that hiring be based on merit rather than politics—by contracting out for janitorial services. Although the contract would clearly have saved the college money, and although a separate statute permitted the state purchasing director to "purchase all materials, supplies, services, and equipment needed for the support, maintenance, and use of" the college (Wash. Rev. Code § 43.19.190), the Supreme Court of Washington voided the contract because "the College has no authority to enter into a contract for new services of a type which have regularly and historically been provided, and could continue to be provided, by civil service staff employees." Three judges strongly dissented, arguing that the majority had intruded upon the prerogative of the legislature in ruling that all state work had to be performed by state employees, even though no statute said so and one statute apparently stated the contrary (§ 43.19.190 above).

Similarly, in *Local 4501 Communications Workers of America v. Ohio State University*, 466 N.E.2d 912 (Ohio 1984), the Ohio Supreme Court (also over a vigorous dissent) held that the university could not contract out for janitorial services during a hiring freeze, while permitting the slow attrition of civil service workers. As in the Washington case, there was no state statute forbidding such a contract, but the court reasoned that the university was circumventing the civil service system; the contracts were thus void. In reaching this result, the court applied the rule from its earlier *Sigall* case, above, but determined that there was sufficient evidence that the university was attempting to thwart the civil service system.

Two years later, however, in *Local 4501 Communications Workers of America v. Ohio State University*, 494 N.E.2d 1082 (Ohio 1986), the same court severely limited its 1984 decision. Noting that the Ohio legislature had in the interim passed a statute permitting public employees to bargain collectively, the court held that civil service employees now had sufficient "protection" through the bargaining table and did not need the additional civil service protection provided by the court's 1984 decision. That decision was thus left to apply only in rare situations where a state agency had attempted to thwart the civil service system but the affected employees had no statutory right to bargain collectively.

As these cases illustrate, the authority of public institutions to outsource services will depend on a variety of factors: the existence of state laws that expressly permit or prohibit particular types of service contracts, the implications that courts may draw from the civil service laws, the impact that a particular contract would have on civil service employment, the presence or absence of collective bargaining in the employment field that would be affected by the service contract, and the provisions of collective bargaining contracts that the institution has entered with its employees. The weight to be given such factors, and the content of applicable statutes and regulations, will, of course, vary from state to state.

One of the newer purchasing contexts, of particular importance, is the purchase of instructional services. A 1997 case, *Linkage Corp. v. Trustees of Boston University*, 679 N.E.2d 191 (Mass. 1997), provides an outstanding example of problems that can arise in this context. The case also illustrates how state statutes, rather than or in addition to state common law of contract or tort, may apply to such purchase arrangements. As explained by the Supreme Judicial Court of Massachusetts, the dispute in the case arose "out of an agreement between Linkage Corporation (Linkage) and Boston University that called for Linkage to create and provide educational, training, and other programs of a technical nature at a satellite facility owned by Boston University." Under this agreement, "Linkage initiated a variety of training programs, conferences, seminars, and other offerings for the corporate market. Boston University also transferred some university courses to [the Satellite Education Center] which Linkage then managed for the university." "Linkage claims that the agreement was renewed by Boston University and then unlawfully terminated; Boston University claims that the agreement was lawfully terminated and never renewed." The court agreed with Linkage and, thus, held the university liable for breaching the renewed contract. The court also agreed that the university's conduct constituted a violation of a Massachusetts unfair practices statute, Mass. Gen. Laws Ann. Ch. 93A. The applicability of this statute was of great importance in the litigation because the statute authorized the court to double the amount of the damages awarded by the jury and, in addition, to award the successful plaintiff attorney's fees and court costs.

The state statute at issue creates new rights, beyond those afforded by the Massachusetts common law of contract and tort. The trial judge found, and the appellate court affirmed, "that Boston University's actions constituted unfair or deceptive practices, and that they constituted willful and knowing violations of the statute." In particular, according to the court, "[t]he University, and its principals, repudiated binding agreements and usurped Linkage's business and work force in order to promote a purely self-serving agenda. The result was to end Linkage's vitality as a going concern, at least until it might be able to reconstitute itself with its main mission still intact."

Before holding the university liable under Chapter 93A, the court addressed two important threshold issues: first, whether the interaction between the parties was "commercial" in character; and second, whether the parties to the dispute were both engaged in "trade or commerce" and, therefore, acting in a "business context." Regarding the first issue, the problem was whether the interaction between the parties was an "intra-enterprise" dispute—such as a dispute between employer and employee or between partners in a partnership—which would not be considered a "genuine commercial transaction" for purposes of the statute. The court held that the transaction was commercial rather than intra-enterprise: "The arrangement between Linkage and Boston University was an arm's-length transaction between two corporations under which Linkage provided services to Boston University and received compensation. Both the base and renewal agreements state that Linkage is 'an independent contractor . . . not an agent or employee of the university,' indicating that, from the very beginning of their relationship, the parties did not intend to be treated as partners or participants in a joint venture."

Regarding the second issue, the problem was whether Boston University, a non-profit corporation, was engaged in trade or commerce when it operated the Satellite Education Center. The court emphasized that an entity's nonprofit or charitable status is not itself dispositive of this question and that "a corporation need not be profit-making in order to profit from an activity." The court also emphasized that fees were charged for the services offered at the Satellite Education Center; that the university was "motivated by a strong desire to benefit as much as possible from its arrangement with Linkage as a means of dealing with the debt service and costs of the [Satellite Education Center]; and that the University sought to 'expand its reach . . . to the corporate market [that] provided a . . . lucrative earnings potential. . . ." The court thus concluded, as to the second issue:

> In most circumstances, a charitable institution will not be engaged in trade or commerce when it undertakes activities in furtherance of its core mission. But when, as in the case here, an institution's business motivations, in combination with the nature of the transaction and the activities of the parties, establish a "business context" . . . G.L. c. 93A will apply because the institution has inserted itself into the marketplace in a way that makes it only proper that it be subject to rules of ethical behavior and fair play [679 N.E.2d at 209].

Thus, having determined that the unfair practices statute applied to the transaction between Boston University and Linkage, and that Boston University had violated the statute, the court doubled Linkage's damage award (from $2,411,852 to $4,823,704) and awarded attorney's fees and costs to Linkage in the amount of $899,382.

15.2.3. Purchase of real estate. While goods are personal property, land and buildings are real property. The U.C.C. is inapplicable to sales of real property; state real property law governs the bulk of the transaction. An institution's real property transactions may include the purchase of title to land and buildings, leasehold interests in land and buildings, and options to purchase or lease land or buildings, as well as easements, rights-of-way, and other interests in land. The title to property transfers only in the first of these types of transactions, and then only at settlement.

Real estate transactions are substantially different from transactions for the purchase of goods or services. The legal documents evidencing the transactions differ, as does the governing law. When an institution purchases land or buildings, for instance, there will be a sales contract with its own special provisions; financing agreements, typically including one or more mortgages or deed-of-trust instruments creating the lender's security interest in the property; and the deed that transfers title to the property. In conjunction with the transaction, the institution may also need to consider local zoning law and the property's zoning classification (see Section 11.2 of this book), as well as the real property tax status of the property under the institution's planned use(s) (see Sections 11.3 & 12.1). For public institutions, there may be various other state law requirements and authority issues to consider. (See generally Carol Zeiner, "Monetary and Regulatory Hobbling: The Acquisition of Real Property by Public Institutions of Higher Education in Florida," 12 *U. Miami Bus. L. Rev.* 105 (2004).) Moreover, because real estate purchases can be part of a larger entrepreneurial or academic endeavor, partnership or joint venture agreements may also be involved, as may other subsidiary real estate transactions, such as purchase options, leases, or lease-backs.

15.2.4. The special case of design and construction contracts

15.2.4.1. General principles. One of the most complex purchasing situations an institution may encounter is that concerning design and construction contracts. Since there are usually more parties involved and more money at stake in these contracts than in other purchase contracts, both counsel and high-level administrators should be directly involved and keenly aware of the difficulties that may arise. (See generally R. Rubin & L. Banick, "The Ten Commandments of Design and Construction Contracts," a paper presented at the 32d Annual Conference of the National Association of College and University Attorneys, 1992, and on file with the Association.)

Before an institution can develop the specifics of the contracts for a major construction project, it must first implement a financing plan. Then, as owner of the future building, the institution will typically contract with an architect or engineer, or both, to design and oversee the plans for construction. Next the institution will solicit bids from general contractors, select a contractor, and negotiate a construction contract. The general contractor will then hire sub-contractors to do masonry work, electrical work, painting, plumbing, and so forth. Numerous suppliers will also be involved, as will insurance companies, bonding companies, and sometimes outside funding sources. Thus, in a standard design and construction arrangement, there are numerous parties that could be liable to the institution and to which the institution could be liable should difficulties arise.

The institution must determine what types of contracts it will seek to negotiate with the architect and general contractor. Construction contracts usually are fixed price contracts resulting from competitive bidding. In such a contract, the entire project is planned from start to finish before any work is done. A price for the project is fixed, and the contractor begins work for that amount (with a possibility of adjustments for unexpected costs incurred during the work, if the contract so provides). A variation of this type of contract is the cost-plus contract, under which the contractor's profit margin is based on a set percentage of overall costs. This type of contract typically contains clauses under which the overall cost may exceed the base bid, taking into account labor and materials costs actually incurred during construction, but may not exceed a specified "guaranteed maximum cost." Yet another type of contract is the "fast-track design" contract, which an institution may use if the project must begin quickly. In such a contract, actual construction starts almost immediately, and details of cost and design are left to be resolved as the project develops—affording the obvious advantage of speed but also the obvious disadvantage of unresolved design issues and an incomplete, potentially escalating, budget for the project.

Various standard form contracts exist for both architectural and construction services. The American Institute of Architects and the National Construction Law Center, among others, offer standardized form contracts for various types of projects, especially private sector projects. Some form contracts tend to favor the architect or contractor, and others the institution, so the institution should be careful in its selection. Moreover, the institution should consider adding terms or deleting particular clauses to make the contract fit the institution's particular purposes and concerns. In negotiating the contract, the institution should also anticipate and cover such problem areas as construction delays, compensation schemes, unsatisfactory work, insurance coverage, employment discrimination, and changes in design or materials. In addition, the contract should specify who may speak for and bind each of the parties and what dispute resolution mechanisms will be used.

Although construction contracts may be more enmeshed in statutory law than other contracts are (see subsection 15.2.4.2 below), the general contract principles discussed in Section 15.1 still apply. As indicated there, however, and as the court explained in *Ames Contracting Co., Inc. v. City University of New York* (cited in subsection 15.2.2 above): "Construction contracts are service contracts providing a combination of labor, skill and materials and are generally exempted from the operation of the Uniform Commercial Code." Making the same point in reference to a subcontractor, the court in *Manor Junior College v. Kaller's Inc.*, 507 A.2d 1245 (Pa. Super. Ct. 1986), noted that, "since . . . [the subcontractor] was hired by [the general contractor] to perform a service, specifically, to provide most of the labor for the installation of a roof, we must reject the assertion of appellant that the U.C.C. is applicable."

Kingery Construction Co. v. Board of Regents of the University of Nebraska, 203 N.W.2d 150 (Neb. 1973), illustrates how general contract principles apply to construction contracts. A general contractor brought an action for declaratory judgment to determine whether, under a contract with the University of Nebraska, it was required to paint exposed pipes in the building under construction. The general contractor's interpretation of the contract was that the mechanical contractor was solely responsible for completing the pipe painting. It did not, however, seek relief from the mechanical contractor; it sought only a declaration from the court that it was not under a contractual duty to the university to do the painting. Relying on basic principles of contract interpretation, the court held that, although "[q]uite possibly the contract, in part, duplicated requirements for painting as pertains to [the general contractor] and the mechanical contractor," the general contractor remained liable to the university to complete the disputed painting. (The court made no comment on possible liability of the mechanical contractor to the general contractor.)

15.2.4.2. Construction contracts in public institutions. Unlike private institutions, public colleges and universities may be statutorily required to use a competitive bidding process in deciding which general contractor to select. Competitive bidding statutes come in many forms. California and New York have statutes pertaining specifically to state universities and construction contracts (Cal. Pub. Cont. Code § 10503; N.Y. Educ. Law § 376). Both statutes require institutions to engage in public bidding before awarding any major construction contract. Other states have more general statutes that apply to any building project the state undertakes (for example, S.H.A. 20 ILCS 3110/0.01 *et seq.* (1994); Tex. Rev. Civ. Stat. Ann. art. 601b). State statutes may also require that contractors or architects for public construction projects meet certain licensing requirements (for example, Fla. Stat. Ann. §§ 481.223 (architects) and 489.113 (contractors)), or may include other particular requirements concerning architectural services (for example, W. Va. Code §§ 5G-1-1 to -4).

Competitive bidding carries its own special baggage. An institution is required to accept the "lowest *responsible* bidder" to do the project. This phrase accords the institution some discretion to look behind the bid and assure itself that the lowest bidder is trustworthy and competent to do the work. Thus, an institution may reject the lowest bidder if that contractor is deemed to be nonresponsible, or it may reject all the bids if no responsible bid is received. Nevertheless, numerous complexities may arise in determining which bidder is the "lowest" bidder, as illustrated by *SE/Z Construction, L.L.C. v. Idaho State University*, 89 P.3d 848 (Idaho 2004). This case arose under Idaho Code § 67-5711C, requiring that "[a]ll construction contracts for public works shall be awarded to the lowest responsible and responsive bidder after receipt of competitive sealed bidding . . ." and Idaho Code § 67-2309, requiring that "all plans and specifications for said contracts or materials shall state . . . the number, size, kind and quality of materials and services required for such contract. . . ." The university solicited bids for renovation of its physical sciences building, and the bids were to include a base price; five alternate prices; and the prices for each of two different packages of audiovisual (AV) systems to be installed in some of the classrooms in the renovated building. Based on the submitted bids, the university awarded the contract to a contractor whose base bid plus alternates was the second-lowest bid received but whose bid prices for the AV packages were the lowest. The bidder with the lowest base and alternate bid price (but not the lowest AV package prices) sued the university, arguing that it was the lowest bidder. Sorting out this complex mix of bid components, and closely examining the provisions of the university's published bid request, the Supreme Court of Idaho determined that the university had not violated the competitive bidding statute and rejected the plaintiff's challenge.

Institutions are also subject to requirements on advertising for bids that can create difficulties in the competitive bidding process. In *Gibbs Construction Co., Inc. v. Board of Supervisors of Louisiana State University*, 447 So. 2d 90 (La. 1984), for instance, a general contractor sued the university after being denied a contract even though it was the lowest bidder. The contractor had not appeared at the pre-bid conference and thus was technically ineligible to submit a bid. The court upheld the lower court's dismissal of the suit because the contractor had not conformed to the advertised specifications that all eligible bidders were required to attend the pre-bid conference.

There may also be issues concerning the type of contracts to which the competitive bidding statutes apply. In *McMaster Construction, Inc. v. Board of Regents of Oklahoma Colleges*, 934 P.2d 335 (Okla. 1997), for example, unsuccessful bidders sought to use Oklahoma's Competitive Bidding Act (Okla. Stat. Title 61 §§ 101–133), to void construction management contracts awarded by the University of Central Oklahoma for the oversight of capital improvements projects on the university campus. The Supreme Court of Oklahoma rejected the plaintiffs' argument that the regents had failed to comply with the Competitive Bidding Act, holding that the construction management contracts were not subject to the Act because they covered personal services requiring professional judgment and did not involve actual construction or supplying materials. The court also rejected the plaintiffs' arguments that the contracts did not comply with the Public Building Construction and Planning Act or with the State Consultants Act; the former Act expressly excluded the regents from coverage and the latter Act covered only architectural, engineering, and surveying services—categories into which the construction services contracts "did not fall."

Another type of issue concerning the applicability of a competitive bidding statute arose in *Associated Subcontractors of Massachusetts, Inc. v. University of Massachusetts Bldg. Authority*, 810 N.E.2d 1214 (Mass. 2004). The university's project was the construction of a dormitory complex. By statute, so long as more than 50 percent of the funds to be expended for the project are from "nongovernmental sources," the University of Massachusetts Building Authority could, with the approval of the Governor, proceed without complying with the state competitive bidding statute (Mass. Gen. Laws Ann. Ch. 75 App. § 1–18). After the building authority demonstrated that at least half of the funds used for the project would be from student fees, "the Governor approved the authority's request, agreeing that the student room and board fees used to fund the construction were 'funds from nongovernmental sources.' . . ." When a state association of subcontractors challenged this interpretation of the key statutory phrase and sued the university and its building authority, the court had to determine, as a matter of first impression, whether the student room and board fees used to repay principal and interest on construction financing bonds were "funds from nongovernmental sources." The court considered the legislative history of the statutory amendment that allowed the university building authority to bypass the competitive bidding process, and also considered other state statutory provisions regarding public funds, and other statutory provisions containing the same terminology as that in the challenged provision. The court emphasized that the student fees were not "raised by State, local, or Federal taxation" and were not part of any "governmental appropriation . . . made for the [construction] project." Moreover, the fees "originate with private individuals who desire to reside in university housing" and are paid by the university "directly to the bond trustee." The fees therefore were funds from "nongovernmental sources" whose use exempted the university building authority from the requirements of the competitive bidding statute.

In an interesting development after the case, however, the Massachusetts legislature amended the statute to overrule the result in the case:

> [T]he term "nongovernmental sources" shall be limited to private donations, gifts, contracts, or grants, including commercial ventures and intellectual property contracts, or grants or contracts from the federal government or the administrative overhead associated with such grants and contracts; but the term shall not mean revenue derived from fees, tuition or charges of any kind paid by students, faculty, or staff [Mass. Gen. Laws Ann. Ch. 75 App. § 1–18 (2004)].

In addition to competitive bidding and licensing statutes, public institutions in some states must also be concerned with minority set-aside statutes. Such statutes "set aside" a certain percentage of state construction work for minority contracting firms. In *City of Richmond v. J. A. Croson Co.*, 488 U.S. 469

(1989), the U.S. Supreme Court indicated that such programs may be constitutional but only if they meet a strict scrutiny standard of review (see Section 5.4). Thus, if the state or a state university seeks to remedy past discrimination through a set-aside program, it will have a heavy burden of justification; a mere general assertion of past discrimination, without specific statistics identifying past discrimination in particular fields and a demonstration of how the set-aside ameliorates that discrimination, is not likely to suffice. Assuming that the statute is valid, the requirements it imposes on the institution will depend on the particular statutory provisions, which vary from state to state. In *Croson,* for example, the set-aside program required that 30 percent of the dollar amount of any contract be subcontracted to minority businesses. Other programs may only establish statewide goals or vest discretion in the institution or statewide system to set its own goals or take other actions favoring minority businesses. In California, for example, the Regents of the University of California may consider whether a "substantially equal" bid is received from a "disadvantaged business enterprise" (Cal. Pub. Cont. Code § 10501); if so, the regents might favor that business over another business that submitted a lower bid. Moreover, under Cal. Pub. Cont. Code § 10500.5(a), the regents are encouraged to adopt measures such as set-aside "targets for utilization of small businesses, particularly disadvantaged business enterprises." The various state statutes include their own definitions of "minority" and may also encompass female-owned businesses (see 30 Ill. Comp. Stat. 575/1 *et seq.*).

An Ohio minority set-aside statute was at issue in *F. Buddie Contracting, Limited v. Cuyahoga Community College District,* 31 F. Supp. 2d 584 (N.D. Ohio 1998). The statute, Ohio Rev. Code § 123.151, requires that 5 percent of contracts on a project be set aside for minority bidders. A second statute, Ohio Rev. Code § 3354.161, applies these requirements specifically to contracts of Ohio community college districts. The community college district had implemented a minority set-aside policy in compliance with the state statute. The federal district court held, however, that the district was also obligated to ensure that its implementation of the policy was "narrowly tailored to advance a compelling government interest"—the constitutional standard used in *Adarand.* The district's failure to meet this requirement violated the equal protection clause of the Fourteenth Amendment. (This case is discussed further in Section 4.7.4 with respect to qualified immunity.)

15.2.4.3. Liability problems. Because of the number of parties involved and the complexities of the contract itself, numerous liability problems can arise with design and construction contracts. The following cases illustrate types of liabilities that may arise, for the institution as well as for other parties, and the ways in which courts may resolve liability issues.

The first case, *Dugan & Meyers Construction Co., Inc. v. State of Ohio Dept. of Administrative Services,* 2003 WL 21640882 (Ohio Ct. Cl. 2003), *affirmed,* 2003 WL 22890599 (Ohio Ct. Cl. 2003), *reversed in part and affirmed in part,* 834 N.E.2d 1 (Ohio Ct. App. 2005), illustrates the complexities, and the clashes among numerous parties, that can arise in construction project litigation, and serves as a valuable cautionary tale for institutions. The case concerned the construction of three buildings for the Fisher College of Business on the campus of the Ohio State University (OSU). After a competitive bidding phase, Dugan & Meyers (D&M) was selected for general trades work and for lead contractor services, and four other companies were selected for additional portions of the work: a heating, ventilation, and air conditioning (HVAC) contractor; an electrical contractor; a plumbing contractor; and a site work company. All parties had agreed to a "baseline schedule" for the work's completion, which stressed the university's need to utilize the completed structures by the start of the fall 1999 academic quarter. The first major disruption of this schedule was a four-week extension, agreed to by the parties, resulting from some difficulty in procuring structural steel for the project. As time passed, the project fell further behind schedule. In July 1999, the university relieved D&M of its responsibilities as lead contractor, employed the construction manager for the project to take over D&M's obligations, and informed D&M that it would be backcharged for the cost of employing the construction manager in its stead. The university further assessed liquidated damages against each of the other contractors for their alleged failures to facilitate the timely completion of the project.

D&M and other contractors sued the university and the state agency responsible for administering the contract. After a lengthy trial that produced voluminous testimony and evidence (seventeen days, more than six thousand pages of testimony, and several thousand pages of exhibits), the court of claims referee found that the principal cause of the delays in construction was "an excessive number of errors, omissions and conflicts in the design documents furnished to bidders by the state and incorporated into the plaintiffs' contracts," which in turn prevented the plaintiffs from "perform[ing] the required activities with the efficiency and productivity reasonably contemplated in the plaintiffs' bids and in the approved baseline schedule" (2003 WL 21640882, at p. 6).

The referee also found that OSU breached its contract with D&M by removing D&M as lead contractor and backcharging D&M for the services of its replacement, and that D&M was entitled to reversal of the charge. The referee recommended that D&M recover over $2.7 million in damages. (In addition, the referee found that the university had breached its contract with the HVAC contractor, and the electrical and plumbing contractors, entitling them to cancellation of the liquidated damages the university had assessed against them.)

On appeal, the reviewing judge on the court of claims adopted much of the referee's report, finding that "[the university's] failure to provide complete, accurate and buildable plans and specifications was a breach of contract, thereby entitling plaintiffs to damages proven by a preponderance of the evidence." Both parties then appealed to the state court of appeals, which affirmed the court of claims' ruling on reversing the "back-charge" but reversed the court of claims' other rulings, on a variety of grounds, and reduced D&M's damage award to $264,000. The Ohio Supreme Court had granted D&M's request for an appeal as this book went to press (840 N.E.2d 202 (2005) (table)).

In *Broadway Maintenance Corp. v. Rutgers, The State University,* 447 A.2d 906 (N.J. 1982), another suit by contractors, the institution prevailed. The contractors requested damages for harm they suffered from delays caused when one subcontractor's work interfered with the timely completion of another's. They claimed that the university was liable because it had failed to "synthesize" the work adequately. The court held that, because the university had entrusted overall responsibility for supervision of the work to a general contractor, the university was not liable to the subcontractors for damages caused by the delays. Since the university had contracted with a general contractor to supervise the work, liability for failure to "synthesize" the work rested entirely on that general contractor. The court noted, however, that "if no one were designated to carry on the overall supervision, the reasonable implication would be that the owner [the university] would perform those duties." The court also noted that subcontractors "may have valid causes of action against each other for damages due to unjustifiable delay."

Similarly, in *John Grace & Co. v. State University Construction Fund,* 472 N.Y.S.2d 757 (N.Y. App. Div. 1984), *affirmed as modified,* 475 N.E.2d 105 (N.Y. 1985), a university construction fund escaped liability to a general contractor because it had fully entrusted the execution of the details of the construction contract to an engineer. The general contractor brought suit against the construction fund for the cost of repairs to a hot water distribution system the general contractor had installed. The contractor installed the system properly to the best of its knowledge, but the engineer hired by the construction fund had allowed improper components to be used in the installation, necessitating the repairs by the general contractor. As in *Broadway,* the court held that the construction fund had hired a third party (the engineer) to be responsible for the overall completion of the contract, and it was that third party, not the university or fund, that was liable to the general contractor for the cost of the repairs.

The university ended up a loser, however, in *Davidson and Jones, Inc. v. North Carolina Department of Administration,* 337 S.E.2d 463 (N.C. 1985), another suit brought by a general contractor. The contractor had encountered unexpected amounts of rock to excavate. The contract clearly stated that the university would pay $55 per cubic yard for any rock excavation in excess of 800 cubic yards. When there turned out to be a 400 percent overrun on excavation, causing a six-month delay, the contractor sued the university, demanding that it pay the agreed-upon $55 per cubic yard plus the additional costs the contractor incurred (such as the cost of keeping personnel at the job site) as a direct result of the delay. The state supreme court held that the university was liable for the additional, duration-related, costs, noting that "[t]he trial court found . . . that [duration-related costs] were customarily budgeted as a function of a project's expected duration and were included as such in a contractor's base bid [and] that it was not customary . . . to make any allowance for such costs in setting unit prices." Thus, because the contract did not provide protection against these costs, and the contractor had no reasonable way of predicting a 400 percent excavation overrun, the court ordered the university to pay the contractor not only the $55 per cubic yard for the overruns but also more than $110,000 for other on-site expenses associated with the extra time spent on the project.

In *United States Fidelity & Guaranty Co. v. Jacksonville State University,* 357 So. 2d 952 (Ala. 1978), it was the university that brought suit, claiming that a general contractor was liable for a subcontractor's breach of contract. The court used standard contract principles in agreeing that the general contractor was liable to the university for the poor workmanship of the subcontractor, even though the architect for the project had specified which subcontractor to use. Although the contract contained conflicting terms regarding the general contractor's responsibility for the work of the subcontractors, the court accepted as controlling a clause stating that the general contractor would be responsible for all project work of the subcontractors. The contract also clearly stated that the subcontractors had no contractual relationship with the university and thus could not be directly liable to it for breach of contract. (Subcontractors would have a contractual relationship with the general contractor, however, who if sued might have the option of impleading the subcontractors, since they would ultimately be liable to the general contractor for their poor workmanship.)

These are but a few examples of the many types of liability issues that may arise from institutional construction contracts. Counsel will need to be heavily involved in the resolution of these problems if they arise, as well as in preventing such problems through careful contract drafting and construction planning.

Sec. 15.3. *The College as Seller/Competitor*

15.3.1. *Auxiliary enterprises*

15.3.1.1. Overview. With increasing frequency and vigor, postsecondary institutions have expanded the scope of "auxiliary" enterprises or operations that involve the institution in the sale of goods, services, or leasehold (rental) interests in real estate.[6] In some situations such sales may be restricted to the members of the campus community (students, faculty, staff); in other situations sales may also be made incidentally to the general public; and in yet other situations the general public or a particular noncampus clientele may be the primary sales target.

---

[6]The phrases "auxiliary enterprises," "auxiliary operations," and "auxiliary activities," as used throughout Section 15.3, refer to a broad range of functions that are claimed to be "auxiliary" to the education and research that are the central mission of a higher education institution. To fall within this Section, such functions must place the institution or one of its subsidiary or affiliated organizations (Section 3.6) in the position of seller and must be (or have the potential to be) income producing. These phrases, however, do not include investment activities generating dividends, interest, annuity income, or capital gains.

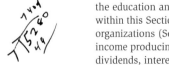

Examples include child care services provided for a fee at campus child care centers; barbering and hairstyling services; travel services; computing services; graphics, printing, and copying services; credit card services; conference management services; and interactive computer conferencing services and related communication services. Other examples concern the sale of goods: the sale of personal computers and software to students; the sale of merchandise by campus bookstores and convenience stores; the sale of refreshments at concession stands during athletic events; the sale of advertising space in university sports stadiums and arenas or in university publications; the sale of hearing aids at campus speech and hearing clinics; the sale of books by university presses; *Yale up* and the sale of prescription drugs and health care supplies at university med- *to* ical centers. Programs and events that generate fees provide other examples, *eyeballs* such as summer sports camps on the campus; training programs for business and industry; entertainment and athletic events open to the general public for an admission charge; and hotel or dining facilities open to university guests or the general public. Leasing activities provide yet other examples, such as rental of dormitory rooms to travelers or outside groups; rental of campus auditoriums, conference facilities, athletic facilities, and radio or television stations; and leasing of campus space to private businesses that operate on campus.

In addition, institutions may sell "rights" to other sellers, who then can market particular products or services on campus—for example, a sale of rights to a soft drink company to market its soft drinks on campus. Similarly, institutions may sell other "rights" for a profit, such as broadcast rights for intercollegiate athletic contests or rights to use the institution's trademarks. Institutions, moreover, may enter corporate sponsorship or corporate partnership arrangements with commercial entities that reap financial benefits for the institution. (The sale (or licensing) of intellectual property rights may also occur in connection with research and development; see Section 15.4.3 below.)

Institutions may engage in such activities for a variety of reasons. The goal may be to provide clinical training opportunities for students (for example, speech and hearing clinics or hotel administration schools); to make campus life more convenient and self-contained, thus enhancing the quality of life (banks, fast-food restaurants, travel services, barber shops and hairstyling salons, convenience stores); to increase institutional visibility and good will with professional and corporate organizations, or with the general public (training programs, conference management services, rental of campus facilities); or to make productive use of underutilized space, especially in the summer (summer sports camps, rental of dormitory rooms and conference facilities). In addition to or in lieu of these goals, however, institutions may operate some auxiliary enterprises in response to budgetary pressures or initiatives that necessitate the generation of new revenues or prompt particular institutional units to be self-supporting.

When the growth in auxiliary enterprises and related entrepreneurial activities is considered alongside the ever-expanding purchasing activities and vendor relationships of institutions, and the increased reliance on outsourcing (see Section 15.2.2 above), a trend toward "commercialization" of college and university operations begins to emerge. Such a trend is further evidenced in the partnerships with industry that institutions increasingly form with respect to scientific research and development (see Section 15.4 below). These developments may affect institutions, their campus communities, and local communities in many ways, some good and some not, and may also raise critical questions about academic values and institutional mission. (See, for example, Jennifer Croissant, "Can This Campus Be Bought?" *Academe,* September–October 2001, 44–48.)

When auxiliary operations are for educational purposes and involve goods, services, or facilities not generally available from local businesses, "commercialization" is generally not evident, and few controversies arise. Those that do arise usually involve tort and contract liability issues fitting within the scope of Sections 3.3 and 3.4 of this book, or issues concerning government licenses and inspections (for example, for a campus food service). But when auxiliary operations extend beyond educational purposes or put the institution in a competitive position, numerous new issues may arise. Critics may charge that the institution's activities are drawing customers away from local businesses; that the competition is unfair because of the institution's tax-exempt status, funding sources, and other advantages; that the institution's activities are inconsistent with its academic mission and are diverting institutional resources from academic to commercial concerns; or that the institution's activities expose it to substantial new risks that could result in monetary loss or loss of prestige from commercial contract and bill collection disputes (see generally Section 15.1) and tort liability claims.

The case of *Heirs and Wrongful Death Beneficiaries of Branning v. Hinds Community College District,* 743 So. 2d 311 (Miss. 1999), illustrates how auxiliary activities can subject an institution to tort liability claims and how a college's structuring of its auxiliary operations can limit its liability for the negligent acts of third parties. In this case, the crash of a private plane had resulted in the deaths of Branning, a passenger in the plane, and Tomlinson, the pilot, and injuries to two other passengers. The defendant, Hinds Community College District (HCCD), acting under a long-term lease from Hinds County (a legal entity separate from the college), served as the airport authority for the airport where the plane had taken off. In fulfilling its responsibilities under the lease, HCCD had contracted with Tomlinson Avionics, Inc., to be its airport manager. Michael Tomlinson, an employee of Tomlinson Avionics, was in charge of implementing the corporation's responsibilities as airport manager, and was also the pilot of the plane that had crashed shortly after takeoff. Tomlinson had met Branning and the other passengers at a bar and had invited them for a ride in his private plane that he kept at the airport. After the crash, Tomlinson was found to have an alcohol content in his blood that was beyond legal limits.

The plaintiffs, representing the deceased passenger, Branning, argued that HCCD had a duty to exercise reasonable care to protect her from the harms she had suffered at the hands of HCCD's own airport manager. The Supreme Court of Mississippi asserted that "[t]o determine whether Hinds [HCCD] owed a duty to take due care to the plaintiffs, the relationship between Hinds and Tomlinson must first be established. . . . The main concern in this case is whether this was an employer/employee relationship or an independent contract." The difference between the two, the court explained, is that, while an employer may be vicariously liable for the acts of its employees, it may not be held vicariously liable for the torts of an independent contractor that it engages "or for the torts of the independent contractor's employees in the performance of the contract." (See generally Sections 2.1.3 & 4.2.1 of this book.) To determine the relationship between HCCD and Tomlinson, the court analyzed the terms of the two contracts between HCCD and Tomlinson Avionics, as well as the conduct of the parties under these contracts, concluding that "the relationship between the two parties is that of independent contractor." HCCD therefore owed no duty of care to the plaintiffs and could not be vicariously liable for the torts of Tomlinson Avionics or of Michael Tomlinson.

In addition to contract and tort liability issues, as in the *Branning* case, commercially oriented or noneducational auxiliary activities may also raise problems in the areas of public relations, government relations (especially for public institutions, and especially with state legislatures), budgets and resources, and insurance and other risk management practices (see Section 2.5). Other types of legal issues may also arise, as discussed in subsections 15.3.1.2 and 15.3.2 through 15.3.4 below.

In some situations, moreover, an institution's activities as a seller will become intertwined with its activities as a purchaser. An institution may outsource the selling of certain products or services on campus to an outside third party, for example, in which case the institution will have "purchased" the services of the third party in order to effectuate sales. The case of *ABL Management, Inc. v. Board of Supervisors of Southern University and Agricultural & Mechanical College,* 773 So. 2d 131 (La. 2000), discussed in Section 15.2.2, is an interesting example of how selling and purchasing may become entwined. When this does occur, the institution may be subject not only to legal requirements pertaining to selling, set out in this Section, but also to some legal requirements regarding purchasing, such as those set out in Section 15.2.

15.3.1.2. Institutional authority to operate auxiliary enterprises

15.3.1.2.1. PUBLIC INSTITUTIONS. The scope of an institution's authority to operate particular auxiliary enterprises may be questioned whether or not the institution's activity puts it in competition with local businesses. As a practical matter, however, competitive activities of public institutions are much more likely to be controversial and to be challenged on authority grounds than are those of private institutions.

For public institutions, the basic question is whether the constitutional and statutory provisions delegating authority to the institution (see generally Section 12.2 of this book), and the appropriations acts authorizing expenditures of public funds, are broad enough to encompass the auxiliary operation at issue. Challenges may be made by business competitors, by state taxpayers, or by the state Attorney General. Challenges may focus on the conduct of a particular activity or the operation of a particular facility, on the construction of a particular facility, or on the financing arrangements (bond issues and otherwise) for construction or operation of a particular facility or activity.

Several important early cases in the period of the 1920s to the 1940s illustrate the problem and lay the foundation for the more modern cases. One of the earliest (and by today's standards, easiest) cases was *Long v. Board of Trustees*, 157 N.E. 395 (Ohio Ct. App. 1926)—a challenge to bookstore sales to students and faculty at Ohio State University. Noting that the sales were "practically upon a cost basis," the court upheld this activity because it was "reasonably incidental" to the operation of the university.

In another early case, *Batcheller v. Commonwealth ex rel. Rector and Visitors of University of Virginia*, 10 S.E.2d 529 (Va. 1940), the issue was whether the university had authority to build and operate a commercial airport. The university offered a course in aeronautical engineering but, without an airport, had been unable to provide its students flight instruction or the ability to take advantage of flight instructors and related benefits that the Civil Aeronautics Authority offered at little or no cost. On the university's application, the State Corporation Commission issued the university a permit to construct, maintain, and operate an airport for civil aircraft involved in commercial aviation. The plaintiffs, adjoining landowners, sought judicial review of the commission's decision, claiming that the commission had no authority to grant the permit because the university had no authority to operate such an airport. The court recognized that the university "has not only the powers expressly conferred upon it, but also the implied power to do whatever is reasonably necessary to effectuate the powers expressly granted." Quoting the commission, the court reasoned that:

> [t]he University in making application for the permit in question was not asking for the right to engage in commercial aviation, but only for the right to operate and conduct an airport for the landing and departure of *civil aircraft engaged in commercial aviation*, upon which there could be given instruction in student flying so necessary and essential to its course in aeronautics. . . . [T]he University will be authorized by the permit to own and operate an airport upon which aircraft engaged in commercial aviation may land or take off, but this would not involve it in a purely commercial or industrial enterprise, but, as has been shown, in an enterprise necessary to and incidental to the full and complete instruction in the course in aeronautics which it has established [10 S.E.2d at 535 (emphasis in original)].

The airport thus fell into the category of "necessary but incidental enterprises," the operation of which was within the university's legal authority.

In *Turkovich v. Board of Trustees of the University of Illinois*, 143 N.E.2d 229 (Ill. 1957), taxpayers sought to enjoin the university from using state funds to construct, equip, and operate a television station. The plaintiffs claimed that: (1) the university had no legal authority to operate a television station; and

(2) there was no valid appropriation of funds for the purpose of building and maintaining a television station, either because the appropriation acts the university relied on were too general to encompass the challenged expenditures or because these acts violated the Illinois constitution's "itemization requirements" governing the legislative appropriation of state funds.

The university had obtained a permit from the Federal Communications Commission (FCC) to construct and operate a noncommercial television station. The station was to be used to train and instruct students in the communications and broadcasting field, to facilitate the dissemination of research on a campus-wide basis, to experiment in the planning and technique of television programming, and to educate the public. (It was not clear from the court's opinion whether the television station would operate in competition with local commercial stations.) Concerning the authority issue, the court determined that, under the statute creating the university, the board of trustees had "authority to do everything necessary in the management, operating and administration of the University, including any necessary or incidental powers in the furtherance of the corporate purposes." Since the challenged activity encompassed "research and experimentation," it was "well within the powers of the University without any additional statutory enactment upon the subject." Regarding the appropriation issues, the court held that "[t]he impracticability of detailing funds for the many activities and functions of the University in the Appropriation Act is readily apparent," and the legislature "cannot be expected to allocate funds to each of the myriad activities of the University and thereby practically substitute itself for the Board of Trustees in the management thereof." The court thus concluded that the board of trustees' expenditures for the television station were consistent with the relevant state appropriation acts and the constitutional mandates concerning appropriation of state monies.

The last of the leading early cases is *Villyard v. Regents of University System of Georgia*, 50 S.E.2d 313 (Ga. 1948). The issue was whether the regents had the authority to operate a laundry and dry cleaning business at one of the system's colleges, the Georgia State College for Women. The customers of the business were the college's students; faculty members, executive officers, staff, and their families; and, apparently, former employees and their families as well. The charges for the laundry and dry cleaning services were lower than those of local commercial dry cleaning and laundry businesses. The plaintiffs, operators of such businesses, sought to enjoin and restrict the college's enterprise. They claimed it was unfair for the college "to use rent-free public property in the operation of said enterprise in competition with the private enterprises of petitioners" and that such activities represented a "capricious exercise of . . . power that thwarts the purpose of the legislature in establishing the University System. . . ." The court recognized that the regent's powers and duties under the Georgia Code "are untrammelled except by such restraints of law as are directly expressed, or necessarily implied. 'Under the powers granted, it becomes necessary . . . to look for limitations, rather than for authority to do specific acts.' *State v. Regents of the Univ. System of Georgia*, 210, 227, 175 S.E.2d 567, 576." Then, suggesting that the college's business was "reasonably related to the education, welfare, and health" of the student body, the court held that the business did not transgress any state constitutional or statutory limitations on the regents' authority. Further, "if the operation of the laundry and dry-cleaning service, at a price less than the commercial rate for the benefit of those connected with the school, is lawful, it matters not that such enterprise is competitive with the plaintiffs' business." In so deciding, the court apparently applied an expansive understanding of the college's educational purposes so as to encompass not only services to students, but also services to faculty, staff, and others with connections to the college. The court did not specify the particular educational benefit that the students gained from the college's provision of services to this expansive group of customers.

The first of the leading modern cases is *Iowa Hotel Association v. State Board of Regents,* 114 N.W.2d 539 (Iowa 1962). The State University of Iowa had planned an addition to its Memorial Union that would include guest rooms, food service facilities for guests, and banquet and conference rooms. The legislature had passed a statute authorizing the addition. The plaintiff hotel association, however, challenged the constitutionality of this statute and the university's financing and construction plans pursuant to the statute. The court rejected the challenge and upheld the university's authority to finance and construct the addition because it was "incident[al] to the main purpose and complete program of the university." In reaching this conclusion, the court noted that university representatives and organizations commonly invite individuals and groups to the campus; that "[f]ood, housing and entertainment are necessary incidents" of such visits; and that "the percentage of those who use [these services] without invitation is small." Although operation of the addition's facilities could put the university in competition with private enterprise, the university did not encourage sales to the general public and any resulting competition would be merely incidental. (In a later case, *Brack v. Mossman,* 170 N.W.2d 416 (Iowa 1969), the same court relied on its *Iowa Hotel Association* decision to uphold the University of Iowa's authority to construct a multilevel parking garage on campus that would be used by campus visitors as well as students, faculty, and staff.)

The case of *Churchill v. Board of Trustees of University of Alabama in Birmingham,* 409 So. 2d 1382 (Ala. 1982), involved a quite different issue: whether the university's speech and hearing clinic had authority to sell hearing aids to its patients. The plaintiffs were private hearing aid dealers and a hearing aid dealers association. They argued that the sale of hearing aids was a commercial rather than educational activity and that neither the university nor other state agencies had authority to engage in commercial activities in competition with the private business sector. This argument rested on Section 35 of the Alabama constitution, which states that "the sole object and only legitimate end of government is to protect the citizen in the enjoyment of life, liberty, and property, and when the government assumes other functions it is usurpation and oppression."

The plaintiffs contended that the university's activity was a profit-making commercial venture that injures private enterprise. The university contended, however, that the sale of hearing aids in its own school clinics allowed students to reap the educational benefits of providing follow-up care to patients and receiving feedback from them—opportunities that would not arise if the clinics had to refer patients to private hearing aid dealers. Reviewing the trial record, including expert testimony presented by both parties, the Alabama Supreme Court sided with the university:

> We believe the evidence before us . . . amply supports the conclusion that the dispensing of hearing aids, although in the broadest sense it is in competition with private enterprise, is a function which is reasonably related to and promotive of the educational, research, and service mission of a modern university [409 So. 2d at 1389].

The court agreed that "[t]he prohibition of Section 35 is not to be taken lightly" and that "each challenged activity [must] undergo careful scrutiny on a case by case basis to avoid the constitutional 'usurpation and oppression' admonition." Applied to this case, the court said, Section 35 would prohibit the university from engaging in the sale of hearing aids "solely for the purpose of raising revenues." On the other hand, under state statutes, the university had clear authority to establish curriculum and provide education—activities that would not violate Section 35. Thus, the question was whether "the commercial aspect, rather than the instructional aspect, was the principal factor in the sale of the hearing aids"—a question the court answered in the negative.

Jansen v. Atiyeh, 743 P.2d 765 (Ore. 1987), involved the authority of the Oregon State Board of Higher Education, acting through Southern Oregon State College, to provide housing, food, and transportation services to groups of nonstudents attending the annual Oregon Shakespearean Festival. The plaintiffs were motel and hotel operators, taxi drivers, and caterers in the Ashland, Oregon, area. The festival, hosted by Ashland and operated by a nonprofit corporation unaffiliated with the college or the state board, offered a series of events running from spring through fall.

The college had devised and implemented a plan to increase revenues by opening college dormitory facilities to outside groups of more than fifteen persons who gathered to pursue an educational objective. Certain groups attending the festival met this qualification and were provided housing and related services for a fee. To accommodate these groups, the college had to renovate some of its residence halls. The renovations were funded with the proceeds of revenue bonds issued pursuant to Article XI-F(1) of the Oregon constitution and Section 351.160(1) of the Oregon statutes. Article XI-F(1) authorized the board to issue revenue bonds "to finance the cost of buildings and other projects *for higher education,* and to construct, improve, repair, equip and furnish buildings and other structures for such purpose, and to purchase or improve sites therefor" (emphasis added). Section 351.160(1), which implements Article XI-F(1), authorized the board to use revenue bonds to "undertake the construction of any building or structure *for higher education* . . . and enter into contracts for the erection, improvement, repair, equipping and furnishing of buildings and structures for dormitories, housing, boarding, off-street motor vehicle parking facilities and other *purposes for higher education . . .*" (first emphasis added). The plaintiffs argued that the college's actions were inconsistent with these provisions because the use of the dormitories to house nonstudents did not satisfy the requirement that the constructed or improved buildings be used "for higher education."

The court recognized that "the crucial issue in this case is whether [the college's] policy of allowing the groups to use the facilities is within the definition of 'higher education.'" This term was not defined in the statute. But in light of the board's broad authority (under other statutory provisions) to supervise instruction and educational activities and to manage campus properties, the court concluded that "the legislature has delegated to the Board the authority to interpret the term." The issue then became whether the board's interpretation "was within its discretion" and consistent "with the constitutional [and] statutory provisions." Concluding that it was, the court thereby rejected the plaintiffs' challenge:

> [T]he statutory scheme relating to higher education contemplates that the system may offer more than traditional formal degree programs. The Board may maintain "cultural development services," ORS 351.070(2)(c), as well as offer "extension" activities, ORS 351.070(2)(a), in its instructions. [The college] has decided that only groups having an educational mission may use its facilities. That use is within those contemplated by the legislative scheme [743 P.2d at 769].

Taken together, the early and modern cases illustrate the variety of approaches that courts may use in analyzing the authority of a public institution to engage in arguably commercial activities or to compete with private business enterprises. Common threads, however, run through these challenges and approaches. In general, courts would consider the particular functions and objectives of the enterprise; the relation of these functions and objectives to the institution's educational purposes (presumably including the creation of a wholesome and convenient residential life environment for students); the particular wording of the statutes or constitutional provisions delegating authority to the institution or limiting its powers; and judicial precedent in that state indicating how to construe the scope of delegated powers.[7] If a court were to find that an auxiliary enterprise serves an educational function or is related to the institution's educational purposes, it probably would conclude that the institution has the requisite authority to operate the enterprise, even if an incidental purpose or result is generation of profits or competition between the institution and private businesses. In contrast, the institution's authority will likely be questionable or nonexistent if the competitive or profit-seeking aspects of its enterprise are not incidental to

---

[7]In some states there may be narrow and specific statutes that expressly authorize the institution to engage in particular entrepreneurial activities. See, for example, 110 ILCS § 75/1 (sale of television broadcasting rights for intercollegiate athletic events). Such a statute, as applied to the specified activity, would alleviate the need for the full analysis suggested in the text.

its educational aspects but instead are the primary or motivating force behind the institution's decision to operate the enterprise. It may be difficult, of course, to separate out, characterize, and weigh the institution's purposes, as all court opinions require. But if an institution carefully plans each auxiliary enterprise to further good-faith, genuine educational purposes, documents its purposes, and monitors the enterprise's operations to ensure that it adheres to its purposes, courts will be likely to construe a public institution's authority broadly and defer to its expert educational judgments.

A more recent case, *Medical Society of South Carolina v. Medical University of South Carolina*, 513 S.E.2d 352 (S.C. 1999), provides an example of how a state institution might handle a situation in which its authority is questionable. The university, Medical University of South Carolina (MUSC), sought to enter a complex affiliation agreement with a private, for-profit health care corporation. As part of the agreement, MUSC was to lease its medical center in Charleston to the health care corporation while MUSC staff continued to provide medical services at the center. A medical society in the state sought to halt the transaction. It challenged the board of trustees' statutory authority to dispose of its real estate. The court agreed that the board, as a statutorily authorized agency of the state, is limited to those powers granted to it by the legislature. Reviewing the South Carolina statutes enumerating the powers of the MUSC Board of Trustees, the statute confirming the charter of MUSC, and the statutes granting powers to state institutions of higher education generally, the court concluded that MUSC had no preexisting authority "to dispose of buildings or personal property" and thus no authority "to consummate its transaction" with the private health care corporation. However, shortly after MUSC had approved this transaction, the state legislature had enacted a provision, Act No. 390, which retroactively authorized the transaction. The court rejected the medical society's contention that this bill was an unconstitutional "special law" and held that it served to validate MUSC's disposition of its buildings as part of the transaction with Columbia/HCA.

15.3.1.2.2. PRIVATE INSTITUTIONS. Private institutions may also encounter issues concerning their authority to operate auxiliary enterprises, although such issues arise less frequently and present fewer difficulties than those regarding public institutions. For private institutions, the basic question is whether the institution's corporate charter and bylaws, construed in light of state corporation law and educational licensing laws, authorize the institution to engage in the particular auxiliary activity at issue (see generally Sections 3.1 and 12.3.1). *State ex rel. [various citizens] v. Southern Junior College*, 64 S.W.2d 9 (Tenn. 1933), provides a classic example. The issue was whether the college had authority to operate a printing business. The state sued the college on behalf of various individuals who operated commercial printing businesses in the college's locale. The college was chartered as a nonprofit corporation and operated under the sponsorship of the Seventh Day Adventist Church. In addition to academic education, the college offered training in various applied arts and occupations. It maintained the print shop and other enterprises (according to the court) in order to "instruct students in such lines of work, to give them practical experience, but also to make these different enterprises self-sustaining, and, if possible, to procure from such operations a profit for the general support of the school." Although the print shop printed the college's catalogs and advertising matter, as well as religious literature for the Seventh Day Adventist Church, the majority of the shop's receipts came from commercial printing, often in competition with local businesses, from which the college realized a profit.

The court held that the operation of the print shop exceeded the college's authority under its charter. No authority could be implied from the charter's express grants of power, "since the carrying on of the business of commercial printing had no reasonable relation to the conduct of the school." Moreover, the print shop ran afoul of a charter provision stating that "by no implication shall [the college] possess the power to . . . buy or sell products or engage in any kind of trading operation." Thus:

> Instead of being an incident, the commercial feature absorbed the greater part of the activities of this printing shop. Without doubt the defendant school was entitled to own a printer's outfit and to use that outfit in giving practical instructions to the students in this art. The institution, however, had no authority to employ this equipment commercially in the printing trade . . . [64 S.W.2d at 10].

The court thereby recognized the private college's authority to operate auxiliary enterprises as long as they served a primary educational purpose but determined that the enterprise at issue went beyond the college's authority because its core purposes were more commercial than educational. In such circumstances, the college's only recourse was to modify its operation so that educational purposes predominated, or to obtain a charter amendment or other additional authority from the state legislature that permitted it to operate the enterprise in a commercial "profit-oriented" fashion.

As the *Southern Junior College* case illustrates, there are parallels between the issues facing private institutions and those facing public institutions. In each circumstance, the all-important factors may be the primary function of the enterprise and the institution's primary purpose for operating it—a difficult inquiry without clear boundaries. Not all courts in all states will pursue this inquiry in the same way as the Tennessee court, according so little deference to the institution's characterization of its purpose; and indeed the inquiry itself and the pertinent factors will differ depending on the particular wording of the institution's charter and the state's corporation laws. Other charters, for instance, may not have restrictive language about "trading" like that in Southern Junior College's charter. In general, it appears that nonprofit private institutions will have at least as much authority as public institutions to operate auxiliary enterprises, and perhaps more—and that private, for-profit (proprietary) institutions may have even more authority than nonprofit institutions.

15.3.2. State noncompetition statutes.
Various states now have statutes that prohibit postsecondary institutions from engaging in certain types of

competitive commercial transactions; and the number of such statutes is increasing. Virtually all these statutes focus on public institutions and do not cover private institutions.[8] Some statutes apply generally to state agencies and boards but include special provisions for state institutions of higher education; other statutes apply specifically and only to state higher education institutions. Some statutes apply broadly to sales of goods and services as well as to the commercial use of facilities, while others are limited to sales of goods. Yet others are even narrower, applying only to a particular type of goods or service—for example, sale of hearing aids (Idaho Code § 54-2902(d)) or leasing of revenue-producing buildings and facilities (Iowa Code § 262.44). Some statutes set out specific prohibitions and rules; others delegate rule-making authority to the state board or individual institutions. University medical centers and health care services often are exempted from these statutes.

An excellent example of the broader type of statute is a 1987 Arizona law on state competition with private enterprise (Ariz. Rev. Stat. Ann. § 41-2751 *et seq.*). The Arizona statute includes a specific section (41-2753) regulating state community colleges and universities; subsection (A)(1) of this section covers sales to "persons other than students, faculty, staff, and invited guests." It prohibits community colleges and universities from selling such persons "goods, services or facilities that are practically available from private enterprise." However, three important exceptions to this prohibition make it inapplicable (1) when the institution is "specifically authorized by statute" to provide a particular type of goods, service or facility; (2) when the "provision of the goods, service or facility offers a valuable educational or research experience for students as part of their education or fulfills the public service mission" of the institution; and (3) when the institution is "sponsoring or providing facilities for recreational, cultural and athletic events or . . . facilities providing food services and sales."

In contrast to subsection A(1) of the Arizona statute, subsection A(3) covers sales to "students, faculty, staff, or invited guests." It prohibits community colleges and universities from providing such persons with "goods, services or facilities that are practically available from private enterprise *except as authorized by the state governing board*" (emphasis added), thus delegating responsibility and discretion regarding such matters to the board of regents and the board of directors for community colleges. Other subsections contain special provisions regarding competitive bidding (§ 41-2753(A)(2)) and special provisions regarding the institution's sale of "products and by-products which are an integral part of research or instruction" (§ 41-2753(B)). The entire section is implemented through rules adopted by the state governing board (§ 41-2753(C)) and is enforced through a complaint process administered by the governing board and through judicial review (§ 41-2753(D)).

Colorado has a statute similar to Arizona's, passed in 1988 (Colo. Rev. Stat. § 24-113-101 *et seq.*). Other states have different types of laws. The State

---

[8]One narrow exception apparently is Idaho Code § 54-2902(d), which prohibits both "state and local governmental entit[ies]" and "nonprofit organization[s]" from selling hearing aids for compensation.

of Washington law requires state higher education institutions, "in consultation with local business organizations and representatives of the small business community," to develop policies and mechanisms regarding the sale of goods and services that could be obtained from a commercial source (Wash. Rev. Code § 28B.63.010 *et seq.*). The Illinois University Credit and Retail Sales Act (110 ILCS 115/1 & 2), restricts sales by any "retail store carrying any line of general merchandise" that is operated by a state higher education institution, or on the institution's property, "when such an operation can reasonably be expected to be in competition with private retail merchants in the community" (with some exceptions). The Illinois statute also restricts credit sales by retail stores operated by state higher education institutions or on institutional property. The Iowa statute (Iowa Code. Ch. 23A) applies broadly to state agencies "engage[d] in the manufacturing, processing, sale, offering for sale, rental, leasing, delivery, dispensing, distributing, or advertising of goods or services to the public which are also offered by private enterprise," but it provides substantial exemptions for public higher education institutions (§§ 23 A.2(2) & 23 A.2(10)(K)). And the Montana statute regulates the use of state higher education institutions' "revenue-producing facilities" by listing the uses that the state regents "may" authorize (Mont. Code Ann. 20-25-302).

Since most of these statutes are relatively new, and since they may not permit enforcement by private lawsuits (see, for example, *Board of Governors of the University of North Carolina v. Helpingstine*, 714 F. Supp. 167, 175 (M.D.N.C. 1989)), there are few court opinions interpreting and applying the statutory provisions. A leading example thus far is *American Asbestos Training Center, Ltd. v. Eastern Iowa Community College*, 463 N.W.2d 56 (Iowa 1990), in which a private training center sought to enjoin a public community college from offering asbestos removal courses in competition with the center. The center relied on Chapter 23A of the Iowa Code (discussed above), arguing that the college's training programs were "services" that could not be offered in competition with private enterprise. The court disagreed. Construing the term "services," as applied to a community college, it held that "[t]eaching and training are distinct from, rather than included within, the meaning of 'services,'" and that the statute therefore was inapplicable to a community college's training programs. Alternatively, the court concluded that, even if training programs were considered "services," the statute still would not apply. The statute does not restrict services that are authorized specifically by some other statute, and other sections of the Iowa Code do specifically authorize community colleges to offer vocational and technical training.

In another case, *Duck Inn, Inc. v. Montana State University-Northern*, 949 P.2d 1179 (Mont. 1997), the court interpreted and applied the Montana statute (above) and rejected a private competitor's challenge to the university's practice of "rent[ing] its facilities to private persons and organizations for parties, reunions, conventions, and receptions." The pertinent provision of the statute specifies "that the regents of the Montana university system may . . . rent the facilities to other public or private persons, firms, and corporations for such uses, at such times, for such periods, and at such rates as in the regents' judgment will be consistent with the full use thereof for academic purposes and will add to the revenues available for capital costs and debt service." The Duck Inn alleged that these rental activities "placed Northern in direct competition with the Duck Inn's business and violated [the Montana Code as well as the Montana State Constitution]." The court rejected the Duck Inn's arguments and held in favor of the university.

The Duck Inn's first argument was that the university's rental of its facilities for private functions was not "consistent with" the "academic purposes" of the institution. The court disagreed, reasoning that the statutory phrase "consistent with" means "compatible with" or "not contradictory to," and did not require (as the Duck Inn had contended) that the leasing be "directly related to" academic purposes. In light of the university's use of the rental income to supplement operating funds and to pay off the bond issues to which the revenue had been pledged, the court concluded that there was no evidence that the "rentals are incompatible with, or contradict, the full use of the facilities for academic purposes." Thus, the court held that the university's leasing activities were authorized by the Montana Code.

The Duck Inn's second argument was that § 20-25-302 is an unconstitutional delegation of legislative authority to an administrative agency (the university) and is also an improper "use of tax-supported facilities for a private purpose—competition with private enterprise—which violates the constitutional requirement that taxes may be levied only for public purposes." The court also rejected both prongs of this argument. Regarding the first prong, it found that the policy underlying the statute was to "increase revenues available for the capital costs of, and debt service on, campus facilities . . . [and] to minimize the tax support necessary to fund units of the . . . university system." Further, the statute "constrains" the university by providing that the rentals must not be inconsistent with the full use of the facilities for academic purposes. Thus, "the regents' discretion is sufficiently limited," and the statute does not constitute an unlawful delegation of legislative authority. Regarding the second prong of the Duck Inn's constitutional argument, the court concluded that the circumstances of the case did not directly implicate the taxation-for-public-purposes provision of the Montana constitution. Even if this provision did apply, the court concluded, § 20-35-302 of the Montana Code and the university's leasing activities have a "public purpose," and would not violate this provision of the constitution. (In a more recent case involving rentals, *In re Appalachian Student Housing Corp.*, 598 S.E.2d 701 (N.C. App. 2004), the court held that the rental of apartments, when the rentals are restricted to students, "is not a service normally provided by private enterprise" and therefore does not conflict with the North Carolina anticompetition statute (N.C. Gen. Stat. § 66-58(a)).)

In light of these statutory developments, business officers and legal counsel of public institutions will need to understand the scope of any noncompetition statute in effect in their state and to ensure that their institution's programs comply with any applicable statutory provisions. In addition, whether or not their state has a noncompetition statute, business officers, counsel, and governmental relations officers of public institutions should monitor state legislative activities regarding noncompetition issues and participate in the legislative process for any bill that is proposed. Some of the existing statutes are not well drafted, and it will behoove institutions faced with new proposals to avoid the weaknesses in some existing statutes. The State of Washington statute, discussed above, appears to embody the best approach and best drafting thus far available. And perhaps most important, both public and private institutions with substantial auxiliary enterprises—whether or not they are subject to a noncompetition statute—should maintain a system of self-study and self-regulation, including consultation with local business representatives, to help ensure that the institution's auxiliary operations serve the institutional mission and strike an appropriate balance between the institution's interests and those of private enterprise.

15.3.3. Federal antitrust law.

Whenever a postsecondary institution sells goods or services in competition with traditional businesses, as in the various situations described in Section 15.3.2 above, it becomes vulnerable to possible federal as well as state antitrust law challenges (see generally Section 13.2.8). Also, in certain circumstances, it might need to invoke the antitrust laws to protect itself from anticompetitive activities of others. In *NCAA v. Board of Regents of the University of Oklahoma*, 468 U.S. 85 (1984), for example, the university successfully invoked the Sherman Act to protect its competitive position in selling the rights to televise its football games (see Section 14.4.4 of this book). Antitrust claims against universities are illustrated by the two cases below. (See also the *Jefferson County Pharmaceutical Ass'n.* case, discussed in Section 15.2.1, which is relevant to postsecondary institutions as sellers of goods as well as purchasers.)

In *Sunshine Books, Ltd. v. Temple University*, 697 F.2d 90 (3d Cir. 1982), a sidewalk discount bookseller (Sunshine) brought suit alleging that the university had engaged in "predatory pricing" at its on-campus bookstore in order to monopolize the market for itself. At the beginning of the fall 1980 semester, Sunshine and the university bookstore engaged in an undergraduate textbook price war. To combat Sunshine's typical price of 10 percent below retail, the university lowered its prices by 15 percent to retain its students' patronage. In retaliation, Sunshine lowered its prices the extra 5 percent plus an additional 25 cents per book and then filed suit in federal district court. To prevail on its claim, according to the court, Sunshine had to show that the alleged predatory prices would not return a profit to the seller. For its proof, Sunshine introduced accounting methods and calculations demonstrating that the university had sold the books below cost. In defense, the university offered its own accounting methods and calculations, which differed materially from the plaintiff's and showed that the university had made a slight profit on its sale of the books. The district court adopted the university's version and granted summary judgment for the university. The appellate court reversed, holding that Sunshine's submissions on allocation of costs were sufficient to create genuine issues of material fact that precluded an order of summary judgment.

In *Ferguson v. Greater Pocatello Chamber of Commerce,* 848 F.2d 976 (9th Cir. 1988), Idaho State University had awarded an exclusive six-year lease to the local chamber of commerce and the *Idaho State Journal* to produce a spring trade show in the university's Minidome. The producers of a similar trade show that had previously been held at the Minidome brought suit against the university, the chamber of commerce, and the *Journal* for allegedly violating the Sherman Act. The federal district court granted summary judgment to the defendants, and the appellate court affirmed, because the plaintiffs were not able to show that the university's lease arrangement unreasonably restrained competition among producers of spring trade shows. The university had awarded the lease through a competitive bidding process, and all producers—including the plaintiffs—"had an equal opportunity to bid on the lease." The university "did not destroy competition for the spring trade show; it merely forced competitors to bid against one another for the one show [it] was willing to house." Moreover, the Minidome could not be considered an "essential facility"—that is, a facility that was necessary to competition in the trade show market and thus had to be accessible to competitors. (For more on the "essential facilities" doctrine in antitrust law, see Section 15.4.5.) The university itself was not a competitor of the plaintiffs, nor had it excluded or refused to deal with the plaintiffs: "It has merely refused to house more than one trade show per spring, and it has decided that the show will be given to the producer who makes the best bid. The [plaintiffs] simply failed to outbid *their* competitors."

As in other antitrust contexts, state institutions involved in competitive activities may escape antitrust liability by asserting the state action exemption as a defense (see Section 13.2.8). An example is *Cowboy Book, Ltd. v. Board of Regents for Agricultural and Mechanical Colleges,* 728 F. Supp. 1518 (W.D. Okla. 1989), another case involving competition between a campus bookstore and a private bookseller. When the bookseller filed suit under the Sherman Act, the court held that the defendant, a state university, was immune from liability and dismissed the plaintiff's complaint. Similarly, in *Humana of Illinois, Inc. v. Board of Trustees of Southern Illinois University,* 1986 WL 962 (C.D. Ill. 1986), a private for-profit hospital brought an antitrust action against a state university and a hospital affiliated with the university's medical school. The court held that the state action immunity covered both the university and the hospital affiliate; it therefore dismissed several parts of the suit challenging alleged anticompetitive effects of medical school policies. Such protection may not always be available to state institutions and their affiliates, however, since there are various limitations on the availability of the exemption, as discussed in Section 13.2.8 of this book.

15.3.4. Taxation of income from entrepreneurial activities.[9] Both
public and private institutions that engage in entrepreneurial activities may face
various taxation issues arising under federal tax laws (see generally Section 13.3
of this book) as well as state and local tax laws (see generally Sections 11.3 and
12.1). These issues may arise both with respect to the institution's own activities and with respect to the activities of captive and affiliated organizations (see
Rev. Rul. 58-194, 1958-1 C.B. 240, and see generally Section 3.6.3 of this book).
The following discussion illustrates the problem and briefly surveys the applicable law.

15.3.4.1. Federal unrelated business income tax. Under the Internal Rev-
enue Code and implementing regulations, an organization that is exempt from
income taxation may nevertheless be subject to a tax on the income derived
from entrepreneurial activities unrelated to the purposes for which the organization received its tax exemption (see Section 13.3.6 of this book). Thus, despite
their tax-exempt status, colleges and universities will need to consider this unrelated business income tax or "UBIT" if they operate auxiliary enterprises or
engage in other entrepreneurial activities that are or may become income-
producing activities. The basic question is whether the entrepreneurial activity
fits within the Internal Revenue Code's test for identifying unrelated business
income (I.R.C. § 512), that is, whether it is (1) a trade or business, (2) regularly
carried on, that (3) is not "substantially related" to the organization's exempt
purposes. The more difficult problems usually concern the third part—whether
the activity generating the income is unrelated to the college or university's educational, scientific, or charitable purposes. (See *Iowa State University of Science
& Technology v. United States,* 500 F.2d 508 (Ct. Cl. 1974) (in which the court
concluded that a university-owned commercial television station's commercial
attributes were "so overwhelming as to make it impossible for the operation of
WOI-TV to be substantially related to the educational purposes of the University," and therefore that income from the station constituted unrelated business
income to the university subject to UBIT).

Various Treasury Department revenue rulings further clarify the statutory concept of unrelated business income. For example, Treasury has ruled in a "dual
use" problem that the fees a university collected from the general public for use
of the university ski slope were taxable as unrelated business income, whereas
income derived from students using the slope was not subject to UBIT, because
student recreational use was substantially related to the university's educational
purposes (Rev. Rul. 78-98, 1978-1 C.B. 167). Treasury has also ruled that the
sale of broadcasting rights to an annual intercollegiate athletic event was substantially related to exempt educational purposes, and income from the sale was
thus not subject to UBIT (Rev. Rul. 80-296, 1980-2 C.B. 195). In contrast, the
leasing of a university stadium to a professional football team—with accompanying services such as utilities, ground maintenance, and security—was a trade

---

[9]This Section was updated and reedited primarily by Randolph M. Goodman, partner at Wilmer,
Cutler, Pickering, Hale and Dorr, LLP, Washington, D.C., and Patrick T. Gutierrez, an associate at
Wilmer, Cutler, Pickering, Hale and Dorr, LLP.

or business unrelated to the university's educational purposes, making the lease income subject to UBIT (Rev. Rul. 80-298, 1980-2 C.B. 197). More recently, Treasury has ruled that income from conducting elementary and secondary school teacher training seminars was not unrelated business income for a university, even though the business was operated through a limited liability corporation (LLC) that the university formed with a for-profit corporation, and the seminars were conducted off campus at sites selected by the for-profit corporation (Rev. Rul. 2004-51, 2004-22 I.R.B. 974).

Similarly, Treasury regulations include examples indicating that a university's sponsorship of theater productions and symphony concerts open to the public is related to the educational purpose of the university, and the income generated is therefore exempt from UBIT (Treas. Reg. § 1.513-1(d)(4)(iv) (Example 2)); and that the solicitation of paid advertising by the student staff of a campus newspaper is substantially related to exempt educational purposes, so that the advertising income is also exempt from UBIT (Treas. Reg. § 1.513-1(d)(4)(iv) (Example 5)).

Even if a particular entrepreneurial activity fits the statutory three-part test for an unrelated trade or business, the income may nevertheless be exempted from taxation under one of the various exceptions and modifications contained in the Code (see Section 13.3.6 of this book). Under the exclusion for activities conducted by an exempt organization "primarily for the convenience of its members, students, patients, officers, or employees" (I.R.C. § 513(a)(2)), for example, the income from sales at a campus bookstore or restaurant or at a university hospital's gift shop or cafeteria may escape taxation (see Treas. Reg. § 1.513-1(e)(2); see also Rev. Rul. 58-194, 1958-1 C.B. 240).[10] The operation of vending machines or laundromats on campus for student and faculty use would similarly fall within the convenience exception (Treas. Reg. § 1.513-1(e)(2)); see also Rev. Rul. 81-19, 1981-3 C.B 353). However, the convenience must be the convenience of members, student, patients, officers, or employees (see Priv. Ltr. Rul. 9720035 (February 19, 1997), ruling that income from the use of a university golf course by students and faculty, but not income from use by alumni and family of students and faculty, qualifies for the convenience exception; and to the same effect, see Tech. Advice. Mem. 9645004 (July 17, 1996)).

Another important exception from UBIT is passive investment income, such as dividends, royalties, and gains and losses from the sale or disposition of property (that is not inventory or property held primarily for sale in a trade or business) (I.R.C. § 512(b)). Determining whether an amount falls within one of these passive income exceptions can be difficult. For example, in *Oregon State University Alumni Association v. Commissioner of Internal Revenue*, 193 F.3d 1098 (9th Cir. 1999), the Ninth Circuit considered the taxability of payments that colleges and universities receive under "affinity credit card" agreements with

---

[10]A bookstore selling items that fall within the "convenience doctrine," however, may still be subject to taxation on the sale of other items, either because they are not "convenience" items or because they are sold to the general public (see Priv. Ltr. Rul. 8004010 (1980) & 8025222 (1980)).

financial institutions. The court concluded that payments from a bank to alumni associations under an affinity credit card program were payments for "the good will associated with the schools' names, seals, colors, and logos" rather than for "mailing list management and promotional services," and were therefore nontaxable royalties and not subject to the unrelated business income tax.

Although Revenue Ruling 80-298, discussed above, provides an example of how leasing campus facilities may create income subject to UBIT, in other instances income from renting campus sports facilities, auditoriums, or dormitories will be exempted from UBIT as passive investment income. The arrangement must be structured carefully, however, so that substantial support or maintenance services are not provided along with the facility, thus complying with the requirements for exclusion from UBIT of income from rents from real property (see I.R.C. § 512(b)(3)(A)(i) and (B)(i); Treas. Reg. § 1.512(b)-1(c)(5)). Entrepreneurial research is also subject to certain key UBIT exemptions and modifications, as discussed in Section 15.4.4 below.

There are a number of important limitations, however, on these UBIT exemptions. As discussed above, the exclusion of royalty income or rental income will be jeopardized if personal services are provided along with the rights licensed or property rented (see the *Oregon State University Alumni Association* case, above; Rev. Rul. 76-297, 1976-2 C.B. 178; and Rev. Rul. 81-178, 1981-2 C.B. 135). The income from rental of *personal* property is generally not exempt (I.R.C. § 512(b)(1)(A)(ii)). Thus, for example, a university could not deduct income from rental of computer time on a computer having excess capacity (see *Midwest Research Institute v. United States*, 554 F. Supp. 1379, 1388 (W.D. Mo. 1983), *affirmed per curiam*, 744 F.2d 635 (8th Cir. 1984)). And the exclusions will not apply to royalty or rental income, dividends, or capital gains derived from debt-financed property (property the institution has acquired with borrowed funds) (I.R.C. § 514; but see Rev. Rul. 95-8, 1995-1 C.B. 107, holding that exempt organizations may sell publicly traded stock short through a broker and not have the income treated as income derived from debt-financed property).

Only net income is subject to UBIT, so typical business deductions "which are directly connected with the carrying on of such trade or business" are permitted. Questions invariably arise, for example, regarding the allocation of deductible expenses between activities exempt from UBIT and those not exempt. In *Iowa State University*, above, for example, the court concluded that the university could not offset the taxable income generated by the commercial operations of the university-owned television station with expenses from the noncommercial operation of two university-owned radio stations, rejecting the argument that the three stations constituted an integrated operation. The court did, however, allow the university to pool the TV station's income and expenses together with those of other trades or businesses that it operated that were also unrelated to the university.

A different type of allocation question was posed in *Rensselaer Polytechnic Institute v. Commissioner*, 732 F.2d 1058 (2d Cir. 1984), another "dual use" case (see generally Treas. Reg. § 1.512(a)-1(c) & 1.513-1(d)(4)(iii)). Rensselaer incurred expenses in operating its field house, which it used partly for exempt purposes (student uses) and partly for nonexempt purposes (commercial ice shows, public ice skating, and similar uses). The court allowed Rensselaer to allocate a percentage of its expenses to the nonexempt use, the calculation to be based on the number of hours the field house was used for the nonexempt purposes compared to the total number of actual hours it was in use.[11]

As these examples suggest, the federal tax issues confronting institutions with auxiliary operations may be complex as well as numerous. In light of the increased attention on UBIT from Congress, the IRS, and the private business community, which has been evident since the mid-1980s, federal tax planning with the assistance of tax experts is a necessity. Institutions or their national education associations also should carefully monitor, and become involved in, congressional and IRS developments.

15.3.4.2. State and local taxation. Even though the property and activities of public and private nonprofit postsecondary institutions are generally exempt from state and local taxation (see generally Section 11.3), particular auxiliary operations may nevertheless subject institutions to property taxes, sales and use taxes, admission and entertainment taxes, and other such levies, depending on the purpose and character of the auxiliary activity and the scope of available exemptions. In *In re Middlebury College Sales and Use Tax* (Section 12.1 of this book), for example, the college's purchases of equipment and supplies for its golf course and skiing complex were subject to state taxes because the golf and skiing operations were "mainly commercial enterprises." And in *In Re University for Study of Human Goodness and Creative Group Work*, 582 S.E.2d 645 (N.C. App. 2003), the university's restaurant was subject to property taxes because it "was being operated predominantly as a business," "there was a material amount of business and patronage with the general public," and "any educational activity occurring on the property was incidental."

Similarly, in *DePaul University v. Rosewell*, 531 N.E.2d 884 (Ill. App. Ct. 1988), the court held that university-owned tennis facilities leased to a private tennis club were subject to local real property taxation. An Illinois statute exempted real property owned by schools from taxation if the schools were located on the property or if the property was "used by such schools exclusively for school purposes, not leased by such schools or otherwise used with a view to profit" (Ill. Rev. Stat. ch. 120, para. 500.1, now 35 ILCS 200/15(35 (1994)). The lease agreement limited the university's use of the tennis facilities (for physical education classes and the tennis team's use) to a fixed number of total hours and to certain times of the day, and permitted additional university use only with the tennis club's permission and for a fee. The university argued that it used the property "exclusively for school purposes," because the tennis club's use did not interfere with the university's own use of the facilities; and that it did not lease the facility "with a view to profit," because the rents were used to support the university's tennis program, a legitimate school purpose. The court

---

[11]In private rulings, the IRS has expressed continuing disagreement with this judicial determination (see Field Service Advice 1999-783 (November 20, 1998); Priv. Ltr. Rul. 9147008 (August 19, 1991); 9149006 (August 12, 1991)).

rejected both arguments. Regarding exclusive use, the court applied the "well-established principle that a property used for more than one purpose, to qualify for an exemption, must be used primarily for an exempt purpose and only incidentally for a non-exempt purpose." Since the tennis club's use was primary, the university could not fit within this principle. Regarding profits, the court applied another established rule: that "'the application of the revenues derived from [school-owned] property . . . to school purposes will not exempt the property producing the revenues from taxation unless the particular property itself is devoted exclusively to such purposes'" (quoting an earlier case).

In other cases, however, institutions have been able to insulate particular auxiliary activities from taxation. In *City of Morgantown v. West Virginia Board of Regents*, 354 S.E.2d 616 (W. Va. 1987) (Section 11.3.3 of this book), for example, ticket sales for university athletic and entertainment events were not subject to a local amusement tax because the revenues generated were "public moneys" and not "private profit."

Similarly, in *University of Michigan Board of Regents v. Department of Treasury*, 553 N.W.2d 349 (Mich. Ct. App. 1996), the court exempted various of the university's sales transactions from state sales and use taxes. The Michigan Department of Treasury had levied sales taxes on the university's sale of photocopies made on machines in the university libraries, dormitories, and the student union; on its sale of replacement diplomas to graduates; and on its charges for meals provided for participants in summer sports camps and an executive development program. The Department of Treasury had also levied use taxes on revenues from rentals of overnight guest rooms and cots in a residence hall. The Michigan appellate court overruled the Department of Treasury's refusal to exempt the board of regents from these various taxes. The court rejected the tax on the photocopying because these sales were not profit making, and were incidental to the operations of an academic enterprise (the library); it rejected the tax on the diplomas because the product was unique, and the sales were not made for reasons of profit; and it rejected the tax on the meals because these sales were to students who, even though they were enrolled in non-degree-granting programs or were students in high schools and elementary schools, were nevertheless considered to be "bona fide enrolled students." Regarding the use tax on the room and cot rentals, the court held that these rentals were exempt because they furthered an educational purpose, were not for purposes of profit, and were not available to the general public.

And in *In re University of North Carolina*, 268 S.E.2d 472 (N.C. 1980), the court relied on an exemption in the state constitution to reject the attempts of two towns and a county to levy taxes on the property a state university used for an airport, an inn, and off-campus electric and telephone systems. The state constitution provided that "[p]roperty belonging to the State, counties and municipal corporations shall be exempt from taxation" (N.C. Const. art. V, § 2(3)). The local governments argued that the exemption did not apply because the property at issue was used for private purposes unrelated to educational activities, and exemption would give the university an unfair competitive advantage over like businesses in the area that are taxed. The court rejected this argument because the only prerequisite for an exemption under the constitution is ownership, not public use; state university property therefore need not be used for wholly public purposes in order to qualify for the exemption.

Such determinations on taxability will vary from jurisdiction to jurisdiction and statute to statute. Administrators and counsel must therefore focus on the relevant state and local tax laws of their jurisdiction, the applicable exemptions, and the relative strictness with which courts of their state construe them. State institutions should also consider the availability of sovereign immunity as a shield against local government taxation (see, for example, *City of Boulder v. Regents of the University of Colorado,* in Section 11.3.3). It is also important to distinguish between auxiliary enterprises that the institution operates itself and those operated by an affiliated organization (see Section 3.6), since the tax exemptions available in the two situations may differ (see, for example, *City of Ann Arbor v. University Cellar,* discussed in Section 11.3.3).

15.3.5. Administering auxiliary enterprises.

As the discussion in subsections 15.3.1 to 15.3.4 suggests, decisions on establishing and operating auxiliary enterprises pose considerable challenges for public and private institutions alike, and involve considerations and judgments different from those that predominate in decision making on academic matters. Administrators should make sure that, through self-regulation and other means, questions about auxiliary enterprises receive high-level and continuing attention. Specifically, administrators should: identify and resolve threshold questions about the institution's authority to operate and to fund particular enterprises (see Sections 15.3.1.2 & 15.3.2); establish procedures and guidelines for reviewing and approving proposals for auxiliary enterprises; consult with representatives of local businesses as part of the review and approval process, in order to alleviate concerns of unfair competition; establish processes for monitoring the operations of auxiliary enterprises; and centralize decision making on major policy issues, so as to promote consistency in institutional objectives and to mobilize all institutional expertise.

Structural arrangements will also be important. An auxiliary enterprise may be operated by the institution itself, either through the central administration or by a school or an academic department. Alternatively, an enterprise may be operated by an outside entity with which the institution negotiates a lease of land or facilities, a joint venture or partnership agreement, or other arrangement; or an institution may establish a subsidiary corporation or other affiliate, either profit or nonprofit (see Section 3.6), to operate an auxiliary enterprise. The various choices may have different consequences for institutional control, availability of business expertise, legal liability, and tax liability.

To attend to the mix of considerations, institutions will need to engage in substantial legal and business planning. Legal counsel, administrative policy makers, business managers, risk managers, and accountants will all need to work together. Lines of communication to the local business community will need to be opened and cooperative relationships cultivated. And involvement and oversight of high-ranking *academic* officers will need to be maintained, to ensure that auxiliary ventures are not inconsistent with and do not detract from the institution's academic mission. Probably the single most important factor for administrators to emphasize—if they seek to minimize legal authority problems and tax liabilities and to maximize good will with the campus community, the local business community, and local and state legislatures—is a correlative relationship between the objectives of the auxiliary enterprise and the academic mission of the institution.

Sec. 15.4. The College as Research Collaborator and Partner

15.4.1. Potentials and problems.

It has become increasingly common for higher education institutions to align themselves with one another or with other outside entities in the pursuit of common entrepreneurial objectives. The primary area of growth and concern is research collaboration involving institutions, individual faculty members, industrial sponsors, and government. The resulting structural arrangements, such as research consortia, joint ventures, and partnerships, are more complex and more cooperative than those for purchasing and selling transactions (discussed in Sections 15.2 & 15.3).

The potentials and problems arising from universities' and faculty members' research relationships with industry have garnered more attention than almost any other higher education development of the past thirty years. This attention has been manifested in a wealth of books, journal and magazine articles, newspaper accounts, op-ed pieces, conference presentations, legislative hearings, and committee and association reports and policy statements. No single book, let alone a section of a book, can cover all the significant developments or all the significant legal and policy questions. The purpose of this subsection is to identify the major themes and issues; subsections 15.4.2 to 15.4.7 relate these themes and issues to legal problems that emerge from them and to leading statutory provisions, regulations, rulings, and cases that apply to these problems.

Universities and faculty members undertake various types of research in collaboration with industry, but the primary focus is on biomedical and biotechnological research. The concerns escalate when such research moves from the pure science realm to the realm of technology transfer and product development, thus potentially placing entrepreneurial considerations in tension with academic considerations. (See generally M. Kenney, *Biotechnology: The University-Industrial Complex* (Yale University Press, 1986).) In this applied research context, questions about compliance with the federal government's environmental requirements (Section 13.2.10) and workplace safety requirements (Section 4.6.1) will often arise. Government also may become involved as a partial sponsor of university research done in affiliation with outside entities, thus raising legal questions about various government grant and contract requirements, such as the scientific misconduct prohibitions attached to research funding (see Section 13.2.3.4). Moreover, since biomedical and biotechnological research sometimes is conducted with human subjects, researchers will be expected to comply with federal requirements for such research (Section 13.2.3.2).

When animals are used, other federal requirements concerning animal research (Section 13.2.3.3) must be followed. States also may place restrictions on medical research under both common law and statute (see Section 12.5.5 and subsection 15.4.2 below). (See generally H. Leskovac, *Research with Human Subjects: The Effects of Commercialization of University-Sponsored Research,* IHELG Monograph no. 89-4 (University of Houston Law Center, 1989).) Research collaborations with industry will also frequently involve the university in complex legal problems concerning contract and corporation law, patent ownership and patent licenses, antitrust laws, copyright and trademark laws, federal and state taxes, federal technology transfer incentives, and conflict of interest regulations, all of which are discussed below. Litigation raising these types of issues can present sensitive questions regarding the scope of judicial review (see D. Sacken, "Commercialization of Academic Knowledge and Judicial Deference," 19 *J. Coll. & Univ. Law* 1 (1992)).

There are many reasons why universities seek to collaborate with business and industry. The financial benefits of such arrangements may be a major motivating factor, as institutions have sought to enhance research budgets that are shrinking because of reductions in federal and state research funding and institutional budgeting pressures. Clearly, however, research relationships can produce benefits other than the purely financial. An institution may seek to broaden the dialogue in which its researchers are engaged, especially to blend theory with practice; to open new avenues and perspectives to its students; to improve placement opportunities for its graduate students, thereby improving its competitive position in recruiting applicants to its various graduate programs; to enhance its ability to recruit new faculty members; or simply to gain access to new equipment and new or improved facilities for research. Institutions may also be motivated by a good-faith commitment to benefit society by putting academic research discoveries to practical use through the transfer of technology.

Various competitive and budgetary pressures also may encourage individual faculty members or their research groups to form their own relationships with industry. Faculty salaries that do not keep pace with those in industry or with inflation may be one factor. Pressures to produce research results in order to meet the demands of promotion and tenure may also encourage faculty members to seek the funds, resources, and technical information available from industrial liaisons in order to boost their productivity. Some researchers may also need particular types of equipment or facilities, or access to particular technology, that cannot be made available within the institution for reasons of cost or scarcity. Faculty members also face pressures to place their graduate students in desirable industrial positions and to have placement prospects that will help in recruiting other new graduate students. (See generally M. Davis, "University Research and the Wages of Commerce," 18 *J. Coll. & Univ. Law* 29, 31–36 (1991).)

In addition, federal and state governments have themselves encouraged university-industry collaboration. By placing new emphasis on economic vitality and technological competitiveness, they have created an increasingly hospitable governmental climate within which such collaborations can expand and flourish.

There are various structural and organizational arrangements by which universities or their faculties may engage in entrepreneurial research activities. The most traditional relationship is the grantor-grantee relationship, under which an industrial entity—the commercial sponsor—makes a grant to a particular university for the use of particular faculty members or departments in return for certain rights to use the research produced. Another traditional form is the purchase-of-services contract, under which the university provides training, consultant services, or equipment or facilities to an industrial entity for a fee. The most basic form, which is of great current importance, is the research agreement, especially the agreement for contracted research (see subsection 15.4.2 below). Another basic form is the patent-licensing agreement (see Section 15.4.3 below). A different type of arrangement is the industrial affiliation, an ongoing, usually long-term, relationship between a particular university and a particular industrial entity, in which mutual benefits (such as access to each other's research facilities and experts) flow between the parties (see Kenney, *Biotechnology* (cited above), at 40–41).

More complicated structural arrangements include partnerships, limited partnerships, joint ventures (a business arrangement undertaken for a limited period of time or for a single purpose, thus differing from a partnership), and the creation (by the institution) of subsidiary corporations to engage in entrepreneurial research functions or to hold and license patent rights. The particular arrangements that may emerge from such structures or a combination of them include the research consortium, the research park, the specialized laboratory, and the patent-holding company. More than one university and more than one business corporation may be involved in such arrangements, and government funding and sponsorship may also play an important role. The legal and policy issues that may arise in such research relationships will depend, in part, on the particular structural arrangement that is used.

Individual faculty members or research groups may form their own independent research relationships with industry. Faculty members may become part-time consultants or employees of a private research corporation; they may receive grants from industry and undertake particular research obligations under the grant; or they may enter contract research agreements of their own with industry. On another level, faculty members may become officers or directors of a private research corporation; they may become stockholders with an equity position in such a corporation; or they may establish their own private research corporations, in which they become partners or sole proprietors.

Virtually all such arrangements, involving either institutional or faculty relationships with industry, have the potential for creating complex combinations of legal, policy, and managerial issues. Perhaps most difficult are the potential conflict of interest issues (see subsection 15.4.7 below) arising from arrangements that precipitate split loyalties, which could detract attention and drain resources from the academic enterprise. Research priorities might be subtly reshaped, for instance, to focus on areas where money is available from industry rather than on areas of greatest academic challenge or need (see Kenney, *Biotechnology* (cited above), at 111–13). Split loyalties may also encourage faculty to give more attention to research than to instruction, or to favor graduate education over undergraduate education. In addition, the university's traditional emphasis on open dialogue and the free flow of academic information may be undercut by university-industry arrangements that promote secrecy in order to serve industrial profit motives (see Kenney, *Biotechnology*, at 121–31). Disputes may also arise over the ownership and use of inventions and other products of research, as well as of equipment and facilities purchased for research purposes. The institution and its faculty may engage in contractual disputes over the faculty's obligations to the institution or freedom to engage in outside activities; the university and its research sponsors or partners may have similar disputes over interpretations of their research agreements. Products liability issues may arise if any persons are injured by the products that are moved to the market. And various other legal, financial, and political risks may be associated with university-industry relationships.

Because of the heightened potential for problems and risks, university or faculty involvement in collaborative research ventures requires the most careful attention. Before the institution enters any collaborative relationship, administrators and counsel should consider carefully all alternatives and options and weigh all possible benefits and risks. When they decide to enter new ventures, they should devise structural arrangements and draft the pertinent contracts with special care. The institution should consider appointing high-level officers to be in charge of sponsored research, technology transfer, and patent management; it might also consider appointing trustees with special sensitivities to the issues and forming a trustee committee to oversee the institution's outside research ventures. Institutions also should make sure that they are served by legal counsel with expertise in the complex problems of technology transfer and the structuring of commercial ventures, as well as by experienced risk managers familiar with commercial risks. Formal institutional policies should be adopted to deal with such matters as faculty conflicts of interest and patent ownership and licensing rights. And above all, administrators and institutional officers and trustees should be sensitive to the value questions that are raised by corporate collaborations (see Sheila Slaughter, "Professional Values and the Allure of the Market," *Academe*, September–October 2001, 22–26); and must maintain a keen appreciation for the institutional mission and the academic enterprise, so that they are not compromised or diluted by such research collaborations (see generally R. Carboni, *Planning and Managing Industry-University Research Collaborations* (Quorum Books, 1992)).

15.4.2. The research agreement. The research agreement is typically the heart of the university-industry research relationship. It is a type of contract, interpreted and enforced in accordance with the contract law of the state whose law governs the transaction (see Section 15.1 above). This agreement may be the entire legal arrangement between the parties, as in contracted research, or it may be part of a broader collaboration that involves other legal documents or other agreements on activities other than research. One or more universities or university research foundations, and one or more industrial sponsors, are typically the parties to the contract. Particular faculty members (or departments or research groups) may be named in the agreement as principal investigators or may occasionally themselves be parties to the agreement. When the research will involve human subjects, there will also usually be subsidiary agreements with them, as discussed later in this Section. The research agreement may be either a short-term or a long-term agreement, or for a specific single project or a combination of projects. Depending on the type of project contemplated and the purposes of the arrangement, threshold questions may arise concerning the institution's authority to enter the agreement (see, for example, Section 15.3.1.2).

The complex process of negotiating and drafting a research agreement requires scientific and technical expertise as well as legal and administrative expertise. Like commercial contracts, the research agreement should include most of the types of provisions suggested in Section 15.1 above. In addition, there are numerous special concerns that will require the insertion of special provisions into the agreement. Such special provisions should normally cover such matters as:

1. Research tasks and objectives—and whether and how the parties may modify them during the course of the project.

2. Supervision of the research—including the responsible researchers and officers within the university and the role, if any, for the corporate sponsor or particular members of the corporate team.

3. Participation in the project—particular members of the university faculty or research staff, or particular departments or research groups, that are obligated to participate in the research.

4. Funding cycles and payment schedules that the sponsor will adhere to and the nonfinancial contributions, if any, that the sponsor will make to the project or the university.

5. Type and frequency of progress reports and oral briefings that the university will provide to the sponsor.

6. Equipment for the research: Who will provide it, and who will retain it when the project is concluded?

7. Inventions discovered during the project: Who will own the patents, and who will have rights to licenses (exclusive or nonexclusive) and to royalty payments? (Similar questions would also arise regarding copyrights in projects that produce copyrightable materials.)

8. University obligations to disclose research results to the industrial sponsor.

9. Researchers' rights to publish their research results—and whether the sponsor may require a delay in publication for a period of time necessary to apply for patent protection.

10. University obligation to protect any trade secrets and proprietary information that the sponsor may release to university researchers or that may result from the project research.

11. Extent of access the sponsor's staff will have to university laboratories and facilities used for the project.

12. Rights of the sponsor to use the university's name, marks, and logos, or prohibitions on their use by the sponsor.

13. Indemnification, hold-harmless, or insurance requirements regarding special matters, such as environmental hazards and products liability.

14. Parties' obligations to protect university and faculty academic freedom and to protect against university or faculty conflicts of interest.

(See generally Donald Fowler, "University-Industry Research Relationships: The Research Agreement," 9 *J. Coll. & Univ. Law* 515 (1982–83).)

If an industrial sponsor or university located in a foreign country is to be a party to the research agreement, the U.S. university will require additional expertise in U.S. laws governing foreign relations—for instance, the export control laws (see Section 13.2.4 of this book)—and in international and foreign law (see Section 1.4.2.5). The university also will need to understand and protect against its potential liabilities (including antitrust liability; products liability; and liability for patent, copyright, or trademark infringement) under the law of any foreign country in which project activities will take place or to which research products will be shipped. Equally, the university will need to understand and be ready to assert its rights under foreign law— for instance, rights to protection against patent, copyright, trademark, and trade secret infringement by others. Taxation and tariff questions may also arise. The applicable law may be found not only in the codes and regulations of particular foreign countries but also in the provisions of treaties and conventions that may apply, such as the Berne Convention for the Protection of Literary and Artistic Works, the Paris Convention for the Protection of Industrial Property, the European Patent Convention, the Patent Cooperation Treaty, the Universal Copyright Convention, or the Beirut Agreement (the Agreement for Facilitating the International Circulation of Visual and Auditory Materials of an Educational, Scientific, and Cultural Character). (See generally Marshall Leaffer (ed.), *International Treaties on Intellectual Property* (2d ed., Bureau of National Affairs, 1997).)

These concerns, among others, should be anticipated in the negotiation and drafting of international research agreements, and may lead to the inclusion of special provisions such as the following: (1) a choice-of-law clause specifying what role (if any) foreign law will have in the interpretation and application of the research agreement; (2) special indemnification, hold-harmless, or insurance clauses dealing with liabilities that arise under foreign or international law; (3) a special arbitration clause, or other dispute resolution clause, adapted to the international context of the agreement (see the New York Convention on the Recognition and Enforcement of Foreign Arbitral Awards; see also *Mitsubishi Motors Corp. v. Soler Chrysler-Plymouth, Inc.*, 473 U.S. 614 (1985), and footnote 1 in Section 15.1.5); (4) clauses regarding the parties' obligations to secure patent, trademark, or copyright protection under foreign or international law;

(5) a clause establishing responsibilities for payment of taxes and tariffs imposed by foreign governments; (6) a clause providing for instruction for project staff in the language, culture, and business practices of foreign countries where project activities will be conducted; and (7) a clause allocating responsibility for paying particular foreign travel and shipping costs.

Whether the research agreement is domestic or international, problems of performance may arise that could result in contract interpretation disputes, claims of breach, or attempts to terminate the agreement (see generally Section 15.1.4 above). In the latter case, the terminating party may argue that it has terminated the agreement because of the breach of the other party. The other party may argue that the terminating party has breached the agreement. In either situation, questions will arise concerning the rights and obligations of the parties upon termination. In general, the answers will depend on interpretation of the agreement's terms in accordance with the contract law of the state whose law governs the transactions. If the termination constitutes or was occasioned by a breach, the answers will also depend on the state law concerning money damages and other remedies for breach of contract (see Section 15.1.4 above).

The case of *Regents of the University of Colorado v. K.D.I. Precision Products, Inc.*, 488 F.2d 261 (10th Cir. 1973), illustrates the types of performance problems that can arise under a research agreement and, by implication, underscores the importance of a comprehensive and clear contract. The case addresses three questions that are likely to be asked when a research agreement is terminated: (1) What constitutes substantial performance under the contract? (2) Which party, or who besides the parties, has the rights to inventions developed or patents obtained under the contract? (3) Which party owns the equipment used in the project? The court looked to the express provisions of the agreement to resolve each of these issues. The University of Colorado, the plaintiff, had entered into a three-year research and development contract with K.D.I., the defendant, under which the university, for remuneration, was to help K.D.I. develop certain scientific devices. After the first year, K.D.I. terminated the contract. The university sued to recover payment for the work it had performed to the date of termination. K.D.I. defended on two grounds: first, that the university had failed to substantially perform its contract obligations and therefore was not entitled to recovery; second, that even if the university did substantially perform the contract, its recovery was subject to a set-off for the value of project equipment the university had allegedly "converted" to its use.

Regarding its first defense, K.D.I. made three arguments. First, it alleged that the university had failed to give it "exclusive" rights to the technical data developed under the research contract, including rights to all the original plans and designs. The court found that the university had specifically agreed to give K.D.I. "unlimited" (rather than "exclusive") rights to use, duplicate, or disclose the technical data and that the university had performed its obligations to extend such "unlimited" rights to K.D.I. Second, K.D.I. alleged that the university did not substantially perform because it failed to complete a prior research contract whose work was continued in the current research contract. The court rejected this argument as well, because the current contract was "complete in itself as to the duties and obligations of the parties thereto. It comprises a separate research contract, and there is no intimation therein of the incorporation by reference to prior contracts." Third, K.D.I. argued that the university did not substantially perform the research contract because it failed to disclose its development of a device called the Optical Communication Link (OCL). The court also rejected this argument, finding that the OCL was not developed under the research contract with K.D.I. Rather, it was developed by two of the university's professors, with the university's money and for use by the university; it was used for the university's own purposes; and it was not necessary to K.D.I.'s purposes. The university therefore had no obligation to disclose the development of the OCL.

Regarding its second defense, K.D.I. argued that certain equipment used by the university for the research project, and retained by the university at termination, was actually the property of K.D.I. The court found that, although K.D.I. had contributed a small amount toward the purchase of one piece of equipment and had made some attempts under the contract to correct problems with another piece, K.D.I. had no legal claim to the equipment. K.D.I. had not loaned or assigned the contested equipment to the university; it had been donated to the project by the university itself and other corporate donors. Moreover, "in the operative and dispositive portions of the contract, as it describes the research to be undertaken, there is no suggestion that title to the equipment was either in K.D.I. or was to vest therein" (488 F.2d at 267). Since K.D.I. did not have legal rights to the equipment, the university could not have converted it; thus, there was no basis for set-off.

In rejecting K.D.I.'s second defense, the court compared the contract's treatment of equipment ownership (where the contract was silent) to the contract's treatment of patent rights—where the contract contained detailed clauses assigning patent rights to K.D.I. and requiring written disclosure by the university of each invention. K.D.I., therefore, did have patent rights under the contract, but not rights to equipment. No issue concerning patent rights arose in the case, however, because the university conceded K.D.I.'s rights in this realm, and K.D.I. did not allege that the university had attempted to assert patent rights belonging to K.D.I.

If the research project is to involve human subjects, the research agreement should contain supplementary provisions covering the special legal and ethical issues that arise in this context. If the parties contemplate using federal funds for some or all of the human subject research, or if the human subject research is to involve drugs within the jurisdiction of the Food and Drug Administration, the research agreement's provisions must satisfy all requirements in the applicable federal regulations (see Section 13.2.3.2 of this book). In addition, whether or not federal regulations apply, the parties should arrange for separate agreements with each of the human subjects that are recruited for the project. These subsidiary agreements may be brief documents whose primary purpose is to document the participants' informed consent, or they may cover in more detail the research subject's duties and the prospective benefits and risks of the research for the subject and for others. (If federal regulations apply, these subsidiary agreements will, of course, need to comply with the federal requirements on informed consent and other matters.)

In a case the court termed one "of first impression," *Grimes v. Kennedy Krieger Institute, Inc.,* 782 A.2d 807 (Md. 2001), Maryland's highest court analyzed many of the legal aspects (and some ethical aspects) of informed consent agreements with human research subjects. The defendant, Kennedy Krieger Institute (KKI), "a prestigious research institute, associated with Johns Hopkins University" (782 A.2d at 811), conducted a research project in cooperation with the university, the federal Environmental Protection Agency (EPA) (which awarded a contract for the project), and the Maryland Department of Housing and Community Development. The research project's purpose was to determine the relative effectiveness of "varying degrees of lead paint abatement procedures" performed on Baltimore low-income housing units, as measured "over a two-year period of time." The plaintiffs were two children who were human subjects in the project; they had lived in two different housing units included in the study and had had their blood tested periodically for evidence of lead contamination. A parent for each of the children had signed a consent form. Subsequently, however, after tests had revealed elevated levels of lead in dust collected from the housing units and in the children's blood samples, each parent, on behalf of her child, sued KKI for negligence. The primary thrust of the claims was that KKI had failed in its duty to fully inform the parents of the study's risks when the consent form was signed and later when the researchers' tests revealed a hazard to the children.

The trial court in each case granted KKI's motion for summary judgment, holding that the consent form was not a contract and that the families had no special relationship with KKI that would give rise to a duty of care. On appeal, the Court of Appeals of Maryland reversed the trial courts' summary judgments for KKI. The appellate court determined that the signed consent form created a "bilateral contract" between the parties: "Researcher/subject consent in nontherapeutical research can, and in this case did, create a contract." The parents' consent was not "fully informed," however, "because full material information was not furnished to the subjects or their parents." The "consent" in the contract was therefore not valid and could not be used by KKI as a defense. The appellate court also determined that the researcher-subject relationship under the contract should, in this circumstance, be considered a "special relationship":

> Trial courts appear to have held that special relationships out of which duties arise cannot be created by the relationship between researchers and subjects of the research. While in some rare cases that may be correct, it is not correct when researchers recruit people, especially children whose consent is furnished indirectly, to participate in nontherapeutic procedures that are potentially hazardous, dangerous or deleterious to their health. . . . The creation of study conditions or protocols or participation in the recruitment of otherwise healthy

subjects to interact with already existing, or potentially existing, hazardous conditions, or both, for the purpose of creating statistics from which the scientific hypotheses can be supported, would normally warrant or create such special relationships as a matter of law [782 A.2d at 845–46].

In addition, the appellate court determined that the research project was subject to "standards of care that attach to federally funded or sponsored research projects that use human subjects." These standards, found in the federal HHS regulations (see Section 13.2.3.2 of this book), imposed a duty of care on KKI. According to the court:

In this case, a special relationship out of which duties might arise might be created by reason of the federally imposed regulations. The question becomes whether this duty of informed consent created by federal regulation, as a matter of state law, translates into a duty of care arising out of the unique relationships that is researcher-subject, as opposed to doctor-patient. We answer that question in the affirmative. In this state, it may, depending on the facts, create such a duty [782 A.2d at 849].

An analysis of state tort law principles provided the appellate court yet another basis for determining that KKI owed a duty of care to the children. Focusing primarily on the foreseeability of personal harm, the court concluded that:

[t]he relationship that existed between KKI and both sets of appellants in the case at bar was that of medical researcher and research study subject. Though not expressly recognized in the Maryland Code or in our prior cases as a type of relationship which creates a duty of care, evidence in the record suggests that such a relationship involving a duty or duties would ordinarily exist, and certainly could exist, based on the facts and circumstances of each of these individual cases. . . . [T]he facts and circumstances of both of these cases are susceptible to inferences that a special relationship imposing a duty or duties was created in the arrangements [at issue] and, ordinarily, could be created in similar research programs involving human subjects [782 A.2d at 842–43].

Based on all these reasons, the Court of Appeals of Maryland stated its conclusion as follows:

We hold that informed consent agreements in nontherapeutic research projects,[12] under certain circumstances can constitute contracts; and that, under certain circumstances, such research agreements can, as a matter of law, constitute "special relationships" giving rise to duties, out of the breach of which

---

[12][Author's footnote] The distinction between "nontherapeutic" and "therapeutic" research projects was important to the court and is also important in the ethics of medical research on human subjects. The former projects, unlike the latter, are not designed to directly benefit the human subjects participating in the project (782 A.2d at 812). This distinction appears to be important primarily for projects in which minors are the human subjects. The court in *Grimes* was unwilling to allow a parent to consent to his or her child's participation in a nontherapeutic research project that involves more than minimal risk to the child (782 A.2d at 858, 862); but the court would apparently be more lenient if the research were therapeutic.

negligence actions may arise. We also hold that, normally, such special relationships are created between researchers and the human subjects used by the researchers. Additionally, we hold that governmental regulations can create duties on the part of researchers towards human subjects out of which "special relationships" can arise. . . .

We hold that there was ample evidence in the cases at bar to support a fact finder's determination of the existence of duties arising out of contract, or out of a special relationship, or out of regulations and codes, or out of all of them, in each of the cases [782 A.2d at 858].

The court therefore remanded the case to the two trial courts for further proceedings consistent with its rulings.

15.4.3. *Application of patent law.*[13] Universities contemplating a collaborative research relationship that could result in a patentable discovery will find that federal patent law may affect their research projects.[14] Patent law will clarify (1) the types of discoveries that are patentable; (2) who will own and have the right to license the patents; (3) how research results will be reviewed and published; and (4) what must be done to avoid infringing *others'* patents. Section 13.2.6 of this book provides a general discussion of these and other issues. This Section focuses in more detail on issues of ownership and infringement that arise in the collaborative research context.

Ownership issues may arise even in the simplest of circumstances. They may become very complex when third-party sponsorship is involved. Fifteen years ago, courts were reluctant to imply an agreement to assign patent rights. Today, the law is much more settled on this subject. The case of *University Patents, Inc. v. Kligman*, 762 F. Supp. 1212 (E.D. Pa. 1991) illustrates the basic problem. The University of Pennsylvania and its patent manager, University Patents, Inc., sued Dr. Kligman and Johnson & Johnson Baby Products Company. They claimed that Kligman breached his employment contract and an implied agreement arising from the university's patent policy when he assigned his rights to an invention to Johnson & Johnson rather than the university, and failed to assign his royalties to the university. Although Kligman and the university had no express contract, the university's patent policy provided that any patentable discoveries made by employees with the use of university equipment, time, and staff belonged to the university. The university published many handbooks that delineated the policy, so the university relied on the professor's knowledge of the patent policy and his continued employment with the university to infer that

---

[13]This Section was updated and expanded by Georgia Harper, Senior Attorney and Manager, Intellectual Property Section, Office of General Counsel, the University of Texas System.

[14]Other federal intellectual property law may also be important. Federal copyright law, for example, protects computer software and other works used or developed in collaborative research ventures (see Section 13.2.5); and the Semiconductor Chip Protection Act of 1984 (17 U.S.C. §§ 901–914) protects the architecture of semiconductor chips (see Edward K. Esping, Annot., "Reverse Engineering Under Semiconductor Chip Protection Act of 1984," 113 A.L.R. Fed. 381). State law may also protect research that qualifies as a "trade secret"; see P. Shockley, "The Availability of 'Trade Secret' Protection for University Research," 20 *J. Coll. & Univ. Law* 309 (1994).

he had agreed to its provisions. The university also claimed that letters written twenty-three years earlier, when Kligman assigned his patent for Retin-A to the university, as well as the patent assignment itself, were evidence that he knew of and accepted the patent policy.

Focusing on general rules of contract formation (see Section 15.1.2) as well as specialized principles regarding employee handbooks and the assignment of patent rights, the district court somewhat reluctantly denied the professor's motion for summary judgment, allowing the university to proceed; but the judge cited the U.S. Supreme Court's opinion in *United States v. Dubilier*, 289 U.S. 178, 188 (1933), that emphasized that courts should be most reluctant to recognize implied contracts to assign patent rights.

Because the university's claim withstood a motion for summary judgment, the *Kligman* ruling seemed to recognize that employment handbooks containing the terms of a patent policy could be enough to imply an agreement to assign patents. The ruling also stood for the proposition, however, that employees should receive the benefit of the doubt. The parties later settled out of court, so *Kligman* ultimately did not answer the questions it had raised. Fortunately, later cases have clarified the law, solidifying the principle that an agreement to assign inventions can be inferred from knowledge of patent policies, and extending the principle to inventions created by graduate students not officially employed by the university. (See *E. I. DuPont de Nemours and Co. v. Okuley*, 2000 U.S. Dist. LEXIS 21385 (S.D. Ohio, December 21, 2000); *Chou v. University of Chicago and Arch Development Corp.*, 254 F.3d 1347 (Fed. Cir. 2001); *University of West Virginia Board of Trustees v. Van Voorhies*, 278 F.3d 1288 (Fed. Cir. 2002); and see also Naoko Ohasi, "The University Inventor's Obligation to Assign: A Review of U.S. Case Law on the Enforceability of University Patent Policies," 15 *J. Ass'n. Univ. Tech. Managers* 49 (2003).)

A patent infringement case brought by the University of Colorado and two professors against American Cyanamid illustrates additional complications that may arise in patent ownership disputes. In the most recent pair of decisions resulting from this lawsuit, *University of Colorado Foundation v. American Cyanamid*, 105 F. Supp. 2d 1164 (D. Colo. 2002), and 216 F. Supp. 2d 1188 (D. Colo. 2002), *affirmed*, 342 F.3d 1298 (Fed. Cir. 2003), the university, its research foundation, and two faculty inventors saw their rights vindicated twenty years after actions constituting fraudulent deception took place—even though the patent had since been invalidated and the product was no longer on the market. The plaintiffs alleged that, although the professors invented an improved formula for Materna, a prenatal vitamin supplement sold by a division of Cyanamid, the company filed a patent application claiming that one of its employees had developed the improved formula. The university sought damages for fraudulent nondisclosure, patent infringement, and copyright infringement, as well as disgorgement of the company's profits from sales of the improved vitamin supplement and equitable title to the patent. The court soundly rejected Cyanamid's claim that its employee actually developed the improved formula. This case strongly supports institutional assertions of rights to employee inventions as against industry collaborators; however, the rather blatant corporate deception that occurred in 1980 seems much less likely to take place in today's more sophisticated university research environment.

Collaborative research raises infringement issues in addition to ownership questions. At times universities may be infringers themselves; other times they must pursue those who violate university rights. Both circumstances are more likely when universities and private industry engage in parallel or overlapping research.

Section 271(a) of the Patent Act states that whoever "makes, uses, offers to sell or sells any patented invention, within the United States . . . infringes the patent." Thus, universities and researchers engaged in collaborative research must obtain a license to use patented inventions. There is no general "research exemption" that excuses infringement for research purposes. The court-created "experimental use exemption" has been construed very narrowly to apply only to purely academic research. (See *Madey v. Duke University*, 307 F.3d 1351 (Fed. Cir. 2002); and see also, Eric W. Guttag, "Immunizing University Research from Patent Infringement: The Implications of *Madey v. Duke University*," 15 *J. Ass'n. Univ. Tech. Managers* 1 (2003).)

The case of *Regents of the University of California v. Eli Lilly & Co.*, 119 F.3d 1559 (Fed. Cir. 1997), illustrates the risks that universities take when they seek to stop third-party infringement. The plaintiff university, owner of two patents regarding DNA technology, claimed that Eli Lilly infringed both patents by manufacturing human insulin. The courts considered the validity of the university's patents, whether Eli Lilly had infringed them, and whether certain university conduct (misrepresenting in its patent application which vector it used in a test of its hypothesis) barred enforcement. After seven years of litigation, the Federal Circuit upheld the district court's determinations that one patent was invalid and that Eli Lilly did not infringe the other, but reversed the district court's determination that the misrepresentation in the patent application constituted inequitable conduct. Thus, the court reversed the district court's finding that neither patent was enforceable.

Technical procedural and evidentiary issues may frequently arise in patent litigation. In the case of *In re Regents of the University of California*, 101 F.3d 1386 (Fed. Cir. 1996), for example, issues arose concerning whether the attorney-client privilege (see Section 2.2.3.3) applied to communications between the university (the patent owner and patent applicant) and the attorneys for Eli Lilly (the university's licensee). The court held that, under the "community of interest" doctrine and the "joint client" doctrine, the privilege applied and protected the communications from discovery by the plaintiff, Genetech, Inc., a biotechnology firm.

15.4.4. *Federal tax exemptions for research.*[15] Like auxiliary enterprises (Section 15.3.4.1 above), income-producing research activities may precipitate numerous federal tax issues. The most common issues concern the

---

[15]This Section was updated and reedited primarily by Randolph M. Goodman, partner at Wilmer, Cutler, Pickering, Hale and Dorr, LLP, Washington, D.C., and Patrick T. Gutierrez, an associate at Wilmer, Cutler, Pickering, Hale and Dorr, LLP.

applicability of the unrelated business income tax (UBIT) (see generally Section 13.3.6 of this book) to the income generated from collaborative research arrangements. Fortunately for higher educational institutions, most of their research-related income can be insulated from UBIT if they engage in careful tax planning that is sensitive to the structure and characteristics of each proposed research activity.

First, any research activity that is "substantially related" to the institution's exempt purposes (that is, the educational, scientific, or charitable purposes providing the basis for the institution's tax exemption) does not fit the definition of an unrelated business, and the income will escape UBIT for that reason alone. Second, even if a particular institutional research activity is not "substantially related" (or its character is unclear in this respect), generated income may nevertheless be insulated from UBIT under a statutory exemption providing that "[i]n the case of a college, university, or hospital, there shall be excluded all income derived from research performed for any person" (I.R.C. § 512(b)(8); see, for example, Priv. Ltr. Rul. 9833030 (May 20, 1998)). Another statutory modification excludes research undertaken for the U.S. government, its agencies or instrumentalities, or a state or local government (I.R.C. § 512(b)(7)). The problem with these two modifications is that the statute does not define the key term "research," thus making the scope of the provisions uncertain. The Treasury regulations (Treas. Reg. § 1.501(c)(3)-1(d)(5)(ii)) help by making clear that both theoretical and applied research may qualify, but that activities "of a type ordinarily carried on as an incident to commercial or industrial operations . . . [such as] ordinary testing or inspection of materials or products" do not qualify as research. Further guidance is available from a smattering of revenue rulings, Tax Court decisions, and federal court decisions. *Midwest Research Institute v. United States,* 554 F. Supp. 1379, 1385–89 (W.D. Mo. 1983), *affirmed per curiam,* 744 F.2d 635 (8th Cir. 1984), clarified the distinction between "research" and "testing or inspection" and stated, among other things, that research may qualify for the exclusion even if it is conducted for a fee for a private sponsor that receives a private benefit, and even if the research arrangement puts the exempt entity in competition with other taxpaying businesses. (See also *IIT Research Institute v. United States,* 9 Cl. Ct. 13 (1985); Priv. Ltr. Rul. 200303065 (October 25, 2002).)

Other UBIT modifications may also apply to research-related activities and provide further assistance in insulating the university from UBIT. Under Section 512(b)(2), for instance, royalty income—that is, payments from third parties for the use of some valuable right, such as a copyright, trademark, or patent—is excludable from taxation. Thus, if a university owns patents, and licenses its patent rights to third parties in return for license fees, the resulting income is excludable as royalty income (I.R.C. § 512(b)(2); see Rev. Rul. 76-297, 1976-2 C.B. 178). Similarly, income from the rental of real property is excludable (I.R.C. § 512(b)(3)(A)(i)). Thus, if a university rents laboratory space, for example, to a corporate organization, the rental income would generally not be taxable under UBIT. Dividends from passive investments are also generally excludable from UBIT (I.R.C. § 512(b)(1)), as are capital gains (I.R.C. § 512(b)(5)), thus excluding certain passive income a university might receive if it held an equity position in a for-profit research corporation.

Whenever an institution moves beyond basic structural arrangements, such as sponsored research agreements and patent-licensing agreements, to more complex arrangements, such as joint ventures and subsidiary corporations, additional considerations may affect UBIT's application to the income generated (see, for example, Priv. Ltr. Rul. 9833030 (May 20, 1998), regarding a research consortium created by a university). If a university contracts with or creates a separate corporation for patent management, this arrangement would make it more difficult to determine whether and to whom the royalty exclusion applies (see Rev. Rul. 73-193, 1973-1 C.B. 262). Or if a university establishes a taxable subsidiary corporation to engage in certain product development functions, this arrangement would raise additional questions concerning the taxability of royalties, rent, or dividend income the university received from its subsidiary (see I.R.C. § 512(b)(13) regarding amounts received from controlled entities). Moreover, such other research arrangements as the establishment of a subsidiary corporation or joint venturing with another separately established corporation may raise questions about whether the subsidiary or other corporation qualifies for tax-exempt status under I.R.C. § 501(c)(3) (see Sections 13.3.2 & 13.3.7 of this book). In *Washington Research Foundation v. Commissioner,* T.C. Memo 1985-570, 50 T.C.M. 1457 (1985), for example, the Tax Court affirmed the IRS's denial of WRF's application for recognition as a tax-exempt organization under Section 501(c)(3). The court rejected each of WRF's characterizations of its purposes and determined that WRF was operated for a substantial commercial purpose, because its primary function was to develop patents to make them available to private industry, it competed with other commercial firms, and it planned its activities so as to maximize profits.[16]

Besides raising questions about the tax status of a subsidiary or separate corporation, some research arrangements could involve the university so deeply in commercial, profit-making activities that its own tax-exempt status would be questioned. Joint ventures and partnerships are the arrangements most likely to raise such concerns and thus to require especially careful tax planning (see Randolph M. Goodman & Linda A. Arnsbarger, "Trading Technology for Equity: A Guide to Participating in Start-Up Companies, Joint Ventures and Affiliates" (Matthew Bender, 1999) (reprinted from the Proceedings of the New York University 27th Conference on Tax Planning for 501(c)(3) Organizations); C. Kertz & J. Hasson, "University Research and Development Activities: The Federal Income Tax Consequences of Research Contracts, Research Subsidiaries and Joint Ventures," 13 *J. Coll. & Univ. Law* 109, 124–45 (1986)).

15.4.5. Application of antitrust law.

Federal antitrust laws (see Section 13.2.8 of this book) apply to and create potential liabilities for universities or their separate research entities when the universities or research entities engage

---

[16]The result in *Washington Research Foundation* was overturned by Congress in Pub. L. No. 99-514 § 1605 (October 22, 1986), which specifically provided for tax-exempt status for an organization introducing into public use technology developed by qualified organizations.

in certain types of collaborative research activities. As with other applications of antitrust law to the campus, the predicate to liability is the existence of concerted research activities that have anticompetitive or monopolistic effects on the market. The risks of such effects are probably greater with applied than with basic research because of the potential competitive market uses for the products of applied research.

Particular activities within or adjunct to an overall research collaboration (joint venture, consortium, or other concerted activity) may make the collaboration vulnerable to antitrust challenges. Such challenges might be made, for example, when patent-licensing and enforcement activities, taken together, allow a research venture to control a certain market or access to a certain technology needed to compete in the market (see generally *SCM Corp. v. Xerox Corp.*, 463 F. Supp. 983 (D. Conn. 1978), *certified question answered*, 645 F.2d 1195 (2d Cir. 1981)); or when the joint operation of a common facility, such as a laboratory or medical treatment facility involving expensive specialized equipment, puts the collaborators in a competitive position in the market and they exclude potential competitors from use of the facility (see generally *MCI Communications Corp. v. American Telephone and Telegraph Co.*, 708 F.2d 1081 (7th Cir. 1983)); or when a computer network is operated under similar circumstances as part of a research collaboration.

Fortunately for higher education, the National Cooperative Research and Production Act of 1993, as amended (15 U.S.C. § 4301 *et seq.*) provides protection from antitrust liability for two or more organizations that wish to enter a collaborative research joint venture. The law was enacted to encourage collaborative research and development, particularly in the area of science and technology, by removing much of the potential for antitrust liability under federal and state law. The Act states that such joint ventures will be evaluated by the rule of reason, "taking into account all relevant factors affecting competition, including, but not limited to, effects on competition in properly defined, relevant research, development, product, process, and service markets" (15 U.S.C. § 4302). The Act also limits the damages recoverable in an antitrust action against a joint venture covered by the Act (15 U.S.C. § 4305). To claim the Act's protections, the joint venture previously must have filed a written notification with the U.S. Attorney General and the Federal Trade Commission, as provided in Section 4305. (See generally D. Foster, G. Curtner, & E. Dell, "The National Cooperative Research Act of 1984 as a Shield from the Antitrust Laws," 5 *J.L. & Com.* 347 (1985).)

15.4.6. Federal government incentives for research collaboration.

The federal government provides numerous types of incentives for technology transfer and university-industry research collaboration. Knowledge of such incentives, and how to obtain and deploy their benefits, will be important for higher education institutions contemplating or participating in collaborative activities.

One type of incentive involves the creation of exemptions from or modifications of federal regulatory requirements. The Patent and Trademark

Amendments of 1980 (94 Stat. 3015), for example, modified federal patent law to facilitate technology transfer and university-industry collaborations involving inventions discovered during federally funded research projects. The National Cooperative Research Act of 1984 (discussed in subsection 15.4.5 above) provides special protections against antitrust liability for "joint research and development ventures." And amendments to export control laws and regulations have been implemented to ease their impact on university research collaborations with foreign scientists (Margaret Lam, "Restrictions on Technology Transfer Among Academic Researchers: Will Recent Changes in the Export Control System Make a Difference?" 13 *J. Coll. & Univ. Law* 311 (1986); but see more recent developments in Section 13.2.4 of this book).

Congress may also build incentives for research collaboration into the federal tax laws. The statutory modifications to UBIT that exclude certain research income and royalty income (see subsection 15.4.4 above) are examples. In addition, special tax treatment for investors in certain research and development ventures may facilitate university participation in such ventures (see J. Bartlett & J. Siena, "Research and Development Limited Partnerships as a Device to Exploit University Owned Technology," 10 *J. Coll. & Univ. Law* 435 (1984)). At various times and in various ways, Congress has provided other tax credits, charitable deductions, expense deductions, accelerated depreciation formulas, and similar devices that encourage involvement of sponsors in university research (see, for example, 26 U.S.C. § 41). Such incentives, combined with the lenient treatment of income from research-related activities, have created a highly favorable tax environment for universities to exploit their expertise in new technologies.

Government also provides direct monetary incentives for biotechnology and biomedical research that may involve or lead to university-industry collaborations. Many National Science Foundation and National Institutes of Health grant programs, for instance, would fall into this category. Government agencies also may provide funds for technology risk assessment projects. The U.S. Department of Agriculture, for example, has awarded grants under its Biotechnology Risk Assessment Research Grants Program (see 57 Fed. Reg. 14308 (April 17, 1992)).

Other legislation and Executive Orders have created yet other types of incentives. The Stevenson-Wydler Technology Innovation Act of 1980 (94 Stat. 2311, 15 U.S.C. § 3701 *et seq.*), as amended, is a primary example. The Act constituted a first step toward development of a comprehensive national policy on technology and acknowledged the role of academia in scientific discoveries and advances. One of its stated purposes is to "encourag[e] the exchange of scientific personnel among academia, industry, and Federal laboratories" (15 U.S.C. § 3702(5)). Another purpose—added by a later amendment, the National Competitiveness Technology Transfer Act of 1989—is to stimulate "collaboration between universities, the private sector, and government-owned, contractor-operated laboratories in order to foster the development of technologies in areas of significant economic potential" (15 U.S.C. § 3701).

The 1980 Stevenson-Wydler Act established Centers for Industrial Technology, since renamed Cooperative Research Centers, to be operated by universities or other nonprofit organizations for the purpose of "enhanc[ing] technological innovation" through various means specified in the statute (15 U.S.C.§ 3705(a)). Among these means are "the participation of individuals from industries and universities in cooperative technological innovation activities" (15 U.S.C. § 3705(a)(1)); and one of the specific activities the centers are authorized to engage in is "research supportive of technological and industrial innovation including cooperative industry-university research" (15 U.S.C. § 3705(b)(1)). These centers were developed under the auspices of the Secretary of Commerce. In later amendments, Congress enhanced the Secretary's functions by creating the Technology Administration in the Department of Commerce (15 U.S.C. § 3704(a)–(c)). Congress has also directed the Secretary to provide financial assistance for "regional centers for the transfer of manufacturing technology," which are to encourage "the participation of individuals from . . . universities [and] State governments . . . in cooperative technology transfer activities" (15 U.S.C. § 278k(a)(2)). "United States-based nonprofit institutions(s)" are eligible for such assistance (15 U.S.C. § 278k(a)). (See also 15 U.S.C. § 278n, establishing an Advanced Technology Program in the Department of Commerce, which facilitates universities' participation in joint ventures with private industry; and 15 U.S.C. § 3710(e), establishing a Federal Laboratory Consortium for Technology Transfer, which is to assist and cooperate with colleges and universities in various ways (see, for example, 15 U.S.C. § 3710 (e)(1)(C), (I), (J)).)

The Federal Technology Transfer Act of 1986 (100 Stat. 1795, codified at 15 U.S.C. §§ 3710a–3710d) added important new provisions to assist in the transfer of commercially useful technology from federal laboratories to the private sector. Under this Act, federally operated laboratories are authorized to enter into cooperative research and development agreements and intellectual property licensing agreements with state and local government agencies, nonprofit organizations (including universities), corporations, partnerships, and foundations (15 U.S.C. § 3710a(a)). The Act also governs the distribution of royalties received from the licensing of inventions under such agreements.

15.4.7. Conflicts of interest. The growth of university-industry research collaborations, with the resultant potential for financial gains and split loyalties (subsection 15.4.1 above), has created an enhanced awareness of ethical issues in research and technology transfer. Increased attention to scientific misconduct (see Sections 6.6.2 & 13.2.3.4) is one manifestation. Another, and perhaps most prominent, manifestation is the emphasis on conflict of interest issues. (See generally H. Leskovac, Comment, "Ties That Bind: Conflicts of Interest in University-Industry Links," 17 *U.C. Davis L. Rev.* 895 (1984).)

The concept of conflict of interest, as applied to higher education, has several important variables. In the traditional conflict of interest situation, an employee or officer of an institution—motivated by an outside financial interest or the prospect of personal financial gain—exerts inappropriate influence on the institution's business judgments or contracting decisions. A newer and more subtle conflict situation is the "conflict of commitment," in which outside commitments (or the search for outside commitments) lead an institutional employee or officer to lessen or subvert commitment to the institution. See generally Association of American Medical Colleges, "Guidelines for Dealing with Faculty Conflicts of Commitment and Conflicts of Interest in Research," *65 Acad. Med.* 487 (1990). In either situation the conflict may be an actual conflict or merely a potential conflict or appearance of conflict; the institution must be concerned about both. Furthermore, conflicts may be occasioned either by an individual employee acting on his own behalf rather than on behalf of the university, or by the university itself acting for itself through its officers and employees. Thus, the university itself may have a conflict, and may need to monitor its own activities as well as the outside activities of its employees if it is to escape the debilitating effects of conflicts of interest.

The potential debilitating effects are numerous. As one author has described: "Among the manifestations of these conflicts are the use of students and university equipment for private gain, the division of working time in such a way as to slight the university, the shifting of research to accommodate corporate sponsors, the transfer of patentable inventions from the university to private laboratories, and the suppressing of research results" (Kenney, *Biotechnology* (cited in subsection 15.4.1 above), 113). Another commentator, focusing especially on conflicts of commitment, has noted three sets of concerns:

(1) the concern that the industrial sponsor will attempt to *improperly control the scientific or technical approach* to the work funded by the sponsor, thereby invading and diminishing the objectivity and independence of the scientific investigator; (2) the problem that faculty investigators, induced by proprietary concerns on the part of the industrial sponsor, may become *improperly secretive about their work,* not only to the detriment of free and open dissemination of any scientific and technological developments, but also to the detriment of interaction with and among their students; and (3) the concern that the industrial sponsor will *improperly attempt to influence or control the choice of, or approach to, future research* in the same or related areas. These problems are generally regarded as particularly acute if the faculty investigators involved (or the university itself) have, or will have, *an equity or some other on-going financial interest in the industrial sponsor* [D. Fowler, "Conflicts of Interest: A Working Paper" (presented at conference of National Association of College and University Attorneys, March 11–12, 1983, at 1–2)].

And yet another commentator has focused on other types of conflicts, called "intellectual conflicts," which may "be less obvious" than conflicts of commitment but nevertheless strike "at the heart of the academic enterprise." Such conflicts may create "[c]ognitive dissonance—the subtle shifting of one's ideas toward those positions favoring personal interests" (R. H. Linnell, "Professional Activities for Additional Income: Benefits and Problems," in R. H. Linnell (ed.), *Dollars and Scholars* (University of Southern California Press, 1982), 43–70, at 62).

Both the legislative and the executive branches of the federal government and of state governments have become increasingly concerned with conflicts of interest in university-industry research relationships, especially for research supported with government funding. In such circumstances, yet another variation on conflict of interest may occur: the "risk of conflict between the private interests of individuals, or of the companies with which they are involved, and the public interest that [government] funding should serve" (National Science Foundation, Investigator Financial Disclosure Policy, 59 Fed. Reg. 33308 (June 28, 1994), amended by 60 Fed. Reg. 35820 (July 11, 1995); supplemental guidelines published at 61 Fed. Reg. 34839 (July 3, 1996)).

At the federal level, some older and more general conflict of interest statutes, such as the Anti-Kickback Act (41 U.S.C. §§ 51 & 54), could apply to research activities. More recently, narrower conflict of interest provisions have appeared in appropriations acts, Office of Management and Budget (OMB) circulars, departmental contracting regulations, and agency grant policies or terms and conditions. Examples include the Department of Defense Federal Acquisition Regulations (48 C.F.R. § 235.017(a)(2), and 48 C.F.R. Part 203: "Improper Business Practices and Personal Conflicts of Interest"); the Department of Energy Acquisition Regulations (48 C.F.R. §§ 909.503–507.2: "Organizational and Consultant Conflicts of Interest"); the National Science Foundation's "Investigator Financial Disclosure Policy," above; the Food and Drug Administration's regulations on "Financial Disclosure by Clinical Investigators" (21 C.F.R. §§ 54.1 *et seq.*); the Department of Health and Human Services' conflict of interest regulations (42 C.F.R. §§ 50.604–606; and the U.S. Department of Health and Human Services (HHS) guidelines on "Financial Relationships and Interests in Research Involving Human-Subject Protection," 69 Fed. Reg. 26393–402 (May 12, 2004). The latter document is specifically for the guidance of research institutions, Institutional Review Boards (see Section 13.2.3.2 of this book), and researchers, and applies to human subject research that is funded by HHS or regulated by the Food and Drug Administration.

At the state level, a number of states have ethics-in-government statutes or administrative regulations that would have some application to state college and university employees and officers and to research activities at state colleges and universities. Under the Illinois Governmental Ethics Act (5 ILCS 420/4A-101 to 4A-107), for example, certain state government employees annually must file a statement of economic interest that lists income, honoraria, gifts, and capital assets, and identifies the source thereof, and that also lists outside employment and professional practice activities. Members of the state board of regents and trustees and employees of the state colleges and universities are expressly covered. Additionally, faculty members are subject to the following conflict of interest requirement:

> No full time member of the faculty of any State-supported institution of higher learning may undertake, contract for or accept anything of value in return for research or consulting services for any person other than that institution on whose faculty he serves unless (a) he has the prior written approval of the President of that institution, or a designee of such President, to perform the outside research or consulting services, such request to contain an estimate of the amount of time which will be involved, and (b) he submits to the President of that institution or such designee, annually, a statement of the amount of actual time he has spent on such outside research or consulting services [110 ILCS 100/1].

Under the Georgia statutes, Ga. Stat Ann. § 45-10-23 *et seq.* ("Conflicts of Interest"), state employees are prohibited from entering business transactions with the agency that employs them (§ 45-10-23) and must also disclose any financial transaction they enter into with any other state agency (§ 45-10-26). Another provision prohibits financial conflicts specifically involving the Board of Regents of the University System of Georgia or the trustees or officers of individual institutions (§ 45-10-40; and see Opin. Atty Gen. Ga. No. 04-7 (July 23, 2004). There are various exceptions (for example, § 45-10-24.1; §45-10-25), some of which focus on employees of the University System of Georgia. One section, for instance, allows such employees to serve "as members of the governing boards of private, nonprofit, educational, athletic, or research related foundations and associations which are organized for the purpose of supporting institutions of higher education in [Georgia]," even though these organizations may transact business with the employee's institution.

Virginia has a statute (Va. Code Ann. § 2.2-3100 *et seq.*) titled the "State and Local Government Conflict of Interests Act." Its provisions apply to all state and local government employees, prohibiting them from receiving gifts, honoraria, fees for services, or any other thing of value in circumstances creating the potential for conflicts of interest. State and local government employees must also file financial disclosure forms under certain circumstances. There are exceptions to the Act's requirements (see, for example, § 2.2-3110), including important exceptions dealing specifically with higher education. Once such exception relates to an employee's involvement "in a contract for research and development or commercialization of intellectual property" between a public higher education institution and a company in which the employee has a personal interest (§ 2.2-3106(C)(7)). Any knowing violation of the Act is a misdemeanor; and upon conviction, a judge may also order the employee to vacate his or her employment position (§ 2.2-3120 to 3122).

Institutions that engage in sponsored research activities, or whose faculty and staff engage in them, will, of course, need to track the continuing debate and developments at all levels and branches of government and in the national educational and professional organizations. Institutions involved in research affiliations with corporations or governments in foreign countries will also need to keep track of developments in those countries and in international forums. The key to success in managing conflicts of interest, however, is effective institutional policies and enforcement mechanisms—whether or not government may require them. Such policies may range from disclosure requirements and confidentiality requirements to prohibitions of certain types of transactions and limitations on outside employment. If sensitively constructed and clearly drafted, such policies are likely to be constitutional. In *Adamsons v. Wharton*, 771 F.2d 41 (2d Cir. 1985), for example, a state medical school enacted a rule limiting the amount of a faculty member's income from private practice. The plaintiff challenged the constitutionality of the regulation on three grounds: that it deprived him of his "property" without due process of law; that, in exempting part-time professors, the regulation discriminated against him in violation of equal protection; and that the regulation violated his First Amendment freedom of association. The court rejected all three claims, calling them "farfetched at best" and noting that the regulation was supported by the medical school's "legitimate interest in promoting devotion to teaching."

Numerous resources are available to guide institutions that are devising or reviewing conflict of interest policies. Among the most helpful are the reports and statements of various national associations. See, for example, the Association of American Medical Schools' Web site on conflicts of interest, http://www.aamc.org/members/coitf/; the AAHC Task Force on Science Policy, *Conflicts of Interest in Academic Health Centers* (Association of Academic Health Centers, 1990); the Association of American Universities' 1985 report on *University Policies on Conflict of Interest and Delay of Publication,* reprinted at 12 *J. Coll. & Univ. Law* 175 (1985); and the 1965 joint statement of the AAUP and the American Council on Education, "On Preventing Conflicts of Interest in Government-Sponsored Research at Universities," along with the AAUP's 1990 "Statement on Conflicts of Interest," both reprinted in *AAUP Policy Documents and Reports* (9th ed., 2001), 144–48. In addition, for helpful governmental guidance, see, for example, Government Accounting Office, *University Research: Most Federal Agencies Need to Better Protect Against Financial Conflicts of Interest* (GAO-04-31, 2003), which includes a survey of the policies of 171 universities; and NIH's "Compendium of Findings and Observations" from two years of compliance site visits, available at http://grants1.nih.gov/grants/compliance/compendium_2002.htm.

State criminal laws may also apply to some conflict of interest problems on college campuses and may prompt criminal prosecutions and convictions in certain situations. The case of *Smith v. State,* 959 S.W.2d 1 (Texas Ct. App. 1997), is illustrative.[17] The defendant had been vice president for finance and administration at Texas A&M University. In that capacity, in 1990, he had negotiated a contract with Barnes & Noble Bookstores, Inc., for the operation of the university's bookstore. In 1993 he made a trip to Barnes & Noble's corporate offices in New York to negotiate an extension of the contract. According to evidence later submitted at trial, Smith either had stated to Barnes & Noble employees that his wife would accompany him on this New York trip, or this arrangement was "understood" from the course of conduct between the parties regarding Smith's previous trips to New York. Barnes & Noble thereupon "provided round trip plane tickets, hotel accommodations, meals, ground transportation, and theatre tickets" for Smith and his wife (and for another university official and his wife).

The state claimed that Smith had solicited a benefit in violation of Texas Penal Code Ann. § 36.08 (d):

> [A] public servant who exercises discretion in connection with contracts, purchases, payments, claims, or other pecuniary transactions of government commits an offense if he solicits, accepts, or agrees to accept any benefit from a person the public servant knows is interested in or likely to become interested in any contract, purchase, payment, claim, or transaction involving the exercise of discretion.

---

[17]See generally, for other criminal and civil cases, John Theuman, Annot., "Validity and Construction of Orders and Enactments Requiring Public Officers and Employees, or Candidates for Office, to Disclose Financial Conditions, Interests, or Relationships," 22 A.L.R.4th 237.

After trial, a jury convicted Smith of this offense. On appeal, the court upheld the conviction, asserting that the trial judge had correctly instructed the jury on the statute's interpretation, and that the statute was neither overbroad nor vague.

Thus, numerous sources of law, and numerous sources of guidance from both governmental and private sources, are now being brought to bear on ethical issues confronting universities involved in biomedical and biotechnological research, technology transfer, and related activities. In this context, and in broader academic contexts as well, ethical issues and issues concerning commercialization and "technologization" are among the cutting-edge issues facing higher education for the present and future.

Selected Annotated Bibliography

General

National Association of College and University Business Officers. *College and University Business Administration* (6th ed., NACUBO, n.d.). A three-volume overview of management and accounting principles designed specifically for use by higher education administrators, especially business officers. Includes a list of resources and government and professional organizations relevant to each chapter's topic. Also available on CD-ROM.

Sec. 15.1 (The Contract Context for College Business Transactions)

Perillo, Joseph M., & Calamari, John. *Calamari and Perillo on Contracts* (West, 2003). A comprehensive discussion of the principles of the law of contracts. Individual chapters are devoted to such subjects as offer and acceptance, consideration, promissory estoppel, breach, and damages.

Sec. 15.2 (The College as Purchaser)

Cole, Elsa Kircher, & Goldblatt, Steven M. "Award of Construction Contracts: Public Institutions' Authority to Select the Lowest Responsible Bidder," 16 *J. Coll. & Univ. Law* 177 (1989). A review of the statutes and case law on when and how institutions may reject an apparent low bidder as nonresponsible. Includes helpful suggestions on factors and processes to be used in making such a decision.

Goldstein, Philip, Kempner, Daphne, Rush, Sean, & Bookman, Mark. *Contract Management for Self-Operation: A Decision-Making Guide for Higher Education* (Council of Higher Education Management Associations, 1993). Examines whether and when institutions should contract out, or outsource, the provision of campus services rather than providing the services themselves; and develops a decision-making approach that can be utilized by managers and business officers facing such questions. Focuses particularly on these functional areas: facilities, bookstores, dining services, administrative computing, child care, and security. Includes six case studies, sample contract language, and a checklist of provisions to be included in outsourcing contracts.

Special Project, "Article Two Warranties in Commercial Transactions: An Update," 72 *Cornell L. Rev.* 1159 (1987). A comprehensive analysis of express and implied warranties applicable to the sale of goods under the Uniform Commercial Code.

Sweet, Justin, & Sweet, Jonathan. *Sweet on Construction Industry Contracts: Major AIA Documents* (4th ed., Wiley Law Pubs., 1999, plus supps.). A thorough and practical analysis of the American Institute of Architects forms used in construction contracting, with advice on selecting forms, drafting contracts, and handling contract disputes.

See Bookman entry in Selected Annotated Bibliography for Chapter 3, Section 3.4.

Sec. 15.3 (The College as Seller/Competitor)

Niccolls, Carol S., Nave, Margaret E., & Olswang, Steven G. "Unrelated Business Income Tax and Unfair Competition: Current Status of the Law," 15 *J. Coll. & Univ. Law* 249 (1989). A discussion of the current and emerging legal issues regarding the unrelated business income tax and its application to colleges and universities. The authors cite numerous IRS and court decisions to illustrate the various income-producing enterprises undertaken by colleges and universities and their treatment by the IRS and the courts. Readers may choose to track subsequent developments.

See Bookman entry in Selected Annotated Bibliography for Chapter 3, Section 3.4; Kirby entry in Selected Annotated Bibliography for Chapter 13, Section 13.2; and Goldstein, Kempner, Rush, & Bookman entry in Selected Annotated Bibliography for Section 15.2 above.

Sec. 15.4. (The College as Research Collaborator and Partner)

Armstrong, Jeffrey R. "Bayh-Dole Under Siege: The Challenge to Federal Patent Policy as a Result of *Madey v. Duke University*," 30 *J. Coll. & Univ. Law* 619 (2004). Discusses the effect of *Madey*, suggesting that it may limit the right of a university to use third-party patented technology for research or educational purposes.

Bok, Derek. *Universities in the Marketplace: The Commercialization of Higher Education* (Princeton University Press, 2003). Focuses in large part on research programs at research-oriented universities and the dangers that may arise from commercial exploitation of university research. Critiques the trend toward more commercialization, its potential effects on the role of faculty, and the potential conflicts with academic values.

Bowie, Norman E. *University-Business Partnerships: An Assessment* (Rowman & Littlefield, 1994). Explores the history, benefits, risks, and other problems of university-business partnerships. Includes a strong emphasis on conflicts of interest. The first part of the book is a lengthy essay by the author; the second part is a select collection of readings and documents, including a model research agreement and several university conflict of interest policies.

Colecchia, Theresa (ed.). *Legal Issues in Sponsored Research Programs: From Contracting to Compliance* (National Association of College and University Attorneys, 2005). A compendium collecting and organizing more than fifty writings and other documents on key sponsored research issues. Provides a basic overview of the field and other sections on "Grants and Contracts," "Responsible Conduct of Research," and "Research in the International Setting." Also provides sample forms and policies for practitioners, and numerous references to additional sources.

Curry, Judith. *Technology Transfer Issues for Colleges and Universities: A Legal Compendium* (National Association of College and University Attorneys, 2005). A collection of pertinent articles, legal documents, and sample policies, primarily for attorneys. Organized into seven sections: "An Introduction to Technology Transfer," "Technology Transfer 101," "Administration of Technology Transfer," "Intellectual Property Licensing," "Special Licensing Issues," "Beyond Licensing—The Entrepreneurial Campus," and "Tax Considerations."

Eisenberg, Rebecca S. "Academic Freedom and Academic Values in Sponsored Research," 66 *Tex. L. Rev.* 1363 (1988). Examines the tripartite relationship among researchers, universities, and research sponsors. Identifies contemporary threats to academic values stemming from sponsored research and suggests that the "traditional American conception of academic freedom . . . is ill-adapted to the task of protecting academic values in sponsored research within universities." See also David M. Rabban, "Does Academic Freedom Limit Faculty Autonomy?" 66 *Tex. L. Rev.* 1405 (1988), responding to the Eisenberg article and disagreeing that there is any actual conflict between academic freedom and the academic values it was designed to advance.

Fairweather, James S. *Entrepreneurship and Higher Education: Lessons for Colleges, Universities, and Industry*. ERIC/Higher Education Research Report no. 6 (Association for the Study of Higher Education, 1988). Discusses economic and academic motivations of institutions competing for government- and corporate-sponsored research projects and the potential ramifications on academic freedom, property rights, facilities use, and recruitment of faculty and students. Provides a cost-benefit framework for use by institutions to determine whether to enter into sponsored-research contracts.

Fowler, Donald R. "University-Industry Research Relationships: The Research Agreement," 9 *J. Coll. & Univ. Law* 515 (1982–83). Identifies and suggests solutions to fifteen potential problems encountered in drafting research contracts between universities and industry. Agreement provisions discussed include the scope of the research project, control over the conduct of the contracted research, funding, receipt of sponsor's proprietary information, intellectual property rights, indemnification and hold-harmless clauses, and potential conflicts of interest.

Gordon, Mark L. "University Controlled or Owned Technologies: The State of Commercialization and Recommendations," 30 *J. Coll. & Univ. Law* 641 (2004). Examines the growth in commercialization of technology transfer activities of universities since passage of the Bayh-Dole Act in 1980, including patent licensing and faculty and institutional collaboration in joint ventures. Provides recommendations for institutions and their counsel, using the policies and practices of several major research universities as examples.

Harrington, Peter J. "Faculty Conflicts of Interest in an Age of Academic Entrepreneurialism: An Analysis of the Problem, the Law and Selected University Policies," 27 *J. Coll. & Univ. Law* 775(2001). As universities increasingly join with private corporations and federal agencies to undertake research projects, the range of issues regarding faculty conflicts of interest increases as well. In this article, the author considers how the issues are being addressed by universities through individually developed policies, and how federal agencies are addressing the problem through regulations aimed at preventing conflicts of interest in federally funded projects.

Leskovac, Helen. "Academic Freedom and the Quality of Sponsored Research on Campus," 13 *Rev. Litigation* 401 (1993–94). Discusses the impacts on the campus of commercialization of academic research. Explores the relationship between private sector research sponsors and the universities conducting the research. Considers the relationship's potential effects on the protections of academic freedom.

Rosenblum, Jerald E., & Fields, Kathy A. "Product Liability Risks of University Research Licensing and How They Affect Commercialization—Is It Time for a Legislative Solution?" 73 *J. Pat. & Trademark Off. Soc'y.* 514 (1991). Examines the effects of the Patent and Trademark Amendments of 1980, under which universities may own the patent on federally funded research results, on the exposure of universities to products liability lawsuits.

Shockley, Pat. "Availability of 'Trade Secret' Protection for University Research," 20 *J. Coll. & Univ. Law* 309 (1994). Analyzes the potential use of trade secret jurisprudence to protect university-generated research. Discusses the effect of Freedom of Information Act requests on the secrecy of research and reviews state laws regarding protection of trade secrets.

Stevens, Ann R. *Ownership and Retention of Data* (National Association of College and University Attorneys, 1997). Discusses ownership of research data generated at universities and other academic institutions, and the attendant questions of what and how long data should be retained, who should retain the data, and when and under what circumstances data can be removed from the university.

Symposium, "Focus on Secrecy and University Research," 19 *J. Coll. & Univ. Law* 197 (1993). Includes the following articles: Peter M. Brody, "The First Amendment, Governmental Censorship, and Sponsored Research"; John Shattuck, "Secrecy on Campus"; Wade L. Robison & John T. Sanders, "The Myths of Academia: Open Inquiry and Funded Research"; and R. Robert Kreiser, "AAUP Perspectives on Academic Freedom and United States Intelligence Agencies." Topics include First Amendment rights of researchers and institutions, problems associated with accepting projects funded by intelligence agencies, and researchers' duties of loyalty in today's economically driven sponsored-research market. For other articles on the same types of concerns, developed from papers presented at the same conference, see Tom L. Beauchamp, "Ethical Issues in Funding and Monitoring University Research," 11 *Bus. & Professional Ethics J.* 5 (1992); Nicholas H. Steneck, "Whose Academic Freedom Needs to Be Protected? The Case of Classified Research," 11 *Bus. & Professional Ethics J.* 17 (1992); and John T. Sanders & Wade L. Robison, "Research Funding and the Value-Dependence of Science," 11 *Bus. & Professional Ethics J.* 33 (1992).

See Harpool entry ("Managing Trustee Conflicts of Interest") in Selected Annotated Bibliography for Chapter 3, Section 3.2.

Statute Index

Cases Index

Subject Index

A

AAAHC (Accreditation Association for Ambulatory Health Care), 893

AACRAO. *See* American Association of Collegiate Registrars and Admissions Officers

AAHE (American Association for Higher Education), 718

AAUP. *See* American Association of University Professors

AAUW (American Association of University Women), 941–42

Abbe, K. H., 1369

Abelson, R., 419

ABOR. *See* Academic Bill of Rights

Abortion, legal issues regarding, 890–892, 1289, 1443–1446

Abstention doctrine, 100

Academic Bill of Rights (ABOR), 746–747, 1018

Academic custom and usage:
faculty contracts, 479–482, 582–586;
overview, 35–37, 1582

Academic deference, 8, 80–81, 126–132

Academic freedom:
Academic Bill of Rights (ABOR), 746–747, 1018;
administrators' authority over, 693–699;
basic concepts and distinctions, 613–615;
claims, methods of analyzing, 648–653;

in classroom, 628–644;
confidential information, privilege for, 699–706;
defamation, defense against, 221;
external versus internal restraints, 622–625;
extramural speech, 688–692;
foundational constitutional law cases, 617–622;
generally, 605–613;
governance matters, speech on, 667–683;
in grading, 644–648;
"institutional" academic freedom, 625–627, 665–685;
intramural speech on extramural public affairs, 683–685;
personnel issues, 700–706;
in private institutions, 653–654;
in private life, 685–692;
professional versus legal concepts, 615–617;
in publication, 654–665;
in religious institutions, 714–716;
in research, 654–665, 706–714;
of students, 737–747;
in teaching, 627–654;
terrorism, war on, effect of, 624;
Title VII, 702

Academic sanctions. *See* Sanctions

Academic senates, authority of, 187–188

Access to campus. *See* Campus access

Accreditation:
agencies, 1530–1534, 1559–1560;
antitrust law, 1546–1549;
bankruptcy law, 1553–1554;
case law, 1534–1538;
common law, 1534–1543;
constitutional requirements, 1543–1546;
courts and, 1534–1554;
defamation law, 1549–1553;
formative developments, 1534–1538;
Secretary of Education, role of, 1532–1533, 1534, 1546, 1554, 1559–1560;
types, 1531;
U.S. Department of Education, role of, 1554–1559

Accreditation Association for Ambulatory Health Care (AAAHC), 893

ACE. *See* American Council on Education (ACE)

ACHA (American College Health Association), 893

Achtenberg, R., 464, 599

ADA. *See* Americans With Disabilities Act

Adams, J. F., 151, 157, 164

Adams, M., 790

Administrative Conference of the United States, 1521

Administrative procedure laws, 1286–1288